Praise for

MILLION DOLLAR MAILING$

"This book is an extraordinary contribution to understanding the how and what of making direct mail pay off. If you have the time for just one book on the inside secrets of successful mailings, this is it. At last, the winners speak and you get a chance to listen."

Stan Rapp
Co-author (with Tom Collins) of *MaxiMarketing* and *The Great Marketing Turnaround*

"*Million Dollar Mailing$* shows you the great mailing packages, and their copy creators tell you what makes the difference in winning mail. It gives you all the straight answers on the successful concepts of great copy. I read it cover to cover in one sitting."

Richard V. Benson
Author of *Secrets of Successful Direct Mail*

"Clear your book shelves of all those tomes on direct marketing theory. Junk all of those 'research' files of other people's mailings. This is the only reliable source of direct mail that really works. Not voted by a panel of self-styled experts, but by customers' checks! Hats off to Denny Hatch for a monumental and truly useful research project."

Robert Teufel
President, Rodale Press

"Want to learn everything you need to know about successful direct mail? How to write and design it? What sells and what doesn't? Who's who? What's what? Why and wherefore? This is the one book to buy, to trust, to follow!"

Bill Jayme
Jayme, Ratahlati, Inc.

Million Dollar Mailings

MILLION DOLLAR MAILING$

The art and science of creating money-making direct mail—revealed by more than 60 direct marketing superstars who wrote, designed, and produced the most powerful mailings of the past decade.

DENISON HATCH

Illustrated with 71 complete mailings!

THE LIBEY BUSINESS LIBRARY

LIBEY PUBLISHING
INCORPORATED
A Regnery Gateway Subsidiary

Washington, D.C.

Library of Congress Cataloging-in-Publication Data

Hatch, Denison.
Million dollar mailings / by Denison Hatch.
p. cm.
Includes index.
ISBN 0-89526-509-5
1. Advertising, Direct-mail—United States. 2. Advertising, Direct-mail—Information services—United States. 3. Advertising, Direct-mail—United States—Awards. I. Title.
HF5861.H35 1992
659.13'3—dc20 92-17544
CIP

Published in the United States by
Libey Publishing Incorporated
A Regnery Gateway Subsidiary
1130 17th Street, NW
Washington, DC 20036

Distributed to the trade by
National Book Network
4720 Boston Way
Lanham, MD 20706

Printed on acid-free paper

Manufactured in the United States of America

10 9 8 7 6 5 4 3 2 1

Copyright Acknowledgments

Epigraph
"The Greatest Copywriter in the World" copyright 1992, Bob Dolman

Chapter 4
"The Direct Mail Package" by Malcolm Decker, copyright by Malcolm Decker

Chapter 5
"Twenty-six Design Tips to Lift Response" by Ted Kikoler, copyright by Ted Kikoler

Chapter 7
Architectural Digest reprinted with permission of Judy Weiss
Lotus reprinted with permission of John Klingel
Islands reprinted with permission of Ken Schneider
Inc. reprinted with permission of Judy Weiss
Business Week reprinted with permission of Judy Weiss
Yankee reprinted with permission of Yankee
Sales & Marketing Management reprinted with permission of Stu Heinecke

Chapter 8
Success reprinted with permission of Ken Scheck
Newsweek reprinted with permission of Newsweek
Advertising Age reprinted with permission of Financial Direct, Inc.
Fortune reprinted with permission of Financial Direct, Inc.

Chapter 9
M reprinted with permission of Milt Pierce
Organic Gardening reprinted with permission of Jim Punkre, Brainstorms, Inc.
Dog Fancy reprinted with permission of Dog Fancy
Harper's reprinted with permission of Nancy Grady

Chapter 10
Bon Appétit reprinted with permission of Linda Wells
W reprinted with permission of Judy Weiss
House & Garden reprinted with permission of Rapp Collins Marcoa

Chapter 11
Science News reprinted with permission of Tom McCormick
The Futurist reprinted with permission of World Future Society
Earthwatch reprinted with permission of Bill Jayme
Audubon reprinted with permission of Peter Gelb
National Wildlife reprinted with permission of National Wildlife Federation
Nature Conservancy reprinted with permission of Frank H. Johnson

Chapter 12
Soviet Life reprinted with permission of Tony Arau
American Spectator reprinted with permission of Laurence Jaeger
The Economist reprinted with permission of Ken Scheck
Foreign Affairs reprinted with permission of Len Berkowe
Passage from *The Solid Gold Mailbox* (New York: John Wiley & Sons, 1987) reprinted with permission of Walter Weintz

Chapter 13
Lear's reprinted with permission of Linda Wells
Utne Reader reprinted with permission of Bill Jayme
Condé Nast Traveler reprinted with permission of Rapp Collins Marcoa

Chapter 14
Mysteries of the Unknown reprinted with permission of Len Berkowe
Time Frame reprinted with permission of Time-Life Books
Singer Sewing Reference Library reprinted with permission of Greg Beaupre

Chapter 15
Book-of-the-Month reprinted with permission of Book-of-the-Month Club and Wunderman Worldwide
Fortune Book Club reprinted with permission of Book-of-the-Month Club
International Preview Society reprinted with permission of BMG Direct Marketing, Inc.
BMG Music Service reprinted with permission of BMG Direct Marketing, Inc.
Literary Guild reprinted with permission of Doubleday Book & Music Clubs, Inc.

Chapter 16
Dr. Chang's Book of Internal Exercises reprinted with permission of Eugene Schwartz
Everyday Health Tips reprinted with permission of Josh Manheimer
Build It Yourself Country Furniture reprinted with permission of Rodale Press
Hints, Tips, Wisdom reprinted with permission of Eugene Schwartz
Encyclopedia of Home Remedies reprinted with permission of Eugene Schwartz
"An Interview with Gene Schwartz" from *Direct Marketing* reprinted with permission of Milt Pierce

Chapter 17
Encyclopaedia Britannica reprinted with permission of Encyclopaedia Britannica
Great Expectations reprinted with permission of Tony Barnard
Institute of Children's Literature reprinted with permission of Institute of Children's Literature

Chapter 18
Gevalia Kaffe reprinted with permission of Wunderman Worldwide
CompuServe reprinted with permission of Sol Blumenfeld
Omaha Steaks reprinted with permission of Herschell Gordon Lewis
Mobil Auto Club reprinted with permission of Robert Haydon Jones

Chapter 19
Aviation Consumer reprinted with permission of Belvoir Publications, Inc.
Aviation Safety reprinted with permission of Belvoir Publications, Inc.
Soundview Executive Book Summaries reprinted with permission of Don Hauptman
"Promotion: Turning a Direct-Mail Flop into a Winner" from *Newsletter on Newsletters* reprinted with permission of Newsletter Clearinghouse

Chapter 20
American Demographics reprinted with permission of Gretchen Fall Burnett, Ph.D.
SRDS Direct Mail Lists and Data reprinted with permission of Elaine Tyson
"Elements of a Successful Direct Mail Package" from *Folio* reprinted with permission of Elaine Tyson
Advertising Age (mug) reprinted with permission of Financial Direct, Inc.
Advertising Age (cartoon) reprinted with permission of Stu Heinecke
Financial World reprinted with permission of Linda Wells

Chapter 21
Book of Inside Information reprinted with permission of Boardroom Reports
Bottom Line/Personal reprinted with permission of Boardroom Reports

Chapter 22
Successful Business Management reprinted with permission of Harry Walsh
SuperInvestor Files reprinted with permission of Alan Schwartz
Successful Investing and Money Management reprinted with permission of Joan Throckmorton
Lead the Field reprinted with permission of Bob Matheo
The Secrets of Power Negotiating reprinted with permission of Don Kanter

Chapter 23
Cinegraph Slides reprinted with permission of Cinegraph Slides, Inc.

Chapter 24
Barron's I reprinted with permission of Dow Jones & Company, Inc.
Barron's II reprinted with permission of Seymour Zogott
Wall Street Journal I reprinted with permission of Seymour Zogott
Wall Street Journal II reprinted with permission of Martin Conroy

Appendix 1
"Positioning" by Dennis S. LeBarron, copyright by Dennis S. LeBarron

To Axel Andersson

whose idea this was, and who has forgotten more about direct mail than all of us represented in this book collectively will ever know

Acknowledgments

Special thanks to:

Tony Arau
Tony Barnard
Greg Beaupre
Paul Bell
Len Berkowe
Sol Blumenfeld
Gretchen Fall Burnett
Ron Burr
Bill Butler
Bill Christensen
Martin Conroy
Jeff Cornish
Tony Cornish
Pat Corpora
Roger Craver
Martin Davidson
Malcolm Decker
Greg Dziuba
Martin Edelston
Lee Eptstein
Heide Follin
Pete Gelb
Paul Goldberg
David Gordon
Nancy Grady
Peggy Hatch
Don Hauptman
Sheldon Hearst
Karen Henkin
Irving Perkins Design
Laurence Jaeger
Bill Jayme
Carla Johnson
Frank H. Johnson
Mark Johnson
Robert Haydon Jones
Don Kanter
Anne Keating
Jane Keiffer
Bill Keisler
Maria Keresey
Ted Kikoler
John Klingel
Dennis S. LeBarron
Herschell Gordon Lewis
Don Libey
Sara Lynn
Beth Maher
Bob Matheo
Tom McCormick
Michael Moroney
Don O'Brien
Milt Pierce
Pamela Poulos
James W. Prendergast
Jim Punkre
Jennifer Reist
John Rettich
Jerry Ricigliano
Ken Schneider
Eugene Schwartz
Robert Scott
Strat Simon
Donn Smith
Emily Soell
Penny Stewart
Martin Tarratt
Robert Teufel
Joan Throckmorton
Elaine Tyson
Frank Vos
Harry Walsh
Karen Weinstein
Walter Weintz
Judy Weiss
Linda Wells
Seymour Zogott

Contents

Acknowledgments viii

Foreword, by Axel Andersson xiii

Part I: The Art and Science of Direct Mail

1. In the Beginning 3

2. Why Direct Mail? 11

3. Direct Mail: The Ultimate *Trompe l'Oeil* 19

4. The Direct Mail Package by Malcolm Decker 23

5. Twenty-six Design Tips to Lift Response by Ted Kikoler 29

6. The Key to Successful Advertising: Interrupt and Keep on Interrupting 35

Part II: The Grand Controls

7. Double Postcards 43

8. The Next Step: The Mini-Package 65

9. Consumer Magazines I: Miscellaneous Special Interest 79

10. Consumer Magazines II: Women's Interest/Home/Shelter 101

11. Consumer Magazines III: Science and Nature 119

12. Consumer Magazines IV: The Nation and the World 157

13. Starting from Scratch: The Launch of a Magazine 179

14. Consumer Publishing I: Continuity Series 203

15. Consumer Publishing II: Negative Option Clubs 223

16. Consumer Publishing III: Individual Titles 251

17. Lead Generators 287

18. Memberships and Merchandise 307

19. Newsletters 327

20. Business and Financial Magazines 345

21. Boardroom Reports 377

22. Home-Study Programs 385

23. The Catalog 419

24. The Dow Jones Story 425

25. Format, Technique, and Offer Grid 443

26. Analysis of the Data 447

Appendices

Appendix 1. Positioning 459
by Dennis S. LeBarron

Appendix 2. The Seventy-one Grand Controls 463

Appendix 3. Names and Addresses of Writers and Designers 469

Bibliography 473

Index 475

The Greatest Copywriter in the World

Whenever I get burned out, I go to visit and watch the greatest copywriter in the world at work, under the portales in the Plaza de Santo Domingo in Mexico City. Oliverio, with his Olympia typewriter made in Brazil, is clearly a king among evangelists, the scribes who sit at card tables behind the old platen presses where you can have your wedding invitations printed while you wait.

Good, plain people who can't write letters for themselves come to Oliverio, and he is much closer to life than I'll ever get. He writes most eloquently about love waiting at home for sons and daughters to return and claim it.

Oliverio always writes from the heart, and his business letters ring with the same truth as his love letters, so people travel from miles around with their problems for Oliverio to solve with his clever typewriter.

Under his fingernails I see a permanent black edge from changing his ribbons. Back home, when I confront my antiseptic computer, I look first at my fingernails and if they are all clean I know my letter would be antiseptic, too.

I wish I could take Oliverio's place at his card table for just one hour, but that would turn into a bitter circus—his clients would believe I was mocking them, and I think they would be right about that. Mocking them or him is something I would never want to do, so I melt into the background and watch and listen while my friend works.

For my own work, the best thing I can do is try to keep Oliverio's human touch in mind every time I write. Lord knows I try.

—Bob Dolman
Freelancer

Foreword

In this book you will find seventy-one of the top mailings in the United States in 1990, 1991, and 1992.

Seventy-one mailings that were controls.

Seventy-one mailings that have not been beaten for three to eighteen years.

Nowhere else will you find so many winners in the marketplace—real winners, controls for so many years.

In this book you can study the most successful direct mail package of all time, Martin Conroy's legendary "Two Young Men . . ." mailing for the *Wall Street Journal.*

To date it has generated sales of $1 billion. I have counted the words in that famous sales letter, 810 words altogether. That means sales of $1¼ million per word.

Think of that—$1¼ million per word. No work of literature, no bestseller has reached one-thousandth of that.

Conroy's letter is probably responsible for more revenue per word than anything else ever printed—except the Bible.

There is one flaw with the *Wall Street Journal* letter—just one flaw.

It never received any award, not a single one.

Why? It was never entered in any award competition.

My impression is that the majority of successful mailers don't want to participate in award competitions. For others, the entry cost is too high.

When did *Reader's Digest,* Publishers Clearing House, American Family Publishers, Easton Press, or Boardroom Reports ever enter a competition?

If many of the mailers spending $10 million a year or more do not enter their controls in award competitions, isn't that like the Olympics without the real star athletes? The real stars are not even allowed to compete?

All other awards are given only to those who want to participate. The Axel Andersson Awards for longevity in the mail—devised by Denny Hatch of *Who's Mailing What!*—many thousands more than were entered in all the award competitions together. That gives everybody, every copywriter, every designer, the right to win, to get the recognition he or she deserves.

Many direct marketing awards have mainly been *pre*-tests—awards given to mailings *before all the results were in.*

The Axel Andersson Award is the only real 100 percent post-test award, a real post-test award because the award is given only after three years' results are in.

We don't know how much more profitable the long-term controls presented in this book are than their predecessors. But we know they have not been beaten—at least not for three or more years. In many cases we also know the mailings that preceded them. The *Who's Mailing What!* archives make it possible to prove conclusively and objectively the success of a particular control and for how many years it has been a control—at least three years up to eighteen years.

To pick the winners we didn't have to rely on claims of success by mailers or agencies, nor on the opinions of judges.

A qualified jury may be able to eliminate the real duds but no panel of judges probably has the ability to pick the real winners—not even in their specific narrow field.

I have spent at least $100 million promoting home-study courses in Germany. For almost fifty years before every single test/split-run I always asked myself which one would be a winner.

I must confess that my batting average in picking winners is not better than 60 percent; and remember, I have done thousands of tests in just one field (home study) in one market (Germany). Still my batting average is no better than 60 percent. What would it be in a field outside the home study? My answer: It would probably be so bad I wouldn't even consider trying to judge insurance promotions, fundraising mailings, or offers of collectibles, for instance, not to mention sweepstakes mailings.

That makes it imperative to judge the judges first. Can you judge a mailing without knowing most of the influencing factors? My answer is no.

For example, for every product and service there are different checklists for different types of mailings. For one-shot mailings, for lead-generating mailings, for mailings introducing a new product, etc.

All the control mailings presented here are cost-effective. That is the only reason they have been controls for more than three years.

In tests some of these controls have probably been beaten on the response rate basis alone—but the bottom line showed the cost of that particular mailing increased more than the response rate. A mailing that costs 40 percent more in the mail but lifts the response rate only 25 percent will probably not remain a control for long.

Cost-effectiveness also involves quality of the order, lead, etc. A more creative and innovative package may reduce the quality of the order as well as the lifetime value of a customer.

Too many mailings, space ads produce bad-quality customers.

My impression is that the award judges don't consider the cost of producing a particular package. A comparison of Axel Andersson Award winners with other award winners may reveal that other award winners cost at least one-third more to produce and to mail. For example, six of the Axel Andersson Award winners (9 percent) are double postcards that cost $250–$300 in the mail. Has a double postcard ever been entered in an awards contest or ever won anything? It's doubtful.

Every mailer knows that when testing new mailings the initial response from a new package will often look good, maybe even beat the present control. But we all know that may be a statistical fluke. In a rollout the old control will stand. So please remember all the award winners in this book have stood the test of time. They have been mailed over at least a period of three years, a proof that statistically valid results are available.

A few of the winners have already been beaten, replaced by new controls. That's also how it should be. The important thing is to study the differences between the old control and the new control and learn from the differences. In some cases the differences are obvious. For instance, the new *Yankee* double postcard has a sticker; the old one does not. That seems to confirm that stickers as a rule lift response—cost-effectively.

In other cases to beat the control you have to change the whole marketing approach; for instance, introduce a sweepstakes.

Will we ever be able to pretest mailings—*and rely on the findings*? Three experts seem to confirm what successful mailers know. From Jim Kobs's *Profitable Direct Marketing* (2d ed.; Lincolnwood, IL: NTC Business Books, 1991):

Even direct marketing professionals with years of experience have difficulty predicting exactly what will strike the consumer's fancy. This point was really driven home to me early in my agency career when I put together a panel session on testing for a Direct Marketing Association conference. My fellow panelists and I presented eight testing case histories, using slides to show the mailings packages or ads that were split-tested. Each member of the audience had a score sheet so he or she could pick his or her favorite before the results were revealed.

When we finished, not a single one of the 400 direct marketing pros in the audience had picked more than six of the eight test winners. But somebody had correctly picked all eight winners, namely, the consumers who had voted by sending in their respective reply cards and coupons.

Even focus groups have failed badly. In their modern classic, *Maxi-Marketing* (New York: McGraw-Hill, 1987), Stan Rapp and Tom Collins write:

In 1981, we had a rare opportunity to compare the accuracy of predictive consumer-interview research and actual direct-response results. A total of 104 respondents were shown eight different ads for RCA Record Club, all featuring essentially the same offer to new members. The respondents were all people who had bought records or tapes within the previous six months, had bought something by mail in the previous three years, and were not totally "turned off" to record clubs.

They were asked to rank eight ad campaigns according to "uniqueness," "interest in reading further," "believability," and "interest in responding." The results of this research predicted that the winners would be ads nicknamed "Guarantee" and "No Fine Print." According to the research, "Headphones" ran a poor fifth and "Cartoon" a miserable last.

However, when we actually ran the ads in an equal eight-way split run, "Headphones" was the clear winner. And "Cartoon," a corny but very effective cartoon ad that had consistently beaten other approaches for years, decisively outpulled the ads which the research respondents had chosen as most likely to interest and persuade them.

If RCA had relied on predictive research, the profitability of their advertising would have been sharply reduced.

I wish I could contradict these three experts sometime in the future, because reliable inexpensive pretesting would be a real breakthrough. It would probably mean the biggest dream-come-true for every direct marketing entrepreneur.

But for now—and for a long time to come—post-test and rollout analysis is the only direct route to profitable direct mail.

For this reason, I believe *Million-Dollar Mailing$* represents a real breakthrough in our understanding of moneymaking direct mail and how to create it.

AXEL ANDERSSON

Part I:

THE ART AND SCIENCE OF DIRECT MAIL

1

In the Beginning

Once a month in the late 1960s a group of direct mail copywriters would get together for lunch at the Blue Ribbon, a German-American rathskeller on West Forty-fourth Street off Times Square in New York City. Drinks were cheap and a very good lunch was served for very little money. Originally called the National Association of Direct Mail Writers, the organization was dreamed up in 1966 by Ed McLean, who was then at Ogilvy & Mather. It was his secretary, Liz Morris, who spent countless hours getting it going, recruiting members, and persuading them to come to the luncheons.

When the Blue Ribbon folded, the venue became the upstairs room at Rosoff's, one block south. Andi Emerson became president and the name was changed to the Direct Mail Writer's Guild. At Rosoff's—where drinks were a buck and there was a great hors d'oeuvres table as well as a superb lunch served on pewter plates—you could meet everyone from young writers just starting out to one of the nicest gentlemen ever to walk planet Earth, the legendary John Caples, whose genius put the direct marketing show on the road. The meetings were terribly important to us, because at that time direct mail was the ugly little stepsibling of general advertising, and we who wrote it were fringe players, sneered at, and dismissed out of hand by those on the Madison Avenue fast track.

At one Writer's Guild luncheon the speaker was Dorothy Kerr, then circulation director of *U.S. News & World Report.* A single sentence of her talk rocketed into my brain and remained etched for all time. It changed my life. Kerr said

To be successful in this business you have to see who's mailing what, really study the mail, look for those mailings that keep coming over and over again which means they are successful, and then steal smart.

Today, Rosoff's is gone. Direct marketing is now the aristocrat of advertising. And direct mail—although still sneered at by the hotshots on Madison Avenue—is the fastest-growing advertising medium and is the linchpin of direct marketing.

And as a result of that meeting where Dorothy Kerr was the speaker, I am proprietor of the largest private library of direct mail samples in the world.

I started slowly, sorting and cataloging my own mail and that of a few friends. Gradually the collection grew from one file drawer to two and then four. Periodically I would hire high school students to come in and help me sort and catalog.

There was no clear thought in my head as to how to turn this collection into a business. But I kept collecting. My wife, Peggy, thought I was cuckoo, but has always supported me in whatever I did.

I did know that the collection was enormously useful to *me* in my freelance copywriting work. For example, one September I received a call from consultant Jerry Gaylord. Victor Kiam of Remington not only wanted to get into the catalog business, but also expected to have a catalog out in time for Christmas. As I said, this was September. Could I write and design a sixteen-page catalog in a week? I said yes.

Gaylord and I met with the Remington people in Bridgeport, Connecticut, and as I was leaving the meeting with two huge shopping bags of merchandise, Gaylord turned to me and said: "Oh, by the way, we'll need an order form, too."

I winced. The order form is perhaps the most important element of a catalog. Screw up the order form so that people have a tough time ordering, and the catalog will bomb. The order form is also a horrendously complex document with many parts. Not only are there lines to write in item numbers, descriptions, sizes, and prices, but also ship-to/bill-to instructions, credit card information, gift shipments with handwritten holiday messages in each one, initials to be engraved on certain items, plus the guarantee and the schedule of shipping charges. The order form must be easy to use and should make the customer feel good about doing business with you.

Mercifully I had a file of catalog order forms. I spread fifteen or twenty on my big desk, chose six that looked relatively simple, and *stole smart*, picking up different elements from each one. In two hours—rather than two days—I had an order form. It was no world beater in creativity. But it was usable; all bases were touched; nothing was left out. It adhered to one of the universal rules of direct mail: Make it as easy as possible for the customer to order.

Only because of my giant swipe file was I able to meet Victor Kiam's impossible deadline. That order form lasted for several years and worked fine; Gaylord built for Kiam a growing and profitable catalog business that lasted for eight years.

Enter Harry Walsh

In the 70s and early 80s there were a few superstar direct mail writers: John Francis Tighe, Robert Haydon Jones, Linda Wells, Frank Johnson, the late Chris Stagg, the late Hank Burnett, Bill Jayme, and Harry Walsh.

Walsh, a gruff, red-haired, six-foot-tall alumnus of Ogilvy & Mather, lived and worked in Westport, Connecticut, just up the Merritt Parkway from my house in Stamford. Every now and again he would call me up to say he had got a new assignment and ask if he could look through my files to see what others had done. After finding what he wanted, and making photocopies, he would invariably offer payment, which I refused. "Okay," he said, "the next time I come down and use the files, I'll buy you lunch."

A month later Walsh and I were settling in for the first of several white ones at La Bretagne in Stamford when he said: "You know, I'd pay to be a member of your archive service so I could come down and use your library."

"If you were a paying member," I replied, "I'd have to send you regular information so you would know what was in there. And that sounds like a newsletter."

I came home and told Peggy I wanted to start a newsletter. She said that cash flow for a newsletter couldn't be any worse than that for a freelancer and immediately agreed.

I wrote a direct mail package for a nonexistent publication called *Who's Mailing What!* and sent out 10,000 pieces. We got 150 subscribers at $99 which brought in enough cash to do a 35,000 mailing and we were in business.

Today I have twenty to thirty correspondents across the country collecting direct mail and forwarding it to me via Federal Express. To create the newsletter, I personally read 4,000 to 5,000 pieces of direct mail a month in some 200 categories: consumer, business, fundraising, and catalogs. The library probably contains 10,000 individual samples. However, we don't save everything. When a duplicate mailing arrives, we note the prior dates received on the new envelope and toss out the old. Thus some envelopes with fifteen or more dates listed on them represent fifteen or more mailing packages. So while there are 10,000 actual pieces in the library, they may represent 40,000 mailings that have been received over ten or more years.

If the average cost of a package in the mail is $500 per thousand and if the average quantity of each mailing is 100,000 pieces, my library of samples representing 40,000 samples, the entire thing is worth some $2 billion in marketing information—money spent in testing and rolling out.

For a small fee, subscribers to *Who's Mailing What!* are automatically members of the library and can phone, fax, or write for copies of mailings so that they, too, can steal smart.

Enter Axel Andersson

Several years ago I met Axel Andersson, who has forgotten more about direct mail technique than I will ever know. Andersson, a Swede, moved to Germany after World War II and built the largest home-study business—writing courses and foreign languages—in Europe. After thirty years he sold out and moved to Florida, where he spends two hours a day walking the beach and the rest of the time studying direct mail and consulting for a roster of international clients.

Axel Andersson is one of the most totally focused men I have met.

Very little gets in the way of his thinking about business in general and direct mail in particular. For years his wife was always stopping him on the way out the door to tell him that his necktie did not go with his shirt and to go put on a different tie. It began to irk him so he came up with a unique solution: whenever he had a shirt made to order, he had a necktie made to match. As a result, Axel is easy to spot at a conference: medium height with a shock of wavy gray hair, a round, cherubic face, with a Terry-Thomas gap between his two front teeth, and his signature outfit of a shirt with necktie of matching material. "Just one problem," Axel says. "Every time I spill on a necktie, I've ruined my shirt!"

Happiness to Axel Andersson is to spend a weekend at the Stamford Marriott where, waiting for him, will be five giant cartons of direct mail purged from my files—the hundreds of dupes and purges that I would have ordinarily thrown away. The routine is invariable. He comes to Stamford on Friday night and we have dinner. Saturday he rises before dawn and spends the entire day in his room reading mail. By Sunday morning he has winnowed the five cartons down to two of material he wants sent to him in Florida for further study. On Sunday morning I load the two cartons and Axel into the car, and he spends the entire day—including lunch and dinner—either going through my library of samples or talking direct mail, or both.

Early in our relationship we struck a deal whereby he would pay me a yearly stipend plus shipping charges for all my discarded mail. So every week we bundle up two or three cartons of mail and ship it via UPS to Axel in Florida.

Whereas my library has mailings cataloged by category and then alphabetically by mailer within each category, Axel files everything by direct mail applications: offers, formats, involvement techniques, sweepstakes, etc. Axel's library is probably larger than mine by now, and he is currently negotiating to buy the house next door to house his massive collection.

The Million-Dollar Mailings

Early in 1991 Axel called. "Why don't you give awards for mailings that are true controls . . . mailings that I keep seeing over and over again?"

It was a brilliant idea.

After all, what is the only true measure of success for a direct mail package?

Efficiency and longevity.

If the same mailing continues to garner responses at the most efficient cost-per-order (CPO), cost-per-paid-order (CPPO), or cost-per-inquiry (CPI) year after year—beating back test after test against it—it is, ipso facto, a masterpiece of this advertising genre.

I started unearthing mailing efforts from my files that had been received over a period of three or more consecutive calendar years—some going back to the early 1970s.

As I started to analyze what they had in common, I began to realize that Axel Andersson had started me on the road to groundbreaking research in the field of direct mail advertising.

These are the supreme examples of direct mail at its level of Million-Dollar Mailings—the Grand Controls—hugely successful efforts that have brought in hundreds of thousands of responses and tens of millions of dollars for the mailers over a period of *years*.

Methodology of Choosing the Winners

Catalogs

Catalogs represent approximately a quarter of my direct marketing library. But catalogs are constantly adding and deleting products and changing covers and formats. At first I assumed that no cataloger would be foolish enough to mail the same catalog three years running, so obviously there could be no catalog awards. It turned out that there was a catalog I had been receiving, and ordering from, for three consecutive years, Cinegraph Slides of Garden Grove, California. It is a masterpiece of inventiveness in that it takes an impossibly complex offer and makes it easy to understand and order.

Financial Services and Fundraisers

Two major categories are not included: financial services and fundraisers (charities, and political action committees, or PACs).

Financial services and fundraisers are direct marketing anomalies. When banks or American Express get an order, they send out a piece of plastic that turns into a cash cow; insurance companies send out a certificate saying that if you land in the hospital you will receive $30 a day, or if you die you will receive $10,000. Either way they fulfill nothing. I once asked Scott Schneider, managing director of First Direct in San Francisco, if a bank could afford $100 cost-per-order for a credit card customer. His one-word answer: "More."

Fundraisers send even less than banks and insurance companies; give to a charity or a PAC and all you get is a promise that most of your money will go for good works, immediately followed by an avalanche of requests for more money—all mailed at nonprofit rates. Because financial services, charities, and PACs operate under different arithmetic, they are not included.

Sweepstakes

With two exceptions, sweepstakes are not included. Virtually all sweeps efforts urge people to enter the sweeps—even if they don't buy the product. Arithmetic has shown that the more nos you get, the more yeses (orders) you'll receive. For this reason, the incredible value of the prizes is hammered home along with the warning that you can't win if you don't enter . . . so, ENTER NOW! Many consumers believe that by ordering, they'll have a better chance at winning a prize, even though this isn't true for legitimate sweepstakes.

Since sweeps are always changing and tend to look alike, I don't analyze them very closely. However, Axel Andersson discovered a *Reader's Digest* sweepstakes package that had come into our various collections some thirty-five times over the course of three years. The outside envelope, entry-order form, and prize information were essentially the same in all of these packages; however, the product was different. The sweeps umbrella was used to sell different books. So under those guidelines, the mailings were different and did not qualify.

The Axel Andersson Awards

This left publishing, merchandise, plus some miscellaneous categories such as correspondence courses, business services and products, and associations.

That first year (1991) I found sixty-seven mailings that had been continuously mailed for three or more calendar years. Since the awards were Axel Andersson's idea, I decided to name them after him.

In the publishing area, the majority were books and magazines (as opposed to newsletters, which tend to be timely and crank out new or updated mailings in response to changing conditions in the world or the markets).

One qualifier did not win an award: a personal computer magazine was marketed via a tawdry sweepstakes for the entire life of the publication before going out of business in 1990. I spoke to the creator of this sweeps and he refused to cooperate because the magazine's demise was an embarrassment.

With the exception of this one judgment call, awards were given based strictly on longevity. Unlike all other awards—the Echos, the Caples, the Clios, the Maxis, the Oscars, the Emmys, the Obies, the Tonys—the only panel of judges or experts was the marketplace.

Since the first group of Axels was awarded for mailings that were received for the three consecutive years of 1988, 1989, and 1990, I have since gone through the library and found a number of additional mailings that qualify. Moreover, new mailings turned up that were first mailed from 1989 through 1992.

I tracked down the creators of these packages, and many of them have agreed to contribute their insights on their own works in particular and on direct mail in general.

The result is a collection of seventy-one Grand Controls that will be fascinating to seasoned professionals and newcomers alike.

A Final Caveat

If you were to take the seventy-one Grand Controls in this book and pin them up on a big wall . . . then do likewise with all the mailings that have won awards for "creativity" and "marketing" (for example, John Caples Awards, Echo Awards, Folio/MPA Awards) . . . and then compare what was on the two walls . . . you would quickly believe you were not only in two different industries, but in two different countries.

As I said earlier, the only judge in the Axel Andersson Award mailings is the marketplace. Many of these mailings are not pretty. If entered in an awards contest, one or two of them might send the judges running from the room clutching their throats and gagging. But they have *proved themselves successful over years.* They are responsible for millions of customers and tens of millions of dollars in revenues.

The way to benefit from this collection is to put aside preconceived ideas about what successful direct mail ought to look like. Instead, study them closely. Ask yourself: What do these Grand Controls have that has made them so successful over a period of years? Why have they beaten back test after test against them? What can I adapt from them to make my own mailings cost less and pull more?

Paul Bell, subscription marketing manager for Dow Jones & Company, said, "These are the workhorses. These are the mailings that are being cranked out at the lowest cost per thousand and bringing in customers at the lowest cost per order."

Or, in the immortal words of Ed McCabe, former president of BMG Direct Marketing, "Every time we get 'creative,' we lose money."

One final point. American direct mail is the very best in the world. No other country or continent can begin to compare with the United States in techniques and technology. This is not self-puffery. There is an overriding and obvious reason: with a population of 250 million, this country has a huge universe of names, all of whom speak the same language. This means American direct mailers are able to test, test, and test. In Europe or the Pacific Rim countries, big lists do not exist. There are privacy strictures. What would be a primitive test here is a full-blown, sophisticated mailing there.

So in the United States, when a mailing arrives month after month, year after year, it has obviously been tested and refined and is bringing in orders at the lowest possible cost.

The seventy-one Grand Controls in this book are the very best of American direct mail because they have proved themselves in the marketplace; they are the very best of the very best.

What's more, people are the same everywhere; we respond to fear, greed, sex, premiums, and low prices whether in Sioux City or Salzburg or Sorrento or Singapore or Sydney. The techniques and copy approaches in this book—when translated and massaged slightly—should work anywhere in the world people can be reached through the mail.

2

Why Direct Mail?

Direct mail . . . advertising mail . . . admail . . . promotional mail . . . is huge business.

Direct mail is the second largest advertising medium. More money is spent on direct mail (Approximately $25.6 billion) than on television . . . or magazine space . . . or radio. Only local newspapers received a larger share of the advertising pie (Approximately $27.9 billion). Last year, 63.7 billion pieces of Third Class mail found their way into mailboxes and corporate in-boxes, more than double the 26.3 billion pieces eleven years earlier. Nearly 92 million Americans, or 51.4% of the country's adult population bought goods or services by mail or phone last year, up from 64.4 million Americans five years before.

According to Arnold Fishman, president of Marketing Logistics of Lincolnshire, Illinois: In 1991, Americans spent $211.1 billion in mail order sales—up from the $200.7 billion the prior year. The breakdown is as follows: Consumer mail, $108 billion; Business Mail, $54.1 billion; Fund raising, $49 billion.

Many Americans depend on catalog shopping for many of their personal needs and gifts. Mail order shopping is especially vital to two-income families where both partners work and simply don't have time to shop.

There are several reasons why direct mail advertising is in the ascendancy and other media—with the exception of local newspapers—are on the decline.

Television

Twenty years ago a television advertiser had four choices: ABC, CBS, NBC, and a buy of independent stations. Today cable has dramatically disbursed the audience. Instead of four or five channels on the home screen, most Americans have a choice of forty or fifty. With forty channels to choose from, how can an advertiser reasonably expect to target a likely prospect?

Second, technology has hurt television advertising. With remote control and a "zapper," or mute button, viewers can silence commercials or flip around the dials when a commercial comes on. The screen within a screen enables viewers to keep an eye on the channel they are watching while they rove the dial during commercials; just as soon as the commercial is over on the screen within a screen, they can switch back.

Writing in *Direct*, Stan Rapp quotes University of Houston media studies professor Jib Fowles:

People scan the television in the way aborigines scan the horizon. They flip channels and never really watch anything. The advertisers know this and they are backing away. They want more targeted media.

Stan Rapp adds:

The waste involved in using mass media to reach ever-smaller markets is reaching truly extraordinary proportions. The cost of advertising paid for and never seen, or that is squandered on an audience that includes fewer than one out of ten real prospects is a recurring nightmare for ad managers.

Finally, the advent of the VCR enables viewers to tape programs and watch them at their convenience; commercials are skipped by running them fast-forward.

For these reasons, leading-edge, award-winning TV commercials seem more like extensions of the programs than the old hard-hitting (and very effective) pitches for laxatives, headache cures, and false teeth stickum. There's just one problem: they're so genteel and clever, they don't sell.

This is substantiated by a 1991 study by Video Storyboard Tests Inc. The study found that 64 percent of people polled in 1986 could cite a favorite television campaign without prompting; by 1991 that figure had dropped to 48 percent. Print advertising was far less effective; only 26 to 31 percent could remember a print campaign.

Telemarketing

The most demanding sound in the world is a ringing telephone. It must be answered or it will keep on ringing. To stop what you are doing—diapering the baby, boiling an egg, watching the news—to answer the phone, only to be hustled for magazine subscriptions, brokerage services, or tickets to the fireman's ball, is a severe irritant. Telemarketing makes enemies. Already Congress has passed laws forbidding the use of robot dialing machines and limiting 900 numbers. More legislation is coming.

Telemarketing scams are rampant. Sweet-talking con men and women set up shops in boiler rooms around the country and prey on gullible consumers who end up revealing their Visa and Mastercard numbers. No merchandise is delivered and the cards are charged several times—often up to and beyond their limit. By the time the scam is discovered, the boiler room has long since closed, and reopened under another name across town.

Magazines

Magazines are struggling. There are just too many of them. All are chasing the same readers and the same advertising dollars, and all are plagued with the same desperate fragmentation that the television industry is experiencing.

The Benefits of Direct Mail

Unlike television and space advertising and radio—which are shotgun media—direct mailers tote a rifle. They can go directly to suburban white families who have 3.7 children, have incomes of $50,000 or more, and drive Lexus cars . . . or any of hundreds of demographic, psychographic, geographic, or financial parameters.

What's more, it is a medium that is coldly logical and measurable within tenths and hundredths of a percent.

Department store mogul John Wanamaker once lamented that half of his advertising was wasted; the problem was, he did not know which half.

Because direct mail requires action—an order, an inquiry, or a donation to be returned by mail, phone, or fax—direct marketers know precisely which of their advertising dollars are effective and which are wasted.

At Its Best, Direct Mail Is Very, Very Good

People complain about the glut of catalogs. Yet the catalog enables any person, rural or urban, to have a complete shopping mall on the bookshelf.

Clothes, jewelry, electronics, furniture, shoes, books, magazines, credit cards, loans and second mortgages, records, gifts, fine art, kitchenware, gourmet food, garden items, camping equipment—the entire range of goods and services is as close to the person at home as the nearest telephone.

The use of an 800 number makes ordering not only convenient, but free. The use of a credit card means automatic charge privileges.

If a purchase is needed in a hurry, Federal Express can deliver it the next day. With reputable mail order merchants, returning merchandise is far easier than being hassled at a department store.

Think of it! You suddenly remember it's your mother's birthday tomorrow. From the "catalog mall on your shelf" you order the perfect gift by phone and know that it will be beautifully wrapped, and delivered by Federal Express amid panache and excitement on the Big Day. Order flowers from Calyx & Corolla and they'll not only get to mom the next day, but also last seven to ten days longer than flowers from the local florist because they come directly from the grower. Instead of being the forgetful and ungrateful child, you are, once again, the apple of her eye. All thanks to direct mail.

Catalog copy is far more informative than the average store clerk (referred to by Poss Pregoff, formerly of Charles Schwab & Co., as a "B-DOT" or "brain-dead order taker").

How dumb are store clerks? Shortly after the death of pianist Vladimir Horowitz, I went into the Sam Goody record store in the Stamford, Connecticut, mall looking for an audiocassette of Horowitz's highly touted final recording. I spoke with a tall, blond, effete-looking young clerk who remarked that I was the third or fourth person who had asked for it that day. "Tell me," he said, "is Horowitz his first or his last name?"

In a 1989 survey of 2,500 adults, Yankelovich Clancy Shulman, market researchers in Westport, Connecticut, found that 66 percent of people who like to shop for clothes found the experience both frustrating and time consuming.

On the other hand, stay home and order by mail and you save time, gasoline, and parking expense. No gook from the exhaust pipe of your car is sullying the ozone. It's good for the environment; it's good for the psyche; it's good for family togetherness.

This is just as true in the business environment as it is for the average consumer.

People LIKE Direct Mail

Many people grouse about "junk mail." Yet they basically like it. People are lonely. Nobody likes to come home to an empty mailbox. If the mailbox is bare, you get a lurking sense in the pit of your stomach that something is very wrong: your mail carrier had a heart attack . . . the Postal Service has collapsed . . . your government has run out of money and can't pay the post office salaries . . . a bomb went off in the main post office. Direct mail is your only daily contact with the federal government; it is the consumer's private check that the system is still working.

Direct Mail Is Secret

Unlike broadcast or space advertising, which becomes public knowledge once the ad goes on the air or the publication hits the newsstands, direct mail is *unseen* by anyone except the sender and the reader. There is no way an outsider can know how many people will receive each mailing . . . or which list it went to.

Send out a wee 10,000 test into the Great Smoky Mountains or Scottsdale, Arizona, and two people will know the quantities: you and a postal clerk. As far as your competitor can tell, you are doing nothing (unless he has relatives around the country collecting and forwarding mail; even so, it's highly unlikely he'd hear about a 10,000 test).

Direct Mail Makes Things Happen

Because direct mail is secret, many organizations use it to influence public opinion with great success. For example, a number of fundraisers have built huge constituencies and communicate with them directly on a one-on-one basis. Recent examples: abortion rights and the Medicare catastrophe bill. Public opinion and Congress have done a flip-flop. Why? Because wheelbarrows full of petitions landed in congressmen's offices and had to be stacked in the hallways. These petitions were the result of fundraising mailings by such groups as National Abortion Rights Action League, Planned Parenthood, National Organization for Women, People for the American Way, National Committee to Preserve Social Security and Medicare, various armed forces and conservative retirees organizations. When he took office, Rep. Christopher Shays (R–Conn.) found *22,000 petitions from senior citizens in his own district* waiting for him on the subject of social security and Medicare.

Traditional media never see these mailings. They make for dull copy. No angry marchers . . . no confrontations at abortion clinics . . . no fiery speeches to an enraged mob. Instead, silently into mailboxes go messages that are read in the quiet of one's home. The readers of these messages take action. Public opinion is changed. Laws are changed. And the press and TV are baffled by unexplainable, fast-moving events.

At Its Worst, Direct Mail Is Very, Very Bad

We are seeing more and more scams: fake charities . . . old pyramid schemes from the 40s and 50s . . . multi-level-marketing schemes . . . instant credit . . . loans you never have to pay back . . . postcards urging you to call 900 numbers because you have won a free vacation and some other prize (which is not free at all because $6.95 a minute will be billed to your phone for the 900 call).

In a recessionary economy, these scam artists prey on those out of work and on fixed incomes, the old and infirm.

In the course of reading up to 5,000 mailings a month, I regularly come across thirty to fifty such fraudulent or near-fraudulent efforts. These are immediately dispatched to the postal inspectors who are doing their level best to combat crime in the mail. I have found the postal inspectors to be dedicated, hard working, and in many cases successful; however, their job is like kicking manure uphill with pointed boots.

The only way to stop scams in the mail is for list brokers to stop renting lists to scam artists, and for consumers to wise up and realize that if an offer sounds too good to be true, it is. Unfortunately, in both cases, greed is a more powerful incentive than common sense.

Why Use Direct Mail?

For a product or service to sell by mail, it must have one or more of these three elements: price . . . service . . . exclusivity.

If the price is lower than in retail stores, a person will buy by mail.

If the mailer offers terrific service, strong guarantees, easy returns policy, a customer will buy by mail.

If the product or service is not available from any other source, those who want it will buy by mail.

This is Universal Rule 1 of direct mail, and is inviolate.

Several years ago a man called asking for information about my newsletter. He said he was going to start a mail order business. We got to talking and he told me his plans. It seems he wanted to sell self-help and instructional videos by mail.

"Are they only available through you?" I asked.

"No, we're going to choose the best of the best and offer them in a catalog."

"At a discount?"

"No, these are really good videos, and people will pay full price for them."

"So then you'll inventory them and ship them out overnight."

"No, actually we plan to have the producers drop-ship the orders."

I told him that he had neither price nor service nor exclusivity going for him, and, in my opinion, he didn't have a mail order business.

He hung up.

I hope I saved him a lot of money.

What Guarantees a Successful Direct Mail Effort?

The late Ed Mayer used to teach that the success of direct mail was dependent upon the following: 40 percent lists, 40 percent offer, 20 percent creativity and presentation. In other words, under Mayer's formula, lists and offer were twice as important as the creative work.

Mayer thought of product and offer as the same. But they are different. The product (or service) is what is ultimately delivered. There can be any number of offers to sell it: different prices, premium with order and/ or premium with payment, sweepstakes umbrella, cash with order, credit card option, installment billing, etc.

My own formula is more stringent than Mayer's. For a mailing to be successful, three elements must be in place: product . . . offer . . . and lists.

Everything else (copy, design, format, paper stock), while important, is secondary to product, offer, and lists.

If any one of these three elements—product, offer, lists—is askew, the mailing will fail.

A farm equipment catalog mailed into the barrios of Los Angeles would bomb. An offer for Omaha Steaks or Godiva chocolates sent to Weight Watchers or subscribers of the newsletter *Cardiac Alert* would almost certainly not work.

This is Universal Rule 2 of direct mail and is inviolate.

Direct Mail and the Environment

Recently I did a call-in radio interview with a truly uppity talk-show host in Chicago. The woman kept up the pressure about junk mail and the environment and the destruction of trees. I did my best to talk about damage to the environment from cars polluting the atmosphere when people go to stores and about the fact that direct mailers advertise only to prospects who have shown relative interest in the same kinds of offers. I assured her that each piece of direct mail can cost from twenty-five cents to a dollar or more, and that unless mailers are very careful about going to the right lists with the right offer, they will be out of business in no time.

Finally, exasperated, she said, "I think people are sick of the waste—of getting a mailbox full of junk and having to throw it out!"

Equally exasperated, I asked: "Do you get the Sunday *Chicago Tribune?*"

She said she did.

I snarled: "Next Sunday, you go through the entire *Chicago Tribune*, page by page. Every time you come across an advertisement that is of no interest to you whatsoever, tear it out, crumple it into a ball, and throw it on the floor. Do this for every ad that you couldn't possibly be interested in—big and small: classifieds, fur coats, trucks, baby carriages, personals, books and records, appliances, real estate. Tear out everything that is of no use to you, ball it and throw it into the middle of the room. Then, while that three-foot-high pile of crumpled newspaper is still sitting there in the middle of your room, call me, and let's have a meaningful discussion about wasted advertising and the destruction of trees!"

The term *junk mail* was coined by the newspaper industry as a result of losing advertising revenue to direct mail. Over the years, to compete with direct mail, newspapers have been forced to slash rates for ROP advertising and for freestanding inserts by as much as 50 percent.

According to a story in *USA Today*, of 227 newspaper publishers, general managers, and advertising executives surveyed by media analyst Ken Berents of Alex Brown & Sons, 60 percent said the biggest competitive threat was advertising mail. Berents said that "advertisers are looking at ways to really target market, and newspapers are realizing it." Survey results indicated that cable television was a distant second, with 13 percent of the executives calling it a major threat.

As a result, many newspapers routinely run vicious editorials and columns about the evils of junk mail and what it does to landfills. Every time there are hearings about a new postal rate increase, the Newspaper Publishers' Association attends in force, urging that postal rates be raised sky high.

What are the facts? Direct mail is responsible for about 2 percent of all landfill waste. Newsprint, on the other hand, takes up 20 percent of landfills. If half the contents of newspapers is advertising, then 10 percent of all landfill rubbish is untargeted, wasted newspaper advertising. Versus 2 percent direct mail.

The battle between direct mailers and newspapers is an ugly one, and will be around for a long time to come.

Along with newspapers, many magazines and television programs decry junk mail, because it does to them what it does to newspapers: cuts into their advertising revenues. In 1990 Mike Riley of the *Time* magazine Washington bureau called to say he had just been assigned to do a big story on junk mail.

"Is it going to be a positive or a negative story on junk mail?" I asked.

"I don't know. I just started, and you are one of the first people I called."

"Well, it better be positive," I said. "Because Time Warner—with its magazines, books and videos—is one of the biggest junk mailers in the world and if you do a negative story, you're all going to look like a bunch of horses' asses."

When the November 26, 1990, cover story ran, in its letter from the editor, *Time* admitted to being one of the biggest direct mailers in the world, and the story itself did not have a negative spin.

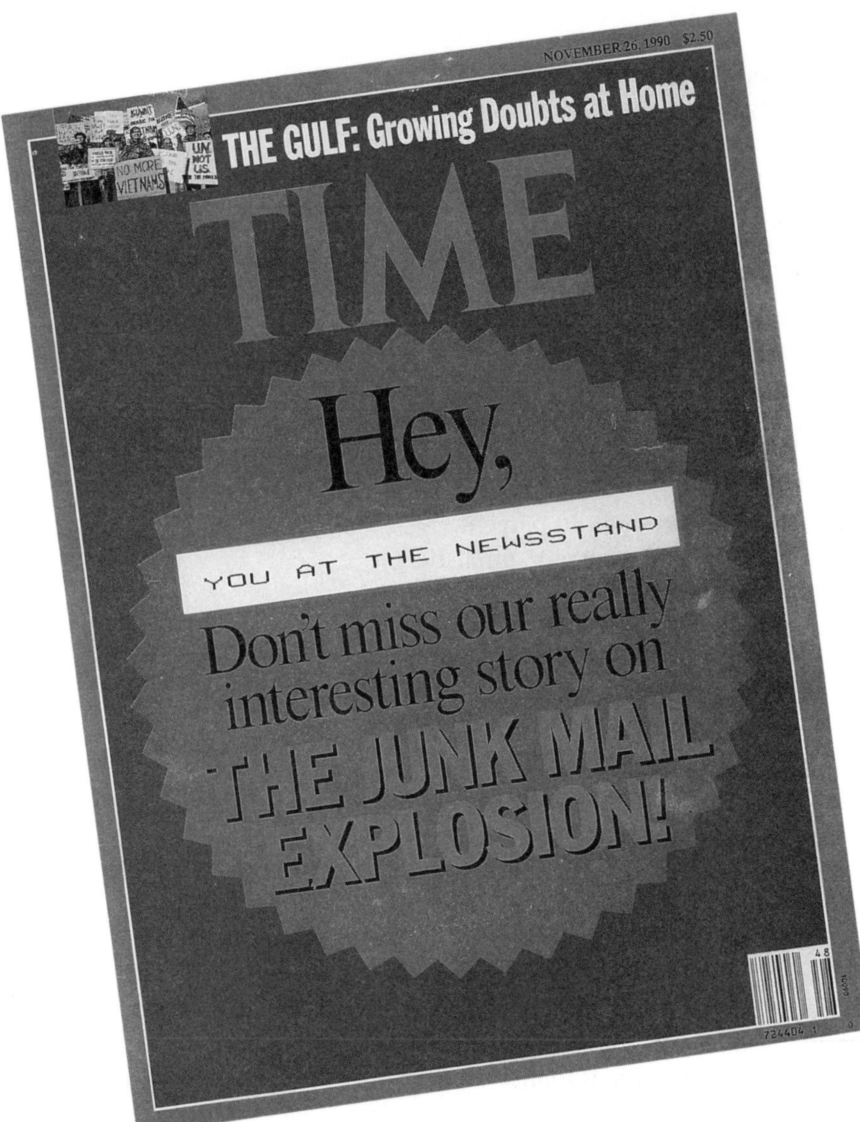

3

Direct Mail:

The Ultimate *Trompe l'Oeil*

One difference between a work of art and a work of advertising is that the artist hopes to sell the painting, whereas the advertiser hopes to sell the subject.

A direct mail package is the only truly participatory art form. You find the envelope in your mailbox and immediately have the option of participating or throwing it away. If you elect to read it, *you* make it happen. You open the envelope, and generally you will find several pieces inside: usually a typewritten letter, a printed illustrated circular or brochure, an order device, and a method for getting the order back to the sender—either a reply envelope or reply information printed on the back of the order card. You can savor each piece at your own pace.

Artistically, direct mail is (as it should be) extremely interruptive. It jerks the eye all over the place . . . highlighting benefits . . . showing the product in a number of different focuses. There is a rhythm to direct mail, a kind of beat you might find in Mondrian's *Broadway Boogie-Woogie* at New York's Museum of Modern Art; when you look at that painting, your eyes climb multicolored ladders, then skitter across to a splotch of red, slide down a bright column of squares, and land with a thump that leads you off in another direction.

The reason for this seeming clutter was best summed up by Lewis M. Smith, former creative director of Wunderman Worldwide and marketing director of Book-of-the-Month. Smith's simple three-word dictum:

"Neatness rejects involvement."

Think about that. If you walk into your office in the morning and your desk is absolutely clean, you'll sit back and have another cup of coffee and ponder the events of the coming day. If your desk is a wreck—piled high with unanswered letters and pink telephone slips—you can't help but start reading . . . foraging around . . . realizing that you have much to do. You are immediately involved. Clutter *invites* involvement.

The direct mail artist—the person who conceives, writes, and designs the work of direct mail—knows direct mail is an impulse sale. Once the envelope is in the prospect's hands, there are perhaps four seconds to grab attention.

Psychologists have discovered that all of us, when not otherwise engaged, walk around holding long conversations with ourselves. There are interruptions: a baby crying, a dog barking, the telephone ringing, the doorbell chiming, the kitchen timer dinging, a pile of direct mail.

Your mailing has to be startling enough to interrupt the day's normal routine and the person's self-conversation. What's more, it has to keep on interrupting until the order device is acted upon then and there. If the mailing is laid aside, chances are it won't be picked up and reconsidered, and the sale will be lost. Thus, if it is too neat—too noninterruptive—it will be rejected.

Not only is direct mail the only participatory art form in which the viewer savors, touches, considers, or rejects each piece at his or her own pace, it is the only one in which the artist can use a lot of words and pictures to tell the story. Unlike the novelist who must decide at the outset whether to use the first or third person and then stick to it, the direct mail artist has the luxury of using all three persons.

Walter Weintz, former circulation director of the *Reader's Digest*, used to say that there is "you" copy, "me" copy, and "it" copy. "You" copy talks about all the benefits to you: why you should buy or subscribe to this product because it will make you rich or beautiful or smart or live longer or whatever. "You" copy naturally falls into the format of the letter, a personal discussion between you (the prospect) and me (the writer). In the letter, you sell the *experience* of owning the product more than you sell the product itself; you talk benefits, not features.

Until recently, there was a basic rule that the letter in direct mail should always be in typewriter type. That's because letters between people are either handwritten or typed (never typeset, which is reserved for mass, not personal, communications) and because handwriting is difficult to read. However, the software company Parsons Technology uses a Times Roman font for the letters that are signed by company president Bob Parsons. When asked why he used Times Roman rather than the traditional typewriter type on letters, the then marketing director Stephen Sorb said categorically that font doesn't matter. "These are all computer people with five fonts on their printers. What's more, we did some research, and the people really believe the letters are written by Bob Parsons."

According to the great Canadian designer Ted Kikoler, a letter should look like a letter; printed formats might be the norm in ten years, but not now. (See Chapter 5 for Kikoler's graphic techniques that he guarantees will kick up a response to your mailings.)

"It" copy describes and shows "it," the product or service, and tends to be what goes into the circular. Here are the illustrations with copy and captions so thoroughly intertwined they are as one. This is akin to cubism, introduced in the early years of the century by Picasso, Gris, Léger, and Braque. It drove the art world somewhat crazy. But cubism wasn't a very complex idea. The artist simply depicted a nude or a still life or a violin from several angles in the same painting. The only way you could see that object in real life from all those angles would be for you to walk around it, which takes time. As a result, cubist paintings had a unique four dimensionality—the three basic dimensions plus time.

A direct mail circular is designed to do the same thing—to show the object from all possible angles, using "it" copy and art.

Some mailings have been tested with and without the circular. Sometimes those without the circular have proved more effective in both numbers of responses and bottom-line cost-per-order, which fact reaffirms the power of the word *you* and the effectiveness of "you" copy and the letter format. However, when mailings are tested with and without a letter, those with no letter almost always lose. Direct mail is a personal medium; letters are personal.

"Me" copy tells the prospect what this product or service has done for "me" . . . the endorsement . . . the testimonial . . . the publisher's letter . . . the words of praise from the user.

The direct mail artist, then, has at his command all the communication techniques that can be reproduced on the printed page—words in all parts of speech, plus illustrations (photographs, drawings, paintings, charts, tables, graphs—anything).

The result: a multifaceted package that assaults the prospect visually, that first and foremost interrupts and then at once charms, amuses, informs, excites, delights, intrigues, creates need, stimulates, and emotionally turns on the reader/viewer. Freelancer George Duncan has the best description for direct mail: "Theater in print!"

Every part of the package is designed to tell a piece of the story. No one thing should tell the whole story. Many practitioners believe that copy on one piece should never be repeated verbatim elsewhere; otherwise the prospect will say, "I've seen this before," and lay the thing down.

The entire effect of these various pieces should be to bring the focus of the prospect down to the most important single part of the package—the order device—which can use all three persons at once ("Reserve IT now" . . . "YOUR personal guarantee: if YOU decide at any time YOU are dissatisfied" . . . "Yes, please rush ME the item and bill ME at the low, low price of . . .").

The direct mail artist has made the product or service so real that the prospect not only believes it exists, but simply *must have it.* The more you study and sift through the various parts of the mailing, the more real the object for sale becomes. Ultimately all the verbiage, wild artistic jumble, and parts of speech melt into the background as this object or service shines forth like a hologram in the prospect's brain—three dimensional, touchable, perhaps even smellable. *You must have it!* (Or at least try it under the risk-free, money-back guarantee.) And so you go through the trouble of ordering it.

In direct mail, the artistry is all the more consummate if the product does not yet exist, such as a new magazine which is not yet published and which, in fact, won't ever be published unless enough people subscribe as a result of this mailing—known as a dry test—that has been executed for one purpose only: to convince the investors to put up the necessary dough.

This is why the direct mail package is the "ultimate *trompe l'oeil*"—that "fool-the-eye" style of painting that makes an object or a scene so real that you cannot tell it's a painting at all. And this is why the direct mail creative professional is a true artist. This is not airy-fairy artistic creativity. It was either David Ogilvy or designer David Wilkison who said: "If it doesn't sell, it's not creative."

The success or failure of this art form is precisely measured by response and cost-per-order. No writer-designer in any other field is as much under the gun to produce actual results. This isn't the business of creating warm, fuzzy feelings about a product that is shotgunned out to the millions in the vague hope that a few hundred thousand will remember it when they get to a store. There is no help from a supersalesman at the dealership or some strong in-store or point-of-purchase backup. No sweet-talking rep is going into an outlet to persuade the manager to put the product on the counter for an extra discount.

The direct mail package goes out with no help from anybody (except, one hopes, a canny list broker), and if the replies don't come back, the sender is out of business, and the artist is out on the street with him.

No other graphic art form in the world is as easily accessible . . . as literate . . . as powerful . . . as totally interruptive . . . as demanding of the viewer's time . . . as effective with its message . . . as direct mail—the ultimate *trompe l'oeil*!

4

The Direct Mail Package

by Malcolm Decker

The direct mail package—especially a full-dress package—is a sales team. First the envelope knocks on the door to see if anyone's home.

Then the major *letter*—the salesman—takes over. Once the envelope is opened, the letter is the most important member of the team. It sells soft or it sells hard. It spins yarns or it spouts facts. It's long (but never long-winded) or it's pithy. However it comes on, it's loaded with customer benefits . . . Customer Benefits . . . CUSTOMER BENEFITS.

Then the demonstrator—the *folder* or *brochure*—goes to work. Like the letter, it can stand on its own. But it's most effective when it demonstrates in graphics what the letter can only say in words. It should convince the reader in images that everything the letter said is true.

The *publisher's letter* (or *lift letter*) is yet another voice backing up the key salesman, the long letter; its job is to convince the waverer and salvage the skeptics. The *order card* restates the offer in the pithiest, most unambiguous language possible. And the *business reply envelope* brings the order home.

When each member of this sales team is performing at his or her best, it's a formidable force. Let's look at the individual elements.

The Envelope

An envelope with a white background is hard to beat. But that doesn't mean you shouldn't try to beat it, because if your envelope doesn't get opened, your package doesn't get read . . . or responded to . . . and we all know what *that* means.

We had great success in a gold stamp offer with a pair of metallic gold wings stretched across the face of the envelope below the caption: ". . . the most brilliant art ever created in gold." I thought we could do better, so we tested it against a jet black version, same gold wings, same caption in knockout white. It was absolutely stunning!

P.S. White won handily.

Envelope copy can help, but it's got to be a bull's-eye. It shouldn't promise or suggest more than the contents can deliver. The outer envelope sets the stage, or strikes the mood for what is to follow, and the copy and design must be "on target." Otherwise, there is a confusion element which could turn off your prospect.

Remember, your envelope stands between you and orders. More prospects see your envelopes than will *ever* see what's inside them. So make sure your envelope not only carries the message, but also does everything possible to set up the sale.

The Main Letter

The letter itself is the pen-and-ink embodiment of a salesperson who is speaking personally and directly to the prospect on a one-to-one basis. It is the most powerful and persuasive selling force in direct marketing once the product, price, and offer are set. The writer creates the salesman, usually from whole cloth, and you must be certain that this sales representative is truly representative of your product or service as well as of your company. He is likely to be the only "person" your market will ever meet—at least on the front end of the sale—so don't make him highbrow if your market is lowbrow and vice versa. Make sure he speaks your prospect's language. If he's a Tiffany salesman, he writes in one style; if he's a grapefruit or pecan farmer or a beef grower, he writes differently. ('Cause he talks diffrunt.) I develop as clear a profile of my prospect as the available research offers and then try to match it up with someone I know and "put him in a chair" across from me. Then I write to him more or less conversationally.

The salesperson in the letter is doing the job he obviously loves and is good at. He knows the product inside and out and is totally confident in and at ease with it and its values and benefits—even its inconsequential shortcomings—and wants to get his prospect in on a good thing. Here is someone with a sense of rhythm, timing, dramatic effect, and possibly even humor—gaining attention . . . piquing curiosity . . . holding interest . . . engaging rationality . . . anticipating and assuaging doubts . . . and ultimately winning the confidence (and the signature on the order) of the prospect.

This personal technique is seen most clearly in long letters. How long should a letter be? The best-known answer to that age-old question is: "As long as it has to be." That doesn't tell you much, but perhaps it suggests two important criteria: economy and—above all—efficiency.

As a sometime angler, I get a better sense of length by remembering a fishing trip to Maine when we used dry flies with barbless hooks. Unless you kept up the tension all the way to the net, you lost the trout. Try it. You should feel the same sort of tension when you write and when you read a letter. If not . . . reel in the slack.

Since the direct mail letter is the most highly personal, intimate form of commercial writing:

- It is *not* a monolithic corporation addressing a computer-generated market profile; it is *not* impersonal in tone, form, or content.
- It is *not* one or more pieces of $8^{1}/_{2}'' \times 11''$ paper with a letterhead on top and a signature on the bottom and the most cherished sales pitch of the VP Marketing sandwiched in between.
- It is *not* set in standard type, is *not* illustrated with photographs, is *not* printed in four-color process, does *not* have a bang-tail or envelope-pocket or other device attached.

A long letter—four pages and especially upward—needs a bit of help, even if you're an expert angler:

- It *can* have an "eyebrow" or "Johnson Box" above the salutation to tease, tantalize, or help the reader preview what's coming in the letter—especially if it's four or more pages.
- It *can* have handwritten notations in the margins, a scrawled P.S. or underlining for emphasis in a second color of the same hue and hand as the signature.
- It *can* be printed on two sides (as long as the stock is opaque). The color, weight, quality, and texture of your letter stock communicate too. Choose them very carefully. They're your salesman's clothes.
- Be sure the right person signs the letter. Recently two investors' newsletters—*Advance Planning Letter* and *Investors World Intelligence Report*—sent out long (12- and 16-page) highly technical promotional letters filled with forecasts and recommendations. The former was signed by Bobbie Bunch, Assistant to the Publisher; the latter was signed by Joan Pendergraft, Executive Assistant to Sid Pulitzer. *Obviously* neither wrote the letter, so believability is out the window.
- Don't overlook the color, size, and vitality of your signature. They're your salesman's handshake. Even people who aren't graphologists pick up a lot from the way a name is signed. It's interesting to compare the signature of Carolyn Davis [*Reader's Digest*] or Carol Wright with that of Salvador Dali or Gloria Vanderbilt. Then ask yourself why the former are so lackluster and the latter are so distinctive.
- The other signature that can work for you is your company name and logotype. Use them to tell your prospect what kind of a company you are: traditional, avant-garde, industrial, financial. Whatever your marketing stance, a good designer can help you express it, and that helps your reader identify you. The objective is individuation—to stand out in the increasingly competitive marketplace of the mailbox—so that when it comes time to toss the me-too mail, yours won't be part of it.
- The letter must be quickly scannable; that is, a reader should get the gist of the proposition simply by reading the (1) eyebrow, (2) lead paragraph, (3) crossheads, (4) wrap-up, (5) P.S. If not, send it back for surgery, because without a strongly integrated skeleton, the body of the argument will slump.
- The letter is easy on the eyes, open, inviting, and varying in its

"texture"—with normal margins . . . individual paragraphs with line space between . . . at least one crosshead or subhead per page (two per page for long letters) . . . occasional variation in paragraph width . . . a quotation, underlined sentence or phrase . . . numbers or bullets to list benefits . . . and/or other bits of "color" to maintain reader interest by promoting visual variety. The longer the letter, the more important these techniques.

The Lift Letter

If your prospect is sitting on the fence, a quick little shove could get him on your side. But be careful—because those already on your side will read it, too. It should be *another* voice, for example, not the person who signed the main letter, but David Ogilvy or Gloria Steinem or Norman Mailer or Madonna speaking very plainly to point up a benefit, reassure a fence-sitter, or disarm a naysayer. It should never introduce anything new; that's the top salesman's job.

The Brochure or Circular

The folder or brochure is "show-and-tell time." It should illustrate what the letter describes. Because it is impersonal, the voice should differ in tone and color from the letter: it is the company—not an individual—talking to the prospect. It shows and demonstrates—it *proves* that everything the very enthusiastic salesman said in the letter is true. Its job is to add visual dimension, and amplify certain points touched on lightly in the letter, thereby gaining further credibility for the offer.

The circular is frequently—but not necessarily—four-color. The pace is much different from that of the driving letter or the greased order card. The reader should be given as much time with this piece as needed or wanted. Although it must be carefully designed to unfold in the way you want to bring your prospect into the offer, he should be able to read every panel or page or spread independent of the others. Think of it as a smorgasbord rather than a seven-course sit-down dinner.

Every panel and spread and broadside of this major illustrated piece has its own particular function. You can't expect the deadfold to do the same job as the cover. Vitally important as the designer is, the organization of the piece—and the decisions of what panel or spread does what job—is still the primary responsibility of the writer.

I read books and articles and any kind of authoritative materials about my subject I can find until I feel comfortable—or, as Frost said, "easy in my harness." Then I take some $8\frac{1}{2}'' \times 11''$ bond (web presses all print multiples of this dimension) and make up as many dummies as I need until I finally "see" all the things I want to say in the right space and in the right relationships. I make notes of all the "pictures" and then I start my *letter.* When I'm through, I go back and write the brochure. I haven't thought about colors or white space or decorative borders or any of the innumerable things that make a brochure sing, but I do have a sturdy piece of architecture in the form of a thumbnail layout to give the designer—with copy that almost fits. The rest of it comes out of working together with the designer all the way down to the signed press sheet.

The Order Device

We give the order card more time and effort per square inch than any other piece in the package. And it's time well spent. It's the net that secures the trout, so it can't have any holes in it. Write it in conjunction with the people who do your order processing, telephone sales, white mail response, and customer service. Give them the final vote. It must be simple, clear, direct, and—if you can possibly imagine it—foolproof. Use the combined talents of your most clever people to write it, but make sure even a fool can understand it.

The order card should also *sell.* But basically it has a particular job to do: it should reprise the essence of the letter *in the reader's voice.* That is, the writer (salesperson) has had his say, and now the prospect (customer) responds.

The order card should contain absolutely nothing new; it should stand on its own feet and crystallize everything that's gone before it. Its purpose is to speed the action. If you're looking for maximum response, it's better to check off or call toll-free than fill in; better to tear off (no pencil required) than check off.

However, you must decide (by testing) whether the fastest order card in the West gives you the quality customer you require.

If you are offering payment by credit card, never use a business reply *card.* No one wants this highly personal and valuable information to go naked through the mails for strangers to see (and steal). Instead, enclose a reply envelope. An envelope also encourages cash.

Finally, it's important to remember that in direct mail, the *word* is king. Copy is the architect of the sale. Design and art are strongly supportive interior designers that often set up the sale.

Because lookers are shoppers while readers are buyers, if you can firmly engage your prospect—and *keep* him engaged—*through reading,* you're on your way to a sale.

5

Twenty-six Design Tips to Lift Response

by Ted Kikoler

1. The desktop publishing trap. If you have a "Mac" (or any other desktop publishing system) don't fall into the trap of making your letters "prettier." If you are using a typesetting font (such as Times, or worse, Helvetica)—instead of real typewriter (Courier or Prestige)—you are giving your letters the kiss of death. I can't stress this point enough. A typewriter-written letter will almost always beat one that's typeset. It's true that more people in business are now using prettier typefaces than typewriter, but it's not the accepted norm. At least not yet. Wait about five to ten years. Until then, give your letters a true typewriter look.

2. The danger of shouting. You tend to back away from people who shout at you. Advertising can easily make the mistake that it has to shout in order to be heard. Don't fall into that trap. Large lettering and lots of color in your direct mail package are perceived as shouting. Some of the best mail comes across like a one-on-one conversation—instead of shouting like a town crier. Try toning your graphics down to a whisper and you'll find it will bring the listener closer.

3. Everyone misses this. Examine ten direct mail packages and you'll see it in nine of them. It's the "feeling" that it's coming from a machine instead of a live human being. There's a total lack of human involvement. Sure, there's a letter from a person but the signature is printed. The reader's name is either a label or computer personalized. It appears as if the only human that ever touched it was the postman. The envelope is full of "printed" things—not things touched by real people. Everything looks too neat . . . too perfect. But if somehow you can give the readers the feeling that the letter was written by a real human, the order form was filled out by someone in the office, the components were folded and inserted by hand, you stand a greater chance of getting them to pay attention to your mailing, and thus lifting response.

4. *How to bring a dying control package back to life.* It doesn't matter how good our control is, it will eventually suffer fatigue and die. As soon as the recipient sees the envelope a second or third time he will recognize it and tune out. Instead of going for brand new copy and design, the first thing you should do is change the outer envelope. Keep the same teaser copy, but give it a new look. When that starts to wear out, take your entire package and give it a whole new look. You'd be surprised how long a control can be kept alive with simple cosmetic changes. That's because we have a harder time remembering what we have read than what we have seen.

5. *A simple personalization trick.* People cannot resist looking at their name. But be careful. Unless you're running a sweepstakes, don't overdo it. The best two places are the letter and the order form. But it can be costly. If you have to make a choice, personalize the order form. A simple trick that helps lift response is to repeat the person's name—or a part of the address—a second time somewhere on the order form. I guarantee this helps.

6. *A simple overlooked response builder: perceived quantity.* If you get an envelope in the mail with two-inch-high letters saying, "YOU ARE OUR $1,000,000,000 WINNER," you know there are millions of these in the mail. That makes yours worthless. On the other hand, if you get an envelope in the mail from your best friend, you know there's just one. That makes it valuable and so you read every word of it. Create the illusion of lower quantity of your mailing and your response will go up.

7. *Benefits of jolting the reader.* Sameness puts people to sleep, whereas a jolt keeps them alert. Jolt them by having as many components as economically feasible in your envelope. It's better to break messages into two or three smaller pieces of paper rather than saving money by crowding it all on one. Give each piece a separate theme such as: guarantee, free bonus, early bird bonus, testimonials, etc. In addition, it's important that every component in your envelope looks different—different size, shape, color, typeface, fold, etc. Yes, it can look like a three-ring circus, but it jolts the reader and that increases your response.

8. *An easy way to get the person to read the letter.* As your prospects open the envelope, they want to know what it's all about in as little time as possible. They make a beeline for the order form or brochure. But these two items spill the beans too fast. Instead, when you direct them to your sales letter first, you have a much better chance of getting the response you want. If you have a strong tease on the envelope—in both words and graphics—duplicate it in the identical manner at the top of your letter. Then, make sure that your letter is folded with the message facing out, and inserted so that the message faces toward

the back of the envelope. It should be the first thing they see when they open the envelope. If your envelope teaser copy did what it was supposed to do, your prospect will eagerly want to know more. As they open the envelope and see the same message, they will start there.

9. Which works best; being homely or cute? Being cute, clever, or showing off can kill response. A homely, even ugly, appearance will many times beat a flashy look. It appears more sincere. Regardless how good your response is from a flashy mailing, it will have a short life in the mail. The longest controls look very plain. With small changes, you can keep them alive for many years.

10. When graphics pay for themselves. Copy is the undisputed king at the creative end of direct mail. The longer you can keep a person *reading*, the higher your response will be. Graphics tend to distract the reader from the words on the page with a *"Hey, look at me"* effect. We all know that a picture is worth a thousand words. But that doesn't work in direct mail. You get higher response when you use graphics that force people to read rather than distract them. Try toning down the color and visuals—especially around large blocks of text.

11. The power of the keyhole view. A lot of people slice open an envelope and view it as looking through a keyhole. They peek inside without removing the contents. Take a look at your mailing this way and you may be surprised what you'll discover. You may find things that give the sales pitch away too soon, or you may see that some of your powerful items—such as a stamp or burst that says FREE—are hidden from view because of the fold. Simply reposition these things to improve the "keyhole view" and draw more people in.

12. Purposely hide part of the headline. It's important to direct and involve the reader, otherwise you lose him. A simple but powerful involvement and direction technique is to purposely hide part of a headline on a fold line, thus forcing the reader to unfold the piece of paper to see the whole message. Designers hate doing it because it looks off balance, but only by throwing your reader off balance do you get him to move. Believe me, it works.

13. Get the product into the reader's hands. This does not mean giving away an actual sample, but visually getting the product closer to the person. The closer the product seems, the more desirable it becomes. Do this by:

- Making photos and illustrations as large as possible.
- Cropping photos to show the essence. Cut away all the unnecessary material. Leave the part of the photo that still tells the whole story. The reader will automatically fill in the missing part of the product in his mind. This technique saves valuable space and can make unexciting photos appear more dynamic.
- Involving the reader in the picture. Have life-sized hands (that could be his) coming in from the sides of the page.
- Showing the product in actual use, if possible.

14. Make the reader's eyes go where you want them to go. His mind will follow. Here are some things that work:

- The eye normally goes from:
  —dark areas to light areas
  —large objects to small
  —bright areas to drab areas
- The eye zeroes in on things that are out of place (color, size, shape and position).
- Have photos and illustrations face the copy or be in the direction you want the reader to go. Every photo has direction.
- The further along in the sales pitch, the smaller the typesize can be. The more interested the reader gets, the easier it is to keep him with you. Therefore, the smaller the type can get. Have your largest type at the beginning for the headlines and lead-in paragraphs.
- Captions and call-outs get high readership.
- If everything looks alike, the reader can make the mistake that he's already seen one of your messages. Make each side of a two-sided piece look different.

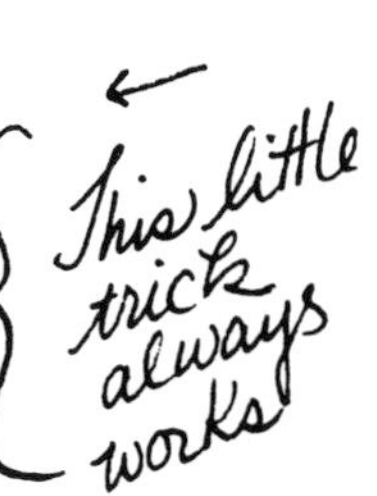
This little trick always works

15. Handwritten messages get noticed. It's an effective way of highlighting special thoughts or teasing a reader into a long letter. But don't overuse them.

16. Make things move. Don't let anything be static. This can be dangerous though. At the same time, too much movement on the page—or movement that takes the eye in the wrong direction—can hurt readability.

17. Break up large areas into smaller visual ones. These smaller chunks are easier to digest and add noticeability. Large, massive blocks of copy look like a lot of work to the reader. Make it easy for your prospect.

18. Make different sections look different. The reader gets bored easily. If he sees something with the same style throughout, it will look like a lot of reading to do—which means work.

19. Talk the reader's language. Use colors, typefaces, layouts, and overall appearances the reader can relate to.

20. Talk the product's language. Masculine products have to look masculine; female products must look feminine, etc.

21. Use serif typefaces for body copy. They're easier to read.

22. Avoid reverse copy—light letters on a darker background. It's much harder to read. But there are exceptions. Reverse headings are fine. Use them for body copy only if they are being knocked out of a photo to attain a larger image area and more dramatic effect.

23. Warm colors get a warm response; cold colors get a cold response. Use bright warm colors on order cards—red, for example.

24. Keep things simple. Make the eye move easily from information to information. Line up as many things as possible. This reduces eye strain and distraction.

25. Avoid a flat look. Try to create dimension. It will look less boring. Varying the weights of typefaces helps—light, medium, bold, and extra bold. Use screen tints for panels to hold copy blocks together and add dimension.

26. Make order cards stand out. If they are part of a larger sheet and must be torn off, either screen the entire area with a tint and leave the card white, or tint the card and leave the rest of the page white. Always add a heavy broken rule along the part where the tint and blank areas meet.

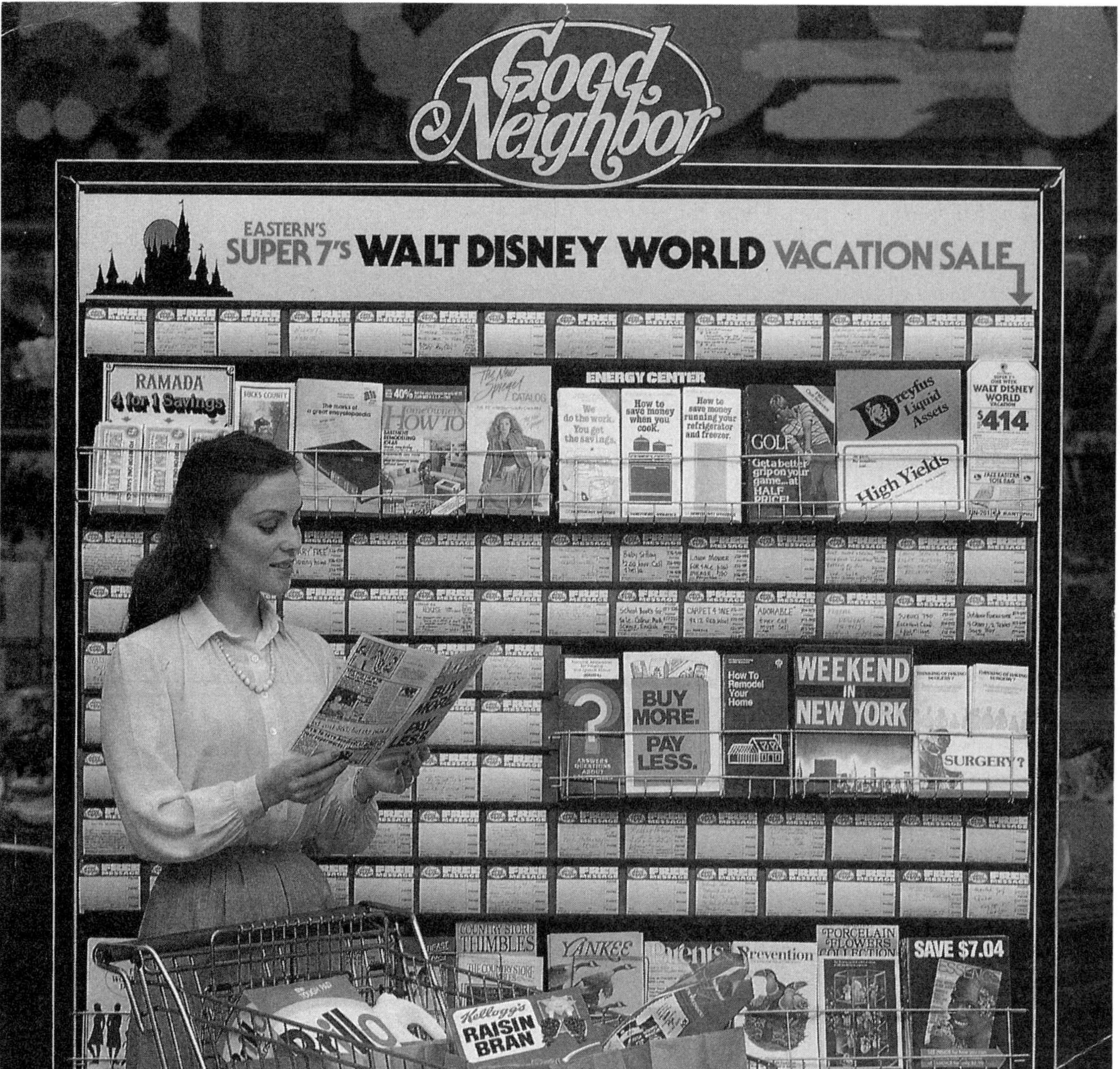
Good Neighbor
EASTERN'S SUPER 7's WALT DISNEY WORLD VACATION SALE
RAMADA 4 for 1 Savings
ENERGY CENTER
We do the work. You get the savings.
How to save money when you cook.
How to save money running your refrigerator and freezer.
GOLF Get a better grip on your game... at HALF PRICE!
Dreyfus Liquid Assets
High Yields
WALT DISNEY WORLD
$414
BUY MORE. PAY LESS.
How To Remodel Your Home
WEEKEND IN NEW YORK
SURGERY?
COUNTRY STORE THIMBLES
YANKEE
Prevention
PORCELAIN FLOWERS
SAVE $7.04
Kellogg's RAISIN BRAN

6

The Key to Successful Advertising: Interrupt and Keep on Interrupting

Most people do not think of supermarkets in the context of direct marketing. Supermarkets generally promote themselves via newspaper ads and freestanding inserts; the package goods crowd relies on couponing and in-store promotions to move its wares.

However, at your local supermarket may well be a "take-one" literature rack that goes to the heart of all advertising—mail, print, and broadcast.

These racks—supplied and stocked by Supermarket Communications Systems of Norwalk, Connecticut—are placed in more than 7,500 stores in thirty-five states and carry the wonderfully warm, fuzzy title, "Good Neighbor Information Center."

Good Neighbor Centers are always near the supermarket exit, taking up space that is outside the cash register area, and therefore not usable for merchandise. Along with flyers for magazines and home-study courses are public service pieces from the federal government, recipes from package food manufacturers, and a host of personal announcements offering everything from firewood and house-sitting services to used cars and cameras. It is a true community bulletin board.

The principle of the take-one is simple: most advertising is wasted. A direct mailer might be delirious with a 4 percent response—which means that a staggering 96 percent of the mailings were thrown away.

The supermarket literature rack prequalifies a prospect. Only people who are genuinely interested in that offer will stop with a cart full of groceries and pause to take a flyer from the rack. Instead of mailing out a hundred pieces in the hopes that four will be looked at, only those interested will take the piece, leaving the rest for the next interested person. The system is efficient and ecologically sound. Rodale Press, publisher of *Prevention* and *Organic Gardening* magazines, has been a long-time user of these supermarket take-one racks. According to Rodale's Larry Hill, the pay-up is not quite as good as direct mail and such subscribers renew at about the same rate as those who came in via package inserts.

Front of the Brain; Back of the Brain

As Sheldon Hearst, president of Supermarket Communications Systems, sees it, people going into a supermarket are thinking, for example, butter, eggs, milk, hamburger, and paper towels. This is what is going on in the front of the brain.

In the back of the brain may be a serious problem at home—a child who is a chronic bedwetter. The child is seven years old and has been given a clean bill of health by batteries of medical specialists and psychiatrists. Yet once or twice a week the child's pajamas and bed are wet in the morning. It is a nagging problem that causes the parents continual distress.

The shopper goes into the supermarket thinking butter, eggs, milk, hamburger, and paper towels . . . plucks the various items off the shelves . . . and goes through the checkout line.

On the way out of the store, the shopper glances up at the Good Neighbor Center and is stopped cold by this take-one flyer.

The headline—so big, so simple, and so directly targeted to her needs—can be seen from across a room. Its power intrudes itself instantly through the front of the brain (butter, eggs, milk, hamburger, and paper towels) and into the back of the brain (seven-year-old bedwetter). The shopper stops in her tracks, then takes one of the brochures, and goes home.

Here is the secret of successful advertising: interrupting what's going on in the front of a prospect's brain with headline and graphics that seize

upon a lurking fear or desire, and exploiting it. It interrupts and keeps on interrupting until action is taken.

Here, the advertiser is the Pacific International Center for Enuresis Control, one of Hearst's longest-term clients.

Many first-time advertisers in Hearst's Good Neighbor Centers believe they can get away with using an existing brochure. Not so. A direct mail piece must capture the prospect's attention within three or four seconds, whereas the supermarket take-one has maybe a millisecond to do its job, often at a great distance.

In the case of this piece, the headline—two words, each made up of just three letters of the alphabet, followed by a question mark—dominates everything around it. A sampling of other successful supermarket headlines:

> Learn Electronics—Microwave Recipes—Train to Be a Computer Technician—Make Money Preparing Tax Forms!—Home Career Opportunity: Full Time, Part Time—Gain Financial Security—Write Children's Books

Nothing clever here. Nothing cute. No humor. Nothing that you have to stop and think through and figure out. Just bold headlines and promises socked to the prospect in a very few words.

In some cases, a picture will accomplish the same thing. This take-one for *Organic Gardening* magazine shows the hands of a dirt-under-the-fingernails gardener holding three absolutely luscious, red, ripe, organically grown tomatoes shown full size. The photograph is a masterpiece.

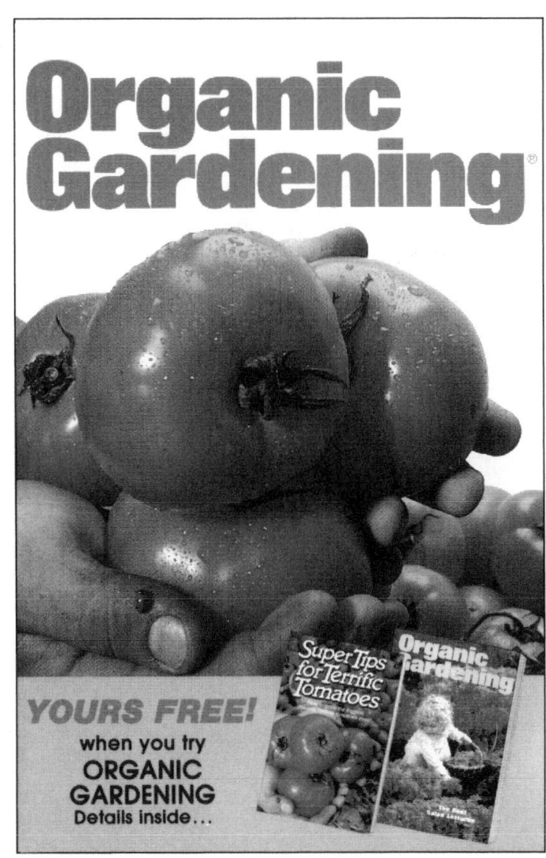

Notice the ladybug on the farmer's right thumb. I asked Rodale's Mike Sincavage how they got the ladybug to pose so nicely. "We put him in a deep freeze for a few minutes," Sincavage replied laconically. "That slowed him up a bit."

The piece is printed on coated stock, and the reproduction is spectacular. Along about January, when we've all had it with mealy, pale winter tomatoes, this photograph will jump right out and grab a serious gardener—or gourmet—by the collar.

Again, the message is direct, unclever, and powerful. Interruptive. Knifing through the front of the brain and getting to the back of the brain, where the things people really care about lurk.

Two Nearly Identical Headlines One a Success, One a bomb

The best example of a winner versus a loser I have ever seen in any medium is the comparison of these two take-ones with nearly identical headlines.

The Rodale offer shows an attractive woman on a scale. The piece is printed in four colors on coated stock and has six powerful promises:

1. LOSE WEIGHT
2. and keep it off!
3. Discover the *fastest* way!
4. FREE BOOK: Reveals the "Secret" of Thinness
5. The No Diet, No Willpower Way to Weight Loss
6. YOURS FREE!

The main promise, "LOSE WEIGHT," is huge, totally out of proportion to the piece itself, and for good reason: it can be seen from ten feet away. Any person whose clothes are too tight or who winced at the most recent reading of the bathroom scale will respond to these promises. This piece was successful for years.

Conversely, this take-one piece from New England Telephone was printed in blue and lavender. The headline makes no sense. In the millisecond a person glances up at the Good Neighbor Center, the benefits of Call Waiting, Call Forwarding, and Speed Dialing are not immediately obvious. This is smartypants stuff, the work of a copywriter trying to be clever. It was the worst bomb in the history of Sheldon Hearst's company.

"Lose wait on the phone" ranks with the 1991 membership drive for the St. Louis Zoo. The directors were sitting around a conference table trying to come up with a catchy slogan to attract members. "Join the Ark in the Park," one suggested. "Don't say Noah," another added.

"Don't say Noah! Join the Ark in the Park" became the theme for the year. It showed up everywhere from solicitation mailings to T-shirts. It was utter gibberish, and membership took a dive.

People's personal and business lives are hectic. They simply don't have the time to figure out what an imprecise copywriter is driving at.

The Prime Interrupter: The Envelope

Direct mail and the supermarket take-one are very much alike. To be successful, both must be so interruptive that they get read and acted upon.

It's amazing to me the number of direct mail professionals who are interested only in seeing what their immediate competition is up to. The fact is, everything in the mailbox—or in the executive's in-box—competes for attention with everything else. The day's mail is a bunch of noisy salesmen shouting for attention. Personal letters, dividend checks, bills, direct mail pieces, catalogs, favorite magazines, lined interoffice envelopes—all are screaming, "Open me! Open me first!"

Sending out a mailing is a crapshoot. There is no way of knowing in advance what kind of company your package will arrive in. If everything else in the box is dishwater dull, you might get opened first; if it is surrounded by powerhouses, you have a problem.

Two Theories

Florida freelancer Gary Halbert maintains that all of us, at home or at the office, have two piles of mail: the "A" pile and the "B" pile.

The "A" pile is the important stuff: letters from the kid in college, notes from the IRS, social security check, insurance premium notices, bills. This is the mail to be dealt with first. Everything else goes in the "B" pile and that can wait.

According to Halbert, if mailers can get their messages into the "A" pile, they will be read. To achieve that, Halbert insists, you must never use a window envelope. Instead, the name and address should be personally typed (or handwritten) on the front of a plain, closed-face (nonwindow) envelope. Always use a stamp (as opposed to a printed indicia). And never put promotional copy on the front of the envelope, because that signals junk mail, something that can be dealt with later.

In the opposite camp is the dean of American copywriters, West Coast freelancer Bill Jayme, who believes that it is wrong to trick a person into putting a promotional mailing into the "A" pile. Yes, it will get read first. But just as soon as the person realizes it is a pitch for a product or service, he or she will become quickly disgusted at the trickery and not only not order, but never want to hear from the mailer again.

"Never disguise the fact that it is advertising mail," Jayme has said. And then, with something less than his usual elegance, he added:

Your outer envelope is where your prospect decides whether to stop, look and listen. It's the come-on—the headline on the ad, the dust jacket on the book, the display window outside the store, the hot pants on the hooker.

According to Jayme, this holds true for the business arena as well. "Any competent secretary can recognize bulk mail. The secret to overcoming the 'secretary barrier' is to create an envelope that looks interesting."

Who's right: Halbert or Jayme?

Of more than 100 mailing packages analyzed for this book—mailings that have proved themselves successful over a period of years—*not one fits the Halbert model.*

Who's right: Halbert or Jayme?

The answer is found in the words of guru Dick Benson, words so often quoted by Malcolm Decker:

There are two rules—and two rules only—in direct marketing. Rule 1: Test everything. Rule 2: See Rule 1.

Part II:

THE GRAND CONTROLS

7

Double Postcards

> One day a man walked into a London agency and asked to see the boss. He had bought a country house and was about to open it as a hotel. Could the agency help him to get customers? He had $500 to spend. Not surprisingly, the head of the agency turned him over to the office boy, who happened to be the author of this book. I invested his money in penny postcards and mailed them to well-heeled people living in the neighborhood. Six weeks later the hotel opened to a full house. *I had tasted blood.*
>
> David Ogilvy, *Ogilvy on Advertising* (Crown, 1983)

The simplest mail format is the postcard. Most people who travel for business or for pleasure pick up local postcards and jot a short greeting to family and colleagues left behind. Other uses of the postcard: announcements or cancellations of meetings, follow-up reminders, recall notices from manufacturers.

Definition

According to the U.S. Postal Service's *Domestic Mail Manual*, a postcard may not be smaller than 3½″ × 5″ or larger than 4½″ × 6″.

To qualify for the special low first-class postage rate, one half the double postcard must be a reply device—either with a business reply face (where postage is paid by the person receiving it) or with a return address and the notation in the upper right corner "PLACE STAMP HERE." In the words of the *Domestic Mail Manual*:

The reply half on a double card must be used for reply purposes only. It must be used to convey a message to the original addressee of the double card or to send statements of account.

The reason the USPS gives the double postcard a break in the first-class postage rates is that it wants the reply half to be mailed back. In that way, the Postal Service collects postage twice on the same card.

Triple, quadruple, and larger postcards are mailable, but at the higher third-class rates or at full first-class postage.

Of the seventy-one original Axel Award-winning packages, six (roughly 9 percent) were postcard-size self-mailers. Four were $3^1/_2'' \times 5''$ double postcards; the fifth was a triple postcard from *Business Week*; the sixth was a $5^1/_2'' \times 8^1/_2''$ double postcard from *Lotus*. *Business Week* (a triple postcard) and *Lotus* (oversized) did not qualify to mail at the first-class double-postcard rate, and so were mailed third class or bulk rate.

Advantages

There are a number of reasons why double postcards are used by savvy direct marketers:

1. *Quick and cheap to produce.*

2. *Benefit of first-class mail.*
Until the recent postage rate increase, the base cost of mailing a double postcard *first class* was 15.0 cents. It was a steal, actually cheaper than basic third-class postage (16.7 cents).

The first-class double postcard gives all the benefits of first-class delivery (speed and address correction at no additional cost, plus perceived importance). The current basic rate of 19.0 cents is still cheaper than the third-class base rate of 19.8 cents; presort discounts can lower the cost of a double postcard to 15.2 cents.

3. *Easy to inventory.*
Since only one piece is involved, you don't have to inventory different elements (letters, circulars, outside envelopes, reply envelopes, order cards, etc.). They are entirely self-contained. When you inventory many different elements, even though you order uniform quantities from the printer, you are invariably left with varying amounts of stock. If a double postcard has proved itself a winner, you can save money by printing large quantities and draw down stocks as needed.

4. *Easy to mail.*
Because only one element is involved, the inserting process is eliminated; they are simply pulled from inventory, laser- or impact-addressed, bagged, and put into the mail stream. Because the format is so simple, you can get the cards into the mail far more quickly—*and cheaply*—than if you had different pieces printed in different plants, delivered separately to a lettershop, and then put through the complex inserting process.

5. *Easily personalized.*
It's possible to use handwriting fonts to make them seem personalized. In addition, they can be metered or stamped to give an even greater sense of personalization. For example, here are two personalized cards from Club Med to a prospective vacationer—part of a three-effort series. Two direct mail professionals—Shelly and Joan (Throckmorton) Satin—were totally fooled and spent much time trying to figure out who Kim and Richard were!

Dear Sheldon,

Richard's talking marriage! Not sure if it was the Caribbean night or this wonderful ship.

This morning we went snorkeling and windsurfing off the special sports platform on the back of the ship.

Tonight is our last night on board and the Captain's party. Can't wait to show you our pictures. See you soon.

Kim

P.S. I've asked them to send you a brochure.

Sheldon B. Satin
P.O. Box

THE CLUB MED 1—With a water sports and recreation platform that literally drops out of the back of the ship, Club Med 1 takes a marina with her wherever she sails. For sailing information and reservations call 1-800-CLUB MED.

Sheldon,

When we went ashore for an afternoon on St. Barths, I wanted to see the nude beach, but Kim wouldn't go for it.

So instead, we found a 4—star restaurant—Les Castelets—on top of the island's highest mountain and had a few sunset cocktails with duck liver appetizers in cherry sauce. May sound strange, but they were great!

Then back to the ship. A real beauty, isn't she? Will write again and tell you more about it.

Best to all...

Richard

Sheldon B. Satin
P.O. Box

THE CLUB MED 1—The world's largest yacht, with five masts and 617 feet in length. A shallow draft (only 16½ feet) gives the ship access to smaller harbors that are out-of-bounds to the larger cruise vessels. Sails the Caribbean October through May.

I use the term *personalized* to mean that the person's name and/or address and/or other intimate information appears more than once in the mailing. On double postcards, personalization is necessary; the name and address are printed on the addressing half (so it will reach its destination) and the reply half (so the mailer will know from whom the order came). On typical third-class mail, the name and address are printed on the order card, which shows through a window; the order card—or "turnaround document"—is then sent back in the reply envelope.

6. Takes color well.
All of these six postcard efforts used four-color process printing on one side. Two (*Architectural Digest* and *Islands*) used coated stock.

Disadvantage

Traditionally, the double postcard brings in a high up-front response and an abysmal conversion (pay-up). It's easy to order the free issue, and many do. But then they fail to pay. Carla Johnson, the capable and outspoken circulation director of *Architectural Digest*, is beginning to find the comp copy offer to be a disaster.

CARLA JOHNSON:
When the comp copy first came into being—and Architectural Digest *was one of the first to use it—conversions were somewhere around 50 percent. Today that's down to 30 to 40 percent, and declining. The public has gotten spoiled. Now a lot of people respond to offers just to get the comp copy and then cancel. In fact, two database companies have created lists of chronic comp copy cancels. I will be able to run this file against rented lists and use it as a suppress file which means my percent response will probably go down, but pay-up should improve dramatically.*

Because it invites tire kickers, the double postcard can be a dicey medium. You can never pronounce a postcard effort a success until you see the net pay-up, which can take six months or more. But the big numbers up front can enable a mailer to net out better than, or equal to, a full-dress package on a cost-per-paid-order basis.

Dealing with Poor Payments

To counter the poor payment syndrome, postcard mailers have to work harder at collecting—get the product and welcoming material into the customers' hands right away . . . put *sell* in each of the billing efforts that rekindle the original excitement.

Four Inviolable Rules

Since there is virtually no room for any in-depth, benefit-oriented sell copy, four inviolable rules must be followed if a double-postcard effort is to be successful. All six Axel winners slavishly adhere to these rules.

Rule 1: A Well-Known Product

Better Homes & Gardens, TV Guide, or *Time* could be sold via a double postcard. Why? Everybody in the country has seen one of these publications at least once—in a dentist's waiting room, at the home of a friend, in the library, or wherever. A long sales pitch might help . . . but it isn't really necessary, since the products are household words.

If the product is not well known, at least the subject should be. For example, as I recall, *Vermont* magazine was launched using a double postcard. How much explanatory copy was needed for *Vermont* magazine, especially when its primary market was Vermonters? The only description needed was: "It's all about Vermont; it has pictures; it has color. Try an issue Free!"

The same would be true for *Yachting, Boating, Wooden Boat, Yacht,* but only if they were offered to the *right lists.* This would also be true of *LAN Technology, Journal of Accountancy, Coin Prices.*

Rule 2: An Irresistible Offer

Three elements must be in place for a direct mail offer to work: (a) product, (b) offer, (c) lists.

If any of these three elements is askew, the mailing will fail, no matter how great the copy, how brilliant the design.

As is instantly apparent, all these double-postcard mailings are for products that are household names. The products are fixed.

The circulation directors know what lists have worked in the past and what new lists are worth testing.

This leaves the offer.

This is a montage of the reply devices of the six postcards. Notice that every one screams "free."

SELECT THE INTRODUCTORY OFFER THAT'S RIGHT FOR YOU!

☐ **6 ISSUES *FREE***
A FREE Trial Subscription.
Please enroll me as a trial subscriber for six issues. If I like the magazine, I will be able to extend my subscription later at the basic rate. To qualify for this free trial offer, I have signed and dated my request, and I have completed the questionnaire.
RRPA

☐ **18 ISSUES AND A *FREE* MACRO GUIDE**
A PREMIUM Subscription.
Yes, please send my free copy of **Macro Library 2.0** and bill me $18 for 18 issues – **just like getting six issues free!** (The basic rate is $18 for 12 issues.) If I'm not satisfied with *LOTUS*, I understand that I'll receive a full refund and that **Macro Library 2.0** is mine to keep.
ORPA2

Wm
P1
Fl 32606

1. Which software program(s) do you use?
☐ 1-2-3 ☐ Symphony

2. In which business or industry are you employed? (check one only)
A. ☐ Construction, mining, or natural resources
B. ☐ Manufacturing
C. ☐ Transportation, utilities, or communications
D. ☐ Wholesale or retail trade
E. ☐ Finance, insurance, or real estate
F. ☐ Business services
G. ☐ Professional or personal services
H. ☐ Government or military
J. ☐ Other

3. Approximately how many employees are in your company or organization?
A. ☐ fewer than 10 E. ☐ 500-999
B. ☐ 10-24 F. ☐ 1,000-4,999
C. ☐ 25-99 G. ☐ 5,000-9,999
D. ☐ 100-499 H. ☐ 10,000 or more

Signature (required for free offer) Date

- Please allow 4-6 weeks for delivery of your first issue.
- This offer is available only in the U.S.
- Basic subscription rate is $18 for 12 issues. Single copy price: $3.
- Lotus Publishing offers one trial subscription per reader. If you have already participated in the Free Introductory Program, and would like to renew – our PREMIUM Subscription offer is just right for you!
- This offer expires June 30, 1990.

A YANKEE FRUGAL OFF
Free Copy Reservation Form
YES! I ACCEPT YOUR OFFER
the next issue of Yankee ... PLUS a copy of *Yankee's Main Supper Cookbook* ... AND a copy of *Yankee's Great New En... off Cookbook*. If I like *Yankee*, I'll pay your invoice for $9.97 a... additional monthly issues (8 in all). If not delighted, I'll mark "... the invoice, return it, and owe nothing. The sample issue ... cookbooks are mine to keep ... FREE!

5021819791
Heide
5

ARCHITECTURAL DIGEST
FREE COPY/RESERVATION CARD
☑ YES! Please send my complimentary copy of *Architectural Digest* (retail value $5.00)–and enter my subscription. If I like it, my special price is just $19.95 for 8 issues (7 issues plus my complimentary copy). These same 8 issues would cost $40.00 on the newsstand. I save $20.05–over 50% off the newsstand price.

058258673
DJP49
NAME BARBA
ADDRESS
CITY NEW YORK STATE NY ZIP 10021

NO OBLIGATION
If I don't choose to subscribe, ...return your subscription ..."Cancel." The ...gift) will

...tion value is $29.95.
...for delivery of your first issue.
...D CARD TODAY

Inc. Free Copy Reservation Card
☐ **Yes!** I'd like to sample the next issue of Inc. I understand that I'll also rec... Inc.'s *Guide to Small Business Success*—FREE—just for trying Inc. If I like my fr... issue, I can subscribe at 47% off the cover price. I'll get a full year (12 issues i... Inc. for just $19—plus I'll also get my Inc. Soft Briefcase and my Inc. Execut... and Pencil Set—free with my paid subscription.
If I don't choose to subscribe, I'll return your subscription bill marked "... The free issue and *Guide to Small Business Success* will be mine to keep. Bu... nothing at all.

Name Ms. Peggy Title

902 03727582 OVEA2

TO RECEIVE YOUR FREE IS...

ISLANDS
Free Copy Reservation Card
☑ YES! Please send me my complimentary copy of ISLANDS (retail value $3.95) and enter my subscription. If I like it, my special price is just $15.97 for 6 elegant bimonthly issues (5 issues plus my complimentary copy). These same 6 issues would cost $23.70 on the newsstand. I save $7.73 – a whopping 33% off the newsstand price!

NO OBLIGATION
If I don't choose to subscribe, I'll return your subscription bill marked "Cancel." The free issue will be mine to keep, but I will owe nothi...

576 00444954 0CA68
State CT Zip 06851
...S POSTPAID CARD TODAY!

BusinessWeek
1221 Avenue of the Americas, New York, New York 10020

POTTSVILLE PA
BLK RT
U.S. POSTAGE
PAID
PERMIT NO. 1013

We have four free issues of Business Week reserved in your name. May we send them to you?

There's no obligation. Our offer lets you sample Business Week and gives you the opportunity to enjoy the magazine for upper management.

Mr. Mike
100 Rd.
Stamford, CT 06905

All six double postcards offer at least one free issue; some offer several.

In addition, *Architectural Digest, Lotus,* and *Yankee* offer free premiums (books) with order.

Inc. offers a book with order . . . *plus* a tote bag and an executive pen and pencil set when payment is received.

Business Week's deal: a solar calculator on payment.

Only *Islands* fails to offer a premium.

Rule 3: Easy to Order

A basic rule of direct marketing: Make it as easy as possible to order.

And double postcards do just that. All that's required is to tear the card in half and drop the reply portion in the mail.

However, careful study of the six postcard efforts shows that the creators have *not made it TOO EASY to order.*

For example, at the bottom of the montage is the reply half of Judy Weiss's double postcard for *Architectural Digest.*

Notice the line of copy at bottom left of this panel:

"To validate order, initial here ________."

It is important to note that all three postcards designed by Judy Weiss (*Architectural Digest, Inc.*, and *Business Week*) require the order to be validated, either by initialing where indicated, or, in the case of *Business Week* and *Inc.*, by checking the "yes" box.

There are two reasons:

1. Asking someone to check a box or initial a line (as opposed to simply tearing off the card and dropping it into the mail) may depress response slightly, but those who do order may be better qualified; if so, chances for conversion (payment) are better.
2. Since these postcards have been successful for so many continuous years, these offers have been *tested.*

Asking for Additional Information

The more information you can learn about your customer or subscriber, the better you can serve that person. As more and more information about purchases or renewals begins to accumulate in the so-called database, a profile of that customer emerges. Not only can you send out more targeted—and therefore more potentially profitable—offers, but you can also charge more for your list rental.

For example, on the reply card of the *Business Week* triple postcard, there is space to write in the name of the subscriber's company as well as a brief description of the product or service; the magazine also wants to know if the magazine is to be sent to a business or residence. With this information, McGraw-Hill (parent of *Business Week*) can offer various "selects" to marketers who want to rent its lists (for example, executives at home or executives in manufacturing companies at home). McGraw-Hill charges and additional $10 per thousand for such selects—tidy business for a quick additional stroke on a computer keyboard.

A Possible Glitch

In the December 1988 *Who's Mailing What!* we reported that a number of our subscribers suddenly began receiving unordered issues of *Magazine Week* and being billed for them.

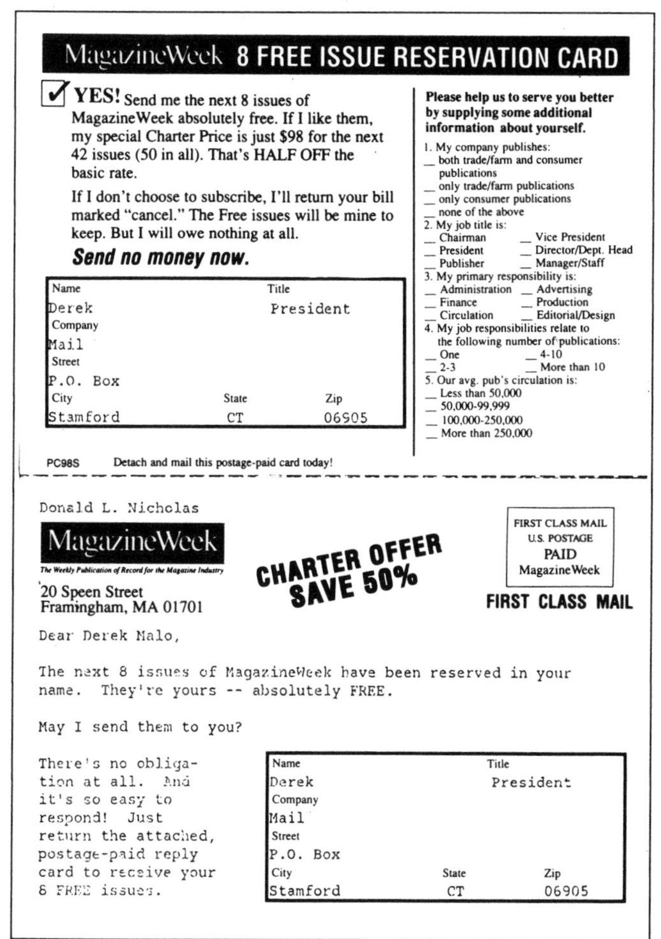

MagazineWeek 8 FREE ISSUE RESERVATION CARD

☑ **YES!** Send me the next 8 issues of MagazineWeek absolutely free. If I like them, my special Charter Price is just $98 for the next 42 issues (50 in all). That's HALF OFF the basic rate.

If I don't choose to subscribe, I'll return your bill marked "cancel." The Free issues will be mine to keep. But I will owe nothing at all.

Send no money now.

Name: Derek — Title: President
Company: Mail
Street: P.O. Box
City: Stamford — State: CT — Zip: 06905

Please help us to serve you better by supplying some additional information about yourself.

1. My company publishes:
 __ both trade/farm and consumer publications
 __ only trade/farm publications
 __ only consumer publications
 __ none of the above
2. My job title is:
 __ Chairman __ Vice President
 __ President __ Director/Dept. Head
 __ Publisher __ Manager/Staff
3. My primary responsibility is:
 __ Administration __ Advertising
 __ Finance __ Production
 __ Circulation __ Editorial/Design
4. My job responsibilities relate to the following number of publications:
 __ One __ 4-10
 __ 2-3 __ More than 10
5. Our avg. pub's circulation is:
 __ Less than 50,000
 __ 50,000-99,999
 __ 100,000-250,000
 __ More than 250,000

PC98S Detach and mail this postage-paid card today!

Donald L. Nicholas
MagazineWeek
The Weekly Publication of Record for the Magazine Industry
20 Speen Street
Framingham, MA 01701

CHARTER OFFER SAVE 50%

FIRST CLASS MAIL
U.S. POSTAGE
PAID
MagazineWeek

FIRST CLASS MAIL

Dear Derek Malo,

The next 8 issues of MagazineWeek have been reserved in your name. They're yours -- absolutely FREE.

May I send them to you?

There's no obligation at all. And it's so easy to respond! Just return the attached, postage-paid reply card to receive your 8 FREE issues.

Name: Derek — Title: President
Company: Mail
Street: P.O. Box
City: Stamford — State: CT — Zip: 06905

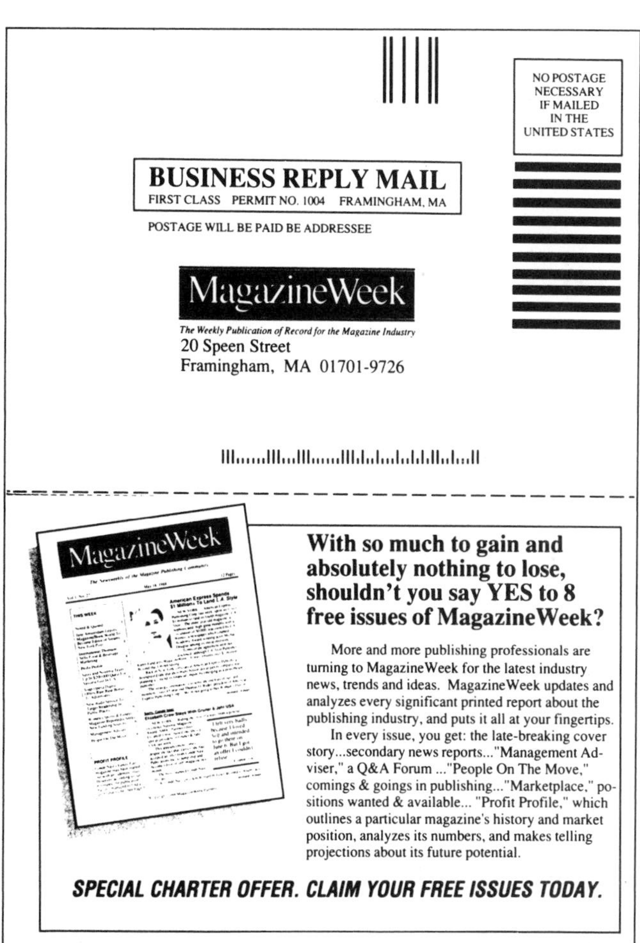

NO POSTAGE NECESSARY IF MAILED IN THE UNITED STATES

BUSINESS REPLY MAIL
FIRST CLASS PERMIT NO. 1004 FRAMINGHAM, MA

POSTAGE WILL BE PAID BE ADDRESSEE

MagazineWeek
The Weekly Publication of Record for the Magazine Industry
20 Speen Street
Framingham, MA 01701-9726

With so much to gain and absolutely nothing to lose, shouldn't you say YES to 8 free issues of MagazineWeek?

More and more publishing professionals are turning to MagazineWeek for the latest industry news, trends and ideas. MagazineWeek updates and analyzes every significant printed report about the publishing industry, and puts it all at your fingertips.

In every issue, you get: the late-breaking cover story...secondary news reports..."Management Adviser," a Q&A Forum ..."People On The Move," comings & goings in publishing..."Marketplace," positions wanted & available... "Profit Profile," which outlines a particular magazine's history and market position, analyzes its numbers, and makes telling projections about its future potential.

SPECIAL CHARTER OFFER. CLAIM YOUR FREE ISSUES TODAY.

According to publisher Don Nicholas, the double-postcard printer had scored the perforations too deeply and the reply cards separated in the mail. The addressing half went to the prospects while the Business Reply Cards came back to the publisher.

Even though there were five questions on the order card, subscriptions were entered in the names of all the cards that came back, whether or not the answer boxes were blank or checked.

The reason, according to publisher Nicholas: "We didn't want to delay sending the magazine to those people who really wanted it; so we filled all the orders that came back to us and figured it would all shake out in the end."

What shook out was a lot of ill will.

So there is a good reason to ask for some kind of validation, and if the reply half of a double postcard comes back blank, it could well pay to call and confirm the order.

Rule 4: Bill-Me Payment Option

All six double postcards offer a "bill-me" option. None gives a cash or credit card option.

The reason: Asking for a credit card number on a reply *card* means that the number is hanging out naked for all to see; not only does this invite credit card theft and fraud; it can depress response. When asking for cash or credit card payment, *always* ensure privacy by using a format that forces the respondent to use a reply envelope, either one that you supply or his own.

MAILER: *Architectural Digest*
PACKAGE: Double postcard
PROJECT MGR.: Carla Johnson
WRITER: Judith Hannah Weiss
DESIGNER: Theo Pappas
FIRST MAILED: Early 1980s

Fancy Labels

If you look at the label areas where the name and address appear, you will notice that four of the six cards (67 percent) have precisely delineated lines and spaces where the name and address should go. They even say: "Name . . . Address . . . City . . . State . . . Zip."

These are called "fancy labels." This fancy label technique has been shown to increase response, and should probably be tested.

The fancy label can be ordered two ways: imprinted on Cheshire computer forms (which are then addressed, cut apart on labeling machines, and affixed to the outside envelope) or printed on the card or envelope, whereupon the name and address are lasered directly on the face.

Variation of the Traditional Package

When all the old direct marketing rules dictate that long letters work better than short letters, that mailings without letters don't work, and that self-mailers don't work, how is it possible that the double-postcard format can be successful?

Direct mail has always relied heavily on the well-crafted letter, the personal communication that makes this medium what Stan Rapp has dubbed "intimate advertising."

In actuality, the double postcard should be looked upon as a miniaturized version of the standard direct mail package, traditionally made up of an outside envelope, letter, circular, order card, and reply envelope.

All of these elements are found in the double postcard, only combined or sharply truncated.

Here is the *Architectural Digest* double postcard opened full and shown front and back. Notice that the bottom panel of the front does double duty.

With the address and indicia, the bottom panel serves as the envelope or carrier through the mail.

It also contains an ever so brief personalized letter.

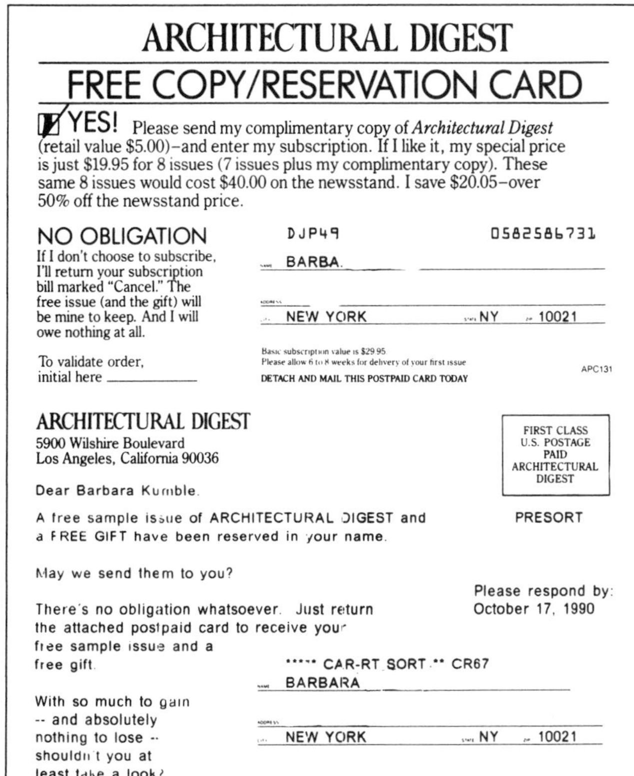

ARCHITECTURAL DIGEST

FREE COPY/RESERVATION CARD

YES! Please send my complimentary copy of *Architectural Digest* (retail value $5.00)–and enter my subscription. If I like it, my special price is just $19.95 for 8 issues (7 issues plus my complimentary copy). These same 8 issues would cost $40.00 on the newsstand. I save $20.05–over 50% off the newsstand price.

NO OBLIGATION

If I don't choose to subscribe, I'll return your subscription bill marked "Cancel." The free issue (and the gift) will be mine to keep. And I will owe nothing at all.

To validate order, initial here ________

DJP49 0582586731

BARBA.

NEW YORK NY 10021

Basic subscription value is $29.95
Please allow 6 to 8 weeks for delivery of your first issue

DETACH AND MAIL THIS POSTPAID CARD TODAY

APC131

ARCHITECTURAL DIGEST
5900 Wilshire Boulevard
Los Angeles, California 90036

FIRST CLASS
U.S. POSTAGE
PAID
ARCHITECTURAL
DIGEST

PRESORT

Dear Barbara Kumble.

A free sample issue of ARCHITECTURAL DIGEST and a FREE GIFT have been reserved in your name.

May we send them to you?

Please respond by: October 17, 1990

There's no obligation whatsoever. Just return the attached postpaid card to receive your free sample issue and a free gift.

***** CAR-RT SORT ** CR67
BARBARA
NEW YORK NY 10021

With so much to gain -- and absolutely nothing to lose -- shouldn't you at least take a look?

NO POSTAGE
NECESSARY
IF MAILED
IN THE
UNITED STATES

BUSINESS REPLY MAIL
FIRST CLASS MAIL PERMIT NO. 225 RED OAK, IA

POSTAGE WILL BE PAID BY ADDRESSEE

ARCHITECTURAL DIGEST
P.O. Box 7194
Red Oak, IA 51591-2194

ARCHITECTURAL DIGEST

PRIVATE LIVES

PRIVATE PLACES

Your invitation to visit some of the world's most beautiful homes...

Every month *Architectural Digest* takes you to the homes of stage and screen stars. Fashion and society leaders. Royalty. Heads of state. Every month *Architectural Digest* takes you to the homes the world's most respected designers have created for others–and for themselves. ...Plus your invitation to receive a sample issue–and a great free gift.

To sample our next issue free, just return the attached postpaid card. Whether or not you choose to subscribe, you'll also receive a free copy of *Private Lives, Private Places* where you'll visit the homes of very famous people. People like Johnny Carson, Julio Iglesias, Liza Minnelli and many more. But quantities are limited, so let us hear from you now.

Although unsigned, it is a little note with a personalized salutation stating the offer in a conversational way.

The top panel is the order device, to be initialed, torn off, and dropped into the nearest mailbox.

Thus, these two panels contain three of the five elements of a standard package: carrier, mini-letter, and reply device.

On the reverse are the two other standard elements of a direct mail effort.

The bottom panel—which backs up to the addressing piece/letter—is the mini-circular. In Chapter 4, "The Direct Mail Package," Malcolm Decker calls the brochure or circular "the demonstrator," that member of the sales team who holds up the product and points out that everything the main salesperson (the letter) says is really true. This mini-circular shows and describes the product and premium in full color.

The top panel, backing on the order device, is the requisite business reply card.

So, contained in this simple four-panel format are the five basic elements of a traditional direct mail package.

Possible Price Point

In these six efforts, the highest price is $24.95. This indicates that in circulation mailings, $25.00 might represent a tested price point in the double-postcard format.

Inc., Architectural Digest, and *Business Week*

Of the original sixty-six Axel Award long-term control mailings, freelancer Judy Weiss was responsible for four of them, more than any other writer. With one of the most inventive and marketing-savvy minds in the business. Weiss is in her ninth year as a freelancer. Previously she was creative supervisor at Grey Direct and spent four years on the staff at Time Inc. Her clients include Condé Nast, Time Warner, Hearst Magazines, *Business Week*, *Forbes*, Fairchild Publications, Consumers Union, and Hachette. She works only for magazines—new-subscriber efforts as well as renewal series, and consulting.

JUDY WEISS:
I don't have any standardized approach to creating a double postcard. I create a double postcard as meticulously as I do a letter. I choose every word precisely, and I am very harsh on myself. I don't care whether it's a double postcard or a letter or anything else, I work until I get it right. What I think pushes my double postcards over the edge is my absolute insistence on getting the strategy, the tone, the rhythm, and every single word right. The less copy there is on the piece, the more important each word is. This holds true for double postcards and for order forms.

Inc.

Here's an offer that piles on the benefits: free issue plus free *Guide to Small Business Success* just for sending in the card. If you decide to sign on as a subscriber and pay the invoice, you receive a free soft briefcase and an executive pen and pencil set, also free.

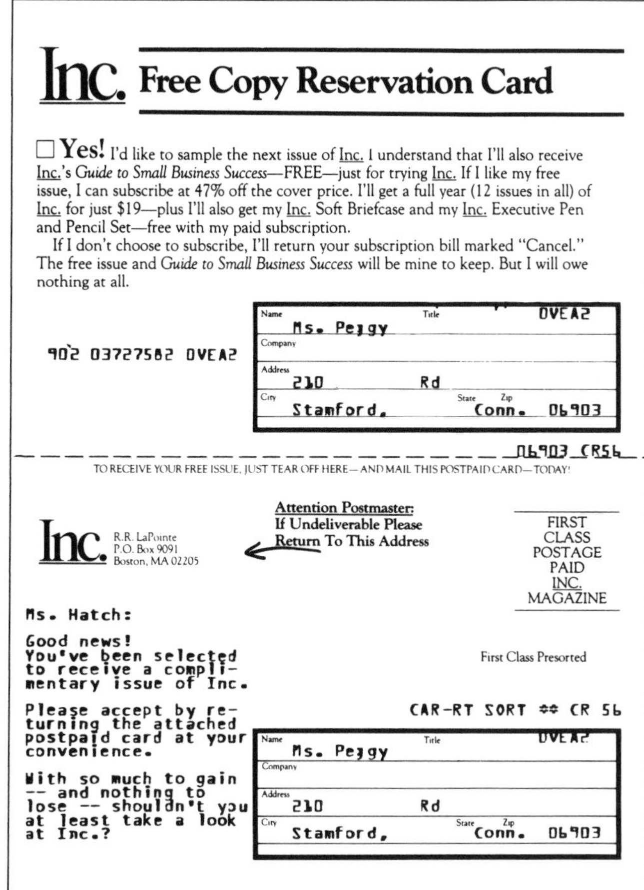

Inc. Free Copy Reservation Card

☐ Yes! I'd like to sample the next issue of Inc. I understand that I'll also receive Inc.'s *Guide to Small Business Success*—FREE—just for trying Inc. If I like my free issue, I can subscribe at 47% off the cover price. I'll get a full year (12 issues in all) of Inc. for just $19—plus I'll also get my Inc. Soft Briefcase and my Inc. Executive Pen and Pencil Set—free with my paid subscription.

If I don't choose to subscribe, I'll return your subscription bill marked "Cancel." The free issue and *Guide to Small Business Success* will be mine to keep. But I will owe nothing at all.

902 03727582 DVEA2

Name Ms. Peggy Title DVEA2
Company
Address 210 Rd
City Stamford, State Conn. Zip 06903

06903 CR56

TO RECEIVE YOUR FREE ISSUE, JUST TEAR OFF HERE—AND MAIL THIS POSTPAID CARD—TODAY!

Inc. R.R. LaPointe
P.O. Box 9091
Boston, MA 02205

Attention Postmaster:
If Undeliverable Please
Return To This Address

FIRST CLASS POSTAGE PAID INC. MAGAZINE

First Class Presorted

Ms. Hatch:

Good news!
You've been selected to receive a complimentary issue of Inc.

Please accept by returning the attached postpaid card at your convenience.

With so much to gain -- and nothing to lose -- shouldn't you at least take a look at Inc.?

CAR-RT SORT ** CR 56

Name Ms. Peggy Title DVEA2
Company
Address 210 Rd
City Stamford, State Conn. Zip 06903

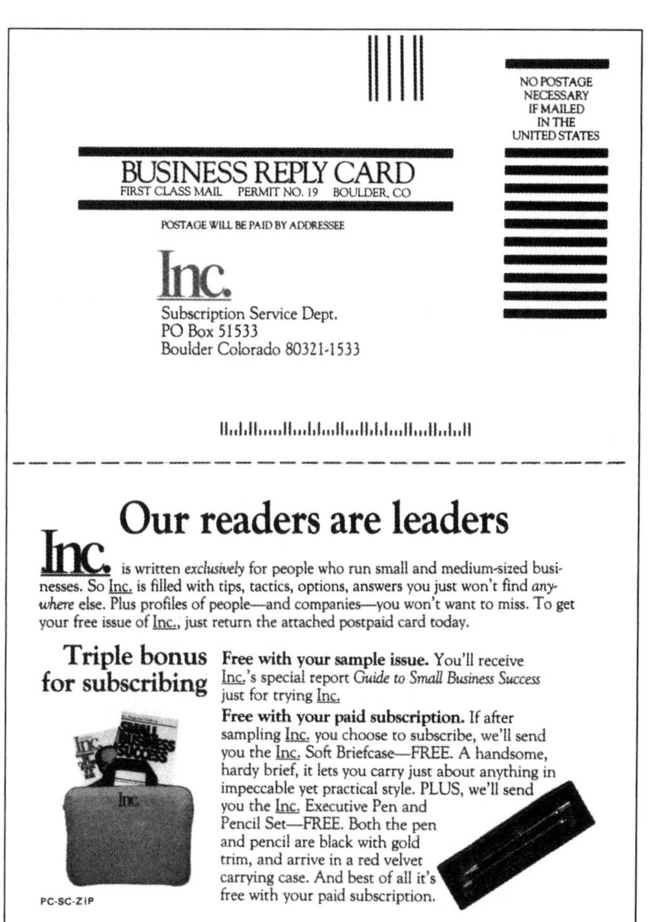

NO POSTAGE NECESSARY IF MAILED IN THE UNITED STATES

BUSINESS REPLY CARD
FIRST CLASS MAIL PERMIT NO. 19 BOULDER, CO

POSTAGE WILL BE PAID BY ADDRESSEE

Inc.
Subscription Service Dept.
PO Box 51533
Boulder Colorado 80321-1533

Our readers are leaders

Inc. is written *exclusively* for people who run small and medium-sized businesses. So Inc. is filled with tips, tactics, options, answers you just won't find *anywhere* else. Plus profiles of people—and companies—you won't want to miss. To get your free issue of Inc., just return the attached postpaid card today.

Triple bonus for subscribing

Free with your sample issue. You'll receive Inc.'s special report *Guide to Small Business Success* just for trying Inc.

Free with your paid subscription. If after sampling Inc. you choose to subscribe, we'll send you the Inc. Soft Briefcase—FREE. A handsome, hardy brief, it lets you carry just about anything in impeccable yet practical style. PLUS, we'll send you the Inc. Executive Pen and Pencil Set—FREE. Both the pen and pencil are black with gold trim, and arrive in a red velvet carrying case. And best of all it's free with your paid subscription.

PC-SC-ZIP

MAILER: *Inc.*
PACKAGE: Double postcard
PROJECT MGR.: Bob LaPointe
WRITER: *Inc.* Staff/Judy Weiss
DESIGNER: Judith Hannah Weiss
FIRST MAILED: 1987

Business Week

The triple postcard allows a bit more for copy and design. For example, Judy Weiss and designer Theo Pappas devote an entire panel to illustrate three issues plus the calculator premium, a luxury not possible within the confines of a double postcard.

MAILER: *Business Week*
PACKAGE: Double postcard
PROJECT MGR.: Kathleen Gallagher
WRITER: Judith Hannah Weiss
DESIGNER: Theo Pappas
FIRST MAILED: 1985

FREE TRIAL RESERVATION CARD

☐ Send me four issues of Business Week—FREE! There is no cost, no obligation. If I like Business Week I can subscribe at 60% off the $2.00 cover price. I'll get 32 issues (including the four sample issues) for the low basic rate of only $24.95—that is only 78¢ an issue. Plus I'll get the Business Week Solar Calculator—free with my paid subscription.

MLD0014

No obligation. If I don't choose to subscribe, I'll simply return your subscription bill marked "Cancel." The free issues will be mine to keep. But I will owe nothing at all.

Mr.
100
Stamford, CT 06905

Your subscription to Business Week may be a tax deduction.

Please allow 4-6 weeks for delivery of your first issue.

IMPORTANT: To insure proper entry of your order, please complete information below.

Company Title

Product or Service ☐ Manufacturer ☐ Non-Manufacturer

Please send Business Week to my ☐ home address ☐ business address
This address is indicated ☐ above ☐ below

Street

City State Zip

BusinessWeek

BWD9PC

BIG PLUS. The Business Week Solar Calculator is your free gift with your paid subscription.

1221 Avenue of the Americas, New York, New York 10020

We have four free issues of Business Week reserved in your name. May we send them to you?

There's no obligation. Our offer lets you sample Business Week and gives you the opportunity to enjoy the magazine for upper management.

Mr. Mike
100 Rd.
Stamford, CT 06905

Subscribe to BusinessWeek with this Free Trial Offer

Business Week is written for people who don't have extra time. So it's precise. Concise. On-target. And so skillfully edited you can *use* and *choose* just what *you need to read.*

FOUR ISSUES FREE

You won't waste time with Business Week. And you won't waste money, either. Because with this special offer, you can *prove it to yourself* just how valuable Business Week is.

Just mail the postpaid card and you'll get *four free trial issues.* With no obligation. No commitment, whatsoever.

BIG PLUS

If, after sampling Business Week, you choose to subscribe, you'll receive a savings of 60% off the $2.00 cover price, and you'll also receive a great *FREE gift.* The Business Week Solar Calculator. It doesn't need batteries. It doesn't need cords. It just needs you to push the keys! And backed by a Life-Long Warranty.

THE UPPER MANAGEMENT MAGAZINE

More successful executives—more chairmen, presidents and top managers—read Business Week than any other business magazine. Join them today. And count yourself in on a really good deal.

See reverse side and mail postpaid card now.

BusinessWeek
Post Office Box 506
Hightstown, NJ 08520-9970

POSTAGE WILL BE PAID BY ADDRESSEE

BUSINESS REPLY MAIL
FIRST CLASS PERMIT NO 42 HIGHTSTOWN, NJ

NO POSTAGE NECESSARY IF MAILED IN THE UNITED STATES

Lotus

The double postcard for *Lotus*, written by magazine consultant John Klingel and designed by Boston art director Paul Baldassini, is a bit of a maverick.

For one thing, it is 5½″ × 8″ (vs. 4½″ or 5″ × 6″ for the others). Klingel also breaks an old rule of direct marketing: don't give too many choices; confuse 'em, ya lose 'em. Whereas the five other double-postcard efforts have a single offer, Klingel gives the choice of six issues free or eighteen issues with a premium with order (as opposed to premium for payment). In addition, he asks for the answers to three questions, which presumably will enhance the *Lotus* customer database, and requires a full signature.

From 1977 to 1990 John D. Klingel was a consultant to approximately 200 magazines in the areas of circulation, financial planning, direct marketing, and new-magazine development. Clients included Time Warner, National Trust for Historic Preservation, CBS, American Express, Scripps-Howard, and Colonial Williamsburg. He is currently vice president, development, for Time Publishing Ventures.

John D. Klingel:

I don't have much to say about how I work because I'm not a copywriter. Lotus *magazine, a consulting client, insisted on my writing their promotion because they wanted something that fit the Lotus Corporation image. Typical copy seemed too pushy to them. They also felt my writing style was more businesslike. So, I kept the important elements of a direct response piece, but toned down the extraneous copy.*

As a consultant, I was responsible for a number of direct response innovations, wrote and edited much order card copy, but did not see myself as a copywriter. Many people in direct response marketing write a lot of copy. In that respect, I've certainly done my share of copywriting.

Mailer: *Lotus*
Package: Double postcard
Project Mgr.: Elizabeth Folsom
Writer: John Klingel
Designer: Paul Baldassini
First Mailed: 1988

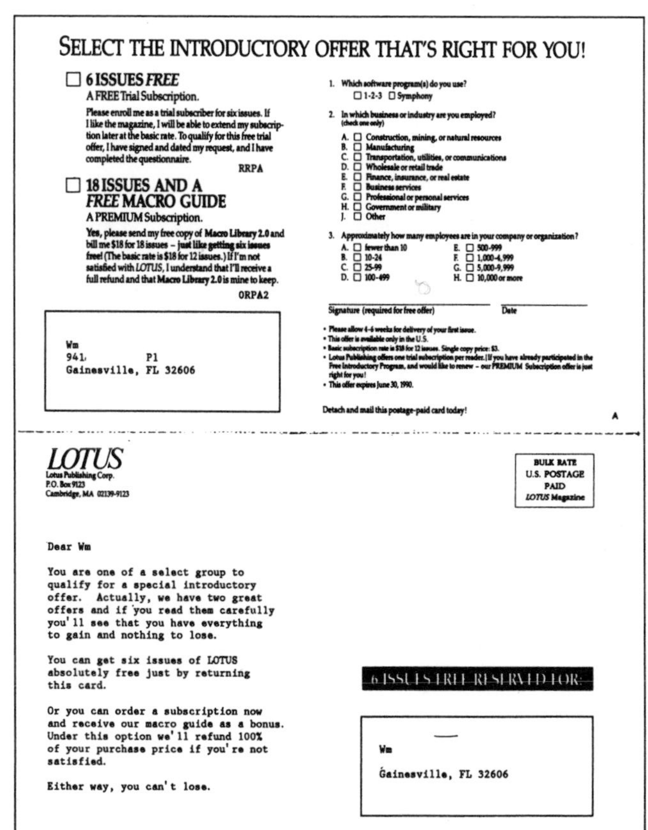

SELECT THE INTRODUCTORY OFFER THAT'S RIGHT FOR YOU!

☐ 6 ISSUES *FREE*
A FREE Trial Subscription.
Please enroll me as a trial subscriber for six issues. If I like the magazine, I will be able to extend my subscription later at the basic rate. To qualify for this free trial offer, I have signed and dated my request, and I have completed the questionnaire.
RRPA

☐ 18 ISSUES AND A *FREE* MACRO GUIDE
A PREMIUM Subscription.
Yes, please send my free copy of **Macro Library 2.0** and bill me $18 for 18 issues – **just like getting six issues free!** (The basic rate is $18 for 12 issues.) If I'm not satisfied with *LOTUS*, I understand that I'll receive a full refund and that **Macro Library 2.0** is mine to keep.
ORPA2

Wm
941 P1
Gainesville, FL 32606

1. Which software program(s) do you use?
☐ 1-2-3 ☐ Symphony

2. In which business or industry are you employed? (check one only)
A. ☐ Construction, mining, or natural resources
B. ☐ Manufacturing
C. ☐ Transportation, utilities, or communications
D. ☐ Wholesale or retail trade
E. ☐ Finance, insurance, or real estate
F. ☐ Business services
G. ☐ Professional or personal services
H. ☐ Government or military
J. ☐ Other

3. Approximately how many employees are in your company or organization?
A. ☐ fewer than 10
B. ☐ 10-24
C. ☐ 25-99
D. ☐ 100-499
E. ☐ 500-999
F. ☐ 1,000-4,999
G. ☐ 5,000-9,999
H. ☐ 10,000 or more

Signature (required for free offer) Date

- Please allow 4-6 weeks for delivery of your first issue.
- This offer is available only in the U.S.
- Basic subscription rate is $18 for 12 issues. Single copy price: $3.
- Lotus Publishing offers one trial subscription per reader. If you have already participated in the Free Introductory Program, and would like to renew – our PREMIUM Subscription offer is just right for you!
- This offer expires June 30, 1990.

Detach and mail this postage-paid card today!

A

LOTUS
Lotus Publishing Corp.
P.O. Box 9123
Cambridge, MA 02139-9123

BULK RATE
U.S. POSTAGE
PAID
LOTUS Magazine

Dear Wm

You are one of a select group to qualify for a special introductory offer. Actually, we have two great offers and if you read them carefully you'll see that you have everything to gain and nothing to lose.

You can get six issues of LOTUS absolutely free just by returning this card.

Or you can order a subscription now and receive our macro guide as a bonus. Under this option we'll refund 100% of your purchase price if you're not satisfied.

Either way, you can't lose.

6 ISSUES FREE RESERVED FOR:

Wm
Gainesville, FL 32606

DISCOVER THE MOST USEFUL, PRACTICAL AND RELIABLE COMPUTING MAGAZINE FOR BUSINESS MANAGERS AND PROFESSIONALS.

LOTUS enhances your ability to use spreadsheets and related products, and helps you get the most out of your computing system. Whether you're an expert, intermediate or novice, you'll get valuable tips, practical suggestions and useful information every month. *LOTUS* also keeps you up-to-date on new products and developments that make spreadsheets faster and more powerful. Its focus on applications makes *LOTUS* the only computing magazine for managers who have integrated technology into their jobs.

Plus you get a special bonus – *FREE*.

It's **Macro Library 2.0**, developed exclusively for *LOTUS* subscribers. Written by noted 1-2-3® author Douglas Cobb and *LOTUS'* macro expert Daniel Gasteiger, **Macro Library 2.0** provides macros and macro-writing instruction for both 1-2-3 and Symphony.® This valuable guide is yours *FREE* when you sign up for 18 issues of *LOTUS*.

1-2-3 and Symphony are registered trademarks of Lotus Development Corp.

Discover what *LOTUS* can do for you – at no risk!

NO POSTAGE NECESSARY IF MAILED IN THE UNITED STATES

BUSINESS REPLY MAIL
FIRST CLASS PERMIT NO. 1264 BOULDER, CO

POSTAGE WILL BE PAID BY ADDRESSEE

LOTUS
Subscription Department
P.O. Box 52349
Boulder, CO 80321-2349

Islands

Of the six postcard efforts, only one fails to show a picture of the product. Instead of a cover of *Islands* magazine, Houston freelancer Ken Schneider opted for a beauty shot of a deserted beach on an idyllic tropical island.

One small point: whereas Judy Weiss forces the respondent to check the yes box, Ken Schneider uses a preprinted checkmark.

Ken Schneider started freelancing in 1981. He began his career writing newspaper ads for the men's and boys' departments of Foleys in Houston and went on to work for McCann-Erickson, Houston; Weekly & Penny, Houston; Ogilvy & Mather, Houston; and The Richards Group, Dallas. His freelance clients have included *American Heritage, Art & Auction, Bon Appétit, Consumer Reports, European Travel & Life, Travel & Leisure, Lotus, PC World, Sail, Ski, Newsweek, Time, U.S. News & World Report, Southern Banker, Elle, Mirabella, Esquire,* Time-Life Books, and the *San Francisco Examiner.*

Ken Schneider:

I think my background . . . as a copywriter in a variety of ad agencies—working on a variety of clients—gave me an extremely strong foundation for working in direct mail as a freelancer. Here's why.

To me, each direct mail package is like a mini ad campaign, combining the disciplines of print, TV, even radio, and a bit of outdoors. The print part is obvious; it's the letter and the brochure copy. The TV aspect is the visual power of the outer envelope and brochure. The radio comes into play in the rhythm of the letter copy, and the images it conjures up in the reader's mind. And many times, the outer acts almost like an outdoor board in quickly grabbing attention in a clever way—with few words.

All put together, it becomes a very calculated piece of marketing that draws on everything I've learned about what motivates people to act.

The double postcard is, though, a bit of a different animal. And frankly, I don't much like using them. Long-time winners like Islands *are more the exception than the rule, I'd wager, even though many of the Axel winners were double postcards. Go figure. We tested two versions: only the four-color back panel changed.*

One version had lots of copy and showed two covers. The other, the winner, featured a color photo of a remote island beach, with very little copy. It was the double-postcard concept doing what postcards normally do so well—evoke a sense of place and escape, perfect for a magazine like Islands.

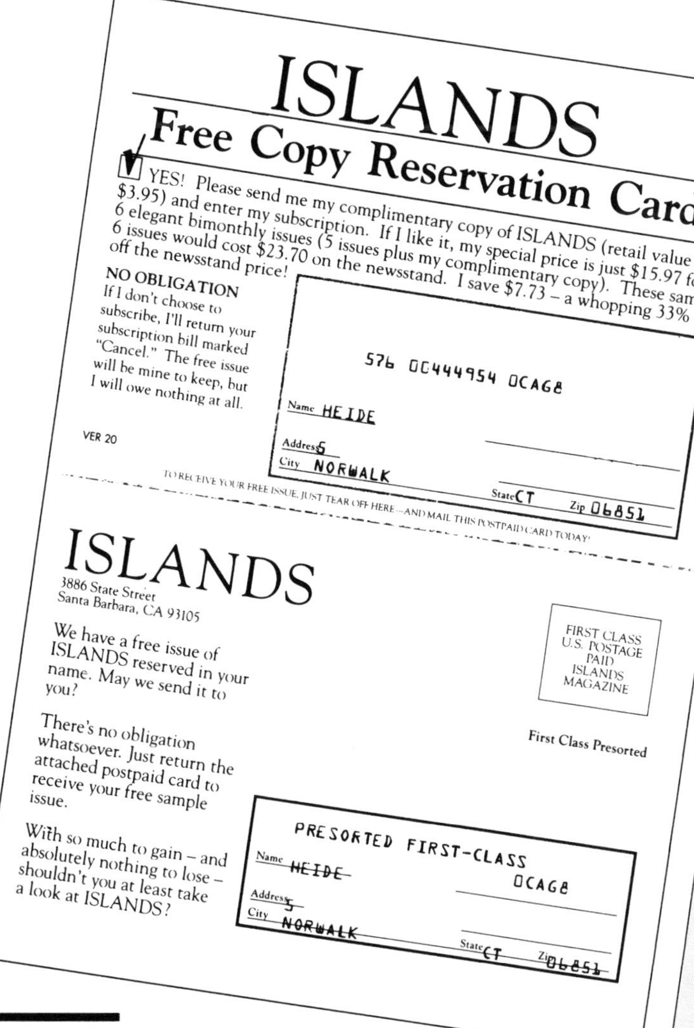

ISLANDS

Free Copy Reservation Card

☑ YES! Please send me my complimentary copy of ISLANDS (retail value $3.95) and enter my subscription. If I like it, my special price is just $15.97 for 6 elegant bimonthly issues (5 issues plus my complimentary copy). These same 6 issues would cost $23.70 on the newsstand. I save $7.73 – a whopping 33% off the newsstand price!

NO OBLIGATION
If I don't choose to subscribe, I'll return your subscription bill marked "Cancel." The free issue will be mine to keep, but I will owe nothing at all.

576 0C444954 0CAG8

Name HEIDE

Address

City NORWALK

State CT Zip 06851

VER 20

TO RECEIVE YOUR FREE ISSUE, JUST TEAR OFF HERE – AND MAIL THIS POSTPAID CARD TODAY!

ISLANDS

3886 State Street
Santa Barbara, CA 93105

FIRST CLASS
U.S. POSTAGE
PAID
ISLANDS
MAGAZINE

First Class Presorted

We have a free issue of ISLANDS reserved in your name. May we send it to you?

There's no obligation whatsoever. Just return the attached postpaid card to receive your free sample issue.

With so much to gain – and absolutely nothing to lose – shouldn't you at least take a look at ISLANDS?

PRESORTED FIRST-CLASS

Name HEIDE

0CAG8

Address

City NORWALK

State CT Zip 06851

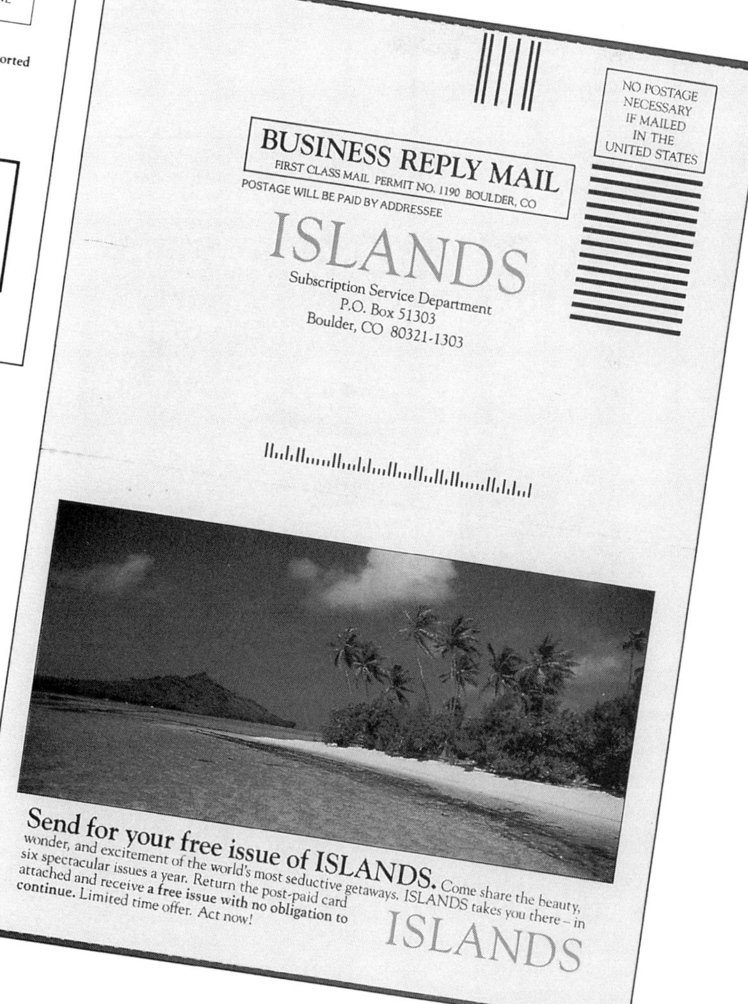

NO POSTAGE
NECESSARY
IF MAILED
IN THE
UNITED STATES

BUSINESS REPLY MAIL

FIRST CLASS MAIL PERMIT NO. 1190 BOULDER, CO

POSTAGE WILL BE PAID BY ADDRESSEE

ISLANDS

Subscription Service Department
P.O. Box 51303
Boulder, CO 80321-1303

Send for your free issue of ISLANDS. Come share the beauty, wonder, and excitement of the world's most seductive getaways. ISLANDS takes you there – in six spectacular issues a year. Return the post-paid card attached and receive **a free issue with no obligation to continue.** Limited time offer. Act now!

ISLANDS

MAILER: *Islands*
PACKAGE: Double postcard
PROJECT MGR.: Tony Theiss (original)
Marcia Scholl (current)
WRITER: Ken Schneider
DESIGNER: Suzette Curtis, A.D.
FIRST MAILED: 1987

Yankee

Of the six postcards, one was written by committee. Sometime in 1985 the folks at *Yankee* became aware of other publications using the (then) new double-postcard format. According to circulation director Mariann Moery (now at *Inc.*), a test panel was scheduled but there was no package to fill it. The circulation department decided that a double postcard really ought to be tested. So the staff analyzed several double postcards from other publications that were state-of-the-art at the time and "stole smart." The staff threw it together, and turned it over to designer Bob Johnson. Collectively they produced an effort that was unbeatable until 1990.

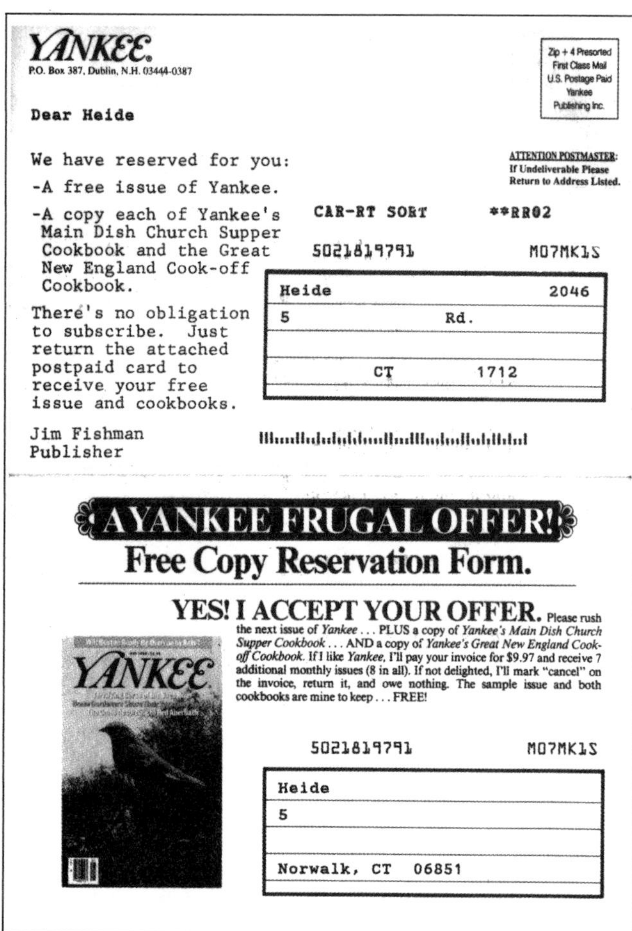

YANKEE
P.O. Box 387, Dublin, N.H. 03444-0387

Zip + 4 Presorted
First Class Mail
U.S. Postage Paid
Yankee
Publishing Inc.

Dear Heide

We have reserved for you:

-A free issue of Yankee.

-A copy each of Yankee's Main Dish Church Supper Cookbook and the Great New England Cook-off Cookbook.

There's no obligation to subscribe. Just return the attached postpaid card to receive your free issue and cookbooks.

Jim Fishman
Publisher

ATTENTION POSTMASTER:
If Undeliverable Please
Return to Address Listed.

CAR-RT SORT **RR02

5021819791 M07MK1S

Heide 2046
5 Rd.
CT 1712

A YANKEE FRUGAL OFFER!
Free Copy Reservation Form.

YES! I ACCEPT YOUR OFFER. Please rush the next issue of *Yankee* . . . PLUS a copy of *Yankee's Main Dish Church Supper Cookbook* . . . AND a copy of *Yankee's Great New England Cook-off Cookbook.* If I like *Yankee*, I'll pay your invoice for $9.97 and receive 7 additional monthly issues (8 in all). If not delighted, I'll mark "cancel" on the invoice, return it, and owe nothing. The sample issue and both cookbooks are mine to keep . . . FREE!

5021819791 M07MK1S

Heide
5
Norwalk, CT 06851

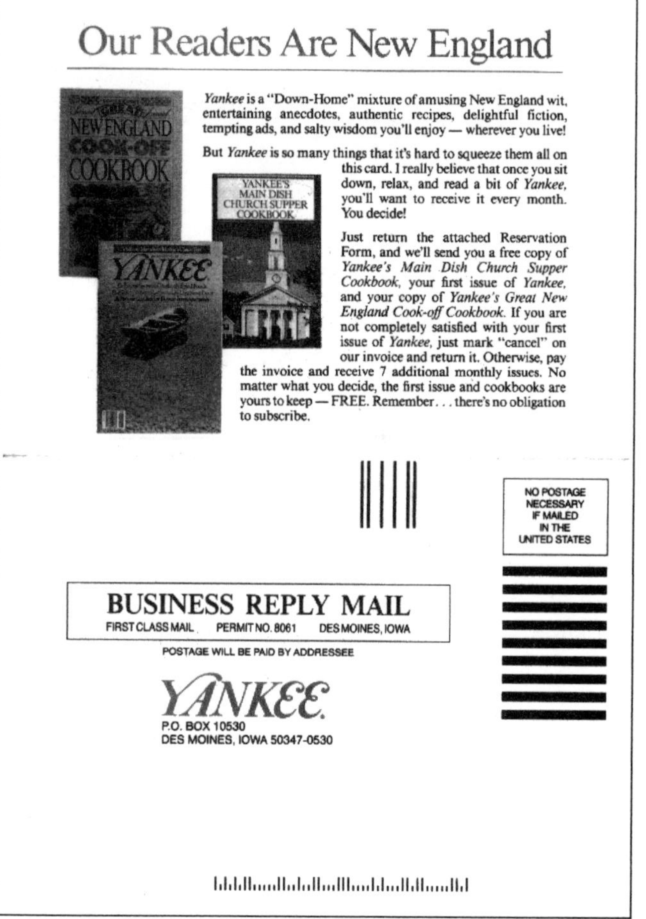

Our Readers Are New England

Yankee is a "Down-Home" mixture of amusing New England wit, entertaining anecdotes, authentic recipes, delightful fiction, tempting ads, and salty wisdom you'll enjoy — wherever you live!

But *Yankee* is so many things that it's hard to squeeze them all on this card. I really believe that once you sit down, relax, and read a bit of *Yankee*, you'll want to receive it every month. You decide!

Just return the attached Reservation Form, and we'll send you a free copy of *Yankee's Main Dish Church Supper Cookbook*, your first issue of *Yankee*, and your copy of *Yankee's Great New England Cook-off Cookbook*. If you are not completely satisfied with your first issue of *Yankee*, just mark "cancel" on our invoice and return it. Otherwise, pay the invoice and receive 7 additional monthly issues. No matter what you decide, the first issue and cookbooks are yours to keep — FREE. Remember. . . there's no obligation to subscribe.

NO POSTAGE
NECESSARY
IF MAILED
IN THE
UNITED STATES

BUSINESS REPLY MAIL
FIRST CLASS MAIL PERMIT NO. 8061 DES MOINES, IOWA

POSTAGE WILL BE PAID BY ADDRESSEE

YANKEE
P.O. BOX 10530
DES MOINES, IOWA 50347-0530

MAILER: *Yankee*
PACKAGE: Double postcard
PROJECT MGR.: Joe Timko
WRITER: *Yankee* staff
DESIGNER: Bob Johnson
FIRST MAILED: 1985

Consumer vs. Business-to-Business Efforts

With the exception of John Klingel's *Lotus* double postcard, notice how closely these efforts resemble one another. All scream FREE (either free issue or free premium or both); all have the mini-letter on the front and the mini-circular on the back; all are printed in four-color and, with the exception of *Islands*, show one or more covers of the magazines.

Direct marketers tend mentally to split the business into two halves: mailings to consumers and mailings to businesses.

But two of these double postcards (*Islands* and *Yankee*) are strictly consumer efforts; two are targeted to businesses (*Business Week* and *Inc.*); and two are aimed at both consumers and businesses (*Architectural Digest* goes to interior decorators, and *Lotus* is a magazine for people who use the Lotus spreadsheet program on either their home or their office PC).

The fact that these postcard efforts and have been working successfully for years indicates something very important:

> People in the workplace are really consumers sitting behind desks in an environment different from their homes. They are *people*, and people respond to the same blandishments whether they are at home or at work.

Many direct marketers seem to think that because mail is going to a business, they have not only the right, but the duty, to be dull. This is absolute nonsense. In the workplace direct mail has to be all the more inventive, because it has to get past the mail room, the secretary in the outer office (who probably screens the mail), and the intended prospect (who may well be extremely busy and therefore will respond only to powerhouse efforts).

What is interesting to a consumer at home can be just as interesting to a person at the office.

Recent Events

Several of these winning double postcards have been displaced as controls. For example, the staff-written *Yankee* winner has been unhorsed by a newer version, this one with a token sticker as the action device. For a long time the sticker or token had been outlawed on double postcards, but is now legal.

The new double-postcard control for *Yankee*. To order, you peel off the "FREE" sticker at bottom left and affix it in the space on the other side of the card. Moving this label from one side of the card to the other is an involvement device; it formalizes the order.

The Snapform

The *Business Week* triple postcard has been upended by—of all things!—this snapform created by the Colligan Group.

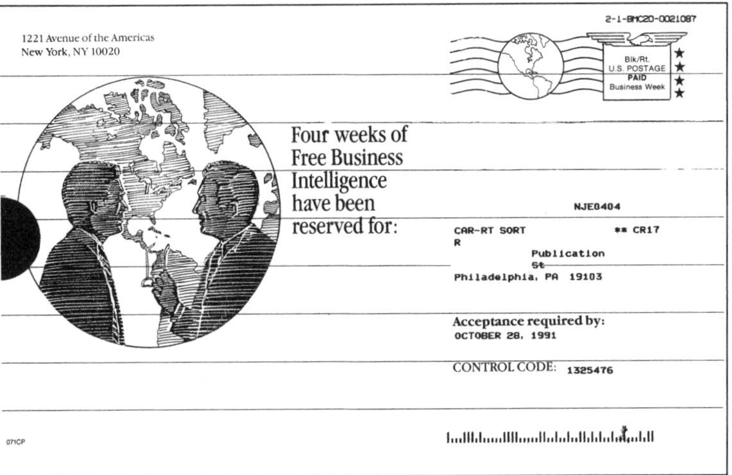

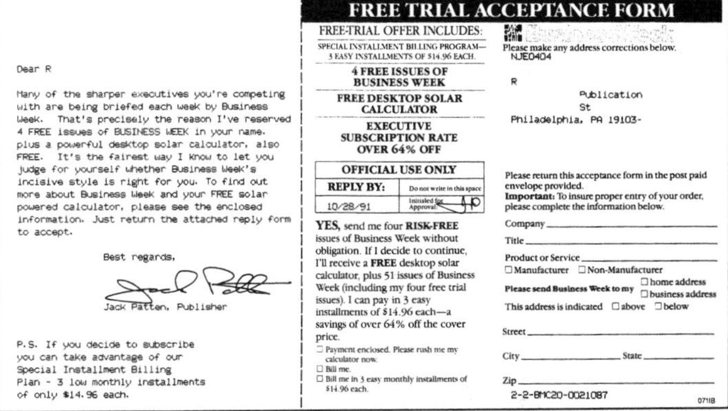

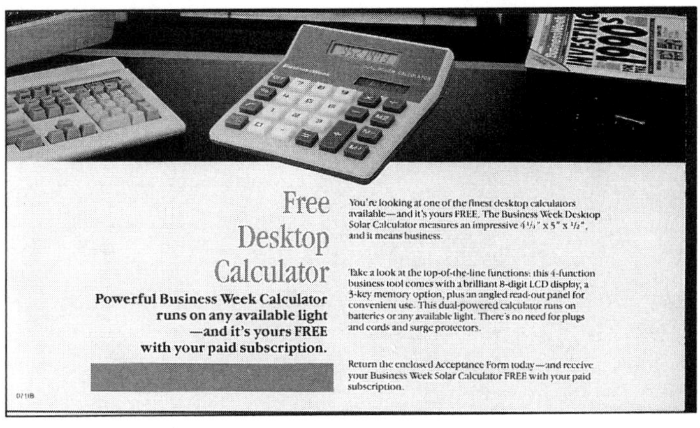

A snapform is a kind of self-mailer that contains a series of elements that are preassembled and enclosed in a sealed carrier. Some snapforms are designed to be addressed with a high-impact printer that bangs the front of the piece hard; inside are carbon or NCR papers which cause the outside form and other pieces. This *Business Week* snapform, printed by UARCO, has computer-generated addresses on the outside and within and includes a 4-color flyer illustrating the magazine and the premiums plus a business reply envelope.

According to circulation director Kathleen Gallagher, this new effort is "incredibly cheap . . . and is responsible for a big leap in cash with order." Remember, there can be no cash with order option on a postcard effort because (1) there is no business reply envelope, (2) asking for a credit card account number on the back of a business reply *card* is dangerous, inviting fraud and depressing response.

Super-Elaborate Personalization

In Chapter 20 you will find details on the use of personalized cartoons in direct mail by the premier practitioner of this technique, Stu Heinecke, head of a West Coast agency that bears his name, in a joint venture with WX Wordtronics.

Two mailers using personalized cartoons on traditional envelope efforts are *Advertising Age* and *Sales & Marketing Management* magazine.

The *Ad Age* package, which has been in the mail for three consecutive years, is described in Chapter 20.

Sales & Marketing Management recently tested a triple postcard with a personalized cartoon. The premium: a "gallery print" suitable for framing with payment. As an incentive to order quickly, the first 200 subscribers would receive their personalized gallery print signed by the cartoonist.

This is the first time we have seen quite such elaborate computer work on a postcard format.

Notice, too, that the cost of *Sales & Marketing Management* is $38 for 15 issues (including 3 additional bonus issues "worth $195"). This price is considerably higher than the highest-priced Million-Dollar Mailing on a double postcard described above (*Business Week*, 32 for $24.95 including a premium).

It may well be that, after testing, the mailers of these six long-term controls discovered that $25 was a price point for this format; if so, *Sales & Marketing Management* might well be wise to test a short-term offer (say, 9 for $24.95) and track both pay-up and lifetime value of the subscriber.

This triple postcard is printed in 2-color; all of the others described in this Special Report have at least one side printed in 4-color.

SALES & MARKETING MANAGEMENT
MAGAZINE

FREE ISSUE/FREE PRINT RESERVATION

GUARANTEE

If you ever decide to cancel your subscription for any reason, your money will be refunded on all unmailed issues. Please allow six to eight weeks for delivery of your first issue.

YES! Please send me my free issue of *Sales & Marketing Management*, so I can look it over at my leisure. If I decide to continue I'll pay only $38 (and save $10 off the basic one year subscription rate) and receive my free gallery cartoon print. But that's just the start, because I'll also receive 11 more regular issues, plus my three free bonus issues, worth $195 alone. If I decide *S&MM* is not for me, I'll write "cancel" on the first bill, return it, and owe nothing. Either way, the first issue is mine to keep.

☐ Payment enclosed (send my free print right away!) ☐ Bill me later

Signature__________ Date__________

Title__________

Please tell me about your business

a [ ] Manufacturing
h [ ] Retailing
d [ ] Distribution
t [ ] Service__________
q [ ] Other__________

Jay

90 St
Ridgefield, CT 06877

M1G46

A BILL PUBLICATION

205
Howard Neibart
633 Third Avenue
New York, NY 10017

I have a free personalized cartoon print and a free issue of *Sales & Marketing Management* reserved in your name. May I send them to you?

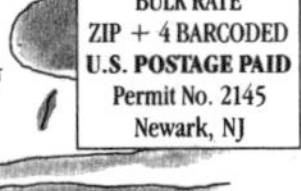
BULK RATE
ZIP + 4 BARCODED
U.S. POSTAGE PAID
Permit No. 2145
Newark, NJ

"I got the idea when I read somewhere that Jay could sell an igloo to an Eskimo..."

CAR-RT SORT ** CR13
Jay

90 St
Ridgefield, CT 06877

SALES & MARKETING MANAGEMENT
MAGAZINE

I have a free issue and a free gallery print of the personalized cartoon above, all reserved in your name. May I send them to you?

Dear Jay ,

What is a customer really saying when he raises an objection? Why is it so important to listen to (as opposed to pitching) a customer? When is it appropriate to drop your prices -- and when isn't it? Obviously, you've had to answer all these -- and much more -- a long time ago. In fact, I'm sure the psychology of selling and marketing is something you know like the back of your hand.

But your sales force may not. And that's where *S&MM* can be so invaluable to you now, as a manager. How can you spot and recruit tomorrow's sales superstars? What more can you do right now to reduce your selling costs? What methods are today's hottest sales trainers using? What do today's marketing gurus say you need to do to prosper in the 90's?

There's only one way to find out, and I've already reserved a **free issue** for you. You have so much to gain and nothing to lose...come on, give it a try!

Howard M. Neibart

Howard M. Neibart, Publisher

P.S. Don't miss out on your free gallery print of the cartoon above -- it's free with your paid subscription!

NO POSTAGE NECESSARY IF MAILED IN THE UNITED STATES

BUSINESS REPLY MAIL
FIRST CLASS PER NO 179 NEW YORK NY

POSTAGE WILL BE PAID BY

Howard M. Neibart
c/o Sales & Marketing Management
Subscription Service Department
Post Office Drawer 1024
Southeastern PA 19398-9974

SALES & MARKETING MANAGEMENT
MAGAZINE

HERE'S HOW TO KEEP YOUR OPPORTUNITIES FROM DRYING UP...

FREE First issue

Like an oasis in the desert, opportunity can show up just about anywhere. But if you and your sales and marketing staff aren't fully prepared to see and act upon them, your opportunities can dry up pretty quickly. Especially in today's economic conditions.

That's where *Sales & Marketing Management* comes in. Each issue is packed with strategies and ideas you can put to profitable use instantly, so you can increase sales revenue while lowering operating expense. You'll hear from experts and peers alike, telling what they're finding effective *now, this year* — not last year.

The fact is, each issue of *S&MM* is full of the kinds of information you'll need to keep your whole company's selling and marketing efforts on target. **That's why I'd like to send you a free issue**, so you can take a look through the magazine and decide for yourself. No risk, and nothing to lose.

If you decide you'd like to continue with a one year subscription, I have lots more good news for you. First, **you'll receive a free three volume bonus** of specially prepared annual market reports worth $195 if sold separately. **"The Sales Manager's Budget Planner"** (published in June, worth $45,) the **"Survey of Buying Power"** (August, $95) and the **"Survey of Media Markets"** (October, $55.)

And then you'll receive your own personalized, suitable-for-framing gallery print of the "Sell igloos to Eskimos" cartoon, absolutely free with your payment. In fact, if you're one of the first 200 with your paid subscription, your print will be *hand signed* by famed cartoonist Stu Heinecke.

Survey of Buying Power
Survey of Media Markets
The Sales Manager's Budget Planner

FREE Three bonus issues worth $195

One free issue, three free bonus issues worth $195 -- fifteen issues in all -- and a free personalized cartoon print...what more could you ask for? How about a discount of $10 off the annual cover price of $48, so you pay only $38 (and save more than 20%!)

So if you were waiting for the perfect time to seize this opportunity, the time is now. Send for your free issue today.

Your name here!
"I got the idea when I read somewhere that ________ could sell an igloo to an Eskimo."

FREE Personalized gallery print

(With your *paid* subscription. And if you're one of the first 200, your print will be *hand signed* by the artist!)

"It starts doing this everytime Albert W. Klein logs on."

"Everytime I ask for help, it reads 'Go ask Joe Enrico.'"

The cartoon on the right raised response by 5 percent. The order device of this double postcard—as with the new *Yankee* control—has a "YES" token that is peeled off from the right and affixed to the box at left.

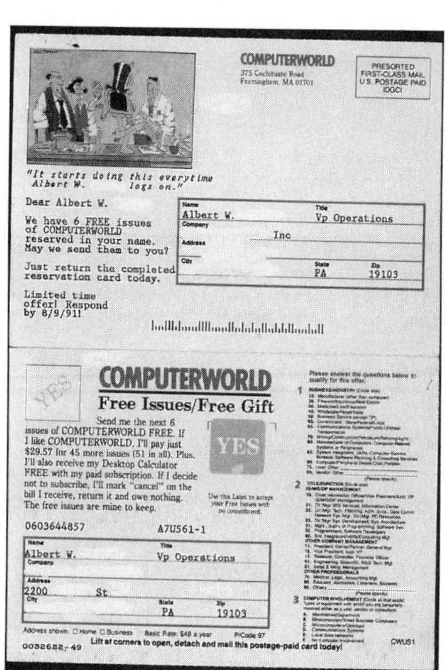

COMPUTERWORLD
375 Cochituate Road
Framingham, MA 01701

PRESORTED
FIRST-CLASS MAIL
U.S. POSTAGE PAID
IDGCI

"It starts doing this everytime Albert W. logs on."

Dear Albert W.

We have 6 FREE issues of COMPUTERWORLD reserved in your name. May we send them to you?

Just return the completed reservation card today.

Limited time offer! Respond by 8/9/91!

Name: Albert W. Title: Vp Operations
Company: Inc
Address:
City: State: PA Zip: 19103

COMPUTERWORLD
Free Issues/Free Gift

YES

Send me the next 6 issues of COMPUTERWORLD FREE. If I like COMPUTERWORLD, I'll pay just $29.57 for 45 more issues (51 in all). Plus, I'll also receive my Desktop Calculator FREE with my paid subscription. If I decide not to subscribe, I'll mark "cancel" on the bill I receive, return it and owe nothing. The free issues are mine to keep.

YES

Use this Label to accept your Free Issues with no commitment.

0603644857 A7U561-1

Name: Albert W. Title: Vp Operations
Company:
Address: 2200 St
City: State: PA Zip: 19103

Address shown: ☐ Home ☐ Business Basic Rate: $48 a year P/Code 97

0032682-49 Lift at corners to open, detach and mail this postage-paid card today! CWUS1

For some time, *COMPUTERWORLD* magazine has been using a double postcard with a personalized cartoon. Unlike *Ad Age* and *Sales & Marketing Management*, which use Stu Heinecke or his stable of well-known cartoon artists (some are published in the *New Yorker*), *COMPUTERWORLD* uses Rich Tennant, the magazine's regular cartoonist. According to circulation director Carol Spach, different cartoons are always being tested.

The double postcards from *Sales & Marketing Management* and *COMPUTERWORLD* both adhered to the rules: household word . . . irresistible offer (free issues plus premiums) . . . easy to order . . . and bill-me option. *Sales & Marketing Management* offered a cash option (as did *Ad Age* in its envelope mailing) so that an eager subscriber could receive the personalized gallery print right away. However, with a postcard effort, this requires the prospect to (1) write a check, (2) find and address an envelope, and (3) supply postage.

Use of Sweepstakes on Double Postcards

Because of the limited size of a double postcard, sweepstakes are difficult to incorporate. Every sweepstakes effort has a space-eating set of rules, plus there must be a description of the sweeps prizes. All this leaves virtually no room to talk about the product. American Express Publishing used sweeps cards briefly but then got out of the double-postcard business altogether.

8

The Next Step: The Mini-Package

Conventional wisdom and years of testing dictate that the letter is the key selling piece in a direct mail package. Malcolm Decker calls it the main salesman.

In her book *Winning Direct Response Advertising: How to Recognize It, Evaluate It, Inspire It, Create It,* Joan Throckmorton describes the letter as being the "center or heart of the direct mail package."

In *The Greatest Direct Mail Sales Letters of All Time,* Dick Hodgson states categorically: "Of all the formats used in direct mail, none has more power to generate action than the letter."

It was the legendary John Caples who said, "Long copy pulls better than short copy." And this is echoed by Walter Weintz in *The Solid Gold Mail Box*:

> *. . . a 4-page letter will generally pull twice as many orders as a one-page letter, provided the copywriter has something to say, and says it with some skill. This isn't just an opinion: it has been proved over and over, by* tests*—where a skeptical client has prepared a one-page letter, in finest prose, and tested it against a long-winded 4-pager.*

Bob Stone, in *Successful Direct Marketing Methods,* also urges direct mailers not to be afraid of long letters: ". . . the longer you hold a prospect's interest, the more sales points you can get across and the more likely you are to win an order."

Flying in the face of all this accumulated wisdom and testing are the mini-packages—small, punchy little efforts that are no more than double postcards in envelopes.

Like the double postcard, there is not much room for selling copy or design, so three of the four inviolable rules apply: (1) household name; (2) fabulous offer; (3) easy to order.

Rule 4, no bill-me or credit card option, can be skipped.

The great advantage these mini-packages have over a double postcard is the inclusion of a business reply envelope; it allows for cash with order and gives the privacy needed for the credit card option. Remember, the double postcard cannot ask for a credit card order because such highly confidential information on the back of a postcard could be seen and stolen anywhere along the mail stream. Requesting a credit card order on a double postcard invites fraud, and very probably would depress response.

Newsweek

One mini-package that has beaten back controls for years is *Newsweek*'s "FREE GIFT/SAVINGS VOUCHER" that was first mailed in 1988 and, as of this writing, is still going strong.

Created in-house and designed by Pierre Volmene, the package has just four elements: plain white 4″ × 8″ window envelope with red printed indicia and blue return address; the personalized voucher with four-color photographs of the three premiums on the detachable lower portion; four-color premium brochure; and business reply envelope. Unlike the double postcards, this effort does not have a mini-letter.

It screams "FREE GIFT" and emphasizes big, big savings. Everybody in America knows the product; what new can be said about the wonders of *Newsweek*? In this case, the offer is everything.

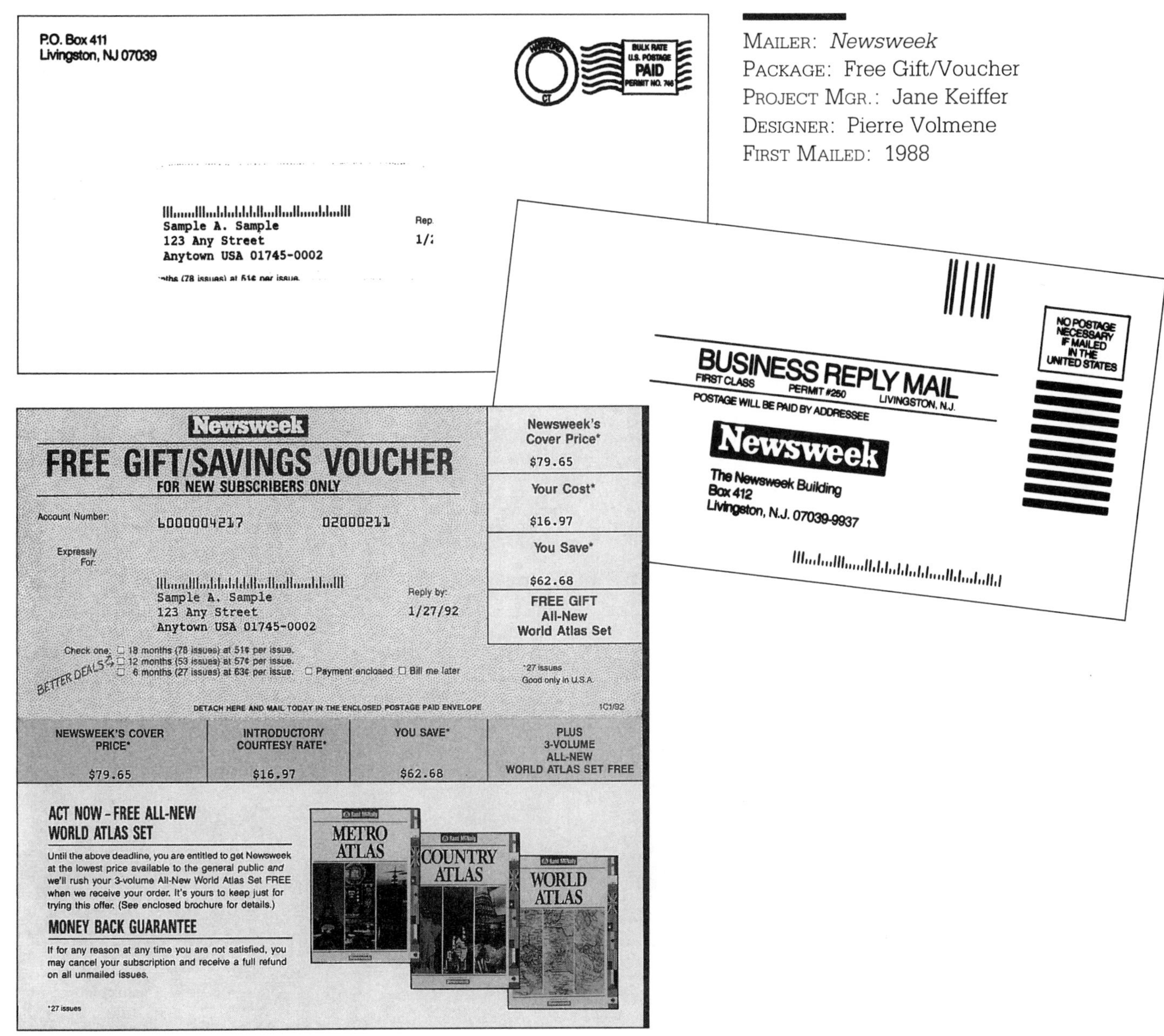

MAILER: *Newsweek*
PACKAGE: Free Gift/Voucher
PROJECT MGR.: Jane Keiffer
DESIGNER: Pierre Volmene
FIRST MAILED: 1988

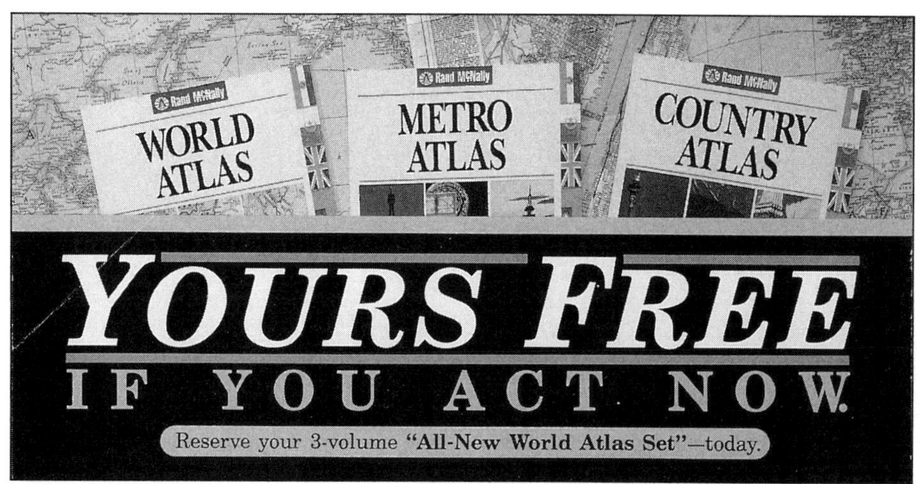

Rand McNally
WORLD ATLAS
METRO ATLAS
COUNTRY ATLAS
YOURS FREE
IF YOU ACT NOW.
Reserve your 3-volume "All-New World Atlas Set"—today.

The Newsweek 4-color mini-brochure shown folded as it comes out of the envelope . . . then unfolded. The back panel is shown below.

If you act now, you'll receive this FREE bonus gift—an indispensable 3-volume set for today's fast-changing world.

It's all the key information and essential maps you'll find most useful to you day to day. . .and it's been carefully compiled and condensed from three comprehensive Rand McNally atlases for your quick-reference convenience. Useful maps, charts and quick facts give complete details about climate, population, languages—from the global picture to the city particulars. And it's all brought together in a manageable, readable format.

You'll travel the globe from the comfort of your home. . .discovering along the way the politics, religions, economic conditions and landmarks of all the places you've always wondered about.

Best of all, this fact-filled set is yours—absolutely FREE—just for ordering Newsweek. Let us hear from you today!

NEWSWEEK presents the "All-New World Atlas Set"

This special 3-volume gift set is YOURS FREE
just for ordering Newsweek. But you must act now.

THE METRO ATLAS
A complete guide to over 60 selected cities from Paris to Peking. . .Rio to Rome. . .including detailed metropolitan maps. . .temperatures and altitudes. . .popular hotels. . .recommended restaurants. . .banking hours. . .information sources—all in one complete guide.

THE COUNTRY ATLAS
Colorful, detailed charts and thematic maps explain the facts behind the headlines—including locations. . .capitals. . .currencies. . .literacy rates. . .ethnic groups. . .religions. . .land use. . .soils. . .climates. . . vegetation. . .geography and environments of continents and nations.

THE WORLD ATLAS
Sixty-four pages packed with indispensable information from around the globe. . .including world political information. . .comparative populations and land areas. . .governments. . .languages. . .cultural, land and water features. . .plus a complete and easy-to-use map index.

METRO ATLAS
COUNTRY ATLAS
WORLD ATLAS

Yours free just for trying Newsweek. But you must act quickly.
This FREE gift set will be sent to you only if we receive your order before the deadline. 3CH1/92

This bright, powerful mini-circular from *Newsweek* is the first example of first-class design of a brochure. It shouts "YOURS FREE if you act now." Notice how the fold of the panel interruptively cuts right across the covers of the three premium books. You are impelled to fold down the flap so you can see the complete covers. It is untidy. Neatness rejects involvement. This mini-circular is involving.

Later on, in full-dress mailings, you will see marvelous circular design where the piece starts small and then unfolds . . . and unfolds . . . and unfolds . . . until you are hit with an explosion of color and copy and promises, an explosion that dominates everything around it.

Newsweek's circulation director, Jane Keiffer:

We have tested it against many new packages and formats, along with a variety of design, copy, and offer variations on the package itself.

It is almost impossible to throw the package away unopened because it looks from the outside as if it contains a check. (The outer envelope is blind and the order form, which shows through the outer envelope, has a checklike background.)

Once inside the package, the offer presentation is simple and clear. It promotes the savings off the cover price and the free gift (a low-cost set of booklets on an editorially related subject). There is no editorial sell or mention of product benefits. The package does not include a sales letter. In addition to the order form, there is a BRE and a small premium brochure.

You remarked that our package is a "cut above a double postcard," or double postcard with BRE. We tried for several seasons to get a double postcard to work. In the one instance where a double postcard lifted response, the absence of a BRE appeared to have a tremendous negative impact on overall pay-up.

Outside

Another mini-package that was first mailed in 1985 and is still successfully bringing in orders seven years later is the control for *Outside* magazine.

Like *Newsweek*, there are just four elements:

1. Small, 4″ × 7½″ white window envelope with printed indicia. Unlike that of *Newsweek*, the cornercard announces the name of the magazine, and there is discreet promotional copy at lower left ("R.S.V.P. Free gift from OUTSIDE . . . details inside!")
2. Personalized "Discount Order Form." To order, you punch out one of two red dots that indicate payment preference.
3. Four-color premium slip. On one side is a picture of the free pocketknife that will be sent on receipt of payment; the reverse shows three issues of the magazine with some selling copy.
4. Business reply envelope.

As with the *Newsweek* effort, and the *Business Week* snapform that knocked off Judy Weiss's triple postcard, the inclusion of a business reply envelope encourages cash with order.

Notice, though, that *Newsweek* offers premium with *order*; the only way you can get the free knife from *Outside* is when you have sent payment.

MAILER: *Outside*
PACKAGE: Discount Order Form
PROJECT MGR.: Ann Mollo-Christensen
AGENCY: In-house
FIRST MAILED: 1985

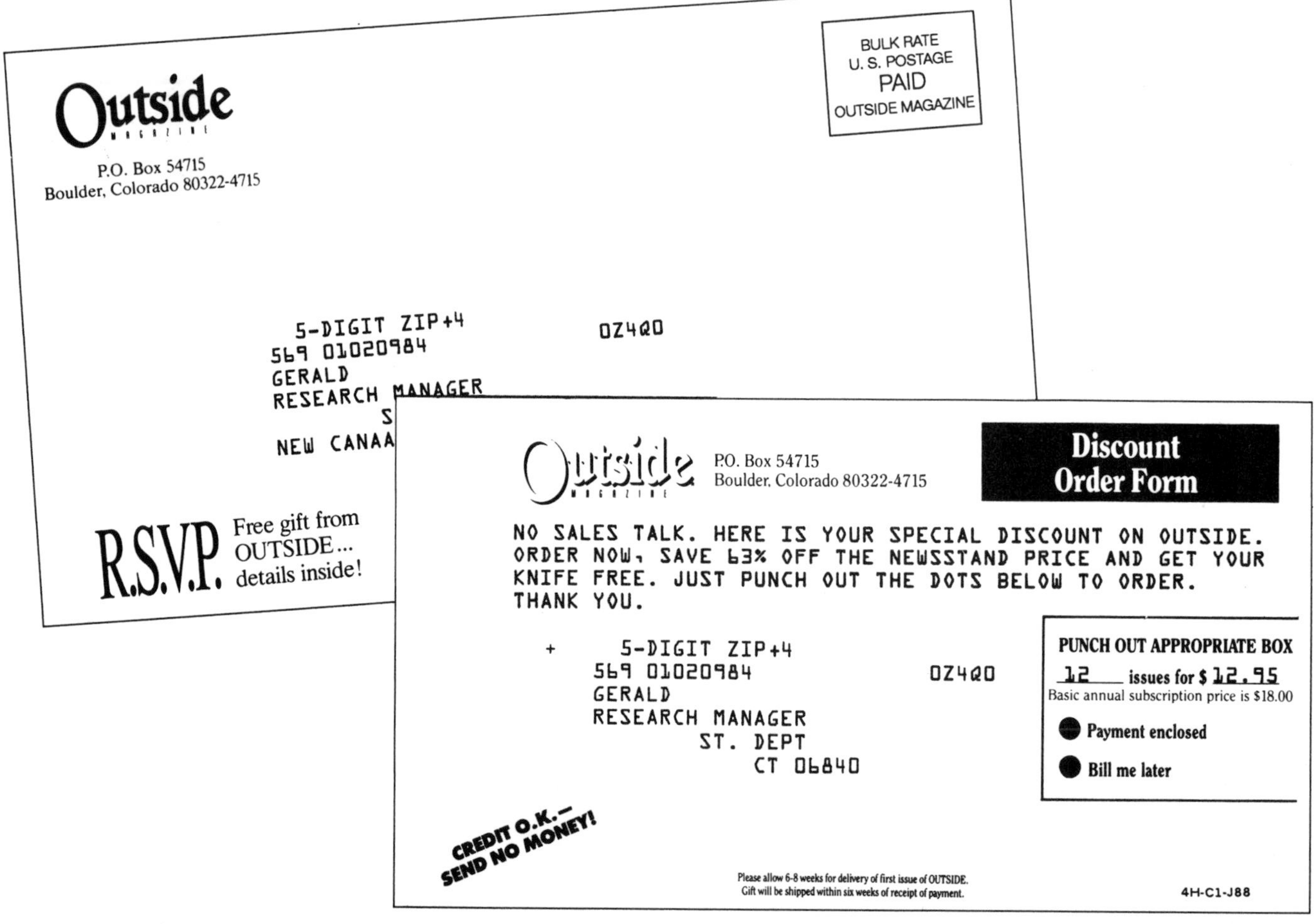

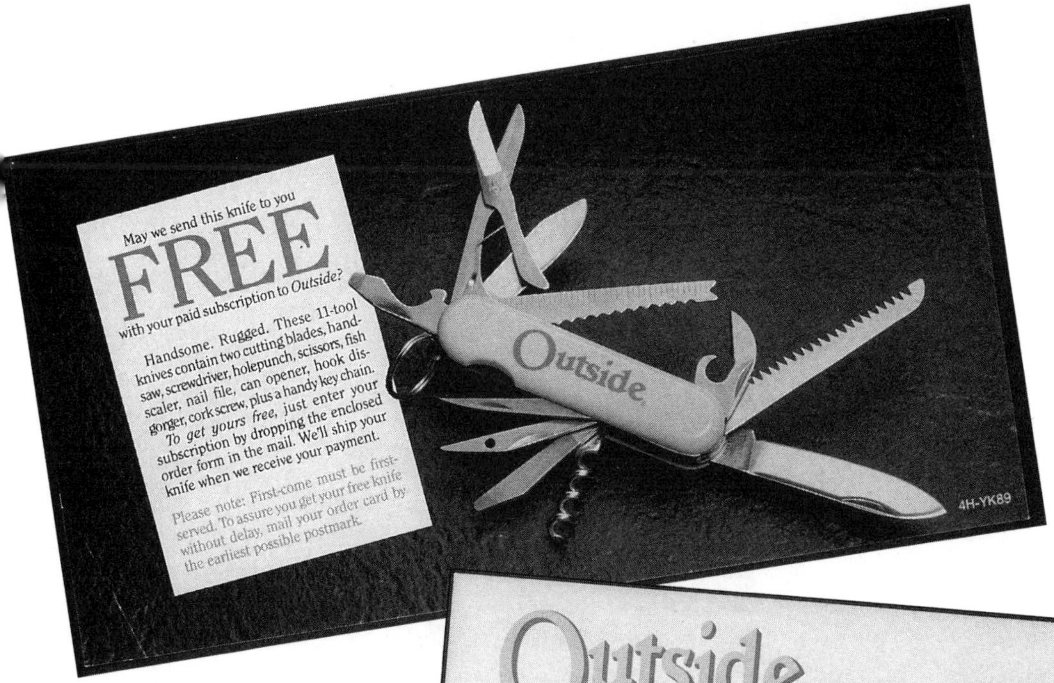

May we send this knife to you

FREE

with your paid subscription to *Outside*?

Handsome. Rugged. These 11-tool knives contain two cutting blades, hand-saw, screwdriver, holepunch, scissors, fish scaler, nail file, can opener, hook dis-gorger, cork screw, plus a handy key chain. *To get yours free,* just enter your subscription by dropping the enclosed order form in the mail. We'll ship your knife when we receive your payment.

Please note: First-come must be first-served. To assure you get your free knife without delay, mail your order card by the earliest possible postmark.

Outside

4H-YK89

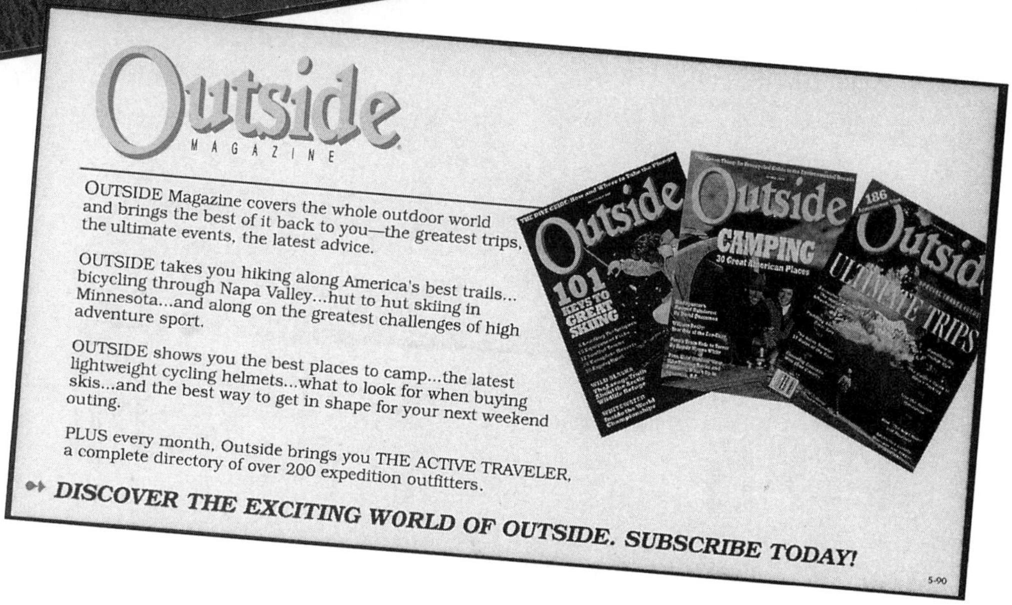

Outside
MAGAZINE

OUTSIDE Magazine covers the whole outdoor world and brings the best of it back to you—the greatest trips, the ultimate events, the latest advice.

OUTSIDE takes you hiking along America's best trails... bicycling through Napa Valley...hut to hut skiing in Minnesota...and along on the greatest challenges of high adventure sport.

OUTSIDE shows you the best places to camp...the latest lightweight cycling helmets...what to look for when buying skis...and the best way to get in shape for your next weekend outing.

PLUS every month, Outside brings you THE ACTIVE TRAVELER, a complete directory of over 200 expedition outfitters.

DISCOVER THE EXCITING WORLD OF OUTSIDE. SUBSCRIBE TODAY!

5-90

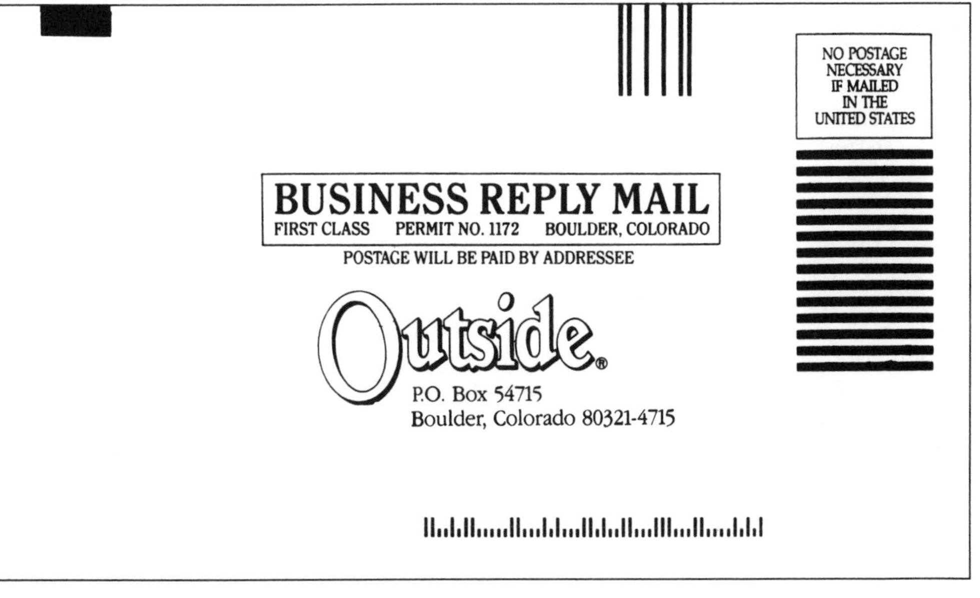

Fortune

Can these mini-packages be mailed with success into the work environment? Of course. We saw the *Business Week* and *Inc.* double postcards, from which the mini-mailing is one step up.

For a number of years my library received this long-term control for *Advertising Age.* It was rested for a year and then mailed extensively beginning in February 1992.

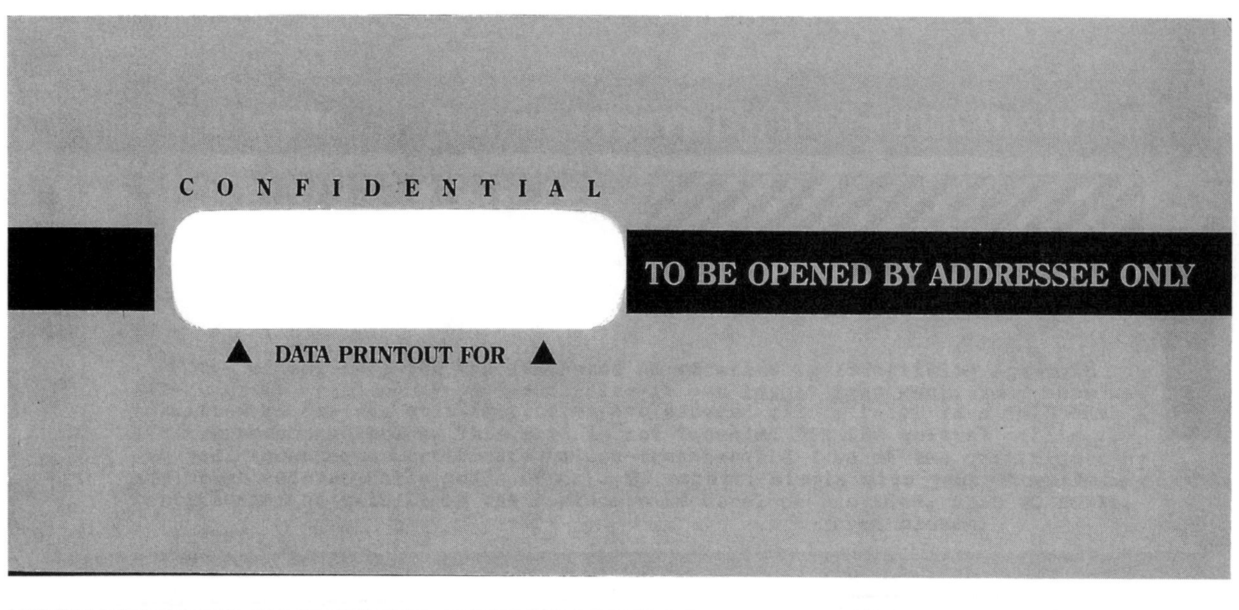

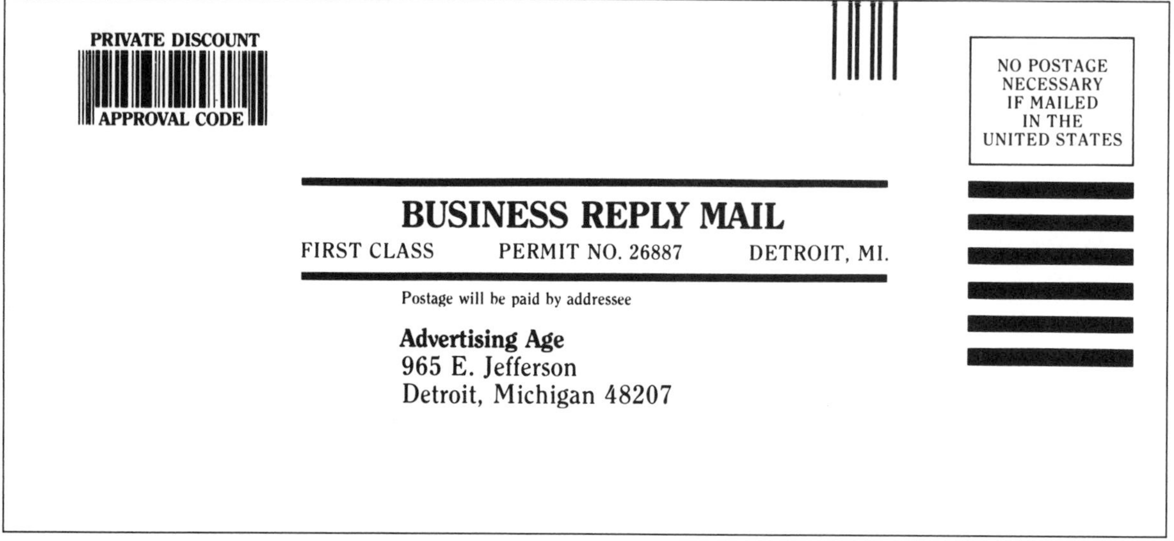

PRIVATE DISCOUNT
APPROVAL CODE
NO POSTAGE NECESSARY IF MAILED IN THE UNITED STATES
BUSINESS REPLY MAIL
FIRST CLASS PERMIT NO. 26887 DETROIT, MI.
Postage will be paid by addressee
Advertising Age
965 E. Jefferson
Detroit, Michigan 48207

A mini-package mailed to the executive at the office, it consists of just three elements: a #10 kraft envelope, a business reply envelope, and a two-piece, official-looking "Qualification Notice" with a half-piece of carbon paper inside that allows for the prospect's name and address to be printed on the order form inside.

QUALIFICATION NOTICE • ADVERTISING AGE • PRIVATE OFFER

VERIFIED RECIPIENT:

MR. BILL
PRESIDENT
FINANCIAL DIRECT, INC.
600
BALTIMORE, MD 21228

DATA PLY ONE

The editor-in-chief has requested an offering of Advertising Age to a select group of industry professionals--at our lowest rate ever. Your name was submitted as one who qualifies. The rate offered ($39 a year) is a full 50% off the newsstand price. This rate is not intended for the general public... and your Acceptance Certificate is non-transferable (use of the certificate by any other automatically voids offer). To accept, simply sign your Acceptance Certificate and mail it in the postage-paid envelope provided. SEND NO MONEY.

(over please)

TEST

You will be billed only after you start receiving your weekly copies of Ad Age. And, your satisfaction is 100% guaranteed. If you'd like to stop your subscription at any time during your one year subscription period just let us know. You'll get a full refund on all unmailed copies--no questions asked.

Due to the special subscription rate available to you at this time, we must request that your Acceptance Certificate be mailed by no later than July 25, 1987. Please don't delay your reply. Remember--send no money.

Sincerely,

Thomas St. Charles
Thomas St.Charles
Director, Special Markets

ACCEPTANCE CERTIFICATE • ADVERTISING AGE • PRIVATE OFFER

VERIFIED RECIPIENT:

MR. BILL
PRESIDENT
FINANCIAL DIRECT, INC.
600
BALTIMORE, MD 21228

▲ Please make corrections if necessary. ▲

Mail this ply only in the postage-paid envelope provided...SEND NO MONEY!

PLEASE RESPOND BY: JULY 25, 1987

Newsstand Price	Private Offer Price	You Save
$78.00	$39.00	$39.00

☐ **Yes,** I accept your private offer of Advertising Age for one year for just $39. I understand that this price is a full 50% off and is the best rate you have ever offered. Please start sending my weekly issues right away.

TITLE ____________ COMPANY ____________

TYPE OF BUSINESS ____________

Signature ____________ Date __/__/__

DATA PLY TWO

Then in 1989 my library started receiving a virtually identical effort on behalf of *Fortune*.

Both were created by Bill Christensen of Financial Direct, Inc., now in his ninth year on his own as a full-service direct mail agency. Among his other clients: Electronic Media Magazine, Security National Bank, Signet Bank, Banner Life, Continental American Life, National Home, and Blue Cross & Blue Shield of Massachusetts and of Maryland.

BILL CHRISTENSEN:

Let's start with the Ad Age *version.*

Ad Age, *by its nature, is attractive to a very limited and select readership. I got to thinking that most of the people* Ad Age *mails to throughout the year are very familiar with the publication in a hands-on way. They already know the style, editorial content, benefits of readership . . . they just aren't subscribers!*

This led me to think that I didn't need to sell the magazine to these folks—what I needed to do was make an offer for them to buy the magazine. *You'll notice that the package does not discuss the product. Instead, it delivers a kind of psychological hook—an ego-stroking reason for tendering this very private offer . . . and it just keeps reinforcing the* validity *of that style of offer as related to pricing, privacy, selectivity of recipient, etc.*

Again, details, comprehensive oversight, and follow-through are very important to this package. The selling style that starts on the OSE carries through each ply of the form and even includes the ''safety screen'' on the back of the second ply. But it doesn't stop there—it continues to the BRE with the bar-coded ''PRIVATE OFFER APPROVAL CODE'' in the upper left.

In fact, you'll see that even the person who signs the letter has a name and title that reinforce the validity of the offer and offer style. The letter begins: ''The editor-in-chief has requested an offering of Advertising Age *to a select group of industry professionals.'' And then it's signed by ''Thomas St. Charles, Director, Special Markets.'' Remember what I kept saying in my first letter to you: DETAILS, DETAILS, DETAILS!*

One more thing: the offer is really only one paragraph long and is finished by the time the reader gets to the end of ply one. That ply ends very intentionally with the capitalized words ''SEND NO MONEY.''

To ensure the execution of those details I purchase and manage the production of the package myself . . . too often little things that mean a lot can slip through the cracks during production. I don't like that . . . so I oversee and buy a lot of production for my clients (I do the production on the Mug package as well).

Anyway, the approach worked very well . . . when this simple package first mailed it even outperformed the numbers on the highly successful ''Award Mug'' package.

Bill Christensen on the *Fortune* package:

I was sitting in my office flipping through a copy of Fortune *when it struck me that the same approach would work for* Fortune. *Again, people who are regularly solicited for subscriptions are very familiar with the magazine and the benefits of readership.*

I met with Ken Godshall and Hala Makowska at Fortune *(Hala has since been hired away by the folks at Forbes as circulation director for* American Heritage)*—and they both agreed with the validity of the approach. By the way, I spoke with Hala while writing this—and she said that they saw the* *package as providing a potential threefold opportunity to (1) take advantage of their highly targeted list selections; (2) reduce package costs; and (3) get away from expensive premium offers.*

It worked. The package moved into the control slot . . . package costs were reduced by 50 percent . . . and for the first time in a long, long time Fortune *had a control that successfully eliminated the costly premiums.*

One further note on the similarities of the *Ad Age* and *Fortune* packages by Bill Christensen. They are virtually identical. Christensen saw the success of *Ad Age* and, with *Ad Age*'s Dave Kelley, who saw no conflict of interests, sold the concept to *Fortune*. Christensen "stole smart"—from himself—to the great benefit of *Fortune* and no detriment to *Ad Age*.

Be sure to see Chapter 20 for the long-running *Ad Age* package offering a personalized coffee mug and Bill Christensen's commentary on it.

MAILER: *Fortune*
PACKAGE: Confidential
PROJECT MGR.: Ken Godshall
Hala Makowska
AGENCY: Financial Direct
WRITER: Bill Christensen
DESIGNER: Bill Christensen
FIRST MAILED: 1988

C O N F I D E N T I A L

CAR-RT SORT **CR30
S R -PRES
RD

GREENWICH CT 06831

TO BE OPENED BY ADDRESSEE ONLY

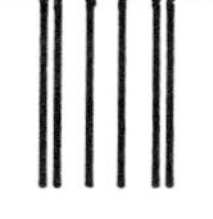

NO POSTAGE
NECESSARY
IF MAILED
IN THE
UNITED STATES

BUSINESS REPLY MAIL
FIRST CLASS MAIL PERMIT NO. 22, TAMPA FL

POSTAGE WILL BE PAID BY ADDRESSEE

FORTUNE
PO BOX 61440
TAMPA FL 33661-1440

QUALIFICATION NOTICE • FORTUNE • PRIVATE OFFER

VERIFIED RECIPIENT:

CAR-RT SORT **CR30
S R
38 RD

GREENWICH CT 06831

DATA PLY ONE

The Publisher has requested an offering of Fortune to a select group of business professionals -- at an exclusive low rate. Your name was submitted as one who qualifies. The rate offered ($19 for 14 issues) is over 65% off the newsstand price. This rate is not intended for the general public ... and your Acceptance Certificate is non-transferable (use of the certificate by any other automatically voids offer). To accept, simply mail your Acceptance Certificate in the postage-paid envelope provided. SEND NO MONEY.

F105B (over please) 1031529 SBCA

You will be billed only after you start receiving your biweekly copies of Fortune. And, your satisfaction is 100% guaranteed. If you'd like to stop your subscription at any time during your subscription period, just let us know. You'll get a full refund, even for copies already received -- no questions asked.

Due to the special subscription rate available to you at this time, we must request that your Acceptance Certificate be mailed by no later than October 23, 1991. Please don't delay your reply. Remember -- send no money.

Sincerely,

Brian Wolfe

Brian Wolfe/Consumer Marketing Director

P.S. I've also been authorized to extend to you a complimentary copy of Fortune's Guide to Successful Investing ... and two extra free issues of Fortune Magazine. See the enclosed yellow slip for details. And mail your Acceptance Certificate right away.

ACCEPTANCE CERTIFICATE • FORTUNE • PRIVATE OFFER

VERIFIED RECIPIENT:

FOAZWF2
S R
38 RD

GREENWICH CT 06831

Cover Price	Private Offer Price	You Save
$55.30	$19.00	$36.30

DATA PLY TWO

☐ **Yes,** I accept your private offer of FORTUNE for 14 issues for just $19.00. I understand that this price is over 65% off the newsstand price. Please start sending my biweekly issues right away. And please send me my extra two free issues as well as my free copy of Fortune's Guide to Successful Investing.

Mail this ply only in the postage-paid envelope provided...SEND NO MONEY!

PLEASE RESPOND BY: OCTOBER 23, 1991

F105B

OFFER DEADLINE

It's a pleasure to extend this private offer to you on behalf of the Publisher. And I know you'll be truly pleased with FORTUNE. With your subscription, you'll also receive a complimentary copy of FORTUNE's Guide to Successful Investing—the authoritative personal investor's reference that's packed with over 80 pages of carefully researched advice on stocks, bonds, real estate, collectibles, limited partnerships, and much more. Plus, you'll get two extra issues of FORTUNE. . . free. That's 16 issues instead of the usual 14. . .with no added obligation on your part whatsoever. Please note that due to the deep discount, valuable free gifts, and private nature of this offer, you must use the enclosed security encoded Acceptance Certificate to reply. We cannot accept any facsimiles or photocopies. Also, you must mail your Acceptance Certificate by no later than the private offer deadline date of: OCTOBER 23, 1991

—SEND NO MONEY—

F105B SBCA

Success

Ken Scheck's 1983 mailing for *Success*, which he did for the Clark Direct Marketing agency, started off as a conventional 6″ × 9″ package. Clark and *Success* decided that it was too expensive to mail and should be cut down to very small size. The original version was a Kurt H. Volk personalized LetterLope with a closed-face (windowless) envelope and a personal salutation on the letter. At some point the mailing was tested with no personalization—just a Cheshire label slapped on the order form and showing through a window in the envelope—and it worked. There was just no good reason to spend the extra money on a closed-face envelope and a personalized salutation.

Success is a magazine that can be mailed to the workplace or to business people at home. Logic dictates that mailings going to offices should be number 10 or larger simply because a tiny mailing on a messy desk can get lost. But there are cases where logic loses: with the *Inc.* and *Business Week* double postcards . . . a tiny mailing from *Official Meeting Facilities Guide* (containing a tiny red pencil so you don't have to reach for a pen to fill out the order form) . . . the American Management Association personalized invitation (see Chapter 17, "Lead Generators") . . . and this demure 4½″ × 6″ mini-mailing from *Success*. And you can't argue with *Success*; nine-year controls don't happen often!

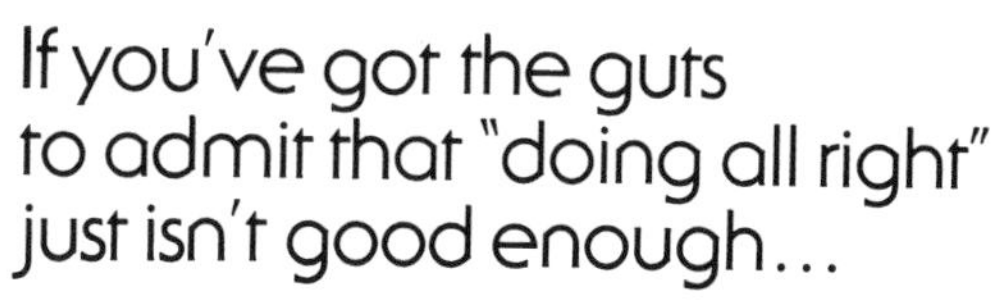

MAILER: *Success*
PACKAGE: "Got the guts . . ."
PROJECT MGR.: Suzanne Pappas
AGENCY: Clark Direct
ACCOUNT MGR.: Meg Fidler
WRITER: Ken Scheck
DESIGNER: Jerry Simon
FIRST MAILED: 1983
To show how diminutive the mailing is, a standard playing card has been photographed next to it.

SUCCESS SAMPLE ISSUE INVITATION

YES, please send me the next issue of SUCCESS for free examination. If I like SUCCESS, I'll pay your bill of only $9.97 for the next 9 issues (10 in all; a full year)—saving me 50% off the regular subscription price.* If not, I'll write "Cancel" on the bill and return it within the month—keeping the trial issue with your compliments.

D3AJ7 0110705605

T A
BOX
HAVERFORD PA 19041

Send no money!

OFFER EXPIRES MAY 15, 1990

▼ DETACH HERE AND MAIL TODAY

*SUCCESS is regularly $19.94 a year by subscription.

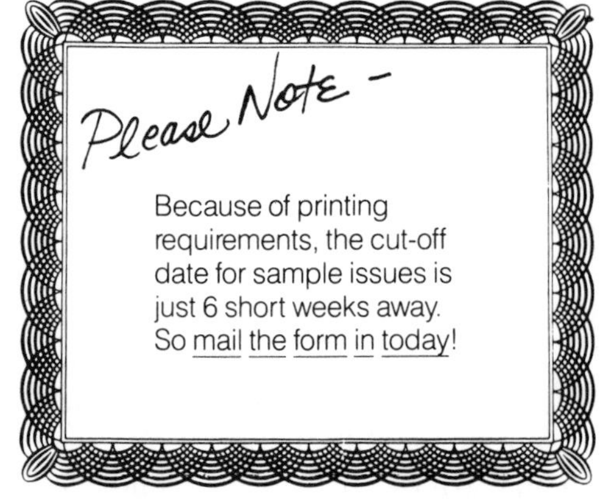

Please Note -
Because of printing requirements, the cut-off date for sample issues is just 6 short weeks away. So mail the form in today!

Dear Friend:

How many times has someone come up to you and asked: "How's it going?" or "How's the job?"

And how many times have you replied: Oh, can't complain. Not so bad. Doing all right.

Just this once ASK YOURSELF:

- Does "doing all right" really mean working long, empty hours at a job that uses only a fraction of your talents and potential?
- Does "doing all right" really mean living backed against the wall by taxes, housing costs, medical bills and fuel bills?

Sure, I know it takes guts to face up to questions like those. But I think you have the courage and that's why...

I want to send you the next exciting issue of SUCCESS MAGAZINE absolutely free!

SUCCESS is really different! SUCCESS gives you tested, proven strategies for improving your life in every way possible!

Each issue, SUCCESS brings you tactics for moving up in your present company.

Plans for shifting jobs or careers.

Techniques for selling yourself and your ideas

Insights on time management, goal setting, entrepreneurship and strategic thinking.

Profiles of super achievers with their "success systems" for going straight to the top.

You'll get expert advice from renowned columnists like Lionel Haines, leading venture capitalist... Roger Ailes, the man behind President Bush's successful campaign... Walter Williams, America's "Champion of Free Enterprise"... plus small business' leading computer hardware and software journalists Dan Gutman, Norman Dolph and Anne Field

Get a taste of SUCCESS! Send me the form at the top of this letter and I'll send you the next issue of SUCCESS absolutely free. There is no obligation -- you don't risk a penny.

Cordially,

Scott De Garmo

SDG/jc

Scott De Garmo
Editor-in-Chief

FM/CT

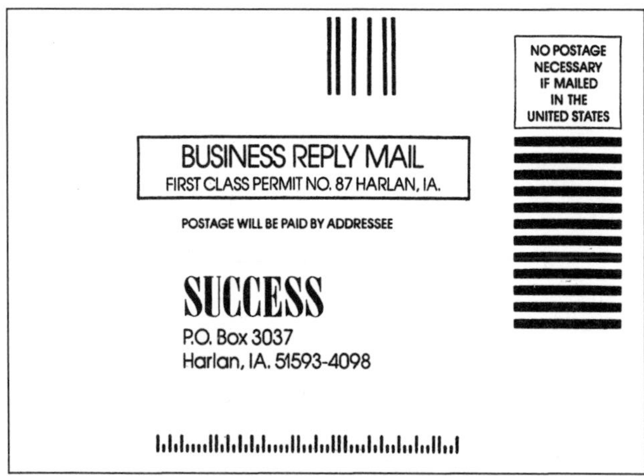

9

Consumer Magazines I:

Miscellaneous Special Interest

Dog Fancy

The next step up from the double postcards and the mini-mailing would be Penny Stewart's effort for *Dog Fancy*. The elements: a white window #9 outside envelope, one-page letter, reply form, and business reply envelope.

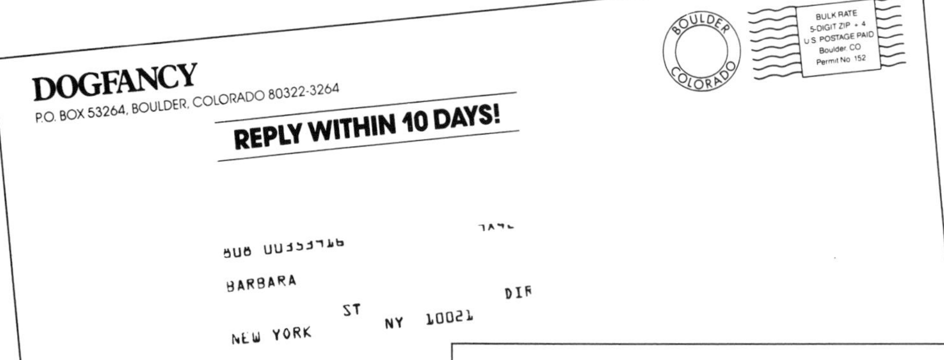

MAILER: *Dog Fancy*
PACKAGE: Reply within 10 days
PROJECT MGR.: Penny Stewart
WRITER: Penny Stewart
DESIGNER: Penny Stewart
FIRST MAILED: 1987

DOGFANCY

Dear Friend:

You'll get the greatest bargain you'll ever find anywhere - for yourself and your dog - by mailing the enclosed card within 10 days. You get:

24 months of DOG FANCY Magazine for only $21.97!

2 years for the price of 1 -- like getting 1 year FREE!

Yes, DOG FANCY, the world's most enjoyable magazine about dogs, will be coming to you every month for the next two years for the cost of a one-year subscription, just $21.97. That's less than 92¢ a copy, instead of $2.50, the regular single-copy price.

But, you get much more than a bargain when you take advantage of this special offer. You get a magazine that provides a wealth of information about the warm, caring world of dogs and puppies, worth many times even the regular low subscription price. And the knowledge you gain will tighten the bonds of trust and affection between you and your dog to a degree you never before believed possible.

There will be articles by veterinarians and other experts on proper diets and feeding, the special characteristics of various breeds, the how-to's of good animal training, and ways to recognize symptoms and prevent various ailments. Also, just for plain enjoyment, there will be some of the most fascinating stories about dogs you've ever read. These tales will entertain you as well as help you understand the antics and distinctive personality traits of your pet.

If you like dogs, you'll love DOG FANCY Magazine. And here's your chance to get it at the greatest bargain price ever offered. But 10 DAYS pass almost before you know it. So don't miss this opportunity. Fill in and mail the enclosed bargain order form TODAY.

Sincerely,

Norman Ridker
Publisher

P.S. Don't forget our guarantee -- if at any time you're not pleased, just let us know. The unused portion of your subscription will be promptly refunded.

P.O. BOX 53264, BOULDER, CO 80322-3264

1M-18-NRPR11

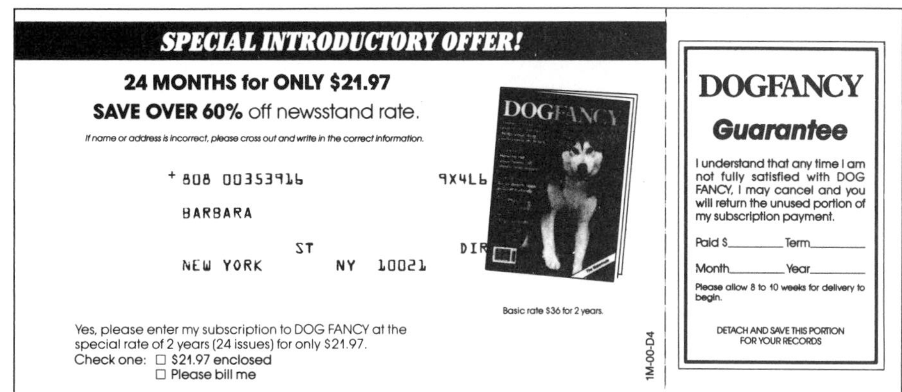

It's a relatively hard offer: no free issue, no premium, no trial, and a minimum term of twenty-four months. The only two concessions to making the customer feel wanted: a bill-me option and 60 percent off the newsstand rate.

How can *Dog Fancy* get away with so hard an offer in an environment of free magazines being given away so profligately? Quite simply, going to the right lists and being the only game in town.

Penny Stewart wrote the package and is circulation director of *Dog Fancy*:

We found the success of this package relied on several factors. First, we had relatively few competitors in the field; second, we enjoyed a reputation for quality and service with the publication; and third, this most basic of direct mail packages was still able to tell our story to dog lovers and give them the best introductory rate besides.

We publish many other special-interest magazines, eight of which are also in the pet field. The formula used for Dog Fancy *direct mail has also been used for years for these other publications. (As a matter of fact, our* Cat Fancy *mailing is older than* Dog Fancy*'s.)*

We are not resting on our laurels, however. We have some tests in the works to see if we can further improve our response. But more important than revising our package is tracking down more targeted lists for these mailings. I believe this is true for all special-interest markets and it is a constant challenge.

Harper's

Of the seventy-one Grand Controls, the *Harper's* effort is one of just two that use a closed-face personalized envelope with a personalized letter and personalized order form.

This inventive effort for *Harper's* was written and designed by Nancy Grady, whose husband is Pete Gelb, creator of the *Audubon* Grand Control, in Chapter 11.

Nancy Grady:

No one needs to be sold on this 142-year-old magazine's distinguished literary tradition. The challenge for this package was to convince prospects that now Harper's *is also provocative, unconventional, and surprisingly* fun *to read.*

The intriguing editorial teasers right on the outer envelope whet the reader's appetite for more inside. The tone of the package is reinforced by the straightforward, low-key design and the upscale look of the closed-face format.

When I originally presented the idea of a closed-face format, the circulation director was all for it. But the publisher suspected direct mail gimmickry. Why *a personalized format? It was tough getting him to accept ''It just* feels *like the right way to go.'' He seemed to want a formula such as ''x dollars spent on computerization will increase your response rate by y percent.'' If formulas like that existed, publishers could write their own controls. A lot of what we get paid for is our gut reactions that tell us when something is right and when it isn't.*

Here's an interesting footnote. Even with terrific results, the publisher was still convinced that gimmickry had won out. He insisted on back-testing his beloved old control in a personalized format. The personalized format actually depressed response on the old control.

Mailer: *Harper's*
Package: Typewriter Typee OSE
Project Mgr.: Lynn Carlson
Writer: Nancy Grady
Designer: Nancy Grady
First Mailed: 1987

John R. MacArthur
HARPER'S
666 Broadway
New York, NY 10012

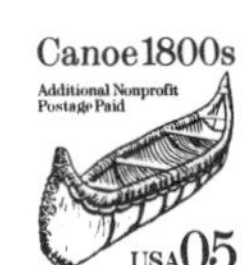

Inside:

The government's secret plan to nationalize your bank.
Christian singles dating questionnaire.
The world according to Oliver North.
How Wall Street stands to profit from AIDS.
A new short story by Margaret Atwood.
The Myth of missing children.
How the Pentagon hides $22 billion.
The actual Baby M contract.
Robert Stone takes a crack at cocaine.

J. T.
Av.
Boston, MA 02124

A fascinating FREE copy of the new
HARPER'S for J. T.

HARPERS

Harper's Magazine Foundation
666 Broadway • New York, NY 10012

DH837

John R. MacArthur
Publisher

We've revolutionized our 138-year-old magazine for you. If you haven't seen the exciting new HARPER'S Magazine, let us send you a complimentary issue.

Dear J. T.

A few choice words describe the new HARPER'S Magazine:

Intriguing. Unconventional. Original. Invigorating. And fun -- a word rarely associated with a serious magazine.

Let me add one more word of interest:

Free.

I'd like to send you a free copy of our next issue, because I suspect you're the kind of person for whom we've revolutionized America's oldest and most respected monthly magazine.

You thrive on independent thinking. You're intrigued by events and ideas. And you read as much as you have time for.

But there is far too much information to cope with these days. Too much disinformation. Too much misinformation. The more you read, the more you wonder what it all means.

The search for meaning is what the new HARPER'S Magazine is all about.

Our mission is not to add to the information explosion, but to help you defend yourself against it ... to rout the propaganda peddlers ... to make sense of a nonsensical world.

To this end, HARPER'S offers you an information implosion -- a concentration of meaningful facts, nuggets of truth, ideas, observations, connectors, and contexts that let you cut through the clutter and get to the meaning in a remarkably short time.

Exactly how do we go about doing this? We start by mining

-- 2 --

scores of interesting papers, books, magazines, manuscripts, press releases, speeches and government memoranda from around the world.

From these, we extract the rough diamonds, and cut them into precious gems of thought, opinion, wit and humor. From recent issues:

The CIA Contra Manual (New, revised edition) ... Johns Hopkins Magazine (Le Carre: Dishonorable Spy) ... The Liberty Report (Pornography causes murder) ... World Policy Journal (Crackpot moralism and U.S. foreign policy) ... Film Comment magazine (Spike Lee on what's wrong with black men in movies) ...

The Autobiography of Sam Snead (As you may suspect, Nixon cheated at golf) ... Coriscope newsletter (Telling right from left, a risk-management guide for surgeons) ... The Village Voice (Chernobyl: the caviar angle) ... Kenyon Review (William H. Gass visits with Yevtushenko) ... The Department of Health and Human Services Office of Adolescent Pregnancy Programs (How to regain your virginity) ...

You may come across a new story by Margaret Atwood. A cartoon from Punch. A speech by John Kenneth Galbraith. An etching from the Jasper Johns retrospective. A memo from the Army Chief of Staff.

The only thing that's predictable about HARPER'S is the incredible diversity of what you'll discover in its pages.

HARPER'S doesn't presume to tell you what to think. We simply tell you what people are thinking. Nor do we preach a particular brand of politics. We'll gladly ruffle feathers on both the left and right wings.

Just a few minutes spent with HARPER'S presents you with an extraordinary diversity of ideas and insights. Just one more example is the exclusive HARPER'S INDEX. Following is a sampling of Index items from recent issues:

Estimated number of Americans who have counterfeit diplomas or credentials : 500,000
Percentage of Americans who know which side the U.S. supports in Nicaragua : 50
Number of pornographic videocassettes released each week : 100
Price of 12 ounces of drug-free urine from

-- 3 --

Byrd Laboratories : $19.95
Chances that a working American has worked at a McDonald's : 1 in 15
Estimated percentage of missing children who have been abducted by strangers : 1
Percentage of Americans who say they have never heard the word "yuppie" : 39
Number of people who try unsuccessfully to get President Reagan on the phone each year : 175,000
Rank of France, Italy, and England among destinations of Congressional fact-finding trips : 1,2,3
Number of New York City police officers who are members of the Screen Actors Guild : 350
People on the waiting list to witness an execution in Florida : 40
Percentage of Americans who say they have been "moved to tears" by a greeting card : 29

Alone, these are random facts. Together, they provide a fascinating, kaleidoscopic view of our paradoxical world.

Like the Index, much of what you'll experience in HARPER'S challenges conventional perceptions. We exposed the myth of missing children. We went back to Ethiopia after the world press had packed up their tents, and took a hard look at what really happened there.

Instead of one-dimensional perceptions favored by the newspapers, the networks, the government, and the cocktail party pundits, HARPER'S offers something more useful. A pair of 3-D glasses for your mind -- an instrument that brings out the hidden dimension, the fine detail.

After all, anyone with a press pass can figure out the "news angle" to a story. HARPER'S helps you look at things at a subtler, infinitely more interesting angle ...

* The Pentagon's secret budget, and the $22 billion dollars-worth of projects blacked out of the public record.
* The government's guide to drug testing, and the insidious implications hidden between the lines.
* The world according to Oliver North -- how much the Colonel has to tell to command the right price on the book market.

And, as we have for the past 138 years, we continue to present

-- 4 --

original stories and essays from some of the leading writers of our time.

... John Barth. Memoirs of a love affair with teaching.
... Walker Percy. On the uses of modern fiction.
... Thomas McGuane. A seasoned angler fishes a new river.
... Bobbie Ann Mason. "State Champions," a short story.
... Cynthia Ozick. The moral necessity of metaphor.
... Tom Wolfe. The worship of art.

These are just a few of the names that join the distinguished HARPER'S tradition of Charles Dickens, Steven Crane, Sinclair Lewis, Rudyard Kipling, Joseph Conrad, Edith Wharton, William Faulkner, and many others.

Overall, I think you'll find that HARPER'S is the most fun you've ever had with "serious" reading.

May I send you a free copy?

There is no obligation attached to my offer. I simply want you to see an issue of the new HARPER'S Magazine, in the belief that it will inspire you to join us as a subscriber.

Please let me know if you'll accept my offer by January 31.

Very truly yours,

John R. MacArthur

JRM:dca

The 4-page letter is printed on the front and back of 2 pages which are then nested and folded. The first page has a personalized salutation. The quality of paper on all elements—outside envelope, letter, lift letter, and reply device—is handsome white linen.

THE IDEA BEHIND OUR FREE ISSUE OFFER...

The lift letter—shown folded and open full—from Lynn Carlson

Lynn Carlson

Dear Reader:

When the editors first unveiled the new HARPER'S Magazine, they were understandably anxious for people to discover it.

It was my idea to offer a free issue. I reasoned that, if the magazine was as exciting as they said, one issue would be enough to convince people to subscribe.

It was a gamble. And it paid off. To date, thousands of readers have sampled the new HARPER'S through our free issue offer. And a gratifying number of them have stayed with us as subscribers.

I hope you'll choose to stay with us as well. However, I want you to understand that you are under no obligation to do so.

Simply return the enclosed acceptance to receive your free issue. If you like it, you can receive the next 11 issues at a savings of 66% off the single copy price. But if you find that HARPER'S isn't for you, you pay nothing, owe nothing, and may keep your free issue with our compliments.

I look forward to sending your free issue soon.

Sincerely,

Lynn Carlson

Lynn Carlson
Vice President,
Subscriptions

LC:pnj

HARPER'S MAGAZINE 666 BROADWAY NEW YORK, NY 10012

A simple 2-color brochure that opens out to ½″ × 14.″ The cover panel.

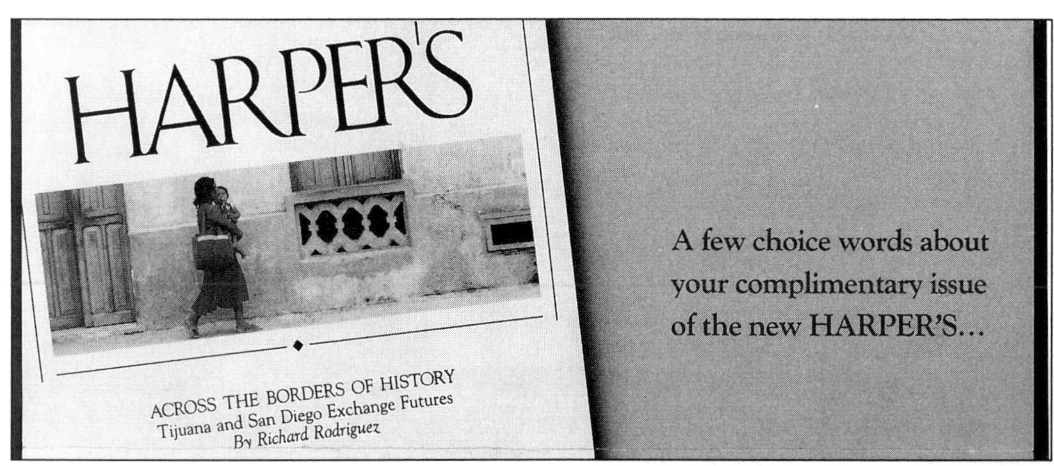

HARPER'S
ACROSS THE BORDERS OF HISTORY
Tijuana and San Diego Exchange Futures
By Richard Rodriguez
A few choice words about your complimentary issue of the new HARPER'S...

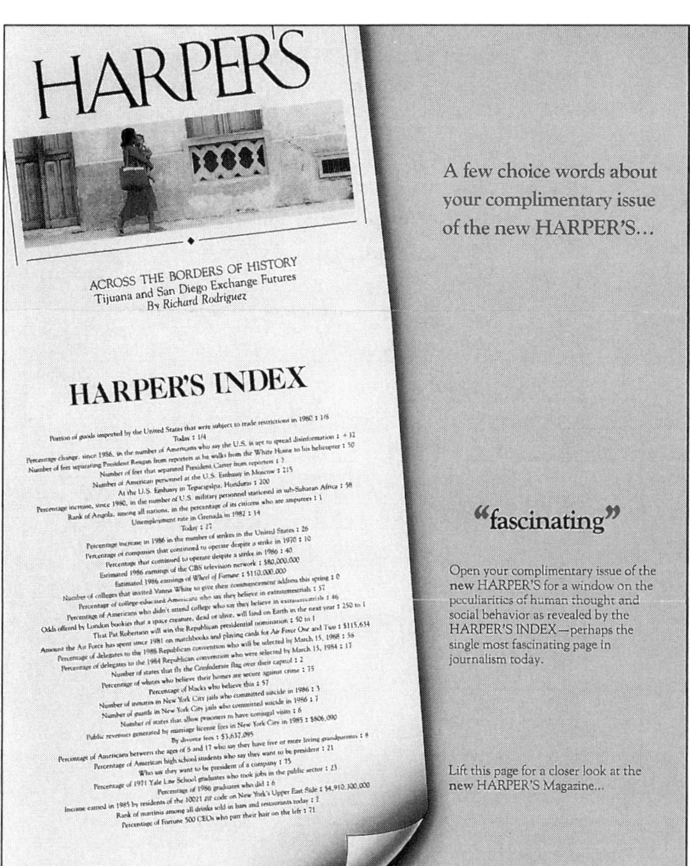

The first inside spread shows the "Harper's Index"—a series of whimsical statistics—which the promotional copy calls "perhaps the single most fascinating page in journalism today."

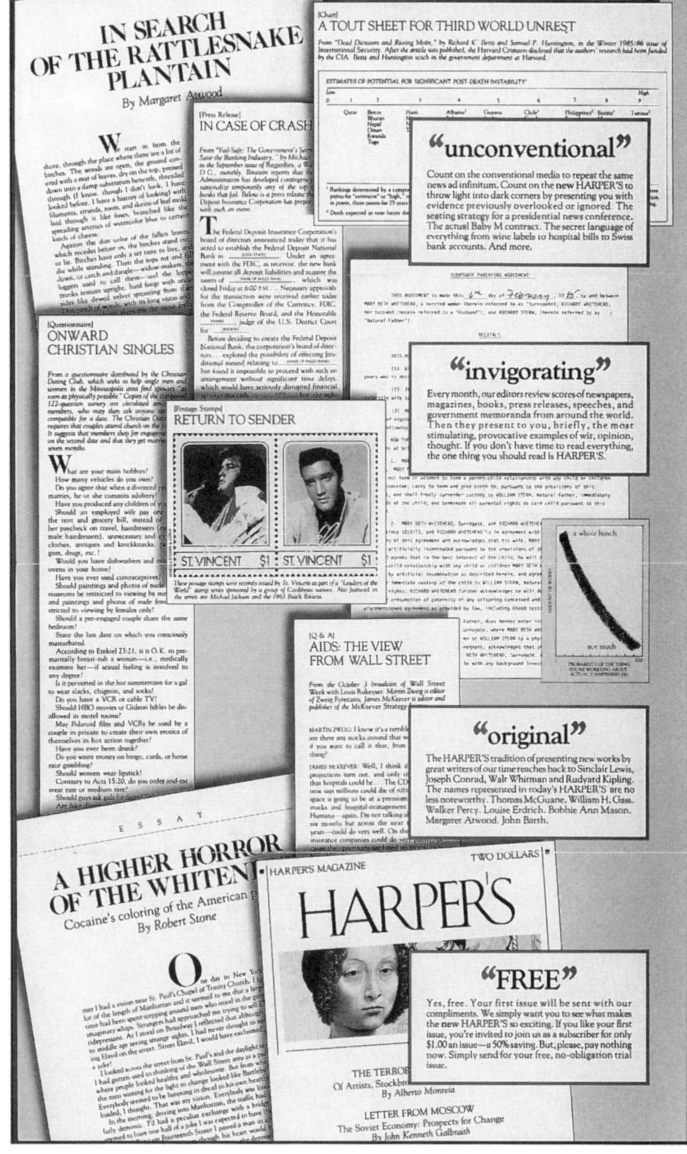

The inside spread shows bits and pieces of various articles and features—A messy hodgepodge of copy and illustrations. It follows Lew Smith's three-word dictum: "Neatness rejects involvement." The only fully readable paragraphs are found in the promotional boxes running down the righthand side of the piece.

FREE ISSUE INVITATION

☐ **I accept. Please send my free issue of the new HARPER'S.** If I like it, I can receive the next 11 issues at half off the single-copy price, paying only $12 for a total of 12 issues. If HARPER'S isn't for me, I'll simply return your bill marked "cancel," pay nothing, and keep my free issue without obligation.

NAME ______________________

ADDRESS ______________________

CITY ______________ STATE ________ ZIP ________

Please send no money. This is a free trial offer. Please allow 6 to 8 weeks for receipt of free issue.

Mail to: HARPER'S

Subscription Services, P.O. Box 1937, Marion, OH 43305

B855H-7

The entire back panel of the brochure is given over to an order coupon—this in addition to the personalized order form. Why an extra coupon? If the personalized form is missing, or if it has been sent in with an order, the mailing would be useless. However, this extra order form gives the mailing passalong value; even if the main order device is missing, a person can order the product. Some years ago *Nation* did a promotion that gave 115 reasons to subscribe (in honor of the 115 years it had been published). The brochure gatefolded vertically until, fully opened, it was probably 4 feet long. On the final fold at the very bottom was an extra order form; *Nation* received a surprising number of orders on that extra coupon. This extra order coupon costs nothing and makes it easy to order.

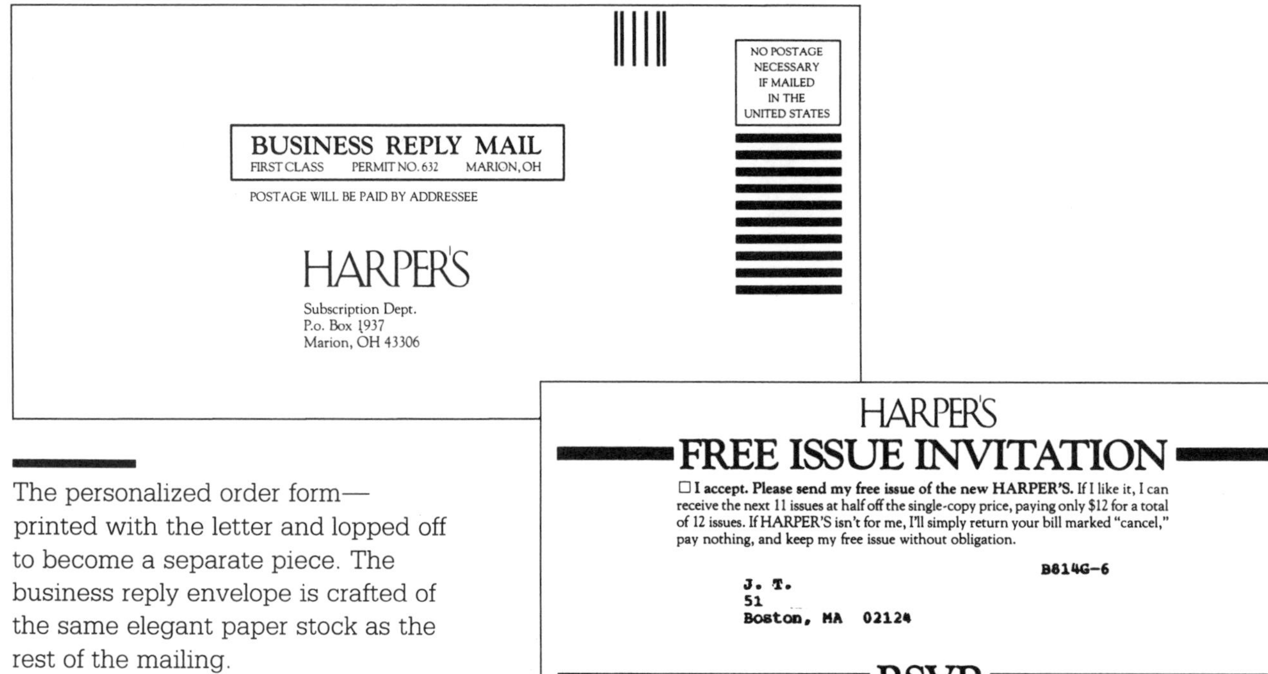

NO POSTAGE NECESSARY IF MAILED IN THE UNITED STATES

BUSINESS REPLY MAIL
FIRST CLASS PERMIT NO. 632 MARION, OH

POSTAGE WILL BE PAID BY ADDRESSEE

HARPER'S
Subscription Dept.
P.o. Box 1937
Marion, OH 43306

HARPER'S

FREE ISSUE INVITATION

☐ **I accept. Please send my free issue of the new HARPER'S.** If I like it, I can receive the next 11 issues at half off the single-copy price, paying only $12 for a total of 12 issues. If HARPER'S isn't for me, I'll simply return your bill marked "cancel," pay nothing, and keep my free issue without obligation.

B814G-6

J. T.
51
Boston, MA 02124

RSVP

Please send no money. This is a free trial offer. *Please allow 6 to 8 weeks for receipt of free issue.*

by January 31, 1988

Subscription Services, P.O. Box 1937, Marion, OH 43305

The personalized order form—printed with the letter and lopped off to become a separate piece. The business reply envelope is crafted of the same elegant paper stock as the rest of the mailing.

M

The *M* offering represents an old approach adapted to new conditions.

In 1960 Ed McLean wrote his first direct mail letter, and in doing so created one of the most successful Grand Controls in history. The client was *Newsweek*, which in the course of fifteen years mailed some 170 million of McLean's letter. It began:

Dear Reader:

If the list upon which I found your name is any indication, this is not the first—nor will it be the last—subscription letter you receive. Quite frankly, your education and income set you apart from the general population and make you a highly-rated prospect for everything from magazines to mutual funds.

At the time he wrote it, McLean was new to the business and became fascinated with the whole concept of list selection while sitting in on meetings with Pat Gardner (later circulation director of the now-defunct Family Media) and the late Red Dembner, then *Newsweek*'s circulation director.

With the current brouhaha over privacy—and *perceived* invasion of privacy—McLean's letter could never be mailed today. Consumers are nervous about the free flow of lists, purchases, and the exchange of personal credit information all over the direct marketing industry. Savvy direct marketers do not want to pour gasoline on the fire by rubbing consumers' noses in how much they know about their private lives. As Ed McLean says, "You can use the information, but you have to dumb down what you know."

MAILER: *M*
PACKAGE: Civilized Man
PROJECT MGR.: Mirta Soto
WRITER: Milt Pierce
DESIGNER: Karen Weinstein
FIRST MAILED: 1988
The outside envelope is black and white with a bright red "M the civilized man," and a red circle around the window.

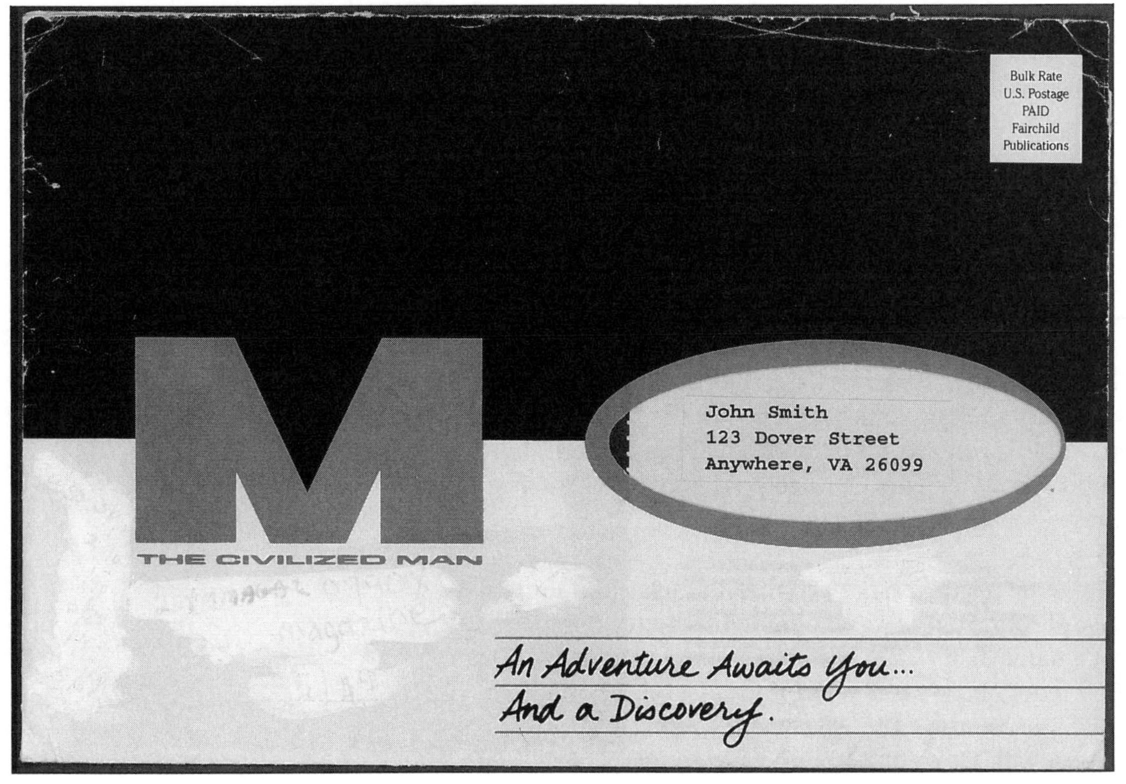

You're educated, successful, well-off, well-traveled, respected, smart.

And that's not guesswork. It's research.

Now I'd like to introduce you to the one men's magazine devoted to making the kind of privileged life you lead actively better.

FREE.

With no obligation to continue.

Dear Reader:

Once you've made something of your life, it's easy to lose patience with the dull and drab, the phony and foolish, the witless and gutless.

So I'd like to introduce you to the one men's magazine in the world that won't waste your time.

No, I can't promise you'll love M. (That's why your introduction to M is at our expense.)

But I can tell you some of the things M will set out to do for you.

Introduce you to the men around the world who are cut from the same uncommon cloth you are. If anyone has anything to say you're likely to find stimulating, provoking, nourishing, amusing, entertaining, they do.

If you'd been with us in recent months, for example, you'd have learned why analyst Peter Drucker is sure the day of the large institutions like General Motors, ITT, and DuPont is over...who sportscaster Jim McKay rates as the greatest athletes of all time...what British SAS veteran John Wiseman advises if you crash-land in the Arctic ("Don't stay in the aircraft -- it becomes a refrigerator").

Peter Beard described what it's like to face an attacking crocodile with a jammed Winchester:

> "That croc's jaws were snapping together so hard and fast it sounded like rifle shots... It was pretty inconvenient."

Art critic John Russell explained the record-breaking bidding at auctions:

> "You'll see the wives and lady friends of the bidders egging them on. 'Show you're a man! Come on! Top his bid!' The poor dope! But he raises his hand in the hope of gaining the favor of the harridan next to him. It's like a public hanging, really, betting when the noose will fall on someone's neck."

And High Plain lawyer Gerry Spense told us what he thinks is wrong with law schools today:

> "They turn out pansy butts. They duplicate academics like themselves who know the law as a textbook but have no understanding of human nature."

You'll seldom find M's people in People. Most of them don't have publicity agents because they don't need or want publicity. They talk to us because they're talking to their peers. And they say what's on their minds.

M will search out the very best the world has to offer you -- particularly the things it's least likely you'll ever hear about anywhere else:

little-known, off-the-trail places you can get away to...
whether it's Thailand's Island of Phuket, where nomadic fishermen supply heaping platters of lobsters for the evening meal, or France's virtually undiscovered coastline of Les Landes, with its pine forests and pristine beaches, its game birds and Armagnac and foie gras;

...and exotic treasures and exquisite fancies you can indulge yourself in.
Like rare maps. Model trains. Vintage wines. A World War II bomber. The world's finest chocolate. A British bike. A pearl of great price. An immaculate fossil from the world's only retail bone shop. (A perfect 12-foot python skeleton: $5,000.)

M will help you look better and dress better and feel better for it. The fashions we show are the kind that last -- investments in good taste, not exercises in conspicuous consumption. And we'll guide you through the intricacies of finding the right look for you.

Milt Pierce's letter for Fairchild's *M* magazine. The 4-page letter is printed in 2 colors on an 11″ × 17″ sheet and folded twice for inserting into the 6″ × 9″ envelope. *M* ceased publication in 1992.

In the opening of his letter for *M* magazine, Milt Pierce says the same thing as McLean did for *Newsweek,* but with far less brashness:

You're educated, successful, well-off, well-traveled, respected, smart.

And that's not guesswork. It's research.

"It's research" is a brilliant euphemism for:

> I rented a bunch of lists which I merged/purged and then ran against your personal credit files at TRW so that I know you make a lot of money, have been late only three times on your $3,700-a-month mortgage, and are current with your payments on the Mercedes and your wife's Jaguar; plus, you are not overdrawn at the bank or up to your eyeballs in hock on your First Chicago gold Mastercard or your American Airlines–Citibank Visa.

"It's research," together with the flattery that follows, sounds as if Chairman of the Board John Fairchild (who signed the letter) happened across the prospect's name in a *Wall Street Journal* article and is writing him a good-ole-boy letter about *M.* It is the quintessential example of dumbing down copy.

New York freelancer Milt Pierce has been on his own for more than

(On the dangers of wearing a hat: "Wearing one makes you conspicuous. Bare-headed, you can stand at the magazine rack and flip through, say, Mud Wrestling, but a hat makes you a man of distinction. Stick to Foreign Affairs.")

We don't take everything that seriously. Because along with everything else...

M is meant to amuse and entertain you. It's a magazine for your leisure hours, after all. And we fill it with morsels you can savor: from the good-humored roasting of The Top 10 Egomaniacs ("George Steinbrenner loves to shoot from the hip, often wounding his foot, which he then puts in his mouth") to a rundown on the BBC's answer to the American TV game show, called Mastermind. (Among the categories submitted by contestants: "routes to anywhere in mainland Britain from Letchworth by road...iron graveslabs of England, and cremation practice and law.")

More?

In no particular order, here are a few of the subjects we've devoted sizable chunks of M to in recent months: Do You Have American Style (including a self-administered test) ...Why Not Change Your Life...Men and Their Toys (private jets, hot cars and fast yachts, to name three)...People Who Have Class (And People Who Don't)...Brains: The Ultimate Asset...Are You A Straight Arrow?...The Right Places (including The Right Jails) and The Wrong Ones...

What does it all add up to?

Style. Original. Independent. Unforced. Self-assured.

M is the only magazine in the world that celebrates the kind of style that a successful man can, at his best, achieve in the world today. And M will help you define yours: refine it...reflect it...perfect it...enjoy it.

As you'd expect, M is an absolutely top quality production, handsomely printed, beautifully illustrated.

As you'd also expect, it's too uncommon to be to everyone's taste.

I'm willing to take the risk that it's perfectly suited to yours.

Return the acceptance form to me in the envelope enclosed. And I'll see that the next issue of M is sent to you, free, with no obligation to continue.

In the tentatively secure hope that you'll like it, I'll also enter a subscription in your name and send along an invoice. If you're unhappy with M in any way, just write "Cancel" on it and return it within two weeks.

The cost of continuing with M?

Again, for you, just $9.00 for the first full year. That's considerably less than the newsstand cost of $36 and half off the regular subscription rate.

But that's for then. For now, I'd just like you to discover how right for you our very uncommon M is.

Do mail your acceptance to me today.

And a hearty "Welcome" to you in advance.

Sincerely,

John B. Fairchild

JF:pc

John Fairchild
Chairman of the Board

P.S. One last anecdote, from an article on Ghurkas, the fearless Nepalese fighting men of the British Army: "There is a story told about a group of Ghurkas told to jump out of an aircraft at about 600 feet. A bit shocked, one of the Ghurkas suggested that it might be better to start at 300 feet. An officer replied that at such a height their parachutes would not open in time. 'Oh,' said a surprised Ghurka, 'we are going to have parachutes?'"

Join us.

twenty years and is the winner of a Gold Echo Award as well as three other Direct Marketing Association awards. He has taught direct marketing at New York University and is a frequent speaker at conferences in the United States and the Far East. It was Milt Pierce, by the way, who came up with the best one-word description of good direct mail. "To be successful," Pierce said, "direct mail has to be *earthy*."

Milt Pierce:
Here's the story behind my M *package. Several years ago I was talking with Leo Yochim, and he told me that he had made an amazing discovery: if you put a bold border around someone's name and address, the response will go up—by a considerable amount.*

"It makes sense," Leo said. "After all, people are in love with their own names."

So I put this little bit of information into my memory bank and used it on the M *package—with slight modification. Instead of putting a border around the name and address, I used an oval window . . . with a bold border. (After all, we were still calling attention to the person's name.) It worked. The envelope got opened and the package did very nicely.*

In subsequent mailings, I used this technique for Archive *magazine—and beat the control by over 60 percent. I also used the concept a few other times—with nice results.*

Thank you, Leo!

Karen Weinstein's 4-color brochure for *M* magazine. The ½″ × 8″ cover panel opens to reveal 2 flaps that unfold top and bottom.

First inside fold. Flaps open top and bottom.

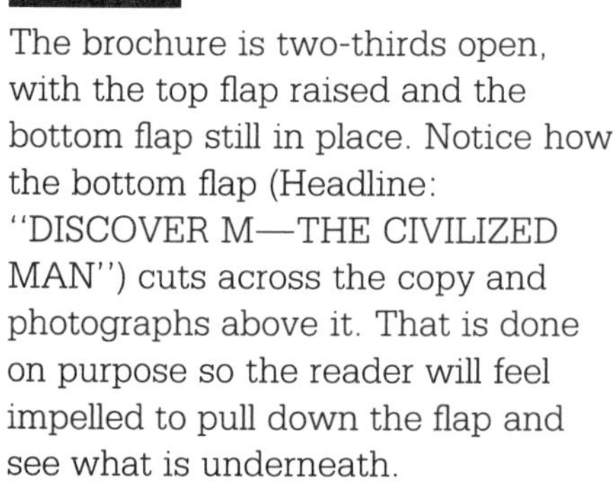

The brochure is two-thirds open, with the top flap raised and the bottom flap still in place. Notice how the bottom flap (Headline: "DISCOVER M—THE CIVILIZED MAN") cuts across the copy and photographs above it. That is done on purpose so the reader will feel impelled to pull down the flap and see what is underneath.

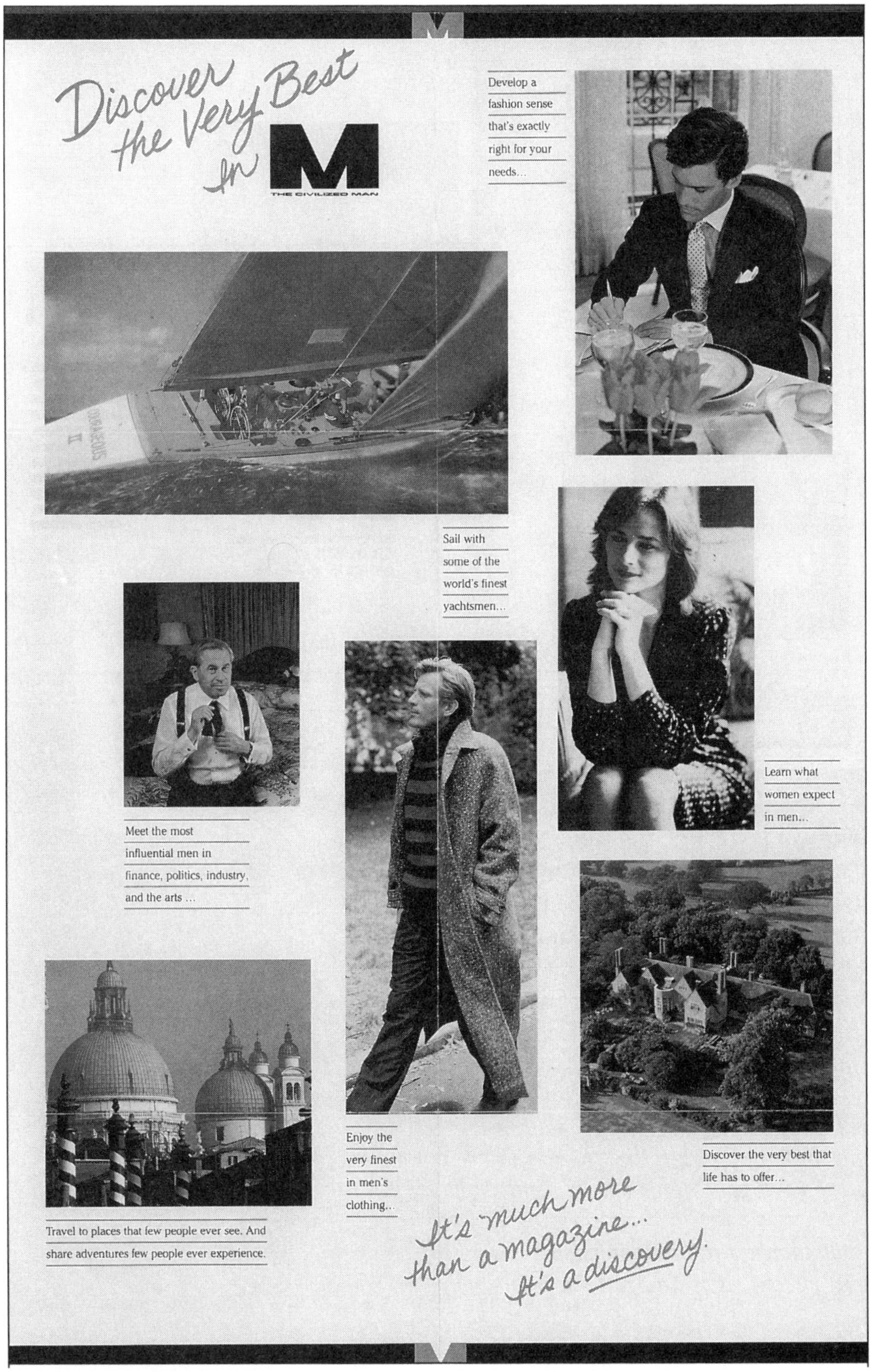

M
Discover the Very Best In
M
THE CIVILIZED MAN
Develop a fashion sense that's exactly right for your needs...
Sail with some of the world's finest yachtsmen...
Meet the most influential men in finance, politics, industry, and the arts ...
Learn what women expect in men...
Enjoy the very finest in men's clothing...
Discover the very best that life has to offer...
Travel to places that few people ever see. And share adventures few people ever experience.
It's much more than a magazine... It's a discovery.

The brochure fully opened.

M
THE CIVILIZED MAN
Who is Hank Kravis?
Great Outdoors Clothes
The Hottest Porsche Ever?
The Best Salmon Fishing
The Big Man at Chrysler
Drug Warrior: Putting the Bad Guys Away
Daniel Day-Lewis
SO INTENSE
M
Discover the joy of travel...
BR90
Forget New York
and the thrill of adventure...

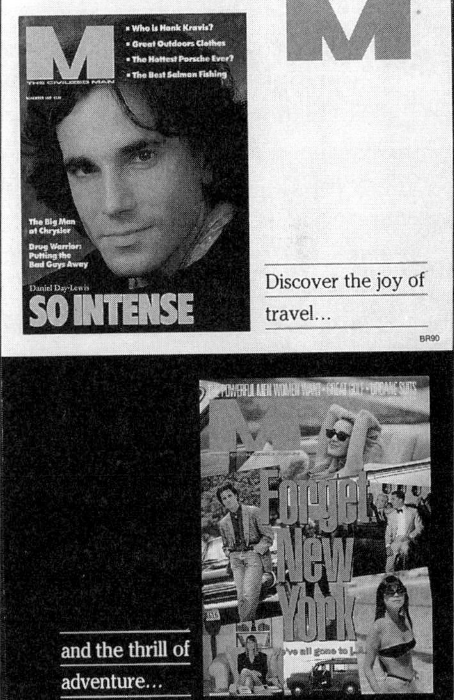

The back panel.

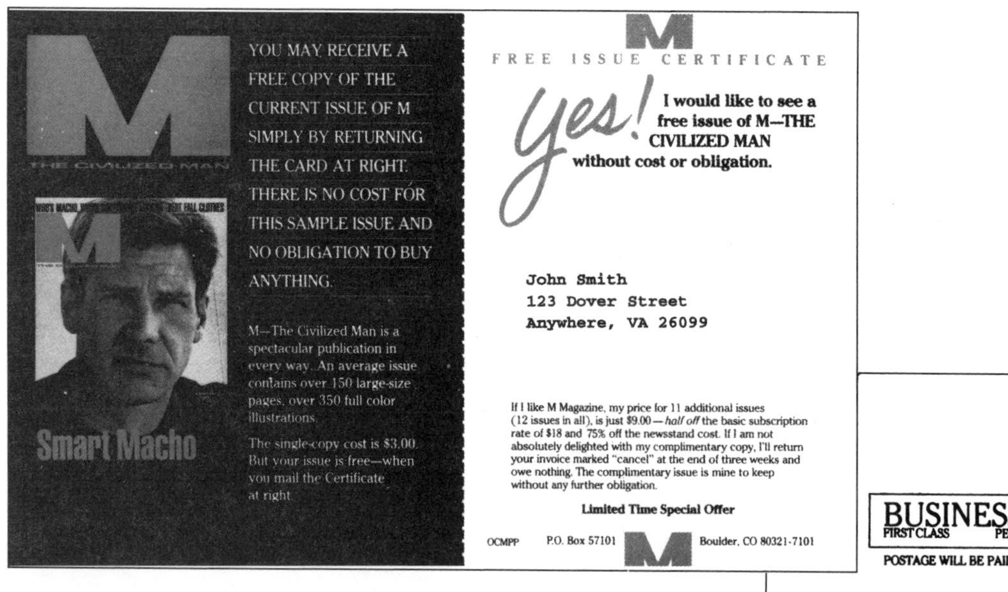

M
THE CIVILIZED MAN

YOU MAY RECEIVE A FREE COPY OF THE CURRENT ISSUE OF M SIMPLY BY RETURNING THE CARD AT RIGHT. THERE IS NO COST FOR THIS SAMPLE ISSUE AND NO OBLIGATION TO BUY ANYTHING.

M—The Civilized Man is a spectacular publication in every way. An average issue contains over 150 large-size pages, over 350 full color illustrations.

The single-copy cost is $3.00. But your issue is free—when you mail the Certificate at right.

Smart Macho

M

FREE ISSUE CERTIFICATE

yes! **I would like to see a free issue of M—THE CIVILIZED MAN without cost or obligation.**

John Smith
123 Dover Street
Anywhere, VA 26099

If I like M Magazine, my price for 11 additional issues (12 issues in all), is just $9.00—*half off* the basic subscription rate of $18 and 75% off the newsstand cost. If I am not absolutely delighted with my complimentary copy, I'll return your invoice marked "cancel" at the end of three weeks and owe nothing. The complimentary issue is mine to keep without any further obligation.

Limited Time Special Offer

OCMPP P.O. Box 57101 M Boulder, CO 80321-7101

NO POSTAGE NECESSARY IF MAILED IN THE UNITED STATES

BUSINESS REPLY MAIL
FIRST CLASS PERMIT NO. 256 BOULDER, CO

POSTAGE WILL BE PAID BY ADDRESSEE

M

Subscription Processing Dept.
P.O. Box 57100
Boulder, CO 80321-7100

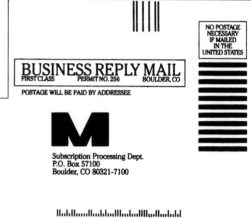

The order form. Karen Weinstein has made the half that is detached and mailed back white, and the stub black. This follows Ted Kikoler's tip 14 in Chapter 5: "The eye normally goes from dark areas to light areas." This is the most important single piece in the mailing, so it must stand out.

The *M* Grand Control was designed by award-winning art director and graphic designer Karen Weinstein, who teaches and lectures on direct response as well as contributes her expertise to national charitable events and associations in her field. Her awards include the Gold Mailbox for Consumer Direct Mail and First Prize for Poster Design by the Printing Industries of Metropolitan New York, as well as an Axel Andersson Award for the *M* magazine Grand Control. Before freelancing, she was with *Newsweek* and was senior circulation art director at Ziff-Davis for all its computer publications and advertising sales independent assignments.

Karen Weinstein:
As an award winner in the direct response industry, I think of myself not as a "designer" but as a marketer using graphic tools. I approach the "person-to-person" challenge of translating visually the goals and needs of my client's audience.

I gather as much marketing, industry, and audience research as possible, as well as production, budget, personalization, offer(s), test, and roll-out information.

Since packages are copy driven, it's my job to get that target person to respond to those words. And, I've been fortunate enough to work with some of the best writers in the business.

As I begin to design, I imagine myself in the target audience. My intuitive, intellectual, and responsive resources interact to design the most effective solution possible. This dynamic process merges art and business into a successful partnership.

Organic Gardening

My advice to anyone who wants to study the very best direct mail being done in America today: buy a book or a magazine from Rodale Press and send $25 each to the Republican National Committee and the National Republican Senatorial Committee.

From Rodale you will see firsthand the finest, most powerful mailings by top writers and designers; these mailings will come to you every month and each one is worth studying closely.

From the Republicans will come leading-edge direct mail technology—dazzling personalization of everything from invitations addressed in Olde English Typeface to lasered certificates of appreciation on parchment paper and elegantly embossed membership cards.

In addition, both organizations will bowl you over with unbelievable offers. Rodale will blitz you with free premiums and ironclad guarantees of satisfaction; the Republicans will set your head spinning with personal invitations to private receptions at the vice president's mansion to dinner with the president and the first lady.

If the three essential elements that ensure a successful direct mail effort are product, offer, and lists, you'll find them in spades from the three Rs—Rodale and the two Republican committees.

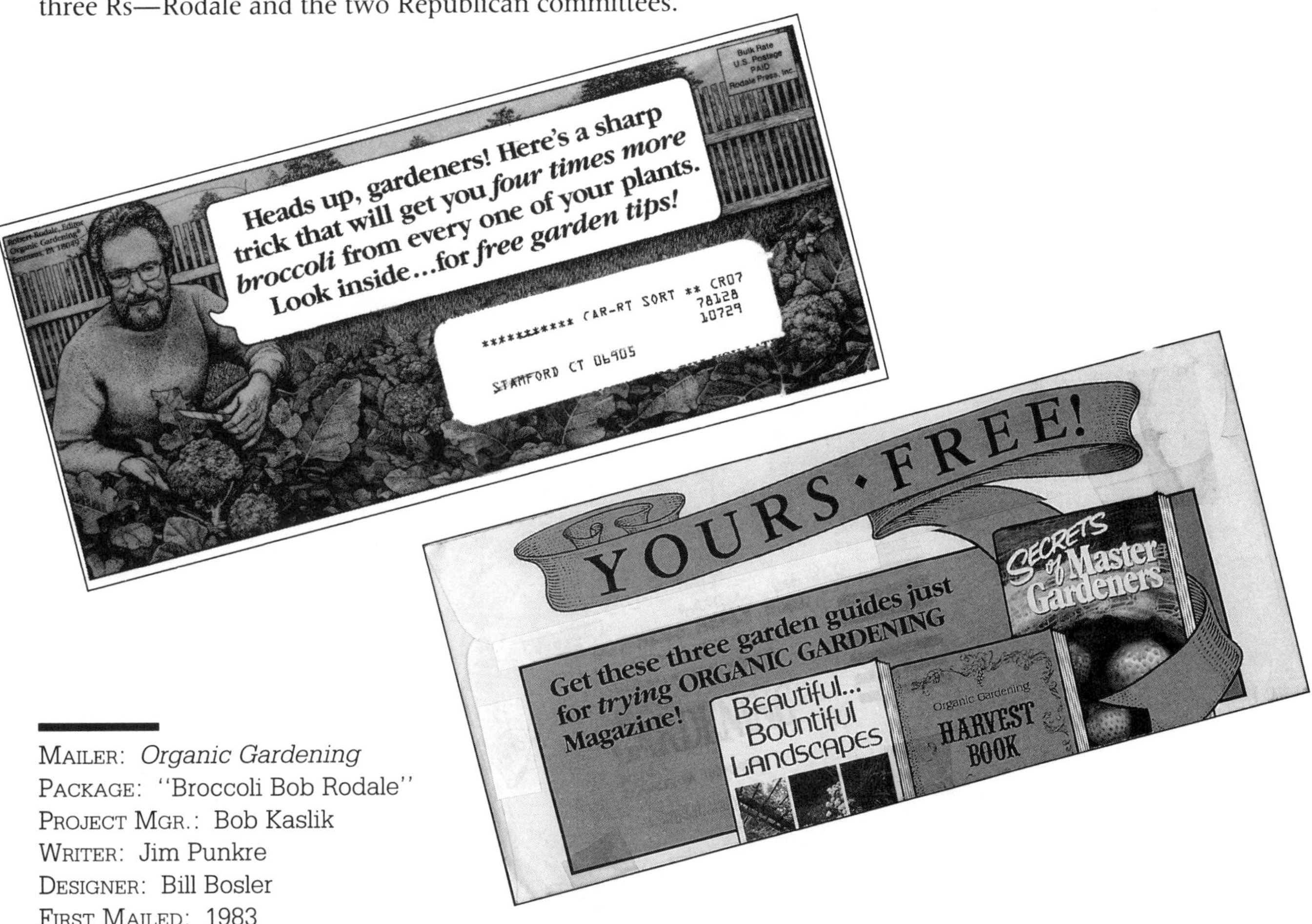

MAILER: *Organic Gardening*
PACKAGE: "Broccoli Bob Rodale"
PROJECT MGR.: Bob Kaslik
WRITER: Jim Punkre
DESIGNER: Bill Bosler
FIRST MAILED: 1983
The front and back of Jim Punkre's envelope for *Organic Gardening*. Rodale never wastes selling space; a typical Rodale outside envelope has powerful selling messages on the front and the back.

A case in point is Jim Punkre's 1983 mailing for Rodale's *Organic Gardening* magazine with a brown and black #10 window envelope featuring a comic-book-like drawing of Rodale's president, Robert Rodale, in the middle of a broccoli patch and luring us to look inside the envelope.

The Rodale offering is akin to the Boardroom Reports mailings in Chapter 21, where you will see two envelopes that have formidable teaser copy:

WHAT NEVER TO EAT ON AN AIRPLANE
WHAT CREDIT CARD COMPANIES DON'T TELL YOU

You tear into these Boardroom envelopes only to discover that the answers will be found in the publication once you buy it.

Whereas the Boardroom writer leaves you titillated and unfulfilled, Punkre delivers in the letter what he promises on the envelope. At the top of the letter he repeats the envelope promise and then shows exactly how to prune broccoli so that four big heads will grow instead of just one.

Many direct mail writers feel that if the mailing gives hard information along with the sales pitch, the reader will feel good about spending time with the piece . . . will feel good about the product and offer . . . will feel good about the mailer . . . and will order.

The *Organic Gardening* 4-page letter, printed in 4-color on an 11″ × 17″ sheet and folded 3 times to fit in a #10 envelope.

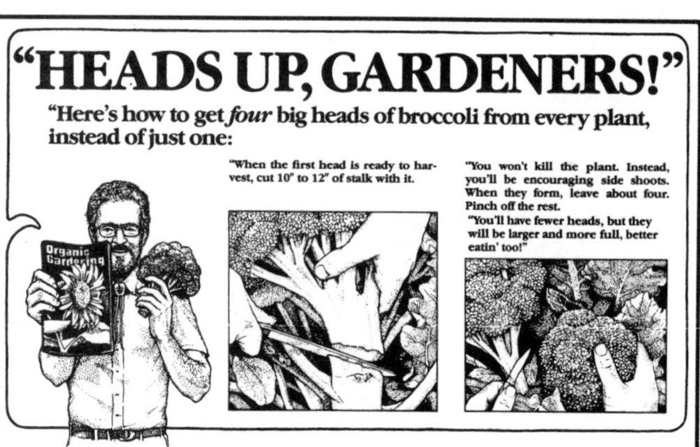

"HEADS UP, GARDENERS!"
"Here's how to get *four* big heads of broccoli from every plant, instead of just one:
"When the first head is ready to harvest, cut 10" to 12" of stalk with it.
"You won't kill the plant. Instead, you'll be encouraging side shoots. When they form, leave about four. Pinch off the rest.
"You'll have fewer heads, but they will be larger and more full, better eatin' too!"
Organic Gardening

Dear Gardening Friend:

Who says you can't teach a good gardener new tricks?

ORGANIC GARDENING magazine does -- every month of the year. Showing good gardeners like you how to grow more food with less effort and fewer mistakes is what has made us the most popular gardening magazine in the entire world!

Every month we pack ORGANIC GARDENING with growing tips that go beyond the basics -- tips that can help you become a master gardener, whether you grow a lot, or a little.

To give you a free sample of how we can help you ...

... we want to send you a collection of the very best gardening ideas we've seen in recent months. These are the "cream of the crop" tips for backyard gardeners ... and we call them "Secrets of Master Gardeners," because they've come to us from some of America's most experienced gardening veterans.

We'd like to send you this -- plus two more books (three in all) just for trying ORGANIC GARDENING -- the magazine that can help you become a better gardener (even if you've been doing it for years!).

That's what makes ORGANIC GARDENING well worth the subscription price. Because issue after issue of the magazine is chock-full of tips and ideas that really deliver the goods. For instance ...

(over, please)

Not long ago we told our readers about ...

... how to get double potato harvests from every plant. The secret is to let your seed potatoes sprout, then you plant the whole potato.

... how to harvest 25 percent more sweet corn! How many times have you heard "it's best to remove suckers from corn stalks because they rob the parent plant and cause the ears to be smaller?" Well, tain't so! In fact, if you forget that extra work and leave those suckers on, you'll have up to 25 percent more ears. On top of that, those ears will be larger and better-formed than those without suckers!

... how to grow cheaper tomatoes and peppers ... earlier! Forget about starting pepper and tomato plants indoors. This master gardener's technique allows you to sow seeds directly in the garden soil for harvests that are up to five days earlier than those started indoors (or bought) and then transplanted. Think of the fuss (and money) this can save you!

You'll find details on all these techniques in "Secrets of Master Gardeners" -- the free better gardening guide we're waiting to send you.

Still think there's "nothing new under the sun" when it comes to gardening?

Believe me, every season brings new discoveries!

Day after day, my editors and I review some truly amazing new gardening methods. And each month it's our job to pick the very best of these new ideas and publish them for our readers ... to make your gardening more enjoyable, more productive, more economical.

Many of our stories are real blockbusters, like the one we recently ran on how to get ...

... 8 to 10 pints of strawberries from a single plant! "Too many plants and too few berries." That's the strawberry grower's lament. But it's not the number of plants that counts. It's how you care for them. One of the biggest stories in ORGANIC GARDENING recently was about a technique that can bring you 8 to 10 pints of plump juicy berries from a single plant! Be sure to send for your free book and read all about this high-yielding technique!

With food prices so high these days, it really pays to grow as much of your food as you can. And with the tips you find in ORGANIC GARDENING every month, you'll save time and make fewer mistakes.

Punkre's letter is noteworthy also for its use of illustrations. We don't think of letters—those intensely personal communications—as being illustrated. Put an illustration on any page, and it immediately loses its intimacy; it announces itself as a piece of mass communication and has the feel of a magazine or newspaper. These days people illustrate letters by enclosing a snapshot or two.

How did letters look before snapshots? How did people communicate with illustrations before George Eastman, inventor of the film roll, came out with his Kodak Brownie Box Camera that put photography into the hands of the masses?

Letters up to the 1920s were frequently illustrated with drawings. The great Lithuanian-born art connoisseur Bernard Berenson used to travel throughout Italy studying and authenticating works of Renaissance art. Was that really a Tiepolo in Pisa or was it "school of . . ."? Berenson would sketch the hand or the arm so he could compare it with that of an authentic Tiepolo in Venice or Rome. Berenson's wife used to do the same, and their letters to each other are filled with drawings—from scribbles to quite good renderings—which were carefully filed in their jewel of a villa, *I Tatti*, outside Florence and referred to in their research and published writings. The advent of the personal camera—and especially the invention of the flash attachment in 1925—obviated the need for sketches on letters.

With the exception of the page-one four-color photograph of the

(After all, it's not how hard you work that determines garden success -- it's how much you know!)

Times are changing. And so are gardening methods. Every day we're discovering a bounty of wonderful new tips that can save you work ... help you eliminate mistakes ... enable you to grow more food ... and extend the growing season further than we used to think was possible!

One of our main jobs is showing you how to get more food from your garden space without increasing your work. The secret to this is intensive gardening techniques that allow you to get more productivity from your garden space -- often with less work. And there's plenty we'd like to show you to help you get a lot more growing on your lot!

Once upon a time a gardener might never have dreamed of yields like four pounds of cucumbers or six pounds of tomatoes per square foot! Or 250 pounds of potatoes from a 10' x 10' patch! But with today's new intensive gardening techniques, now you can.

Cut a cardboard triangle with sides the length of the spacing you want.

And every issue of ORGANIC GARDENING will show you how!

Yes, even if you own just a little land you can grow practically all your own food. And you'll learn all about how to do it in your copy of "Secrets of Master Gardeners." Be sure to send for it today!

I could go on and on, because so does "Secrets of Master Gardeners" -- 14 helpful chapters of great gardening ideas in all.

Use the triangle to set plants or seeds (here shown as dots) at exact spacing.

You'll find "best ideas" on starting seeds right ... harvesting and storing fruits and vegetables ... saving more time, money ... and avoiding mistakes and unnecessary work in nearly every aspect of your garden operation.

Even if you're already a good gardener, you can become a better gardener thanks to this "best ideas" book.

I'd like to send you a copy of "Secrets of Master Gardeners" free. Here's why ...

> We're certain that once you see how much easier and enjoyable your gardening can be ... you'll want to go deeper and deeper into the fulfilling and rewarding experience of the organic gardening world. And that's where ORGANIC GARDENING magazine comes in. Because no other magazine can get you more personally involved in the world beneath your feet.

(over, please)

Each and every issue of the magazine is chock-full of the best gardening ideas from our research center ... the latest discoveries and techniques ... and the plots and patches of some of the world's most experienced gardeners.

> So send in the enclosed order card today to start ORGANIC GARDENING coming your way and I'll send off your three free gifts: "Secrets of Master Gardeners" plus "Beautiful ... Bountiful Landscapes" and "The Harvest Book." (See the enclosed flyer for information about these extra free gifts.)

One look is worth a thousand words of advertising, so I'll spare your time. But, please, don't miss this opportunity.

So act right now. The postage is paid and you've got nothing to lose and a great garden to gain!

Waiting to mail your book,

Robert Rodale
Editor

P.S. REMEMBER, this special offer for ORGANIC GARDENING® magazine brings you these three free gifts. Each one is chock-full of some of the best tips money can't buy. So use the easy order card today for a start on your best garden ever.

Printed in USA

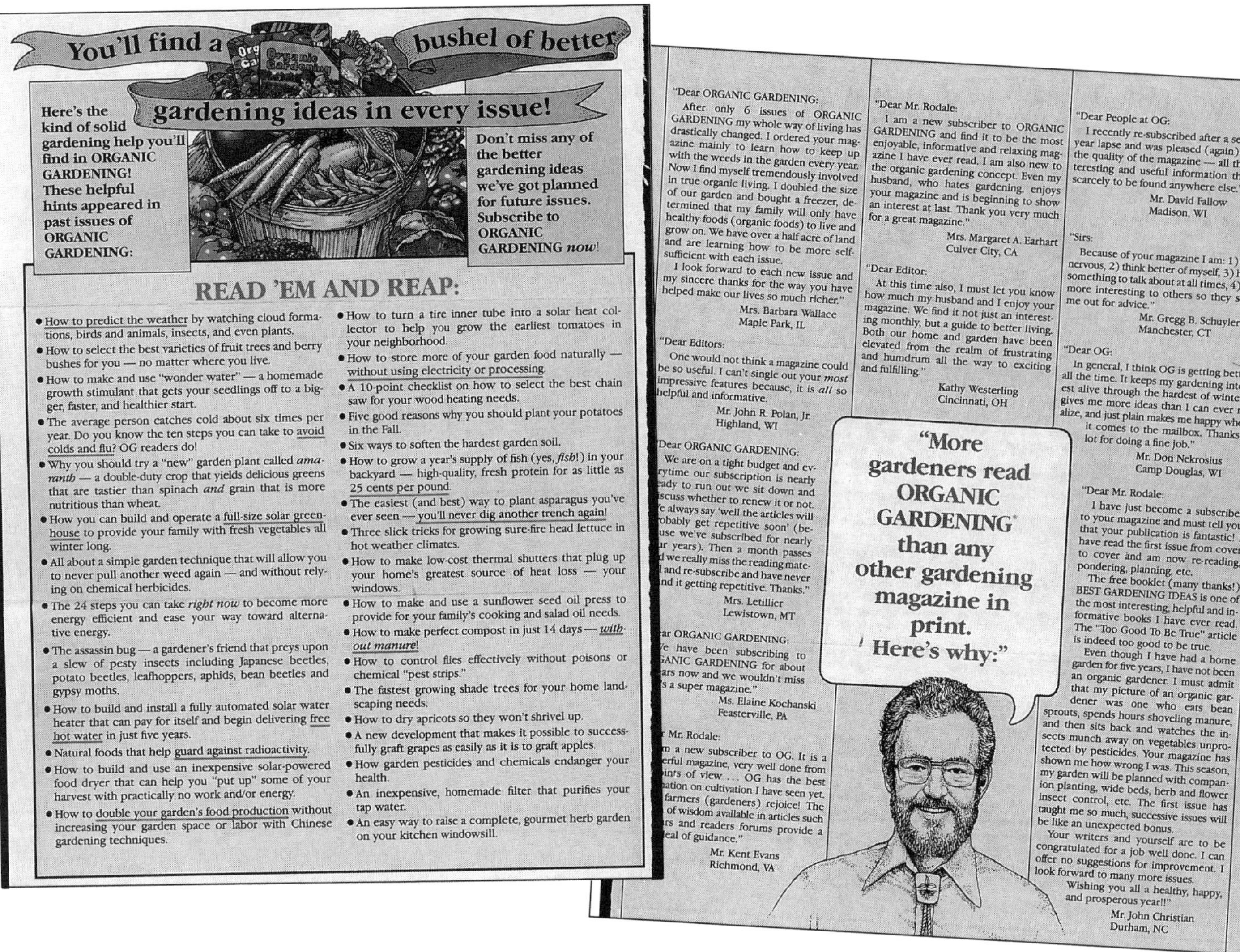

You'll find a bushel of better gardening ideas in every issue!

Here's the kind of solid gardening help you'll find in ORGANIC GARDENING! These helpful hints appeared in past issues of ORGANIC GARDENING:

Don't miss any of the better gardening ideas we've got planned for future issues. Subscribe to ORGANIC GARDENING *now*!

READ 'EM AND REAP:

- How to predict the weather by watching cloud formations, birds and animals, insects, and even plants.
- How to select the best varieties of fruit trees and berry bushes for you — no matter where you live.
- How to make and use "wonder water" — a homemade growth stimulant that gets your seedlings off to a bigger, faster, and healthier start.
- The average person catches cold about six times per year. Do you know the ten steps you can take to avoid colds and flu? OG readers do!
- Why you should try a "new" garden plant called *amaranth* — a double-duty crop that yields delicious greens that are tastier than spinach *and* grain that is more nutritious than wheat.
- How you can build and operate a full-size solar greenhouse to provide your family with fresh vegetables all winter long.
- All about a simple garden technique that will allow you to never pull another weed again — and without relying on chemical herbicides.
- The 24 steps you can take *right now* to become more energy efficient and ease your way toward alternative energy.
- The assassin bug — a gardener's friend that preys upon a slew of pesty insects including Japanese beetles, potato beetles, leafhoppers, aphids, bean beetles and gypsy moths.
- How to build and install a fully automated solar water heater that can pay for itself and begin delivering free hot water in just five years.
- Natural foods that help guard against radioactivity.
- How to build and use an inexpensive solar-powered food dryer that can help you "put up" some of your harvest with practically no work and/or energy.
- How to double your garden's food production without increasing your garden space or labor with Chinese gardening techniques.
- How to turn a tire inner tube into a solar heat collector to help you grow the earliest tomatoes in your neighborhood.
- How to store more of your garden food naturally — without using electricity or processing.
- A 10-point checklist on how to select the best chain saw for your wood heating needs.
- Five good reasons why you should plant your potatoes in the Fall.
- Six ways to soften the hardest garden soil.
- How to grow a year's supply of fish (yes, *fish*!) in your backyard — high-quality, fresh protein for as little as 25 cents per pound.
- The easiest (and best) way to plant asparagus you've ever seen — you'll never dig another trench again!
- Three slick tricks for growing sure-fire head lettuce in hot weather climates.
- How to make low-cost thermal shutters that plug up your home's greatest source of heat loss — your windows.
- How to make and use a sunflower seed oil press to provide for your family's cooking and salad oil needs.
- How to make perfect compost in just 14 days — *without manure*!
- How to control flies effectively without poisons or chemical "pest strips."
- The fastest growing shade trees for your home landscaping needs.
- How to dry apricots so they won't shrivel up.
- A new development that makes it possible to successfully graft grapes as easily as it is to graft apples.
- How garden pesticides and chemicals endanger your health.
- An inexpensive, homemade filter that purifies your tap water.
- An easy way to raise a complete, gourmet herb garden on your kitchen windowsill.

"Dear ORGANIC GARDENING:

After only 6 issues of ORGANIC GARDENING my whole way of living has drastically changed. I ordered your magazine mainly to learn how to keep up with the weeds in the garden every year. Now I find myself tremendously involved in true organic living. I doubled the size of our garden and bought a freezer, determined that my family will only have healthy foods (organic foods) to live and grow on. We have over a half acre of land and are learning how to be more self-sufficient with each issue.

I look forward to each new issue and my sincere thanks for the way you have helped make our lives so much richer."

Mrs. Barbara Wallace
Maple Park, IL

"Dear Editors:

One would not think a magazine could be so useful. I can't single out your *most* impressive features because, it is *all* so helpful and informative.

Mr. John R. Polan, Jr.
Highland, WI

"Dear ORGANIC GARDENING:

We are on a tight budget and ev-rytime our subscription is nearly eady to run out we sit down and iscuss whether to renew it or not. e always say 'well the articles will obably get repetitive soon' (beuse we've subscribed for nearly ur years). Then a month passes d we really miss the reading mate-l and re-subscribe and have never nd it getting repetitive. Thanks."

Mrs. Letillier
Lewistown, MT

ar ORGANIC GARDENING:

e have been subscribing to ANIC GARDENING for about ars now and we wouldn't miss s a super magazine."

Ms. Elaine Kochanski
Feasterville, PA

r Mr. Rodale:

m a new subscriber to OG. It is a erful magazine, very well done from ints of view ... OG has the best ation on cultivation I have seen yet. farmers (gardeners) rejoice! The of wisdom available in articles such rs and readers forums provide a eal of guidance."

Mr. Kent Evans
Richmond, VA

"Dear Mr. Rodale:

I am a new subscriber to ORGANIC GARDENING and find it to be the most enjoyable, informative and relaxing magazine I have ever read. I am also new to the organic gardening concept. Even my husband, who hates gardening, enjoys your magazine and is beginning to show an interest at last. Thank you very much for a great magazine."

Mrs. Margaret A. Earhart
Culver City, CA

"Dear Editor:

At this time also, I must let you know how much my husband and I enjoy your magazine. We find it not just an interesting monthly, but a guide to better living. Both our home and garden have been elevated from the realm of frustrating and humdrum all the way to exciting and fulfilling."

Kathy Westerling
Cincinnati, OH

"More gardeners read ORGANIC GARDENING® than any other gardening magazine in print. Here's why:"

"Dear People at OG:

I recently re-subscribed after a several year lapse and was pleased (again) with the quality of the magazine — all the interesting and useful information that is scarcely to be found anywhere else."

Mr. David Fallow
Madison, WI

"Sirs:

Because of your magazine I am: 1) less nervous, 2) think better of myself, 3) have something to talk about at all times, 4) am more interesting to others so they seek me out for advice."

Mr. Gregg B. Schuyler
Manchester, CT

"Dear OG:

In general, I think OG is getting better all the time. It keeps my gardening interest alive through the hardest of winters, gives me more ideas than I can ever realize, and just plain makes me happy when it comes to the mailbox. Thanks a lot for doing a fine job."

Mr. Don Nekrosius
Camp Douglas, WI

"Dear Mr. Rodale:

I have just become a subscriber to your magazine and must tell you that your publication is fantastic! I have read the first issue from cover to cover and am now re-reading, pondering, planning, etc.

The free booklet (many thanks!) BEST GARDENING IDEAS is one of the most interesting, helpful and informative books I have ever read. The "Too Good To Be True" article is indeed too good to be true.

Even though I have had a home garden for five years, I have not been an organic gardener. I must admit that my picture of an organic gardener was one who eats bean sprouts, spends hours shoveling manure, and then sits back and watches the insects munch away on vegetables unprotected by pesticides. Your magazine has shown me how wrong I was. This season, my garden will be planned with companion planting, wide beds, herb and flower insect control, etc. The first issue has taught me so much, successive issues will be like an unexpected bonus.

Your writers and yourself are to be congratulated for a job well done. I can offer no suggestions for improvement. I look forward to many more issues.

Wishing you all a healthy, happy, and prosperous year!!"

Mr. John Christian
Durham, NC

Organic Gardening's brochure, printed 4 colors over 3.

premium, all the illustrations in this letter are drawings in the tradition of the Berensons.

The design and efficient use of paper in Jim Punkre's package are extraordinary. The 11″ × 17″ letter is printed in four-color; the top area is printed in bright yellow with the headline "HEADS UP, GARDENERS!" printed in red. The letter itself is printed in black typewriter type against a light brown background. Only the photograph of the premium makes use of four-color process printing.

The brochure is an 8½″ × 11″ single sheet, printed front and back and packed with copy. The four-color illustration on the front shows a farm basket filled with beautiful vegetables and surrounded by others. The copy is made up of thirty-one specific promises of the kind of information to be found in every issue of *Organic Gardening*; they are printed against a bright yellow background.

The back—printed in three colors on the same bright yellow background—is made up of testimonials from happy readers.

One thing is for sure: no reader will doze off looking at these yellows and reds.

The $4^{3}/_{4}'' \times 11''$ premium slip is also printed in four colors.

What makes this entire effort so efficient is that all three pieces were printed together on one sheet of paper, slit, folded, and inserted.

The great Canadian designer Ted Kikoler insists that designers and copywriters should know the basics of printing and the kinds of presses used. More than once Kikoler has found that in the course of printing a particular piece, the entire sheet of paper going through the press would not be used; rather an excess piece of it would be sheared off and sent to a landfill.

The premium slip, front and back.

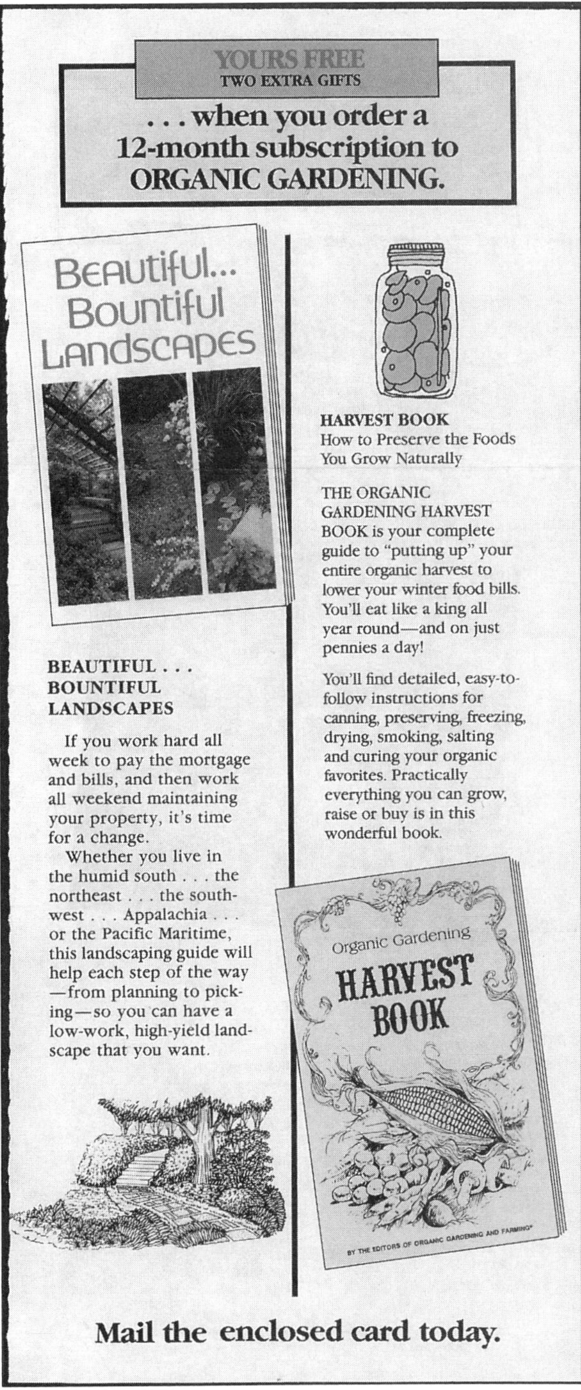

Instead of wasting that paper, Kikoler will design a lift piece to those specifications. The only cost is in the creation: copy, design, photography, separations, and mechanical. The printing of it is free, since it is going through the press anyway. The shape might be a little odd, but so what? An extra little surprise in the package will usually raise results. And the cost per thousand is unchanged.

According to Jim Punkre, this *Organic Gardening* effort fit the Kikoler model: the letter, circular, and lift piece were all printed at once on the same sheet of paper, which certainly fits Rodale's guiding philosophy of ecological responsibility.

Notice on the order card that the price is 10 issues for $12.97 (plus $1.97 delivery). *Reader's Digest* first came up with the idea of burying a

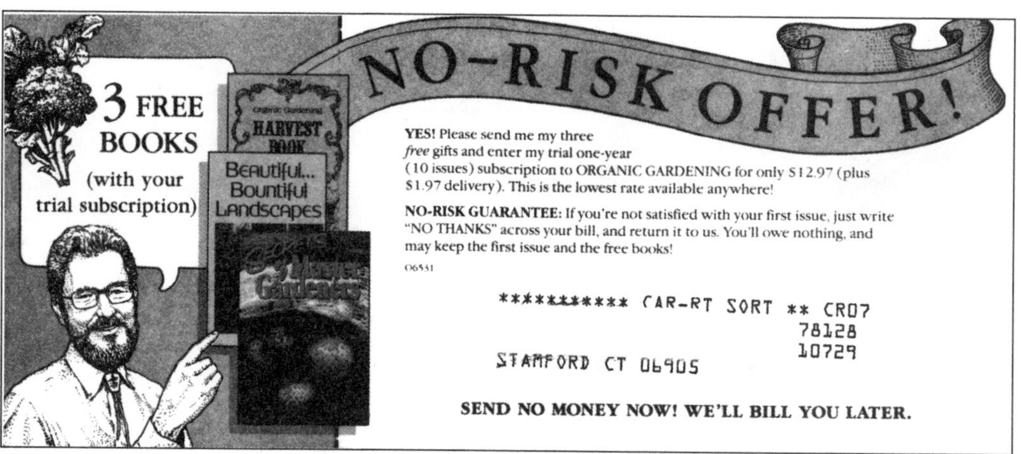

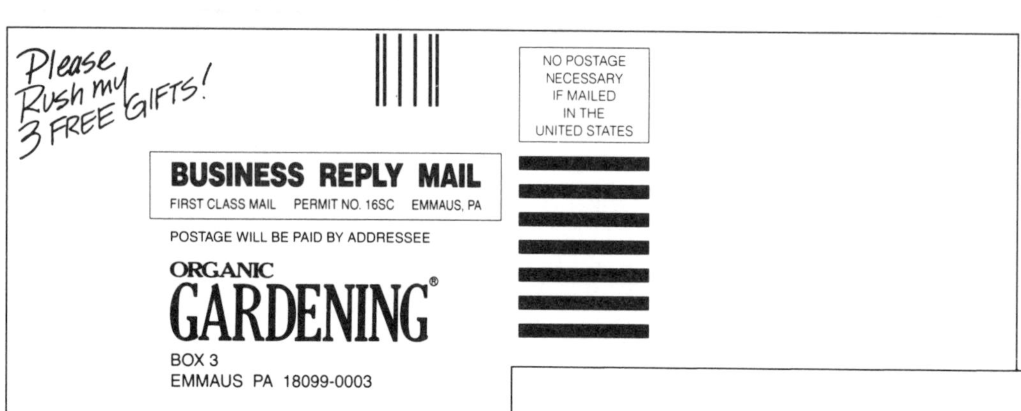

The order form, front and back, and the business reply envelope.

price increase by charging for postage. This is rare, but presumably works for Rodale as well as the *Digest.*

Another feature of this mailing is the use of two business reply elements. The back of the order card has a business reply face, which means that you can simply tear off the stub and drop the card into the mail. In addition, a business reply envelope is enclosed in case you are inclined to send some cash or if you prefer the privacy that an envelope ensures.

This effort—known at Rodale as the "Broccoli Bob Rodale package"—would most probably be control today. It was forced into retirement by the tragic death of Bob Rodale in a bus accident at the Moscow airport in the late fall of 1990.

Ever resourceful, the designers at Rodale deleted Bob Rodale's picture

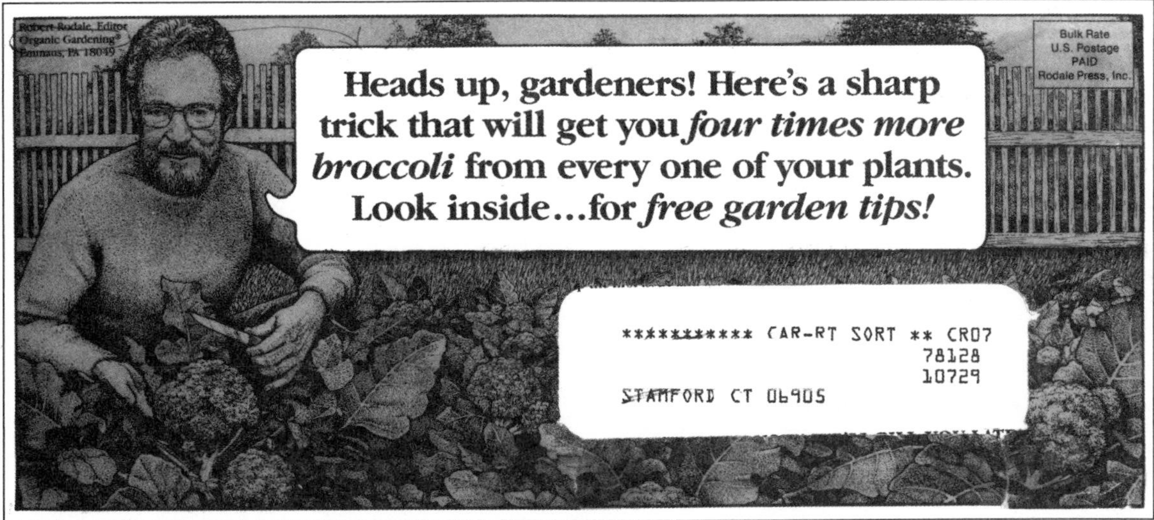

The "Broccoli Bob Rodale" mailing shown before Bob Rodale's death.

The mailing after Bob Rodale's death.

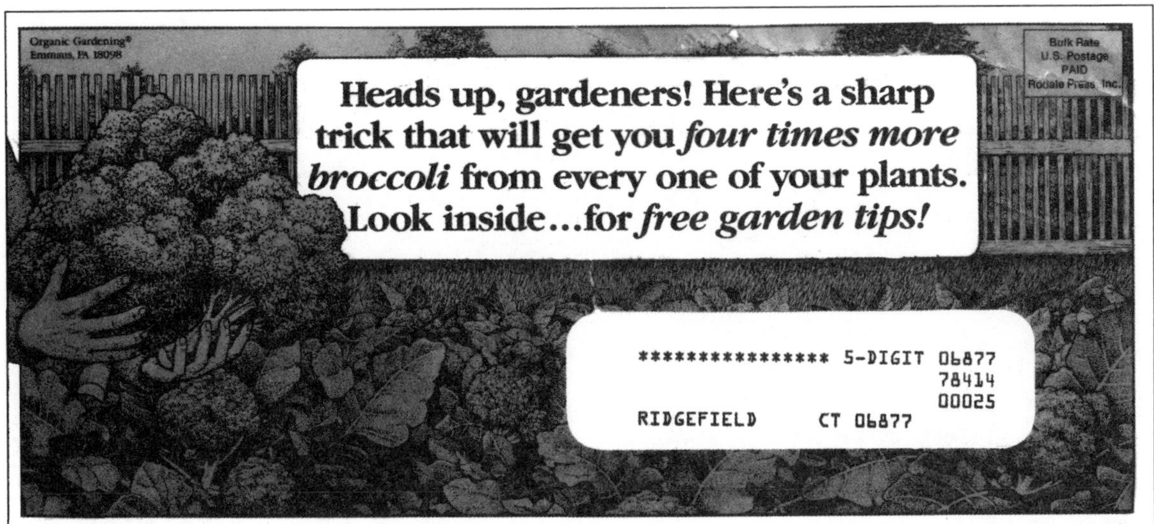

throughout the package and it resumed its control status. It has apparently since been beaten.

Jim Punkre spent thirteen years as chief copywriter for Rodale Press before starting his own West Coast creative service, Brainstorms, Inc. Among his clients: *Esquire*, *Playboy*, Democratic Party, Oxmoor House, *U.S. News & World Report*, Sunset Books, *Bicycling*, *Consumer Reports*, and Girls Clubs of America.

JIM PUNKRE:
As far as the way I work . . . I think the current Nike theme (''Just Do It!'') says it all. My belief system can be summed up in Punkre's ten laws:

1. *People want to know ''what's in it for ME?'' first and foremost.*
2. *Negativity repels; positivity ATTRACTS.*
3. *Inspiration reveals itself in the midst of PERSPIRATION.*
4. *Research, research, RESEARCH!*
5. *It's more important to know the MARKET than the product.*
6. *Our job is to make the new feel FAMILIAR, and the familiar feel suddenly NEW.*
7. *Clients would rather have mediocre copy on time than outstanding copy LATE.*
8. *Great design will frequently SAVE bad copy—but bad design will always destroy even the most brilliant text.*
9. *A copywriter is the BRIDGE between things and dreams.*
10. *Possession is nine-tenths of the FLAW. Spending too much on self-promotion and fighting over ownership or who did and did not do what tends to thwart creativity.*

10

Consumer Magazines II:

Women's Interest/Home/Shelter

Bon Appétit

In his commentary on his Omaha Steaks mailing in Chapter 18, Herschell Gordon Lewis compares creating a direct mail package to method acting. A good direct response writer not only gets inside the head of the person who will receive the mailing, but *becomes* that person, as Marlon Brando became Don Corleone in *The Godfather* and Meryl Streep became Karen Blixen in *Out of Africa*. On becoming that person, the writer then has to imagine all possible objections that could be raised to the product and offer, and then overcome those objections in the course of the copy and design. It's a head game, pure and simple. Fats Waller's "I'm Gonna Sit Right Down and Write Myself a Letter" is truly the direct mail writer's theme song.

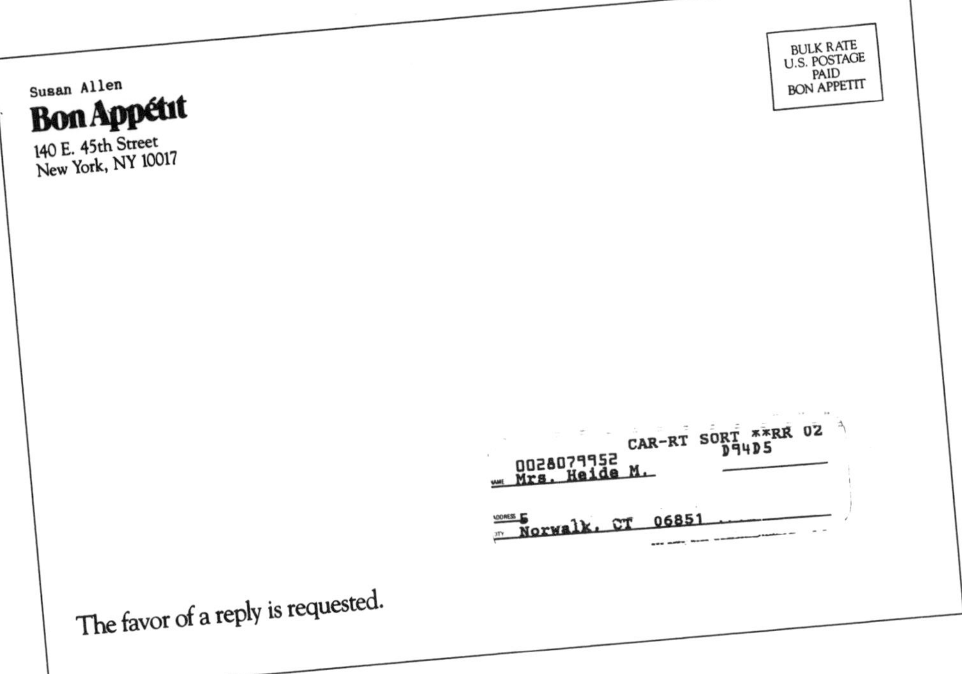

MAILER: *Bon Appétit*
PACKAGE: "Pick of the crop!"
PROJECT MGR.: Susan Allyn
WRITER: Linda Wells
DESIGNER: R. L. Polk
FIRST MAILED: 1986
The *Bon Appétit* outside envelope.

What distinguishes a great actor is the same thing that distinguishes a great direct mail writer. Just as Dustin Hoffman can become Willie Loman, Ratso, an idiot savant in *Rain Man,* and even a bumptious, buxom woman in *Tootsie,* so a direct mail writer must be able to change roles. In Chapter 20, the late Hank Burnett alludes to the discomfort he felt in knowing so much about thirteen- and fourteen-year-old girls when he was writing the *Sassy* magazine package.

Linda Wells can be equally chameleonlike, jumping inside the skin of a food lover (*Bon Appétit*), a middle-aged woman (*Lear's*), a nurse (*American Journal of Nursing*), a collector (*Art & Auction*), a child (Children's Television Workshop), or an investor (*Financial World*).

The offer arrives in a simple, white 6″ × 9″ window envelope. In the upper left corner—the so-called cornercard—are the magazine logo and address. It's a real address on East Forty-fifth Street in New York. Even though the business reply envelope is addressed to a post office box in Red Oak, Iowa, the letter comes from a real address.

It comes from a real person, too. Circulation director Susan Allyn's name is over the magazine's name in typewriter type, as though it were hand-typed. This personalizes the mailing; even though the addressee's name is on a Cheshire label, the mailing *appears* to come from a real person as well as a real street address. This is subtle stuff; but maybe it makes a difference of a tenth of a percentage point.

There is a single line of copy on the envelope: "The favor of a reply is requested."

At first glance, this seems to be an innocuous, weak teaser. However, Linda Wells uses the same line on the envelope of her launch package for *Lear's* (Chapter 13), so she knows what she is doing. More to the point, this line of copy is used very frequently. Audrey Ridley of R. L. Polk reported that the original Jayme-Ratalahti long-term control for the *Harvard Medical School Health Letter* had a belt and belt buckle going across the face of the envelope with this copy:

Yes or No.
Food is more fattening
when you eat it
late at night.

There was other copy as well. This was tested against "The favor of a reply is requested," and the latter won handily.

Another Linda Wells signature is to start a letter with "Congratulations!" You'll find it in the *Lear's* Grand Control in Chapter 13. Right off the bat, she makes readers feel good about themselves.

The cover panel of the circular depicts a delectable dish of peach ice cream; it is so beautifully printed on coated paper that you can almost take a spoon to it. The desserts shown on the first inside panel are equally inviting. They follow Meredith's rule of never showing small pictures of food.

The inside of the brochure explodes open with a beautiful dessert table and cover of the magazine and the word "FREE" all over the place. The back panel shows covers and spreads from the magazine and screams "FREE!"

Bon Appétit

BON APPETIT! It's the pick of the crop! The freshest, most colorful food, travel and entertaining magazine published! The one that's tenderest on your time and budget! The one that blossoms with over 100 new kitchen-tested recipes every month! The one that's yours to sample and savor

FREE!

Dear Reader:

Congratulations!

You know more about sound nutrition and smart consumer shopping than any generation before. You cook with more imagination. You serve with more style. Busy as you are with everything else, you entertain so gracefully and graciously, you make it all look easy.

Congratulations!

Keep it up! Do it even better and faster with the issue of BON APPETIT we'd like to send you free. That's right, free! We want you to taste-test BON APPETIT the same way our editors taste-test the 100-plus recipes in every issue. We want you to try it, to use it, to enjoy it. We want you to find out for yourself if it can help you live more beautifully and bountifully for less.

If your free copy of BON APPETIT makes you hungry for more, join us at savings of half off the regular subscription value for 12 issues. If it's not to your taste, pay nothing -- and keep the issue absolutely free!

More about our peach of an offer in just a minute. First, let me describe BON APPETIT -- its style, its sophistication, its savvy and its place in your fast-paced life.

New Times. New Foods. New Fun!

When the publishers of Architectural Digest and HOME bought BON APPETIT in 1975, it was obvious that folks like you had left traditional food magazines far, far behind.

They were still printing 863 ways to cook hamburger. You were experimenting with new ingredients. Traveling and bringing back new food combinations. Discovering new gadgets that helped you make recipes you never dared to try before. Cooking lighter and healthier. You weren't throwing the old ways out -- just updating them for now.

So BON APPETIT shrugged off its old gingham apron, tipped on a new toque blanche and traveled the world to find you the best new products, foods, wines, appliances, chefs, restaurants and holiday destinations. We quickly became America's favorite food magazine -- with a happy following of more than 5,600,000 readers.

Today, our friends use BON APPETIT as a kind of international meeting place where good cooks trade great ideas for making fine foods fast.

In a recent RSVP column, a New York reader told us about a Pennsylvania restaurant where she had the lightest, brightest bisque. We asked the chef for his recipe...and here it is. Terrific! Try it!

Honeydew and Lime Bisque

Peel, seed and dice a large honeydew melon. In your food processor or blender, mix it with a pint of lime sherbet and the juice of one large lime. Puree until smooth. Divide among bowls set into crushed ice. Garnish with fresh mint.

In Too Busy to Cook?, another BON APPETIT exclusive, readers exchange recipes for days when you're simply rushed off your feet. For instance...

Mary's Spicy Apple Syrup

In saucepan, combine 1 cup cold water, 1 6-ounce can of frozen unsweetened apple juice (thawed), 1/4 cup sugar, 1-1/2 tablespoons cornstarch, 1/2 teaspoon cinnamon and 1/2 teaspoon vanilla. Stir over medium heat until mixture simmers and clears, about 10-12 minutes. Serve warm over ice cream, pancakes or crepes -- and listen to the raves!

Every month in Shortcuts with Style, you get complete menus, recipes and techniques for using your food processor and microwave creatively. In Cooking for Friends, you get elegant and easy entertaining ideas -- menus and recipes for marvelous meals like this...

Caribbean Festival Dinner

Chilled Avocado Lime Cream Soup
Chicken and Chorizo Stew
Cheese Corn Sticks
Tossed Salad Tropicale
Pina Colada Cake
Red Rioja Wine

In Bon Vivant, you learn who's who in the world of wine and food. In Wine Press, experts answer your questions from grape to glass. With BON APPETIT's useful, practical, helpful columns, you get countless ideas and complete plans for faster, more flavorful feasts.

But that's not all! Every month, BON APPETIT brings you at least six full-color photo features, all complete with recipes and finished, mouth-watering photographs. And every recipe is kitchen-tested so even a beginner can get perfect results the first time -- and every time!

Try these! California bistro menus. Fabulous cheesecakes. Delicious Asian flatbreads. Fast one-dish dinners. Vintage desserts. Cozy informal suppers. New wave sandwiches. Curry classics. Ethnic entrees. Buttermilk baking. Dazzling dessert buffets. Fast gifts from your kitchen. A New Orleans jazz brunch. A dessert chef's perfect pastries.

Try these! Romantic dinners for two. Sky-high spiced chocolate cake. Warming chowders from New England. A spirited Halloween dinner (from Transylvania, where else?) Recipes from La Cote Basque in New York...Le Francais in Illinois... Robuchon in Paris...the Mandarin in Singapore...Girardet in Switzerland...Kiccho in Tokyo...Berowra Waters near Sydney.

New Culinary Worlds to Conquer

In every issue of BON APPETIT, the world's greatest chefs give you a complete, step-by-step cooking class. Home cooks and cooking couples open up their kitchen doors and give you masterplans for perfect parties. Galloping gourmets escort you around the whole, wide world of food, wine and travel adventure. BON APPETIT! Bon voyage!

Come! Come with BON APPETIT to the beautiful back roads of Holland. Send postcards from Kauai, where the sun, the fun and the food are first-rate. Eat your heart out in the restaurants of Lyons. Cruise the high seas for the hautest cuisine afloat. Let Seville cast its colorful spell. Be a guest at the great wine estates of Germany.

Be our guest in a free preview of America's wisest, wittiest and worldliest magazine of fine food, travel and entertaining...

BON APPETIT! Your First Issue is FREE!

All you do to get your free copy of the current issue is to return the enclosed card in the postpaid envelope today.

As soon as you answer YES, we'll send off the magazine and enroll you as a subscriber, entitled to get eleven additional issues -- 12 issues in all -- for only $9.00. That is half off the regular subscription value for 12 issues.

If BON APPETIT isn't the most luscious food magazine you have ever seen, write "cancel" across the bill when you get it, return it and keep the issue absolutely free. It's a gift with our sincerest compliments!

And if you subscribe, then change your mind, you can always cancel. Let us know, and we'll send you an immediate and unquestioned refund -- 100% money back -- on full amount paid.

SEND NO MONEY NOW! But please mail your card today! Reap the pick of the magazine crop! Harvest a hundred new kitchen-tested recipes from BON APPETIT -- FREE!

Sincerely,

William J. Garry
Editor

WG:ccr

P.S. This half-price offer is the lowest rate available. We may not be able to offer it again, so don't miss the opportunity. Mail your order today! Thanks -- WJG

Bon Appétit 140 E. 45th Street, New York, NY 10017

WL2

IT'S Bon Appétit – YOURS FREE!

Will it be love at first bite? Will a taste of *Bon Appétit* ripen into a lasting romance? We'd like to send you a mint-fresh copy of the current issue to find out. *Free.*

In your free issue, you'll find more than 100 recipes for new adventures in eating. Quick and easy recipes when you've no time to cook. Food processor and microwave recipes when you want fine food fast. Recipes from restaurants readers like you have discovered. Recipes from great home cooks and cooking couples. Recipes and illustrated, step-by-step cooking classes from name professionals. A world of glamorous ethnic recipes from around the globe – all translated into American ingredients and American ways of home cooking.

They're all taste-tested in our *Bon Appétit* kitchen. You'll have more fun cooking than ever before because you can't go wrong!

FREE STARTERS!

In your free issue of *Bon Appétit*, you'll learn to shop smarter, faster and thriftier. You'll get tips and techniques for achieving top quality quickly. You'll find make-ahead meals you can fix and freeze.

For starters, you'll get recipes like Chicken Wings Cumberland – crispy, crunchy, broiled chicken wings with a sauce of oranges, red currant jelly, mustard, ginger, shallots and red wine vinegar. What a happy, high-flying combination! What a way to make a party take flight!

FREE SOUPS!

Take Quick Borscht, for instance. All you do is combine a jar of red cabbage, a can of diced beets, a can of beef bouillon, white wine vinegar and a dash of ground red pepper. Cover and chill until ready to serve. Then garnish this rosy red soup with a swirl of sour cream and a pretty sprig of fresh green dill.

FREE SALADS!

You'll find the most colorful combinations in your free issue of *Bon Appétit*! Brown rice with vegetable salad. Orange chicken salad with cashews. Romaine and grapefruit salad with pine nuts. Asparagus salad with cucumbers. Mozzarella, tomato and basil pesto salad. Red pepper pasta salad with shrimp and snow peas. Provençal potato salad. Warm chicken and walnut salad. Main dish salads. Side dish salads. He-man salads. Salads for ladies who lunch!

FREE MAIN DISHES!

You get new, fun-to-fix ideas for every meal of the day – and every day of the year! Most *Bon Appétit* recipes use fresh, natural foods in season when prices are at their lowest. For instance, this fall you might like to try: Brisket with prunes. Duck with plum sauce. Moroccan lamb tajine with dates. Polenta and sausage casserole. Polynesian flank steak. Quick chicken curry. Red snapper Szechuan. Reuben casserole. Stuffed breast of chicken with Chinese vegetables. Sole Wellington. Veal chops with artichokes. Zucchini lasagna.

FREE VEGGIES!

Having a Meat-and-Potatoes Person over to dinner? Take an ordinary meal out of this world with vegetables from your free *Bon Appétit*! With ham, try a cheese and green bean casserole. With pork, try a quick corn savory. With lamb, try saffron rice. With barbecued burgers, try mixed grilled vegetables. With fish, try spinach Catalonian style. With roast beef, try Cumberland sausages.

FREE SWEETS TO THE SWEET!

Your free issue – and every issue – of *Bon Appétit* brings you the most delectable desserts and pastries in all the world. Some are as quick as sundae sauces you whiz up in the blender. Some are so spectacular you'll enjoy the time they take. But even the most complicated come easy with the crisp, clear instructions and step-by-step full-color illustrations you get in *Bon Appétit*.

So feast your eyes on bon bon *Bon Appétit* today! Send for your free copy now!

Linda Wells's 4-page letter for *Bon Appétit*.

Bon Appétit
Light, Easy and Fast
Bon Appétit
It's the pick of the crop – America's freshest food, travel and entertaining magazine from the Knapp Communications Corporation family of publications, which includes *Architectural Digest* and *HOME*. And the big, bountiful current issue is yours
FREE!
© 1988 Bon Appétit Publishing Corporation

R. L. Polk's brochure for *Bon Appétit*.

SPECIAL

HALF-PRICE OFFER

We invite you to subscribe to **Bon Appétit**

This half-price offer is the lowest rate available. We may not be able to offer it again, so don't miss the opportunity. Mail your order today!

BON41HP

The *Bon Appétit* mini-lift piece and order card with fancy label and "YES" token. On the business reply envelope, the *Bon Appétit* logo is printed in bright red, as is the "Special Money-Saving Offer" in the circle. There's no reason why a BRE can't have some *sell* on it; it's the last thing the new customer sees before it goes into the mail, and some reassurance—such as "Special Money-Saving Offer"—can make a person feel good about ordering.

The lift piece is a nuts-'n'-bolts restatement of the half-price offer.

The four-color order card is cute, with the sweet, succulent peach serving as a "YES" token and the word "NO" below it on a sour lemon. The peach is a detachable, pressure-sensitive token. The lemon is simply printed on; you cannot affix the "NO" token to the reply card and return it.

Linda Wells is one of the legendary freelancers, along with John Tighe, the late Hank Burnett, the late Chris Stagg, Judy Weiss, Robert Haydon Jones, Frank Johnson, Walter Weintz, and Bill Jayme.

Before freelancing, Linda Wells had a successful corporate career at J. Walter Thompson, McCann-Erickson, BBDO, Condé Nast Publications, and Citibank. A freelancer since 1971, she has written winning packages for just about *everybody*: Alexander Hamilton Institute, Bantam Books, Boardroom Reports, Columbia House, Figi's, *Food & Wine*, *Money* magazine, Smithsonian Books, Time-Life Books, *University of California Wellness Letter*, and a slew more. Wells splits her time between New York and London.

Linda Wells:

It is my hope that the Axel Awards inspire a return to classic direct response packages that work up front, work at the bottom line, and work for years to come.

I like to see outer envelopes with wonderful headlines instead of freefreefree . . . letters that look and read like letters from one human being to another instead of one corporate robot to another . . . brochures that track and build in excitement instead of the current hodgepodge . . . order cards that make purchasing easy instead of aggravating. I like to see packages that sell product benefits instead of premiums—packages that are thoughtful, intelligent, and informative.

I think that in the nervous nineties, too many people are trying to sell too many different things in one package—with the result that they are selling almost nothing at all. Instead of testing, they're second-guessing and the result is, in my opinion, a very real decline in quality. We can do better. And with the encouragement of the Axel Awards, I believe we will.

House & Garden

The *House & Garden* "White Sale" mailing by Jerry Ricigliano of Rapp Collins Marcoa is elegant, demure, and literate. The outside envelope and simple two-page letter are printed on coated white stock and printed with black and gold. The only illustration in the mailing is a small four-color cover on the order form. The lift piece—a screaming exhortation in blue type on a white background to "ACT NOW"—breaks the otherwise subdued mood and reminds you that the point of the mailing is to send in an order.

Jerry Ricigliano:

For me, having to beat your own control package stirs up overwhelming feelings of mixed emotion. (I think of that old joke that equates mixed emotion with "seeing your mother-in-law drive off a cliff in your new Mercedes.")

On the one hand, the opportunity to push your creative prowess to new

HG

.LK RATE
U.S. POSTAGE
PAID
PERMIT NO. 121
TRENTON, NJ

HOUSE & GARDEN
IS HAVING
ITS OWN VERY SPECIAL
WHITE SALE

□YES

ONLY $1.00 AN ISSUE

388 01496761 CAR-RT ST CR56
Peggy BKL
Rd. OS53
Stamford, CT 06903

Valid until August 15, 199C

Mailer: *House & Garden*
Package: Special White Sale
Project Mgr.: Kim Doneker
Agency: Rapp Collins Marcoa
Account Mgr.: Cindy Abrams
Writer: Jerry Ricigliano
Designer: Jerry Genova
First Mailed: 1986

The elegant #9 *House & Garden* outside envelope with 3 windows. Through the lefthand window appears the word "YES"; through the bottom window is the cutoff date. Should you use a cutoff date? It can stimulate orders by imposing a time limit. At the same time, third-class delivery is chancy. If the mailing arrives after the deadline, it will die; if you allow for this possibility by having a cutoff date in the distant future, the urgency is lost. You may want to mail first class.

HOUSE & GARDEN

Share the excitement of creative living. Now for just $1 an issue.

Dear Reader,

Something exciting has happened to House & Garden that's turning heads...raising eyebrows...and eliciting "oohs" and "ahs" from discriminating people across the country...and around the world.

House & Garden has grown! Because we have created a fresh, new format that presents all the surprise and fascination of today's design world like you've never seen it before!

And right now you can be among the first to share in the brand-new excitement of HG, available to you through a very special offer.

To make it as enticing as possible for you to try the "new look" House & Garden, we are holding our own very special "Summer White Sale."

Just as your favorite department stores have "white sales" to help you fill your home with beautiful possessions at greatly reduced prices--so will House & Garden. Bringing you the best style in interiors, the finest furniture, the rarest art and antiques--all provocatively displayed on bigger pages with more full-color photography--for you to "take home" every month.

> And it's all yours, not at our regular cover price of $4, but for only $1 an issue. We urge you to use the Savings Certificate enclosed before August 15, 1990, to obtain a full year's subscription at this low introductory price. And save a full $3 per issue for the very finest of creative living...

Romantic splendor
Discover the latest trends in design--like the mixture of simplicity and ornate decoration dramatically represented by a New York City apartment that has gilt mirrors and highly ornamented tables set in a background of stark white walls.

Artful expressions
Enjoy the singular vision of David Hockney--his Hollywood house is an extension of his art with walls, ceilings and floors painted in brilliant primary colors.

Engaging eccentricity
Be surprised by the unusual--a house and studio encased in corrugated steel, accented with tree-stump coffee tables and a spectacular all-glass bathtub illuminated by fluorescent lights

(over, please)

--owned by maverick actor, Dennis Hopper.

Extraordinary views
When you open the thick and beautiful pages of HG, you'll have an extraordinary inside view of private homes like these, captured in vivid photographs and intelligent commentary. Lavishly printed on fine, glossy paper...

...so you can examine today's finest interiors in glowing detail. Such as Bette Midler's divine combination of Bloomsbury and Southern California in her Los Angeles house. The sumptuous château of the Rothschild family. The ever-changing face of The White House. HG will bring you the wide, wonderful world of fine living as no other magazine can.

Celebrated personalities
We not only show you fascinating places, we introduce you to the designers, architects, and celebrated tastemakers who create them. So you can discover how their visions and ideas bring rooms to life. Be inspired by their striking combinations of fabrics and furniture. Intrigued by the effects of color and texture.

Art, antiques, decorative accessories...and more
You'll be captivated by every aspect of HG. By exquisite collections of art and antiques (we recently photographed an authentic Victorian shell-back chair dating back to 1870). Enlightening insights on architecture (we'll show you the flamboyant new designs of Helmut Jahn). Essays on style (what's new about checks and stripes)...to accessories (the latest look in tableware: faux tortoise shell fashioned in glass)...to travel (find out where to rent a castle in the British Isles).

Add to that a glorious panorama of breathtaking gardens ...and you've got the fun and impact of every aspect of the design world to help expand and enhance your own potential for living.

Come explore the rare and special places where life is lived with refreshing imagination in the "new look" HG. It's yours to enjoy for just $1 an issue--when you send us the Savings Certificate enclosed.

What's more, you have our assurance of satisfaction. If at any time, for any reason, House & Garden fails to meet your expectations, you may cancel your subscription and receive a full, unquestioned refund for all unmailed issues.

So indulge--in so much excitement, for so little! Please take advantage of our **"Summer White Sale"** and save on a subscription to HG today.

Sincerely,

Nancy Novogrod
Editor-in-Chief

P.S. Our "Summer White Sale" is only running until August 15, 1990. To make certain your Savings Certificate is valid, please post it before that date. No need to send payment now. If you prefer, we'll bill you later.

HLWP

The 2-page letter, printed front and back on glossy paper to match the envelope stock.

heights and achieve another creative triumph is exhilarating. On the other hand . . . fear and dread. (You'd rather be in the plummeting Mercedes with your mother-in-law than take on the Herculean challenge of creating another winning package.)

That's what associate creative director Jerry Genova and I were feeling when we had to come up with a new package for Condé Nast's House & Garden (HG) *magazine. A package everyone was counting on to knock the control out of the box.*

Briefly, here's what we were up against. We had tested our way into a strong ''savings'' position. The current HG *control was a simple turnaround approach that offered the opportunity to ''activate a valuable $36* HG *Savings Certificate'' enclosed in the package. (That was the amount the prospect would save off the newsstand price by accepting our $12 subscription offer.)*

Jerry and I started our creative problem-solving session in a rather unusual way—by not allowing each other to put a pen to paper or a marker to pad. We were set on establishing a creative strategy (without writing a headline or making a pretty picture!) . . . and analyzing the control position led us quickly to it. If savings continued to push the prospects' hot buttons in test after test . . . we would take that position, but do it better.

We started free-forming ideas to come up with ways of communicating ''savings.'' (Tough task, because, face it, guys, it's all been done before.) In our initial brainstorming, a ''sale'' concept emerged. Not totally original, yet it was *a classic way to get someone's attention and to dramatize saving money.*

We agreed to explore it, but established parameters: this sale could not sound forced, overly promotional, or expected. (Fire Sale, Sample Sale, and Sale-a-Thon were obviously out!) Our sale had to appeal to HG*'s upscale audience and fit with its ''art book'' quality. In other words, we needed a sale with image.*

We agonized. Then it hit us. There was one kind of sale that hoity-toity stores like Bloomingdale's and Saks felt comfortable *running. That didn't detract from their image. That didn't say ''bargain basement.''*

The White Sale.

It was a perfect solution, especially for a magazine like HG. *After all, a White Sale was an attention-getting event that ran only for a limited time. It was related to the home. It definitely communicated savings. It had image. (And maybe it was even a bit intriguing in its ambiguity—how could a magazine have a White Sale anyway?)*

*This all worked to our advantage. So we started putting pen to paper and marker to pad. We created an outer envelope that announced that ''*HG *was having its very own special White Sale.'' We tailored a letter opening that made the case simply . . . and convincingly. The hook with* HG *was a natural: ''Just as your favorite department stores have white sales to help you fill your home with beautiful possessions at greatly reduced prices—so will* House & Garden. *Bringing you the best style in interiors, the finest furniture, the rarest art and antiques—all provocatively displayed on bigger pages with more full-color photographs—for you to 'take home' every month. And it's all yours . . . for* only $1 an issue.''

Jerry Genova purposefully came up with a clean, understated design for the package. Every piece was pure white, with black type and accented with gold hot stamping. It had a rich, upscale, elegant feel to it that was in sync with the magazine.

Although the package looked great, had just the right image, and presented a strong, focused case in the copy—we believe that the White Sale idea was king here. Jerry and I labored long to hit on that idea. And once we did, the execution seemed to come easily.

The HG *White Sale package did beat control (as if you couldn't guess). It held up for a few years, in fact. During that time, Jerry and I never teamed up to beat it. Other writers and art directors in the agency took their shots without success. However, the time did come when we were asked to beat our own control again . . . but that is another story!*

One-color (blue) lift piece, 4-color order card shown front and back, and business reply envelope.

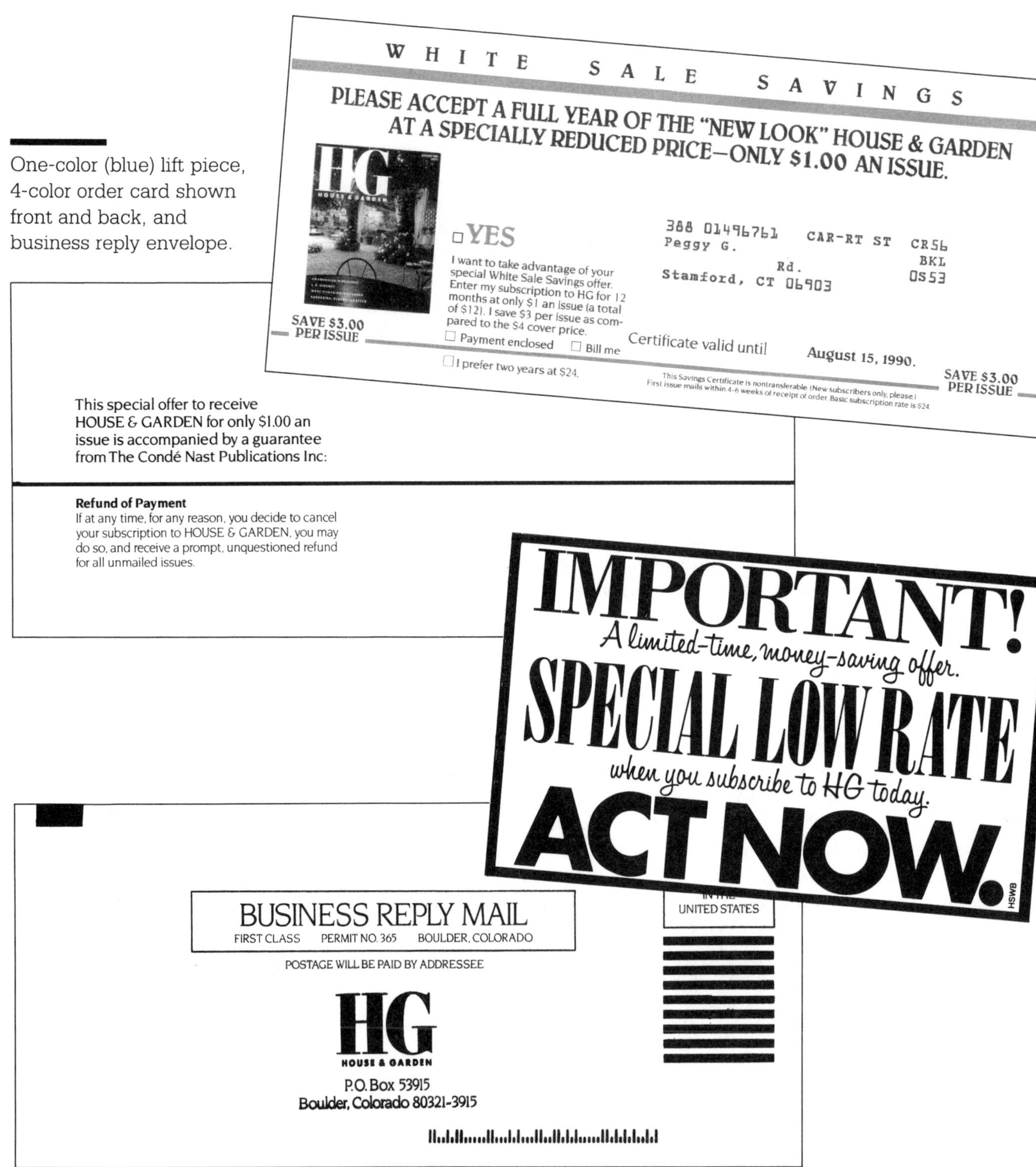

WHITE SALE SAVINGS
PLEASE ACCEPT A FULL YEAR OF THE "NEW LOOK" HOUSE & GARDEN AT A SPECIALLY REDUCED PRICE—ONLY $1.00 AN ISSUE.
HG
□YES
I want to take advantage of your special White Sale Savings offer. Enter my subscription to HG for 12 months at only $1 an issue (a total of $12). I save $3 per issue as compared to the $4 cover price.
□ Payment enclosed □ Bill me
□ I prefer two years at $24.
388 01496761 CAR-RT ST CR56
Peggy G.
Rd. BKL
Stamford, CT 06903 0S53
Certificate valid until August 15, 1990.
SAVE $3.00 PER ISSUE
SAVE $3.00 PER ISSUE
This Savings Certificate is nontransferable (New subscribers only, please.) First issue mails within 4-6 weeks of receipt of order. Basic subscription rate is $24.
This special offer to receive HOUSE & GARDEN for only $1.00 an issue is accompanied by a guarantee from The Condé Nast Publications Inc:
Refund of Payment
If at any time, for any reason, you decide to cancel your subscription to HOUSE & GARDEN, you may do so, and receive a prompt, unquestioned refund for all unmailed issues.
IMPORTANT!
A limited-time, money-saving offer.
SPECIAL LOW RATE
when you subscribe to HG today.
ACT NOW.
HSWB
BUSINESS REPLY MAIL
FIRST CLASS PERMIT NO. 365 BOULDER, COLORADO
POSTAGE WILL BE PAID BY ADDRESSEE
HG
HOUSE & GARDEN
P.O. Box 53915
Boulder, Colorado 80321-3915
UNITED STATES

W

If there is a direct mail superstar these days, it is Judy Weiss. Of the original seventy-one Axel Andersson Awards, Weiss was the winner of four. Whereas most project managers and circulation directors like to pigeonhole writers (for example, consumer vs. business), Weiss has demonstrated the ability to create successful mailings to both markets. For example, her winning mailings were: *Business Week* and *Inc.* (business), *Architectural Digest* (consumer/business), and *W* (consumer). Weiss is also one of those rare talents who can move comfortably between direct mail and broadcast; she does TV and radio direct response.

From an extended interview with Judy Weiss on how she goes about creating a direct mail package:

When I get an assignment there is usually a long lead time. When the time comes for me to start work (let's say for a monthly magazine) I want one and a half to two years of issues plus samples of other mailing packages—those that have worked and those that have not. I also want a basic look at who is reading the magazine: male, female, age, income, and what lists my mailing will be going out to. I need to get a handle on who subscribes and who renews. And I want to know what the distinction is between regular readers of the magazine and those I am trying to interest in it.

I spend three weeks on every package: one week looking at the magazine, one week roughing out the copy, and one week polishing it.

The first week I look at every issue and take notes. I am always thinking about the people I will be writing to. I make notes by hand on yellow legal pads.

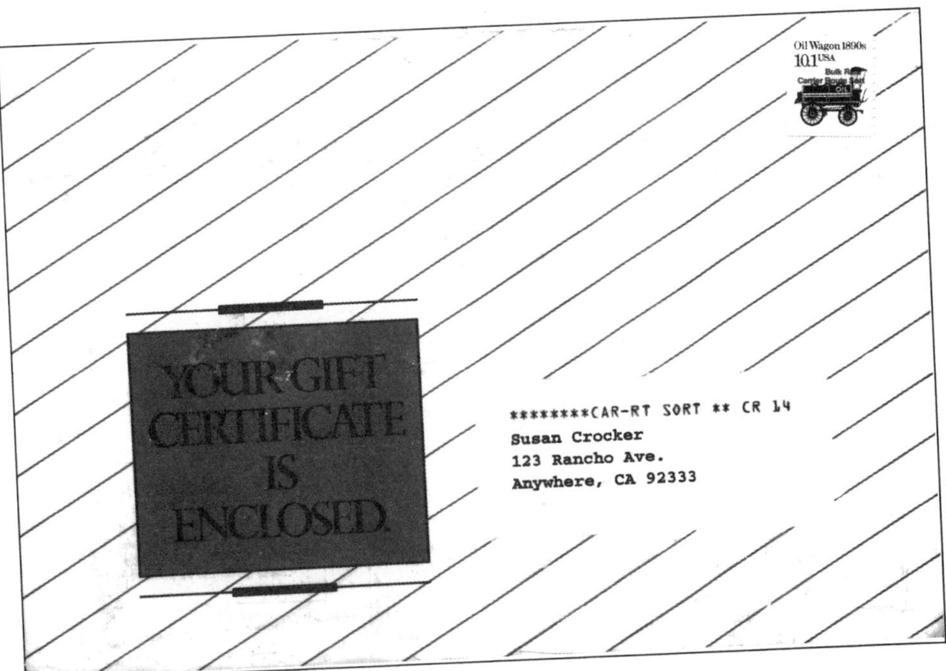

MAILER: *W*
PACKAGE: Gift Certificate Enclosed
PROJECT MGR.: Mirta Soto
WRITER: Judith Hannah Weiss
DESIGNER: Davidson & Maltz
FIRST MAILED: 1981

FASHION. BEAUTY. SOCIETY. STYLE.

Dear Friend:

You are among a very small group of women invited to use the Gift Certificate we've enclosed.

It effectively reduces the 12-month single issue price of W from $76.70 to $16.50. It's absolutely the lowest price available anywhere.

> That is like getting 20 issues of W -- absolutely free.
>
> Your Gift Certificate has your name on it. And it is only for your personal use.

You see, we are not "mass" publishers here at W. Or at Fairchild, either. On the contrary, W is published for a very select number of women. Women who lead -- where others follow.

> It's not just your clothes. It's also your face. Your figure. Your frame of mind.
>
> When you walk into a room, you make a statement -- with polish, presence and impact to spare!

You're the kind of woman W speaks to. You're the kind of woman W wants.

W. It's fashion -- with dash. Splash. Flash. Flair. It's what's striking, what's stunning in every place, every mood. From the ballroom glamor of haute couture to the street-smart savvy of ready-to-wear, it's the pursuit of pleasure. Treasure. Panache.

The best of the best

W is published every two weeks. So it brings you news while it is news. News on fashion. Society. Parties. Style. W. It's the fastest way to keep up with it all. The best way to be first to know the new looks. The new books. Temptations. Retreats. And first to go to the new hot spots. The new restaurants. The best experts on skin.

But let's be precise. At W, we don't bring you all the new fashion. Nor do we bring you all the new films. Shows. Books. Places.

(over please...)

A FAIRCHILD PUBLICATION 7 EAST 12TH STREET NEW YORK, NY 10003

At W, we bring you only the best of the best.

The best of the brightest

At W, we bring you the best and the brightest finds of our time. And the best and the brightest minds of our time. From L.A. to London, Paris, Tokyo, Manhattan, Milan, we bring you the world's most talented designers, decorators, actors, artists, writers, chefs.

> Plus the new discoveries. The soon-to-be-stars. And the people they'll be talking about.

In every issue of W, you'll come with us to the showrooms. The galas. The previews. The opening nights. And to the parties everyone wants to attend.

> You'll know who said what. Who did what. Who wore what. You'll know what was served. How the table was set. And just how it all came off.

Behind the seams

In W, you'll learn who's talking. Who's walking. Who's staying fit. You'll learn who's IN. Who's OUT. Who's so far OUT, they might just be IN again.

In W, you'll meet the six hardest-working women in Washington. They work around the clock, juggling their roles as hostess, actress, general, aide-de-camp, mother, wife.

In W, you'll spend a weekend with Ralph and Ricky Lauren in their Caribbean hideaway -- and you'll see how this fashion legend enjoys "the closest thing to heaven."

In W, you'll come with us to meet Gianni Versace. Liza Minnelli. Albert Finney. Herbert von Karajan. Kathleen Turner. In W, you'll meet Bill Blass and Claude Montana. Meryl Streep. Prince Charles. Princess Anne. In W, you'll meet Nancy Reagan. Baroness Phillipine de Rothschild. Jessica Lange. Sir John Gielgud. La Belle Helene Rochas.

Take advantage of our connections

W is brought to you by the people at Fairchild, who also publish Women's Wear Daily, the "Bible" of the fashion world. W shares the enormous contacts and unerring fashion sense of WWD. Plus it also brings you its own staff of 70 top-of-the-league reporters. They're everywhere important just as soon -- or before -- anything important happens. And every two weeks, they bring you their inside, in-depth, indispensable writing.

> You'll learn what's new, what's next, what's not to be seen anymore. You'll learn who's coming, who's going. What's IN. What's OUT.

In W, you'll find reports on *the season's best California wine *the best hotel in Dallas *the three most beautiful homes in L.A. *great gifts for men *the elegant table of Noel *great beauty tips for when you travel

Judy Weiss's 4-page letter for *W*, printed on an 11″ × 17″ sheet and folded twice, fit into the 6″ × 9″ envelope. Note the staccato, breathless prose.

I never know where the notes will lead or if or where I'll use the copy. In the course of taking notes, something may hit me as possible copy for an element. I stick a Post-It note on it with a thought as to where it may go. I am getting into the magazine this first week, and I find it very relaxing and really wonderful.

On Monday of the second week I start working on the piece. This is the scary part. I have all these notes, many of them covered with Post-Its. Much of it is stream of consciousness—just thoughts or bites of copy that came to me as I read the magazine.

I think of a magazine as a theater piece. There is an entirely different language that propels every magazine, whether it's Vogue *or* Allure *or* Business Week *or* New Yorker. *My job is to get inside the skin of the magazine and live in it for three weeks to understand that language and evoke it. In writing the piece, my tone must sound exactly right for the magazine.*

At the same time I have the sense that I am writing to a real person—a reader of Allure *or* Entertainment Weekly *or* Business Week. *Focusing on that real person gives a tone to my copy too.*

For every magazine constituency there is a hot button. For instance, the hot button for Sassy *and* YM (Young & Modern) *is boyfriends. The publishers of* YM *have positioned it as a fashion magazine. But I think that's secondary to features on guys. And in my copy I will go out on a limb on this. Because of my past work, most magazines go along with me, and I think I'm usually right.*

The process of writing copy is really shaping all these notes. I often put down ten to twenty outer envelope ideas and come up with eight or ten possible heads to the lift memo.

By the end of the second week, it is all in rough form. There is always way too much stuff and I have to start carving away the excess.

*the evening face *having your money and making it, too.

Bigger, faster, more luxurious

W. It's sleeker, slicker and more sophisticated than anyone else in the field.

But it's not only better. It's bigger, too.

Open it up. It's more than double the size of any other magazine -- big enough to dwarf the competition. Big enough so when you see fashion in W, you really see the fashion. Big enough so when you see the latest makeup for eyes, you really see how it's done. Big enough so you can really visualize yourself in each new look.

You see, W is printed in newspaper format -- so we can rush it off the presses and get it to you in a flash. That's why W comes to you every two weeks, not every four weeks like the other magazines.

And that's why W women get their news first. Fast. Ahead of the rest.

But in W, they don't just get news fast. They get it in lavish, luxurious form. Because in W, the reproduction of colors is masterly, meticulous, rare. The quality of the photography is absolutely top-of-its class. And even the texture of the paper is heavy. Silken. Sumptuous. Smooth. It feels good to hold W, to turn each page...

Good news

W is good news cover to cover. In fact, it's the best news in fashion. Beauty. Hair. The best news on star-quality people, giving their best to all they do. The best news on the best places, too.

From sipping hot white chocolate at Downtown's Dean & DeLuca to dancing the night away at Der Dschungel, the two-tiered "jungle" of West Berlin -- every two weeks W takes you to special playgrounds, haunts and hideaways of the worldly. The rich. And the wise.

Find out why New Zealand is the world's best-kept travel secret (enjoy it now before everyone else goes there!) Come with us to Marrakesh at Easter. To Brittany -- anytime at all. Follow stamping heels and strains of enchanting flamenco guitars through all-night dinners in Puerta Hierro, the posh suburb of passionate, awakening Madrid. Join us at midday at the Brasserie Lipp in Paris -- where Yves Montand, Jean-Paul Belmondo, Princess Caroline of Monaco, Yves Saint-Laurent and Karl Lagerfeld are lunching, too.

Great looks every day

W doesn't stop at haute couture. For as Rosemarie Bravo, President at I. Magnin says: "Today, no one need dress expensively every day."

In W, you'll see fresh, relaxed looks that are as affordable as they are versatile. In W, you'll really learn how to create a look. Better still, in W, you'll learn how to use accessories to give each look a multiple life. And, in W, you'll find our What's in Store feature -- where to find all the best

(over please...)

things in all the best stores all over the world.

How to join us now

It's simple. And with this special offer, it's more attractive than ever before.

Use your W Gift Certificate. This is like having 10 months of W -- 20 issues -- absolutely free. And it saves you $60.20 off the cover price. Just check the "Yes" box on the Gift Certificate and place it in the postage-paid envelope we've enclosed.

Try W before you fully decide. We know that a bargain is only a bargain if it is what you truly want. So we make this suggestion. Order W now -- and simply try a free issue. If you don't like it, you won't owe us a cent. Just write "Cancel" on the invoice, mail it back to us and that will be that. No strings. No fooling. No obligation at all.

Money-Back Guarantee. If you are ever dissatisfied with your subscription, you will receive a full and prompt refund on all unmailed issues.

This offer may not last long. So order W now -- and see what you think of your free issue. After all, with so much to gain -- and with absolutely nothing to lose -- shouldn't you at least take a look?

Cordially,

John B. Fairchild

JF:ns

John Fairchild
Chairman of the Board

P.S. As mentioned before, your Gift Certificate bears your name and may not be used by anyone else. A mailing like this -- for a publication like W -- must remain quite selective.

It's at the end of the second week also that I take a look at the samples of the other packages. Until that point I don't want to be influenced by what others have done. But it's imperative to see if I missed any copy points that others might have thought of. I owe it to the client to know about these and include them if I think they will help sales.

In the third week I really polish. I knock the hell out of the copy. Really attack it. Nine out of ten headlines might get thrown out. If I've come up with a list of sixteen editorial references, I will pick the best six or seven. Twenty or thirty adjectives will become ten or twelve.

I tell people that I write by the ''rhythm'' method. This may sound cute, but it's true. I wrote broadcast before I wrote print, so I get very intense about timing and rhythm. Every sentence and every word has to sound *right. I use alliteration and rhyme on occasion. Even puns. Two headlines in my* W *package are examples: ''Behind the Seams'' and ''Fashion with Passion.''*

I'm told that direct mail should not be ''clever.''

But the magazines themselves are clever. If they weren't clever, readers would fall asleep and would not renew. I want my work to be as clever and well written as the magazine itself. I respect the titles I work for. If I didn't respect them, I wouldn't work for them. I try to make my copy clever, entertaining, enjoyable, and appropriate to the magazine.

I am very untutored in this. What I do is based on instinct. For example, I don't study direct mail. I don't receive much direct mail to speak of. Most of my magazines comp me, so I'm not on promotable lists. If I am derivative, it is only of myself.

The copy for a particular piece of direct mail reads at a certain speed, just as a magazine reads at a certain speed. The New Yorker *doesn't read that quickly.*

Martin Davidson's stylish brochure starts off $6^{1}/_{2}'' \times 5^{1}/_{2}''$ and ends up $16^{3}/_{4}'' \times 11''$. The three dots that follow the copy line on the cover panel ("It's good news . . .") point the way to opening the brochure. Thereafter, each of the next two short folds cuts across artwork, forcing you to open it and open in again. These short folds are untidy. Neatness rejects involvement. The back panel restates the guarantee, and calls it a "Gift Guarantee." By slipping in the word "gift," Judy Weiss has added some *sell* to what is normally a perfunctory piece of copy.

W
PARIS IS HOT
COOL ARMANI
AMERICAN FASHION
HOT TIMES
IT'S GOOD NEWS...

FROM COVER...
SPECIAL DOUBLE ISSUE
PARIS THE GREAT NEW COUTURE
NEW YORK CLOSEUP
Paris says short
TO COVER.
UNGARO ON FIRE
IN OUT
W

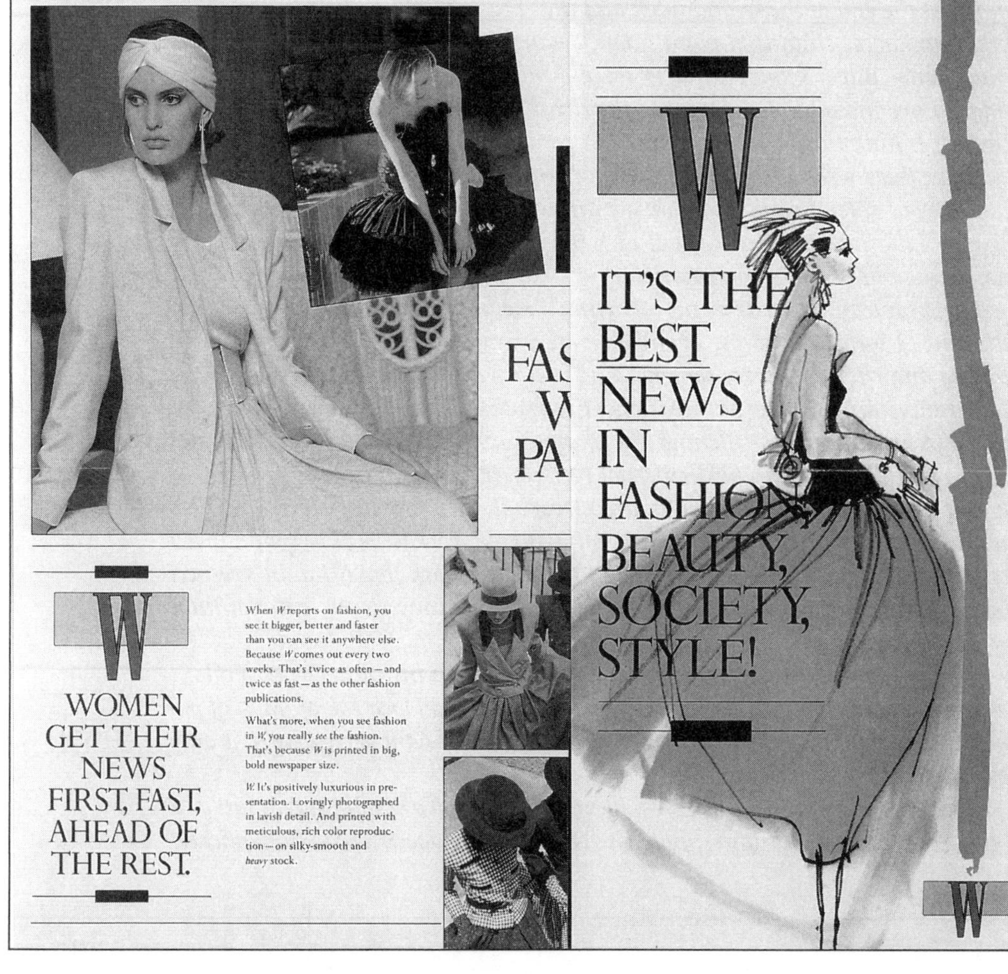
W
WOMEN GET THEIR NEWS FIRST, FAST, AHEAD OF THE REST.
When W reports on fashion, you see it bigger, better and faster than you can see it anywhere else. Because W comes out every two weeks. That's twice as often—and twice as fast—as the other fashion publications.
What's more, when you see fashion in W, you really see the fashion. That's because W is printed in big, bold newspaper size.
W. It's positively luxurious in presentation. Lovingly photographed in lavish detail. And printed with meticulous, rich color reproduction—on silky-smooth and heavy stock.
IT'S THE BEST NEWS IN FASHION, BEAUTY, SOCIETY, STYLE!

FASHION WITH PASSION.

W—a Fairchild publication—is the sister of *Women's Wear Daily*, the "Bible" of the fashion pros. *W* shares the international contacts and the unerring fashion sense of *WWD*. Plus it also adds its own team of 70 top-flight reporters to bring you *the in-depth, inside, indispensable* report on fashion. Beauty. Society. Style.

From what's IN and what's OUT (people, places, fashion, things) to the finest looks in haute couture and the freshest looks in pret-a-porter, *W* tells you what's new, what's next, what's not to be seen anymore.

THE BEST OF THE BEST.

At *W*, we don't bring you all the new fashions. At *W*, we bring you only the best. The best in new looks. New books. Films. Shows. Restaurants. Hotels. Spas. Resorts. The best hair and skin regimes. The best work from the fashion legends. And the best from the soon-to-be fashion stars.

W. It's *The evening face *Attractive Australians *Great retreats *Beauty tips for when you travel *It's Marrakesh—with Yves Saint-Laurent *A cozy picnic with Bill Blass *An intimate chat with Claude Montana *It's what's really big in Paris Sportive *Women and money *Great gifts for men *The Morgan—an haute couture automobile *The season's best California wines *It's Portofino. Positano. Newport. Nantucket. Cancun. Cozumel. *It's absolutely not-to-be-missed!

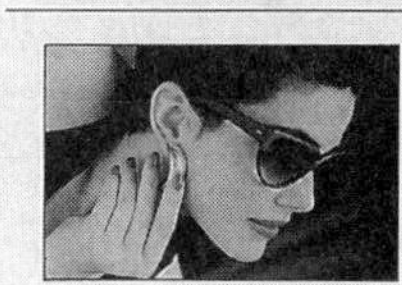

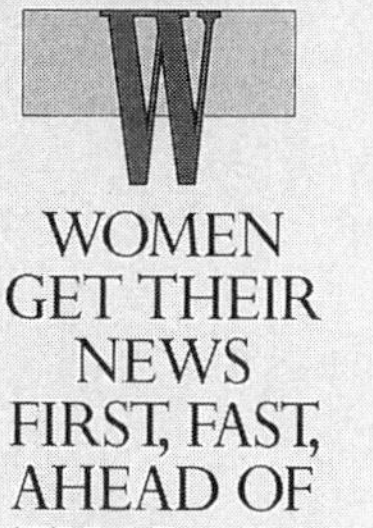

W WOMEN GET THEIR NEWS FIRST, FAST, AHEAD OF THE REST.

When *W* reports on fashion, you see it bigger, better and faster than you can see it anywhere else. Because *W* comes out every two weeks. That's twice as often—and twice as fast—as the other fashion publications.

What's more, when you see fashion in *W*, you really *see* the fashion. That's because *W* is printed in big, bold newspaper size.

W. It's positively luxurious in presentation. Lovingly photographed in lavish detail. And printed with meticulous, rich color reproduction—on silky-smooth and *heavy* stock.

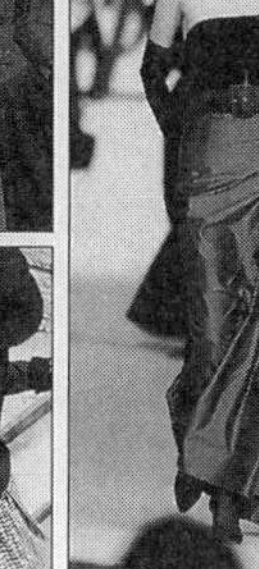

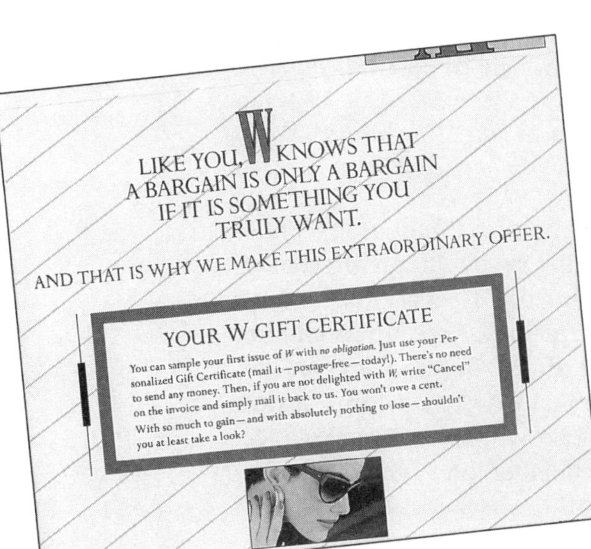

LIKE YOU, W KNOWS THAT
A BARGAIN IS ONLY A BARGAIN
IF IT IS SOMETHING YOU
TRULY WANT.
AND THAT IS WHY WE MAKE THIS EXTRAORDINARY OFFER.
YOUR W GIFT CERTIFICATE
You can sample your first issue of W with no obligation. Just use your Personalized Gift Certificate (mail it—postage-free—today!). There's no need to send any money. Then, if you are not delighted with W, write "Cancel" on the invoice and simply mail it back to us. You won't owe a cent.
With so much to gain—and with absolutely nothing to lose—shouldn't you at least take a look?

So my current control for the New Yorker *goes at a slower pace. Copy for other magazines—such as* Elle *or* Entertainment Weekly*—should have more syncopation, a quicker rhythm like bop or jive. To me these things are not accidental. My copy has the pace appropriate to each magazine. It's all part of my process. I want to speak as the magazine would speak. It's blend of sales and benefits, but in the language of that magazine. And if cleverness speaks to those people, I want my copy to be clever. If cleverness keeps people reading, or if rhythm keeps people reading, I'll pull out all the stops. I have to keep people reading to get them to act on the order form.*

In addition, copy that sounds great—and sounds like the magazine—is a good introduction to the product.

The direct mail package is like a symphonic thing, with each element adding a new theme.

The order form has to be clean. I don't use tokens or gimmicks. Like the double postcard, the less copy I am able to write, the greater the importance I attach to every word.

I spend a lot of time on lift memos. I think the lift memo is extremely significant in bringing in higher responses.

I prefer to do a brochure only if the client agrees to test the package with and without it. If you write great copy, you may not need a brochure. If great copy paints a picture in the reader's mind, a brochure with pictures may well be superfluous. If that is the case, it will not pay for itself and simply isn't necessary. I never create a huge brochure, even when I'm launching something. I don't think that much paper is required.

For design I work almost exclusively with Marty Davidson. Sometimes I give him thumbnail sketches. But more likely we talk about the package. I give him my ideas on typography and look and feel. We know each other really well. Even when I suggest something, Marty may well ignore me and do it his way. In no sense do I try to be Marty's boss. Marty and I both work for the client, and I am not his boss.

Vince Lombardi once said that if you're not fired with enthusiasm, you will be fired with enthusiasm. I love what I do. And I love magazines. I have a passion for this. This is why I give each piece so much time. This is what allows me to find the right tone, the right words, and the right strategy.

Designer Martin Davidson began working in direct mail in 1965 and formed Davidson & Maltz in 1972, specializing in circulation direct mail for the publishing industry. Major clients include Hearst Publications, Condé Nast Publications, Time Warner magazines, Consumers Union, New York Times magazines; K-III magazines, Book-of-the-Month Club, Walt Disney publications, and Columbia House. Davidson teams up with such leading freelancers as Len Berkowe, Steve Finkel, Grace Garguilo, Tom Gillett, Ken Scheck, Ken Schneider, and Judy Weiss. He works quickly, turning out a record eighty-three packages in 1990, and claims to have had forty controls in the mail simultaneously.

MARTIN DAVIDSON:
We like our package to have the feel and look of the magazine. Our motto is, "It doesn't have to be ugly to sell." Our packages have a real clean look to them; we try to evoke excitement; we use typefaces that are easily read; I work with the best writers . . . best designers . . . best mechanical people. When you put a team together where everyone is the best, more often than not you can create a winner. It's worked for me now for twenty years.

short message from . . .
ADRIENNE CLEERE

The "short message from . . . Adrienne Cleere" unfolds to reveal a 1-page lift letter.

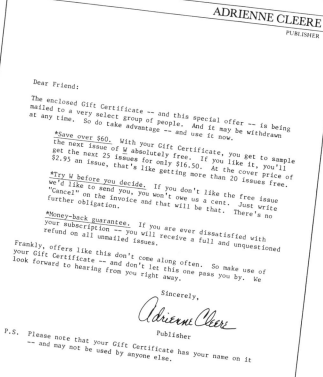

ADRIENNE CLEERE
PUBLISHER

Dear Friend:

The enclosed Gift Certificate -- and this special offer -- is being mailed to a very select group of people. And it may be withdrawn at any time. So do take advantage -- and use it now.

*Save over $60. With your Gift Certificate, you get to sample the next issue of W absolutely free. If you like it, you'll get the next 25 issues for only $16.50. At the cover price of $2.95 an issue, that's like getting more than 20 issues free.

*Try W before you decide. If you don't like the free issue we'd like to send you, you won't owe us a cent. Just write "Cancel" on the invoice and that will be that. There's no further obligation.

*Money-back guarantee. If you are ever dissatisfied with your subscription -- you will receive a full and unquestioned refund on all unmailed issues.

Frankly, offers like this don't come along often. So make use of your Gift Certificate -- and don't let this one pass you by. We look forward to hearing from you right away.

Sincerely,

Adrienne Cleere

Publisher

P.S. Please note that your Gift Certificate has your name on it -- and may not be used by anyone else.

LLK9A

NO POSTAGE NECESSARY IF MAILED IN THE UNITED STATES
BUSINESS REPLY MAIL
FIRST CLASS PERMIT NO. 256 BOULDER, CO
POSTAGE WILL BE PAID BY ADDRESSEE
W
Subscription Department
P.O. Box 56180
Boulder, CO 80321-6180

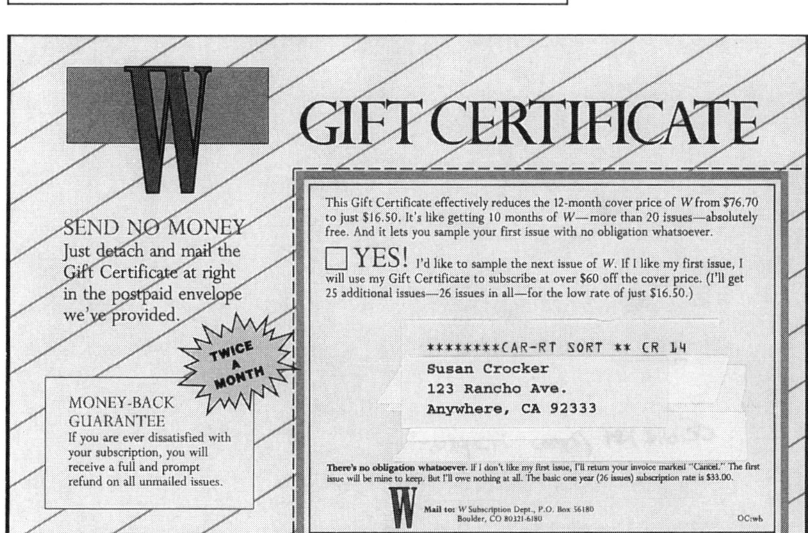
W GIFT CERTIFICATE

SEND NO MONEY
Just detach and mail the Gift Certificate at right in the postpaid envelope we've provided.

TWICE A MONTH

MONEY-BACK GUARANTEE
If you are ever dissatisfied with your subscription, you will receive a full and prompt refund on all unmailed issues.

This Gift Certificate effectively reduces the 12-month cover price of *W* from $76.70 to just $16.50. It's like getting 10 months of *W*—more than 20 issues—absolutely free. And it lets you sample your first issue with no obligation whatsoever.

☐ YES! I'd like to sample the next issue of *W*. If I like my first issue, I will use my Gift Certificate to subscribe at over $60 off the cover price. (I'll get 25 additional issues—26 issues in all—for the low rate of just $16.50.)

********CAR-RT SORT ** CR 14
Susan Crocker
123 Rancho Ave.
Anywhere, CA 92333

There's no obligation whatsoever. If I don't like my first issue, I'll return your invoice marked "Cancel." The first issue will be mine to keep. But I'll owe nothing at all. The basic one year (26 issues) subscription rate is $33.00.

W **Mail to:** *W* Subscription Dept., P.O. Box 56180
Boulder, CO 80321-6180 OC:wb

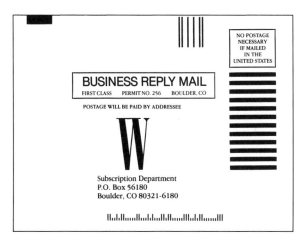

Order card and business reply envelope. This order card doesn't simply ask for the order; it *sells*. Look at these selling elements: "Send No Money" . . . "Twice a Month" . . . "Money-Back Guarantee" . . . "Gift Certificate" . . . "effectively reduces the 12-month cover price of *W* from $76.70 to just $16.50. It's like getting 10 months of *W*—more than 20 issues—absolutely free. . . . no obligation whatsoever."

11

Consumer Magazines III: Science and Nature

Some of the most effective direct mail is to be found in the arena of magazines that appeal to consumers' love of nature and science. With the exception of *Science News*, what makes these Grand Controls different from traditional magazine offers is that the magazine is the by-product of a nonprofit organization. All mail at nonprofit rates and that fact gives them a tremendous edge over their competition; they can afford to mail more and/or charge less and/or settle for poorer results than magazines mailing at full third-class rates.

The mailings are powerful in two ways: they either make an irresistible offer or call to something deep within all of us to know more about our world and somehow make it a better place for our having responded to the offer.

Audubon

The first two things you see in the 1985 subscription effort is a red and black peel-off sticker offering a free backpack and a handsome, personalized membership card in the National Audubon Society. Inside, Pete Gelb's letter is filled with a series of images that both tug at your heartstrings and raise your ire. By the end of the letter, you feel that the least you can do for the planet is to send for your free backpack and trial membership. The backpack, by the way, is free with the order, as opposed to other offers where the premium is "free" only when payment has been made.

This *Audubon* effort has two involvement devices. The peel-off sticker on the outside envelope is supposed to be placed in the circle at the bottom of the order form; that bottom part is then detached and mailed. The second involvement element is the personalized temporary membership card which you are urged to detach and keep.

For years, Pete Gelb and Carl Bloom operated the highly successful direct response agency Bloom & Gelb. In 1986 they parted, and Gelb set up shop as Grady & Gelb in the bucolic setting of eastern Long Island. The other half of the partnership is Nancy Grady, who created the *Harper's* package (discussed in Chapter 9), and who is also known as Mrs. Pete Gelb.

The 4-page letter, printed on an 11″ × 17″ sheet in 2 colors, folded twice to fit in a 6″ × 9″ envelope. At the bottom of the letter is the notice: "Printed on Recycled Paper." This copy line also appears on the order form, business reply envelope, and the lift letter. At first blush it may seem like a positive statement that will make the reader feel good about *Audubon*. However, this is an extraneous thought—a non sequitur that can interrupt the flow of the letter. It interrupts the interruption. A number of mailers have reported that announcing recycled paper in a mailing actually depresses results. It should be tested.

MAILER: *Audubon*
PACKAGE: Risk-Free Membership
PROJECT MGR.: Trish Edelman (Original)
Celia Tennenbaum (Current)
WRITER: Pete Gelb
DESIGNER: David Gordon
FIRST MAILED: 1985

National Audubon Society

950 THIRD AVENUE NEW YORK NY 10022

Dear Friend:

The members of the National Audubon Society constitute only a fraction of one percent of America's population.

But they are a very important fraction.

My hope is that you will want to join them. And for this reason I have enclosed an interim membership card already inscribed in your name.

You are invited to accept this free trial membership, including a free issue of AUDUBON magazine, for two months without obligation. Simply peel the token from the envelope, place it on the enclosed invitation, and return it as soon as possible. Later, if you wish to continue as a member, you may do so simply by paying our bill for only $20. Or you may cancel your membership and owe us nothing.

As an Audubon member, you will experience the wonders of our planet in a magazine widely considered to be the most beautiful published anywhere. At the same time, you will be helping to preserve those wonders through your support of America's most effective conservation group. There are other benefits as well, which I will outline in a moment.

<u>AUDUBON</u> ... <u>the beauty of a fine art book,</u>
<u>the excitement of an adventure story</u>.

In a world of throwaway publications, AUDUBON magazine is truly unique. Reading it makes you feel the same way you do after a walk in the deep woods, or a swim in a crystal lake. You are rewarded. Enriched. Uplifted.

AUDUBON is a magazine that radiates with magnificent color photographs, reproduced in the highest possible quality on rich lustrous paper. For almost 20 years it has been the premier showcase for the world's finest nature photographers and writers, and has won the prestigious National Magazine Award four times.

AUDUBON will expand the scope of your world, bring the magnificence of nature's most breathtaking creations into your home, and alert you to progress and problems in the environmental war zone ...

Snowbound in a remote Minnesota cabin, you hear a thump at the window. You freeze in your tracks as your flashlight picks up the blazing yellow eyes of a wild timber wolf. He is leaning weakly

Printed on Recycled Paper

- 2 -

against the window. Is he hurt? Would he attack? As you cautiously approach, he stares at you, unmoving. You pick him up, carry him inside, lay him by the fire. You wait and watch as the wolf wheezes, gasps and dies. You learn, later, that the wolf was starved, his hunting impeded by a foot mutilated in a fox trap. That he died of pneumonia. That starving wild animals sometimes do approach people near the end. And as you share the experience with the AUDUBON writer who actually lived it, you understand why we must save our few remaining wolves -- and all of wild America.

The U.S. senator, decked out in his hunting togs and toting a shotgun, headed warily towards the illegally baited Maryland duck pond. Then, sensing something amiss, he suddenly turned back to the house -- just barely averting a collar by agents of the U.S. Fish and Wildlife Service. Who warned the senator to beware? None other than the director of the FWS. AUDUBON revealed how Washington's poaching politicos -- and other fat cats -- dodge the game laws honest hunters respect.

With an otherworldly shriek and clatter, an immense flock of sandhill cranes explodes into the sky over Nebraska's North Platte River. For a million years and more, this spectacle has been one of nature's most awesome. Now the once mighty Platte, already 70% drained, is threatened by new water projects that could drain it dry -- to keep suburban lawns green. AUDUBON detailed the devastation this would bring, not only to the cranes but to millions of other birds that need the Platte to stay alive.

Why do Maine blueberry growers need rifles? To kill the bears. Why must the bears be killed? Because they raid the beehives. Why are there beehives? Because the growers have killed all the native pollinating insects with chemicals. What's the point, asks AUDUBON? In our taming of the wild blueberry, both nature and reason seem to have gone awry. Especially now that all the pesticides and herbicides are only bringing new insects and plant diseases to the blueberry barrens.

Where do the beautiful aquarium fish come from? Dive with AUDUBON beneath tropical waters to the coral reef and watch the fish collectors at work. Driven by desperate poverty, these divers squirt sodium cyanide from a detergent bottle into the

- 3 -

coral, and grab the fish as they try to escape. But nine out of ten fish die. And so, eventually, do some of the divers, killed by their own poison, and so does the coral reef. Worldwide, the resplendent reefs of tropical oceans are being decimated by man. AUDUBON explored the wonders of the reefs -- and the efforts of determined scientists to save them.

Will the administration live up to its promises on clean air and wetlands protection? Can the last of our ancient forests be saved from the chainsaw? Is an economy based on non-fossil energy sources an achievable dream? What can be done to prevent more catastrophic oil spills like the wreck of the <u>Exxon Valdez</u>? AUDUBON keeps you in touch with the vital issues being tackled by the environmental movement.

<u>You cannot touch, see, or hear</u>
<u>the most important benefit of</u>
<u>your Audubon membership</u>.

There is one benefit of your National Audubon Society membership that gives you nothing immediately tangible in return.

Nothing, that is, except the peace of mind of knowing that you are doing your part to stop the senseless destruction of Earth's precious natural resources.

Your dues directly support active and vital programs to protect wildlife, promote energy conservation, and help ensure a healthier environment.

Quite simply, very few organizations do more (or more important) work to save the balance and beauty of nature, including the acquisition and maintenance of wildlife sanctuaries all over America.

<u>Free visits to Audubon Nature</u>
<u>Centers are another advantage</u>
<u>of membership</u>.

You and your family will be awestruck by the sights and sounds along Audubon's nature trails, where birds and wildlife exist in undisturbed natural environments, protected from depredation by man.

The six Audubon Nature Centers, located in Ohio, Connecticut, California, New Mexico and Wisconsin, are among the most serene and pristine places on Earth.

-4-

<u>Local chapter membership,</u>
<u>exciting adventure tours, special purchase</u>
<u>opportunities, and more</u>.

Your National Audubon Society membership also gives you the opportunity to be a part of the Audubon network. If one of our 500 chapters is in your area, you can participate in enjoyable, worthwhile activities with some very interesting people.

You will have opportunities to purchase books, gifts, and artwork of special interest to nature lovers. And you can travel with fellow members to fascinating places like Africa, Antarctica or Chilean Patagonia at reasonable costs.

To begin receiving AUDUBON at once and to enjoy all the other benefits of membership in the National Audubon Society, simply return the enclosed form.

You will be joining over 500,000 of the most concerned, interesting, and informed people on the face of this struggling Earth. I look forward to welcoming you.

Sincerely,

Peter A.A. Berle
President

P.S. Remember, to reserve your FREE BACKPACK and become a temporary member of the National Audubon Society, just place the token from the envelope on your RISK-FREE invitation and return it in the envelope provided. You'll be joining the group doing so much to help save our threatened planet Earth. And you'll enjoy AUDUBON magazine, free visits to Audubon Nature Centers throughout the United States, and other benefits. That's more value for less money than I've heard of in a long, long time! So, please become an Audubon Society member now!

LTR-90

David Gordon's evocative 4-color circular that opens to 20″ × 7½″ is, quite simply, a masterpiece of elegance and beauty.

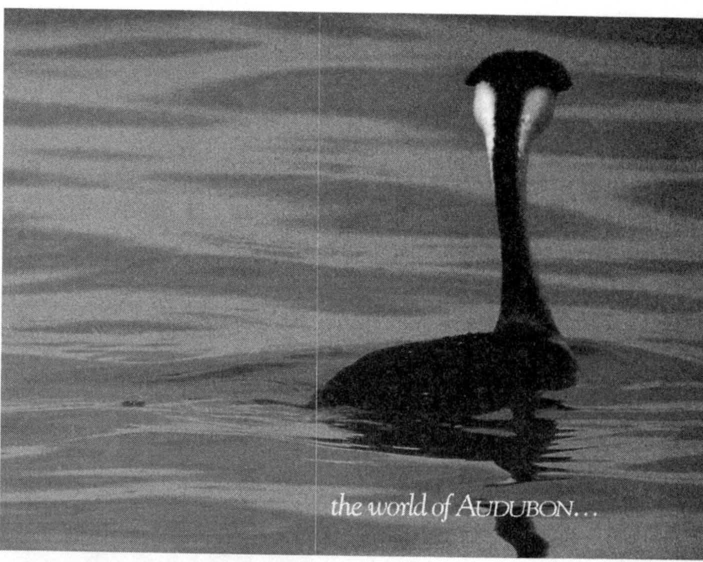

the world of AUDUBON...

Experience the world's most beautiful magazine...

AUDUBON
AUDUBON
AUDUBON
YOU'LL DISCOVER A WHOLE NEW WORLD of beauty and wonder as captured by some of America's foremost nature photographers. AUDUBON has been called the most beautiful magazine in the world. And browsing through this exquisitely printed journal is like taking an expertly guided tour of the natural world.
But AUDUBON'S award-winning graphics are just the beginning. Our distinguished group of contributing nature writers can make you feel the sting of a bitter Antarctic windstorm . . . taste the pleasant tartness of a barely ripened wild persimmon . . . breathe the fresh and cool smell of a North American forest after a summer storm . . . hear the white-breasted nuthatch's clever imitation of a cracking tree branch. Like no other magazine in the world, AUDUBON displays an uncanny ability to put you in the picture.
AUDUBON satisfies your wide-ranging curiosity about nature and her many secrets. An issue of AUDUBON might unfold to you anything from why the Raven is nature's most intelligent bird to how man has neglected some of the "better qualities" of the leech.
Yet AUDUBON'S stimulation of your mind does not end with mere facts. AUDUBON is the principal forum of the National Audubon Society and one of the major voices of the environmental movement in America. Six times a year, you'll find controversy, criticism, philosophy, essays, news and humor. Nowhere will the thoughtful conservationist find a more provocative and stimulating journal—in itself a compelling reason for joining the National Audubon Society.

...and a great deal more
1. Unique Purchase Opportunities
Enjoy special offers of nature-oriented books, gifts, and collectibles.
2. Local Chapter Membership
Get to know local animals, plants, and birds, and meet interesting new friends, through activities sponsored by one of the 500 local Audubon chapters near you.
3. Audubon Nature Centers
You and your family are invited to walk along beautiful nature trails and observe birds and other protected wildlife in their natural surroundings.
4. Ecology Camps and Workshops
One- and two-week sessions are offered at Audubon camps and workshops in Connecticut, Maine, and Wyoming.
5. Audubon Tours
Fabulous opportunities to embark on dream vacations to exotic destinations from Australia to the Amazon.
Perhaps your most important membership benefit

This world...

or this world?
As a member of the National Audubon Society, you'll know that your dues are helping to rescue endangered species, educate the public on environmental issues, and protect our planet from the pollution and destruction of our natural resources. Join us today and help choose the more beautiful, bountiful world we all want to live in.

PETE GELB:
Working methods: nothing very different about them. I try to collect lots of information about the product and the market, including what has worked and what hasn't worked in the past.

I try a little harder than most writers to fit the copy to the situation, instead of creating the same formula package for everybody, as direct mail writers commonly do.

The Audubon *package is a good example. It looks and sounds right to its middle-aged, upscale prospects. Test packages with inappropriate copy or design have repeatedly failed to equal it. Don't hire Crazy Eddie to sell a Rolls-Royce.*

If you can look at a package and tell who wrote or designed it, you're looking at a formula package. It will work for some people some of the time, but that's all it will ever do.

The *Audubon* package was designed by David Gordon, a direct marketing graphic designer for over thirty years. Among his clients: AARP, AT & T, Avon, *Esquire*, Franklin Mint, GAF, Jackson & Perkins, Meredith, Metropolitan Opera, PBS, Rodale Press, Sotheby's, Time-Life Books, and *Women's Wear Daily*.

Lift here for the most important reason to join Audubon now...

National Audubon Society
801 Pennsylvania Avenue SE
Washington, DC 20003

Dear Member-elect:

You'll soon find that Audubon membership is a wonderful way to enhance your appreciation of the beauty and balance of nature.

But the most important reason to join Audubon is that it's a wonderful way to help preserve that beauty and balance.

Audubon's Washington, D.C. office is the launching ground for important programs designed to protect endangered species and preserve our natural resources by . . .

. . . speaking up for urgently needed new wildlife refuges and against commercial exploitation of public lands and national forests.

. . . speaking up for stronger clean air laws with tough controls on acid rain pollution.

. . . proposing and promoting rational policies on energy, recycling and toxic waste disposal, and global warming.

These are just a few examples of the issues we're working on. Day by day, we're in the center of government decision-making where we can react quickly and effectively to vital developments in environmental legislation. And Audubon research, made possible by our members, enables us to support our opinions with solid evidence.

So while you're enjoying the spectacle of nature through AUDUBON magazine and the other benefits of membership, know that you're also helping to preserve it through your support of these efforts.

We'll keep you informed of our progress. In the meantime, we look forward to welcoming you as a member.

Sincerely,

Elizabeth Raisbeck

Elizabeth Raisbeck
Senior Vice President
Regional and Government Affairs

P.S. There really is no risk when you accept this trial membership. It's your chance to get a glimpse of AUDUBON magazine, and a taste of the satisfying feeling that comes from helping to save our planet -- and everything that lives on it.

Printed on Recycled Paper

The 2 lift elements. The lift letter also states that it is printed on recycled paper. The salutation ("Dear Member-elect") may seem stiff, but not nearly as cumbersome as the salutation in the main letter in the long time control of the National Trust for Historic Preservation: "Dear Initiate Elect." The 4-color flyer depicting the backpack premium is printed on one side only.

NATIONAL AUDUBON SOCIETY
Wherever you go take your Audubon backpack with you. It's your carry-all for work and play; walking to the office or on the trail, to school or on a picnic.
The Audubon backpack is very roomy (16X12X4). A zippered main compartment and a generous front pocket provide plenty of room for belongings big and small. The adjustable straps are fully padded for real comfort on long walks; there's even a fabric loop from which your nylon backpack can be hung.
FREE WITH YOUR AUDUBON MEMBERSHIP
But best of all, this is unmistakably an Audubon backpack. An embroidered patch proudly displays your logo.
To receive our handsome navy blue backpack free, please fill out the enclosed form. Upon receipt of membership payment, we'll mail your backpack.
NATIONAL AUDUBON SOCIETY
Please allow 6-8 weeks for delivery from receipt of payment.
BSP-ROL

DAVID GORDON:

My "secret" is not just unstoppable energy and enthusiasm, but the ability to work from a marketing basis, keeping creativity centered on "marketing realities" throughout the development process. Indeed, understanding these "marketing realities" is the foundation for any good direct mail campaign, for it is then, and only then, that one is able to fully meet the needs of both client and audience.

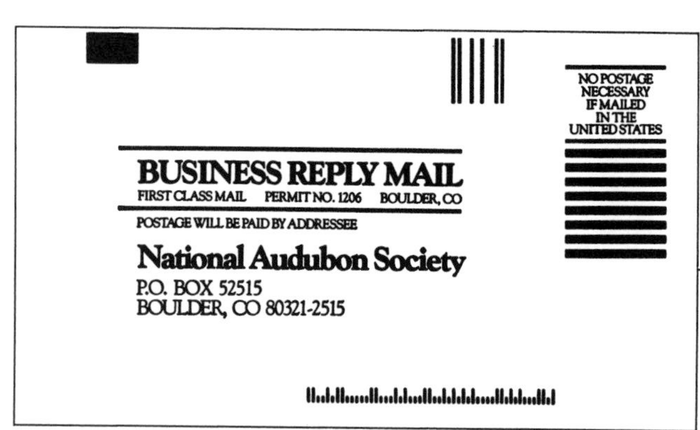

The order form and business reply envelope.

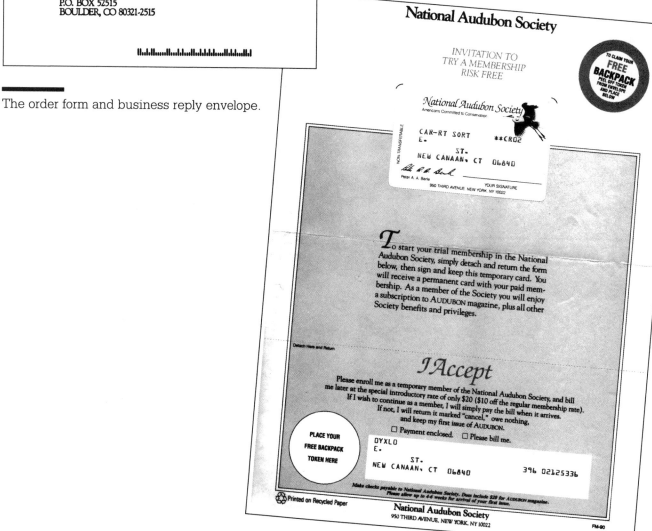

National Audubon Society

INVITATION TO TRY A MEMBERSHIP RISK FREE

TO CLAIM YOUR FREE BACKPACK PEEL OFF TOKEN FROM ENVELOPE AND PLACE BELOW

National Audubon Society
Americans Committed to Conservation

NON-TRANSFERABLE

CAR-RT SORT **CR02
E.
ST.
NEW CANAAN, CT 06840

Peter A. A. Berle
YOUR SIGNATURE
950 THIRD AVENUE NEW YORK, NY 10022

To start your trial membership in the National Audubon Society, simply detach and return the form below, then sign and keep this temporary card. You will receive a permanent card with your paid membership. As a member of the Society you will enjoy a subscription to AUDUBON magazine, plus all other Society benefits and privileges.

Detach Here and Return

I Accept

Please enroll me as a temporary member of the National Audubon Society, and bill me later at the special introductory rate of only $20 ($10 off the regular membership rate). If I wish to continue as a member, I will simply pay the bill when it arrives. If not, I will return it marked "cancel," owe nothing, and keep my first issue of AUDUBON.

☐ Payment enclosed. ☐ Please bill me.

PLACE YOUR FREE BACKPACK TOKEN HERE

OYXLO
E.
ST.
NEW CANAAN, CT 06840 396 02125336

Make checks payable to National Audubon Society. Dues include $20 for AUDUBON magazine. Please allow up to 4-6 weeks for arrival of your first issue.

Printed on Recycled Paper

National Audubon Society
950 THIRD AVENUE, NEW YORK, NY 10022

FM-90

Earthwatch

For any person with a wanderlust, a love of nature, and the desire to do some hands-on good works, the outer envelope for *Earthwatch* by Bill Jayme and designer Heikki Ratalahti is a stopper:

Got some free time?
A week? A month? A summer?

Inside, Jayme's letter socks you with a sequence of staccato paragraphs that describe the essence of a series of irresistible adventures. What's more, the copy makes it clear that these exploits can be enjoyed for real by the incipient Indiana Jones or by the armchair traveler for whom "roughing it" is sleeping with the window open at the Holiday Inn.

With each unfolding of Ratalahti's magnificent four-color brochure, you are bombarded with a new and evocative group of images right up to the final spread where a beautiful mountain scene is depicted on the magazine cover, together with seven benefits of membership. The back panel contains a series of testimonials with perhaps the best testimonial of all: a photograph of a group of very happy campers.

In the current incarnation of the mailing, the brochure has been halved; the entire piece, front and back, has been picked up from the center spread of the brochure shown here.

NonProfit Org.
U.S. Postage
PAID
Frederick, M.D.
Permit #377

Got some free time?
A week? A month? A summer?

Come volunteer for
a conservation project in the wilds.
An environmental study in the tropics.
An archaeological dig abroad.

Or, if you're busy now,
cheer us on from the sidelines.

INVITATION TO EARTHWATCH

MAILER: *Earthwatch*
PACKAGE: "Got some free time?"
PROJECT MGR.: Robin Schweikart
WRITER: Bill Jayme
DESIGNER: Heikki Ratalahti
FIRST MAILED: 1989

EARTHWATCH

Come with us to Maya ceremonial caves,
China's bustard haunts, Florida's dolphin playgrounds,
Majorca's Bronze Age sanctuaries.

Invitation to membership

Dear Membership Candidate:

I'm writing to offer you a job.

It's not a permanent job, understand. You'll be working for only as much time as you find it rewarding and fun.

It's not even a paying job. On the contrary, it will cost you money.

But if you're willing to travel to offbeat places all over the U.S. and abroad ... to meet fascinating new people of all ages and nationalities ... to open your mind to new perspectives and ideas ... and in the process to help make this planet of ours a better place for us all ...

... then please accept this invitation to become a member of EARTHWATCH and prepare yourself to enjoy some of the richest rewards that human existence offers.

Adventure. Fellowship. Challenge. Growth. A feeling of personal fulfillment like you may have never experienced before.

EARTHWATCH is a nonprofit organization that works a bit like the Peace Corps. We organize expeditions to research sites all over the world for leading scholars and scientists. We then recruit interested men and women like yourself who are willing to lend a hand by serving as staff volunteers.

We've recently been supporting archaeological digs in Mexico,

(over, please)

2.

Spain, Israel, Brazil.

We're involved in environmental and conservation programs in the U.S. and abroad.

We not long ago opened cultural bridges linking America with China and Russia.

We're also helping to preserve endangered species and habitats.

Worthy goals, don't you agree? And if you'd like to play a more active role in seeing them come to fruition, a good place to start is with a membership in EARTHWATCH.

By returning the enclosed acceptance form, you'll immediately become eligible to participate in any and all expeditions.

You'll also enjoy all other member benefits including a lively and beautiful magazine.

You'll be invited to special outings, lectures and receptions in your area so you can meet your fellow members, and rub shoulders with scholars, scientists, authors. At the beginning of each year, you'll receive a colorful and handy desk diary that doubles as an expedition planner.

In addition, you'll also start getting the magazine EARTHWATCH -- a publication that's been characterized as a cross between the National Geographic, Smithsonian, and the departures board at the airport for the way it reports on scientific and cultural phenomena of all kinds ...

... then also binds into each issue a special section that lists and describes all the different expeditions you can go on. Pick your date! Pick your place! Pick your project!

How much time do expeditions require? As many days or weeks as you care to give. It's entirely your decision. Recent issues of EARTHWATCH have listed an extraordinary variety of choices:

. A week or two at North Carolina's Pisgah Bear Sanctuary to help determine what the animals do with themselves all day now that they no longer have to be on the run

. A few more weeks at Fort Peck Reservoir in Montana trying to find out why there were dinosaurs still on the prowl half a million years after they were supposedly

3.

all wiped out by a falling asteroid

. A month or so in the Auvergne region of France, helping to dig up from underneath vineyards and Romanesque churches new revelations about Stone Age settlements

. A winter getaway to Punta Gorda, Belize collecting and analyzing Caribbean artifacts to learn what role ceremonial caves played in Maya life and religion

. Spring breaks in Majorca exploring sanctuaries that hold clues to life in the Bronze Age, or in the waters off Florida making new entries in the dictionary of the language of dolphins

. A summer odyssey in the Gulf of Alaska to record weather patterns from ocean vessels that can determine how often you'll need to carry your umbrella once you get home

. An entire season in China's Beidaihe headland helping ornithologists from all over the world survey native great bustards, cranes, pied harriers, Oriental white storks.

Tempted? Want to learn more? Once you locate a project that fits your schedule, interests and budget, you can send for a detailed Expedition Briefing Kit containing maps, background information, biographies, goals and scenarios, requirements.

These dossiers make such good reading that many stay-at-home members order them to pore over purely for pleasure, the way armchair globe-trotters curl up with Fodor and Fielding guidebooks. Other members use them as teaching aids.

How much money will an expedition cost you? It all depends. Certainly less than you'd have to budget for crowding onto the Interstate highways and checking in and out of motels. And far less than you'd probably need to pay to see the world on your own -- the great cities, deserts, seas, mountains, jungles, wildlife preserves.

What keeps your costs low is sharing expenses with others who make up your team. Informal hostels and camps instead of pricy hotels. Native cooks and foods. Too, all reasonable expedition costs are tax-deductible, including getting there and returning back home.

What special skills will you need? Few that you don't have already. The ability to measure wildflower growth in our burned-out national

(over, please)

4.

parks. To brush the dust off an Egyptian tomb that's lain buried for over three thousand years. To count the shining cuckoos remaining in New Zealand's Kowhai Forest.

The ability to explain to an African mother, through a village translator, how to prepare a formula that's more nourishing. To record the song of a humpback whale from a skiff idling off the beaches of Hawaii.

The ability to gaze up into the heavens and discover a new comet, a new star, a new galaxy, and to see it christened with your own name ...

Since its founding in 1971, EARTHWATCH has provided a meeting ground for like-minded men and women. Young people and retirees who share a common concern for the planet. Doctors, architects, lawyers looking to contribute to the betterment of the world.

Business people seeking worthwhile outlets for their own specialized skills and know-how. Technicians. Carpenters. Teachers. Photographers. Mechanics. Nurses. Librarians.

If our organization sounds like something that you too would take pleasure in being a part of -- whether by participating actively, or cheering us on from the sidelines -- I urge you to send in the membership form at your earliest convenience ... so your adventure can begin with the very next issue of EARTHWATCH.

May we look for your acceptance by return mail? Thanks from all of us here, and welcome!

Faithfully yours,

Brian Rosborough
President

P.S. Important tax benefits. Like virtually all EARTHWATCH contributions, membership is tax-deductible. Note too that you can charge your donations to your credit card.

EARTHWATCH
680 Mt. Auburn Street · Box 403
Watertown, Massachusetts 02272

The 4-page letter, printed on an 11″ × 17″ sheet and folded twice. Although the letter is 2-color (red and black), the only red is to be found in the ruled lines below "EARTHWATCH" and above "Invitation to membership."

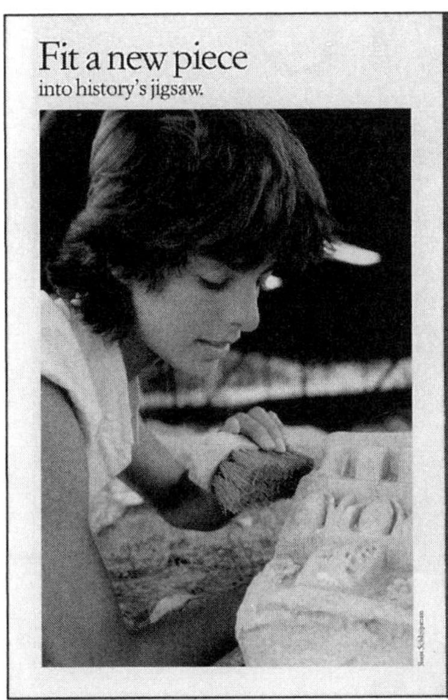

Fit a new piece
into history's jigsaw.

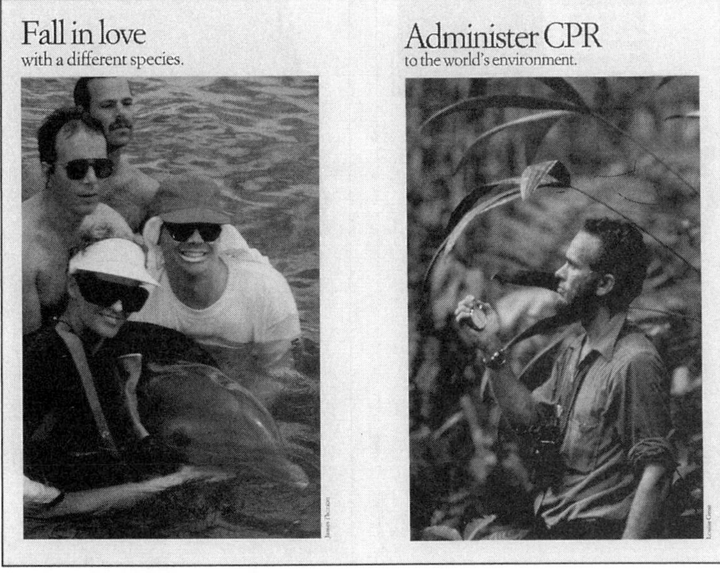

Fall in love
with a different species.
Administer CPR
to the world's environment.

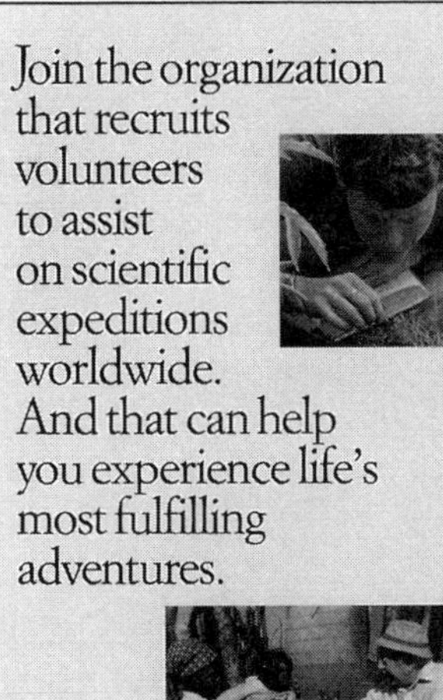

Join the organization
that recruits
volunteers
to assist
on scientific
expeditions
worldwide.
And that can help
you experience life's
most fulfilling
adventures.

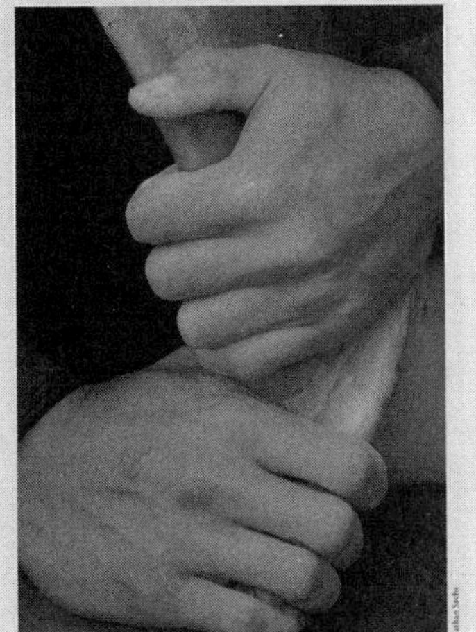

Lend a hand
to this glorious planet of ours.

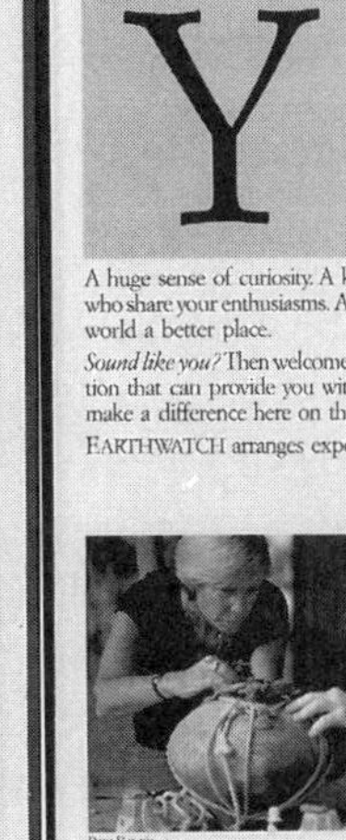

You don't need special training or skills. You can be almost any age. You don't have to invest a great deal in the way of time, or money or physically demanding work.
All that is required are some personality traits that you're probably already blessed with. A willingness to travel. A hankering for adventure. A huge sense of curiosity. A knack for working with people who share your enthusiasms. And a burning desire to make this world a better place.
Sound like you? Then welcome to EARTHWATCH, the organization that can provide you with an unparalleled opportunity to make a difference here on the planet.
EARTHWATCH arranges expeditions throughout the U.S. and in 60 countries abroad for researchers involved in environmental and conservation studies, archaeological digs, cultural programs, projects in every major scientific field. It then recruits from its membership volunteer "team members" who want to lend a hand – men and women willing to collect data, make observations, conduct interviews, do whatever may be required in order to come up with insights, answers, solutions.
EARTHWATCH was founded in 1971. It is non-political. It is not-for-profit. And whether you actively take part in expeditions, or prefer to cheer from the sidelines, membership can bring a new dimension to your life – exciting, enriching, fulfilling.
Presenting
EARTHWATCH

Heikki Ratalahti's magical circular that starts at $5^{1}/_{2}'' \times 8^{1}/_{2}''$, unfolding 3 times . . .

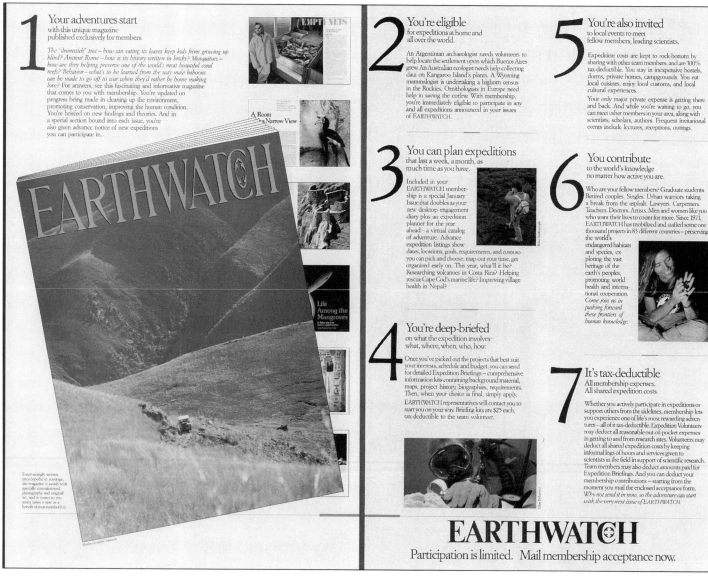

1 **Your adventures start**
with this unique magazine
published exclusively for members.

The "drumstick" tree – how can eating its leaves keep kids from growing up blind? Ancient Rome – how is its history written in bricks? Mosquitoes – how are they helping preserve one of the world's most beautiful coral reefs? Behavior – what's to be learned from the way male baboons can be made to go off to war when they'd rather be home making love? For answers, see this fascinating and informative magazine that comes to you with membership. You're updated on progress being made in cleaning up the environment, promoting conservation, improving the human condition. You're briefed on new findings and theories. And in a special section bound into each issue, you're also given advance notice of new expeditions you can participate in.

EMPTY NETS

A Room a Narrow View

EARTHWATCH

Life Among the Mangroves

Entertainingly written, encyclopedic in coverage, the magazine is awash with specially commissioned photographs and original art, and it comes to you seven times a year as a benefit of your membership.

2 **You're eligible**
for expeditions at home and all over the world.

An Argentinian archaeologist needs volunteers to help locate the settlement upon which Buenos Aires grew. An Australian ecologist needs help collecting data on Kangaroo Island's plants. A Wyoming mammalogist is undertaking a bighorn census in the Rockies. Ornithologists in Europe need help in saving the curlew. With membership, you're immediately eligible to participate in any and all expeditions announced in your issues of EARTHWATCH.

3 **You can plan expeditions**
that last a week, a month, as much time as you have.

Included in your EARTHWATCH membership is a special January Issue that doubles as your new desktop engagement diary plus an expedition planner for the year ahead – a virtual catalog of adventure. Advance expedition listings show dates, locations, goals, requirements, and costs so you can pick and choose, map out your time, get organized early on. This year, what'll it be? Researching volcanoes in Costa Rica? Helping rescue Cape Cod's marine life? Improving village health in Nepal?

4 **You're deep-briefed**
on what the expedition involves: what, where, when, who, how.

Once you've picked out the projects that best suit your interests, schedule and budget, you can send for detailed Expedition Briefings – comprehensive information kits containing background material, maps, project history, biographies, requirements. Then, when your choice is final, simply apply.

EARTHWATCH representatives will contact you to start you on your way. Briefing kits are $25 each, tax-deductible to the team volunteer.

5 **You're also invited**
to local events to meet fellow members, leading scientists.

Expedition costs are kept to rock-bottom by sharing with other team members, and are 100% tax-deductible. You stay in inexpensive hostels, dorms, private homes, campgrounds. You eat local cuisines, enjoy local customs, and local cultural experiences.

Your only major private expense is getting there and back. And while you're waiting to go, you can meet other members in your area, along with scientists, scholars, authors. Frequent invitational events include lectures, receptions, outings.

6 **You contribute**
to the world's knowledge no matter how active you are.

Who are your fellow members? Graduate students. Retired couples. Singles. Urban warriors taking a break from the asphalt. Lawyers. Carpenters. Teachers. Doctors. Artists. Men and women like you who want their lives to count for more. Since 1971, EARTHWATCH has mobilized and staffed some one thousand projects in 83 different countries – preserving the world's endangered habitats and species, exploring the vast heritage of the earth's peoples, promoting world health and international cooperation. *Come join us in pushing forward these frontiers of human knowledge.*

7 **It's tax-deductible**
All membership expenses.
All shared expedition costs.

Whether you actively participate in expeditions or support others from the sidelines, membership lets you experience one of life's most rewarding adventures – all of it tax-deductible. Expedition Volunteers may deduct all reasonable out-of-pocket expenses in getting to and from research sites. Volunteers may deduct all shared expedition costs by keeping informal logs of hours and services given to scientists in the field in support of scientific research. Team members may also deduct amounts paid for Expedition Briefings. And you can deduct your membership contributions – starting from the moment you mail the enclosed acceptance form. *Why not send it in now, so the adventure can start with the very next issue of EARTHWATCH.*

EARTHWATCH

Participation is limited. Mail membership acceptance now.

. . . until it turns into a 17″ × 22″ bedsheet.

"Wish you were here".
Postcards from some of the members.
Urban warriors. "Keeps us in touch with what's really important – nature, people, ideas."
Retired Couple. "Working with younger folks keeps us on our toes."
Undergraduate. "It's what a true education is all about – intellectual adventure."
Parents. "Unparalleled way to keep on growing and learning."
Baby Boomer. "Same satisfactions I got from the Peace Corps – helping out, doing good."
Scientist. "Membership is an 800-number to what's happening in other disciplines."
Newlyweds. "EARTHWATCH was our first date."

680 Mt. Auburn Street, P.O. Box 403, Watertown, MA 02272

This technique is sometimes called the "Direct Mail Strip Tease." In a test and rollout situation, you want to give the mailing every chance of working, so you go full tilt. Once it has proved itself, the object is to begin to lower the cost-per-thousand by cutting down—or eliminating altogether—various elements with as little sacrifice of results as possible. Will a #10 envelope work just as well as the 6″ × 9″? Can the size of the circular be cut down? Can the circular be eliminated completely? The idea of having a control mailing that continues to generate responses at an acceptable cost-per-order, but at a lower cost-per-thousand, is tantalizing, and should always be tested if the test seems logical.

If you'd rather cheer us on from the sidelines right now...

Maybe you've just started a new job. Gotten married. Had a baby. Moved. Retired. Whatever. But for the foreseeable future, you just want to catch your breath.

Does this mean you should wait to join EARTHWATCH? Not at all. *Sign on now as a member anyway, and you'll still have the time of your life.* You can follow expeditions from your armchair through stories in the magazine, through your handy desk diary/expedition planner, and through Briefing Kits you may order. You can take part in local invitational events, and broaden your circle of friends.

Come April 15, you can also take tax deductions for your annual membership dues and contributions. And throughout the year you can bask in that nice, warm feeling that comes from knowing you're doing good – supporting research that will ultimately and significantly improve the quality of human life.

MEMBER BENEFITS

1. EARTHWATCH Magazine.
Illustrated member magazine brings you science updates, announcements of new expeditions.
2. Eligibility.
Membership automatically qualifies you for any and all expeditions.
3. Desk Diary.
Special January Issue lists expeditions and events for coming year, serves as your planner.
4. Get-Away Kits.
At cost, detailed expedition briefing kits tell what, where, when, who, how.
5. Invitational Events.
Meet leading scientists, fellow members at regional gatherings.
6. Make a Difference.
Whether you go, or cheer from the sidelines, you help advance the frontiers of knowledge.
7. Tax Deductions.
Membership contributions and shared expedition expenses are fully tax deductible except for $3 applied to magazine subscription.

DATE ____ $ ____ DEDUCTION

CHECK# ____ CREDIT CARD ____

Detach and mail in postpaid envelope

I accept your invitation with anticipation.

Please put me down to receive all benefits – EARTHWATCH Magazine, eligibility for all expeditions, desk diary issue, get-away kits, invitational events, plus the satisfaction of making a difference.

☐ Check for my $25 dues contribution is enclosed.

☐ Please charge my credit card:
☐ VISA ☐ MasterCard ☐ American Express

CARD # ____ EXP DATE ____

☐ HURRY! Please rush last-call information on expeditions I might go on in the immediate future. No extra cost or obligation.

Postmark Early. Participation limited. Be on the safe side. Mail card now in postage-paid envelope to make next pick-up.

EARTHWATCH

Membership Services · P.O. Box 8037 · Syracuse, NY 13217

P0X

NO POSTAGE NECESSARY IF MAILED IN THE UNITED STATES

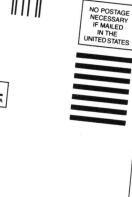

BUSINESS REPLY MAIL
FIRST CLASS PERMIT NO. 45600 BELMONT, MA

POSTAGE WILL BE PAID BY ADDRESSEE

Director of Membership Services
EARTHWATCH
Membership Services
680 Mt. Auburn Street
P.O. Box 403
Watertown, MA 02272

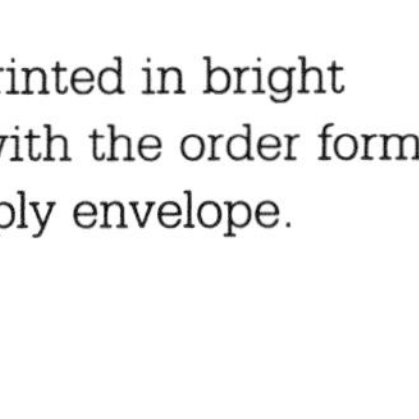

The lift piece, printed in bright yellow, shown with the order form and business reply envelope.

Jayme's lift piece is there to reassure armchair travelers and ecologists that they are every bit as welcome as the incipient Indiana Jones.

Notice that the seven benefits on the order card either are phrased differently from those on the circular or are new benefits altogether. Also notice Jayme's caveat that encourages action under the name and address:

Postmark Early. Participation limited. Be on the safe side. Mail card now in postage-paid envelope to make next pick-up.

Bill Jayme:

A nonprofit organization, Earthwatch serves as a kind of Peace Corps for history, science, the environment, civilization itself.

Through its membership program and magazine, it matches researchers who need temporary help on field projects with volunteers looking for ways to "get involved." Naturalists in rain forest, jungle, veldt who need observers to track vanishing species. Archaeologist requiring willing hands in excavating clues to our cultural DNA.

The concept is at once revolutionary, serendipitous, and complicated. It raises myriad questions in the prospect's mind that must be answered all at once.

Where might I work? When? For how long? How would I get there? What would I be doing? What qualifications must I have? What are the living conditions? Who pays for what?

Of all practical advertising media, only direct mail offers a sufficiently large canvas for telling such a complex story. The assignment was a writer's and designer's dream—a product that packages the nobility of all creation, addressed to prospects who are still hopeful about the human condition.

Futurist

On the outer envelope of the *Futurist*, Tony Cornish promises to reveal "Social & Technological Forecasts for the Next 25 Years" and repeats the promise on the first page of his eight-page letter. Rather than pique your interest and leave you hanging, he delivers what is promised—plastic cars, the collapse of Japan, a NASA-designed aerospace vehicle that will carry passengers halfway around the world in two hours.

A feature of the letter worth noting is the list of directors going down the left margin of page 1. These are important people; many of their names and works will be known to the reader. The mere listing of their names is a powerful endorsement—the equivalent of a testimonial—for the product.

The World Future Society is a family affair. Edward Cornish is president; Jeff Cornish is business manager; Tony Cornish is in charge of circulation.

Edward Cornish, President

World Future Society
4916 Saint Elmo Avenue
Bethesda, Maryland 20814

NONPROFIT
U.S. POSTAGE
PAID
WORLD FUTURE
SOCIETY

INSIDE:

Social & Technological Forecasts for the Next 25 Years

3A53
S. R.
ST
NEW CANAAN, CT 06840

PLUS:

Details on how you can receive a valuable book on the last decade of the twentieth century — a $7.95 value — absolutely FREE. See inside!

MAILER: *Futurist*
PACKAGE: Forecasts for next 25 yrs.
PROJECT MGR.: Jeff Cornish
WRITER: Tony Cornish
DESIGNER: Tony Cornish
FIRST MAILED: 1985
Outside envelope, 2-color, 6″ × 9″.

An Association for the Study of Alternative Futures

Publisher of THE FUTURIST: A Journal of Forecasts, Trends and Ideas About the Future

SOCIAL AND TECHNOLOGICAL FORECASTS FOR THE NEXT 25 YEARS

Forecast #1: By the year 2000, the average car will be mostly plastic and will last an average of 22 years.

Forecast #2: The economy of Japan, envied worldwide today, is in for a period of turmoil and decline during the 1990s. Subsequently, Japan will not regain its current overpowering presence in world trade in the foreseeable future.

Forecast #3: "Electronic immigrants" could become a hot international trade issue by the late 1990s. These new service workers who "telecommute" across borders via computers will perform a variety of services electronically and compete against workers in affluent countries.

Forecast #4: By the year 2000, 52% of the world's people will reside in urban centers. That number may leap to 90% by the end of the twenty-first century.

Forecast #5: A worldwide economic collapse is extremely likely in the next few years. Those unprepared may stand naked before a crisis unseen in the U.S. since the Civil War.

Forecast #6: NASA plans the first flight of the National Aero-Space Plane before 1995. A short ten years from now, NASA scientists believe, civilian aerospace vehicles will travel at Mach 12 and carry travelers half-way around the world in two hours.

Dear Reader:

These are some of the latest forecasts from members of the World Future Society and its magazine THE FUTURIST.

In this letter, I will share other forecasts with you and tell you how you can receive--completely without risk--a volume on the last decade of the twentieth century

(over, please)

4916 Saint Elmo Avenue • Bethesda, Maryland 20814 • U.S.A. • 301/656-8274

absolutely FREE with an introductory membership.

At the outset, let me say that futurists do not predict the future. And there's good reason for this. If we could predict the future, it would mean that the future could not be changed. We could not consciously create it. Yet this is the main purpose of studying the future: to look at what may happen if present trends continue, decide if this is what is desirable, and, if it's not, work to change it.

You'll Get a Unique Perspective on Our Rapidly Changing World.

Our world changes so quickly that it has become increasingly difficult to keep up with new developments--much less to understand their implications to society. Through World Future Society publications and activities, you'll understand what new technologies, new values, and social change will mean to you.

Since 1966, when the World Future Society was founded, we've worked hard to share information on new developments, possibilities, forecasts, trends, and scenarios. This information helps individuals, governments, and businesses participate in creating a better future for themselves and the world as a whole. Thirty thousand people in 80 countries find membership essential.

As a nonprofit organization, we've put all our effort into sharing this information with everyone--not just governments or corporations. The World Future Society is totally independent, offers no official view of what the future will or should be like, embraces no creed or ideology. Only in this way can we give you the unbiased information you need about the most important subject there is: Your Future.

Whether we are on the threshold of a Golden Age or on the brink of a global cataclysm that will extinguish our civilization is, I believe, not only unknowable, but undecided. The decision will emerge through what we do in the years ahead, for each of us will create a piece of the common future of all mankind.

We can do nothing to change the past, but we have enormous power to shape the future. Once we grasp that essential insight, we recognize our responsibility and capability for building our dreams of tomorrow and avoiding our nightmares. Of course, we feel abysmally ignorant of how to proceed, but as we join together, forming networks of human concern about the future, we will find the strength and wisdom needed to create a better future world.

This is some of the thinking that went into forming the World Future Society more than 20 years ago. And now for more thought-provoking forecasts:

2

Forecast #7: Scientists have succeeded in synthesizing the human growth hormone, enabling parents to increase the height of their children. Wilt Chamberlain, watch out!

Forecast #8: Mexico City, which already has nearly 20 million residents, is adding more at the rate of 2,000 each day. By the year 2000, Mexico City will have 28 million people and be the largest city in the world.

Forecast #9: "Copreneurs"--married couples who work together--may be the wave of America's business future. Hiring working couples as a team could be a logical step for corporations. And more married couples are expected to start their own businesses.

Forecast #10: During the 1990s, animal and plant species could disappear at the rate of 10,000 per year, largely due to the destruction of tropical forests. Every hour, one species will become extinct, some biologists believe.

As you can see, the future offers us many opportunities as well as dangers. If we can look ahead, and decide what kind of future is desirable, we can make the right decisions ... for tomorrow is built today!

You'll Learn to Forecast Your Own Future.

The best person to forecast your future is you. Why? Because you can influence and change your future in ways that no one else can. By learning about trends, forecasts, and scenarios, you can do a lot to build a better future for yourself, your family, your business, and your investments.

And when you accept our invitation to join the World Future Society today, we'll send you a valuable bonus book to help you and your family make the right choices to create a better future for yourselves--THE 1990s & BEYOND. This information-packed volume, 160 well-illustrated pages, is yours absolutely free.

Outstanding Benefits Available Only to Members

Your membership entitles you to a fantastic array of exclusive benefits to help you learn about tomorrow and understand today. As a World Future Society member you will receive:

THE FUTURIST: A Journal of Forecasts, Trends, and Ideas About the Future. This lively, independent magazine will keep you informed and enlightened with the latest developments, scenarios, technologies, trends, recommendations, and more. You'll learn of new ways of doing things, radical proposals, and solutions--ideas to create a better tomorrow.

THE FUTURIST is filled with articles and features that capture

(over, please)

3

your imagination and fill you with ideas, visions, and opportunities. You can position yourself and your business to take advantage of important trends that are occurring now and will continue in the coming months and years. Each issue is packed cover to cover with departments and features:

TOMORROW IN BRIEF -- provides a quick update of unique and remarkable developments you can't find anywhere else. In each issue you'll learn about provocative new ideas and developments such as:

* The Superfish -- how scientists are using genetics to breed a 100-pound trout.
* Mind-Reading Computers -- that will pick up your thoughts and place them before you on a computer screen--the ultimate in data entry.
* The New Gold and Silver Prospectors -- who aren't digging in the ground, but rather are running a computer scrapyard in England and mining $10 million a year in gold, silver, and platinum from junk computer circuit boards.

And in each issue you'll receive WORLD TRENDS & FORECASTS. You'll explore stimulating ideas, visions, new ways to live and work, and remarkable happenings now on the horizon, such as:

* The Junkyard in Space -- how communications satellites face increasing hazards from burned-out rocket shells, old payloads, and abandoned malfunctioning satellites.
* The New Achievers -- how corporations are working on developing their people not just as workers but as individuals, encouraging them to grow personally in the workplace for increased job satisfaction and productivity.
* Why Computers Worry Doctors -- how some M.D.'s fear that computer diagnosis may change the doctor's role from esteemed decision-maker to a paramedic technician and forever change the doctor/patient relationship.

... If even one of these ideas sparks your imagination, read on ... your membership and THE FUTURIST offer you so much more...

FUTURE VIEW -- a thoughtful essay by a distinguished thinker. Leading futurists identify important issues and place developments in a broader context. You'll get a fascinating overview to help you make sense of our changing world. You'll read items such as:

* The Need for "Knowledge Processing" -- how computers are generating mountains of data, but making sense of it is becoming increasingly difficult.
* A New Silver Age -- a remarkable comparison of Western history examined in relation to the stages of early Greco-Roman civilization and what this may portend for the future.

4

An 8-page letter, printed on two 11″ × 17″ nested and folded sheets.

* New Challenges for the Information Age -- surveys project a tenfold growth both in personal computers and their processing capability. "Expert systems" will allow us to have the knowledge of the most-renowned heart surgeons, scientists, and even cooks, available to anyone, anywhere in the world.

Book Reviews. Leading futurists give you expert evaluations of new works especially selected for their impact and originality.

And, of course, feature articles you will find nowhere else.

Each issue is packed with 8-10 feature articles by leading thinkers, scientists, researchers, economists, politicians, and experts from virtually every field who know that the actions we take today create the world of tomorrow.

A small sampling of well-known futurists whose ideas have appeared in THE FUTURIST includes: Alvin Toffler, John Naisbitt, B.F. Skinner, John Diebold, Senator Albert Gore, Jr., theologian Harvey Cox, sociologist Amitai Etzioni, Nobel Prize-winning chemist Glenn Seaborg, Star Trek originator Gene Roddenberry, author and employment expert Richard Bolles, Hazel Henderson, health expert Dr. Anthony Fauci, Willis Harman, former Colorado Governor Richard Lamm, Herman Kahn, Bertrand de Jouvenel, science fiction writer Frederik Pohl, economist E.F. Schumacher, educator Harold Shane, public opinion expert Daniel Yankelovich, Gerard K. O'Neill, visionary Fritjof Capra, forecaster Marvin Cetron, and far too many more to mention. Through the pages of THE FUTURIST, you'll meet creative, dynamic individuals like these, whose thoughts and ideas are changing the way people think, live, work, and play.

Some recent articles include:

Weapons in Space: A "Star Wars" debate between Lt. General James A. Abrahamson and astronomer Carl Sagan.

The Kondratieff Cycle and War: How long-wave economic cycles can predict more than economic trends.

Automate, Emigrate, or Evaporate: America's choices in the global economy -- why the U.S. must regain a substantial lead in productivity to compete in the global economy.

The Robot Revolution: The "robotization" of business is proceeding rapidly, driven by increased labor costs and the plummeting price of technology.

Telecommuters: The Stay-at-Home Work Force of the Future -- how many workers in the "information age" may earn their living on their home computers.

Window of Opportunity: How advances in communications, biotechnology, and space are creating hope for the future.

(over, please)

5

Emerging Careers: Occupations for Postindustrial Society -- The future holds in store a multitude of exciting new occupations, from treasure hunting to moon mining, says a careers expert.

Schools of the Future: Why schools must stay open longer, pay teachers better, and open their doors to adult workers in need of retraining.

Skynet 2000: Raising Global Productivity Through Space Communications -- By the year 2000, a new system of communicating via space could enable mankind to make great jumps in productivity even in isolated areas of the Third World.

But THE FUTURIST is only one benefit of your membership ...

You can attend World Future Society conferences and seminars at special members' rates, such as the Society's Sixth General Assembly, "Future View: The 1990s and Beyond" (July 16-20, 1989, Washington, D.C.). WFS conferences bring together leaders from many fields and many nations to share ideas and forecasts, to view exciting new technologies, and to establish networks of common concern.

Often these conferences serve as forums for world leaders to announce their plans. You can get an exclusive advance view. For example, at our 1989 conference, Senator Albert Gore, Jr., presidential candidate in 1988, spelled out many of his newest ideas. And, at an earlier conference, Congressman Newt Gingrich outlined his ideas for a "conservative opportunity society."

Speakers have included Arthur C. Clarke, Gerald R. Ford, Walter Mondale, Marshall McLuhan, Herman Kahn, Edward M. Kennedy, Hubert Humphrey, B.F. Skinner, Betty Friedan, Buckminster Fuller, Alvin Toffler, John Naisbitt, Maurice Strong, Charles Schultze, and many others prominent in their respective field or country.

From presidential candidates to radical poets, World Future Society conferences provide an open forum to leading thinkers and doers of every point of view. You'll meet and hear these thought-leading individuals at what has been referred to as "the greatest intellectual show on earth." And you will receive advance notice of these happenings as well as special members-only rates.

But that's not all. You'll also receive the following ...

A Free Subscription to NEWSLINE, the WFS Members' Newsletter that will give you late-breaking news about individuals and events of the Society.

The Opportunity to Join Local Chapters--Now in Over 120 Cities. As a member, you'll be able to join groups of forward-looking individuals in your area to share your common interests and learn more about future-oriented issues at special workshops, meetings,

6

conferences, and luncheons, many of which feature distinguished speakers.

The Semi-Annual Bookstore Catalog and Discounts on Over 300 Books, Videos, and More. Your membership entitles you to receive the World Future Society's Bookstore Catalog containing the largest single collection of books on the future available anywhere.

What's more, as a member, you'll receive a 10% discount on everything in the catalog. You'll save on best-sellers like MEGATRENDS, but you'll also save on hard-to-find books like ISSUES MANAGEMENT. You'll enjoy browsing through this "bookstore of the future" in the comfort of your own home and save off what you'd pay in ordinary bookstores--if you could find the book.

And, as a special bonus, you'll also get two exclusive reports--

The Annual OUTLOOK Report. Each year, the World Future Society assembles forecasts from more than 50 authoritative sources to form a general outlook of trends to look for in the coming years. You will receive the latest issue in your introductory membership kit.

... and THE ART OF FORECASTING -- a special primer on the scientific techniques used by futurists. Discussing terminology and showing the most valuable methods, this bonus report will give you a solid introduction to this important new field.

Now here's the most important part. Your membership will give you the satisfaction of knowing that you make it possible for leading thinkers and doers from all over the world to participate in studying the future and helping to create a better tomorrow. The world faces enormous challenges. We need to work collectively to develop the wisdom and consensus to build a world worth handing over to our children. A better tomorrow truly depends on your support.

Won't you join us? Enclosed with my letter you'll find an introductory membership application. Dues are just $30 for a full year. And you'll receive all the membership benefits described above.

To sum up, your membership entitles you to:

* A one-year subscription to THE FUTURIST (six issues).
* Special Discounts on Conferences and Seminars.
* A Free Subscription to NEWSLINE.
* The Opportunity to Join Local Chapters.
* The Twice-Yearly Bookstore Catalog.
* Special Discounts on Books, Tapes, and More.
* The Exclusive OUTLOOK Report.
* The ART OF FORECASTING Report.
* and the knowledge that you are helping to build a better tomorrow.

(over, please)

7

You'll receive all this for only $30--just 58 cents a week! Many newsletters or professional associations charge many times this amount.

And if you are not 100% satisfied with your introductory issue and other benefits, you may simply write me personally, and I will see that you receive a full and immediate refund with no questions asked. And you may keep everything we've sent you, including your free book, THE 1990s & BEYOND.

If you agree that the future consists of a variety of alternatives, that choice is unavoidable, and that refusing to choose is itself a choice, you have taken the first step toward a more active role in your own future.

The World Future Society can make a major contribution to creating a better future for all of us. Thanks to you, we may be able to halt the present trends toward calamity and move human civilization toward the happy future that exists within our imagination and capability. RSVP today!

Sincerely,

Edward Cornish

Edward Cornish
President

P.S. Remember, you will also receive, absolutely free, THE 1990s & BEYOND, an information-packed book on the last decade of the twentieth century. This 160-page, well-illustrated volume (a $7.95 value) is yours free when you join.

Forecast #11: Water shortages in the United States may become severe, due to excessive demand and contaminants from toxic wastes. But new technologies could head off the threatened crisis--and bring new life to arid regions.

Forecast #12: Between now and the end of the century--just a few short years away--the U.S. economy will generate $4 to $5 trillion in new capital assets, assets that will embody the next generation of applied technology. But unless current financing techniques are altered, small business may find access to credit even more limited in the future than today.

For independent views of the World Future Society and THE FUTURIST, please see the back of your membership application.

8

The 11″ × 17″ brochure has a marvelously futuristic cover from the magazine—a series of computer images thrust forward from deep space.

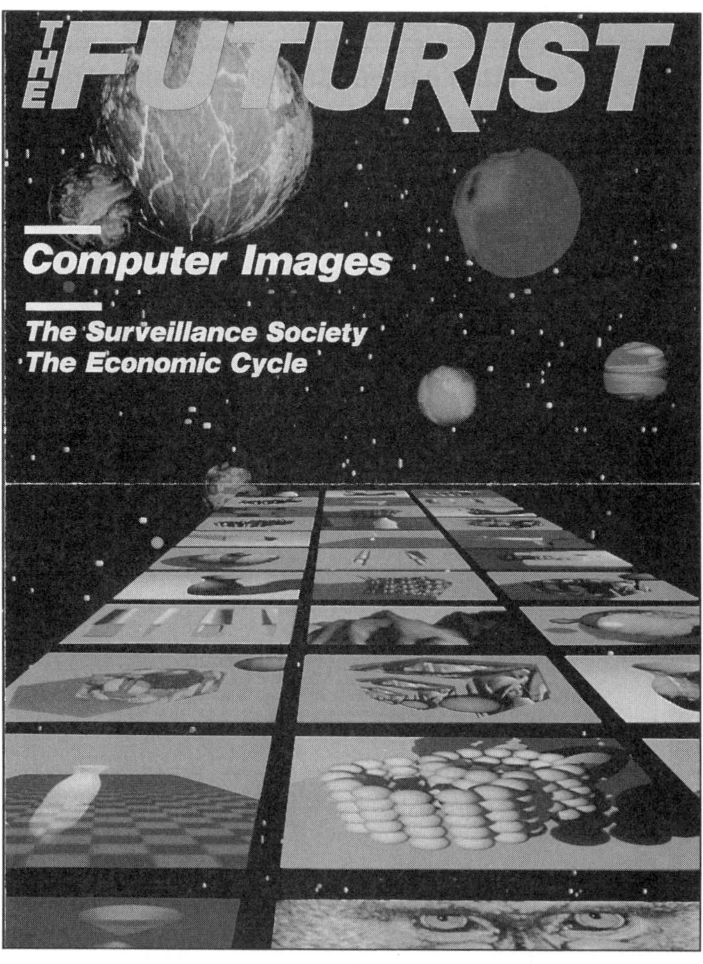

JEFF CORNISH:

My first note about our package is that we consider it a membership *in the World Future Society rather than a* subscription *to the* Futurist, *and that change was important to the success of the package over our previous efforts.*

The package was first mailed December 31, 1985. Our early efforts tested a discount price and the value of the color brochure. The discount lost—not even winning on percent response on most lists. The color brochure won. We later tested and added the lift note.

Though the carrier is a 6″ × 9″, we fold the letter to number 10. This began in the original test mailing when I received a call at home to tell me that the letters had accidentally been folded to number 10—could they go ahead and use them or would they have to reprint. I told them to go ahead and use them. We continued to have them folded number 10 for several years before finally testing it against 5¹/₆″ × 8¹/₂″. When we finally did, the number 10 fold provided an 8 percent lift—not necessarily significant, but we're still folding them number 10.

Our biggest blunder with the package was when we decided to update the forecasts and articles mentioned in the letter. We felt the changes were small and would not affect response, so on we went with a mailing scheduled for October 21, 1987. When the stock market crashed October 19th, we wondered if we should delay the mailing. With all the money spent already, we decided to go on with the scheduled drop date. A few weeks later I was looking at response

The 1990s & Beyond
Edited by Edward Cornish
BIG — 8½" × 11" — 160 pages
Over 100 Illustrations — 26 Information-Packed Chapters
YOURS FREE!
This Essential Volume on the last decade of the twentieth century is your FREE GIFT when You Join at Absolutely No Risk.

Highlights From THE 1990s & BEYOND

"There seems to be no a *priori* reason for rejecting the possibility of nonhuman mechanisms possessing the same kinds of intelligence humans do."

— John Baer

"The desire to prolong life and relieve suffering is . . . creating a revolution in so-called biomaterials — artificial tissues and organs made of plastics, ceramics, glasses, and composites that can augment or replace bodily tissues and parts."

— Tom Forester

"Some people . . . may decide that robots are so much easier to get along with than people that they will refuse to interact with people anymore. We may need 'robot-abuse' clinics, just as we already have drug- and alcohol-abuse clinics."

— Mike Higgins

This valuable book is yours free with a no-risk introductory membership!

OUR NO-RISK GUARANTEE

You must be completely satisfied with your first issue of THE FUTURIST and membership in The World Future Society or you may simply write us and receive a full and immediate refund of your membership dues, no questions asked. And keep this guarantee. You must be continually satisfied or we will refund the unused portion of your membership dues.

WORLD FUTURE SOCIETY • 4916 ST. ELMO AVENUE, BETHESDA, MD 20814

C2

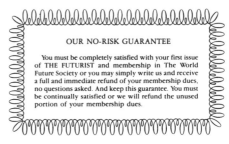

TABLE of CONTENTS

5 Introduction
By Edward Cornish
Exploring the possibilities of the future helps us make better choices as we go about the task of shaping the world of tomorrow.

8 Issues for the 1990s
By Edith Weiner and Arnold Brown
Should robots pay taxes? Can Africa be saved? Do people have a right to quiet? These could be among the major issues of the 1990s.

12 Nine American Lifestyles: Values and Societal Change
By Arnold Mitchell
A noted social scientist portrays nine adult lifestyle groups and shows how they may change in response to future economic, social, and political conditions.

23 The American Family in the Year 2000
By Andrew Cherlin and Frank F. Furstenberg, Jr.
There will be more divorces, single-parent families, and mixed families from remarriages, but the ideal of marrying and having children is still very much a part of the American experience.

31 Age Wars: The Coming Battle Between Young and Old
By Phillip Longman
Current economic trends and fiscal policies forbode a future of generational wars.

35 Death of the University
By Herbert I. London
Changes both within and outside the university system will make its end inevitable.

41 Class of 2000: The Good News and the Bad News
By Marvin J. Cetron
The high-school graduating class of 2000 has already begun its journey through the American educational system. Will the journey prepare these students for the future they will face?

48 Health Care Tomorrow
By Roy Amara
Medical, technological, and social trends will force major changes in American health care by the turn of the century.

53 The Future of AIDS
By John Platt
By the end of this century, AIDS could have the impact of a world war, producing recession and a stay-at-home society at the same time that it transforms world health and demographics.

60 Medical Breakthroughs: Cutting the Toll of Killer Diseases
By Theodore J. Gordon
Fewer people will die from heart attack and stroke in the future, but more will die from cancer, say medical experts.

63 The Materials Revolution
By Tom Forester
New man-made materials such as high-performance plastics and superconducting ceramics are the driving forces behind key technological advances that are shaping the future.

68 Hyperintelligence: The Next Evolutionary Step
By George Bugliarello
A dramatic extension of the power of the brain, made possible by worldwide computer networks, will help to create a new and better global society.

74 Artificial Intelligence: Making Machines That Think
By John Baer
Most computer experts agree that a true "thinking" computer is a long way away–and some argue that it can never be.

80 The Future of Personal Robots
By Mike Higgins
Personal robots may be able to do more for us than we can even imagine today. But "super-robots" may develop that cause all sorts of problems for people.

84 Living on the Moon: Will Humans Develop an Unearthly Culture?
By Philip R. Harris
In adapting to their new environment, lunar settlers will develop new lifestyles, new values, and a new vocabulary.

90 The Future Course of International Terrorism
By Brian Michael Jenkins
The world will face continued growth in terrorist attacks in the next decade, and large-scale incidents involving hundreds of deaths will become more common.

96 Crime and Punishment: Forces Shaping the Future
By Gene Stephens
The changing social and technological environment will lead to new definitions of crime and new challenges for the criminal justice system.

105 Downtown 2040: Making Cities Fun!
By John Fondersmith
The historic buildings of downtowns will take on new importance as "cities of the future" enhance their individual characters.

114 Going Height Crazy: Super Skyscrapers of the Future
By Hans-Gerhard Kauschke
Mile-high skyscrapers are technically feasible. But is bigger better?

118 Tourism: A Vital Force for Peace
By Louis J. D'Amore
Tourism has the potential to be the world's great "peace industry," as people meet face-to-face and establish strong, personal ties with one another.

124 "Dream" Vacations: The Booming Market for Designed Experiences
By Philip Kotler
Got a dream? Live it! "Designed experience" brokers will help you make your dreams come true–for a price.

131 The 21st Century Economy
By William Van Dusen Wishard
The global economy is in rapid transition. A U.S. Department of Commerce official describes key trends that warrant especially close scrutiny.

137 Earth's Vital Signs
By Lester R. Brown, Christopher Flavin, and Edward C. Wolf
The earth's vital signs reveal a patient in declining health. Policy makers can ill afford to postpone making the investments needed for a preventive health-care plan for the planet.

145 Do We Owe Anything to Future Generations?
By Robert B. Mellert
The actions we take today will shape the world that future generations live in. What is our responsibility to them?

150 John Elfreth Watkins, Jr.: Forgotten Genius of Forecasting
By Harold G. Shane and Gary A. Sojka

150 What May Happen in the Next Hundred Years
By John Elfreth Watkins, Jr.
An all-but-forgotten journalist wrote some surprisingly accurate forecasts at the turn of the century.

156 The 1990s in Brief
Selections from THE FUTURIST's "Tomorrow in Brief" column include test-tube forests and clothes with a built-in thermostat.

What You'll Learn . . . In This Valuable Bonus Volume

- **The earth's troubling "vital signs," and what can be done to improve the health of the "patient." See page 137.**
- **How school–business partnerships can improve education and produce more-employable graduates. See page 41.**
- **Why international terrorist incidents are likely to grow in numbers and in violence in the future. See page 90.**
- **A baker's dozen of trends that will shape the twenty-first-century economy. See page 131.**
- **How personal robots could help solve the problem of caring for our elderly population. See page 80.**
- **What sorts of "designed experiences" are available to the adventure-minded consumer. See page 124.**
- **Why birth defects will be *the* environmental and occupational health and safety issue of the 1990s. See page 8.**
- **How "participatory justice" could create a cheaper, faster, and more-equitable criminal justice system. See page 96.**
- **A provocative scenario of generational conflict, with a "Youth Machine" pitted against aging baby boomers. See page 31.**
- **How a new space culture may develop as people begin living on the moon. See page 84.**

— and much, much more.

YOURS FREE WHEN YOU JOIN TODAY!

There are 2 lift pieces: a $5^1/_2$" × $8^1/_2$" 2-color brochure offering the 160-page premium book, *The 1990s & Beyond*, and a letter from the membership secretary offering a *"full and immediate refund."* This is a far stronger guarantee than the usual promise of a refund on all undelivered issues. The *Futurist* is truly a no-risk offer.

OPEN THIS ONLY IF YOU'RE STILL UNDECIDED
ABOUT MEMBERSHIP IN THE WORLD FUTURE SOCIETY

World Future Society

Dear Reader:

If you have an interest in the future, if you're fascinated by new technology, new ideas, new ways of doing things...if you are concerned about some of the disturbing trends in our world and would like to help...then there's no reason not to give membership a try. Because...

If, for any reason, you are not 100% satisfied, you can cancel your membership and get a full and immediate refund with no questions asked. And you may keep your Outlook Report, "The Art of Forecasting," and your free book THE 1990s & BEYOND.

That's how sure we are you'll be glad you accepted our invitation.

So if you're looking for knowledge, a rewarding adventure, and the advantage a future perspective can offer, mail the enclosed card today!

Sincerely,

Susan Echard
Membership Secretary

P.S. To receive your free copy of THE 1990s & BEYOND, please respond within ten days.

4916 SAINT ELMO AVENUE
BETHESDA, MARYLAND 20814 U.S.A.
TELEPHONE: 301/656-8274

PUBLISHER OF THE FUTURIST: A JOURNAL OF FORECASTS, TRENDS, AND IDEAS ABOUT THE FUTURE

figures that were way off earlier mailings. Was it the Crash? Or was it the change in forecasts? It took several months to get a small test mailing together to test the new package against the old one. The revised forecasts were the primary culprit! Although the crash may also have depressed response. By the time we had another—our most responsive—mailing out, six months had passed. Lesson learned: Even if it seems like a minor change, test it!

I'm optimistic about the near-term future of the direct marketing industry. In any business, a period of success brings many marginal players in. The years 1987 and 1988 were great for response, so we all mailed more pieces to less responsive lists. It's no wonder response rates and profitability fell. (Postal rate increases certainly didn't help, either.) In the past two years, most of us have cut back on the number of pieces mailed and the weakest firms have folded. This should make room for solid increases in response rates and profits. Our 1991 response rates are up from 1990.

There will always be up and down markets, but, if we can deal with the public's concerns about privacy and the environment—which are more perception than reality—direct mail will last many more years.

Tony Cornish:

Here are a few of my thoughts on creating the World Future Society control package.

Value-added advertising. *I tried to give the reader a reward simply for reading the copy. In this case, the reader learned what leading futurists*

MEMBERSHIP APPLICATION

For Your FREE 1990s Volume and Other Membership Benefits, Mail This Card Today!

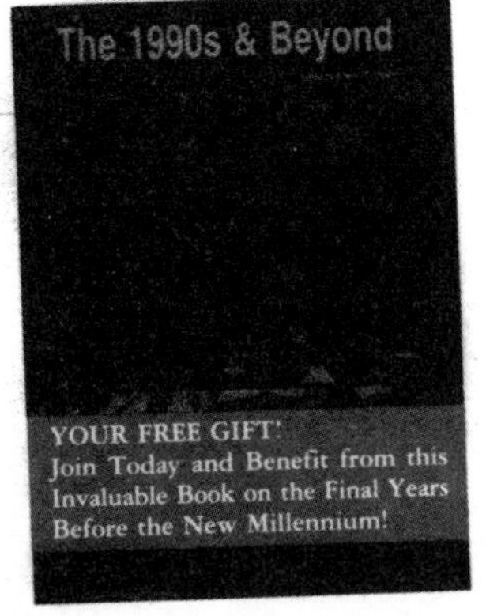

The 1990s & Beyond
YOUR FREE GIFT!
Join Today and Benefit from this Invaluable Book on the Final Years Before the New Millennium!

The World Future Society 4916 Saint Elmo Avenue Bethesda, Maryland 20814

☑ YES! I accept your invitation. Please sign me up for a one-year membership in the WORLD FUTURE SOCIETY at $30. My membership entitles me to a one-year subscription to THE FUTURIST, a Free Subscription to NEWSLINE, special notices and substantial discounts on conferences, 10% discounts on any of over 300 books, and my twice-yearly Resource Catalog. Also please send my FREE BONUS copy of THE 1990s & BEYOND, an exclusive volume on the decade preceding the turn of the century, and my two bonus reports, OUTLOOK '91 AND BEYOND and THE ART OF FORECASTING. If I'm not fully satisfied with my first issue, I'll let you know and you will send a full refund. The FREE BONUS 1990s book and the two special reports will be mine to keep.

3A53

S. R.
ST
NEW CANAAN, CT 06840

☐ Please sign me up for a two-year membership at $54. I save 20% off the second year's dues.

☐ My payment is enclosed. ☐ I am adding $ ______ as a tax-deductible contribution to your work.

☐ Charge my ☐ MasterCard ☐ Visa ☐ American Express

Acct. No. ________________ Exp. Date________ Sig.____________

What Others Say About the World Future Society:

"You are to be congratulated on the zeal with which you are engaging problems of the future."
Jonas Salk
Developer of the Polio Vaccine

"I find THE FUTURIST an absorbing, authoritative and useful publication in my work and circulate it to a number of other reporters and editors concerned with planning problems."
Fred Poland, President
International Science
Writers Association

"I am a subscriber to THE FUTURIST and find it to be an absolutely fascinating publication—containing solid data to support conclusions but still very readable, even for a layman."
Paul Jannesch
Publisher
Pollution Abstracts

"If I had to give up every periodical I take, except one, that one would be THE FUTURIST..."
D'Etta Leach
Public Affairs Producer
WTVI-TV
Charlotte, North Carolina

"Many thanks for sending me THE FUTURIST which I read with great interest...I enclose cheques for myself and Stanley Kubrick."
Arthur C. Clarke, author
2001: A Space Odyssey

"You deserve all of the accolades for turning THE FUTURIST into an outstanding journal—the preeminent publication in the futures field."
Robert W. Prehoda
Author

"Your journal continues to fascinate me. It is excellent. Also impressive is the general scope of work which you undertake."
Joel Burdin
Editor
Journal of Teacher Education

"These FUTURIST magazines for me are like martinis would be to some others, I become so excited, so turned on, that sometimes I find it hard to go to sleep. I find I am reading every article in every magazine and that because of these articles, I am changing an enormous amount of my approaches to things."
Rita Shaw
KTCA-TV
Minneapolis, Minnesota

"I have never had a journal 'swiped' as much as my copies of THE FUTURIST."
Dr. Charles W. Case
University of Vermont

"As one who has trouble planning a week in advance, I find the whole philosophy of the World Future Society exciting and challenging."
Ray E. Abbott, Director
Community Development
Temple, Texas

"...I hate to be without even one issue."
David B. Koth
Lakehurst, New Jersey

"The World Future Society can become an important institution with a firm influence on shaping the great events of our time. I look forward to working with you in building a better and stronger society which can contribute even more importantly to a better future for all mankind."
Orville L. Freeman
former U.S. Secretary of Agriculture

"I hope the World Future Society will continue to lead the way in promoting responsible research, and I hope you will bring your considerable talents to the complex task of finding solutions to the critical problems likely to confront us within the next 5, 10 and 15 years. If we are to enhance the prospects for human survival and well-being, we must be able to anticipate, evaluate, and respond to critical problems. Your forum, with its interdisciplinary and international exchange of information, will help decision-makers see the potential consequences of the decisions they make today. In addition, you are helping us explore alternative, innovative approaches to critical world problems. For this, we in Congress owe you great thanks."
Rep. Bob Edgar
U.S. Congressman
Pennsylvania

R2

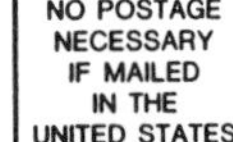

NO POSTAGE
NECESSARY
IF MAILED
IN THE
UNITED STATES

BUSINESS REPLY MAIL
FIRST CLASS MAIL PERMIT NO. 10485 BETHESDA, MD

POSTAGE WILL BE PAID BY ADDRESSEE

WORLD FUTURE SOCIETY

4916 SAINT ELMO AVENUE
BETHESDA, MD 20897-1406

The order form shown front and back and the business reply envelope. Ecologically sound and not wasteful, the back of the order form is used for testimonials.

considered to be the most significant forecasts for the next twenty-five years. Forecasts had worked well for many financial mailers and seemed a natural for this project.

Long letter. *The letter copy was eight pages. The offer was cash-with-order only so we didn't want to leave any questions unanswered. (A bill-me option will probably be tested soon, per the results of your analysis.)*

Pile on the benefits. *I tried to bring out every feature and corresponding benefit that went along with membership from each department of the magazine to saving on book sales to the importance of helping to create a better future.*

Enhance the offer. *We created a new report to accompany this offer and added another report. These, along with the free book and other enhanced benefits, were combined into a ''New Member Kit.''*

Add inexpensive premiums. *World Future Society had used books as premiums for years. These anthologies of popular articles from the magazine were simple to produce, enhanced the offer, and provided a valuable introduction for new members.*

Strong guarantee. *Here our guarantee allowed new members to cancel if unsatisfied and keep everything we sent them; the magazines, free book, and reports. We used the lift memo basically to play up this guarantee as well as restate the basic proposition.*

National Wildlife

The *National Wildlife* mailing is made up of four small main elements that all say pretty much the same thing. Whereas the *Earthwatch* copy platform is on the benefits of working in the field for the betterment of humanity—or of reading about it—Don O'Brien's offer focuses almost exclusively on the offer: six issues of a full-color magazine free when you pay for six issues of another. The offer is restated in the letter, the brochure, the lift piece, and on the order form, which is itself a kind of mini-brochure or lift piece.

Two interesting elements of the mailing are to be found on the back page of the brochure.

1. Brief mention is made of "Summit Vacations—in the Rockies, along the Pacific Coast, and in the Green Mountains of Vermont." This throwaway benefit here is what Jayme pinned the *Earthwatch* mailing to.
2. There is an order coupon on the circular *in addition to* the order form. Nancy Grady used this technique in her package for *Harper's* (Chapter 9). This follows the basic rule of direct marketing: "Make it as easy as possible to order."

   If the regular order form is missing—or if it has been used to place an order—the extra order form on the back of the circular means the mailing package is still viable.

Incidentally, this effort is textbook correct in that it includes the address of the magazine on every single element; thus if a person happens to see just one single element and becomes interested, there is an address to write for further information.

MAILER: *National Wildlife*
PACKAGE: Best Free Bonus Gift
PROJECT MGR.: Susan Hord (original)
Susan Harford (current)
WRITER: Don O'Brien
DESIGNER: Muriel Ebitz
FIRST MAILED: 1988
Outside envelope, #10 window.

G9032

Working for the Nature of Tomorrow.

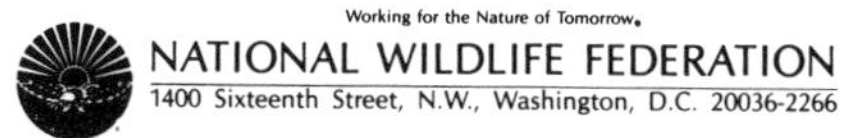

NATIONAL WILDLIFE FEDERATION
1400 Sixteenth Street, N.W., Washington, D.C. 20036-2266

The 6 issues of International WILDLIFE magazine are free, but the opportunity to get them may not last too long.

Dear Friend,

Let me explain.

Usually when you become an Associate Member you choose either National WILDLIFE or International WILDLIFE magazine to go along with your Membership.

Normally, if you want to receive both magazines, the dues are higher.

Nothing unusual in any of that...until you take a quick look at the offer in front of you right now.

Here it is...

Join today as an Associate Member. We'll send you the 6 issues - a full year - of National WILDLIFE magazine every other month just as we usually do. But, if you order before October 15th, 1990, there's a Bonus that goes along with your Membership. We'll also send you 6 issues of International WILDLIFE in the months between.

They will be sent Free. There's no cost at all for them -- and so you'll enjoy a full year of Membership, get all the usual benefits (which I'll detail for you in a moment) -- and you'll get a magazine every single month all year long - National WILDLIFE one month and International WILDLIFE the next!

All of this comes to you at the usual National Associate Membership dues of only $15.00. And it's quite a bargain, let me tell you. Those benefits I mentioned are part of this special opportunity, too -- so let me give you the particulars...

- You'll enjoy valuable discounts on a wide selection of nature books, video-tapes, and records. Good values --

and it's a handy benefit when gift-giving time comes along.

- You'll have the opportunity to join us in our summer vacation program. Sites range from Vermont with comfortable accommodations and a panoramic view of the historic Green Mountains to the scenic Pacific North-west with its famous coastal and mountain recreation areas. These programs are for Members only, and are exclusive.

- You'll get a personalized Membership card, an official NWF emblem for your car, special mailings and updates through the year to keep you posted on the effective conservation work you're helping us accomplish -- and other benefits, too.

You see, the National Wildlife Federation is America's largest conservation group, working for clean air, wildlife habitat, and the other natural resource concerns which you and I share. Our Members include people from all walks of life -- naturalists, teachers, homemakers, sportsmen, scien-tists, students, doctors, senior citizens, children...everyone with an interest in nature and a desire to work on its behalf.

I think you'll enjoy your new Membership. I know you'll enjoy your WILDLIFE magazines and the benefits that will be yours. So let me repeat my offer.

...Join today. You'll get all the usual Membership benefits -- plus, we'll add those six issues of International WILDLIFE at no extra cost to you at all. They are free!

FREE. But, time is limited. Your chance to take me up on this offer will be over soon. So, with all the information and ordering materials in-hand right now, check a box on the order card, and drop it into the mail to us today.

And in addition to the fun, enjoyment and good reading ahead of you...you'll be happy with the knowledge that you are directly helping the environment and the wildlife all across the country.

Sincerely,

Bill Howard

William W. Howard, Jr.
Executive Vice President

P.S. You'll be pleased with your decision, your 2 magazines, your Membership and all your other benefits!

Printed on recycled paper

Two-page letter.

The order form is an oddity in that it is personalized (the person's name and city appear in more than one place) for no apparent reason. The personalizing does not match the printed type, so it was obviously done by a computer—and a rather inept one at that. This is one of just four of the seventy-one Grand Controls that used personalization for the sake of personalizing.

The *National Wildlife* Grand Control was written by Donald D. O'Brien, a graduate of Emerson College, Boston, where he triple-majored in broadcasting, English, and speech. He worked on-air during the last two and a half years in college and then continued as a disk jockey for a few years after that. By learning how to "talk" as a radio person, O'Brien believes he was helped in his subsequent career. "Writing radio advertising is a great start for a direct mail professional—listen to some of the ads you like most and analyze them. You'll find they're similar in construction to the best direct marketing copy. (A secret has been revealed!)" O'Brien has also taught public speaking and writing for the business person; but his love is direct response writing.

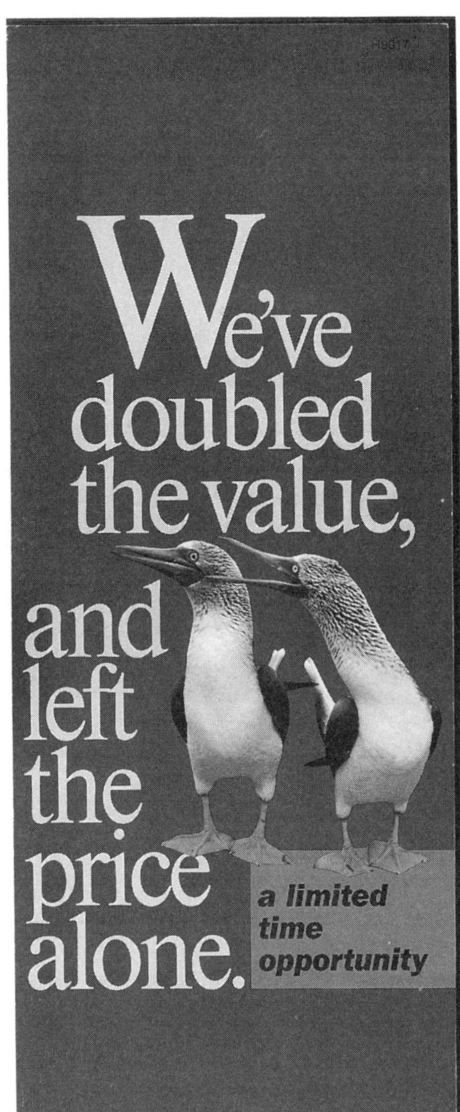

We've doubled the value, and left the price alone.
a limited time opportunity

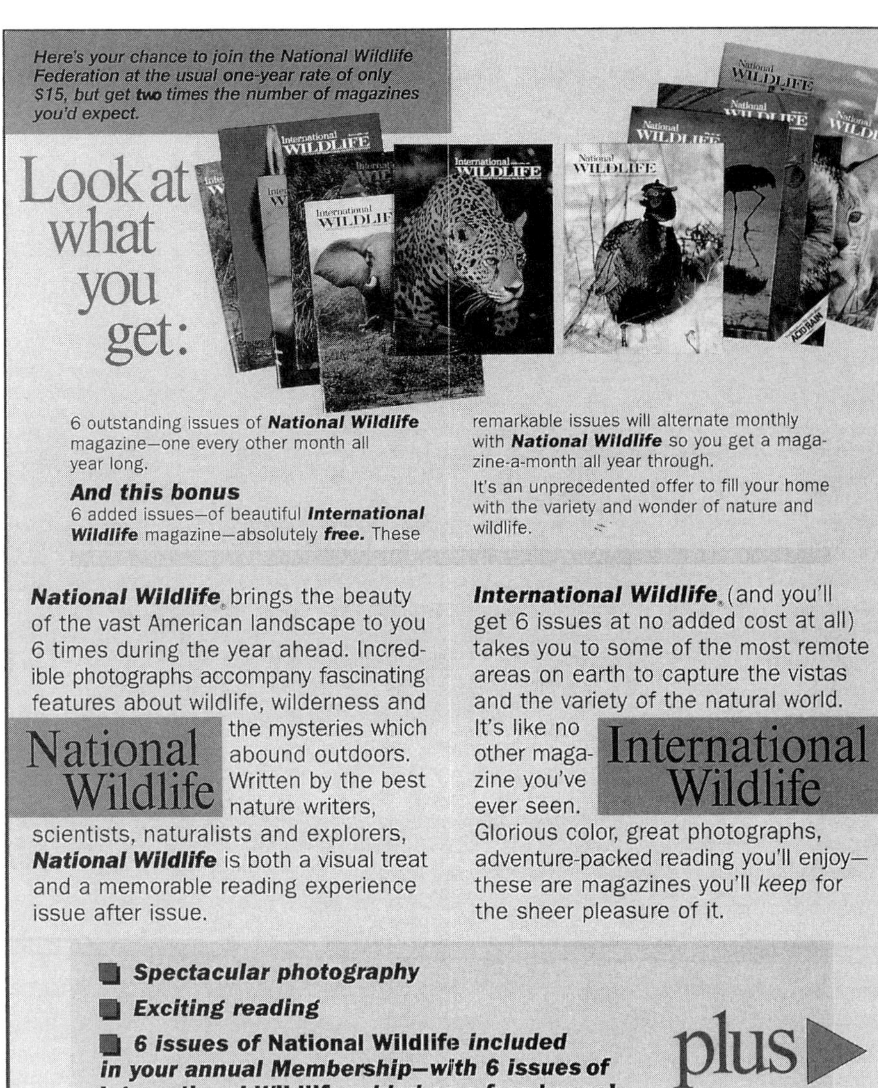

Here's your chance to join the National Wildlife Federation at the usual one-year rate of only $15, but get two times the number of magazines you'd expect.
Look at what you get:
6 outstanding issues of National Wildlife magazine—one every other month all year long.
And this bonus
6 added issues—of beautiful International Wildlife magazine—absolutely free. These remarkable issues will alternate monthly with National Wildlife so you get a magazine-a-month all year through.
It's an unprecedented offer to fill your home with the variety and wonder of nature and wildlife.
National Wildlife brings the beauty of the vast American landscape to you 6 times during the year ahead. Incredible photographs accompany fascinating features about wildlife, wilderness and the mysteries which abound outdoors. Written by the best nature writers, scientists, naturalists and explorers, National Wildlife is both a visual treat and a memorable reading experience issue after issue.
National Wildlife
International Wildlife (and you'll get 6 issues at no added cost at all) takes you to some of the most remote areas on earth to capture the vistas and the variety of the natural world. It's like no other magazine you've ever seen. Glorious color, great photographs, adventure-packed reading you'll enjoy—these are magazines you'll keep for the sheer pleasure of it.
International Wildlife
Spectacular photography
Exciting reading
6 issues of National Wildlife included in your annual Membership—with 6 issues of International Wildlife added as a free bonus!
plus

Don O'Brien:

The "We've doubled the value . . ." package has been one of a number of control packages I've written at the National Wildlife Federation over the past few years. As copy director there I wrote the various components, but cannot take total responsibility for the success it has enjoyed—as with any significant project in this business, it's the result of a team effort. Designers, list managers, and creative input from a variety of people made this package work initially, and keep it working today.

Let me start at the start.

The Federation's director of membership at the time this mailing was devised was Susan R. Hord, now retired. She and I, along with others in her department, wanted to increase the number of new-start members for the Federation (surprise). This would broaden the Federation's ability to show the values of nature to those who may not realize its worth (through our magazines and other educational materials), and develop renewal and contribution support later on. Our traditional approach to membership solicitation in those days was to offer only *our* National Wildlife (NW) *magazine, published every other month, along with the various benefits which are part of all membership plans*

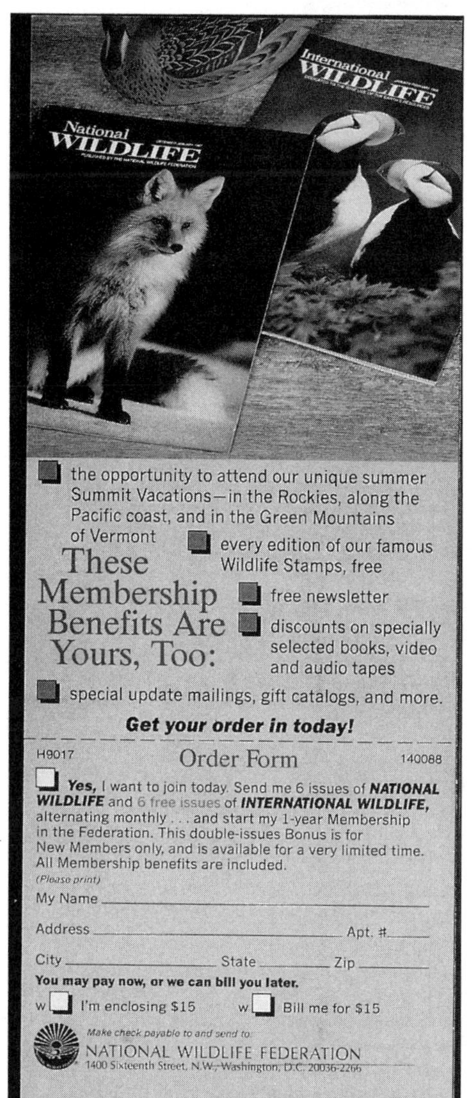

International WILDLIFE
National WILDLIFE
the opportunity to attend our unique summer Summit Vacations—in the Rockies, along the Pacific coast, and in the Green Mountains of Vermont
These Membership Benefits Are Yours, Too:
every edition of our famous Wildlife Stamps, free
free newsletter
discounts on specially selected books, video and audio tapes
special update mailings, gift catalogs, and more.
Get your order in today!
H9017
Order Form
140088
Yes, I want to join today. Send me 6 issues of NATIONAL WILDLIFE and 6 free issues of INTERNATIONAL WILDLIFE, alternating monthly . . . and start my 1-year Membership in the Federation. This double-issues Bonus is for New Members only, and is available for a very limited time. All Membership benefits are included.
(Please print)
My Name
Address
Apt. #
City
State
Zip
You may pay now, or we can bill you later.
I'm enclosing $15
Bill me for $15
Make check payable to and send to:
NATIONAL WILDLIFE FEDERATION
1400 Sixteenth Street, N.W., Washington, D.C. 20036-2266

The 3¾″ × 9″ brochure, 4-color, printed on coated stock.

From the editor

you get two magazines for the price of one!

Dear Friend,

With NATIONAL WILDLIFE magazine in hand, you'll enter the incredible world of grizzly bears and alligators, wolves and whooping cranes, bobcats and bluebirds.

But now, as a FREE bonus, you'll travel even further with a year of INTERNATIONAL WILDLIFE. Its glorious pages will take you to the land of pandas, the jungles of jaguars -- discover the underwater kingdom of the great blue whale and the realm of Japanese snow monkeys. And along the way, you'll see some old favorites, from storks to elephants, plus animals you'd never dream existed.

Right now, get your FREE bonus gift -- a year of INTERNATIONAL WILDLIFE. That's both magazines for the price of one, and double the number of animals for you to enjoy!

Send in the enclosed order form today. Get a wildlife magazine every month. You'll thank me for the adventure, I promise you.

Sincerely,

Jon Fisher

Jon Fisher
Editor
INTERNATIONAL WILDLIFE

Lift piece, cover and inside, printed in blue and black.

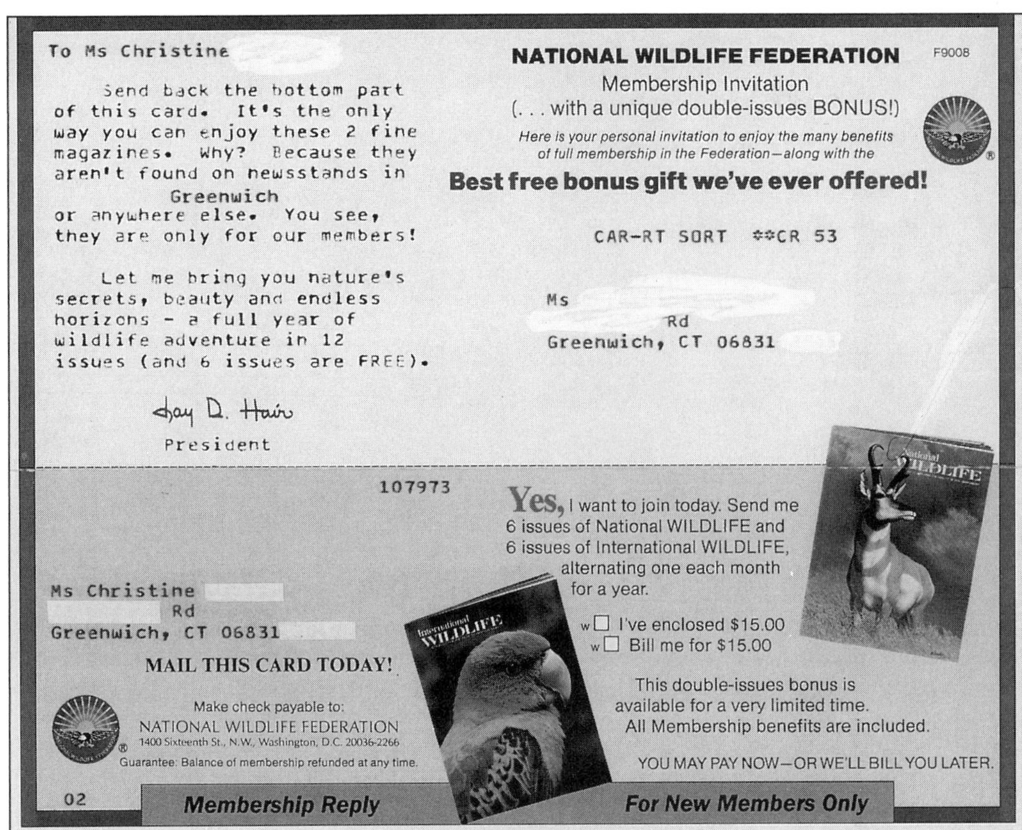
To Ms Christine

Send back the bottom part of this card. It's the only way you can enjoy these 2 fine magazines. Why? Because they aren't found on newsstands in Greenwich or anywhere else. You see, they are only for our members!

Let me bring you nature's secrets, beauty and endless horizons - a full year of wildlife adventure in 12 issues (and 6 issues are FREE).

Jay D. Hair
President

NATIONAL WILDLIFE FEDERATION F9008
Membership Invitation
(. . . with a unique double-issues BONUS!)
Here is your personal invitation to enjoy the many benefits of full membership in the Federation—along with the
Best free bonus gift we've ever offered!

CAR-RT SORT **CR 53

Ms
Rd
Greenwich, CT 06831

107973

Ms Christine
Rd
Greenwich, CT 06831

MAIL THIS CARD TODAY!

Make check payable to:
NATIONAL WILDLIFE FEDERATION
1400 Sixteenth St., N.W., Washington, D.C. 20036-2266
Guarantee: Balance of membership refunded at any time.

Yes, I want to join today. Send me 6 issues of National WILDLIFE and 6 issues of International WILDLIFE, alternating one each month for a year.

w☐ I've enclosed $15.00
w☐ Bill me for $15.00

This double-issues bonus is available for a very limited time. All Membership benefits are included.

YOU MAY PAY NOW—OR WE'LL BILL YOU LATER.

02 Membership Reply For New Members Only

Top, 4-color addressing piece and order form, personalized on both halves with a personalized salutation. Below, the reverse side, also 4-color, and the business reply envelope.

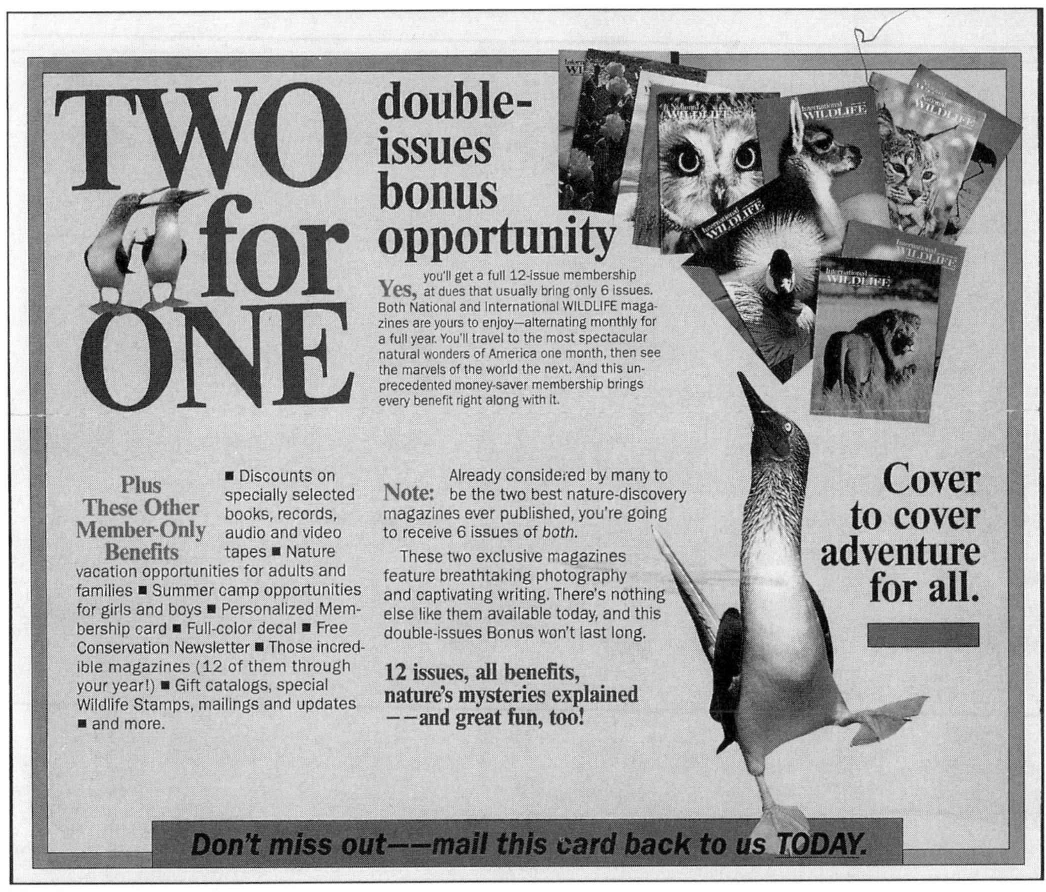
TWO for ONE

double-issues bonus opportunity

Yes, you'll get a full 12-issue membership at dues that usually bring only 6 issues. Both National and International WILDLIFE magazines are yours to enjoy—alternating monthly for a full year. You'll travel to the most spectacular natural wonders of America one month, then see the marvels of the world the next. And this unprecedented money-saver membership brings every benefit right along with it.

Plus These Other Member-Only Benefits ■ Discounts on specially selected books, records, audio and video tapes ■ Nature vacation opportunities for adults and families ■ Summer camp opportunities for girls and boys ■ Personalized Membership card ■ Full-color decal ■ Free Conservation Newsletter ■ Those incredible magazines (12 of them through your year!) ■ Gift catalogs, special Wildlife Stamps, mailings and updates ■ and more.

Note: Already considered by many to be the two best nature-discovery magazines ever published, you're going to receive 6 issues of *both.*

These two exclusive magazines feature breathtaking photography and captivating writing. There's nothing else like them available today, and this double-issues Bonus won't last long.

12 issues, all benefits, nature's mysteries explained —and great fun, too!

Cover to cover adventure for all.

Don't miss out—mail this card back to us TODAY.

at NWF. Many of our mailings also gave the option to take the companion magazine, International Wildlife (IW), *for an additional fee—but the combination was always offered at less than if a person bought both separately. (Thus, you could buy both at a saving, but the primary offer was for* NW.)

As time and experience moved along, we'd occasionally test a premium for accepting a one-year membership. (We call them Bonus Gifts.) *One of the best we ever used was the* Rand McNally Road Atlas. *This book was imprinted with our name, and the words "Members Edition." It was a natural—the* Atlas *had an extensive National Park Guide within it, along with information about natural areas and scenic spots along the way to almost any destination. New Members liked it . . . and we still use it from time to time.*

But the best premium we ever devised surfaced at one of our copy meetings: money. And who can argue that? So, as this "value . . ." package clearly shows, you can get both NW *and* IW *for the price of one.*

But I didn't position this money saver in any of the time-tested, traditional ways: neither "Get 2 for the Price of 1" nor "Buy 1, Get 1 Free" seemed to tell the story from my point of view. Moreover, anyone can use lines like that. We wanted to be unique. We've doubled the value, and left the price alone *said it best. No one had said it that way before. Plus, it tied up the money-saving opportunity directly to the worthwhile nature of the offer: membership.*

The mailing beat our existing control (by a handsome margin), unfortunately unavailable for publication in your book! It continues to do so today. And while I keep trying to beat it (it doesn't look so great if you can't beat your own best effort after three or four years, does it?), so far no luck.

You asked for some personal comments on direct mail in general and "how you work."

I work best with the door closed, my Macintosh humming along, and research notes at hand. (By the way, research *for me is a low-priority item. I need to know the offer and the product, of course, and have a profile of the person to whom the mailing is directed . . . but I rely on instinct, an understanding of human nature, and a monomaniacal love of unisyllabic words.)*

I write very fast—but will often put off starting a project until the last day or so. During the interval from receipt of request for copy until I put finger to keyboard the project rolls around inside me. Sometimes I'll make a penciled note or two and stick it in the folder, but usually not. When the deadline is at hand I put every other late job aside and plow ahead, finishing an entire mailing in a day or so. Then I'll let the thing sit unattended for twenty-four to forty-eight hours, then open it and read as if I'd never seen it before.

That's when the truth comes out. Is it clear? What is the offer? Am I interested at all*? Did the "writer" follow the usual rules of clear, motivating, and persuasive copy? Do the various components hang together?*

My reason for speed is twofold . . .

. . . first, I believe that if you know the product and offer well enough you ought to be able to tell someone quickly. If you had to say *the mailing out loud, as if it was a radio commercial, could you do it in sixty seconds? If not, why? This is not to say that you should be able to read an entire package in a minute, but that you must be able to reduce the offer and major benefits into a tight bundle which most folk could follow and understand in a brief span of time.*

. . . second, I can't *write slowly! (Good reason, huh?) I save* slow *for editing, and I am a merciless editor of my own work. I rewrite somewhat, surely, but my major editing task is to* physically *arrange copy on a page (especially letters), and tighten the flow of words into a clean and swiftly understandable flow. I try to think as a designer does, being convinced that mechanical organization—both through the formatting of typography and the sequencing of words, sentences, paragraphs, and sidebars on a page or in a brochure—is an essential of persuasive direct marketing. It is a concept frequently bypassed by writers.*

The old saying that "you've got only five seconds to capture a reader's attention" is true. So, putting a variety of attractive and interesting elements on a page increases the span from three seconds to ten to sixty . . . and to an order*. So no matter where the eye falls, the arrangement and variety sitting there spark interest—which the words amplify at once.*

The Nature Conservancy

One of the greatest direct mail writers is Frank H. Johnson, who is widely credited—falsely, he swears—with "inventing" the "Johnson Box," the typewritten headline on the direct mail letter that is frequently surrounded by a rectangle made up of asterisks. But he admits he has often used lead-ins above a letter's salutation that were sometimes boxed with lines or asterisks. "No one invents such doodles," he says; "they just occur to most writers as we try to focus on the glazing eye of a reader in two seconds before we lose him."

Johnson learned direct mail in twenty years at Time Inc., mostly doing promotion for *Fortune*, then joined American Heritage Publishing Co. as its founding promotion VP. He retired after another twenty years,

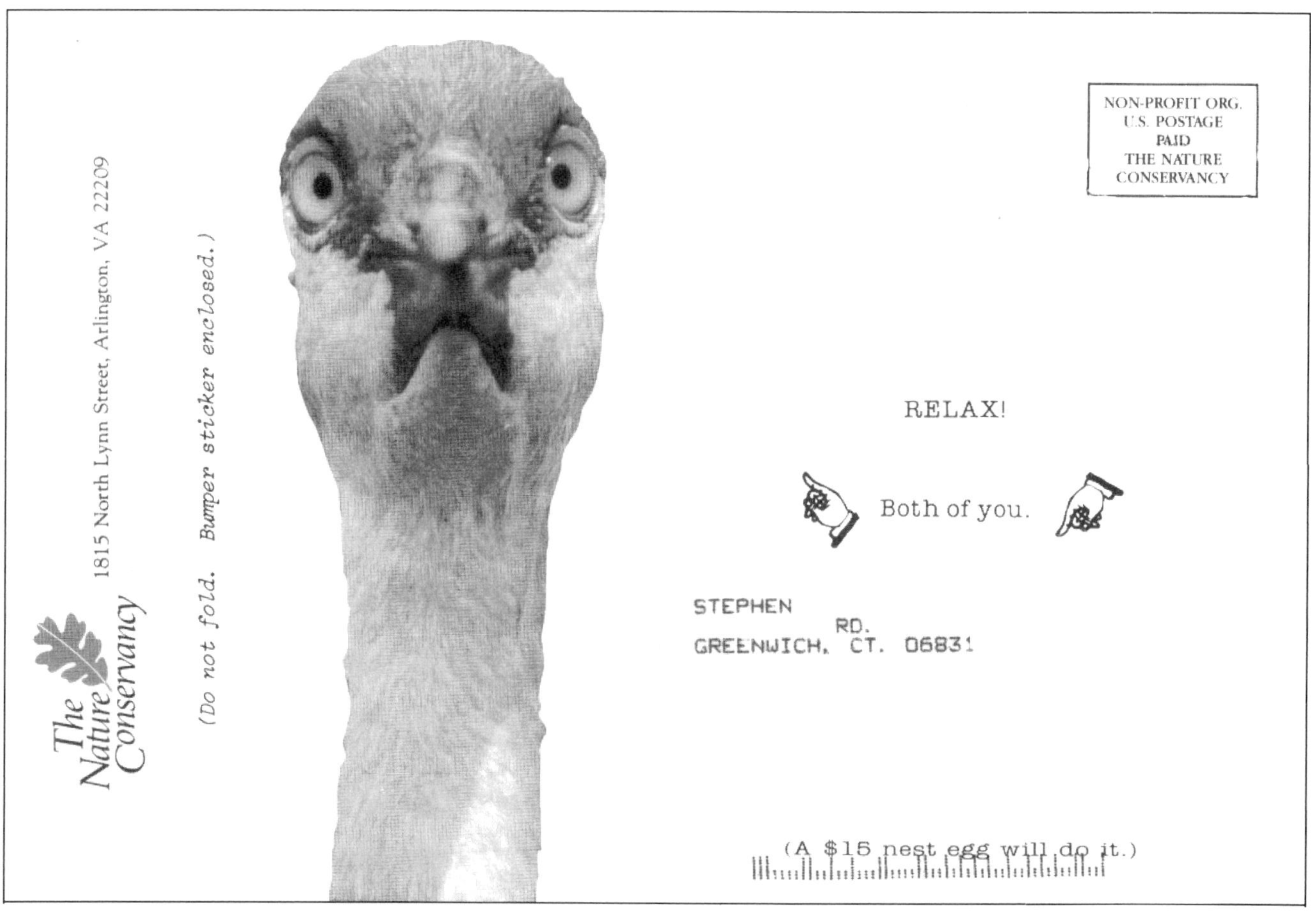

MAILER: Nature Conservancy
PACKAGE: Crane Package
PROJECT MGR.: Michael Coda
WRITER: Frank H. Johnson
DESIGNER: Frank H. Johnson
FIRST MAILED: 1985
The splendid 4-color envelope designed by Frank Johnson. In the P.S. of the letter, Johnson relates where he found the photograph. This is the only 4-color element in the mailing.

then freelanced for ten more, almost exclusively for so-called cultural products: the Metropolitan, Modern, and Guggenheim Museums; the Nature Conservancy, *Audubon*; plus Boardroom Reports.

Frank Johnson:
For all fifty of those years, writing copy was snail-slow, grubby, worrisome, hard *work. The brief fun came when the proofs had been read, color corrected, the presses were rolling. So for five minutes I'd look at it, realize I was a Successful Poet, feel great . . . then look again, and see two dozen idiotic errors.*

Frank Johnson knows it's hopeless to deny birthing the box, but still would rather be remembered for the improbably successful package format he worked out in the early days of *American Heritage*, along with the then circulation director, famed Dick Benson, and art director Irwin Glusker (now art director of *Gourmet*), which they used to sell many tons of illustrated history books: a 6″ × 9″ color envelope, four-page letter, and 17″ × 22″ bedsheet full-color folder with two-color order form and business reply envelope. For some years it couldn't fail, despite its expense, and was imitated by everyone from Stuttman to Time-Life Books.

If Frank Johnson's copy has the same superb urbanity as Bill Jayme's, it's because Jayme is a Johnson protégé; both are among the most elegant and literate writers ever to work in direct mail, as well as two of the best conversationalists.

Johnson acquired the Nature Conservancy as a client after his long-time friend Thomas Beers retired as VP and circulation director of *National Geographic.* Beers began advising the Nature Conservancy on direct mail, and brought Johnson in as a writer. The "Crane Package" (figs. 11.29–11.32) became the control for four years, 1982–86. For a couple of years it was displaced by a Webcraft effort. In 1991 it was retested and promptly became the control again, which it continues to be as of this writing.

Besides pulling well, the Crane letter has had a rare ability to inspire fan mail. Thousands of notes, from scrawled order forms to engraved stationery, have expressed amazement and joy that this "junk mail" letter was thoroughly read *and* enjoyed.

Johnson admits he loves fan mail, but regrets that no one has yet noted, in writing, what he considers the only truly original line in the letter, its last, which he added to comply with a legally required notice about where to send for a financial report. It turns a dull legality into a promotional plus by saying, "If you like to read financial statements, this one is a beauty. We're rather vain about it. Do ask."

The 4-page letter, printed on an 11″ × 17″ sheet of paper. Only the leaf in the Nature Conservancy letterhead is printed in a second color—green. We saw this very restrained use of a second color in Heikki Ratalahti's letter for *Earthwatch*.

Nancy C. Mackinnon
Membership Director

The Nature Conservancy

1800 North Kent Street
Arlington, Virginia 22209

Dear Investor:

The bug-eyed bird on our envelope who's ogling you with such distemper has a point. He's a native American sandhill crane and you may be sitting on top of one of his nesting sites.

As he sees it, every time our human species has drained a marsh, and plowed it or built a city on it, since 1492 or so -- there went the neighborhood. It's enough to make you both a bit edgy.

So give us $10 for his nest egg and we'll see that a nice, soggy spot -- just the kind he and his mate need to fashion a nest and put an egg in it -- is reserved for the two of them,undisturbed, for keeps. Only $10. (Watch those cranes come in to land, just once, and you're paid back. Catches at your throat.) Then the cranes can relax, and so can you. A bit.

> How will we reserve that incubator with your $10?
> Not by campaigning or picketing or suing.
>
> We'll just BUY the nesting ground.

That's the unique and expensive and effective way The Nature Conservancy goes about its non-profit business. We're as dead serious about hanging on to nature's precarious balance as the more visible and vocal conservation groups. But our thing is to let money do our talking.

> And we buy a whopping lot of land: starting with 60 acres of New York's Mianus River Gorge in 1951 (now 395 acres), we have protected over 2,200,000 acres -- about the area of Rhode Island and Delaware combined. The plots are spotted coast to coast and from Canada deep into the Caribbean, 3,469 of them sized from a quarter of an acre to hundreds of square miles.

All of it is prime real estate, if you're a crane or a bass or a sweet pepperbush or a redwood. Or a toad or a turtle. And a lot of

-2-

it's nice for people, too -- lovely deserts, mountains, prairies, islands. (Islands! We own huge Santa Cruz, off the California shore, and tiny Dome Island in Lake George, and most of the Virginia Barrier Islands, and dozens more.)

So besides being after your $10, we invite you to see a sample of our lands. We have 38 chapters in 32 states. Check your phone book. If we're not there yet, call me at (703) 841-5388. We'll guide you and yours to a nearby preserve where you're most welcome to walk along one of our paths, sit on one of our log benches, look about, and say to the youngster we hope will be with you, "This will be here, as is, for your grandchildren." Nice feeling.

We do ask that you don't bother the natives. E.g., there's a sign in one preserve that says "Rattlesnakes, Scorpions, Black Bear, Poison Oak/ARE PROTECTED/DO NOT HARM OR DISTURB." For $10, you're privileged not to disturb a bear or stroke a poison oak. Bargain.

> Bargains in diverse real estate are what we look for and find. Not just any real estate. We've been working for years to make and keep a huge ongoing inventory of the "natural elements" in each of the United States (so far, 35 are done). These "State Natural Heritage Programs" identify what's unique, what's threatened, what's rare or a rare natural sight to see in each state: animals, birds, plants, bugs, lakes, river systems, swamps, waterfalls, woods ... and cranes' nests.

Then we try to acquire those places that desperately need protection and preservation. We think big. The Richard King Mellon Foundation has given us the largest single grant ever for private conservation: $25,000,000 -- if we can match that sum in other gifts by 1988. We will, believe us.

The revolving fund this will give us can protect outstanding examples of threatened aquatic and wetland systems, from Augusta to Attu. We're well along already, copying some of our recent successes.

For example, Elder Creek in northern California is safe, sleep well tonight; so is the winter habitat of the gentle, pudgy manatees in Crystal River, Florida; and we (and you, soon, for $10) own the whole Canelo Hills cienega in Arizona. (We're impressed if you already know a cienega is a desert spring marsh.)

But we don't just shovel cash at these projects. We buy some lands, trade for others, get leases and easements, ask to be mentioned in wills. Then we give or, preferably, sell up to 40 percent of what we buy to

-3-

states, cities, universities, other conservation groups -- any responsible organization which wants and loves the land so much that it doesn't mind our clever lawyers making it very difficult for anyone to "improve" any part of it, ever. Unless the someone can build nests or eat acorns.

That cash flow replenishes our revolving fund, every dime of which is plowed into the unpaved and as yet unplowed. All this activity generates a lot of fascinating true stories, and lovely photos. These we put into a small (32 pages) but elegant, sprightly and adless magazine, our report to our 245,000 members every other month: The Nature Conservancy News.

Here you may find that the land you and the rest of us have just bought is harboring a four-lined skink, or a spicebush, or boreal chickadees, or kame and kettle topography. You've a lot to learn and see that's most intriguing, as you'll discover.

The Nature Conservancy News also describes well-led tours of our various properties, tells you what we're doing in your state, and shows you how you can help and have some healthy fun at the same time.

You see, the millions of acres we own are mostly watched over by volunteer stewards -- wonderful men and women who are proud to show off their lovely charges. These likely include bats, salamanders, toadstools and such. Or cranes. You'll be invited to Nature Conservancy chapter meetings nearest you.

And if you paste the complimentary white-oak-leaf sticker we've enclosed with this letter on your bumper, backpack, boat, hang glider, pool, bicycle, wheelchair ... wherever, you'll attract grateful grins from your fellow cognoscenti.

> Now, you may think it's disproportionate to brag about how we're raising millions for our projects and then ask you for only $10. Who needs you?
>
> We need you, very much! Those hard-headed foundations and corporations and ranch owners and such who give us money or property must be convinced that our ranks include a lot of intelligent, concerned, articulate citizens: people who know we ought to let nature alone to tend to much of this finite earth and all its creatures ... if we're to be among the creatures.

Yes, we need you and your ear and your voice -- and your $10 ($10 times 245,000 members buys a lot of acres.) Please join us today, like so: Get a pen. Check and initial the "membership application" form that

-4-

your hand is touching. Tear off the Interim Membership stub, sign and pocket it, and wait six weeks or so for your first magazine and permanent card. Enclose a check for $10 in the return envelope (more, if you can spare it.) NOTE that it's tax-deductible. Mail the form. Go.

Thank you, and welcome!, dear wise fellow investor in nest eggs. For your fanfare, listen for the wondrous stentorian call of that sandhill crane.*

Sincerely,

Nancy C Mackinnon

Nancy C. Mackinnon
Membership Director

* We borrowed his picture from Country Journal magazine where he illustrated an article about the International Crane Foundation of Baraboo, Wisconsin. The photo is by brave Cary Wolinsky. And we don't actually know if the crane is as upset as he looks. Maybe he's smiling? Certainly he will if, when he leaves the Foundation, his first motel stop has been reserved with your $10.

NCM/al

The most recent Nature Conservancy financial report filed with the Department of State may be obtained by writing to: New York State, Department of State, Office of Charities Registration, Albany, New York 12231, or The Nature Conservancy, 1800 North Kent Street, Arlington, Virginia 22209.

If you like to read financial statements, this one is a beauty. We're rather vain about it. Do ask.

1815 North Lynn Street • Arlington, Virginia 22209

Dear Skeptical Investor,

If putting a landing pad under a crane's egg, as Mr. Coda's letter urges, seems too dank an investment for your $15, there are plenty more flora and fauna that can use all the acreage we can buy for them. Because right now, they're losing ground.

Please help, by joining us today. There's reason to hurry. At least one of the world's five to ten million species is dying out every day, and soon it will be one an hour, and then when will it be our turn? We simply don't know.

Nor do we know, any of us (yet), just how our lives and survival may rely on the survival of hackberry trees and piping plovers, Indiana bats, wild orchids, golden-cheeked warblers, needle-and-thread grass, an insignificant little fish called the Panaca Big Spring spinedace (*Lepidomeda mollispinis pratensis*), or most of the thousands of other rare living things now thriving on the lands the Conservancy cares for.

But you and I both know we must treasure that diversity of nature -- and we're losing time. If enough of us get together, fast, maybe we can gain it back. The Nature Conservancy -- as you'll learn when you read our magazine and talk to any of our people -- is doing an intelligent, large-scale job of identifying and locating threatened species, as well as protecting the lands and waters they occupy.

Yet we're not always able to act quickly enough, or to be everywhere. We need your voice, your thought, your contribution. Now. And thank you!

Sincerely,

John C. Sawhill
President and Chief
Executive Officer

JCS/sgr

Recycled paper

If you prefer other kinds of feathers or fur . . .

The lift letter—another voice added to the sales team.

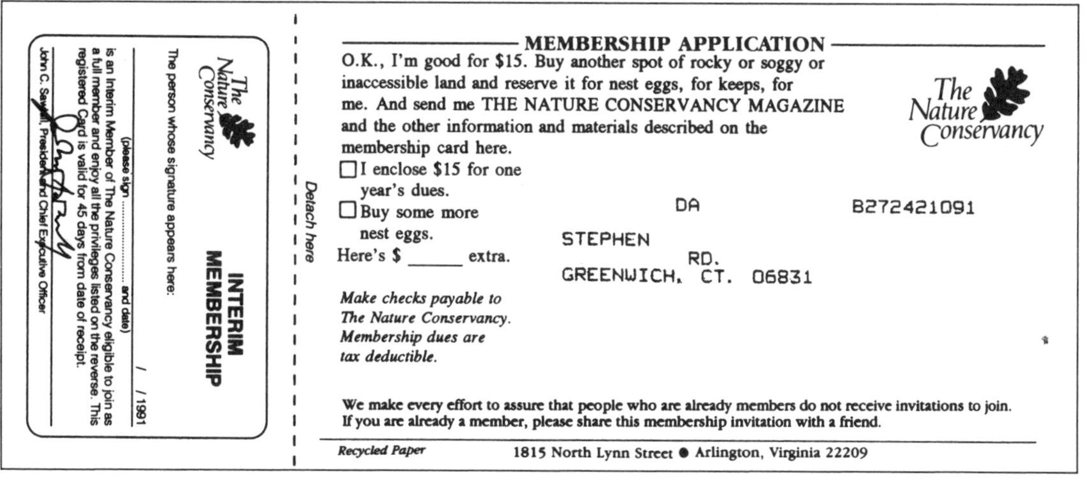

The Nature Conservancy

INTERIM MEMBERSHIP

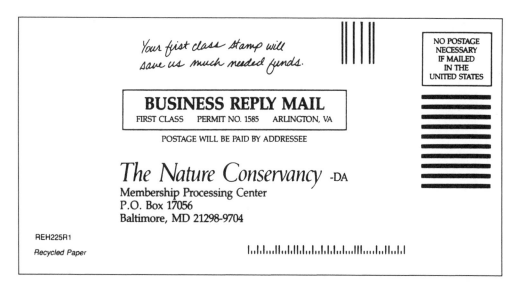

The person whose signature appears here:

(please sign .... and date) / / 1991

is an Interim Member of The Nature Conservancy eligible to join as a full member and enjoy all the privileges listed on the reverse. This registered Card is valid for 45 days from date of receipt.

John C. Sawhill, President and Chief Executive Officer

Detach here

MEMBERSHIP APPLICATION

O.K., I'm good for $15. Buy another spot of rocky or soggy or inaccessible land and reserve it for nest eggs, for keeps, for me. And send me THE NATURE CONSERVANCY MAGAZINE and the other information and materials described on the membership card here.

☐ I enclose $15 for one year's dues.

☐ Buy some more nest eggs. Here's $ ______ extra.

The Nature Conservancy

DA B272421091

STEPHEN
RD.
GREENWICH, CT. 06831

Make checks payable to The Nature Conservancy. Membership dues are tax deductible.

We make every effort to assure that people who are already members do not receive invitations to join. If you are already a member, please share this membership invitation with a friend.

Recycled Paper 1815 North Lynn Street ● Arlington, Virginia 22209

A copy or summary of the current Financial Statement, or Annual Report, and Registration filed by The Nature Conservancy may be obtained by contacting: The Nature Conservancy, 1815 N. Lynn St., Arlington, VA 22209 (703/841-5300); Office of Secretary of State, Statehouse, Annapolis, MD 21401; Office of Charities Registration, 162 Washington Ave., Albany, NY 12231; Pennsylvania Department of State, toll free number within the state 1-800-732-0999; Division of Consumer Affairs, Department of Agriculture and Consumer Services, P.O. Box 1163, Richmond, VA 23209; Charities Division, Office of the Secretary of State, State of Washington, Olympia, WA 98504-0422 (1-800-332-4483); and Secretary of State, State Capitol, Charleston, WV 25305. The Nature Conservancy is registered with the State of Utah, Department of Commerce, Division of Consumer Protection, Permit #C29. Registration does not imply endorsement by any state.

MAH225R2

Keep this Interim Membership card. Your permanent membership card will be mailed immediately upon receipt of your $15 dues, will entitle you to:

- **The Nature Conservancy Magazine.**
- **Invitations to field trips and special events at Conservancy preserves.**
- **Opportunities to participate in local chapter activities.**
- **Newsletters from your state Conservancy program.**

Your first class stamp will save us much needed funds.

NO POSTAGE NECESSARY IF MAILED IN THE UNITED STATES

BUSINESS REPLY MAIL

FIRST CLASS PERMIT NO. 1585 ARLINGTON, VA

POSTAGE WILL BE PAID BY ADDRESSEE

The Nature Conservancy -DA
Membership Processing Center
P.O. Box 17056
Baltimore, MD 21298-9704

REH225R1

Recycled Paper

Bumper sticker, order form shown front and back, and business reply envelope. The stub of the order card is an "Interim Membership" card that—unlike those of *Audubon* and the BMG compact disk clubs in Chapter 15—is not personalized. The order card is only half as tall as the envelope. With a small order card in a big envelope, there would appear to be danger that the card might float around inside to the point where the name and address won't show through the window, making the entire piece undeliverable. This does not happen. Once inserted, the card stays in place. However, for the half-size card to be inserted, a *bottom flap envelope* is preferable, which this one is.

Science News

Freelancer Tom McCormick's Grand Control for *Science News* breaks so many rules of direct mail that it's a wonder the rules exist at all. In an era of the comp copy or free issue offer, *Science News* asks for $1. As Tom McCormick said, "The offer was my idea; I wanted to get rid of the tire kickers." The offer is highlighted in the Johnson Box area of the letter and on the order form.

Testimonials should be an integral part of every direct mail effort; however, it is extremely rare to see them take up most of the front page of a letter. Malcolm Decker calls the letter "the main salesman," and salesmen talk directly to *you*. Testimonials, traditionally, are more the province of the "demonstrator"—a piece of the brochure or a separate lift piece that reinforces everything the main salesman has said in the letter.

The second color on the outer envelope, letter, and order card is purple-lavender. Traditional direct mail practice suggests that if the second color on a letter is blue, then the signature at the end can be blue to simulate blue ink. If the second color is red or green, the signature should be in black, because nobody signs letters in red or green (unless it's a Christmas mailing); putting an oddly colored signature depersonalizes a letter, because it is jarringly obvious that the signer was a printing press. In the case of this *Science News* letter, the signature is in lavender.

MAILER: *Science News*
PACKAGE: 12 for $1
PROJECT MGR.: D. R. Harless
WRITER: Tom McCormick
DESIGNER: Ernie Kunz
FIRST MAILED: 1986
The #10 outside envelope.

The Weekly Newsmagazine of Science
1719 N Street NW, Washington DC 20036

May I send you twelve issues of SCIENCE NEWS, America's only weekly science report, for just $1.00?

They're yours without any further cost or the least commitment.

Dear Reader:

Frankly, twelve issues of SCIENCE NEWS are worth a lot more than $1.

However, I have a good reason for making you this no-strings-attached introductory offer.

> You see, once someone with your demonstrated interest in science has spent three months with SCIENCE NEWS, I'm fairly sure we'll have gained another regular subscriber.

Why? Consider what a few of our current (and better known) readers have written about our unique weekly:

From Wilbur E. Garrett, Editor of the "National Geographic" . . .

> "In no other publication can the intelligent layman get so quick and accurate a summary of the latest findings and the latest thinking in all the sciences. Perhaps the greatest tribute to you is the commendations one often hears from the scientists themselves."

From Isaac Asimov, noted science author and futurist . . .

> "The existence of SCIENCE NEWS spans sixty years . . . I am pleased that for one-third of this stretch of time, I have been (and still am) a subscriber."

From Walter Sullivan, science writer for the "New York Times" . . .

> "I feel compelled to clip something from almost every issue of SCIENCE NEWS for my files. How can one ignore a source that offers us Jonathan Eberhart, Janet Raloff, and all the others?"

From Stephen J. Gould, Professor of Geology at Harvard University . . .

> "SCIENCE NEWS has long distinguished itself as America's finest journal of general and accessible science. It

(over, please)

> should be everybody's starting point to a necessary understanding."

Finally, I'd like to pass along this comment by the "Columbia Journalism Review" . . .

> ". . . by far the best source of science news is a weekly magazine called SCIENCE NEWS. It offers prompt, witty reporting to readers who are not put off by a few such basic scientific terms as ion or hormone. Evidently writers of other science magazines read SCIENCE NEWS; uncredited echoes of its stories often appear elsewhere."

As you can see, while many of our readers are practicing scientists, you don't have to be one of them to enjoy and benefit from SCIENCE NEWS.

But you will have to be a bit above average in intellect and interest.

Still, the rewards you'll gain from each of our concise weekly issues will be of far greater value to you than any you may occasionally pick up from the current plethora of pseudo-science magazines.

You'll get them far sooner, too.

To illustrate, long before any of those other publications got around to announcing the existence of an artificial heart . . . the threat to our defense communications of "EMP" generated by nuclear blasts in space . . . or the use of bone marrow transplants to save children lacking natural immunity to infections, SCIENCE NEWS readers already knew the essential details.

How is SCIENCE NEWS able to "scoop" other science periodicals and keep serious readers like you so exceptionally well informed? Because it gives you a combination of three advantages you simply can't get in any similar-seeming publication.

SCIENCE NEWS is uniquely authoritative. Published for over 60 years by the non-profit Science Service, SCIENCE NEWS is the product of a respected editorial team that constantly monitors more than 200 specialized sources to capture the essence of progress for you.

SCIENCE NEWS is delivered to you fresh every week. Keeping you fully current on the fast-breaking advances in fields like biomedicine and the space sciences means getting this news to you with the least delay possible. As a weekly publication, SCIENCE NEWS updates you four times faster (and more often) than any monthly magazine can.

SCIENCE NEWS gives you only the facts you want. With its trim 16-page format, SCIENCE NEWS doesn't waste your time. Each issue is a brisk, tautly telegraphic report that brings you the truly important news from science's many and varied frontiers -- with a maximum of fact and a minimum of words.

Yet, for all its businesslike brevity, this authoritative weekly will definitely never bore you!

For while each SCIENCE NEWS article and feature is carefully prepared for fast, easy, informative reading, we keep a tight rein on technical jargon and make every illustration count.

Then too, there's the breadth of our science coverage. To demonstrate, here are just a few examples of what our readers learned recently. (Don't be surprised if some of them still come as "new" news to you.)

> PAVING THE WAY FOR SPACE-AGE CEMENT. Thanks to a growing interest in the chemistry and physics of concrete, scientists are now exploring specialty cements for us in turbine blades, springs, nuclear waste storage, even substrates for ICs.
>
> TARGETED DRUG DELIVERY. As geneticists create highly specific drugs of extreme effectiveness, the call is for delivery systems to match. Recent answers include biodegradable wafer implants, radiation-emitting glass beads, antibiotic-releasing contact lenses, and the amazing "microsponge" with 240,000 miles of pore-lengths per gram.
>
> NEW VIEW OF VISION. The brain may process visual information much as an FM radio receives broadcasts say two government scientists. According to their theory, visual nerves transmit images to the brain as multiplexed, encoded signals. If true, it could revolutionize thinking about the brain.
>
> ART DETECTIVES. The use of carbon-14 dating, isotope analysis, and other such aids is helping art experts trace the evolution of artists, peg the materials used -- and spot frauds. Pottery forgers are getting wise to thermoluminescent dating, though. They're dosing fakes with X-rays to gain the effect of lengthy radiation exposure.
>
> ALCOHOLISM'S ELUSIVE GENES. Researchers studying the role of heredity in alcoholism are dubious about the extent of that role. They now see alcoholism as an interaction of nature and nurture, with nature not necessarily the dominant factor.
>
> SOLAR SURPRISES. While many see our sun as a dull star, today's astrophysicists don't. They've found that different parts of it rotate at different rates. It quivers, too. And it resonates like a bell at specific frequencies, emitting its own acoustic signature. What's it all mean? Our sun has a lot to teach us!
>
> CHILLING NEWS ABOUT GREENHOUSE WARMING. Citing temperature records and backed by computer models, a NASA climatologist has expressed a 99% certainty that global warming over the last decade is due to the buildup of "greenhouse" gases.

As you can see, SCIENCE NEWS covers all areas of science for you in a way that is not only informative but genuinely interesting as well.

And now you can try twelve weeks of it for just $1.

(over, please)

All you have to do is initial the enclosed Acceptance Form and mail it back to us -- together with your dollar -- in the postage-paid envelope provided.

> Please notice that there are no strings attached to this offer. When we receive your acceptance, we will send you the following twelve weeks of SCIENCE NEWS. And that, if you wish, will be all you need be concerned about.

While there is a provision in the Acceptance Form's wording for a 52-week SCIENCE NEWS subscription at just $29.87 (a savings of 13% off our regular $34.50 annual rate), this does not obligate you in any way at all!

For if you choose not to take advantage of this special discount opportunity after receiving your twelve trial issues -- you have only to write the word "cancel" across the invoice we'll send you and return it.

In that case, the matter will be immediately and fully closed.

> Obviously, though, I'm quite confident that after spending twelve weeks at the cutting edge of the sciences and technologies with SCIENCE NEWS, you will decide to take us up on that money-saving invitation.

However, we'll leave that decision to you.

As you can see, I've tried to make our "twelve trial issue offer" as attractive as possible. So naturally, I hope you won't put off accepting it for even one minute.

Thank you for reading my letter. I look forward to hearing from you soon.

Sincerely,

E. G. Sherburne, Jr.
Publisher

P.S. SCIENCE NEWS is not sold at newsstands or bookstores. It is available only to those who order subscriptions and, for a limited time, through this special introductory offer.

The 4-page letter, printed on an 11″ × 17″ sheet, folded 3 times.

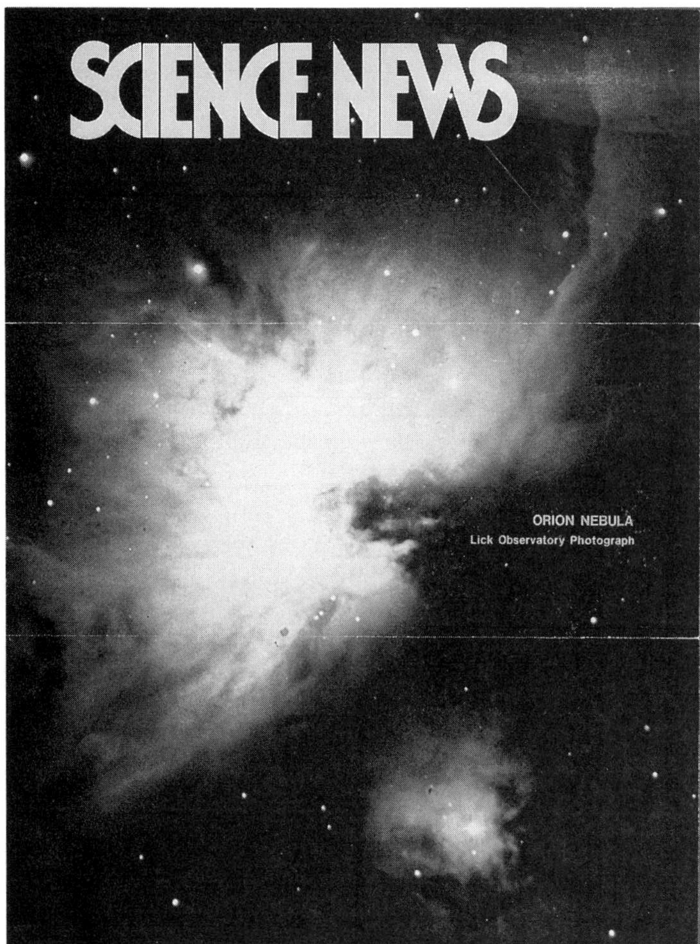

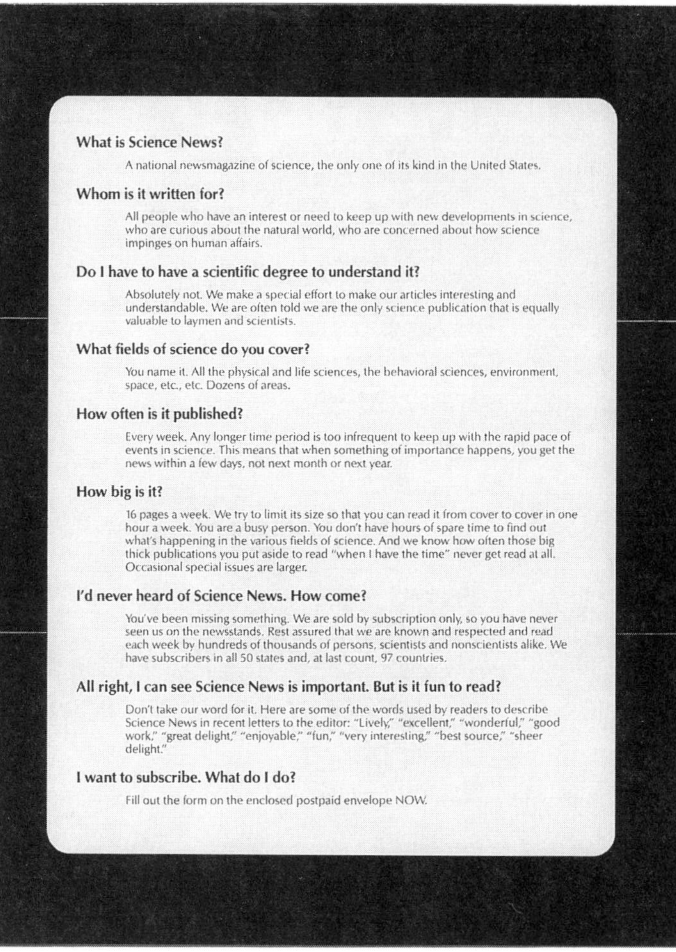

What is Science News?

A national newsmagazine of science, the only one of its kind in the United States.

Whom is it written for?

All people who have an interest or need to keep up with new developments in science, who are curious about the natural world, who are concerned about how science impinges on human affairs.

Do I have to have a scientific degree to understand it?

Absolutely not. We make a special effort to make our articles interesting and understandable. We are often told we are the only science publication that is equally valuable to laymen and scientists.

What fields of science do you cover?

You name it. All the physical and life sciences, the behavioral sciences, environment, space, etc., etc. Dozens of areas.

How often is it published?

Every week. Any longer time period is too infrequent to keep up with the rapid pace of events in science. This means that when something of importance happens, you get the news within a few days, not next month or next year.

How big is it?

16 pages a week. We try to limit its size so that you can read it from cover to cover in one hour a week. You are a busy person. You don't have hours of spare time to find out what's happening in the various fields of science. And we know how often those big thick publications you put aside to read "when I have the time" never get read at all. Occasional special issues are larger.

I'd never heard of Science News. How come?

You've been missing something. We are sold by subscription only, so you have never seen us on the newsstands. Rest assured that we are known and respected and read each week by hundreds of thousands of persons, scientists and nonscientists alike. We have subscribers in all 50 states and, at last count, 97 countries.

All right, I can see Science News is important. But is it fun to read?

Don't take our word for it. Here are some of the words used by readers to describe Science News in recent letters to the editor: "Lively," "excellent," "wonderful," "good work," "great delight," "enjoyable," "fun," "very interesting," "best source," "sheer delight."

I want to subscribe. What do I do?

Fill out the form on the enclosed postpaid envelope NOW.

The brochure, printed 4 colors over 1 color on a single $8\frac{1}{2}'' \times 11''$ coated sheet.

The brochure is a simple, undated cover of the publication—a handsome four-color photograph of an exploding heavenly body deep in black space. The back of the brochure is printed in one color (black) with a funereal border that resembles a giant mass card. Direct mail tradition says to stay away from black.

The order form breaks three rules:

1. Most direct mail designers will use sans serif type in headlines, but avoid it in body copy; it is the most difficult type of all to read.
2. Responders are encouraged to put a $1 bill into the business reply envelope. Everyone—from the Postal Service to the overwhelming majority of direct marketers—urges mailers *not to ask for cash*; it can be pilfered.
3. There are no clear instructions to detach the stub and no clear perf marks. More to the point, traditional direct mail designers will never allow a perforation to cut through an object because people instinctively don't like to destroy things. In this case, to detach the stub, you have to tear through the picture of the envelope and the $1 bill. According to all the old rules of direct mail, this will inhibit ordering.

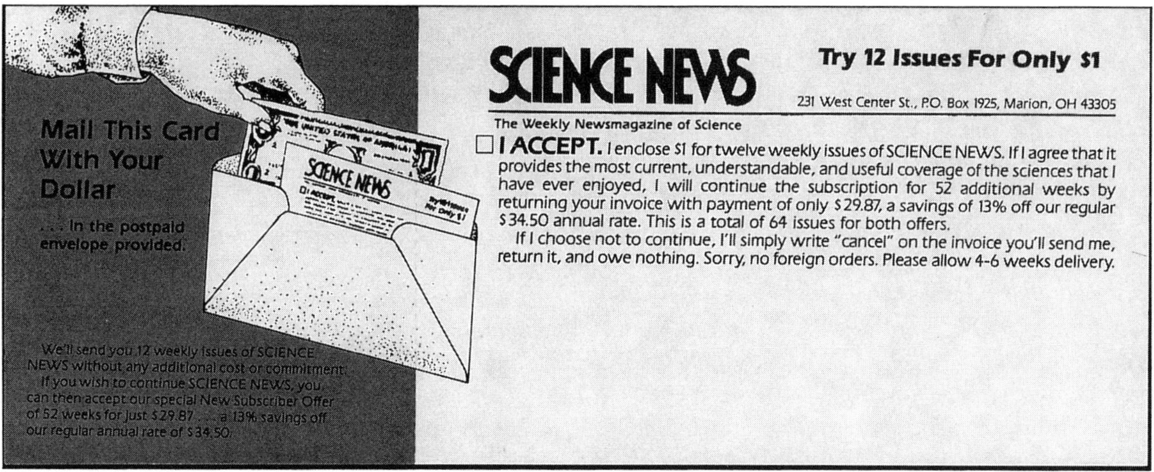

Order form and business reply envelope.

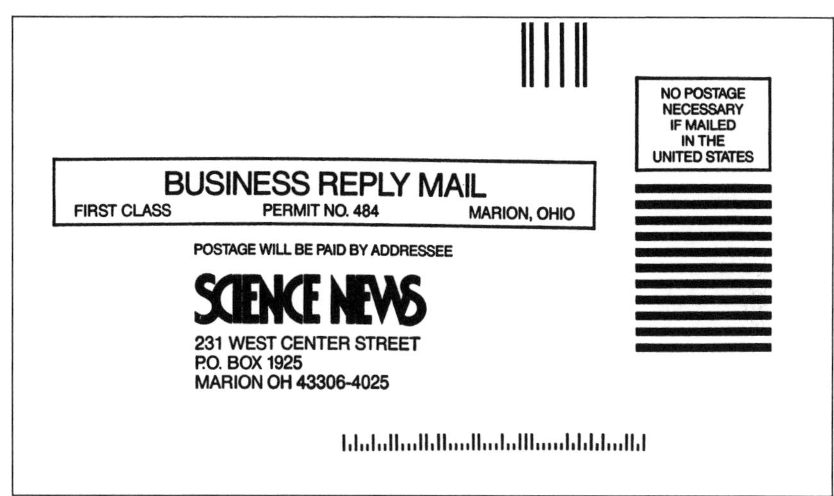

Notwithstanding, this effort has been control for seven years. Just as contrarian investing can pay off big, so can contrarian direct mail copy and design.

Tom McCormick has been a freelancer for twelve years with clients that include *Smithsonian* magazine, *Kiplinger's Personal Finance*, the Nature Conservancy, *Harrowsmith Country Life*, American Diabetes Association, *Nation's Business*, and National Arbor Day Foundation.

Tom McCormick:

When I was assigned to do a package by this client, they had tried comp offers and gotten poor results. Seems that up-front pull was okay, but the conversion to first-year paid was pretty dismal.

As I recall, the mailings they'd been using weren't too specific about what Science News *actually was. And I think that many recipients imagined it to be more along the lines of, say,* Popular Science. *Given the foregoing, and the actual nature of the publication, the client inevitably wound up with lots of uninterested comp-offer takers—and not enough qualified respondents.*

My answer to the problem was copy focusing on the true benefits of Science News *(a weekly digest of news and noteworthy events in the sciences that's an honestly fast, intriguing "read"—IF you have more than a passing interest in the subject area), topped off by the $1 offer and followed by heavyweight testimonials.*

Rationale? It was my expectation that the $1-for-4-issue offer (now 12 issues) would accomplish two things. First, it would cut down on the idle curious free-takers. Second, it would help convey a well-deserved perception of value to a weekly ''magazine'' that consisted of just sixteen pages.

The purpose of putting those testimonials on page 1 of the letter was to reinforce that intended perception, real fast!

After that, everything depended on the support and continued judicious list selection of Science News*'s business/circulation manager, Don Harless. With rare understanding, this very able professional recognized immediately what I was doing, and delivered beautifully on his end—standing firmly behind what is, admittedly, a highly unorthodox mailing.*

But as history and subsequent testing continue to show, it sometimes takes an unconventional approach to sell an unconventional product.

There are, of course, other areas where my Science News *mailing strays, perhaps unnecessarily, from traditional direct mail formulae. On the order form, for example, the hand-dollar-envelope illustration protrudes out of the stub and into the actual form. After almost nixing the original design, I decided that since we already had a thoroughly maverick package going, that eye-grabbing illustration at the ''decision point'' could only help to support my primary objectives. So caution was thrown to the wind.*

On other matters such as colors and typefaces, the package has been reproduced with minor alterations so often that I can no longer recall what the original looked like. I suspect, however, that it hasn't changed much.

12

Consumer Magazines IV:

The Nation and the World

American Spectator

MAILER: *American Spectator*
PACKAGE: "Not since the heyday"
PROJECT MGR.: Ron Burr
WRITER: Laurence Jaeger
DESIGNER: Lucy Durand Sikes
FIRST MAILED: 1985

The 6″ × 9″ front-flap outer envelope shown front and back. All elements of the mailing are printed on tan colored stock with a rust/red second color.

Like Jim Punkre's letter for *Organic Gardening*, this subscription package by Laurence Jaeger also uses an illustrated letter that acts as a combination letter-circular.

Laurence Jaeger has worked in mail promotion for nearly forty years, twenty-five of which were spent as a freelancer. He has specialized in the concoction of space advertising and mail package for, mainly, books, book clubs, periodicals, and various kinds of subscriptions.

LAURENCE JAEGER:
What I like most, and do best, are high-type offerings: things that flatter the intellect, appeal to our inflated notions of our own taste, cultivation, or aesthetic sense, or serve the needs of tony professional people.

How I work: I start every job by asking myself (as though I were my prospect), "Why on earth should I want this anyway? What will it do for me?" Then every word I write is an answer to those questions.

By the way, if you're going to reproduce any of that package for the American Spectator, *do know that I am probably the only one who has the original, authentic, unaltered version from which all subsequent mailings have, inevitably, had to depart because of topicality.*

Ron Burr, publisher of the *American Spectator*, has a B.A. in government and economics and an M.B.A. in finance, both from Indiana University. He has been with the *American Spectator* since its founding as an off-campus student publication in 1967. He is also a director of Lemley, Yarling Investment Company in Chicago.

RON BURR:
First, in advertising one should not be timid about describing the product, even if it means lengthy copy. Potential buyers want to know as much as possible about a product and they will read copy.

Accurate description, without exaggeration, is also important. At the Spectator, *we are interested in repeat business and we want readers to make the right decision when making their initial purchase. We seek new subscribers who will enjoy the magazine enough to renew. As you know, because advertising expenses are usually quite high, it is difficult to make money in direct mail on initial orders. But once customers are found, advertising costs are much lower and repeat orders are profitable.*

Our business relies heavily on repeat business, and our new-subscriber prospect campaign is based on the amount of money we can invest to obtain a new subscriber, taking repeat orders into account. Because we are purchasing future cash flow, the cost of obtaining a new subscriber can exceed the amount of revenue initially received. To determine how much money we can spend to obtain a new subscriber we calculate how much money an average subscriber generates from renewals over a five-year period, discount the cash flow for time and risk, and arrive with an amount we can spend to obtain a new subscriber.

It is the same calculation corporate treasurers use when deciding if a capital investment in a machine is warranted, only instead of purchasing a machine to produce cash flow, we are purchasing customers who produce cash flow.

THE AMERICAN SPECTATOR®
2020 N. 14th Street, P.O. Box 549
Arlington, Virginia 22216-0549

Nonprofit Org.
U.S. Postage
PAID
Indianapolis, Ind.

Subscribe now to

while our money-saving
Introductory Offer
remains in force.

J928

THOMAS
ST
CRTN ON HUDSO NY 10520

THE AMERICAN SPECTATOR®

writes about politics, ideas, and the state of American culture as no other monthly does. Though we're frankly intellectual, we're also funny, earthy, and irreverent. We hold to old-fashioned notions like self reliance, the family, an honest day's work, plaintalking prose, a strong defense, a sound currency, and two distinctively different sexes. We're against meddlesome bureaucrats, spineless diplomats, and fools, knaves, or hypocrites anywhere in public life. Most of all, we abhor those Americans who continually take potshots at their country—while shielded by the freedom she guarantees.

If The American Spectator sounds good to you, look inside for a money-saving subscription invitation.

E93

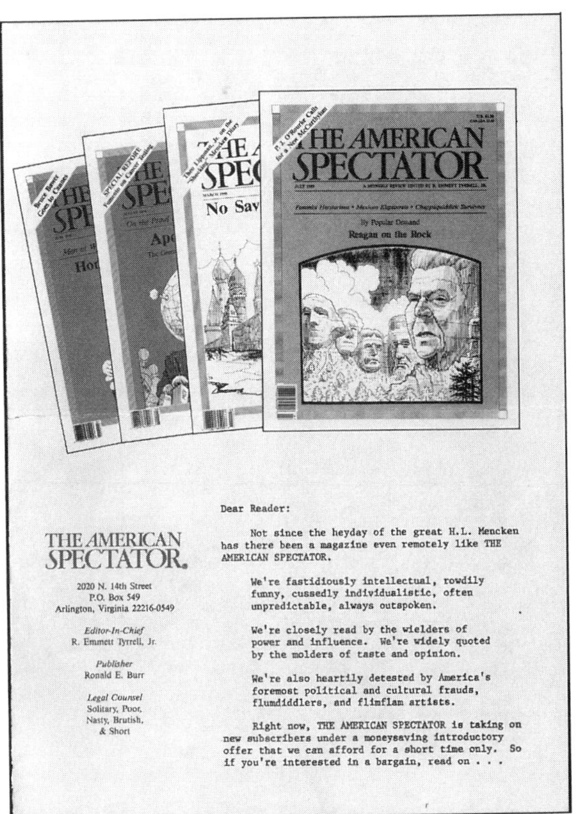

THE AMERICAN SPECTATOR

2020 N. 14th Street
P.O. Box 549
Arlington, Virginia 22216-0549

Editor-In-Chief
R. Emmett Tyrrell, Jr.

Publisher
Ronald E. Burr

Legal Counsel
Solitary, Poor,
Nasty, Brutish,
& Short

Dear Reader:

Not since the heyday of the great H.L. Mencken has there been a magazine even remotely like THE AMERICAN SPECTATOR.

We're fastidiously intellectual, rowdily funny, cussedly individualistic, often unpredictable, always outspoken.

We're closely read by the wielders of power and influence. We're widely quoted by the molders of taste and opinion.

We're also heartily detested by America's foremost political and cultural frauds, flumdiddlers, and flimflam artists.

Right now, THE AMERICAN SPECTATOR is taking on new subscribers under a moneysaving introductory offer that we can afford for a short time only. So if you're interested in a bargain, read on . . .

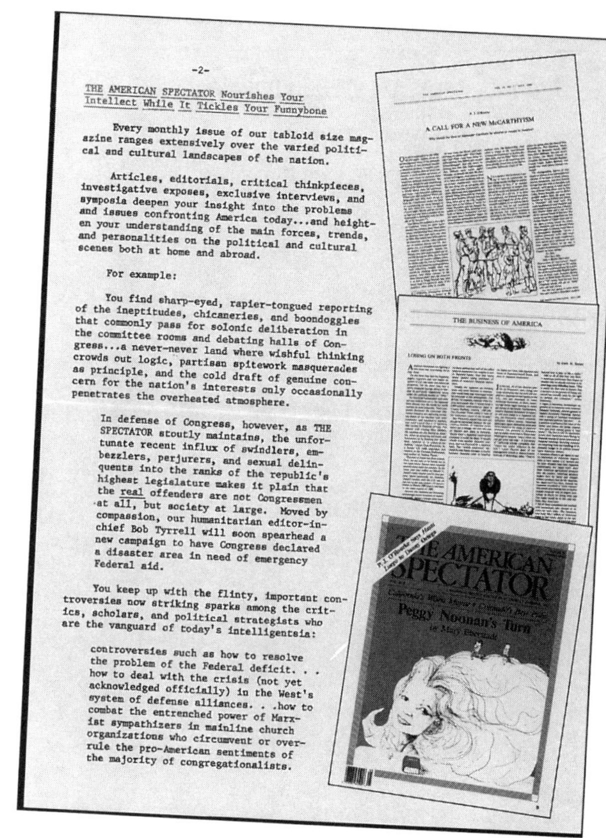

-2-

THE AMERICAN SPECTATOR Nourishes Your Intellect While It Tickles Your Funnybone

Every monthly issue of our tabloid size magazine ranges extensively over the varied political and cultural landscapes of the nation.

Articles, editorials, critical thinkpieces, investigative exposes, exclusive interviews, and symposia deepen your insight into the problems and issues confronting America today...and heighten your understanding of the main forces, trends, and personalities on the political and cultural scenes both at home and abroad.

For example:

You find sharp-eyed, rapier-tongued reporting of the ineptitudes, chicaneries, and boondoggles that commonly pass for solonic deliberation in the committee rooms and debating halls of Congress...a never-never land where wishful thinking crowds out logic, partisan spitework masquerades as principle, and the cold draft of genuine concern for the nation's interests only occasionally penetrates the overheated atmosphere.

In defense of Congress, however, as THE SPECTATOR stoutly maintains, the unfortunate recent influx of swindlers, embezzlers, perjurers, and sexual delinquents into the ranks of the republic's highest legislature makes it plain that the real offenders are not Congressmen at all, but society at large. Moved by compassion, our humanitarian editor-in-chief Bob Tyrrell will soon spearhead a new campaign to have Congress declared a disaster area in need of emergency Federal aid.

You keep up with the flinty, important controversies now striking sparks among the critics, scholars, and political strategists who are the vanguard of today's intelligentsia:

controversies such as how to resolve the problem of the Federal deficit. . . how to deal with the crisis (not yet acknowledged officially) in the West's system of defense alliances. . .how to combat the entrenched power of Marxist sympathizers in mainline church organizations who circumvent or overrule the pro-American sentiments of the majority of congregationalists.

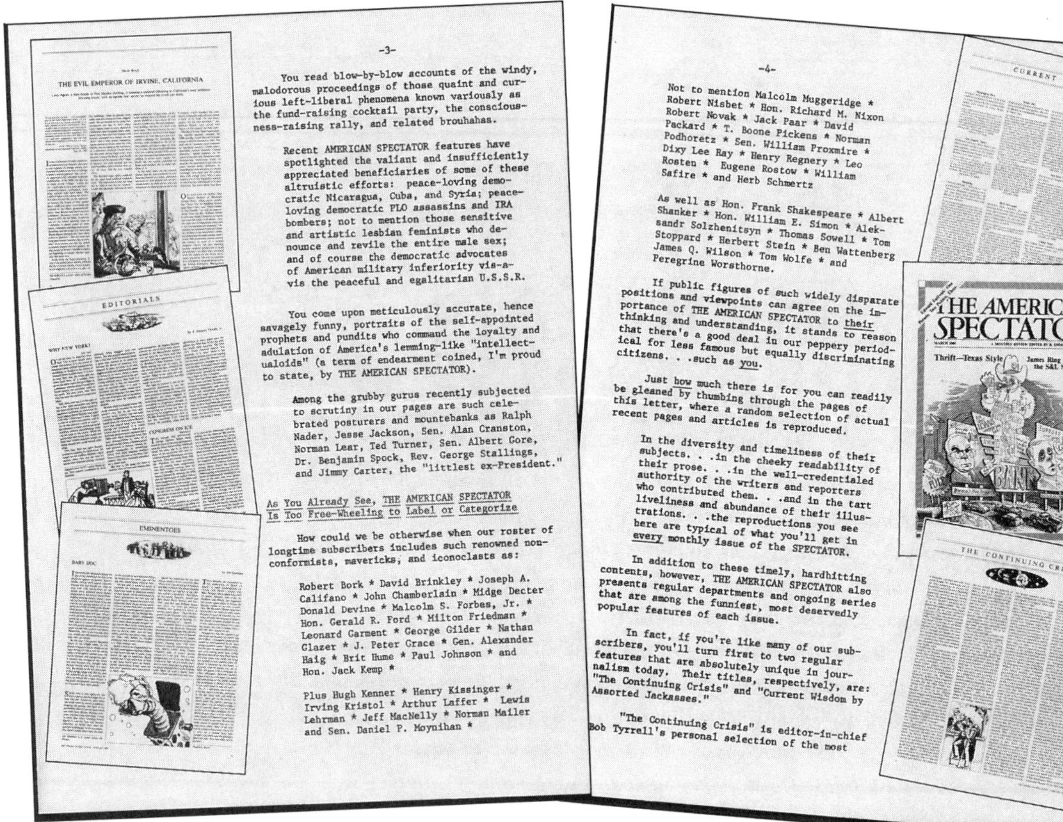

-3-

You read blow-by-blow accounts of the windy, malodorous proceedings of those quaint and curious left-liberal phenomena known variously as the fund-raising cocktail party, the consciousness-raising rally, and related brouhahas.

Recent AMERICAN SPECTATOR features have spotlighted the valiant and insufficiently appreciated beneficiaries of some of these altruistic efforts: peace-loving democratic Nicaragua, Cuba, and Syria; peace-loving democratic PLO assassins and IRA bombers; not to mention those sensitive and artistic lesbian feminists who denounce and revile the entire male sex; and of course the democratic advocates of American military inferiority vis-a-vis the peaceful and egalitarian U.S.S.R.

You come upon meticulously accurate, hence savagely funny, portraits of the self-appointed prophets and pundits who command the loyalty and adulation of America's lemming-like "intellectualoids" (a term of endearment coined, I'm proud to state, by THE AMERICAN SPECTATOR).

Among the grubby gurus recently subjected to scrutiny in our pages are such celebrated posturers and mountebanks as Ralph Nader, Jesse Jackson, Sen. Alan Cranston, Norman Lear, Ted Turner, Sen. Albert Gore, Dr. Benjamin Spock, Rev. George Stallings, and Jimmy Carter, the "littlest ex-President."

As You Already See, THE AMERICAN SPECTATOR Is Too Free-Wheeling to Label or Categorize

How could we be otherwise when our roster of longtime subscribers includes such renowned nonconformists, mavericks, and iconoclasts as:

Robert Bork * David Brinkley * Joseph A. Califano * John Chamberlain * Midge Decter Donald Devine * Malcolm S. Forbes, Jr. * Hon. Gerald R. Ford * Milton Friedman * Leonard Garment * George Gilder * Nathan Glazer * J. Peter Grace * Gen. Alexander Haig * Brit Hume * Paul Johnson * and Hon. Jack Kemp *

Plus Hugh Kenner * Henry Kissinger * Irving Kristol * Arthur Laffer * Lewis Lehrman * Jeff MacNelly * Norman Mailer and Sen. Daniel P. Moynihan *

-4-

Not to mention Malcolm Muggeridge * Robert Nisbet * Hon. Richard M. Nixon Robert Novak * Jack Paar * David Packard * T. Boone Pickens * Norman Podhoretz * Sen. William Proxmire * Dixy Lee Ray * Henry Regnery * Leo Rosten * Eugene Rostow * William Safire * and Herb Schmertz

As well as Hon. Frank Shakespeare * Albert Shanker * Hon. William E. Simon * Aleksandr Solzhenitsyn * Thomas Sowell * Tom Stoppard * Herbert Stein * Ben Wattenberg James Q. Wilson * Tom Wolfe * and Peregrine Worsthorne.

If public figures of such widely disparate positions and viewpoints can agree on the importance of THE AMERICAN SPECTATOR to their thinking and understanding, it stands to reason that there's a good deal in our peppery periodical for less famous but equally discriminating citizens. . .such as you.

Just how much there is for you can readily be gleaned by thumbing through the pages of this letter, where a random selection of actual recent pages and articles is reproduced.

In the diversity and timeliness of their subjects. . .in the cheeky readability of their prose. . .in the well-credentialed authority of the writers and reporters who contributed them. . .and in the tart liveliness and abundance of their illustrations. . .the reproductions you see here are typical of what you'll get in every monthly issue of the SPECTATOR.

In addition to these timely, hardhitting contents, however, THE AMERICAN SPECTATOR also presents regular departments and ongoing series that are among the funniest, most deservedly popular features of each issue.

In fact, if you're like many of our subscribers, you'll turn first to two regular features that are absolutely unique in journalism today. Their titles, respectively, are: "The Continuing Crisis" and "Current Wisdom by Assorted Jackasses."

"The Continuing Crisis" is editor-in-chief Bob Tyrrell's personal selection of the most

The 8-page illustrated letter with pictures of covers and pages of the publication cascading down the gutter side of each inside page. The letter was printed on two 11″ × 17″ sheets that were nested and then folded twice to fit in the 6″ × 9″ outside envelope.

-5-

delicious follies, frauds, and flubdubberies committed during the month just ended.

Uproarious in its satire, deadly in the accuracy of its aim, "The Continuing Crisis" is best described by letting you read a typical recent excerpt:

"To relieve the sorrow of the October 17 quake there was the arrival of CBS's Mr. Dan Rather, who again demonstrated in his inimitable way that insanity can be vastly entertaining. Initially, he covered the story from a newsroom somewhere, his demeanor earnest to the point of neurasthenia, his toupee awry, his raiment suggestive of the haberdashery sold in the menswear section of a large drugstore--an obvious clip-on tie attached to his wash-and-wear shirt. Then he donned military attire and stood in the open air, betraying ludicrous Schadenfreude whilst murmuring dire prognostications. It is possible that Mr. Rather wears clip-on ties in response to doctors' orders to keep his hands away from his throat. Mr. Rather returned to New York without further incident."

As for "Current Wisdom by Assorted Jackasses," it epitomizes THE AMERICAN SPECTATOR style of humor: a straightfaced recitation of some of the most egregiously idiotic statements and judgments disseminated during the previous month by the nation's news media.

What funnier, more effective device could be provided for quacks and simpletons to hang themselves upon? Take, for example, this recent gem from "Assorted Jackasses," originally appearing in the New York Times Book Review:

"Human rights violations against the English language, as committed by a Mr. Arthur C. Danto whilst arguing the case for Cro-Magnon Man, whose eloquence the moron seems to be emulating:

'The fictiveness of the concept can be deduced from the very meaning of the term, which connotes simplicity, basicness, the zero-degree of cultivation, mankind in its so-called natural state. In truth, there are no primitive cultures: just as everything can be expressed in natural language,

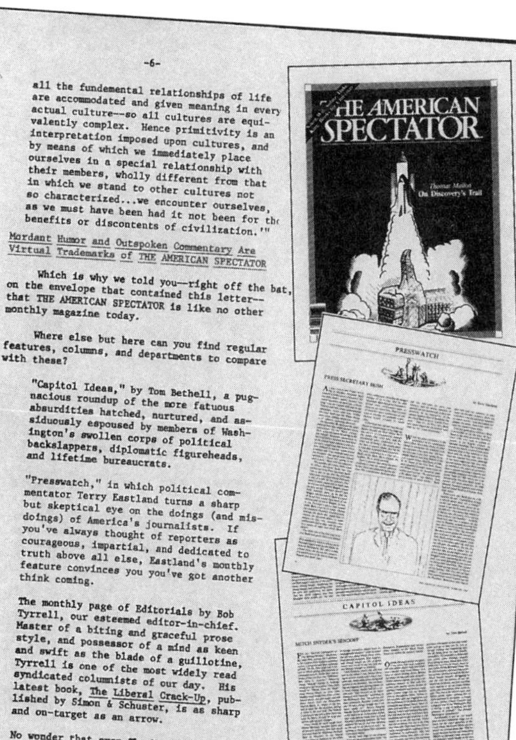

-6-

all the fundamental relationships of life are accommodated and given meaning in every actual culture--so all cultures are equivalently complex. Hence primitivity is an interpretation imposed upon cultures, and by means of which we immediately place ourselves in a special relationship with their members, wholly different from that in which we stand to other cultures not so characterized...we encounter ourselves, as we must have been had it not been for the benefits or discontents of civilization.'"

Mordant Humor and Outspoken Commentary Are Virtual Trademarks of THE AMERICAN SPECTATOR

Which is why we told you--right off the bat, on the envelope that contained this letter--that THE AMERICAN SPECTATOR is like no other monthly magazine today.

Where else but here can you find regular features, columns, and departments to compare with these?

"Capitol Ideas," by Tom Bethell, a pugnacious roundup of the more fatuous absurdities hatched, nurtured, and assiduously espoused by members of Washington's swollen corps of political backslappers, diplomatic figureheads, and lifetime bureaucrats.

"Presswatch," in which political commentator Terry Eastland turns a sharp but skeptical eye on the doings (and misdoings) of America's journalists. If you've always thought of reporters as courageous, impartial, and dedicated to truth above all else, Eastland's monthly feature convinces you you've got another think coming.

The monthly page of Editorials by Bob Tyrrell, our esteemed editor-in-chief. Master of a biting and graceful prose style, and possessor of a mind as keen and swift as the blade of a guillotine, Tyrrell is one of the most widely read syndicated columnists of our day. His latest book, The Liberal Crack-Up, published by Simon & Schuster, is as sharp and on-target as an arrow.

No wonder that even The Washington Post

-7-

--which has often felt the sting of Bob Tyrrell's barbed criticisms--pays tribute to him as a "sassy, erudite, conservative gadfly."

Other characteristically SPECTATOR features and departments include "Eminentoes," in which personalities as diverse and entertaining as good ol' Sally, the Quinn-tessential Washingtonian wit, and Dr. Leo Buscaglia are profiled; "Politique Internationale," which presents unconventional communiques from our footloose foreign correspondents; "Among the Intellectualoids," in which THE SPECTATOR cheerfully provides a petard for the convenience of America's idiots savants in need of a hoist.

Not least among our regular features is that sterling travelogue, "The Great American Saloon Series," which presents fearless, on-the-spot assessments by our roving editors of the bibulous paradises hidden away in some of the most unlikely corners of our fair land.

Plainly One Can See Why THE AMERICAN SPECTATOR Is Such a Widely Quoted and Influential Journal

That circumstance is one of the most gratifying by-products of our publishing enterprise. For, as you can readily understand, though we're pleased when our readers enjoy and appreciate us, we're tickled silly when we get bouquets from our peers in the profession.

USA Today, for example, recently praised us for our "literate, witty, and provocative writing." And the number of citations of and quotations from AMERICAN SPECTATOR articles which appear in other newspapers and magazines in the course of any given month is little short of staggering.

From the Wall Street Journal to the Orange County (California) Register...from the New York Times to the Marine Corps Gazette. . .THE AMERICAN SPECTATOR's comments, observations, and editorial judgements are noted and quoted. And respected.

By Now You Know As Much About THE SPECTATOR As You Can Know Without Reading It Yourself

And that, of course, is the point of this long letter now nearing its close.

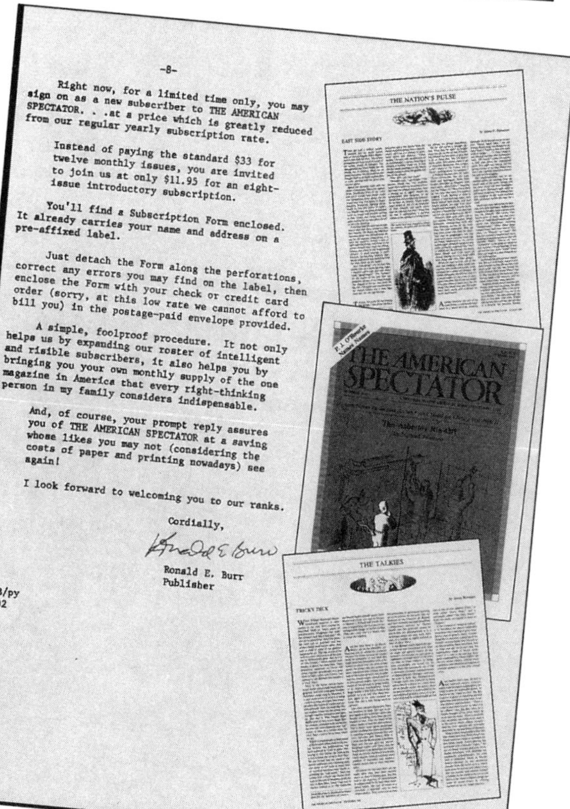

-8-

Right now, for a limited time only, you may sign on as a new subscriber to THE AMERICAN SPECTATOR. . .at a price which is greatly reduced from our regular yearly subscription rate.

Instead of paying the standard $33 for twelve monthly issues, you are invited to join us at only $11.95 for an eight-issue introductory subscription.

You'll find a Subscription Form enclosed. It already carries your name and address on a pre-affixed label.

Just detach the Form along the perforations, correct any errors you may find on the label, then enclose the Form with your check or credit card order (sorry, at this low rate we cannot afford to bill you) in the postage-paid envelope provided.

A simple, foolproof procedure. It not only helps us by expanding our roster of intelligent and risible subscribers, it also helps you by bringing you your own monthly supply of the one magazine in America that every right-thinking person in my family considers indispensable.

And, of course, your prompt reply assures you of THE AMERICAN SPECTATOR at a saving whose likes you may not (considering the costs of paper and printing nowadays) see again!

I look forward to welcoming you to our ranks.

Cordially,

Ronald E. Burr
Publisher

REB/py
302

To start your subscription to

THE AMERICAN SPECTATOR.

while our big money-saving introductory offer remains in force . . .

. . . make use of the pre-addressed return portion alongside. Detach along the perforations, enclose your check, and mail in the postage-paid reply envelope provided.

THE AMERICAN SPECTATOR
is regularly available at $33
for a year of 12 monthly issues

YOURS—WHILE THIS INTRODUCTORY SPECIAL LASTS—AT ONLY $11.95

for a 8-issue Trial Subscription.
Outside United States, add $4 for postage.

THE AMERICAN SPECTATOR

☐Please open my subscription under the terms of your money-saving Introductory Special: 8 monthly issues for only $11.95, instead of the regular yearly rate of $33 (outside U.S., add $4 for postage).

☐Enclosed is my check for $11.95 payable to *The American Spectator.*

Charge my: ☐MasterCard ☐VISA
Card #: __________
Exp. Date: __________
Signature: __________

J928

THOMAS
ST
CRTN ON HUDSO NY 10520

No-Risk Guarantee. If displeased, I may cancel at any time and receive a full refund for the unused portion of my subscription.

THE AMERICAN SPECTATOR
P.O. Box 549, Arlington, VA 22216-0549

O289

The order card and business reply envelope.

E92

NO POSTAGE NECESSARY IF MAILED IN THE UNITED STATES

BUSINESS REPLY MAIL

FIRST CLASS PERMIT NO. 6978 ARLINGTON, VA

POSTAGE WILL BE PAID BY ADDRESSEE

THE AMERICAN SPECTATOR.
2020 NORTH 14TH STREET
P O BOX 549
ARLINGTON VA 22216-9850

Economist

One of the oldest Grand Controls is Ken Scheck's masterpiece of pure snob appeal and elitism. It is as simple as a mailing can be: absolutely blank white outer window envelope, six-page letter, order card, and business reply envelope. Even though it is going to highly paid and wealthy individuals, it uses the word "free" prominently throughout. Rich people like a bargain just like everybody else; maybe that's why they're rich.

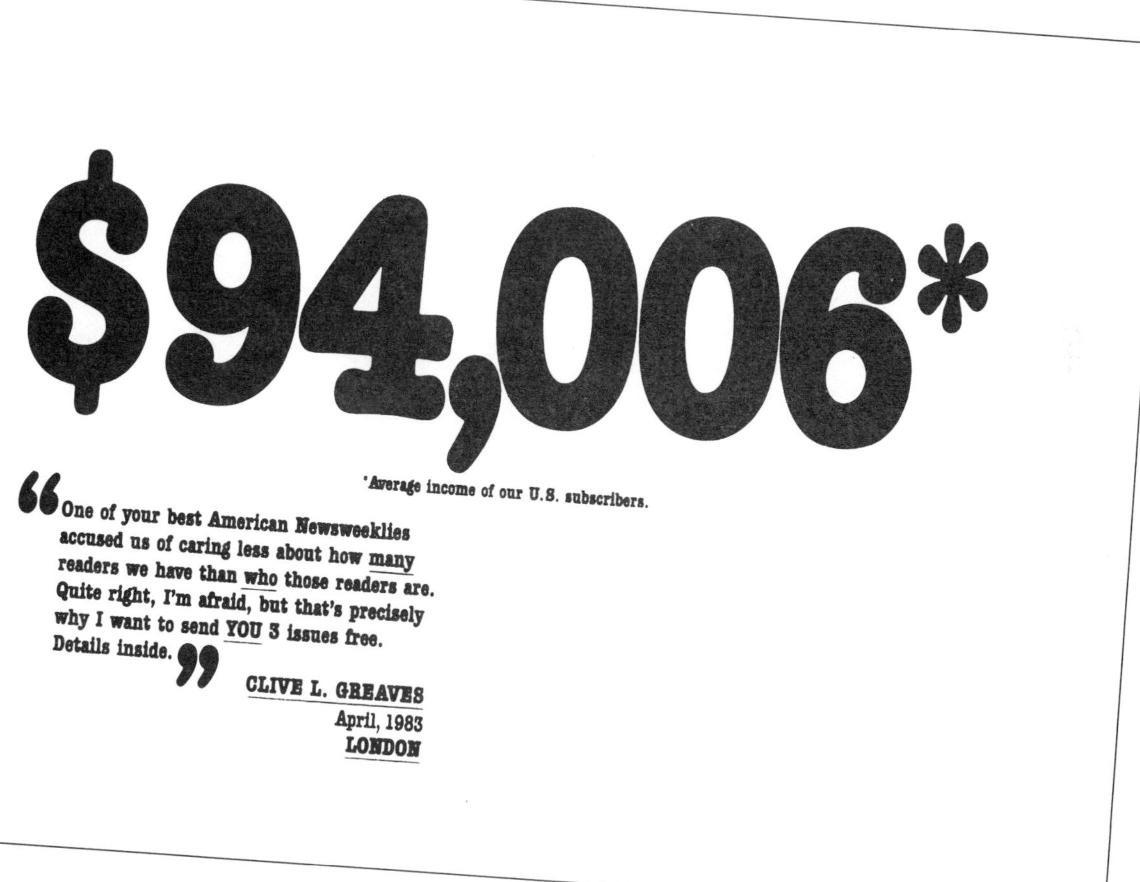

$94,006*
*Average income of our U.S. subscribers.
"One of your best American Newsweeklies accused us of caring less about how many readers we have than who those readers are. Quite right, I'm afraid, but that's precisely why I want to send YOU 3 issues free. Details inside."
CLIVE L. GREAVES
April, 1983
LONDON

MAILER: *Economist*
PACKAGE: 3 Free Issues
PROJECT MGR.: Beth Maher
WRITER: Ken Scheck
DESIGNER: Ken Scheck
FIRST MAILED: 1981

Two versions of the *Economist* outer envelope. The 6″ × 9″ piece with "$94,000*" was the original envelope. In her commentary, *Economist* vice president Beth Maher reveals why they soon changed to the plain white #10 window outer. On the #10 version, the return address is printed on the flap on the back; that address is the P.O. box of the fulfillment house in Boulder, CO.

732 02446032 0U135

10309/25 CAR-RT SORT **CR07

T F
61 St
Croton Hdsn NY 10520

Ken Scheck's 6-page letter, printed on an 11″ × 17″ sheet with an 8½″ × 11″ sheet nested inside, folded 3 times to fit in the #10 envelope.

May I send you

3 FREE ISSUES

of what may be the most influential

(as well as selectively distributed)

newsweekly in the world?

Dear Colleague,

Every Monday morning, a rather unusual publication arrives at the desks of a select circle of individuals in positions of power and influence.

The readers of this discreetly (one is almost tempted to say reluctantly) publicized newsweekly include presidents (of countries, banks, universities and Fortune 500 companies), ranking executives (in business, government and industry) and prominent thinkers (in law, science, economics and military strategy).

Now, it may not surprise you to learn that the average income of North American subscribers to this singular periodical exceeds $117,000 per annum. However, it may surprise you to discover that despite the enormous clout and affluence of its world renowned readers...

> only a relative handful of Americans are aware of the existence of this exclusive publication, much less the intelligence it provides.

But now, with this letter, you are cordially invited to join the extremely select circle of men and women who wouldn't think of beginning each business week without the incomparable insight and reporting of... The Economist.

> Enclosed you will find a non-transferable order card. Return it to me and I will send you three absorbing issues of The Economist to read at my expense. These three issues will be yours to keep free whether or not you decide to become a subscriber.
>
> However, should you wish to join our distinguished roster of American subscribers, I will then reduce the $3.00 cover price to just $1.33 for each of your 30 issues. This will save you up to 56% on newsstand costs -- 31% on regular subscription costs.

But why The Economist? Why you?

- 2 -

First, let me make it plain that I am not writing to you today because I think you may not be earning $117,000-a-year, or at least not yet. (Of course, many of our most distinguished subscribers earn considerably less than our reader-average -- this makes them no less distinguished in our eyes.)

However, allow me to assume that The Economist is not exactly a "household name" with you. Perhaps you've never even heard of us at all! It is possible, of course, that you have heard vague references to us as an erudite publication read only by an elite cadre of professional economists and other exotic abstractionists.

Well, nothing could be further from the truth!

> The Economist is much more than just a magazine of economics and finance -- it is, in fact, the only true worldclass newsweekly expressly compiled to increase your understanding of the critical inter-relationships between global affairs and the tough realities of today's marketplace.

Indeed, as the events of the past decade underscore, the "global village" has become reality. To put it another way, when the Mideast shudders ... the world shivers. And so on. But that's just part of it.

Relatively a short time ago, it was universally assumed that U.S. management techniques were decades ahead of the rest of the world. It was, afterall, just under 30 years ago that French author Servan-Schreiber touched off an international bombshell with his sweeping indictment of Europe's antiquated approach to business. Since then, there have been changes, to say the least.

> Today, many of the most revolutionary management and productivity innovations are being put to the test in Western Europe, Japan and elsewhere. Smart American businessmen -- those with a global perspective -- are gaining an extra edge by keeping close tabs on developments in world business. The Economist is their potent "secret weapon".

But it's not an ironclad secret. In the often cut-throat world of news-gathering The Economist is that rarest of all media species -- a universally admired and astonishingly respected publication -- as is remarkably demonstrated by these comments from the press:

The Wall Street Journal: "It (The Economist) should be bound in leather and made required reading..."

- 3 -

Time Magazine: "...exerting an influence far beyond its circulation... its calm authoritativeness has made it a favorite of political and business leaders in the U.S. as well as Britain."

The New York Times: "May be the most sensible publication in the English language."

International Herald Tribune: "This unique journal...in which sheer intellect, backed by integrity and a bold welcoming of new ideas has held such sway over statesmen and governments."

Newsweek: "Abroad it is required reading at the pinnacles of power. In the U.S. The Economist is a week-end habit on Wall Street and in the White House."

Very well. We're pleased to know The Economist is considered required reading at 1600 Pennsylvania Avenue. But how does our publication relate to you?

Perhaps I can answer this best by pointing out that most men and women in business will never receive the letter you have in your hands right now. They will, of course, receive solicitations galore to subscribe to run-of-the-mill business newspapers, magazines and news-letters. But not The Economist. Why not?

The reason is simply that most managers, throughout their careers, will never be called upon to handle the critical information or make decisions of the scope and magnitude of those who require The Economist. I believe you have already made or will soon be called upon to make such critical decisions. I can't put it more bluntly than that.

> But what, exactly, can you expect to find in the pages of The Economist?

For starters, do not expect to find a rehash of what's already been covered by The Wall Street Journal, The New York Times, Fortune, Forbes or Business Week. Unlike these otherwise splendid periodicals, The Economist's reporting is in a class by itself -- worldclass.

Instead, count on discovering a clear and penetrating picture of how the forces at work today are shaping the world in which you will work tomorrow. For example...

Feel jittery about the effects of continuing world turmoil? Who in his right mind doesn't? Terrorism. Revolutions and threatened invasions. Nuclear sabre-rattling. It's a wonder the world is able to absorb and survive as many shocks as it does!

- 4 -

The Economist can sort it all out for you. Each week we bring you six to eight indepth articles that clearly define and analyze the week's critical developments. It's tough-minded, clear-headed observation that brings the world down to size.

Wonder what's going on in other business capitals? You should. Exciting things are happening in virtually every corner of the world. Never before has it been so important to stay abreast of so many business developments in so many different places!

Here, again, The Economist is your key. Whether it's the prospect of another bumpy ride for the auto industry, trade restrictions and protectionism affecting the U.S. market, the problems of investing in gold, the potential for factories in space, or the promise of superconductors.

Afraid of missing out on new ideas, new breakthroughs? Welcome to the club. After all, who among us hasn't dreaded the possibility of being rendered obsolete by a microchip!

Rest easy. The Economist, in its widely-acclaimed "Science and Technology" section, keeps you up-to-the-minute on what's being discovered, invented or just plain dreamed about! Computers that think. Drugs that boost brain power. Microchips (never turn your back on one!) which pack nearly 100 million components on a sliver of silicon. Telecommunications that are bringing the whole world into the office and living room.

But be forewarned. You'll see a very different America when you look at your country through the "eyes" of The Economist.

Maybe it's a kind of "hothouse" effect. Or maybe it's simply a case of being too close to the action to see it clearly. Whatever the reason, it is our opinion that domestic news media often present a somewhat feverish overwrought picture of what's really going on in the United States. Pity, really.

You see, someone once said that when America sneezes the world catches pneumonia. We tend to (cough) agree. And so, every week, The Economist devotes six full pages to a close look at America... but from a distance, of course. We call it our "American Survey" and, believe me, you'll find the perspective positively refreshing!

- 5 -

In recent issues, for example, we have cautioned of the impending economic impact of America's "twin deficits" and Bush's insistence on no tax increases.

We've analyzed SDI and America's future in space; commented on the effects of drug smuggling and cocaine economies on foreign policy; defined key foreign investment trends as 1992 approaches; and discussed how the advent of LBO's are forcing the restructuring of corporate America.

Whether you agree with our conclusions or not, I think you'll come to agree with the experts -- that our weekly "American Survey" is simply the most cool and level-headed appraisal of the U.S. political and business scene in print today!

The final judgement, however, is best left to you. And in the paragraphs that follow I intend to make it as enticing as possible for you to agree to sample several issues of The Economist.

Why I must insist that you read your first three issues of The Economist absolutely free!

It has nothing, I assure you, to do with spending too much time "in the mid-day sun" or any of those alleged Anglo-Saxon quirks! You may, if you like, chalk it up to my sense of fair play.

You see, it's simply that I'm very conscious of the fact that in all likelihood, you've never seen anything remotely resembling The Economist. And so it just wouldn't be reasonable to ask you to subscribe to our publication sight unseen.

Of course, you may look over your free issues as you wish but, frankly, I rather hope you'll read The Economist with a decidedly jaundiced eye. In other words, be as skeptical as you like! Doubt our every word! Make us prove to you that our predictions and surveys give you an extraordinarily accurate look at where our confusing world is headed.

Then, if the first three issues leave you unimpressed, if you decide for any reason at all that The Economist is not the remarkable source of invaluable intelligence I promised it would be, simply write "cancel" across your bill and owe not a cent.

- 6 -

Should you decide, on the other hand, that our magazine is a truly unique addition to your regular reading, just remit by check. You'll then receive a total of 30 weekly issues of The Economist at our special introductory rate of only $39.90 -- a savings of up to $50.10 on newsstand costs.

But, putting savings aside for the moment, I sincerely hope you'll take this opportunity to experience one of the world's most distinguished and respected weekly publications.

Find out how stimulating it can be to read a worldclass newsweekly that gives you a perspective you simply can't get anywhere else.

Yes, try The Economist.

Try The Economist now while this special invitation to read three absorbing issues at our monetary risk is still in effect. All it takes is a checkmark on the enclosed card!

Cordially,

M. M. Scardino
President

MMS:csb

P.S. As mentioned earlier, this invitation is not-transferable. It is valid in your name only. If you decide not to accept my offer, please do not pass it along to anyone else. I would prefer you simply discard it. Thank you.

P.O. Box 58524, Boulder, CO. 80321-8524

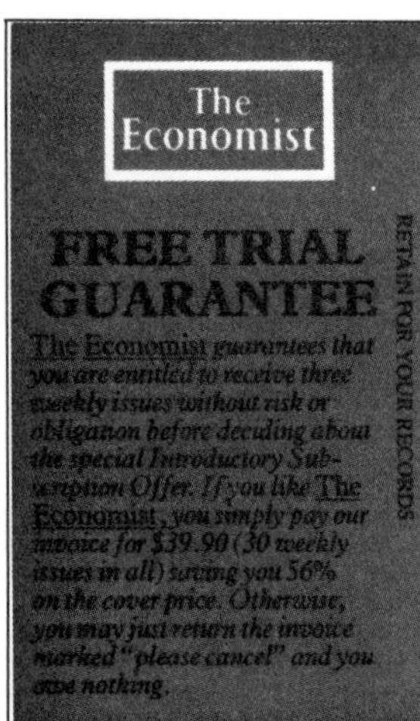

The Economist
FREE TRIAL GUARANTEE
The Economist guarantees that you are entitled to receive three weekly issues without risk or obligation before deciding about the special Introductory Subscription Offer. If you like The Economist, you simply pay our invoice for $39.90 (30 weekly issues in all) saving you 56% on the cover price. Otherwise, you may just return the invoice marked "please cancel" and you owe nothing.
RETAIN FOR YOUR RECORDS

The Economist FREE Trial Offer

The Economist
What we need is a good recession

☐ **YES,** please send me my first three issues of The Economist risk free. If I like The Economist, I'll pay your invoice for $39.90 and receive 27 additional issues (30 weekly issues in all) and save 56% off the cover price.

732 02446032 OU135
10309/25 CAR-RT SORT **CR07

T F
St
Croton Hasn NY 10520

The Economist by regular subscription is $57.60 for 30 issues. Newsstand cost is $90.00. These rates payable in U.S. dollars only. CJN

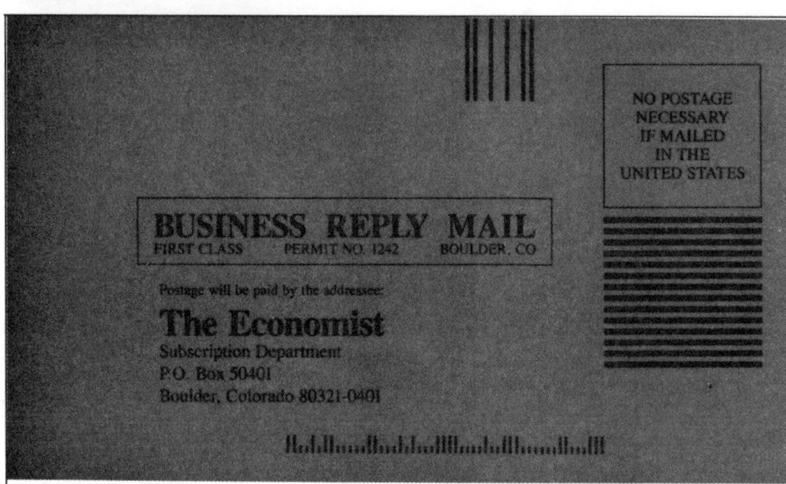

The benefits of getting acquainted with The Economist NOW!

1. You receive three *free* issues of The Economist.
2. You send no money now.
3. If you decide to continue, you can take advantage of a special low subscription price reserved for new subscribers that saves you up to $50.10 on the newsstand price.

C

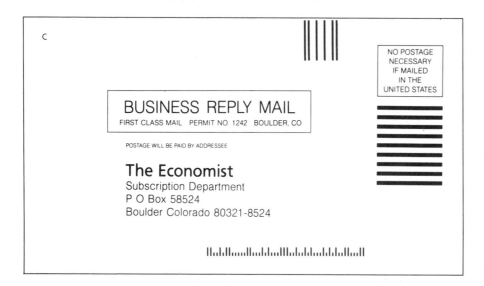

NO POSTAGE
NECESSARY
IF MAILED
IN THE
UNITED STATES

BUSINESS REPLY MAIL
FIRST CLASS MAIL PERMIT NO. 1242 BOULDER, CO

POSTAGE WILL BE PAID BY ADDRESSEE

The Economist
Subscription Department
P O Box 58524
Boulder Colorado 80321-8524

The order card shown front and back and the business reply envelope. The stub on the order card is red with black surprinting—leading the eye from dark to light so that the order card stands out. The business reply face is red with a white stub. This is one of several Grand Controls that include both a business reply *card* and a business reply *envelope.*

Beth Maher, vice president of circulation and marketing for the *Economist,* is a thoroughgoing professional who knows how to buy copy and how to get the best out of a copywriter. Before signing on with the *Economist,* she worked for *New York, Esquire,* and *Prime Time.*

From an interview with Beth Maher:

When we hired Ken Scheck to create this package, it was obvious at the outset that he had an immediate and absolute understanding of the Economist *and what our ideas were on how to market it. We were trying to find American subscribers for a then relatively unknown British publication—a newsweekly international in scope with an audience difficult to target.*

When the package was written, we changed maybe one or two words at most. His copy perfectly described the product and reached out to and for the audience. Our instincts were right; Ken's package has been the Economist's *control for eleven years.*

The original package had a 6" × 9" outer envelope that was positively revolutionary at the time—so revolutionary that other magazines instantly started copying it. As a result, Ken's original envelope got tired very quickly.

So we decided to go with the plain #10 window envelope. Over the years we've tested other envelopes, but this version keeps coming up a winner.

People often ask about finding and hiring copywriters. There's no mystery about it. I hear of someone . . . or see a package that impresses me and find out through the grapevine who did it . . . and I call the person up. I ask for samples of prior packages. If I like what I see, then we talk, either in person or by phone. If the writer seems to understand what we have in mind and wants to tackle the assignment, I give out the assignment.

Generally I like to know the overall approach the writer has in mind, so that we are in sync about the objectives. Then I give the writer free rein.

Some writers submit finished copy and artist's comprehensives that are so beautiful that they look like the finished package. I don't need that. I'm happy with copy and thumbnails. I can visualize what the package will look like. The important thing is the words. Do they flow? Does the letter sell*?*

I don't like to make copy changes. Editors and publishers love to change copy, but I believe that's the worst thing that can happen to direct mail copy; it's downhill from there. You'll never stop publishers and editors from taking the punch out of copy, but I think you're always much better off going with what the writer has done. After all, direct mail writers have real marketing sense; editorial people do not.

In getting a writer to make changes, I don't say: ''Change this; this is the way I want it.'' I find it's better if there's a disagreement to say, ''I'm looking at this and this from a certain perspective and this is what I get out of it, and I don't think this is what either of us has in mind, is it? Could you take another crack at it?''

One other thing I've learned: if the writer comes back a second time and it's still not quite right, the writer will never get it. It's not worth spending any more time on.

Foreign Affairs

Whereas Ken Scheck's *Economist* effort appeals to the snob in all of us, Len Berkowe is the ultimate name dropper, banging home the unrivaled credentials of *Foreign Affairs*. On the outer envelope he calls it "the most influential periodical in print" and backs up his claim in the Johnson Box of the letter.

FOREIGN AFFAIRS
58 East 68th Street, New York, N.Y. 10021

Should *you* be reading "the most influential periodical in print"?

(You can try it now — at just half the regular price — with your satisfaction guaranteed!)

UVGF4

JAMES
ADDRESS ST DIR
CITY NEW YORK NY 10028

MAILER: *Foreign Affairs*
PACKAGE: Should *you* be reading?
PROJECT MGRS.: Doris Forest
Dave Kellogg
George Fisher
Margaret Kable
WRITER: Len Berkowe
DESIGNER: Vincent Gallipani
FIRST MAILED: 1982

The 6″ × 9″ outside envelope, printed in 1-color (black). All elements of this package are printed on expensive textured stock.

The 4-page letter, printed on an 11″ × 17″ sheet and folded twice. The *Foreign Affairs* logos on the front and back pages, and David Kellogg's signature, are printed in a smoky blue. There is an unusual amount of white space around the letter, in keeping with the upscale look of the package and the upscale audience it is going to.

FOREIGN AFFAIRS

It's welcomed wherever foreign policy decisions are made — in the White House, the State Department, the halls of Congress.

It's quoted in corporate boardrooms — and major news rooms — from coast to coast.

For *Newsweek*, it's the "pre-eminent journal of its kind." *Time* calls it "the most influential periodical in print."

But once you try FOREIGN AFFAIRS, you may come to regard it as something else — simply one of the most fascinating, eye-opening and rewarding magazines you'll ever read.

Dear Reader:

Not everyone has a vested interest in understanding world affairs. Many people — millions, in fact — get along quite nicely with just daily headlines, the TV evening news and maybe a once-a-week news magazine.

But not, I suspect, you.

Chances are, you've already discovered, from personal experience, what a truly interdependent world we live in. How often even far-off events can affect your pocketbook, your investments, your future planning.

Or perhaps you simply enjoy "being in the know" — with a firm grasp of not only what's happening, but why.

Whatever the reason, I hope you'll accept my invitation to join those perceptive and demanding readers — all over the world — who emphatically rely on FOREIGN AFFAIRS to keep them fully informed.

With the enclosed card you can now try FOREIGN AFFAIRS under truly advantageous terms — and with no risk whatsoever! But before I go into details, let me take just a moment to tell you a bit more about us — and especially what you can expect to find in every issue of FOREIGN AFFAIRS.

First and foremost, a chance to be briefed on major world events by the brightest, best informed minds around . . .

U.S. foreign policy makers and their advisors, world political leaders, celebrated journalists, distinguished economists, renowned scholars — experts of every kind who willingly share their latest information and insights with you.

Starting with your first issue, you'll see what a difference FOREIGN AFFAIRS can make in your own understanding of today's news. You'll view major world events in their proper historical perspective. With the essential facts in place. And all the available policy options fully discussed.

Indeed, just one article in FOREIGN AFFAIRS is likely to tell you more about the state of our world than a score of newspaper or magazine reports.

You'll be surprised, too, at how much easier it is to interpret the latest headline developments, once you have the basic background information FOREIGN AFFAIRS so skillfully provides.

And unlike many other magazines, FOREIGN AFFAIRS won't bring you just one point of view, no matter how well informed it may be.

For we have no axe to grind, no ideology to preach. FOREIGN AFFAIRS is an independent, non-profit publication, open to all shades of opinion — provided only that they are intellectually honest, and based on a decent regard for the facts.

If we delve into the future of world trade, you will hear from protectionists as well as free traders. On arms control, we give equal space to the pessimists and the optimists. And when it comes to the Middle East, you'll get appraisals from Arab and Israeli as well as U.S. experts.

So you can always count on the full-range of viewpoints you need to make up your own mind on the most important international questions of the day.

And since our contributors are people who either closely observe or actively participate in major policy decisions, you're likely to be forewarned of important new developments — long before they become public knowledge.

Over the years, in fact, we've compiled a rather impressive record of journalistic "firsts."

It was in FOREIGN AFFAIRS that George F. Kennan first unveiled the idea of "containment" that was to become U.S. policy during the Cold War.

And it was in FOREIGN AFFAIRS that Henry Kissinger first argued for a new attitude that would later lead to detente and the dramatic opening to China.

Before the current international focus on safeguarding the environment, Pulitzer Prize-winning author and scientist Carl Sagan first forewarned of the catastrophic devastation of the global climate that would follow a nuclear war in an award winning article for FOREIGN AFFAIRS that sparked a controversial debate.

As unprecedented progress with the Soviet Union moved the world closer to a more stable peace, former President Richard Nixon advocated taking advantage of this historic opportunity without making concessions that would prove unwise if superpower relations were to deteriorate.

And it was in FOREIGN AFFAIRS that Henry Kissinger and Cyrus Vance, writing together for the first time, formulated foreign policy recommendations — and warnings — for the Bush administration.

Throughout the coming year, FOREIGN AFFAIRS will offer you fascinating, informative articles such as these. And included with your subscription will be our special year-end issue, "America and the World" — a review of the basic foreign policy challenges facing our country, and their ongoing significance for the year ahead.

As you can see, FOREIGN AFFAIRS is something rare indeed. A rich source of information and enlightenment. A reliable guide to what is being thought and debated at the highest levels of world affairs.

Ordinarily, our four regular issues plus the "America and the World" special issue would cost you $32.00 by subscription, even more on newsstands. But if you accept this invitation, you can try FOREIGN AFFAIRS for as little as $16.00, or exactly half the regular price!

Naturally, we make such an offer to only a limited number of people — those who, in our opinion, will find both pleasure and profit in reading FOREIGN AFFAIRS. And it may be some time before you hear from us again.

So why not use the enclosed card, while it's still at hand, to enter your own trial subscription? There's no need to enclose payment — we'll be happy to bill you later. Or you may charge your trial subscription to your preferred credit card.

And remember, as a new subscriber you are entitled to the unconditional guarantee: if at any time you are disappointed in FOREIGN AFFAIRS, simply write to us. We'll cancel your trial order and send a full refund for the entire cost of your subscription. With no questions asked.

We look forward to hearing from you today.

Cordially,

David Kellogg

David Kellogg
Publishing Director

P.S. For a sampling of our recent articles — and some reader comments on the value of FOREIGN AFFAIRS — take just a moment to look through the enclosed brochure. But please don't delay too long before returning your reply card. Our next issue will soon be on press, and we'd very much like to reserve a copy for you.

FOREIGN AFFAIRS
58 East 68th Street, New York, NY 10021

990-CEF-LT

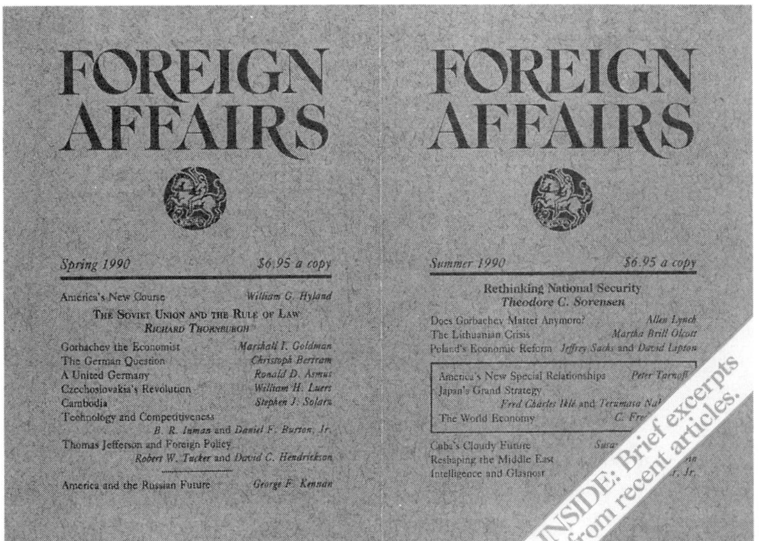

The 4-panel brochure is printed on card stock in black. The only color is the red banner and type within it slashing across the bottom right of the cover panel. The cover and back panels—shown together here—are the same gray as actual magazine covers, but one-half the size. Illustrated here are the gatefolds as they progress from 2 . . . to 3 . . . to 4 panels.

The first inside page of Berkowe's brochure amplifies the publication's pedigree by giving its venue—a townhouse just off New York's fashionable Park Avenue.

. . . to this Manhattan address comes a year-round stream of manuscripts bearing such noteworthy names as Andrei Sakharov, Cyrus Vance, William F. Buckley, Jr., Yitzak Shamir, Robert S. McNamara, Peter F. Drucker, Arthur Schlesinger, Jr., Martin Feldstein, Zbigniew Brzezinski, George P. Shultz, Leonard Silk, Henry Kissinger.

On a facing panel are testimonials from Diane Sawyer, John Chancellor, Peter Drucker, and Tom Brokaw.

Like Tony Cornish's package for the *Futurist,* which lists a distinguished group of directors on the letter, this assemblage of international luminaries is very persuasive in making readers feel that by subscribing, they will be in exalted company and have a private pipeline to leading-edge thinking.

LEN BERKOWE:
The creative challenge in my Foreign Affairs *assignment was to convince an audience of nonspecialists that this was really the magazine for them. So I tackled it right from the start—with a question on the outer envelope—and then used the rest of the mailing to provide a variety of answers.*

In general, I like to work this way: starting off with one central idea and carrying it through the entire package. The toughest part is coming up with the ''big idea.'' The second toughest part is spelling it out, clearly and convincingly, in a letter. It took about twelve drafts to get the Foreign Affairs *letter into good shape.*

Although Foreign Affairs *has no graphics, I decided to add a brochure to ''illustrate'' selling points that could not be conveyed as well in the letter—namely the quality of writing and insights that* Foreign Affairs *gets from its biggest name contributors.*

The home of the "most influential periodical in print."

58 East 68th Street, New York, New York

To a casual observer, it might seem like just another stately townhouse bordering New York's fashionable Park Avenue.

And yet, to this Manhattan address, comes a year-round stream of manuscripts bearing such noteworthy names as Andrei Sakharov, Cyrus Vance, William F. Buckley, Jr., Yitzhak Shamir, Robert S. McNamara, Peter F. Drucker, Arthur Schlesinger, Jr., Martin Feldstein, Zbigniew Brzezinski, George P. Schultz, Leonard Silk, Henry Kissinger.

Why do so many of today's best-informed minds agree to share their latest thoughts in the pages of FOREIGN AFFAIRS?

It surely has something to do with our 68-year-old reputation as an open forum of ideas. And much to do with the special caliber of our readers.

With this invitation, you are invited to join us now. Come enjoy spirited discussions on the pros and cons of current U.S. policies. Learn about bold new proposals for the future. Be alerted to emerging global trends. And discover the challenges—and opportunities—that await us in the months and years ahead.

Should *you* be reading FOREIGN AFFAIRS? The following brief excerpts from recent articles will, we hope, provide some additionally persuasive reasons why you may want to return the enclosed card, and start your trial subscription today.

The home of the "most influential periodical in print."

58 East 68th Street, New York, New York

To a casual observer, it might seem like just another stately townhouse bordering New York's fashionable Park Avenue.

And yet, to this Manhattan address, comes a year-round stream of manuscripts bearing such noteworthy names as Andrei Sakharov, Cyrus Vance, William F. Buckley, Jr., Yitzhak Shamir, Robert S. McNamara, Peter F. Drucker, Arthur Schlesinger, Jr., Martin Feldstein, Zbigniew Brzezinski, George P. Schultz, Leonard Silk, Henry Kissinger.

Why do so many of today's best-informed minds agree to share their latest thoughts in the pages of FOREIGN AFFAIRS?

It surely has something to do with our 68-year-old reputation as an open forum of ideas. And much to do with the special caliber of our readers.

With this invitation, you are invited to join us now. Come enjoy spirited discussions on the pros and cons of current U.S. policies. Learn about bold new proposals for the future. Be alerted to emerging global trends. And discover the challenges—and opportunities—that await us in the months and years ahead.

Should *you* be reading FOREIGN AFFAIRS? The following brief excerpts from recent articles will, we hope, provide some additionally persuasive reasons why you may want to return the enclosed card, and start your trial subscription today.

Zbigniew Brzezinski

POST-COMMUNIST NATIONALISM

The time has come for the West to confront as a policy issue a problem that for years most Western scholars have tended to ignore and that all Western policymakers still consider to be taboo: the rising tide of nationalism in Eastern Europe and especially in the Soviet Union itself. Indeed, whereas Marx once described the tsarist Russian empire as the prison of nations, and Stalin turned it into the graveyard of nations, under Gorbachev the Soviet empire is rapidly becoming the volcano of nations.

Winston Lord

CHINA AND AMERICA: BEYOND THE BIG CHILL

The Big Chill has descended over China. Sino-American relations are suffering. While we assess the ramifications, we must also look beyond the crisis and sketch blueprints for a warmer climate, for the present season will not long endure . . . To be sure, the revival of broad cooperation will not be automatic or facile even with a moderate government in the future. Scars will remain. Trust will have to be rebuilt. Traders and investors will be more prone to hedge their bets and to swerve to other markets. Cultural and academic leaders will harbor uneasiness about future winds of xenophobia.

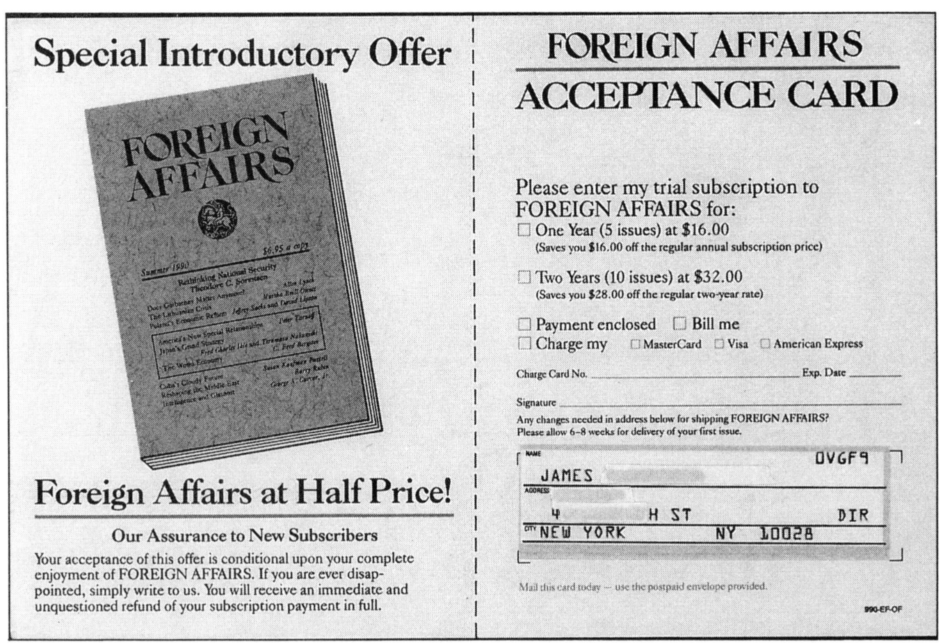

Special Introductory Offer

Foreign Affairs at Half Price!

Our Assurance to New Subscribers

Your acceptance of this offer is conditional upon your complete enjoyment of FOREIGN AFFAIRS. If you are ever disappointed, simply write to us. You will receive an immediate and unquestioned refund of your subscription payment in full.

FOREIGN AFFAIRS

ACCEPTANCE CARD

Please enter my trial subscription to FOREIGN AFFAIRS for:

☐ One Year (5 issues) at $16.00
(Saves you $16.00 off the regular annual subscription price)

☐ Two Years (10 issues) at $32.00
(Saves you $28.00 off the regular two-year rate)

☐ Payment enclosed ☐ Bill me
☐ Charge my ☐ MasterCard ☐ Visa ☐ American Express

Charge Card No. ______ Exp. Date ______

Signature ______

Any changes needed in address below for shipping FOREIGN AFFAIRS?
Please allow 6–8 weeks for delivery of your first issue.

OVGF9
JAMES
4 H ST DIR
NEW YORK NY 10028

Mail this card today — use the postpaid envelope provided.

990-EF-OF

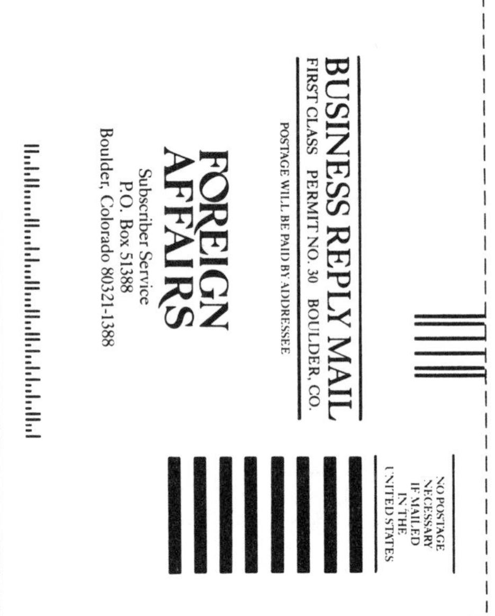

The order card shown front and back and the business reply envelope. This is another mailing that provides both a business reply *card* and a business reply *envelope* for those who wish privacy or prefer to enclose cash with order.

Soviet Life

A number of the mailings described so far have tokens or action devices. Among them: *Audubon* and *Bon Appétit*.

The token in direct mail was first conceived by Walter Weintz, the dynamic postwar circulation director of *Reader's Digest*. He describes his first use of it, in his book *The Solid Gold Mailbox*:

By 1955 my circulation department had expanded considerably, and I was becoming more of an administrator and less of a copywriter. I had even acquired a copywriter, Marie Hill, who helped with both Digest *and condensed book promotions, and helped me puzzle over new ways to get attention.*

One morning Marie came into my office with a fundraising mailing someone had sent her for some worthy charitable cause. The mailing had a shiny new penny in it—"for luck," as the accompanying letter said. And Marie suggested that we should try out a penny in our Digest *mailings.*

Sticking a penny in a mailing just to get attention seemed a weak crutch to me. But it suddenly occurred to me that in my search for new attention-getting

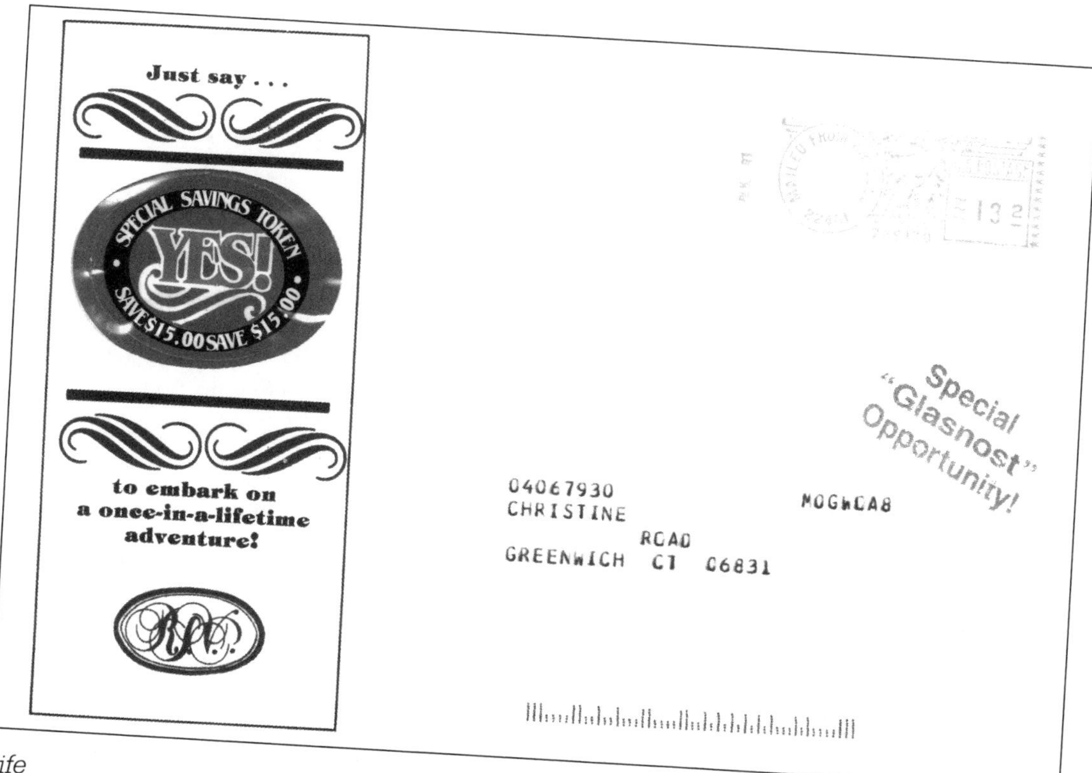

MAILER: *Soviet Life*
PACKAGE: Just Say YES!
PROJECT MGR.: Victor Karasin
WRITERS: Tony Arau
Marlene Lewis
DESIGNER: Lonnie Rossi
CONSULTANT: Arau Associates
FIRST MAILED: 1983
The 5½" × 8" outer envelope for *Soviet Life*. Tony Arau's dramatic red "YES" token, ringed in blue on a gold background, shows through an oval window. The back of the envelope has a witty rubber stamp effect: "Had your 'Glasnost' this month? You'd better see inside!"

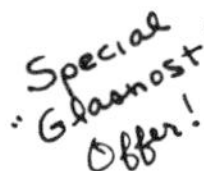

4 Zubovsky Blvd., Moscow, USSR

....

What country occupies about 8.6 million square miles -- nearly 15% of the earth's dry land -- contains over 270 million people, and is now waiting for you to get to know it . . . for just $1.00 a month?

....

Dear Reader:

The correct answer, of course is the Soviet Union. If you said "Russia", you were almost right, because Russia covers three-quarters of our country's territory, and Russian is spoken throughout all 15 Soviet republics. But, the Russians are only one of more than a hundred distinct nationalities that make up the U.S.S.R.!

That's what makes SOVIET LIFE magazine so interesting! And that's what this letter is all about.

The Soviet Union has always been a fascinating place -- and SOVIET LIFE has for more than 30 years been a fascinating magazine. But now, under the twin policies of "glasnost" and "perestroika", dramatic changes are taking place in the Soviet Union, changes you'll find detailed and illuminated in the pages of SOVIET LIFE!

Each month, in wonderfully colorful, in-depth feature articles, with vivid color photos, SOVIET LIFE takes you across the U.S.S.R.'s vast -- and swiftly changing -- panorama of human and physical geography! . . . A journey that will help satisfy your curiosity about "those Russians" and, we hope, whet your desire to know us better!

And, starting this year, SOVIET LIFE will be published in a handsome new, more "modern" format -- with more color photos and illustrations than ever before!

If you act now, you can receive the next 12 big issues of our spectacular magazine for only $12.00. (That's a Very Special Trial Offer, which saves you $15.00 off the single copy price -- $6.00 off the regular subscriber price!)

So come, let us transport you across steppe and plain and tundra and forest . . . into our modern cities . . . into our timeless villages. See the charming churches of Suzdal -- masterpieces of medieval Russian architecture; visit one of the ungainly (but clever) yurta -- portable dwellings of the rugged Kirghiz shepherds; visit Kiev's Palace of Sports -- an extraordinary "Madison Square Garden" in the 1500-year-old capital of the Ukraine! . . .

(over, please)

Come learn, for example, of the colorful marriage customs, the favorite foods and entertainment of our various republics . . . get a frank and fresh insight into some of the problems caused by our famous Russian winters . . . discover the challenge of farming lands north of the 50th parallel (i.e., somewhat higher than the line dividing the U.S. and Canada) -- and much, much more!

And discover, too, a wealth of facts and insights on the Soviet economy not often published elsewhere . . . learn of Soviet achievements in science and medicine, of new developments in Soviet industry . . . learn how the Soviet Union copes with worldwide problems such as environmental protection and overcrowding . . .

Get to know, at first hand, both the genius of our traditional folk arts and crafts -- and the brilliance of contemporary Soviet artists, writers and musicians -- as well as the overflowing treasures of our great museums, such as the Hermitage, and so many more!

And here's something else: By subscribing to SOVIET LIFE, you'll be taking part in a unique cultural exchange program that's been in existence between our two governments for over 30 years! (While you're enjoying SOVIET LIFE in the United States, Soviet citizens will be enjoying the American Russian-language magazine, AMERICA ILLUSTRATED, published every month in the Soviet Union!)

For just $1.00 a month, just over 3¢ a day -- you and your family can not only tour our land and meet our people at work and play -- but you'll be helping to build a vital bridge of understanding between our two peoples . . . between the two nations who today may shape the destiny of our increasingly fragile world!

To start your personal "armchair visit", simply detach the "YES" token from the stub of the enclosed RSVP Trial Offer Card, affix it in the space provided, then return the Card in the postage-paid envelope enclosed. There's no need to send any money -- we'll be pleased to bill you later.

But, to embark on your personal "adventure of a lifetime" -- don't delay. Mail your Special Trial Offer Card, today!

Yours truly,

Robert Tsfasman

Robert Tsfasman
Editor in Chief
SOVIET LIFE

P.S. Don't delay! Make sure you get your personal introduction to "glasnost", today!

gimmicks, like savings stamps and plastic coins, I had gradually gotten away from the basic thing I was trying to sell: the rewards a reader would enjoy from a subscription to Reader's Digest. *I had gotten away from the basic story of what a wonderful magazine the* Reader's Digest *was—the story told in the old Persian Poet letter.*

That letter carried Reader's Digest *circulation up from next to nothing to a circulation of more than five million. And the letter started out:*

> *Dear Friend:*
>
> *An Ancient Persian Poet said, ''If thou hast two pennies, spend one for bread. With the other, buy hyacinths for thy soul.''*

The 2-page letter with blue letterhead, handwritten note at upper left on the front page, and blue signature on the back.

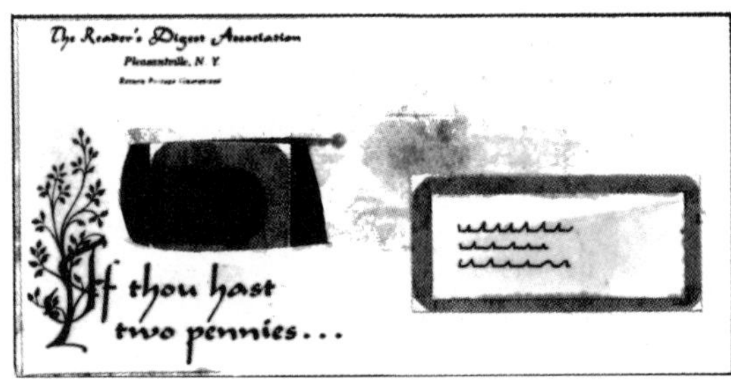

The trouble with the old Persian Poet mailing was that it did not *dramatize the offer with a* physical *object. The offer was there but you had to read the copy, and the communication of ideas through the written word is always difficult. The obvious wedding of Persian Poet and pennies came in an instant flash. I fished out the old Persian Poet letter and modified it slightly. I put together a mailing with two bright, shiny pennies showing through a second window in an envelope. And the copy on the envelope said: ''If thou hast two pennies . . .''*

On the letter inside, I went on: ''Keep one penny for bread,'' I said. ''Or for luck. Send back the other penny as a down payment on a subscription to the Reader's Digest*—a penny to seal the bargain! You'll get 8 months (a $2 value) for $1.01. You'll save 99 cents. So the penny is worth 99 cents to you,* if you use it now. *We'll bill you for the balance of $1.00.''*

We tested this mailing in 1955. The test was extremely successful. It increased returns from about 6 to over 9 percent.

Probably the greatest practitioner of the use of the token in direct mail today is Tony Arau. He is to the token what Charles Goren was to contract bridge. Arau was copy and creative director of the *Reader's Digest* Book & Record Division for five years before going on his own in 1962. He is president of Arau Associates in Valley Forge, Pennsylvania. In 1985 I asked Arau to jot down some thoughts on the concept of the order token in direct mail for *Who's Mailing What!*

Tony Arau:
In the beginning was the penny. And Walter Weintz saw that the penny was good and said, hey, let's put a penny or two on all Reader's Digest *mailings. And so it came to pass, and all over America people received lucky pennies (''Here's your change—in advance!'') from the kindly folks in Pleasantville.*

And then came the ''advanced'' token, and knocked the penny on its ear. And Walter Weintz saw that that was pretty good, too, and he said, by jingo, we may be on to something here! And so it, too, came to pass. And for the next several years a few million fortunate Americans received more plastic savings tokens—''Yes'' tokens,'' ''Yes'' and ''No'' tokens, cardboard book tokens of all sizes, shapes, colors, and materials—than even Walter Weintz would care to shake a stick at. And Walter shook a stick at more than a few.

And then came the Reader's Digest *Sweepstakes and knocked the token on its ear—at least in Pleasantville.*

But the token showed incredible stamina, and outside the ivy-covered walls at Pleasantville, the ''age of the token'' really hit its stride. And proved its viability as a marketing tool in situations far removed from the Digest.

Sometimes marketers ''disguised'' tokens—as a ''Credit Card'' for TV Guide *and an ''RSVP Card'' for* Better Homes & Gardens *in the early sixties. But they were still action devices. Still tokens. Some personalized, some numbered, some not.*

We devised computer-personalized punch-out ''Yes'' and ''No'' tokens for McCall's *and* Redbook *in the early sixties. And a computer-numbered Sweepstakes ''Key'' token for the* Saturday Evening Post *after that. And even a quietly elegant ''seahorse'' token for the* Atlantic Monthly *. . . and a tongue-in-cheek punch-out ''Armed Robbery'' token for* True *. . . and a ''Passport'' token for Time-Life Books.*

And many, many more.

SOVIET LIFE
Your Invitation to a Land of more than 100 Different Peoples! . . .
Where dramatic changes are now taking place!...
SPECIAL "GLASNOST" INTRODUCTORY OFFER!
1 Year (12 Issues) Only $12.00

SOVIET LIFE
Learn of the Extraordinary Achievements of Modern Soviet Industry!
From the new towns of the once-empty Siberian wilderness to astonishing hydro-electric projects on the Dnieper, the Volga and the Don . . . from the bustling steel mills of the Ukraine, to the mighty ship-yards of Leningrad and Nikolayev . . . Soviet industry is on the move!
Famous landmarks and revered shrines.
The theater, the circus, the opera, and comedy, too.
Take part in the unique cultural exchange program that makes this exceptional magazine available in the U.S. and America Illustrated available in the U.S.S.R.
Mail your special trial offer card today!
12 BIG ISSUES/$12.00
A Savings of $15.00 Off the Regular Price

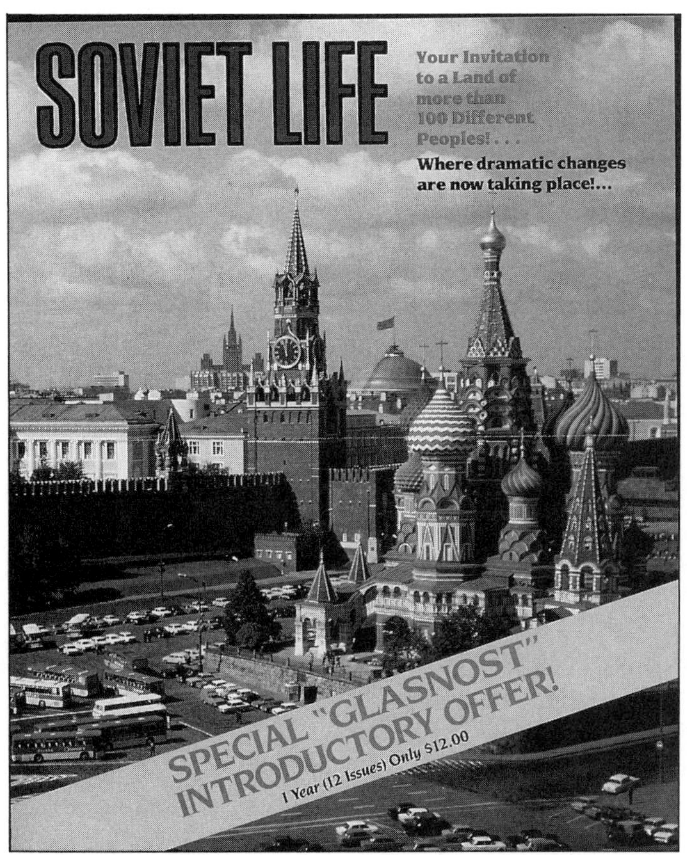

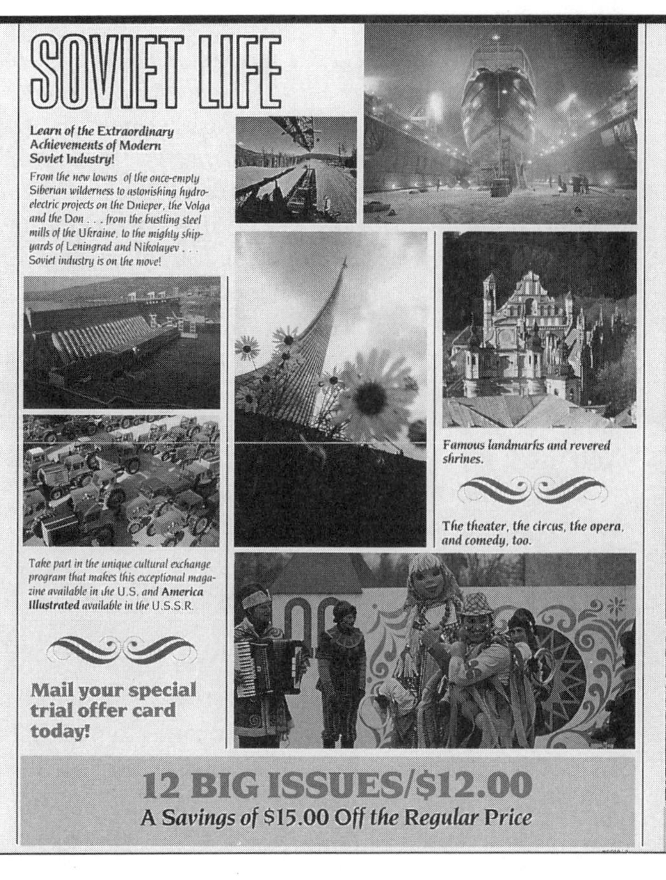

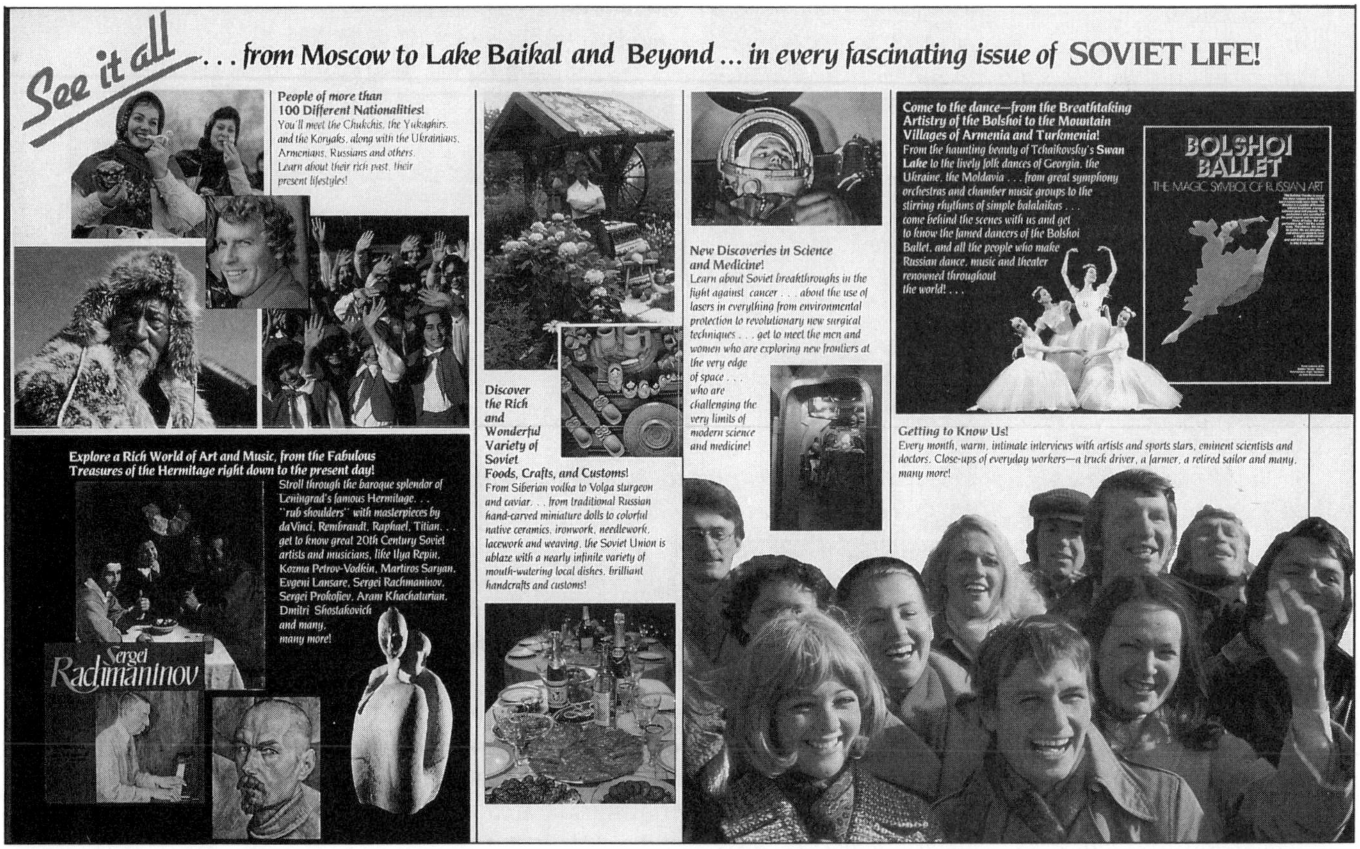

See it all . . . from Moscow to Lake Baikal and Beyond ... in every fascinating issue of SOVIET LIFE!
People of more than 100 Different Nationalities!
You'll meet the Chukchis, the Yukaghirs, and the Koryaks, along with the Ukrainians, Armenians, Russians and others. Learn about their rich past, their present lifestyles!
Explore a Rich World of Art and Music, from the Fabulous Treasures of the Hermitage right down to the present day!
Stroll through the baroque splendor of Leningrad's famous Hermitage. . . "rub shoulders" with masterpieces by daVinci, Rembrandt, Raphael, Titian. . . get to know great 20th Century Soviet artists and musicians, like Ilya Repin, Kozma Petrov-Vodkin, Martiros Saryan, Evgeni Lansere, Sergei Rachmaninov, Sergei Prokofiev, Aram Khachaturian, Dmitri Shostakovich and many, many more!
Sergei Rachmaninov
Discover the Rich and Wonderful Variety of Soviet Foods, Crafts, and Customs!
From Siberian vodka to Volga sturgeon and caviar. . . from traditional Russian hand-carved miniature dolls to colorful native ceramics, ironwork, needlework, lacework and weaving, the Soviet Union is ablaze with a nearly infinite variety of mouth-watering local dishes, brilliant handcrafts and customs!
New Discoveries in Science and Medicine!
Learn about Soviet breakthroughs in the fight against cancer . . . about the use of lasers in everything from environmental protection to revolutionary new surgical techniques . . . get to meet the men and women who are exploring new frontiers at the very edge of space . . . who are challenging the very limits of modern science and medicine!
Come to the dance—from the Breathtaking Artistry of the Bolshoi to the Mountain Villages of Armenia and Turkmenia!
From the haunting beauty of Tchaikovsky's Swan Lake to the lively folk dances of Georgia, the Ukraine, the Moldavia . . . from great symphony orchestras and chamber music groups to the stirring rhythms of simple balalaikas . . . come behind the scenes with us and get to know the famed dancers of the Bolshoi Ballet, and all the people who make Russian dance, music and theater renowned throughout the world! . . .
BOLSHOI BALLET
THE MAGIC SYMBOL OF RUSSIAN ART
Getting to Know Us!
Every month, warm, intimate interviews with artists and sports stars, eminent scientists and doctors. Close-ups of everyday workers—a truck driver, a farmer, a retired sailor and many, many more!

The 4-color brochure, printed on a coated 9″ × 15″ sheet of paper that folds down to 4½″ × 7½″.

NO POSTAGE NECESSARY IF MAILED IN THE UNITED STATES

BUSINESS REPLY CARD
First Class Permit No. 15, Fredericksburg, VA 22404

Postage will be paid by addressee

SOVIET LIFE
Magazine
P.O. Box 578
Fredericksburg, VA 22404-9989

NOTE:
Soviet Life Magazine is published under a special reciprocal agreement between the governments of the United States of America and the Union of Soviet Socialist Republics. You are cordially invited to be included among a limited number of United States citizens privileged to receive one of the world's most colorful and exciting publications.

The reply card shown front and back, along with the business reply envelope. Yet another effort with both a business reply *card* and a business reply *envelope*.

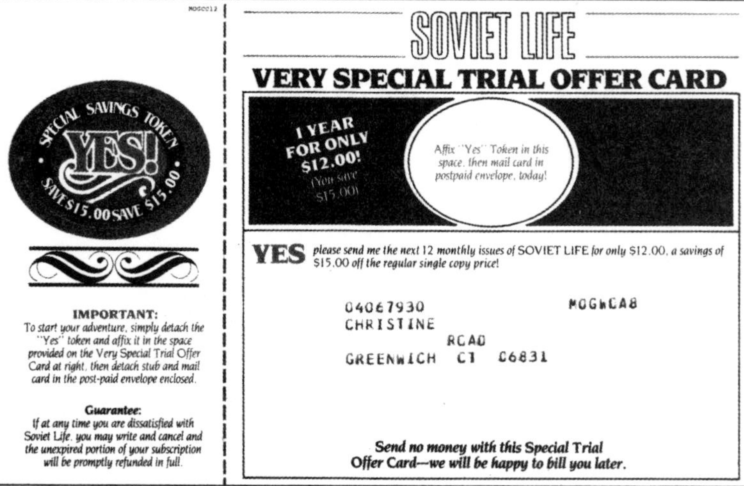
SPECIAL SAVINGS TOKEN
YES!
SAVE $15.00 SAVE $15.00

IMPORTANT:
To start your adventure, simply detach the "Yes" token and affix it in the space provided on the Very Special Trial Offer Card at right, then detach stub and mail card in the post-paid envelope enclosed.

Guarantee:
If at any time you are dissatisfied with Soviet Life, you may write and cancel and the unexpired portion of your subscription will be promptly refunded in full.

SOVIET LIFE
VERY SPECIAL TRIAL OFFER CARD

1 YEAR FOR ONLY $12.00! (You save $15.00)

Affix "Yes" Token in this space, then mail card in postpaid envelope, today!

YES please send me the next 12 monthly issues of SOVIET LIFE for only $12.00, a savings of $15.00 off the regular single copy price!

04067930 MOGWCA8
CHRISTINE
RCAD
GREENWICH CT 06831

Send no money with this Special Trial Offer Card—we will be happy to bill you later.

There were Savings Tokens, of course, and Discount Tokens, Free Book Tokens, Special Privilege Tokens, Guarantee Tokens, First Edition Tokens, Validation Tokens, Extra Bonus Tokens, Bonus Gift Tokens, and even "Maybe" Tokens. At least twenty-eight different flavors in all.

Initially, we tested a tip-on gold-foil "Mickey Mouse" token for Mondadori—and got the highest response they've ever had on a book promotion. In France, we developed computer-personalized "Oui" and "Non" tokens for L'Express, *the French news magazine—and achieved startling results. The potential of the token, the most versatile of direct action devices, seemed limited only by copywriters' and creative directors' fertile imaginations.*

In the mid-seventies, the popularity and use of the token began to decline—a decline that has continued until the present time. Yet the decline seems due more to creative exhaustion or indifference than to any falling off of response or appeal. We discovered early on that a well-conceived and executed action device—plain and simple token or thinly disguised token—can usually outpull nearly identical mailing pieces without them. The token is, in fact, quite alive, very well, and flourishing in places where they take direct mail seriously—and measure response carefully.

When we helped to launch Smithsonian books, we were at first hesitant to use tokens or action devices of any kind, not because we thought they wouldn't work, but because of our concern that both readers of Smithsonian *magazine, and members of Congress—who act as watchdogs over the activities of the* quasi-public Smithsonian Institution—might object to their use as "too commercial." We couldn't have been more wrong. On our third Smithsonian book promotion, offering a book on the National Zoo, we tried a rather charming pen-and-ink "Panda" token—and results were spectacular. Because the token was executed tastefully, and because it was appropriate to the marketing situation, it worked and worked well. Later, we even developed a four-color "Johann Sebastian Bach" token for Smithsonian's nine-record album of Bach's music (the rest of the mailing piece was executed in two colors only)—and achieved another lively success. Since then, tokens of one kind or another have been the mainstay of most Smithsonian book promotions.

As the Ubiquitous Sweepstakes, the plastic insurance card, and ever more sophisticated computer formats have come to dominate the direct mail scene in the late seventies and early eighties, the humble token seems to be more and more relegated to the back seat. Worse still, when tokens are used nowadays, concept, design, and execution are usually painfully uninspired—there are probably more totally boring, tacky, and tedious tokens in the mail than ever before. And that's a pity, because it needn't be that way.

In recent years we've developed highly successful ink-jet personalized tokens for L'Express and both Free Gift "Scuba Diver" tokens and ink-jet personalized "Membership Card" tokens for the International Oceanographic Foundation.

Take a look at Walter Weintz's winning Sweepstakes mailing piece for Great American magazines. The action device is a thin, plastic, numbered, and personalized "Verification Card"—that you keep. A variation on the insurance card. But, essentially, it's still a special kind of action device. A kind of token, if you will.

Our current control piece for Soviet Life, the U.S./U.S.S.R. cultural exchange magazine, is a brisk and colorful "Yes" token—it outpulled the previous control by better than 100 percent. And our first two renewal efforts for Soviet Life utilized a "Da!" token!

Of course, tokens and action devices don't always work, aren't always appropriate, sometimes shouldn't be used—and used inappropriately they can even decrease response. For example, in the late 1960s we did a mailing for Holiday magazine. Figuring that if a penny worked well, an actual Austrian 5-groschen coin would work better. Ah but alas, it seems people kept the coin as a souvenir and threw the order card away; twenty years later we're still waiting for our first response.

The truth is, the token is not only NOT dead, it's not even slightly wounded. Action devices still work. And can be made to work better than ever—by utilizing them to work in harmony with all the exciting new technical developments available to us today. All that's required, after all, is imagination, creativity, and sound marketing know-how. And a sense of taste and appropriateness sometimes helps, too. That's all. It doesn't seem too much to ask.

13

Starting from Scratch: The Launch of a Magazine

One of the tidiest assignments a writer-designer team can have is to be hired to create a new subscriber package for a magazine. Here is the background material a seasoned professional will ask for:

1. *A full year of issues*
2. *A media kit*

This is the material sent out by the sales reps to potential advertisers. The media kit tells you how the people at the magazine describe it to outsiders—in effect, how they see themselves.

Every now and then a copywriter will read through back issues and form an opinion of what the magazine is all about, only to discover that the people who created the media kit see it as something completely different. When this happens, the writing assignment can turn out to be difficult—if not impossible. You may want to consider turning down the assignment; otherwise, you could find yourself in snarling fights and with horrendous revision problems.

An example. I used to be a subscriber to the *Economist.* It was (and is) a British weekly magazine that does what *Time, Newsweek,* and *U.S. News & World Report* do, but without any of the flash and dynamic graphics. International coverage is far more detailed and there are no gossip or people features. Where the writing in its American counterparts has been purposely dumbed down over the years until it is currently at about the fifth- or sixth-grade level so as to appeal to the widest possible audience, the *Economist*'s prose is dense, almost scholarly.

Curiously, the folks at the *Economist* see themselves as direct competitors of *Forbes, Fortune,* and *Business Week.* When I first started publishing *Who's Mailing What!* Beth Maher, the *Economist*'s circulation director, refused to subscribe until I would agree to list her publication with business and financial magazines rather than with the newsweeklies. (I refused and she subscribed anyway.)

3. The four bestselling newsstand covers
Magazines sell at newsstands because of the power of the cover. If a direct mail package contains a brochure that shows covers of the magazine, it makes sense to use those covers that have proved their effectiveness by evoking the most response on the newsstand.

4. A sample of the current control mailings

5. Samples of past mailings that have worked

6. Samples of past mailings that have bombed

7. A list of lists
(the people to whom you will be writing)

With these elements in hand, a copywriter has just about everything needed to create a direct mail subscription package. The job of the writer is to get to know everything about the magazine—and its many features—and then *turn those features into benefits* to the person opening the mailing.

For example, a feature of *Gourmet* might be bread recipes from the greatest bakeries in the world. The *benefits* of such a feature: "Forget all your cares and woes as you have the satisfaction of kneading this wonderful dough, watching it rise like magic, and then getting out all your aggressions by punching it down again. . . ." "Imagine the heavenly smells coming out of your kitchen as you create magnificent bread for a fraction of what Parisians gladly pay. . . ." "Your friends and family will be dazzled—not only by the buttery, melt-in-your-mouth taste, but with your culinary wizardry. . . ."

When the Magazine Does Not Yet Exist

What is a copywriter to do when there are *no* issues in print and when, in fact, the magazine exists only inside the heads of a publisher and an editor? There might be an editorial policy statement, a list of possible articles and features, perhaps a dummy cover, and maybe a dummy spread or two. But not much more.

The challenge: turn that amorphous nothing into a living, breathing magazine. Create a mailing that makes the magazine seem so real, so important, and so full of benefits that anyone who opens the envelope not only believes it really exists, but *has to have it* (or at least send for a free issue under the no-risk trial offer).

The copywriter's job in a start-up situation is infinitely more complex than creating a package for an existing magazine. First, the copywriter must get inside the heads of the people who will be receiving the mailing and *become those people*; the next step is to figure out exactly what they want and then come up with a string of benefits based not on an existing magazine, but—on the vague hopes and dreams of the publisher and editor. And all the while the writer has to be inside the heads of the publisher and editor so as not to stray too far from what they have in mind.

Bill Jayme, probably the best-known freelancer in the world, has created a slew of winning packages over the years for nonexistent magazines. Because of his reputation, Jayme's clients do what he tells them to do. The features, the article titles, the benefits, and the look and feel of the magazine—all are as much Jayme's (and that of his enormously gifted partner, designer Heikki Ratalahti) as the editor's and publisher's.

Frequently, the launch process can be a mine field. Remember, the copy and artist's comprehensives may be the first time the publisher and editor have actually "seen" their magazine in the flesh. A typical reaction: "This isn't my magazine."

"Why isn't it?" the writer will ask.

"I don't know. This just isn't the magazine."

"Could you be specific?"

The publisher glances through the copy. "For example, I never said this."

"Actually you did. Here are my notes from the interview."

"Well, that's not what I meant."

"What did you mean?"

"I don't know. All I know is that this isn't my magazine."

For writer and publisher alike, the encounter can be a nightmare.

I remember once the founding publisher of *Working Woman*, Beatrice Buckler, had an idea for a magazine for older women. Buckler and her consultant, Paul Goldberg, hired renowned freelancer Linda Wells to write the launch package. Wells submitted copy and design and Buckler was totally dissatisfied. The mailing package did not reflect what she had in mind. Suddenly two very strong-willed people had different ideas as to what this magazine was to be.

Wells met with Buckler, who gave her a line-by-line critique. Wells then went away, incorporated all of Buckler's changes, and resubmitted the copy. It was rejected as being more wrong than the original version.

Consultant Paul Goldberg asked me to read the copy and critique it; in my opinion, it was weak. I asked to see Wells's original version, and it bowled me over. It was powerful, energetic, filled with marvelous imagery and benefits. It was as brilliant a direct mail effort as I had ever read. But it was Buckler's magazine, not Wells's.

I knew immediately what had happened. Wells had attacked this challenge with gusto, enthusiasm, and love, putting the very core of her being into it. When Buckler started nitpicking it to death, it was like a kick in the stomach to Wells, who probably lost enthusiasm, simply typed in Buckler's changes, and went on to other work.

Neither of Wells's versions was ever mailed; the magazine never got off the ground.

Lear's

In 1987 three different mailing packages were mailed to launch a magazine for older women. All three packages had a lift letter from Frances Lear that started:

Dear Friend:

Five years ago, on a brilliantly sunny day in October, I left Los Angeles and a 28-year marriage to the television producer, Norman Lear.

I landed in New York, my hometown as a young woman, with two suitcases of the only clothes I really wore and a few sheets of paper on which I had scribbled an idea for a magazine. A magazine for women like myself, for the "woman who wasn't born yesterday." For the woman who did not have a magazine of her own.

LEAR'S

655 Madison Avenue
NY, NY 10021-8043

Bulk Rate
U.S. Postage
PAID
LEAR'S

A special invitation to a woman who has reached the interesting age

CAR-RT.SORT.** CR38
894 67454805 ORZEL
R L
ST
NEW YORK NY 10022

The favor of a reply is requested

MAILER: *Lear's*
PACKAGE: "Congratulations"
PROJECT MGR.: Mirta Soto
CONSULTANT: Dick LaMonica
WRITER: Linda Wells
DESIGNER: John Wagman Design
FIRST MAILED: 1988
Linda Wells's 6″ × 9″ 2-window envelope.

LEAR'S

Congratulations! You've been a daughter, perhaps a student, a bride, a mother, a career woman, a community leader. You've cared, shared and nurtured. One thing is certain--you've reached that interesting age when you can make the most of yourself!

Congratulations! Now there's a magazine for women like you--women with your character, courage and sense of fun. Women who are exploring their own possibilities and changing their lives for the better. It's LEAR'S. And this is your Special Invitation to preview your first issue

FREE!

Dear Reader:

Some women love it.

Some women loathe it.

Some women shut their eyes and endure it.

No, I'm not talking about sex--yet! I'm talking about the inevitability of change in your future. Sometimes, a health crisis sparks the change. Sometimes, a financial windfall--or sudden financial need. Sometimes, a career success--or burnout. Sometimes, children growing up. And sometimes, a divorce or widowhood shocks you into a new lifestyle.

In my case, it was divorce. After 28 years, my marriage to television producer Norman Lear cracked open at the thin lines of its discontent. On a brilliantly sunny day in October, 1985, I left Los Angeles for New York and an unknown future. But soon, I found old friendships. Lunched with "the ladies." But soon, I found myself silently screaming, "IS THIS ALL THERE IS?"--and decided I'd better take command of myself and control of my life.

I turned to women's magazines for advice. Some

(over please)

advice! "How To Lose your Wrinkles at Lunch." "How To Open a Checking Account." "Why Be Thigh Shy?" "Sex and the Married Boss." "457 Ways to Cook Hamburger." "How to Redo your Kitchen for under $20."

As I leafed through page after page of this fatuous nonsense, I realized I had found a job worth doing. I decided to start the first magazine for stylish, sophisticated and civilized adult women--women who are mature enough to be interesting.

LEAR'S is a magazine for you, I hope!

A magazine for you, as a woman with a past. A magazine for you, as a woman who could use intelligent help with present problems. A magazine for you, as a woman with a growing range of future possibilities. A magazine about your health and fitness, beauty and fashion, education and career, money and investments, relationships and love life, social life and cultural interests.

Your Body, Your Mind

Come with LEAR'S to the world's leading spas, salons, health clubs and medical centers, where you'll meet experts who specialize in the physical and emotional changes mid-life brings.

Talk with researchers who have exciting news about life and longevity from the cutting edge of science. Let therapists work out moderate exercise programs you can fit into your busiest day. Have nutritionists plan commonsense diets that don't devastate your social life. Listen to people like Dr. David Zigond, a London psychotherapist and authority on psychosomatics who believes that power is the most potent medicine of all.

"There is a great deal of evidence to show that a sense of hope and purpose influence the immune system of the body, and that people who have them are less likely to get ill than those with hopeless feelings about themselves...those who feel powerless and not in control of their lives."

With LEAR'S your body will soon know who's boss. You'll join the ranks of women who have made the most of themselves, regardless of age...the women you'll admire on the cover of LEAR'S.

Prime Minister Margaret Thatcher might be a LEAR'S "cover girl." So might Barbara Jordan, Diane Sawyer, Elizabeth Dole, Doris Lessing, Joanne Woodward, Erma Bombeck and a host of women from Savannah to Seattle.

Your Beauty, Your Style

Coco Chanel started it. Katherine Hepburn Americanized it. Grace Kelly personified it. Tina Turner has brought it up to

The 4-page main letter, printed on 11″ × 17″ sheet and signed by Frances Lear.

The story of the letter—and the launch of *Lear's*—is fascinating. For starters, there was more to the second paragraph than meets the eye. In addition to two suitcases and a few sheets of paper, Frances Lear landed in New York with another little piece of paper—a check for $140 million, which was one-half of Norman Lear's fortune.

Frances Lear sounded like a woman who wasn't born yesterday, but then, neither were her predecessors—three enormously gifted, but woefully undercapitalized women who put their fortunes on the line to start similar magazines, only to be chewed up and spat out by money men: Beatrice Buckler, Judy Daniels, who founded *Savvy*, and Barbara Hertz, who bet everything on *Prime Time* for people over forty, and took a huge personal financial bath. Unlike Buckler, Daniels and Hertz, Lear had the cash to turn her dream into reality.

The original *Lear's* mailing package was one of two created by Clark Direct. The third was written by the late Hank Burnett.

At the time, I talked to Penny Marsh and Mark Liu at *Lear's* and to Meg Fidler at Clark Direct. The consensus was that all three packages date. By "it," I mean elegance with individualism--a look that tells the world you are about making the most of yourself.

"It" is easy and fun to come by with LEAR'S. Our fashion and beauty editors will cover international openings and shop the world's best shops to help you meet the challenge of your changing private and public life.

Our models will be marvelously mature adults like you, photographed in places you go and would love to go. The office, the committee room, the country club, the private party, the charity gala, the week-end getaway, the once-in-a-lifetime vacation.

You'll travel far and wide with LEAR'S. To the most interesting places. To the most interesting houses. To the most interesting parties and major events. En route, you'll see how other interesting women decorate their homes, design their gardens and display such poised perfection as hostesses, no one would ever guess they had full-time outside commitments.

Your Finances, Your Career

If you're like most of us at LEAR'S, you've not only had to take command of your life, you've had to learn to control your finances. You're bombarded with advice from bankers, brokers, real estate agents, estate planners and other money men who use big words to make you feel like "the little woman" again.

Phooey! In LEAR'S, the nation's top money managers and lawyers treat you with the respect your intelligence and experience demand. They tell you how they choose their own advisers...how they evaluate recommendations...what really goes on in backrooms and boardrooms that should affect your decisions.

Regardless of how your personal numbers crunch, you may have decided to go to work, return to work or start a new business. And who can help you better than women who've already done it themselves?

So in every issue of LEAR'S you'll connect with entrepreneurs and other successful women. A woman who went from secretary to Secretary of State of Texas. The housewife who started Access Philadelphia. A mother who makes millions from toys. A divorcee who found two new careers when she moved from mainland U.S.A. to St. Barts in the Caribbean.

Your Family, Your Friendships, Your Loves

In LEAR'S, interesting men and women talk to you from their minds--their hearts--in articles that are as comic, tragic, silly,

(over please)

serious and surprising as your own life has become.

Carol Matthau opens up about love, pain, sex, William Saroyan, Walter Matthau, hope and more. Mercedes Gregory reveals a story of quiet courage --how she saved her marriage and career without being consumed by the powerful theatrical personalities all around her.

Colonial Africa provides the background for Doris Lessing's drama of a daughter learning to understand her mother. John Leonard remembers his. Elinor Klein speaks out in praise of younger friends. Roger Rosenblatt discusses the wounds and blessings of age.

In future issues of LEAR'S, we'll cover mature love, sex and sensuality from every possible point of view. Some articles will be based on important new scientific findings. Others will come from personal experience. But LEAR'S will never trivialize the subject with the kind of inane how-to articles that assume you are an infant, an acrobat--and an idiot.

Your Magazine
With my Compliments
And sincerest Congratulations!

I know you're no fool. You weren't born yesterday. So I want you to try LEAR'S before you buy it. If you accept my invitation today, I will send you a free preview issue of LEAR'S and enter your subscription at no risk or obligation. If it's your kind of magazine, join us as a subscriber at Special Savings of 50% off the single copy price.

You'll pay only $18.00 for 11 more issues (12 in all). That is a savings of $18.00 off the single copy price. And with it, you will get a Special Money-Back Guarantee--if at any time you decide to cancel, you get a refund on any unmailed issues.

If you don't like LEAR'S, just write "cancel" across the bill when you get it, return the bill unpaid and keep your FREE Preview issue with my compliments.

Please do not send any money now! We'll bill you later, after you've made up your mind. In the meantime, I'd just like to say CONGRATULATIONS on being the interesting woman you are. It's our goal at LEAR'S to help you enjoy the challenge of change in your life and make every day more interesting than the last!

Sincerely,

Frances Lear

Frances Lear
Founder and Editor-in-Chief

were so heavily edited and rewritten by Buckler and her consultant, Robert Shnayerson, that no one is sure who did what.

The result of all this client diddling was predictable; the packages were so much alike there was no clear winner. Results all fell within 10 percent of one another.

Unlike Buckler, Daniels, and Hertz, Frances Lear had plenty of capital. So she hired Linda Wells to create a package. This was during the start-up of the magazine, so Wells, once again, did not have a year's worth of issues to work from. Maybe Wells was lucky enough to have seen a prototype plus an issue or two.

You see several elements from Linda Wells's *Bon Appétit* package in Chapter 10: "The favor of a reply" on the outer envelope . . . the letter starting with "Congratulations!" . . . and the "Accept/Decline" tokens.

One rule breaker in this package: it is very rare to see a main letter and a lift letter signed by the same person, but both are signed by Frances Lear.

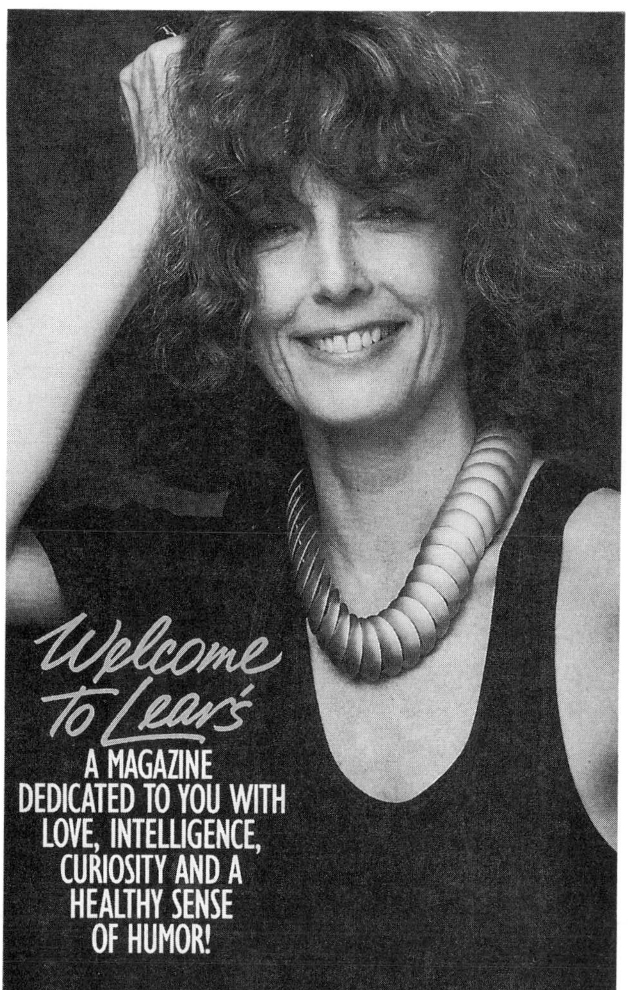

The $5\frac{1}{4}'' \times 8''$ brochure cover features an attractive "older" woman with an impish smile, printed in black and white. The inside of this brochure is printed in 4-color. It opens . . .

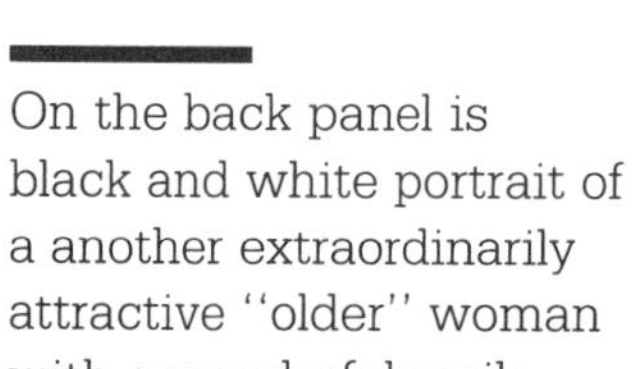

On the back panel is black and white portrait of a another extraordinarily attractive "older" woman with a wonderful smile.

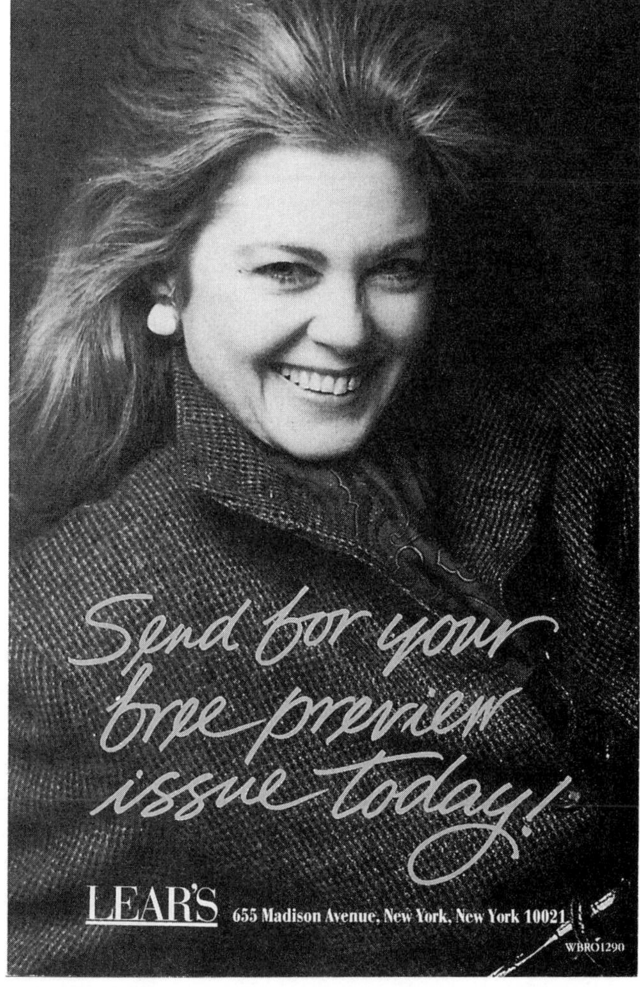

And opens . . .

And opens.

And opens . . .

And opens . . .

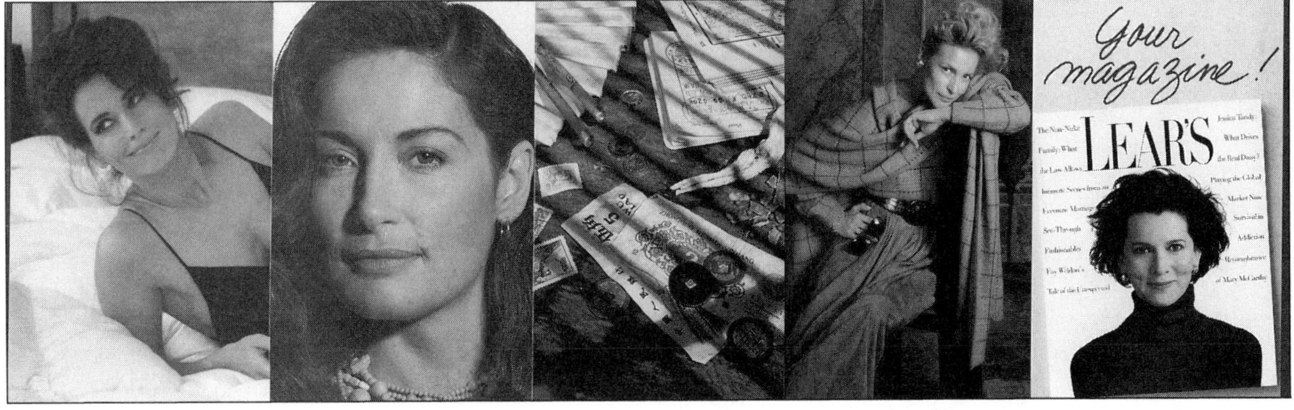

FRANCES LEAR

Dear Friend:

Five years ago, on a brilliantly sunny day in October, I left Los Angeles and a 28-year marriage to the television producer, Norman Lear.

I landed in New York, my hometown as a young woman, with two suitcases of the only clothes I really wore and a few sheets of paper on which I had scribbled an idea for a magazine. A magazine for women like myself, for the "the woman who wasn't born yesterday." For the woman who did not have a magazine of her own.

Something had happened to magazines (or something had happened to me) in the last few years that made my old favorites seem out of touch with my life.

I could not, as one magazine wrote on its cover, "lose my wrinkles at lunch." I could never look like Linda Evans. Articles that directed me to invest in this idea or save in that plan were either dense with technical terms or patronizingly simple.

The women's magazines were urging me to travel, but every resort showed pictures of slim young women in bikinis sipping tropical drinks with slim young men in bikinis. There was no room on those beach chairs for me -- even if I had been married.

The magazines I had been reading all my life seemed to have stood still -- filled with ads for rejuvenating creams on 17-year-old faces -- while I had gone on, the way all of us have.

We are more serious about ourselves and much more interesting. The dreams of women I know are about expressing their creativity, not competing in the tropics with teenagers.

That's why I decided to publish LEAR'S,
a magazine for "the woman who wasn't
born yesterday."

Women like you and me have lived in two very different worlds. We spend much of our lives tending, nurturing, encouraging and supporting others. To abandon this role would deprive us, for it is a truly wonderful one, but sooner or later the time comes for each of us to turn the central focus of our lives around to ourselves.

The ubiquitous "Frances Lear. . . ." lift letter.

-2-

We were brought up to believe in family and community and country and most of us had pretty definite ideas about what a woman's life was about. We questioned our role for 20 years and finally came to the conclusion that being traditional was fine. As a matter of fact, it was the way we wanted it as long as we also had the opportunity to create an identity of our own that was separate from others. That, essentially, is the purpose of LEAR'S.

LEAR'S will illuminate the growing range of possibilities now open to women -- in work, education, entertaining, fashion, beauty, travel, health, the arts, relationships, sexuality.

LEAR'S will meet your requirements for information -- about managing your money, changing careers or entering the work force for the first time, about looking great and feeling great, starting new relationships, going to new places and learning new things.

LEAR'S will encourage you in your pursuit of happiness -- wherever it takes you -- and help you to see every day from the best vantage point you can.

Won't you join us?

Use the order form and postpaid reply envelope enclosed to receive your first issue absolutely free.

Sincerely,

Frances Lear

FL:3JJ

Frances Lear
Founder and Editor-in-Chief

I'm
INTERESTING!
I'm
INTERESTED!

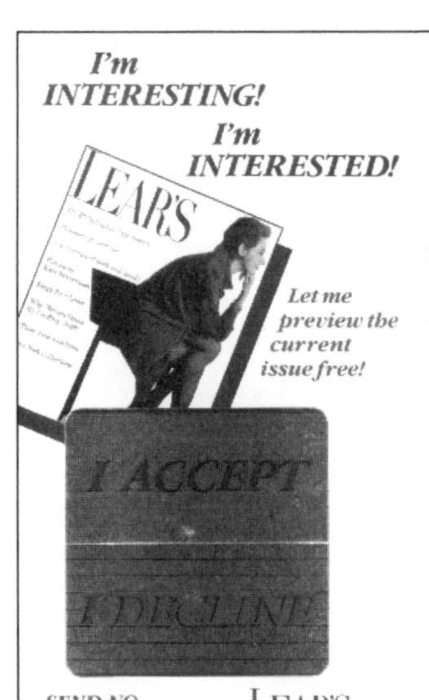

Let me preview the current issue free!

Detach here and mail in postage paid envelope provided.

Free Preview Issue

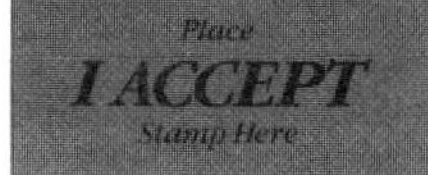

YES, send me the current issue of LEAR'S to preview free. If I'm interested, I'll join you as a Special Subscriber at savings of 50% off the single copy rate of $36. I'll pay just $18 for one full year (11 additional issues, 12 in all). If LEAR'S is not for me, I'll write "cancel" across the bill when I get it, pay nothing, owe nothing and keep the issue absolutely free.

No, thank you. I am not interested now. Please keep me in mind for future offer.

CAR-RT-SORT.** CR38
894 62454805 ORZE1
R L
ST
NEW YORK NY 10022

SEND NO MONEY NOW!
Mail this card to:

LEAR'S
P.O. Box 53216
Boulder, CO 80321-3216

WOC1290A

NO POSTAGE
NECESSARY
IF MAILED
IN THE
UNITED STATES

BUSINESS REPLY MAIL
FIRST CLASS MAIL PERMIT NO. 1208 BOULDER, COLORADO

POSTAGE WILL BE PAID BY ADDRESSEE

LEAR'S
P.O. BOX 53216
BOULDER, COLORADO 80321-3216

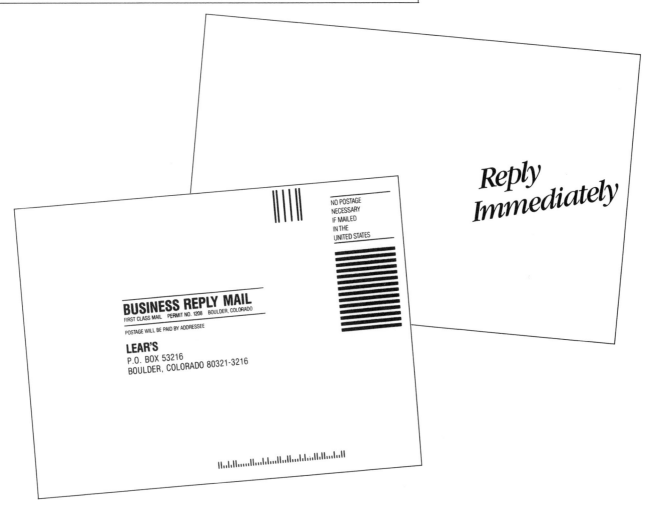

Reply Immediately

The order form with silver metallic "I Accept/I Decline" pressure sensitive token and business reply card.

Condé Nast's *Traveler*

The 4-page letter, printed in 2 colors on an 11″ × 17″ sheet and folded 3 times.

Whenever Condé Nast starts a magazine, there is one writer S. I. Newhouse insists on creating the launch package: Emily Soell, who operates under the official title of vice chairman and COO of Rapp Collins Marcoa, the great New York direct response agency founded by the legendary Stan Rapp and Tom Collins. In actuality, Soell is one of the greatest direct mail writers at work today.

EMILY SOELL:

When the package for Condé Nast's Traveler *magazine was created there was no magazine.*

There was no copy for the magazine. No art for the magazine. There was only a concept. A competitor. A target audience. And a very engaging editor whose desk was heaped with itty bitty pieces of paper upon which he had scribbled a host of ideas.

But, the shortage of data made no difference. Because the package isn't about the product. It's about the prospect. From the line on the envelope to the opening of the letter, to the fluency of the brochure . . . it's about YOU—your preferences, your passions, your needs and dreams, all captured in your kind of travel magazine.

MAILER: *Condé Nast Traveler*
PACKAGE: Launch effort
PROJECT MGR.: Joanne Wallenstein
AGENCY: Rapp Collins Marcoa
ACCOUNT MGR.: Cindy Abrams
WRITER: Emily Soell
DESIGNER: Jerry Genova
FIRST MAILED: 1987
The 6″ × 9″ outside envelope.

Bulk Rate
U.S. Postage
PAID
Permit No. 1187
Philadelphia, PA

ANNOUNCING

A magazine for people who love to travel but don't care much for travel magazines.

850 07662142 CAR-RT ST CR17
DNU
0E67
Susan
The
2300 St. 519
Philadelphia, PA 19103

Special
$1 AN ISSUE
offer enclosed

Condé Nast
Traveler

From the publishers of *Vogue, Gourmet, House & Garden, GQ* and *Vanity Fair*...

...something new and completely different in travel magazines, for people who demand the unique—both when they travel and when they read magazines.

NOW ONLY $1 AN ISSUE

Dear Friend:

We know you...

...You find a few extra dollars in your pocket--a crack in your impossibly busy schedule--and what do you do?

Take off, that's what! For a Greek Island, a Caribbean beach, a Colorado ski slope...for a French pension, a Spanish posada, a New England inn...for carnival in Rio or Venice or New Orleans...to see the beautiful people in today's new hot spots or find a spot where you'll see almost no one at all.

In many ways we are you...

...Not satisfied only with guided tours and main attractions, but always poking around in the nooks and crannies of the places you go.

...Endlessly curious about the culture, the history, the people--how they live, how they make their living, where they make their homes. Wondering what it would be like to live there yourself.

...Wanting to know how to get around easily, independently, to see the real place, interact with the people, be welcomed, be able to take home--not just photographs--personal experiences.

You don't get much help from conventional travel magazines.

BUT...now there is a new magazine that leads you to the back roads, down side streets and cobblestone lanes...to colorful shops, pubs, local restaurants...food, flower, antique markets...docks and pocket parks and small churches you love to explore. Tells you how much it costs to buy a cottage there, rent a condo, own a chalet in the mountains or a villa on the sea.

A magazine that makes the history of a place come alive in its

(over, please)

pages. And maps a route so you can relive history when you go. To see the 39 houses where Beethoven lived in Vienna...walk the same Dominican beach that dazzled Columbus...visit the "love pavilions" outside Paris where Madame du Barry conducted her amours.

A magazine that tells you how to take the subway in Stockholm... make a phone call in Paris...how much to tip the taxi driver in St. Thomas, the porter in Palm Beach, the concierge in Cannes...whether to tip for great service if service is already included in the bill.

In short, a magazine created by people like you, for people like you. It's called Condé Nast Traveler. And we (the folks who created it) are so excited about it, so eager for you to see it, judge it, and conclude it's like no other travel magazine, that we're going to make you a wonderful offer:

Right now, you can subscribe for only $1 an issue. $12 for 12 issues--a 60% savings off the newsstand price.

What makes us so sure we'll be able to delight and enchant you where others may have failed? Three main reasons.

FIRST--our creators and contributors--an unbeatable combination! We formed an alliance with the respected, reliable travel experts at Fodor's--publishers of over 120 travel guidebooks--as well as with Paul Grimes, originator of "The Practical Traveler" column in the Sunday New York Times, who is our Editor at Large. That means you'll find each issue of our magazine is packed with real inside information --the kind only experienced, well-connected, professional travelers have access to. And of course, Condé Nast--the people who bring you Vogue, Gourmet, House & Garden, Gentlemen's Quarterly, Vanity Fair, is our publisher. That means our magazine is stylish, elegant, knowing, provocative, gossipy, beautiful to look at--quality!

SECOND--our continuing goal is to give you a magazine that is magnificently entertaining--whether you need to make immediate travel plans or not. Filled with fascinating information you won't find anywhere else. With inspiration and intelligence to enable you to know and enjoy our world more--even when you're staying home.

AND FINALLY...a magazine that's designed to be useful, usable! With articles and features you'll want to keep and refer to. With detail-packed pieces you'll want to take along. With digest summaries of the salient points in each issue, so you can have the facts you need at a glance.

What can you count on every month in Condé Nast Traveler! Well...

*Places--from our destination scouts...BUT, virtually unknown to the ordinary American traveler: Australia's mysterious Daintree rain forest; an Arabian night's oasis in Tunisia; unspoiled beaches and great prices on the tiny Caribbean island of Providencia.

*Prices--from our field correspondents: what souvenirs, crafts, clothing, etc. you should shop for; what $1,000 will buy you in Paris, London, Zurich, New York; what you can expect to pay for a week in a chateau, or a weekend in a hotel suite, or a night in a pension.

*The best (and sometimes worst) from our travel critics: the best small hotels, spas, ski runs, Caribbean beaches, dude ranches, safaris, cruises, air/tour travel packages, the best 50 restaurants in the world, best and worst duty-free deals.

*Charts--to show you current money rates, the weather, what to wear in major travel destinations worldwide.

*A three-month calendar--will alert you to exciting events you may want to travel to see. (Also, how to get tickets.)

*Maps--of important cities with key streets, sights, buildings accented. (Collect them! Soon you'll have a walking plan to the major cities in the world.)

*File articles--on an important place and what to see if you only have a short time to spend. The Vatican, the Metropolitan Museum, the Houses of Parliament--with floor plans. (Collect them! Soon you'll have a visiting plan for every major site in the world.)

*Drawings with callouts--of Bond Street or Rodeo Drive, for example--with all the stores captioned as to name, product, price. Or Greek Islands, identified--historic islands, beach islands, shopping islands--to help you make a choice.

We guide you to hideaways and getaways. Suggest escapes and escapades. Lead you off the beaten path, or...just off beat!

*The hot spot of the month--where the people who know are going.
*America's vanishing hideaways--places to go now(!) before the gawkers and graffiti writers ruin everything.
*The ultimate escape--going places where you can't be reached.
*Doing something different--feeding giraffes from your bedroom window in Kenya...going hot air ballooning over Newport... crossing India in a "Palace on Wheels" designed for maharajas.

We deal with the special travel challenges:

SINGLES: Advice on where to go, what to take, how to meet people, find resorts, hotels, tours, cruises that make you feel comfortable.

SPONTANEOUS TRAVELERS: Strategies for people who go without plans.

TIME AND MONEY CHALLENGES: How to see a place in two months, two weeks, two days, on a budget or with a bundle on hand.

(over, please)

PACKING: We bring you the pros' packing methods plus new gadgets to help you have everything but still travel light.

FOR BUSINESS TRAVELERS: Where to go if you only have evenings. What to see in an adjacent weekend. Daytime plans for a spouse.

We bring you places from the perspectives of some of today's most exciting writers, artists, personalities...

...and explore places from the perspectives of the classic travel writers themselves.

Flaubert's Brittany...Sir Harold Acton's Italy...
Dame Freya Stark's Arabia.

...but when it comes to recommendations, critiques, we do them from one perspective--yours, our readers. For your pleasure alone.

We invite you to participate in our magazine. To write us with your comments. To share your secrets. (We'll print them!) To be part of our family of people who love to go...and also love to know.

We promise integrity, candor, lack of bias. Our only responsibility is to you.

So, if you're intrigued by the magazine I've described to you, or curious to see if we can give you all the things we say--why not decide to try us? Right now you can lock in a $1-an-issue price!

Simply return the enclosed card and we'll put you down for a special introductory subscription--12 issues $12. (People who buy it on the newsstand will pay $2.50 an issue--more than double the price.) Your risk is nil. We GUARANTEE your satisfaction. If you're ever unhappy, just tell us. WE'LL REFUND EVERY PENNY ON ISSUES WE HAVEN'T MAILED.

The enclosed card is all we need to secure this special rate. There's no need to send money now unless you wish. We'll be happy to bill you later.

Send the card today and be among the first to see Condé Nast Traveler. For people who travel, it's a magazine that must be seen!

Sincerely,

Harold Evans

Harold Evans
Editor in Chief

KLAO

Like the circular for *Lear's*, the 4-color *Condé Nast Traveler* starts off $5^{1}/_{2}'' \times 7^{1}/_{2}''$ . . .

And it opens . . .

THE SECRET PLACES...

THE INSIDE STORIES...

And opens . . .

THE SECRET PLACES...
AND PEOPLE WHO WANT TO GO...
OFF THE BEATEN PATHWAYS...

And opens.

THE SECRET PLACES...
AND PEOPLE WHO WANT TO GO...
IN GRAND AND GENUINE STYLE...
INTO THE REAL LIFESTYLE
OF A PLACE

DREAMING... PACKING... READING...

HISTORIC PLACES...

OFFBEAT PLACES...

PLACES OFF THE BEATEN TRACK...

PEOPLE PLACES...

MAPPING...

DINING... SHOPPING...

UNDISCOVERED PLACES...

VANISHING PLACES...

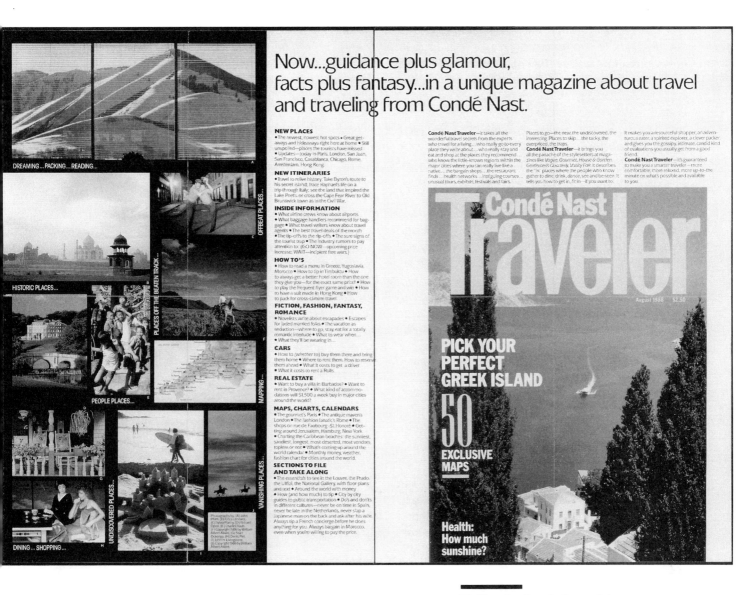

Now...guidance plus glamour, facts plus fantasy...in a unique magazine about travel and traveling from Condé Nast.

NEW PLACES

• The newest, nowest hot spots • Great get-aways and hideaways right here at home • Still unspoiled—places the tourists have missed • Updates—today in Paris, London, San Juan, San Francisco, Casablanca, Chicago, Rome, Amsterdam, Hong Kong.

NEW ITINERARIES

• Travel to relive history: Take Byron's route to his secret island; trace Raphael's life on a trip through Italy; see the land that inspired the Lake Poets, or cross the Cape Fear River to Old Brunswick town as in the Civil War.

INSIDE INFORMATION

• What airline crews know about airports • What baggage handlers recommend for baggage • What travel writers know about travel agents • The best travel deals of the month • The tip-offs to the rip-offs • The sure signs of the tourist trap • The industry rumors to pay attention to: (GO NOW—upcoming price increase; WAIT—incipient fare wars.)

HOW TO'S

• How to read a menu in Greece, Yugoslavia, Morocco • How to tip in Timbuktu • How to always get a better hotel room than the one they give you—for the exact same price! • How to play the frequent flyer game and win • How to have a suit made in Hong Kong • How to pack for cross-climate travel.

FICTION, FASHION, FANTASY, ROMANCE

• Novelists write about escapades • Escapes for jaded married folks • The vacation as seduction—where to go, stay, eat for a totally romantic interlude • What to wear when... • What they'll be wearing in...

CARS

• How to (*whether to*) buy them there and bring them home • Where to rent them. How to reserve them ahead • What it costs to get a driver • What it costs to rent a Rolls.

REAL ESTATE

• Want to buy a villa in Barbados? • Want to rent in Provence? • What kind of accommodations will $1,500 a week buy in major cities around the world?

MAPS, CHARTS, CALENDARS

• The gourmet's Paris • The antique maven's London • The fashion fanatic's Rome • The shops on rue de Faubourg-St. Honoré • Getting around Jerusalem, Hamburg, New York • Charting the Caribbean beaches: the sunniest, sandiest, longest, most deserted, most vendors, topless or not • What's coming up around the world calendar • Monthly money, weather, fashion chart for cities around the world.

SECTIONS TO FILE AND TAKE ALONG

• The *essentials* to see in the Louvre, the Prado, the Uffizi, the National Gallery, with floor plans and text • Around the world with money • How (and how much) to tip • City by city guides to public transportation • Do's and don'ts in different cultures—never be on time in Spain, never be late in the Netherlands, never slap a Japanese man on the back and ask after his wife. Always tip a French concierge *before* he does anything for you. Always bargain in Morocco, even when you're willing to pay the price.

Condé Nast Traveler—it takes all the wonderful travel secrets from the experts who travel for a living... who really go to every place they write about... who really stay and eat and shop at the places they recommend... who know the little-known regions within the major cities where you can really live like a native... the bargain shops... the restaurant finds... health networks... intriguing courses... unusual tours, exhibits, festivals and fairs.

Places to go—the new, the undiscovered, the interesting. Places to skip... the tacky, the overpriced, the traps.

Condé Nast Traveler—it brings you all the panache of the stylesetters at magazines like *Vogue, Gourmet, House & Garden, Gentlemen's Quarterly, Vanity Fair.* It describes the "in" places where the people who know gather to dine, drink, dance, see and be seen. It tells you how to get in, *fit in*—if you want to.

It makes you a resourceful shopper, an adventurous eater, a spirited explorer, a clever packer, and gives you the gossipy, intimate, candid kind of evaluations you usually get from a good friend.

Condé Nast Traveler—it's guaranteed to make you a smarter traveler—more comfortable, more relaxed, more up-to-the minute on what's possible and available to you.

Condé Nast Traveler

August 1988 $2.50

PICK YOUR PERFECT GREEK ISLAND

50 EXCLUSIVE MAPS

Health: How much sunshine?

Unlike the *Lear's* flyer, this one explodes into a 15″ × 21″ broadside.

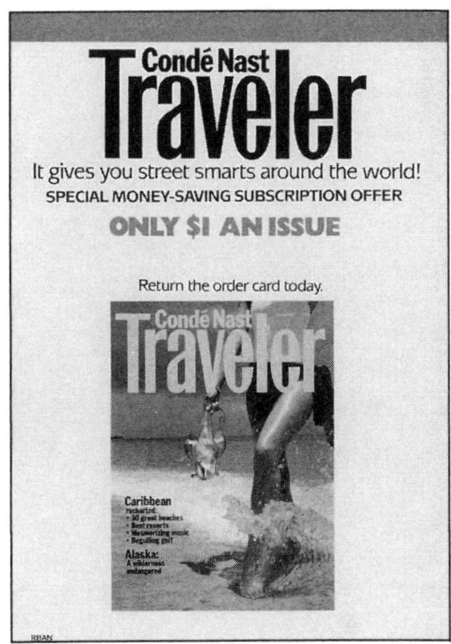

The back panel brings you back down to earth and offers all these wonders for only $1 an issue.

It is my conviction that if a direct mail package (or print ad, or television commercial . . .) can convince a reader that he is known and understood and valued *it is nine-tenths of the way to selling its wares.*

To me, the strength of this mailing turns on the envelope line. I have a personal method for coming up with envelope lines. It's really dumb. But it's mine.

After inundating myself with whatever material is available about the project, exhaustive discussions with the art director and a lot of nonsense doodling on a yellow pad (words . . . phrases . . . the beginnings of headlines . . . big pictures of eyes . . . small pictures of fish . . . ugly little stick figures stamping their feet . . .) I draw twelve $\frac{1}{2}$" × $2\frac{1}{4}$" *rectangles on a concept pad page. In each square I write a unique envelope line. I reflect as many different concepts, positionings, offers as I can think of, suspending, for the moment, good judgment, good taste, intelligence, experience, and sanity. I fill two or three pages if I can. Then I throw out all but three and hone those into the sharpest, most provocative, involving, and irresistible statements I can craft.*

The envelope line on this package was created thusly and it has proved itself over time. We have learned not to mess with it. Whenever we encumber it with a photo . . . or fool with the wording . . . we depress response.

Moreover, whenever the package starts to fatigue, we have managed to revive it simply by changing the color of the envelope. It started out red. Since then we have run it on green, blue, and yellow.

The 4-color order form and business reply envelope. The order form sells hard: "Special Money-Saving Offer" . . . A list of its distinguished sibling publications . . . "Only $1 an Issue—Save 60%" . . . "Satisfaction Guaranteed." Nowhere is a free issue offered. However, "Send no money now! We will bill you after you receive your first issue" is kind of a "buried comp copy" offer.

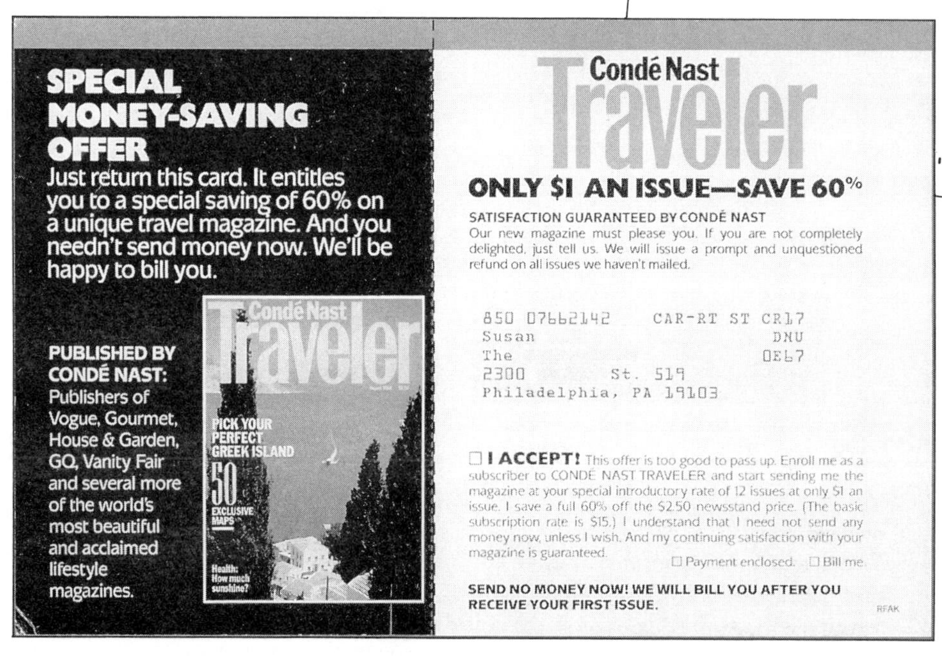

Utne Reader

Stan Rapp calls direct mail "intimate advertising." When a direct mail effort arrives in the mailbox, it is in the company of the most highly personal correspondence: wedding invitations, letters from the kid stationed in Germany, refunds from the IRS, social security checks, bills from the plastic surgeon. In the workplace environment, a direct mail effort is right there among memos from the field, job performance ratings, your new stripped-down health insurance benefits, the notice of a raise, and a "suggestion" from the boss that you spend the first week in February at that convention in Chicago.

To wander through the exhibit hall of any direct marketing conference is to go by booth after booth representing printers and fulfillment houses whose names start with *Auto-* . . . *Data-* . . . *Scan-* . . . *Info-* . . . *Compu-* . . . *Response-*. Pause for a split second and earnest young reps will engage you in deep conversation about how their system alone will enable you to create mailings so exquisitely personalized that they seem more real than the handwritten note from your snotty seven-year-old nephew who was pistol-whipped into scrawling a thank-you for the birthday present you sent him six months ago.

These days it seems the direct marketing industry is besotted with technology. Never mind the product or the offer. If the effort seems personal enough, prospects will be so appreciative of the seemingly special attention that they will order. The medium is the message. And more and more, the message is trickery.

As Bill Jayme has said:

Personalize indiscriminately at your peril. Do you really want as a customer some boob who gets turned on by seeing his own name repeated nine times in a single page?

The secret of successful direct mail is (1) reaching the right person, (2) dramatizing an offer that is important and believable, and (3) making each customer feel good about doing business with you.

Believability is the key. Consumers and business people are becoming more wily, seeing through the hype and fakery that are disguised in elaborate personalization.

Another kind of personalization is not accomplished by technology, but found within the copy. An example is in the personalized thank-you letter from Bill Bonner of Agora Marketing to new subscribers of his newsletter, *International Living.* In the course of the letter Bonner writes:

. . . And please do not hesitate to call on our TOLL FREE customer service line (800) 433-1528, if there is any problem. If the product you've purchased, or anyone in my organization fails to meet with your complete approval, I would like to know about it.

Our company specializes in two areas—investment and travel. To a large extent, these areas reflect my personal interests. Perhaps you share these interests. If so, please allow me to take a moment more of your time to tell you about an organization I am involved with called The Passport Club. It's a very useful group that appeals to both my desire to travel and my interest in financial topics . . .

. . . In short, I've found membership in the club to be a source of a lot of fun as well as a lot of profit.

What Bonner has done is inject himself personally into the correspondence with the new subscriber. It's obvious that Bonner (1) is a real person, (2) cares about excellence and customer satisfaction, (3) loves travel, (4) loves what he does, (5) is delighted to communicate that enthusiasm and share the benefits.

I call this "Reflexive Personalization" whereby the writer's personality comes through. The result: tremendous believability. You are made to feel that a real person has communicated with you; Bonner has created a mental image of himself as, perhaps, a boulevardier sipping an apéritif in a Parisian café or an amateur archaeologist in Indiana Jones hat and hiking boots prowling the ruins of Petra.

When a letter comes from a real person—and you can *see that person* in your mind—it closes the loop. Use Reflexive Personalization, and there may not be any need to spend a lot of money on elaborate computer work; the intimacy is there thanks to the copy, not the technology.

Reflexive Personalization, then, is giving your product or service personality by using a real person or situation. An analogy can be found in the 1991 U.S. Open Tennis Championships. In a sport dominated by sullen, scowling, serve-and-volley machines, many of them foreign, Jimmy Connors was the quintessential wild and crazy American kid (Kid? The man was thirty-nine years old!) who exploded onto the court

The #10 outside envelope for the *Utne Reader*, printed in 2 colors (the "FREE" circle is bright red).

THE ALTERNATIVE PRESS
READING & DINING SALON

invites you to sample the bill of fare of

UTNE READER

by sending for the next issue without cost or obligation

FREE

Dear Reader:

If you believe that exercise will help you live longer...that small companies are better to work for than big ones...and that you can't possibly make money while maintaining your principles...

...there's something you should know. It won't. They aren't. You can. And if revelations like these contradict axioms you learned at your mother's knee, there are more surprises to come. Just open UTNE READER to any page. Overturned truisms. Shattered shibboleths. Debunked bromides. Truth!

UTNE READER? Yes, UTNE READER. It's the new magazine that rekindles the kind of intellectual excitement we all enjoyed here in America before complacency set in. The magazine that's got people making up their own minds again instead of swallowing ideas whole. The magazine that gives you perspective. Opens your eyes. Saves you time and money.

Free issue. When you mail the enclosed card promptly, you'll get the next issue of UTNE READER with our compliments. No cost. No commitment. Free. If you like it? Subscribe and save yourself some silver. Read on!

UTNE READER was created a little over five years ago to bring you the best of the alternative press. Economic forecasts like you find in Dollars and Sense. Lifestyle how-to like you get from Mother Earth News. Politics -- American Spectator, Mother Jones, The Nation. Activism -- Ms., Earth First!, Dissent. Commentary -- The New Statesman, Foreign Policy, The Guardian.

The Cutting Edge -- The Village Voice, Washington Monthly, Rolling Stone. Fitness and Health -- Medical SelfCare, American Health, Whole Life Times. Science, Technology and the Environment --Audubon, Resurgence, Orion. Any and everything you ought to know about that you won't find in mainstream media.

UTNE READER isn't slick -- no glossy paper, no centerfolds, no scratch-and-sniff perfume packets -- but it is designed to please the eye as well as the mind. It's where more and more of the brightest movers and shakers are congregating. And what our magazine is doing for them, it can also do for you.

(over please)

Bill Jayme's 2-page letter, printed on a single 8½″ × 11″ sheet, front and back.

UTNE READER adds to your perspective. Here's Barbara Ehrenreich on today's crazed pursuit of "excellence." Ken Kesey on coming to terms with the death of his 20-year-old son. Alice Walker on saying goodbye to a dying friend. Gary Snyder on life in general. The meaning of marathoning according to Hunter Thompson. The jogger's prayer according to Tom Wolfe.

Here's Chris Mullin on Vietnam today. Allen Ginsberg on Nicaragua. Deena Metzger on careers in prostitution. Jonathan Rowe on Ralph Nader. Noam Chomsky on disarmament. Garrison Keillor on porches. "A good porch," Keillor observes, "lets you smoke, talk loud, eat with your fingers...without running away from home."

UTNE READER opens your eyes. Child abuse -- how parents can scar their kids worse than any molester. Dieting -- why are health authorities now telling you to forget it? Central America -- how is the administration censoring the news? Nazis -- if you think that they're ancient history, why should you think again? AIDS -- what's more dangerous than the disease?

Family farms -- how does saving them start at your supermarket? World peace -- what might you be doing? Stress -- how can you lessen it by taking on more responsibility? All these have been the focus of UTNE READER stories that reveal the facts without bias, pull no punches, help you get at the truth.

UTNE READER saves you time and money. The New York Times notes that the Lord's Prayer contains 56 words, the 23rd Psalm 118 words, the Gettysburg Address 226 words, and the Ten Commandments 297 words, while the U.S. Department of Agriculture directive on pricing cabbage weighs in at 15,629 words.

If you go for gospel over gobbledegook, brevity over bombast, pith over prolixity, our magazine can save you hours in reading time. It can also save you big bucks. Instead of paying $18, $24, $30 a year apiece for all the publications that interest you, you get the best of all of them with a single subscription to UTNE READER.

Send no money. To get a taste of UTNE READER, just mail the enclosed card. If the magazine goes down easy, your introductory price for a full year's subscription (6 bimonthly issues in all) is only $18. Single copy costs come to $24. You save a full $6.00.

Owe nothing. If UTNE READER doesn't sit well, though, just return the subscription bill marked "cancel," and that's the end of the matter. You've spent nothing. You owe nothing. You're under no further obligation. The issue is yours to keep with our thanks.

Early postmark. Only so many copies of each issue are published, and no more. In fairness, first come, first served. Avoid disappointment. Mail card quickly. Our gratitude. And bon appetit.

Cordially yours,

Carolyn Adams
For the Alternative Press
READING & DINING SALON

Utne Reader **• P.O. Box 1974 • Marion, Ohio 43306**

AB9LR

like a smart bomb from the Iraqi war. Late in the fifth hour of his quarterfinal match with Aaron Krickstein, with the crowd screaming at every point, Connors looked directly into a courtside television camera and shouted: "This is what they come for! This is what they want!" At that moment he had the television audience eating out of his hand along with the stadium crowd. Connors had put his unique stamp on the proceedings; he *personalized* them. Did the TV audience respond? The match garnered a 7.7 in the Nielsen overnights for 25 markets, giving CBS a 6.9 rating, up 22 percent from the comparable night the prior year.

Washington-based freelancer Richard Armstrong echoed these sentiments in a letter responding to a *Who's Mailing What!* article on Reflexive Personalization:

Your last newsletter, which focused on the issue of personalization, substantiated a long-standing theory of mine: Namely, that the most important word in direct mail copy (aside from "free" of course) is not "you"—as many of the textbooks would have it—but "I."

What makes a letter seem "personal" is not seeing your own name printed dozens of times across the page, or even being battered to death with a never-ending attack of "you's." It is, rather, the sense that one gets of being in the presence of the writer . . . that a real person sat down and wrote you a real letter. A heavily computerized letter, by contrast, seems less personal than it does robotic.

The direct-mail recipient, after all, doesn't need to be reminded that he is a real human being and that he has a real name. To the contrary, he needs to be assured that the letter he is reading comes from a human being—not a computer. And not a committee either.

Ironically, it is sometimes harder for professional copywriters to write this kind of copy than it is for our clients! (Although Frank Johnson, Tom Collins, and Ed McLean were and are masters of it.) Often it is the entrepreneurs and activists themselves—people like Joe Sugarman [JS & A], Gary Halbert [copywriter], Father Bruce Ritter [former head of Covenant House], Howard Ruff [publisher of Ruff Times*], and many others—who have the gift for putting their persuasive personalities on the printed page.*

A delicious example of Reflexive Personalization is to be found in the lift letter that Bill Jayme wrote for Eric Utne's signature. You can see in your mind's eye the motley assortment of eccentrics who create the magazine. *You're there* in that Minneapolis loft!

Before moving to California and freelancing, Bill Jayme was an executive with Time Inc., CBS, and McCann-Erickson in New York City. Among the magazines he and Ratalahti have launched over the past two decades: *Smithsonian, Bon Appétit, New York, Food & Wine, Mother Jones, Cooking Light,* and *California.*

BILL JAYME:

Why is Ben and Jerry's causing meltdowns in the sales of other ice cream manufacturers? Because everyone knows that these two guys not only make the stuff themselves by hand, but also personally examine each scoop.

Why is L. L. Bean the envy of Macy's? Same reason. Because everyone knows that old L. L. not only sews the shoes himself, but also sees that they fit.

Two basic tenets of selling are that (1) people buy from other people more

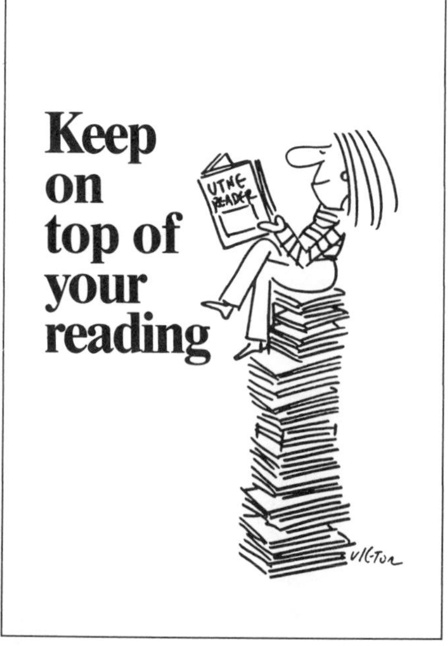

Keep on top of your reading
UTNE READER

Heikki Ratalahti's mini-circular that starts out at $3\frac{3}{4}'' \times 5\frac{1}{2}''$ . . .

Utne Reader
The best of the alternative press
THE SECRET THIRD WORLD WAR
HI. MY NAME IS OPUS, AND I AM A HERRINGHOLIC. I ADMIT I AM POWERLESS OVER FISH INNARDS AND THAT MY LIFE HAS BECOME UNMANAGEABLE...
ARE YOU ADDICTED TO ADDICTION?
A skeptical look at AA and other 12-step programs
HERRINGHOLICS ANONYMOUS

"The refinement, compression and focus of each issue make it the Swiss army knife of periodicals."
—GARY SNYDER, NEVADA CITY, CA.

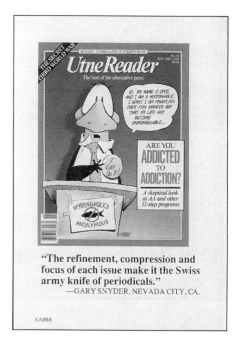

Fold it all up, and this is the back panel.

Introducing an easy and effective way to monitor the most innovative, challenging and unconventional viewpoints of the alternative press . . .

*Utne Reader**

It's the first and only magazine devoted to bringing hard-to-please readers the best of over 1,000 independent, small-circulation magazines, journals and newsletters.

Here's where to look for the most incisive commentaries and most perceptive analyses of issues and subjects that matter. Discerning readers are aware that the *real* energy in periodical publishing these days comes not from the mainstream publications, but from these spiritual heirs to the underground press of the '60s and '70s.

Problem is, you can't keep up with more than 1,000 publications no matter *how* rewarding they may be. Or at least you couldn't until now. Because now, at last, there's a magazine that does this *for* you.

*"Utne" rhymes with "chutney" and means "far out" in Norwegian.

Utne Reader, *P.O. Box 1974, Marion, OH 43306.*

"A magazine junkie's heaven . . . it slogs through the newsstand muck to save you the trouble, and picks out the delectable and provocative for your attention."
—CHARLES TRUEHEART, *USA TODAY*

And it opens . . .

Introducing an easy and effective way to monitor the most innovative, challenging and unconventional viewpoints of the alternative press . . .

*Utne Reader**

It's the first and only magazine devoted to bringing hard-to-please readers the best of over 1,000 independent, small-circulation magazines, journals and newsletters.

Here's where to look for the most incisive commentaries and most perceptive analyses of issues and subjects that matter. Discerning readers are aware that the *real* energy in periodical publishing these days comes not from the mainstream publications, but from these spiritual heirs to the underground press of the '60s and '70s.

Problem is, you can't keep up with more than 1,000 publications no matter *how* rewarding they may be. Or at least you couldn't until now. Because now, at last, there's a magazine that does this *for* you.

*"Utne" rhymes with "chutney" and means "far out" in Norwegian.

Utne Reader, *P.O. Box 1974, Marion, OH 43306.*

. . . the most exciting writing from publications you haven't even *heard* of . . . brought to you every other month in the pages of a lively, intelligent new magazine.

Every other month, ***Utne Reader*** editors sift through over 1,000 publications, unearth the most important, most interesting and most intriguing articles, condense and refine them into a coherent yet delightfully varied smorgasbord of commentary, clippings, reviews, first-hand reports, interviews and cartoons. The ***Utne Reader*** is *one* digest that manages consistently to be much more than the sum of its parts.

Look for these departments and features in every issue of the *Utne Reader* . . .

In Brief Short takes on the latest trends, ideas and developments as reported in the alternative press. Through more than two dozen capsule interviews, we keep you abreast of significant articles in America's leading non-establishment, small-circulation news and opinion magazines. This valuable survey lets you range

"With a flair for prophecy . . . UTNE READER aims to chronicle the intellectual voice of the Baby Boom generation."
—*ASSOCIATED PRESS*

And opens . . .

Introducing an easy and effective way to monitor the most innovative, challenging and unconventional viewpoints of the alternative press . . .

*Utne Reader**

It's the first and only magazine devoted to bringing hard-to-please readers the best of over 1,000 independent, small-circulation magazines, journals and newsletters.

Here's where to look for the most incisive commentaries and most perceptive analyses of issues and subjects that matter. Discerning readers are aware that the *real* energy in periodical publishing these days comes not from the mainstream publications, but from these spiritual heirs to the underground press of the '60s and '70s.

Problem is, you can't keep up with more than 1,000 publications no matter *how* rewarding they may be. Or at least you couldn't until now. Because now, at last, there's a magazine that does this *for* you.

*"Utne" rhymes with "chutney" and means "far out" in Norwegian.

Utne Reader, *P.O. Box 1974, Marion, OH 43306.*

. . . the most exciting writing from publications you haven't even *heard* of . . . brought to you every other month in the pages of a lively, intelligent new magazine.

Every other month, ***Utne Reader*** editors sift through over 1,000 publications, unearth the most important, most interesting and most intriguing articles, condense and refine them into a coherent yet delightfully varied smorgasbord of commentary, clippings, reviews, first-hand reports, interviews and cartoons. The ***Utne Reader*** is *one* digest that manages consistently to be much more than the sum of its parts.

Look for these departments and features in every issue of the *Utne Reader* . . .

In Brief Short takes on the latest trends, ideas and developments as reported in the alternative press. Through more than two dozen capsule interviews, we keep you abreast of significant articles in America's leading non-establishment, small-circulation news and opinion magazines. This valuable survey lets you range

far and wide, get an indispensable overview of news and issues that may never be covered by the mainstream press.

Recommended Reading This reader's guide introduces you to elusive, little-known newsletters and journals you've probably never heard of but may want to investigate. Each is reviewed briefly; complete ordering information is included. (Every article excerpted and reviewed in ***Utne Reader*** comes with the information you'll need to order subscriptions or back issues.)

Some of a Kind Want to know who's publishing what in a particular field of interest? This department sharpens the focus.

"A literate 'Lifestyles of the Rich in Spirit' . . . the UTNE READER is a must . . . a masterful job."
—*THE NEW YORK TIMES*

And opens . . .

Introducing an easy and effective way to monitor the most innovative, challenging and unconventional viewpoints of the alternative press . . .

*Utne Reader**

It's the first and only magazine devoted to bringing hard-to-please readers the best of over 1,000 independent, small-circulation magazines, journals and newsletters.

Here's where to look for the most incisive commentaries and most perceptive analyses of issues and subjects that matter. Discerning readers are aware that the *real* energy in periodical publishing these days comes not from the mainstream publications, but from these spiritual heirs to the underground press of the '60s and '70s.

Problem is, you can't keep up with more than 1,000 publications no matter *how* rewarding they may be. Or at least you couldn't until now. Because now, at last, there's a magazine that does this *for* you.

*"Utne" rhymes with "chutney" and means "far out" in Norwegian.

Utne Reader, *P.O. Box 1974, Marion, OH 43306.*

. . . the most exciting writing from publications you haven't even *heard* of . . . brought to you every other month in the pages of a lively, intelligent new magazine.

Every other month, ***Utne Reader*** editors sift through over 1,000 publications, unearth the most important, most interesting and most intriguing articles, condense and refine them into a coherent yet delightfully varied smorgasbord of commentary, clippings, reviews, first-hand reports, interviews and cartoons. The ***Utne Reader*** is *one* digest that manages consistently to be much more than the sum of its parts.

Look for these departments and features in every issue of the *Utne Reader* . . .

In Brief Short takes on the latest trends, ideas and developments as reported in the alternative press. Through more than two dozen capsule interviews, we keep you abreast of significant articles in America's leading non-establishment, small-circulation news and opinion magazines. This valuable survey lets you range

far and wide, get an indispensable overview of news and issues that may never be covered by the mainstream press.

Recommended Reading This reader's guide introduces you to elusive, little-known newsletters and journals you've probably never heard of but may want to investigate. Each is reviewed briefly; complete ordering information is included. (Every article excerpted and reviewed in ***Utne Reader*** comes with the information you'll need to order subscriptions or back issues.)

Some of a Kind Want to know who's publishing what in a particular field of interest? This department sharpens the focus.

gives you reviews of periodicals in areas such as the feminist press, bioregional publications, "punkzines," American Buddhist periodicals, baseball fanzines, pop music magazines, renewable agriculture, peace and disarmament, mind research, the new right, the radical right, animal rights and much more.

Plus . . . U.N.C.L.E. (Utne Network for Communications, Letters & Epistles), one of the liveliest most provocative letters to the editor departments you'll ever read . . . cartoons . . . original commentary and opinion pieces . . . excerpts and reviews of important new books . . . useful introductions to excerpted articles that place issues and ideas in context.

Where can you read these superb writers on these provocative topics?

Frances Moore Lappé on the politics of eating • Tom Wolfe on the 21st Century • Alice Kahn on the modern parent • Ram Dass on how to help • Michael Ventura on William Irwin Thompson • Joani Blank on outercourse Ken Kesey on death • Winona La Duke on the frontier mentality • Ray Bradbury on management from within Brenda Euland on walking • Keith Schneider on Jeremy Rifkin • Deena Metzger on the holy prostitute • Andrew Kopkind and Alexander Cockburn on the left • Dana Ullman on wellness macho • Doug Henwood on business ethics • Alice Walker on animal rights • Garrison

"With so much to read, how do you sift the good from the goofy? . . . the *Utne Reader*."
—THE WALL STREET JOURNAL

And opens . . .

Introducing an easy and effective way to monitor the most innovative, challenging and unconventional viewpoints of the alternative press . . .

*Utne Reader**

It's the first and only magazine devoted to bringing hard-to-please readers the best of over 1,000 independent, small-circulation magazines, journals and newsletters.

Here's where to look for the most incisive commentaries and most perceptive analyses of issues and subjects that matter. Discerning readers are aware that the *real* energy in periodical publishing these days comes not from the mainstream publications, but from these spiritual heirs to the underground press of the '60s and '70s.

Problem is, you can't keep up with more than 1,000 publications no matter *how* rewarding they may be. Or at least you couldn't until now. Because now, at last, there's a magazine that does this *for* you.

*"Utne" rhymes with "chutney" and means "far out" in Norwegian.

Utne Reader, *P.O. Box 1974, Marion, OH 43306.*

. . . the most exciting writing from publications you haven't even *heard* of . . . brought to you every other month in the pages of a lively, intelligent new magazine.

Every other month, ***Utne Reader*** editors sift through over 1,000 publications, unearth the most important, most interesting and most intriguing articles, condense and refine them into a coherent yet delightfully varied smorgasbord of commentary, clippings, reviews, first-hand reports, interviews and cartoons. The ***Utne Reader*** is *one* digest that manages consistently to be much more than the sum of its parts.

Look for these departments and features in every issue of the *Utne Reader* . . .

In Brief Short takes on the latest trends, ideas and developments as reported in the alternative press. Through more than two dozen capsule interviews, we keep you abreast of significant articles in America's leading non-establishment, small-circulation news and opinion magazines. This valuable survey lets you range

far and wide, get an indispensable overview of news and issues that may never be covered by the mainstream press.

Recommended Reading This reader's guide introduces you to elusive, little-known newsletters and journals you've probably never heard of but may want to investigate. Each is reviewed briefly; complete ordering information is included. (Every article excerpted and reviewed in ***Utne Reader*** comes with the information you'll need to order subscriptions or back issues.)

Some of a Kind Want to know who's publishing what in a particular field of interest? This department sharpens the focus.

gives you reviews of periodicals in areas such as the feminist press, bioregional publications, "punkzines," American Buddhist periodicals, baseball fanzines, pop music magazines, renewable agriculture, peace and disarmament, mind research, the new right, the radical right, animal rights and much more.

Plus . . . U.N.C.L.E. (Utne Network for Communications, Letters & Epistles), one of the liveliest most provocative letters to the editor departments you'll ever read . . . cartoons . . . original commentary and opinion pieces . . . excerpts and reviews of important new books . . . useful introductions to excerpted articles that place issues and ideas in context.

Where can you read these superb writers on these provocative topics?

Frances Moore Lappé on the politics of eating • Tom Wolfe on the 21st Century • Alice Kahn on the modern parent • Ram Dass on how to help • Michael Ventura on William Irwin Thompson • Joani Blank on outercourse Ken Kesey on death • Winona La Duke on the frontier mentality • Ray Bradbury on management from within Brenda Euland on walking • Keith Schneider on Jeremy Rifkin • Deena Metzger on the holy prostitute • Andrew Kopkind and Alexander Cockburn on the left • Dana Ullman on wellness macho • Doug Henwood on business ethics • Alice Walker on animal rights • Garrison

Keillor on porch-sitting • Suzi Gablik on socially conscious art • Daniel Zwerdling on the farm crisis Ivan Illich on ritual's dark side • Thich Nhat Hanh on Buddhism and social change • Bernard Nietschmann on the Third World War • Robert Burrows on New Age nonsense • Wendell Berry on the risk of marriage Myra Macpherson and Robert Bly on Vietnam • Carl Jensen on news not fit to print • George Leonard on erotic limits • Patrick Breslin on legendary Irish storytellers • Harvey Cox on politics and religion Kirkpatrick Sale on the bioregional urbanite • Judith Guest on family systems • Farley Mowat on snow Robert Heilbroner on advertising • Christine Downing on menopause • Bob Black on abolishing work Charlene Spretnak and Fritjof Capra on the Greens Gerri Hirshey on the tyranny of couples • Todd Gitlin on hot postmodernism • Jonathan Rowe on Cuban baseball Calvin Trillin on politically correct cuisine • Barbara Ehrenreich on blue collar feminism • Walter Truett Anderson on rethinking liberalism • Starhawk on community rituals • Salim Muwakkil on black males Laurens Van Der Post on the wilderness within Wallace Shawn on getting comfortable • Thomas Martin on devolution • Michael Lerner on reforming psychotherapy • John Avedon on Tibet • Jim Hightower on grassroots prosperity • Ellen Herman on addiction to addiction • Hazel Henderson on phony economics • Paul Fussell on tourist angst • Bertand Russell on idleness Jim Swan on sacred places • I. F. Stone on muckraking and the effects of pissing on a boulder . . .

In 1,000+ alternative publications such as these . . .

Against the Current • American Demographics • American Spectator • Anima • Artpaper • Audubon • Chicago Reader • Christianity and Crisis • The Churchman Country Journal • Cultural Survival Quarterly • Dissent Dollars and Sense • Earth First! • East West Journal Environmental Action • Erospirit • Family Therapy Networker • Grand Street • Granta • Green Letter • The Guardian • Harper's • Harrowsmith • Heresies • In Context Inside Joke • In These Times • Islands • Jewish Currents L.A. Weekly • MediaFile • Mother Earth News • Multinational Monitor • The Nation • National Catholic Reporter • New Age Journal • New Farm • New Internationalist • The New Republic • The New Statesman • The New York Review • Nutrition Action • Orion • Phoenix New Times • Processed World • Progressive • Spy Reason • Resurgence • Rolling Stone • San Francisco Bay Guardian • Santa Barbara News and Review • Science for the People • Skeptical Inquirer • Socialist Review Sojourners • Southern Exposure • Technology Review Texas Observer • Threepenny Review • Vajradhatu Sun Vegetarian Times • Vermont Vanguard • Village Voice Washington Monthly • Westword • Wigwag • Whole Earth Review • World Watch • Yellow Silk • Yoga Journal • Zeta . . .

. . . or in the *Utne Reader!*

And opens . . . until it stretches 22″ long, while remaining 5½″ high. It's like a dachshund which someone once described as "a dog and a half long by half a dog high."

SEND NO MONEY
Just mail card to get issue

Utne Reader
P.O. Box 1974 • Marion, Ohio 43306

Detach and return this card

AAØFM

PLEASE SEND MY FREE COPY and reserve my one-year subscription.

Save $6. If I like UTNE READER, you'll send me 5 more issues (6 in all) for only $18. The cover cost is $24. I save a full $6.

Owe nothing. If I decide not to continue, I just write "cancel" on the subscription bill, return it within two weeks and that's that. I've spent nothing. I owe nothing. The issue is mine to keep, free.

BMJW9-5
JAY
48
NEW
CT 06840

Guarantee. If UTNE READER ever fails to give me perspective, open my eyes, or save me time and money, I can cancel and get a full refund on all copies still to go.

The order card and business reply envelope.

happily than from faceless corporations, and that (2) in the marketplace as in the theater, there is indeed a factor at work called "the willing suspension of disbelief."

Who stands behind our pancakes? Aunt Jemima. Our angel food cake? Betty Crocker. Our coffee? Juan Valdez. Anyone over the age of three knows that it's all a myth. But like Santa Claus, the tooth fairy, and Jesus, the myths are comforting.

This package was an attempt to establish a persona *for an uncommonly cheerful and readable alternative magazine that would differentiate it from such impenetrable competitors as the* Nation *and from such relentlessly carping ones as* Mother Jones.

At the time Heikki Ratalahti and I created the mailing, a mere handful of people improvised the magazine more or less as described in the copy. Today, with a circulation of over a quarter million—much of it secured with this package—the masthead lists a staff of thirty-something.

ERIC UTNE

Dear Reader:

Utne rhymes with chutney. In Norwegian, it means far out
out!" is what you'll probably say when I tell you how we
READER.

The magazine comes to you six times a year from a conve
here in Minneapolis. We have an editorial staff of fou
Our executive editor, Jay Walljasper. Our task-master
Our resident generalist, Helen Cordes. And in the bes
feisty little journals, our friends and relatives vol
help plan the magazine.

There's Nina, my bemused wife. There's a Buddhi
activist. There's a socially responsible philan
dream analyst. An Amish quilt merchandiser. A

Why the "Utne Reader"?
Why "Utne"?

Why the "Alternative Press Reading & Dining Salon"?

ERIC UTNE

Dear Reader:

Utne rhymes with chutney. In Norwegian, it means far out. And "far out!" is what you'll probably say when I tell you how we publish UTNE READER.

The magazine comes to you six times a year from a converted warehouse here in Minneapolis. We have an editorial staff of four. Myself. Our executive editor, Jay Walljasper. Our task-master, Lynette Lamb. Our resident generalist, Helen Cordes. And in the best tradition of feisty little journals, our friends and relatives volunteer time to help plan the magazine.

There's Nina, my bemused wife. There's a Buddhist anti-nuclear activist. There's a socially responsible philanthropist. A Jungian dream analyst. An Amish quilt merchandiser. An anarcho-punk theorist. A hog farmer. Plus a dozen or so other stalwart media junkies who are nice enough to lend a hand.

For two months, we all read and clip whatever we find of interest in more than 1,000 alternative publications. Political exposés. How-to lifestyle pieces. Money advisories. Interviews with unusual people. Stories about the environment, survival, shenanigans in high places. Any and everything that you're not likely to find in mainstream newspapers and magazines.

Then, round about deadline time, we all get together in an all-night gathering that's come to be known as The Alternative Press Reading & Dining Salon. We discuss what we've read. We talk. We argue. We nibble on pizza and popcorn. And by dawn's early light, we've got it -- what we feel is one of the most exciting, yet useful, magazines you can read today.

UTNE READER is independent, unbiased, revealing, irreverent, comprehensive, authoritative, spirited, visionary, forthright, honest, and a blueprint for social betterment. It's also fun to read in the tub...

...but <u>come see for yourself on us</u>. When you mail the enclosed card promptly, you get the next issue free. If you like it, you'll save $6.00. If you don't, just say so and that's that. You've spent nothing. You owe nothing. No nerd will knock at your door to try to change your mind. No computer will bug you. You have the oath of a Viking Son. <u>Jeg lover</u> -- I promise!

<u>May we look for your reply by return mail</u>? There's not much storage space here in the office, and we have only so many copies to hand out free. Avoid disappointment by mailing the card before sundown. Thank you,

Cordially yours,

Eric Utne

AB9LL

The lift piece, with two headlines—one on each outside fold.

Does anybody out there care? Apparently not. They simply suspend belief, then buy from a struggling young editor named Eric Utne. They want to help him out.

An Intriguing Similarity

One common design feature these three launch packages share is an unfolding four-color brochure that opens . . . and opens . . . and opens . . . and opens . . . with each succeeding gatefold containing a surprise of some sort.

The direct mail creative teams had to disguise the fact that, at the time, these magazines existed only inside the heads of their editors and publishers. The three designers came up with the concept of making the publications seem real by the technique of literally making them unfold before the reader's eyes.

14

Consumer Publishing I: Continuity Series

There are three ways of engineering automatic multiple sales in direct marketing: continuity efforts, "til-forbid" offers, and negative option clubs.

Typically, a continuity series is a set of books or records to be sent automatically at the rate of one or two a month until the set is complete.

Til-forbid offers are the same as continuity series except there is no set number of volumes in the series. Sign up with Fleetwood for stamps and first-day covers, and you'll keep receiving products *ad infinitum* un*til* you *forbid* the company to send any more—til forbid.

In both cases, customers receive no mechanism in advance that warns of an impending shipment and gives the opportunity to reject it.

Negative option book and record clubs will be discussed in the next chapter.

Initial Offer

Before the Federal Trade Commission took an active interest in the practices of mail order merchants, the typical continuity series offer and fulfillment went as follows:

> Take Volume I Free. In about four weeks you will receive Volume II. If dissatisfied, return the second volume with your bill marked "Cancel" and you owe nothing and are under no further obligation. Otherwise, you will receive a new volume approximately every four to six weeks—always on approval—always at the same low price. You may return any book; you never pay for a book you do not wish to keep; you may cancel anytime.

What Really Happened

Volume I would be shipped free with a welcome letter. Volume II would be shipped four weeks later with a bill. When the bill was paid, Volume III would be shipped. When that bill was paid, a giant box containing

Volumes IV through XXIV were sent with a letter that said: "Guess what, you lucky person. Because the books are all ready, we assumed that you want them now, rather than having to wait for them on a month-by-month basis. It's a great deal; you have full use of the books, and you pay for them at the affordable rate of just one book a month. What's more, since we shipped them all at once, you save on postage. Here's your monthly payment book and reply envelopes."

Shipping all of the remaining volumes at once is called the "load-up." In the situation illustrated above, where the books came as an unordered surprise, it was known as the "dirty load-up." Although there were objections, most people found it was more trouble to ship the books back than to keep them and pay the low monthly rate. Profit or loss on a continuity program is measured by the average number of paid items (books, records, first-day stamp covers) per starter. If you can get someone to accept an entire box of books and pay for it, the number of paid books for that starter is far higher than the average of five or six or seven, which is where most people cancel when receiving shipments at the rate of one book a month. The load-up was sent only to those people who paid for the second and third volumes; their payment qualified them as likely candidates for the dirty load-up.

So many complaints resulted from the dirty load-up that the Federal Trade Commission stepped in and took action against this practice. Publishers got around that by writing a letter saying: "Guess what, you lucky person. All of the books are ready and we are going to send them to you all at once *unless you tell us you want them on a one-a-month basis."*

This was the negative option load-up. Unless the person said no, the books were shipped. The FTC caught on to this and said that consumers did not have pay for unordered merchandise and were under no obligation to return it; books sent under the negative option were emphatically unordered.

Publishers started sending letters following the payment for Volumes II and III that said: "Guess what, you lucky person. All of the books are ready, and you can have them all at once just by initialing the enclosed form and returning it to us."

This was the positive option; the load-up was actually ordered. Some people ordered them; others canceled. The net result is that most continuity series today are shipped at the rate promised on the original order form.

Singer Sewing Reference Library

Direct marketing guru Dick Benson states categorically that self-mailers do not work and are not worth testing. Dick Hodgson, author of *The Greatest Direct Mail Sales Letters of All Time*, says that self-mailers should be used in two areas, both in the workplace: for promoting seminars and for selling goods and services to people with stand-up jobs (barbers, shop stewards, etc.).

With the exception of postcard efforts, only one self-mailer has been continually received for three or more years—an eight-page effort written by Greg Beaupre of Minneapolis. In relation to all the other mailings, it is a true maverick—letter as part of the brochure, two side-by-side reply cards (the second one for a friend), more space devoted to sewing lessons than to selling the product and its benefits. Two possible reasons for its success: Singer is the premier name in home sewing, and in eight

MAILER: Cy DeCosse Incorporated
PACKAGE: Singer Sewing Reference Library
PROJECT MGR.: Al Anderson
WRITER: Greg Beaupre
DESIGNER: In-house
FIRST MAILED: 1984
The 7½″ × 11″ 4-color self-mailer cover.

We guarantee you'll sew your next project faster and better, or we'll refund your money.

Examine Vol. I, *Sewing for the Home*, for two weeks FREE!

Now you can learn the tips and techniques that will help you sew faster, with more professional results. The SINGER® SEWING REFERENCE LIBRARY® shows you how! Expert techniques, from sewing perfect tucks to the quickest way to install a zipper, are shown with step-by-step photos. So there's no guesswork!

Singer is a registered trademark of the Singer Company.

Step-by-step projects for your home

Sewing for the Home, Volume I of the Singer Sewing Reference Library, is your complete guide to sewing home decoration projects. You'll begin by learning the basics of fabric and color selection and how to use your sewing machine and standard equipment to achieve the best results.

Sewing for the Home, is divided into four exciting project sections — Windows, Pillows, Tables, and Beds. Everything you need to know for each project is contained in this amazing book, from basic construction to designer customizing hints.

A new idea in sewing books

Sewing for the Home, represents a completely new kind of sewing book. The hard-to-understand line drawings that fill most sewing books have been replaced by clear, precise color photographs, so you get expert guidance through every step of your project. The information contained in the Singer Sewing Reference Library makes the series an invaluable reference source for every home sewer, beginner or advanced.

A complete library

Your subscription to the Singer Sewing Reference Library begins with *Sewing for the Home*, followed by books such as *Sewing for Style, The Perfect Fit, Sewing Essentials, Timesaving Sewing, Sewing Activewear*, and other exciting volumes. As you acquire each book, you'll be building a valuable sewing library you'll turn to again and again for all your sewing projects.

FREE trial offer

Examine *Sewing for the Home* for two weeks, FREE!

Use the card inside to order your copy of *Sewing for the Home*. Examine and use the book for two weeks: if for any reason you don't want to keep it, return it to us. We even pay the postage!

SINGER
SEWING REFERENCE LIBRARY
5900 Green Oak Drive P.O. Box 3040 Minnetonka, MN 55343

Announcing the Singer® Sewing Reference Library® — your photo-filled "how-to" guide to better sewing success. I double guarantee it! Start with one of these volumes:

Dear Friend:

I'm writing to you today with some important news. It's about a guaranteed way to have even more fun on your sewing machine and improve your sewing results, regardless of your level of experience!

We designed the Singer Sewing Reference Library to help every new sewer achieve professional results quickly, and every experienced sewer achieve even better results! I'm so sure of this, I'm offering you an unheard-of double guarantee. But first I want to tell you about this impressive library.

You can choose Sewing for the Home as your first volume, and learn home decorating projects (like Roman and balloon shades, ruffled pillows and tufted quilt comforters) step-by-step. Every project keeps cost, simplicity, easy-care and coordinated style and color in mind.

Or if you wish, examine Quilting by Machine or Timesaving Sewing as your first volume. You'll learn how to quilt wonderful creations quickly and easily . . . or save time and work on all your sewing projects with a variety of helpful tips and techniques.

Helpful, step-by-step photos (like those following in this brochure) fill every page of every volume and show you exactly how to sew like a pro. In fact, there are over 450 color photos in each handsomely bound, hardcover book.

That leads me to my double guarantee offer:

#1. Soon after ordering, you'll receive your book choice to examine for two weeks free. If this book fails to meet your expectations, return it to us at no charge! You can cancel your subscription to the series at any time.

#2. If you do like what you see in those first few weeks, keep the book and continue using it on your sewing projects. If you later decide your choice isn't helping you achieve better results, return it to us and receive a full refund guaranteed.

To receive Volume 1 for your free two-week examination, simply return the order card attached to the brochure. If Sewing for the Home, Quilting by Machine or Timesaving Sewing lives up to all I've said, keep it and pay just $13.95 (plus shipping and handling). It will pay for itself many times over! Order today!

Sincerely,

James B. Maus
President

Surprise FREE GIFT!

Turn page for FREE SAMPLE INSTRUCTIONS

P.S. We'll send you a SURPRISE FREE GIFT just for examining your first volume. This valuable gift is an exciting innovation that will help you sew faster and better. And it's yours to keep, FREE, even if you decide not to purchase the book.

First inside spread.

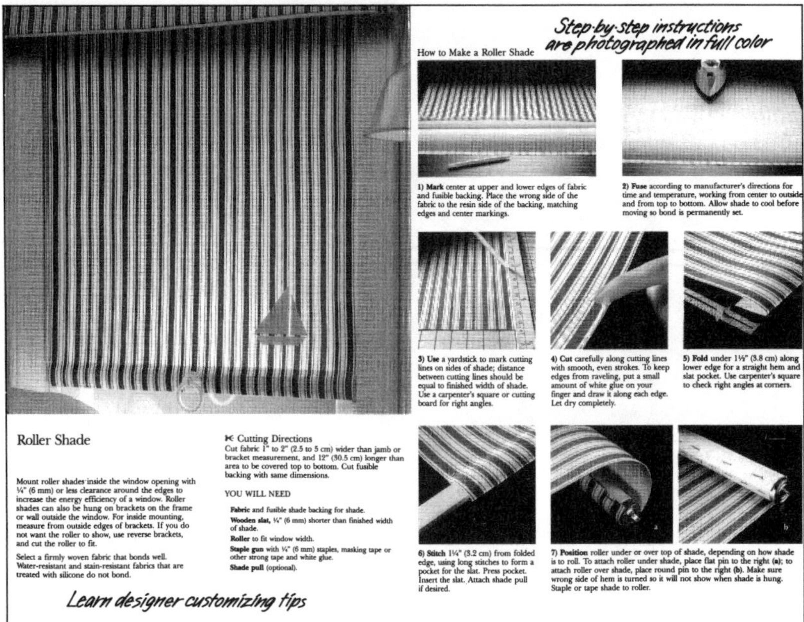

Step-by-step instructions are photographed in full color

How to Make a Roller Shade

1) **Mark** center at upper and lower edges of fabric and fusible backing. Place the wrong side of the fabric to the resin side of the backing, matching edges and center markings.

2) **Fuse** according to manufacturer's directions for time and temperature, working from center to outside and from top to bottom. Allow shade to cool before moving so bond is permanently set.

3) **Use** a yardstick to mark cutting lines on sides of shade; distance between cutting lines should be equal to finished width of shade. Use a carpenter's square or cutting board for right angles.

4) **Cut** carefully along cutting lines with smooth, even strokes. To keep edges from raveling, put a small amount of white glue on your finger and draw it along each edge. Let dry completely.

5) **Fold** under 1½" (3.8 cm) along lower edge for a straight hem and slat pocket. Use carpenter's square to check right angles at corners.

6) **Stitch** 1¼" (3.2 cm) from folded edge, using long stitches to form a pocket for the slat. Press pocket. Insert the slat. Attach shade pull if desired.

7) **Position** roller under or over top of shade, depending on how shade is to roll. To attach roller under shade, place flat pin to the right (**a**); to attach roller over shade, place round pin to the right (**b**). Make sure wrong side of hem is turned so it will not show when shade is hung. Staple or tape shade to roller.

Roller Shade

Mount roller shades inside the window opening with ¼" (6 mm) or less clearance around the edges to increase the energy efficiency of a window. Roller shades can also be hung on brackets on the frame or wall outside the window. For inside mounting, measure from outside edges of brackets. If you do not want the roller to show, use reverse brackets, and cut the roller to fit.

Select a firmly woven fabric that bonds well. Water-resistant and stain-resistant fabrics that are treated with silicone do not bond.

✂ Cutting Directions
Cut fabric 1" to 2" (2.5 to 5 cm) wider than jamb or bracket measurement, and 12" (30.5 cm) longer than area to be covered top to bottom. Cut fusible backing with same dimensions.

YOU WILL NEED

Fabric and fusible shade backing for shade.

Wooden slat, ¼" (6 mm) shorter than finished width of shade.

Roller to fit window width.

Staple gun with ¼" (6 mm) staples, masking tape or other strong tape and white glue.

Shade pull (optional).

Learn designer customizing tips

Second inside spread.

years of looking at some quarter of a million mailings, I can't recall a single competitor. And there is a huge universe of home sewers that is reachable by renting lists.

Since 1989 Greg Beaupre has been with BBDO Minneapolis, where he currently works on accounts ranging from US West Cellular and Group Health to Surdyk's and Hormel Meat Products. Prior to joining BBDO, he worked as creative director at Lee & Riley writing and supervising targeted advertising and direct marketing campaigns for Network Systems, Lee Data, Xerxes Computer Corporation, and First Banks. He has also worked at Fallon McElligott, and Fallon subsidiary McCool & Co.

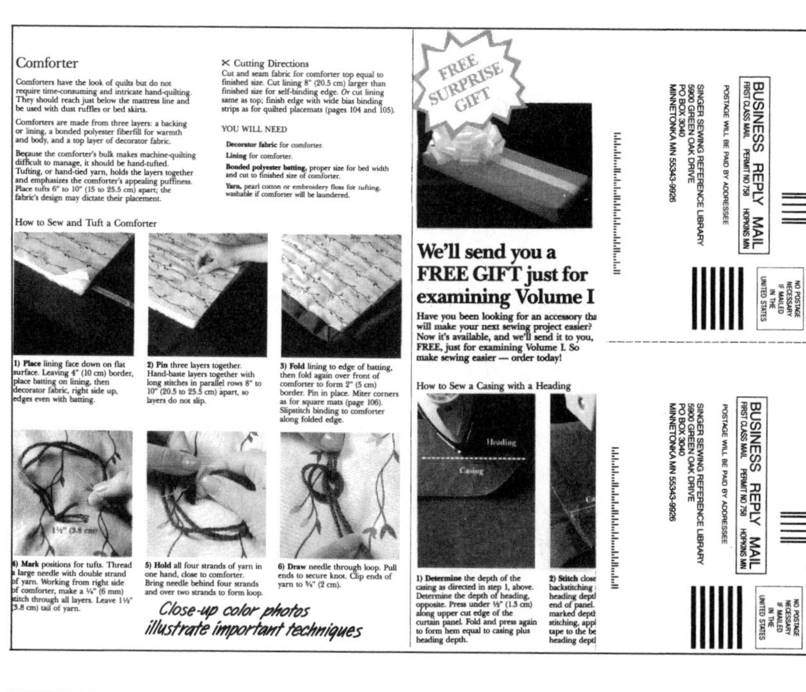

Inside back cover spread. The side-by-side reply cards folded in. The name and address on one of the cards show through the back cover window.

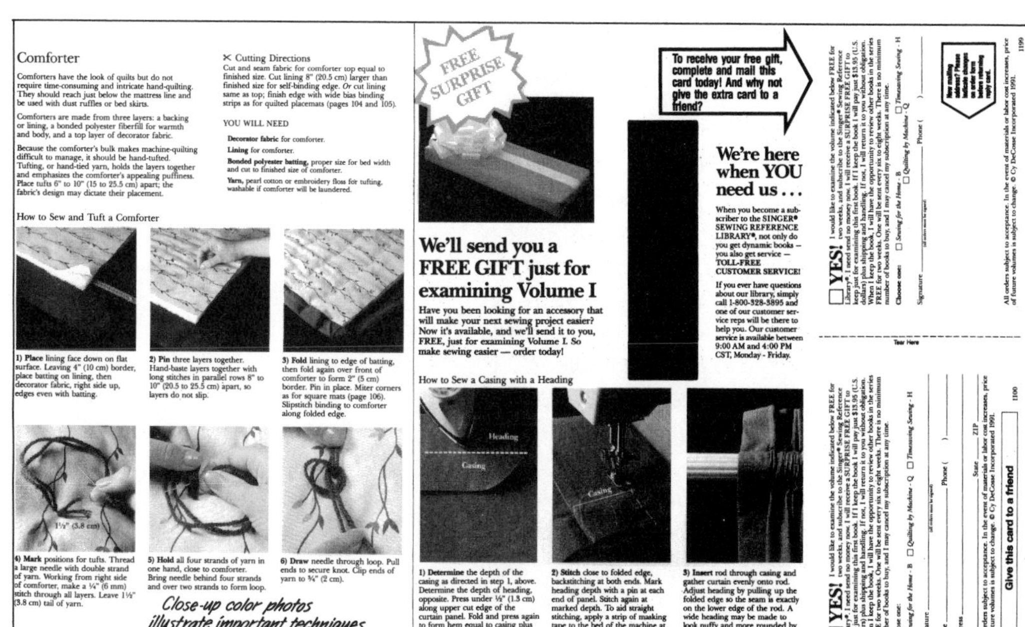

Inside back cover spread with side-by-side reply cards unfolded.

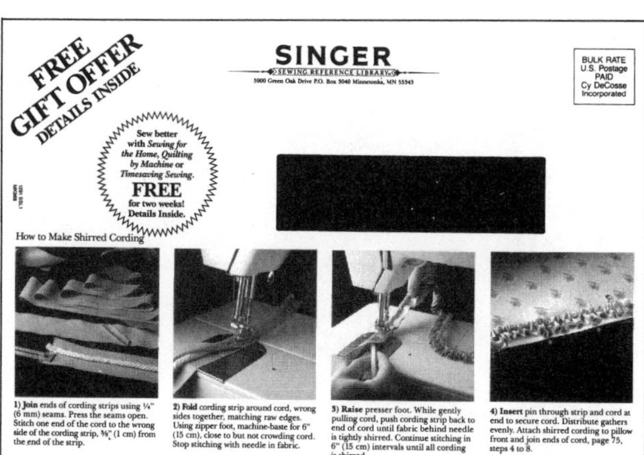

The back cover of the self-mailer.

Greg Beaupre:

My thoughts on the Singer mailing: In a nutshell, if I were to do it all over again, I'd do it differently, despite the mailing's success. As conceived, the control mailing to me represents ''good enough.'' Incremental success. A solid, traditionally written self-mailer with a predominantly buckeye-minded layout, all of which gives the basic poop in rather pedestrian fashion, presumably hitting a healthy percentage of the ''right'' people with a good offer on a well-perceived product. So the classic direct-mail triumvirate of list, offer, and creative must be working to the right mix for this mailing to continue to be effective. (I also saw a recent piece in the Minneapolis Star Tribune *that suggests the growing popularity of home sewing might have something substantial to do with it, too. Of course, that would be a constant across all mailings, control and tests alike, but would certainly help put the overall effort in the ''Win'' column.)*

At any rate, if it ain't broke, why fix it, right? Well, the answer's a long one that I'll try to make short. First, my contention regarding direct mail (and other areas of advertising as well) is that this kind of workmanlike, unsurprising, no-bullshit approach tested with other unremarkable, essentially similar packages gives you only a narrow view of success. That is (and this is based on my own conjecture since I have no idea what the real numbers on this mailing and its tests have netted), control and test mailings all hovering in the 1.59–3.27 percent response range type of thing, with the control winning out. As opposed to something designated to thrust the whole effort upward into the richly successful ranges—3.5–6 percent and beyond. I participated in a ''Kings of Copy'' conference in New York a few years back and a fellow presenter said it better than I can in this letter, to the effect that fewer and fewer companies can afford the kind of incremental, leave-well-enough-alone success this kind of control mailing achieves. Production costs go up, consumers' wallets continue to shrink, competition inevitably creeps up on you and overtakes you if you're not willing to take a few more chances than you have in the past. What worked well enough in the past will be your death sentence in the marketplace tomorrow.

Now that I've stopped to reread and proofread this, I realize I'm doing a pretty good job of making a long subject longer, not shorter. So I'll wind this down.

This whole subject seems always to devolve into a discussion—or heated argument, as was the case in New York—of creativity vs. effectiveness, as if the two were somehow mutually exclusive. I've got a whole portfolio of direct mail advertising that has won awards for effectiveness and *creativity, suggesting the cause-and-effect relationship between the two that I believe is there. And the nut of it is, I don't believe the Singer piece is ''creative'' at all. I don't believe it takes the greatest possible advantage of the creative variable in the mix. And I do believe, given the chance, I could beat the control applying the greatest possible creative leverage to the task. More refreshing, surprising, compelling headlines. A more conceptually thought-out approach on the cover. More appealing graphics. Get in the free, but do it more tastefully. Project a less predictable, more progressive image for the company itself. Etc., etc., etc.*

Time-Life Books

Probably the most successful mail order book publishing operation in history is Time-Life Books, founded in 1961 by an authentic publishing genius, Jerome Hardy, formerly of Doubleday. At the time, Hardy had two choices: use the fabulous Time-Life photographic archives to put together a cut-and-paste series, or create real books from scratch, tapping into the parent company's material only where the fit was absolutely correct. Hardy wisely opted for the latter course and built what was to become the largest book publisher in the United States. Foreign operations were added in 1971 and today Time-Life books are printed in many languages and marketed throughout the world.

Time-Life Books is a prodigious force in mail order. To get new customers it uses space ads, insert programs, and a slew of direct response television commercials. According to one source, over 100 new direct mail packages are tested in the course of a year. With this kind of constant tinkering and testing, long-term direct mail controls are rare; somebody is always beating the last winning package. However, two Time-Life efforts qualify as Grand Controls.

Writers who work on Time-Life projects have an enormous advantage over those of other publishers in that Time-Life spends a fortune on market research and focus groups before committing to a new series. As a result, writers can know in advance what consumers' "hot buttons" are in relation to the product being sold and can highlight those throughout the effort.

Notice, by the way, that the order cards for both Time-Life packages use a token as an involvement device.

Mysteries of the Unknown

MAILER: Time-Life Books
PACKAGE: *Mysteries of the Unknown*
PROJECT MGR.: Martin Tarratt
WRITER: Len Berkowe
DESIGNER: Ron Wilcox
FIRST MAILED: 1987

Starting with the metallic silver and blue of the envelope, progressing through the haunting copy on the letter that is printed on speckled gray stock, and culminating in the gargantuan four-color circular that seemingly won't quit, freelancer Len Berkowe and the design team at Time-Life have pushed through to the back of the reader's brain and stirred up curiosity and emotion lurking deep within all of us.

Len Berkowe has been a freelancer for the past twenty-three years and has written for just about every major publisher of consumer magazines, book clubs, and book continuity programs. He works almost exclusively in consumer publishing. He cut his teeth on direct mail as an agency copywriter and circulation manager for the *New York Times* and Scholastic magazines. For what he describes as "one wild and woolly year," he headed up the first U.S.-based direct mail agency operating throughout Western Europe.

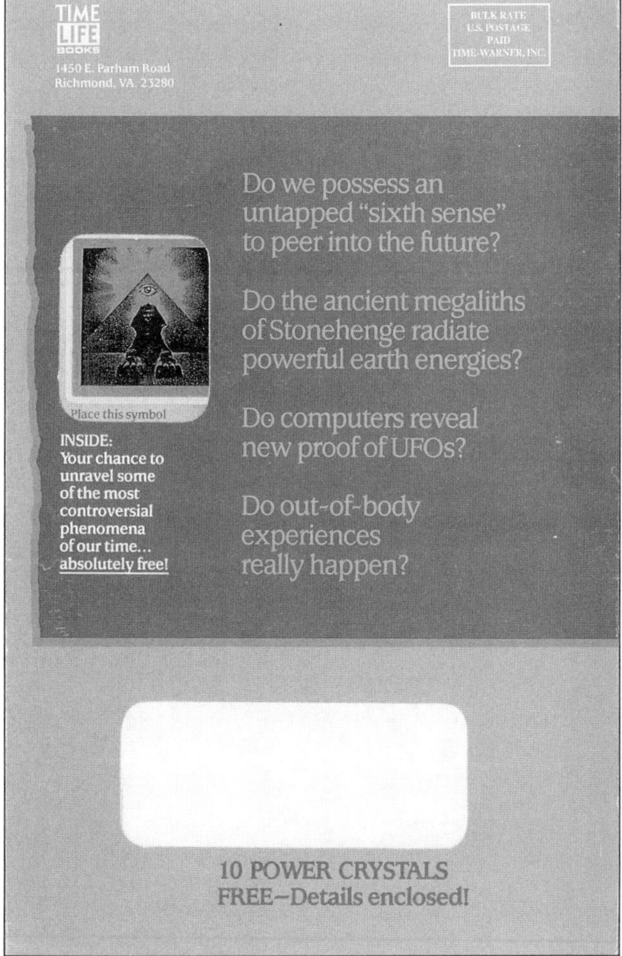

The 6″ × 9″ outside envelope of metallic silver and grayish blue shown front and back. The order token—action device—shows through the small square window at upper middle left.

Have you ever entered an unfamiliar room and somehow felt you'd been there before? Or known absolutely that something was going to happen–before it actually did?
Or perhaps you've experienced even more puzzling examples of extrasensory perception?
If so, you're not alone. According to recent surveys, more than two-thirds of all Americans now claim they've had brushes with ESP, at least once in their lives!
Are these tricks of the mind? A product of over-heated imagination? Or something else...still waiting to be explained?
Now you can decide for yourself as you venture into the extraordinary new series that's yours to sample and ponder–for 10 exciting days–absolutely free!

MYSTERIES OF THE UNKNOWN

Dear Reader:

On an autumn day, not too long ago, sociologist Robert Harner visited the Great Serpent Mound of Ohio.

As he stood on this sacred Indian ground, the air was oddly still--not even a breeze.

Then suddenly, Harner froze with fear. Inexplicably, the leaves at his feet began to swirl around him--as if energized by some mysterious force!

The spell lasted only a few minutes. Yet this sober-minded scholar could never shake it from his mind. Was it an illusion? Or did it happen exactly as described by Harner himself?

Since time immemorial, people have whispered about mystic places. And strange encounters with "another world"--preserved in legends that remain with us even today.

Yet only recently have scientists begun to probe these age-old mysteries--with all the tools of modern technology!

What have they learned? What still puzzles them? What new frontiers of the unknown are now being explored?

You'll find out some truly extraordinary answers in our new series, MYSTERIES OF THE UNKNOWN!

Never before have you enjoyed access to so wide a range of information: new clues...documented evidence...first-hand experiences...authenticated findings...unanswered questions...

...all designed to help you make up your own mind about some of the most controversial phenomena of our time!

And if you act now, you can examine the introductory volume --Mystic Places--at no cost and with absolutely no obligation. Absolutely free!

So come with us to sites, all over the world, that have long been shrouded in mystery. Probe their secrets through rare photographs, specially commissioned art, the latest research. Then see if you can find your own answers to...

The Great Pyramid of Egypt. What ancient wisdom remains locked inside this seventh wonder of antiquity? Is it a mammoth tomb? If so, why has no pharaoh been found within its walls?

The Awesome Megaliths of Europe. Were they erected on earth energy centers known long ago, but since forgotten? Why do powerful magnetic fields and ultrasound continue to be recorded near them?

The Sacred Indian Mounds of North America. Can we ever decode the hidden meaning of Ohio's Great Serpent Mound...Wyoming's giant spoked wheel...the strange rock circles of Arizona?

The Nazca Earth Pictures of Peru. Why have they been etched high on a plateau in the Andes? By whom? And for what purpose?

The Lost Continent of Atlantis. Will new archaeological discoveries help us find it, at long last?

From the great Avebury Circle in Britain to the deadly Bermuda Triangle...from lost cities in the jungles of Brazil to legendary openings in the core of the earth...Mystic Places takes you on a supreme adventure of mind and spirit!

And that's just the beginning. Because, as our new series unfolds, you'll venture even further into realms of mystery that, until now, have defied human understanding.

Remember all those stories and pictures of UFOs that were the rage a few years ago? Well, now you can probe more deeply into this fascinating subject--with The UFO Phenomenon!

Read amazing first-hand accounts, with details never published before, of UFO encounters. See actual sketches made on the spot. Learn what computers now reveal about some famous UFO photographs. And ponder Project Blue Book, the Air Force's monumental study of UFOs that may raise more questions than it answers.

Then, in Psychic Powers, take a look at some of the most unusual cases of ESP ever recorded. Lincoln's famous dream of his own assassination. Edgar Cayce's inexplicable exploits of psychic healing. The Swedish scientist who accurately described a fire raging near his home--almost 300 miles away--as verified by 15 witnesses!

And join us at universities all over the world where psychic powers are being rigorously tested to determine their reality--and outer limits.

And in Psychic Voyages, you'll travel into even stranger realms of psychic phenomena! Out-of-body experiences, as reported by Charles Lindbergh, Ernest Hemingway and many others. Accounts from people who have hovered on the brink of death and returned to describe their experiences in vivid detail. Stories of reincarnation that have stood up even under the most exhaustive investigations!

And in such future volumes as Mind over Matter, Phantom Encounters and Visions and Prophecies, you'll come face to face with questions that have intrigued humankind down through the centuries!

Send for your first free-trial volume now... without risking a penny.

That's right! When you return the accompanying certificate, you'll receive your introductory book, Mystic Places, absolutely free for a 10-day examination.

Leaf through it at your leisure. Enjoy more than 100 photographs, illustrations, diagrams and maps. Join new explorations and see what exciting new vistas they open up!

If you're as thrilled by Mystic Places as we think you'll be, it's yours to keep for just $14.99, plus shipping and handling.

You can then examine future volumes on the same free-trial basis. Each book will be delivered to you, one about every month. (Prices are guaranteed for as long as you choose to subscribe.) There is no club to join. You keep only the books you want...

...and you're free to cancel your subscription if you are ever less than satisfied!

So come, open your mind to new discoveries and fresh possibilities--to extraordinary glimpses of a reality far beyond our everyday lives!

Return your Free Examination Certificate today. You really have nothing to lose--and a world of wonders to gain!

Cordially,

Robert H. Smith

Robert H. Smith
Publisher

P.S. Take a look at your certificate now for news of a special gift of welcome! 10 power crystals, from amethyst to snow quartz, plus a guide to their legendary mystic qualities. Use them to meditate or relieve stress. Or enjoy them for their natural beauty. We'll send you all 10 power crystals free, plus a carrying bag, when you purchase Mystic Places.

L/MTU192

The letter, printed on 11″ × 17″ sheet and folded twice.

The brochure for *Mysteries of the Unknown* is a typical Time Life spectacular. It starts off with a $5^1/_2' \times 9''$ cover.

The inside gatefold pictures are purposely spooky and other-worldly—images seen through a haze. It opens . . .

And opens . . .

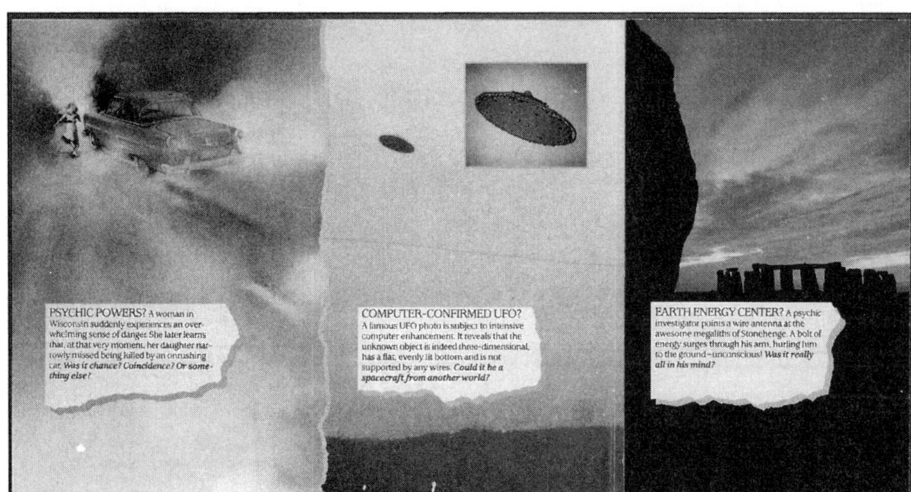

And opens again . . .

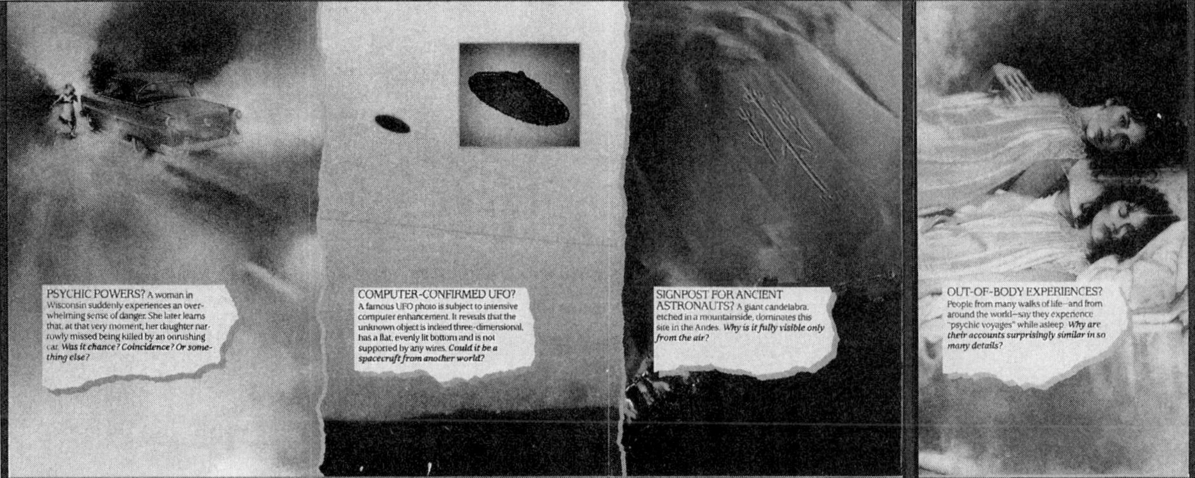

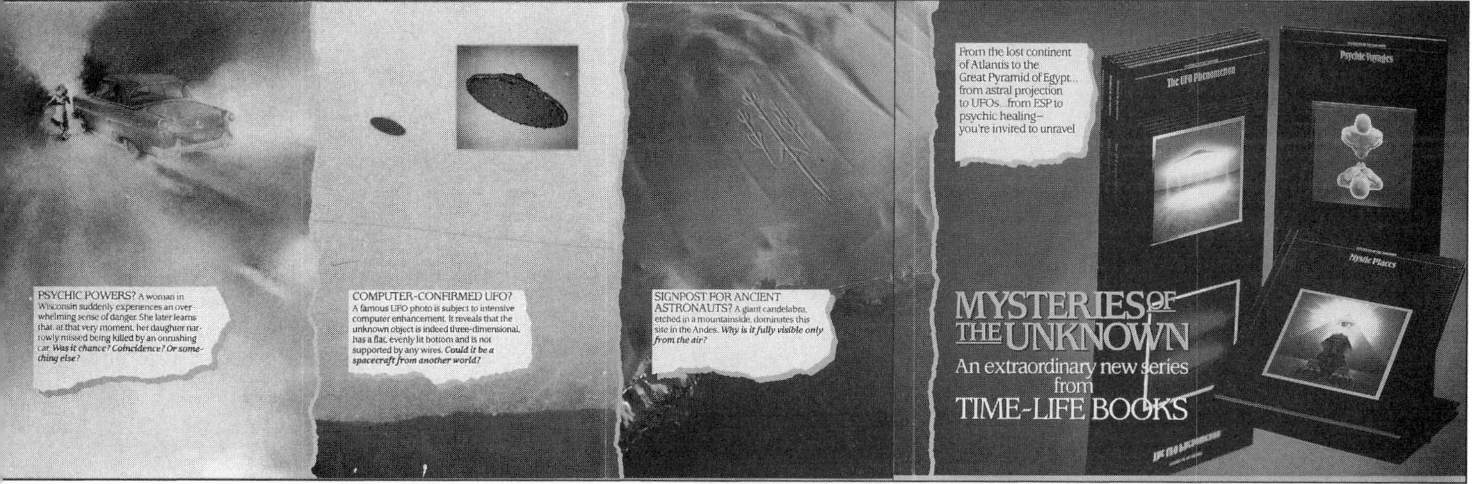

And opens one more time lengthwise . . .

MYSTERIES OF THE UNKNOWN

For 10 days free, travel to the new frontiers of paranormal phenomena–and beyond!

If you suspect there's more to life than meets the eye... If you've experienced psychic phenomena yourself, or heard of experiences from others...

Above all, if you possess an open mind and an adventurous spirit...

then you'll find MYSTERIES OF THE UNKNOWN fascinating!

INFORMATION & INSIGHTS

This extraordinary new series brings you fresh information... startling insights... the latest scientific findings–all to help you make up your mind about some of the most controversial phenomena of our time!

Why, for example, do the legendary "healing stones" of England radiate so high a level of electromagnetism–the very same energy now used by modern medicine to speed up bone healing!

Can we believe the detailed sketches made by an airline pilot who claims he sighted UFOs high over Alaska?

What do the latest tests reveal about extrasensory perception–a "second sight" to see far-off events... a "third eye" to look back at the past... a "sixth sense" to peer into the future?

With MYSTERIES OF THE UNKNOWN, you'll venture to the very threshold of human understanding–reincarnation, astral projection, psychic healing–and beyond!

Rare photographs and specially commissioned art will guide you on your way. And at every step you'll be briefed on what science now knows... what is merely guessed at... what still remains unanswered.

SEE FOR YOURSELF

The enclosed certificate will bring you a free-examination copy of your introductory volume, *Mystic Places*. There's no risk, no obligation. And if you decide to keep it, you'll be able to examine future volumes in this exciting series –on the same no-risk basis.

"SKIN SIGHT." *While blindfolded, child psychic Bogna Stefanska fingers a pane of glass and accurately describes the size, shape and color of objects that lie beneath.*

EXPERIMENT IN ESP. *In one room, a psychic lies relaxed, his eyes covered and soft sounds emanating from his earphones. In another room, a researcher flashes a film about two fire-eaters on a TV monitor. Incredibly, the psychic begins to describe flames he cannot see–but adds with surprise: "I have no feeling of heat."*

LINDBERGH'S GHOSTLY FLIGHT. *At one moment during his historic transatlantic flight, Lindbergh sensed that his spirit was leaving his body. An illusion brought on by deep fatigue, claim some. But the famed aviator always maintained that his out-of-body experience was real.*

UFO SIGHTING. *In 1986, Japan Air Lines pilot Kenju Terauchi described his encounter with three UFOs over Alaska. His sketch shows how the largest UFO dwarfed his 747. It also reveals the location of the UFOs and when they were first sighted on his radar screen.*

Mystic Places

A Dreadful Day of Reckoning

TIME LIFE BOOKS Satisfaction Guaranteed!

Examine each volume on a 10-day free-examination basis. Keep only the books you want. Cancel your subscription at any time!

Start off with a fantastic journey to the most mysterious places on earth!

Come explore the awesome, puzzling Great Pyramid of Egypt. Is it a giant sundial? A mammoth astronomical observatory? A storehouse of age-old wisdom, as yet untapped?

Or gaze at the majestic megaliths of Stonehenge and other strange stone circles scattered across Europe. Who built them? And why do they emit ultrasound and other energy readings–just before sunrise?

FROM STONEHENGE TO NAZCA...

Venture into the sacred Indian mounds of North America. Are eyewitnesses right when they say ancient spirits linger there still?

Or decode, if you can, the sprawling Nazca pictures, etched high on a plateau in Peru. Who drew them? And why are they fully visible only from the air?

Then try your hand at unraveling the enigma of the Bermuda Triangle, where dozens of planes and ships have disappeared–never to be found again!

Or sift through archaeological finds that may hold the key to discovering Atlantis, the fabled lost continent of antiquity.

...EXPLORE ANCIENT EARTH MYSTERIES!

Mystic Places is indeed something special: an endlessly exciting voyage of discovery–into the unknown!

You'll want to read and ponder it, again and again. Show it to your family and friends. Talk about it with all those who share your spirit of adventure–and your inquiring mind!

So why not join us now? Sample this unique book as our guest–for 10 exciting days–absolutely free!

MYSTIC PLACES

Send for your free-examination copy today!

SECRETS OF ANCIENT WISDOM. *Long ago, when the Sphinx was buried in sand, visitors sought wisdom from its lips. Modern experts believe that ancient wisdom is embodied in the Great Pyramid of Egypt–a marvel of mathematical construction whose secrets have yet to be fathomed!*

GOLDEN CLUE. *For centuries, scholars and mystics have speculated about Atlantis, the fabled lost continent said to have been swallowed up by the sea. New archaeological finds may help pinpoint the actual location of Atlantis–some 2,500 years ago!*

TRUTH SEEKER. *Using the latest monitoring devices, Paul Devereux tracks earth energies at megalith sites all over Britain where unexplained events have allegedly occurred.*

MISSING MISSION. *In a famous 1945 incident, five Navy planes disappeared over the Bermuda Triangle after reporting compass trouble. Not a scrap of wreckage from any of the planes was ever recovered–or from the search planes sent to find them!*

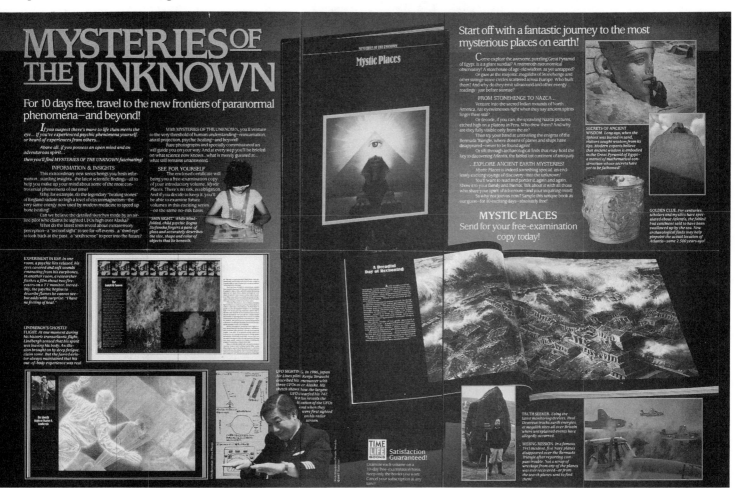

The giant inside spread explodes into an 18″ × 26″ bedsheet. Virtually all designers shy away from body copy reversed out of dark backgrounds; it is extremely difficult to read. However, given the subject matter of the series, it is appropriate; the words seem to be coming out of eerie dark backgrounds, enhancing the aura of mystery.

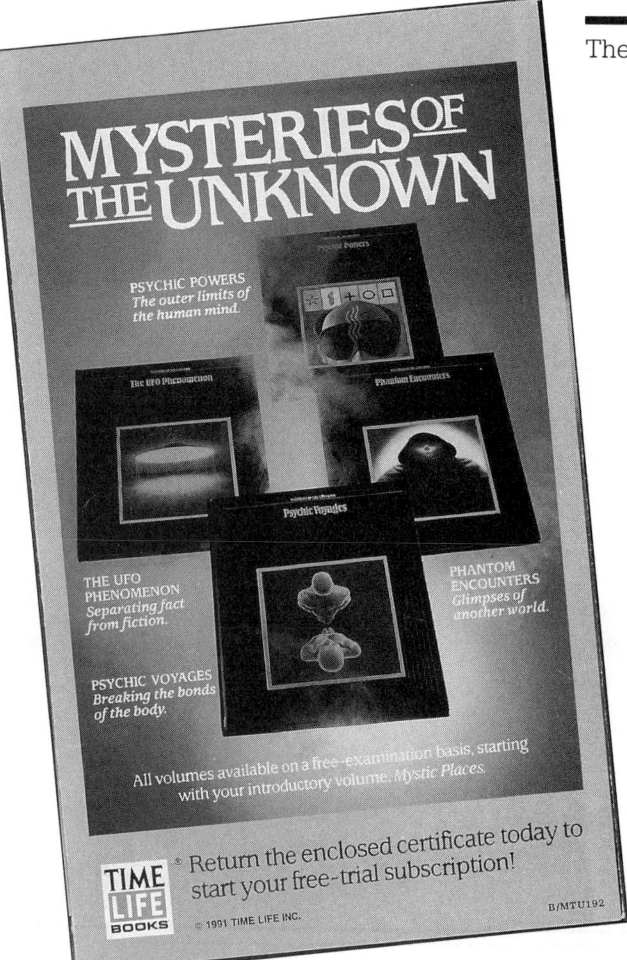

The back panel of the circular.

Len Berkowe:

Mysteries of the Unknown *was launched at a time when "New Age" culture had enormously heightened public interest in the occult. The market was crowded, indeed overcrowded, with materials. So we had to forge a unique selling claim that would immediately set this book series apart.*

Our solution: Provocative new answers to questions about the supernatural—based on the latest scientific investigations!

The tone of the package was important. We had to avoid any suggestion that the supernatural was merely titillating entertainment. Occult fans take it seriously, and so did we.

But given the inherent sensationalism of the subject, I was tempted to go with big, "blockbuster" teaser copy on the outer envelope. There was, however, a problem. Market research revealed that occult fans usually zero in on a specific area of interest like psychic powers or UFOs. If we didn't hit the right button, we could lose a lot of readers. Hence, the list of questions on the outer envelope to cover all four of the most popular subject areas.

We also felt that the free-trial offer, the premium, and some examples of the kind of information Mysteries of the Unknown *offered were powerful selling points. Too powerful to bury inside the package. The result was a lot of copy on the outer envelope. The trick, of course, was to avoid that cluttered look that could easily land the envelope in the nearest wastepaper basket.*

The letter, too, aims to reach the broadest possible audience. That's why we started off with the psychic phenomenon most people are familiar with—the feeling of ''deja vu.'' And bolster it with the fact that, in a nationwide survey, two-thirds of all Americans claim to have experienced the supernatural in their personal lives.

Like all good direct response advertising, this package is anchored firmly in what worked in the past. The brochure, for example, owes much to the TV commercial that tested best for Time-Life Books. The opening panels, like the frames of the winning commercial, reveal a series of startling case histories and the puzzling questions they raise. Indeed, when it comes to graphics, I think all of us in direct mail can learn from successful TV techniques.

In doing this package, I had the advantage of working with real direct-response pros—people like Ron Wilcox and Martin Tarratt at Time-Life Books. Because they shared their market research, test results, and personal insights, I was able to sell effectively in an area almost totally unfamiliar to me.

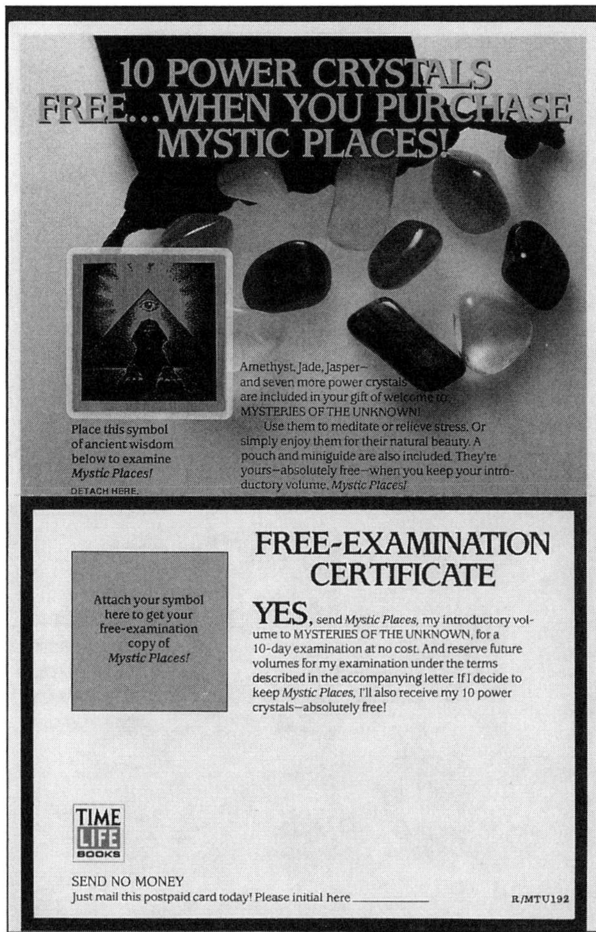

The back of the order card. Since this is a free trial offer—with no cash or credit card option—the order device is a business reply card. No need for an envelope. Above the business reply face is the guarantee. This top portion is to be torn off and contains a very positive message on each side: the guarantee and the free premium.

The front of the 4-color order card. The lift piece/premium slip is the top half of the order card. It offers a free goodie at the very point when you are deciding whether or not to order.

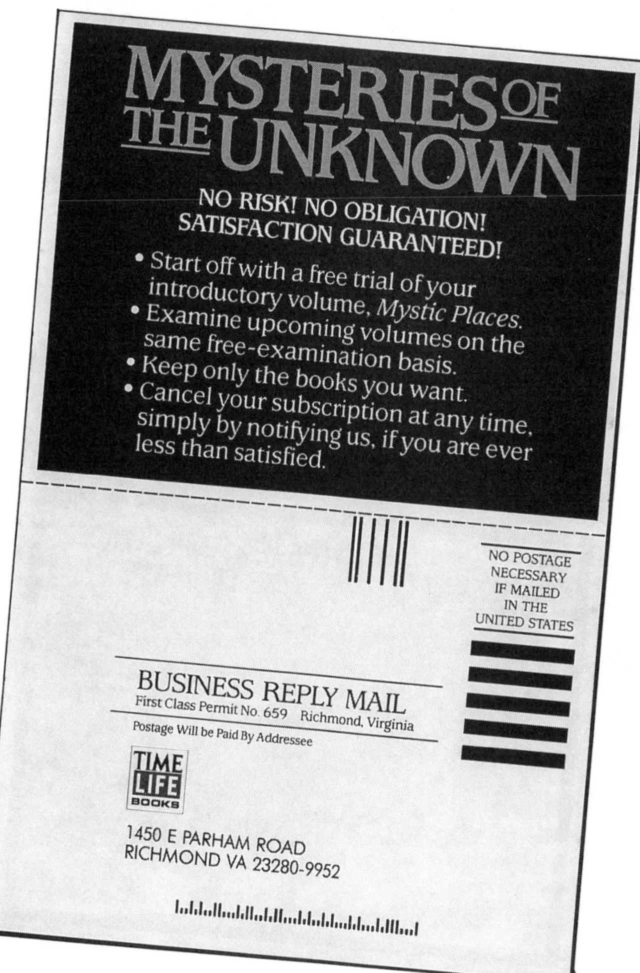

Time Frame

MAILER: Time-Life Books
PACKAGE: *Time Frame*
WRITER: Martin Tarratt
DESIGNER: Lynda Chilton
FIRST MAILED: 1988

My archives have been receiving Martin Tarratt's *Time Frame* effort in two formats: 9″ × 12″ and 6″ × 9″. With the 1991 increase in postage rates, "flats" (mailing pieces and catalogs larger than 6⅛″ × 11½″) are whacked with a $50-per-thousand penalty. As a result many mailers are downsizing both catalogs and letter mail to avoid the extra postage. In some cases results do not suffer; in others, the additional penalty is worth the increased results. In the case of *Time Frame*, the most recent versions are the 9″ × 12″ size.

British born and Cambridge educated, Martin Tarratt began as a junior copywriter in London with no love for direct mail. But after working on such accounts as Cunard and Honda, "the challenge of learning a highly specialized writing technique and of having each performance measured by response became as addictive as a roulette wheel."

In 1973, after a brief stint with BBDO in Amsterdam, Tarratt joined the Amsterdam office of Time-Life Books. Since 1976 he has been with Time-Life in New York and Alexandria (Virginia) as a copywriter and creative director.

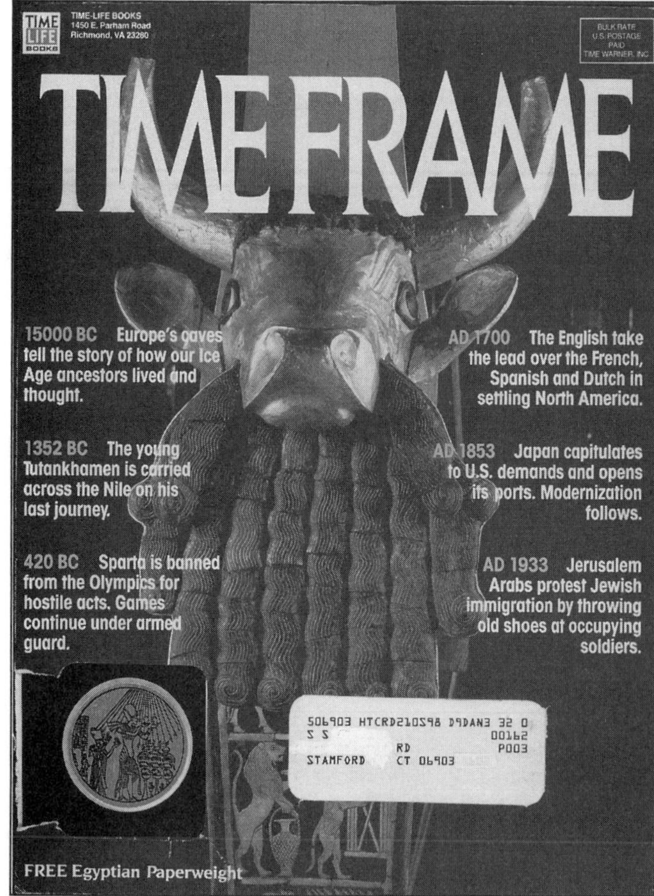

The 9″ × 12″ 4-color envelope, shown front and back. As with *Mysteries of the Unknown*, the order token shows through a small window, this one to the left of the addressing window.

TIME-LIFE's
journey through time
takes you back to

THE AGE OF GOD-KINGS
3000-1500 BC

Dear Reader,

The land is Egypt. A god-king rules ancient cities along the Nile and plays a game called hounds and jackals.

He is Khafre, lord of the land, master of the fields. And he lives in gilded, glittering splendor among many wives.

His is the face of the Great Sphinx. His word is law. And even in death, his power is absolute.

In Egypt you will live again forever, for death is not an end but a beginning. And you'll learn to count in thousands, not hundreds of years, because your world is already unthinkably old.

Let the past live again
in your free-trial introduction to

TIME FRAME

A unique world view of 5,000 years
of civilization from TIME-LIFE BOOKS

THE AGE OF GOD-KINGS 3000-1500 BC is your first volume. In it, you'll find the story of how a 500-mile cleft in the

Sahara became the richest, most fascinating culture in the ancient world.

In the same TIME FRAME, you'll return to the Sumerian metropolis of Ur. Throw dice in its bazaars. Climb its holy ziggurat. And wander through a warren of houses where people are writing, accounting and using the first books of law.

Then unlock the secrets that lie buried in the palace-cities of the Minoans: a love of sports, a horror of flab... feats of engineering, a talent for seafaring and trading.

Next take a shower in a bathroom complete with plumbing in the well-ordered cities of what is now Pakistan. Follow astonishing breakthroughs in technology along the Mekong...

Observe life at the court of China's first emperors and see why, of all the world's first civilizations, only the Middle Kingdom would endure with its traditions intact.

> Complete with original maps, specially commissioned art, time lines, hundreds of artifacts and a detailed narrative, each TIME FRAME's wealth of information is arranged so that you can extend your knowledge of global history at your own pace...

In THE AGE OF GOD-KINGS, full-color picture essays show you the first use of the written word (and the world's first-known love letter) in Sumer and Egypt...

...and the last rites of royalty--from Ur to the Great Pyramid. Minoan princes, priestesses and bull-leaping acrobats spring from the vivid frescoes of Crete and Thera.

Stonehenge, New Grange, ziggurats, pyramids, fortresses, palaces, villas and whole cities are restored to their original splendor in dramatic three-dimensional reconstructions.

Each one is authentic down to the last detail and specially commissioned in close consultation with eminent historians, curators, archaeologists, cartographers...

...so that you can share an intimate, you-are-there, cross-cultural view of history that entertains as it informs.

Keep THE AGE OF GOD-KINGS
then continue your
worldwide journey through time...

TIME FRAME can take you almost anywhere you want to go over the past 5,000 years...

...to cover events, meet personalities, follow the spread of ideas and inventions, examine lifestyles, works of art and watch ancient imaginations at work--and play.

> You can close the gaps in your knowledge with THE MARCH OF ISLAM AD 600-800.

Track the desert whirlwind that carried Muslim banners from Spain to India in less than a century...and the barbarian tides that swept Europe into the twilight of the Dark Ages.

This one-volume guide to history's missing centuries also takes you inside the cosmopolitan melting pot of T'ang China. To India as it discovers the atomic nature of the universe...

And to a Japan so open to the outside world that its emperor wore silk shirts with Greek designs twelve centuries ago.

> Or sail the distance between the Middle Ages and the modern world of globes and atlases in VOYAGES OF DISCOVERY AD 1400-1500.

Learn why, after Columbus crossed the unknown sea in three patched-up caravels and da Gama reached India, the world would never be the same again.

And in the same TIME FRAME, return to Renaissance Italy as a new urban elite masters the art of doing business and living in cities as we know them...

...witness the fall of Constantinople to a glory-seeking, 21-year-old Ottoman sultan...

...and travel to Cuzco where the imperial Inca provides for the old, the sick and the hungry, and sends messages along all-weather roads that run from Ecuador to Argentina.

Continued...

Return to THE AGE OF GOD-KINGS now:
Without obligation or commitment!

You need send no money today to examine your first TIME FRAME. Look through it at your convenience. Enjoy this unique global view of the ancient world, then decide.

If TIME FRAME 3000-1500 BC does not offer you a rewarding, informative experience, return it. It's that simple!

But if you keep it, just send us your payment of $16.99 plus shipping and handling. (Prices are guaranteed for as long as you choose to subscribe.)

> Future volumes--BARBARIAN TIDES 1500-600 BC, A SOARING SPIRIT 600-400 BC, EMPIRES ASCENDANT 400 BC-AD 200--will be sent, one about every month, always with the same free-examination privilege.
>
> Remember too, that with TIME-LIFE, there is no club to join. That means no risk and no commitment. You can buy as many or as few books as you wish--there is no minimum number. And you are free to cancel your subscription if you're ever less than satisfied!

So come, let the past live again in THE AGE OF GOD-KINGS. View the fabulous royal treasures that accompanied the pharaohs on their journey to the afterlife...

Meet the Egyptians themselves--hunters, sailors, viziers, scribes, embalmers, dancing dwarfs and priests who managed the cults of more than 2,000 fearsome gods. Then travel to Sumer, Crete, Mohenjo-daro, Ban Chiang and China as you see the world through TIME FRAME 3000-1500 BC.

Sincerely,

Robert H. Smith
Robert H. Smith
Publisher

P.S. Take a look at your certificate now to see your handsome Egyptian Paperweight! When you keep THE AGE OF GOD-KINGS, it will be your Gift of Welcome. This unusual pewter-finish disk features an exquisite engraving taken from the temple of Akhenaten.

L/TFR192-1

The 4-page letter, printed in 3 colors on an 11″ × 17″ sheet.

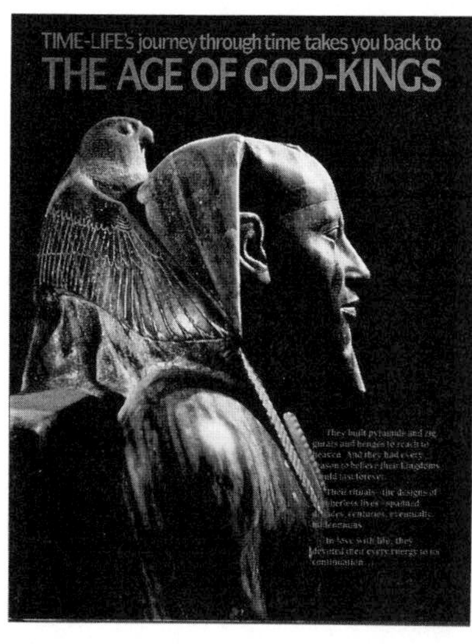

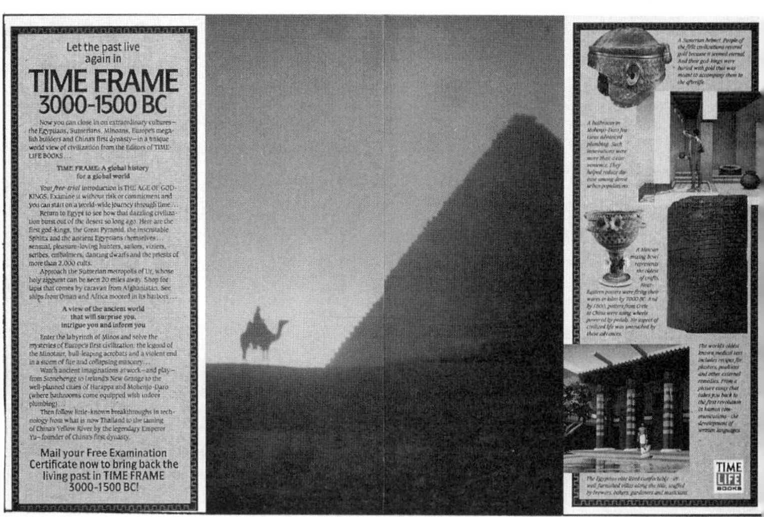

The first inside spread. The right- and left-hand panels are short gatefolds.

Lynda Chilton designed the *Time Frame* brochure to look like a magazine, with a powerful cover, a series of intriguing inside spreads, and gatefold surprises at the beginning and end.

The first inside spread with the gatefolds open to the full 11″ × 26″.

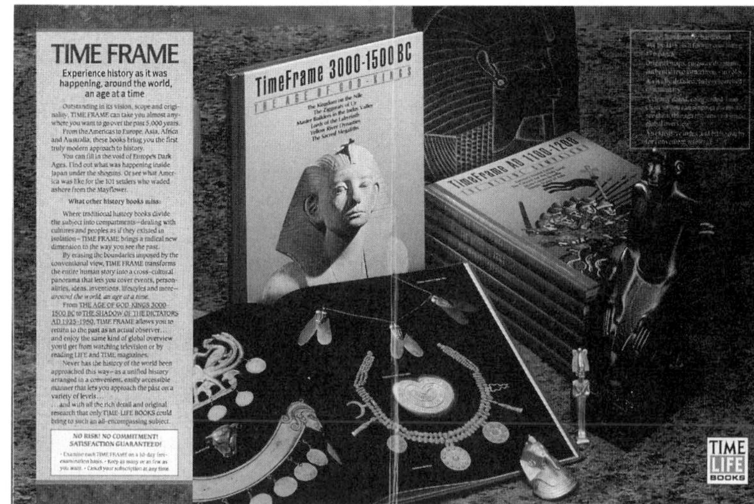

The middle spread.

The inside back spread. Both pages are full gatefolds.

The inside back spread with both gatefolds extended to the eye-stretching 39″.

Martin Tarratt:

This Time Frame *package, first mailed in 1988, offered a special challenge. The series was already several mailing seasons old, but still tied to a control package created long before the first book came off press.*

The books represented a unique editorial concept—history as it was happening around the world an age at a time. But few marketing people then at Time-Life believed world history could be sold to an American audience.

By 1988, and with few books in the series published, Time Frame *was being dismissed as unprofitable, a loser, a dog that would never hunt.*

It was time for a fresh approach—a new envelope test. What emerged is the concept on the front of the envelope—a hybrid of Time *and* People *as such a magazine might have looked had it been in circulation since, say, about 3000 B.C.*

We took this and other envelope ideas into focus groups—with mixed results. The groups did not tell us what we wanted to hear.

The back cover of the mini-magazine/circular.

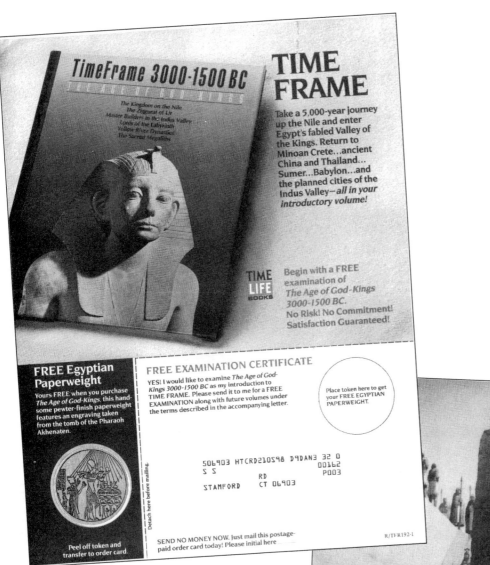

TimeFrame 3000-1500 BC

THE AGE OF GOD-KINGS

The Kingdom on the Nile
The Ziggurat of Ur
Master Builders in the Indus Valley
Lords of the Labyrinth
Yellow River Dynasties
The Sacred Megaliths

TIME FRAME

Take a 5,000-year journey up the Nile and enter Egypt's fabled Valley of the Kings. Return to Minoan Crete...ancient China and Thailand... Sumer...Babylon...and the planned cities of the Indus Valley—*all in your introductory volume!*

TIME LIFE BOOKS

Begin with a FREE examination of *The Age of God-Kings 3000-1500 BC.*
No Risk! No Commitment! Satisfaction Guaranteed!

FREE Egyptian Paperweight

Yours FREE when you purchase *The Age of God-Kings*, this handsome pewter-finish paperweight features an engraving taken from the tomb of the Pharaoh Akhenaten.

Peel off token and transfer to order card.

Detach here before mailing.

FREE EXAMINATION CERTIFICATE

YES! I would like to examine *The Age of God-Kings 3000-1500 BC* as my introduction to TIME FRAME. Please send it to me for a FREE EXAMINATION along with future volumes under the terms described in the accompanying letter.

Place token here to get your FREE EGYPTIAN PAPERWEIGHT.

506903 HTCRD210598 D9DAN3 32 0
S S 00162
RD P003
STAMFORD CT 06903

SEND NO MONEY NOW. Just mail this postage-paid order card today! Please initial here _____

R/TFR192-1

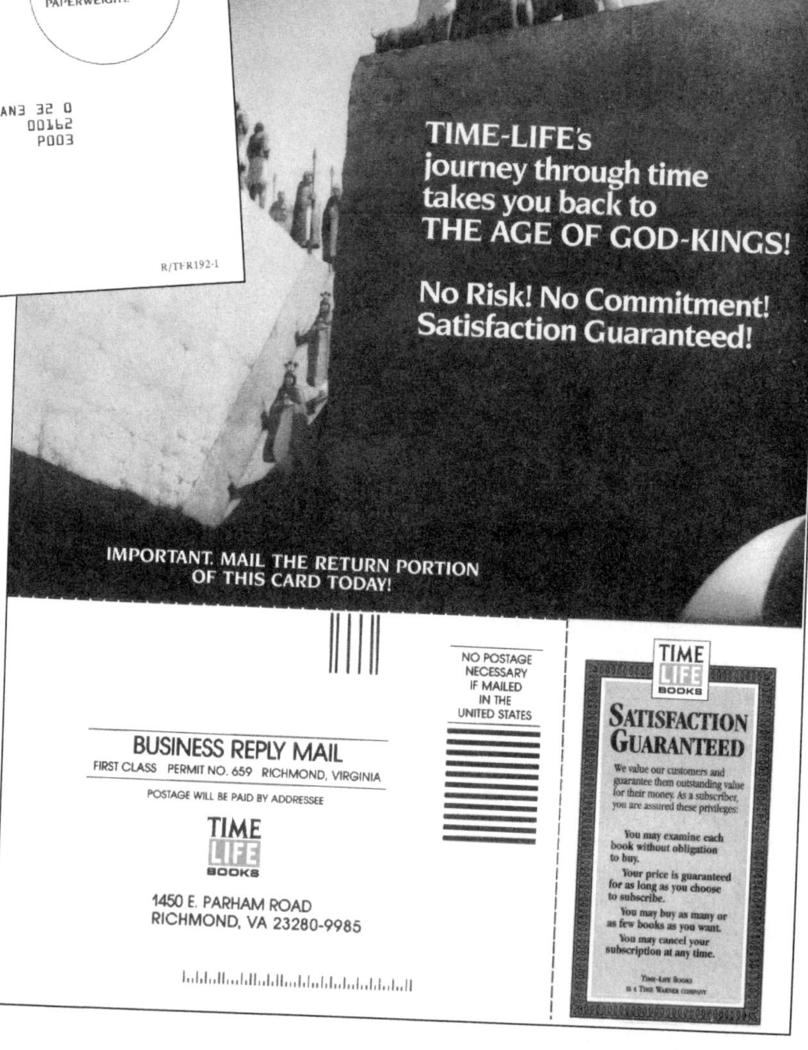

TIME-LIFE's
journey through time
takes you back to
THE AGE OF GOD-KINGS!
No Risk! No Commitment!
Satisfaction Guaranteed!
IMPORTANT. MAIL THE RETURN PORTION
OF THIS CARD TODAY!
NO POSTAGE
NECESSARY
IF MAILED
IN THE
UNITED STATES
BUSINESS REPLY MAIL
FIRST CLASS PERMIT NO. 659 RICHMOND, VIRGINIA
POSTAGE WILL BE PAID BY ADDRESSEE
TIME
LIFE
BOOKS
1450 E. PARHAM ROAD
RICHMOND, VA 23280-9985
TIME
LIFE
BOOKS
SATISFACTION
GUARANTEED
We value our customers and guarantee them outstanding value for their money. As a subscriber, you are assured these privileges:
You may examine each book without obligation to buy.
Your price is guaranteed for as long as you choose to subscribe.
You may buy as many or as few books as you want.
You may cancel your subscription at any time.

The 4-color order form, front and back. As with *Mysteries of the Unknown*, a token is removed from the stub and affixed to the order form. This token is a reproduction of the premium which will be sent on payment.

This left us with intuition based upon fifteen years of living inside other people's mailboxes. The magazine concept seemed the way to make 5,000 years of world history accessible, palatable—even enjoyable.

Taking the envelope from concept to words was the easy part. Finding the Sumerian ram's head to anchor the copy was a stroke of luck—or genius. Credit for this goes to art directors Ron Wilcox and Lynda Chilton.

In addition, the die-cut and premium sticker were involvement devices we'd never tried at Time-Life Books. (With only one test cell at our disposal, we were never to learn what part of the new thinking was driving the response.)

The new envelope and BRC (the brochure and letter remained the same as control) generated an 89 percent lift. A brief epidemic of astonishment ensued.

Time Frame lived. The edit staff was able to continue producing books—up to the Nuclear Age. And, with an average take of eight to nine books, the series would become one of the most lucrative in Time-Life's portfolio. But that is not quite the end of the story . . .

The creative breakthrough liberated funds for subscriber research. The conclusions drawn from that study overwhelmingly confirmed the creative instincts that had gone into the envelope test.

As we'd suspected, our subscribers were mature, affluent, and well educated. They saw history as a way of escaping the grim realities of their own century. And when asked where they'd most like to spend ten free days, Tutankhamen's Egypt was the clear favorite.

The way was open to create a new brochure and letter—and Egypt the direction. Just one catch . . .

The introductory volume, The Age of God-Kings, had a resonant title but stopped at 1500 B.C., long before the better-known god-kings—Akhenaten, Tutankhamen, Ramses II—made Egypt what we now think of as Egypt.

But we built an Egypt package anyway, creating a journey through time with pyramids, dancing dwarfs, reconstructions, time lines, and all the gold we could find.

We chose a booklet format for the brochure, making it harder for the prospect to throw away (and with an eye toward our back end).

And we built the letter around a real pharaoh, Khafre, whose face is on the Great Sphinx. We replaced our traditional four-page sea of words with a quicker, lighter, larger read. (Mature pairs of eyes were a consideration here!) Its tone and detail were designed to dispel any lingering historyophobia.

The new components gave us a further 20 percent lift up-front and maintained the unusually high average book take.

15

Consumer Publishing II: Negative Option Clubs

A negative option club offers an irresistible premium up front and then a commitment to buy a minimum number of additional books at discount on a "negative option" basis. Well before a book is shipped, the member receives a notice describing the book and a "rejection slip"—an instruction form that tells the club whether or not the main selection is wanted. If no action is taken by a specified date, the main selection is shipped. If the book is not wanted, or if the member wants an alternate title, the rejection slip is returned with the instructions.

The first negative option club was Book-of-the-Month, dreamed up by Harry Scherman, Maxwell Sackheim, and Robert K. Haas. Its first selection was shipped in April 1926; Literary Guild came hot on its heels in March, 1927.

Originally Book-of-the-Month was just that: an offering twelve times a year. Now most book clubs have expanded that to fifteen cycles a year, with occasional extras such as special holiday offerings.

In fulfillment and scheduling, the negative option club is the most demanding of all direct marketing operations. At any time there can be three different items in the mail *to* the member (monthly announcement with rejection slip, book shipment with bill, and statement of account); at the same time, there can be as many as four different items being sent simultaneously *from* the member: rejection slip or order for alternate selection, order for a bonus book, payment of statement, and return of a book. The fulfillment director of a negative option club and the data processing manager are necessarily master jugglers.

All the successful negative option Grand Controls have one common element: a powerful offer. The usual come-on is a menu of books or records with a very high retail value that can be yours for a token payment or even free. In turn, the new member must agree to buy a certain number of books through the club at discount prices off retail. For every book purchased after the commitment, the club will issue "a dividend" or "bonus certificate"—a credit toward purchasing bonus books at very low prices.

In the book club business the ideal situation is to have several different clubs under one roof, such as Doubleday. The Literary Guild can sign a contract with a publisher for a main selection in one club; that same book can become an alternate in another club. When the title has run its course, leftover books can be used in the low-price Doubleday Book Club. Finally, titles can end up as book dividends for all clubs.

In the early days of book clubs, a dividend certificate was sent with each selection. When the members had two or three certificates, they could order a book dividend. The paper certificates were cumbersome; people who returned books often kept the certificates and then illegally cashed them in for bonus books. At the same time, members often lost the certificates, and so the club did not have to fulfill so many claims.

At some point the data processing people came up with the idea of tallying the book dividend credits on the monthly rejection slip; the members could be kept up to date on their bonus status every month, just as frequent flyers are continually reminded of their accrued mileage. It appeared to be an ideal solution: no more bits of paper (ecologically sound); no more cashing in of unearned certificates.

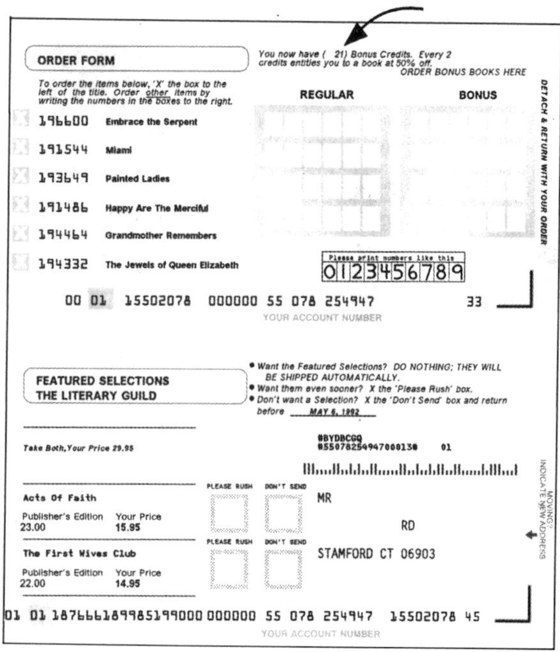

ORDER FORM

You now have (21) Bonus Credits. Every 2 credits entitles you to a book at 50% off.
ORDER BONUS BOOKS HERE

To order the items below, 'X' the box to the left of the title. Order other items by writing the numbers in the boxes to the right.

REGULAR | BONUS

DETACH & RETURN WITH YOUR ORDER

196600 Embrace the Serpent
191544 Miami
193649 Painted Ladies
191486 Happy Are The Merciful
194464 Grandmother Remembers
194332 The Jewels of Queen Elizabeth

Please print numbers like this 0123456789

00 01 15502078 000000 55 078 254947 33
YOUR ACCOUNT NUMBER

FEATURED SELECTIONS
THE LITERARY GUILD

- Want the Featured Selections? DO NOTHING; THEY WILL BE SHIPPED AUTOMATICALLY.
- Want them even sooner? X the 'Please Rush' box.
- Don't want a Selection? X the 'Don't Send' box and return before MAY 6, 1992

Take Both, Your Price 29.95

#BYDBCGQ
#55078254947000130 01

Acts Of Faith
Publisher's Edition 23.00 Your Price 15.95
PLEASE RUSH DON'T SEND

The First Wives Club
Publisher's Edition 22.00 Your Price 14.95
PLEASE RUSH DON'T SEND

MR
RD
STAMFORD CT 06903

MOVING? INDICATE NEW ADDRESS

01 01 187666189985199000 000000 55 078 254947 15502078 45
YOUR ACCOUNT NUMBER

There was just one problem: the marketing departments of the book clubs never thought through the consequences. A case in point is my own membership in the Literary Guild where I have built up 21 dividend credits. The bonus books offered are seldom of interest to me; yet every time a monthly mailing comes and I think about buying the main selection or an alternate, I am whacked in the nose by the fact that I have twenty-one book dividend credits. Instead of ordering a book, I send in the rejection slip, vowing not to buy anything until I work off some of those dividends. I'm told there are members with hundreds of such dividends.

Savvy consumers will join a negative option club for the free offer, buy the minimum number of books or records required, and then resign and join again later.

BMG Music Service

Here are two Grand Controls, both written by BMG's director of creative services, Strat Simon. The first is a classical club, International Preview Society, with an offer of 3 for $1. The second is a derivative effort for the popular Compact Disc club—presumably going to a less upscale universe—with a far stronger offer of 8 CDs, cassettes or records for the price of half; this effort dramatizes the value by including a "Music Voucher" that looks like a check and is worth up to $63.92.

Strat Simon worked for over twenty-five years as copywriter, copy chief, marketing director, and creative director. Most recently he was director of creative services for Bertelsmann Music Group's direct marketing subsidiary where he directed the transition of the creative group to electronic publishing. He has also held copywriting and copy chief positions at Doubleday Book Clubs, Grey Advertising, and *Highlights for Children* where he developed the first insert to wrap around the *outside* of a magazine.

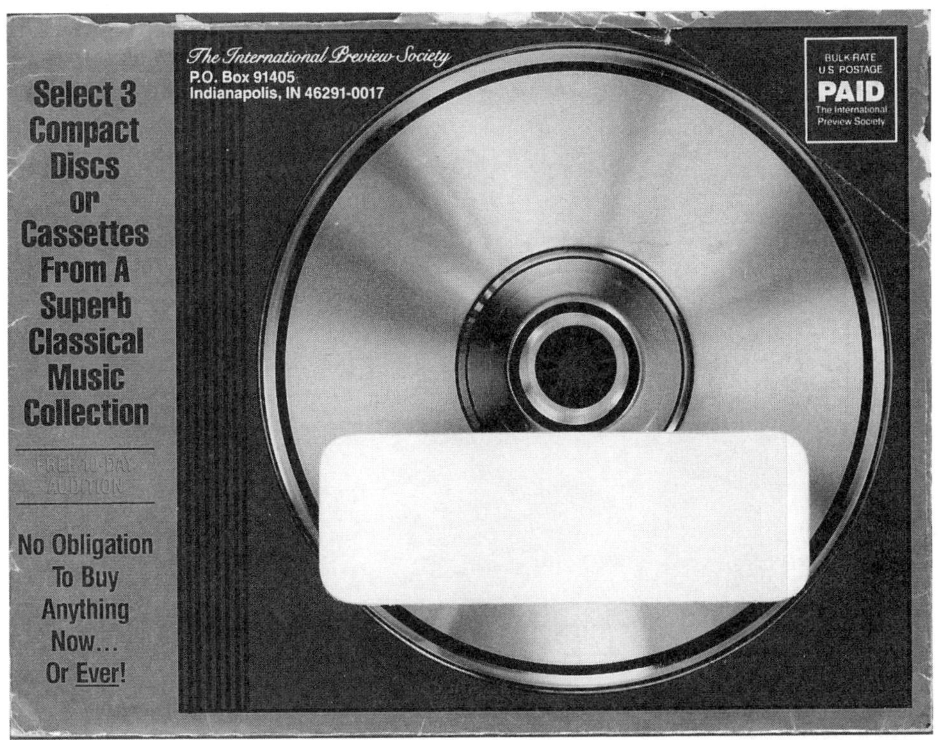

MAILER: International Preview Society
PACKAGE: Free 10-Day Audition
PROJECT MGR.: Stratis Simon
AGENCY: In-house
WRITER: Stratis Simon
DESIGNER: Joseph Pontevolpe
FIRST MAILED: 1988
The 5″ × 6½″ 4-color outside envelope of metallic silver and black with a rainbow effect on the compact disc. The design of the back of the envelope is identical to the front. Subsequent mailings have since eliminated 4-color on the envelopes.

The International Preview Society

P.O. Box 91406, Indianapolis, Indiana, 46291-0005

You are invited to take

3 Classical Compact Discs or Cassettes

for only $1*

... with no obligation to buy
another album again!

Dear Music Lover,

The monumental genius of Beethoven ... the excitement of Vivaldi ... the sensuousness of Tchaikovsky ... the thrills of hallmark performances by Pavarotti and Galway ... such pleasures are creating new and growing demand for quality recordings of classical music.

That's why The International Preview Society was founded more than a decade ago: to bring classical music lovers the finest new releases of classical recordings ... at prices members could afford.

And to introduce new members to the Society, we are extending a truly extraordinary introductory membership offer ...

Any 3 Classical Compact Discs
or Cassettes for Only $1*

Yes, up to $47.94 worth of classical CDs or Cassettes are yours for just $1 -- and here is the best part:

You Need Never Purchase Another Album
From The Society Ever Again!

We hope you do, of course ... and we believe you will once you learn all the many benefits of membership. But The International

* plus shipping & handling (over, please)

A WORD ABOUT RECORDING QUALITY

The Society features albums on the world's most respected labels -- RCA Red Seal, Deutsche Grammophon, Philips, London, Angel, Nonesuch and Newport Classic, to name a few. Compact disc recordings, employing laser-accurate digital technology, sound so real and flawless, it's like being there "live" at a concert. And the Society's cassette recordings are also magnificent. Many of the cassettes are mastered on superior quality chrome tape using the most advanced noise reduction systems. No matter which format you choose, your classical selections will never cease to thrill you with their superb audio quality.

All the Main Selections are chosen by the distinguished Selection Committee. They must be judged superior in choice of music, performance and quality of sound to be offered to members. Many Main Selections and alternates are multi-album sets which offer still more value in classical music. Most of these sets come complete with:

-- An illustrated booklet with commentary about the composer and performers.

-- A handsome presentation case to protect and display your recordings.

SUBSTANTIAL SAVINGS NOW -- AND IN THE FUTURE!

Decide to keep your 3 introductory albums and pay just $1! Then, in addition to the significant savings you'll enjoy on many future single and multi-album sets, you'll immediately qualify for our Half-Price Bonus Plan!

ABOUT THE SOCIETY'S HALF-PRICE BONUS PLAN

You receive one Bonus Certificate with every single album you purchase, two with every multi-album set you purchase. Use your Certificates to get

Preview Society believes you should purchase only the recordings you want -- when you want. And this special offer has no minimum purchase agreements or time limitations. Here, at last, is a music club for adult sensibilities!

THE ENCLOSED STAMP SHEET HAS
JUST A SAMPLING OF THE ENORMOUS
NUMBER OF CHOICES DISPLAYED IN
THE SOCIETY'S BULLETIN

The International Preview Society features such artists as Vladimir Horowitz ... James Galway ... Itzhak Perlman ... Neville Marriner ... Sir Georg Solti ... Herbert von Karajan ... Luciano Pavarotti ...Andrés Segovia ... Van Cliburn ... Jascha Heifetz ... Leonard Bernstein ... Christopher Hogwood --- and hundreds of other world-renowned classical performers.

Select any 3 now -- for only $1 -- then sit back and enjoy your introductory selections, knowing that literally hundreds of other outstanding albums will be offered to you in the months ahead through the Society ... many at substantial savings.

You'll receive the Society's bulletin, Preview, about every four weeks ... 13 exciting shopping opportunities in a year! Each issue highlights a Main Selection and an impressive array of alternate albums. But remember, there is no obligation to accept any offering. In fact, there is absolutely no obligation to purchase anything at any time.

If you'd like the Main Selection, you need do nothing. It will be sent automatically. If you'd like another album, or none at all, just return the Notification Card to us by the date specified. Should you ever have less than 10 days to decide, return the shipment at our expense.

compact discs or cassettes of your choice at half price! Imagine ... you can receive some of the world's greatest classical recordings at savings of 50%! (Shipping & handling, plus any applicable sales tax, are added to all shipments.) I think you'll agree you'd be hard pressed to find a record store to offer you such incredible half-price discounts.

MAIL YOUR AUDITION CERTIFICATE TODAY!

You just can't lose as a Society member! You get a tremendous variety of albums to choose from, superb quality, fabulous savings, the Half-Price Bonus Plan and NO MINIMUM PURCHASE. And you may cancel at any time, simply by writing to us.

Begin your membership now by choosing 3 classical albums from the enclosed stamp sheet. Affix them to the certificate and mail in the post-paid envelope provided. The 3 CDs or cassettes you select are yours for only $1, plus shipping & handling; you save as much as $46.94 off regular Club prices.

Send no money now. Enjoy the 3 recordings you select for 10 days. If not delighted, feel free to return your 3 albums at the end of 10 days without obligation. But I believe you will keep the three you select ... music you'll enjoy for a lifetime!

Sincerely yours,

William Crowley

William Crowley
Music Director

P.S. Do look over the enclosed stamp sheet now, from Pavarotti At Carnegie Hall to Galway's Greatest Hits, from Sir Georg Solti to Itzhak Perlman... any 3 of the world's greatest artists and performances are available now for your 10-day free audition.

The 4-page letter printed on 2 nested, folded sheets.

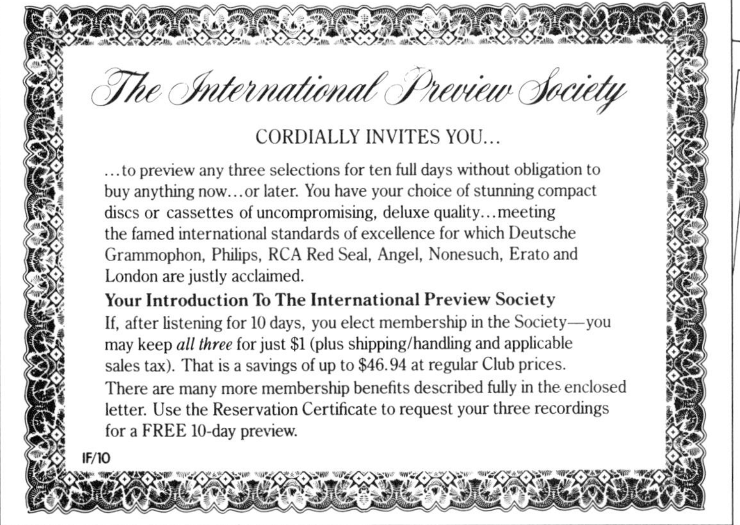

The International Preview Society

CORDIALLY INVITES YOU...

...to preview any three selections for ten full days without obligation to buy anything now...or later. You have your choice of stunning compact discs or cassettes of uncompromising, deluxe quality...meeting the famed international standards of excellence for which Deutsche Grammophon, Philips, RCA Red Seal, Angel, Nonesuch, Erato and London are justly acclaimed.

Your Introduction To The International Preview Society

If, after listening for 10 days, you elect membership in the Society—you may keep *all three* for just $1 (plus shipping/handling and applicable sales tax). That is a savings of up to $46.94 at regular Club prices.

There are many more membership benefits described fully in the enclosed letter. Use the Reservation Certificate to request your three recordings for a FREE 10-day preview.

IF/10

The International Preview Society was founded more than a decade ago to provide its members with a selection of the finest new releases of classical recordings...at prices members could afford.

And what better way to introduce new members to the Society than with these superior performances by the world's most renowned performers in the field of classical music, and this special offer that does not obligate you to purchase anything else, ever. It is a unique opportunity to acquire the nucleus of a great and lasting classical musical library—at remarkable savings.

There is a Free audition privilege with this introductory offering. So do accept this no-risk opportunity today. You will not be disappointed.

The Selection Committee

The lift piece, printed in 2 colors.

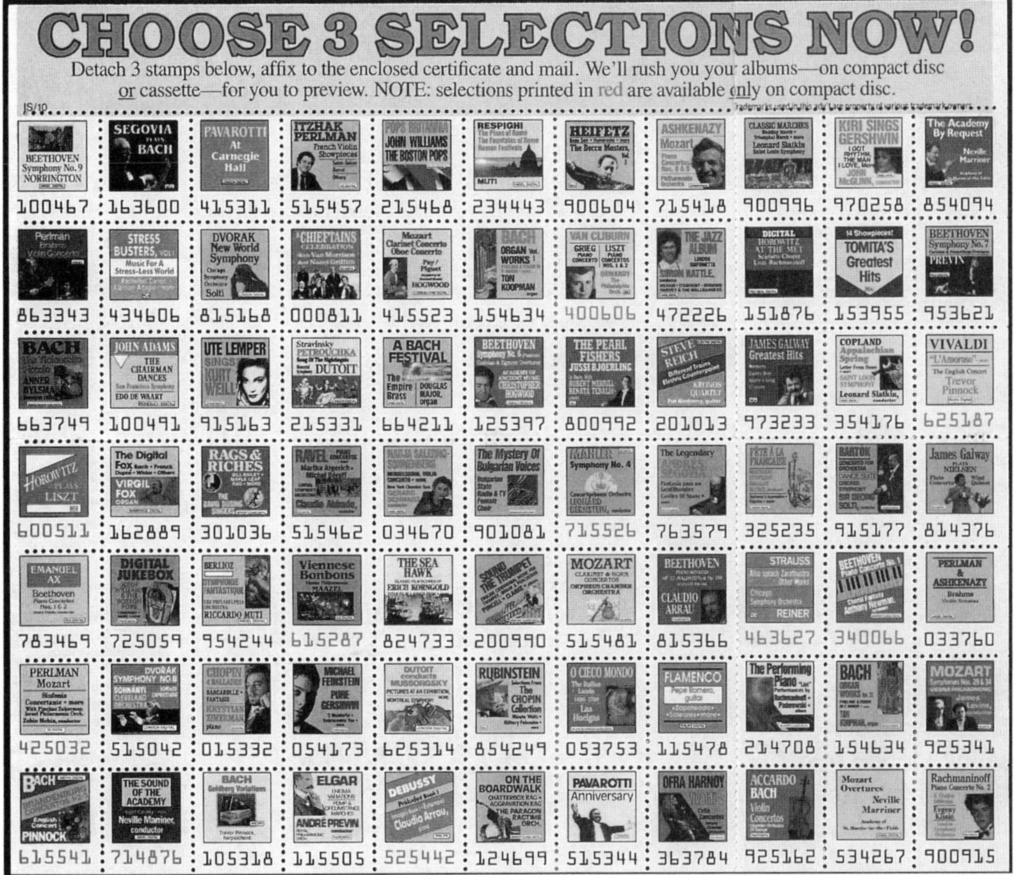

The stamp sheet, printed in 4 colors. Each stamp is just 3/4″ square, so you must have good eyes. To order, you detach 3 stamps representing the premiums of your choice and affix them to the order card. With all the different album covers shown in full color, this is the jolliest, most involving piece in the package.

Strat Simon:

I used to say I was the world's second best copywriter with everybody else tied for first place, so it's good to be included in this collection.

What makes a copywriter? In my case many things came together. I was introverted, learned English as a second language so I was better at expressing myself on paper rather than verbally. I was a prolific letter writer while away at college, and I liked the freedom of working on an assignment basis rather than in a structured nine-to-five office.

More important, you have to love writing copy that motivates a reader as an end to itself. I was so serious about it that after a year in my first job at Prentice-Hall, I left for a job in the midwest because all my fellow New York associates were talking to themselves. Unlike the novelty store maps that show New York

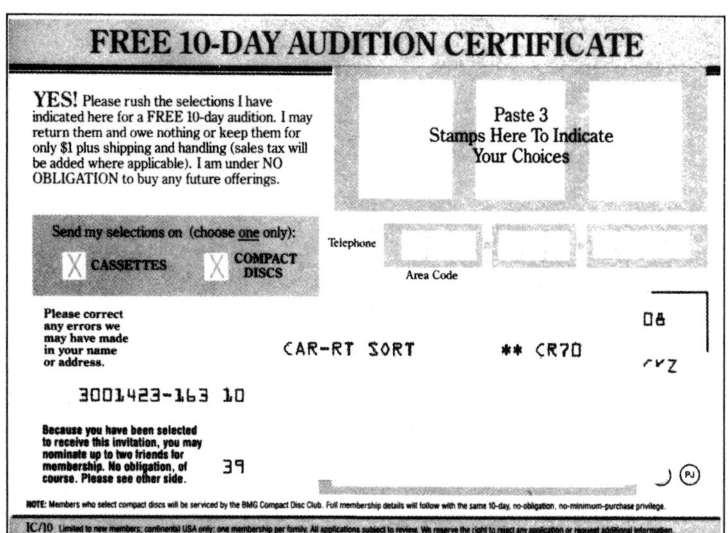

FREE 10-DAY AUDITION CERTIFICATE

YES! Please rush the selections I have indicated here for a FREE 10-day audition. I may return them and owe nothing or keep them for only $1 plus shipping and handling (sales tax will be added where applicable). I am under NO OBLIGATION to buy any future offerings.

Paste 3 Stamps Here To Indicate Your Choices

Send my selections on (choose one only):

X CASSETTES X COMPACT DISCS

Telephone

Area Code

Please correct any errors we may have made in your name or address.

CAR-RT SORT ** CR70

08

3001423-163 10

Because you have been selected to receive this invitation, you may nominate up to two friends for membership. No obligation, of course. Please see other side.

39

NOTE: Members who select compact discs will be serviced by the BMG Compact Disc Club. Full membership details will follow with the same 10-day, no-obligation, no-minimum-purchase privilege.

IC/10 Limited to new members; continental USA only; one membership per family. All applications subject to review. We reserve the right to reject any application or request additional information.

You may introduce up to two special friends to the greatest classical recordings in the world.

If you have friends who enjoy classical music as you do, simply write their names and addresses in the spaces below. We'll send them a similar invitation, so that they, too, may decide to accept membership in The International Preview Society. No obligation on your part...just the opportunity to share the splendid advantages of membership.

Name

Address Apt.

City State Zip

Name

Address Apt.

City State Zip

The order card shown front and back along with the business reply envelope, also shown front and back. The back of the order card is a Member-Get-a-Member (MGM) effort, which is unusual for a cold solicitation. One of the most profitable sources of membership in book and record clubs is referrals. Virtually every monthly mailing contains an MGM and offers a premium to both the prospective member and the member if the referral becomes an active member. But it could be argued that asking for the referral on the cold solicitation could interrupt the ordering process and cost sales. This should be tested. On the back of the BRE is a recap of the ordering instructions.

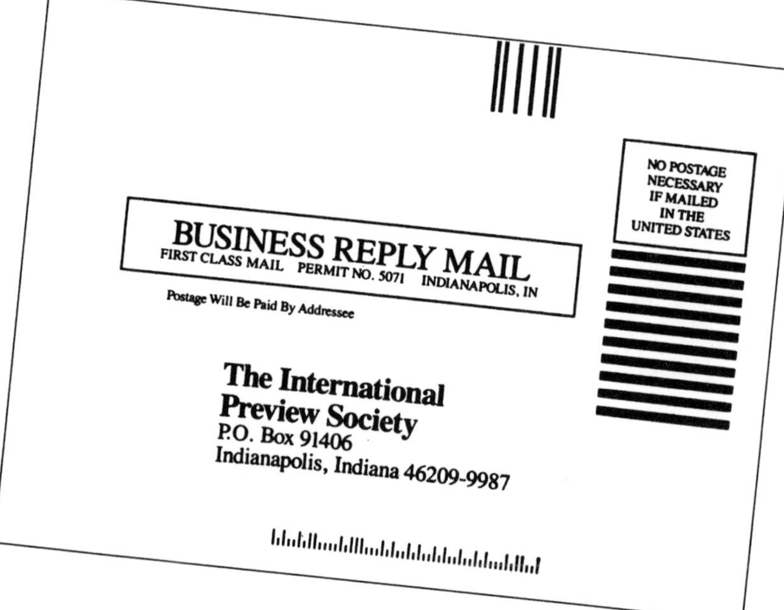

NO POSTAGE NECESSARY IF MAILED IN THE UNITED STATES
BUSINESS REPLY MAIL
FIRST CLASS MAIL PERMIT NO. 5071 INDIANAPOLIS, IN
Postage Will Be Paid By Addressee
The International Preview Society
P.O. Box 91406
Indianapolis, Indiana 46209-9987

City spread over three-fourths of the United States and the rest of the country on the other side of the Hudson River, New York was not America, and to "reach" my audience, I felt I needed to live among the people I was writing to.

The two direct mail packages in this book are conceptually related. As with most creative ideas, they occur through interaction, and in this case, the club president, Raju Puthukari, was looking for a method of giving the recipients the sense of receiving a compact disc in their hands.

Since the CD case was almost the shape of an envelope, it was only a matter of a few words and thoughts between Raju, myself, and Joe Kreiser, our list and mailing expert who was present at the time. We pushed, pulled, and stretched the idea into the International Preview Society piece. The mail piece was just slightly smaller than an actual CD case. The concept was further enhanced by embossing the four-color envelope with ridges representative of those on a CD case and adding a silver metallic ink. The copy itself, although adapted from earlier offers, "romanced" the advantages of the Compact Disc—so new at the time, the major CD purchasers were classical music buffs.

The #10 piece for BMG Music Service was based on the same strong visual portrayal of the CD, extended one step further by our art director, Joe Pontevolpe, who created a series of overlapping discs to fill out the new dimensions.

The copy was totally offer driven. As with all mass market book and record club offers, it appealed to the timeless, basic (and base) instinct of getting something for nothing . . . or as close as we could profitably make it. A realistic voucher, representative of the value of the up-front offer, was included and from prior uses, was known to be strong; there was no need—indeed it was detrimental—to include a brochure of the many stars and recording labels available through the club. This piece ran for several years until we developed equally productive but less expensive packages.

8
COMPACT DISCS,
CASSETTES OR RECORDS
FOR THE PRICE OF
1/2
...with nothing more to buy EVER!
SEE INSIDE FOR DETAILS
Raymond Johnson
P.O. Box 91001
Indianapolis, IN 46291-0002
BULK RATE
U.S. POSTAGE
PAID
BMG Music Service
********CAR-RT SORT **CR09
HEATH
LANE
HOUSTON TX 77074
NOW THE BEST MUSIC OFFER IS ON SALE
THIS OFFER EXPIRES FEBRUARY 23RD.
AND WILL NOT BE REPEATED IN 1990!
When you do buy your one album, we'll bill you at just one half the regular Club price.

The outside #10 4-color envelope for the nonclassical club. The offer is much stronger than that of the classical club; the addressing voucher is on bank-check-like paper with a saving of "up to $63.00" showing through. Like that on the International Preview Society's envelope, the design on the back is identical to the front.

VL/10

BMG Music Service
6550 E. 30th St., Indianapolis, IN 46219-1194

December 22, 1989

Enclosed...

... is your voucher worth up to $63.92, which I ask you to return to me – for 4 compact discs, cassettes or records of your choice from the BMG Music Service.

Yes, this voucher is actually good for up to $63.92 worth of top-star, top-hit selections at regular Club prices. It enables you to try the Music Service without risk ... to hear the quality of our compact discs, cassettes or records, to test our membership services and benefits. All I ask in return is that you buy only 1 selection within the next year (something you would probably do anyway) and pay – not our regular Club prices – but half that! Then you can choose 3 more compact discs, cassettes or records FREE (shipping/handling added to each shipment). After that, you may cancel your membership at any time simply by writing to us.

This special offer is really incredible when you consider you're getting 8 smash-hit compact discs, cassettes or records for the price of JUST HALF of one hit ... with nothing more to buy ever!

REMEMBER -- THIS OFFER WILL NOT BE REPEATED IN 1990.
THIS OFFER EXPIRES FEBRUARY 23rd, SO, DO ACT NOW!

Please take a look at the stamp sheet enclosed. It has 140 top-star selections by fantastic artists like Guns N' Roses, Richard Marx, Janet Jackson, U2, The Beach Boys, Vladimir Horowitz, Tracy Chapman, Bon Jovi, Alabama, The Traveling Wilburys, Kenny Rogers, James Galway, Madonna, ZZ Top, Kenny G, Randy Travis, Van Halen, Elvis Presley and more. And you'll find every music category represented, too, from pop, rock and country ... to classical and easy listening.

Just pick your 4 favorites now! Detach the appropriate stamps and paste them in the spaces provided on your personal voucher/order form. Then complete, sign and mail it to us postage-free. Your music voucher is worth the price of 4 hit compact discs, cassettes or records of your choice – you pay only shipping/handling – when you choose to mail it in today.

Sincerely,

Raymond Johnson

Raymond Johnson
Membership Director

The 1-page, 2-color $6^{1}/_{2}'' \times 8^{1}/_{2}''$ letter. Note the lack of a salutation.

"Is this voucher for 4 hit compact discs, cassettes or records for real?"

The lift piece. The headline is on the outer fold.

OFFICE OF THE VICE PRESIDENT
BMG Music Service

Dear Music Lover,

Let me make a prediction–

I predict that many, many thousands of people who really love music will not mail in their vouchers for the 4 compact discs, cassettes or records we offer – simply because they're suspicious!

"There's got to be a catch," they'll say. "Getting up to $63.92 worth of compact discs, cassettes or records for nothing is just too good to be true."

But there is no catch, I assure you. Our offer is exactly as described in Mr. Johnson's letter.

We make this offer simply because experience has shown that it is a sound, economical way to acquire new friends for the Music Service. Many of the trial members will continue with us for three, five, even ten years. We'll make a fair profit while you keep on saving.

So set your suspicions to rest and redeem your voucher today for great music and great value.

Cordially,

Paul Finn

T. P. Finn

P.S. We will not repeat this offer in 1990. Please act now. This offer expires on February 23rd!

The multicolored stamp sheet.

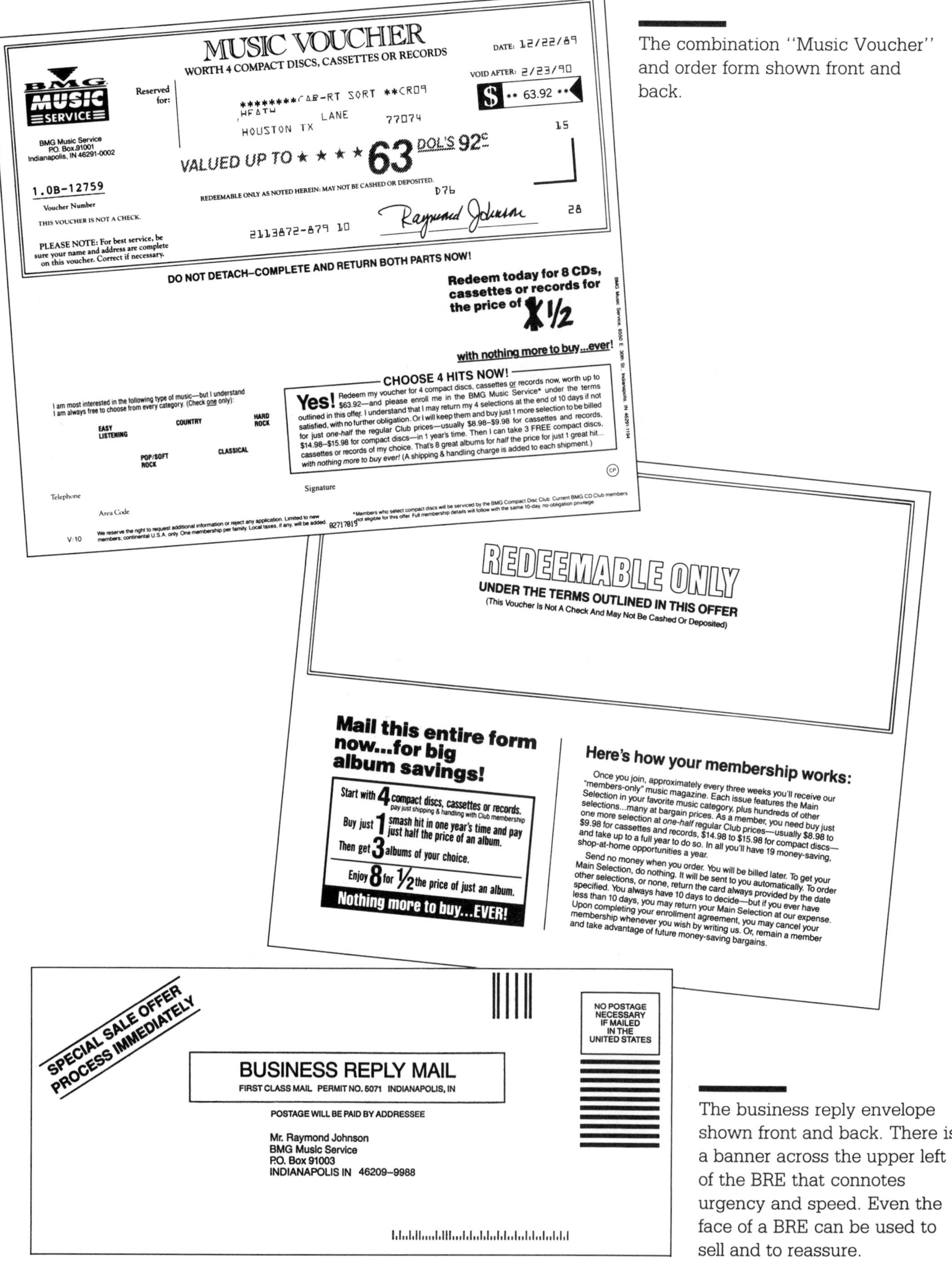

MUSIC VOUCHER
WORTH 4 COMPACT DISCS, CASSETTES OR RECORDS

DATE: 12/22/89
VOID AFTER: 2/23/90
$ ** 63.92 **

BMG MUSIC SERVICE

Reserved for:
********CAR-RT SORT **CR09
HEATH LANE
HOUSTON TX 77074
15

BMG Music Service
P.O. Box 91001
Indianapolis, IN 46291-0002

VALUED UP TO ★ ★ ★ ★ 63 DOL'S 92¢

1.0B-12759
Voucher Number

REDEEMABLE ONLY AS NOTED HEREIN: MAY NOT BE CASHED OR DEPOSITED.
D76

THIS VOUCHER IS NOT A CHECK.

2113872-879 10
28

PLEASE NOTE: For best service, be sure your name and address are complete on this voucher. Correct if necessary.

DO NOT DETACH–COMPLETE AND RETURN BOTH PARTS NOW!

Redeem today for 8 CDs, cassettes or records for the price of ~~1~~ 1/2

with nothing more to buy...ever!

BMG Music Service, 6550 E. 30th St., Indianapolis, IN 46291-1194

I am most interested in the following type of music—but I understand I am always free to choose from every category. (Check one only):

EASY LISTENING | COUNTRY | HARD ROCK | POP/SOFT ROCK | CLASSICAL

CHOOSE 4 HITS NOW!

Yes! Redeem my voucher for 4 compact discs, cassettes or records now, worth up to $63.92—and please enroll me in the BMG Music Service* under the terms outlined in this offer. I understand that I may return my 4 selections at the end of 10 days if not satisfied, with no further obligation. Or I will keep them and buy just 1 more selection to be billed for just *one-half* the regular Club prices—usually $8.98–$9.98 for cassettes and records, $14.98–$15.98 for compact discs—in 1 year's time. Then I can take 3 FREE compact discs, cassettes or records of my choice. That's 8 great albums for *half* the price for just 1 great hit... *with nothing more to buy ever!* (A shipping & handling charge is added to each shipment.)

CP

Telephone

Area Code

Signature

V/10

We reserve the right to request additional information or reject any application. Limited to new members; continental U.S.A. only. One membership per family. Local taxes, if any, will be added. 02717019

*Members who select compact discs will be serviced by the BMG Compact Disc Club. Current BMG CD Club members not eligible for this offer. Full membership details will follow with the same 10-day, no-obligation privilege.

REDEEMABLE ONLY
UNDER THE TERMS OUTLINED IN THIS OFFER
(This Voucher Is Not A Check And May Not Be Cashed Or Deposited)

Mail this entire form now...for big album savings!

Start with 4 compact discs, cassettes or records.
pay just shipping & handling with Club membership
Buy just 1 smash hit in one year's time and pay just half the price of an album.
Then get 3 albums of your choice.
Enjoy 8 for 1/2 the price of just an album.
Nothing more to buy...EVER!

Here's how your membership works:

Once you join, approximately every three weeks you'll receive our
"members-only" music magazine. Each issue features the Main
Selection in your favorite music category, plus hundreds of other
selections...many at bargain prices. As a member, you need buy just
one more selection at *one-half* regular Club prices—usually $8.98 to
$9.98 for cassettes and records, $14.98 to $15.98 for compact discs—
and take up to a full year to do so. In all you'll have 19 money-saving,
shop-at-home opportunities a year.

Send no money when you order. You will be billed later. To get your
Main Selection, do nothing. It will be sent to you automatically. To order
other selections, or none, return the card always provided by the date
specified. You always have 10 days to decide—but if you ever have
less than 10 days, you may return your Main Selection at our expense.
Upon completing your enrollment agreement, you may cancel your
membership whenever you wish by writing us. Or, remain a member
and take advantage of future money-saving bargains.

SPECIAL SALE OFFER
PROCESS IMMEDIATELY

NO POSTAGE NECESSARY IF MAILED IN THE UNITED STATES

BUSINESS REPLY MAIL
FIRST CLASS MAIL PERMIT NO. 5071 INDIANAPOLIS, IN

POSTAGE WILL BE PAID BY ADDRESSEE

Mr. Raymond Johnson
BMG Music Service
P.O. Box 91003
INDIANAPOLIS IN 46209–9988

The combination "Music Voucher" and order form shown front and back.

The business reply envelope shown front and back. There is a banner across the upper left of the BRE that connotes urgency and speed. Even the face of a BRE can be used to sell and to reassure.

Book-of-the-Month

Guru Axel Andersson has said that if you want to increase response dramatically, change the offer. In the case of Book-of-the-Month, the offer has gotten very soft—four books (worth up to $100 retail) for $1 each and *no commitment* to purchase any more books. Obviously this offer raised up-front response; and while it enabled people to rip off the club by purchasing no additional books, more responders up front means more buyers later on. Since the mailing was control for six years, the arithmetic must have worked.

One curious aspect of the mailing is the personalized letter. A window envelope with promotional copy on the front states loud and clear that it is a piece of advertising mail. Showing through this window are the name and address from the top of the personalized letter (not the order card); over the person's name is the following:

*BLK RT CAR-RT SORT ** CR17*

It's obvious on three counts (window envelope, promotional copy on outer envelope, and carrier-route sort postal discount over the person's name) that this is *in no way* a personal letter.

Why bother with a personalized letter?

Presumably because it worked for Book-of-the-Month in terms of the lifetime value of a member.

BOMC Book-of-the-Month Club, Inc.
Camp Hill, PA 17012

Tractor Trailer
Additional Presort 1930s
Postage Paid
USA 10

BULK RATE

BLK RT CAR-RT SORT ** CR93
James

New York, NY 10028

(Please don't tell your friends)
We have a special offer for you: choose 4 books for $1 each with *no obligation* to buy any more.

MAILER: Book-of-the-Month Club
PACKAGE: "Don't tell your friends"
PROJECT MGR.: Michael Moroney
AGENCY: Wunderman Worldwide
WRITER: Bill Kaisler
DESIGNER: Wunderman Worldwide
FIRST MAILED: 1985
The #10 outside envelope, printed on gray stock flecked with blue. The script copy in parentheses is in blue; everything else is printed in black.

Book-of-the-Month Club, Inc.
Camp Hill, PA 17012

BLK RT CAR-RT SORT ** CR93
James

New York, NY 10028

Dear Mr.

This letter is going to be short and to the point. We don't want to make a big thing of it. Not yet, anyway.

We'd like to invite you to take advantage of what we call our "no-strings" membership.

This offer extends our typically generous introduction to you: choose any 4 books for $1 each.

But it omits the usual obligation to buy four more books. You don't have to buy even one more book.

In other words, you can join Book-of-the-Month Club, take your welcoming package of 4 books (saving up to $100 or more), and never buy another thing from us.

It's an experiment for us. Will this attract the kind of reader who will appreciate our other Club benefits as well as the introductory offer?

It's an experiment for you. A way to try us without tying yourself down to a commitment.

So enjoy all the Club benefits you wish. Just as if you were a committed member. We've put it all in writing. Take any 4

1091/0

books for $1 each, plus shipping and handling, with no obligation to buy anything else. The rest is up to you.

I can't imagine a bigger bargain for the reader. Can you?

Sincerely,

James Mercer
President

P.S. This offer isn't available to everyone. It isn't transferable. But, if you do decide to join and become a member of the Club, we can understand why you might want to share the news of your "no-strings" membership with a special friend or two. In that event, ask them to write me and mention your name.

The 2-page letter printed front and back on an $8^{1/2}'' \times 11''$ sheet that matches the outside envelope.

The creative director at Book-of-the-Month is Michael Moroney, who began his direct marketing career as a copywriter in the great apprentice factory, Prentice-Hall. In 1979 he moved to Book-of-the-Month as a direct mail copywriter and since then has held a variety of positions, most recently that of vice president, promotion. He is a recipient of two Echo Leader Awards and a first place John Caples Award.

MICHAEL MORONEY:

This is a deceptively simple and quiet package: just a letter/application form and a brochure. The brochure is mostly books with little copy. The letter is a short two-pager. Except for a self-mailer, nothing could be simpler.

But that's part of its strength. We're asking people to choose four books—a fairly complicated process compared to other direct response offers—so a brochure that doesn't get in the way of selecting the books makes sense.

Also, we're offering a no-commitment membership. The whole psychology of no commit is that you don't have to fear entanglements or commitments after you join. So the copy doesn't say much about what happens after you join, but focuses almost entirely on the up-front, no-commit offer. The shortness of the copy reinforces the message, as if to say, ''Look, there's really nothing to be afraid of.''

The letter is a masterful and friendly piece of writing by Bill Keisler. The hook, of course, is ''Please don't tell your friends,'' and the copy throughout hits the exclusive nature of the offer. The hook is nicely ''closed'' in the P.S. of the letter.

'When we say "no strings" we mean it....'

The lift piece.

When you choose 4 books for $1 each you make no commitment whatsoever.

Dear Reader,

I wouldn't blame you if you didn't believe us when we say "no strings." There are many confusing schemes out there with more strings than you have fingers to count them on.

But this isn't one of them.

When we say no strings we mean no catches, no hidden traps, no fine print to fool you.

For just $4, plus shipping and handling, we'll send you 4 honest-to-goodness, quality hardcover books.

You have no obligation to buy another book — ever.

And that's the truth.

Sincerely,

Brigitte Weeks
Editor-in-Chief

In my years as a creative director, I've seen countless examples of weak, muddled copy. So my creative philosophy is a simple one. I believe in good writing. And I believe in clarity, content, and credibility.

I also agree with Lew Smith who says that the role of a creative director is simply to determine if an ad is ''quickly coherent'' and ''ultimately persuasive.''

Enough said.

The Book-of-the-Month Grand Control was written by Bill Keisler, now retired from Wunderman.

Bill Keisler:

Admittedly, a direct mail package is a complicated project, an ad of many parts. That can be intimidating.

One piece of advice I received early on was first to write and put into place all the mandatories: the outer envelope, offer, guarantee, nuts-and-bolts, order form. Then, I was told, fill in the leftover space with ''copy.''

Fortunately, I ignored this well-intentioned advice. I began with the view that direct mail—even more than other media—can be, simply, one human being talking to another human being. With Book-of-the-Month, it is also one avid reader talking to another avid reader. Keeping that in mind, everything (including the nuts-and-bolts) represents in tone and content pretty much what I'd say in person to a suitable prospect. Reading it aloud helps me determine how well I've achieved this.

If I've done my job, the package will communicate well with the right prospects. I also believe that readers who join as a result will become better performing members, and further, that the mailing piece itself will enjoy a longer, more prosperous life.

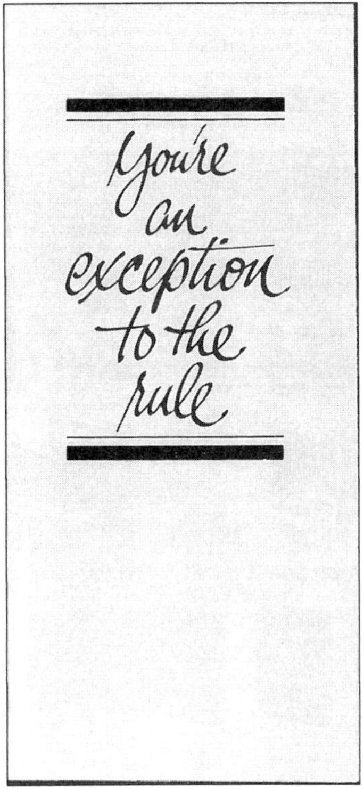

The brochure cover is gray with blue type. When you open it . . .

The back of the brochure with 9 more titles.

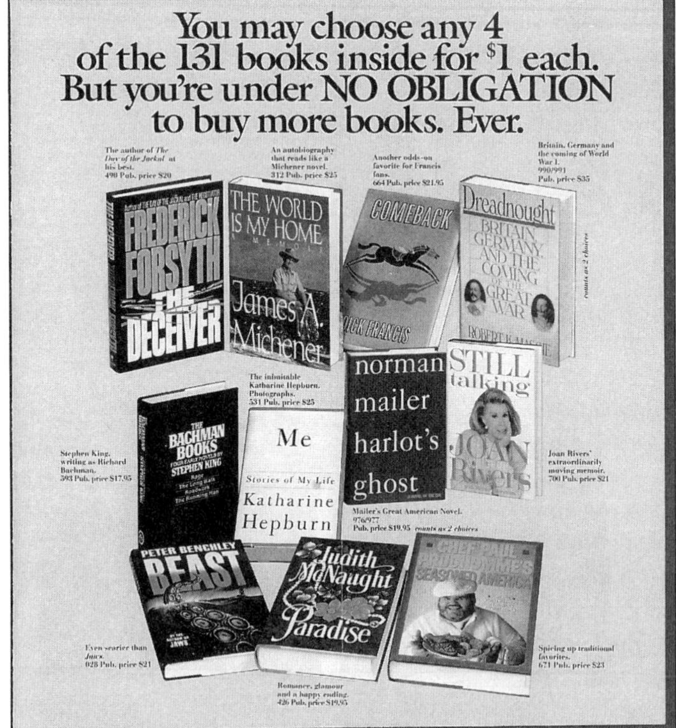

. . . you are hit with a lot of color and a headline that restates the "no obligation" offer.

Open it again and the brochure becomes tall and skinny (7¾″ × 17″) and repeats the no obligation offer in the superhead and again in the headline.

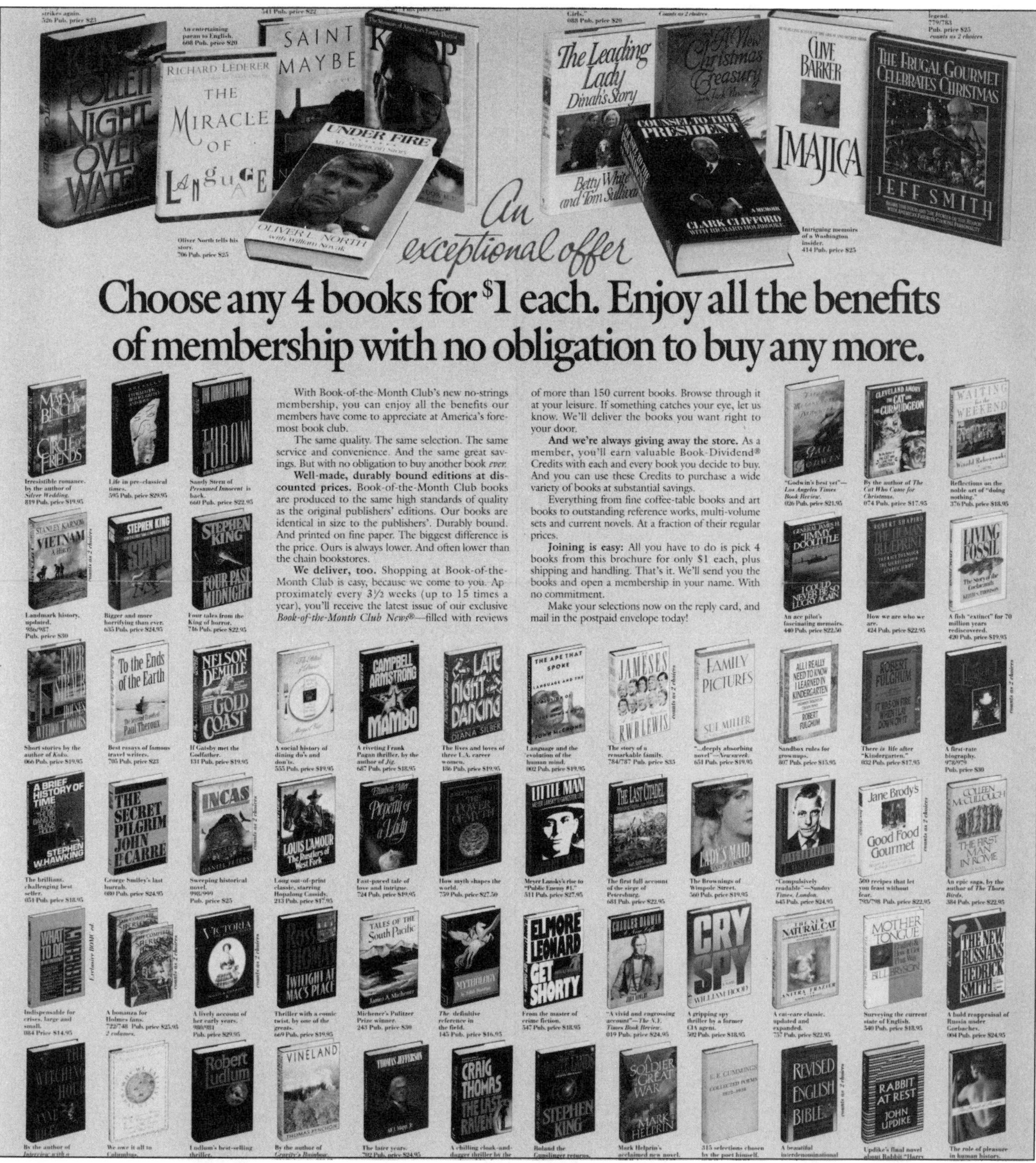

Finally the brochure opens to 15½″ × 17″, revealing a dazzling selection of additional books. Repeated in the headline is the no obligation offer.

Return this form to receive your choice of 4 books for $1 each with no obligation to buy another book.

PLEASE DETACH HERE.

Yes Please enroll me as a member of Book-of-the-Month Club and send me the 4 choices I've listed below, billing me only $1 for each, plus shipping and handling charges. I understand that I'm not required to buy another book. You will send me the *Book-of-the-Month Club News®* (if my account is in good standing) for at least six months. If I have not bought at least one book in any six-month period, you may cancel my membership. A shipping and handling charge is added to each shipment.

Indicate by number the four books you want.

1091/0

All orders subject to approval.

1-11

V96-10-0

James 351002 060433

New York, NY 10028

SEND NO MONEY NOW. Just mail in the enclosed postpaid envelope today.

See other side for facts about membership.

The order device with the nuts-'n'-bolts information on how the club works on the back. Also shown is the BRE.

Here's how your no-strings membership works:

1. *The deal:* We offer you 4 books for $1 each, plus a charge for shipping and handling. You have no obligation to buy another book.
2. *What you get:* We offer good books in well-made, high-quality, durably bound editions. We always price below the publisher's price, and the books are delivered to you. You pay only for the books you want, plus a charge for shipping and handling.
3. *Keeping in touch:* We'll send you the *Book-of-the-Month Club News®* every 3½ weeks (15 times a year). In it we review our main Selection and more than 150 other good books.
4. *Freedom of choice:* If you want the Selection, do nothing. We'll send it to you automatically. If you want another book, or nothing at all, send us the Reply Form by the given date.
5. *Never fear:* If the *News* is delayed and you receive the Selection without having had 10 days to notify us, just return it for credit.
6. *Breaking up is easy:* If at any time you find that we're not serving your needs, you can end your membership. We reserve the right to cancel your membership if you choose not to buy at least one book in any six-month period.
7. *Staying is better:* Stay with us and you'll get lots of benefits, like our Book-Dividend® plan that offers you a variety of fine books at savings of 50%–80% off publishers' prices.
8. *You mean a lot to us:* If at any time we can do anything to make you happier, please let us know.

NO POSTAGE NECESSARY IF MAILED IN THE UNITED STATES

BUSINESS REPLY MAIL

FIRST CLASS MAIL PERMIT NO. 224 CAMP HILL, PA

POSTAGE WILL BE PAID BY ADDRESSEE

BOOK-OF-THE-MONTH CLUB, INC.
CAMP HILL PA 17011-9970

Fortune Book Club

One of the most startling envelopes to come down the pike was the replica of an interoffice envelope created by Greg Dziuba for the Fortune Book Club, a division of Book-of-the-Month. The interoffice envelope is almost always opened immediately because the contents can directly impact the recipient's future: approval or disapproval of a marketing plan . . . notice of an important meeting . . . announcement of a new boss coming in. The holes punched in the body of the envelope let you see whether there are any contents—a kind of tantalizing peek at what may be inside. Late in their careers, these envelopes are wonderful-looking things—with dozens of handwritten names scratched out all over the front and back. The mailing package beat control by 50 percent.

MAILER: Fortune Book Club
PACKAGE: Interoffice Correspondence
PROJECT MGR.: Kathy Bloomfield
WRITER: Greg Dziuba
DESIGNER: Elizabeth Dipalma
FIRST MAILED: 1988
The #11 outside envelope, front and back. This was the first time an interoffice envelope was re-created and used as an outside envelope.

FORTUNE BOOK• CLUB
485 Lexington Avenue, New York, N.Y. 10017

Bulk Rate
U.S. Postage
PAID
Book-of-the-Month Club, Inc.

Note: Trial Membership Offer:
3 Books—Just
$2 Each.

No Sealing Unless Confidential

Use Until All Spaces Are Filled

INTER-OFFICE CORRESPONDENCE

TO	TO	TO
~~JAMES L. MERCER~~		
~~PRESIDENT~~		
	F.Y.I.	
	ALL MANAGERS:	
	IMPORTANT—SEE INSIDE!	

F791/0

After he left Book-of-the-Month, Greg Dziuba freelanced for a while before joining International Masters as creative director in 1991.

Greg Dziuba:

''So what exactly do you intend to do, Son, now that you've been to journalism school?''

''Well, Dad, I thought newspapers would be a great place to start. Then maybe magazines. Eventually novels or screenplays.''

Five years later.

''So how's the writing career going, Son?''

''Dad, let me explain what it means to beat a control.''

Actually, I did work in newspapers and magazines before being seduced by advertising. In fact, a hard-bitten veteran of the Daily News *finally wrote ''Good lead'' on a story I rewrote half a dozen times. I still consider that one of the highest compliments of my writing.*

I can't imagine anyone starting out to be a direct mail writer. But I remember that it actually happened to me after reading a magazine circulation renewal package for Cycle *magazine. After briefly skimming and tossing lots of junk mail, here was something that stopped me cold. I remember thinking, ''Whoever wrote this really understands my passion for motorcycles. And by the way, the person can really write! I wonder how much this kind of writing pays? What a neat way to make a living!''*

After ten or fifteen years in this field I've had a number of winning packages and several long-term controls. And every one of them has been built on my very best understanding of the person I'm talking to through the package. Marketing managers call that ''Psychographics.''

When I submitted the concept for my ''Interoffice Mail'' package it wasn't very well received by my boss. He thought it was ''too gimmicky and got in the way of the offer.'' So I did what I always do when I don't get my own way: I threatened to quit.

Fortunately, he had just hired me and was tired of interviewing. So first, I convinced him that was the right gimmick. And besides, no one to my knowledge had ever received an interoffice envelope at home. There should be some power in that.

Well it turned out that it was a very powerful and long-lived package. But I really believe that the power comes as much from the writing as from the novelty of the gimmick. I'm still proud of the letter lead:

> *You've got enough people trying to waste your time with things you don't really want or need.*
>
> *I'm not one of those people.*

I worked very hard on talking to middle managers in a way that demonstrated an understanding of their motivations and concerns. There's really no substitute for making a fundamental connection with your reader. And for me, that takes some genuine and substantial understanding of the person you're talking to.

All that sounds pretty trite until you actually do make a fundamental connection with your reader. You know when it happens, because that's the beauty of direct response. And that's the territory where I invest most of my time, because great gimmicks don't score as consistently in my experience as making that one-to-one connection.

INTEROFFICE MEMO

TO: All Managers

FROM: James L. Mercer, President

SUBJECT: TRIAL MEMBERSHIP OFFER:
Any 3 books for only $2 each. Take up to 6 months to buy one more book (or take advantage of our Bonus Offer and have no obligation to buy whatsoever)

You've got enough people trying to waste your time with things you don't really want or need.

I'm not one of those people.

First of all, here's an exceptional offer you'll want to take advantage of:

> Choose from over 60 of the best-selling books shown in the enclosed brochure. Start with any 3 for just $2 each. Take up to 6 months to buy one additional book, or take a 4th book now at 50% off the Club price and have absolutely no obligation to buy more books.

Here's a small sample of the important business books you can choose from right now: • The Disney Touch: How a Daring Management Team Revived an Entertainment Empire by Ron Grover • Europe 1992: The New World Power Game by Michael Silva and Bertil Sjogren • Financial Self-Defense by Charles Givens • The Portable MBA by Eliza G.C. Collins and Mary Anne Devanna • The McGraw-Hill Guide to Starting Your Own Business by Stephen Harper.

You will find these and 55 more of the best-selling business books to choose from in the enclosed brochure. These are not books that will sit on your shelf...these are the best tools for taking charge of your career, your business and your money right now!

Great, but now that I've told you how to invest in the solid foundation of an impressive professional library, what more could you want?

Let's, for a moment, talk about something you need.

For example: You're having lunch with a few colleagues and someone, maybe your boss, brings up an important new book that everyone at the table has read. Everyone except you.

Are you, your career and your business missing out on the best thinking... the newest strategies...and the most vital information available? You need to stay current. But who has got the time to do the research, read all the reviews, then shop around?

That's the point. No one really has the time. So why not have a team of experienced business professionals do the work for you? Especially if this invaluable service is available to you absolutely free.

Here's how it works. Each month, your "consultants" at Fortune Book Club will send you a Newsletter at no additional charge. Every issue represents an exhaustive search and review of all the best business, investment and personal interest literature being published. One important Selection is recommended, along with a variety of other fine choices. But the final word is always yours.

All it takes to get started is for you to drop the "Quick Response Card" in the mail today. I look forward to serving you as a valued member of Fortune Book Club.

James L. Mercer
President

* Still unsure? Here's a New Member Bonus Option to help you make the right decision. After you choose your 3 books – pick a 4th book at 50% off the Club price shown and I'll eliminate all book-buying obligations from your membership. That's right, you'll never have to buy another book. Obviously, I'm pretty confident about our books and the real contribution Club membership can make toward your success. I hope you'll take me up on my offer!

F791/0

FORTUNE BOOK CLUB®
485 Lexington Avenue, New York, NY 10017

The $8^{1}/_{2}'' \times 14''$ sales letter that continues the theme of interoffice correspondence. The red token at upper right should probably have instructions to detach and affix to order card.

Interoffice Memo: Addendum

Per today's meeting with the editors of Fortune Book Club, here are some of the important titles that will be reviewed for members very shortly:

The Elements of Business Writing
Strategic Focus: A Gameplan For Developing Competitive Advantage
Recession-Proof Your Business
Getting Past No: Negotiating With Difficult People
Selling To The Giants

If you want to take advantage of the special member prices on these and many other vital, new books for managers, please be certain that your "Quick Response Card" is in the outgoing mailbox in time for early pickup!

***

The lift piece. "Important Update" is on the folded flap of the letter.

The front and back cover of the brochure.

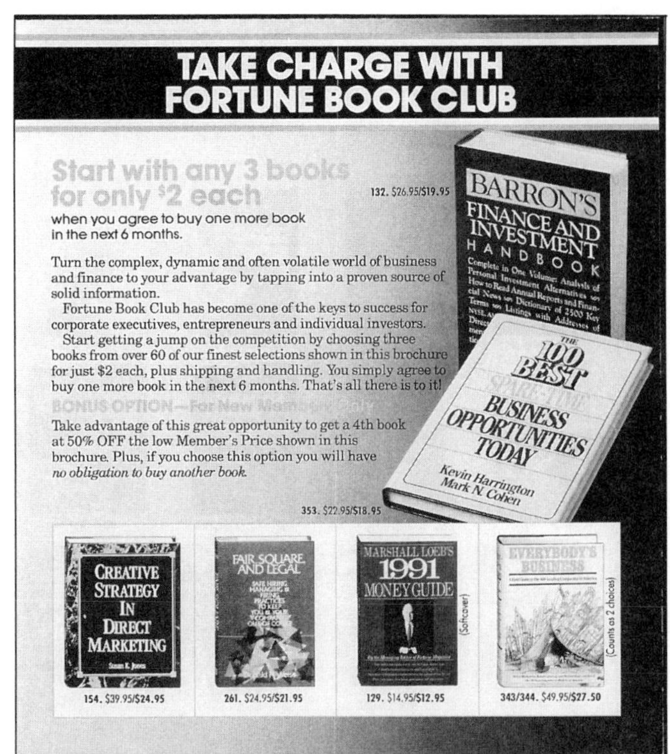

The first fold. The flap with the "Take Charge" headline cuts across the inside copy and book jacket, so that you have to open it. The book covers throughout are 4-color. This is purposely untidy design. Neatness rejects involvement.

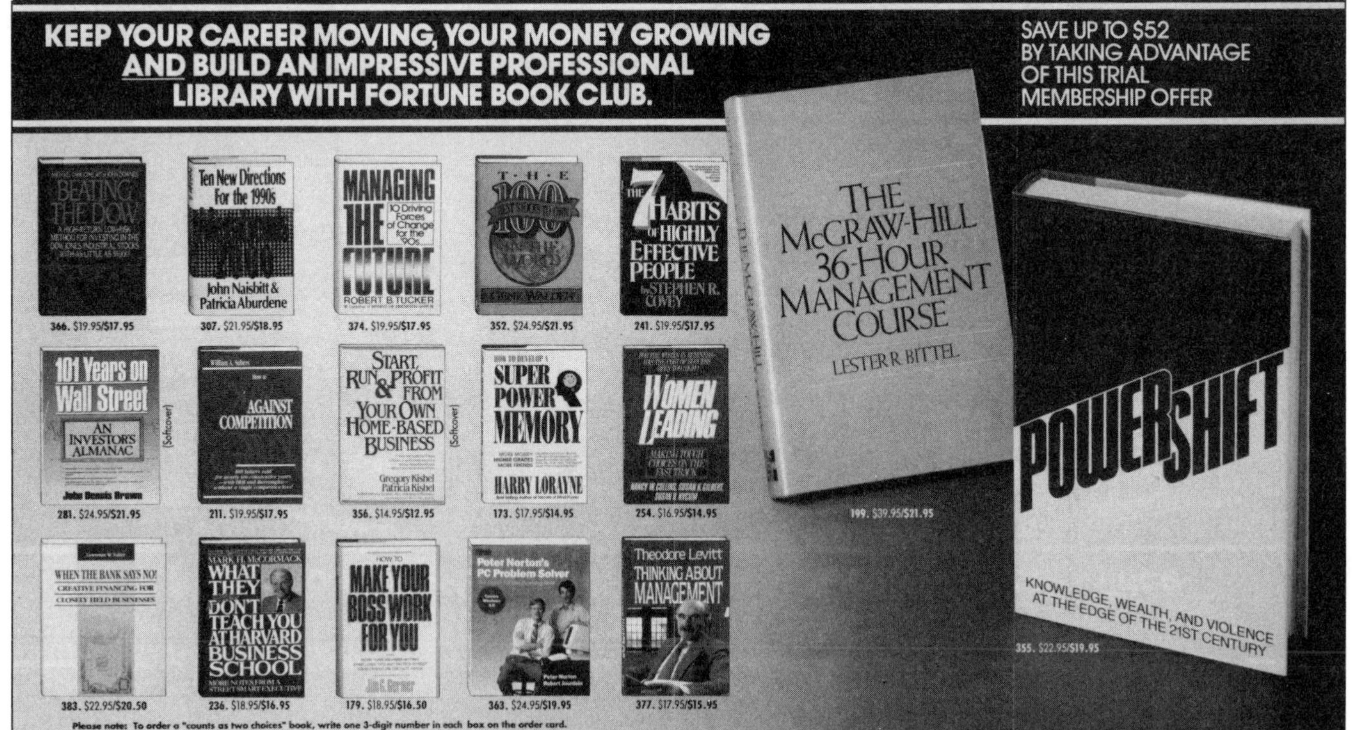

The flap opens, revealing this second spread.

3 BOOKS FOR $2 EACH—

Plus the option to buy a 4th book at 50% OFF Member's Price

322. $22.95/$19.95
332. $24.95/$19.95
217. $22.95/$19.95
346. $19.95/$18.95* (Softcover)
381. $24.95/$19.95
368. $27.95/$21.95

329. $22.95/$19.95
339. $24.95/$18.95

All the important books in one place.

With Fortune Book Club you'll never miss an important business book again. Every 3½ weeks, the *Fortune Book Club Newsletter* presents you with the best new books available in every area of business, management and personal finance.

Each issue of the *Newsletter* reviews a special Selection recommended by our editors, plus dozens of other invaluable books. You'll enjoy reading each review from our knowledgeable staff of experts and save yourself the aggravation of having to shop around for the books you really want. And the cost of books that you purchase from *Fortune Book Club* for use in your trade or business may be tax deductible.

Easy membership—on your own terms.

Remember, you're always in control. You decide how many books you buy, if any at all. Your membership only requires that you buy one more book in the first 6 months of membership. (Unless you choose the New Member Bonus Option, and then you have no obligation to buy ever.)

So why not put the business publishing experts at Fortune Book Club to work for you? Especially if their invaluable service is available to you absolutely free. All it takes to get started is for you to drop the postage-paid "Quick Response Card" in the mail today!

110. $14.95/$12.95 (Softcover)
385. $14.95/$11.95 (Softcover)
335. $24.95/$21.95
144. $19.95/$16.95 (Softcover)
240. $22.95/$19.95
327. $22.95/$17.95

131. $13.95/$11.95 (Softcover)
176. $19.95/$17.95
204. $14.95/$12.95 (Softcover)
369. $22.95/$19.50
333. $24.95/$21.95
351. $22.95/$19.95
380. $22.95/$19.95
340. $22.95/$18.95

280. $19.95/$16.95
251. $29.95/$22.95
297. $29.95/$22.95
283. $40/$25.95 (Revised)
337. $11.95/$10.95 (Softcover)
221. $19.95/$15.95
143. $14.95/$13.50
358. $24.95/$21.95

313. $18.95/$15.95 (Softcover)
379. $9.95/$7.95 (Softcover)
375. $26.95/$24.95 (Softcover)
196. $17.95/$15.95 (Softcover)
386. $24.95/$21.95
382. $17.95/$14.95
158. $19.95/$16.95
259. $17.95/$14.95 (Softcover)

Please note: To order a "counts as two choices" book, write one 3-digit number in each box on the order card.

First price is Publisher's List. **Boldface is Member's Price.**

The main inside spread measuring 11″ × 17″

QUICK RESPONSE CARD

Send No Money Now—Just mail this postage-paid card today.

Affix
Seal Here
To Take Advantage
of Our
BONUS OPTION
A 4th book at
50% off
Members' Price

Choose 3 Books for $2 Each when you agree to buy one more book in the next 6 months.*

YES! Please send me the 3 books as indicated below. Bill me $2 each, plus shipping and handling. I simply agree to buy one more book within the next six months. A shipping and handling charge is added to each shipment.

***New Member Bonus Option:** Take advantage of this great opportunity to get a 4th book at 50% OFF the low Members' Price. Plus, if you choose this option you have no obligation to buy another book.

Indicate the 3 books you want by number: | | | |

BONUS OPTION: Indicate your 4th choice at 50% off. | |

Note: The cost of books you buy for business or professional use through Fortune Book Club may be tax deductible.

HOW YOUR MEMBERSHIP WORKS

Start your membership by choosing 3 books for just $2 each, plus shipping and handling. You have up to six months to buy one additional book.

You'll receive the *Fortune Book Club Newsletter* 15 times each year (about every 3½ weeks), plus up to 4 more offers of special Selections. Each issue reviews a new Selection, plus scores of other good books, most at discounts off publishers' prices.

If you want the Selection, do nothing. It will be shipped to you automatically. If you want one or more other books—or no books at all—just indicate your decision on the Reply Form provided with each *Newsletter* and return it by the date specified. A shipping and handling charge is added to each shipment.

Guaranteed Service. If the *Newsletter* is delayed and you receive the Selection without having had a full 10 days to notify us, you may return it for credit. No questions asked.

Membership may be canceled, by either you or the club, at any time after you have purchased three additional books.

All orders subject to approval.

1-69 F791/0

NO POSTAGE
NECESSARY
IF MAILED
IN THE
UNITED STATES

BUSINESS REPLY MAIL

FIRST CLASS MAIL PERMIT NO. 224 CAMP HILL, PA

POSTAGE WILL BE PAID BY ADDRESSEE

FORTUNE BOOK® CLUB

OPERATED BY
BOOK-OF-THE-MONTH CLUB, INC.
CAMP HILL PA 17011-9919

The order form and business reply envelope.

Literary Guild

The Literary Guild Grand Control has a truly seductive promise on the outer envelope: "WE'RE GOING TO SPOIL YOU!" It was written by Alan Friedenthal, who was a freelancer for many years; when he went to work for Grey, one of his clients called me up and wailed, "Why did Alan do it? We love his work! We would have given him a retainer, regular work, anything!"

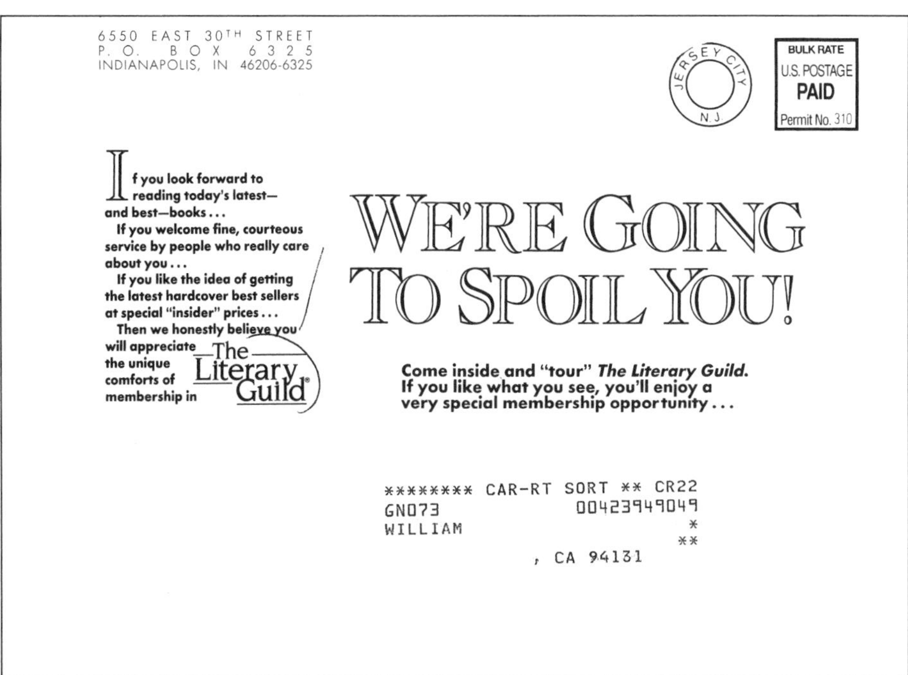

MAILER: Literary Guild
PACKAGE: "We're Going to Spoil You"
AGENCY: Grey Direct
CREATIVE DIR.: Karen Henkin
WRITER: Alan Friedenthal
ART SUPVR.: Judi Kolstad
SR. ART DIR.: David Micklewright
FIRST MAILED: 1988
The 6″ × 8″ outside envelope, in 2 colors (black and peach), shown front and back.

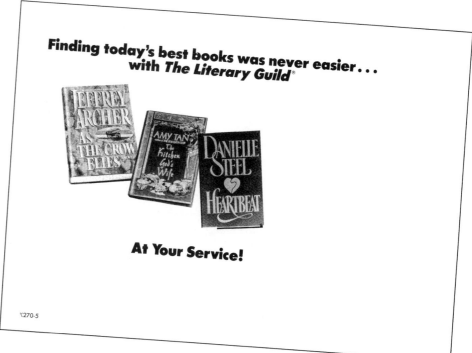

K270-2

You're Going To Get Spoiled!

With great reading . . . Great service . . . And great insider prices . . .
It's membership "As You Like It" courtesy of The Literary Guild

Dear Friend,

Frankly, membership in *The Literary Guild* is not for everyone.

But . . . if you're the type of person who enjoys the excitement of "getting into" a really good book . . .

. . . If you look forward to that special time each day when you can relax with a terrific novel . . . fascinating biography . . . or edge-of-your-seat mystery . . .

. . . If you wait—eagerly—for the newest book by a favorite author . . . because you just know you're going to love it . . .

Then you sound like the type of person who's ready to be "spoiled" by *The Literary Guild*!

How will we spoil you? Introducing "Membership As You Like It!"

First, we're going to spoil you with a very special membership offer:

Pick any 5 books now for just $2 (and buy 4 more books within 2 years) . . .

You'll enjoy tremendous savings—as much as $50 . . . $75 . . . even $100 or more off the cost of bookstore editions when you join *The Literary Guild* right now.

But there's more. For a limited time, we're giving you a special opportunity to sample our "members only" savings immediately.

If you wish, you may order your first Club Selection on the enclosed form. You'll be billed just $4.95, plus shipping and handling. You'll automatically reduce the number of books you need to buy as a member—only 3 books, instead of 4.

This special "first selection" purchase will save you as much as $20 off the publisher's edition price of a current best seller of your choice from the enclosed brochure.

And if you love browsing for books, you'll love our brochure. It's overflowing with the latest, most entertaining and thought-provoking books . . . specially selected by our editors as being among the "very best reads" in America today!

We'll spoil you with our selection.
Not just right now, but from now on!

The 150 books shown here are just a taste of the wonderful choices coming your way in our colorful Club magazines—available exclusively to our members!

You'll always have your pick of the best in contemporary Fiction. Plus Adventures . . . Suspense . . . Classics . . . the hottest Biographies, too . . . the newest Cookbooks . . . noteworthy Diet and Fitness books . . . books especially for you . . . for the whole family . . . delightful Children's books . . . superb References . . . breathtaking books on Travel, Art, Fashion and Photography . . . all carefully screened, selected and recommended by our editors.

From the hundreds we bring you, choose only the books you want, when you want them. You'll always have at least 10 days to make any selections from your Club magazine.

We'll spoil you with special insider prices, too.

Imagine being able to buy all the books you want at up to 40% off publishers' edition prices. Well, now you can—every time you buy!

You'll save on the books you want most because we print Club editions for our members. Always hardcover (except for certain books available only in paperback) . . . always in the complete uncut form—the way we know you want them!

And the more you read, the more you'll save. You can "reward" yourself with our exclusive Bonus Plan. Using your Bonus Credits, you'll be able to choose bonus books from your Club magazine—at half off our already low prices!

Are you ready to be spoiled by the unique comforts of membership? Then welcome to *The Literary Guild*—at your service!

To start your membership, simply turn to the enclosed book brochure and browse to your heart's content. Then take your pick—any 5 books for just $2 (with membership).

Use the special New Member Acceptance Form to tell us your choices. Don't send any money now—we'll bill you later for the $2 (and $4.95, if you wish to order your first Club selection), plus shipping and handling.

You don't even need a postage stamp. Just drop your New Member Acceptance Form in the mail. Then sit back and relax—and get ready for the most luxurious reading experience of your life—thanks to the unique comforts of *The Literary Guild*!

At your service,

Lee Sommers

Membership Director

P.S. I nearly forgot to mention one more unique comfort of membership . . . our exclusive tapestry-print Floral Tote. It's stylish, sturdy, practical and—best of all—FREE (with membership). In fact, it's yours to keep, even if you choose not to remain a member.

The 2-page letter, printed front and back on one 7½" × 11" sheet.

Karen Henkin, creative director, Grey Advertising:

The creative strategy for this mailing was twofold: (1) to effectively communicate that the Literary Guild offers access to a wide selection of today's bestselling books at very attractive prices via convenient at-home shopping . . . and (2) emphasize value-added services. These include expert editors, extraordinary selections, and personal service.

This strategy comes to life in a creative execution that is the ultimate ''what's in it for me'' features-and-benefits direct marketing. In this package, ''you'' are the focus. ''We're going to spoil you'' is our promise. ''Membership as You Like It'' is our offer. The tone and manner of this package make it seem as if we're not selling—we're just agreeing. ''If you believe'' certain features are important in a book club, ''then we believe'' you'll find them in the Literary Guild.

The sense of personal service relationship gives the Literary Guild a perceived benefit that goes beyond the home delivery of good books at discount prices. Most importantly, beyond what the main competitors had to offer. Finally, it makes the Literary Guild a brand instead of a commodity.

The basic principles and subtle influences that make this mailing work reflect the Grey Direct approach to creating successful mailings. Quality photography and innovative design are essential to supporting the quality service described in the copy. Writing about the product in a way that lets the reader know we think alike is also the key. It's directed toward the prospect's aspirations and establishes the connection that this service is "for people like me." We find that building this kind of bond or relationship not only gets an up-front response but works toward keeping a customer long-term.

The 4-color lift piece.

YOURS FREE
with membership
A rich tapestry-print Floral Tote travels in style.
Beautifully detailed like the season's most costly tapestry accessories, our exclusive Tote is really a sturdy helper. With strong leatherette handles, it holds everything from weekend essentials to paperwork. And it's your gift, even if you decide not to remain a member.
The Literary Guild

The 4-color brochure starts out with a 5″ × 7½″ cover and opens . . . and opens . . . and opens . . . and opens . . . until it becomes a massive 15″ × 20″ bedsheet of book covers in full color, producing somewhat the same effect as a BMG Music Club stamp sheet; the book covers are larger than the BMG stamps, and the coated paper stock makes the colors pop.

K370-1
The books you want . . .
The service you expect . . .
The special insider prices
you've been looking for . . .
THE LITERARY GUILD PRESENTS
MEMBERSHIP
AS YOU LIKE IT!
You're about to discover why The Literary Guild is not just another book club. If you like what you see, we genuinely hope you'll join us.
Your membership begins by choosing any 5 books for just $2.
Order your first selection now and save . . .

IF YOU BELIEVE

that reading a good book is one of life's greatest joys . . . but that all too often choosing a good book—the right book—is a "hit-or-miss" proposition that leaves you frustrated or unhappy . . . then you'll be pleased to know that *The Literary Guild* has perfected the art of selecting good books!

Our editors read thousands of books and manuscripts each year, in order to select the ones that are truly worthy of your time and interest. The books that people are talking about . . . or will be talking about . . . the books they know will provide you with the type of reading pleasure you want most.

With *The Literary Guild*, it's easier than ever to find—and enjoy—entertaining, thought-provoking "must-reads" every time!

IF YOU BELIEVE

that joining a book club should entitle you to preferential treatment . . . with benefits and privileges available only to members . . .

Now *The Literary Guild* is going to spoil you with "Membership As YOU Like It" starting with . . .

- A special generous Membership Plan . . .
- Savings of up to 40% on each and every book you buy . . .
- An exclusive free magazine that makes shopping for great books a pleasure . . .
- Pressure-free membership that lets you say "no" to books you don't want . . .
- A special New Member Reading Profile that lets you tell our editors about your personal reading preferences . . .
- An exclusive Bonus Plan that lets you choose extra books at 50% off our already low Club prices . . .
- A generous "Extra Savings" option that gives you the chance to order your first book as a member for only $4.95 . . .
- And so much more.

IF YOU BELIEVE

that a book club needs to understand the wants and needs of its members . . .

that its editors should share your passion for the best in today's reading . . .

that it should be staffed by people who genuinely care about keeping you happy (with great selections, great service and great savings) . . .

THEN WE BELIEVE

that you've never been more ready to take advantage of a very, very special opportunity from *The Literary Guild* . . .

LIFT HERE

Come Join Us

AND ENJOY THE UNIQUE COMFORTS OF MEMBERSHIP IN *THE LITERARY GUILD*®

TAKE ANY 5 books for $2 and buy 4 more whenever you want in the next 2 years

Act now and get this stylish tapestry-print Floral Tote as your FREE GIFT!

EXTRA SAVINGS! If you wish, ORDER YOUR FIRST SELECTION RIGHT NOW FOR ONLY $4.95. Then buy only 3 more books in the next 2 years.

Here at *The Literary Guild*, we believe you deserve the freedom to enjoy the kind of membership that lets you take your time selecting your reading. So we're offering you a special "no-hurry" membership plan.

Choose any 5 books in this brochure for just $2. Then, you have 2 full years to select only 4 more books from the hundreds offered in your *Literary Guild Magazines*.

Start enjoying "members only" savings right away by ordering your first Club selection now for just $4.95. Please note: Books that count as 2 choices are not included in this offer. We'll bill you later, plus shipping and handling. You'll immediately reduce the number of books you need to buy as a member from 4 to only 3.

Either way, we'll treat you to this free gift: a rich, tapestry-print Floral Tote. It's beautiful but durable, perfect for carrying books and other essentials wherever you go. The gift is yours to keep, free, even if you decide not to remain a member.

Treat yourself to the reading experience of your life — choose the books you want from the 150 shown here and tell us your choices on your Acceptance Form.

Then sit back and relax and start enjoying the unique comforts of membership in *The Literary Guild*!

The Literary Guild®

A Special Guarantee of Satisfaction, Courtesy of *The Literary Guild*:

Select your books with confidence. We're sure you're going to love them! But if you're not satisfied—for any reason whatsoever—simply return them within 10 days (at our expense, not yours). We'll cancel your membership, you'll owe nothing, and the Floral Tote is still yours to keep with our compliments—FREE. It's just one more example of the unique comforts you'll enjoy as a member of *The Literary Guild*!

Prices shown are for publishers' editions. Literary Guild editions are always discounted—up to 40% off publishers' edition prices.

*Denotes explicit sex, language and/or violence.

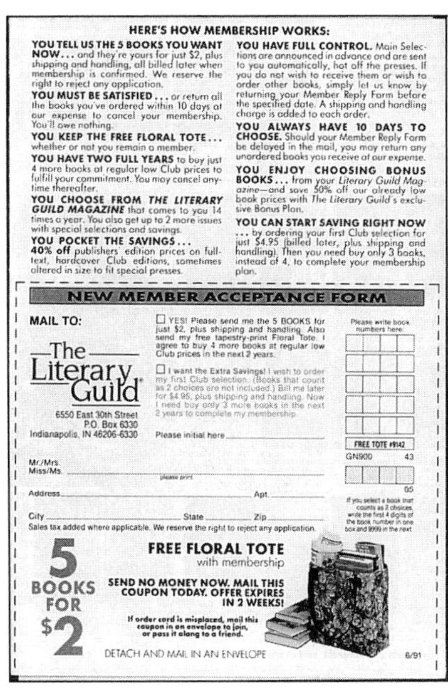

HERE'S HOW MEMBERSHIP WORKS:

YOU TELL US THE 5 BOOKS YOU WANT NOW... and they're yours for just $2, plus shipping and handling, all billed later when membership is confirmed. We reserve the right to reject any application.

YOU MUST BE SATISFIED... or return all the books you've ordered within 10 days at our expense to cancel your membership. You'll owe nothing.

YOU KEEP THE FREE FLORAL TOTE... whether or not you remain a member.

YOU HAVE TWO FULL YEARS to buy just 4 more books at regular low Club prices to fulfill your commitment. You may cancel anytime thereafter.

YOU CHOOSE FROM *THE LITERARY GUILD MAGAZINE* that comes to you 14 times a year. You also get up to 2 more issues with special selections and savings.

YOU POCKET THE SAVINGS... 40% off publishers' edition prices on full-text, hardcover Club editions, sometimes altered in size to fit special presses.

YOU HAVE FULL CONTROL. Main Selections are announced in advance and are sent to you automatically, hot off the presses. If you do not wish to receive them or wish to order other books, simply let us know by returning your Member Reply Form before the specified date. A shipping and handling charge is added to each order.

YOU ALWAYS HAVE 10 DAYS TO CHOOSE. Should your Member Reply Form be delayed in the mail, you may return any unordered books you receive at our expense.

YOU ENJOY CHOOSING BONUS BOOKS... from your *Literary Guild Magazine*—and save 50% off our already low book prices with *The Literary Guild*'s exclusive Bonus Plan.

YOU CAN START SAVING RIGHT NOW... by ordering your first Club selection for just $4.95 (billed later, plus shipping and handling). Then you need buy only 3 books, instead of 4, to complete your membership plan.

NEW MEMBER ACCEPTANCE FORM

MAIL TO:

The Literary Guild®
6550 East 30th Street
P.O. Box 6330
Indianapolis, IN 46206-6330

☐ YES! Please send me the 5 BOOKS for just $2, plus shipping and handling. Also send my free tapestry-print Floral Tote. I agree to buy 4 more books at regular low Club prices in the next 2 years.

☐ I want the Extra Savings! I wish to order my first Club selection. (Books that count as 2 choices are not included.) Bill me later for $4.95, plus shipping and handling. Now I need buy only 3 more books in the next 2 years to complete my membership.

Please initial here ________

Please write book numbers here:

FREE TOTE #9142

GN900 43

05

If you select a book that counts as 2 choices, write the first 4 digits of the book number in one box and 9999 in the next.

Mr./Mrs.
Miss/Ms. ________ (please print)

Address ________ Apt. ________

City ________ State ________ Zip ________

Sales tax added where applicable. We reserve the right to reject any application.

5 BOOKS FOR $2

FREE FLORAL TOTE with membership

SEND NO MONEY NOW. MAIL THIS COUPON TODAY. OFFER EXPIRES IN 2 WEEKS!

If order card is misplaced, mail this coupon in an envelope to join, or pass it along to a friend.

DETACH AND MAIL IN AN ENVELOPE 6/91

The back panel of the brochure. Whereas International Preview Society added a Member-Get-a-Member option on the back of the order form, Literary Guild gives an extra order form so that an additional person can take advantage of the offer and become a member. Book-of-the-Month could not do this, because one of the themes is "Please don't tell your friends."

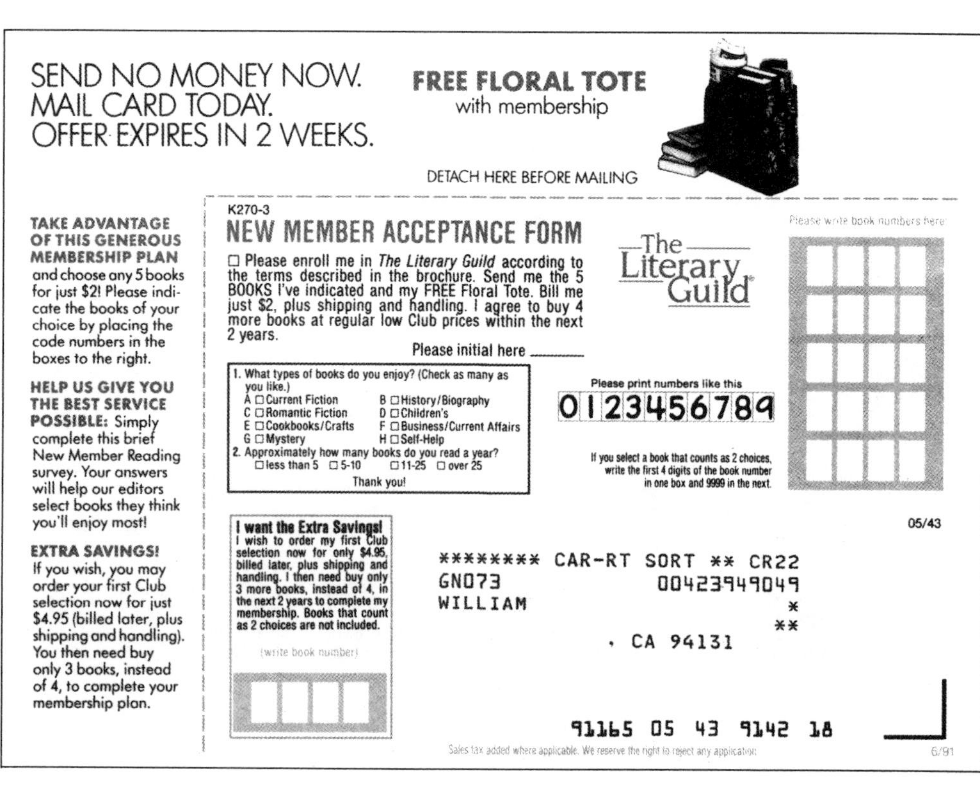
SEND NO MONEY NOW.
MAIL CARD TODAY.
OFFER EXPIRES IN 2 WEEKS.

FREE FLORAL TOTE
with membership

DETACH HERE BEFORE MAILING

TAKE ADVANTAGE OF THIS GENEROUS MEMBERSHIP PLAN and choose any 5 books for just $2! Please indicate the books of your choice by placing the code numbers in the boxes to the right.

HELP US GIVE YOU THE BEST SERVICE POSSIBLE: Simply complete this brief New Member Reading survey. Your answers will help our editors select books they think you'll enjoy most!

EXTRA SAVINGS! If you wish, you may order your first Club selection now for just $4.95 (billed later, plus shipping and handling). You then need buy only 3 books, instead of 4, to complete your membership plan.

K270-3

NEW MEMBER ACCEPTANCE FORM

The Literary Guild®

☐ Please enroll me in *The Literary Guild* according to the terms described in the brochure. Send me the 5 BOOKS I've indicated and my FREE Floral Tote. Bill me just $2, plus shipping and handling. I agree to buy 4 more books at regular low Club prices within the next 2 years.

Please initial here ______

Please write book numbers here

1. What types of books do you enjoy? (Check as many as you like.)
A ☐ Current Fiction B ☐ History/Biography
C ☐ Romantic Fiction D ☐ Children's
E ☐ Cookbooks/Crafts F ☐ Business/Current Affairs
G ☐ Mystery H ☐ Self-Help
2. Approximately how many books do you read a year?
☐ less than 5 ☐ 5-10 ☐ 11-25 ☐ over 25
Thank you!

Please print numbers like this
0 1 2 3 4 5 6 7 8 9

If you select a book that counts as 2 choices, write the first 4 digits of the book number in one box and 9999 in the next.

I want the Extra Savings!
I wish to order my first Club selection now for only $4.95, billed later, plus shipping and handling. I then need buy only 3 more books, instead of 4, in the next 2 years to complete my membership. Books that count as 2 choices are not included.
(write book number)

05/43

******** CAR-RT SORT ** CR22
GN073 00423949049
WILLIAM *
**
. CA 94131

91165 05 43 9142 18

Sales tax added where applicable. We reserve the right to reject any application.

6/91

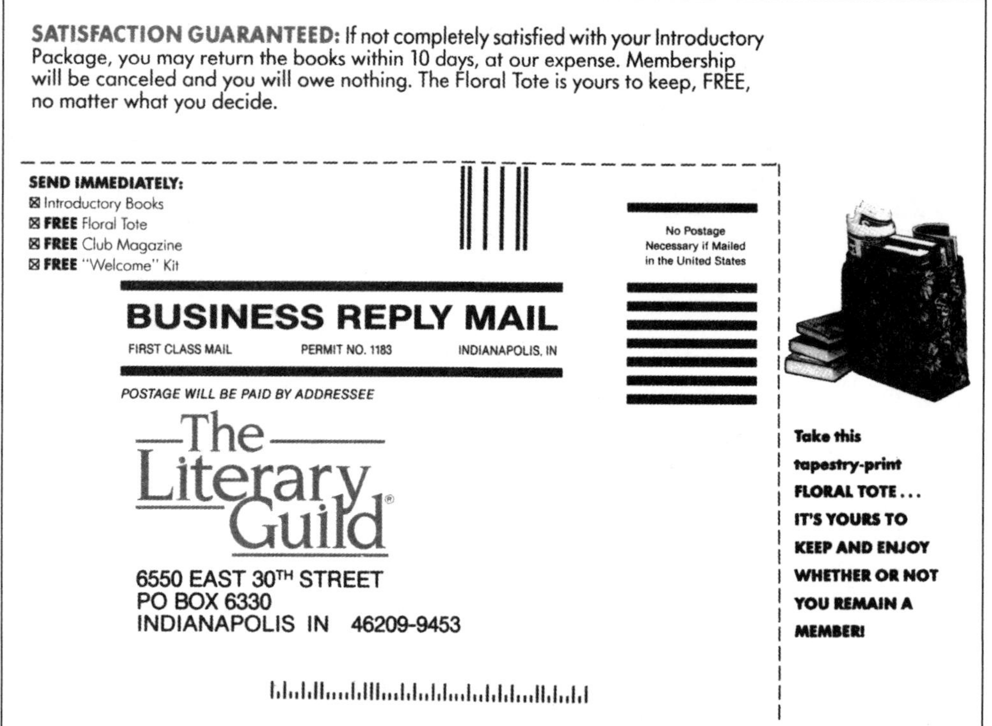
SATISFACTION GUARANTEED: If not completely satisfied with your Introductory Package, you may return the books within 10 days, at our expense. Membership will be canceled and you will owe nothing. The Floral Tote is yours to keep, FREE, no matter what you decide.

SEND IMMEDIATELY:
☒ Introductory Books
☒ **FREE** Floral Tote
☒ **FREE** Club Magazine
☒ **FREE** "Welcome" Kit

No Postage Necessary if Mailed in the United States

BUSINESS REPLY MAIL
FIRST CLASS MAIL PERMIT NO. 1183 INDIANAPOLIS, IN

POSTAGE WILL BE PAID BY ADDRESSEE

The Literary Guild®

6550 EAST 30TH STREET
PO BOX 6330
INDIANAPOLIS IN 46209-9453

Take this tapestry-print FLORAL TOTE... IT'S YOURS TO KEEP AND ENJOY WHETHER OR NOT YOU REMAIN A MEMBER!

The order card shown front and back. Since the offer is bill-me only, there is no need for a business reply envelope.

16

Consumer Publishing III:

Individual Titles

Dr. Chang's Book of Internal Exercises

There are many adjectives to describe the envelope you see here. Before turning the page to go on, STOP! LOOK! READ! STUDY!

If any writer has set the tone and style for successfully marketing books to consumers, it is New York freelancer/publisher Eugene Schwartz. Mark Johnson at Rodale said that Gene Schwartz's packages not only sell millions of books for them, but also provide an inspiring model for everyone at the company. No writer in the business can match

MAILER: Instant Improvement, Inc.
PACKAGE: *Dr. Chang's Book of Internal Exercises*
PROJECT MGR.: Eugene M. Schwartz
WRITER: Eugene M. Schwartz
DESIGNER: Ed Jastrom
FIRST MAILED: 1979
The 9″ × 12″ outer envelope.

How Modern Chinese Medicine Helps Both Men and Women

BURN DISEASE OUT OF YOUR BODY

using nothing more than the palm of your hand!

"How to treat high blood pressure, bursitis and arthritis — and prevent them from degenerating further, or even reverse them — simply by massaging the outside of the legs in a downward way."

"This pose helps reduce water retention and excess weight."

"...cures and prevents hemorrhoids, and cures problems of the prostate, such as weakness, enlargement and cancer."

"Eventually throw your glasses away, and never need to see an eye doctor again, simply by rubbing around the eyes for a few minutes every day."

"If one has strong sexual glands, one may never grow old."
(To find out how, see page 64)
FREE
NO RISK
SNEAK PREVIEW

INSTANT IMPROVEMENT
FULFILLMENT DIVISION
250 Lexington Avenue
P.O. Box 2788
Grand Central Station
New York, NY 10163

BULK RATE
U.S. POSTAGE
PAID
INSTANT
IMPROVEMENT

FREE: HOW TO RUB YOUR STOMACH AWAY

"THE SIMPLEST AND MOST NATURAL WAY TO LOSE WEIGHT IS BY THIS EFFORTLESS TWO-MINUTE EXERCISE."

"By applying the exercise faithfully, he regularized his bowel movement, lost 40 pounds, and was filled with new energy."

"In just a few weeks, she had lost five inches in her waist, hips and thigh area."

MAIL ENCLOSED CARD FOR FREE COPY...

"I got a call from him a month later, and he told me gleefully that he had already lost three notches on his belt."

"By such apparently simple means, the superflous areas of the stomach and abdomen are literally rubbed away."

Jay
48
New
06840
R901
AHB

How modern Chinese Medicine helps both men and women

BURN DISEASE OUT OF YOUR BODY

...lying flat on your back, using nothing more than the palm of your hand!

This may be the most startling health news you have ever read, dear friend—

And we are going to let you prove its merits to yourself, without risking a single penny. It is that different. That powerful. That provocative and controversial.

Let us explain:

THE CHINESE DO NOT BELIEVE IN SURGERY OR MEDICINE FOR MAJOR ILLNESSES. THEY PREVENT SUCH ILLNESSES INSTEAD—WITH A SERIES OF MILD, ALMOST EFFORTLESS INTERNAL EXERCISES.

If you do not have an open mind, please stop reading here. For this letter is about to introduce you to a new (although it is 4,000 years old), and different type of self-healing. Born in China over 40 Centuries ago, it is called Taoist medicine. And we will let the foremost practitioner of it in the Western world—Dr. Stephen T. Chang—give you a brief and startling introduction to these effortless exercises:

"Primary symptoms of old age are often experienced as coldness or numbness in the legs and feet due to the deterioration of the circulatory system at the extremities of the body, stiffness of the joints, and the lack of sexual energy. This exercise is designed to reverse these and other degenerative problems of the lower trunk, thus restoring youthfulness to the body."

AND HERE ARE MORE RESULTS DR. CHANG PROMISES YOU —PERHAPS STARTING WITH YOUR VERY FIRST DAY...

"Solar plexus exercise." The exercise described in the headline of this letter, in which the Chinese help BURN DISEASE OUT OF THEIR BODIES...lying flat on their back, using nothing more than the palm of their hand. As Dr. Chang says, "Building up this fire will help to burn out every disease associated with this area of the body, including diarrhea, constipation, flatulence, diverticulitis, cancer, and other disorders."

"...with consistent practice, the muscles in the abdomen and body will tighten and become toned and strengthened. Excess fat, water and flesh will be eliminated, and the belly will shrink."

"The heart exercise may be practiced morning, noon and night, depending upon the seriousness of the problem. If you have a weak heart, practice it once a day. If there are palpitations of the heart or angina, practice it at least twice a day. If you have had a heart attack, then this exercise needs to be performed at least three times a day. The exercise may also be practiced as preventative medicine to keep a strong heart healthy."

YOURS TO KEEP FREE — "HOW TO RUB YOUR STOMACH AWAY"... even if you return "Internal Exercises" for every cent of your purchase price back. **Read full details in enclosed brochure—**

"...Many diseases of the ears, such as ringing and partial deafness, can be helped or cured by using this exercise."

"This way, invading germs do not have a good environment in which to settle and germinate...Then it is not easy to get diseases."

"...Clicking the teeth—as shown to you on page 59—will help tighten the joints of the body, and keep the teeth healthy."

SPECIAL FOR MEN: "...The in-flow of energy will help to heal any injury or disease you may have in your arms or shoulders."

SPECIAL FOR WOMEN: "The pose increases the circulation to the toes, feet and legs as well as the organs throughout the abdomen....It works to cure...menstrual problems of the female system such as cramps and excessive bleeding. It is also an excellent exercise for pregnant women as it opens up the pelvis and assures an easy delivery."

"The exercise strengthens the muscles of the rectum and prevents and/or cures hemorrhoids."

BUT WHY, DR. CHANG ASKS, DO SUCH EFFORTLESS INTERNAL EXERCISES HAVE SUCH AMAZING EFFECTS UPON YOUR BODY? HERE ARE HIS ANSWERS:

"Stress...breeds fear and disease. Presently, growing old conjures images of high blood pressure, arterial sclerosis, embolisms, cancers and diseases of all imaginative types. Until recently, Westerners have been given few alternatives for dealing with these stresses. We have allowed our bodies and minds to weaken with only cursory hopes of slowing down the aging process and deterring disease for a time. However, the main emphasis of the Internal Exercises, is on strengthening our bodies and minds...by performing these simple exercises on a daily basis we can look forward to growing old with a sense of ease and excitement, knowing that we carry an aliveness which comes only from living a life free from the anxiety of future illnesses and the weakness due to present diseases."

"It was Western scientists who ingeniously verified the existence of electromagnetism providing thereby a means for the logical explanation for many of the previously unexplained phenomena resulting from acupuncture therapy...as well as the health-enhancing benefits obtained through the practice of the Internal Exercises."

"By learning the Internal Energizing Exercises we are thus able to gain control over the vast energy upon which all life depends. We can then use this energy to heal ourselves as well as others, and insure our continuing health and spiritual growth..."

"THE ANCIENT TAOIST UNDERSTOOD THAT...DISEASE OCCURRED WHEN THERE WAS A STATE OF ENERGY DEPLETION OR WEAKNESS."

In other words—

"Disease of the body can be eliminated by readjusting the energy imbalance that is the unseen cause..."

"...weakness is the first step toward disease. If we have no weakness, then it will be impossible to contract a serious illness..."

"...SELF-HEALING, WHICH IS THE NATURAL RESULT OF DOING THESE EXERCISES ON A REGULAR BASIS, IS GUARANTEED."

ABOUT THE AUTHOR

Stephen Chang, M.D. (China), Ph.D. comes from a family which has practiced medicine for more than 400 years. Dr. Chang's great grandfather was personal physician to Empress Chih Shee and also the first Ambassador to the United Kingdom. Dr. Chang has a Ph.D. in philosophy, holds two law degrees and received his medical degree in China, from Yung Chi University Medical School, where he was trained in both Western and Chinese medicine.

Currently, he is on the faculty, or has consulted or conducted classes and lectures in Chinese medicine (which he has been practicing for more than 30 years) in such universities and organizations as: The University of California, at Berkeley...The University of Oslo, Norway...U.S. Public Health Service Hospital, San Francisco...The University of Oregon...College of San Mateo...Golden West College...Center for Chinese Medicine, Continuing Education...and many more.

In addition, Dr. Chang has given many workshops for registered nurses. When held in California, for example, each workshop provided Continuing Education Credit by: California State Board of Registered Nursing...American Medical Association Category II...and California State Board of Dental Examiners.

"The Internal Exercises are easily performed, require no strenuous activity, and do not require a great deal of time to perform."

"They are the very opposite of an external exercise. While external exercises...may produce an attractive outer figure, they often do so by depleting the energy of the internal organs, thereby causing not only any number of illnesses, but also premature aging."

"Internal Exercises encourage the circulatory system without speeding up the heart rate. All the exercises are done slowly, without effort. You see, the number of times our heart beats during our lifetime indicates the length of our life. We do not want the heart to wear out prematurely. The heart rate does not increase during the practice of these exercises and, yet, through their practice the heart rate actually slows down."

FOR EXAMPLE, LET US GIVE YOU THE SIMPLE INTERNAL EXERCISE THAT ENERGIZES THE HEART.

This exercise shows you immediately how incredibly simple, how incredibly easy, how incredibly comfortable these Internal Exercises are. When you receive Dr. Chang's book, to prove or disprove at our risk, turn immediately, without preliminary reading, to page 82. There you will be shown the exact way to hold your body while energizing your heart. No movement—we repeat, no movement—is required. All you do instead is this:

Sit, or stand, in a comfortable position, with your hands simply extended in front of your chest at the level of your shoulders. Make sure that the fingertips of each hand almost touch—but keep about a quarter of an inch distance between them. Keep your eyes focused on the tops of your fingers. THAT IS ALL THERE IS TO THE ENTIRE EXERCISE. Nothing else. no further effort. Not even the simplest movement of the body is required.

Nothing more. Nothing more to do. Not a single strain on any part of your body. Your heart beat doesn't rise a single beat. And yet, what happens, is this—

"This exercise creates a flow of energy, which comes in through the fingers of the right hand, comes across the chest and into the heart, then passes through the left arm, hand and fingers. As the energy passes through the heart, IT STRENGTHENS THE HEART TISSUES AND SURROUNDING BLOOD VESSELS. If at first you are unable to perceive this energy flow, develop your patience and keep practicing the exercise. You will quickly begin to perceive a tingling sensation in the fingertips. With practice, you will be able to feel the entire circle of energy as it passes through your arms, body and heart. Then you will know that you are building a stronger heart."

BUT THERE IS FAR MORE. FOR EXAMPLE—

How to treat high blood pressure, bursitis and arthritis—and prevent them from degenerating further, or even reverse them—simply by massaging the outside of the legs in a downward way. How to check stomach sag, merely by concentrating on the heels of your feet. Brain cleansing—by breathing.

How to reach the state of inner vision, so that no one will be better equipped than you to diagnose your own state of physical health. In other words, helps you see all the signs before a disease begins to take hold in your body.

How to wash out the heart, with healing-air, so that it becomes strong and revitalized again.

AND REMEMBER, YOU LEARN THE HEALING INTERNAL EXERCISES LISTED ON THE BACK COVER OF THE ENVELOPE AS WELL...

AS DR. CHANG SAID, "IF ONE NEVER HAS A MILD ILLNESS, THEN A SERIOUS DISEASE WILL NEVER DEVELOP."

Many years ago, most medical men would have laughed at the Taoist medical invention of acupuncture. Now thousands of doctors all over America are using it for their own supplementary treatment. Will the same story now be repeated with these Internal Exercises?

No one knows, but already they are being used by thousands of people to heal themselves, through this great new book by the leading practitioner of Taoist acupuncture and Taoist medicine in the United States—Dr. Stephen T. Chang.

We know that these exercises are so unusual, so different, so simple, so easy, and so remarkable in their promised results, that we cannot expect you to take our word for them in advance. Therefore, we ask you to prove them, or disprove them, entirely at our risk.

Here's all you do. Send in the no risk order blank today. Try these Internal Exercises, on your own body, in the privacy of your own home, for as long as you wish, entirely at our risk. If they do not do everything that Dr. Chang says, if you are not delighted beyond belief, simply return that book at any time, and every cent of your purchase price will be refunded immediately, without quibble or question.

What could be fairer? Are you tired enough of the failure of conventional techniques, conventional medicines, to help your particular ill or ailment? If so, why not try these Internal Exercises—without risking a penny, today?

Sincerely,

Barbara Schwartz

Eugene M. Schwartz

Barbara Schwartz and Eugene M. Schwartz
for Instant Improvement

The 4-page letter, printed on an 11″ × 17″ sheet.

FREE... HOW TO RUB YOUR STOMACH AWAY—

YOURS TO KEEP *FREE*, EVEN IF YOU RETURN "INTERNAL EXERCISES" FOR EVERY CENT OF YOUR PURCHASE PRICE BACK.

Sound impossible? Then let us quote directly from Dr. Stephen Chang—
"What is going to be discussed here is a disarmingly simple method to lose weight and inches. This same method also promotes proper digestion, sound sleep and a healthy heart."

"This weight loss method does not come from Western medicine. No, its source is the wisdom of the ancient Chinese sages. . . arrived at through literally 6,000 years of observation and study of the natural principles of healing. It is only now that this ancient wisdom of the body is becoming available to you in the West."

"THE SIMPLEST AND MOST NATURAL WAY TO LOSE WEIGHT IS BY THIS EFFORTLESS TWO-MINUTE EXERCISE."

"There are two principal components to this exercise. The first part begins by lying flat on your back. Relax. Put the palm of your hand on your navel. Then simply rub—nothing more—in exactly the way I am going to show you. (See Page 5 of Dr. Chang's Confidential Report.)"

"What is really taking place while you are rubbing your stomach away is this. When the hand is gently passed over the body this way, energy invisible to the naked eye passes from that hand through the skin. So. . . you are actually 'brushing with energy' the cells and tissues, throughout the stomach area. Your own bodily electricity, like a fine and gentle brush, shoots out into the skin and underlying tissue."

"In the first part of the exercise, then, this electricity from your own hand gently massages the intestines, the blood vessels, and the digestive and eliminatory system. Fatty accumulations and deposits are disturbed from their resting places and eventually broken up. They are then passed into the eliminatory system and out of the body."

"BY SUCH APPARENTLY SIMPLE MEANS, THE SUPERFLUOUS AREAS OF THE STOMACH AND ABDOMEN ARE LITERALLY RUBBED AWAY."

"What I must impress upon you is that losing weight is largely a matter of increasing the efficiency of the digestive organs. Have you ever tried cutting down on your food intake, or changed your diet overall, and still found yourself unable to lose weight? This is most probably because your digestive and eliminatory processes are not what they should be."

"Well, this exercise is a kind of gentle and natural colonic irrigation. . . excess fat is being burned off. Fatty tissues around the stomach and intestines are metabolized and then discarded."

"The usefulness of the exercise has nothing to do with rubbing the skin with great pressure. The movements of your hand are simply a mechanism to pass your own bodily energy, which is an electrical force in itself, back into your lower extremities. The key is that energy. Relax the body. Let it do its own healing work. Physicians don't heal others; they simply find ways to allow the body to heal itself."

"YOU NEEDN'T FEEL YOU MUST DO IT FOR MORE THAN TWO MINUTES AT A TIME FOR IT TO BE EFFECTIVE."

"The exercise should be performed twice a day (or more if you like) while lying on your back. The best times to do it are the first thing in the morning upon awakening, and then again just before you go to sleep."

"If you persist, you will reap other benefits as well. It will improve the condition of your heart, because you will have reduced its burden. The blood vessels will be gradually strengthened. . . You will improve your digestion. You may very well notice an upswing in your level of vitality."

AND, ONCE AGAIN—"THE SUPERFLUOUS AREAS OF YOUR STOMACH AND ABDOMEN ARE LITERALLY RUBBED AWAY."

Dr. Chang's confidential report, "How to Rub Your Stomach Away", can be obtained nowhere else but through this advertisement.

And—best of all—it is yours ABSOLUTELY FREE . . . even if you return "Internal Exercises" for every cent of your purchase price back.

Why not send for this startling Free gift. . . today?

VITAL NOTE: The guaranteed promises on this page are so startling, so unexpected to those who are not familiar with Eastern medicine, **that it is imperative that you read Dr. Chang's credentials.** These are given to you, in a brief outline, on page 3 of the accompanying letter.

READ DR. CHANG'S THRILLING CASE HISTORIES ON BACK OF THIS PAGE!

P12

If you still don't believe in these "Internal Exercises" *Including How To Rub Your Stomach Away* then read Dr. Chang's thrilling case histories below.

As told in Dr. Chang's own words.

1.

I lecture frequently on college campuses, and was one day in up-state New York. The dean of studies, who was very overweight, looked much older than her years, and was in poor physical health generally. I suggested the exercise, demonstrating it for her. In just a few weeks she had lost five inches in her waist, hips, and thigh areas, and her color had come back to "normal." She became a younger, more vibrant woman, and is today head of one of the most important academic institutions in the nation.

2.

John a bank president, was overweight, sluggish, constipated. And, at age 55, he was almost ready to give up. His secretary, urged him to try the simple stomach rubbing exercise. By applying the exercise faithfully, he regularized his bowel movement, lost 40 pounds, and was filled with a new energy.

3.

A very pretty, but extremely overweight young woman of 29 came up to me after a lecture session to say that she feared she'd never shed her excess inches—she was wearing a size 18 dress and that was tight on her. She didn't think she could stick with the stomach exercise—so I tried to get her to see how easy it is, and how well it keeps me in shape. After trying the exercise, she realized that it is actually fun to do anyway, and within two weeks she noticed how loose her size 18 dress was becoming. So she stuck with the exercise, doing it daily no matter where she happened to be, and today she is down to a size 11. When I first met her, she appeared to be in her 40's—and today she can easily pass for her very early 20's.

4.

Mrs. Rosario ran a successful Italian restaurant in Chicago, and she nibbled at everything. Her husband was dead, and she was convinced that she'd never attract the attention of any suitors at her age (she was 47) and with her weight (5′4″, 175 pounds). Oddly, the stomach-flattening exercise not only slimmed her down, it seemed to help direct her interests away from the food with which she was surrounded daily. Today she is happily remarried, and she keeps her stomach flat and her hips trim by doing this simple exercise every day.

5.

Although I wouldn't recommend that a person continue to eat and drink excessively, let me give you an example of a man who did just that and still managed to lose inches. Paul C. is an acquaintance of mine who attended one of my lectures in Phoenix, Arizona. Now, this man was nothing short of obese, and he was still gaining weight. He told me that eating was his chief pleasure in life and he didn't see that he would be willing to give it up. "But is there a way for me to lose this stomach?" he asked me, pointing to his distended belly. Mr. C. was obviously a "hard case," but I recommended that he do the exercise. I got a call from him a month later, and he told me gleefully that he had already lost three notches on his belt! He continued to lose weight until he had stabilized into a normal range, but he still shows his friends his old belt.

6.

Morgan was one of my most difficult cases. He'd come to me just after he'd lost his influential job as head of a major airline; partly because he was under so much stress, he had become a compulsive eater, and was getting no exercise—drinking large quantities of beer at the local bar, too. One day he heard that he'd lost out on a major executive position with a Fortune 500 company—and it was only because of his sloppy appearance. Then he determined to stay faithfully with the exercise, did in fact slim down and firm up, and shortly thereafter was hired as president of a major food concern. I see him often, and he looks younger today than he did ten years ago.

7.

Several years ago I spoke to a group of overweight wives of physicians. After my talk, one young woman turned to me and said, "Dr. Chang, I don't think my marriage is going to last. I love my husband, and he loves me, but I'm more than pleasingly plump. What can I do?" Well, she was about 5′9″, and weighed about 210 pounds. But I noticed that her weight was mostly in her mid-sections, front and back. I suggested the exercise. Several weeks later the young wife called me to say that her figure was "straightening out." I saw the couple quite recently, and she is nicely proportioned. Her husband now paid her close attention (as did all other men in her presence), and they were obviously quite happy.

The $8\frac{1}{2}'' \times 11''$ lift piece, printed front and back.

Schwartz's energy, intensity, and ability to pile benefits on top of benefits on top of benefits. In a guest column for *Who's Mailing What!* Malcolm Decker reported on two of Schwartz's packages—for Dick Benson's *Wellness Encyclopedia* and Rodale's *Secrets of Executive Success*—and counted an astonishing 299 separate and distinct benefits to the buyer in the former and 237 in the latter.

With this package, you have the unique opportunity to see what Gene Schwartz writes *for himself*, for he is not only the copywriter but also the publisher of *Dr. Chang's Book of Internal Exercises.*

Nothing whispers in a Gene Schwartz package; it screams for attention, as can be seen in this effort. It is jarring; it is offensive; it is hokey. Yet this package has been in the mail continuously since 1979. Think of it! *Thirteen years old and still going strong*! All you can do is study a package like this and ask over and over again, "What has this got that mine ain't got?"

Incidentally, when the postal rates put a \$50-per-thousand penalty on "flats"—mailings larger than $6\frac{1}{8}'' \times 11\frac{1}{2}''$—Schwartz tested this package in a $6'' \times 9''$ and a number 10 size; the *net* results on the number 10 were equal to the original $9'' \times 12''$ (fewer orders, but also less cost per thousand). The $6'' \times 9''$ did not work as well.

It should be added here that many of the promises, benefits, and claims found in Schwartz's copy may seem suspect; in fact, you sometimes wonder how they got by the FTC or the FDA. Pat Corpora once told me that Rodale's philosophy is that if a claim is made in the product itself, it can be used in the direct mail piece.

Eugene Schwartz and his wife, Barbara, are proprietors of a small publishing company, Instant Improvement, Inc. Schwartz is also one of the greatest—yet least known—copywriters in America. Of the first sixty-six Axel Andersson Awards, Schwartz was the winner of three, one for his own title, *Dr. Chang's Book of Internal Exercises*, and two for Rodale Press. Two of the eight books he has authored—*Breakthrough Advertising* and *Mail Order*—are must-read classics for all direct marketers. His mailing piece for *The Encyclopedia of Natural Healing* reportedly sold nearly two million books at $25 per book (an eye-popping $50 million gross). For the August 1987 issue of *Direct Marketing*, Gene Schwartz sat for an interview with Milt Pierce (creator of the *M* magazine package, discussed in Chapter 9), and it is reprinted here with permission of Milt Pierce.

PIERCE: What do you consider the most important characteristics of a copywriter?

SCHWARTZ: There are four: indefatigability, clarity, craziness, and humility. Let me explain: When I talk about indefatigability, I mean that copywriting is research. You can always determine the ad that has had the best research; it has something I call "claim density." It's packed with facts, with information, with ideas. You can't get that without doing a lot of research.

PIERCE: What about clarity?

SCHWARTZ: It's quite simple. Clear writing is strong writing.

PIERCE: Craziness?

SCHWARTZ: The copywriter is the person who looks at things that other people don't see. As a result, the copywriter writes in a way that's strangely fascinating . . . offbeat . . . and somewhat crazy.

PIERCE: Humility?

SCHWARTZ: Yes, humility. The copywriter puts himself last. The customer comes first. The product comes second. The writing is what comes last. But above all, the copywriter has got to have integrity. He—or she—must never write an ad just to please the client . . . or to make money . . . or to meet a deadline . . . and never, never write an ad for a bad product.

PIERCE: What made you decide to go into this business?

SCHWARTZ: Hunger. I came to New York after getting out of the University of Washington. I wanted to write the Great American Novel. Got a job as a messenger boy for Huber Hoge Advertising. That was 1949. I went from messenger to copy cub to copywriter to copy chief. Worked at Huber Hoge from 1949 to 1954. Then I started out on my own. In 1959 I started Information Incorporated.

PIERCE: Would you say that Cecil Hoge was your mentor?

SCHWARTZ: Yes. Without a doubt.

PIERCE: Do you have any special techniques that you use to get ideas?

SCHWARTZ: Yes, research. When I write copy for a book, I generally know more about that book than the editor.

PIERCE: What do you like most about being a copywriter?

SCHWARTZ: I like the aloneness of this business. I like the fact that I can sit at a desk and make money. I like the intelligent gambling that's so much a part of direct marketing. I like the mathematics of direct marketing. Most of all, I like the feeling I have of helping people by selling good products.

PIERCE: What do you like least?

SCHWARTZ: Clients who change copy without telling me. Or who don't let me see layouts. And I *hate* people who steal my ads and my ideas.

PIERCE: Is there a relationship between your best work and the sales that resulted from it?

SCHWARTZ: Yes, one-to-one. I'm a copywriter. My best work is the copy that sold best.

PIERCE: Is there any ad you feel particularly happy about?

SCHWARTZ: I wrote a direct mail package for Marty Edelston. In effect, this was the package that started Boardroom Reports and put Marty into business.

PIERCE: What was so special about that package?

SCHWARTZ: The headline for that was "How to Get the Guts out of 300 Business Magazines in 30 Minutes." I think that's one of the best I have ever written.

PIERCE: How long does it take you to write a direct mail package?

SCHWARTZ: Usually about six hours. But I like to work on a project for two hours a day . . . three days in a row.

PIERCE: Do you do much rewriting?

SCHWARTZ: With a word processor, that's a thing of the past, because you can write and rewrite at the same time. I'm now involved in creating and selling software for computers. In my opinion, that's the future of our business.

PIERCE: Do you enjoy listening to music?

SCHWARTZ: Yes. I think there's a connection between music and writing. It's a certain rhythm that exists in good writing as well as in good music.

PIERCE: What are your favorite ads?

SCHWARTZ: I love that Ogilvy ad for Rolls-Royce—"At 60 Miles an Hour the Loudest Noise Is the Clock Ticking." And Gary Halbert's ad, "The Amazing Diet Secret of a Desperate Housewife." And Ed McLean's letter for Mercedes, the one that begins, "Forget it Heinz. . . ." And that classic by Maxwell Sackheim, "Do You Make These Mistakes in English?"

PIERCE: Which books have influenced you the most.

SCHWARTZ: Hopkins's *My Life in Advertising.* And *How I Raised Myself from a Failure to Success in Selling.* And the new book by Rapp and Collins, *MaxiMarketing.* Of course, those classics by Caples and Ogilvy and Robert Collier and Victor Schwab. That almost goes without saying.

PIERCE: Would you rather write a direct mail piece or an ad?

SCHWARTZ: I prefer direct mail; it's where I get the best results.

The order form, front and back.

FOR WOMEN • FOR MEN • FOR BOTH MEN AND WOMEN

"This outward circular rubbing motion of the hands (shown on page 19 of the book described inside) is called **DISPERSION**, and helps to prevent lumps and cancer of the breasts. One may reverse the motion of the hands.... This is called **STIMULATION** and its effect is to enlarge the breasts."

"This pose strengthens and tones the thighs, calves and ankles. It makes the abdominal muscles strong and increases the circulation in the legs and body, as well as strengthening the back and the nerves in the body. It also stimulates the meridians of the bladder, gallbladder and stomach. These meridians lie along the legs, and so it helps to reduce water retention and excessive weight and lowers the blood pressure."

"Thus one secret of maintaining youth into one's old age is to exercise glands and keep them strong."

"...and it is said that if one has strong sexual glands, one may never grow old."

"This exercise cures and prevents hemorrhoids and cures problems of the prostate, such as weakness, enlargement and cancer (all by using a simple sitting exercise that doesn't cause you even to take one extra breath)."

How to eventually throw your glasses away, and never need to see an eye doctor again, simply by rubbing around your eyes for a few minutes each day.

How to keep your lungs strong, acquire fewer colds, allergies, and sinus conditions, simply by stimulating certain points about your nose.

How to use natural healing water as a form of medicine, so powerful that it may be used to treat cuts and other infections. And so powerful, indeed, that, when properly used, it helps prevent tooth decay.

Stephen Chang, M.D. (China), Ph.D.

And dozens more...Read the full details inside. Prove them all yourself, in the privacy of your own home, entirely at our risk.

DOUBLE GUARANTEE
KEEP THIS FOR YOUR RECORDS!

You are fully protected by this 100% No-Risk Double Guarantee:

1—If you don't like this amazing new book when it arrives, return it for a full refund—no questions asked.

2—Or, keep and use it for ONE FULL YEAR. You are still protected. You MUST get all we've promised—or send it back ANYTIME DURING THAT ENTIRE YEAR. You still get every penny of your purchase price back.

DR. CHANG'S BOOK OF INTERNAL EXERCISES..... $29.98

Instant Improvement, Inc.
Fulfillment Center
250 Lexington Avenue
P.O. Box 2788
Grand Central Station
New York, NY 10163

Cut here and Mail in Enclosed Envelope

MAIL THIS NO-RISK COUPON TODAY!

Please rush me a copy of DR. CHANG'S BOOK OF INTERNAL EXERCISES by Dr. Stephen T. Chang! I enclose $29.98. In addition, I understand that I may examine this revolutionary new book for ONE FULL YEAR, since I am fully protected by your 100% No-Risk Double Guarantee shown at left.

Also rush me my free gift copy of "HOW TO RUB YOUR STOMACH AWAY." I understand that it is mine to keep, even if I return the main book for every cent of my purchase price back.

Send check or money order (U.S. currency only) payable to *Instant Improvement, Inc.* New York residents, please add appropriate tax.

Charge my credit card:
☐MasterCard ☐VISA

Credit Card No.

Exp.

Signature

Jay
48
New 06840
R901
AHB

SEE OTHER SIDE...

From
FORTUNE MAGAZINE—

in the April 27, 1987 article on

WHAT BOSSES READ—

"Wall Streeter George L. Ball, 48, of Prudential Bache Securities, applies Taoist teachings from *The Book of Internal Exercises* by Stephen T. Chang... "This is a compilation of ancient Chinese Yoga exercises that energize body and mind in concert," explains Ball... "These exercises help you avoid stress and concentrate."

From Two Continents—
Unsolicited Letters Of Thanks Pour In

From America—

"...though I have only had it for six weeks, I have had several good results. My glaucoma is much improved—over ten points.

"Forty five years ago I was injured in a fall—job-related—and my left foot has plagued me ever since. After using Toe Wiggling several times a day, I can get up in the night without pain. I am eighty years old, and I can work in the garden again.

"My wife, seventy one years old, had had constipation troubles for sixty five years. She had tried everything on the market to no avail. After rubbing her solar plexis for two weeks, she is now able to go almost every day. Great..."

Jack J.... Hoquim, Washington 98550

"The book saved me from having a plastic disk put in my back as advised by my doctors.

"It worked for others, so I'm sure it wasn't just me.

"I will buy any and all books by the author—just let me know..."

Helen E.... Mendata, Illinois 61342

"It has helped me so much. I am seventy three years old... This is my second book. I gave the other to an aunt who is older than me..."

Ruth R.... North Highlands, California 95660

From France—

"Dr. Chang's book has allowed me to resolve many health problems, without medicine. No more tachychardia, no more swelling in the ankles, two duodenal ulcers in the process of healing. I no longer wear glasses and I see better than before."

Mme Presse, Grenoble

"Since the age of twenty, I had great nervous disorders. Things were aggravated by hypertension and cardiac problems. No medicine supressed the cause of the illness. By contrast, since I applied the very simple methods of Dr. Chang, I no longer have any nervous or cardiac problems."

M Derudder, Coudekerque

"I experienced 'a complete sense of well being,' a better physical and mental equilibrium. I have made the students of my Yoga course (from eleven to eighty years old) benefit from your Internal Exercises, and everyone finds that they feel so good."

Mme Germaine, Montmorillon

NO POSTAGE NECESSARY IF MAILED IN THE UNITED STATES

BUSINESS REPLY MAIL
FIRST CLASS MAIL PERMIT NO. 2472 NEW YORK, NY

POSTAGE WILL BE PAID BY ADDRESSEE

INSTANT IMPROVEMENT, INC.
250 Lexington Avenue
P. O. Box 2788
Grand Central Station
New York, NY 10164-1252

The business reply envelope.

PIERCE: What kind of results are we talking about?

SCHWARTZ: I get a success rate of 80 percent in my direct mail. In space ads, it's about one out of three.

PIERCE: Do you have samples of your favorite ads to share with our readers?

SCHWARTZ: No. I don't save my ads. That would be living in the past. I'm interested in tomorrow . . . not yesterday.

PIERCE: Do you have any words of advice to our readers?

SCHWARTZ: Yes. We're undergoing a profound revolution. The mail order firm is now able to serve its customers more completely than the retail store. Consequently, the copywriter now concentrates as much on delivery as he does on claims. He no longer makes a sale, but invites his prospect to a lifetime of borrowing products before having to buy them.

Rodale—The Quintessential Direct Marketer

No publisher is more in tune with its market than Rodale Press. The company was founded in 1930 by J. I. Rodale, a devout believer in organic farming and gardening as well as in consuming only natural foods and vitamins and living in harmony with the earth.

Rodale was a true Renaissance man: publisher, inventor, gardener, playwright, and author of a number of books, including *The Synonym Finder*, an infinitely more valuable and easy-to-use guide to the English language than *Roget's Thesaurus*.

Although many considered Rodale a "health nut," he never varied from his philosophy of natural living and achieved a devoted following through his magazines *Organic Gardening* and *Prevention*.

With the publication of Rachel Carson's *Silent Spring* and the collective consciousness raising of the environmental movement, it turned out that J. I. Rodale was right on the money—a man ahead of his time, totally in tune with the 1970s and 1980s. But he never lived to see the sprawling media empire that bears his name. In a well-publicized demise during a guest appearance on the Dick Cavett television show in 1971, Rodale fell asleep during a commercial break and never woke up.

A great deal of credit for Rodale's success goes to the extraordinary group of executives that were nurtured by the Rodale family. Among them: Bob Teufel, who started in circulation and is now president and CEO, and Pat Corpora, president of the book division.

Pat Corpora has been with Rodale Press since 1980 where he has risen from product accountant in the Finance Department to president of the Book Division. A native of the Lehigh Valley, he earned a B.A. degree from Moravian College. Corpora is the ideal Rodale representative: He is both a bicyclist and an avid runner who has competed in thirteen consecutive Boston Marathons; at his home in Upper Saucon Township, Center Valley, Pennsylvania, he maintains a large organic garden with his wife, Sandy.

PAT CORPORA:

There are four elements in our business that have allowed us to grow and succeed. The first is an extremely powerful editorial product that meets our customers' needs. We encourage our editorial group to be as creative as possible in developing ideas and concepts for new book titles. We give them no boundaries as long as the concept fits our division mission: "To publish books that empower people's lives."

We then take these new editorial concepts and put them through a very rigorous quantitative and qualitative testing process. The combination of creative editorial thinking and solid research methodology has consistently ensured that we bring new, exciting, and salable books to market.

The second element in our direct mail process is powerful creativity. We work with the best copywriters and designers, often encouraging them to break the rules in search of new creative breakthroughs. One of the best examples I can provide was the creative idea of enclosing the merchandise label in our mailing package to reassure the customers that if they were unhappy for any reason, they could simply return our book at no charge.

We have also developed a multistep creative process that brings the marketing and creative people together to brainstorm concepts and approaches and review the mail package before it goes into production.

The third aspect of success is the attention we pay to our lists. We view our lists in two areas. The first is the acquisition of new customers; the second, the enhancement and manipulation of our house file. We are willing to lose money on the acquisition of a new Rodale book customer—whether that customer comes from direct mail, television, or space advertising. Adding new customers to our house file is viewed as an essential element for our future growth. We then enhance our customer file and use the most sophisticated selection methodologies to put the right offer into the right mailbox.

The fourth element of success, and one that is often overlooked, is the efficient and responsive fulfillment, customer service, and distribution functions. The best products and promotions can be rendered useless if this ''unglamorous'' aspect of our business is overlooked.

Those are the four items that I think all direct marketers should be paying attention to and constantly trying to improve upon.

One aspect that distinguishes Rodale's direct marketing efforts is the use of freelancers: just about anybody who wants a shot at a package—from cubs just starting out to top writers and designers who command huge fees—will get one. In addition, it does extensive testing on both product and direct mail packages. Of the original sixty-six Axel Andersson winners, Rodale had five of them, more than any other company.

What follow are the two Axel winners by Gene Schwartz for Rodale Press. They are incredibly copy heavy, filled with bits and pieces of paper—lift notes, premium slips, first-person narratives, benefits, benefits, benefits. Every element is more interruptive than the next, more filled with reasons to buy—and buy *now*.

This is mail order copy at its most intense and most masterful. In the words of Malcolm Decker:

The rite of passage for everyone entering this industry should be to memorize one of [Gene Schwartz's] packages after understanding the marketing, creative, and copy strategy underlying it.

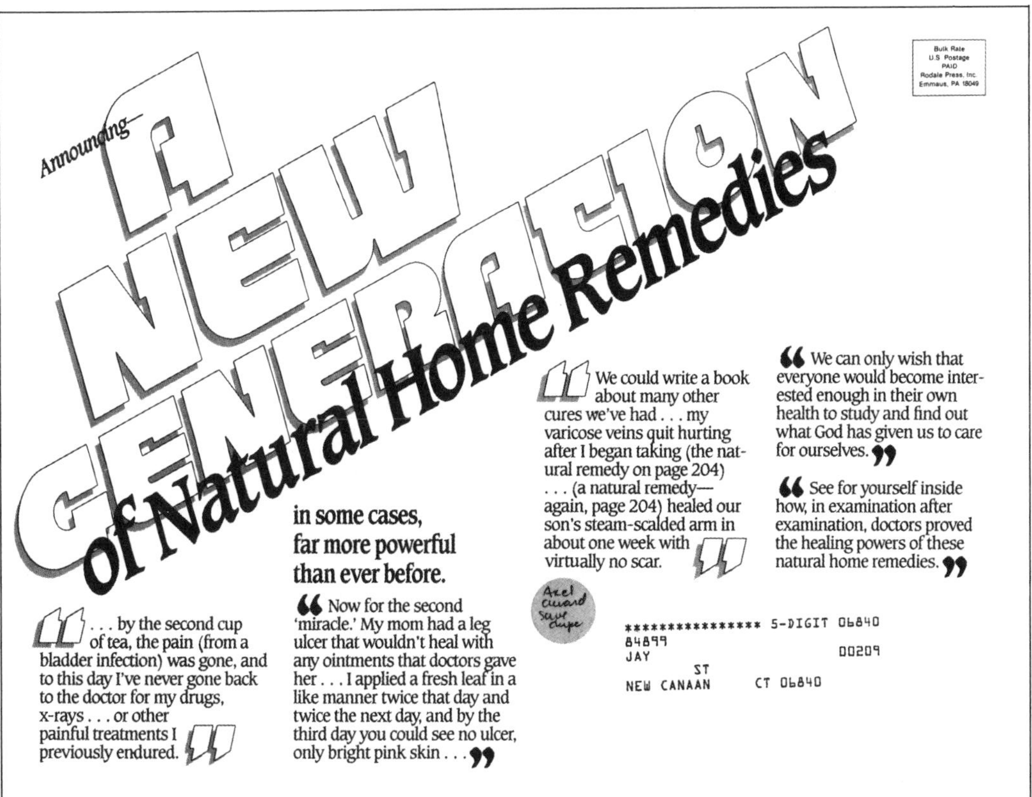

Mailer: Rodale Press
Package: *Encyclopedia of Natural Home Remedies*
Project Mgr.: Pat Corpora
Writer: Eugene M. Schwartz
Designer: Maureen Logan
First Mailed: 1986
The 9″ × 12″ outside envelope in bright yellow, shown front and back.

WHY THIS ENCYCLOPEDIA OF NATURAL HOME REMEDIES

IS SO DESPERATELY NEEDED TODAY

"Major medical bills are now prohibitive to almost any nonwealthy person without a governmental or insurance subsidy, and often even for people with these buffers."

"And although America spends more money per person on health care than any other country in the world, 14 countries lead the United States in male life expectancy . . . despite all the billions of dollars spent on medical research and technology, the life expectancy of an American who has already reached the age of 60 is today only three or four years longer than it was in 1900."

"According to one expert, 'At least 25 percent of the prescriptions dispensed by the modern-day physician contain active ingredients from plants.' Furthermore, says Norman R. Farnsworth, Ph.D., a pharmacy scientist at the Illinois Medical Center in Chicago, 'Essentially all of the plants yielding useful drugs, or which are found in prescriptions as extracts, are rich in medicinal folklore."

"What happens when doctoring simply doesn't work? . . . Some of us go to doctor after doctor, and still no help. Is that the end of the line? Do you spend the rest of your life waiting for the Medical Miracle Train to arrive . . . or do you start walking—cautiously—on your own two feet?"

"You and I will live in the first generation in the history of the world that has been all but entirely cut off from this age-old tradition of self-reliance. Healing and health care have become—almost—the exclusive province of duly licensed physicians. . . . But is it really progress, or have we in effect sold our birthright for a mess of pills?"

If you have the slightest agreement with the logic expressed above . . . if you would like to read for yourself what today's scientifically based home remedies have actually accomplished . . . then simply open this envelope.

Printed in U.S.A.

Because it is impossible to reproduce the vast wealth of *natural remedies* contained in this 512-page volume, we have had to limit ourselves to only one or two case histories for each of the major maladies listed below.

"Much of that time I had to walk with a cane, could not carry anything heavy, and literally crawled up stairs, holding onto the bannisters with both hands. I was told by the M.D.s that I'd have to learn to 'live with it.' After six months on (the natural remedy given you on page 12), the pain vanished completely, and has not returned. My health is excellent -- my back's straight and very strong, and I can run up stairs."

How two desperate alcoholics found their way back to sanity -- page 5.

"I had a very bad infection -- labeled 'athlete's foot' by a specialist ... It itched severely and I scratched it until it bled almost every day for a year and a half. Almost everyone thought it was incurable, including myself. But by late December (after starting to take the natural remedy on page 27), I noticed my foot looking good, and it did not itch anymore. Looking at it now, one would never think that it was as infected as it was."

How to soothe away arthritis pain with your own body heat -- page 14.

"On the third day I could feel an improvement in my bladder condition and on the seventh day there was no soreness. In addition, I had a chronic lung infection which also cleared up." (See page 37.)

Recipe for a "good breath" tea -- page 29.

"One year ago, I started my mother-in-law on (the regimen given you on page 47). She was born in 1898. She could hardly dress herself and was having trouble walking and sleeping due to severe pain from arthritis. Her doctor prescribed Tylenol and 'learn to live with it.' Within three months' time, she was remarkably better and now she has no pain and can outwalk a young woman ... Then on Easter Sunday she was knocked to the pavement by a Volkswagen turning the corner as she was crossing. The sum amount of damages to her was a nasty bruise behind her right ear and a spasm in her neck ... Before ... she had a history of broken bones from falls -- her arm and hips -- but since then, although she still falls occasionally, she has no more broken bones. Not even from the Volkswagen."

The modern miracle for burns -- page 54.

"I am happy to report that after several months on the regimen ... I can see amazing results: one breast is now free of lumps, and two very large lumps in the other are less than half their former size. An added benefit has been the absence of monthly swelling and tenderness." (See page 48.)

The new natural healer for eczema -- page 133.

"At a senior center recently, boiling water was accidentally poured over my hand ... I was stunned by the pain, and there was no ointment on hand to apply to the burn. I got into my car, scarcely able to grasp the wheel. My left thumb and forefinger were beginning to turn a grayish white and I thought of going directly to the hospital. Then I remembered that I had my (natural healing) supplements in my purse. I quickly ... spread the contents over the burned skin. The pain subsided within minutes." (See page 55.)

Other emergency natural-healing first aid -- page 138.

"I then visited my doctor. Upon examining my foot, which was a bluish purple color, he informed me that I had poor circulation in my leg. He then prescribed medication ... No improvement was forthcoming even though he changed the prescription from time to time. I then (started on the natural remedy on page 76) ... The ulcer under my large toe began to heal and my foot lost some of its bluish purple color. After about 12 months I felt reasonably sure that I had either arrested or cured my Buerger's disease and my angina pectoris."

A chemist's home natural-healing remedies -- page 202.

"I am in my sixties and have always been constipated ... I have been operated upon for hemorrhoids twice and a severe anal fissure once. I've been stabbed, spliced, sewed and repaired, yet despite all that, my troubles continued ... Luckily, I had to go to my dentist for my usual checkup, and ... he suggested (the combination formula on page 89). I am happy to state that within a day or so my fears of hospitalization for another repair job were completely eliminated. It's only been six months but the word 'constipated' is no longer in my vocabulary."

The contributions of Biblical medicine and modern science -- page 225.

"From November 1970 until June 1971, I suffered with bronchitis. I ... spent most of my time coughing. I was going to doctors regularly, but with no success. A friend of mine told me to drink (the natural healing tea on page 95). Within a week, my seven-month-long illness was gone!"

The revival of an ancient cure by modern medicine -- page 225.

"For many months I had a small cyst on the lower eyelid. Then it started growing at a great rate. The doctor suggested that I could have an ophthalmologist remove it. He described the procedure which would be used. I was not enchanted. That night I grabbed (the natural remedy from page 102) ... and put some of the liquid on the cyst. The next morning it was down by nearly half. Now, a week later, one can hardly see the cyst ... It does beat surgery!"

Natural remedies for hair loss -- page 247.

"A few months ago my dry, itching, sore facial skin sent me to a dermatologist. It didn't take him long to tell me that the condition was eczema. He prescribed a medicated cream and charged me $25. But it didn't help at all. Then ... I tried (the natural remedy on page 133). Soon not one of those little blisters or pimples remained. I discontinued the medicated cream and still my complexion was clear."

A "Biofeedback" cure for headaches at the kitchen sink -- page 255.

"I have been biting my fingernails since the second grade. Fifteen years later and a graduate student in college, I was still biting those nails. Needless to say, I have always been very embarrassed by my hands ... I am now very proud to say that in the last month and a half, my nails have grown and are very strong. My body needed (the natural remedy on page 191) and this I now believe is what was causing the nail biting all those years."

Natural insect repellents -- page 284.

"Our young son, who suffered petit mal seizures for three years [despite the conventional anticonvulsant therapy] was not relieved until we (tried the natural remedy from page 194). It worked. One week after ... our boy was seizure-free and has been for one year."

Natural remedies for rectal itching -- page 294.

"I have suffered with an aching, throbbing knee for almost two years. After going to several doctors, chiropractors, and having x-rays and taking bottles of aspirin, I was about to give up. With two children and many years ahead of me [I'm 29], I had to find something. I immediately bought several cans of (the natural remedy from page 238 that is found in all food stores). I ate them for about a week, and all the swelling and stiffness disappeared! It was a miracle!"

Banishing creepy-crawlies from your home -- page 286.

"I became prone to vaginal infections of various sorts in my late twenties. From that point on, although I was given a variety of prescriptions and pills ... nothing helped. As I grew older and near menopausal time, the condition worsened. Ultimately the infection from the vagina would lodge in the bladder, causing me much discomfort from frequency of urination. I purchased (the natural remedy on page 245, making sure it was freshly dated) ... Almost immediately my bladder symptoms abated and much of the vaginal irritation I had experienced for so long disappeared ... I have been delighted to find that I can travel, work and engage in activities without the constant desire to urinate, caused by vaginal infection. I have not been back to a doctor in this time."

A natural cure for malaria -- page 322.

"I am nearing age 85. Fifteen years ago, the doctor told me that I had heart disease. I called at his office once or twice each month for the next two years without much improvement. My blood pressure ranged from 160/100 to 180/110. If I walked up stairs, up a slight grade, or a little too fast, I would get a very heavy pressure in my chest. Then one day I began taking (the all-natural regimen on page 262) ... Now after 14 years, no chest pain and a blood pressure of 130/70. The doctor that I mentioned above said: 'The natural remedy described above) has been tried and found to be useless, but ... it's your money.' He dropped dead from a heart attack before he reached 60."

Major drugs that come from natural remedies -- page 324.

"When I was 17, I developed an extreme case of herpes simplex 2 in the vaginal area. Due to the tiny ulcers, it was extremely painful to urinate. My doctor told me that there was nothing he could give me to heal it, but that it had to run its course. So for seven days I suffered. At 21, I had a return visit of herpes. I took (the all-natural regimen on page 270) ... By the next morning there was no pain. The following day the sores were gone. I told my gynecologist the story and he said it was impossible. He is no longer my doctor."

For those who are allergic to antibiotics, the natural remedy that could be a real lifesaver -- page 344.

"I've been treated for high blood pressure for two years. My doctor wanted me to stay on medication for the rest of my life. Then I started taking (the natural remedy from page 272) three times a day. I was able to reduce my medication from a pill every day to two pills a week. Four months ago I started taking larger capsules (of this natural remedy) -- one a day. I've been off medication ever since and my blood pressure has been normal."

Home remedies for fertility problems -- page 375.

"I suffer from varicose veins, and many nights, I could not get any sleep because of severe pains and cramps in my legs. The doctor told me to give up my job -- I had to be on my feet all day long -- and find a sitting job ... Then, one day ... I ordered a supply of (the natural remedy on page 318) and took it regularly. Since then have I experienced a wonderful change. Those cramps have practically disappeared. I no longer wear support hose but regular panty hose. I no longer need those ointments, and my legs feel almost like they did a long time ago."

Healing cracked skin -- page 399.

"For years, I had been plagued with severe, incapacitating menstrual cramps. I could not even get out of bed during the first day or two of my period. The pain was so horrible I once passed out from it. During my first period after beginning (the natural remedy on page 328), my cramps were somewhat bad, but not at all incapacitating

... The second period there were no cramps at all. In fact, I didn't know I was going to begin my cycle ... And I have never had cramps since then."

Victory over rashes, even the worst -- page 404.

"I went to my doctor because I was having pain and difficulty controlling my urination. He said it was my prostate, and that I would probably have to have surgery. That was the only way out. But I postponed it. Then I read something about (the all-natural regimen on page 382) ... I started taking one after each meal and within a month the results were unbelievable. Things are now normal, as far as I am concerned. I have no pain and no control problems."

Stress relievers in everyday life -- page 445.

"My sinus condition began in the fall of 1977, and became more acute last year. My doctor gave me antibiotics and irrigation. Neither gave me any relief. Then he suggested surgery. I hesitated. For the past two months I have been taking (the natural remedy on page 396). Now, I can happily relate that ... After more than a year using up a dozen handkerchiefs a day, I am down to less than one a day. It's great being able to breathe freely again."

Unsuspected food allergies as a cause of illness -- page 473.

"When I was pregnant with my son, I had the most unsightly stretch marks across my entire abdominal areas that I have ever seen. So, about two or three times daily I rubbed (the simple natural remedy on page 407) into the reddened areas. Within two weeks my stretch marks had completely disappeared, and did not return. The women in my natural childbirth class refused to believe me, and were convinced that nothing can get rid of stretch marks. But the skin on my abdominal area is now as smooth as the day I was born, and I am proud to say I am the new owner of a bouncing blue string bikini."

Herbs that whip warts -- page 487.

"After spending 12 months and over $200 with a foot doctor unsuccessfully treating my ingrown toenails, I decided to give (the natural remedy on page 464) a try. A few weeks later I noticed the color coming back in the nails. They were growing fast ... Now after six months of careful treatment ... The nails are healthy ..."

The leading herbal remedy for arthritis -- page 16.

"At the age of 90, my grandmother was told she was developing cataracts and would, eventually, have to have an operation to save her sight. We started her on (the all-natural regimen on page 482). This was two years ago and grandma's general health has improved considerably, and her eyesight has improved to the point where she sits and plays cards with us and has no more 'weeping,' which had caused her so much discomfort."

These are only some of the vital health stories in RODALE'S ENCYCLOPEDIA OF NATURAL HOME REMEDIES. But you can read them all before you decide to buy.

To take advantage of our "free take-a-look offer," here's all you need to do:

1. Just drop the enclosed postage-paid card in the mail today.

When your copy arrives, be our guest: examine it ... use it should pain and injury strike ... show it to an ill friend or relative ... discuss it with your family doctor.

2. If it isn't all and more than we claim it to be -- if it fails to prove itself ...

... send it back to us within 15 days and owe nothing.

But ...

... if you agree that this big, helpful encyclopedia is the book that you and your family will use with confidence time and again, keep it. We will bill you later in three easy monthly payments of $7.32 each (plus postage and handling), with no interest or finance charges.

And keep it handy. Even though this book is not a substitute for a doctor's care, you'll be reaching for this up-to-date source of natural help instead of reaching for sometimes dubious medicines.

Can it help you save money? Take greater control over your family's health? Bring your body into greater harmony with its natural strengths?

Truly, what a book this is, if it does! And we believe it will!

But, please, you be the judge. Mail the enclosed card right now, to examine RODALE'S ENCYCLOPEDIA OF NATURAL HOME REMEDIES FREE for 15 days.

Sincerely,

Mark Bricklin

Mark Bricklin
Executive Editor
PREVENTION Magazine

P.S. ACT NOW AND GET THIS FREE GIFT! To help introduce you to the world of NATURAL HOME REMEDIES, we'd like to send you "Easing Aches and Pains" -- a booklet written to help you draw on your body's own natural resources to relieve the aches and pains of everyday life. And the booklet is yours FREE whether you decide to purchase RODALE'S ENCYCLOPEDIA OF NATURAL HOME REMEDIES or not. Supplies are limited, so please act soon. Mail the enclosed card today.

B9896

Printed in the USA

The 6-page letter printed in blue and black on a 11″ × 17″ sheet with an 8½″ × 11″ sheet inserted. Key phrases are highlighted in blue (e.g., "the pain vanished completely" . . . "a chronic lung infection which also cleared up" . . . "she has no more broken bones" . . . "swelling and stiffness disappeared! It was a miracle!").

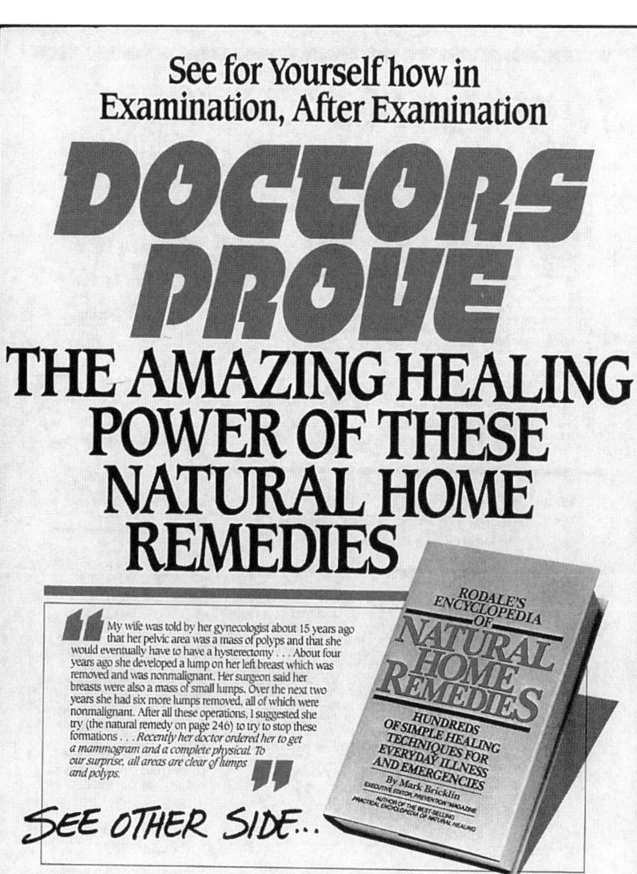

See for Yourself how in Examination, After Examination
DOCTORS PROVE
THE AMAZING HEALING POWER OF THESE NATURAL HOME REMEDIES
My wife was told by her gynecologist about 15 years ago that her pelvic area was a mass of polyps and that she would eventually have to have a hysterectomy . . . About four years ago she developed a lump on her left breast which was removed and was nonmalignant. Her surgeon said her breasts were also a mass of small lumps. Over the next two years she had six more lumps removed, all of which were nonmalignant. After all these operations, I suggested she try (the natural remedy on page 246) to try to stop these formations . . . Recently her doctor ordered her to get a mammogram and a complete physical. To our surprise, all areas are clear of lumps and polyps.
SEE OTHER SIDE...
RODALE'S ENCYCLOPEDIA OF NATURAL HOME REMEDIES
HUNDREDS OF SIMPLE HEALING TECHNIQUES FOR EVERYDAY ILLNESS AND EMERGENCIES
By Mark Bricklin

You can imagine our joy when he (the doctor) said the operation wasn't necessary. (See page 390)
Years ago, I received weekly treatments from my doctor for an 'unhealthy' prostate. The doctor said that there was no help available except sitz baths and his treatments. I started taking (the natural remedy on page 384) . . . and I realized there was a definite improvement . . . After nearly a year . . . the same doctor examined that area again and remarked, 'Wow! You seem to have a healthy prostate now. What have you been doing?' I proudly told him . . . I happened to see him recently . . . he said, 'By the way, what did you say you took for that prostate problem you had?' I told him once again. I believe he was having problems of his own in that area and was eager to avoid the usual treatments.
Following x-rays of my neck and spine 12 years ago I was told that I would soon be stiff and bedridden because the entire area was so heavily calcified. I began taking (the natural remedy on page 14) . . . Two sets of x-rays very recently revealed no calcification of the spine or pelvic area and no arthritis. After a thorough examination I was told I had the heart, heart valves, veins, arteries, and blood pressure of a 25-year-old. (I'm almost 70).
I have been having problems with bleeding gums since I was a teenager . . . about five years ago a dentist warned me that I would probably lose my teeth in my forties because of gum disease . . . My mother suggested taking (the natural remedy on page 240) . . . Three months later I returned to the dentist for a cleaning . . . There wasn't any pain this time, and the bleeding was slight. After the cleaning, the hygienist and dentist smiled and said the gums looked normal. 'What have you been doing?' they asked. I told them . . . 'Keep it up,' said the dentist.
. . . my blood pressure was down to 110/76, so I discontinued medication entirely. Since then and for well over a year now, my pressure averages 130/74 as long as I take two (of the natural remedy on page 272) a day. Three will bring it down under 130/70. When I finally told my doctor what I was doing, he admitted he had heard (that natural remedy) could help high blood pressure.
When I went over to the doctor at that time he said, 'What happened?' I told him and he said, 'Well whatever you did, keep it up,' and now he believes. (See page 263)
. . . in Denmark . . . I came down with a severe case of diarrhea during the early months of pregnancy. Our regular doctor was out of town, so we contacted another doctor, an older man who had practiced his own variety of medicine along with the orthodox variety for many years. He said I should not take any medication for fear of harming the baby. His instructions, instead, were to (follow the simple natural procedure on page 112) . . . I was almost back to normal within 24 hours and completely well soon after.
My doctor says he would now recommend this treatment to his other patients. (See page 393)
Some years back (I am now 83), when living in St. Louis, there seemed to be something dreadfully wrong with my kidneys. Three doctors having taken an x-ray which showed the lower half of one kidney completely black, decided there must be an operation, at least exploratory. Deciding not to have the operation, I took my family to the country, bag and baggage, and drank (the natural remedy on page 299) instead of water for a year. Upon my return to the city one of the doctors called upon me and asked, 'How are you?' I answered, 'Just fine!' . . . Another x-ray showed an entirely clean kidney.
We were fortunate to have a young orthopedic surgeon come to this area. As I felt things could not get much worse, I went to see him. More x-rays. Three days later, he called me to this office and—now what I call the 'miracle'—he ordered (the natural remedy on page 13) . . . The first month I discarded the back brace and sling. . . . The only pain I have now is occasionally in my right elbow.
Prove it yourself—just as these professionally skeptical medical people have! Read RODALE'S ENCYCLOPEDIA OF NATURAL HOME REMEDIES from cover to cover, entirely at our risk.

Lift piece 1.

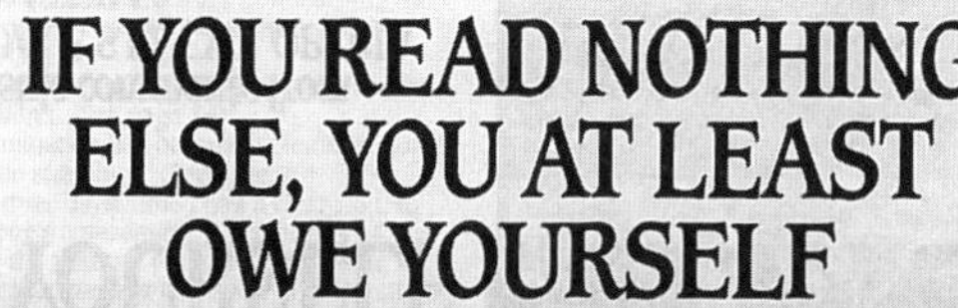

IF YOU READ NOTHING ELSE, YOU AT LEAST OWE YOURSELF THIS HOPE:

Capsule comments from RODALE'S ENCYCLOPEDIA OF NATURAL HOME REMEDIES—

". . . before the bottle was finished, her warts were gone." (See page 488)

"I have not taken one Fiorinal tablet since that time." (See page 255)

"As a bonus my hair stopped falling out." (See page 3)

"Doctors and nurses are now learning the technique in unparalleled numbers." (See page 305)

"This winter my whole family had the flu, but I didn't. (See page 78)

"Elimination has become a pleasure. No pain, no straining." (See page 90)

"In three days' time I had a clear skin, to everyone's amazement." (See page 4)

"By the time my husband came home for dinner that evening there was only the slightest tinge of pink, no soreness whatsoever, and my hand never did peel or blister!" (See page 55)

"After five years of parental anguish you must pardon us if we act like a miracle has occurred to our family." (See page 195)

"I took two in the evening, two the next morning, and my painful ordeal was over." (See page 266)

"However, the best testimony was unsolicited and direct from my daughter: 'Mommy, I don't feel all wiggly inside.' " (See page 275)

And now listen to Mark Bricklin—executive editor of PREVENTION® magazine, and author of this ENCYCLOPEDIA OF NATURAL HOME REMEDIES:

"If one plant could be called jack-of-all-trades in healing, it would be the (one given to you on page 428)."

". . . of 2,959 responses, 1,379 reported bone or joint pain had been either relieved or entirely abolished after taking (the natural remedy on page 121)."

"Tested by time, entirely without side effects, and free for the taking, these stress relievers are, for my money, worth more than all the tranquilizers and mood elevators ever bottled." (See page 446)

"According to several physicians, this (no-cost natural treatment from page 60) is more effective (and cheaper!) than any drug treatment. Such enthusiastic endorsements, however, do not necessarily mean that it is going to find its way into medical textbooks."

And this is just a "quick taste" of the treasures awaiting you in this 512-page Encyclopedia! Quite truthfully . . . HELP MAY BE JUST A PAGE AWAY. It costs you nothing—not a single penny—to prove this to yourself in the privacy of your own home. Why not take another moment to scan the thrilling case histories enclosed? And then enjoy every page of this massive "compendium of hope" . . . entirely at our risk.

39899

Lift piece 2.

Why do we proudly call this
A NEW GENERATION
of Natural Home Remedies
IN SOME CASES, FAR MORE POWERFUL THAN EVER BEFORE.
Let Mark Bricklin—executive editor of PREVENTION magazine—give you the thrilling facts:

Lift piece 3.

" . . . the remedies of the past, often calling for complicated formulas and exotic or potentially dangerous ingredients, are simply not very practical for modern use."

"Today's home remedies reflect the tenor of our own time, with its high regard for good nutrition, good living habits and good medical care, along with an appreciation of the importance of individual differences, safety in all remedies (medical and nonmedical) and—yes—convenience, too."

"This search for specific evidence of the guiding principles of nature as they relate to physical health has become the mission of 20th-century naturopaths. Using contemporary diagnostic and evaluative equipment, much of it computerized, and modern medical procedures, they chart the effects of natural remedies. In so doing, they have departed from the purely empirical mode and have embarked upon establishing a new science of natural healing."

The following are just three examples of this new generation of natural home remedies:

"Recently I came down with a blazing sore throat that felt like it was going to turn into a cold. *Taking vitamin C kept down the severity of the resultant illness, but what really kept it from spreading into my head was (the natural remedy on page 80)*."

"I've been a sufferer of psoriasis for over eight years. It covered about 15 percent of my body from the scalp to my kneecaps . . . Various doctors prescribed diverse creams and ointments—including a $35 visit to a dermatologist prescribing a cortisone cream—but to no avail, just temporary removal of the scales. *I've even tried applying vitamin E oil—but again, no success. I happened to mention this problem to a woman and she casually mentioned (the home remedy on page 385) . . . Believe it or not, within 90 days, all the scales from all of my body disappeared. Unbelievable.*"

"My nails would 'peel' off in layers. They were brittle, too, and would break easily. Three or four years of gelatin capsules and over-the-counter preparations of several kinds were to no avail. *Then . . . I began with (the simple natural regimen on page 206). In less than three months my nails were strong and flexible again! I have waited about three years to make sure it is not just a temporary situation. But now I am convinced it is permanent.*"

And there are dozens upon dozens of other startling examples in the enclosed pages. Read those that touch closest to your own life . . . that offer you thrilling new hope that you might have imagined was gone forever. *And then send for this new ENCYCLOPEDIA OF NATURAL HOME REMEDIES—to read from cover to cover, entirely at our risk.*

Mark Bricklin

Printed in USA

B9897

YOURS FREE
When you order RODALE'S ENCYCLOPEDIA OF NATURAL HOME REMEDIES for a No-Risk, 15-day Examination.
Easing
by the editors of the Prevention Total Health System
Aches & Pains

Lift piece 4—announcing the premium.

EASING ACHES AND PAINS

How to draw on your body's own natural resources to relieve the aches and pains of everyday life

INCLUDING:

- Four ways to stimulate the body to release its own natural painkillers.
- How to *avoid* many headaches *before* they can happen, instead of having to deal with them later.
- But if it does occur, here's how to brush your headache away.
- If you have a tension headache, here's why you should forget your scalp, and concentrate *on your toes.*
- When doctors took 500 women with migraines, and gave them a simple food supplement, in 80 percent the migraines disappeared, no matter how long they'd been present.
- Migraine prevention? A heartening possibility! See the section on "The Antimigraine Diet."
- How a doctor at the UCLA School of Medicine found that many of his patients headaches could be *washed right down the drain.*
- Earaches and toothaches—nondrug measures you can take.
- The no-surgery method for doctoring an ingrown toenail.
- The natural anesthetic for the murderous tooth . . . so powerful that you must use it with caution.
- Two nutrients and a simple exercise that can help banish cramps.
- No more exercise cramps.
- Quick, *soothing* relief for monthly menstrual cramps.
- The nutritional supplement combination that doctors have now come up with that may ease uterine cramping.
- Why *the vast majority* of backaches can be treated with simple, at-home methods . . . and some of the best of them.
- From a world-renowned doctor: "(This is) the single most important thing you can do to protect your back."
- How to give a great backrub.
- Eight ways to bid a backache goodnight.
- And much, much more.

YOURS FREE just for taking a 15-day look at RODALE'S ENCYCLOPEDIA OF NATURAL HOME REMEDIES. Why not send in the enclosed No-Risk Order Card . . . *today.*

Easing Aches & Pains

Printed in the U.S.A.

B9898

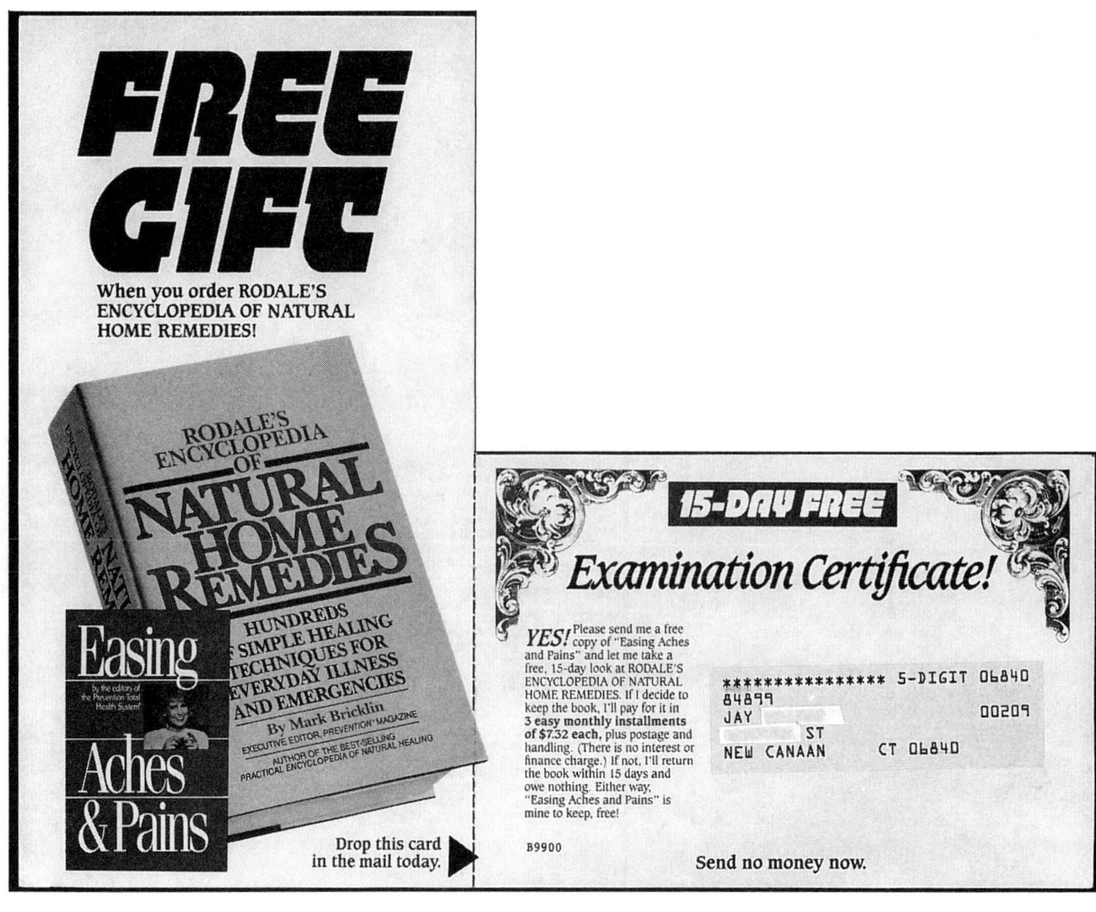

The L-shaped order card with business reply face on the back.

Hints, Tips & Everyday Wisdom

YOURS FREE...perhaps the most important book you may ever own.

See Inside!

Rodale Books
Emmaus, PA 18098

Bulk Rate
U.S. Postage
PAID
Rodale Press, Inc.

TRICKS OF THE TRADE

A form of ordinary water that, by itself, can relieve cold symptoms -- page 273. Simple do-it-yourself ways to not only burglarproof your door, but also have invincible windows -- page 159. A way to vacuum dust from drawers without removing their contents -- page 71. A way to prevent 60 percent of all accidents that kill children with just one 10-second action -- page 249. A three-step strategy that can save you hundreds of dollars when you buy a used car -- page 252.

SO POWERFUL

An adjustment to your TV set that can save up to half the cost of running it -- page 136. A new way to plant strawberries so they'll be heavier, larger and ready to pick in only eight weeks -- page 188. A way to make torrid 87-degree air feel like a comfortable 77 degrees, throughout your entire house, without spending a cent on an air-conditioner -- page 139. A simple, legal way to speed up the approval on a bank loan -- page 162. A trick with vinegar that will take the shine right out of old worsted garments -- page 84.

THEY CAN CHANGE

Seeds from ordinary plants that can provide the same pick-me-up and calming effect as tobacco -- see page 271. Never deal with muddy shoes or boots again -- page 222. Why it's no longer necessary to buy special insurance on your credit cards -- page 166. How to use vitamin C to give you quick biscuits that are almost as fluffy, and healthier, than yeast biscuits -- page 4. An almost trouble-free way to turn an ordinary closet into a cedar closet -- page 108.

YOUR LIFE!

Why relieving an agonizing headache may now be as easy as swinging your arms -- see page 264. The simple, no-cost trick of storing your tools that keeps them rust-free and shiny-clean -- page 218. How to use ordinary water to evaporate static cling -- page 85. How to avoid probate, and still keep control over your assets -- page 168. An instant way to remove baked goods that don't want to leave their pans -- page 7. Why the worst place in the world to keep your will is a safe deposit vault -- page 168. And nearly 1,000 more inside ...

****************** 5-DIGIT 77074
4177074 WIT730RWR-7 95584
02563
LA
HOUSTON TX 77074

How do you tell a professional from an amateur?

Because the professional's tricks are so powerful they startle you!

For example, Dear Friend,

A New York City policeman was once asked, "What's the worst thing you can cry out if you're attacked by a man in the hall of a strange building?"

He replied at once, "'Help' ... because that will make everyone in the building double-lock their apartment doors."

"Then what should you yell out?" he was asked.

"'Fire,'" he responded immediately. "Because that will make everyone run out of their apartments into the hall with you."

Think about these answers for a moment. First of all, the policeman said that the amateur's common sense was completely wrong -- and might very well get him (or her) killed.

Secondly, the expert answer -- the professional 'trick of the trade' -- was exactly the opposite of naive common sense. Why? **Because it took a lifetime of being on the firing line to know what made that trick work.**

In every field -- in every area of living -- this is what makes the difference between the smooth-as-silk grace of the true professional, and the bungling attempts of the amateur.

There are thousands of experts out there -- real pros -- and wouldn't it be wonderful if YOU could borrow all of their tricks, shortcuts, wisdom and insight?

(over, please)

Well, now you can. Because three brilliant young editors of Rodale Press have spent two years collecting the combined wisdom of such 'real pros' as this:

Every other editor at Rodale Press.

Horticultural experts at the Rodale farms.

Researchers and staff at Prevention®, Organic Gardening®, Practical Homeowner, and Bicycling® magazines and Executive Fitness® newsletter.

Many of our favorite authors and consultants.

Our magazine and book club readers who volunteered their most powerful discoveries that they had proven (sometimes for 20 or 30 years).

But this was just the beginning. Every one of these tricks was sent to a Rodale staffer -- tops in his or her specialty -- to be approved, tested and checked out.

Only then were they allowed in here. Two years later. Over 1,000 startling, shocking, tested, proven expert secrets that you may never have dreamed existed.

We want you to read every one of them without cost or risk. It doesn't cost you a penny to receive this book in your home. You risk not one cent to examine every word of it. And -- after that no-risk examination -- if you want to return it, you pay absolutely nothing to return it. Our enclosed prepaid shipping label assures you of that.

What could be fairer? A single professional trick from this book could save your life, or that of someone you love, or your savings, or your home from burglary ... or simply enormous amounts of time, energy and wasted everyday effort.

Just glance at these secrets. Which do you want to know -- without cost or risk -- **tomorrow?**

Sincerely,

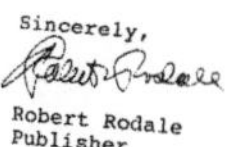

Robert Rodale
Publisher

Here are the three experts who guided this immense search for these proven, professional tricks of the trade.

Printed in the U.S.A. 810354

MAILER: Rodale Press
PACKAGE: Book of Hints, Tips
PROJECT MGR.: Brian Carnahan
PROMOTION MGR.: Kris Rice
WRITER: Eugene M. Schwartz
DESIGNER: Maureen Logan
FIRST MAILED: 1988
The 9″ × 12″ outside envelope—shown front and back—printed in bright yellow and black.

The 2-page letter, printed on a single 8½″ × 11″ sheet. Top of letter is white type reversed out of purple.

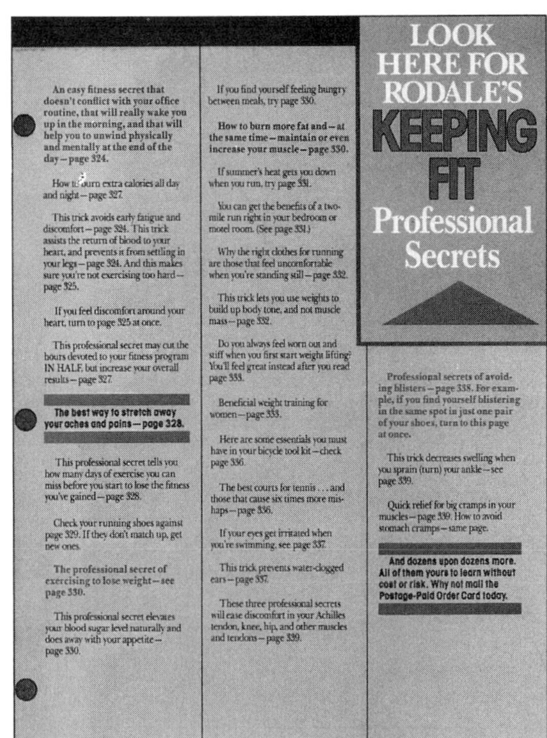

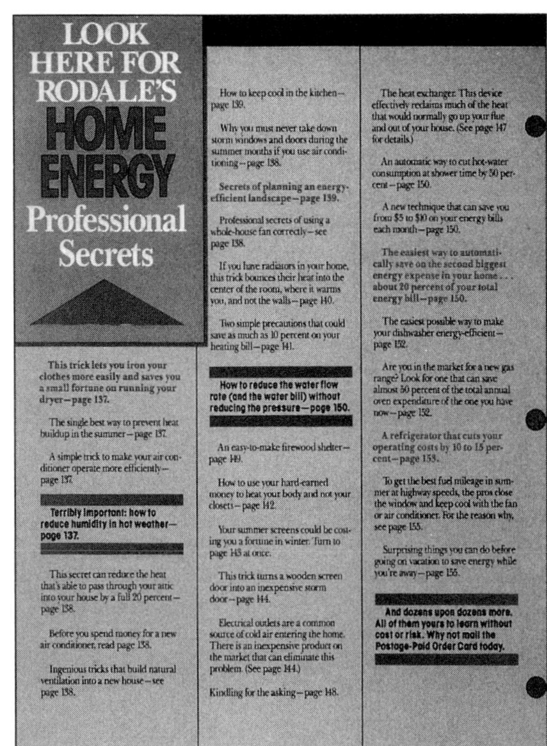

First of four 8½″ × 11″ lift pieces—shown front and back—that looks like loose-leaf pages from a notebook. The holes are printed. The dominant colors: orange, green, and purple, printed on gray stock.

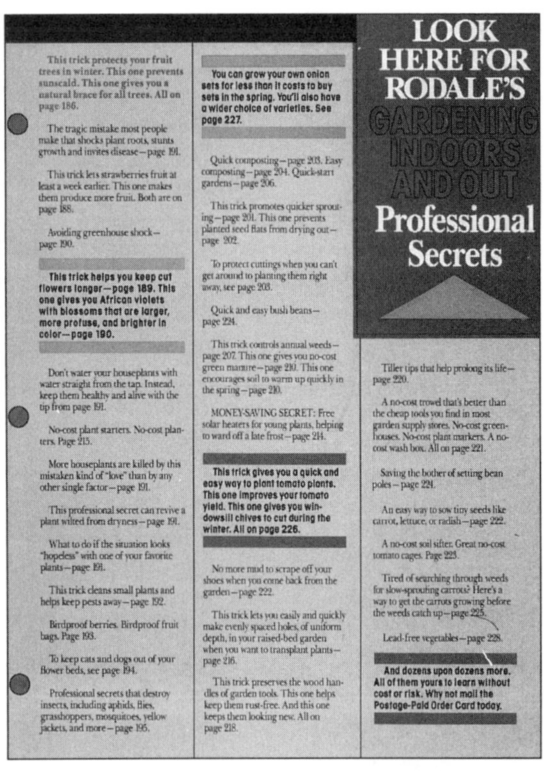

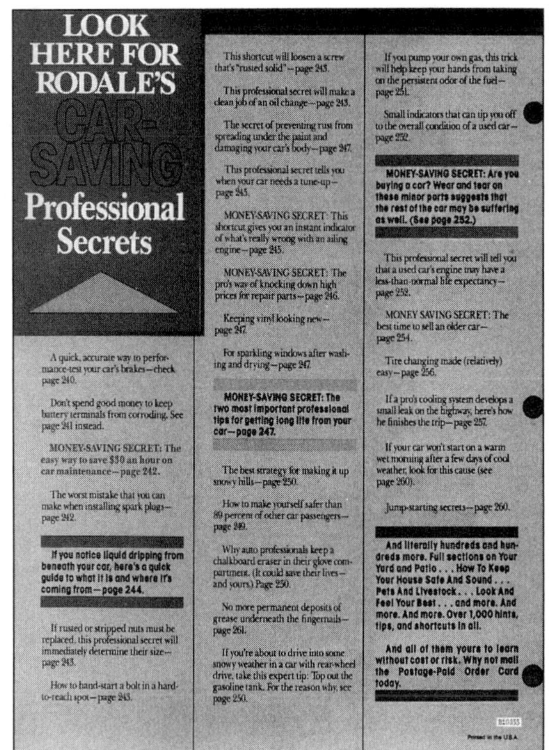

"Loose-leaf" lift piece no. 2 shown front and back. The dominant colors: green, purple, and orange on gray stock.

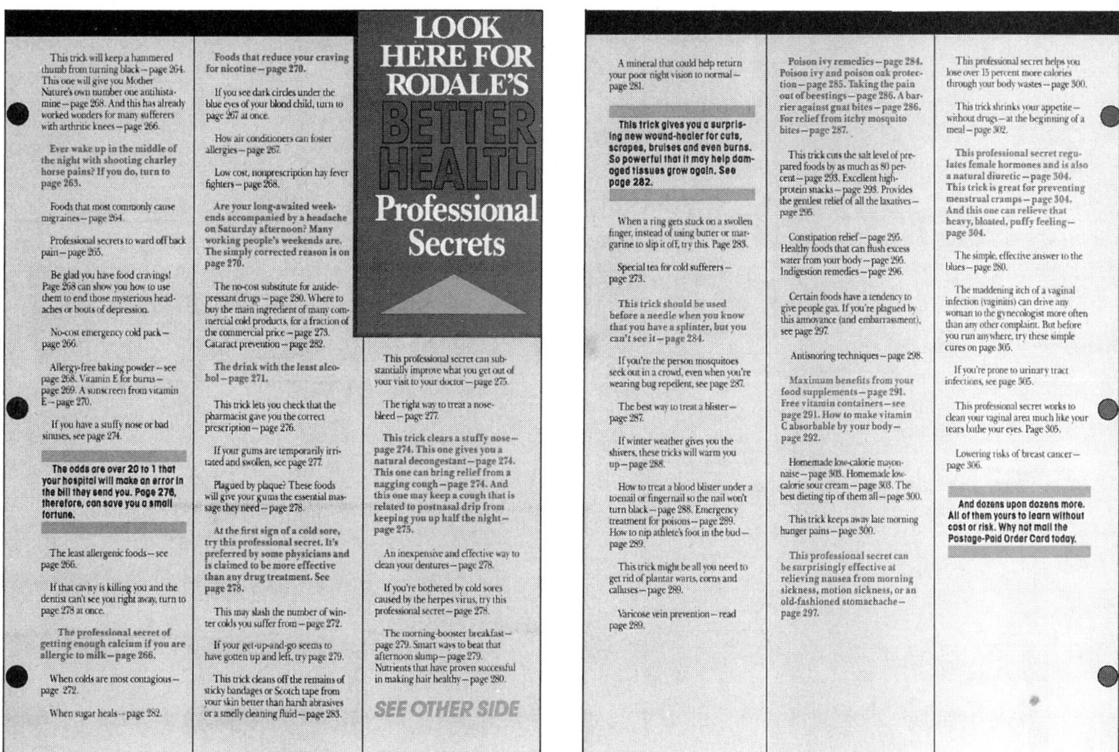

"Loose-leaf" lift piece no. 3 shown front and back. Dominant colors: purple with orange on light green stock.

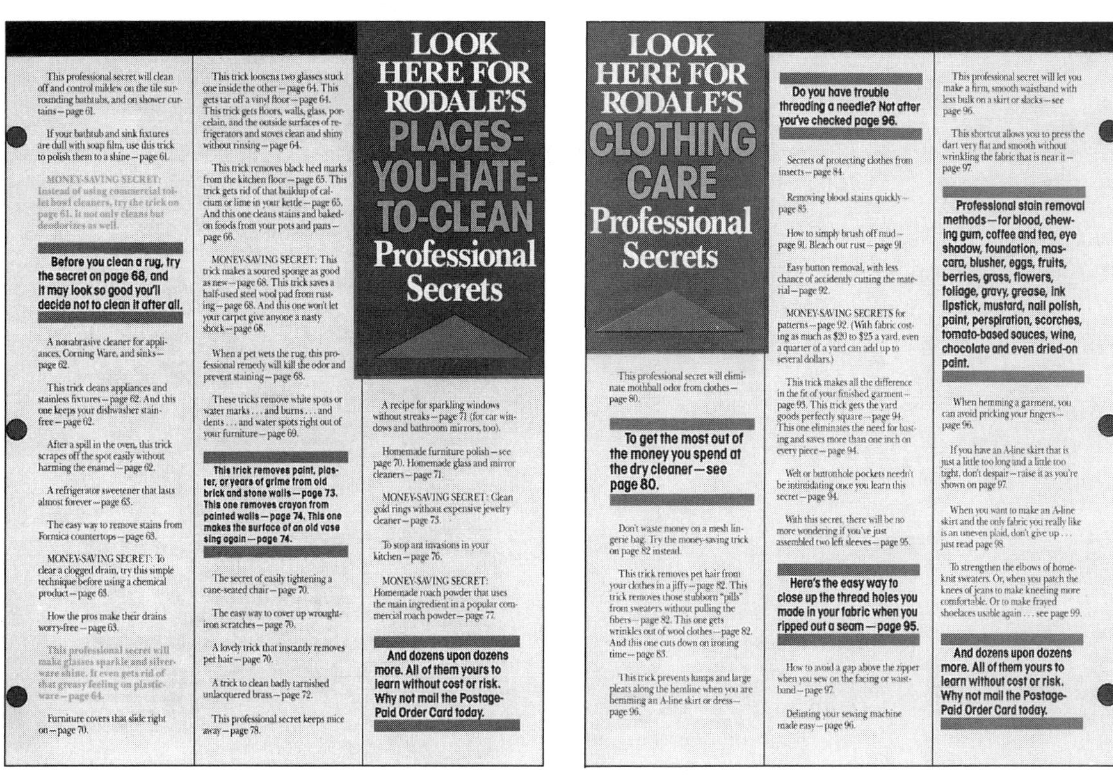

"Loose-leaf" lift piece no. 4 shown front and back. Dominant colors: green and purple on salmon stock.

LOOK HERE FOR RODALE'S KITCHEN WISDOM Professional Secrets

This trick makes whole wheat bread rise higher and feel lighter. This one gives you moister bread. This one gives the bread an extra rising. All on page 1.

A sweetener-free bread. No more flour-stained kitchens when the phone rings. Page 2. Easier kneading. Page 3.

Just-baked bread whenever you want it—page 3. Rx for dried-out breads—page 4. An instant moistener for stale bread or rolls . . . and quick but fluffy biscuits—page 4.

No more moldy cheese in the refrigerator—page 10.

Excellent salt substitutes—page 25.

MONEY-SAVING SECRET: No need to buy a fancy baking tile to produce a crisp bottom on your pizza and French bread. See page 3.

This trick tenderizes a tough piece of meat—page 29.

Quick, natural, light desserts—page 18. Freeze peaches and other fruits without sugar—page 18. Keep cut fruits from browning—page 19. Speed up the soaking time for beans—page 19. Get rid of gas in beans—page 19. Non-sticky pasta—page 20.

This professional secret gives you a shiny crust on pastry—page 6. This one protects the edges of a piecrust from overbrowning while it is baking—page 7. This one keeps dark cakes brown and beautiful—page 7. And this gets rid of the smell of chlorine in your tap water—page 9.

Get almost twice the amount of juice out of a lemon or lime—page 15.

Forget about those nondairy creamers that are filled with a laboratory's worth of chemicals. If you run out of fresh milk, just see page 9.

No-fail cooked rice—page 22.

An instant way to tell whether eggs are fresh or not—page 11. How to store raw eggs without the help of a refrigerator—page 11. Directions for a no-fault hard-cooked egg—page 12.

A free egg poacher—page 12.

This trick gives you more volume from beaten eggs—page 12. A no-fail way to separate eggs—page 12. Smoother homemade ice cream—page 12. How to have "sour cream" on your baked potatoes without extra calories—page 13.

A wonderful use for ripe bananas—page 14.

This professional secret keeps apple skins from cracking while they bake—page 13. This one ripens an avocado faster—page 13. This one keeps refrigerated avocado dip or half a sliced avocado from turning dark quickly—page 14.

How to roast meats so they'll shrink less, be more tender, and be easier to carve—page 29.

Hurry-up hamburgers—page 31.

This trick eliminates the strong flavor of bluefish—page 26. This one gives you a low-calorie fish dressing—page 26. This one prevents flabby and flavor-poor fish of any kind—page 26.

An easy way to skim the fat from soup or gravy—page 40.

This professional secret keeps oil and vinegar dressing from separating—page 38. This one keeps lettuce fresh for more than a week in the refrigerator—page 39. This one lets you make a molded gelatin salad even though you have no mold—page 39.

An electrical fire extinguisher for your kitchen that costs pennies—page 55.

This professional secret shows you how to store poultry safely—page 27. This one eliminates the need to thaw frozen chicken parts before you cook them—page 27. This secret gives you the no-mess way to stuff poultry—page 28.

Homemade cashew butter—page 42.

If you must interrupt roasting because dinner is delayed—what to do page 29. If you want to reheat meat but don't want it to dry out, see page 31.

Ground meat substitutes—more healthful than beef, and usually also cheaper. See page 31.

Free picnic plates—page 55. Free candles—page 59. Homemade non-stick spray—page 60. Free oil dispenser—page 60.

Cracking nuts without using a nutcracker—page 41.

This trick makes it easier to find foods packed into a freezer—page 32. This bit of advice saves on freezer containers—page 34. This one gives you a no-cost root cellar—page 37.

This trick gives you an easy way to cook long stalks of asparagus without having to cut them into little pieces and without having to use a very large pot—page 42. This one frees you from ever peeling carrots and potatoes again—page 43.

Easy ways to prepare fresh hot chilies—page 47. To remove silk from corn—page 47. To peel garlic cloves each time you need them—page 47. To save time when you're cutting onions—page 48. To cut an onion painlessly—page 49.

Stubborn lids now come off jars with little effort—page 56.

Some easy ways to peel tomatoes—page 52. To ensure that tomato slices stay firm and intact—page 52. To get great tomato spaghetti sauce without peeling a single tomato—page 53. To restore the tomato's vitamin C content—page 53. To speed up the ripening process of mature green tomatoes brought in from the garden—page 53.

How to cool children's hot soup quickly and easily, and add more nutrition to it—page 55.

And dozens upon dozens more. All of them yours to learn without cost or risk. Why not mail the Postage-Paid Order Card today.

LOOK HERE FOR RODALE'S MIND-YOUR-MONEY Professional Secrets

In 1983, five billion dollars in forgotten money was sitting in the nation's banks. Could some of it be yours? Check page 163 at once.

This trick gives you free investment advice that other people pay $500 a year for—page 174.

Can your state require your bank to turn over your savings account to it? Sound impossible? Not after you read page 163.

This professional secret shows you how to discover which money market deposit account or money market mutual fund really offers you the best deal. Page 163.

How long will it take to double your money? Page 163.

The professional way to provide for your nest egg—page 165.

A large-corporation secret for running your family finances—page 165.

The best way of speeding up a loan if you need to borrow money—page 162.

WARNING: Too much credit can hurt you in some cases where you want to borrow money. Page 166.

This trick lets you know when someone—who wants to charge you good money to prepare your taxes—won't dig hard enough for every tax break you may have coming. Page 181.

How to have an instant inventory of your credit cards—page 166.

How to get your homeowner's coverage to automatically rise. How to pay less for that policy—page 171.

THIS IS A FINANCIAL MUST: Each member of your family must establish his or her own credit. (If each of you don't have a separate credit record today, put page 167 to work.)

How to save bank charges and brokerage commissions on your savings—page 172.

This trick in taking a vacation could pay for a large part of that vacation—page 177. How to cut down on finance charges—page 167.

Estate planning—page 168. How to make sure that all your family affairs remain private after you die, rather than being made part of a public record—page 168. On page 169, how to make sure that your will can't be declared invalid.

These tricks show you how to survive financially if you have to cosign a loan—page 164.

Self-employment after retirement, without losing any Social Security benefits—page 176.

This professional secret lets you look beyond advertised interest rates, and proves to you that one money market account may be far superior to another—even though both say they have the same rate. Page 163.

This trick can mean cutting your yearly insurance premium by as much as 30 percent—see page 170. On the same page, how to know when collision insurance on your car just isn't worth the money.

This trick gives you a quick and easy record of all your possessions—for maximum return from your insurance in case of burglary or fire—that no one else can see if you don't want them to. Page 171.

Most insurance policies pay you far less, if your things are stolen, than it costs now to replace them. Page 171 can correct that.

Is your bank getting away with not paying interest on some of your older savings accounts? They recently got away with it on 10 million different accounts in one year. See page 163 to make sure.

Why the shorter tax form may be costing you big money—page 180. How to persuade Uncle Sam to chip in with a tax break when you search for a new job—page 180. Deducting volunteer expenses—page 181.

Could your bank be charging you a yearly fee to keep your money there? They do exact this charge from millions of people—even though these depositors don't know it. Wake up! See page 163.

This professional secret allows you to start receiving interest on an investment within weeks—but not to be taxed on that interest for a full year. Page 172.

Even if you have only $100 or $200 set aside at a time, you, too, can tap into high yields—page 173.

High-yield investments that are insured for safety—page 173. Senior citizen discounts that are available for the asking—page 175.

How one student in your family can equal two $1,000 tax exemptions—both perfectly legal—page 178.

How to deduct the cost of your children's summer camp, even if it comes to as much as $4,800—page 178.

Do you suspect that Social Security monies are being taken away from you? Then turn to page 179 at once.

Perfectly valid reasons for not reporting some deposits as income—page 179.

Running a little short of cash toward the end of the year? Here's how to get the IRS to unknowingly, but legally, help out. Page 180.

When service contracts on appliances and products really aren't necessary—page 176.

How to save up to $5,000 on funeral expenses—page 184.

A money saving alternative to legal fees—page 183. How to give Christmas gifts that cost nothing, but that often are appreciated more than anything you could buy at a store—page 183.

And literally hundreds and hundreds more. Full sections on Your Yard and Patio . . . How To Keep Your House Safe And Sound . . . Pets And Livestock . . . Look And Feel Your Best . . . and more. And more. And more. More than 1,000 hints, tips, and shortcuts in all.

And all of them yours to learn without cost or risk. Why not mail the Postage-Paid Order Card today.

Printed in the U.S.A. 810356

Lift piece no. 5 that resembles the loose-leaf pieces but is 8½″ × 14″ The dominant color: green on light green stock.

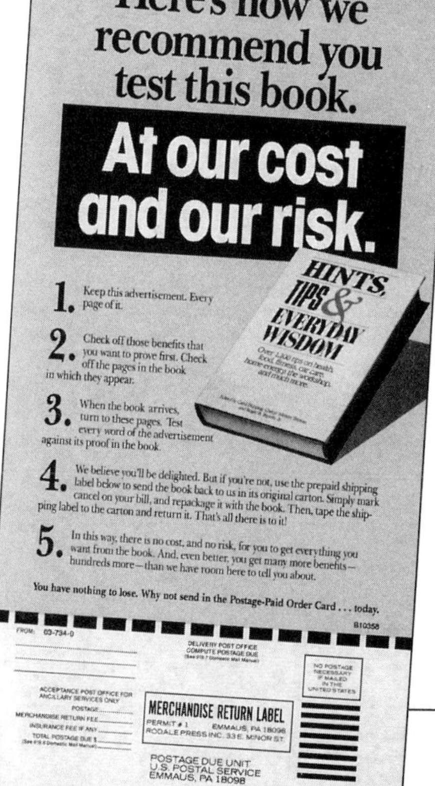

Here's how we recommend you test this book.

At our cost and our risk.

1. Keep this advertisement. Every page of it.

2. Check off those benefits that you want to prove first. Check off the pages in the book in which they appear.

3. When the book arrives, turn to these pages. Test every word of the advertisement against its proof in the book.

4. We believe you'll be delighted. But if you're not, use the prepaid shipping label below to send the book back to us in its original carton. Simply mark cancel on your bill, and repackage it with the book. Then, tape the shipping label to the carton and return it. That's all there is to it!

5. In this way, there is no cost, and no risk, for you to get everything you want from the book. And, even better, you get many more benefits—hundreds more—than we have room here to tell you about.

You have nothing to lose. Why not send in the Postage-Paid Order Card . . . today.

810358

Lift piece no. 6—the prepaid merchandise return label. This reassures prospects that if they want to return the book, they can use this label and Rodale will pay postage.

Lift piece no. 7—the premium slip. Dominant color: bright yellow.

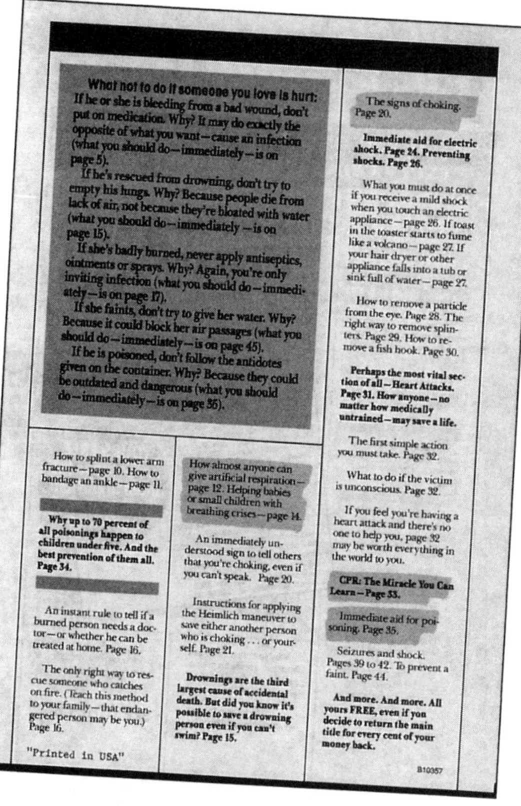

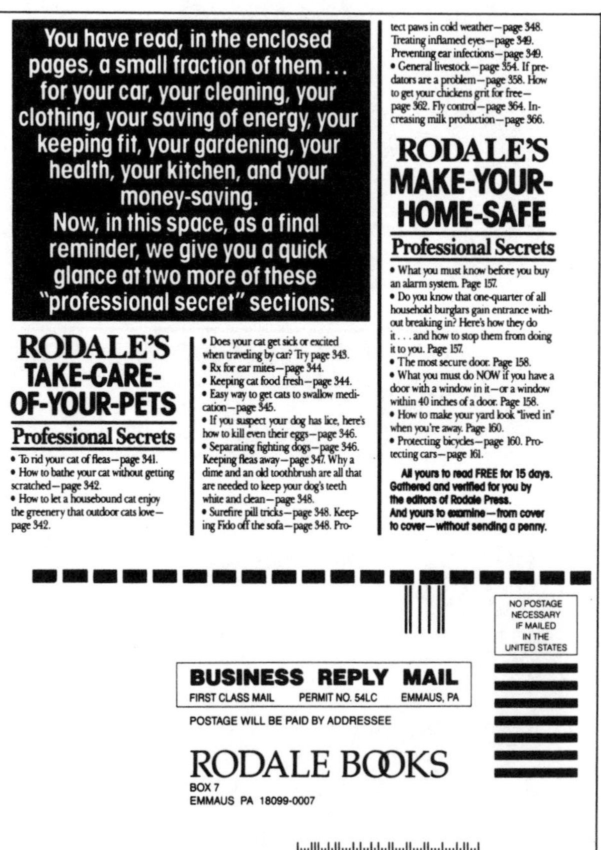

The order card shown front and back.

Build-It-Better-Yourself COUNTRY FURNITURE

While Rodale uses a great many freelancers, it has also built up a stable of great copywriters and designers who are always being pitted against the outsiders. Any one of them who chose to turn freelance could probably do so and make a grand living. In fact, the copywriter for *Build-It-Better-Yourself COUNTRY FURNITURE*, Mark Johnson, did just that early in 1992.

What distinguishes this package is that the two major pieces—the letter and the circular—are both simply huge, the letter printed on a 14″ × 22″ sheet and the four-color circular printed on a 17″ × 22″ sheet.

The 2-color letter. The back page of the letter contains the same merchandise return label used in *Hints, Tips, & Everyday Wisdom* described above.

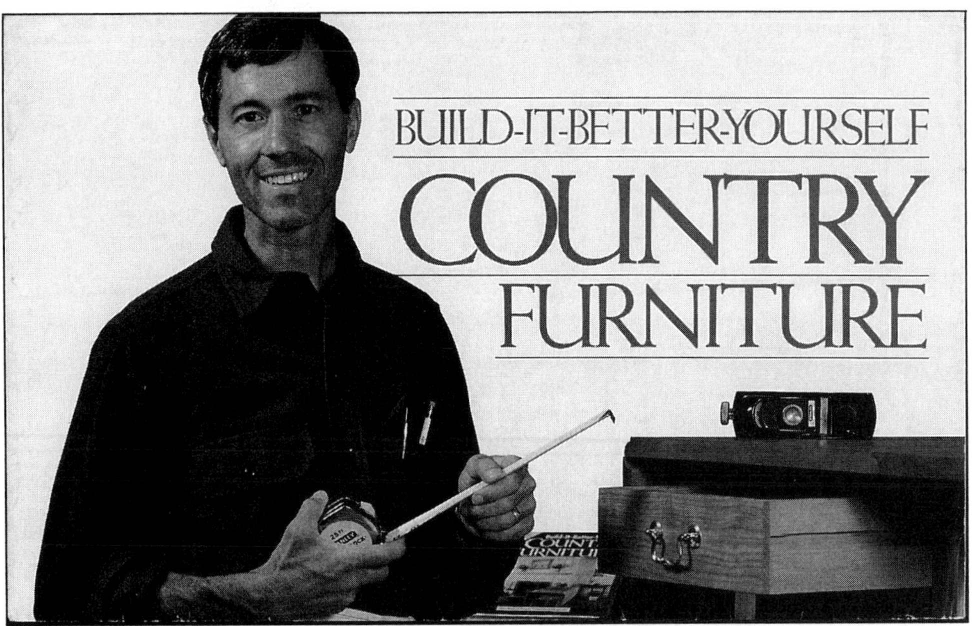

MAILER: Rodale Press
PACKAGE: *Country Furniture*
PROJECT MGR.: Brian Carnahan
WRITER: Mark Johnson
DESIGNER: Linda Camana
FIRST MAILED: 1986
The $7^{1}/_{2}$″ × 12″ 4-color envelope shown front and back.

BUILD-IT-BETTER-YOURSELF

COUNTRY FURNITURE

Build better country furniture yourself...and save!

Dear Home Woodworker:

I have taken the liberty of reserving a free-trial inspection copy of **BUILD-IT-BETTER-YOURSELF COUNTRY FURNITURE** in your name.

I believe this may be the best country furniture book you've ever seen ... and the one you've been waiting for ...

> Here in one sturdy, hardcover volume are fully detailed plans and instructions to help you build over 100 beautiful country furniture projects ...
>
> ... lovely pieces that will add your personal "signature" to the decor of your home.

To take advantage of this free-inspection, no-obligation opportunity, simply drop the enclosed Shipment Authorization card in the next mail. Your copy of **COUNTRY FURNITURE** will be shipped to your home promptly for your guaranteed 15-day no-risk inspection.

> **GUARANTEE**
>
> Take 15 days to examine **BUILD-IT-BETTER-YOURSELF COUNTRY FURNITURE** in your home. If the book isn't 100% satisfactory to you in every respect (or if you simply change your mind), return the book at our expense and owe nothing. Period.

(over, please)

Quality is the reason I can offer you this rock-solid guarantee. **COUNTRY FURNITURE** is a quality book that will give you real enjoyment and outstanding finished furniture from your own workshop.

COUNTRY FURNITURE features so many quality furniture plans, you may have a difficult time deciding which piece you want to build first.

Perhaps you'll choose the **Shaker Trestle Dining Table.** This period reproduction is a reflection of the 19th century Shaker movement, and it's a very functional piece of furniture.

The **Country-Style Sewing Cabinet** is another functional piece that is sure to please the seamstress in your household. The classic design dates from about 1840.

Or create a family heirloom that will be passed from generation to generation by choosing a **Colonial** or **Early American Cradle.**

Solve storage problems beautifully with a **Colonial Bookcase,** and **Early American Hutch,** a **Bed Chest,** or a **Country-Style Corner Cupboard.**

Display collections of what-have-you in a **Curio Cabinet,** in a **Collector's Cabinet,** or on a **Curio Shelf.**

Add a useful item to your home or workshop with a **Cobbler's Workbench.**

Enhance your home's entryway with a **Victorian Hall Butler,** a **Coat-Rack Hall Mirror,** or a simple **Letter Box.**

For outdoor relaxation, choose the **Rustic Chaise Lounge,** the **Lawn Swing,** or an all-time favorite, the **Porch Swing.**

> You get all these plus over 80 more plans for a complete variety of country furniture projects in your favorite styles. Including Colonial, Traditional, Early American, Shaker, and antique reproductions.

The plans for each piece include ...

* step-by-step instructions
* a materials list
* an exploded illustration
* photographs

Best of all, each piece is functional, economical, and easy to build, even if you don't have a great deal of woodworking experience.

Because the furniture in **BUILD-IT-BETTER-YOURSELF COUNTRY FURNITURE** has been designed especially for the at-home do-it-yourselfer, not for furniture factories or mass-production shops.

You'll also find a full chapter devoted to finishing techniques ... sanding, buffing, and staining your furniture to give it just the look you want.

"Bring Out Your Best"

BUILD-IT-BETTER-YOURSELF COUNTRY FURNITURE will help you bring out the best in your woodworking skills.

Let's face it -- your knack for woodworking and for building things yourself makes you a special person in today's pre-fab society. In a world of formica and plastic, you are one person who still appreciates the beauty of natural wood.

Because you take pride in your handmade projects, we wouldn't offer you a build-it book that was anything less than the best. In fact, Rodale Books has a proven "track record" of producing quality, popular books for the home woodworker and do-it-yourselfer.

Tens of thousands of satisfied readers have enjoyed our previous "Build It Better Yourself" books.

One reader wrote to us about one of the "Build-It" books and said, "This book is super. I wish I had a copy of it five years ago."

Another wrote, the book is "fantastic. It is better than you said."

A reader from California wrote us to say, "after looking at the book, I probably saved $2,000 .... Thanks to Rodale."

I believe you will be as happy with **BUILD-IT-BETTER-YOURSELF COUNTRY FURNITURE** as these and many other readers have been with Rodale's other fine build-it books.

Of course if you aren't completely satisfied, your 15-day in-home examination of **COUNTRY FURNITURE** costs you nothing -- not even return postage (see the Return Privilege Label at the end of my letter). That's our guarantee that you will be happy with your book.

If you've shopped in an antique shop or a fine furniture store lately, you know what it might cost to purchase just one piece of quality country furniture ... maybe $150 for a small piece, $300, $500, $750 or more for a larger item, and $1,000 and up for a full-sized piece that's really special.

You'd be "out of pocket" several hundred dollars for a store-bought item ... and there's no way you are going to have the same kind of satisfied feeling that comes only from lovingly and carefully "building it yourself."

Furniture that you have built to last in your own workshop is your personal statement of creativity, artistry, and beauty.

Your eye for quality leads you to shun products that are substandard, slipshod, and "disposable." Enduring value and pride of craftsmanship are your standards.

In **COUNTRY FURNITURE** you'll get plans for over 100 sturdy country pieces whose designs are faithful to these principles. You'll be hard pressed to find this many quality designs in any other single book, with complete plans and without skimping on details.

I think you'll want to take a look at the copy of **BUILD-IT-BETTER-YOURSELF COUNTRY FURNITURE** that I have reserved for you. Along with your book, I'll send you a ...

*** F R E E G I F T ***

(over, please)

The booklet "Working with Stained Glass" is yours free when you agree to take a 15-day trial look at **COUNTRY FURNITURE.**

> In this booklet you'll learn the secrets of creating beautiful glasswork in your own workshop. With just a few relatively inexpensive simple tools, you can make stained glass windows, elegant inserts for your cabinetry, even spectacular Tiffany-style lamps. All the techniques are thoroughly explained for the beginner.

Best of all, "Working with Stained Glass" costs you nothing. It's our gift to you for simply accepting our free inspection offer for **COUNTRY FURNITURE.**

Our shipping department has been alerted to this offer. They will ship your book and your free gift promptly upon receipt of your Shipment Authorization card.

You'll then have a full 15 days to inspect **COUNTRY FURNITURE** at your leisure, in the comfort of your own home. If you feel the book isn't everything I've described and more, or if you simply decide that it isn't for you, you may return it and owe nothing. Here's all you do: 1. Repackage the book in the carton it came in, or in another secure type of package. 2. Clip the Return Privilege Label below and affix it to the package. 3. Drop the package in any mailbox. No need to affix postage.

As you can see, you've got nothing to lose by mailing back your Shipment Authorization card today. Since your credit is pre-approved, there's no need to send money now.

But I urge you to act promptly. Your reserved copy of **BUILD-IT-BETTER-YOURSELF COUNTRY FURNITURE** can be held for only 30 days. After that, we may extend this offer to others, and your order will be handled on a first-come, first-serve basis.

So please drop your Shipment Authorization card in the mail today. You don't risk a penny, and I guarantee you'll be delighted with the fine furniture plans in **COUNTRY FURNITURE.**

Sincerely,

Ray Wolf
Senior Editor

P.S. Save this postage-paid Return Privilege Label as your 15-day free examination guarantee. If you aren't delighted with **BUILD-IT-BETTER-YOURSELF COUNTRY FURNITURE,** simply repackage the book, attach the return label, mail it back, and owe nothing. The free gift, "Working with Stained Glass," is yours to keep regardless.

B6840

DETACH AND SAVE THIS RETURN LABEL

FROM

DELIVERY POST OFFICE
COMPUTE POSTAGE DUE
(See 919.7 Domestic Mail Manual)

NO POSTAGE NECESSARY IF MAILED IN THE UNITED STATES

ACCEPTANCE POST OFFICE FOR ANCILLARY SERVICES ONLY
POSTAGE
MERCHANDISE RETURN FEE
INSURANCE FEE IF ANY
TOTAL POSTAGE DUE $
(See 919.6 Domestic Mail Manual)

MERCHANDISE RETURN LABEL
PERMIT #1 EMMAUS, PA 18049
RODALE PRESS INC 33 E MINOR ST

POSTAGE DUE UNIT
U.S. POSTAL SERVICE
EMMAUS, PA 18049

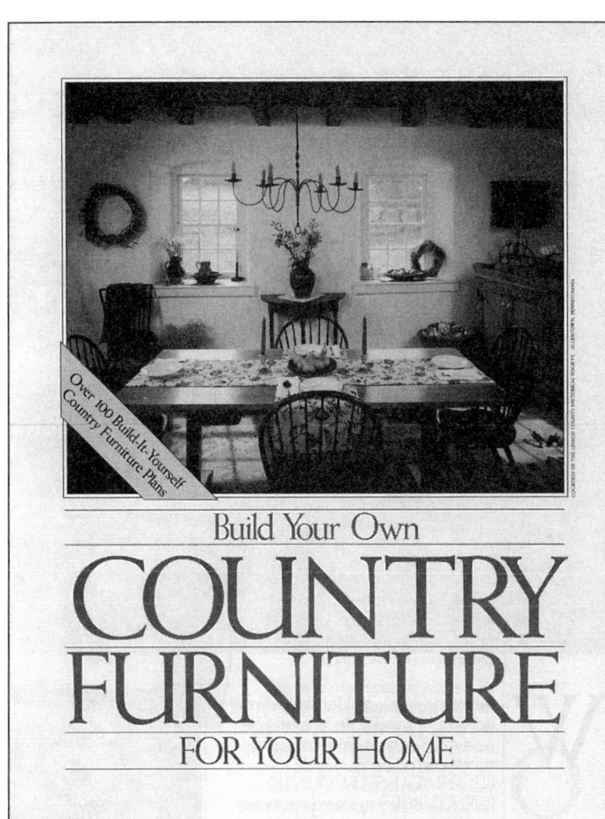

Over 100 Build-It-Yourself Country Furniture Plans
Build Your Own
COUNTRY
FURNITURE
FOR YOUR HOME

The giant 4-color brochure cover.

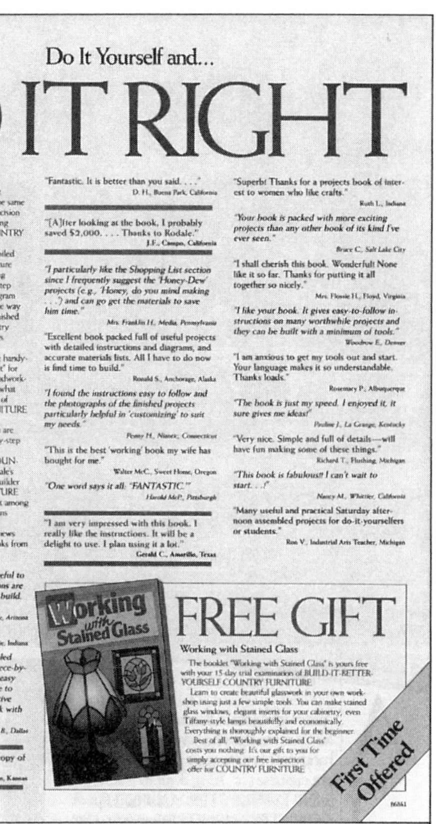

The back of the brochure.

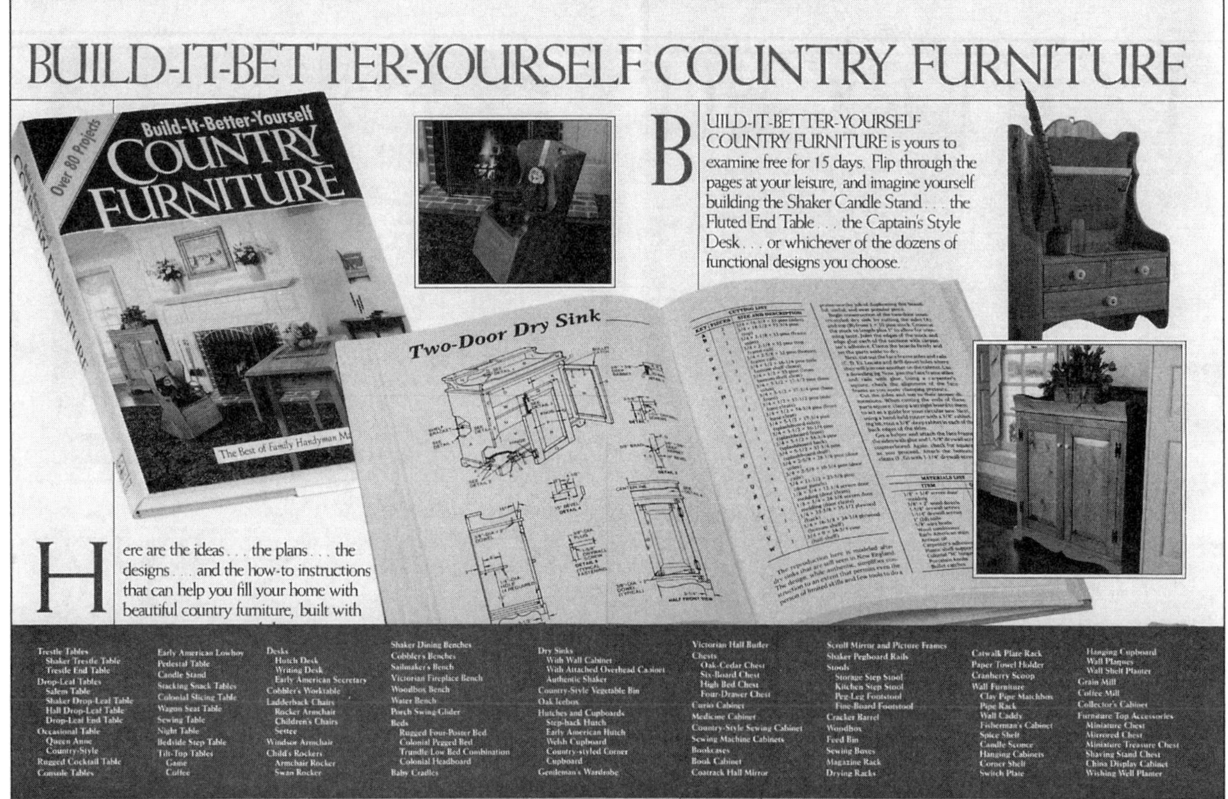

BUILD-IT-BETTER-YOURSELF COUNTRY FURNITURE
Build-It-Better-Yourself
COUNTRY FURNITURE
Over 80 Projects
BUILD-IT-BETTER-YOURSELF COUNTRY FURNITURE is yours to examine free for 15 days. Flip through the pages at your leisure, and imagine yourself building the Shaker Candle Stand . . . the Fluted End Table . . . the Captain's Style Desk . . . or whichever of the dozens of functional designs you choose.
Two-Door Dry Sink
Here are the ideas . . . the plans . . . the designs . . . and the how-to instructions that can help you fill your home with beautiful country furniture, built with

At the bottom of the center spread of the brochure is a flap that cuts across copy and design.

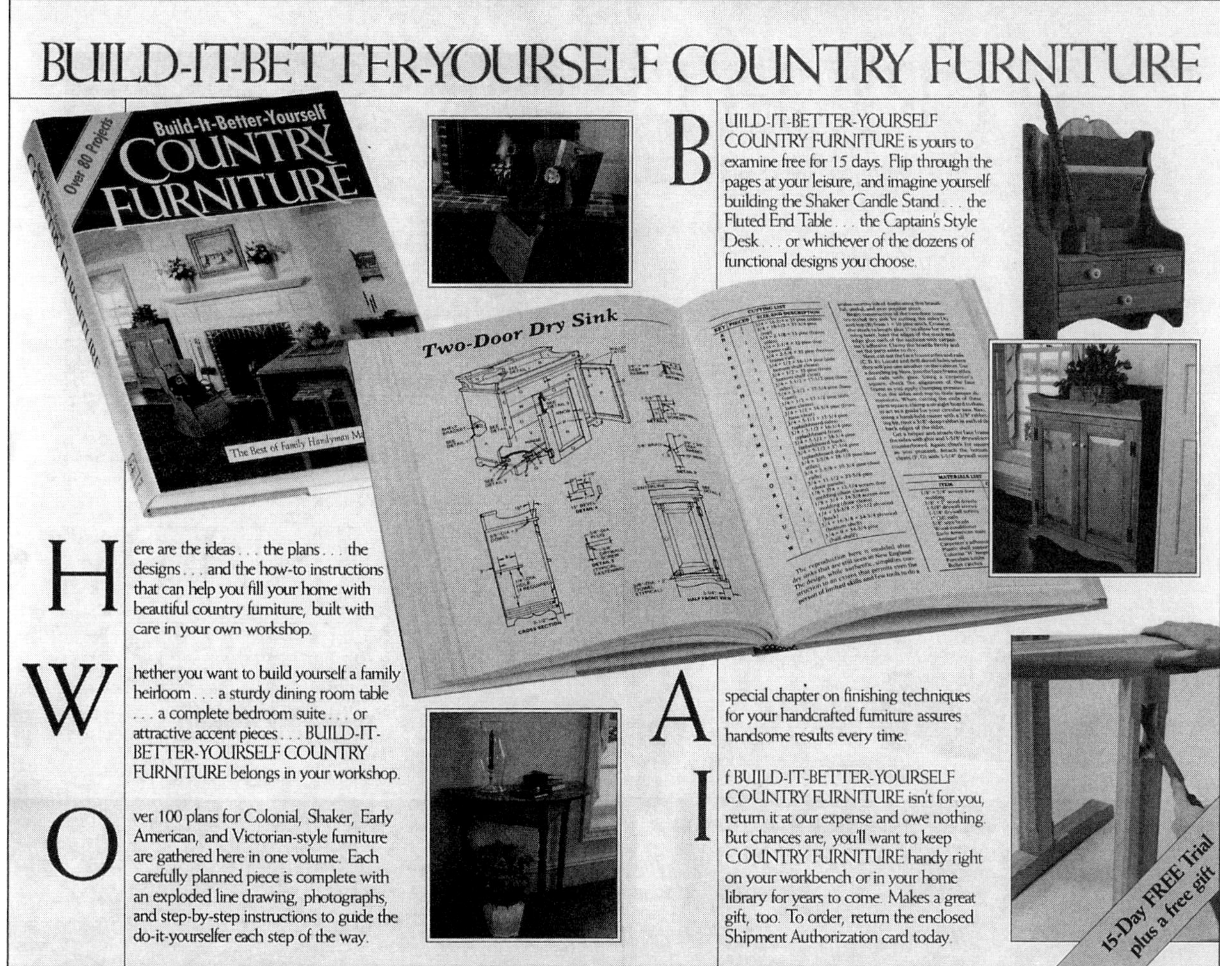

BUILD-IT-BETTER-YOURSELF COUNTRY FURNITURE
Build-It-Better-Yourself COUNTRY FURNITURE
Over 80 Projects
Two-Door Dry Sink
BUILD-IT-BETTER-YOURSELF COUNTRY FURNITURE is yours to examine free for 15 days. Flip through the pages at your leisure, and imagine yourself building the Shaker Candle Stand . . . the Fluted End Table . . . the Captain's Style Desk . . . or whichever of the dozens of functional designs you choose.
Here are the ideas . . . the plans . . . the designs . . . and the how-to instructions that can help you fill your home with beautiful country furniture, built with care in your own workshop.
Whether you want to build yourself a family heirloom . . . a sturdy dining room table . . . a complete bedroom suite . . . or attractive accent pieces . . . BUILD-IT-BETTER-YOURSELF COUNTRY FURNITURE belongs in your workshop.
Over 100 plans for Colonial, Shaker, Early American, and Victorian-style furniture are gathered here in one volume. Each carefully planned piece is complete with an exploded line drawing, photographs, and step-by-step instructions to guide the do-it-yourselfer each step of the way.
A special chapter on finishing techniques for your handcrafted furniture assures handsome results every time.
If BUILD-IT-BETTER-YOURSELF COUNTRY FURNITURE isn't for you, return it at our expense and owe nothing. But chances are, you'll want to keep COUNTRY FURNITURE handy right on your workbench or in your home library for years to come. Makes a great gift, too. To order, return the enclosed Shipment Authorization card today.
15-Day FREE Trial plus a free gift

The inside spread opened fully.

Mark E. Johnson spent six and a half years at Rodale Press as copy chief, creative director, and copy director before striking out on his own. Prior to Rodale, he worked for the Viguerie Company, America's premier conservative fundraiser.

Mark E. Johnson:
This package has had tremendous staying power in the mail. Here's why I think it's been so successful:

- *This book has a simple, benefit-oriented title. People* do *judge books by their covers, and products by their names. This book's title instantly conveys both its content and the benefit to the consumer; it is used as a headline five times in the package.*
- *The photography involves the reader. This package uses fourteen photos, only three of which are of the book (and one of those is a page spread). All the other photos show the furniture projects, the warm, homey environments the projects help create, plus hands-on photos the reader can project himself into. The photos have the effect of inviting the prospect to read the copy and explore the offer.*

- *Offer lead: the letter could easily have started out by romancing the wonderful qualities of country furniture and the fine art of woodworking. Instead, it follows good direct mail strategy by leading with the offer, in this case a free, no-obligation trial. The warm, feel-good copy is left for the body of the letter.*
- *The package design is wonderfully efficient—only three inserts. The art showcases the product and lets the copy come through. In-house art director Linda Camana made each piece bold yet simple, elegant yet hands-on. This is a nice package to look at.*

In the end, a successful direct mail promotion means that we have served our customers well. Those who received this offer have long forgotten the direct mail package, but they and their families will enjoy for years the fine handcrafted furniture that has been built because of it.

The order card shown front and back.

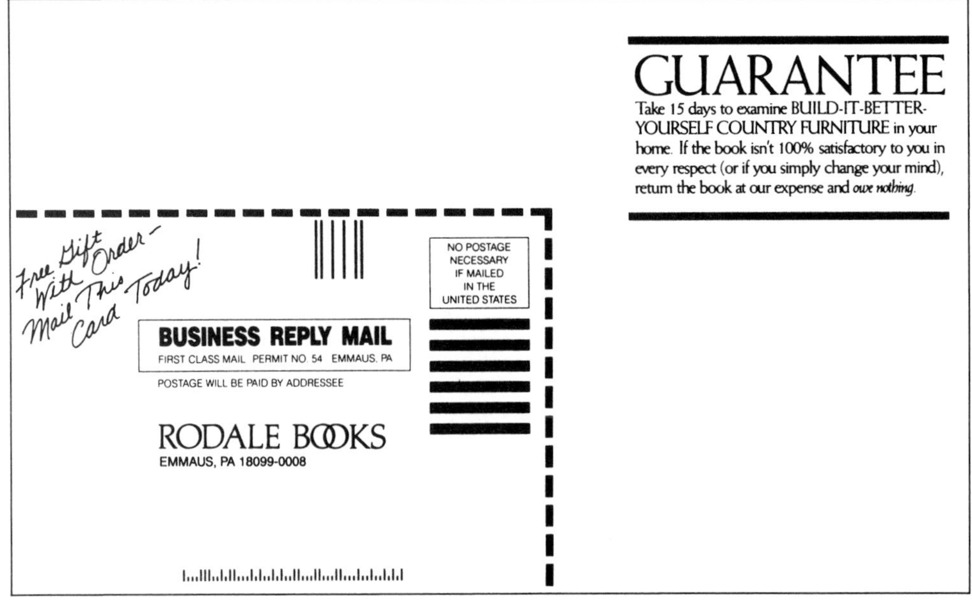

Rodale's *Everyday Health Tips*

Writer-designer team Josh Manheimer and David Wise exploded onto the freelance scene with a series of spectacular efforts for *Playboy, Art & Antiques, British Heritage,* and *U.S. News & World Report.*

Their mailing for Rodale's *Everyday Health Tips* was brilliant—a true breakthrough. It was not accomplished using the CPP (clean piece of paper) approach to copywriting. Rather, Manheimer and Wise astutely built the package on proven techniques—some radical, others traditional—devised for Rodale by other copywriters.

Who's Mailing What! has followed, and written about, Rodale book mailings since its inception, and many of the breakthroughs incorporated in this hugely successful effort were flagged in early issues of the newsletter.

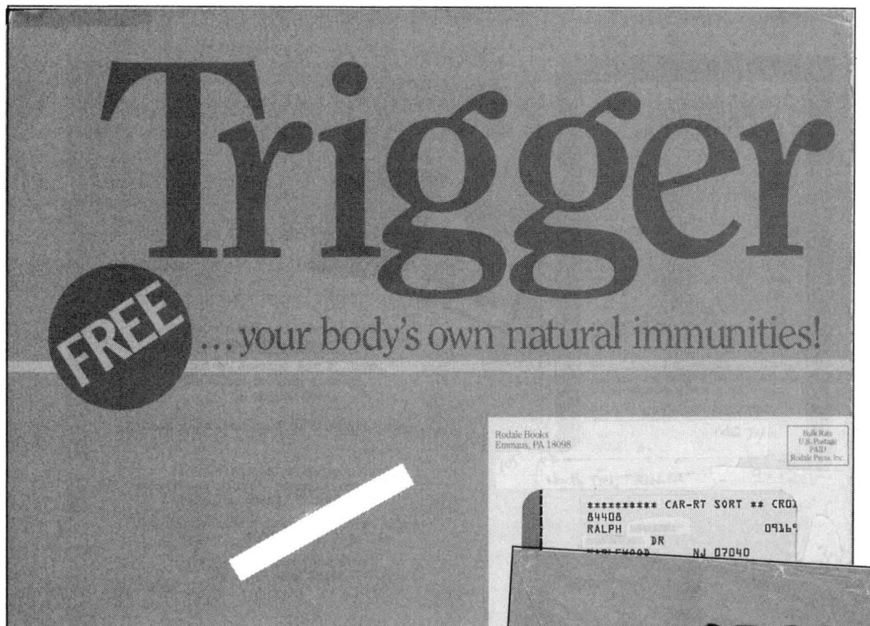

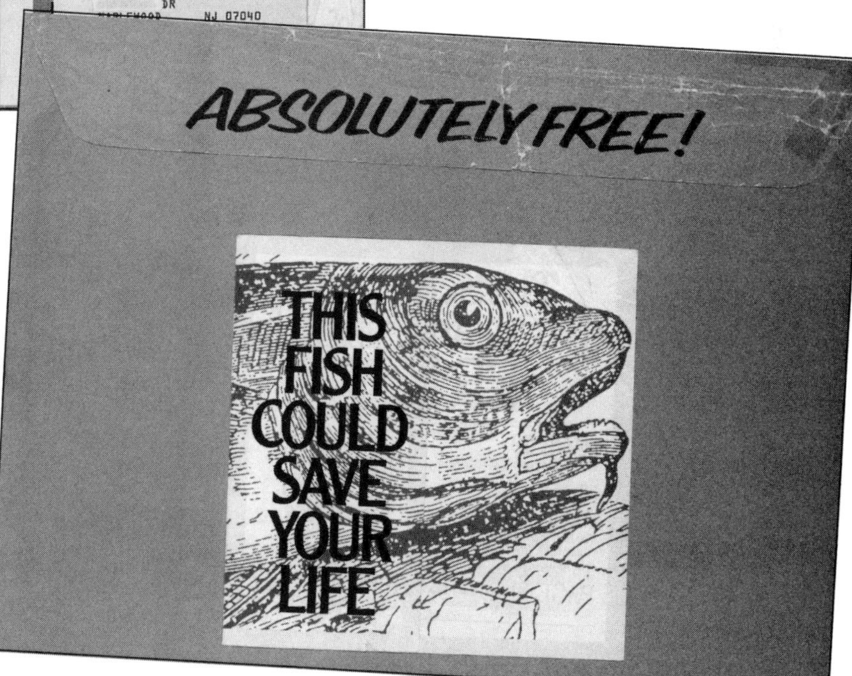

MAILER: Rodale Press
PACKAGE: *Everyday Health Tips*
PROJECT MGR.: Brian Carnahan
WRITER: Josh Manheimer
DESIGNER: David Wise
FIRST MAILED: 1988
The powerful 9″ × 12″ outside envelope, printed red on pink with yellow as the second color.

For example, in January 1985 we reported on a 9″ × 12″ envelope full of bold promises and a six-page letter jam-packed with "tease" copy by Gene Schwartz offering the raging bestseller (1.75 million copies sold up to that time), *Encyclopedia of Natural Healing*.

Manheimer and Wise refined this down to two big promises on the outside envelope: "Trigger your body's own natural immunities" and "Free."

In March 1986 Alan Friedenthal came up with an extraordinary "lift" device—a business reply merchandise return label and letter affixed to the back of a 9″ × 12″ outer envelope. The message: "Read this first. If you don't like the book use this label to return it at our expense." It raised response 30 percent.

In the September 1987 issue of *Who's Mailing What!* we reported on a 9″ × 12″ Rodale mailing by Jim Punkre, with confirmation from Brian

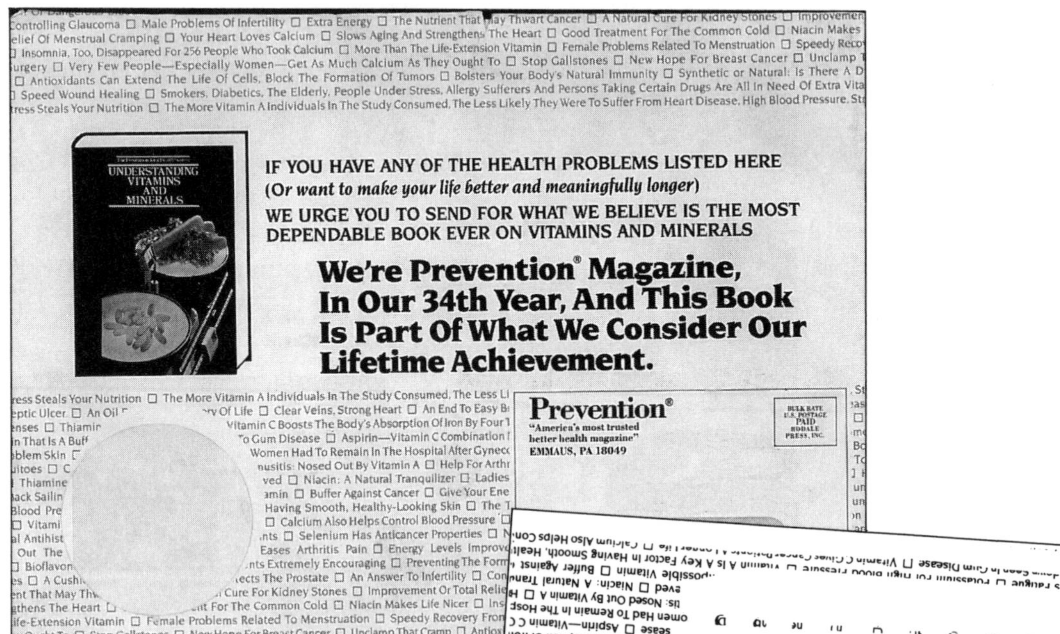

Alan Friedenthal's breakthrough lift piece attached to the back of an envelope. It was Friedenthal, incidentally, who wrote the "We're going to spoil you" package for Literary Guild.

The lift piece attached to the back of Josh Manheimer's "Trigger" package.

ABSOLUTELY FREE!
THIS FISH COULD SAVE YOUR LIFE

ABSOLUTELY FREE!
AN EXCLUSIVE REPORT prepared for you by the Rodale Division of Health Services
YOURS ABSOLUTELY FREE!

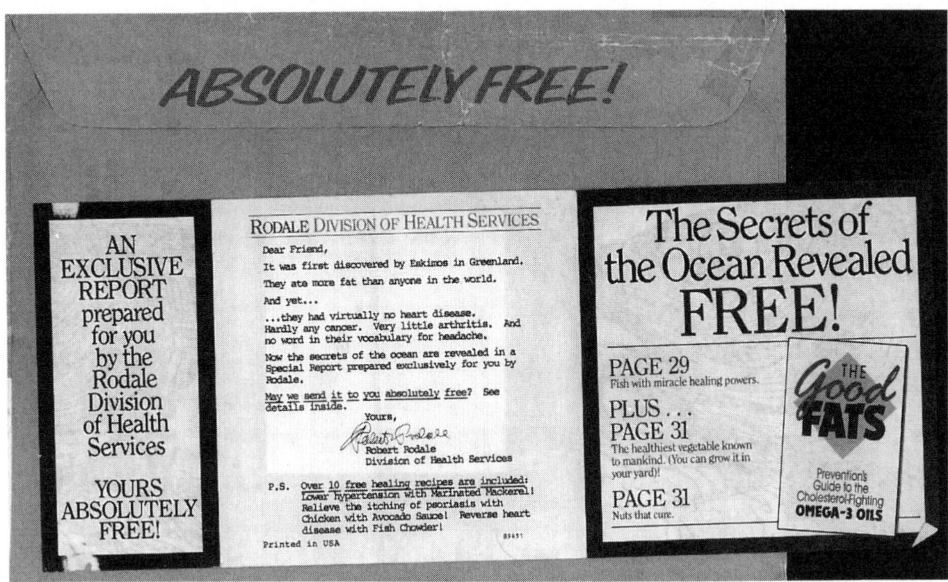

ABSOLUTELY FREE!
AN EXCLUSIVE REPORT prepared for you by the Rodale Division of Health Services
YOURS ABSOLUTELY FREE!

RODALE DIVISION OF HEALTH SERVICES

Dear Friend,

It was first discovered by Eskimos in Greenland.

They ate more fat than anyone in the world.

And yet...

...they had virtually no heart disease. Hardly any cancer. Very little arthritis. And no word in their vocabulary for headache.

Now the secrets of the ocean are revealed in a Special Report prepared exclusively for you by Rodale.

<u>May we send it to you absolutely free?</u> See details inside.

Yours,

Robert Rodale
Division of Health Services

P.S. <u>Over 10 free healing recipes are included: Lower hypertension with Marinated Mackerel!</u> Relieve the itching of psoriasis with Chicken with Avocado Sauce! Reverse heart disease with Fish Chowder!

Printed in USA 89451

Carnahan at Rodale that 90 percent of Rodale's book mailings went out in this large size because it lifted response by 25 percent—"more than enough to pay for itself." Today, with a fat $50-per-thousand postage rate penalty on jumbo-size mailings (flats), Rodale mails at the largest allowable size that qualifies as a letter (6⅛" × 11½").

In the November 1987 *Who's Mailing What!* we commented on a Rodale offer: "3 easy monthly installments of $8.32 each plus postage and handling." Nowhere are you told how much the book will cost nor the postage and handling. Robert Rodale, president, defended the wording:

Detroit has been selling cars like this for years. It costs so much per month. I don't have a problem asking the consumer to multiply $8.32 by 3. Most people think the American consumer is stupid. But the American consumer is smart. Look at the rising percentages of people who take a comp copy offer and never pay for it.

Pat Corpora explained the rationale:

Our entire object is to break down every argument—via benefit-oriented copy and design—that would prevent a customer from seeing the book for fifteen days free trial . . . and then let the excellence of the editorial product stand on its own. Meredith and Reader's Digest *price this way. Obviously it is easier to pay $5 a month than see a big $18 total plus shipping and handling. We even send a prepaid return label with the mailing, so the offer is truly risk-free.*

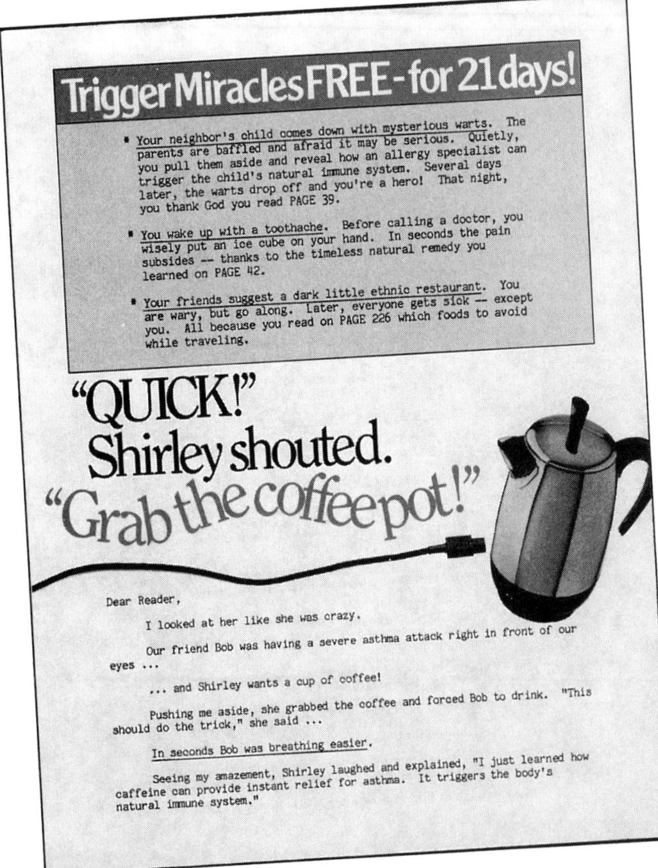

Trigger Miracles FREE - for 21 days!

* Your neighbor's child comes down with mysterious warts. The parents are baffled and afraid it may be serious. Quietly, you pull them aside and reveal how an allergy specialist can trigger the child's natural immune system. Several days later, the warts drop off and you're a hero! That night, you thank God you read PAGE 39.

* You wake up with a toothache. Before calling a doctor, you wisely put an ice cube on your hand. In seconds the pain subsides -- thanks to the timeless natural remedy you learned on PAGE 42.

* Your friends suggest a dark little ethnic restaurant. You are wary, but go along. Later, everyone gets sick — except you. All because you read on PAGE 226 which foods to avoid while traveling.

"QUICK!" Shirley shouted. "Grab the coffee pot!"

Dear Reader,

I looked at her like she was crazy.

Our friend Bob was having a severe asthma attack right in front of our eyes ...

... and Shirley wants a cup of coffee!

Pushing me aside, she grabbed the coffee and forced Bob to drink. "This should do the trick," she said ...

In seconds Bob was breathing easier.

Seeing my amazement, Shirley laughed and explained, "I just learned how caffeine can provide instant relief for asthma. It triggers the body's natural immune system."

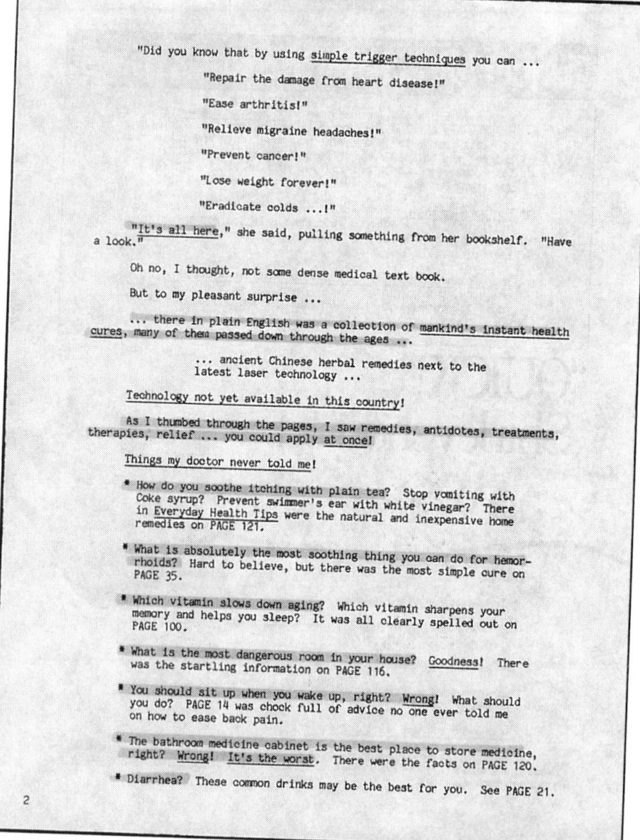

"Did you know that by using simple trigger techniques you can ...

"Repair the damage from heart disease!"

"Ease arthritis!"

"Relieve migraine headaches!"

"Prevent cancer!"

"Lose weight forever!"

"Eradicate colds ...!"

"It's all here," she said, pulling something from her bookshelf. "Have a look."

Oh no, I thought, not some dense medical text book.

But to my pleasant surprise ...

... there in plain English was a collection of mankind's instant health cures, many of them passed down through the ages ...

... ancient Chinese herbal remedies next to the latest laser technology ...

Technology not yet available in this country!

As I thumbed through the pages, I saw remedies, antidotes, treatments, therapies, relief ... you could apply at once!

Things my doctor never told me!

* How do you soothe itching with plain tea? Stop vomiting with Coke syrup? Prevent swimmer's ear with white vinegar? There in Everyday Health Tips were the natural and inexpensive home remedies on PAGE 121.

* What is absolutely the most soothing thing you can do for hemorrhoids? Hard to believe, but there was the most simple cure on PAGE 35.

* Which vitamin slows down aging? Which vitamin sharpens your memory and helps you sleep? It was all clearly spelled out on PAGE 100.

* What is the most dangerous room in your house? Goodness! There was the startling information on PAGE 116.

* You should sit up when you wake up, right? Wrong! What should you do? PAGE 14 was chock full of advice no one ever told me on how to ease back pain.

* The bathroom medicine cabinet is the best place to store medicine, right? Wrong! It's the worst. There were the facts on PAGE 120.

* Diarrhea? These common drinks may be the best for you. See PAGE 21.

2

The 6-page letter, printed on an 11" × 17" sheet with extra page inserted.

* Which of your friends can be helped by having skin removed from behind his ears, grafted onto his face and fine-sanded? PAGE 36.

* Travelers: How do you drag a spare tire out of a car trunk, stuff a briefcase into an airplane's overhead compartment -- without back pain? For latest techniques, read PAGE 14.

* When should you choose a sauna over a steambath? When is it best you choose neither. PAGE 17.

* An ancient Oriental treatment better than acupuncture? Yes! PAGE 17 tells you why so few have heard of it.

As I leafed through this remarkable publication, I grew more excited.

Bob was not our only friend with health problems.

Here on PAGE 26 was a way I could help my sister Gladys with her eye problem. PAGE 72 offered new hope for my nephew with his bad heart. PAGE 24 gave surprising new advice for my husband's allergies.

Whom could you help?

Did you know ...?

* Moles can turn into skin cancer. PAGE 40 tells you the warning signs and the 100 percent solution if you catch the symptoms early.

* You could be swallowing air instead of breathing it. For the side effects and how to stop, see PAGE 18.

* Gas pains? These seemingly healthy foods may be the cause. See PAGE 18 for fast relief.

* 5 steps that conquer constipation every time. PAGE 20.

* The 10 best foods for zinc. PAGE 110.

* Regulate your blood pressure with fruits and vegetables. PAGE 71.

* The vitamins you should be taking to fight off aging ... cancer ... cataracts ... respiratory disease ... bleeding gums ... infertility. PAGE 100.

"Where did all this come from?" I asked Shirley.

"Rodale Press," she replied. "You know them. They publish Prevention and Organic Gardening magazines."

"Some time ago the folks at Rodale realized there was no one place you could turn for instant home remedies.

"So, with their vast resources, Rodale assigned a team of researchers to gather together the most effective health tips currently known to mankind.

"Finally, after years of research, here is the fruit of their labor. Instantly, you can get your hands on over 2,000 trigger methods ... hints ... tips -- all bound within the covers of one over-sized, illustrated volume.

3

"It is the most important book they've ever published."

I nodded my head, fascinated ... and read on.

There was everything from avoiding colds ... to removing molds.

* What are the 3 factors that determine if you will catch someone else's cold? How do you "short-circuit" just one to remain healthy? PAGE 2.

* You should turn on your air conditioner in the summer, right? No! A brief burst of mold contamination can lie hidden inside the filter. How to clean it? PAGE 25.

* Can eyeglasses give you a facial rash? Yes. PAGE 24.

* How do you prevent the crippling deformities of arthritis? PAGE 22.

* The 3 factors that make an exercise program successful? (Otherwise, don't bother.) PAGE 260.

There were dozens of helpful "do's! ..."

* Why you should get up at the same time every morning -- no matter how badly you've slept! PAGE 28.

* Why you should take fewer showers. PAGE 37.

* Why you should take faster showers. PAGE 37.

* Why you should garden in the evening. PAGE 25.

* When you should drink more water than your thirst calls for. PAGE 45.

And the most eye-opening "don'ts ..."

* Why you should not read in the bathroom. PAGE 21.

* Why you should not use a wash rag when treating poison ivy (or poison oak)! PAGE 25.

* Who should not use soap anywhere but under the arms and on the genitals. PAGE 37.

* The absolute worst time for your body to do paperwork or read? PAGE 26.

* Over-the-counter corn-removal medications? No! Soaking and sand-paper for corns? No! An easy way to avoid them? Yes! PAGE 46.

If you have questions, the easy-to-grasp explanations spell out all the answers clearly.

* What is "palming?" PAGE 27.

* What is a better alternative to eyedrops? PAGE 26.

* What is the secret to healing cuts twice as fast? PAGE 32.

* What is the "S" stance? How can it help an aching back? PAGE 12.

4

* How can a canvas-covered device filled with a mixture of sand and silicone help you? See PAGE 16.

If you have a specific problem, the handy index takes you right to the solution.

* Prostate problems? Sex may be the best prevention. PAGE 52.

* Athlete's foot? First, dust with cornstarch inside your shoes. Then turn to PAGE 47 for the key to picking perfect socks.

* Age spots? Lighten them. PAGE 40.

* Gastric ulcer or duodenal ulcer? What not to do! PAGE 19.

* Blister? Sterilize a sewing needle with 70 percent isopropyl alcohol. Clean the blister with antiseptic. Make small holes to release fluid. Final critical step -- PAGE 47.

* When should you skip the above advice and rush immediately to your doctor? PAGE 47.

See through myths ... and shibboleths.

* Sneezing into a tissue prevents colds, right? Wrong! PAGE 2 explains why.

* You should cut a "V" in the center of an ingrown toenail, right? Wrong, again. PAGE 49 tells you what does work.

* "Unscented" products have no scent? Sorry. Many are masked with a chemical that can cause allergic reactions. PAGE 24.

* You accidently knock out a tooth. Should you wrap it in a tissue and drive right to a dentist? No. First, put it back inside your mouth. Then get in your car. PAGE 43.

* If your gums are pink and clean, are you okay? Not necessarily. Hidden bacteria can eat away at the bone supporting the tooth. Stop it cold. PAGE 43.

How do you know ...?

* Is the same sales clerk selecting the best pair of shoes for you? Six critical things to watch for. PAGE 48.

* Which is really better? Chocolate or carob? Sugar or honey? PAGE 67 has some surprises in store for you.

* Your friend has painful swelling in her big toe. You tell her it's because she eats too many sardines. She looks at you like you're Marcus Welby, M.D. Quietly, you thank PAGE 48.

When I finally put the book down, I was afraid to ask Shirley my next question.

"What does a book like this cost? It must be outrageous."

Shirley laughed and said, "Believe it or not ...

5

"You get to sample it free for 21 days."

"How?" I asked.

"Easy," Shirley replied, "mail in your Free Trial Certificate. When the book arrives, pour yourself a cup of tea, sit down, and thumb through it. You're encouraged to try out several of the instant trigger health hints and see how well they work.

"Only then, if you decide to keep your personal volume, do you pay in three low, easy monthly installments."

You and I know, a visit to the doctor can really cost. Just one tip from Everyday Health Tips could pay for itself many times over.

"Remember, don't send them any money now," Shirley added.

"And if for any reason you do wish to return the book, Rodale will gladly pay the return postage. (A return shipping label is enclosed in this package. Just affix it to the box the book comes in. And that's that.)

"And ... I almost forgot ..." Shirley said.

"You also get a free Special Report prepared exclusively for you by the much-respected Division of Health Services at Rodale.

"It's a breakthrough study you won't find in any store.

"Inside, Rodale health experts reveal for you the miracles of the high seas. Miracles that have kept the Greenland Eskimos free from heart disease, cancer, arthritis, diabetes and headaches!

"The advice alone is worth hundreds. And they give it to you as a free gift, which is yours whether you keep Everyday Health Tips or not!"

When Shirley was done, you can bet I sent for both books immediately. You feel better just knowing that instantly, you can get your hands on over 2,000 trigger methods ... hints ... tips -- whenever you (or your friends!) need one.

Cordially,

Kathi Fry

Kathi Fry

P.S. About Bob, the friend I mentioned at the start of this letter. He's all better thanks to Shirley's instant remedy.

Whom will you help save with over 2,000 instant trigger cures at your fingertips?

P.P.S. Because only so many copies of Rodale's free Special Report can be prepared at one time, first-come must be first-served.

Therefore, to avoid any chance of delay, return your Free Trial Certificate by the earliest possible postmark. Thanks! K.F.

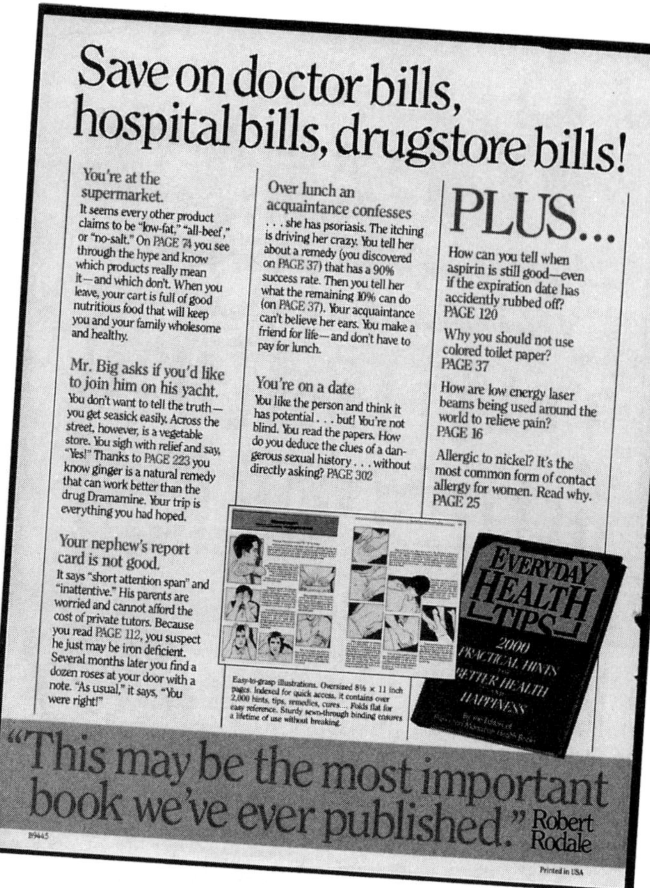

Lift piece no. 1 in 4 colors, shown front and back.

When asked if Rodale had ever done an A/B split—full price disclosure vs. so much per month—Corpora said he had tested a cash option: pay so much per month plus shipping and handling, or send cash now and we'll pay postage and handling. The cash option measurably depressed response. "This is a lot more honest than what Time-Life Books is doing," Corpora added. "They don't put any price on the order form."

Many writers think the only way to hit a grand slam home run is to do something completely different from anything done before. Manheimer and Wise show us otherwise. They slipped easily into the Rodale groove, employing all these techniques that were tested and known to raise response. Then they added some razzle-dazzle of their own (including yellow highlighter through strategic sentences in the six-page letter, truly compelling "tease" copy, and a nifty lift piece titled "The extraordinary discovery of AcuPinch"). The result? In a letter to designer David Wise, Kathi Fry-Ramsdell of Rodale wrote:

The "Trigger" package now tops our winners list—as the best-ever package for Rodale books with results two to one over the standard which was written by a long-time Rodale writer. Your package is a real breakthrough for Rodale. . . . In fact, response was so high we had to change the print run for the book as well.

The message here: If you've found something that works, urge your copywriters to use it, build upon it, and improve on it.

Lift piece no. 2—printed in green, red, pink, orange, yellow and black—which picks up the theme from the attachment on the back of the envelope. Shown front . . . then with left flap open, and finally fully opened.

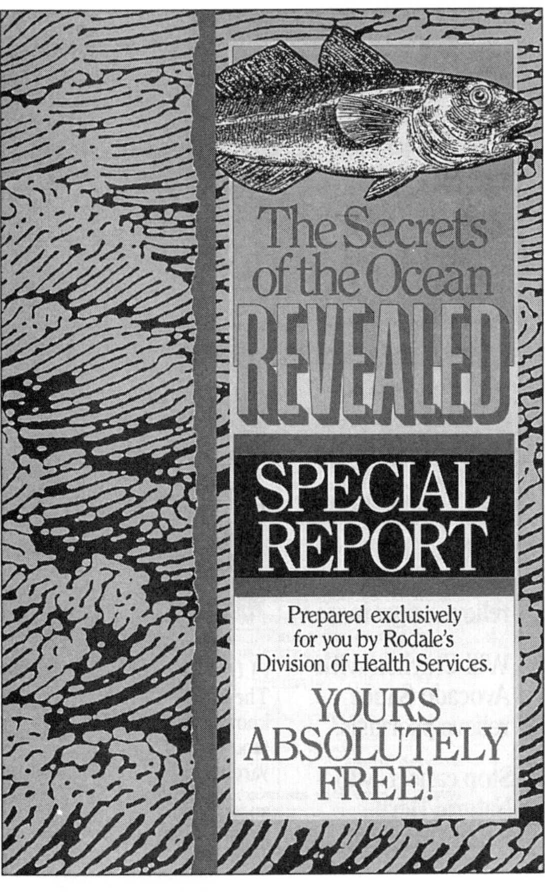

The Secrets
of the Ocean
REVEALED
SPECIAL
REPORT
Prepared exclusively
for you by Rodale's
Division of Health Services.
YOURS
ABSOLUTELY
FREE!

* You should cook fish only after it has thawed, right? Wrong! SEE PAGE 33

* You can reach for chunk white tuna or chunk light. The difference? SEE PAGE 25

* Frozen fish is preserved longer when dipped in this household ingredient. SEE PAGE 33

* Should you pan-fry? Bake? Poach? Steam? PAGE 34 tells which method is best for which fish. Plus how to make sure fish is done.

HEAL WITH MEALS

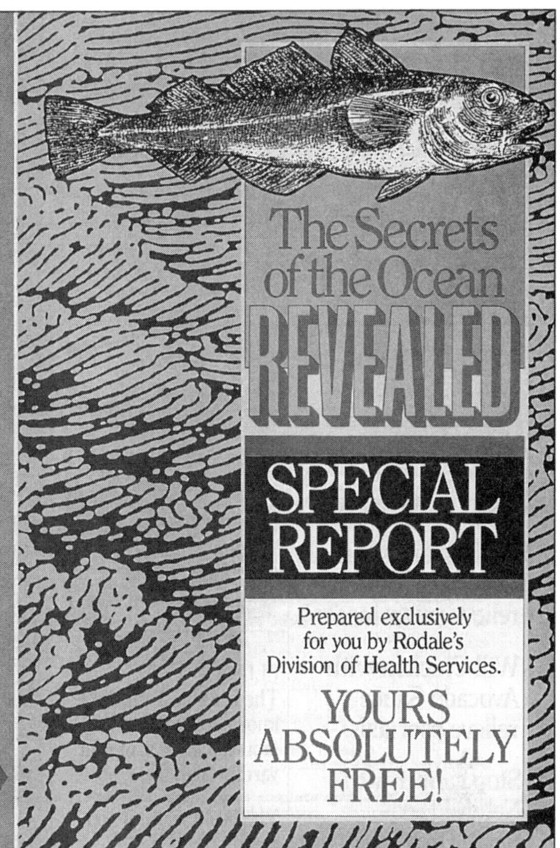

The Secrets
of the Ocean
REVEALED
SPECIAL
REPORT
Prepared exclusively
for you by Rodale's
Division of Health Services.
YOURS
ABSOLUTELY
FREE!

* You should cook fish only after it has thawed, right? Wrong! SEE PAGE 33

* You can reach for chunk white tuna or chunk light. The difference? SEE PAGE 25

* Frozen fish is preserved longer when dipped in this household ingredient. SEE PAGE 33

* Should you pan-fry? Bake? Poach? Steam? PAGE 34 tells which method is best for which fish. Plus how to make sure fish is done.

HEAL WITH MEALS

RODALE DIVISION OF HEALTH SERVICES

Dear Friend,

The Greenland Eskimos ate more fat than anyone in the world. And yet...

...they had virtually no heart disease. Hardly any cancer. Very little arthritis. And no word in their vocabulary for headache.

Why? How?

Now the mysterious healing properties of the ocean are revealed in a Special Report prepared exclusively for you by Rodale.

May we send it to you absolutely free?

Inside you too will discover the amazing curative powers of the high seas and how you can take instant advantage of this remarkable breakthrough to...

* Calm hyperactive children. PAGE 11
* Remove the fatty globules that clog arteries. PAGE 13
* Ease the pain of rheumatoid arthritis. PAGE 15
* Help the itching caused by psoriasis. PAGE 18
* Relieve the pressure of migraine headaches. PAGE 16
* Protect yourself against breast cancer. PAGE 17
* Minimize the complications of diabetes. PAGE 17

Not available in any store, this Special Report is yours -- absolutely free — simply for agreeing to sample your personal volume of Everyday Health Tips in your own home for 21 days.

To get it, just drop the enclosed Free Trial Certificate in the mail today. There's no obligation. No commitment.

And you can keep the free report even if you decide to return Everyday Health Tips. It's our way of saying, "Thanks for at least giving us a try."

Cordially,

Robert Rodale

Robert Rodale
Division of Health Services

P.S. Your free report comes complete with over 10 tasty, easy-to-prepare gourmet recipes. Recipes that can literally save a life!

Printed in USA

May we rush you this Special "Life-Saving" Report absolutely free?

Lower blood pressure with Marinated Mackerel!

Unclog arteries with Fish Chowder!

Will Creamy Tuna Broccoli Soup relieve migraines?

Will Chicken with Avocado Sauce relieve psoriasis?

Stop cancer with Natural Herb Salad Dressing!

THE
Good
FATS
Prevention's
Guide to the
Cholesterol-Fighting
OMEGA-3 OILS
YOURS TO KEEP FREE
No matter what!

PLUS
The healthiest vegetable known to mankind? (You can grow it in your yard!) PAGE 31

The healthiest nuts on earth? PAGE 31

Lift piece no. 3 with a bright yellow cover and pink lips; opens into the letter from Mark Bricklin.

The extraordinary discovery of

AcuPinch

b

c

Prevention

Dear Friend,

It was the national collegiate wrestling championships.

Dr. Donald Cooper was one of the tournament physicians, closely watching the young, determined competitors give it their all, when...

"This student just bent over double with pain," said Dr. Cooper.

"He had real bad cramps in his arms and legs, and he couldn't move. I went over to him to get his attention, and I said, 'Listen! I'm going to pinch your upper lip. Just hold on.'

"He probably thought I was a little crazy. But I pinched his lip between my thumb and index finger, and the pain began to subside almost right away.

"That kid went ahead and won his match!"

Oddly enough, Dr. Cooper first discovered acupinch in a letter from a man who "learned" of the technique in a dream.

Dr. Cooper threw the letter away and dismissed the idea until his own leg cramps revived his memory. He tried the technique and it worked. Now he prescribes it for his athletes.

"It works 80 to 90 percent of the time," says Dr. Cooper. "And anything in medicine that works 90 percent of the time is extraordinary!"

That's the true story behind just one of our health hints in this exciting new book.

For more than 2,000 instant tips, cures, remedies... return your Free Trial Certificate for Everyday Health Tips today!

Cordially,

Mark Bricklin

Mark Bricklin
Editor, Prevention

P.S. Don't miss Kathi's letter. She tells you about the Special Report that's included with your book -- absolutely free.

Printed in the U.S.A.

B9448

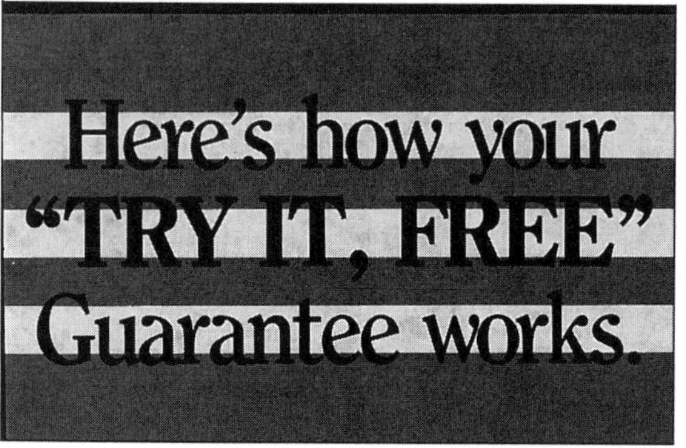

Here's how your
"TRY IT, FREE"
Guarantee works.

Lift piece no. 4—with merchandise return label.

1 WE SEND YOU BOTH BOOKS FREE—FOR THREE FULL WEEKS. After you mail in the enclosed Free Trial Certificate, we'll rush you *Everyday Health Tips* and *The Good Fats*—absolutely free for three full weeks.

2 TRY THE 2,000 CURES AND SEE FOR YOURSELF IF THEY WORK. When your two books arrive, pour yourself a cup of tea, curl up, and enjoy. You have 21 days to thumb through the book so take your time.

You can try out any of the 2,000 cures and hints you'll discover. You may want to talk over some of your exciting new findings with friends. Or discuss some of the health tips with your doctor. Maybe even prepare some of the exciting "healing" recipes you'll learn about. We don't mind. If it's not everything you expected, return it within 21 days at no cost to you.

3 YOUR HANDY RETURN SHIPPING LABEL MEANS WE PAY POSTAGE. So far you haven't spent 1 dime! Now, if you wish to return *Everyday Health Tips*—for any reason whatsoever—just tape the handy label below onto the box the book comes in. Then, drop it into your nearest mailbox. It's that easy! *No* phone calls. *No* paying for postage. *No* waiting in line at the post office.

4 YOU KEEP YOUR FREE GIFT...REGARDLESS. *Best of all!* You can still keep your free gift—*The Good Fats* as our way of saying, "Thanks for giving *Everyday Health Tips* a try."

B944

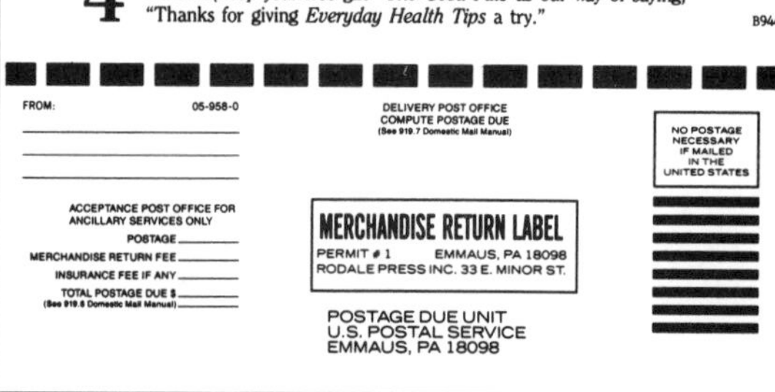
FROM: 05-958-0

DELIVERY POST OFFICE
COMPUTE POSTAGE DUE
(See 919.7 Domestic Mail Manual)

NO POSTAGE NECESSARY IF MAILED IN THE UNITED STATES

ACCEPTANCE POST OFFICE FOR ANCILLARY SERVICES ONLY
POSTAGE ______
MERCHANDISE RETURN FEE ______
INSURANCE FEE IF ANY ______
TOTAL POSTAGE DUE $ ______
(See 919.6 Domestic Mail Manual)

MERCHANDISE RETURN LABEL
PERMIT # 1 EMMAUS, PA 18098
RODALE PRESS INC. 33 E. MINOR ST.

POSTAGE DUE UNIT
U.S. POSTAL SERVICE
EMMAUS, PA 18098

Order card shown front and back.

17

Lead Generators

When do you sell a product or service using a lead generator and then a series of follow-ups? Direct mail guru Axel Andersson, who built a huge home-study business in Germany, believes that anything costing over $350 should be a two-step sale. Certainly anything more than $450 requires this technique, with the exception of continuity series; you can hide the full price of a twenty-four-volume set by offering it at the rate of one or two volumes a month.

But a big ticket item usually requires a lot of explanation, either in print or in person. Examples: investing in a mutual fund, membership in a trade association, a timeshare condo or vacation home, an office copier, an automobile, a home-study course.

Some lead generators ask you to send for more information; others are after appointments for their sales reps; still others, such as real estate developers or automobile manufacturers, try to lure you to their venue to talk to a representative.

The object here is to reach potentially interested prospects and get them simply to raise their hands by writing, phoning, or faxing for more information or an appointment.

Robert Hacker of the Hacker Group in Seattle heads an agency that specializes in lead generation. Hacker's philosophy of getting leads is opposite that of traditional direct marketing. "The more you tell, the more you sell," is the rationale for the traditional direct mail package of long letter, brochure, lift piece, order form, etc.

According to Hacker, in the business of generating leads, "The more you tell, the less you sell. Avoid giving your prospect reasons NOT to buy."

Hacker's philosophy of lead generation: give them enough information to rouse and excite them—an irresistible promise—but not enough to make a decision.

The next step is the follow-up—either the phone call for an appointment in the home or office . . . or the sales rep's treatment of the hand raiser down at the automobile showroom or the timeshare condo . . . or the material sent in the mail in response to the inquiry.

For the follow-up efforts, Axel Andersson came up with rules of thumb based on years of testing in Germany. Axel's axioms transcend language or country of origin; they deal with cold logic and common sense:

With a high-ticket item (such as a correspondence course) never put the prospect's name on the order form. Otherwise, the first thing he will see is a bunch of huge prices right next to his name, and this will discourage him. Instead, use a pressure-sensitive label that can be transferred from the addressing document to the order form . . . and bury the order form in the middle of the mailing. Let the prospects get excited about their new career and new life before hitting them with the bad news that they will be in hock for years.

Andersson also believes American direct marketers don't do enough follow-ups. In Germany he would do as many as nine follow-up efforts to a prospect who requested information about his courses. Each follow-up would have a different approach and a different offer. After a lot of testing, he found every effort was profitable. One technique he used for a writing course: send a mailing out on the one-year anniversary of receiving the inquiry and ask the person how life has been over that year . . . and suggest that if he had started the writing course back then, he might be a successful author by now.

On Axel's inquiry forms were such questions as: "For what purpose are you interested in this course?" There would be boxes to check for vocational information on hobbies, etc. On the basis of those answers, Axel would add a specific paragraph to the follow-up efforts emphasizing that particular part of the course. If you ask for the person's age, you can refer to it in the follow-up letters: "At 29, you are just the right age to learn . . ." "At 49, you have the maturity to . . ."

American Management Association

The American Management Association mailing is one of the classics of direct mail. It was created by the old Schwab & Beatty agency in 1973 and was only recently discontinued because the personalization got too expensive. Every element, including the business reply envelope, is printed on lovely cream-colored vellum paper, so it looks and feels like a real invitation, such as the kind you would receive to a wedding or a bar mitzvah.

Most personalized mailings preprint the reply device so nobody has to go through the trouble of filling in name, address, and other information. This AMA package forced the person to fill in a lot of data. There is a double benefit here: (1) AMA's follow-up material will be sent to the correctly spelled name and precise address; (2) people who take the trouble of filling the form out completely are thereby qualified as being really interested in the AMA.

Notice there is no request for a phone number; it may be that asking for the phone number scares prospects into thinking a telemarketer will call.

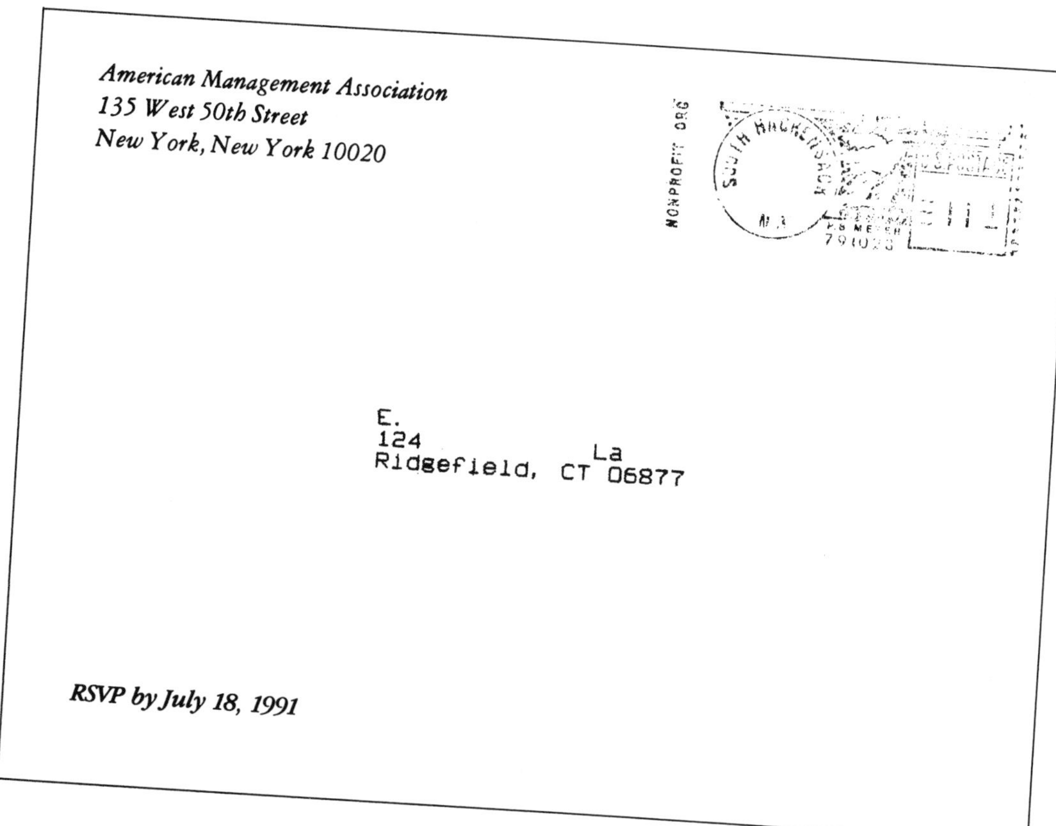

MAILER: American Management Association
PACKAGE: Handwritten Invitation
PROJECT MGR.: Eileen Lewis
AGENCY: Schwab & Beatty
WRITER: Unknown
DESIGNER: Unknown
FIRST MAILED: 1973
The $4\frac{1}{2}'' \times 6\frac{1}{2}''$ outside envelope.

The invitation cover with the addressee's name written by hand.

Diane Laurenzo
Director of Membership
on behalf of all its members,
cordially invites

to become a member
of the
American Management Association

By accepting this invitation,
you join a select group of business and government leaders
in a common cause: to produce the highly skilled professional managers
America needs.

AMA membership gives you the opportunity to meet, influence and be influenced by these successful, experienced professional managers. It makes available to you the largest pool of information ever assembled on management problemsolving. It assures a continuous flow of published material to alert you to new ideas and new techniques.

For over 65 years, AMA training has played an important role in the personal growth and professional development of thousands of executives.

If you would like to know more about AMA, please fill out and return the RSVP card as soon as possible.

The invitation opened.

The front of the reply form. On the reverse is the apology for the possible inconvenience of a duplicate.

American Management Association

Please send me more information regarding membership in your association and reserve my place for sixty days.

PLEASE PRINT NAME

TITLE

DIVISION

ORGANIZATION

ADDRESS APT/FLOOR/SUITE

CITY STATE ZIP

RSVP by July 18, 1991 **591G**

Please note: Try as we do to avoid duplication and waste, the process we use to identify and eliminate duplication is not perfect, so the occasional error will occur. If you are a member, our apologies.

NO POSTAGE NECESSARY IF MAILED IN THE UNITED STATES

BUSINESS REPLY MAIL
FIRST CLASS PERMIT NO. 7172 NEW YORK, NY

POSTAGE WILL BE PAID BY ADDRESSEE

American Management Association
Attn: Director of Membership
P.O. Box 1025
Saranac Lake, New York 12983-9987

The business reply envelope.

Encyclopaedia Britannica

I cannot remember a month going by in the last fifteen years without seeing a mailing package in some incarnation or other—either from Britannica or from some third-party mailer offering it.

According to Bill Butler, founder of Perkins/Butler Direct Marketing, he wrote the *Encyclopaedia Britannica* package for the Frank Vos Company back in 1975 or 1976 for what was, at that time, known as the "salvage package." It was Britannica's attempt to sell books directly to prospects after they had already seen an EB sales rep but decided not to buy. The original package was 9″ × 12″. The letter was later adapted to EB's third-party endorsed format.

The entire point of the Britannica effort is to persuade people that they will get a nifty reference set—with no obligation to buy the encyclopedia—if only they will talk to a salesman. A sales rep is the key ingredient here. Unlike, say, a Time-Life series wherein each book is an

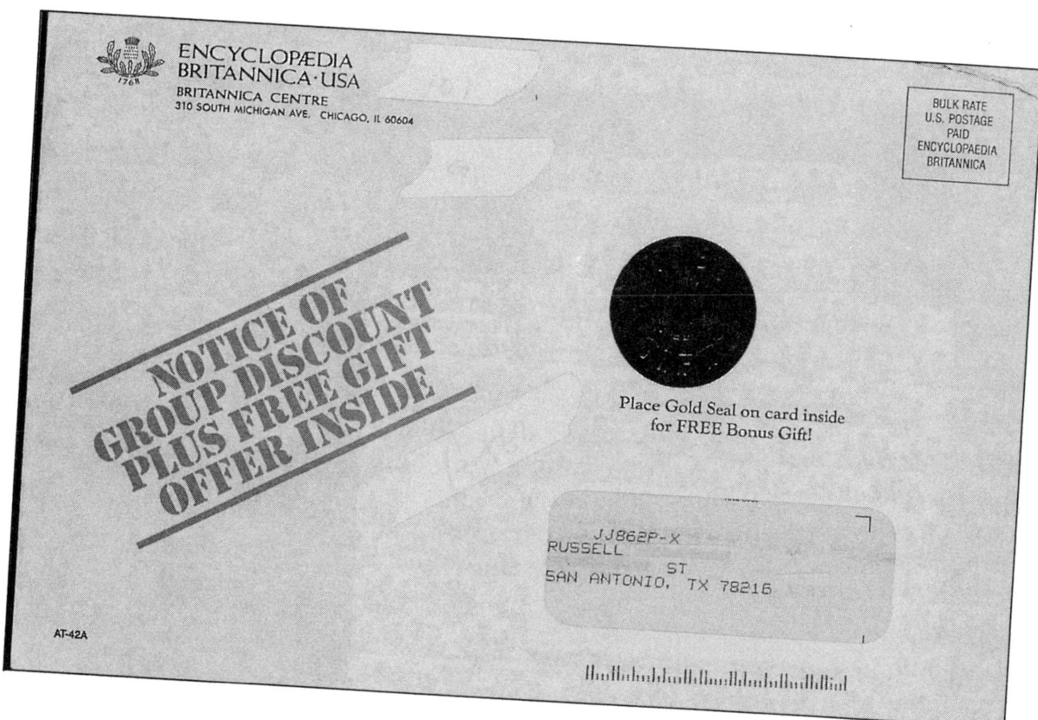

MAILER: *Encyclopaedia Britannica*
PACKAGE: "If money were no object"
PROJECT MGRS.: Ray Markman
Harold Silver
Alan Boyer (Current)
AGENCY: Frank Vos Company
PROJECT DIR.: Frank Vos
ACCOUNT MGR.: Mitch Hisiger
WRITER: William A. Butler
COPY CHIEF: Joe Morrone
DESIGNER: Winnie Young
FIRST MAILED: Mid-1970s
The 6″ × 9″ outside envelope with gold foil token on the front.

SL-71-EBF

ENCYCLOPÆDIA BRITANNICA USA

1768

Now...we've overcome
the last reason for not owning
The New Encyclopaedia Britannica.
Money.

Dear Friend:

If money were no object, would you own Encyclopaedia Britannica?

Of course! Most people would. And that's particularly true now, because today's Britannica is better than ever! But more about that in a moment . . .

Right now I'm happy to tell you that you can acquire Encyclopaedia Britannica for far less than you ever thought possible. You can do so . . . direct from the publisher . . . at a substantial Group Discount.

Just mail the enclosed postage-free card, and you'll receive a big, full-color booklet--FREE. You'll also get the full details of this Group Discount Plan we have arranged for you.

That's right. Through this Group Discount Plan you are entitled to obtain Britannica at a price that is substantially lower than the retail list price.

When you receive this full-color booklet, you'll learn how--after more than 200 years as the outstanding reference work in the entire world --Encyclopaedia Britannica has achieved another first in publishing leadership--a revolutionary approach to a family reference library.

Britannica--with its expanded format--is not just a latest edition--but a completely unique encyclopaedia which outmodes all other encyclopaedias. Never before has so much knowledge, so readily accessible, so easily understood--been made available as a complete home library.

With Britannica, every member of your family will profit; for it is unequaled as a source of daily help in school, business, home management, hobbies and recreation, and social activities as well.

BRITANNICA CENTRE
310 SOUTH MICHIGAN AVE. CHICAGO, IL 60604

Easier to use . . . easier to read . . . easier to understand! Today's 32-volume Britannica is America's only encyclopaedia that offers you this unique format:

Two-volume Index--contains over 200,000 entries with over 440,000 references which quickly guide you to any of the tens of thousands of articles in Britannica.

Ready Reference--designed to help you find facts fast . . . covering just about every field of knowledge in twelve volumes of short, easy-to-understand entries. Perfect for homework!

Knowledge in Depth--for people who want to learn more about a subject in all its depth. Seventeen volumes of articles of the kind that make Britannica the best reference work in the world.

Outline of Knowledge--surveys major fields of study . . . and much more! With this outline, any member of your family can learn at his or her own speed--you can follow your own interests as far as your curiosity takes you.

Plus, for Britannica subscribers, the unique and invaluable Britannica World Data Annual. This single volume gives you instant access to the latest statistical information on over 200 countries of the world. And your first copy of this year's exciting volume is yours as a FREE GIFT from Britannica Home Library Service, Inc., when you acquire Britannica.

Also included is the Britannica Instant Research Service that gives you up to 100 research reports on almost any subject of your choice. See inside of brochure for details.

We urge you to send today for your booklet which pictures and describes Britannica and shows how this revolutionary Home Learning Center can provide the entire family with a reservoir of knowledge unequaled by any other reference in the world.

To get your free full-color booklet, just complete and return the enclosed postage-free reply card. You'll also get the exciting details of this outstanding Group Discount Plan.

Please do it promptly. There's no cost or obligation, of course.

Sincerely,

James D. Battin
Vice President

P.S. I think you'll discover that the Group Discount Plan makes it easier than you'd dreamed to own today's incomparable Britannica!

The 2-page letter, printed front and back on an $8\frac{1}{2}'' \times 11''$ sheet.

entity and can be enjoyed on its own, there is no way a traditional encyclopedia can be sold as a continuity program on a one- or two-volume-a-month basis; there are so many cross-references to unshipped volumes that the customer would spend months feeling the set was useless.

Another aspect of the *Encyclopaedia Britannica* that makes it different from an ordinary continuity series: when all the books are in place in the home, they are handsomely bound and do not take up a lot of space. The "beauty shot" on the inside spread of the circular shows the books as "furniture."

There is a logical progression in the mailing. *Outside envelope*: savings plus free gift offer inside and a gold seal that proclaims FREE GIFT. *Letter*: special group discount plan . . . great home reference library to benefit every member of the family . . . send for free full-color booklet. *Circular*: savings and free booklet offer on cover . . . knowledge benefits for the entire family on first inside spread . . . spectacular piece of furniture that will impress friends and neighbors on the main inside spread. In fact, all fine-binding sets, such as the Franklin Mint or Easton Press leather-bound volumes, are sold as furniture, not books.

So the Britannica message is multifaceted: big savings, knowledge, affirmation, and furniture.

Lift piece no. 1—cover flap and letter inside.

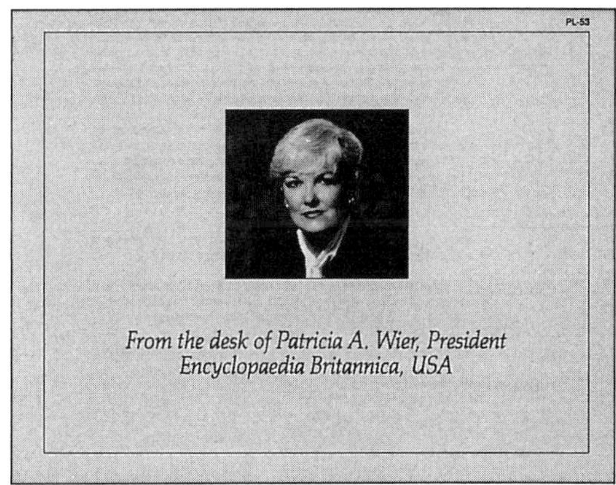

PL-53
From the desk of Patricia A. Wier, President
Encyclopaedia Britannica, USA

From the office of the President

Dear Reader,

Several years ago, the members of our distinguished Board of Editors came to me with a plan to make Britannica easier to use, easier to read, and easier to understand than ever.

Frankly, I didn't think it could be done. I didn't think it was possible to improve what I felt was the world's finest encyclopaedia.

But you'll see for yourself as I did: today's Britannica stands alone as a masterpiece. Its 2-volume Index and unique organization make it easier than ever to find the facts you need. Authoritative and up to date, it is your key to the Information Age . . . truly, the ultimate family library!

If you're a person with a love of learning -- one who values personal achievement -- and I have every reason to believe you are -- then you really should take advantage of this opportunity to preview The New Encyclopaedia Britannica. You'll receive a 3-volume Desk Reference Set, worth $14.40, free and without obligation to buy anything. And when you peel the Gold Seal off the envelope and put it on the reply card, you'll also receive a second free gift -- a wonderful hardcover book with a retail value of up to $20.00.

But there are other more compelling reasons to welcome Britannica into your home: a desire for achievement; your willingness to give your children the best encyclopaedia available; or simply, the satisfaction of having the world's finest home reference set there in your own home.

Won't you take the first step now by mailing the enclosed card? We look forward to hearing from you.

Sincerely,

Patricia A. Wier

Patricia A. Wier
Encyclopaedia Britannica, USA

P.S. If money concerns you, as it does everyone these days, please keep this in mind: with your Group Discount savings and the convenient payment plan we offer, you'll find Britannica is easier to own than you'd guess. But there's no reason to decide anything right now. Find out for yourself. There is absolutely no obligation. Simply mail the card today.

BRITANNICA CENTRE
310 SOUTH MICHIGAN AVE CHICAGO, IL 60604

NOTICE!

THERE IS A LIMIT OF ONE DESK REFERENCE SET TO A FAMILY.

If you have not yet requested yours, please mail the enclosed Reply Card promptly. Thank you for your cooperation.

HS-13

Lift piece no. 2, printed in black on bright red paper.

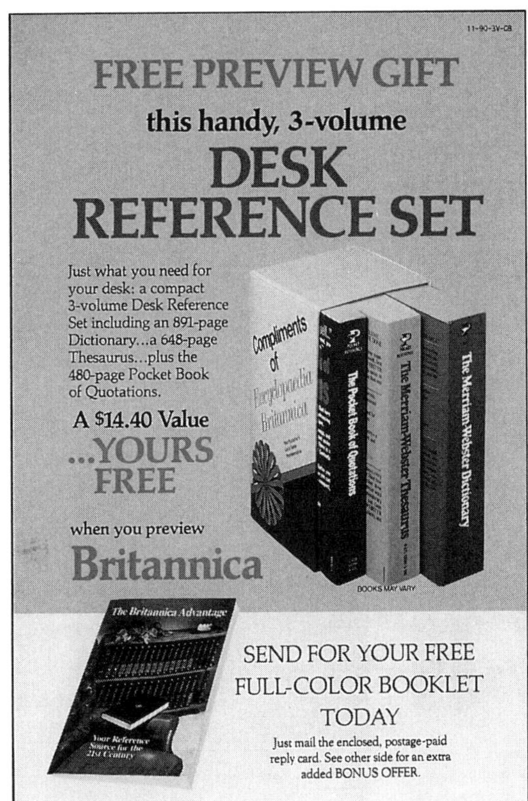

FREE PREVIEW GIFT
this handy, 3-volume
DESK REFERENCE SET
Just what you need for your desk: a compact 3-volume Desk Reference Set including an 891-page Dictionary...a 648-page Thesaurus...plus the 480-page Pocket Book of Quotations.
A $14.40 Value
...YOURS FREE
when you preview
Britannica
Compliments of Encyclopaedia Britannica
The Pocket Book of Quotations
The Merriam-Webster Thesaurus
The Merriam-Webster Dictionary
BOOKS MAY VARY
The Britannica Advantage
SEND FOR YOUR FREE FULL-COLOR BOOKLET TODAY
Just mail the enclosed, postage-paid reply card. See other side for an extra added BONUS OFFER.

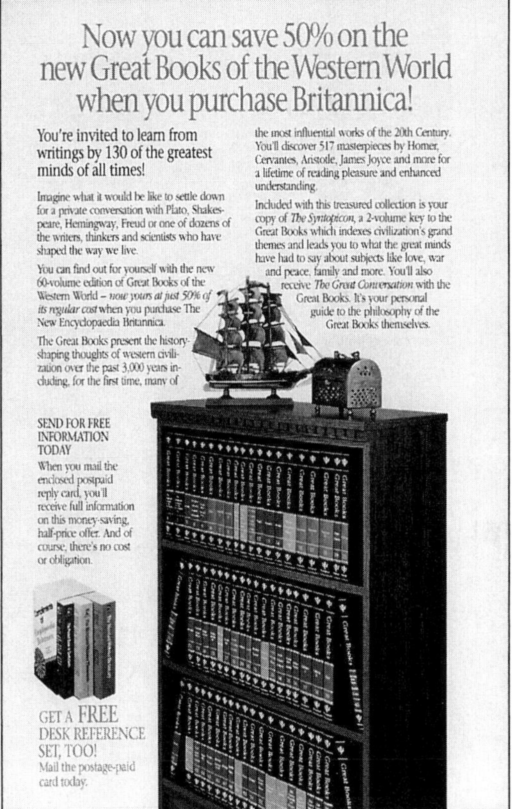

Now you can save 50% on the new Great Books of the Western World when you purchase Britannica!
You're invited to learn from writings by 130 of the greatest minds of all times!
Imagine what it would be like to settle down for a private conversation with Plato, Shakespeare, Hemingway, Freud or one of dozens of the writers, thinkers and scientists who have shaped the way we live.
You can find out for yourself with the new 60-volume edition of Great Books of the Western World – now yours at just 50% of its regular cost when you purchase The New Encyclopaedia Britannica.
The Great Books present the history-shaping thoughts of western civilization over the past 3,000 years including, for the first time, many of the most influential works of the 20th Century. You'll discover 517 masterpieces by Homer, Cervantes, Aristotle, James Joyce and more for a lifetime of reading pleasure and enhanced understanding.
Included with this treasured collection is your copy of The Syntopicon, a 2-volume key to the Great Books which indexes civilization's grand themes and leads you to what the great minds have had to say about subjects like love, war and peace, family and more. You'll also receive The Great Conversation with the Great Books. It's your personal guide to the philosophy of the Great Books themselves.
SEND FOR FREE INFORMATION TODAY
When you mail the enclosed postpaid reply card, you'll receive full information on this money-saving, half-price offer. And of course, there's no cost or obligation.
GET A FREE DESK REFERENCE SET, TOO!
Mail the postage-paid card today.

Lift piece no. 3, 5½″ × 8″, printed in 4-color and shown front and back.

SB-54
Britannica
can now be yours
for less than you ever
thought possible.
Much less.
(But only through this substantial
group discount offer...direct
from the publisher.)
Send
for details
and
FREE
BOOKLET
See inside for details...

The 8½″ × 11″ 4-color circular cover.

Whatever your interests,
you'll find the answers in
Britannica!
The New Encyclopaedia Britannica is a complete Home Learning Center...with over 44 million words that give you more up-to-date information on more subjects than you'll find anywhere else.
And the 2-volume Index with over 200,000 entries and over 440,000 references makes it easier to put your hands on just what you need! And Britannica's 23,000 maps, illustrations, photographs and works of art add so much—they're designed not to decorate, but to illustrate and clarify the fascinating articles.
Discover Britannica for yourself—and see how it can help you and your children achieve your highest goals.
Preview
Britannica...
take advantage of your
Group Discount
savings now!
©1990 Encyclopaedia Britannica, Inc.

The back cover.

The first inside spread, 11″ × 17″.

Preview the world's finest Home Learning Center

THE NEW ENCYCLOPAEDIA BRITANNICA

It's yours now at a substantial Group Discount!

There's no obligation when you preview Britannica and it's a perfect opportunity to learn what a tremendous difference it can make in how well you achieve your goals.

Why? Because Britannica is a totally unique approach to learning that's just right for today's more advanced school work and more competitive work world.

Britannica covers more subjects in greater detail. It lets youngsters do better work faster because it puts the information they need at their fingertips. And it's just as useful to you, because it gives you important information you need in your business and personal life, and to follow up your personal interests and hobbies as well.

Politics...business...religion...art...music...science...literature...sports...health... biography...history...Britannica covers them all, in clearly written, easy-to-understand articles that give you all the facts you need for total learning.

PREVIEW BRITANNICA NOW.

Because Britannica is so unique—its four-part arrangement alone sets it apart from all other encyclopaedias—we have created an interesting, colorful booklet that describes the encyclopaedia in far greater detail than we can here. You'll also receive full details on your Group Discount Savings and convenient payment plan. **Please read the reply card carefully.** You'll see there's no obligation. Send for your FREE booklet today.

Dreaded Gray Shark
—terror of the sea—
as pictured
in Britannica.

Grass-Pink
Orchid lures
bees and traps
them with its
falling petal.

2-Volume Index
...makes the Britannica
easier to use than ever.

Britannica
World Data Annual
...this valuable book gives you
up-to-date information on over
200 countries of the world!

Britannica
...an incomparable Home
Learning Center you'll turn
to again and again...for
information and for
fascinating reading.

Get the facts about your Group Discount savings on

Britannica

Included with Britannica...these unique learning aid options:

1. **Britannica World Data Annual***
   Two books in one, the Britannica World Data Annual gives you the major events of the year in review plus all the latest statistical facts on all the countries of the world!

2. **Yearbook of Science and the Future***
   No better way to keep abreast of the latest developments in the field and keep your home reference library right "up to the minute."

3. **Medical and Health Annual***
   Britannica owners keep on top of the newest advances in health and medicine with this authoritative volume complete with its own family first aid supplement.

4. **10-Year Britannica Instant Research Service**
   ★ This unique service, available only to Britannica subscribers, provides you with detailed, authoritative research reports on any of hundreds of thousands of subjects.

   ★ We'll register 100 Research Coupons in your name. Any time that you want an Instant Report—up to 10 a year for 10 full years—just call or mail in your request from our catalog and we'll speed it to you!

   ★ Add a personal dimension to the wealth of information already in Britannica and keep yourself up-to-date on topics ranging from hobbies to money management to world problems.

   ★ You'll receive full details on this important benefit when you acquire Britannica.

Television
Observation
Satellite TIROS 7
helps meteorologists
track and forecast storms.

Four-Eye Butterfly Fish
displays biological coloration to confuse predators.

Bird-Watchers
will recognize this
4-colored Bush Shrike as
pictured in Britannica.

*From Britannica Home Library Service, Inc.

The main inside spread, a 17″ × 22″ broadside.

The only price mentioned anywhere in the mailing is the $14.40 value of the three-volume desk reference set that is "yours, free, when you preview Britannica for yourself."

Bill Butler calls himself "the legendary, almost mythic former chairman of Chiat/Day Direct Marketing." After learning his craft under the guidance of the master, Frank Vos of Altman, Vos & Reichberg, Butler went to Wunderman Worldwide, where he became creative director, arguably the most important creative job in direct marketing at the time. In 1989 he was picked by Jay Chiat to cofound and lend his name to Perkins/Butler Direct—later to become Chiat/Day Direct Marketing, which went from $0 to $60 million in three years. Accounts include American Express, National Car Rental, AT & T, and Nissan Motor.

Bill Butler:

I start from the proposition that all good direct mail must answer the question "Why am I writing you?" That is to ask, why you instead of your neighbor? And why mail instead of print or broadcast?

All great direct mail seems to deal with that question, and in doing so, helps explain why mail packages without letters do so poorly. They just don't answer the "Why am I writing you?" question very well for consumers, at least to this observer.

I value clarity over cleverness.

I like dealing with letters, though increasingly, nontraditional direct marketers insist on wasting money on lavish brochures and outside envelopes to make them "strategically" acceptable. They miss the point that most direct response advertising, particularly direct mail, has its roots in retailing and not mass marketing. Hence, direct response advertising is normally best used as a tactical, targeted retail or sales promotion tool rather than an instrument of grand strategy.

Next to letters, I find order cards most rewarding, I think because they are most overlooked, especially by agencies. Too bad for them. It's where the results live for me.

I most appreciate the kind of creative development that goes into advertising whose results are carefully measured, then used to plan future advertising. Such is no longer always the case in the industry as direct response advertising is co-opted to meet other agendas, often with embarrassing results. Actuaries beware. Lifetime value calculations now frequently assume Biblical lifespans just to finance questionable "relationships" most consumers don't know what they want.

Frank Vos, founder and president of the Frank Vos Company, is urbane and literate, with one of the most wide-ranging and eclectic intellects ever to grace the direct marketing stage. Born in New York City in 1917, he graduated magna cum laude from Columbia University with a B.A. in 1982 [sic], earned his M.A. in 1984, and a master's in philosophy in 1989. Vos's incipient career with the old Schwab & Beatty Company was interrupted by service as a lieutenant in the U.S. Army in Italy during 1943–46. There he won the Bronze Star and became fluent in everything Italian—language, wine, gastronomy, cinema, art, and history. While at Schwab & Beatty—along with such fledgling legends as Walter Weintz, Tom Collins, and Len Reiss—Vos learned the craft of direct mail copy. In 1948 he became sales promotion manager of the

The 4-color order card shown front and back.

Doubleday Book Clubs. In 1957 he founded the direct marketing agency of Vos & Co., serving such clients as Greystone Press, Capitol Record Club, Encyclopaedia Britannica, Grolier Enterprises, the World of Beauty, National Liberty Insurance, Lenox China, Vanguard Funds, and the Meredith Book Division. Over the years the agency went through a series of metamorphoses until it was finally sold to the Interpublic Group in 1984 and became part of SSC & B (now Lintas). Vos is semi-retired and working on his doctoral thesis at Columbia. The subject: the decline of political bosses in New York City. Now in his seventies, he remains the best conversationalist in the state of Connecticut.

Frank Vos:

First of all, list selection and the structure of the offer are far, far more important than copy and artwork. But, even when lists, offer, and presentation are well done, at least ninety-five of every hundred pieces which one mails generally become landfill, usually unread.

A substantial portion of these unheeded mailing pieces are thrown away simply because the offer is too easily and quickly understood by those not seeking the product at the moment. Therefore, I often tried to include in the forefront of each mailing a physical device of seeming value (or usefulness) which was not immediately rejectable. With this technique I was able to compel prospects to read my sales story in order to discover the purpose of the dissonant element in the mailing. I reasoned that if my product had merit, a broader readership would produce greater sales.

Let me give you just a few examples from the precomputer age.

When I was in my twenties I tipped an important-looking blank shipping label to the top of a very brief letter. Until you read the letter, you could not understand what to do with the label. The recipient was instructed to write his name and address on the label in order to receive an attractive ''on approval'' item which was the basis of this client's recruitment offer. This was a very simple involvement idea, but it pulled so much better than the client's conventional and more elaborate control that it became part of my thinking forever after.

In my thirties I invented, for the Doubleday Book Club, a perforated sheet of some twenty ''value stamps.'' This was during the heyday of ''S & H Green Stamps'' and no one was about to throw away a lot of value stamps until he knew what they represented. Each of my book stamps pictured a bestseller, and displayed its retail value. The prospect was invited to affix three stamps to the enrollment card, representing the three books he could select as a membership gift. This device was extraordinarily effective, doubling the results of the venerable control which merely asked the prospect to check three product numbers. During the next few decades the stamp concept was copied by so many book and record clubs that it eventually lost its mystery.

In my forties, we were the first to send ultrarealistic, individually embossed plastic ''membership cards'' to those ''eligible'' for hospital insurance. Credit cards were just then beginning to gain popular acceptance, and a bit of similar plastic would not be discarded until it was understood. That is how we forced people to read our benefits-and-offer copy. The heavy plastic card added substantially to the mailing's cost, but the tremendously enhanced results paid for the increment many times over.

I guess the most important promotion, dollarwise, which I developed in those days was the broad marketing of insurance policies which were deliberately restricted to military veterans and their families. This concept came out of my own wartime experiences; I realized that millions of veterans had been taught (correctly) that GI insurance was the cheapest and best coverage to be had. It took no more than five minutes for me to convince the late Arthur S. DeMoss, founder of National Liberty, that he could cash in on this belief. Our direct mail results were so phenomenal that Art, at first, kept the offer out of space and TV so that his competitors would not immediately discover how successful it was. They found out eventually, and then everybody got into the act. Nothing I ever created made so much money for so many others.

By this time I had become successful. So had many of our clients, and some of them thereupon replaced entrepreneurship with hydra-headed bureaucracy. As a result, I'm afraid that our mailings became better looking but less inventive, simply because the more unusual they were, the harder it now became to get them okayed. In any case, the agency could make more money collecting commissions on space and TV.

Great Expectations

Tony Barnard's lead generator to this video dating service includes a board of advisers, a list of the local chapters, a one-page letter, and a detailed application. As with the other lead generators, there is no mention of price.

Tony Barnard has been a freelance direct response copywriter for more than twenty years with clients such as Xerox, Time Inc., the *New York Times*, Carte Blanche, Johns-Manville, McGraw-Hill, Petersen Publishing, Columbia Records, and *Kiplinger Washington Letter*.

TONY BARNARD:

Great Expectations is today's largest video dating service with offices in some thirty cities across the U.S. They mail approximately sixty million lead generation mailers a year, designed to attract single men and women to the various offices for closing by in-house sales people. Because of the heavy volume, keeping the per-piece mailing cost to a minimum is critical.

Their control had been a standard #10 package with an 8½" × 11" two-sided letter/questionnaire and a #9 BRE inside a #10 envelope. Larger packages and self-mailers had been tested against this control with weak results.

I had a hunch that an involvement device would heighten response. The Great Expectations logo is a double heart, one overlapping the other. I designed a #10 window envelope with a peel-off red heart showing through the win-

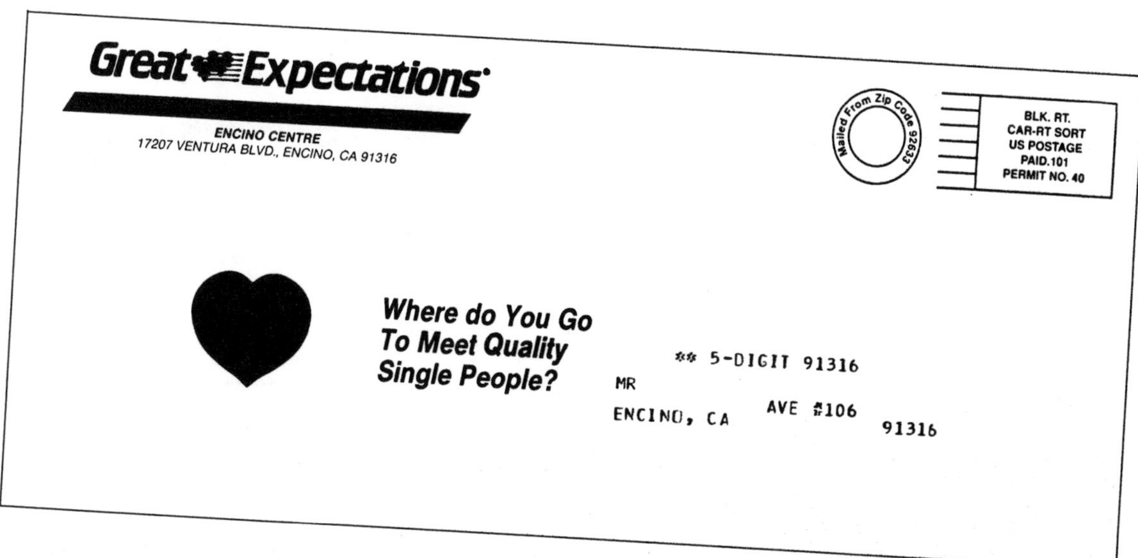

MAILER: Great Expectations
PACKAGE: Meet Quality Singles
PROJECT MGR.: Janice Mayo
WRITER: Tony Barnard
DESIGNER: Tony Barnard
FIRST MAILED: 1986
The no. 10 outside envelope with the red heart token showing through a round window.

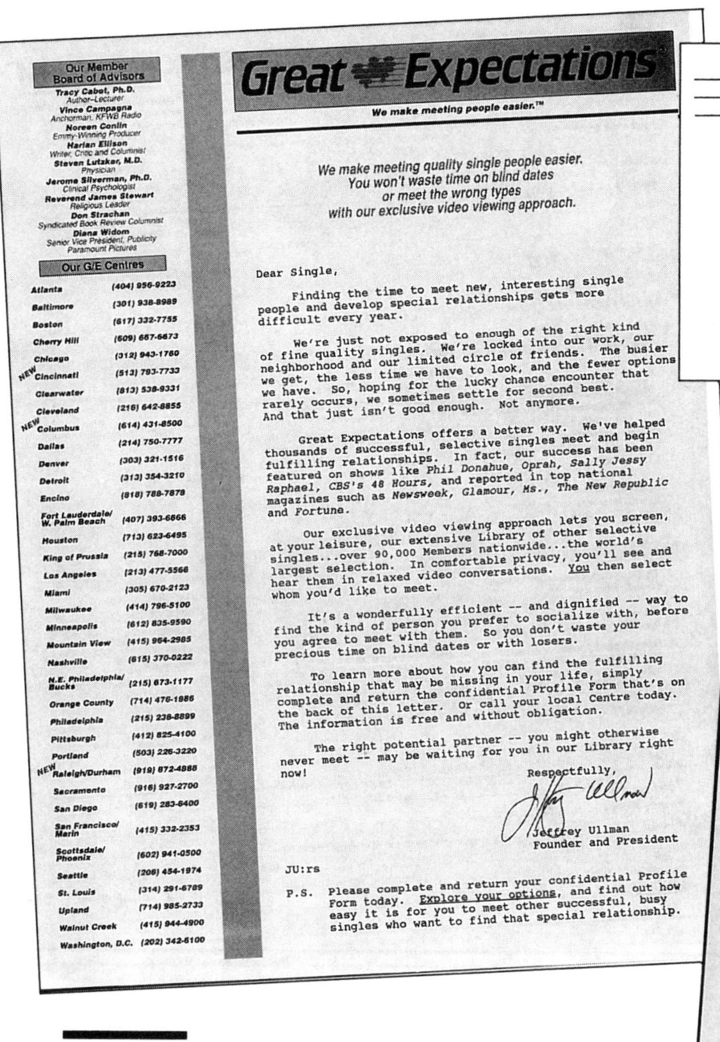

Our Member Board of Advisors

Tracy Cabot, Ph.D. — *Author–Lecturer*
Vince Campagna — *Anchorman, KFWB Radio*
Noreen Conlin — *Emmy-Winning Producer*
Harlan Ellison — *Writer, Critic and Columnist*
Steven Lutzker, M.D. — *Physician*
Jerome Silverman, Ph.D. — *Clinical Psychologist*
Reverend James Stewart — *Religious Leader*
Don Strachan — *Syndicated Book Review Columnist*
Diana Widom — *Senior Vice President, Publicity, Paramount Pictures*

Our G/E Centres

Atlanta	(404) 956-9223
Baltimore	(301) 938-8989
Boston	(617) 332-7755
Cherry Hill	(609) 667-6673
Chicago	(312) 943-1760
NEW Cincinnati	(513) 793-7733
Clearwater	(813) 538-9331
Cleveland	(216) 642-8855
NEW Columbus	(614) 431-8500
Dallas	(214) 750-7777
Denver	(303) 321-1516
Detroit	(313) 354-3210
Encino	(818) 788-7878
Fort Lauderdale/ W. Palm Beach	(407) 393-6866
Houston	(713) 623-6495
King of Prussia	(215) 768-7000
Los Angeles	(213) 477-5566
Miami	(305) 670-2123
Milwaukee	(414) 796-5100
Minneapolis	(612) 835-9590
Mountain View	(415) 964-2985
Nashville	(615) 370-0222
N.E. Philadelphia/ Bucks	(215) 673-1177
Orange County	(714) 476-1986
Philadelphia	(215) 238-8899
Pittsburgh	(412) 825-4100
Portland	(503) 226-3220
NEW Raleigh/Durham	(919) 872-4888
Sacramento	(916) 927-2700
San Diego	(619) 283-6400
San Francisco/ Marin	(415) 332-2353
Scottsdale/ Phoenix	(602) 941-0500
Seattle	(206) 454-1974
St. Louis	(314) 291-6789
Upland	(714) 985-2733
Walnut Creek	(415) 944-4900
Washington, D.C.	(202) 342-6100

Great Expectations®

We make meeting people easier.™

We make meeting quality single people easier.
You won't waste time on blind dates
or meet the wrong types
with our exclusive video viewing approach.

Dear Single,

Finding the time to meet new, interesting single people and develop special relationships gets more difficult every year.

We're just not exposed to enough of the right kind of fine quality singles. We're locked into our work, our neighborhood and our limited circle of friends. The busier we get, the less time we have to look, and the fewer options we have. So, hoping for the lucky chance encounter that rarely occurs, we sometimes settle for second best. And that just isn't good enough. Not anymore.

Great Expectations offers a better way. We've helped thousands of successful, selective singles meet and begin fulfilling relationships. In fact, our success has been featured on shows like *Phil Donahue, Oprah, Sally Jessy Raphael, CBS's 48 Hours,* and reported in top national magazines such as *Newsweek, Glamour, Ms., The New Republic* and *Fortune.*

Our exclusive video viewing approach lets you screen, at your leisure, our extensive Library of other selective singles...over 90,000 Members nationwide...the world's largest selection. In comfortable privacy, you'll see and hear them in relaxed video conversations. You then select whom you'd like to meet.

It's a wonderfully efficient -- and dignified -- way to find the kind of person you prefer to socialize with, before you agree to meet with them. So you don't waste your precious time on blind dates or with losers.

To learn more about how you can find the fulfilling relationship that may be missing in your life, simply complete and return the confidential Profile Form that's on the back of this letter. Or call your local Centre today. The information is free and without obligation.

The right potential partner -- you might otherwise never meet -- may be waiting for you in our Library right now!

Respectfully,

Jeffrey Ullman
Founder and President

JU:rs

P.S. Please complete and return your confidential Profile Form today. Explore your options, and find out how easy it is for you to meet other successful, busy singles who want to find that special relationship.

NO POSTAGE NECESSARY IF MAILED IN THE UNITED STATES

ZIP

LSS

BUSINESS REPLY MAIL
FIRST CLASS MAIL PERMIT NO. 64003 LOS ANGELES CA

POSTAGE WILL BE PAID BY ADDRESSEE

Great Expectations®
ENCINO CENTRE
16830 VENTURA BLVD SUITE P
ENCINO CA 91499-3527

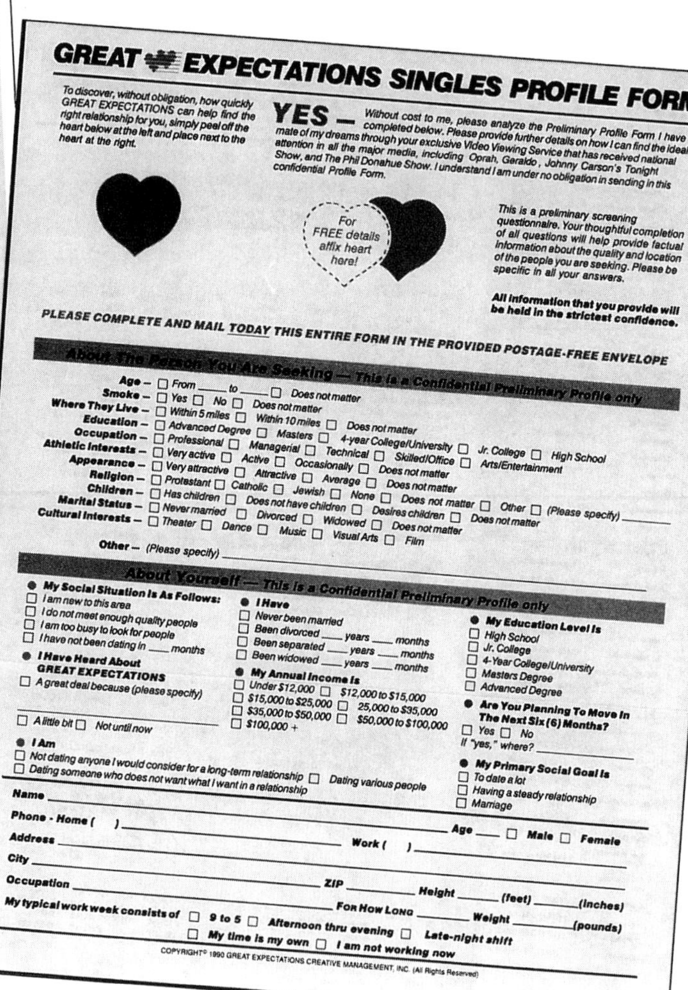

GREAT EXPECTATIONS SINGLES PROFILE FORM™

To discover, without obligation, how quickly GREAT EXPECTATIONS can help find the right relationship for you, simply peel off the heart below at the left and place next to the heart at the right.

YES — *Without cost to me, please analyze the Preliminary Profile Form I have completed below. Please provide further details on how I can find the ideal mate of my dreams through your exclusive Video Viewing Service that has received national attention in all the major media, including Oprah, Geraldo, Johnny Carson's Tonight Show, and The Phil Donahue Show. I understand I am under no obligation in sending in this confidential Profile Form.*

For FREE details affix heart here!

This is a preliminary screening questionnaire. Your thoughtful completion of all questions will help provide factual information about the quality and location of the people you are seeking. Please be specific in all your answers.

All information that you provide will be held in the strictest confidence.

PLEASE COMPLETE AND MAIL TODAY THIS ENTIRE FORM IN THE PROVIDED POSTAGE-FREE ENVELOPE

About The Person You Are Seeking — This is a Confidential Preliminary Profile only

Age — ☐ From ___ to ___ ☐ Does not matter
Smoke — ☐ Yes ☐ No ☐ Does not matter
Where They Live — ☐ Within 5 miles ☐ Within 10 miles ☐ Does not matter
Education — ☐ Advanced Degree ☐ Masters ☐ 4-year College/University ☐ Jr. College ☐ High School
Occupation — ☐ Professional ☐ Managerial ☐ Technical ☐ Skilled/Office ☐ Arts/Entertainment
Athletic Interests — ☐ Very active ☐ Active ☐ Occasionally ☐ Does not matter
Appearance — ☐ Very attractive ☐ Attractive ☐ Average ☐ Does not matter
Religion — ☐ Protestant ☐ Catholic ☐ Jewish ☐ None ☐ Does not matter ☐ Other ☐ (Please specify) ___
Children — ☐ Has children ☐ Does not have children ☐ Desires children ☐ Does not matter
Marital Status — ☐ Never married ☐ Divorced ☐ Widowed ☐ Does not matter
Cultural Interests — ☐ Theater ☐ Dance ☐ Music ☐ Visual Arts ☐ Film
Other — (Please specify) ___

About Yourself — This is a Confidential Preliminary Profile only

● **My Social Situation Is As Follows:**
☐ I am new to this area
☐ I do not meet enough quality people
☐ I am too busy to look for people
☐ I have not been dating in ___ months

● **I Have Heard About GREAT EXPECTATIONS**
☐ A great deal because (please specify) ___
☐ A little bit ☐ Not until now

● **I Am**
☐ Not dating anyone I would consider for a long-term relationship ☐ Dating various people
☐ Dating someone who does not want what I want in a relationship

● **I Have**
☐ Never been married
☐ Been divorced ___ years ___ months
☐ Been separated ___ years ___ months
☐ Been widowed ___ years ___ months

● **My Annual Income Is**
☐ Under $12,000 ☐ $12,000 to $15,000
☐ $15,000 to $25,000 ☐ 25,000 to $35,000
☐ $35,000 to $50,000 ☐ $50,000 to $100,000
☐ $100,000 +

● **My Education Level Is**
☐ High School
☐ Jr. College
☐ 4-Year College/University
☐ Masters Degree
☐ Advanced Degree

● **Are You Planning To Move In The Next Six (6) Months?**
☐ Yes ☐ No
If "yes," where? ___

● **My Primary Social Goal Is**
☐ To date a lot
☐ Having a steady relationship
☐ Marriage

Name ___
Phone - Home (   ) ___ **Age** ___ ☐ **Male** ☐ **Female**
Address ___ **Work (   )** ___
City ___
Occupation ___ **ZIP** ___ **Height** ___ **(feet)** ___ **(inches)**
___ **For How Long** ___ **Weight** ___ **(pounds)**
My typical work week consists of ☐ **9 to 5** ☐ **Afternoon thru evening** ☐ **Late-night shift** ☐ **My time is my own** ☐ **I am not working now**

The letter/questionnaire reply form shown front and back of an $8^{1/2}$" × 11" sheet. The only other piece in the mailing is the business reply envelope.

dow. To say yes, the recipient simply peeled off the heart and affixed it to the reply form next to the second preprinted heart—thus forming the company's double-heart logo, and, of course, suggesting a romantic link between man and woman.

In addition, I rewrote the letter, punching up the copy.

The resulting package clobbered the control in both test and rollout. My package has reigned supreme now as the control for over five years, beating every test package handily (including another of my own creations which came closest).

Institute of Children's Literature

Malcolm Decker's direct marketing career spans thirty years and includes stints with Famous Artists Schools, Walt Disney Productions, Young & Rubicam, and McCann-Erickson. He learned his craft from many of the greatest practitioners. Among them: Tom Collins, the Wundermans, and Ben Ordover. Among his awards: DMA Gold Mailbox, Silver Mailbox, and the Axel Andersson Award for his long-time control for the Institute of Children's Literature. His letters have been featured in Bob Stone's *Successful Direct Marketing Methods* and Dick Hodgson's *The 100 Greatest Direct Mail Letters.* You will find Decker's landmark article for *Who's Mailing What!* on "The Direct Mail Package"—a classic on the philosophy and execution of direct mail—reprinted as Chapter 4.

MAILER: Institute of Children's Literature
PACKAGE: Looking for People
PROJECT MGR.: Malcolm Decker
WRITER: Malcolm Decker
DESIGNER: David Gordon
FIRST MAILED: 1977
The advertisement from which the direct mail package was adapted.

"We're looking for people to write children's books"

by Alvin Tresselt, *Dean of Faculty*

"Writing for children is the perfect way to begin," says the author of 53 children's books. "Your ideas come right out of your own experience. And while it's still a challenge, it's the straightest possible line between you and publication—if you're qualified to seek the success this rewarding field offers."

IF YOU WANT TO WRITE and see your work published, I can't think of a better way to do it than writing books and stories for children and teenagers. Ideas flow naturally right out of your own life. And while it's still a challenge, the odds of getting that first unforgettable check from a juvenile publisher are better than they are from just about any other kind of publisher I know.

Later on, you may get other checks from other publishers. But right now, the object is to begin, to break into print, to learn the feeling of writing and selling your work and seeing your name in type. After that, you can decide if you want your writing to take another direction.

But after 40 years of editing, publishing and teaching (and 53 books of my own), I can tell you this: You'll go a long way before you discover anything as rewarding as writing for children.

Your words will never sound as sweet as they do from the lips of a child reading your books and stories. And the joy of creating books and stories that truly reach young people is an experience you'll never have anywhere else.

The soaring children's market

But, that's not all. The financial rewards go far beyond most people's expectations because there's a surprisingly big market out there for writers who are trained to tap it. More than $1 *billion* worth of children's books are purchased annually and more than 300 of the 500 publishers of books related to children welcome manuscripts from aspiring writers. And over 400 magazines rely on freelancers to fill their issues.

Yet two big questions bedevil nearly every would-be writer..."Am I really qualified?" and "How can I get started?"

"Am I really qualified?"

This is our definition of a "qualified person": it's someone with an aptitude for writing who can take constructive criticism, learn from it, and turn it into a professional performance. That's the only kind of person we're looking for. The reasons are simple: Our reputation is built on success and if prospective students don't have the aptitude it takes, we probably can't help them. And we tell them so; it's only fair.

Alvin Tresselt, Dean of Faculty, was Executive Editor of Parents' Magazine Press, the first editor of *Humpty Dumpty's Magazine* for children, and a board member of the Author's Guild. His 53 books for young readers have sold over two million copies.

An old mansion nestled deep in the woods of Connecticut is the home of the Institute of Children's Literature. It was founded in 1969.

To help us spot potential authors, we've developed a revealing test for writing aptitude. It's free, and we don't charge for our evaluation. But no one gets into the Institute of Children's Literature® without passing it. Those who pass and enroll receive our promise:

You will complete at least one manuscript ready to submit to a publisher by the time you finish the course.

One-on-one training with your own instructor

This is the way I work with my students, and my fellow instructors—all of whom are experienced writers or editors—work more or less the same way.

- When you're ready—at your own time and your own pace—you send your assignment to me.
- I read it and reread it to get everything out of it you've put into it.
- Then I edit your assignment just the way a publishing house editor would—if he had the time.
- I return it along with a detailed letter explaining my comments. I tell you what your strong points are, what your weaknesses are, and just what you can do to improve.

It's a matter of push and pull. You push and I pull and between us both, you learn how to write and how to market your writing.

The proof of the pudding

This method really works. I wouldn't spend five minutes at it if it didn't. The proof of the pudding is that some of our students break into print even before they finish the course.

"My how-to article that sold to 4-H Magazine for $75 was my rewrite of a course assignment," says Jeanne Shoemaker, Birmingham, AL. "My beloved instructor has made this course one of the highlights of my adult life!"

"The thing that gives me the most satisfaction," writes Brandy S. Wells, Greensboro, MD, "is the idea that my story will be read by 150,000 Sunday school children—my dream come true."

Marilyn Day, Marissa, IL, says, "I am no longer a housewife. I am a *writer!*"

"Most importantly, the course has allowed me to explore my creative writing skills without committing myself to a strict classroom environment with immediate deadlines and meeting schedules," reports Jeanne Nickerson, Washington, DC. "I needed the flexibility of a correspondence course and I have enjoyed dealing on a one-on-one basis with my instructor."

Free Writing Aptitude Test offered

To find qualified men and women with an aptitude for writing, the faculty and consultants to the Institute of Children's Literature have prepared an intriguing Aptitude Test. It is offered free and will be professionally evaluated at no cost to you.

You'll also receive our free 28-page illustrated brochure describing our course, faculty, and the current market for children's literature. If you demonstrate a true aptitude for writing, you will be eligible to enroll. But that's up to you.

There is no obligation.

Writing Aptitude Test

Writing for Children and Teenagers

Get both FREE

Institute of Children's Literature
93 Long Ridge Road
West Redding, CT 06896-0812

Yes, I'm interested in your program to help new writers get started. Please send me your free Writing Aptitude Test and 28-page brochure. I understand I am under no obligation whatever and no salesman will visit me.

Please circle one and print name clearly:
Mr. Mrs. Ms. Miss MD9

Name ______

Street ______

City ______

State ______ Zip ______

Founded in 1969 • APPROVED BY THE CONNECTICUT COMMISSIONER OF EDUCATION

*The testimonials in this ad were provided without remuneration and voluntarily by the Institute's students between 1985 and 1990.

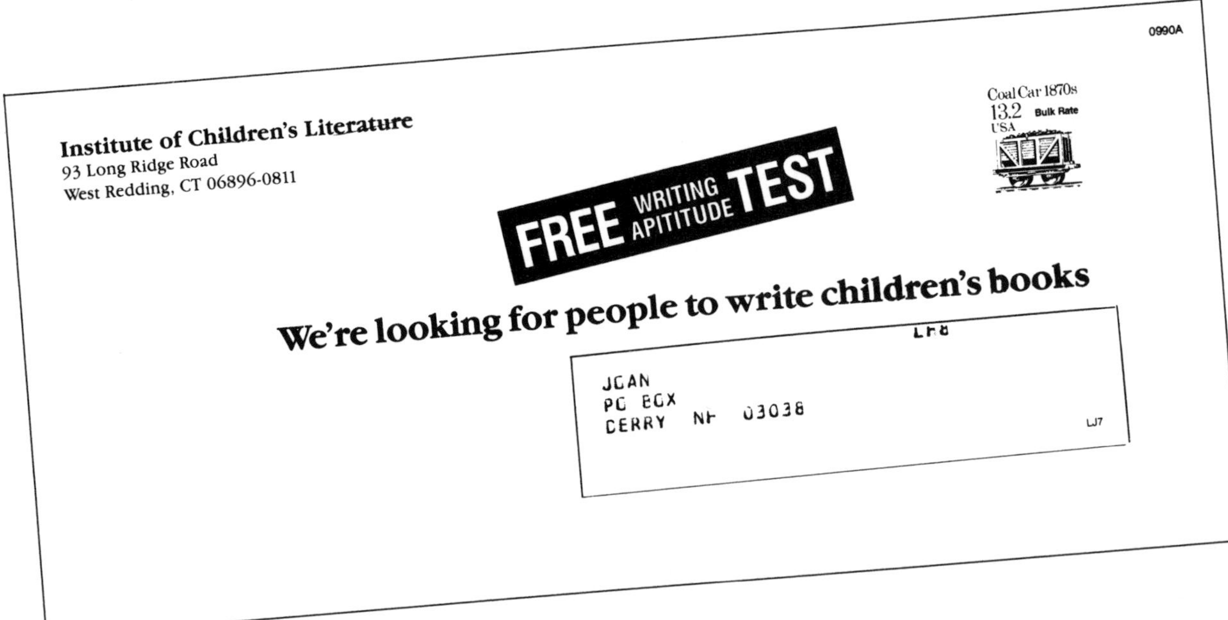

The #10 outside envelope.

Malcolm Decker:

The Institute of Children's Literature was established in 1969 in Westport, Connecticut, in the shadow of the Famous Writer's School, to offer a correspondence course in juvenile writing. FWS did not offer such a course. The Institute wisely distinguished and distanced itself from FWS by using no ''famous'' writers, and by converting leads by mail rather than by salespeople. The result was a product that was profitable at half the cost to consumers.

In 1976 the Institute asked me to write some direct mail packages for a test, and while one or two were modestly successful, none measured up to our expectations. Nevertheless, the Institute was encouraged and asked me to write some ads to test in Parade. *They had made three attempts to beat their control without coming close. I wrote three, and I got Harry Redler to design them.*

The best of the three pulled 28.3 percent more inquiries, 45.7 percent more aptitude tests, and 3.8 percent more signed-up students than the ''unbeatable'' control. My ad was retested in Family Weekly *against the old control and it did even better: 31.7 percent more coupons, 32.7 percent more tests, 28.6 percent more sign-ups!*

After some additional refinements, the final version outpulled the original control by a cumulative total of 66.1 percent more inquiries, 73.9 percent more aptitude tests, and 59.9 percent more signed-up students.

Their next step was to turn the winning ad into a letter, word for word, and mail it. The headline became the envelope caption, the offer was printed in reverse in a box on the envelope, the ad's subhead was turned into a Johnson Box, and—except for the ''Dear Friend'' and sign-off—it was 100 percent ad copy. The ad coupon became the order card.

By that time, it had gotten to be 1977. Both the ad and the direct mail package have been control ever since. This copy also runs in package inserts,

The Institute of Children's Literature®
93 Long Ridge Road, West Redding, Connecticut 06896-0811

Alvin Tresselt
Dean of Faculty

Writing for children is the perfect way to begin.

Your ideas come right out of your own experience. And while it's still a challenge, it's probably the straightest possible line between you and publication -- if you're qualified to seek the success this rewarding field offers.

Read on and find out how to get your writing aptitude tested and evaluated -- free of any cost or obligation!

Dear Friend:

If you want to write and get published, I can't think of a better way to do it than writing books and stories for children and teenagers. Ideas flow naturally right out of your own life.

While it's still a challenge, the odds of getting that first unforgettable check from a juvenile publisher are better than they are from just about any other kind of publisher I know.

Later on, you may get other checks from other publishers. But right now, the object is to begin -- to break into print -- to learn the feeling of writing and selling your work and seeing your name in type. After that, you can decide if you want your writing to take another direction.

But after 30 years of editing, publishing, and teaching (and 53 books of my own) I can tell you this: You'll go a long way before you discover anything as rewarding as writing for children.

Your words will never sound as sweet as they do from the lips of a child reading your books and stories. And the joy of creating books and stories that truly reach young people is an experience you'll never have anywhere else.

The soaring children's market

But, that's not all. The financial rewards go far beyond most people's expectations because there's a surprisingly big market out there for writers who are trained to "tap" it. Over $1 billion worth of children's books are purchased every year and some 4,000 different titles share in this bonanza -- many by new authors.

Of approximately 500 publishers of books related to children, over 300 of them welcome manuscripts from aspiring writers. And more than 400 magazines rely on freelancers to fill their issues. You can imagine how much writing that takes!

Yet two big questions bedevil nearly every would-be writer...

(1) "Am I really qualified?" and (2) "How can I get started?"

"Am I really qualified?"

This is our definition of a "qualified person": It's someone with an aptitude for writing who can take constructive criticism, learn from it, and turn it into a professional performance. That's the only kind of person we're looking for at the Institute of Children's Literature. The reasons are simple: Our reputation is built on success, and if prospective students don't have the aptitude it takes, we probably can't help them. And we tell them so. It's only fair to both of us.

To help us spot potential authors, we've developed a revealing test for writing aptitude. It's free, and we don't charge for our evaluation. But no one gets into the Institute without passing it.

Those who pass and enroll receive our promise:

You will complete at least one manuscript ready to submit to a publisher by the time you finish the Course.

I've learned a lot about writing for children and I love it. Now I'm passing my knowledge on to my students so they can profit from what I've learned. When I'm not writing my own books, I spend my time at the Institute, a children's literature workshop for new writers that does one thing and does it better than any other educational institution I know of: It trains qualified people to write for the young reader.

Learn at your own pace

This is the way I work with my students, and my fellow instructors -- all of whom are published writers or seasoned editors -- work more or less the same way:

- When you're ready -- at your own time and your own pace -- you send your assignment to me.
- I read it and reread it to get everything out of it you've put into it.
- Then I edit your assignment just the way a publishing house editor would -- if he had the time.
- I return it along with a detailed letter explaining my comments. I tell you what your strong points are, what your weaknesses are, and just what you can do to improve.

It's a matter of push and pull. You push and I pull and between us both, you learn to write.

The proof of the pudding

This method really works. I wouldn't spend five minutes at it if it didn't. The proof of the pudding is that some of our students break into print even before they finish the Course.

"My how-to article that sold to 4-H Magazine for $75 was my rewrite of a Course assignment," says Jeanne Shoemaker, Birmingham, AL. "My beloved instructor has made this Course one of the highlights of my adult life!"

"Most importantly, the Course has allowed me to explore my creative writing skills without committing myself to a strict classroom environment with immediate deadlines and meeting schedules," reports Jeanne Nickerson, Washington, DC. "I needed the flexibility of a correspondence course and I have enjoyed dealing on a one-to-one basis with my instructor."

" -- my dream come true!"

"The thing that gives me the most satisfaction," writes Brandy S. Wells, Greensboro, MD, "is the idea that my story will be read by 150,000 Sunday school children -- my dream come true."

"Seeing my story in print, and knowing that some child out there is reading it and maybe enjoying what I have to say is all the reward I'll ever want," says Win Simpson, New Providence, NJ.

Free Writing Aptitude Test offered

To find qualified men and women with an aptitude for writing, the Faculty and Consultants of The Institute have prepared an intriguing Aptitude Test. It is offered free and will be professionally evaluated at no cost to you.

You'll also receive our free 28-page illustrated brochure describing our Course, Faculty, and the current market for children's literature. If you demonstrate a true aptitude for writing, you will be eligible to enroll. But that's up to you.

Just sign and return the enclosed reply card. Do it now before you forget it. It does not obligate you in any way.

Sincerely,

Alvin Tresselt

Alvin Tresselt

P.S. If you teach or write professionally, please turn page.

The 3-page letter, printed on an 11″ × 17″ sheet. On the bottom of the back page is the small notice to teachers and professional writers.

WHAT STUDENTS SAY (continued)

"I danced, cried, whooped and just about hugged everybody that didn't run and hide. How nice that a manuscript left my house and never returned. Who would have imagined a story on its first time out would be purchased?

"Thank you for making ICL available at such a reasonable price. It has helped me unlock the door to the dreamland I thought I could never enter. You can't put a nack in a person, but you can draw it out."

Peggy Adams, Oklahoma City, OK

"The material I sold was my Assignment #2 in your Course.

"The editor added, 'We will also be happy to receive additional manuscripts you would like to send us for consideration. Keep writing!'"

W.J. Holmes, Jr., Crossville, TN

"After rewriting Assignment #3 according to my instructor's suggestions...*The Friend* accepted it...I will shortly receive a check for $84.00! Think of that!"

Annabelle Sumera, Birmingham, MI

"My story sold the very first time I submitted it. I give the credit for the sale to my instructor...I submitted it to *Probe* magazine under her direction after redoing it using her suggestions.

"I now have seven stories out in the marketplace, and one I just received back with suggestions for resubmittal. I am on top of the clouds and I plan to stay there."

Charles Gillenwater, Coral Springs, FL

"My first article was accepted. The second was turned down. Then the 3rd and 4th were accepted. I've made $145.00 now and I'm *so* thankful."

Debbie J. Sharpe, Ketchikan, AK

"I don't know which felt nicer—seeing that check with my name on it, or seeing my name under the story title in the magazine. I do know this; it's an unbeatable combination! Thanks for everything!"

Cari Koerner, Bethany, CA

"Your Course has helped me a great deal to organize my work, to write regularly, and to locate markets for my work. My library does not stock your market guides; they should! The guides are the best I've seen for the serious children's writer."

Rinda M. Byers

"My first submission to *Highlights for Children* was accepted.

"I have gone from being the Institute's number one skeptic to number one fan. I highly recommend the Course."

Marian Costello, Arlington Hts., IL

"After I get my check from *Ranger Rick* I will probably have made back all the money I spent taking the Course..."

Elaine Ostrander, Corpus Christi, TX

"...the Course was excellent in teaching me the who, what, when, where, why, and how as well as the do's and don'ts of writing, querying, and submitting. My instructor was positive, supportive, and caring about my writing efforts."

Susan M. Winstead, Augusta, GA

"It's been a rich, rewarding personal experience for me. My first book–'Peel, the Extraordinary Elephant'–and a series of magazine articles were published in 1985. People say I'm lucky. I say, the harder you work, the luckier you get. Special thanks to my instructor and all of you at the Institute...you make learning fun! I will continue to recommend your outstanding program to 'could-be' writers."

Susan Joyce (Horowitz), Lincoln City, OR

"Most importantly, the Course has allowed me to explore my creative writing skills without committing myself to a strict classroom environment with immediate deadlines and meeting schedules. I needed the flexibility which a correspondence course provided, and I have enjoyed dealing on a one-to-one basis with my instructor."

Jeanne Nickerson, Washington, D.C.

"The time I spent working on my Course with the Institute was special. I looked forward to the feedback it provided and valued the fact that someone else was finally willing to help me get through the problems I was pouring my sweat and blood into. None of the problems were easy to solve but with my instructor's help, they were at least solvable.

"In short, the Course is worth the money. It provides you a shortcut through the long haul."

Mike Allen, Elizabethtown, KY

"Seeing my story in print, and knowing that some child out there is reading it and maybe enjoying what I have to say is all the reward I'll ever want."

Win Simpson, New Providence, NJ

IMPORTANT NOTICE FOR TEACHERS AND PROFESSIONAL WRITERS

TAX DEDUCTIBILITY The Internal Revenue Code permits the deduction as a business expense of tuition payments for education if it is designed to improve one's skills in the conduct of a trade or business. Accordingly, individuals such as professional writers, teachers, and others whose business skills are enhanced by the writing techniques developed in our Course may qualify for a tax deduction. You should consult your tax advisor to determine if a deduction of our tuition would be available in your particular case.

EDUCATIONAL CREDIT Educational credit may be granted at the discretion of your local school board or, if you are currently matriculated in a degree program, by the registrar of your college or university. We will be happy to forward on request any required information on content and hours for submission to your board or college.

Approved by the Connecticut Commissioner of Education

9890A

Welcome to the Institute

IN 1969, A GROUP OF WRITERS AND EDITORS of children's literature met in New York to work out the final details of a Course in writing for children and teenagers. It was designed to offer the finest instruction available, and since it was conceived as "a workshop without walls," it would be open to aspiring writers everywhere—provided they could demonstrate an aptitude for writing.

It was named "the Institute of Children's Literature," and dedicated to the development of superior writing for young readers.

The founding group of published writers and seasoned editors knew the agony of rejection as well as the chronic frustration of finding publishable material and they felt that many of their "hard knocks" could have been avoided with expert guidance. They wanted to give beginners the benefit of their hard-won knowledge and experience and school them in the special skills they themselves used to win success. If they could make their dream a reality, the Institute would enrich the entire field of children's literature—and children.

The Institute of Children's Literature, founded in 1969, is the *Alma Mater* of more than 3,000 published students and writers.

The cornerstone of the Course that has evolved through a series of refinements and enrichments since 1969 is its one-on-one method of teaching: each student is assigned his own instructor—a published writer or experienced editor—and they work together until the student completes the Course and produces a minimum of one professional-quality manuscript suitable for publication. This pairing of a beginner with an accomplished instructor—the classic master-apprentice relationship—gives aspiring authors the finest training available anywhere.

The results have been remarkable! In less than 20 years, students and graduates of the Institute have published more than 5,000 books, stories and articles!

The Institute also encourages its faculty to write and publish, lecture, and conduct and participate in writer's workshops so that by enriching themselves as writers and editors, they will pass on ever-richer insights to their students. The faculty has compiled a record of more than 1249 published books and 10,700 stories and articles—a record unmatched by any writing faculty in the world!

The remarkable success of the Institute and the students who complete its now-famous Course of one-on-one instruction is measured in various ways. For many students, publication is the yardstick of success. For others, it is the gratifying power they feel in being able to communicate in writing more effectively than they ever thought possible. Still others use their skills in business or professional life, and some pursue their lifelong dream of writing a family history. In the words of one student, "Truly, the Institute with its wealth of teaching methods and materials, and my instructor, have both contributed much toward making this one of the most exciting adventures of my life."

Whatever your writing objective may be, if you pass our Writer's Aptitude Test and enroll in the Course, we will help you achieve it.

This is our promise: *You will complete at least one manuscript suitable to submit to a publisher by the time you finish the Course.*

THE FACULTY

Alvin Tresselt

Teri Martini

Rubie Saunders

Patricia Windsor

THE INSTITUTE OF CHILDREN'S LITERATURE has a large faculty of published writers and seasoned editors with national reputations. They have worked for virtually every publisher of children's literature in America as well as *Time, Newsweek, Woman's Day, Reader's Digest, National Geographic, Smithsonian* and hundreds of other publications. Following are a few of these outstanding instructors.

Alvin Tresselt is our Dean of Faculty. His 53 books for young readers have sold over two million copies. He is the former Vice President and Executive Editor of Parents' Magazine Press, a past editor of *Humpty Dumpty's Magazine for Little Children* and has served on the Board of Directors of the prestigious Author's Guild.

Teri Martini is a brilliantly successful example of a school teacher-turned-writer-turned-writing instructor. She has published a wide range of fiction and non-fiction in both the adult and juvenile markets including romances, histories, gothic novels, short stories and articles. Teri is a guiding light at the Institute of Children's Literature: her students have already sold more stories, books and articles for children and adults than she has!

Rubie Saunders has nearly 30 years of editing experience, most recently as Editorial Director of *Children's Digest, Humpty Dumpty's* and *Young Miss*. Ms. Saunders is also the author of 12 books and over 150 magazine stories and articles for young people.

Patricia Windsor's seven books have been published in this country and abroad, and in 1986 her writing career reached a new pinnacle when she was awarded an Edgar—the highest award given by the Mystery Writers Association of America—for *The Sandman's Eye*. She has also written 17 short stories for young adults.

The Institute's prolific faculty has published over 1,249 books and 10,700 stories and articles for children and young adults. As instructors, they have helped over 3,000 of the Institute's students and graduates become published authors. We are proud of the contributions to the field of children's literature made by our faculty and students.

Because writing is a very personal endeavor, we believe that the teaching of writing must be tailored to your individual needs. That is why you will have your own personal instructor to guide you, individually, throughout the Course.

That personal guidance is, perhaps, the greatest single value our Course offers the beginning writer: the experience and judgment of a personal instructor who is a published author or seasoned editor with substantial credits—a true professional who knows the publishing standards that must be met, knows your aspirations, and knows the market for which you are writing.

THE COURSE

THE INSTITUTE OFFERS A MULTIPLE-assignment Course in writing for children and teenagers to those aspiring authors who pass our Writing Aptitude Test. You train under the personal guidance of one of our experienced faculty members who works with you throughout the Course. You begin writing immediately. You send your manuscripts to your instructor who reads, and rereads them, before editing your work and preparing his critique. Then your instructor returns your edited assignment with a detailed personal letter which explains his editorial suggestions and criticisms. This one-on-one relationship between student and instructor is the cornerstone of the Institute's unique Course.

The faculty and staff at the Institute have developed a 400-page Course Manual and the supplementary materials used in the Course. Selected textbooks and our comprehensive and exclusive two-volume, 622-page market guide to children's book and magazine publishers are also supplied at no additional cost. We firmly believe it is our job to teach our students how to write and—at the same time—how to go about selling what they have written. As a result, the majority of student sales are made to markets listed in our Guides, many of them recommended by instructors.

Your instructor will show you how to use this exclusive two-volume 622-page guide to market your manuscripts.

WHAT STUDENTS SAY

Following is a selection of excerpts from the dozens of letters the Institute receives every month.

"The publisher's acceptance notice for my first story arrived on our 35th Wedding Anniversary. The pride in my husband's eyes was a sight to behold!"

Laura Lee Marques, PA

"I have taken a course at a local university which would not begin to compare with the information in your textbook and the outside reading you include in the Course."

Sheila D. Brown, IN

"The Course gave me the confidence, and *Ebony Jr.* bought the story for $125. The money was great, but nothing could compare with the thrill of seeing my own story in print."

Thomas Lee, MD

"Thanks to your Course I not only know how to write, prepare, and produce a suitable manuscript, but most importantly, I know how to get published..."

James A. Worth, Ventnor City, NJ

"...although the Course is aimed specifically at writing for children, the basic values of the Course will serve any writer..."

V.L. Townley, Abilene, TX

"The thing that gives me the most satisfaction, is the idea that my story will be read by 150,000 Sunday School children—my dream come true."

Brandy S. Wells, Greensboro, MD

"...Congratulations on giving me the background and, most importantly, the self-confidence to write the article and send it in. The article I sold to *Ranger Rick* for $350 was written for Assignment #9. Thanks to you, and me, I am now a paid-and-soon-to-be-published writer. We did it!"

Judy O'Rourke, Madison, GA

"I am delighted about the publication of my children's book 'The Adventures of Bad Sam.'

"The first check I received was for a thousand dollars, with a promise of more to come."

Raz Autry, Raeford, NC

"The Institute gave me the edge I needed to become a published writer."

Mary Sue Seymour, Heuvelton, NY

"Assignment #2 sold the very first time I sent it out. I was so excited, I began to cry. I ran back and told the postmistress, 'They bought my story! I *am* a writer!'"

Diane H. Watts, Mountainair, NM

"The amount of money is small but the feeling of accomplishment is at least a million dollars high. Seeing something I wrote in print, having my peers comment on it, knowing that 20,000 members all over the world, will receive a copy of it and getting paid as well—what a giant boost to the ego!"

Lafern E. Porter, Detroit, MI

The 1-color brochure, printed on an $8^1/_2'' \times 13''$ sheet.

To help us spot potential authors, we've developed a revealing test for writing aptitude. It's free, and we don't charge for our evaluation. But no one gets into the Institute without passing it. Those who pass and enroll receive our promise: You will complete at least one manuscript suitable to submit to a publisher by the time you finish the course.

Alvin Tresselt, *Dean of Faculty*

Approved by the Connecticut Commissioner of Education

DETACH AND MAIL

Dear Mr. Tresselt:

I am interested in your program to help new writers get started. Please send me your free Writing Aptitude Test and 28-page illustrated brochure describing the Institute, its Course, Faculty and the current market for children's literature.

I understand that if I demonstrate a true aptitude for writing I will be eligible to enroll. I also understand that I am under no obligation whatsoever and I have your assurance that no salesman will visit.

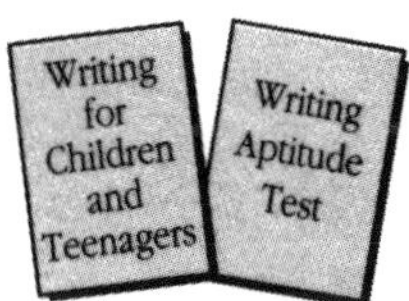

Get both FREE

Circle one: **Mr. Mrs. Ms. Miss** ____________________

Please Sign Above

LH8

JOAN
PO BOX
DERRY NH 03038

LJ7

Place Stamp Here

Institute of Children's Literature
93 Long Ridge Road
West Redding, Connecticut 06896-1100

The reply device and reply envelope. This is one of the few reply envelopes that force respondents to use their own first-class stamp. Failing to pay return postage can hurt up-front results; but anyone who is willing to pony up cash for a stamp is more than a tire kicker and more likely to enroll in the course.

statement stuffers, supermarket take-ones, and elsewhere. Copy cuts and other adjustments are sometimes necessary because of the formats of these media. The testimonials of current students replace older students on a regular basis, a few facts and figures have to be updated periodically, and the type style and illustrations have changed over the years, but the basic copy is unchanged.

Quite a few writers have taken a crack at this copy, but most efforts have fallen far short. I've tried and come close, but not close enough; my original copy is still king—for now.

One final word: every direct marketing pro knows there's no such thing as an unbeatable ad or package or commercial. There are only temporary winners.

18

Memberships and Merchandise

One good reason to personalize a mailing is the inclusion of a temporary membership card, such as the one found in Pete Gelb's effort for *Audubon* or Robert Haydon Jones's Mobil Auto Club mailing described later in this chapter.

The two mailings that follow—Sol Blumenfeld's effort for CompuServe and Robert Haydon Jones's Mobil Auto Club effort—both employ this technique. The reason behind the temporary membership card is somewhat akin to Tony Arau's token philosophy (see Chapter 12), an attention-getting device that appears to be of value. Like Walter Weintz's penny token, the temporary membership card is a hot potato—you have to do something with it. In this case, instead of using it to order the product, you retain it, presumably in a safe place.

CompuServe

CompuServe is an electronic supermarket, offering everything from business, academic, health, and personal information; news; weather; travel and shopping services; *Consumer Reports* product ratings; movie reviews; and games.

The cost of all these services sounds like a pittance: $25.00; and for that, you receive a series of premiums that would cost far more than that if bought at retail. Throughout the mailing, Sol Blumenfeld hypes the many benefits.

On the last page of the four-page letter he alludes to additional costs:

Your CompuServe membership and everything listed above are yours for $25.00 (plus postage and handling of the kit). Your initial payment entitles you to lifetime membership and access while your account is in good standing. CompuServe will charge you only for use you make of its facilities plus a minimal monthly $1.50 membership support fee (after your third month of membership).

To find out the bottom line—how much the so-called use charges are—you are forced to read the entire mailing and go through all four folds of the circular. Finally, on the last fold-out gatefold panel of the circular is the per-hour fee structure. Blumenfeld has illustrated the technique Axel Andersson propounded in the previous chapter: get prospects excited about the offer before hitting them with the bad news about money.

Sol Blumenfeld started in direct marketing as a copywriter with Wunderman, Ricotta & Kline, Inc., in 1961. After thirteen years at Rapp &

MAILER: CompuServe
PACKAGE: Preferred Acceptance/ $25 Cert.
PROJECT MGR.: Regina Brady
WRITER: Sol Blumenfeld
DESIGNER: Sol Blumenfeld
FIRST MAILED: 1987
The 6″ × 9″ 4-color envelope with 2 windows; one is for the address, and the second window—cutting into the eyes and brain of the profiled head—shows the name and membership number.

No. Y02A1

FREE USAGE

CompuServe
PREFERRED MEMBERSHIP CREDIT

$25.00

Please credit: Twenty-Five Dollars

To the account of: **************** 5-DIGIT 19103
Russell
Publications
St.
Philadelphia, PA 19103

APPROVED for FREE BRIEFCASE gift!

Please return this credit slip with your Acceptance form below. When your membership is processed, your account will automatically be credited for the amount shown and you may use it immediately. Membership credit for new members only.

EXPIRATION DATE: March 31, 1991

PREFERRED MEMBER

CompuServe
INFORMATION SERVICE CARD
P.O. Box 20212 / Columbus, Ohio 43220

Russell
Preferred Y02A1

Please keep this card confidential to prevent unauthorized use of your user I.D. and password.

DETACH AND SAVE the above service card for your reference.

Detach and return this Acceptance with Credit Slip above.

PREFERRED

CompuServe
New Order Department 815/P.O. Box 20212/Columbus, Ohio 43220

ACCEPTANCE OF MEMBERSHIP

☐ **Yes! I want access to CompuServe.** Please enter my name as a Preferred Member and rush me a Membership Kit. I understand that my one-time payment of $25.00* (plus $3.00 shipping and handling) gives me Lifetime Access to CompuServe while a member in good standing. I am enclosing my Preferred Credit Certificate entitling me to free usage for the amount shown. I understand that I may return the Membership Kit within 10 days for a full refund of the purchase price if I am not satisfied for any reason. Please include the free briefcase with my kit.

Y02A1

Include gift for--
Russell
Publications
St.
Philadelphia, PA 19103

(Please check)
☐ My check is enclosed.
Please charge my: ☐ MasterCard ☐ Visa ☐ American Express
Expiration Date: ___/___
Account Number:
My computer type is: ☐ IBM/compatible (3 1/2") ☐ IBM/compatible (5 1/4") ☐ Macintosh ☐ Apple ☐ Atari ☐ Commodore ☐ Other
Home Phone: (____)________
SIGNATURE:________________

*Plus applicable sales tax.

BS/1OC
Printed in USA

MEMBERSHIP INCLUDES:

Complete 263-Page Users Guide with binder and slipcase ($14.95 value).
Quick Reference Booklet to help you quickly access special areas of interest.
Confidential Signup Booklet containing your signup User ID and Secret Password.
Free monthly subscription to COMPUSERVE MAGAZINE, ($30.00 a year value).
Free $25.00 Online Usage Credit as your "get acquainted" introduction to CompuServe.
Lifetime Access to CompuServe for members in good standing.
Poster Size Wall Chart which depicts the organization of our services.

To order by phone, call toll free 1-800-368-3343. Ask for Operator 20.

After removing the contents of the envelope, the 4-color addressing piece and cardboard personalized membership card dominate the reader's attention. Next to the order form are a photograph of all the elements of the product and a list of benefits and value (users guide, $14.95; magazine, $30.00; free $25.00 on-line usage; lifetime access). Look to the right and you see all of this is yours for just $25.00 plus $3.00 shipping. At the bottom is one of the very few toll-free 800 numbers in this entire collection. CompuServe can afford the cost of an inbound 800 number—unlike books or magazines—because the yearly usage could amount to hundreds of dollars.

CompuServe

You're invited to discover how CompuServe can help you advance your career, manage your money more effectively, provide educational resources and entertainment for your family ... build a more productive and successful you.

Dear Friend,

If we're not mistaken, you're already quite familiar with computers and how to use them.

We believe you're also interested in ways your computer "know how" can help improve your life and the lives of those close to you.

That's why we invite you to accept Preferred Membership (under especially attractive terms) in CompuServe, the nation's largest electronic information service.

Simply return the enclosed Acceptance. It entitles you to enroll in CompuServe with lifetime access privileges, while a member-in-good-standing. And, if you act now, you also receive $25.00 WORTH OF COMPUSERVE USAGE ... FREE!

With CompuServe, you join over 610,000 computer-users nationwide, sharing a nearly endless source of online information, guidance, entertainment ... even companionship.

Open your own electronic "letter box" and communications center.

Exchange instant messages with friends, customers, colleagues across the street or across the country through CompuServe's Electronic Mail system. Upload and download documents and files. Tie into MCI Mail®, the Telex Network, or the fax system.

Tap into huge business, reference, professional and academic databases.

In just seconds, CompuServe brings up product ratings from Consumer Reports or full information on 3,000 colleges or universities or key articles from leading computer magazines.

Let the students in your family use IQuest℠ or the online edition of Grolier's® Academic American Encyclopedia for better schoolwork (and better grades).

Make smarter investment decisions.

Put the latest securities quotes on your screen. Look up facts like the experts do with data from MicroQuote II, Standard & Poor's, Value Line Data Base II, Disclosure II and more. Place your buy-sell orders with CompuServe's online brokerages.

Go pleasure shopping or bargain hunting in The Electronic Mall®, Shoppers Advantage and Software Exchange.

Get great buys on everything from teddy bears and specialty chocolate to spreadsheet programs, automotive accessories and even automobiles. No parking problems, sore feet, crushing crowds, heavy packages. You enjoy home delivery, while saving time and money!

Make travel arrangements (and save money, too!).

Information on airline fares, flight schedules, hotel accommodations are no further away than your computer keyboard. Just key in the Official Airlines Guide (OAG EE) or Travelshopper℠ or Eaasy Sabre. Make reservations, if you wish, at the same time.

Find help with your computing problems.

Just post your message on the electronic "bulletin board" devoted to your hardware (there are more than 60 of them from Apple® and Atari®, through IBM® and Kaypro®, to Macintosh®, Tandy® and Zenith®). You'll have an answer in no time.

Having trouble with WordPerfect®, Lotus® 1-2-3®, dBASE IV®, Turbo Pascal® or any other popular software? CompuServe gives you a direct link with those who developed the program. You can talk directly with Borland, Microsoft and over 100 others. They'll be pleased to hear from you.

Need a special accounting program, utility or other program? Just browse through CompuServe's enormous files of public domain software and copy those you want.

Get together with your kind of folks for good talk.

Do you build model airplanes? Love science fiction? Raise tropical fish? Follow auto racing? Like casino games? There are over 60 CompuServe special interest forums ranging from art and business to human sexuality and rock music (recently, for example, RockNet, a music forum, had Foreigner's Lou Gramm online ... Apple users met John Sculley ... science fiction buffs looked to the future with Isaac Asimov).

(Note: You can also join in a lively CB Simulator conversation with members from coast to coast and over 80 countries worldwide.)

Keep up with the news, weather, sports.

With access to the Associated Press, UPI, and other news wires, you learn of major events as fast as newspapers and TV stations. The Executive News Service gives you a competitive "edge" on the job with additional sources and an exclusive clipping service, which will extract and save items of interest to you. AP Sports covers your favorite sports. And weather reports, forecasts, and maps are there for the asking.

Join the fun and games any hour of any day.

What do you turn to when you want to unwind ...when the kids are bored ... when you want to "break the ice" at a get-together? Now, you can turn to CompuServe and trivia quizzes, role playing adventures, puzzles, etc. Or be an armchair warrior commanding your own squad of soldiers in SNIPER!™.

And there's more ... much more to CompuServe. You could spend weeks ... even months ... in the CompuServe network, continually discovering exciting and helpful areas of information (including how to use your new camera lens!).

You'll find CompuServe easy to use.

With so much data on call, you might think CompuServe requires special hardware and expertise.

Nothing could be further from the truth. The only equipment you need is a computer (yours will do just fine), telephone and a modem. With these simple tools plus a basic communications program, you're all set.

(If you do not yet have a modem and communications program, you'll find them available everywhere at reasonable prices.)

Navigating through CompuServe requires no special programming knowledge. Thanks to simple menus, command structures, and help provisions, you can start using it effectively the day it arrives.

You get a valuable Membership Kit.

When we receive your completed Acceptance form, we'll rush your CompuServe Membership Kit. It contains everything you need to gain access to CompuServe and get the most out of your membership.

- Access telephone numbers in your area which connect you to CompuServe facilities. Plus a special toll-free phone number for additional information. Note, over 85% of the country can access CompuServe with a local phone call.
- Your personal identification number and confidential password. For your protection, do not reveal your password to anyone.
- A copy of the CompuServe Information Service Users Guide including binder and slipcase. This comprehensive volume (Value: $14.95) details the structure of CompuServe and provides instructions on how to navigate the various services.
- A quick reference booklet which gives you a quick start in using the most popular CompuServe services and lists the most commonly used commands.
- A monthly subscription to *CompuServe Magazine* (Value: $30.00) is automatically yours when you start using CompuServe. In addition to software reviews, problem solving articles and new product announcements, each copy gives you valuable guidance on how to use and get the most out of your CompuServe membership.
- Poster Size Wall Chart which graphically depicts the organization of our services.

Lifetime membership for a small enrollment fee.

Your CompuServe membership and everything listed above are yours for $25.00 (plus postage and handling for the kit). Your initial payment entitles you to lifetime membership and access while your account is in good standing. CompuServe will charge you only for use you make of its facilities plus a minimal monthly $1.50 membership support fee (after your third month of membership.)

With its low enrollment cost, CompuServe is possibly the best buy in computing today. It will pay for itself the first time you download a program. And it could reward you hundreds of times over its price in savings, increased earnings, and other benefits for you and your family.

You get $25.00 in free usage if you join now.

As your welcome to CompuServe, you will receive $25.00 in free usage. That amounts to several hours of online time—plenty of time to explore and try new things. We've even arranged a special free online "tour" for new users like yourself. You will not be billed until you use up this initial credit.

The only limitation is that you return your Acceptance form or call 1-800-368-3343 (and ask for Operator 20) before the date indicated.

Don't miss out on this opportunity.

Act now! There is little risk or obligation. You can cancel CompuServe at any time or return your Membership Kit within 10 days for a full refund (less shipping and handling), if you are dissatisfied for any reason. Please note, you would be responsible for any online usage billing beyond your $25 in free usage. Don't wait! Invest in your future today.

Make a more successful you. Join CompuServe while these materials and this opportunity are in front of you.

Sincerely,

John E. Meier
Vice President,
Market Development and Services

P.S. Be sure to indicate your computer type on the order form so that you'll receive the membership kit designed for your computer. Plus, you're entitled to receive a free CompuServe briefcase as described on the enclosed flyer.

B8/1L
Printed in USA

The 4-page letter; an 11″ × 17″ sheet.

The 4-color brochure starts off 8¼″ × 8½″.

It opens to 16½″ wide.

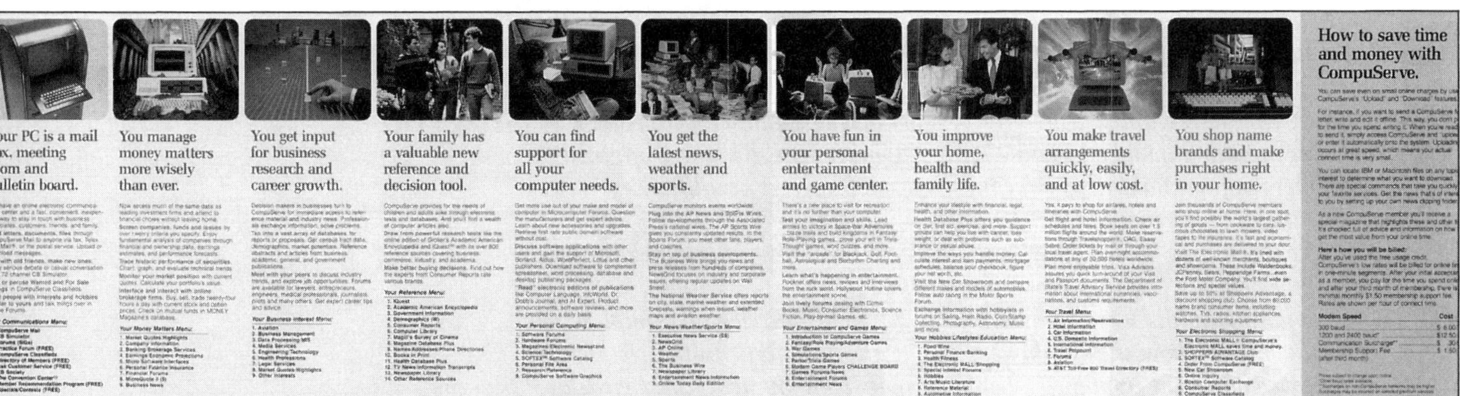

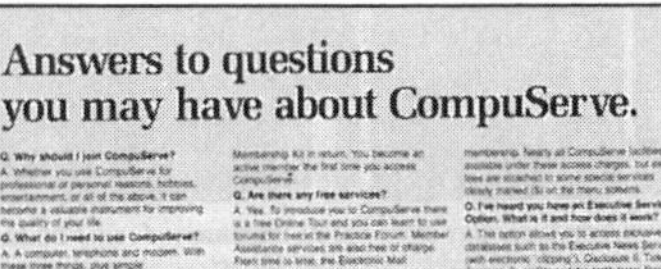

The 2 gatefolds open to reveal the inside spread, a whopping 32″ long.

The back panel with questions and answers about CompuServe.

Keep Important Issues
In Black & White.
CompuServe
Free soft-sided briefcase
with purchase of a
CompuServe Membership Kit.
Take issue with any matter, anywhere, with this bonus briefcase.
Made of durable, black, water-resistant canvas, it has a zippered front pocket with convenient storage areas. Inside, a document pocket keeps important papers safe, and closes with a velcro tab.
With padded handles and a comfortable shoulder strap, this is the perfect alternative briefcase. And it's yours absolutely free with your paid CompuServe membership. Just return the enclosed reply card in its postage-paid envelope, or to order direct, call 1-800-368-3343.
Reserve your briefcase today. And make an issue out of it.
Yours free with purchase.

The lift piece describing the premiums.

Collins—where he served as senior vice president and creative director—he briefly joined TLK Direct before going on his own in 1977. Other clients include Time-Life Books, MCI Telecommunications Corporations, Boardroom Reports, Columbia House, Merrill Lynch, Citicorp, and Dow Jones.

Sol Blumenfeld:

This particular CompuServe mailing was created very much in response to the marketing imperatives prevailing at the time.

CompuServe, until recently, was directed at the "technically proficient" market. They now wanted to impact a broader business market, using lists with both business and home addresses. The positioning was to make CompuServe seem more approachable and relevant to recipient careers and lifestyles.

The theme of the mailing was "success."

Photographically we led off with the attractive sweater-clad couple dividing their time between CompuServe and some Chablis.

Copy and graphics were both themed to a panoramic view of CompuServe applications and how they could very specifically contribute to the recipient's health, wealth, and happiness. Long copy, in both the letter and circular, spelled out literally dozens of potential benefits.

As in many of my mailings, I try to use involvement (membership card, coupon), incentives ($25.00 free on-line time) and urgency (with a cutoff date).

More abstractly, I wanted this package to be a "hot potato" for individuals tuned into computing . . . creating enough tension to overcome inertia. That it did . . . beating the control handily, with individual list response improvements starting at 30 percent and going up to about 140 percent.

This mailing has run its course and CompuServe presently has a new control again answering some very new marketing imperatives.

Mobil Auto Club

In his article "The Direct Mail Package" (Chapter 4), Malcolm Decker suggests that black is not the ideal color for direct mail. Rules are made to be broken, and Robert Haydon Jones has broken them not only with a black envelope but also with a black "Instant Membership Card" that shows through a second window on the outside envelope.

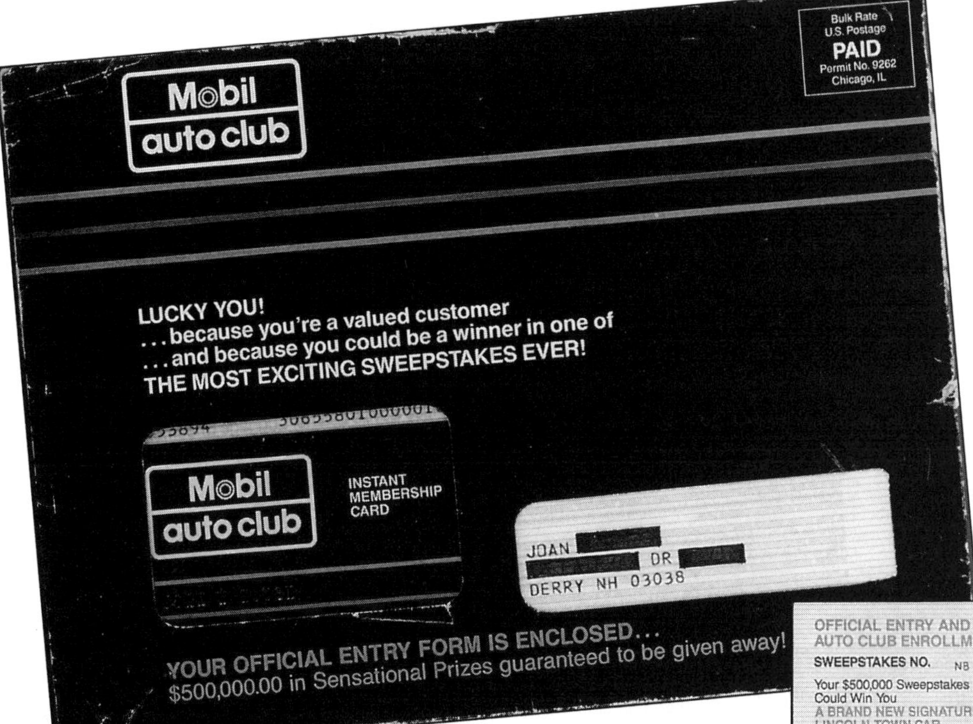

MAILER: Mobil Auto Club
PACKAGE: Instant Card/Sweeps
PROJECT MGR.: Cynthia Morgan
WRITER: Robert Haydon Jones
DESIGNER: Harold Strauss
FIRST MAILED: 1987
A dramatic black 6″ × 9″ outside envelope with narrow red, purple, and blue stripes and reversed out copy. The address window is at right; at left is a large window with an embossed "Instant Membership Card" showing through. Unlike the CompuCard membership card, this one is heavy plastic and, like Visa, connotes substance. Shown at right is the card carrier/order form. Below, a personalized letter begins.

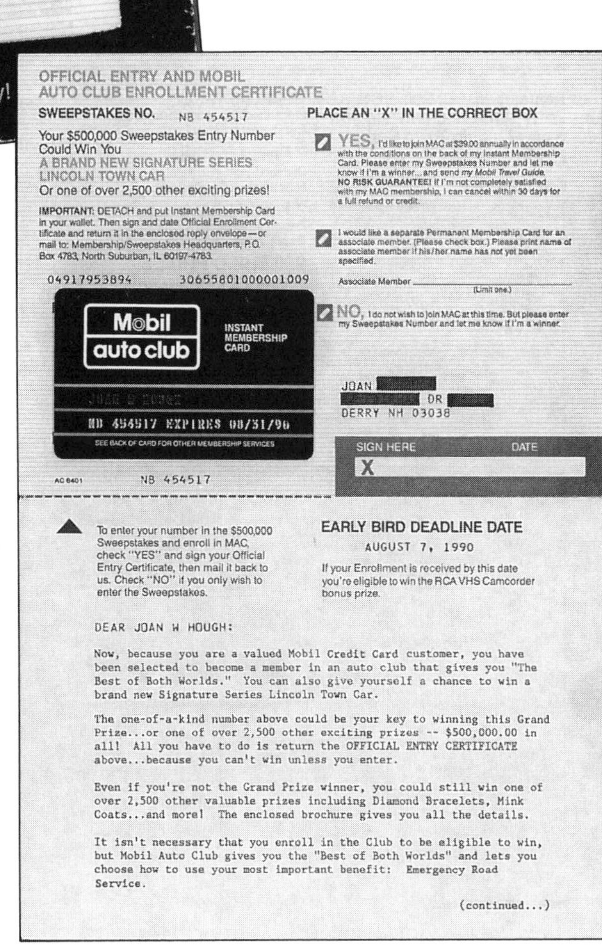

OFFICIAL ENTRY AND MOBIL
AUTO CLUB ENROLLMENT CERTIFICATE

SWEEPSTAKES NO. NB 454517

Your $500,000 Sweepstakes Entry Number Could Win You
A BRAND NEW SIGNATURE SERIES LINCOLN TOWN CAR
Or one of over 2,500 other exciting prizes!

IMPORTANT: DETACH and put Instant Membership Card in your wallet. Then sign and date Official Enrollment Certificate and return it in the enclosed reply envelope—or mail to: Membership/Sweepstakes Headquarters, P.O. Box 4783, North Suburban, IL 60197-4783.

04917953894 30655801000001009

Mobil auto club INSTANT MEMBERSHIP CARD

454517 EXPIRES 08/31/90

SEE BACK OF CARD FOR OTHER MEMBERSHIP SERVICES

AC 6401 NB 454517

PLACE AN "X" IN THE CORRECT BOX

YES, I'd like to join MAC at $39.00 annually in accordance with the conditions on the back of my Instant Membership Card. Please enter my Sweepstakes Number and let me know if I'm a winner...and send *my Mobil Travel Guide*. NO RISK GUARANTEE! If I'm not completely satisfied with my MAC membership, I can cancel within 30 days for a full refund or credit.

I would like a separate Permanent Membership Card for an associate member. (Please check box.) Please print name of associate member if his/her name has not yet been specified.

Associate Member ____________ (Limit one.)

NO, I do not wish to join MAC at this time. But please enter my Sweepstakes Number and let me know if I'm a winner.

JOAN
DR
DERRY NH 03038

SIGN HERE X DATE

To enter your number in the $500,000 Sweepstakes and enroll in MAC, check "YES" and sign your Official Entry Certificate, then mail it back to us. Check "NO" if you only wish to enter the Sweepstakes.

EARLY BIRD DEADLINE DATE
AUGUST 7, 1990

If your Enrollment is received by this date you're eligible to win the RCA VHS Camcorder bonus prize.

DEAR JOAN W HOUGH:

Now, because you are a valued Mobil Credit Card customer, you have been selected to become a member in an auto club that gives you "The Best of Both Worlds." You can also give yourself a chance to win a brand new Signature Series Lincoln Town Car.

The one-of-a-kind number above could be your key to winning this Grand Prize...or one of over 2,500 other exciting prizes -- $500,000.00 in all! All you have to do is return the OFFICIAL ENTRY CERTIFICATE above...because you can't win unless you enter.

Even if you're not the Grand Prize winner, you could still win one of over 2,500 other valuable prizes including Diamond Bracelets, Mink Coats...and more! The enclosed brochure gives you all the details.

It isn't necessary that you enroll in the Club to be eligible to win, but Mobil Auto Club gives you the "Best of Both Worlds" and lets you choose how to use your most important benefit: Emergency Road Service.

(continued...)

-2-

MOBIL AUTO CLUB

This protection is the heart of any good auto club, but all auto clubs are not alike! As a member, you choose the kind of service that's best for you whenever you need help...car won't start, mechanical breakdown, out of gas, flat tire or accident.

24 HOUR SERVICE

You can call our 24-hour emergency dispatch service toll-free and we'll arrange to have help sent from the closest available facility. When the truck arrives, just show your membership card and sign for the service. We'll pay the service facility directly for all expenses covered by your Membership.

FREEDOM OF CHOICE

Or, if you prefer, call the service facility of your choice and we'll reimburse you for up to $70.00. You have complete freedom of choice.

Fortunately, you are already eligible for membership in our Club -- a club that's the envy of the others. And, as you'll see, we offer you so much more for the money. We offer you some truly impressive privileges.

AN AFFORDABLE AUTO CLUB

In fact, when you read the privileges of your membership, the natural thing to do is to wonder how on earth you can get all these unique benefits at such an astonishingly low cost -- literally pennies a day.

It's really quite simple. We created our Club as a service especially for conscientious drivers like you. We wanted to offer the best Auto Club protection in the nation at the lowest possible price.

That's one of the basic reasons for MAC's existence, and that's why we're better than other auto clubs you may have heard about or even joined. Here are some of the ways our Club treats you better:

When utilizing the reimbursement option of your road and tow benefit, you can call any garage, service station, repair shop, towing or wrecker service that you wish, and we'll reimburse you. So it stands to reason that you're better off with the widest possible choice of road service.

TOW WHERE YOU WANT TO GO

Another important difference: Most other clubs will tow only to their stations, in effect encouraging you to have repairs, body work, etc., done there. If you decide you want another repair shop to do the work, you may have to pay to be towed a second time. But we encourage you to call the shop you want. You save time and money, and avoid inconvenience and possible embarrassment.

NO MATTER WHOSE CAR YOU DRIVE

Yes, we're a true service. You'll be delighted by the difference. We'll cover you to the fullest extent of your membership for the delivery charges of emergency gasoline anywhere you need it, even your driveway ...we'll cover you for the servicing of snowbound vehicles...we'll cover you for the servicing of a vehicle that's disabled in any area that's regularly traveled. Any car you own, borrow or rent!

(continued...)

Some benefits may vary by state. Please see notes on back of the enrollment certificate and Instant Membership Card.

-3-

Compare what we offer with what you have now -- you'll switch to Mobil Auto Club!

STAY OUT OF JAIL CARD

As a member of Mobil Auto Club, you'll also enjoy peace of mind with up to $1,000.00 Arrest Bond and up to $10,000.00 Bail Service Protection. Should you be stopped for a traffic violation (other than driving while intoxicated, while under the influence of narcotics, without a valid operator's license or for a felony), your Membership Card could keep you or your associate member from spending a night in jail.

AS OFTEN AS YOU WANT

If you're planning a vacation or a business trip, we'll supply you with the maps and routing you need -- as often as you need them -- as a privilege of membership. We will provide you with a personally routed Tour Kit showing the best route with full-color, easy-to-follow maps.

Your Custom Tour Kit includes state-by-state maps, along with local points of interests; hunting, fishing and traffic regulations; state park and camping guides; and a mileage guide. All this -- as often as you request it -- as a benefit of membership.

And you can request this information at any hour of the day or night simply by calling our toll-free help line phone number! You can also call for instant weather reports that cover every major U.S. city.

If you've ever left your keys locked in your car, you know how frustrating -- and expensive -- it can be to get back in. As a Mobil Auto Club member, you'll be reimbursed up to $60.00 for a locksmith's service call to open the vehicle.

AD&D PROTECTION

What's more, with us you get Accidental Death and Dismemberment protection as a member benefit. We provide $5,000.00 all-risk coverage that protects you 24 hours a day, anywhere in the world. You can even split this protection with your spouse. (Not available to residents of NC or to associate members.)

Other clubs typically limit their coverage to accidents in cars or "common carriers" -- buses, trains, planes, etc. MAC covers you for any type of accident -- on the job, in your car, even in your home!

EMERGENCY TRAVEL EXPENSES

If you should have a collision that disables your car more than 50 miles from home, we'll reimburse you up to $1,000.00 for expenses incurred within 72 hours of the accident -- such as motel accommodations, meals, car rentals or commercial transportation. This extra protection could save your vacation from turning into a nightmare!

YOU CHOOSE, WE PAY

You'll also be entitled to up to $1,000.00 in Legal Defense Reimbursement for traffic violations, should you want to be defended in court. You choose your attorney and we reimburse you for his fee according to a payment schedule in your Member's Handbook.

(continued...)

-4-

SAVE ON YOUR NEXT NEW CAR

Save up to $1,000.00 off the sticker price on the purchase of your next new car. MAC's optional, low-cost New Car Pricing Service gives you confidential pricing information on most current-model cars, vans and pickup trucks.* Armed with this information, you can make the best deal at the lowest possible price for the new vehicle you really want.

ACCIDENT AMBULANCE EXPENSE

And, if you and/or your associate member are driving anywhere in the world, and should require an ambulance due to a motor vehicle accident, we'll reimburse you up to $50.00 each for ambulance charges. That includes any motor vehicle accident -- in any car you own, borrow or rent.

STOP THEFT!

Plus, there are many more membership features: What if a thief steals your car? We will pay a reward totaling $5,000.00 for information leading to the arrest and conviction of the guilty party. In addition, we will send you a Theft Reward Sticker to place on your car. This extra measure of protection serves as a warning to potential thieves.

To give you even more protection, we'll reimburse you up to $500.00 for attorney's fees* if you take legal action against uninsured motorists. We also pay a reward totaling $1,000.00 (or $5,000.00 if death of member or associate member occurs) for information leading to the arrest and conviction of the hit-and-run driver who injures you or your associate member, or who damages the car you own.

GET TRAVELERS CHEQUES FROM HOME

Mobil Auto Club could help protect your money too -- with BankAmerica Travelers Cheques. You can order your Travelers Cheques through our Club Headquarters, and they'll be delivered directly to you (via certified mail) to insure safety. Fee? Not a penny for Mobil Auto Club members.

CAR AND TRUCK RENTAL DISCOUNTS PLUS OTHER SAVINGS

As a member of Mobil Auto Club, you're entitled to significant car and truck rental discounts at National, Hertz, Avis and Hertz/Penske ...plus up to 40% discounts at hundreds of fine hotels and motels nationwide...plus special discount prices available through MAC's Film Processing Service. So your membership can pay for itself many times over through these special club discounts, even if you never have to use the motoring benefits.

What's the cost of membership in this remarkable Auto Club? That's the best news of all, since one of our goals is to offer more advantages at the lowest cost. Both you and your associate member can enjoy the benefits and services for less than 11 cents a day -- only $39.00 a year --billed annually on your Mobil credit card account. There's no initiation fee and no extra fee for your associate member (some clubs charge an extra $10.00 or more for these features).

On the first page of my letter there's an Instant Membership Card already made out in your name. If you want to become a member of Mobil Auto Club, sign it and place it in your wallet while waiting for your Permanent Membership Cards (one for you and one for your associate member) to arrive.

(continued...)

-5-

The whole package of Club benefits becomes effective on the date you receive your Permanent Membership Cards. In the meantime, from the moment we receive your Enrollment Certificate at Club Headquarters, your Instant Card offers you protection on all Club benefits except Arrest Bond and Accidental Death and Dismemberment protection.

NOW IS THE TIME!

As soon as you join MAC, a Member's Handbook will be mailed to you, which provides details on the simple and easy procedures for filing claims. But it's important that you act promptly so that you will receive your Handbook and your Permanent Membership Cards -- entitling you to all club benefits -- just as soon as possible.

So please enroll now, while you're thinking of it. And, if we receive your Enrollment Certificate before the sweepstakes closing date, we'll send you a current year's Mobil Travel Guide for your region, yours to keep as a free gift. It'll take but a few moments for you to join one of the finest Auto Club in the country. I know you'll enjoy being with us.

Sincerely,

W. B. Blackwell

W. B. Blackwell
President
Mobil Auto Club

P.S. If you don't mail your $500,000.00 SWEEPSTAKES entry, the prize that you might have won will go to someone else. That won't happen if you return the Official Entry Certificate in the envelope provided.

Some benefits may vary by state. Please see notes on back of the enrollment certificate and Instant Membership Card.

The letter continues on 4 individual nested sheets with red "handwritten" notes in the margins.

Don't drive another mile without MAC's "Best of Both Worlds" Emergency Road Service. Help is only a phone call away with the MAC emergency dispatch service. Or, call the service facility of your choice—we'll reimburse you up to $70.

Mail your enrollment card today.

AC 4305

Lift piece no. 1, printed in red, one side.

AC-5970-1
Mobil Travel Guide
Great Lakes
Yours as a member of the Mobil Auto Club... 1990 Mobil Travel Guide for your region
...and get a minimum of $150 in money-saving discount coupons for popular sightseeing attractions, amusement parks and museums in your part of the country.
INCLUDES $150.00 OR MORE DISCOUNT COUPONS
Just mail in your Enrollment Certificate
and you'll have a 275+ page directory of motels, resorts, restaurants and points of interest. Another benefit of membership.
Your Mobil Travel Guide can save you time, money and gasoline
Make the most of every auto trip you take.
(see back for more details)

Read in detail about the benefits your Mobil Travel Guide will give you

Lists and rates a cross-section of food and lodging establishments in a wide price-range... choose the kinds of places you like and can afford.

Ratings: Food & Lodging

- ***** one of the best in the country
- **** outstanding—worth a special trip
- *** excellent
- ** very good
- * good, better than average;
- ✓ in addition an unusually good value, relatively inexpensive

- **Local points of interest and special events** listed city by city, town by town. It's an easy-to-use format. Just pick your spot and plan your fun—before you leave home. Save on admission fees with discount coupons that come with your Guide.
- **Maps, mileage and driving time** to help you plan a quick, direct, gas-saving route.
- **Vacation planning tips** to help make your travels go more smoothly and economically.
- **Car care recommendations** help you make sure your car is running safely and efficiently.
- **Coping with emergencies on the road**—your Mobil Travel Guide tells how to avoid some of the most common problems. But if you do get stalled or stuck, have a flat tire or run out of gas—even if you have an accident—the Mobil Auto Club is the best friend you can have. As a Mobil Auto Club Member, just call our toll-free Helpline and a dispatch operator will have help sent from the nearest participating facility. Or, if you prefer, call the station of your choice and MAC will reimburse you up to $70 for every emergency road service call. (See reference notes on back of enrollment form.)

Lift piece no. 2 shown front and back; it promises a Travel Guide with $150 worth of discount coupons.

PLACE STAMP HERE

Membership Services/Sweepstakes Headquarters
P.O. Box 4783
North Suburban, IL 60197-4783

ENCLOSE SWEEPSTAKES ENTRY FORM AND MAIL TODAY!

Don't miss this chance to be a winner in the exciting $500,000 SWEEPSTAKES!

Sign your Enrollment Certificate, enclose in this envelope and mail today!

The business reply envelope shown front and back—one of the very few that does not prepay postage. The reason: this is a sweepstakes mailing, and you never supply a business reply envelope with a sweepstakes, because everyone will enter without buying the product.

This effort just one of two sweepstakes in these seventy-one Million Dollar Mailings. Virtually all sweeps efforts urge people to enter the sweeps, even if they don't buy the product. Arithmetic has shown that the more nos you get, the more yeses (orders) you'll receive. For this reason, the incredible value of the prizes is hammered home along with the warning that you can't win if you don't enter . . . so, ENTER NOW!

Traditional sweepstakes efforts (*Reader's Digest*, Publishers Clearing House) jump up and down and scream and yell WIN! WIN! WIN! . . . PRIZES! PRIZES! PRIZES! . . . so loudly that it is difficult to find out what the offer really is. Many consumers believe that by ordering, they'll have a better chance at winning a prize, even though that isn't true in legitimate sweepstakes.

This effort for Auto Club is emphatically *not* a traditional sweeps. For example, the embossed plastic membership card is the same size and weight of a Visa or Mastercard, and as such, dominates the entry-enrollment form; since this form is the top half of page one of the letter, it also dominates the letter. Throughout the mailing, the benefits of membership in the club are emphasized; the prizes are almost an afterthought.

The rest of the letter is made up of four additional nested pages (individual pages, printed on one side only, folded and arranged in proper sequence). Notice the handwritten notes in the margin; Ted Kikoler talks about this technique as one of his twenty-six design tips in Chapter 5.

Robert Haydon Jones began his career in general advertising with David Ogilvy, serving as group head for Bristol Myers, General Foods, Zippo Lighters, British Travel, Rolls-Royce, and Cunard. As the youngest creative director in J. Walter Thompson's history, Jones directed creative and broadcast production for Pan Am, Ford, and Kodak. After serving as president of Interpublic Direct Response Marketing, he opened in 1974 his own creative shop, Robert Haydon Jones & Associates, where he has launched *Ms.* magazine, American Film Theatre, Xerox Learning Systems, Montgomery Ward Pre-Paid Legal Services Plan, Citytrust Money Market Account, and Frank Lewis Ruby Red Grapefruit.

ROBERT HAYDON JONES:

Thanks for your notice on the Axel Award on our package for the Auto Club and their direct marketing managers at the Signature Group.

I must confess that, at first, this very good news brought me down a peg. You see, what I remember most about this package is that it was nothing but hard slogging.

Frankly, of the hundreds of packages I've done over the years—in my mind's eye—this one was perhaps the least *''creative!''*

So, when ''Jones the Word'' here got noticed about this award—not for one of my oh-so-creative efforts—but rather for a project that almost literally required bib overalls and work boots—I had mixed emotions. My Ugly Duckling had become one of the Belles of the Ball!

Wake-up Calls don't often come with such a sugarcoat. And wake-up *is the bottom line for me on this. Where do I get off forgetting what this business is all about?*

It is not about ''Creativity.'' It is about response and sales and profits. That's precisely why I value the Axel Award over all the others.

To hammer out marketing and develop packages that make profits for my client. That's what my job description is. Ugly, long, short, ''creative,'' or ''dull''—who cares?

The Auto Club package was not so much created *as it was carefully* assembled—*mainly by my son, Evan Owen Jones, who is now a freelancer in his own right in Atlanta, and a number of Signature people, especially Paul Misniak.*

We looked over at least a decade of mail for Auto Clubs and determined that successful packages had certain factors in common. Briefly, the keys we saw were positioning, benefit priority, and practicality of usage.

We then set out to assemble an ''idea'' package along these lines. It was a lot easier said than done! In fact, it took us months *longer than usual to come to finish. By the time we dropped our test, I hated the bugger!*

Earl Weaver, the feisty baseball manager, has a line that sure seems to fit:

It's what you learn—after you know it all—that counts!''

You asked for comments on how I work. Here goes. I approach every assignment as if it were a launch. First I interrogate *the assignment. Often it is way off base—in terms of a practical business reality. There's precious little upside for yours truly—or my client—if that's so.*

Many Moons ago, I broke in with David Ogilvy [*D.O.*] *and his merry crew on the ''straight'' side of the biz as a writer-producer. D.O. was* (*and is*) *a* fanatic *about product and market knowledge. ''Know at least as much about the product as the client.'' That's D.O.'s war cry.*

I think he is dead right. Deep background is still the key for me. And, frankly, it is still the hardest *discipline of my craft to follow faithfully.*

But it's the linchpin for all good work. Without careful research, you may do well because you are clever—but even so, as far as I am concerned, you are indulging in the Original Amateur Hour!

One more thing. David Ogilvy keeps the most *important key to success on a sign that hangs above his desk. It reads:*

''Oh God, please give us smart *clients!''*

Gevalia Kaffe

The Gevalia Kaffe promotion is a til-forbid continuity series. Because it is a food offer, it was included in this group rather than in Chapter 14, which comprises books.

Mary Ann Donovan of Wunderman Worldwide:

First of all, Jane Walsh, the art director, and I, the copywriter, worked as a team from beginning to end—under the watchful eye of our creative director, Jim Infantino.

In 1985 we were asked to do a new Gevalia Kaffe campaign consisting of a print ad and a direct mail piece. (I have to talk about both, because they're inextricably linked since we did them at the same time.)

I was very pleased to get the assignment as I had recently come to Wunderman from a background in general advertising and had a lot of experience working on food accounts, which I've always loved.

I prepared by reading all the available research on coffee and studied the previous advertising. And we met with Account Management to make sure we all agreed on the strategy.

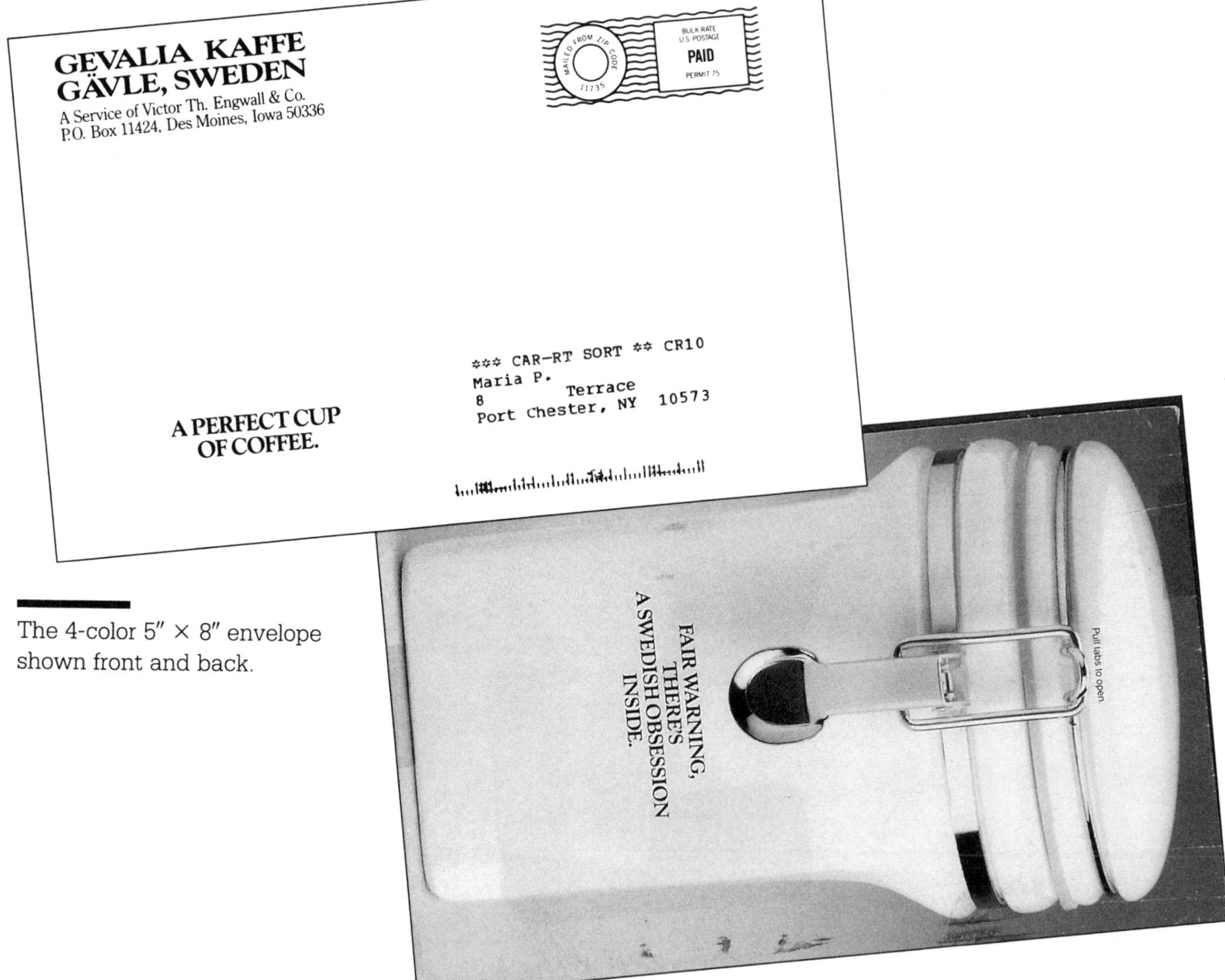

The 4-color 5″ × 8″ envelope shown front and back.

Then armed with a Creative Work Plan (a one-page Wunderman document listing the prospects, the competition, the problem the advertising must solve, the benefit, the reasons why, and the offer), Jane and I sat down in the same office and worked together day after day until we felt we had solved the problem and had headlines and layouts that were on strategy and that we really liked. Although she was the art director and I the writer, there was no rigid demarcation. We both came up with the ideas and sometimes she would think up a headline and I a visual.

This was our thinking as we went along. For the direct mail, we wanted to do a package that wasn't promotiony. We felt the product—a superb Swedish

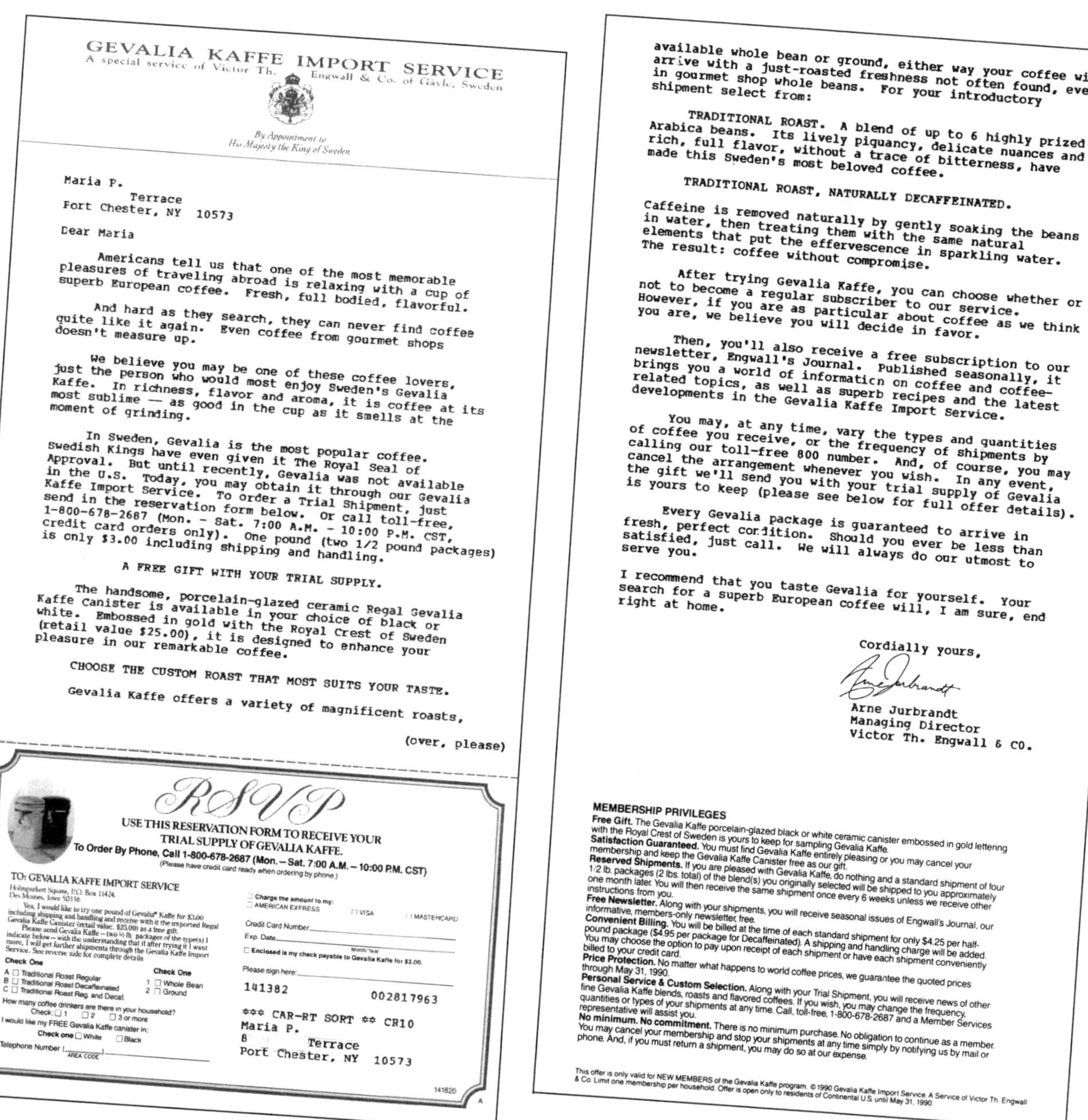

GEVALIA KAFFE IMPORT SERVICE
A special service of Victor Th. Engwall & Co. of Gavle, Sweden

By Appointment to His Majesty the King of Sweden

Maria P.
Terrace
Fort Chester, NY 10573

Dear Maria

Americans tell us that one of the most memorable pleasures of traveling abroad is relaxing with a cup of superb European coffee. Fresh, full bodied, flavorful.

And hard as they search, they can never find coffee quite like it again. Even coffee from gourmet shops doesn't measure up.

We believe you may be one of these coffee lovers, just the person who would most enjoy Sweden's Gevalia Kaffe. In richness, flavor and aroma, it is coffee at its most sublime — as good in the cup as it smells at the moment of grinding.

In Sweden, Gevalia is the most popular coffee. Swedish Kings have even given it The Royal Seal of Approval. But until recently, Gevalia was not available in the U.S. Today, you may obtain it through our Gevalia Kaffe Import Service. To order a Trial Shipment, just send in the reservation form below. Or call toll-free, 1-800-678-2687 (Mon. - Sat. 7:00 A.M. - 10:00 P.M. CST, credit card orders only). One pound (two 1/2 pound packages) is only $3.00 including shipping and handling.

A FREE GIFT WITH YOUR TRIAL SUPPLY.

The handsome, porcelain-glazed ceramic Regal Gevalia Kaffe Canister is available in your choice of black or white. Embossed in gold with the Royal Crest of Sweden (retail value $25.00), it is designed to enhance your pleasure in our remarkable coffee.

CHOOSE THE CUSTOM ROAST THAT MOST SUITS YOUR TASTE.

Gevalia Kaffe offers a variety of magnificent roasts,

(over, please)

RSVP

USE THIS RESERVATION FORM TO RECEIVE YOUR TRIAL SUPPLY OF GEVALIA KAFFE.

To Order By Phone, Call 1-800-678-2687 (Mon. – Sat. 7:00 A.M. – 10:00 P.M. CST)
(Please have credit card ready when ordering by phone.)

TO: GEVALIA KAFFE IMPORT SERVICE
Holmparken Square, P.O. Box 11424,
Des Moines, Iowa 50336

Yes, I would like to try one pound of Gevalia® Kaffe for $3.00 including shipping and handling and receive with it the imported Regal Gevalia Kaffe Canister (retail value: $25.00) as a free gift.

Please send Gevalia Kaffe – two ½ lb. packages of the type(s) I indicate below – with the understanding that if after trying it I want more, I will get further shipments through the Gevalia Kaffe Import Service. See reverse side for complete details.

Check One
A ☐ Traditional Roast Regular
B ☐ Traditional Roast Decaffeinated
C ☐ Traditional Roast Reg. and Decaf.

Check One
1 ☐ Whole Bean
2 ☐ Ground

How many coffee drinkers are there in your household?
Check: ☐ 1 ☐ 2 ☐ 3 or more

I would like my FREE Gevalia Kaffe canister in:
Check one ☐ White ☐ Black

Telephone Number (AREA CODE) ____

☐ Charge the amount to my:
☐ AMERICAN EXPRESS ☐ VISA ☐ MASTERCARD

Credit Card Number ____
Exp. Date ____ Month/Year

☐ Enclosed is my check payable to Gevalia Kaffe for $3.00.

Please sign here: ____

141382 002817963

*** CAR-RT SORT ** CR10
Maria P.
8 Terrace
Port Chester, NY 10573

141820

A

available whole bean or ground, either way your coffee will arrive with a just-roasted freshness not often found, even in gourmet shop whole beans. For your introductory shipment select from:

TRADITIONAL ROAST. A blend of up to 6 highly prized Arabica beans. Its lively piquancy, delicate nuances and rich, full flavor, without a trace of bitterness, have made this Sweden's most beloved coffee.

TRADITIONAL ROAST, NATURALLY DECAFFEINATED.

Caffeine is removed naturally by gently soaking the beans in water, then treating them with the same natural elements that put the effervescence in sparkling water. The result: coffee without compromise.

After trying Gevalia Kaffe, you can choose whether or not to become a regular subscriber to our service. However, if you are as particular about coffee as we think you are, we believe you will decide in favor.

Then, you'll also receive a free subscription to our newsletter, Engwall's Journal. Published seasonally, it brings you a world of information on coffee and coffee-related topics, as well as superb recipes and the latest developments in the Gevalia Kaffe Import Service.

You may, at any time, vary the types and quantities of coffee you receive, or the frequency of shipments by calling our toll-free 800 number. And, of course, you may cancel the arrangement whenever you wish. In any event, the gift we'll send you with your trial supply of Gevalia is yours to keep (please see below for full offer details).

Every Gevalia package is guaranteed to arrive in fresh, perfect condition. Should you ever be less than satisfied, just call. We will always do our utmost to serve you.

I recommend that you taste Gevalia for yourself. Your search for a superb European coffee will, I am sure, end right at home.

Cordially yours,

Arne Jurbrandt

Arne Jurbrandt
Managing Director
Victor Th. Engwall & CO.

MEMBERSHIP PRIVILEGES

Free Gift. The Gevalia Kaffe porcelain-glazed black or white ceramic canister embossed in gold lettering with the Royal Crest of Sweden is yours to keep for sampling Gevalia Kaffe.
Satisfaction Guaranteed. You must find Gevalia Kaffe entirely pleasing or you may cancel your membership and keep the Gevalia Kaffe Canister free as our gift.
Reserved Shipments. If you are pleased with Gevalia Kaffe, do nothing and a standard shipment of four 1/2 lb. packages (2 lbs. total) of the blend(s) you originally selected will be shipped to you approximately one month later. You will then receive the same shipment once every 6 weeks unless we receive other instructions from you.
Free Newsletter. Along with your shipments, you will receive seasonal issues of Engwall's Journal, our informative, members-only newsletter, free.
Convenient Billing. You will be billed at the time of each standard shipment for only $4.25 per half-pound package ($4.95 per package for Decaffeinated). A shipping and handling charge will be added. You may choose the option to pay upon receipt of each shipment or have each shipment conveniently billed to your credit card.
Price Protection. No matter what happens to world coffee prices, we guarantee the quoted prices through May 31, 1990.
Personal Service & Custom Selection. Along with your Trial Shipment, you will receive news of other fine Gevalia Kaffe blends, roasts and flavored coffees. If you wish, you may change the frequency, quantities or types of your shipments at any time. Call, toll-free, 1-800-678-2687 and a Member Services representative will assist you.
No minimum. No commitment. There is no minimum purchase. No obligation to continue as a member. You may cancel your membership and stop your shipments at any time simply by notifying us by mail or phone. And, if you must return a shipment, you may do so at our expense.

This offer is only valid for NEW MEMBERS of the Gevalia Kaffe program. © 1990 Gevalia Kaffe Import Service. A Service of Victor Th. Engwall & Co. Limit one membership per household. Offer is open only to residents of Continental U.S. until May 31, 1990.

A very different letter—personalized with the detachable order form at the bottom—shown front and back. Size: 7½″ × 14″

The cover of the brochure is a 4-color box of Gevalia coffee.

BECAUSE 137 YEARS AGO, ONE STUBBORN SWEDE WAS OBSESSED WITH CREATING THE PERFECT CUP OF COFFEE.

In 1853, in the little seaport town of Gävle, Sweden, Victor Theodor Engwall sorted and roasted and tasted and tested. Tirelessly, he experimented with all the best, most exotic coffees that came into port until, at last, he achieved what he so stubbornly sought: a uniquely perfect coffee.

THE KING APPROVES.

It is said that one chilly day, Gustav V, King of Sweden, stopped in Gävle and tasted it. So enchanted was he that he appointed Gevalia Kaffe coffee to His Majesty and the Royal Court of Sweden.

Whole Bean.

Ground.

Today, this remarkable coffee is still made in Gävle by people imbued with Engwall's obsession for perfection. Generations of Swedish kings have awarded it the Royal Seal of Approval, and Gevalia has become Sweden's most popular, most beloved coffee. That's quite an achievement since Swedes are extremely sophisticated about coffee. They drink more than any other people in the world, and feel as passionately about coffee as the French do fine wine. They appreciate that up to 6 varieties of highly prized Arabica beans must be blended and balanced with infinite care in order to create the high flavor notes, the delicate nuances in Gevalia.

There's yet another secret to Gevalia's flavor: its impeccable freshness. Even the finest whole beans rapidly grow stale when exposed to air in gourmet shop bins. But Gevalia is roasted in small quantities and immediately vacuum sealed in golden foil ½ lb. pouches to preserve the just roasted freshness.

WHOLE BEAN, GROUND, REGULAR & NATURALLY DECAFFEINATED.

Gevalia® Kaffe comes in several magnificent whole bean roasts, which we will grind for you if you prefer. But perhaps the biggest revelation is Gevalia Decaffeinated. Caffeine is removed naturally by gently soaking the beans with water, then treating them with the very same elements that put the effervescence in sparkling water. The result: coffee that maintains full coffee flavor. Drinking decaffeinated is no longer a compromise.

A REGAL BRIBE.

Now this exceptional Swedish coffee may be bought in the U.S., but not in the usual manner. As Gevalia is not available in mass market quantities, the only way to order it is from our Import Service. Just fill out the enclosed reply form. With your trial supply, we'll send you, free, the porcelain glazed ceramic Regal Gevalia Canister in your choice of black or white embossed in gold with the Royal Crest of Sweden. (Retail value $25.00.) It's yours whether or not you continue our service.

But, fair warning. Once you sip superbly fresh, rich Gevalia, you're likely to become obsessed with it.

By Appointment to His Majesty the King of Sweden.

GEVALIA
KAFFE
THE COFFEE FAVORED BY KINGS

The cover isn't really a cover; the brochure is folded like a Z and is shown here front and back.

The business reply envelope.

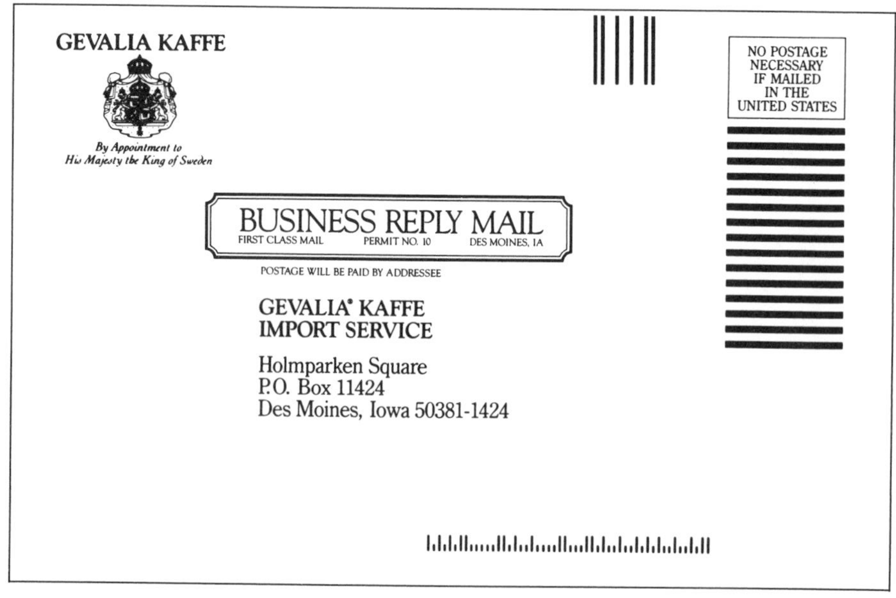

coffee made in small quantities and only available by mail—deserved an upscale, elegant package that would differentiate it from mass market coffees. We also wanted to attract prospects by making the package intriguing and fun.

For both the ad and the package, we kept the basic image and storyline that had been established in the very successful first magazine ad: ''The Magnificent Obsession that produced coffee favored by kings.'' And took it into a second phase.

Instead of the storybook quality of the original, we decided to bring Gevalia's inventor, Victor Theodor Engwall, to life. We did it in the main photography by giving the reader the feeling of his presence—showing the coffee in ''his'' study on his desk next to his pipe and pocket watch. Through the window, you see his little town in Sweden. And we made the headline about his real-life struggle to invent a great cup of coffee (and benefit): ''Because 132 years ago, one stubborn Swede was obsessed with creating the perfect cup of coffee.''

We now had the basic idea, which became the ad as well as the two inside pages of copy in the brochure. We then moved on to the other elements of the package.

The client had asked us to feature the white canister. So we made the whole envelope the canister. And like the real canister, you could pull the coffee out—this time the ''coffee'' being the package photograph on the cover of the brochure.

Then we realized it would also be neat if you could pull out real coffee and prospects could try it for themselves. So Jane designed it to work two ways: as a box with a four-cup coffee sample and as an envelope without the sample. And it was later produced and mailed both ways.

Our next job was to do a provocative teaser line to go on the canister on the envelope. ''Fair Warning, there's a Swedish Obsession inside.'' Then Jane went to her drawing board to do tight layouts and I went to my typewriter to write body copy.

Jane also tackled the order form for the ad, and invented something new and very effective which has been called ever since the ''Janevelope.''

And I tackled the letter. I wrote it right from the heart, basing it on my own experience when traveling abroad of tasting European coffee for the first time. And then trying and trying to find a brand of coffee that tasted as good when I got back home.

Our clients, Art Trotman and Jerry Maxson, liked the package immediately and approved it. It was produced in 1985, and has been running ever since.

I'd like to tell you that during the process, some magic thing happened, that suddenly one of us leapt up from her chair shrieking, ''I've got it!'' It would make things more exciting. But actually, it was all very quiet and workmanlike. I think the creative process was a success because we had the right experience for the job, were provided with good information, worked well together, had fun doing it, and took the time we needed to think it all out.

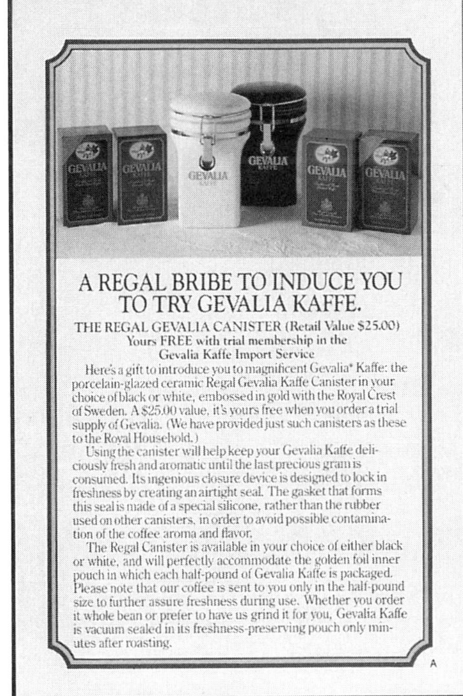

The 4-color lift piece, $4^1/_4$" × $6^1/_4$".

Omaha Steaks

Just as Sol Blumenfeld and Robert Haydon Jones created "hot potatoes" with their temporary membership cards for CompuServe and the Mobil Auto Club, Florida freelancer Herschell Gordon Lewis did likewise with his "Gourmet Gift Certificate" for Omaha Steaks.

Omaha Steaks is responsible for a magnificent product—filet mignon better than anything you've every eaten before and so tender it can be cut with a butter knife.

The trick to selling Omaha steaks is to compare their cost with that of eating in a fine restaurant, and *not* compare them with steaks found in the supermarket, or even at your local butchershop. This effort by Herschell Gordon Lewis is a masterpiece of creating benefits and, at the same time, burying the true cost of the product, which is about $20 per pound.

In his book *Power Copywriting* Lewis writes: "Nitpicking does pay off in a business that measures effectiveness the right way—by fractions of a percent response."

No one in the world has mastered the nuances of how to use the English language to *sell and persuade* like Florida freelancer Herschell Gordon Lewis. An example of Lewis's thinking is found in his *Power Copywriting*, which contains hundreds of tips and techniques to make just about every sentence stronger, more readable, and *more persuasive*:

4400 SOUTH 96TH STREET
P.O. BOX 3300
OMAHA, NEBRASKA 68103

Your Reply Will Really Be Appreciated!

PAY TO THE ORDER OF **$28 dol's 00 cts**

```
 CAR-RT SORT        **CR09
Mr. Larry
          Ln.
Houston, TX  77074
```

MAILER: Omaha Steaks
PACKAGE: Very Special Person . . .
WRITER: Herschell Gordon Lewis
DESIGNER: Jim Spangler
FIRST MAILED: Early 1980s
The no. 10 outside envelope with a savings certificate showing through the window. Where Linda Wells uses "The favor of a reply is requested," Herschell Gordon Lewis is a lot more informal—and enthusiastic!

Your Reply Will Really Be Appreciated!

A Private Message To a Very Special Person

Dear Friend,

This private invitation is going out to just a handful of people, yourself included. I hope you'll accept my invitation. But even if you decide not to, I want to send you a gift... **ABSOLUTELY FREE.**

Yes. An attractive, acrylic salt shaker/pepper mill will be delivered right to your door. It's easy and fun to use. And it will create a lovely accent on your table. It can be yours - without any obligation - simply by telling us that you'd like to have it.

Why I'm Writing to You

I believe you're someone who travels well, eats in fine restaurants --- and appreciates the difference between dinner at a four-star restaurant and a hamburger on the run.

You know, of course, it isn't unusual to pay a day's wages for a steak dinner. Fine, cornfed beef is impossible to find in many areas. We at Omaha Steaks International® know this well, because many of the most famous restaurants in the nation buy their gourmet steaks from us.

I'm writing to invite you to have those same gourmet steaks --- steaks you never on earth could get at any supermarket, steaks most restaurants can't even buy because there just aren't enough of them to go around. I want you to try some of our Special Filet Mignons, and I'm prepared to do what I have to do to convince you they're the gourmet treat of your lifetime.

Six (6 oz.) Omaha Steaks® Filets, flash frozen, packed with dry ice, and shipped to you in our marvelous reusable container, are regularly $57.95. I've enclosed a discount certificate, good as cash for $28.00, which means the steaks are yours for an introductory offer price of $29.95, plus $6.50 shipping and handling.

Back in 1917, my family began selling cornfed, Midwestern Beef to a couple of the swanky restaurants in Omaha.

Soon word got around about the tenderness, juiciness and flavor of Omaha Steaks®. Before long we expanded to serve some of the great restaurants in America. We still do.

Naturally, individuals began asking for our steaks by name. That's how we began sending steaks direct, and I can tell you that our list of customers is a real Who's Who.

What Can You Expect?

First of all, our steaks look marvelous, as well they should. Line one up alongside an ordinary filet and you'll instantly see the difference in beautiful marbling, close, hand trimming and sturdy, vacuum packaging. It's like putting an elegant limousine alongside a stripped-down economy car.

But the real test "is in the eatin'." If you're serving to guests, surprise them: for the first time in their lives, they'll be able to slice steaks with their forks, because that's just how tender an Omaha Steaks® Filet Mignon is.

That tenderness comes from slow, natural aging. It requires 21 days. And during the process, the beef must be maintained at a very exact temperature. Most beef suppliers are in too big a hurry to bother with aging. That's why the melt-in-your-mouth tenderness of these Filets will amaze you.

Ah, but now the ultimate way of judging a steak...taste...

It's the corn feeding, along with the natural aging, that sets these steaks apart from the beef available for mass consumption through supermarkets and most butcher shops. Corn feeding beef gives the meat a wonderful interior marbling. The marbling dissolves during cooking.

It makes the meat sensationally juicy ... with a flavor you'll crave once you've tasted it!

This cornfed beef is chosen with the care you'd give to a lifetime treasure. (That's what it is, to us, because our reputation is right on the line with every single Omaha Steaks® Filet Mignon.)

When I tell folks we guarantee our steaks, I often hear, "How in the world can you do that? Your customers can't return any steaks because they eat them."

Well, I certainly hope you eat them, but that doesn't affect our Guarantee.

Just about every guarantee you've ever seen includes the word "return." You have to return the merchandise, or the unused portion, or whatever, in order to get your money back. Not ours! You can keep the remaining steaks and still get your money back.

So order your steaks today. You'll get them in perfect condition, shipped in a container you can reuse for years, when you go on picnics or take an automobile trip or spend a day at the beach or decide to visit someone and bring the steaks with you (they'll be talking about it for weeks). I'll include a copy of our Cookbook, yours to keep. It's loaded with tips most cooks don't know about. Your steaks will be registered by actual serial number; in fact, you'll get a numbered Certificate verifying the Gold Seal of Approval.

When you order, you'll have our promise...

IF YOU'RE NOT ABSOLUTELY THRILLED WITH YOUR ORDER FROM OMAHA STEAKS® - FOR ANY REASON AT ALL - WE'LL CHEERFULLY REPLACE YOUR ORDER OR REFUND YOUR MONEY (TO THE PENNY) WHICHEVER YOU PREFER.

I think you deserve this wonderful treat. I think I've proved, by sending you this exclusive private invitation, that we at Omaha Steaks® believe you should have the same fantastic steak the rich and famous enjoy.

Do you agree you should sample Omaha Steaks®, especially since you can have them at more than 48% off the usual price? Do you agree you should give me the opportunity to prove my point: that you deserve the best, and this is it? Do you agree you can't lose, since I'm taking all the risk as proof that we do want you in the select group we regard as "family" --- those who have tasted the royalty of fine steaks?

I hope you do. I want you to taste our steaks and test my Guarantee.

I'm counting on your experiencing one of the great gourmet events of your lifetime (and the lifetimes of your fortunate guests, as well). You'll never have a better opportunity.

Sincerely,

Frederick J. Simon

Frederick J. Simon

P. S. Don't wait until the expiration date on your certificate is on top of you. We guarantee your satisfaction. What can you lose? Call now TOLL FREE 1-800-228-9055.

P.P.S. Remember, to add even more zest to your first meal of Omaha Steaks®, you'll receive - ABSOLUTELY FREE - an acrylic salt shaker/pepper mill. Even if you decide not to place your order for luscious, fork-tender Omaha Steaks® right away, the pepper mill is yours FREE. Read about it on the enclosed insert.

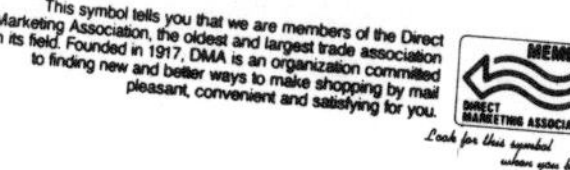

G4876-0291

The 4-page letter, printed on an 11″ × 17″ sheet.

"Understand" is weaker than "figure out."

"I understand" (or "Do you understand?") is passive and therefore less emphatic than "I figured it out" (or "Have you figured it out?").

"Figuring out" is more reader-involving, implying more active participation than "understand," which suggests acceptance.

This is subtle stuff, a series of complex rules to commit to memory. But Lewis employs them in his own copy. And because he writes with absolute precision—having thought through all possible shades of meaning—he has had a legion of controls over the years. If using a more powerful word or phrase raises the response rate to a mailing by one-tenth of a percent, and there are a hundred such techniques used, the mailing will pull 10 percent better.

Herschell Gordon Lewis is a direct marketing creative source, a direct response writer, and a consultant with clients throughout the world. The author of fourteen books on direct marketing, copywriting, and public relations, he is the "Curmudgeon-at-Large" for *Direct* as well as a regular columnist for *Direct Marketing* magazine, *Catalog Age*, and *Direct Marketing International* in the United Kingdom. Lewis is a frequent, and very popular, lecturer, seminar presenter, and after-dinner speaker all over the world.

The 4-color brochure shown front and back.

For that special occasion...
Filet Mignons from
Omaha Steaks
Omaha Steaks International
Questions and Answers About Omaha Steaks
Q. Is there really a difference between these Filet Mignons and the very best steaks I can buy in a supermarket?
A. You bet there is. You'll not only taste the difference, you actually can see it. It's the difference between good commercial-grade steaks and filets the very rich or world-famous gourmets usually can enjoy whenever they wish.
Q. Do people buy Omaha Steaks Filet Mignons as a gift?
A. They're a much-wanted gift, because throughout the world Omaha Steaks Filet Mignons are known as the very best.
Q. What makes them the best?
A. Every Omaha Steaks Filet is USDA inspected and cut from the finest cornfed beef, selected before any commercial market even sees it. Omaha Steaks International offers this unconditional guarantee:
Guarantee...
If you are not absolutely thrilled with your order from Omaha Steaks® - for any reason at all - we'll cheerfully replace your order or refund your money (to the penny), whichever you prefer.
Unbelievable? Not for the finest filets in the world.
REGISTERED
Nº 877870
THE ULTIMATE SYMBOL OF GOOD TASTE...
Omaha Steaks International®
4400 South 96th Street • P.O. Box 3300 • Omaha, NE 68103
CALL TOLL FREE 1-800-228-9055
TURN OVER FOR MORE INFORMATION

F•I•L•E•T M•I•G•N•O•N•S
from
Omaha Steaks International®
Unlike Any Steak You've Ever Tasted
No "supermarket" steak, regardless of cut, can begin to equal the perfect taste and tenderness of a genuine Filet Mignon from Omaha Steaks.®
No, these superb filets aren't everyday fare! They're for the person you want to impress. They're for you when you want to serve the best filets money can buy. They're elegant gifts for the person who "has everything" — and who, enjoying the filets' good taste, will appreciate your good taste.
Omaha Steaks® Filet Mignons are flash-frozen at just the right moment of aging. They're shipped in a reusable insulated chest, protected by dry ice so that wherever in the world they go, they're absolutely perfect when they arrive.
Each filet is a genuine "Gold Seal" filet; your shipment is registered and numbered, and the Registration certificate is your assurance that each filet is Omaha Steaks®-inspected for perfection.
* Included FREE
The Omaha Steaks® Cookbook... full of tips for preparing steaks and other delicacies the way the great chefs do, including exclusive recipes by the great gourmet expert James Beard.
BY INVITATION ONLY
Six Perfect Omaha Steaks® 6 oz. Filet Mignons — $57.95
Only $29.95 with your certificate.
You'll find no finer filets anywhere in the world.
SAVE $28.00
$29.95 special price (+ $6.50 shipping)
Limited Offer!
TURN OVER FOR MORE INFORMATION

FREE Ask for Gift #8156

A Striking, 3½" Salt Shaker/Pepper Mill

Add elegance and sparkle to your dinner table! And enjoy the special zest and flavor of fresh peppercorns ground by hand as you dine.

Right now, with (or even without) your Introductory Order from Omaha Steaks,® you'll receive a 3½" acrylic salt shaker/pepper mill with the light-catching look of crystal. It's attractive and fun to use. Best of all, it's yours FREE!

Order now! Return the order form enclosed, using the envelope included.

Omaha Steaks International® 4400 South 96th Street P.O. Box 3300 Omaha, Nebraska 68103

The lift piece offering a premium.

OUR "MINIATURE MAILABLE FREEZER"

No matter how hot the weather, your Omaha Steaks® will arrive in excellent condition, thanks to our packaging which serves as a portable "deep freeze." We guarantee safe arrival!

This proven "deep freeze" package gets response:

"Shipment was excellent. Packaging perfect and quality superb!"
Robert Rushlow
Atlanta, Georgia

"I order your products with confidence. I know the packaging and delivery will always be satisfactory. And the quality is always AAA #1!
Josephine Washington
Bronx, New York

4400 South 96th Street • P.O. Box 3300 • Omaha, Nebraska 68103

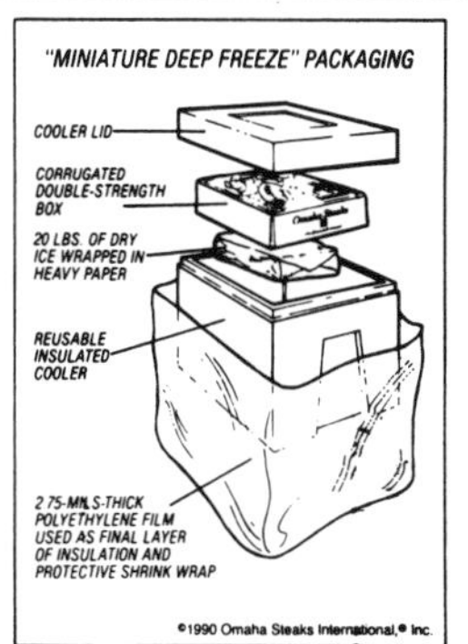

HERSCHELL GORDON LEWIS:

My successful copywriting ''secret'' isn't a secret at all: It's a combination of the two most logical conclusions any professional communicator should reach.

Conclusion one: Inject yourself inside the brain of your typical target.

Using this simple formula, I've written many a package as a woman . . . as a member of an ethnic or religious or political or philosophical group to which I don't belong or subscribe . . . as a plain ol' country boy. The process parallels ''Method Acting.''

Conclusion two: Don't show off for your peer group (I hate that term).

One reason so many writers of ''conventional'' advertising fail as direct marketers is their insistence on showing the reader (or viewer or listener) how clever they are, or how huge a vocabulary they can command. To me, this is a horrendous mistake.

For direct mail copy to work, it must have verisimilitude. Verisimilitude is the appearance *of truth. Raw truth has weeds in it; verisimilitude is an unblemished garden.*

Truth: ''Although the survey shows that readers spend more time with Fortune, *and* Forbes *attracts greater advertising response, this magazine has shown a greater percentage of circulation growth.'' Verisimilitude: ''The marketplace knows what's best! We outstrip both* Fortune *and* Forbes *in rate of circulation growth.''*

Verisimilitude also is a brake on claims. I call this The Ballooning Number Rule:

> *The farther a number rises beyond the typical reader's personal experiential background, the less emotion the number generates.*

*So referring to the national debt in trillions of dollars has less impact than ''*You owe *. . .''; computer monitor manufacturers whose copy talks about 16 million colors may be truthful, but they're outside the verisimilitude loop.*

One more point about verisimilitude: It thrives on specificity. Example:

Instead of, ''We've been in business a long time . . .'' a verisimilitude-conscious writer would say, ''My father opened his first store at 30th and Main, 32 years ago. . . .''

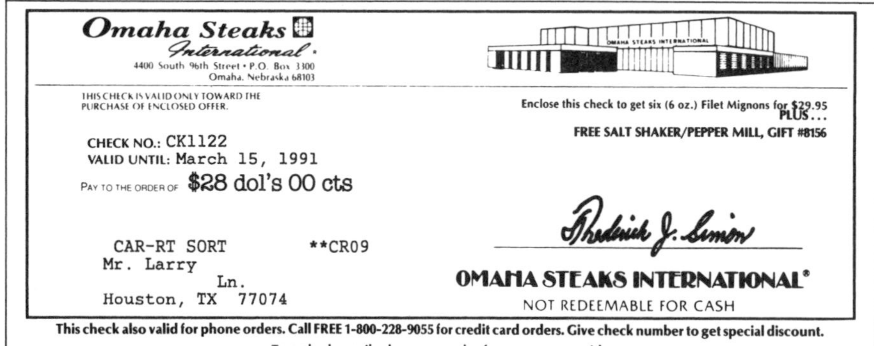

Omaha Steaks International
4400 South 96th Street • P.O. Box 3300
Omaha, Nebraska 68103

THIS CHECK IS VALID ONLY TOWARD THE PURCHASE OF ENCLOSED OFFER.

Enclose this check to get six (6 oz.) Filet Mignons for $29.95 PLUS...
FREE SALT SHAKER/PEPPER MILL, GIFT #8156

CHECK NO.: CK1122
VALID UNTIL: March 15, 1991
PAY TO THE ORDER OF $28 dol's 00 cts

CAR-RT SORT **CR09
Mr. Larry
Ln.
Houston, TX 77074

OMAHA STEAKS INTERNATIONAL®
NOT REDEEMABLE FOR CASH

This check also valid for phone orders. Call FREE 1-800-228-9055 for credit card orders. Give check number to get special discount.
To order by mail, please use order form on reverse side.

Yes, please send me:
SELECTION #460
☐ **plus Free Salt Shaker/Pepper Mill, Gift #8156**
Six (6 oz.) Filet Mignons at the special introductory discount price of $29.95. (Regular price is $57.95, less your $28.00 discount check = $29.95 plus $6.50 shipping and handling for a total of $36.45.) A savings of $28.00. Limit of two packages at this special price.

NO:
☐ I'm going to ask that you wrap, package and ship to me the Free Salt Shaker/Pepper Mill only.

You Must Be Thrilled GUARANTEE
If you are not absolutely thrilled with your order from Omaha Steaks® - for any reason at all - we'll cheerfully replace your order or refund your money (to the penny), whichever you prefer.

DISCOUNT APPROVED

PLEASE, we must have your phone number to verify your order!
Area Code ☐☐☐ Phone Number ☐☐☐ ☐☐☐☐
Order with cash or any charge card listed below. Please X proper box. When using charge card, give appropriate card number.
☐ Check or Money Order $______
☐ VISA ☐ MasterCard ☐ American Express ☐ Discover
Credit Card No. ☐☐☐☐☐☐☐☐☐☐☐☐☐☐☐☐
Card Expiration Date Month ☐☐ Year ☐☐
PLEASE CHECK/CORRECT ADDRESS ON CHECK.
We'll deliver your steaks to the address shown — unless you tell us otherwise. If you use a P.O. Box, please give us a street address or phone number.
☐ Ship at once (Allow 10-14 days from date you mail your order.)
☐ Ship to arrive by______
Additional charge for shipment to Alaska/Hawaii. Call for details.
Prices subject to change.

G4877-0291

Omaha Steaks International®
4400 SO. 96TH STREET
P.O. BOX 3300
OMAHA, NE 68103-0300

The discount certificate/order device shown front and back, and the business reply envelope.

I have an insurance client whose business began in 1784. In almost every mailing I add to that date, "That's five years before George Washington became president," which in my opinion is considerably stronger than "That's well over 200 years ago."

Now, how I work:

When I start a project, I start writing at once. I'm lucky: I'm able to write as fast as I can type. I don't *delve deeply into the technical aspects of what I'm marketing until I've written the key selling piece—usually, the letter. This enables me to stay inside the reader's experiential background.*

Too often, we run afoul of the appreciation-differential separating the seller and sellee. The vendor cares about what it is. The buyer cares about what it will do for him or her. I've found this to be especially true in electronics and computer software. Lord knows how many millions of dollars software developers waste, trying to sell programming *to a buyer. The typical buyer cares less about how it works than about what its benefits are.*

After I have the sales appeal on paper, I'll inject any salesworthy technical details to validate the claims. This technique prevents me from falling into the slough of ignoring what the reader wants to see in favor of what the vendor wants to say.

My opinion—and please categorize this as opinion, not fact: Components of a mailing should have a synergistic effect on one another but not *parallel one another. Thus, the letter exhorts; the brochure explains; a validating enclosure authenticates both the exhortation and the explanation.*

19

Newsletters

Newsletters don't lend themselves to long-term promotional efforts. They are by definition *news* and *letters*, private pipelines into the expertise of an editor or a research organization. They generally go to a narrowly defined audience that would quickly get tired of seeing the same envelope over and over and throw succeeding copies of the same effort away. (One technique to revive flagging controls: change your envelope.)

Plus . . . as industries and opportunities change, newsletters change, and those changes must be reflected in the promotional copy to make the publication and its editor seem *au courant.* For example, an investment letter that made people rich on stocks in the mid-80s would have had dramatically to change its story to attract new subscribers (and keep old ones) after the 501-point crash of the Dow on October 17, 1987.

I remember creating a mailing for the Fidelity Investments *Mutual Fund Letter* that landed on the desks of Fidelity investors *the very week of the crash.*

Several weeks later I called circulation manager Bill Baird (now with Ziff-Davis) to ask how the mailing fared in light of the Dow Jones debacle. "You beat control," Baird said.

"I did? Really?"

"Yeah, you got one order."

I quickly rewrote the package, citing the various Fidelity Funds that actually gained in the crash and how, as a member of the Fidelity family, an investor could switch money around without paying commissions or penalties; it was remailed and became control.

That said, five newsletter promotions qualify as Grand Controls. Three are by Donn Smith of Belvoir Publications, Inc.; two of those are identical-looking efforts for two very different products.

One of these efforts—for the Boardroom Reports publication, *Bottom Line/Personal*—is covered in Chapter 21. Boardroom mailings are so distinctive and revolutionary—and so much is to be learned from them—that the two Boardroom Grand Controls have a chapter of their own.

Belvoir Publications

Aviation Consumer and *Aviation Safety* fall into a category somewhere between a magazine and a newsletter. When cataloged by me or my staff, half the time these publications wind up as special-interest magazines and the other half they fetch up in the newsletter files.

When I called Donn Smith to tell him that he had won an Axel Andersson Award for his *Practical Sailor* package, he asked which particular package. When I described it to him, he said, "Ah, my knock-off of the old *Consumer Reports* "Which should you buy?"

Smith "stole smart." The "Which Would You Buy?" Grand Control was a masterpiece that brought in hundreds of thousands of new subscribers for *Consumer Reports* over a period of years.

Aviation Consumer

Donn E. Smith began at Time Inc. in its corporate training program in 1967 and went on to take a position with Time-Life Records, a fledgling offshoot of the book division. Later he was circulation promotion director of the old *Life* magazine and, with its pending demise, moved a few blocks east to become circulation manager at *Newsweek*, and then on to the same job at the *Harvard Business Review* and *New Times*. Since Harvard encourages outside consulting by staff and faculty, Smith developed a relationship with Belvoir Publications, a multititle newsletter publisher in Greenwich, Connecticut, where for the past dozen years he has been executive vice president. Throughout his career, Smith has

MAILER: *Aviation Consumer*
PACKAGE: "Which . . . ?"
PROJECT MGR.: Donn E. Smith
WRITER: Donn E. Smith
DESIGNER: John Rettich
FIRST MAILED: 1985
The *Consumer Reports* mailing that was the inspiration for the bright yellow 9" × 12" *Aviation Consumer* mailing below it.

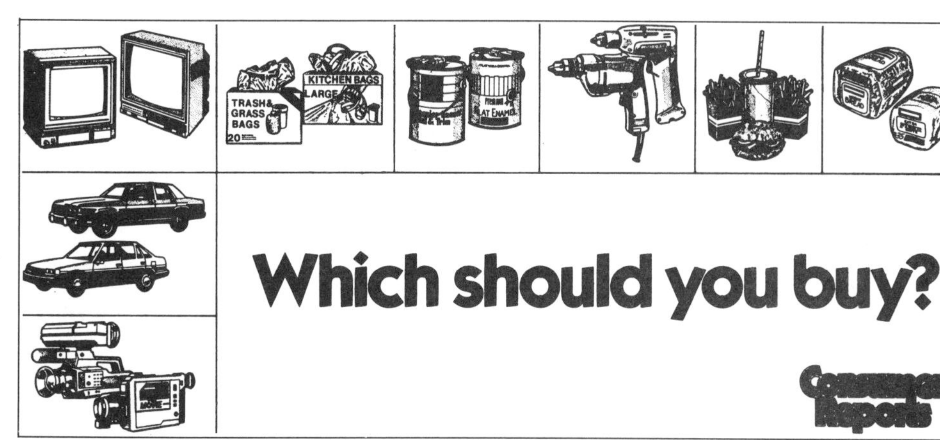

The Aviation Consumer.

CESSNA SKYLANE RG

PIPER PA-32R

Dear Pilot,

Say the words "general aviation" and what kind of planes come to mind?

More than likely, single engine retractables. The wheels-up, one-fan class is general aviation's most popular. It is also the class where buying the wrong plane can be a fatal mistake.

Among single engine retractables, a huge gulf exists between the safest and the most dangerous models. In fact, when AVIATION CONSUMER last evaluated accident rates for singles, we discovered that you're four times -- 400% -- more likely to get killed in the worst than the best. The worst? The Piper PA-32R.

Can You Believe You Just Read That?

Stop for a second. Think about that last paragraph. You were just told -- flat-out -- that one airplane is more dangerous than another. The offending plane was named. There were no excuses, no sugarcoating. Instead, there was a solid, straightforward, and honest answer.

Refreshing, isn't it? A real answer. A statement that actually states something. These days that's a rare commodity.

AVIATION CONSUMER is a rare publication. AVIATION CONSUMER is different. AVIATION CONSUMER's editors say what should be said. Whenever the choice of a plane or product affects your flying safety, budget, or well-being, you can count on AVIATION CONSUMER to provide the straight answers you're looking for.

With this letter you are invited to find out just how valuable AVIATION CONSUMER's ratings and evaluations can be for your flying.

You're invited to accept the next two issues of AVIATION CONSUMER -- absolutely free -- No strings. No obligations.

When you receive your two free issues you'll quickly discover that

AVIATION CONSUMER's premise is simple: honesty. You'll also discover that its purpose is clear: to give you the facts and recommendations you need to make intelligent, careful and confident buying decisions.

Written with no nonsense and no-holds barred

At AVIATION CONSUMER we do just one thing. We test. We test the equipment and the planes you fly. We test them rigorously. We test them relentlessly. And we test them thoroughly.

We fly them. We shake them. Bake them. Freeze them. Turn them inside out and upside down. We find which can take it -- and which can't.

And then we tell our readers. Loud and clear. Yes or no. Buy or don't buy. There's no pussyfooting. Just honest answers.

Because AVIATION CONSUMER accepts no advertising, we're free to evaluate planes and products fairly, fully, and frankly.

FOR PILOTS EVERYWHERE. THE AVIATION CONSUMER CAN BE YOUR BEST FLYING INVESTMENT.

AVIATION CONSUMER earns its keep. It's one publication that pays for itself from the very first information-packed issue.

Recently AVIATION CONSUMER readers discovered an IFR-approved loran that offered twice the data at half the price of its competition!

Are you in the market for a handheld? With the results of AVIATION CONSUMER's six-way handheld transceiver shootout, you'd be able to zero in on the best buy for under $500. (The winner was the easiest to use and had the lowest price tag of all!)

Does your state owe you money? AVIATION CONSUMER showed readers which states offer avgas tax refunds and how to apply. (One reader followed-up with his state and collected $7,000!)

In the pages of AVIATION CONSUMER you would have been warned about a famous flight academy that's overpriced and offers instruction no better than what you can get at your local FBO. Or you could have read how the price of a single strobe could jump from $1048.65 (exorbitant already!) to $2724.90 overnight! (Happily, AVIATION CONSUMER found three other companies willing to supply suitable replacement strobes for $141 to $321 each.)

AVIATION CONSUMER regularly shows readers how to shop for everything from headsets to deicing boots ... from mikes to maps ... from the newest electronic instruments to the most comprehensive insurance packages.

Money is only one part of the story.

Time is the other. AVIATION CONSUMER's purpose is to see that you waste as little time as possible on broken parts and busted promises.

We test equipment for its reliability, its durability, and its longevity. If a pump's TBO is just a pipe dream -- you'll find out before you buy.

When AVIATION CONSUMER looks at aircraft -- as we do each month in our famous USED AIRCRAFT GUIDE -- we look at every element which could cost you irreplaceable airtime. How long does an average annual take? Does the powerplant have a solid performance record? How many ADs have been issued -- and how many are likely to follow? Is there an affordable and adequate parts inventory?

We never forget the importance of reliability

As a buyer you've found that manufacturers believe you shouldn't worry about reliability. After all, right along with their product they're giving you "the best warranty in the business." Big deal.

What you really want is a product that doesn't break! There's no such thing as a free replacement -- not when it's costing you valuable time for every installation, removal, and reinstallation.

Each issue of AVIATION CONSUMER gives you rigorously-researched assessments that take nothing for granted. When we heard that a certain engine was spalling tappets and destroying camshafts, we warned our readers immediately.

When we unearthed the story about a cheap canopy cover that was causing unrepairable windshield crazing, we quickly gave our readers the clear picture.

Thinking about an altitude-reporting transponder? Soon you may not be able to leave home without one. But which black box should you buy? King, Collins, and Narco all make good sets, but one's durability is less than half that of the others!

All equipment is not created equal

As our transponder survey revealed, most manufacturers are trying to bring good products to the marketplace, but some succeed far better than others. Inevitably, one set will outperform the rest, one oil will break down before the others, or one battery will outlast the competition.

AVIATION CONSUMER provides the necessary information for its readers to make informed buying choices -- to make the right choices. Our aim is to make sure that you know -- in no uncertain terms -- which equipment

is best (and which is not) before you fly and before you buy.

We believe your flying investment should never be jeopardized, and your safety never be compromised, by equipment unable to meet its promise and your expectations.

If this all sounds great -- here's the clincher!

You are cordially invited to accept the next two issues of AVIATION CONSUMER absolutely free!

You see, just as we want you to be fully informed before you fly, we want you to be fully convinced that AVIATION CONSUMER is for you, before you buy.

Take our next two issues and see if they are all I've promised. If you agree that THE AVIATION CONSUMER is a valuable addition to your aviation reading and its unbiased evaluations can save you time, money, and quite possibly, your life, you may then sign up as a regular subscriber to receive the next 12 issues for just $16 -- a $20.00 savings from our regular subscription rate!

But, if after examining your two free issues, you feel our publication is not for you, simply write "cancel" on the subscription bill and owe us nothing. No questions. No strings.

And that's it. A great opportunity to try the most important and influential consumer aviation publication available ... entirely at our risk.

So, before you do anything else today, send for your two free issues of THE AVIATION CONSUMER. Thank you.

Cordially,

Donn E. Smith
Executive Vice-President

DES:cjl

P.S. Because we can distribute only a limited number of free review invitations annually, this may be your only opportunity to try AVIATION CONSUMER this year. I sincerely urge you to take advantage of this offer. There is no risk; we've even paid the postage for your reply.

P.P.S. When you become a subscriber to AVIATION CONSUMER, you will receive The 1991 Pilot's Yearbook. This just-published guide is loaded with our latest evaluations, ratings and buying tips. The Yearbook is a $9.95 value, but it's yours free as a new subscriber.

The 4-page letter, printed on an 11″ × 17″ sheet.

"been fortunate to learn from the best, from attending the late Ed Mayer's fabled Basic Direct Mail Course, to having such mentors as Joan Manley [of Time-Life Books], Wendell Forbes [renowned magazine circulation consultant], Bob Riordan [publisher of Family Media], and George Hirsch [magazine publisher]."

Although Smith has worked for such clients as the *Wall Street Journal, Barron's, Penthouse, Art & Auction,* and *Newsweek,* he currently limits his work almost exclusively to Belvoir's many newsletters and book projects.

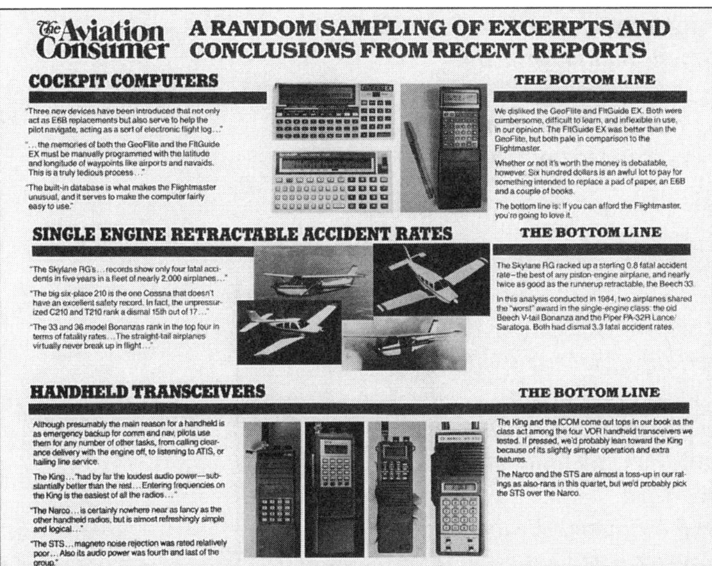

The Aviation Consumer

A RANDOM SAMPLING OF EXCERPTS AND CONCLUSIONS FROM RECENT REPORTS

COCKPIT COMPUTERS

"Three new devices have been introduced that not only act as E6B replacements but also serve to help the pilot navigate, acting as a sort of electronic flight log..."

"...the memories of both the GeoFlite and the FltGuide EX must be manually programmed with the latitude and longitude of waypoints like airports and navaids. This is a truly tedious process..."

"The built-in database is what makes the Flightmaster unusual, and it serves to make the computer fairly easy to use."

THE BOTTOM LINE

We disliked the GeoFlite and FltGuide EX. Both were cumbersome, difficult to learn, and inflexible in use, in our opinion. The FltGuide EX was better than the GeoFlite, but both pale in comparison to the Flightmaster.

Whether or not it's worth the money is debatable, however. Six hundred dollars is an awful lot to pay for something intended to replace a pad of paper, an E6B and a couple of books.

The bottom line is: If you can afford the Flightmaster, you're going to love it.

SINGLE ENGINE RETRACTABLE ACCIDENT RATES

"The Skylane RG's...records show only four fatal accidents in five years in a fleet of nearly 2,000 airplanes..."

"The big six-place 210 is the one Cessna that doesn't have an excellent safety record. In fact, the unpressurized C210 and T210 rank a dismal 15th out of 17..."

"The 33 and 36 model Bonanzas rank in the top four in terms of fatality rates...The straight-tail airplanes virtually never break up in flight..."

THE BOTTOM LINE

The Skylane RG racked up a sterling 0.8 fatal accident rate—the best of any piston-engine airplane, and nearly twice as good as the runnerup retractable, the Beech 33.

In this analysis conducted in 1984, two airplanes shared the "worst" award in the single-engine class: the old Beech V-tail Bonanza and the Piper PA-32R Lance/Saratoga. Both had dismal 3.3 fatal accident rates.

HANDHELD TRANSCEIVERS

Although presumably the main reason for a handheld is as emergency backup for comm and nav, pilots use them for any number of other tasks, from calling clearance delivery with the engine off, to listening to ATIS, or hailing line service.

The King..."had by far the loudest audio power—substantially better than the rest...Entering frequencies on the King is the easiest of all the radios..."

"The Narco...is certainly nowhere near as fancy as the other handheld radios, but is almost refreshingly simple and logical..."

"The STS...magneto noise rejection was rated relatively poor...Also its audio power was fourth and last of the group."

THE BOTTOM LINE

The King and the ICOM come out tops in our book as the class act among the four VOR handheld transceivers we tested. If pressed, we'd probably lean toward the King because of its slightly simpler operation and extra features.

The Narco and the STS are almost a toss-up in our ratings as also-rans in this quartet, but we'd probably pick the STS over the Narco.

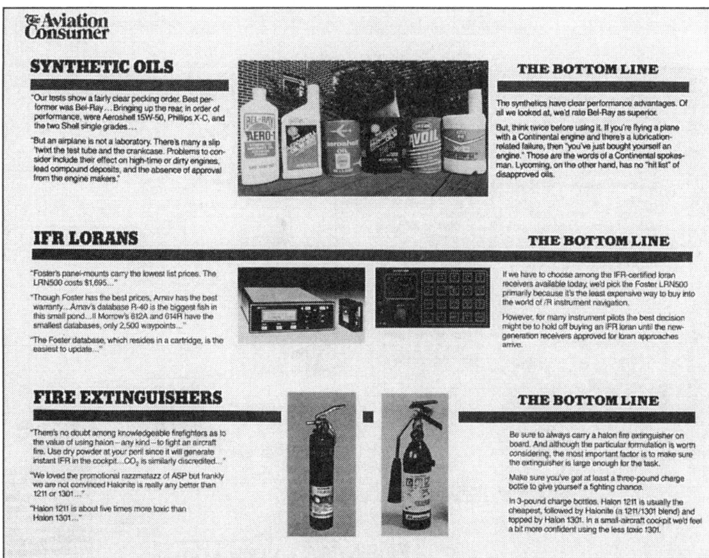

The Aviation Consumer

SYNTHETIC OILS

"Our tests show a fairly clear pecking order. Best performer was Bel-Ray...Bringing up the rear, in order of performance, were Aeroshell 15W-50, Philips X-C, and the two Shell single grades...

"But an airplane is not a laboratory. There's many a slip 'twixt the test tube and the crankcase. Problems to consider include their effect on high-time or dirty engines, lead compound deposits, and the absence of approval from the engine makers."

THE BOTTOM LINE

The synthetics have clear performance advantages. Of all we looked at, we'd rate Bel-Ray as superior.

But, think twice before using it. If you're flying a plane with a Continental engine and there's a lubrication-related failure, then "you've just bought yourself an engine." Those are the words of a Continental spokesman. Lycoming, on the other hand, has no "hit list" of disapproved oils.

IFR LORANS

"Foster's panel-mounts carry the lowest list prices. The LRN500 costs $1,695..."

"Though Foster has the best prices, Arnav has the best warranty...Arnav's database R-40 is the biggest fish in this small pond...II Morrow's 612A and 614R have the smallest databases, only 2,500 waypoints..."

"The Foster database, which resides in a cartridge, is the easiest to update..."

THE BOTTOM LINE

If we have to choose among the IFR-certified loran receivers available today, we'd pick the Foster LRN500 primarily because it's the least expensive way to buy into the world of /R instrument navigation.

However, for many instrument pilots the best decision might be to hold off buying an IFR loran until the new-generation receivers approved for loran approaches arrive.

FIRE EXTINGUISHERS

"There's no doubt among knowledgeable firefighters as to the value of using halon—any kind—to fight an aircraft fire. Use dry powder at your peril since it will generate instant IFR in the cockpit...CO_2 is similarly discredited..."

"We loved the promotional razzmatazz of ASP but frankly we are not convinced Halonite is really any better than 1211 or 1301..."

"Halon 1211 is about five times more toxic than Halon 1301..."

THE BOTTOM LINE

Be sure to always carry a halon fire extinguisher on board. And although the particular formulation is worth considering, the most important factor is to make sure the extinguisher is large enough for the task.

Make sure you've got at least a three-pound charge bottle to give yourself a fighting chance.

In 3-pound charge bottles, Halon 1211 is usually the cheapest, followed by Halonite (a 1211/1301 blend) and topped by Halon 1301. In a small-aircraft cockpit we'd feel a bit more confident using the less toxic 1301.

Lift piece 1.

THINK OF US AS YOUR "GROUND SUPPORT" TEAM... *A final word from the editor*

The Aviation Consumer

Dear Pilot,

From our experience we have found that, except for a few out-and-out charlatans, most aircraft and equipment manufacturers endeavor to produce decent products.

However, the unfortunate truth is that some succeed far better than others. And no matter how good a manufacturer's intentions, you can't afford to bet your life on his equipment if it's less than 100% airworthy.

And some are far from it. Recently we've discovered lorans that fail in cold weather, additives loaded with contaminants, and a plane so prone to disaster that nearly 10% of the fleet has crashed due to engine failure!

You certainly never want to trust your life to instruments, lubricants, or aircraft like that. And our job is to see that you never do!

As "ground support" for your flying, THE AVIATION CONSUMER will point you to those planes and products which are the best of the breed. We'll help you select equipment that's safer, more efficient, and more reliable.

I can assure you that no other publication will work harder for your flying safety and enjoyment.

So, please, take this no-risk opportunity to sample the added measure of flight protection that's yours with THE AVIATION CONSUMER. Thank you!

Cordially,

Richard B. Weeghman

Richard B. Weeghman
Editor

RBW:ioi

Lift piece 2.

Donn Smith:

Being my own copywriter—being both the assigner and the assignee—gives me the luxury of having a long lead time to "think" about a project. Unlike many of my freelance colleagues who learn the details of a project only days before the deadline, I have the luxury of time.

With a package, I work from the outside in. The outer envelope comes first. The inspiration—the grabber—can come at any time and place—stuck in I-95 traffic, at the dinner table, at 3 A.M.

Once I have the hook, the rest of the package flows. Next the order card, then the letter, etc.

I think it extremely important for a writer to monitor and partake of American culture at its broadest—to get in the car, to go to the mall, to grab the remote and flip channels.

That's where you find the lingua franca, *the common threads and shared concerns that hold this diverse society together. A writer must understand those hopes and fears if his copy is to be evocative and effective.*

More from Donn Smith:

We all know about the Sports Illustrated *jinx—that whenever a player or team is featured on the cover, that athlete's fate is certain to take a swift, catastrophic turn.*

Perhaps we should consider the jinx of the Axel Andersson in those same terms. Since we received the award for Practical Sailor*'s "Evaluations" mailing, that package has taken a precipitous turn downward.*

Interestingly, I cannot attribute the decline to format, for although Evaluations is now a 6″ × 9″, that smaller configuration had earlier tested out dead-even with the jumbo.

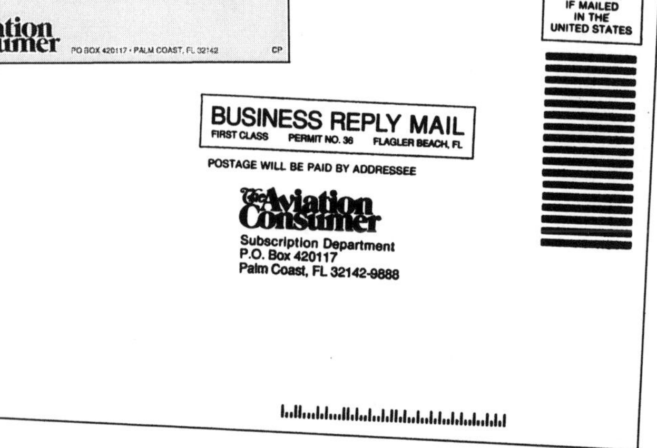

The order card and business reply envelope. The order card is 5″ × 11½″—only half as high as the envelope. In order for it to be inserted into a 9″-high envelope and stay in place, an envelope must have a bottom flap, which this one does.

As you may know, we use this same format for promoting two other newsletters, Aviation Consumer *and* Powerboat Reports. *There too a similar fall-off has occurred. It's as if there has been a seachange in what motivates a buyer this year.*

Fortunately we have found new packages which are faring well, but it is interesting to note that even the sturdiest of controls can suddenly and dramatically weaken.

> *P.S. Willing to challenge fate, however, I do enclose a package for consideration in the next round of Axels. This* Aviation Safety *control has been in use, and unconquered, since 1987.*

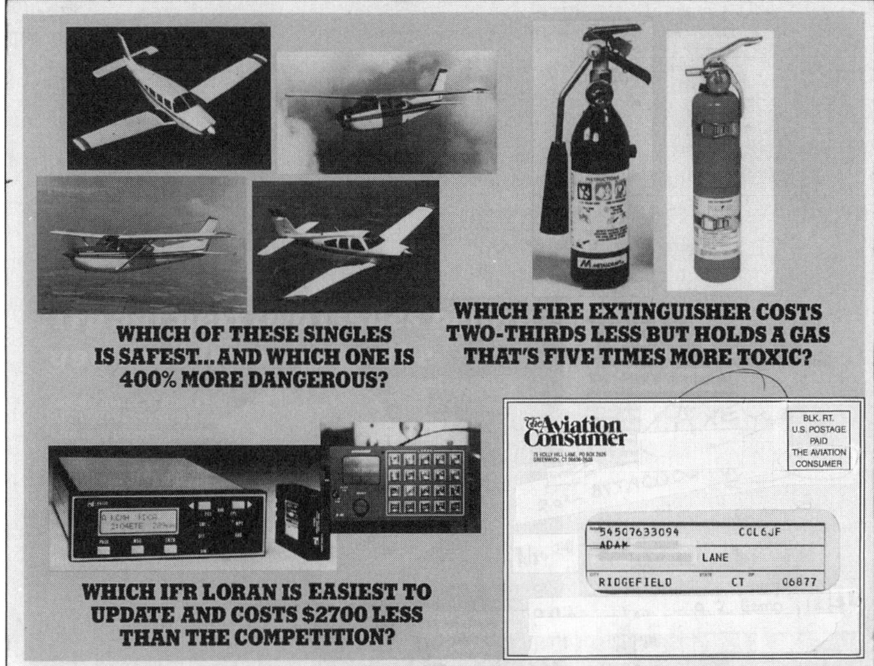

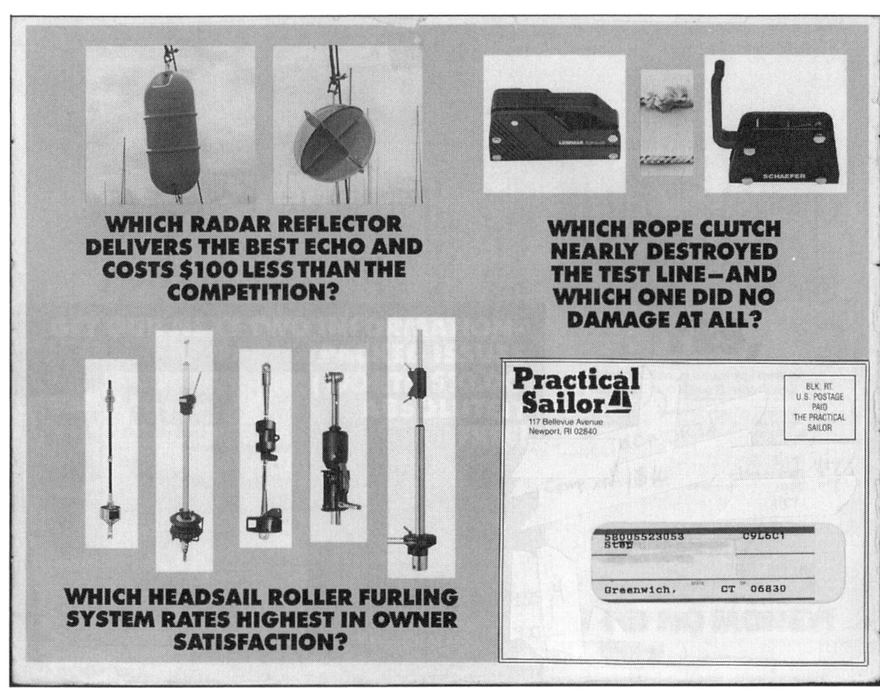

Not only did Donn Smith "steal smart" from *Consumer Reports*, he went on to do likewise from himself. The *Aviation Consumer* package is a precise knock-off of *Practical Sailor* (or vice versa, since no one is sure which came first). This shows that if a format and copy approach works in one universe, you can change the illustrations and the descriptive copy, and use it in another universe.

Aviation Safety

This *Aviation Safety* sweeps is a splendid maverick. Like Robert Haydon Jones's Grand Control for Mobil Auto Club, Smith's five-year-old control for *Aviation Safety* flouts tradition. Unlike any sweeps we've ever seen, the letter discourages nonpilots from entering and even disparages the value of the grand prize, a forty-five-year-old restored Piper Cub.

Smith doesn't totally turn off the NO entrants. The grand prize winner could opt for $10,000 cash, plus there are over 1,000 other prizes ranging from a Sony camcorder to a Coleman flashlight. But the centerpiece is the classic plane.

According to Donn Smith, he is following in the footsteps of the early *New York* magazine sweeps where the grand prize was dinner with (then) Mayor John Lindsay and second prize was a bench in Central Park with your name on it. "You had to be a dedicated New Yorker to appreciate it," Smith said. "Same thing here."

So far there have been two grand prize winners. A young student pilot won it and really wanted the plane; but Smith spoke to the kid's mother and after running the numbers by her on what it would cost for insurance, they opted for the $10,000 cash. The other winner really wanted the plane and told Smith that his neighbor down the street was trying to sell precisely that model for $11,000. So *Aviation Safety* bought the Piper from the neighbor and presented it to the winner.

Is this sweeps still working after six years? Smith just mailed it to the Aircraft Owners and Pilots' Association (AOPA) list and it pulled a mind-blowing 10½ percent gross.

CONGRATULATIONS!
YOU MAY HAVE ALREADY WON OUR SWEEPSTAKES GRAND PRIZE.
WHAT IS IT?
HERE'S A CLUE: IT'S SOMETHING 98 OUT OF 100 PEOPLE WOULDN'T EVEN WANT.
AND YOU MAY HAVE WON IT?
YES!
BLK. RT. U.S. POSTAGE PAID AVIATION SAFETY
Adam W
Ridgefield, CT 06877

MAILER: *Aviation Safety*
PACKAGE: Piper Cub Sweeps
PROJECT MGR.: Donn E. Smith
WRITER: Donn E. Smith
DESIGNER: John Rettich
FIRST MAILED: 1985
The #10 outside envelope for *Aviation Safety* in bright orange-yellow with a red "CONGRATULATIONS!" and black type below.

Aviation Safety
"WE'VE GOT YOUR NUMBER" SWEEPSTAKES II
75 Holly Hill Lane
Greenwich, CT 06836-2626

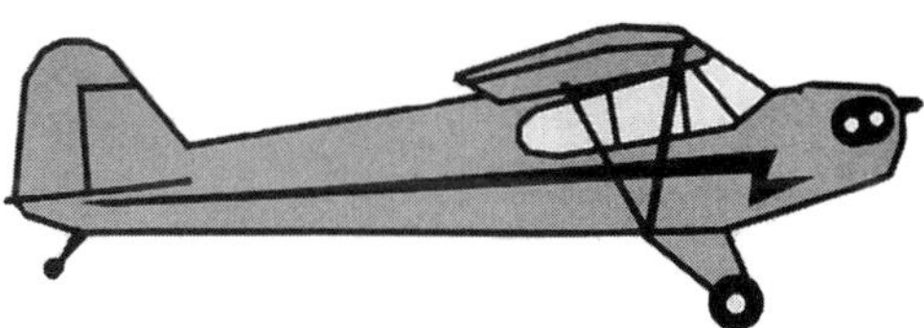

Dear Reader,

That's right. This is it. A Piper J-3 Cub. It's the Grand Prize in our "We've Got Your Number" Sweepstakes II and you may have already won it!

The Cub is a classic. In all, 19,978 were built. The last was in 1947. And now they're getting scarce. But this one could be yours. Meticulously restored, our Cub is still not fast, or quiet, or roomy -- it's just pure enjoyment -- all the pleasures of flight wrapped in a beautiful yellow package.

<u>If you don't want our Cub,</u>
<u>there's only one thing for you to do</u>.

98 out of 100 people are not pilots. Never have been. Never will be. For them a Piper Cub is about as useful as wings on a blimp.

So, if you're not a pilot, get out now! You shouldn't even be seen with an entry certificate. Tear it up and throw it away. Unless you're looking forward to having a seven hundred pound yellow lawn ornament with wings, don't return that card!

BUT, if you are a pilot, if you love planes and delight in the simple joy of flying -- send back your Entry Certificate immediately!

<u>Your chances of winning</u>
<u>have never been better</u>!

Here's why. As we said, 98% of the country isn't interested in flying. And we're not interested in having them in our Sweepstakes either. Zap! We just eliminated about 241,000,000 entries right there.

Now we're down to pilots. And frankly, we're not so hot about all of them.

We're only looking for pilots who take their flying seriously...who

- 2 -

accept the responsibility of command...and who want to be around long enough to win our Sweepstakes and fly the Grand Prize home.

We're encouraging only a select group of pilots like yourself to enter this Sweepstakes. That means that your odds of holding a winning number are far better than in just about any sweepstakes you've ever seen.

And here's a clincher. It's a fact that most people do not return sweepstakes entries. So, even if you don't have the winning number, chances are that whoever does won't return it! So then what happens? We then select the Grand Prize winner from those entries we do receive. And if one of those is yours, you've got a second chance to be the winner!

So, enter! The Piper J-3 Cub could be yours. (If you already have a Cub, you can take $10,000 cash instead. Even if you don't, you can take the cash; we won't mind keeping the Cub for ourselves.)

And the Grand Prize is just one of the 1,043 pilot-perfect prizes we have waiting. You could win a Sony 8mm Camcorder...a Jason celestial telescope...a Sony Mega Watchman...a 76-piece mechanics tool set...or one of One Thousand other runner-up prizes.

<u>Say "YES" and you'll also receive</u>
<u>the next two issues of AVIATION SAFETY</u>
<u>absolutely free</u>!

This is a special sweepstakes. It's just for pilots. It costs nothing to enter. And you'll get two issues of AVIATION SAFETY <u>free</u>! The issues are an $8.00 value, and they're yours just for saying "YES".

We're doing all this to introduce you to <u>the one aviation publication whose purpose is to make your flying safer than ever before</u>.

AVIATION SAFETY, in a little over eight years, has become <u>the</u> most respected and influential accident and safety report in the United States. Our readers aren't merely plane buffs -- they're active <u>pilots</u>.

Among its intensely loyal readers, AVIATION SAFETY is becoming something of an institution. Although we're certain that our subscribers would much rather <u>fly</u> than read about flying -- we believe them when they tell us that AVIATION SAFETY is absolute <u>must</u> reading.

Fine. But why should you, as a pilot, go out of your way to read AVIATION SAFETY?

First, AVIATION SAFETY is your most indispensable source of vital accident information. Twice every month, we focus on recent accidents that deserve close scrutiny not only for their causes -- but also for the implications for <u>you</u>.

You see, we figure the bottom line is this:

<u>When a plane like the one you're flying suffers a serious malfunction or -- even worse -- goes down, you want to know the reasons WHY as soon as possible</u>.

- 3 -

Every issue of AVIATION SAFETY is like strapping yourself into the right seat of a dozen or more aircraft headed for hot water. You'll share the build-up, the crisis, the pilot's reactions, the outcome -- everything but the consequences. Instead, you'll walk away ... with valuable, life-saving information to keep similar trouble away from your own flying.

With comprehensive analysis, AVIATION SAFETY directs special focus on those accidents with inescapable significance for every pilot. You'll get the full details on accidents resulting from a whole spectrum of causes -- human and otherwise.

Each issue is a practical seminar in understanding the hows and whys of mishaps caused by mechanical breakdowns, sloppy maintenance, defective parts, pilot error, horrible weather, rotten luck, and, all too often, plain, old-fashioned stupidity.

You'll find that AVIATION SAFETY's editors give rare clarity to the most complex difficulties, to those problems which can develop in the rigors of a demanding instrument environment or may occur in the operation of today's sophisticated and advanced aviation equipment.

Through AVIATION SAFETY <u>you'll be reminded</u> by those accidents which still happen for all the classic reasons. <u>You'll be informed</u> about those crashes resulting from just-discovered problems or defects. And <u>you'll be forewarned</u> by those accidents occurring from yet unknown causes.

Because "what you don't know" CAN hurt you, AVIATION SAFETY tells you more ... and more often.

We don't think you should have to wait for information that is vital to your flying safety. That's why we publish <u>two</u> issues every month. As soon as we know something, you'll know it too.

And, to make sure that you're kept up-to-date on all aspects of flying safety, every issue includes, not only AVIATION SAFETY's insightful accident analysis, but detailed articles on safe aircraft <u>operations</u> and <u>procedures</u>. Subjects as important and as varied as ...

* Preventing an in-flight airframe failure
* How good is the FAA's weather data?
* Firefighting in the air
* The dividends of an extra-effort pre-flight inspection
* Dealing with the epidemic of misrigging
* A model-by-model comparison of stall spin rates
* How to beat the risk of a wire-strike accident
* Cutting the odds of a mid-air collision

Plus, a new AVIATION SAFETY feature assesses the safety of

- 4 -

individual aircraft. Our comprehensive <u>Aircraft Safety Ratings Guides</u> are designed to help prospective owners of new and used aircraft. We examine the accident records, handling qualities, powerplant problems, design, cockpit layout and more. Altogether 115 factors are considered, resulting in a safety rating that lets you compare fairly and fully before you buy.

It's all information every pilot can use and the savviest pilots refuse to be without.

Judge AVIATION SAFETY for yourself.
Say "YES" and examine our next two issues
with no cost or obligation.

You can't lose! When you return your Sweepstakes Entry not only will you be immediately eligible to win any one of the 1,043 prizes, but you'll also receive the next two issues of AVIATION SAFETY -- <u>absolutely free</u>!

You can put AVIATION SAFETY through your own stringent "flight check." See for yourself how effectively this unique, serious and lively publication delivers the essential safety information that will save you money, time and -- quite possibly -- could save your life.

Then, if you'd like to become a regular subscriber to AVIATION SAFETY, you can .. and at a very special savings! All you have to do is pay the bill we'll send and you'll get 10 additional issues for just $18.

If, on the other hand, you decide not to become a subscriber, simply write "cancel" on the invoice and send it back to us and owe nothing. No further issues will reach your mailbox. The complimentary issues are yours to keep and you'll still be eligible to win the Sweepstakes.

But remember: <u>You must say "YES" to enter the Sweepstakes and receive the two free issues of AVIATION SAFETY</u>.

There's nothing to lose. And there's a lot to win -- starting with that Grand Prize Piper Cub or $10,000.00 cash! So don't wait. Put us to the test. And put yourself into the Sweepstakes today!

Good luck and good flying,

Donn E. Smith
Executive Vice-President

DES:np

The 4-page letter, printed on an 11″ × 17″ sheet.

The circular shown front and back—4-color on the front, 3-color on the back.

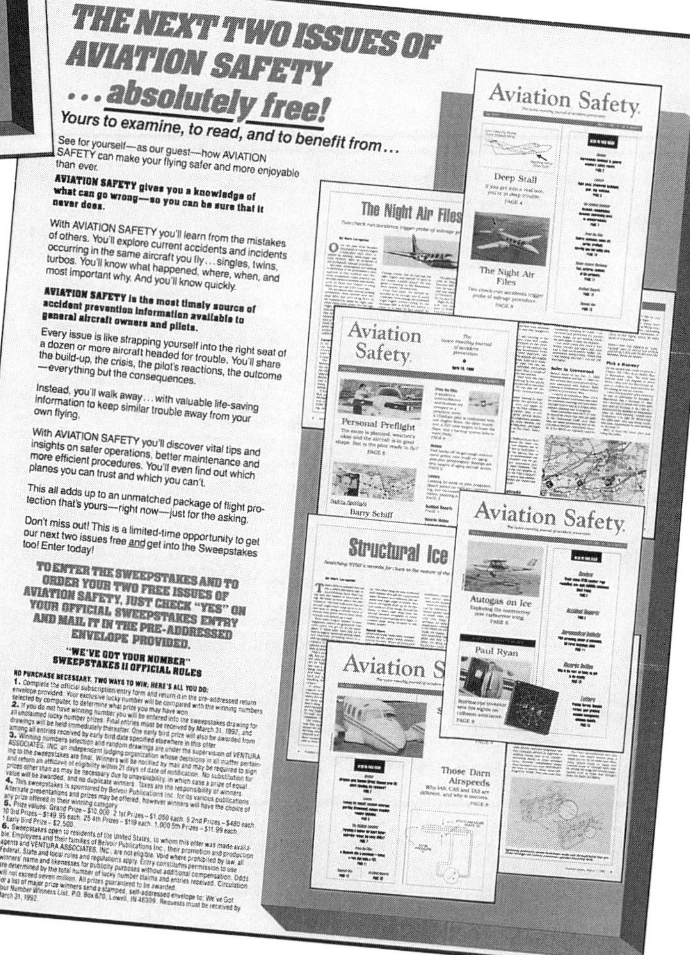

A SERIOUS REASON TO SAY "YES"...

The lift piece.

Aviation Safety

Dear Reader,

There are really two reasons for you to say "YES" when you enter our Sweepstakes.

The first reason is for the fun of it. For the prizes. The Cub...the cash...and 1,042 other prizes all specially selected for pilots. And every one a good reason to get out of the house and get your Entry into the mailbox.

But wait. There's also a serious reason: Two free issues of AVIATION SAFETY.

You see, as pilots we know flying is fun. But we also know it's serious business. And that's how we write AVIATION SAFETY.

AVIATION SAFETY is different. There's no fluff. No fly-ins. No filler. No ads. And no nonsense.

AVIATION SAFETY will tell you what is safe and what is not, be it aircraft, avionics, accessories, airports, or instruction. And we'll tell you why.

From cover to cover every issue is filled with insightful and important safety information you can use every time you fly.

Two issues of AVIATION SAFETY regularly cost $8.00, but they're yours -- with absolutely no cost -- when you say "YES"!

So now get to the mailbox. Enter the Sweepstakes and send for your two free issues!

Sincerely,

Marvin Cweibel
Circulation Director

MC:rev

The sweepstakes entry/ order form.

HAVE YOU ALREADY WON THIS AIRPLANE?

A902125
YOUR ENTRY NUMBER

There's only one way to find out: Enter the Sweepstakes! You may have already won a Piper Cub, or $10,000 cash or one of 1,042 other pilot's dream prizes.
To claim your prize you must return the attached card.
Don't delay—find out if your number has won! Send in your entry today!

OFFICIAL SWEEPSTAKES ENTRY CERTIFICATE # A902125

☐ **YES!** Tell me if I've won! Enter me in the Sweepstakes with the Piper Cub Grand Prize plus 1,042 other prizes and send me the next two issues of AVIATION SAFETY absolutely free!

If I'm impressed with Aviation Safety I may then become a regular subscriber and receive 10 additional issues for just $18. If I decide not to subscribe, I'll just write "cancel" on my bill and owe nothing.

55504543293 OOL1JY

Adam

Ridgefield, CT 06877

☐ No, I will give up my chance to review two free issues, but I would like to enter the Sweepstakes.

AVIATION SAFETY, "WE'VE GOT YOUR NUMBER" SWEEPSTAKES II, PO BOX 420121, PALM COAST, FL 32142

☐ **YES,** enter me in the Sweepstakes and send my two free issues of AVIATION SAFETY.

☐ No, I do not wish to try AVIATION SAFETY. But please enter me in the Sweepstakes.

Aviation Safety
"WE'VE GOT YOUR NUMBER" SWEEPSTAKES II
PO BOX 420121
PALM COAST, FL 32142-0121

The reply envelope. Because this is a sweepstakes offer, the mailer will not pay reply postage. If you want to enter the sweepstakes, it will cost a first-class stamp.

Soundview Executive Book Summaries

"Read all the current important business books—and know what's in them—in fifteen minutes each," is the seductive promise of this service for harried executives. It's not quite a book club, nor is it exactly a newsletter; but it's closer to a newsletter than anything else.

Generally, in direct mail you don't want to repeat the copy or design in one element of a mailing in some other element of the mailing. The logic: a prospect will see it the second time and say, "Whoops, I've seen this before . . ." and lay the entire mailing aside. Once a mailing is laid aside, other pieces of paper are put on top of it and the order is lost.

This effort, written by Don Hauptman and designed by Ted Kikoler, breaks that rule. The copy and design motif on the outer envelope reappear on the first page of the letter. There are two reasons.

MAILER: *Soundview Executive Book Summaries*
PACKAGE: Stopwatch
PROJECT MGR.: Rob Carter
WRITER: Don Hauptman
DESIGNER: Ted Kikoler
FIRST MAILED: Mid-1980s
Don Hauptman's first envelope for *Soundview Executive Book Summaries* which bombed and Ted Kikoler's revision which became a Grand Control.

SLASH
YOUR BUSINESS READING TIME!
Finally—an ingenious, positively ruthless new solution to the chronic complaint *"There's just too much to read!"*
See inside.

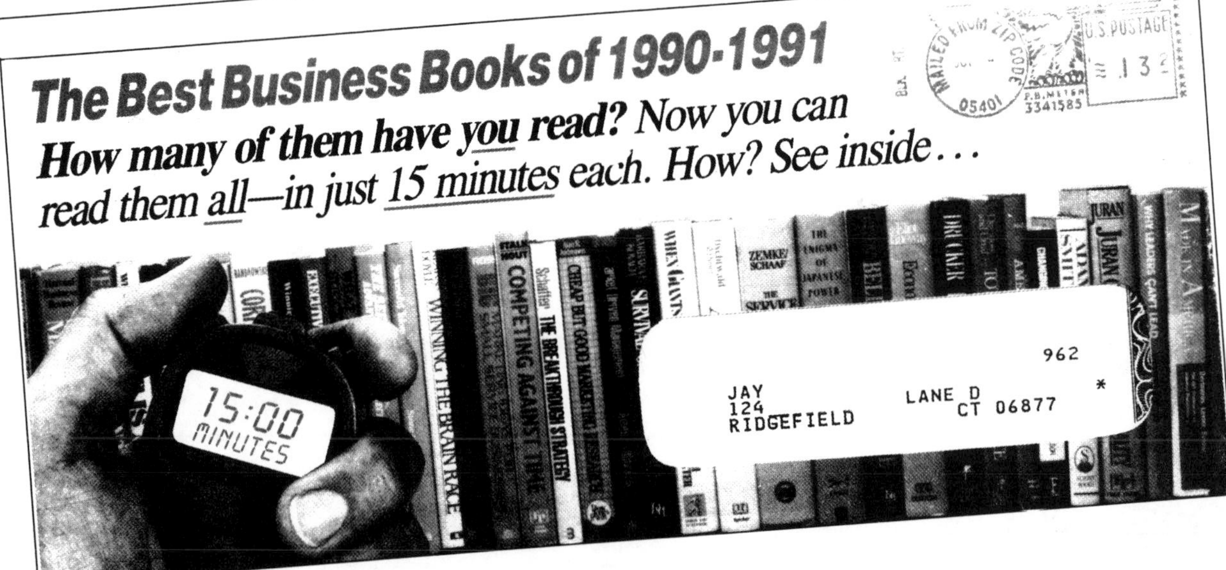

First off, a great deal of time and thought goes into the outer envelope. Yet, in the business environment, the outside envelope may not be seen by the person to whom the mailing is addressed. There may be a secretary or assistant in the outer office who opens the mail, discards the outer envelope, prioritizes the mail, and sends it to the boss unfolded and clipped together along with all the other advertising mail. In the 1960s we used to refer to the secretary as "Whitefang," and spent many hours trying to figure out how to get the mailing past Whitefang (who was always female). Today Whitefang can be of any sex; there are many male secretaries and assistants. I am reminded of the two high-powered women executives wanting to arrange a lunch date; one of them said, "Have your boy call my boy."

If Whitefang discards the envelope, all that powerful copy and design are wasted. Hauptman and Kikoler dealt with this possibility by using the headline from the envelope at the top of the first page of the letter and the design—the stopwatch motif—at the bottom.

In addition, Kikoler believes that if the envelope is opened by the addressee, the repetition of the copy and design on the letter subconsciously leads the person to read the letter first, which is the hope of every direct mail writer, since the letter is (in Malcolm Decker's words) the main salesman.

Unlike most direct response writers who learned their craft working for mailers or agencies, Don Hauptman got out of the Navy in 1974 and went directly "from unemployment to self-employment" as an independent copywriter and consultant, specializing in the marketing of information—newsletters, books, conferences, seminars, computer software, and instructional tapes. He may be best known for his Audio-Forum ads with the long-running headline: "Speak Spanish Like a Diplomat!"

Recently Hauptman published *Cruel and Unusual Puns*, a celebration of spoonerisms, shaggy dog stories, and broadcast bloopers. He calls it the perfect stuffing stocker—er, stocking stuffer. Or, as Bill Bailey might have opined: "It's nothin' but a fine couth tome!"

Don Hauptman:
Here are five principles and techniques for writing direct mail:

1. Start with the prospect instead of the product. *Avoid superlatives and brag-and-boast language. Wherever possible, incorporate anecdotes, testimonials, success stories, and other believable elements of human interest.*
2. Do research. *Interview customers, ask questions, listen carefully. My favorite question is: "What are your (the prospect's) greatest problems, needs, and concerns right now?" At least half the time spent on an assignment is pure research—before attacking the blank page or computer screen.*
3. Use specifics to add power and credibility. *Use precise, documented figures and facts in advertising. Cite data or opinions from outside, impartial sources. A lot of copy is anemic and ineffective because it's superficial, vague, and unspecific. Concrete statements and detail supply the ring of truth. But to find this kind of material, you've often got to dig for it.*

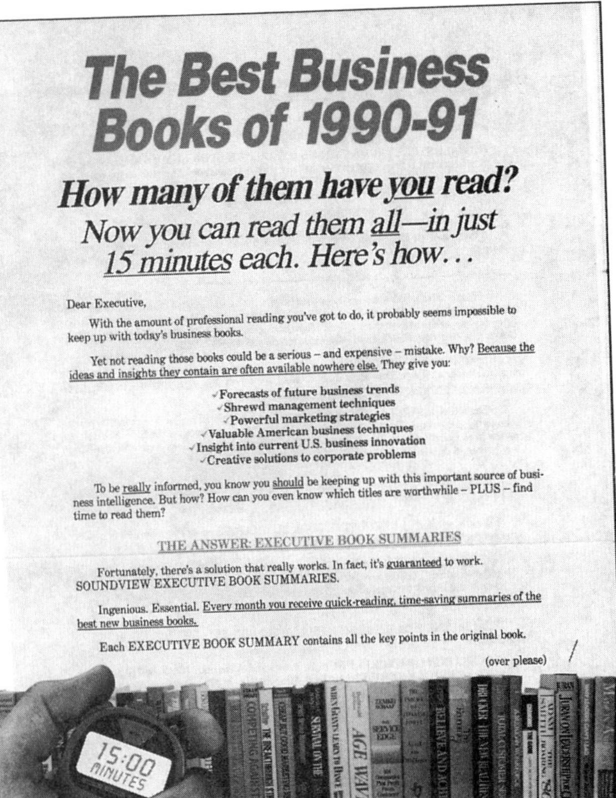

The Best Business Books of 1990-91

How many of them have you read?

Now you can read them all—in just 15 minutes each. Here's how...

Dear Executive,

With the amount of professional reading you've got to do, it probably seems impossible to keep up with today's business books.

Yet not reading those books could be a serious – and expensive – mistake. Why? Because the ideas and insights they contain are often available nowhere else. They give you:

- ✓ **Forecasts of future business trends**
- ✓ **Shrewd management techniques**
- ✓ **Powerful marketing strategies**
- ✓ **Valuable American business techniques**
- ✓ **Insight into current U.S. business innovation**
- ✓ **Creative solutions to corporate problems**

To be really informed, you know you should be keeping up with this important source of business intelligence. But how? How can you even know which titles are worthwhile – PLUS – find time to read them?

THE ANSWER: EXECUTIVE BOOK SUMMARIES

Fortunately, there's a solution that really works. In fact, it's guaranteed to work. SOUNDVIEW EXECUTIVE BOOK SUMMARIES.

Ingenious. Essential. Every month you receive quick-reading, time-saving summaries of the best new business books.

Each EXECUTIVE BOOK SUMMARY contains all the key points in the original book.

(over please)

The big difference: instead of 200-500 pages, the summary is only 8 pages. Instead of taking five, ten or more hours to read, it takes just 15 minutes!

The SUMMARIES are the ideal length for the traveling executive. They take up little room in a briefcase and turn wasted commuting time into productive learning time.

The WALL STREET JOURNAL hails EXECUTIVE BOOK SUMMARIES as "An inventive answer to what is becoming an increasingly irksome management problem: too much to read."

HOW MANY BUSINESS BOOKS SHOULD YOU READ

Of the thousands of business books published each year, only a handful are really worth reading.

We know it.

We're specialists. We're the business book people. We've summarized hundreds of business books. Each of those summaries is available to help you save time. And that's our job, to save you time. So we search out every new title of interest to executives. Our highly professional Editorial Board reads through them all and eliminates roughly 99 out of 100 titles.

Our criteria is rigorous. "Is this book truly useful to our subscribers? Does it say something new and important? Are there ideas that will help executives save time, increase profits, avoid problems, work more productively, advance their careers?"

When a book meets all our tests, it is assigned to a professional business writer who reads it thoroughly, several times, extracting every useful idea. Then he prepares the SUMMARY. Not a review (somebody's opinion). Not a digest (book excerpts strung together). A skillful distillation that preserves the content and spirit of the entire book.

HOW MANY OF THESE OUTSTANDING BUSINESS BOOKS HAVE YOU READ?

The titles selected by EXECUTIVE BOOK SUMMARIES cover every subject of concern to international business people today:

Management techniques. . .Advertising and marketing. . .Productivity. . .Leadership and motivation. . .Career advice. . .Effective communication. . .Hiring and firing. . . Health and fitness. . .Negotiation. . .Time management. . .Small business tactics. . . Computers. . .Strategic planning. . .And much more.

Here's just a sampling of the many superb business titles we summarized for our subscribers:

- **IN SEARCH OF EXCELLENCE**, by Peters and Waterman. (Book: ~~360~~ pages)
- **AT AMERICA'S SERVICE!**, by Karl Albrecht. (Book: ~~175~~ pages)
- **MADE IN AMERICA**, by MIT Commission. (Book: ~~344~~ pages)
- **THRIVING ON CHAOS**, by Tom Peters. (Book: ~~561~~ pages)
- **TOTAL CUSTOMER SERVICE**, by Davidow and Uttal. (Book: ~~287~~ pages)

- **WORK SMART, NOT HARD**, by George Sullivan. (Book: ~~245~~ pages)
- **WHEN GIANTS LEARN TO DANCE**, by Rosabeth Kanter. (Book: ~~415~~ pages)
- **THE NEW REALITIES**, by Peter Drucker (Book: ~~276~~ pages)
- **THE SERVICE EDGE**, by Zemke and Schaaf. (Book: ~~584~~ pages)
- And many more

Important books. New Books. Best sellers. Books people talk about. Books that broaden your business knowledge and sharpen your management skills. Books with useful ideas, answers and solutions that bring results for you – every business day. And of course, we include the business classics you've never had a chance to read – wise, enormously useful books that have never been equalled.

Because we're concerned with bringing you the background and the ideas you need – we're not about to send you useless time-wasters.

Each SUMMARY takes 15 to 20 minutes to read. And remember: you're getting the concentrated essence of the whole book – not selected chapters or excerpted passages.

5 KEY BENEFITS YOU'LL RECEIVE

International executives have discovered this unique new method for keeping totally informed in today's competitive business environment. Join them and you'll realize these 5 important advantages:

1. **Get ideas you can use.** Our subscribers tell us they regularly discover a wealth of ideas in the SUMMARIES. Ideas they put to work immediately. Because of its concise form, the content is far more accessible than it is when buried in a book.

2. **Increase your business confidence.** EXECUTIVE BOOK SUMMARIES give you a "talking knowledge" of the latest and the best business books. The next time someone mentions "Time Is Money: Save It" or the latest Peter Drucker book – you'll know what the book is all about. And you'll be prepared to respond intelligently.

3. **Learn more, remember more.** Unfortunately, even books with the best ideas are not always well written or well edited. But in an EXECUTIVE BOOK SUMMARY, the author's ideas are presented in the simplest, clearest, most logically organized way. Readers tell us the SUMMARIES are less repetitious, easier to comprehend. (According to a scientific study, the ideas in a summary are more easily remembered than the same ideas in a book.)

4. **Reduce your reading time by hundreds of hours.** Think of what would happen if you could get the essence of a book in minutes instead of hours! You'd clear your calendar for more important projects, for yourself, for your family.

5. **Never waste money on books you'll never read.** How many times have you bought a book that sounded good, but turned out to be useless. Our screening process separates the winning titles from the losers that do nothing but absorb your precious time. You'll never again throw away valuable time – or money – on an uninformative title.

Take 2 months. See next page →

SPECIAL INTRODUCTORY OFFER
2 MONTHS FREE

But no matter what I say, nothing can take the place of experiencing EXECUTIVE BOOK SUMMARIES for yourself. Try it. Over the next 12 months, you'll receive 30 summaries – two or three per month. The 30 best business books of the year. Reading time: 15 to 20 minutes apiece.

The regular price for a one-year subscription is $96. But our special introductory price is just $69.50 – a 28% savings. Tax-deductible to you or your company.

What's more, if you act now, you can take advantage of our special offer of 2 months free (5 SUMMARIES) to try at no risk – and you'll also receive the amazingly useful bonus book "SKILLS FOR SUCCESS: BUSINESS EXPERTS SHOW YOU THE WAY".

Add up your savings:

Two free months (5 SUMMARIES)	$ 16.00
One year subscription (30 SUMMARIES)	96.00
BONUS BOOK: **"Skills for Success"**	12.95
TOTAL VALUE	~~$124.95~~
YOU PAY ONLY	69.50

You save $55.45

Today, the average cost of a business book is $22.50. To buy the 30 books we'll be summarizing over the next year would cost you around $675.00. And would you have the time to read even half of them?

You risk nothing. If you're not 100% pleased with your first SUMMARIES, let us know and we'll send you a full refund. Fair enough?

There's nothing else like Soundview's Executive Book Summaries. Executives coast to coast, in every field, have discovered this unique time – and money – saving solution. Shouldn't you join them and find out what all the excitement is about?

A subscription certificate is enclosed. Please complete and mail it today.

Sincerely

Cynthia Langley Folino
Publisher

P.S. Don't forget your extra free gift. Send in the subscription certificate right away and we'll send you, FREE, a copy of "SKILLS FOR SUCCESS: THE EXPERTS SHOW THE WAY" – the book with hundreds of terrific ideas from past SUMMARIES. Whether or not you stay with us as a subscriber, you still keep this enormously handy reference tool! Subscribe now!

SOUNDVIEW Executive Book Summaries
5 Main Street, Bristol, VT 05443 USA

The 4-page letter, printed on an 11″ × 17″ sheet. Notice how Kikoler uses handwritten notes in the margins.

4. Don't try to change behavior. *It's time-consuming, expensive, and often futile. It's usually wise to capitalize on existing motivations. In other words, preach to the converted. Unless you have an unlimited budget, avoid products and services that require the buyer to be educated or radically transformed.*
5. Be a "creative plagiarist." *You can learn by studying the work of others. But don't imitate, emulate, or re-create. When you see an idea you admire, try to identify the principles behind it, then apply those principles in a fresh, original way to your own work.*

In *The Newsletter on Newsletters,* editor and publisher Howard Penn Hudson reported on the story of Hauptman's control for *Soundview Executive Book Summaries.* It is reprinted here with permission.

Turning a Direct Mail Flop into a Winner

Do copywriters ever make mistakes? Does a mailing sometimes bomb? You'd better believe it. But occasionally, even a promotional catastrophe can have a happy ending.

Copywriter Don Hauptman tells us an intriguing story of a strategic error he committed in a subscription promotion campaign—and the strikingly different results of the two sets of tests that followed.

The brochure shown front and back.

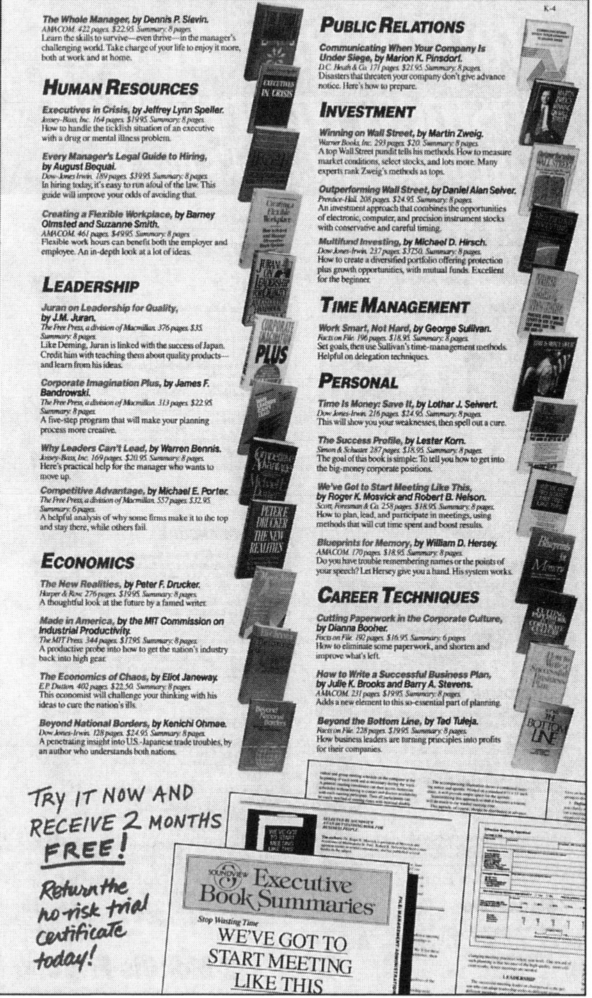

Soundview Executive Book Summaries *is an unusual publication. The editorial consists largely of condensations of business and management books—the object being to save time for busy executives. Yet despite its novel format,* Soundview *has ''newsletter economics'' in all respects. The monthly has a paid circulation of 25,000. The subscription price is $59.50* [*currently $69.50*] *annually. There is no bill-me option; all subs are paid in advance via check or credit card.*

The first package Hauptman wrote had this carrier shown at the beginning: ''SLASH your business reading time.''

The control beat it by 23 percent.

''I went back to the proverbial drawing board and realized I had made a mistake,'' Hauptman confesses. [*The late*] Soundview *editor Harold Longman had warned me that books have to be emphasized up-front. I ignored his advice. Instead, I tried to be provocative, intentionally disguising the nature of the product in an attempt to entice a larger number of people inside.*

''What probably happened is that the executive assumed from the teaser that we'd help him with his routine *reading tasks: correspondence, memos, reports, trade publications. When he opened the envelope, we lost him. Meanwhile, many 'book people'—genuine prospects—never got inside.*

''I should have targeted the book-oriented *executive from the start,'' Hauptman concludes. He called the client and offered to do a revision. He created a new carrier and rewrote the opening of the letter.*

The result? This time, Hauptman's revision outpulled the control by 27 percent. It's now the publisher's new control package.

Comments Soundview *publisher Cynthia Langley Folino: ''When his first effort didn't work, Don was eager to go back and try again, without charge. We were impressed. Not every copywriter would be willing to do that.''*

The moral of the story? There probably isn't a publisher or copywriter on earth who hasn't made some giant mistakes. The real question is whether you can acknowledge a blunder, analyze why it happened, learn from the experience, and recycle that knowledge back into your marketing to improve future results.

Howard Hudson is dead on. No copywriter likes to create a loser. Why not go back to the copywriter with the results and ask what might be done to salvage the package and turn it into a winner?

When Hemingway was producing novels, he would create a first draft and then stick it in a drawer for six months while he went hunting in Africa or followed a matador and his cuadrilla around Spain. After the long hiatus, he could look at the manuscript with absolutely fresh eyes and start rewriting.

Copywriters seldom have that luxury. And chances are good that between the time a writer completes the assignment and several months later when the results are in, the writer will immediately see some changes that he or she would have made if only there had not been those impossible deadlines at first.

Freelancer Richard Silverman and I once talked about this, and we both agreed that if a client came back to us for ideas on how to make a losing package a winner—and was willing to give it another shot—we'd gladly make revisions, and for no additional charge.

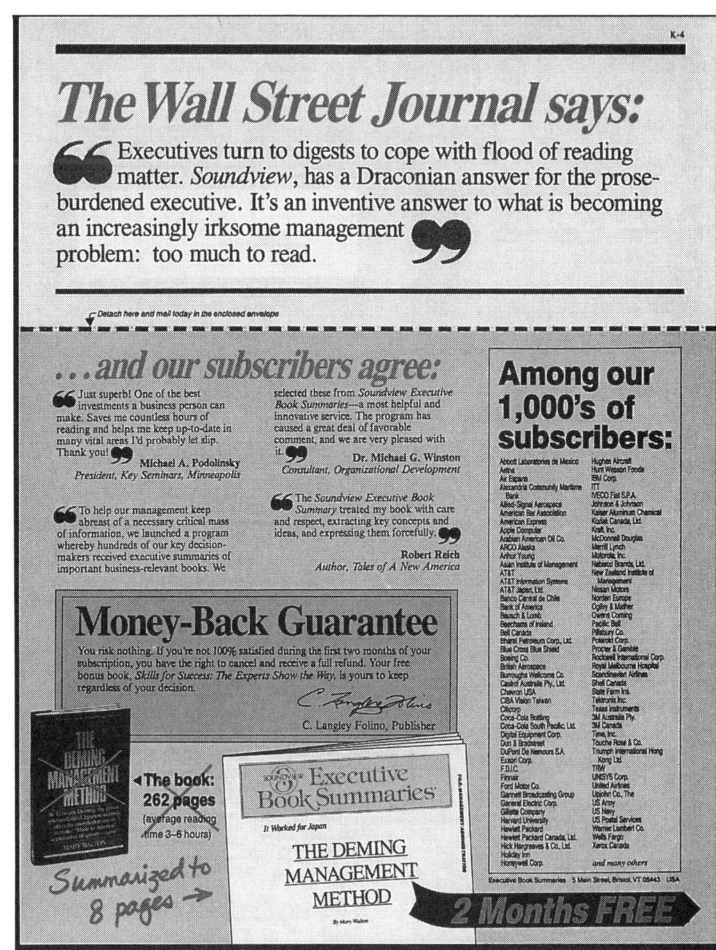

The order form shown front and back. Hauptman and Kikoler have "sell" all over this piece. Notice the testimonial from the *Wall Street Journal* on the back; the name of the publication is set large and the quote small. The reason: if you have a testimonial from a big name person or organization, scream it to the skies; the source is more important than the testimonial. Also shown, the business reply envelope.

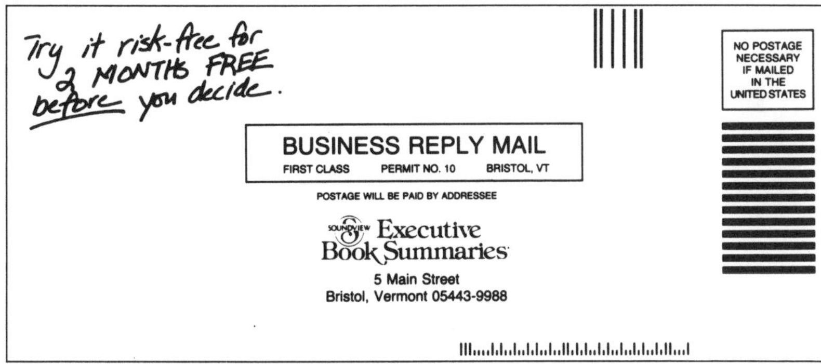

20

Business and Financial Magazines

Of all the direct mail I read, the most tedious, boring junk is from mailers trying to sell products and services to people at their place of business. For me, the term *junk mail* is too kind to describe 95 percent of the business-to-business mail I see; because of the boredom factor, there are other four-letter words that more aptly describe it.

There is a reason: *business-to-business* is a misnomer.

At one point I was thinking of writing a book on business-to-business direct mail and was having severe trouble with the title. Business-to-business direct mail sounds as though a business were talking to a business. The image runs through my mind of great megalithic computers grunting out unreadable MBA yuppietalk messages that could only be read by some other great megalithic computer. Much of the mail going to the workplace fits that model.

At Seattle Direct Marketing Day in 1990 I was sitting at lunch with freelancer Herschell Gordon Lewis and Nancy Haug, director of direct marketing for Airborne Express. I said that the term *business-to-business* direct mail was misleading. Businesses don't write letters to other businesses. Mailings go to *people*; people in the workplace happen to be consumers sitting behind a desk or wandering around the factory floor or standing behind a sales counter. I wanted to call the book "Business to People."

"That's not very good," Lewis said. "You don't write letters to people; in direct mail you are talking to each individual *person*."

"Call the book 'Business to Ralph,' " Nancy Haug volunteered.

She was on to something. At least there was acknowledgment that a *person* would be receiving the message. But calling that person Ralph was sexist; the workplace was full of women.

"How about 'Business to Ralph and Nancy,' " I suggested.

That was not very strong either. The implication was still there that a business was creating the mailing, that it was totally impersonal. After some discussion, we came up with a title: "Ralph and Nancy at the Office: The Art & Science of Reaching People in the Workplace and Persuading Them to Act."

The book has yet to be written, but the concept embodied in the title is with me always whenever I write a direct mail package aimed at the business environment as well as whenever I report on one.

I say glibly that a person in the office is a consumer sitting behind a desk and should therefore respond to all the techniques tested in the consumer arena. It's not quite that easy.

Yes, the person behind a desk responds to all the basic human needs and wants: fear, greed, power, lust, self-worth, a bargain, something for nothing. But any mailing to the workplace must also deal with the following circumstances:

1. The mailing must get past the mail room and past "Whitefang"—the secretary or assistant. If the outside envelope looks like Marvel Comics or a *Penthouse* cover, it may offend, not be taken seriously, and be discarded before the right person sees it.
2. The person in the office is different from the same person at home. At home, people can lie around on the sofa in grubby clothes munching potato chips and watching the tube, while taking pointed barbs from the in-laws who are visiting. At the office, this person dresses up and, like Rodney Dangerfield, hopes to get some respect. A wild mailing might intrigue the consumer at home but make the same person feel diminished at the office.
3. In the workplace people are spending the company's money, not their own. Offers mailed into the business arena cannot simply gratify a personal need; they have to demonstrate a value to the business as well.
4. The decision to purchase may not rest with the person receiving the mailing. A group decision or the okay from someone higher up may be involved. This is especially the case of a high-priced item. If so, the mailing will most certainly be passed along. After all, if someone thinks enough of an offer to forward it to someone else in the company, isn't that a tacit testimonial from a stranger in behalf of the product or service?
5. People at work spend their time absorbing information and figuring how to put that information to work for them. They want quick fixes, not long, boring diatribes. If a person in the office can grasp the benefits and their importance in one minute instead of three minutes, response should be higher. There is no place for dull, copy-heavy junk mail anywhere, anytime, but most especially in the workplace. This is borne out by comparing the length of direct mail letters of consumer magazines that of such letters of business and financial magazines. If you study the statistical grids in Appendix 1, you will see that the average letter length of consumer magazines is 3.3 pages while business and financial magazine letters average only 2.1 pages, or 36 percent less. What's more, 64 percent of business magazine mailings have window envelopes; 79 percent of them announce that they are advertising mail by having promotional copy on their envelopes; and 71 percent of these mailings use the word *free* prominently.

In *Who's Mailing What!* I once reported on a small side business of Publishers Clearing House (PCH)—getting magazines into the reception rooms of doctors and small companies. Everybody in the country receives giant PCH mailings with huge window and dazzling personalized headlines that scream $10 million in sweepstakes prizes. When the company mails into the business arena, the outside envelope is discreet enough to get through the mail room and into the hands of Whitefang. Once inside the package, however, you find all the traditional PCH bells and whistles from their consumer efforts—albeit a bit muted: stamp sheet, $10 million sweeps entry-order certificate, prize brochures, a flyer touting those magazines where you save the most, a personalized letter with a personalized Post-It-like piece stuck on, and a fake check for $50 to illustrate the amount you'll win if you are among the first fifty respondents.

In the words of Robin Smith, the perceptive and articulate president of Publishers Clearing House: "We tried upscale mailings to businesses and they didn't do any better than downscale mailings to businesses."

Advertising Age I

Personalizing a mailing is more expensive than simply printing a label and slapping it on an order card. As we have pointed out, very few of these seventy-one Grand Controls use personalization for no apparent reason—Book-of-the-Month, *Harper's*, *National Wildlife*, and *Financial World*.

The two *Advertising Age* packages in this chapter stretch personalization techniques to the outer limits of effectiveness. Since both offer personalized premiums, the direct mail solicitations are themselves personalized to show off precisely what the free goodies are.

Just about everybody has received mailings with personalized cartoons on the #10 envelopes from *Advertising Age* and *Sales & Marketing Management*. There has been much media coverage lately about the use of these devices in direct mail. Yet, for all that has been written about them, two questions have remained unanswered: Do they hype response? How much do they cost?

The premier practitioner of the personalized cartoon is Stu Heinecke, head of a West Coast agency that bears his name, in a joint venture with WX Wordtronics. Heinecke, bespectacled, with a long, craggy John Carradine face, makes no secret of his love for what he calls his Project X. "My God, I get to work with my heroes—Gahan, Arnie, Eldon, Cullum!" he enthuses. He has assembled a stable of world-class cartoonists and a library of their cartoons—along with many of his own—on a variety of themes: general business-to-business, lawyers, doctors, restaurateurs, banking, travel, investments. All can be personalized.

When we asked Heinecke for information, he sent a sheaf of thirty personalized cartoons, each more fun than the next. My favorite: an executive on the phone saying, "Put Donald Trump on hold; I need to talk to Denny Hatch."

Do they increase response?

MAILER: *Advertising Age*
PACKAGE: Cartoon Letter
PROJECT MGR.: David Kelley
WRITER: David Kelley
DESIGNER: Stu Heinecke
FIRST MAILED: 1990
The #10 outside envelope, closed face, with a personalized cartoon.

Advertising Age
965 East Jefferson
Detroit, Michigan 48207

"We need someone with vision, creativity, and great marketing instincts... someone like A. Walker."

October 29, 1991

A. A.
Lane
Ridgefield, CT 06877

Dear A. A. Walker:

The Publisher of Advertising Age asked me to make a very special subscription offer to a small, select group of advertising and marketing professionals. Your name was submitted to me as one who qualifies.

So ... here it is -- a private invitation to subscribe to Advertising Age at the best discount I can offer -- a savings of $20 off the regular subscription price. And, if you send in your subscription order by November 25, 1991, you will also receive an 8 X 10, suitable-for-framing gallery print of the cartoon above, personalized with your name.

This limited edition cartoon by famous New Yorker cartoonist Leo Cullum will be personalized with your name, and mailed to you absolutely free and with our compliments.

This opportunity to subscribe to Advertising Age at such a low rate is being offered to you A. A. Walker, because we are sure that you will benefit from the advertising, marketing, and media news and analysis which Advertising Age provides each week.

You see, just because you're reading this letter we know this much about you -- in one way or another you're in the business of making products or services move. That tells us you're different.

You've made a decision to put up with a unique set of demands and challenges. You want to move your business ahead. You want to move your career ahead. And you're willing to pay the price to fulfill your ambitions.

You're also a busy person. Long hours. Short deadlines. High expectations. And intense commitment. Few people realize what you go through

next page please...

Advertising Age

2

every day. And only a couple of business publications even come close to meeting your unique information requirements.

That's because -- to deliver the knowledge you need -- a publication would have to live inside your world. Understand your job. And feel the pulse of every segment of the industry that impacts yours.

That's Advertising Age -- and that has been our only mission for over 60 years.

In each weekly issue, Ad Age delivers news, features and analysis on every aspect of the marketing process. Nothing important is skipped. Market research and testing. New product development and packaging. Ad budgets, media strategy, media buying. Sales Promotion. Direct Marketing. International marketing news. Accounts up for grabs. The key players -- people making the key decisions. People on the way up -- people on the way out. Client news, brand news, agency news, media news.

You'll be among the first to discover the closely guarded marketing strategies of the world's leading companies and agencies. Then you'll see the competitors develop their counter-strategy. It all unfolds in the pages of Ad Age every week.

You'll get the latest, hottest advertising and marketing news from around the world, and in your own backyard. You may even get your next job from "The Advertising Marketplace," the most widely read classified section in the entire world of advertising.

You'll be inspired by the international creative brilliance which Advertising Age covers like no one else. You'll see the latest creative trends and market-shaking promotions. You'll see what's working ... and who's creating it.

You'll get special reports on Newspapers, Magazines, Cable, Network Programming, Hispanic Marketing, Retailing, Automotive Marketing, Travel Marketing, Sports Marketing, Computer Marketing, Grocery Marketing, Licensing, and on, and on.

Everything essential is covered -- and covered intelligently. In fact, we guarantee that you'll never be at a loss for the most current news, information, and knowledge in the business. If you're ever not 100% satisfied, just let us know. We'll stop your subscription, and you'll get a full refund -- no questions asked.

Along with your weekly issues of Advertising Age -- you'll receive two special bonus issues at no extra charge. First, you'll get our annual Advertising Agency Profiles issue in March. This valuable reference examines every agency in the country with measurable income. It lists agency officers,

next page please...

Advertising Age

3

department heads, and other key personnel. It ranks every agency by income, billings and size, and reports on accounts gained and lost during the past year.

You'll also receive The 100 Leading National Advertisers issue in September. This jumbo reference issue has been an industry standard for over 30 years. In it you'll get a close up look at the biggest companies with the biggest budgets. Key personnel are listed by name, along with precise data on corporate budgets and budgets for every brand and service offered. You'll get to look at the marketing strategies of these companies and see how, where, and why they are spending over $32 billion on advertising this year.

These annual reference issues will provide you with some of the most valuable data in the advertising marketplace. Many people pay separately for these issues, but for you they are included with your subscription to Ad Age at no extra charge as part of this special offer.

You are invited to subscribe to Advertising Age at this time at a special private offer subscription rate. Your rate -- just $64 for an entire 52 issue year -- is a full $20 off the regular price.

To activate your subscription please complete the enclosed Acceptance Certificate and mail it in today in the postage-paid envelope provided. That's all you need to do. I'll make sure that your own personal copy of Ad Age shows up on your desk every week.

But please, make sure you reply today. This is a special private offer. As a result, we must request that your Acceptance Certificate be mailed no later than November 25, 1991.

Sincerely,

Dave Kelley

Dave Kelley
Subscription Manager

P.S. If you liked seeing yourself in the cartoon on this letter, you'll enjoy seeing it in the 8 X 10 suitable-for-framing gallery print I have reserved in your name. Simply send in your completed Acceptance Certificate in the enclosed postage-paid envelope. It's perfect for the office.

The 3-page letter, printed on 3 nested $8^{1}/_{2}'' \times 11''$ sheets; the personalized cartoon is repeated at the top of page 1.

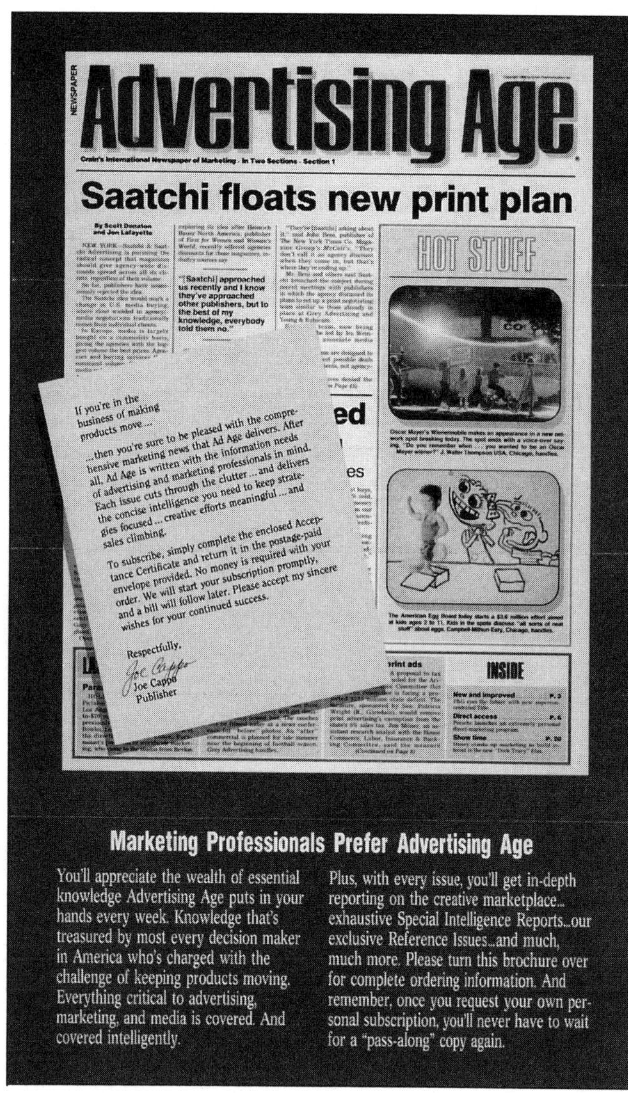

NEWSPAPER
Advertising Age
Crain's International Newspaper of Marketing · In Two Sections · Section 1
Saatchi floats new print plan
"[Saatchi] approached us recently and I know they've approached other publishers, but to the best of my knowledge, everybody told them no."
HOT STUFF
INSIDE
If you're in the business of making products move...
...then you're sure to be pleased with the comprehensive marketing news that Ad Age delivers. After all, Ad Age is written with the information needs of advertising and marketing professionals in mind. Each issue cuts through the clutter ... and delivers the concise intelligence you need to keep strategies focused ... creative efforts meaningful ... and sales climbing.
To subscribe, simply complete the enclosed Acceptance Certificate and return it in the postage-paid envelope provided. No money is required with your order. We will start your subscription promptly, and a bill will follow later. Please accept my sincere wishes for your continued success.
Respectfully,
Joe Cappo
Publisher
Marketing Professionals Prefer Advertising Age
You'll appreciate the wealth of essential knowledge Advertising Age puts in your hands every week. Knowledge that's treasured by most every decision maker in America who's charged with the challenge of keeping products moving. Everything critical to advertising, marketing, and media is covered. And covered intelligently.
Plus, with every issue, you'll get in-depth reporting on the creative marketplace... exhaustive Special Intelligence Reports...our exclusive Reference Issues...and much, much more. Please turn this brochure over for complete ordering information. And remember, once you request your own personal subscription, you'll never have to wait for a "pass-along" copy again.

Advertising Age

Helping you keep strategies focused, creative efforts meaningful, and products moving each and every week of the year.

UP TO THE MINUTE NEWS

Every week you'll discover that your copy of Ad Age is packed with late breaking news that's unavailable from any other single source...at any price. You'll stay fully informed with the concise summaries of "Global News Roundup" and "U.S. Newswatch." Plus you'll profit from exclusive, colorful, and revealing investigative reports on the companies, personalities and strategies that affect us all.

36 SPECIAL REPORTS

You'll get a wealth of essential knowledge with "36 Special Reports." Each report singles out and covers in detail just one segment of the industry. And whether the topic is direct marketing, auto marketing, publishing, or radio, you'll know what makes it tick when you're done.

MEDIA WORKS

You'll get the right ammo for smart media decisions from "Media Works." All the major media are covered. And so are the unknowns, the start-ups, and the alternate media that can help you put together a brilliant media plan.

GLOBAL GALLERY

Every week, "Global Gallery" gives you a chance to look at, dissect, inspect and understand the best creative in the world. You'll see what's working. You'll find out who's creating it. And you'll know what it's achieved.

ADVERTISING MARKETPLACE

Ad Age is proud to feature the most widely read classified section in the world of advertising, sales promotion, and marketing. The weekly "Advertising Marketplace" is your personal guide to new business opportunities...important industry contacts...hot creative resources...and profitable employment possibilities.

PEOPLE

The advertising and marketing community is full of colorful personalities who shape industry direction each day. Ad Age gives you a close look at the players who make big news...and force big change. You'll gain important insight from their successes...and avoid the pitfalls of their failures.

VIEWPOINT

"Viewpoint" is your opportunity to consider the opinions, editorials, and essays of respected industry leaders each week. It's a thought-provoking sounding board that often calls the industry insider to a sober consideration of our methods, responsibilities, and power.

SALES PROMOTION NEWS

Sales promotion continues to command massive budgets in a vast array of product categories. That's why Ad Age remains committed to keeping you fully informed of the new strategies and creative talents behind todays market shaking promotions.

ADREVIEW

Each week, Bob Garfield gets the last word with his critique of a notable campaign, ad, or commercial. His column is always insightful...sometimes disturbing... and most enjoyable. Of course, once you get in the habit of reading "ADREVIEW" you won't want to stop. After all, you never know when one of your campaigns will win a well-deserved "four stars" from Bob.

INTERNATIONAL NEWS

In today's world, chances are that your professional future is taking shape beyond your own national borders. A lot is changing quickly. Walls are breaking down. Borders are opening up. International mergers are increasing. And restrictions are easing. It all spells opportunity for the well informed Ad Age reader.

ANNUAL REFERENCE ISSUES

Each year we publish "The 100 Leading National Advertisers," and "U.S. Advertising Agency Profiles." Between them you'll see major advertisers spending billions of dollars. And now you'll know exactly how, where and why. Of course, we urge you to be thorough in your use of these two reference issues. After all, you just might find some very critical ammo for your next client presentation... or essential competitor data for your next product launch.

Subscribing Is Easy

Simply complete the enclosed Acceptance Certificate, and return it in the postage-paid envelope provided. Or fax the card to 313-446-0961.

ADVERTISING AGE

Circulation Department • 965 E. Jefferson • Detroit, Michigan 48207

The 8½″ × 14″ brochure shown front and back; front is 4-color, back 3-color.

Dave Kelley of *Ad Age* is delighted with his results. His package has the personalized cartoon on the #10 outer and then repeats it twice inside—at the top of the letter and on the order card. Kelley's offer: a $40 discount on a subscription and—free with payment—an 8″ × 10″ limited edition of a personalized cartoon by *New Yorker* cartoonist Leo Cullum, suitable for framing. According to Kelley, this was the most successful test of the year, with great up-front response, okay pay-up, and the highest cash with order in the history of *Ad Age*. Apparently prospects are so excited about seeing their name on the personalized cartoon premium, a disproportionate number write a check on the spot.

Judy Samuels at *Sales & Marketing Management* reported great up-front response, but less-than-terrific pay-up. Her package repeated the envelope cartoon only on the letter but did not offer the premium suitable for framing. She is currently testing the personalized cartoon suitable for framing plus a "nifty fifty" wrinkle: if your order is among the first fifty to be received, you will receive your personalized cartoon signed by the artist a cartoon postcard has replaced this # 10 effort as control.

As for costs, Stu Heinecke had been charging as much as $25,000 for conception, copy, design, and an original *exclusive* cartoon, but found that prospective clients were balking at that high front-end risk. So now he offers a menu of choices. There is a minimum-use fee of $3,000 for mailings of 5,000 or less, with the per-piece rate falling to 7 cents at 100,000, all the way down to a penny on huge rollouts. For an additional $2,500, an original *nonexclusive* cartoon can be created that will then go into the Image Bank (library) after first use by a client; an exclusive design is $5,000, plus all royalties. If Heinecke does the creative, there is a $2,500 fee for full copy and $2,500 for full design. According to Dave Kelley, the 8″ × 10″ personalized premium cartoon is in the mail for $3. Project X mailings are marketed and produced exclusively by WX Wordtronics. According to Howard Strome of Wordtronics, a 100,000 #10 cartoon mailing with personalized cartoon on the OSE, letter and order form, three-page letter, BRE, cartoon royalty, and inserting and mailing would be approximately $400 per thousand; to this must be added the cost of any additional flyers, postage, and list rental. Not cheap, but it can more than pay for itself.

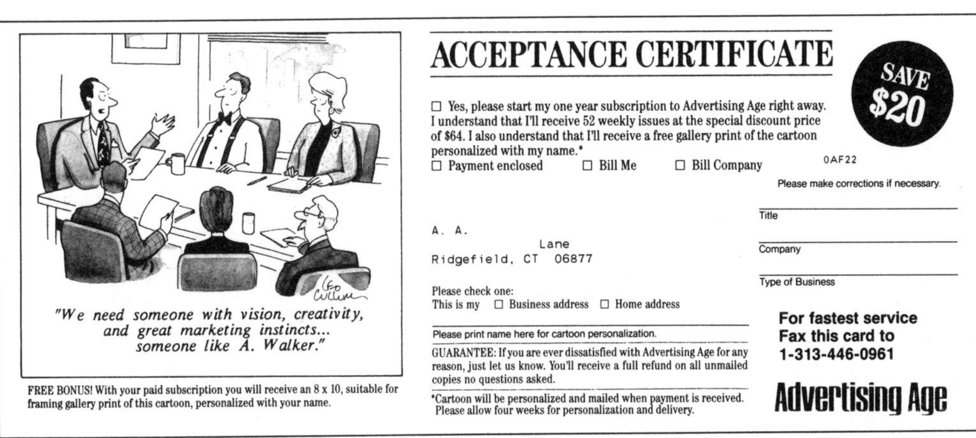

"We need someone with vision, creativity, and great marketing instincts... someone like A. Walker."

FREE BONUS! With your paid subscription you will receive an 8 x 10, suitable for framing gallery print of this cartoon, personalized with your name.

ACCEPTANCE CERTIFICATE

SAVE $20

☐ Yes, please start my one year subscription to Advertising Age right away. I understand that I'll receive 52 weekly issues at the special discount price of $64. I also understand that I'll receive a free gallery print of the cartoon personalized with my name.*

☐ Payment enclosed ☐ Bill Me ☐ Bill Company

0AF22

Please make corrections if necessary.

A. A.
Lane
Ridgefield, CT 06877

Title

Company

Type of Business

Please check one:
This is my ☐ Business address ☐ Home address

Please print name here for cartoon personalization.

GUARANTEE: If you are ever dissatisfied with Advertising Age for any reason, just let us know. You'll receive a full refund on all unmailed copies no questions asked.

*Cartoon will be personalized and mailed when payment is received. Please allow four weeks for personalization and delivery.

For fastest service
Fax this card to
1-313-446-0961

Advertising Age

The order card with personalized cartoon repeated.

NO POSTAGE NECESSARY IF MAILED IN THE UNITED STATES

BUSINESS REPLY MAIL
FIRST CLASS PERMIT NO. 26887 DETROIT, MI

Postage Will Be Paid By Addressee

Advertising Age
Subscription Department
965 East Jefferson
Detroit, Michigan 48207-9901

The business reply envelope.

Advertising Age II

The second *Ad Age* package relying heavily on computer wizardry is Bill Christensen's "Marketing Genius Award." What makes the package unusual is that the laser personalization is done on the circular, enabling you to see exactly how the coffee mug premium will look with your name on it. The personalized order device—called an "Award Acceptance Certificate"—was printed on the same piece of paper as the personalized circular, burst, and inserted separately. In addition, the package includes a two-page letter (printed front and back), a BRE, and two lift elements—a bright yellow "Offer Deadline" notice and a four-color piece offering the free supplement, *Creativity*.

When this *Ad Age* package was first launched, it beat control by 251 percent.

MAILER: *Advertising Age*
PACKAGE: Coffee Mug Premium
AGENCY: Financial Direct
WRITER: Bill Christensen
DESIGNER: Bill Christensen
FIRST MAILED: 1985
The 6″ × 9″ kraft outside envelope with "DO NOT BEND!" in red.

Advertising Age

The enclosed Award
Acceptance Certificate bearing
your name verifies that . . .

. . . as a potential new subscriber recommended to us by a third party -- you are eligible at this time to receive Advertising Age at a full $15 off the regular subscription price. Very important, it also verifies that, should you reply by February 28, 1991, you will receive the "Marketing Genius Award" mug -- personalized with your name -- absolutely free and with our compliments.

Your opportunity to obtain this indispensable publication at such a low rate should be seriously considered. You'll discover it offers marketing and advertising intelligence unavailable from any other single source. The kind of information that will help you keep products moving . . . and creative juices flowing each and every week of the year.

Remember, to activate your subscription . . . and receive your free "Marketing Genius Award" mug, all you need do is complete and return the enclosed Award Acceptance Certificate. You need send no money.

Please take a moment, right now, to read over the following extraordinary benefits you'll receive from Advertising Age each week:

1. You'll get in-depth exclusive reports -- on every facet of the business. Nothing important is skipped. Media Buying, Sales Promotion, Corporate Management, Direct Marketing, Trend Analysis . . . it's all covered. And much, much more. Best yet, it's all covered in depth. You'll never lack for intelligent development of the critical facts.

2. You'll get a regular creative explosion. Here's your opportunity to look at, dissect, inspect, and understand the best creative in the marketplace. You'll meet who's producing it. You'll know what it's achieved. And, where things are going next. You'll love having this once a week inspiration and brainstorming partner on your desk.

3. You'll get 36 important Special Reports. These thorough reports, included in select issues, each focus on a different segment of the industry. And whether it's newspaper publishing, network programming, or cola marketing, you'll find it broken down into meaningful components -- with all the details on personnel, dollars, budgets, demands and challenges. You'll discover new movements in your own business and gain revelation from ideas sparked in somebody else's.

4. You'll get our essential Reference Issues -- no extra charge. These authoritative issues include "The 100 Leading National Advertisers" issue and, the "Advertising Agency Profiles" issue. Between them you'll see the world's major advertisers . . . spending billions of dollars. And now you'll know how, where, and why. You'll see budgets and breakdowns of budgets. Together with a close-up view of the big products, key players, and dynamic strategies. Plus . . .

. . . over please

Circulation Department • 965 E. Jefferson • Detroit, Michigan 48207

. . . you'll peruse facts on every ad agency in the United States with measurable income -- including annual billings and names and titles of agency officers together with their account responsibilities. These comprehensive reports will place some of the most meaningful data in the entire marketplace in your hands.

5. You'll get your own personalized "Marketing Genius Award" mug -- for free and with our compliments. You'll appreciate seeing your name headlined on the cover of Advertising Age -- after all, you deserve that kind of recognition. The thing is, now everybody else will know you deserve it too. And, whether you display it proudly on a shelf, stuff it with a fistful of pencils, or actually drink coffee out of it, it's guaranteed to give you a lift. Remember, it's our free gift to you with your paid subscription . . . and there is no further obligation.

6. All this, and much more -- for only 64 dollars a year. That's only $1.23 a week! And best yet, it's a full $15 off the regular subscription price. Just think about it . . . where else can you get this kind of information -- so vital to what you do each day for so little money? The fact is, you can't get it anywhere else. But, you can get Advertising Age now . . . and you don't even have to send any money with your reply.

7. Your satisfaction is absolutely guaranteed. In fact, if you'd like to stop your subscription at any time during your one year subscription period, just let us know. You'll get a 100% refund on all unmailed copies -- no questions asked and no further obligation whatsoever. Of course, you keep the "Marketing Genius Award" mug -- it's our free gift to you either way.

There you have it -- 7 smart reasons for saying "yes" to this important offer. And saying yes couldn't be easier. Simply complete the enclosed Award Acceptance Certificate and mail it in the postage-paid envelope provided. That's all there is to it. And remember, send no money. We'll make sure you start receiving you own copy of Advertising Age -- and your personalized "Marketing Genius Award" mug right away.

But please, say yes today. Due to the nature of this free offer . . . and the special subscription rate available to you at this time, we must request that all Award Acceptance Certificates be mailed no later than February 28, 1991. Please don't delay your reply.

Sincerely,

Dave Kelley

David J. Kelley
Circulation Manager

P.S. You've always known your marketing wizardry bordered on genius. Now let the rest of the world (or at least the rest of the office) know too. Send for your free "Marketing Genius Award" mug right away.

The 2-page letter, printed front and back on an 8½" × 11" sheet.

One basic rule that Christensen breaks regularly is designing an order form that is larger than the business reply envelope. Traditionalists say that you should never have to fold the order form to fit the BRE; it requires action that allows for one more slip between cup and lip. On at least two mailings for *Ad Age,* Christensen has disregarded this rule. And given the longevity of this "Marketing Genius Award" effort—strong performance every year since 1985—who's to argue?

Bill Christensen:
The creative process is a lot more than a rewrite of copy and a re-do of graphics. I ask the client lots of questions about the offer itself. If I find weak spots in the offer I like to eliminate them. I question the client on terms, pricing, length of contract, guarantees, and much more. A lot of these things are never ques-tioned *by other creatives . . . because they are perceived as cast-in-stone standard client operating methods. A good creative person should dig into all of this . . . because this is where you find ways to simplify the offer . . . and boil things down to a quick "yes" decision.*

By the way, one way I have dramatically lifted response for a lot of clients (and simultaneously saved tons of operating dollars) is by removing *the toll-free phone number as a reply option.*

This kind of up-front thinking and research is just the first step in putting

"Marketing Genius Award" Mug awaits
DENNISON HATCH
--Advertising Age editors await reply--

Good news -- you are now eligible to receive Advertising Age hot off the press and fresh on your desk...every week for a full $15 off the regular subscription price! Now, you'll stay right on top of the most comprehensive and authoritative advertising and marketing news available anywhere in the world...at any price. News that'll help you keep strategies focused...creative efforts meaningful...and products moving.

But, that's not all. You'll also get the handsome personalized "Marketing Genius Award" mug--like the one pictured above--absolutely free with your paid subscription.

This is the famous mug that touts you as a marketing wizard...and announces it to the rest of the world. Whether or not you drink coffee, it's guaranteed to pick you up. Remember, the mug is free...and you don't have to send any money with your reply. Please read the enclosed letter for complete details on this important free offer.

OFFICIAL NOTIFICATION FOR:

DENNISON
PO BX
STAMFORD, CT 06903

NON-TRANSFERABLE

The 4-color addressing piece with personalized name up big on the mug premium. This is one of the very rare mailing efforts where the personalization is done on the brochure rather than on the ordering device.

Advertising Age

Crain's International Newspaper of Marketing

Helping you keep strategies focused, creative efforts meaningful, and products moving.

You'll appreciate the wealth of essential knowledge Advertising Age puts in your hands every week. Knowledge that's treasured by most every decision maker in America who's charged with the challenge of keeping products moving. Best yet, as part of this offer, you can have a one year subscription to this important publication for a full $15 off the regular subscription price.

You're also sure to be pleased with the free gift we'll send your way. It's the Advertising Age "Marketing Genius Award" mug--personalized with your name in headlines on the front. Getting your award mug--and your low rate subscription is easy. All you need do is return the enclosed Award Acceptance Certificate in the postage-paid envelope provided. You need send no money.

Here's what else you'll get with Advertising Age:

All the News and Information you need.

That's right, if there is something important to report, expose, explain, or develop, you'll find it in Advertising Age each Monday morning. Everything critical to making products move is covered. And covered intelligently. Plus, you'll receive in-depth reporting on the creative marketplace. You'll see what's working...and who's creating it. And you'll get a first look at new trend-setting ads and market shaking promotions.

But it doesn't stop there--you'll also get 36 Special Intelligence Reports a year. Each report singles out...and covers in great detail just one segment of the industry. And, whether the business is radio, sweepstakes, direct marketing, or magazines, you'll know what makes it tick when you're done.

And, there's even more!--because you'll get--at no extra charge--our essential annual reference issues. You'd be hard-pressed to find an advertising professional who doesn't keep these two valuable issues handy. You'll get "The 100 Leading National Advertisers" issue and, the "Advertising Agency Profiles" issue. They're recognized as solid reference standards in the industry...and will be your guide to how and where billions of dollars are being spent by the world's top marketers. Plus, you'll get to look into every advertising agency in the country with measurable income.

The Marketing Genius Award Mug.

Just like the mug pictured, it announces you as the winner of the prestigious Advertising Age "Marketing Genius" Award. You know you deserve it. The thing is, now everybody else will know it too--after all, it says so in print. Remember, this fun "Award" is yours absolutely free with your paid one year subscription.

A Price that can't be beat.

Just $64 for a one year subscription gets you everything you've just read about. That's only $1.23 a week--and a full $15 off the regular subscription price. Plus, you don't even have to send any money with your reply--we'll bill you later and you can choose from several convenient payment methods (personal check, company check, or major credit card.)

To subscribe simply complete and mail the enclosed Award Acceptance Certificate in the postage-paid envelope provided. Send no money. Remember, to be eligible for this special offer you must mail your Award Acceptance Certificate by no later than February 28, 1991. Please reply right away.

**Subscribing to Advertising Age is easy.
And your Marketing Genius Award Mug is FREE.
Please respond today!**

together what should always be a unified *presentation of the offer that starts with the outside envelope and carries all the way through to even subtle details on the BRE. Everything in a direct mail package should work together toward the one common goal of ''yes.'' And, at the same time, every element in a package should also stand on its own, possessing its own ability to trigger the reply. This point relates directly to what I see as the biggest single weakness when I review direct mail packages for other people:*

> Most packages simply don't ask for the order aggressively enough, often enough, and in a sufficient variety of ways.

A package that makes a single request for the order in the last paragraph of the letter is like a salesman with a cold, weak handshake. If he's not confident . . . neither am I.

One more thing I like to do is create substance *where there once was none. This is particularly important for lead offers. Instead of asking the prospect to send for more free information from Mid-American Life (no substance, too vague), I'll have him ''send for Information Packet No. 17'' (the word ''packet'' automatically denotes* tangible *substance . . . and adding ''No. 17'' implies the existence of an established consumer information bureau). In fact,*

REMEMBER
...to activate your subscription and receive your free "Marketing Genius Award" mug simply complete and mail the attached Award Acceptance Certificate.
(Award Certificate attached)

Advertising Age
Crain's International Newspaper of Marketing
YOUR NAME HERE
WINS "MARKETING GENIUS" AWARD

CODE A-3

Award Acceptance Certificate

☐ Yes, I want Advertising Age. Hot off the press. Every week--while all the news is still fresh and meaningful. Please start my one year subscription (for a low $64) right away. And please send me my own personalized "Marketing Genius Award" mug. **I understand that my Award Mug is free with my paid subscription and that I am under no further obligation whatsoever.** I also understand that I need send no money with this Acceptance Certificate, and, that I will be billed at a later time (once billed payment can be conveniently made by personal check, company check, or major credit card.)

Signature

Indicate here exactly how you'd like your name to appear on your Award Mug. PLEASE PRINT.

ISSUED TO:

DENNISON
PO BX
STAMFORD, CT 06903

Please make corrections if necessary.

☐ Please send *creativity* each month for free.
Title
Company
Type of business
0XW64

Order form, also printed in 4-color. The 2 personalized 4-color pieces are printed on a single sheet, burst, and inserted separately.

OFFER DEADLINE

It's a pleasure to make this free "Marketing Genius Award" mug offer to you. And you're sure to be truly pleased with your personalized coffee mug. Most important though, we know you'll be delighted with your own subscription to Ad Age. You'll never have to wait for a "pass-along" copy again. And you'll always get comprehensive marketing news--from the world's most authoritative source--while it's still fresh, hot, and meaningful. We do ask, however (due to the nature of this free offer) that you mail your Award Acceptance Certificate by no later than the offer deadline date of: **FEBRUARY 28, 1991**

Lift piece no. 1, printed in black on a bright yellow slip of paper with the deadline date in red. Forcing a deadline can be dangerous, especially if the mailing gets delayed in any way. It may give urgency, but virtually all orders will cease at the deadline date. Never use a deadline without testing.

I'll carry this through to the offer copy and even the BRE . . . with the offer reading something like:

> *Information Packet No. 17 is available to you—for free—from Mid-American Life Information Service Group. The Group is operated as a complimentary service to people like you—to make sure you have all the knowledge you need to plan a brighter, more dynamic future.*

I'll then carry that to the BRE . . . with the first address line reading, "Information Service Group."

Here's a little on what went into creating the Advertising Age *package.*

The previous control was a classic (for its era) 9″ × 12″ poly bag with four-color inserts, letter, perf-off reply piece, and BRE. More important, the old package offered several subscription-length options, several payment options

Lift piece no. 2, printed in 4-color.

creativity
ALL THE CREATIVITY YOU'LL EVER NEED!
see inside...
DESIGNER'S SHOWCASE

Truly brilliant creative . . .

It starts out as a simple idea.
Sometimes born of pure inspiration.
And often, the product of brain-taxing labor . . .

But, when it comes to fruition, it motivates . . . causes action . . . and ultimately changes the purchasing behavior of your audience. There's a good chance that your own career revolves around the need for a consistently great creative product.

That's why I'm so pleased to let you know that you'll now get a regular creative explosion -- every month -- from a full color Ad Age supplement called "*creativity*". It's the only magazine I know of that's dedicated 100% to the creative side of the business. And, there's no extra charge to you whatsoever for receiving it.

In every single issue you'll get to take a look at the major players in the creative marketplace. You'll discover first hand insights on philosophy, technique, and style. Plus, you'll stay tuned to all kinds of hot sources: Producers who produce. Jingles that sell. Writers who inspire. Directors with focus. Artists who illustrate. Studios that accomodate. Photographers with flash. Even direct mail gurus with "pull". You find out what's working. And what's not. With concise insights on why. Best yet, you'll have a lot of fun in the process.

This valuable monthly creative resource won't be found on newsstands. There's only one way to get it . . . FREE . . . with your one year subscription to Ad Age.

Please make sure you reply by no later than the offer deadline.

Sincerely,

Dave Kelley
Dave Kelley
Circulation Manager

P.S. Please let me recap all that's yours when you reply. You get Advertising Age at a full $15 off the regular subscription price. You get two industry standard jumbo reference issues for free. You get the free "Marketing Genius Award" mug, personalized with your name. And, "*creativity*" 12 times a year, also free. Please return your Award Acceptance Certificate today.

The business reply envelope. The urgency of the deadline is repeated in the upper left corner.

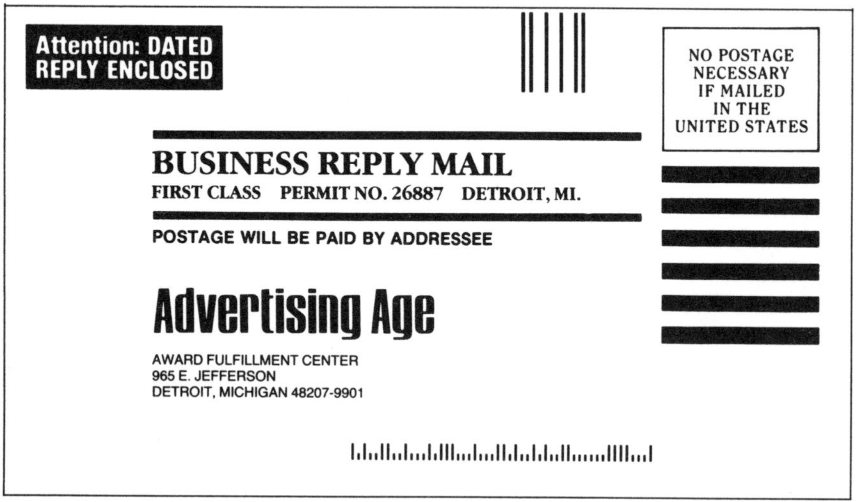

(check, major credit cards, and ''bill me later''), and three reply options (mail, toll-free, and local phone). I asked Dave Kelley at Ad Age *if such a vast array of options was dictated by forces beyond his control, and, if not . . .*

. . . what was the most popular payment method, subscription length, and reply method. The answer came back, ''bill me later,'' one year, and reply-by-mail. The responding public had spoken . . . and as a result I determined that Dave's new package would incorporate that one simple reply formula only.

Next, I thought about my target audience. ''Hmm . . . largely people in advertising and marketing. I'm one of those guys myself. Let's see, if the rest of them are like me, there's a lot of self-importance to play with here . . . and some pretty big ego considerations . . . a desire for recognition . . . and, of course, the sure knowledge that they are the greatest thing since David Ogilvy. Awards! . . . that's it. We all deserve one. The outer envelope will say ''Award Acceptance Certificate Enclosed'' . . . if that doesn't generate a 99 percent 'openage' rate, nothing will.''

And that's how it went. I decided to key in on the Marketing Genius Award mug . . . and incorporate it into a format that would allow me to use personalization in a way that really showed it off. As a result, what ultimately got featured in the package was the recipient . . . who is, by the way, the single most important element in any direct mail package. *I coupled the mug offer with copy and graphic elements that communicated a high degree of selectivity . . . with that selectivity qualifying the recipient for both the ''Award'' mug and a* fantastic *price offer.*

I then made sure that this was all carried through on every piece of paper in the package . . . and incorporated prominently featured classic techniques like a reply deadline (communicated several times with an urgent, credible tone) and a P.S. that uses the central hook to provoke the recipient to read the whole letter, etc., etc. Basics. Basics. Basics.

And, to refer back to an earlier point, I ask for the order, sometimes repeatedly, on every panel of every piece of paper. I ask first in the first paragraph of the letter . . . then I ask again by the third paragraph . . . and it continues on from there, over and over again. (I can't emphasize this enough as a help to folks who want to learn direct mail selling.)

Good direct mail is created by using good common sense. Stick to the basics. And follow through on the details. Every detail counts. Make sure the letter looks and reads like a letter. Use a classic format . . . but use it well *by motivating the buyer with every piece of paper in it. Ask for the order a lot. Keep things simple.* A well-executed classic format stands out in the mailbox. *That's because—to this day—*most *of what comes in the mail is, in fact, not classic . . . it has not been fully thought through.*

One more thing—for most clients the day of the single ''cure-all'' control-package-that-can-be-rolled-out-to-most-of-America is over. Break your lists down. Segment. And write well-targeted offers for each segment. It takes a lot more elbow grease. But it pays off big.

American Demographics

One of the consummate masters of the direct mail writing craft was the late—and very beloved—Hank Burnett of Santa Barbara, California. A graduate of Harvard, Burnett worked as director of special projects and account supervisor at Dickie-Raymond (later the D-R Group of Boston and New York) and as creative director (New York), and vice president and director of West Coast operations (Los Angeles) for Benson, Stagg & Associates. In 1968 Burnett created one of the greatest direct mail efforts of all time—a seven-page typed letter that began:

As Chairman of the Admiral Richard E. Byrd Polar Center, it is my privilege to invite you to become a member of an expedition which is destined to make both news and history. It will cost you $10,000 and about 26 days of your time. Frankly, you will endure some discomfort and may even face some danger.

On the other hand, you will have the rare privilege of taking part in a mission of great importance for the United States and the entire world. A mission, incidentally, which has never before been attempted by man.

MAILER: *American Demographics*
PACKAGE: Yes-No-Maybe
PROJECT MGR.: Michael Edmondson
WRITER: Hank Burnett
DESIGNER: David Gordon
FIRST MAILED: 1987
The plain 9″ × 12″ outside envelope, gray with tiny blue flecks.

American Demographics
108 N. Cayuga Street
Ithaca, NY 14850

HOWARD LAKE MINN
U.S. POSTAGE 16.7
791796

Heidi 7INH
Road
Norwalk, CT 06851

American Demographics

Why do people buy what they buy?

Two reasons, according to one marketing guru: "To get what they don't have -- and to keep what they've got."

There you have it.

But if that's not quite enough; if you still have a few questions about who, what, where, when and at what price; you should get to know the lively, authoritative magazine that fills in these details. It's called

American Demographics

... and this is your chance to get the next issue FREE!

Dear Marketing Professional:

Exasperating, aren't they?

I'm talking about human beings. Americans. Consumers. The public. The markets. The crazy-making jury out there you're paid to understand -- and whose whims and flights of fancy you're rewarded for predicting.

Just what do they want? And what will they want tomorrow?

My guess is that like most of us in this line of work, you could use all the reliable help you can get -- not only in digging out the facts about what really is going on, but what's likely to go on in the future.

Fortunately, there's a bright, incisive magazine that specializes in this kind of help. A magazine that cuts through hype, fantasy, and wishful thinking -- and that gives you the figures and analyses you need to distinguish received wisdom from reality.

A magazine, what's more, devoted to helping you see around corners.

It's American Demographics, The Magazine of Consumer Trends and Lifestyles, and if you've been looking for a publication that can breathe life, substance and meaning into statistics ... one that keeps you up to date on the most important and most interesting new demographic research and helps you connect it with your own areas of concern ... you're in luck.

[Over, please]

And you're invited to try out American Demographics free, to appraise before you decide to buy. I'll give you the specifics on this offer in a moment. First, let me tell you more about what you'll find in this intriguing, engaging magazine.

Chances are, your intuitive function is pretty well developed or you'd be in a different business. But how often have you noticed that what makes perfect sense to you, what feels right intuitively, turns out to be off the mark, once you measure and quantify it?

American Demographics gives you the hard information you need to confirm your observations and perceptions. Or sometimes to disconfirm them; much of what you'll find in our pages is astonishingly counter-intuitive. Take, for example, those questions on the outer envelope:

- Americans are slightly silly about their dogs, as anyone selling to the pet market can attest. But doggies aren't eating as much filet mignon as you might think. Only about 13% of leftovers carried home in doggie bags actually goes to the dogs.

- If you think Mississippi leads the country in illiteracy, you're right. Sort of. It actually shares the top spot with Louisiana, Texas and -- get this -- New York!

- Despite the big bucks TV evangelists generate in donations, it's not even close: Americans spend 15 times more on gambling than they give to churches.

- People implicitly equate money with sex -- but only 34% of Americans think they'd have better sex if they had more money.

- Not only does food consume a larger share of a traveler's budget than lodging, it also consumes more than transportation, entertainment or anything else.

Count on American Demographics to intrigue and entertain you, even as it informs you. And as it gives you new clues to the wants, needs, hopes, dreams and fears of consumers.

With the help of American Demographics, you'll better understand the interconnections and interactions among factors such as age, education, geography, income, wealth, lifestyles and spending. You'll find new ways to identify, define, segment and approach markets, new systems and methods for refining the techniques you use now.

How are other businesses using demographics in their marketing plans? What's new and what's coming in the field? Which new ideas and innovations show the most promise -- and how can you utilize them? How can you capitalize on the opportunities offered by entirely new ways to slice up the population -- and your markets?

American Demographics will keep you in touch -- and keep you reliably informed -- every month. And by so doing, provide you with the best possible insurance against your own obsolescence.

What's ahead over the next five, ten or fifteen years? By helping you see around corners, American Demographics will help you take your organization -- and yourself -- into the future. Here you'll find exclusive, invaluable insights and perspectives on the latest developments, issues, changes and trends that promise to shape our world and society in the years to come.

For instance, what's likely to happen to the near-equal male-female sex ratio when people can choose the sex of their child? Probably not much; people still want a boy and a girl. But most want the boy first, so there may be a significantly higher percentage of first-born males.

Checkless banking is the coming thing? Maybe in time -- but you'd never guess it from the methods by which Americans pay now: 57% with checks, 36% with cash, only 6% with credit cards.

What can we do about the rising crime rate? It'll probably come down all by itself, once the number of people likely to commit crime -- young men aged 15 to 29 -- decreases. The crime rate may be due in part to drugs, decline of the family and the impact of the Vietnam War, but the fact is that it fluctuates in direct proportion to the size of this age group -- and in this country, there will be four million fewer by the year 2000. Makes you wonder why we're building all those new prisons, doesn't it?

Why -- in this video age -- does the future look especially rosy for book publishers? Because the fastest growing age group is 35-49, which happens to be the age group that buys and reads the most books.

Why should we start planning now to open America's borders at some point in the relatively near future? Because once the huge baby-boom and echo-baby-boom generations move past childbearing ages, our population will decline by about 1.5 million per year. We'll need immigrants just to stay even.

Does this mean new impetus for bilingual education? Maybe, but attitudes will have to change. Now 45% of whites and 43% of blacks oppose it -- but 56% of Hispanics are against the idea. Hard to understand why some political activists are pushing to preserve ethnic identity while a majority of Hispanics seem to prefer to integrate. Just another instance where American Demographics observes that the emperor wears no clothes -- and backs it up with figures.

[Over, please]

And there's much, much more to this indispensable journal. In recent issues, you'd have heard about the explosive growth of out-of-store retailing. About the occupations that will gain the most new jobs between now and 1995. About the counter-intuitive finding that VCR owners and cable TV subscribers are more likely to attend movies in theaters than other people.

You'd have been alerted to the cooling of America's passion for small town life. Which markets are likely to be affected most by our aging population and why. Who spends the most on clothing (working women without children). All about time-use diaries and why the key to knowing what people will buy is knowing how they spend their time.

It's common knowledge that about 20% of Americans move per year, right? Not any more -- it's down to 17%. And what opportunities may lie in a curious (if understandable) statistical discrepancy: 86% of parents expect their kids to go to college, but only 54% are saving to help pay for it.

Can American Demographics give you the timely, reliable and usually exclusive information you need to make crucial marketing decisions with greater confidence? Can it be your DEW (Distant Early Warning) Line on trends and changes destined to alter our society -- and thus your markets?

Our implicit guarantee is that it can. But there's no need to accept my word for it, because now you can get the next issue with our compliments (and without obligation to subscribe) and judge for yourself.

Send no money now. Just return the token order card in the postage-paid reply envelope. We'll send you the next issue, absolutely free. If you like it, pay just $58 for one year of American Demographics (your complimentary issue + 11 monthly issues). If your verdict is negative, no problem. Just write "cancel" on the bill, return it unpaid, keep your issue free and that will be the end of it. No cost to you, no obligation now or ever. Fair enough?

Sincerely,

Doris L. Walsh

Doris L. Walsh, Publisher

P.S. Suppose disenchantment sets in later on? Still no problem. Then you can take us up on our explicit guarantee: Cancel any time, for any reason, and we'll send you a full refund of your subscription price!

American Demographics

A Dow Jones Publication • P. O. Box 58184 • Boulder, CO 80322-8184

LS893

The 4-page letter, printed on at 11″ × 17″ sheet.

Can this bright, lively, indispensable magazine help you see around corners? Get the next issue FREE…and see!
Can AMERICAN DEMOGRAPHICS help take you—and your marketing plans—into the future? Can it give you the insights and perceptions you need to understand better the opportunities your markets present now and tomorrow? Can it supply ideas that become the raw material for your own creativity?
• Here's how to find out—at our risk. Just return the coupon below (or the separate token order card) in the postage-paid reply envelope. We'll send you the next issue of AMERICAN DEMOGRAPHICS on a complimentary basis. Then you decide whether or not to confirm your subscription.
• If you like AMERICAN DEMOGRAPHICS, pay just $58 for one full year (your free issue + 11 monthly issues). If your verdict is negative, no problem. Just write "cancel" on the bill, return it unpaid and keep your copy of AMERICAN DEMOGRAPHICS free. No cost to you, no obligation now or ever.
Suppose your negative verdict comes later? Still no problem. In that case, you can take us up on our long-term guarantee:
Your money back in full. Tell us to cancel—anytime, any reason—and we'll send you an immediate, unquestioned refund of your full subscription price. Fair enough?
American Demographics
A Dow Jones Publication
P. O. Box 58184, Boulder • CO 80322-8184
Yes I'll take you up on your offer of a FREE look at AMERICAN DEMOGRAPHICS. Please send me the next issue on a complimentary basis. If I like it, I'll pay just $58 and receive 11 additional issues (total of 12 monthly issues). If I'm not pleased, I'll write "cancel" on the bill, return it unpaid, keep my complimentary copy FREE and not be obligated further in any way.
Send no money now. Just fill in this coupon, clip it out and return it in the postage-paid reply envelope, or use the separate order card enclosed.
Name (please print)
Company
Address
City
State
Zip Code
American Demographics
A Dow Jones Publication
P. O. Box 58184
Boulder, CO 80322-8184

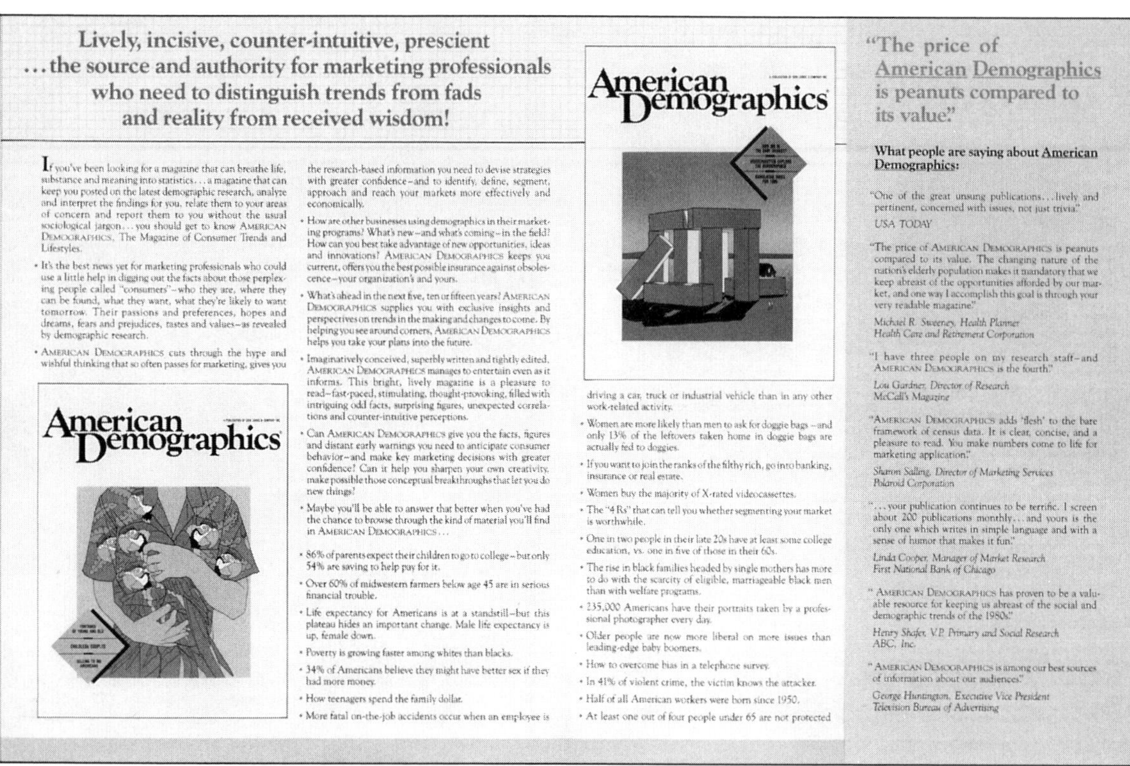

The brochure that starts off 8½″ × 11″ and opens to 11″ × 17″ At right is a flap; when completely opened, the brochure is 11″ × 22″. On the back panel is an extra order coupon.

Lively, incisive, counter-intuitive, prescient ...the source and authority for marketing professionals who need to distinguish trends from fads and reality from received wisdom!

If you've been looking for a magazine that can breathe life, substance and meaning into statistics . . . a magazine that can keep you posted on the latest demographic research, analyze and interpret the findings for you, relate them to your areas of concern and report them to you without the usual sociological jargon . . . you should get to know AMERICAN DEMOGRAPHICS, The Magazine of Consumer Trends and Lifestyles.

- It's the best news yet for marketing professionals who could use a little help in digging out the facts about those perplexing people called "consumers"–who they are, where they can be found, what they want, what they're likely to want tomorrow. Their passions and preferences, hopes and dreams, fears and prejudices, tastes and values–as revealed by demographic research.
- AMERICAN DEMOGRAPHICS cuts through the hype and wishful thinking that so often passes for marketing, gives you the research-based information you need to devise strategies with greater confidence–and to identify, define, segment, approach and reach your markets more effectively and economically.

- How are other businesses using demographics in their marketing programs? What's new–and what's coming–in the field? How can you best take advantage of new opportunities, ideas and innovations? AMERICAN DEMOGRAPHICS keeps you current, offers you the best possible insurance against obsolescence–your organization's and yours.
- What's ahead in the next five, ten or fifteen years? AMERICAN DEMOGRAPHICS supplies you with exclusive insights and perspectives on trends in the making and changes to come. By helping you see around corners, AMERICAN DEMOGRAPHICS helps you take your plans into the future.
- Imaginatively conceived, superbly written and tightly edited, AMERICAN DEMOGRAPHICS manages to entertain even as it informs. This bright, lively magazine is a pleasure to read–fast-paced, stimulating, thought-provoking, filled with intriguing odd facts, surprising figures, unexpected correlations and counter-intuitive perceptions.
- Can AMERICAN DEMOGRAPHICS give you the facts, figures and distant early warnings you need to anticipate consumer behavior–and make key marketing decisions with greater confidence? Can it help you sharpen your own creativity, make possible those conceptual breakthroughs that let you do new things?
- Maybe you'll be able to answer that better when you've had the chance to browse through the kind of material you'll find in AMERICAN DEMOGRAPHICS . . .

- 86% of parents expect their children to go to college–but only 54% are saving to help pay for it.
- Over 60% of midwestern farmers below age 45 are in serious financial trouble.
- Life expectancy for Americans is at a standstill–but this plateau hides an important change. Male life expectancy is up, female down.
- Poverty is growing faster among whites than blacks.
- 34% of Americans believe they might have better sex if they had more money.
- How teenagers spend the family dollar.
- More fatal on-the-job accidents occur when an employee is driving a car, truck or industrial vehicle than in any other work-related activity.
- Women are more likely than men to ask for doggie bags–and only 13% of the leftovers taken home in doggie bags are actually fed to doggies.
- If you want to join the ranks of the filthy rich, go into banking, insurance or real estate.
- Women buy the majority of X-rated videocassettes.
- The "4 Rs" that can tell you whether segmenting your market is worthwhile.
- One in two people in their late 20s have at least some college education, vs. one in five of those in their 60s.
- The rise in black families headed by single mothers has more to do with the scarcity of eligible, marriageable black men than with welfare programs.
- 235,000 Americans have their portraits taken by a professional photographer every day.
- Older people are now more liberal on more issues than leading-edge baby boomers.
- How to overcome bias in a telephone survey.
- In 41% of violent crime, the victim knows the attacker.
- Half of all American workers were born since 1950.
- At least one out of four people under 65 are not protected against catastrophic medical bills.
- 45% of whites, 43% of blacks–and 56% of Hispanics–oppose bilingual education.
- Without immigration–legal and illegal–U.S. population will decline by 1.5 million per year, once the huge baby-boom and echo-baby-boom generations move past their childbearing years.
- Retirement income from IRAs may not amount to much–52% of married couples now aged 25-34 would have an IRA income at age 67 of less than $3000 a year (in 1985 dollars).
- The five occupations that will gain the most jobs between now and 1995: cashiers, registered nurses, janitors and maids, truck drivers, waiters and waitresses.
- During the past month, 24% of the general public went to a movie–but 27% of cable TV subscribers and 31% of VCR owners did.
- Eight out of ten Americans live near a source of toxic wastes or a toxic waste dump.
- Americans don't move as much as they used to–only 17% each year now, compared to 20% in 1960.
- Why marketers who understand regional and local differences are likely to find themselves riding a cultural wave.
- Time-use diaries: the key to knowing what people will buy is knowing how they spend their time.
- New Sunbelt migration patterns.
- Who gives to charity.
- The probability that a newly married couple will remain married for at least 20 years, have two children (one boy, one girl) spaced three years apart: 6 out of 100.
- Massachusetts, New York and Michigan should rank among the top ten population gainers over the next 15 years.
- The proportion of people who sleep seven or eight hours a night rises with income.
- Eating–not transportation or lodging–consumes the largest chunk of a traveler's budget in the U.S.
- Why retailers who don't clearly define their target markets risk fading into obscurity.
- Women control the checkbook in three out of four households.
- Americans spend 15 times more money on gambling than they donate to churches.
- Businesses marketing to youth should look for countries whose median ages fall between 20 and 30 (those with sizeable youth populations, but developed enough to supply paying customers for American products).
- Direct correlation: the longer the commercial, the better the chances for recall.
- Why Americans' love affair with small towns may be over.

Want more? Take a look at the next issue FREE!

Can AMERICAN DEMOGRAPHICS give you the monthly briefings you need to make high-stakes marketing decisions with greater confidence? Why not get your complimentary copy of the next issue and see? No cost to you, no obligation. The risk is ours, as it should be. Check out the details of this trial offer on the back of this brochure.

As Dick Hodgson writes in *The Greatest Direct Mail Sales Letters of All Time* (Dartnell):

The Admiral Byrd letter is more than just a great letter. It is a classic example of how a great letter alone can do a selling job. The total marketing budget for this project was $5,000, which ruled out use of the usual four-color brochure included in almost every travel mailing. So Hank Burnett, and his associates, Dick Benson and Christopher Stagg, had little choice but to let a letter do the job. And, thanks to Hank Burnett's challenging copy, this single seven-page letter completely sold out all 60 seats available and raised $600,000 for the Admiral Richard E. Byrd Polar Center.

Burnett was a freelancer for twenty years, and his many clients included AARP, Amnesty International, *Atlantic Monthly*, Boardroom Reports, *Consumer Reports*, the Cousteau Society, Hearst Magazines, MADD, *New York Review of Books*, *Psychology Today*, *Sassy*, Sierra Club, *Smithsonian*.

I wrote Mrs. Hank Burnett to ask if she could jot down some memories of how Burnett worked, and back came some fascinating material, including letters from writer to client about his *American Demographics* package.

Burnett's Yes-No-Maybe package for *American Demographics* was first mailed in 1987 and has been control ever since. We have seen it in both 9″ × 12″ and 6″ × 9″ formats.

Gretchen Fall Burnett:

First, Hank was a voracious reader, always on the lookout for anything that might apply to his life and work. He culled newspapers, magazines, books, etc., marking relevant facts, passages and observations.

Always a stickler for grammatical correctness and the consummate wordsmith, Hank's library consisted of any number of dictionaries, books devoted to the English language, synonyms, quotations, etc., which he consulted when necessary or out of curiosity. He also collected famous—and perhaps not so famous—quotations relating to any number of topics to be used when and if appropriate.

His love for and extraordinary mastery of the language, not to mention his proper and emotionally engaging use of it, is summed up well, I think, by Milt Pierce's observation that Hank ''didn't blast out his ideas'' when other writers expounded ideas with ''olympian grandeur,'' but instead waited for a pause in the shouting and would modestly speak ''with a softness that stood out of the din. And we were all suddenly silent, listening to Hank. He had ideas. He had style. And he knew the craft of copywriting better than any of us. In his understated way he said more than any of us.''

Second, upon receiving background materials from a client, Hank would review them in depth, thoroughly grounding himself in, for example, previous copies of the magazines (pictures which were often used in his rough layouts for the artist), previous fundraising efforts and/or direct mail subscription efforts. In this sense Hank was a researcher who really did his homework.

Then he would begin the letter. Enter the creative leap! How Hank then came up with a new *approach is a mystery. I often wondered how he was able, on so many occasions, to come up against one of his* own *control packages and beat it! Sometimes again and again. This happened several times with some clients he did work for over the years.*

Third, I do know Hank wrote painstakingly, choosing every word very carefully, and did not proceed to paragraph 2 until paragraph 1 was in his mind perfected and so on throughout the letter and the rest of the package. Needless to say, some clients and their products/causes were easier than others with respect to the time it took him to ''knock out'' a package.

Fourth, Hank's thoughts on direct mail. He obviously had many throughout his long and distinguished career, many of which I learned through sheer exposure/osmosis—too many to share given my time constraints at this point. However, one of his oft-quoted statements comes readily to mind: ''Never forget that you are trying to reach and persuade one human being, no matter how many millions of pieces you mail. And if you would better know that human being, take a close look in your mirror.''

Personalize and convince the reader that he/she needs the product, that his/her life will be improved and enriched by whatever/whoever is being promoted.

I think Hank was an author who was able to tap into the collective unconscious of his readers. He had an uncanny and intuitive intellect and was able to be in many places simultaneously. For example, I am reminded of how he launched Sassy *for adolescent girls and immediately launched* Lear's *for women over age forty-five.*

I once wrote Burnett to ask him for his thoughts on the *Sassy* launch package and he replied:

It was not an assignment I approached with my usual confidence; what do I know about that age group of that sex? I have a difficult enough time figuring

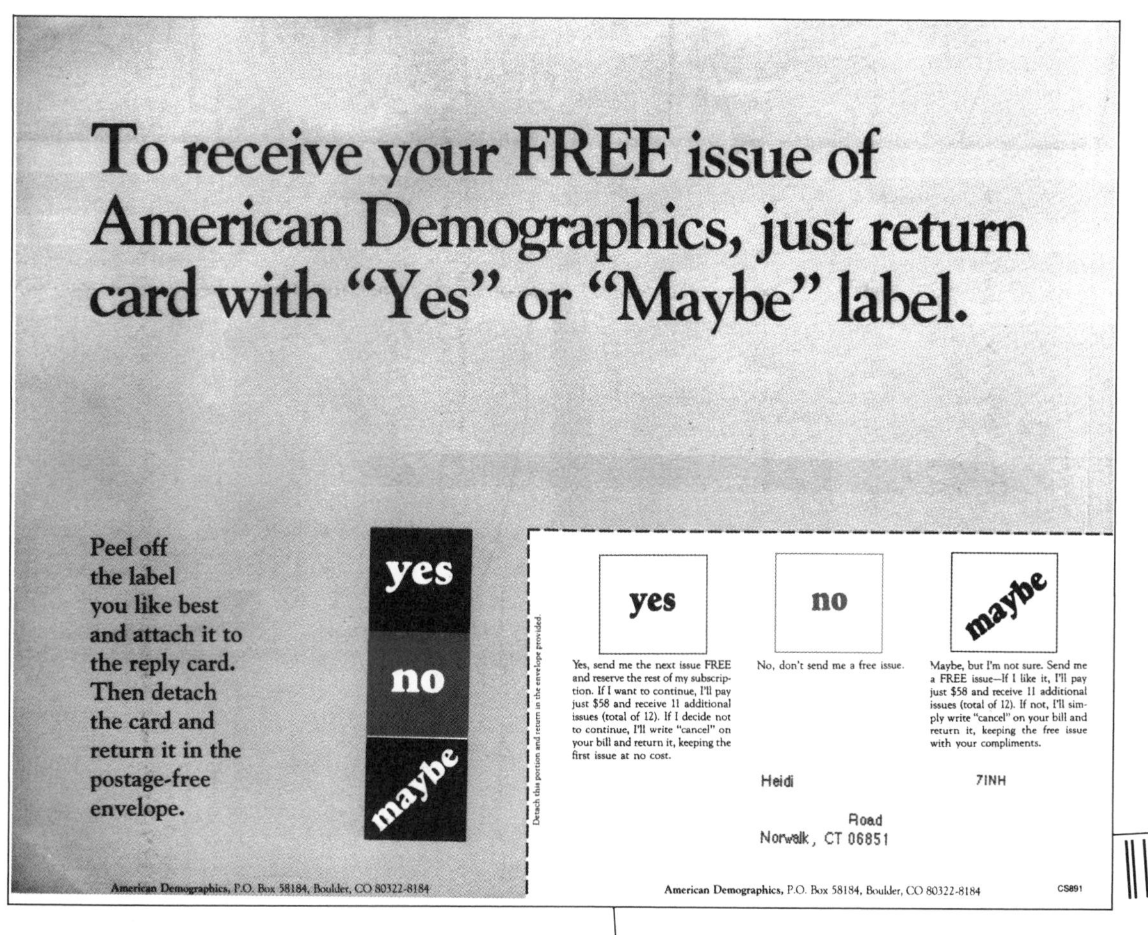

To receive your FREE issue of American Demographics, just return card with "Yes" or "Maybe" label.
Peel off the label you like best and attach it to the reply card. Then detach the card and return it in the postage-free envelope.
yes
no
maybe
American Demographics, P.O. Box 58184, Boulder, CO 80322-8184
Detach this portion and return in the envelope provided.
yes
no
maybe
Yes, send me the next issue FREE and reserve the rest of my subscription. If I want to continue, I'll pay just $58 and receive 11 additional issues (total of 12). If I decide not to continue, I'll write "cancel" on your bill and return it, keeping the first issue at no cost.
No, don't send me a free issue.
Maybe, but I'm not sure. Send me a FREE issue—If I like it, I'll pay just $58 and receive 11 additional issues (total of 12). If not, I'll simply write "cancel" on your bill and return it, keeping the free issue with your compliments.
Heidi
7INH
Road
Norwalk, CT 06851
American Demographics, P.O. Box 58184, Boulder, CO 80322-8184
CS891

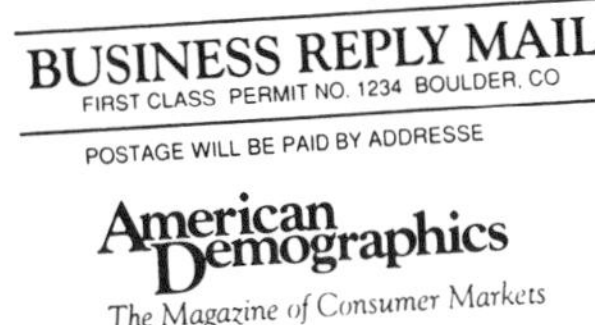

NO POSTAGE NECESSARY IF MAILED IN THE UNITED STATES
BUSINESS REPLY MAIL
FIRST CLASS PERMIT NO. 1234 BOULDER, CO
POSTAGE WILL BE PAID BY ADDRESSE
American Demographics
The Magazine of Consumer Markets
P.O. Box 58184
Boulder, CO 80321-8184

The order card with the Yes-No-Maybe tokens and the business reply envelope.

out adult women. *And besides, I have the lurking impression that it is not only unseemly but faintly illegal for a man of my age to know too much about thirteen- to fourteen-year-old girls.*

That launch mailing to 96,000 names pulled 6.02 percent overall, with five lists pulling two digits, including one list that pulled a whopping 80.05 percent.

Hank Burnett to Catherine Elton, circulation director of *American Demographics*, March 27, 1987:

Here's my direct mail subscription package—copy and organizational rough layouts for the outer envelope, four-page letter, lift letter, 11″ × 21¼″ brochure, and order card (with token).

As I think I mentioned to you on the phone, I've conceived this as a 9″ × 12″

package, to help it not *get lost in the great pile of direct mail these people get. I'm just a bit ambivalent about this. On the one hand, I want to be sure the package gets every possible chance. On the other, of course, I'm keenly aware of the cost.*

So ideally, I guess, I'd like to see it tested also in a 6″ × 9″ version. I think the only component that might be a bit difficult to transform into that format would be the order card. So let me offer to redo the order card—at no additional cost to you—if you decide you'd like to test a 6″ × 9″.

I'm afraid I got a bit carried away on my roughs. Sometimes that happens if, as in this case, I develop fairly strong feelings about how the package ought to look as I'm writing it (I have a tendency to think both visually and verbally at the same time). What I intended to convey was sort of the tone and feeling of the package, but in this case I more or less ended up designing it. It really isn't my intention to get in the way of whatever Dave Gordon's ideas may be; he is after all a designer, and I am not. So he may take exception to this. If he does, I won't mind in the least (though I would like to retain the tone and feeling).

I invariably end up feeling a bit awkward about this, but being able to see *it really does help me write it.*

Incidentally, your editors may want to alter the list of articles and topics in the brochure. I have no problem with that; they may well have strong opinions about which articles have aroused the most interest and controversy.

Anyway, I hope you like it. And please don't hesitate to give me a call if you have questions.

Hank Burnett to Catherine Elton, April 10, 1987:

I hope you're recovering nicely from your brush with mortality. My own left me with slightly altered driving habits, a good thing; I'm a bit more cautious, a bit less inclined to take things for granted on the road. And I guess those new habits are pretty durable; it's been about seventeen years.

Anyway, here's material for the 6″ × 9″ package version. This didn't pose as many problems as I thought it might. What I've done—as you'll see in the enclosed roughs—is to reduce the components (and do a minor bit of shifting around on the order card). The idea is to introduce as few new variables as possible, so that you get as accurate a reading as possible on the effect of the different size. Incidentally, I didn't go as far, in terms of design, as I did on the original layouts, but the colors should remain as close to the 9″ × 12″ as possible. Almost as if this were a miniature of that format.

Please don't hesitate to give me a call if you have questions—and be well.

Financial World

To create a package for *Financial World,* Linda Wells had to get inside the head of an entrepreneur/investor, which she did with enormous success. The package—written by Wells and designed by John Rettich—was first mailed in 1986 and became control in 1987. Although the package has been tested with and without personalization, the most recent efforts have been personalized; this is one of the very few of the seventy-one Grand Controls that use elaborate data processing for no particular reason beyond the fact that it apparently works better than the plain version.

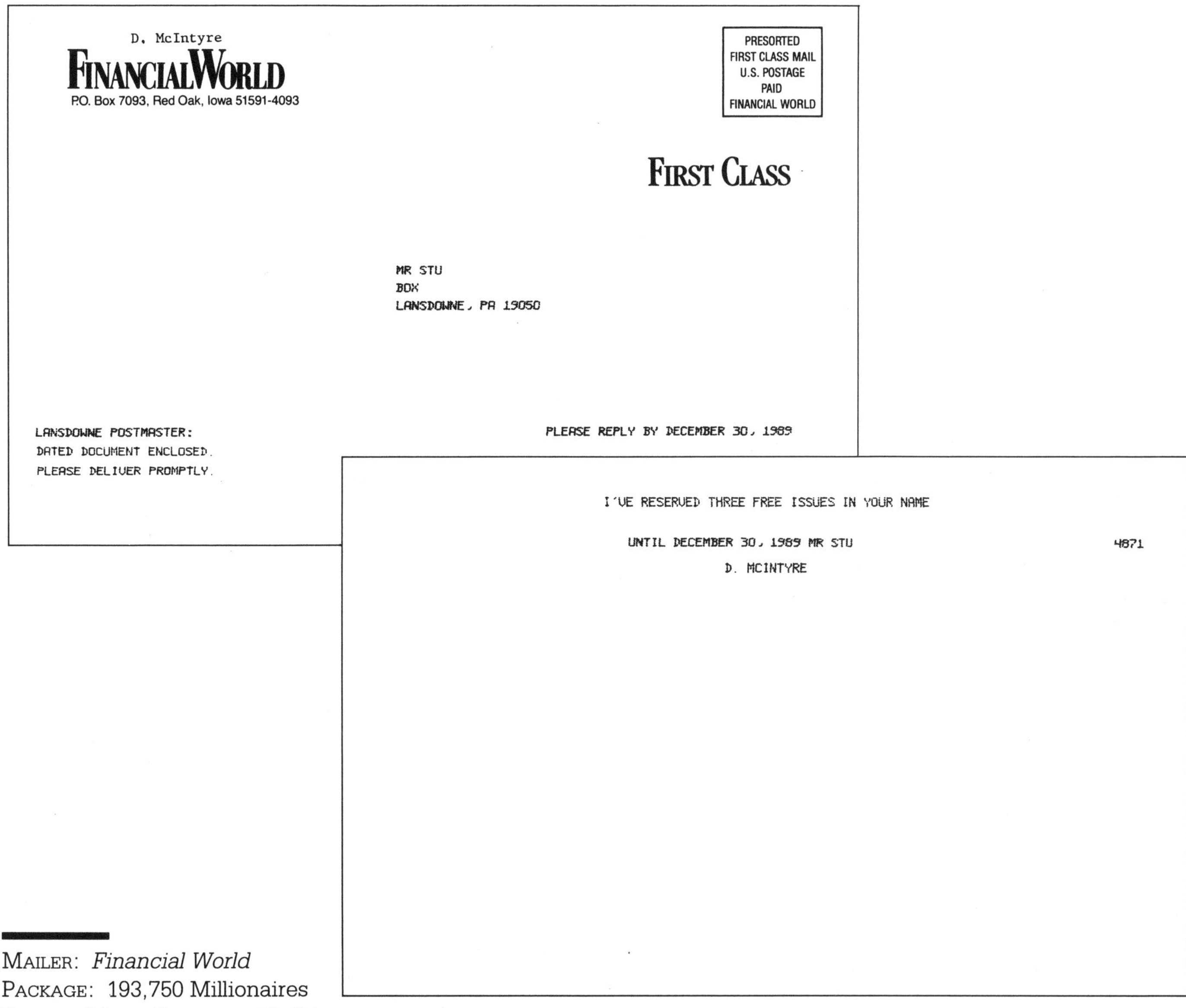

MAILER: *Financial World*
PACKAGE: 193,750 Millionaires
PROJECT MGR.: Laurence Hedblom
WRITER: Linda Wells
DESIGNER: John Rettich
FIRST MAILED: 1986
The closed-face, personalized $5^1/_2'' \times 8^1/_2''$ outer envelope shown front and back, with personalization on the flap. Copy at lower left and right is in red.

FINANCIAL WORLD

****

193,750 READERS OF FINANCIAL WORLD ARE ALREADY MILLIONAIRES. WITH $835,175 AVERAGE NET WORTH, THE REST WILL PROBABLY MAKE IT SOON.

AND NOW YOU, STU ARE INVITED TO JOIN THIS GROUP OF INVESTMENT INSIDERS AT NO RISK, OBLIGATION OR COMMITMENT.

IN FACT, IF YOU'LL GIVE US A "YES" OR EVEN A "MAYBE" TODAY, WE'LL SEND YOU THREE ISSUES OF FINANCIAL WORLD FREE.

****

DEAR MR STU

Can one-third of all the millionaires in America be wrong?

I can't answer that for you. But I can send you three free issues of FINANCIAL WORLD, the investment magazine they trust, respect and use to make their most important decisions. If your three free issues convince you they're right about FINANCIAL WORLD, I can guarantee you a 74% saving off the single-copy price and a 48% saving off the regular subscription rate.

This is the story. For most investors, it's a jungle out there. A jungle of financial analysts, stock promoters, investment whizzes, public relations operatives, media pundits and government bureaucrats all disgorging a deluge of paper that confuses, rather than clarifies, the market situation. It's a jungle of out-of-date statistics, factual errors, biased reporting and out-and-out fraud that makes investment decisions difficult, if not actually dangerous.

But America's most serious--and successful--investors don't waste their high-priced time on this hype and hoopla. They rely on FINANCIAL WORLD for up-to-the-minute investment news they need. They trust it for accurate, unbiased information that helps them outperform the averages and substantially increase their net worth.

Investments--and the World of Investing

FINANCIAL WORLD is the premier magazine in America today that focuses on the needs of the active investor. While other magazines like Business Week and Forbes offer general business background, FINANCIAL WORLD alone hones in on the factors that affect your specific investment options.

It's published 26 times a year to keep you on top of investment opportunities in today's multi-faceted markets. It covers every type of investment vehicle and related subjects of special interest to professional and individual investors like you--co... industries, specific investment situations, important inves... nds and profiles of people whose activities may affect your plans and decisions.

For instance . . .

Performance Ratings--clear, comparable numbers and independent, objective ratings of companies, mutual funds, brokers, money managers and more . . .

Company and Industry Spotlights--inside stories on major companies . . Dow Jones, Xerox and Citicorp . . . guides to investing in real estate and auto stocks, health care, space technology and cable TV . . . finding undervalued banks . . .

Investment Techniques--how you can lock in profits . . . investing in foreign markets . . . using puts and calls to reduce risk . . making money with option funds . . .

Personal Finance and Estate Planning--the new shelter game . . . interviewing a money manager . . . tax-free real estate swaps . . retirement payout plans . . .

Whether it's a major corporate merger or hidden values in Maine real estate, FINANCIAL WORLD provides the hard numbers and analysis you need to make profitable buying and selling decisions. When we like--or don't like--an investment, you'll know exactly why. And, of course, our recommendations are fully independent . . . and unbiased.

Special Issues for Alert Investors

Every year, FINANCIAL WORLD schedules over a dozen special issues that often become the Talk of the Street.

- Two Annual Forecast Issues. At year's beginning and at midyear, FINANCIAL WORLD polls the leading economists, money managers, analysts, corporate leaders and government officials compiling an exclusive overview of the months ahead. Prospects for the markets, the economy as a whole and 24 separate industries are examined to keep you not just in the game--but ahead of it.
- The Financial World 500. Growth Company Directory. An exclusive ranking of companies with an outstanding record of earnings growth during the past five years.
- Discount Brokerage. A complete survey of the discount brokerage industry--including comparative fees and commissions.
- The Futures Industry. The exchanges. Commodities. Indexes. Options. How professionals and individuals put various futures to use in their portfolios and investment strategies--and you can use them, too.
- Regional Financial Institutions. A guide to the major regional securities exchanges, brokerage firms and banks.
- The Year-End Financial Planner. A November special to help you get your house in order--with investment and tax strategies galore.

Every Issue is Loaded!

You'll hear the strategies of the chief financial officer of a major corporation in "The CFO" interview . . . pick up timely warnings in "Sell Signals" . . . explore new markets in "Global Investing." It's all useful, all practical.

And it's authoritative, too. Our experts are well-known on the Street. You get sage advice and investment savvy from the likes of Robert H. Stovall in "Market Comments," Harry W. Laubscher in "Technical Talk," and David S. Leibowitz in "Special Situations."

Extra Bonus

Every month, you'll receive FW's Independent Appraisals of Stocks and Mutual Funds. Our stock guide gives you comprehensive performance figures on all 3,000 common stocks on the NYSE, Amex and NASDAQ national market. Our fund guide evaluates over 1,000 mutual funds of all types and rates them by return, yield and assets. Our Independent Appraisals are separately bound from the magazine for easy reference and mailed to you with every other issue.

As a subscriber to FINANCIAL WORLD, you'll receive the same timely, accurate and unbiased information that has helped our readers/investors make their millions. But we want you to try it before you buy it, receiving your first three issues at no risk or obligation.

HOW TO GET YOUR THREE FREE ISSUES, STU

Give us a "yes" or even a "maybe" on the enclosed card, mail it in the postpaid envelope today, and you'll receive . . .

1. Three Issues Free. You'll receive three issues of FINANCIAL WORLD to find out if it's for you. If you think it could make your next million easier, sign on as a subscriber. If not, just let us know or write "cancel" across the bill when you get it, owe nothing, pay nothing and keep the three issues absolutely free.
2. Savings of 74%. If you decide to subscribe, you pay only $19.95 for 23 additional issues (making 26 in all). That is a 74% saving off the single-copy price, a 48% saving off the regular subscription rate.
3. A Pro Rata Money Back Guarantee. If you ever wish to cancel your subscription, simply let us know. We'll send you an immediate and unquestioned refund—your money back—on all unmailed issues.

You don't need to send any money now. We'll bill you after you've had a chance to read and use your three free issues and see for yourself why a third of all American millionaires are fans of FINANCIAL WORLD.

Sincerely,

Douglas A. McIntyre

Douglas A. McIntyre
Publisher

P.S. FIRST, STU , YOU GET THREE FREE ISSUES. THEN YOU GET A CHANCE TO SUBSCRIBE AT SAVINGS OF 74%. AND, IF DURING YOUR SUBSCRIPTION, YOU DECIDE THAT FINANCIAL WORLD ISN'T FOR YOU, WE'LL SEND YOU A FULL REFUND ON ANY UNMAILED ISSUES. SO HURRY AND MAIL YOUR CARD TODAY. POSTAGE IS ON US!

The 4-page 7″ × 10″ letter, printed front and back on 2 nested pages, with the first page personalized.

Notice that the order device uses the Yes-No-Maybe token that Hank Burnett employed in *American Demographics.* Years ago Yes-No stickers were tested. It was a daring concept, because if the person said No and sent it back in your business reply envelope, you were paying postage for No order. It wasn't a total loss: the list of people who responded No could be profitably rented to mailers with contrarian products such as burglar alarms and guard dogs. More to the point, it was found that even though giving the Yes-No option did bring in some Nos, it also raised the number of Yeses, and so was profitable.

The Yes-No-Maybe wrinkle was invented by freelancer John Francis Tighe. While a basic rule of direct marketing is not to give the prospect too many choices ("Confuse 'em, you lose 'em"), this technique seems to work in some instances. It's all the more remarkable here, because of the crummy personalization—a dot matrix typeface that doesn't match the rest of the letter. But it works!

Designer John Rettich has over twenty years' experience in direct response marketing, predominantly consumer magazine circulation, but with wide experience in other areas as well. Awards include the 1987 Gold Mailbox (with Karen Weinstein and Milt Pierce), silver Folios, and four Axel Andersson Awards for (*Aviation Consumer*, *Aviation Safety*, *Practical Sailor*, and *Financial World*). He teaches and lectures on direct response design.

PRIVILEGED INFORMATION FOR:

MR STU

Lift piece no. 1, personalized on the flap: "PRIVILEGED INFORMATION FOR: MR. STU SO-AND-SO."

Financial World
1450 BROADWAY, NEW YORK, N.Y. 10018

...That's what you get in every issue of FINANCIAL WORLD. Accept our FREE offer and see for yourself how we can help you beat the averages.

Dear Investor:

If you're about to say "No" to our FREE offer, I'd like you to reconsider. Saying "Yes" or "Maybe" gives you an opportunity to get three issues of FINANCIAL WORLD FREE without obligation. Three FREE issues to put to use to make money - save money - and beat the averages.

That's because FINANCIAL WORLD covers the gamut of investment opportunities - from Mutual Funds to Real Estate - from Mergers to New Issues - and everything that's in between. We pack each issue with the kind of facts you need to help you make important decisions.

If, after examining your three FREE issues, you don't agree this is the magazine that can help you increase your investment yield, just tell us. You'll pay nothing. Your three FREE issues are yours to keep, no matter what.

But if you do want to become a subscriber, you'll get a fabulous low rate too!

With every reason in the world to say "Yes" or "Maybe", and no good reason for saying "No", I urge you to return the Order Card and take full advantage of this No-Risk, profit-making opportunity while it lasts.

Sincerely,

Lawrence Hedblom

Lawrence Hedblom
Circulation Director

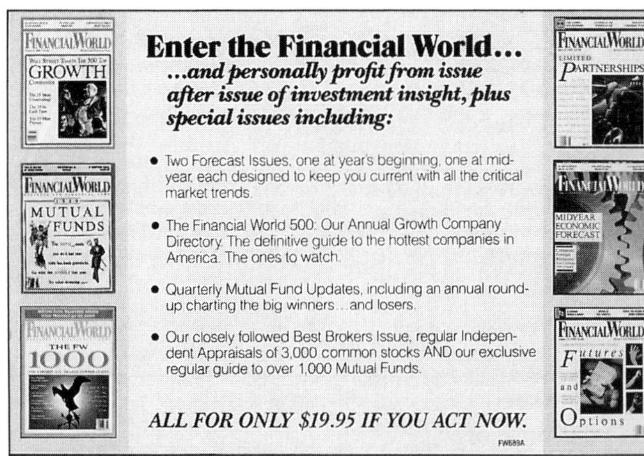

Lift piece no. 2, printed in 4-color.

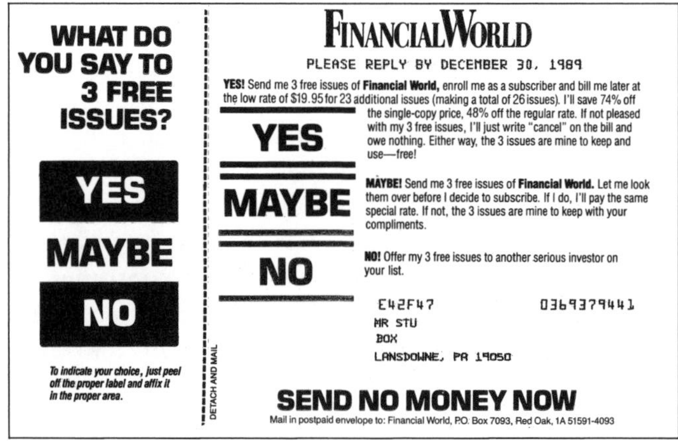

The order card with Yes-No-Maybe tokens.

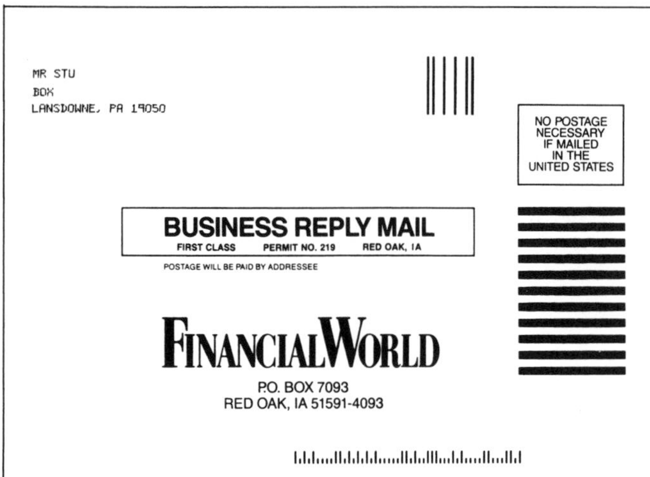

The business reply card, personalized with the person's name and address in the upper left.

JOHN RETTICH:

It's difficult for me to analyze a process I've spent my whole working career internalizing.

Most important, I try not *to be a designer; I try to become the consumer of the product that I am going to promote.*

I try to find out who uses it, who purchases it, its place in the market, its competition, its perceived benefits to the individual consumer or business, and as much else as possible to make my perceptions realistic.

I then get all the production parameters . . . budget constraints, if successful, rollout quantity, lists (whole audience range), personalization, etc.

Although a picture is worth 10,000 words, I have yet to see a successful direct mail effort that does not depend on copy to make the promotion and *the sell! The essence of my design is how I make the copy readable and graphically effective (e.g., how my choice of type makes the message and therefore the product ''feel''). That's also why I usually draw a very strong line between typography and typesetting.*

This doesn't mean that I don't believe in excellent design or even opulent visuals when appropriate. And I certainly advocate depicting the product. But I do thoroughly believe that the words are what are really deeply perceived and acted on by this society.

I also believe firmly in the sanctity of the consumer. We are there only at the consumer's indulgence, and I believe the consumer has the absolute right to a clear, thorough presentation that is as easy as possible to understand. This doesn't rule out humor or entertainment, or the wonderful complexities of ''bells,'' ''whistles,'' and personalization in a sweeps—but it does guide my handling of them.

With all this in mind and the information at hand, I simply let my internal tools take over and hope for the best!

SRDS Direct Mail List Rates and Data

Elaine Tyson is president of Tyson Associates, Inc., a Connecticut-based direct response agency and consulting firm. Clients include both business and consumer magazines. Prior to forming her own company, she was an account executive with Throckmorton/Zolfo, a New York direct marketing agency, and the director of circulation planning and development for the Periodicals, Directories, and Catalogs Division of Macmillan.

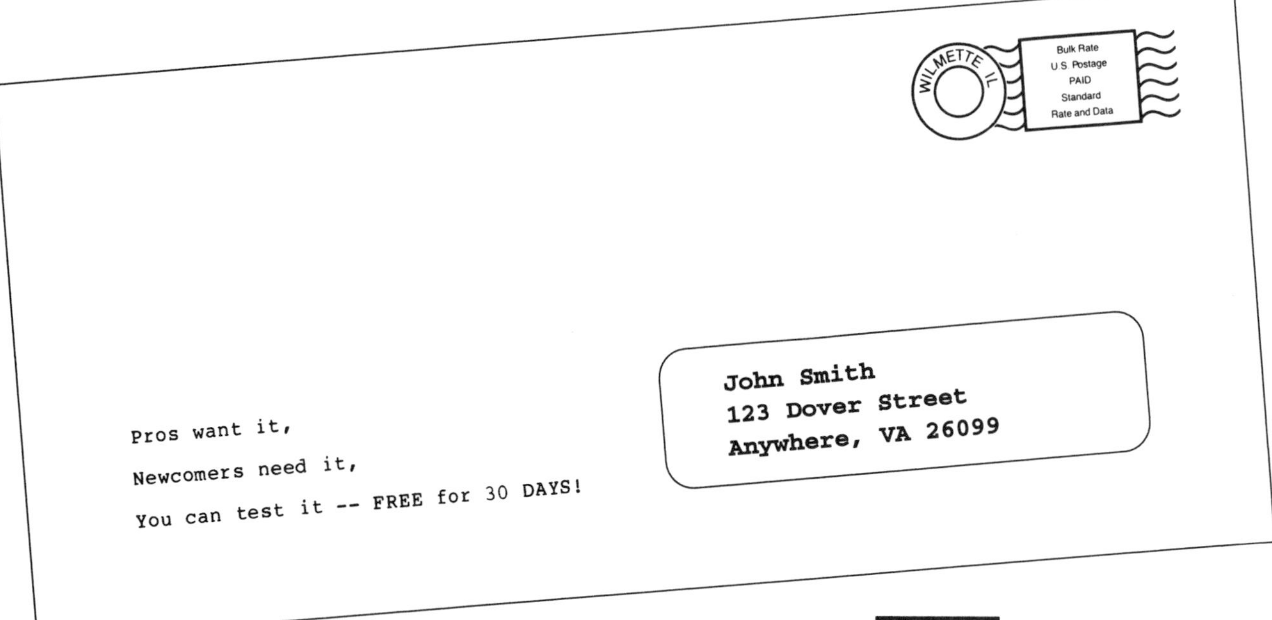

MAILER: Standard Rate and Data
PACKAGE: *Direct Mail List Rates and Data*
AGENCY: Tyson Associates, Inc.
PROJECT MGR.: Frank Paulo
WRITER: Dennis S. LeBarron
DESIGNER: Bill Iller
FIRST MAILED: 1985
The #10 outside envelope with typewriter type printed on blue lined stock.

ELAINE TYSON:

It's not at all unusual for direct mail packages to wear out quickly in finite markets where the same mailing lists are used frequently. For many limited-universe publications—particularly business and trade magazines—sneaking a subscription solicitation onto a prospect's desk has, of necessity, become an art form.

Direct mail packages for Standard Rate and Data Service (SRDS) products have an average life expectancy of about twelve to fourteen months. SRDS mails into relatively small market segments for all their media planning and buying catalogs. So, imagine the surprise at possessing an eight-year-old control for SRDS Direct Mail List Rates and Data.

For the past eight years, this subscription direct mail package has beaten everything thrown at it—including two completely new test packages (a #10 and 6" × 9" format), a premium version of the existing #10 control, and an envelope test version of the control.

This winning package is a circulator's delight—simple to produce, economical to mail. It has some well-thought-out features; and it's worthwhile to study each package component for clues to its seeming invincibility.

What makes this direct mail package so successful?

Direct Mail List Rates and Data
3004 Glenview Road, Wilmette, Illinois 60091

Subscribe now to the NEW 1985 SRDS DIRECT MAIL LIST RATES AND DATA -- the answer to making your direct marketing program more profitable. Try it FREE for 30 days.

Dear Direct Marketer:

I was having lunch the other day with some friends who are also in our business. One of them is well-known -- a veteran direct marketer. The other person is just starting out in our field.

Naturally, we soon got around to "talking shop". And I asked them to make a list of what they considered to be indispensable tools for today's direct marketing decision-maker.

To my surprise, on top of both of their lists was the SRDS DIRECT MAIL LIST RATES AND DATA.

I guess I shouldn't have been surprised because anyone whose success even partly hinges on the success of their direct mail program needs and wants this unique catalog.

NOW -- You can examine the most recent issue in your office or home -- FREE for 30 days. At no risk or obligation.

Your winning lists are right here. Because the 1985 SRDS DIRECT MAIL LIST RATES AND DATA is the most complete and comprehensive catalog of mailing list information available anywhere. Only SRDS puts over 55,000 business, consumer, and farm list selections in 228 markets all at your fingertips.

It's the most accurate and timely information you can get. You can be confident that you're making critical decisions based on up-to-minute facts, because these catalogs are revised and updated six times a year -- plus you'll receive 24 twice-monthly Update Bulletins at no extra charge. You'll know instantly about any list news that affects you and your business!

The most important element in your marketing program is now even easier to find. You know that the right list can be your ticket to success in direct mail. Now you can find that "break-through" list faster using the NEW "Subscribers Guide to Efficient Use" in the front of all 1985 issues. Just one of the many ways SRDS saves you priceless time!

For about 42 cents a day, you can reach the whole direct mail world. Besides giving you instant access to over 55,000 mailing list selections, the 1985 DIRECT MAIL LIST RATES AND DATA also puts you in touch with experts on co-op programs, package insert programs, computer services, lettershops, plus list managers and list brokers -- virtually everyone you need to ensure the success of your mailing program.

A full-year subscription to SRDS DIRECT MAIL LIST RATES AND DATA -- six issues and 24 Update Bulletins -- is only $170. That's about 42 cents a day -- about the price of a cup of coffee.

But there's no need to send money now. You can examine your first issue at our risk, not yours.

Test it yourself -- if it doesn't pay for itself -- you owe nothing.

Direct mail is a testing business. So we invite you to test us -- FREE for 30 days. Please hurry if you want a copy of the most recent issue -- there are only a limited number of each issue printed.

Whether you make only a few mailings a year, or mail every week, you'll save time and make more money with this catalog. You'll discover a wealth of new marketing ideas... what products are moving and in what numbers... keep an eye on your competition... work more effectively with your broker.

To order the 1985 DIRECT MAIL LIST RATES AND DATA, at no risk, simply complete and mail the enclosed postpaid card today. Or if you're in a hurry, call toll-free 800-323-4588.

We'll rush your copy right out to you. Then, you can examine it ... use it ... browse the many lists and services. Decide for yourself how it will help put more hard cash in your pocket. If you don't think it will pay for itself over and over, return it within 30 days and owe nothing.

Direct response is booming! And I'm sure you want to grab a bigger piece of the action. Let SRDS help you.

Do it now -- don't let this precious opportunity slip by.

Sincerely,

Frank N. Paulo
Circulation Director

P.S. In 1984 we reported over 2,000 new mailing lists. Anyone of these lists might unlock thousands of potential new dollars for you, but only if you are aware.

The 2-page letter printed front and back on an 8½″ × 11″ sheet of blue paper with thin light-gray lines that match the envelope.

1. The Outer Envelope

I think the envelope has a lot to do with the success of this package. Some solid direct marketing savvy went into its creation.

The teaser copy reads: "Pros want it, Newcomers need it. You can test it—FREE for 30 days!" This approach accomplishes a couple of things. It targets every prospect, both novice and veteran. It also piques curiosity about the package contents and promises a free trial. And because the copy makes prospects wonder what's inside, it's hard not *to open the envelope for a peek at the contents.*

The graphics carry the copy to its logical conclusion. As it should, the design works with the teaser to intrigue. The envelope is pale blue with light gray lines overprinted to suggest laid paper without the expense of using special paper.

Beyond this, typewriter repro is used as the typeface to suggest a personal appeal. A return address, again in typewriter repro, is printed on the flap rather than in the usual lefthand corner. And, the return address used the circ director's name only. No company logo is shown. This is a deliberate decision made to enhance the overall mystery of the envelope by refusing to telegraph the package contents.

How to get almost 23 feet of mailing lists facts into a 2-inch package!

The brochure starts at 3¾″ × 8½″: it opens and opens again to 8½″ × 14″, printed in red and black.

The preprinted third-class bulk indicia in red is "designed" to look like a postage meter. Very often, mailers find metered envelopes outpull ones with preprinted indicias. So, the envelope makes use of this knowledge without the increased expense of metering the mail in the lettershop. The indicia also maintains the subtle suggestion of a personal solicitation by looking as though it might have run through a company's postage meter.

2. The Sales Letter

Johnson Box copy above the letter salutation states the sub offer immediately and reinforces the free trial offer mentioned on the outer envelope.

The salutation—"Dear Direct Marketer"—targets the prospect very specifically. This technique tells the prospect that SRDS knows something about him/her and is writing to the prospect personally rather than to an amorphous mass of prospects.

The copy begins with a short story about a luncheon the SRDS spokesperson had with two direct marketing colleagues. Taking a story approach for the sales letter works for several reasons: It's not too long; it's interesting and involving; it's completely believable; and it ties back to the copy on the outer envelope. Almost anyone reading the letter can imagine being at such a luncheon meeting.

In addition, this letter answers every conceivable question about the subscription and states product benefits clearly. It tells how to order (by mail or

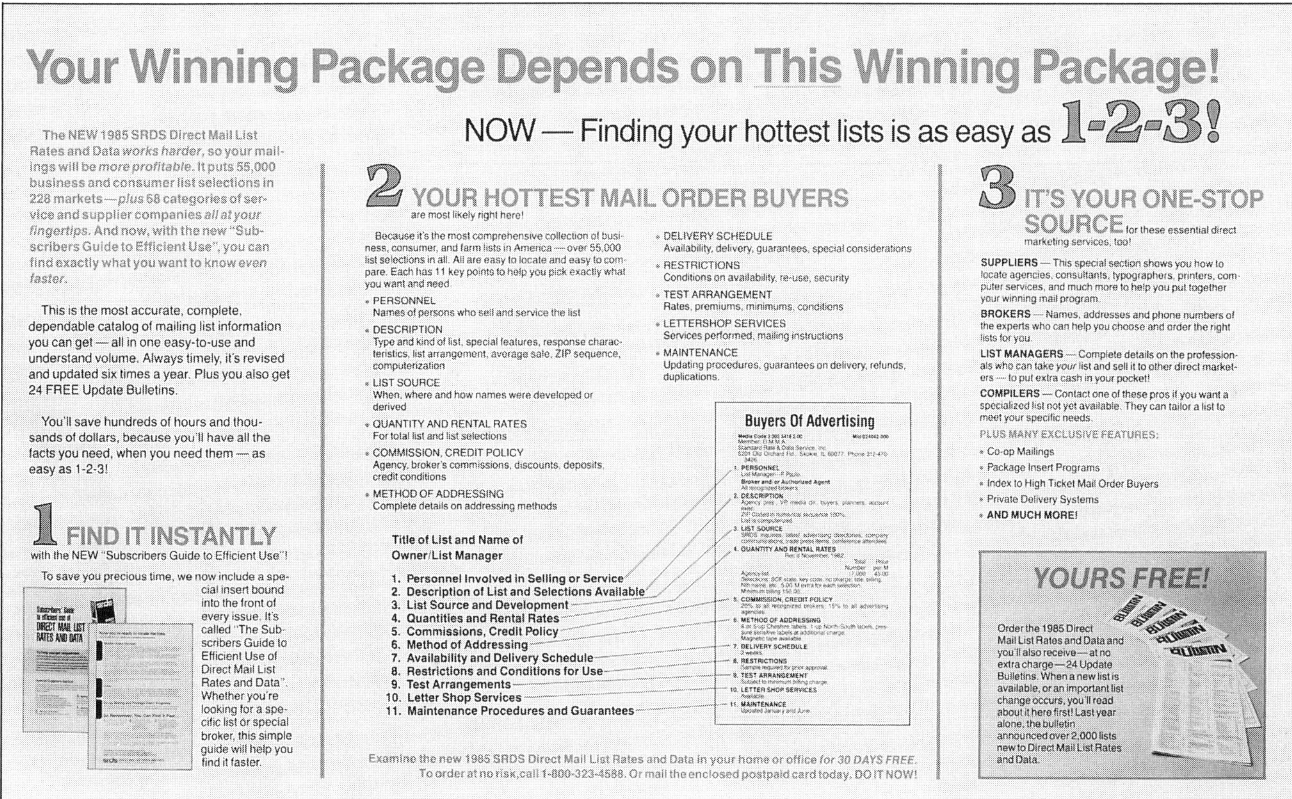

telephone), asks for the order, and uses a postscript to offer a new benefit.

The letterhead is printed to match the outer envelope. And, the letter itself is graphically appealing and easy to read because of the judicious use of subheads, underlining, and short, unintimidating paragraphs.

3. Testimonials Lift Letter

Everyone, I think, understands the importance of testimonials in terms of building credibility for a product. Testimonials can be used anywhere in a direct mail package. SRDS uses them in the lift letter.

Copy on the outside fold targets prospects who may be undecided about ordering. This copy directs those prospects to the inside of the lift letter, where testimonials from satisfied subscribers are discussed. One testimonial is from a large, well-known firm, the other from a smaller company. This reinforces the sales point that Direct Mail List Rates and Data *is for every mailer, regardless of the mailer's size.*

The lift letter folds vertically—not horizontally, as most prospects have come to expect. This is an unusual and attention-getting use of a component that may be becoming passé—depending upon which direct marketing guru you subscribe to. I personally like lift letters and think the jury is still out on whether using one improves response. I never hesitate to use a lift letter if a logical reason presents itself.

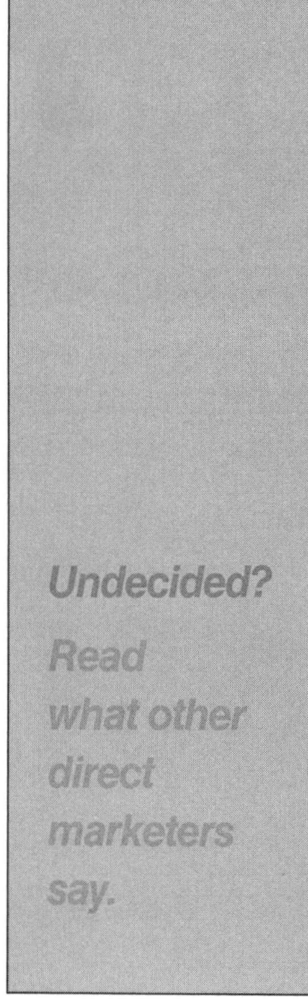
Undecided?
Read
what other
direct
marketers
say.

srds

Dear Direct Marketer:

Both novice and pro are well acquainted with the direct marketing Golden Rule -- the most important part of any direct mail effort is the list.

After thousands of dollars and hundreds of hours are spent worrying about every line of copy and the presentation of the offer, this effort results in bottom line profits only when the right list is used. Direct Mail List Rates and Data will help you find the right mailing list.

Here's what Joe Clark, Marketing Director of the Franklin Mint, has to say, "Direct Mail List Rates and Data? It's my ready reference tool when making list decisions in house, and in reviewing list recommendations from my brokers."

Other direct marketers use Direct Mail List Rates and Data for the very same reasons. Just ask Herb Oughton of Binks Manufacturing. "Direct Mail List Rates and Data has enabled us to target the right people more quickly."

I hope you'll take advantage of our special 30-day FREE TRIAL OFFER -- and see for yourself how it helps you be a more successful marketer.

All you have to do is mail the enclosed card or call today. Even the call and postage are on us.

Try it -- and you'll wonder how you ever got along without it.

Thank you,

Rick Botthof

Rick Botthof
Market Development Director

The lift piece.

4. The Order Card

What could be more appropriate as an involvement device for a direct marketer than a third-class bulk indicia? The use of a token that simulates such an indicia makes this simple order card effective. The prospect is instructed to move the token to the return portion of the card to say "Yes" to the free trial offer.

The guarantee is repeated in the offer copy and, as a way to satisfy those prospects with a need for instant gratification, a toll-free number is included.

There is a reply side on the order card and a business reply envelope is also included—even though the offer stresses "no need to send money now." The reason? Some prospects like to pay up front and others like privacy. This order card does ask for a signature and phone number. So, giving prospects a reply envelope eliminates any possible frustration.

The order card is well designed and a snap to use. It fulfills the requirements for making an order card appear important.

5. The Package Brochure

The SRDS control benefits from the inclusion of a brochure even though many direct marketers are somewhat familiar with the product.

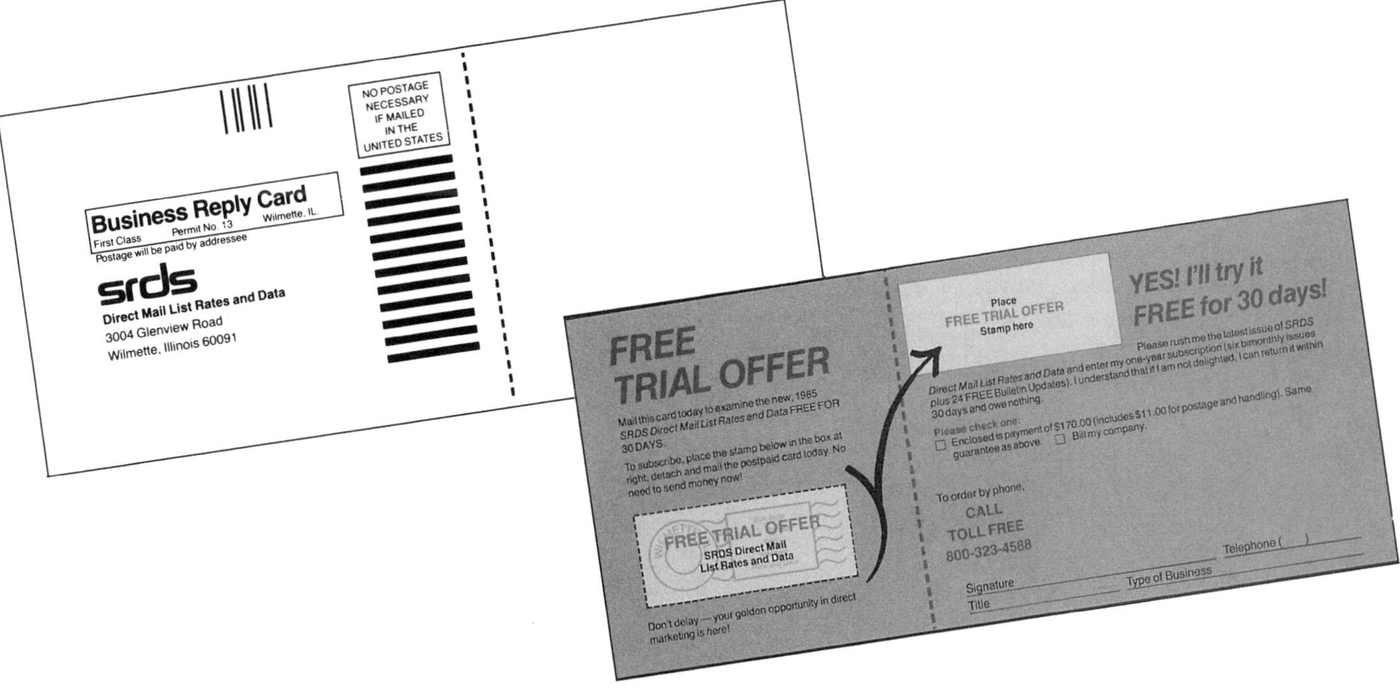

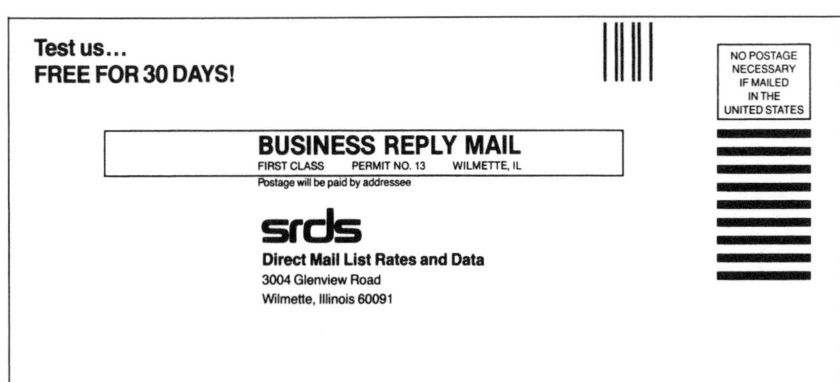

The order card shown front and back and the business reply envelope. The mailing uses both a business reply card and, for those who want privacy, a business reply envelope. Notice the reply card asks for a signature, title, and telephone number. This may cut up-front response, but it also may inhibit tire kickers.

As with all good brochures, this one is able to stand alone. It contains only the strongest and most visual product benefits and reinforces those benefits and features already described in the sales letter.

Additionally, the piece injects some gentle humor into the package with copy on the cover that states: ''How to get almost 23 feet of mailing lists facts into a 20-inch package!''

When the brochure is opened to the first small spread, it shows the product and explains, ''We estimate it would take a stack of thin direct mail list data cards over 23 feet high to give you just a part of the information you get in the new Direct Mail List Rates and Data.*''*

This copy puts into perspective the wealth of information offered relative to the subscription price. If you need the list information available from SRDS, this kind of benefit makes you think. It also graphically illustrates the comprehensiveness of the product, plus the hard versus easy work-saver copy.

The large inside spread has a compelling headline that uses a play on words to convey a benefit: ''Your Winning Package Depends on This *Winning Package.''*

Copy goes on to describe editorial features and benefits, and shows a listing from Direct Mail List Rates and Data *with call-outs detailing each element of the listing. The brochure's back panel urges the prospect to take immediate action, and repeats the SRDS guarantee in a certificate border. It also thanks the prospect for ordering—something too many direct marketers overlook.*

The exact trim size of the brochure is 8½" × 14"—and this one takes maximum advantage of limited space by using interesting folds. It is folded first to 7" × 8½", then short folded again to 3⅝" × 8½". This results in the illusion of more color on the first panel because of the short fold, and creates a small and large spread for copy and graphics.

This brochure also does something else: It tracks. By that I mean it is designed so the prospect's eyes move logically from the brochure cover, to the small spread, right on to the large spread, then to the back panel and, presumably, on to the order card.

There isn't anything worse than a jumbled, confusing brochure. When you look at one that is poorly executed, you know immediately, because you can't decide where to look first and its folds don't seem to work logically. The confusion created by a poorly designed brochure results in slowing down and possibly turning off a prospect.

The Direct Mail List Rates and Data *brochure, on the other hand, leaves room for copy to breathe and makes it easy for prospects to understand exactly what is being offered and specifically what benefits will accrue as a result of subscribing.*

Overall, this control package concept is clear. There is continuity throughout by virtue of great attention to detail. Each component reinforces the package concept, and all the components work together to create a sum greater than its parts.

Proven Bells and Whistles

The creative team took advantage of many proven direct mail bells and whistles. But these tried-and-true techniques were used in a fresh, appealing way. None was stifled by the use of two-color, by budget limitations, or the "unsexy" nature of the product. This package proves that a little imagination will go a long way toward overcoming difficult or unexciting subject matter.

21

Boardroom Reports

In the previous chapter I mentioned that so-called business-to-business mail is the dullest. And the most stupifyingly dull comes from the publishers of business and financial books. If I had the choice of reading a month's worth of this category of mail or spending the day at the local barbershop watching haircuts, there would be no contest.

The two mailings that follow are the exceptions rather than the rule. Maybe that is why they are so long-lived and so effective.

One of the all-time modern success stories in the arena of business books and newsletters is Martin Edelston, who, prior to starting his own company, had been a lifeguard, dishwasher, advertising salesman, book club manager, and circulation director. In 1972 he founded Boardroom Reports, which he built into an empire of newsletters and books with more than one million active customers. Three copywriters helped catapult Edelston into the first rank of publishers: Eugene Schwartz, Pat Garrard, and a secret copywriter whose name Edelston will reveal to no one.

MAILER: *Bottom Line/Personal*
PACKAGE: Eat on Airplane
PROJECT MGR.: Laurie Mellon
AGENCY: In-house
WRITER: Declined to reveal
DESIGNER: Declined to reveal
FIRST MAILED: 1987
The #10 outside envelope.

WHAT NEVER TO EAT ON AN AIRPLANE

SIDNEY OHIO
U.S. POSTAGE 10
P.B. METER

CAR-RT SORT **CR53
Chris
38 Rd.
Glenville, CT 06831

OE-BLPB

What never to eat on an airplane

How to outwit mugger in self-service elevator

TRY IT FREE

- **Legal way to take tax deduction for cost of commuting to work**
- **How thieves deactivate burglar alarms. Changes you should make in yours**
- **What never to keep in your safe deposit box. *Never.* And how to stop the state from sealing it**
- **How to detect marked cards and loaded dice**
- **Cost not listed in health insurance contract can be covered if you know the ropes**
- **Add up what you spend on daughter's wedding and use it to reduce your income tax**
- **How to avoid a tax audit. What the IRS computers are looking for on your return and how to put them off the scent**
- **Intensity of pain in dentist's office depends on time of day. New discovery: Hours when it hurts least**
- **How to deduct cost of hobby as business expense even if you never show a profit**

Dear Business Colleague:

So much is changing so fast these days that you need to be an expert on everything. And now you can try having the world's leading experts on everything working for you -- free. Know it all.

. How to deduct all your medical bills without first subtracting 7.5% of gross income. Lots of people do it and never get in trouble. What's more, their ploy is perfectly legal.

. Quick look at sticker price plus simple arithmetic reveals minimum figure car dealer will accept.

. Bank offers discount for early repayment of low-interest mort-

Two famous cold remedies that make you sicker if taken together.

gage. Grab it, right? Wrong.

. Cancelled check for fire insurance premium proves you're covered, right? Wrong.

. How to translate medical jargon on patient's hospital chart.

. Withdraw IRA money before age 59 1/2 if needed, and pay penalty. Beats any other form of saving.

. How to deposit check marked "payment in full" from someone who still owes more money without losing your right to collect the rest.

. How to deduct family vacation as business expense. Possibilities your accountant never showed you.

. How stockbrokers unload securities from their own inventory at higher than market price. Evidence is buried in fine print on confirmation slip.

. How much to tip so you'll never look like a sucker or a tightwad.

. When to sue a lawyer for malpractice.

All in plain English for people who want to do everything right.

It's all in BOTTOM LINE/PERSONAL, the biweekly executive update that puts your personal affairs on a businesslike basis.

And you can try it free.

. How to make money in a declining stock market. (Done all the time by Wall Street professionals, and easier than it sounds.)

. How to use sleeping pills without becoming addicted.

. How to take parent as dependent without providing 50% of support.

. How to collect interest from two money market funds at same time on same spare cash.

. Numbers that should never be used for combination lock. (Professional burglars try them first.)

. How to know when it's time to sell a stock, recognize a real downward trend, get out before issue takes big tumble.

. What never to tell an insurance adjuster. First thing said after loss can be worst mistake.

. Why couples who have signed mutual wills should tear them up

-2-

Skin caught in zipper. Quick fix.

and draft separate ones.

. Promises not to believe in package tour brochure.

. Best times to get standby seat on any airline.

. How vasectomy changes body chemistry.

. How to beat the high interest rate on unpaid credit card balance.

. How to check in and out of crowded hotel without standing in line.

. What surgeons don't tell you. Seven questions to ask before consenting to an operation.

. Legal way to deduct gambling losses.

. What you don't have to tell a tax auditor. How to prevent a "fishing" expedition through your records.

. Best time of year to look for bargains at auction houses and art galleries.

. Most dangerous tax audit comes right after you die. How to fight back from the grave.

. How to choose the right vacation cruise. New insiders' rule of thumb for predicting average age of fellow passengers. Best cabins on any ship if you don't want to be seasick.

. Wife deeds assets over to dying husband. This is estate planning at its shrewdest.

. Credit cards that can start charging interest before you even get your bill.

. How to choose a real estate broker today. Difference between exclusive agency, exclusive right to sell, open listing, multiple listing. How property you put up for sale can be taken off the market without your knowledge. How broker can collect commission even if property is never sold.

All straight from the great experts through BOTTOM LINE/PERSONAL.

Try it free. See what you could have been missing.

What it's your business to know about the travel business, the insurance business, the nursing home business, the bank business.

What doctors and hospitals don't tell you. What the IRS doesn't tell you. What brokerage houses don't tell you.

How to distinguish the facts from the hype in health foods, computers,

-3-

Safest place in any hotel room to hide valuables.

pension plans.

How to pick the right wines, the right exercises, the right stereo system, the right credit card.

. How to choose a nursing home. Smartest time for inspection tour. What to look at and how to evaluate what you see. Extra charges that may not be mentioned unless you ask about them.

. Stop a headache by pressing the right spot on your wrist. (Try it and see for yourself.)

. How to make your keys hard to duplicate and your signature almost impossible to forge.

How to do everything right. Taxes. Investments. Budgeting. Travel. Health. Fitness. Insurance. Banking. Estate planning. Managing your finances, your household, your career. Making your money grow and getting the best value when you spend it. Sample BOTTOM LINE/PERSONAL's inside information now, while you can do it free.

See for yourself why more than a quarter-million knowledgeable people read every word of every issue.

BOTTOM LINE/PERSONAL
TENTH ANNIVERSARY OFFER

Act now and we will send you three issues of BOTTOM LINE/PERSONAL -- absolutely free -- plus a one-year (24 issues) trial subscription at a big discount.

If I'm wrong, and BOTTOM LINE/PERSONAL is not for you, just return the bill marked canceled.

You simply can't lose.

It pays to mail the free trial form today. And many thanks.

Very truly yours,

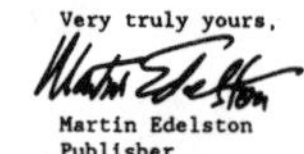

Martin Edelston
Publisher

ME:lnp

P.S. When not to fly first class -- in this age of airline disintegration.

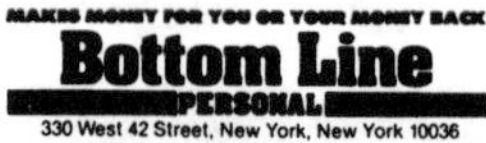

The 4-page letter, printed front and back on two 8½″ × 11″ nested sheets.

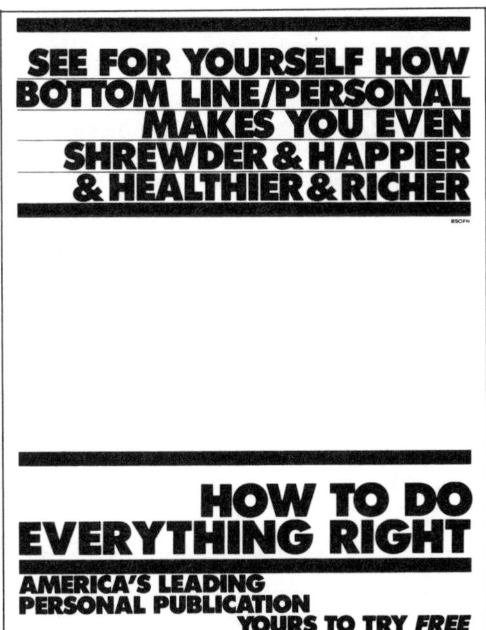

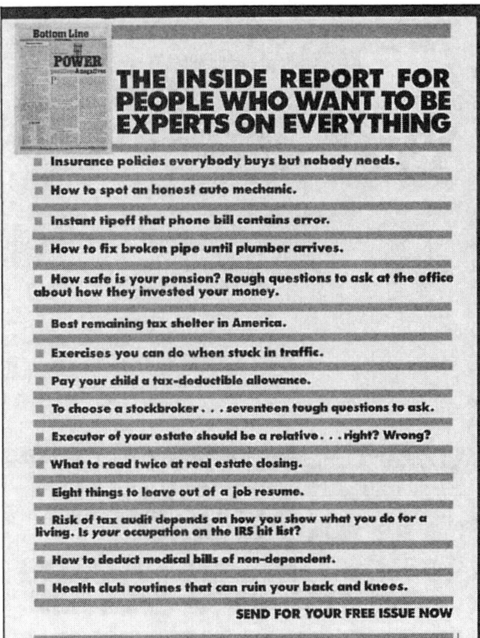

THE INSIDE REPORT FOR
PEOPLE WHO WANT TO BE
EXPERTS ON EVERYTHING
Insurance policies everybody buys but nobody needs.
How to spot an honest auto mechanic.
Instant tipoff that phone bill contains error.
How to fix broken pipe until plumber arrives.
How safe is your pension? Rough questions to ask at the office about how they invested your money.
Best remaining tax shelter in America.
Exercises you can do when stuck in traffic.
Pay your child a tax-deductible allowance.
To choose a stockbroker . . . seventeen tough questions to ask.
Executor of your estate should be a relative . . . right? Wrong?
What to read twice at real estate closing.
Eight things to leave out of a job resume.
Risk of tax audit depends on how you show what you do for a living. Is your occupation on the IRS hit list?
How to deduct medical bills of non-dependent.
Health club routines that can ruin your back and knees.
SEND FOR YOUR FREE ISSUE NOW

The brochure. The 2 separated headlines appear on the 2 folds as you open it.

Edelston believes that long-term controls are not winners; they are losers. When I announced the Axel Andersson Awards and sent Edelston certificates for *Bottom Line/Personal* and *The Book of Inside Information,* he sent me a note on his screaming yellow 14″ × 17″ stationery with the following in big black caps at the top:

ASYOUWANDERONTHROUGHLIFE
FRIENDWHATEVERBEYOURGOAL
KEEPYOUREYEUPONTHEDONUT
ANDNOTUPONTHEHOLE

Edelston scrawled:

Re: Awards. Longtime controls are, I think, a sign of failure—failure to beat The Control. And—that, too, is dangerous to one's health. As controls diminish—and they all do—it hurts not to have a replacement. Fortunately we have new winners emerging at last for the two winners (losers) that you sent us awards for. Crazy—crazy times!

In a fax to Edelston, I pointed out that the original 1991 Axel Awards comprised just sixty-six mailings out of the 50,000 a year that I review.

His comment: "49,934 winners and 66 losers—and I have two of those . . . ouch!"

He was gleeful that his long-term controls were finally beaten.

The *Bottom Line/Personal* Grand Control that follows is vintage Boardroom. The envelope screams: "WHAT NEVER TO EAT ON AN AIRPLANE."

You tear into the mailing only to find that this is the kind of information you will get if you send for a free trial of the publication. Reading a Boardroom mailing is like eating peanuts: you can't stop. The entire promotion—letter and circular—is a series of splendid teasers that have you salivating by the end.

Another extraordinary aspect of this effort: there is no price mentioned *anywhere.*

Bottom Line
PERSONAL
GUARANTEED
TO MAKE MONEY FOR YOU
OR YOUR MONEY BACK
INSIDE
INFORMATION

READING BOTTOM LINE'S INSIDE INFORMATION IS THE NEXT BEST THING TO HAVING A RELATIVE IN THE IRS

AND A RELATIVE INSIDE YOUR BANK	**AND A RELATIVE INSIDE THE BEST INVESTMENT HOUSE IN AMERICA**
AND A RELATIVE INSIDE YOUR INSURANCE COMPANY	**SEND FOR YOUR FREE SAMPLE AND SEE WHY. . .**

The lift piece.

DON'T SEND MONEY

YES

NO

FREE Yes, please send *free* three issues of BOTTOM LINE/PERSONAL. If I like the free issues, I may subscribe at a big saving off the regular subscription rate. If I don't like BOTTOM LINE for any reason, I'll simply return the bill, owe nothing and keep my three free issues.

738 02057247 7EAK7

CAR-RT SORT **CR53
Chris
38 Rd.
Glenville, CT 06831

THREE FREE ISSUES

BOTTOM LINE/PERSONAL, Box 58432, Boulder, CO 80321-8432

OC.BLNP90

The order card shown front and back. The Yes-No tokens are gold foil. The back of the card is in screaming red.

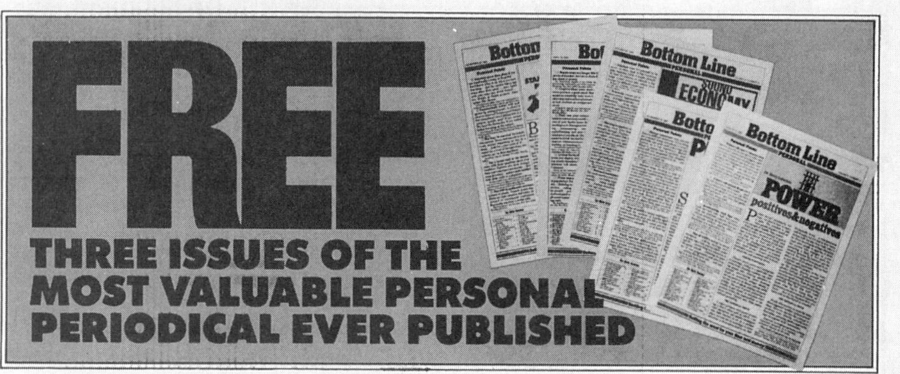

The business reply card.

BUSINESS REPLY MAIL
FIRST-CLASS MAIL PERMIT NO 1216 BOULDER CO

POSTAGE WILL BE PAID BY

Bottom Line
PERSONAL
Subscription Service Center
PO Box 58433
Boulder CO 80321-8433

The Book of Inside Information

Like the effort for *Bottom Line/Personal*, this Grand Control for *The Book of Inside Information* is vintage Boardroom Reports.

Part of Martin Edelston's genius as a publisher is that he takes existing editorial material from his newsletters and repackages it and sells it to the same audience that wants all these pearls of wisdom in the permanent format of a book.

This effort closely parallels that of *Bottom Line/Personal*: a screamer of an outer envelope promises to reveal "What credit card companies don't tell you." Inside, you discover that the answer to the teaser can only be found on page 10 of the book. The letter then goes on to list dozens of other such teasers and on what pages of *The Book of Inside Information* the answers will be found.

There is even a P.S. that implies the price of the book is tax deductible, but you have to see page 75.

Also notice the lift piece, obviously a real testimonial letter—complete with typo—enlarged to fill the entire page with copy. Brilliant design!

If you skip back to Chapter 16 and reread Gene Schwartz's copy for the two Rodale books and then read these Boardroom efforts, you'll see a lot of similarity. If Schwartz did not write these packages, at least you can see how he set the tone and style for Martin Edelston's entire enterprise.

What credit card companies don't tell you.
BLK RT
SIDNEY OHIO
A33M52
J. A.
251 E ST
NEW YORK, NY 10022

MAILER: Boardroom Reports
PACKAGE: *Book of Inside Information*
PROJECT MGR.: Michael Weil
AGENCY: In-house
WRITER: Declined to reveal
DESIGNER: Declined to reveal
FIRST MAILED: 1987
The #10 outside envelope.

What credit card companies don't tell you. Page 10

THE BOOK OF INSIDE INFORMATION

Dear Friend:

These must be 1,688 of the best kept secrets in America:

- You miss your April 15 deadline and don't get around to filing until mid-August. No IRS penalty. Lots of taxpayers just like you are quietly getting away with it. Their perfectly legal ploy is explained on page 107.
- How to fight back when health insurance claim is denied. And win. Costs not listed in contract can be covered if you know the ropes. Page 429.
- Work after retirement and earn all the money you want without giving up a cent of your Social Security. (You have to be 70, right? Wrong! Legal for any retired person.) Page 2.

(continued...)

What hospitals don't tell you. Page 421

- Quick look at sticker price plus simple arithmetic tells how much dealer paid for car and minimum figure he will accept for it. Page 349.
- How auto repair shops pad their bills. Inside strategy for getting honest total. Page 362.
- You walk into an empty self-service elevator late at night and press the button. Before the door has a chance to close, you get back out fast. Why? (Nine ways to outwit a mugger.) Page 380.
- Insider's guide to new-style mortgages. Comparison of adjustable mortgage loan, variable-rate mortgage, lease-buy agreement, interest-only mortgage, land lease, equity sale, balloon mortgage, and more. Page 258.
- How to read a condominium prospectus. Tip-off that floor plan is deliberately misleading and costs will escalate fast. Page 264.
- Mistakes the phone company makes in its bills. How to spot them on yours. Page 306.
- What never to eat on an airplane. How insiders bend the rules on carry-on luggage. When not to fly first class. And more. Page 367.

Did anybody ever explain all this to you before? Your accountant? Your travel agent? Your mechanic? Mine never did.

Consider the question of exercise. Did anyone ever tell you that three widely recommended forms of calisthenics can ruin your back and knees? See page 453 for this and a lot more you may never hear at your health club.

THE BOOK OF INSIDE INFORMATION comes with a one-year money-back guarantee. I'm betting you never ask for a refund.

- A simple exercise you can do in the house gives you all the benefits of jogging and works three times better. Page 460.
- Best real estate profits are in Sun Belt, right? Wrong. Where to buy property instead. Page 49.
- Inside life insurance. Five signs that life insurance salesman should not be trusted. Questions to ask about any insurance company before you take out a policy. Formula for calculating how much life insurance you really need. Life insurance bargain for husband and wife who both need coverage (not likely to be mentioned unless you specifically ask about it.) Page 136.
- How to prepare for insurance physical when not in best shape. Page 138.
- Homeowner mistake permits fire insurance company to give you 20% less protection than you're paying for. (Page 267.) What not to tell an

-2-

What the IRS doesn't tell you. Page 115

insurance adjuster. (First thing said after loss can be worst mistake.) Page 268.

- Inside the credit-card business. Cards that can start charging interest before you even get your bill. (Page 10.) Which cards to use abroad for best break on currency conversion. What never to reveal when you report loss of credit card. Never. Page 10.
- Inside Wall Street. Best way for small investor to play stock market. How to evaluate price/earnings ratio, yield, growth rate, relation of market price to book value. How insiders read ticker tape and market averages. How to evaluate high technology stocks, venture stocks, growth stocks, new issues by established companies, foreign stocks, utility stocks. Page 19.
- How to choose a mutual fund. Open-end vs. closed-end. Page 39.
- How to choose a money market fund. Short vs. long maturities. Page 40.
- Options, warrants, T-bills, municipal bonds, convertibles, "junk" bonds, foreign currencies, commodities. (Worst mistake commodities trader can make after big win -- or big loss. Page 46.)
- Inside the IRS. How government computers select tax returns for audit. Percentage of returns audited at each income level. The two kinds of IRS agents and which one means more trouble. The four kinds of audit and which is worst. Figures you don't have to show a tax auditor. Questions you are not required to answer. Page 109.
- Who gets charged with tax fraud and who gets convicted. IRS statistics on cases involving business owners, corporate officers, doctors, dentists, lawyers. Page 113.
- Advice you get by phone from IRS protects you against later claim of tax deficiency, right? Wrong. To protect you, advice must be in writing. Wrong again. Page 115.
- Inside banking. Bank is responsible for valuables in safe deposit box, right? Wrong. Where to keep them instead. How bank can be forced to honor bad check. How to deposit check marked "payment in full" from someone who still owes more money. When a check is too old to cash. You run out of checks and pay bills by writing a simple letter the bank will cash. Page 8.

1,688 inside ways to protect your earnings, your assets, your health, your life style, your heirs. How to be more secure in troubled times.

All in plain English from 600 inside experts on investment, insurance, taxes, real estate, medical care, fitness, nutrition. How insiders read a manufacturer's warranty, a mortgage agreement, a hotel bill, a financial statement, a sales

(please turn...)

-3-

What the airlines don't tell you. Page 367

contract, a nursing home contract, a lawyer's bill, a phone bill--and what they look at twice.

What insiders look for when they're deciding on a pension plan, a dentist, a surgeon, a California wine, a moving company, a dry cleaner.

How to get the most for your money from a tax accountant, an investment firm, an appliance dealer, a public utility, a private school.

- Life expectancy of new TV sets, refrigerators, washer-dryers, dishwashers. Best refrigerator design--freezer on top, bottom, or side? Freezer works best full of food, right? Wrong. Page 305.
- How insiders select stereo equipment. Best value for money. When to avoid pre-recorded tapes. Page 313.
- How to get a store's best price. Most shoppers start bargaining a few minutes too early in the game. Page 299.
- Why it's smart to buy low-priced microwave oven and high-priced garbage disposal. Page 305.
- The two kinds of down and which one makes a warmer jacket. Page 317.
- How to spot a well-made pair of jeans. Five signs. Page 317.
- How to buy Western boots. City slickers get the wrong size. Page 318.
- How to buy caviar and champagne like an expert. Page 309.
- How to buy diamonds. If you own good ones, you should wash them. Dry them, too. Instructions on page 343.
- How to select a vacation cruise. Predict average age of passengers. Best cabin location if prone to seasickness. How to get top accommodations on best ships at minimum rate. Page 368.
- How to read a package-tour brochure and when to be skeptical. People paying by check should put special wording on front and back as precaution. Page 367.
- Quick way to check accuracy of complicated hotel bill when you've been charging lots of meals and drinks to your room. How to make crowded hotel honor your reservation. Page 371.
- Where insiders buy furs wholesale. You can, too. (Page 320.) Furs should be stored in cedar closet, right? Wrong. Page 321.
- Advice for hay fever sufferers. Sleep late in the morning and stay out of swimming pools. For reasons why see page 404.
- 15 ways to make your marriage work. How children, in-laws can sabotage

-4-

The 6-page letter, printed on 6 nested 8½″ × 11″ sheets.

What car dealers don't tell you. Page 347

marriage. Secrets of successful 2-career marriages. One habit all married couples should never get into - ever. Times when it's advisable to have honest-to-goodness fight. Insights so valuable they can affect long term prospects for marriage success. Page 220.

- How to check a doctor's credentials, understand medical jargon on a patient's hospital chart, cut through hospital red tape, and get courteous treatment from floor staff. Page 421.

How not to be intimidated by a hospital administrator, a custom clothier, a head waiter, a bank loan officer, a county assessor. Inside ways to separate facts from hocus-pocus. When it's your business to know about other people's business.

Know-how you need at your fingertips in an increasingly complex world where you have to be an expert on everything.

- Eight things to leave out of your resume. Page 209.
- Burglar alarms that smart thieves can deactivate. What to install instead. Page 290. How to choose a watchdog. Page 292.
- Best lock for front door. Best lock for windows. Page 289.
- Fire detection devices. Smoke alarm vs. heat detector. Page 287.
- Best place in hotel room to hide valuables. Best place in home to keep valuables if you don't own a safe. How to buy a safe; best choices if you want protection against fire as well as theft. Page 307.
- Instant way to spot fake ID. Page 9.
- How aluminum cooking utensils can poison you. When to discard them. Page 383.
- Health hazard in non-stick cookware. Danger signal to watch for. Page 384.
- What to read twice at a real estate closing. Page 261.
- How to prove your property is assessed too high. Page 277.
- People with circulatory problems should not sleep under electric blankets. People with heart trouble should not drink ice water. Why? Page 384.
- How to service your own refrigerator, air conditioner, washer and dryer. Page 295.
- Options to turn down when you buy a new car. Page 35.
- Birth control method to avoid if you plan on having children later. Page 412.
- Antibiotic that should be avoided when you're going to be out in the sun. Page 416.

-5-

(continued...)

What banks don't tell you. Page 6

- Best men's clothes for each body build. Who looks good and who looks bad in pinstripes, double-breasted jackets, short jackets, layered clothes, turtlenecks. And more. Page 316.
- Best time of year to find bargains at top auction galleries. What never to bid on. Page 329.
- Common mistake in wording of will can give bulk of estate to those who should get least. Page 146.
- How professional gamblers spot marked cards and loaded dice. Page 377.
- How insiders buy custom-made suits and custom shoes. Page 316.
- Easy way to remember names and numbers. Page 171.

Information you never expected to see in print. Loopholes your lawyer never told you about or showed you how to use. More about insurance than most policyholders learn in a lifetime.

Send for a copy of THE BOOK OF INSIDE INFORMATION at my risk. Keep it as long as twelve months and see how much cold cash it saves you.

All I ask is that you consult it regularly and judge the results for yourself. You get a prompt refund if you can honestly say it isn't worth a hundred times the low price.

Regularly $50.00. Executive discount price $29.95.
And a one-year money-back guarantee from Boardroom Classics.

Is it a deal? Then please mail your order form today. And many thanks.

Sincerely,

Martin Edelston
Publisher, Boardroom Classics

ME:jclda

P.S. Executive discount price is tax deductible as permitted by the Tax Reform Act of 1986. See page 75.

MAKES MONEY FOR YOU OR YOUR MONEY BACK
BOARDROOM CLASSICS
330 West 42 Street, New York, New York 10036

A critical customer says it best...

Board Room Books
P.O. Box 1026
Millburn, NJ 07041

Gentlemen:

I received my copy of your book, The Book of Inside Information this morning. This book is class from cover to cover. I started to read a few paragraphs and I have been reading for several hours. I find this book very hard to put down. Everything I have read so far is very clear and to the point. I wish I had a book like this about thirty years ago. I have six children, 4 boys and 2 girls. I think the greatest thing I could do for them at the present time is to give each one of them a copy of this book.

Enclosed please find an order for 6 (six) more books.

Very truly yours,

Lift piece 1.

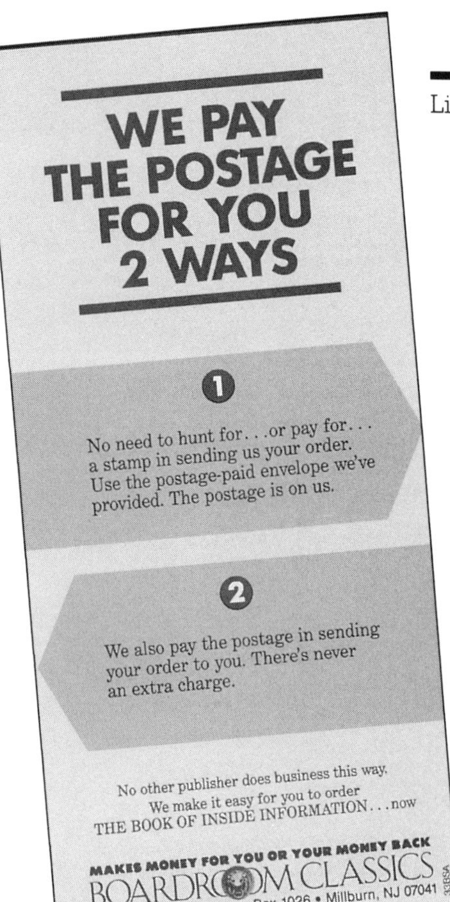

WE PAY THE POSTAGE FOR YOU 2 WAYS
1
No need to hunt for. . .or pay for. . . a stamp in sending us your order. Use the postage-paid envelope we've provided. The postage is on us.
2
We also pay the postage in sending your order to you. There's never an extra charge.
No other publisher does business this way.
We make it easy for you to order
THE BOOK OF INSIDE INFORMATION. . .now
MAKES MONEY FOR YOU OR YOUR MONEY BACK
BOARDROOM CLASSICS
Order Fulfillment Center • Box 1026 • Millburn, NJ 07041

Lift piece 2.

The business reply envelope.

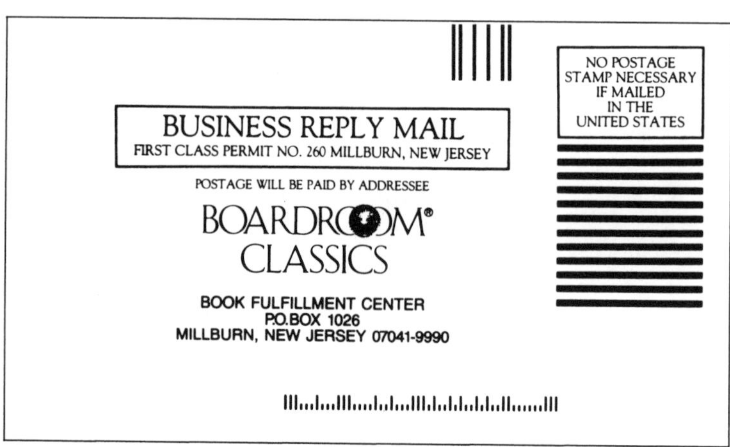

NO POSTAGE STAMP NECESSARY IF MAILED IN THE UNITED STATES
BUSINESS REPLY MAIL
FIRST CLASS PERMIT NO. 260 MILLBURN, NEW JERSEY
POSTAGE WILL BE PAID BY ADDRESSEE
BOARDROOM® CLASSICS
BOOK FULFILLMENT CENTER
P.O.BOX 1026
MILLBURN, NEW JERSEY 07041-9990

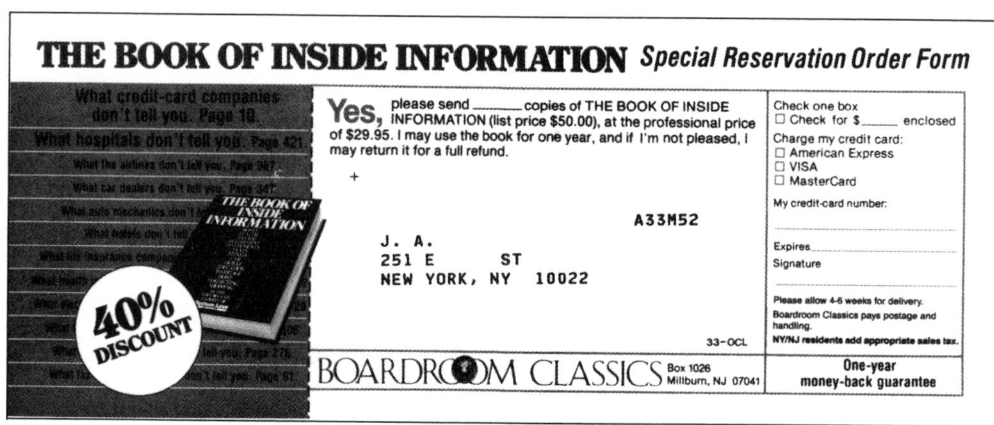

THE BOOK OF INSIDE INFORMATION Special Reservation Order Form
What credit-card companies don't tell you. Page 10.
What hospitals don't tell you. Page 421
THE BOOK OF INSIDE INFORMATION
40% DISCOUNT
Yes, please send ______ copies of THE BOOK OF INSIDE INFORMATION (list price $50.00), at the professional price of $29.95. I may use the book for one year, and if I'm not pleased, I may return it for a full refund.
A33M52
J. A.
251 E ST
NEW YORK, NY 10022
33-OCL
BOARDROOM CLASSICS Box 1026 Millburn, NJ 07041
Check one box
☐ Check for $_____ enclosed
Charge my credit card:
☐ American Express
☐ VISA
☐ MasterCard
My credit-card number:
Expires
Signature
Please allow 4-6 weeks for delivery.
Boardroom Classics pays postage and handling.
NY/NJ residents add appropriate sales tax.
One-year money-back guarantee

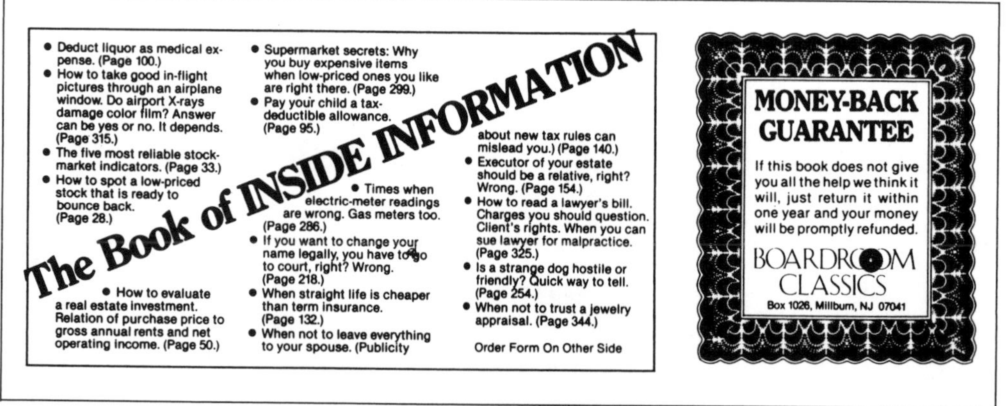

The Book of INSIDE INFORMATION
• Deduct liquor as medical expense. (Page 100.)
• How to take good in-flight pictures through an airplane window. Do airport X-rays damage color film? Answer can be yes or no. It depends. (Page 315.)
• The five most reliable stock-market indicators. (Page 33.)
• How to spot a low-priced stock that is ready to bounce back. (Page 28.)
• How to evaluate a real estate investment. Relation of purchase price to gross annual rents and net operating income. (Page 50.)
• Supermarket secrets: Why you buy expensive items when low-priced ones you like are right there. (Page 299.)
• Pay your child a tax-deductible allowance. (Page 95.)
• Times when electric-meter readings are wrong. Gas meters too. (Page 286.)
• If you want to change your name legally, you have to go to court, right? Wrong. (Page 218.)
• When straight life is cheaper than term insurance. (Page 132.)
• When not to leave everything to your spouse. (Publicity
about new tax rules can mislead you.) (Page 140.)
• Executor of your estate should be a relative, right? Wrong. (Page 154.)
• How to read a lawyer's bill. Charges you should question. Client's rights. When you can sue lawyer for malpractice. (Page 325.)
• Is a strange dog hostile or friendly? Quick way to tell. (Page 254.)
• When not to trust a jewelry appraisal. (Page 344.)
Order Form On Other Side
MONEY-BACK GUARANTEE
If this book does not give you all the help we think it will, just return it within one year and your money will be promptly refunded.
BOARDROOM CLASSICS
Box 1026, Millburn, NJ 07041

The order card shown front and back.

22

Home-Study Programs

There are two kinds of home-study program offers: (1) a one-shot shipment of tapes and/or books; (2) a continuitylike arrangement where one or two lessons are sent every three or four weeks. Unlike the curricula of Malcolm Decker's Institute for Children's Literature—an interactive program between student and an assigned instructor who reads, coaches, and rates the student's work by phone and mail—these products from Hume Publishing and Nightingale-Conant require no instructor.

Hume Publishing

One of the strangest business sagas of the 1980s is the story of Canadian Ronald Hume and his publishing company's spectacular rise and meteoric collapse.

Hume, a high school dropout, worked his way up to become vice president of the trade book division of McGraw-Hill Canada. In 1965 he met a doctor and part-time investor named Morton Shulman who he persuaded to write a book, *Anyone Can Make a Million*; it became an international bestseller and, with the royalties, Shulman reportedly made his first million.

In 1972 Hume created his first proprietary product, the *Successful Investing & Money Management* (*SIMM*) course which became hugely successful. A *SIMM* premium was *The MoneyLetter*, a newsletter for investors that kept the *SIMM* course current. In 1976 Hume launched *The MoneyLetter* as a separate service with an advisory board that included Shulman and investment adviser Andrew Sarlos; the publication quickly grew to a circulation of 80,000 and was generating revenues of $7 million a year.

Other Hume cash cows: *Successful Business Management* and *The Super-Investor Files* dreamed up by copywriter Alan Schwartz. It has been estimated that in the past twenty years, Hume Publishing had revenues of $500 million.

How did Ron Hume snatch defeat from the jaws of victory? He started the Hume Fund and the Hume RSVP Fund, and in just eighteen months he had acquired 40,000 investors and $230 million under management. The managers were Sarlos and Shulman; by 1986 both funds were at the bottom of the *Financial Times* rankings. After the crash of 1987, the funds were down to $140 million in assets as a result of sales, redemptions, and bad investments. Hume started three additional courses which bombed: *Success over 50* for retirees, *School Success* for parents, and a course based on Nathan Pritikin's diet. By 1990 the Hume Group had lost $11.4 million on sales of $60.3 million. Ron Hume has been eased out by disgruntled stockholders and is off on another venture.

In its heyday, Hume hired the very top American and Canadian creative talent and did brilliantly innovative testing. Three of the original packages are still being mailed full tilt and keeping the U.S. subsidiary profitable with about 100,000 enrollees under the capable direction of Suzanne Eastman and Ben Ordover.

Successful Investing & Money Management

Joan Throckmorton has more than thirty years' experience in direct marketing, twenty of which were as head of her own agency. Her "Winning Direct Mail" seminar for the DMA is legendary for its extraordinary combination of strategy, tactics, and solid nuts-'n'-bolts copy and design technique. Throckmorton's *Winning Direct Response Advertising* (Prentice-Hall, 1986) is an essential addition to any direct marketer's library. As a freelance writer, her clients include IBM, Rodale Press, Bankers Trust, AT & T Long Lines, *Southern Living*, Avon Products, *Parents*, and Metropolitan Life. Her mailing for Meredith's *Metropolitan Home* unseated Carol Larson's Grand Control and is expected to win an Axel Award in 1993.

Want to be financially independent?

It takes only 2 things—
and neither one of them is money.

You don't need a fancy education either—or business contacts, or expensive advisors. And you don't have to give up a thing, but a little of your leisure time.

As a matter of fact, you may already be half-way there.

Too good to be true?

See inside, then decide for yourself.

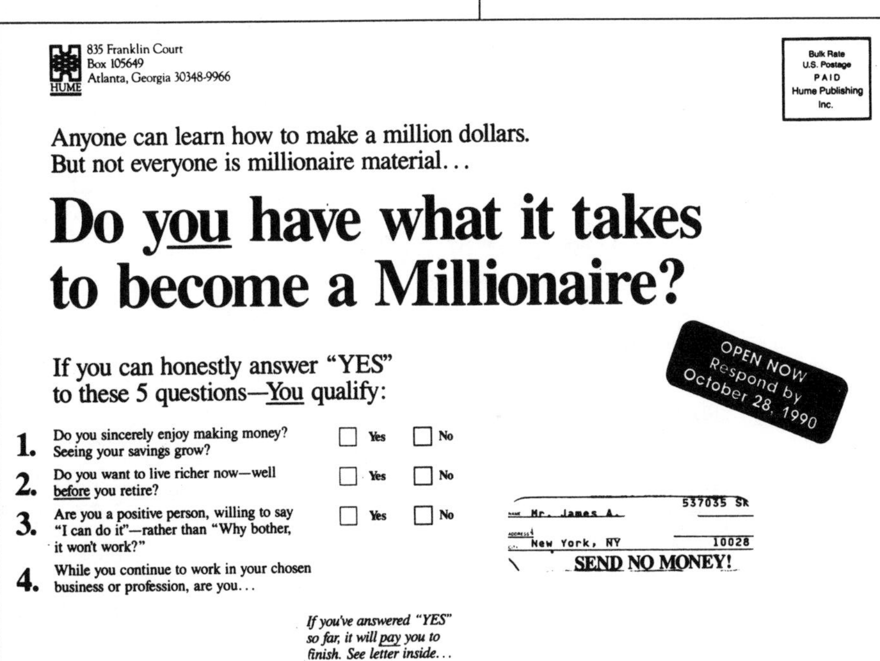

MAILER: Hume Publishing I
PACKAGE: *SIMM* Course
PROJECT MGR.: Kate Bryant
WRITER: Joan Throckmorton
DESIGNER: Unknown
FIRST MAILED: 1986
The 9″ × 12″ outer envelope shown front and back. Cornercard and type in black; headlines in green. This has also been mailed in a 6″ × 9″ size.

Ronald C. Hume
Founder
HUME PUBLISHING
Atlanta • Los Angeles • Toronto
Publishers of Financial Educational
Materials since 1974

Anyone Can Learn How to Make a Million.
But Not Everyone is Millionaire Material. . .

Do you have what it takes to become a Millionaire?

If You Can Honestly Answer "YES" to These 5 Questions—You Qualify:

1. Do you sincerely enjoy making money? Seeing your savings grow? ☐ Yes ☐ No
2. Do you want to live richer now—well before you retire? ☐ Yes ☐ No
3. Are you a positive person, willing to say "I can do it"—rather than "Why bother, it won't work?" ☐ Yes ☐ No
4. While you continue to work in your chosen business or profession, are you willing to give some of your leisure time to making money—and keep at it as your money grows? ☐ Yes ☐ No
5. Do you want to try first before you commit, because you prefer to judge and decide for yourself? ☐ Yes ☐ No

If you can say "Yes" to these five questions—good. You'll find this letter of great importance—as a matter of fact, it could change your life!

Dear Reader:

There are two basic requirements for every self-made millionaire. I believe you may already have one of them.

> This first requirement is the right attitude. If you've got it, you're halfway there. And if you answered "Yes" to the 5 questions, it's likely you do.

The second requirement is knowledge. This is something I can give you. Actually, it's something a group of self-made millionaires can give you because I've brought them together in an exceptional

-2-

program called SUCCESSFUL INVESTING & MONEY MANAGEMENT. (Your financial friends, if you join us, are people like Dr. Morton Shulman and Andrew Sarlos; I'll tell you more about them and their amazing achievements in a minute.)

Learn from those who have actually done it themselves.

You will be guided on your journey by those who've already made their money practicing principles of wealth accumulation. These are not theorists -- no ivory-tower seers with empty bank accounts. And no get-rich-quick schemers.

These individuals are part of a small circle of self-made millionaires -- friends, advisors, educators -- who practice what they preach. Each has his own area of expertise. Each has his technique.

I first brought them together over 10 years ago with the thought that it would be fun for them to exchange trade secrets, share proven methodologies.

Then it occured to me -- why not work together to pass this combined knowledge to other individuals with the desire and motivation to build a fortune. Individuals like you, I suspect.

The result, SUCCESSFUL INVESTING & MONEY MANAGEMENT, a program by millionaires for those aspiring to great wealth and financial freedom.

You may be wondering, "If such information is readily available, why doesn't everyone use it? Why hasn't everyone achieved wealth beyond their wildest dreams?"

And you are right to be skeptical. But the answer is quite simple. Although anyone can learn -- and start without a single penny -- few have that first basic requirement.

If, as I believe, you have the right qualifications, let me tell you how you can join the ranks of the individuals who have gained impressive wealth by developing their own investment techniques.

We're Looking for People Who Enjoy Making Money. You?

You are invited to join an exclusive group of men and women dedicated to accumulating considerable wealth in their spare time. Let them share with you all the methods, rules, caveats and tricks of the game that have helped them achieve their fortunes.

Join them without risking all the things you've already worked hard for...without giving up your present job, profession or life-style.

Join them by simply doing what they do -- by giving a few hours of your time each week and by deciding irrefutably that you want to

-3-

be among the first truly wealthy.

There are only two essential ingredients:

- Our ability to provide you with the proper information
- Your determination to use that information

The first I absolutely guarantee you. The second is up to you.

Understand right off, none of our contributors boasts extra-ordinary financial degrees. They achieved their goals with no "inside" business contacts or famous advisors. Most of them did it working in their spare time at home -- almost as a hobby -- little by little, simply because they enjoyed it.

Take Dr. Morton Shulman; he's a practicing physician and many times a millionaire, but he started with only $400. He lost that $400, but went on to develop a technique that's worked for him ever since.

Or Andrew Sarlos, a frequent advisor to our program. He landed in North America as a World War II refugee with $500 in his pocket. He built a very successful multimillion dollar investment group, thanks to methods he developed himself and continues to use to this day.

Why You Are So Important

Making a fortune is, quite literally, a do-it-yourself occupation. You, in the final analysis, will be the best advisor you can have.

Let me explain this.

Ironically, until you actually are very wealthy, sound advice on building your fortune is rather hard to come by.

The cold facts are:

- Few investment advisors really care about helping a small nest egg grow, no matter how precious it may be to its owner.
- Few bank officials are looking to assist in building or preserving a modest estate.
- And no mass market dispenser of financial assistance, be it magazine, book or newspaper, is going to interpret its news in light of its effects on you, or in consideration of your goals.

In the long run, it's up to you to take care of #1. Otherwise, the advice you get will seldom be given with any serious thought to your personal requirements.

Here's an example that illustrates this well:

You've saved $2,000 and you want to invest it, but you need advice. Obviously, you're looking for a good return. You take your money to a broker. He spends a fast half-hour telling you about

-4-

stocks. He explains why now is a good time to go into the market. He gives you the current recommendations from his research department. And he stresses why it's in your best interest to do business through him.

Next, you take your money to a banker. The banker rules out the market. He discusses interest rate fluctuations and the value and security of CDs. He suggests a certificate of deposit or a money market fund as an alternative. But strongly urges you to do this through him and his bank. His bank is well established and reliable.

Last, you take your $2,000 to a bond specialist who recommends a high-yield bond fund. The specialist explains in detail the advantages and security of this type of mutual fund. He finds it inconceivable that you could consider any other investment.

This story, in one form or another, occurs all the time. Everyone talks a good "deal." About his own speciality. And even if everyone's sincere -- no one's thinking about your overall financial picture.

How to Get Help You Can Trust --
When You Don't Have a Bundle in the Bank

Hume Financial Education Services' SUCCESSFUL INVESTING & MONEY MANAGEMENT has only one purpose, one interest:

> To enable each person enrolled in the program to achieve security and financial independence with just those investments most suitable to their particular circumstances.

We're not a brokerage or insurance company, nor do we make any financial offering of any kind to the public. We are an independent educational service offering a unique, completely practical course and successful method of acquiring wealth.

In plain English, this means we win when you win. Our vested interest is your success. Because if you're satisfied, you'll continue the program -- and send others who aspire to wealth our way. We count on this. And we're not often disappointed.

What's more, if you truly want to accumulate riches, but you haven't got the money in the bank to start with, we've thought of that, too. There are 10 simple things you might do to get up to $2,000 right now.

And we'll show you how each and every one of them work before you commit to spending a cent! Too good to be true?

Not necessarily. There is a catch...and that's why I asked that you qualify yourself before reading this letter.

You Are Going to Make Money

And blind luck never enters into it. We can give you proven methods. We can show you how to handle every conceivable investment

The 8-page letter, printed on two 11″ × 17″ nested sheets.

-5-

opportunity, every economic swing -- but only you can do it.

And you can do it!

The secret of every self-made millionaire is that at one time or another -- usually after a series of setbacks or losses -- he or she claims, "I'm going to get rich." They make a conscious decision to accumulate wealth.

Once you make this decision, apply sound, tested strategies and stick to it -- you can succeed.

And you won't be alone. Others with the same attitude you have are already working their way to financial success. For example:

"This course gave me the information and background knowledge to increase my net worth over the past year by $100,000."
Edwin L. Snyder, Wisconsin

"In just six months I made enough to pay for this course - and I'm only halfway through the course."
Robert W. Page, Indiana

"This program's informal style of teaching has given me the insight to not only prepare for a profitable future and greatly enhance the chances for success, but also helped me to find out that I do have assets with which to invest."
Roberto Villa-Real, California

"The $300 investment in the course has made it plausible for me to earn $24,000 in a little over six months, investing in stocks and bonds."
Wilbur L. Smith, Illinois

"With SUCCESSFUL INVESTING & MONEY MANAGEMENT I was able to increase my net worth by $70,000 and also was able to make very profitable decisions in stocks and bonds."
Joseph Louis, Louisiana

"My new perspective has allowed me to triple my savings rate without reducing my lifestyle in any way. Thanks for the impetus to a more financially secure future!"
Christopher A. Lin, Illinois

"I found the program not only motivated me but gave me the steps to take in reaching my goals in financial security. While taking the course, I set a goal to become a millionaire within 5 years. I finished the course and already I have almost reached the halfway point of my goals."
Tommy C. Cole, Georgia

-6-

"I have been able to increase my personal wealth in a very short period of time and am now becoming involved in real estate investing. This course was one of my best investments."
Kenneth L. Clark, Pennsylvania*

These people all enjoy making money. They have become confident and willing to act because they have the knowledge and judgement to do so. They are already on the road to building their fortunes.

I'm counting on you joining them.

How Your Life Can Change
As You Enlarge Your Horizons Through Knowledge

All hobbies enrich your life. And the more you do them -- like tennis, golf, gardening or model building -- the better you get.

If you like making money, this is one hobby that's doubly enriching. You give it a few hours every week and the better you get, the more it pays you back with financial success and confidence. After a while, you'll begin to see real opportunities everywhere!

What now may seem like meaningless economic data will gradually become the material for your new hobby -- the hobby of making money in your spare time. Knowledgeably. With confidence. Here's the sort of thing you'll be able to spot, just by reading the daily paper:

Dr. Morton Shulman began to follow the Australian dollar closely in 1983. He and other shrewd investors predicted a rise in spending and currency devaluation if the Socialist Labor Party won Australia's last national election. This was no secret.

When he learned the Party had a commanding lead, he and others went to the bank and sold Australian dollars for delivery after the election. The result: The Labor Party won, the dollar was devalued by 10% and Dr. Shulman cleared over $100,000.

You will have many opportunities like this when you learn where to find them and how to look.

Whether interest rates go up or down, in a bull or bear market -- you'll know how to react. What a feeling of accomplishment to be sure your investments are sound! And growing! Often by using other people's money, with the use of leverage!

You can sit back free of worries and enjoy life's comforts, plan trusts for your children, vacations for yourself and other luxuries beyond the reach of ordinary people.

Few can realize this security. You can if you resolve to make the accumulation of wealth your leisure-time hobby.

*These comments are selected from our files. You may do better than these people—or you may not do as well, but if ever you are not 100% satisfied with *your own rate of success*, you may drop out of the program at any time.

-7-

What's more -- if you've honestly answered "Yes" to the five questions, then...

You'll Want to Say "Yes" to This FREE Trial Offer Too.
Simply respond by October 28, 1990!

Evaluate and use SUCCESSFUL INVESTING & MONEY MANAGEMENT FREE of charge or obligation to continue.

I'll give you lesson 1. That's right -- give it to you. And with it comes...

- Key ways to immediately improve your financial standing,
- Why compounding is one of the single most powerful tools to multiply your wealth.
- How to use all your money all of the time -- and this is just the beginning!

Respond now and you'll also get -- with our compliments -- "63 Ways to Cut Your Taxes - Now" by tax specialists Karl H. Loring and William M. Ruddy. This guide includes all the latest tax-bill revisions.

I'll also send you Lesson 2 on approval. Look it over, too. Without risk. If you are not completely satisfied and if you decide not to continue -- return only Lesson 2 within 15 days at my expense. You'll have no further obligation. (And, naturally, no salesman will ever call on you.)

Now Let Me Tell You Why This Offer Is Good For Both Of Us

You may wonder why someone like me, wise in the ways of making money, is literally giving away valuable programs.

Think about it this way: If you have the right attitude (and I believe you do), you'll take Lessons 1 and 2 and start right in making money.

By the time your next lessons arrive you may have already amassed $1,000...$2,000 -- even more -- in "found" monies. You will have begun to build your fortune.

And if you truly enjoy making money and making it work for you -- why would you possibly want to stop? Just when you are learning how easy it is?

So you see, I risk very little. Because you gain so much.

Remember, I didn't get rich giving things away.

Each year about 100,000 new millionaires are created. With the right qualifications, the right attitude, the right knowledge, you have a better chance than most of adding your name to that list.

So stop reading about other people's financial successes. Stop

wishing and start winning. Cut yourself in.

America is still the land of opportunity for those who know how to take advantage of that opportunity. Come join us.

Sincerely,

Ronald C. Hume
Founder

RCH:sk

P.S. A smart investor right now is probably asking what all of this costs. You're going to be surprised when you learn how little it is.

Each lesson is $10 (plus a small shipping and handling charge). There is one free lesson plus 28 lessons that you pay for, sent to you two at a time. And you're not committed to accept any set number.

Why don't we charge more? We don't want qualified prospects to be put off by the price or by terms that create obligations to continue purchasing.

We want as many as possible to try our program, then continue with us solely because of "satisfaction received". It's the best way that we know to run a business.

Here is what other smart investors tell us about *Successful Investing & Money Management*...

"*Successful Investing & Money Management* is exactly what I needed to help myself start controlling, monitoring and maximizing my finances permanently. The course had immediate benefits: When I enrolled last May, I owned a 5-year-old Japanese subcompact car and owed well over $6,000. I even had a negative net worth! Today I drive a new BMW and have no installment debt at all. And my net worth is growing fast. But the course not only has immediate benefits, it also provides basic, in-depth principles that last over time. Having completed all the lessons, I'm now using the materials as the start of my own 'library' of financial references and information. Thank you *very* much!"

Norman E. Thomas, Washington

"This is a comprehensive, results-getting course! Your commitment to produce 'the best' training possible is, in fact, as you advertise it. What a refreshing experience!! Thanks!"

Jim Richardson, Missouri

"*Successful Investing & Money Management* is informative and complete. It gave me an excellent background on many types of investments and strategies that I knew little or nothing about. I was able to make use of much of the covered information shortly after completing the lessons.

The course was most enjoyable and practical. It will also serve as an excellent reference for years to come."

David F. Loomis, California

"*Successful Investing & Money Management* has helped me to learn more about investing and money management than I could have ever imagined. I have already put to work what I have learned and am now well on my way to becoming a self-made millionaire."

Bruce E. Elsner, Illinois

"Since completing this course my brokers now refer to me as a 'sophisticated investor' and I do take more control and get better information from them. Thanks to Hume, I make and *keep* more money."

C. Alan Smith, Florida

These comments are selected from our files. Naturally, everyone who participates in the Successful Investing & Money Management program will not have the same sort of experience...but I do guarantee that if you are not 100% satisfied with *your own rate of success*, you may drop out of the program at any time.

Ronald C. Hume
Founder, Hume Publishing

FOR YOUR SAKE—BE SURE TO

READ THIS SECTION

IF YOU HAVE ANY QUESTIONS ABOUT THE NEED TO ACT NOW

TO PRESERVE WHAT YOU ALREADY HAVE...

AS WELL AS BUILD FOR YOUR FUTURE.

TAX REFORM AND INFLATION:

THE TWO GREATEST FORCES THAT WILL AFFECT YOUR MONEY IN THE NEXT 5 YEARS —CONTROL THEM TO YOUR ADVANTAGE— AND PROSPER...

If you do nothing else in the months ahead, use SUCCESSFUL INVESTING & MONEY MANAGEMENT to help you cope with the far-reaching effects of tax reform and inflation on your money.

The 1980s have produced sweeping changes in our tax laws. And more changes are coming. Be ready to take advantage of them. Here is information that can radically alter your planning and help you move wisely in the next 12 to 14 months.

How to Live With a Brand New Set of Money-Making Rules

Washington's tax reforms, the most sweeping reforms in half a century, have already changed many of the ways we build our wealth. And where we find it. Some areas of investing are booming. Others have been "taxed" away.

The old "smart" ways for lowering -- or even eliminating some of your own taxes -- are ruled out. But new money-saving strategies are taking their place. Opportunities are impressive. (Attractive tax shelters have faded, for example, while stocks with healthy dividends look better than ever.)

With Successful Investing & Money Management you'll be able to start

-2-

planning to take advantage of new money-making techniques. We'll help you turn the consequences of the Tax Reform laws into real profit opportunities.

And, because tax reduction is essential to your wealth, as an active subscriber you'll also receive, free of charge, THE HUME TAX BULLETINS -- special reports published on a must-know, as-needed basis to help you cope with any future tax law changes.

Inflation -- Ever-Lurking in the Wings

Not all experts agree exactly when inflation will return, but all agree 100% that inevitably it will return. Oil prices could take off again at any time and government spending continues at all-time highs.

You must be ready for change. SUCCESSFUL INVESTING & MONEY MANAGEMENT will see that you are.

We'll show you how to track inflation indicators so you'll know well in advance when to take action. Instead of sitting idly by watching your profits fade, you'll move in quickly.

You'll recognize major new opportunities for making money and building on what you have already accumulated. And now is the time to start planning your strategies.

4 Wealth-Building Principles We Urge You to Adopt Immediately

1. You can keep on building right through inflation, disinflation, stagflation, no inflation. There are no bad times for the astute investor. In other words, you can profit at all times. SUCCESSFUL INVESTING & MONEY MANAGEMENT will show you how.

   For example: Say you have $5,000 invested in a mutual fund specializing in high-growth stocks. Then inflation hits and interest rates rise -- and your stocks slow down.

   So, you change horses midstream, before your fund dips, and ride off with a money market mutual fund. Then, as interest rates peak, you invest in bonds -- always a good buy when rates run high.

   When interest rates finally drop and inflation levels off, you could have a small fortune in bonds. And, you'll be ready to reverse procedures when rates again start to rise.

   Rising interest, war scares, recession, energy crisis, strong or weak dollar -- at no time do you lose upward impetus on your investments because you know when to act. And, you're not afraid to do so.

2. Do it with other people's money!

   The entrepreneurs, the major corporations and the super rich make billions this way -- it's called leveraging. And it's a smooth way

-3-

to build fast, if you know what you're doing.

As a matter of fact, leveraging can be magic for you and SUCCESSFUL INVESTING & MONEY MANAGEMENT will show you why and how. In real estate, stocks, commodities -- you can make big profits on other people's money, once you've carefully evaluated your proposed investment.

Say you laid out $5,000 to buy 100 shares of a stock at $50 per share. You sold at $60 for a $1,000 profit. Or a 20% return.

But if you leveraged, and bought 200 shares on margin, paying only $5,000...you'd double your profits when the stock went to $60. And even if you paid 12% interest on your loan -- or $600, you'd still be ahead with a $1,400 profit or 28% return!

Once you have the knowledge to choose your investment wisely by weighing the key factors that make up sound investments (and SUCCESSFUL INVESTING & MONEY MANAGEMENT helps you here), then do it with OPM (Other People's Money).

3. If leveraging is "Magic" -- Compound Interest is your "Miracle."

   Never let your money rest. Even starting with a modest sum you can accumulate good money by making it work for you. The important thing is to get started.

   For example: By investing just $119 a month, or $1,428 a year, starting at age 30, you can have over a million dollars by the time you're ready to retire if you average a return of just 13% -- possible with any number of investments currently available.

   And you can move even faster if you can invest more than $119 a month...or if you can do better than 13%. Returns of up to 25% on some investments are possible, once you learn the investing techniques in the course...and if you know how to make some of your investment dollars have the "leverage" of $5 or $10 (which you'll also learn).

4. The best investment you'll ever make is right in your own backyard. And owning your own home is only the first step.

   As it increases in value -- and many homes have increased 5 and 10 times over their original price -- you'll have new opportunities. Homes that once sold for $40,000 are now going for $150,000, $200,000, or more.

   New homes (condominiums and single-family dwellings) going for $90,000 today will be selling for two and three times these prices when inflation returns.

   So if you're already a home owner, learn how to leverage a vacation

-4-

home, a second or retirement home with little investment, good tax advantages plus possible rental income.

If you don't already own your home, SUCCESSFUL INVESTING & MONEY MANAGEMENT will show you how to use leverage to your best advantage to get the home of your dreams.

Start Living Better RIGHT NOW

Now is the time for you to start enjoying a better, more comfortable life. You don't have to wait for retirement.

Find hidden cash every month!

SUCCESSFUL INVESTING & MONEY MANAGEMENT will show you how you can begin today with many ways to save hundreds -- even thousands -- of dollars while improving your lifestyle.

For example: How, when and where to buy the best products at the best prices -- food, appliances, clothing...avoid soaring medical costs without reducing the quality of your care...make sure you get a fair dealer's price next time you buy a car...enjoy a deluxe vacation without paying deluxe prices!

Start investing with as little as $1,000

Because you're a busy person, while you live better and save money you'll also learn how to manage that savings on a limited-time budget...how to get started with small-scale investing...what your three most suitable investments are...where to use your time and put your money for the highest returns.

Plan now to make sure you don't "outlive" your retirement income

SUCCESSFUL INVESTING & MONEY MANAGEMENT also helps you with financial planning to prepare you for a secure retirement, filled with all the advantages you've ever dreamed about -- because you'll know in advance how to set retirement goals and make your retirement goals and make your retirement income last...maximize your pension/profit-sharing plans...start a retirement "career"...continue profitable investing...coordinate income and social security ...evaluate your insurance requirements and plan your estate.

If you ever thought about or hoped or aspired to becoming comfortably rich, there has never been a better time for you to act. Let our self-made millionaires give you the know-how and techniques to become the best advisor you've ever had. After all, no one cares as much about your money as you do. And no one will ever care for it as well as you will.

HUME FINANCIAL EDUCATION SERVICES 835 Franklin Court Box 105627 Atlanta, Georgia 30348

A 4-page insert printed on a bright yellow 11″ × 17″ sheet and inserted in the middle of the letter.

The mailing for the Hume *SIMM* course is a classic in piling benefits on top of testimonials on top of benefits until you can positively smell the leather interior of your first Rolls-Royce and the silence of the Concorde as it passes Mach 1 on the way to a deluxe holiday in Paris and the south of France. Count the number of times Throckmorton uses the word "millionaire," "million," or "multimillion."

JOAN THROCKMORTON:

The Hume package was a tough one. The previous control was excellent; it had never been beaten, and, as I remember it, the package itself had been going strong for several years.

As I saw it, my job was to first get into the market's head. What kind of people enroll in self-taught financial programs that can go on for a year or more? Not simple demographics but an examination of their deepest drives, aspirations, desires, and dreams.

Next, an analysis of the control. Why was it successful; how did it fulfill their desires and dreams; how did it create credibility, involve, and motivate?

Then, how could this have been done in a stronger way—a way that would be even more compelling, yet, at the same time, bring in quality customers who would stick around and pay out. After all, anyone can create a gold rush with

OTLINE • TAX HOTLINE • TAX HOTLINE • TAX HOTLINE • TAX HOT

Announcing a Complimentary Service...

The Hume Tax Bulletins

Our experts, advisors and consultants are daily at work making sure every aspect, every detail of *Successful Investing & Money Management* is timely and thoroughly up-to-date.

Because our job is to help you take advantage of economic changes—and prosper from them as they happen—we are fully dedicated to keeping you informed and ahead on one of the momentous financial changes of the last 50 years—tax reform.

To do this adequately in this change-over tax year, we have made special provisions to send you, **absolutely free** with our compliments, the *Hume Tax Bulletins.* They will be sent to subscribers, while they are enrolled in the course, on a strictly must-know, as-needed basis; they will be timely and analytical, providing you with necessary data to start planning early for major strategy changes, as they relate to future tax law changes.

Every important move in Washington is being monitored—the House, the Senate, special interest groups and lobbyists, the Oval Office. Our tax analysts have prepared detailed explanations of the new tax laws and their effects—how to shift your strategies to take advantage of these laws in terms of preserving income and seeking out emerging investment opportunities.

Don't miss out. Changes are coming that can wipe out your present tax advantages and set your current planning on its ear.

2010A WA

Lift piece no. 1, printed on bright orange paper.

Dr. Morton Shulman,
the medical doctor and "amateur" investor
who turned $400 into a
multimillion-dollar investment fortune
in his spare time.

**Some people will throw this letter away.
A few will go on to make a fortune.
Where do you stand?**

Dear Friend:

Ron Hume tells me that fewer than 1 in 100 people will take advantage of our "no strings" offer. Many won't even bother to read this letter.

I was a little surprised when I first learned this -- then two things occurred to me.

> First -- most people simply aren't what we call "millionaire material."

Everyone would like to be given a million dollars or so. Sure. But few actually believe they can go out and get it for themselves.

These people profess skepticism, but what they really have is self-doubt and fear. They'll always be part of the lazy mass, watching with envy and dissatisfaction as others get ahead.

So let them, I say. If you've gone this far, I believe you can go the distance. You're qualified.

> Second -- when something sounds too good, too easy -- we are all subject to honest skepticism.

Be skeptical -- that's healthy. I'd be so myself, if I weren't living proof that an average human being can take $400 and build it into millions.

Now you will have access to the exact same information that enabled me to move ahead -- so there's really nothing stopping you, but you.

Believe in yourself. Have confidence. The sooner you get started, the sooner you will join those of us who enjoy self-accumulated riches.

And as for that honest skepticism -- look at the investment deal you've already got. Recognize it!

> An opportunity to try without risk. A chance to make your first $500, $1,000, $2,000 -- even more -- before you pay a cent.

I wouldn't resist an offer like that. If I were in your shoes, I'd act now and return the No-Risk Enrollment Form today. It's the surest way to put yourself in my shoes!

Sincerely,

Morton Shulman

Morton Shulman, M.D.

MS:wa

P.S. When you get it -- use it. Start right in with Lessons One and Two. Because if you answered "Yes" to those 5 questions, I know you'll find at least one new idea, one strategy or technique, that alone could pay you back tenfold the price of this program.

Lift piece no. 2, printed on light blue paper.

STOP:
Please open this after you read Ron Hume's letter! M.S.

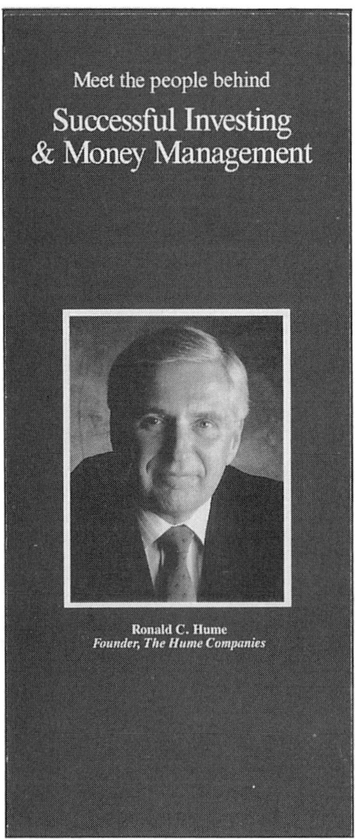

Meet the people behind
Successful Investing & Money Management
Ronald C. Hume
Founder, The Hume Companies

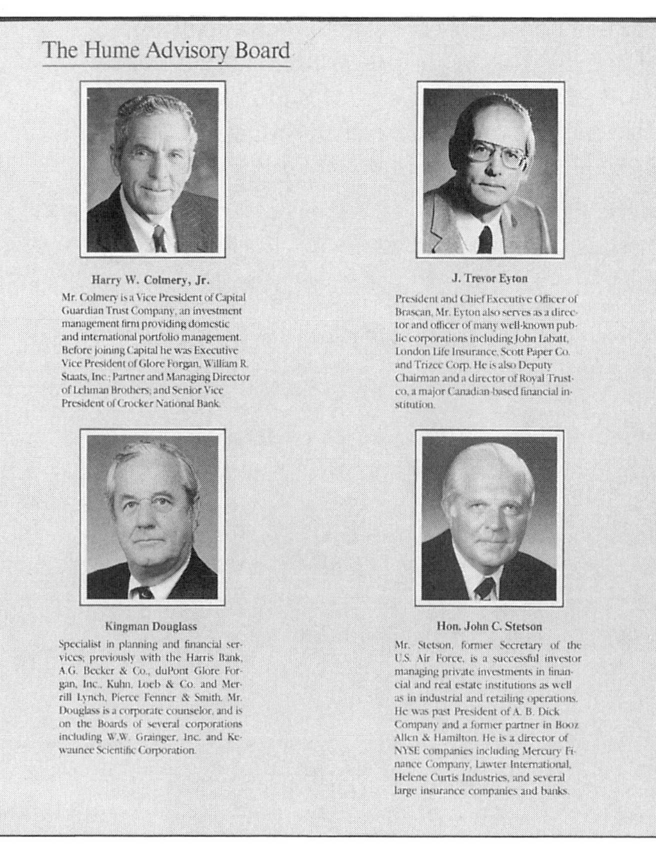

The Hume Advisory Board

Harry W. Colmery, Jr.

Mr. Colmery is a Vice President of Capital Guardian Trust Company, an investment management firm providing domestic and international portfolio management. Before joining Capital he was Executive Vice President of Glore Forgan, William R. Staats, Inc.; Partner and Managing Director of Lehman Brothers; and Senior Vice President of Crocker National Bank.

J. Trevor Eyton

President and Chief Executive Officer of Brascan. Mr. Eyton also serves as a director and officer of many well-known public corporations including John Labatt, London Life Insurance, Scott Paper Co. and Trizec Corp. He is also Deputy Chairman and a director of Royal Trustco, a major Canadian-based financial institution.

Kingman Douglass

Specialist in planning and financial services; previously with the Harris Bank, A.G. Becker & Co., duPont Glore Forgan, Inc., Kuhn, Loeb & Co. and Merrill Lynch, Pierce Fenner & Smith. Mr. Douglass is a corporate counselor, and is on the Boards of several corporations including W.W. Grainger, Inc. and Kewaunee Scientific Corporation.

Hon. John C. Stetson

Mr. Stetson, former Secretary of the U.S. Air Force, is a successful investor managing private investments in financial and real estate institutions as well as in industrial and retailing operations. He was past President of A. B. Dick Company and a former partner in Booz Allen & Hamilton. He is a director of NYSE companies including Mercury Finance Company, Lawter International, Helene Curtis Industries, and several large insurance companies and banks.

Hume Faculty Contributors

Among the key contributors are...

Ben Branch, *Course Reviewer:* A professor of finance at the University of Massachusetts School of Management, Mr. Branch has published extensively in financial and economic periodicals including *Barron's*, *The Wall Street Journal* and *Harvard Business Review*. He has also written several books on investing and finance, including *Investments: A Practical Approach*.

Michelle Bekey, *Writer:* Ms. Bekey's articles on business, investing and money management have appeared in a wide array of national publications, including *Time, Money, Fortune, Venture, The Economist* and *Sylvia Porter's Personal Finance*.

David Myers, *Writer:* A business and real estate writer for more than ten years, Mr. Meyers is also a licensed real estate salesperson and an active investor. He speaks publicly on real estate investing, and is a former spokesman for the California Association of Realtors.

Richard Sherer, *Writer:* Mr. Sherer has written professionally for 25 years and has operated his own public relations agencies and written for a number of business publications. In 1986 he coordinated the tax reform revision of Hume's *Successful Investing & Money Management* course. He has written and edited extensively on the new tax law.

Statement of Principles

WHAT WE ARE NOT—We are not a brokerage or insurance company nor do we make any financial offering of any kind to the public.
WHAT WE ARE—We are an independent educational service offering a unique, completely practical course and successful method for acquiring wealth.
OUR OBJECTIVE—Our objective is to enable each person enrolled in the program to achieve security and financial independence with just those investments most suitable to their particular circumstances.

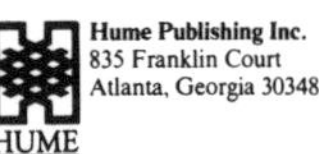

Hume Publishing Inc.
835 Franklin Court
Atlanta, Georgia 30348

HUME PUBLISHING, INC., LOS ANGELES, ATLANTA, TORONTO. REPRESENTED BY DELOITTE & TOUCHE, CERTIFIED PUBLIC ACCOUNTANTS. ATTORNEYS: HISHON & RANNEY, ATLANTA

SJ

The $3^5/_8''$ × $8^1/_2''$ 4-color brochure—cover and back page and inside spread.

hype. It takes hard work to get miners in who are willing to go on panning for years.

This is basically a letter package. But the outer envelope is the key. It perfectly selects the right prospect and pulls him into the package with question 4. The letter finishes off the job.

Both the letter and the lift letter also play heavily on perceived self-image.

By the way, the letter originally ran twelve pages. I decided to revise it and break out four pages as a separate section in the middle to make it easier to read and a little more dramatic.

The only other relevant thing I can remember is that it took the 20 percent inspiration and 80 percent perspiration.

And, oh, yes—I seldom have a real winning package like this with clients who fiddle around and make a lot of changes. My winners infallibly come from those clients who say, ''It's up to you. We're paying you because you're supposed to know what you're doing.''

Bless their hearts.

The $8^{1/2}'' \times 11''$ order form shown front and back with bright red Yes-No tokens.

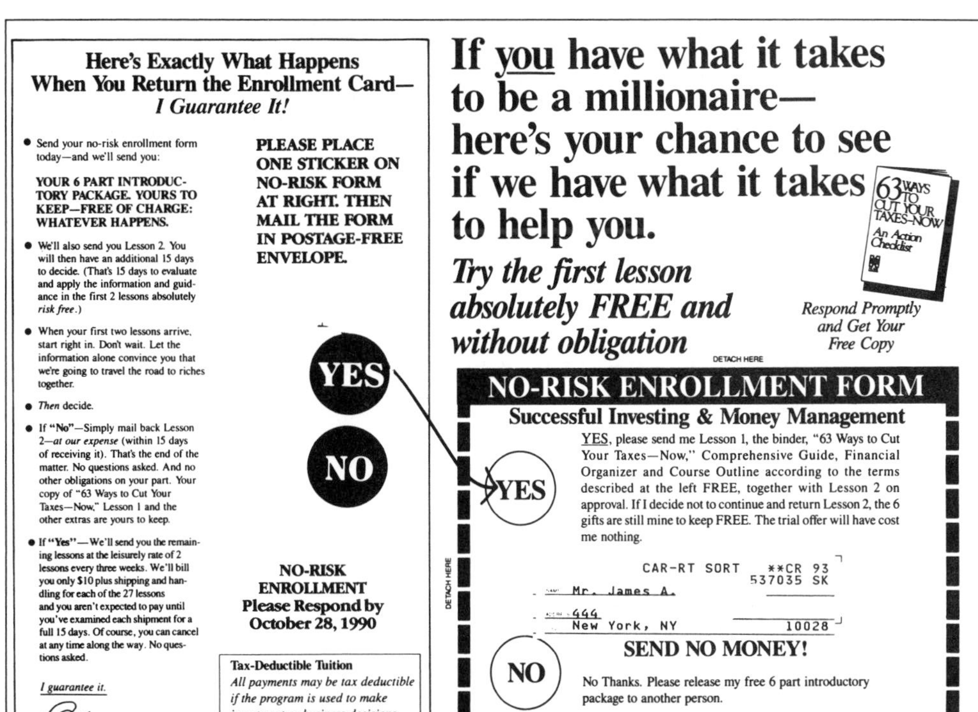

Here's Exactly What Happens When You Return the Enrollment Card—*I Guarantee It!*

- Send your no-risk enrollment form today—and we'll send you:

YOUR 6 PART INTRODUCTORY PACKAGE. YOURS TO KEEP—FREE OF CHARGE: WHATEVER HAPPENS.

- We'll also send you Lesson 2. You will then have an additional 15 days to decide. (That's 15 days to evaluate and apply the information and guidance in the first 2 lessons absolutely *risk free.*)
- When your first two lessons arrive, start right in. Don't wait. Let the information alone convince you that we're going to travel the road to riches together.
- *Then* decide.
- If **"No"**—Simply mail back Lesson 2—*at our expense* (within 15 days of receiving it). That's the end of the matter. No questions asked. And no other obligations on your part. Your copy of "63 Ways to Cut Your Taxes—Now," Lesson 1 and the other extras are yours to keep.
- If **"Yes"**—We'll send you the remaining lessons at the leisurely rate of 2 lessons every three weeks. We'll bill you only $10 plus shipping and handling for each of the 27 lessons and you aren't expected to pay until you've examined each shipment for a full 15 days. Of course, you can cancel at any time along the way. No questions asked.

I guarantee it.

Ron Hume

PLEASE PLACE ONE STICKER ON NO-RISK FORM AT RIGHT. THEN MAIL THE FORM IN POSTAGE-FREE ENVELOPE.

YES

NO

NO-RISK ENROLLMENT Please Respond by October 28, 1990

Tax-Deductible Tuition
All payments may be tax deductible if the program is used to make investment or business decisions, depending on your personal tax situation.

If you have what it takes to be a millionaire—here's your chance to see if we have what it takes to help you.

Try the first lesson absolutely FREE and without obligation

Respond Promptly and Get Your Free Copy

DETACH HERE

NO-RISK ENROLLMENT FORM

Successful Investing & Money Management

YES, please send me Lesson 1, the binder, "63 Ways to Cut Your Taxes—Now," Comprehensive Guide, Financial Organizer and Course Outline according to the terms described at the left FREE, together with Lesson 2 on approval. If I decide not to continue and return Lesson 2, the 6 gifts are still mine to keep FREE. The trial offer will have cost me nothing.

CAR-RT SORT **CR 93
537035 SK
Mr. James A.
444
New York, NY 10028

SEND NO MONEY!

NO — No Thanks. Please release my free 6 part introductory package to another person.

Hume Financial Education Services
835 Franklin Court • Box 105627 •
Atlanta, Georgia 30348

California and Georgia residents: State sales tax will be charged as applicable. SK

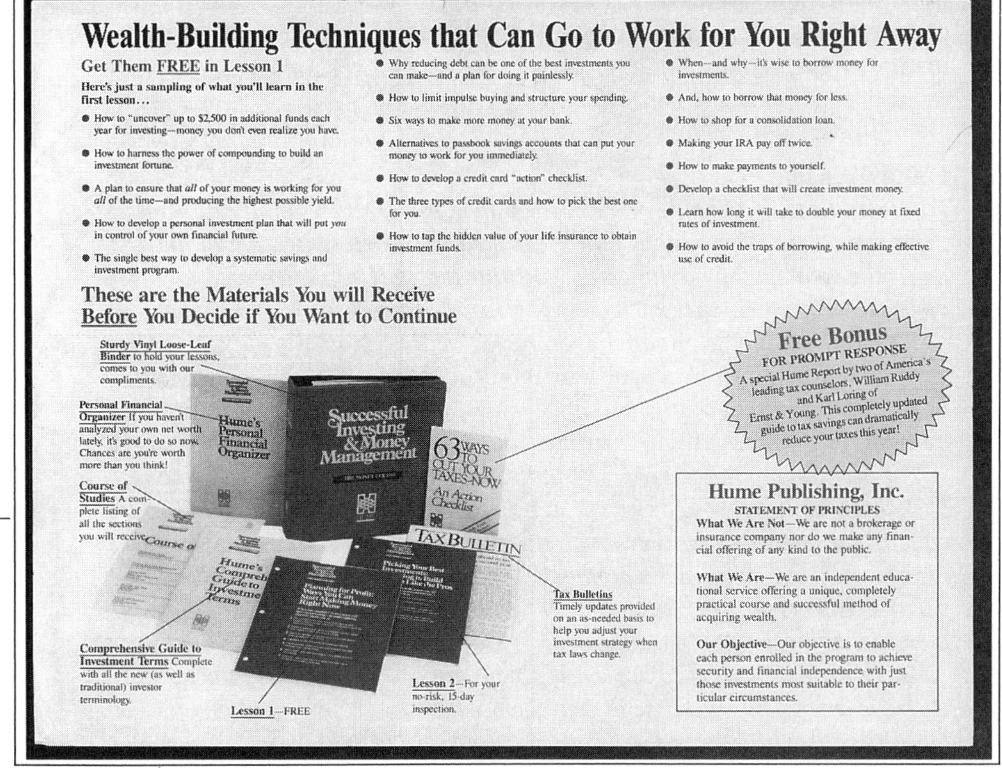

Mail today for your free lesson. There's no risk, no obligation.

BUSINESS REPLY MAIL
FIRST CLASS MAIL PERMIT NO. 10938 ATLANTA, GA

POSTAGE WILL BE PAID BY ADDRESSEE

Hume Financial Education Services
835 Franklin Court
Box 105627
Atlanta, Georgia 30348-9966

The business reply envelope. The second color throughout the mailing is money green; this BRE is printed in the same green. Notice the sales message at upper left; Joan Throckmorton even puts the BRE to work as a sales tool.

Successful Business Management

MAILER: Hume Publishing II
PACKAGE: *Successful Business Management*
PROJECT MGR.: Randy Levin
WRITER: Harry Walsh
DESIGNER: Gia Felis Watkins/ Giagraphics
FIRST MAILED: 1987
The 9″ × 12″ outside envelope shown front and back with pressure-sensitive name label and I ACCEPT/I DECLINE tokens on the front. To order the product, you must peel the pressure-sensitive label with your name on it and the I ACCEPT token onto the order card. This is a closed-face envelope (no window), but the mailing is not personalized since the addressee's name appears only this once in the package.

During the time Harry Walsh was starting out in the advertising business "as a conventional copywriter in a conventional Madison Avenue agency," he launched a little mail order company from his kitchen table. His product was a carbon steel knife which he knew took an edge better than the stainless steel variety found in most American kitchens. He rewrote the copy for the little one-column-by-five-inch ad fifty times and used a tried and true mail order headline: "Who else wants a really sharp knife?"

I picked it up from one of John Caples's early books in which he listed mail order headlines. "Who else wants a whiter wash?" was the daddy of mine, I think.

The ad worked, and Walsh was hooked by direct marketing. "The mail order business fascinates people," he writes. "The prospect of finding dozens of checks from total strangers in your morning mail is irresistible. It certainly attracted me."

Eventually Walsh became creative director of the direct response division of Ogilvy & Mather, and freelanced extensively. Today, as a full-time freelancer and proprietor of the Walsh Company in Weston, Connecticut, the bulk of his time is spent writing for large mailers around the country. He is a generalist whose clients include magazines, newsletters, insurance companies, book publishers, music clubs, fundraisers, investment firms, and many others.

HARRY WALSH:
I consider the letter to be the prime element in nonsweepstakes mailings. And in this element, which is usually four to six pages, the first sentence and the first page take up half of my writing time. Because if I can't get the prospect to finish page one, I've surely struck out.

The brochure is of secondary importance. I've written many winners with a letter and no brochure, but none with a brochure and no letter. Sometimes, as in the Hume mailing that follows, it is a key factor. Other times it contributes nothing. Occasionally it even depresses response!

The lift memo, or second letter, usually strongly restates the no-risk, money-back guarantee. Years ago the creative director of a huge mailer of negative-option book offers told me they had tested this element in all sizes, shapes, and forms, and it always, always produced a lift in response of between 10 and 12 percent. Mailers for other products don't perceive so uniform a benefit, but a lift memo is well worth testing.

There are many ways to approach a new project. Most writers like to start with the letter. Others choose the envelope—first things first, you know. The late Chris Stagg believed in last things first, and started with the order form. He claimed this gave him an absolutely clear concept of the offer which, after all, is what all the other copy must focus on.

Good idea. But before writing anything at all, I usually go through a routine I borrowed from Bertrand Russell, the English philosopher and mathematician.

First I read all the material pertaining to the project. Most of this will come from the client; some I may get from my own outside researchers. I jot down

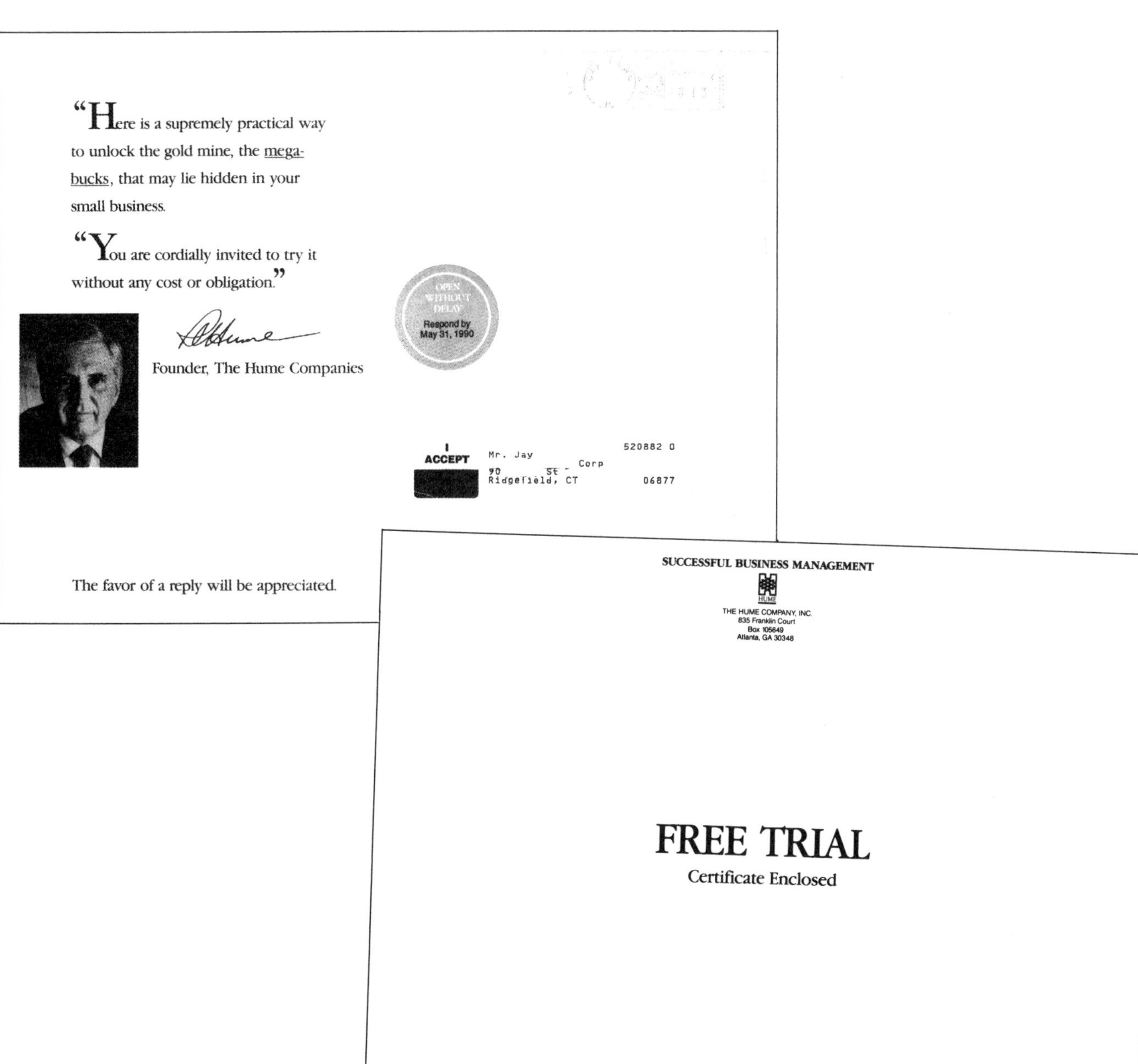
"Here is a supremely practical way to unlock the gold mine, the mega-bucks, that may lie hidden in your small business.
"You are cordially invited to try it without any cost or obligation."
Founder, The Hume Companies
OPEN WITHOUT DELAY
Respond by May 31, 1990
I ACCEPT
Mr. Jay
Corp
Ridgefield, CT
520882 0
06877
The favor of a reply will be appreciated.
SUCCESSFUL BUSINESS MANAGEMENT
HUME
THE HUME COMPANY, INC
835 Franklin Court
Box 105649
Atlanta, GA 30348
FREE TRIAL
Certificate Enclosed

every thought and idea that comes to me, then put all into a file, mentally command the work to proceed underground, and turn my attention elsewhere.

A week or ten days later I reopen the file and find that new, more practical ideas have sprouted in my mind during the hiatus, and even organized themselves to some extent. The work isn't finished, of course, but the path has been smoothed. (Darn clever, these philosophers!)

Finally, some random thoughts about direct mail . . .

The tone of a good direct mail letter is as direct and personal as the writer's skill can make it. Even though it may go to millions of people, it never orates to a crowd, but rather murmurs into a single ear. It is a message from one *letter writer to* one *letter reader.*

When assigning a project to a writer, (1) allow adequate time for reflection, writing, and revisions, and (2) set a deadline. I know from dire experience that

Presenting today's "bible" for small business owners.
Get acquainted with it entirely without risk or obligation to continue.
Ronald C. Hume
Founder, The Hume Companies

Dear Reader,

I have a montage picture of you in my mind's eye.

I see you running an independent business with a payroll of three or four people.

Or perhaps you're farther along now, and have dozens or even hundreds of people working for you. (In most statistical classifications, though, you're still a small business.)

Or maybe you haven't even begun yet. Your business is so far just a gleam in your eye, but you know in your heart that you'll get it started some day.

If you fit anywhere into this picture, then the loose-leaf binders pictured above were written especially and specifically for <u>you</u>!

<u>A priceless resource for people like us!</u>

There is nothing else like SUCCESSFUL BUSINESS MANAGEMENT on the market today. It is by far one of the most comprehensive and completely <u>practical</u> guides to the fascinating and rewarding task of running a business that I've ever encountered.

If it were on the desk of every owner of a small or closely held or family-owned or entrepreneurial business (choose your favorite designation) I think our gross national product would go zoom -- right through the roof!

I only wish it had been on my desk fifteen years ago when I started what is now The Hume Companies.

I'd have made more money faster, not made dozens of costly mistakes, and saved oceans of time if I'd had before me the precise, proven guidelines and techniques which are now available to you exclusively in the pages of SUCCESSFUL BUSINESS MANAGEMENT.

Back in 1971 I was an executive with one of the world's largest publishing houses, and was doing pretty well. I was

(over, please)

making my mark in the business and earning good money. And it looked as if there would be plenty more down the road.

But I had this itch, this idea in the back of my head that I ought to have my own business. It was an idea that got hold of me and wouldn't let go. And what drove me was not the lure of big money, but rather the prospect of independence, of being able to set my own agenda and call the shots.

I think you know exactly what I mean. In fact I'm willing to bet that you, like almost every other entrepreneur I've met, started (or plan to start) your business for the same reason: independence rather than money.

That instinct is sound. For people like us, the psychological rewards of being able to run your own show are beyond computation. But the monetary rewards can be outsized, too!

<u>Unlock the megabucks that lie hidden in your small business!</u>

Inside almost every viable small business lies a potential gold mine, a flowing bonanza of revenue and profits for the owner. It can easily dwarf both the rewards and the security that a lifetime of faithful service to a large corporation might reasonably be expected to generate.

It takes two keys to unlock the door to these megabucks. First, your business must be founded on a sound product or marketing opportunity, or fill a service niche. And second --

> -- it must be operated according to management principles and practices that are <u>proven effective</u>, not by windy talk or theorizing, but by actual results.

In the process of building my new business from scratch, I learned the truth of this second rule the hard way.

I started out in the best entrepreneurial tradition, doing my initial planning and projections after hours on the kitchen table.

When I finally opened my company's doors, I did so with a tiny staff and huge hopes.

But the actual management of the business proved more difficult than I had anticipated. I brought more hands-on managing experience to the job than most new entrepreneurs do. But providing the total top management for an entire business that was rapidly growing in complexity was a task I had never faced before.

What I needed was sound, on-the-spot advice and plenty of

2

it. And that is hard to come by. Bankers, accountants, board members and friends pitched in and contributed some much appreciated tips and insights.

But I needed much more than friendly help. Every day I was wrestling with things like finding and keeping good people, and getting rid of not-so-good people; relating with customers and suppliers; finding sources of capital; regulating and monitoring my cash flow; trying to keep the tax burden at a minimum; tracking company operations with ratios and financial statements.

I had to watch my competition to keep them from passing me, and watch the government to keep from being strangled in red tape. I had to make marketing decisions, pricing decisions, advertising decisions, credit decisions; make sure that purchasing and inventories weren't getting out of hand, check constantly on company and personal liability, be effective at both planning and managing -- and much, much more.

Eventually, by trial and error, I developed a management style that enabled me to handle such matters with relative ease. (At that point, the profits of The Hume Companies really took off!) But it was a costly education.

<u>A remarkable program for business success!</u>

Why, I wondered, wasn't there some sort of course or "encyclopedia" that would provide me and all the millions of other entrepreneurial business people in America with practical, easily accessible advice on how to handle the management problems and opportunities we constantly face?

A good-sized library will contain hundreds of books on small business management, but I have never found one that responded well to that perceived need.

Then, not long ago, a proposal for the new SUCCESSFUL BUSINESS MANAGEMENT came across my desk.

Here was exactly what I had been seeking for my business for many years! Frankly, I was so impressed with how much this program helped me, I decided to buy it from the publisher, had my editors bring it up-to-date, and I'm now ready to share it with you. And if I read your situation correctly, it's precisely what you need to operate (or start) your own small business.

SUCCESSFUL BUSINESS MANAGEMENT is <u>not</u> a theoretical treatise by professors or eggheads. It is not written by multimillionaires who struck it rich overnight.

Every word comes from working businessmen and professionals who have worked and sweated with the very same problems that now confront you, or who have specialized in personally advising business people on the management strategies, practices and techniques that have evolved to solve these problems.

3

(over, please)

The program is structured as a series of 29 sections, which total approximately 1,000 pages. If you accept the no-risk free trial offer I'll describe later, each section will be sent to you on approval. You will have 15 days in which to examine it and decide whether to keep it and pay its modest cost or return it and pay nothing.

A handsome and extremely sturdy three-ring binder that holds the sections will be sent to you free. It will stand up to the constant reference and thumbing through that SUCCESSFUL BUSINESS MANAGEMENT will inevitably receive.

A typical section consists of (1) thirty to forty pages of text covering the topic of the section and citing many actual case histories (2) a summary of the text (3) additional features, which may include sample forms, plans, analyses, journals, checklists and the like that you will be able to use for your own business (4) questions and answers with which you can check and reinforce your comprehension of the material.

And there are no complicated formulas to work out or big words to look up in SUCCESSFUL BUSINESS MANAGEMENT. Operating a business is a complex task, to be sure, but these supremely practical sections explain it simply. Here are a few of the sections you will receive --

STRATEGIES FOR SUCCESS -- What separates the winners from the losers.

OTHER PEOPLE'S MONEY -- How to raise capital for your business.

PLANNING FOR SUCCESS -- How to define and achieve your business objectives.

WHY KEEP RECORDS -- How good information can keep you in the driver's seat.

AVOIDING THE CASH CRUNCH -- How to budget and forecast your cash flow.

MAXIMIZING YOUR MARKETING POWER -- How to find and define a secure niche in the market.

WORKING WITH YOUR BANKER -- How to capitalize on your banker's knowledge and services.

SUCCESSFUL TAX STRATEGIES -- How to lighten your tax burden.

NEGOTIATING THE BEST DEAL -- How to get the most from your negotiations.

BUILDING YOUR ORGANIZATION -- How to find the best people and get the most from them.

4

The 6-page letter, printed on an 11″ × 17″ sheet with and 8½″ × 11″ sheet inserted in the centerfold.

And what is the cost of the complete, comprehensive, authoritative SUCCESSFUL BUSINESS MANAGEMENT program? It is actually less than you would pay for many business seminars that provide only a fraction of its broad coverage. It is certainly less than you would pay to go to business school or college -- or even enrolling part-time!

And once the course has given you a broad understanding of business principles, strategies, techniques and practices, the sections remain in your ring binders as a permanent desk reference you'll find yourself turning to again and again.

Wayne O'Neil, owner of his own company, described his experience this way:

"When I read about SUCCESSFUL BUSINESS MANAGEMENT it seemed to cover most of what I envisioned as my weak areas. Since there was no obligation I subscribed and received the start-up kit, which was far beyond my expectations.

"I feel that the course paid for itself more than ten times over in the first three or four months. Its practical discussions of just about every aspect of business have helped me make some very successful business decisions.

"I now use the course as a basic business reference library referring to it two or three times every week to assist me in the day-to-day operation of the corporation. I strongly recommend that every entrepreneurial businessman or would-be entrepreneur take the course. I'm sure that they, like myself, will appreciate its complete practicality. Even the forms provided are worth the price of the complete course!"

Please respond by May 31, 1990.
Just mail your Free Trial Certificate today!

Now you can get acquainted with SUCCESSFUL BUSINESS MANAGEMENT on the same no-cost, no-obligation to continue basis as Mr. O'Neil did. Just be sure to mail your Free Trial Certificate. You will then receive the following:

1. FREE! - Section 1, "Strategies for Success." Covers the rewards of business ownership; why it's worth the effort; the advantages of being small; how to stay in command as your business grows; how to grow without pain; the best sources of information and help; a 12-point plan for getting help. Plus three case histories, four special exhibits, and question-and-answer review section.

2. FREE! - Handsome, heavy-duty three-ring binder that will hold your SUCCESSFUL BUSINESS MANAGEMENT sections.

5 (over, please)

3. FREE! - How to Cut Government Red Tape." A valuable 48-page handbook that suggests many ways to handle this serious business problem. (It is described in detail on the enclosed yellow flyer.)

4. FREE! - "Problem-Solver Index" that directs you to topics throughout your 29 sections that will help you solve day-to-day business problems. Also a "Program Content List" and "Guide to Key Business Terms and Concepts."

You'll also receive on approval Section 2, "Other People's Money," which tells how to find capital and approach its sources; how to create an effective proposal; how the risk-reward ratio will affect your costs; how to use the SBA, trade credits, credit unions and many other sources. And much more.

If you decide to keep Section 2, you will receive a bill shortly. If you decide to return it, you may do so within 15 days and owe nothing. All four of the free items listed above, however, will still be yours to keep -- free!

One business mistake nobody should make.

In business terms, the free trial offer just outlined has absolutely no downside risk. All that is assumed by The Hume Company, Inc. And the upside potential is almost unlimited.

Improving your management skills will not only make your business more successful, it will also make your whole life more pleasant. You'll find you have more free time for family, friends, hobbies and leisure.

And as I've already pointed out, there is a potential gold mine hidden in many small businesses. Honing your management skills will make good things happen to your business. It is the most practical, direct way to unlock those megabucks and, perhaps, become wealthier than you've ever thought possible.

So don't make the mistake of turning down a can't-lose proposition. Mail the enclosed Free Trial Certificate today!

Sincerely,

Ronald C. Hume
Founder

RCH:sbo

P.S. You'll find I ACCEPT and I DECLINE stickers on the envelope. Please place one or the other on your Certificate along with your address label, and mail it promptly. Even your negative answer will help us as we have only printed a limited number of FREE trial materials.

6

the writer needs the second of these elements as much as the first. It was Peter Drucker, I believe, who said that work without a deadline is work toyed with. To which I add a heartfelt "amen."

Avoid using costly paper stocks in an effort to give your mailing a "quality" look. Countless tests show that they almost never pay for themselves. People will judge your product by what you print on your paper, rather than by what paper you print on.

The future of direct mail? It seems to me to be uncertain. We who write it know from experience that length is strength, and that the more you tell the more you sell. But to understand and respond to this kind of advertising, you have to be able to read.

Back in the early years of this century, virtually every American could read. We were the world's most literate country. Today, of the thirteen major industrialized nations, we are a poor thirteenth in literacy, and are still losing ground. I'm sure there are Third World countries that surpass us.

Thirty-seven years ago Rudolph Flesch put his finger on this problem and on its stunningly simple solution in a historic little volume entitled Why Johnny Can't Read. *But the educational powers-that-be have resolutely ignored his insights, and the dumbing-down of America continues apace.*

I and the other writers featured in this book will, of course, keep giving our best efforts to selling with the written word. But our audience will, I fear, keep dwindling.

HUME
The Hume Company, Inc.
presents
SUCCESSFUL BUSINESS MANAGEMENT

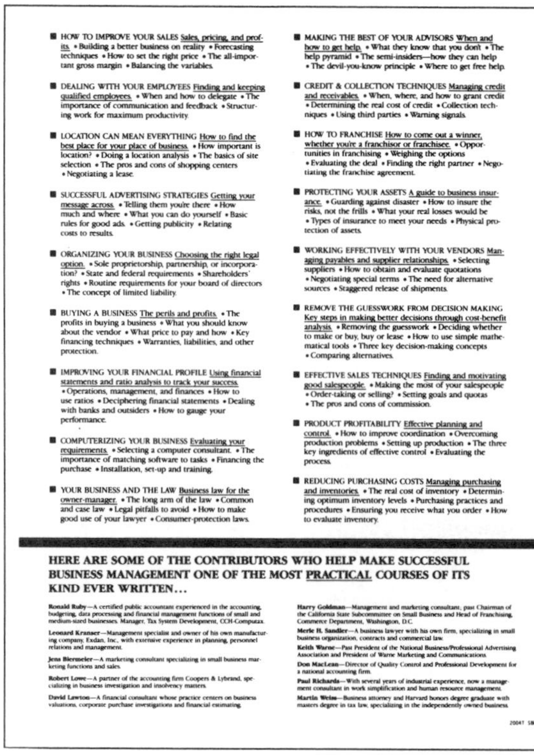
■ HOW TO IMPROVE YOUR SALES Sales, pricing, and profits. • Building a better business on reality • Forecasting techniques • How to set the right price • The all-important gross margin • Balancing the variables.
■ DEALING WITH YOUR EMPLOYEES Finding and keeping qualified employees. • When and how to delegate • The importance of communication and feedback • Structuring work for maximum productivity.
■ LOCATION CAN MEAN EVERYTHING How to find the best place for your place of business. • How important is location? • Doing a location analysis • The basics of site selection • The pros and cons of shopping centers • Negotiating a lease.
■ SUCCESSFUL ADVERTISING STRATEGIES Getting your message across. • Telling them you're there • How much and where • What you can do yourself • Basic rules for good ads. • Getting publicity • Relating costs to results.
■ ORGANIZING YOUR BUSINESS Choosing the right legal option. • Sole proprietorship, partnership, or incorporation? • State and federal requirements • Shareholders' rights • Routine requirements for your board of directors • The concept of limited liability.
■ BUYING A BUSINESS The perils and profits. • The profits in buying a business • What you should know about the vendor • What price to pay and how • Key financing techniques • Warranties, liabilities, and other protection.
■ IMPROVING YOUR FINANCIAL PROFILE Using financial statements and ratio analysis to track your success. • Operations, management, and finances • How to use ratios • Deciphering financial statements • Dealing with banks and outsiders • How to gauge your performance.
■ COMPUTERIZING YOUR BUSINESS Evaluating your requirements. • Selecting a computer consultant. • The importance of matching software to tasks • Financing the purchase • Installation, set-up and training.
■ YOUR BUSINESS AND THE LAW Business law for the owner-manager. • The long arm of the law • Common and case law • Legal pitfalls to avoid • How to make good use of your lawyer • Consumer-protection laws.
■ MAKING THE BEST OF YOUR ADVISORS When and how to get help. • What they know that you don't • The help pyramid • The semi-insiders—how they can help • The devil-you-know principle • Where to get free help.
■ CREDIT & COLLECTION TECHNIQUES Managing credit and receivables. • When, where, and how to grant credit • Determining the real cost of credit • Collection techniques • Using third parties • Warning signals.
■ HOW TO FRANCHISE How to come out a winner, whether you're a franchisor or franchisee. • Opportunities in franchising • Weighing the options • Evaluating the deal • Finding the right partner • Negotiating the franchise agreement.
■ PROTECTING YOUR ASSETS A guide to business insurance. • Guarding against disaster • How to insure the risks, not the frills • What your real losses would be • Types of insurance to meet your needs • Physical protection of assets.
■ WORKING EFFECTIVELY WITH YOUR VENDORS Managing payables and supplier relationships. • Selecting suppliers • How to obtain and evaluate quotations • Negotiating special terms • The need for alternative sources • Staggered release of shipments.
■ REMOVE THE GUESSWORK FROM DECISION MAKING Key steps in making better decisions through cost-benefit analysis. • Removing the guesswork • Deciding whether to make or buy, buy or lease • How to use simple mathematical tools • Three key decision-making concepts • Comparing alternatives.
■ EFFECTIVE SALES TECHNIQUES Finding and motivating good salespeople. • Making the most of your salespeople • Order-taking or selling? • Setting goals and quotas • The pros and cons of commission.
■ PRODUCT PROFITABILITY Effective planning and control. • How to improve coordination • Overcoming production problems • Setting up production • The three key ingredients of effective control • Evaluating the process.
■ REDUCING PURCHASING COSTS Managing purchasing and inventories. • The real cost of inventory • Determining optimum inventory levels • Purchasing practices and procedures • Ensuring you receive what you order • How to evaluate inventory.
HERE ARE SOME OF THE CONTRIBUTORS WHO HELP MAKE SUCCESSFUL BUSINESS MANAGEMENT ONE OF THE MOST PRACTICAL COURSES OF ITS KIND EVER WRITTEN...
Ronald Ruby—A certified public accountant experienced in the accounting, budgeting, data processing and financial management functions of small and medium-sized businesses. Manager, Tax System Development, CCH-Computax.
Leonard Kranser—Management specialist and owner of his own manufacturing company, Exdan, Inc., with extensive experience in planning, personnel relations and management.
Jens Biermeier—A marketing consultant specializing in small business marketing functions and sales.
Robert Lowe—A partner of the accounting firm Coopers & Lybrand, specializing in business investigation and insolvency matters.
David Lawton—A financial consultant whose practice centers on business valuations, corporate purchase investigations and financial estimating.
Harry Goldman—Management and marketing consultant; past Chairman of the California State Subcommittee on Small Business and Head of Franchising, Commerce Department, Washington, D.C.
Merle H. Sandler—A business lawyer with his own firm, specializing in small business organization, contracts and commercial law.
Keith Warne—Past President of the National Business/Professional Advertising Association and President of Warne Marketing and Communications.
Don MacLean—Director of Quality Control and Professional Development for a national accounting firm.
Paul Richards—With several years of industrial experience, now a management consultant in work simplification and human resource management.
Martin Weiss—Business attorney and Harvard honors degree graduate with masters degree in tax law, specializing in the independently owned business.
20041 SBM

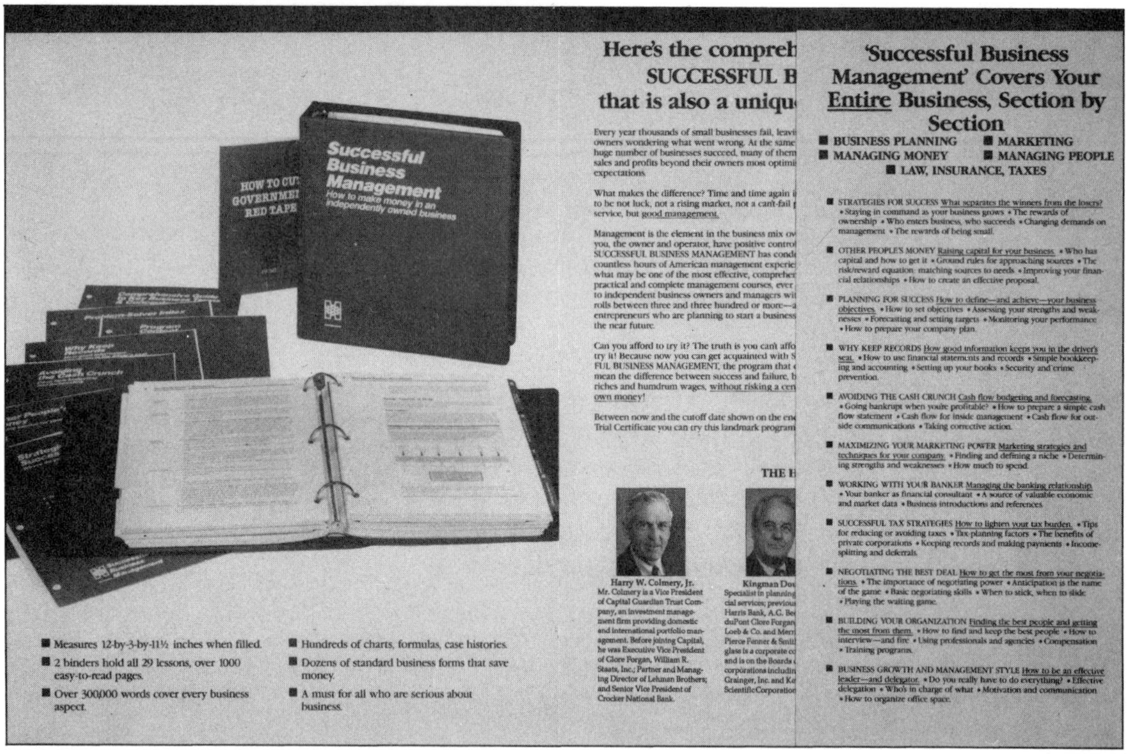
Here's the compreh
SUCCESSFUL B
that is also a uniqu
Every year thousands of small businesses fail, leavi
owners wondering what went wrong. At the same
huge number of businesses succeed, many of them
sales and profits beyond their owners most optimi
expectations.
What makes the difference? Time and time again i
to be not luck, not a rising market, not a can't-fail
service, but good management.
Management is the element in the business mix ov
you, the owner and operator, have positive contro
SUCCESSFUL BUSINESS MANAGEMENT has cond
countless hours of American management experie
what may be one of the most effective, comprehe
practical and complete management courses, ever
to independent business owners and managers wi
rolls between three and three hundred or more—a
entrepreneurs who are planning to start a business
the near future.
Can you afford to try it? The truth is you can't affo
try it! Because now you can get acquainted with S
FUL BUSINESS MANAGEMENT, the program that
mean the difference between success and failure, b
riches and humdrum wages, without risking a cen
own money!
Between now and the cutoff date shown on the en
Trial Certificate you can try this landmark program
THE H
Harry W. Colmery, Jr.
Mr. Colmery is a Vice President of Capital Guardian Trust Company, an investment management firm providing domestic and international portfolio management. Before joining Capital, he was Executive Vice President of Glore Forgan, William R. Staats, Inc.; Partner and Managing Director of Lehman Brothers; and Senior Vice President of Crocker National Bank.
■ Measures 12-by-3-by-11½ inches when filled.
■ 2 binders hold all 29 lessons, over 1000 easy-to-read pages.
■ Over 300,000 words cover every business aspect.
■ Hundreds of charts, formulas, case histories.
■ Dozens of standard business forms that save money.
■ A must for all who are serious about business.
'Successful Business Management' Covers Your Entire Business, Section by Section
■ BUSINESS PLANNING ■ MARKETING
■ MANAGING MONEY ■ MANAGING PEOPLE
■ LAW, INSURANCE, TAXES
■ STRATEGIES FOR SUCCESS What separates the winners from the losers? • Staying in command as your business grows • The rewards of ownership • Who enters business, who succeeds • Changing demands on management • The rewards of being small.
■ OTHER PEOPLE'S MONEY Raising capital for your business. • Who has capital and how to get it • Ground rules for approaching sources • The risk/reward equation: matching sources to needs • Improving your financial relationships • How to create an effective proposal.
■ PLANNING FOR SUCCESS How to define—and achieve—your business objectives. • How to set objectives • Assessing your strengths and weaknesses • Forecasting and setting targets • Monitoring your performance • How to prepare your company plan.
■ WHY KEEP RECORDS How good information keeps you in the driver's seat. • How to use financial statements and records • Simple bookkeeping and accounting • Setting up your books • Security and crime prevention.
■ AVOIDING THE CASH CRUNCH Cash flow budgeting and forecasting. • Going bankrupt when you're profitable? • How to prepare a simple cash flow statement • Cash flow for inside management • Cash flow for outside communications • Taking corrective action.
■ MAXIMIZING YOUR MARKETING POWER Marketing strategies and techniques for your company. • Finding and defining a niche • Determining strengths and weaknesses • How much to spend.
■ WORKING WITH YOUR BANKER Managing the banking relationship. • Your banker as financial consultant • A source of valuable economic and market data • Business introductions and references.
■ SUCCESSFUL TAX STRATEGIES How to lighten your tax burden. • Tips for reducing or avoiding taxes • Tax planning factors • The benefits of private corporations • Keeping records and making payments • Income-splitting and deferrals.
■ NEGOTIATING THE BEST DEAL How to get the most from your negotiations. • The importance of negotiating power • Anticipation is the name of the game • Basic negotiating skills • When to stick, when to slide • Playing the waiting game.
■ BUILDING YOUR ORGANIZATION Finding the best people and getting the most from them. • How to find and keep the best people • How to interview—and fire • Using professionals and agencies • Compensation • Training programs.
■ BUSINESS GROWTH AND MANAGEMENT STYLE How to be an effective leader—and delegator. • Do you really have to do everything? • Effective delegation • Who's in charge of what • Motivation and communication • How to organize office space.

The 8½″ × 11″ brochure cover—printed on deep blue background,—and the back panel. Below is the first inside spread printed in red and black. At right a 5″ flap cuts across copy, forcing the reader to open it. Neatness rejects involvement.

- Measures 12-by-3-by-11½ inches when filled.
- 2 binders hold all 29 lessons, over 1000 easy-to-read pages.
- Over 300,000 words cover every business aspect.
- Hundreds of charts, formulas, case histories.
- Dozens of standard business forms that save money.
- A must for all who are serious about business.

Here's the comprehensive, practical program in SUCCESSFUL BUSINESS MANAGEMENT that is also a unique, permanent desk reference!

Every year thousands of small businesses fail, leaving their owners wondering what went wrong. At the same time a huge number of businesses succeed, many of them delivering sales and profits beyond their owners most optimistic expectations.

What makes the difference? Time and time again it turns out to be not luck, not a rising market, not a can't-fail product or service, but good management.

Management is the element in the business mix over which you, the owner and operator, have positive control. And now SUCCESSFUL BUSINESS MANAGEMENT has condensed countless hours of American management experience into what may be one of the most effective, comprehensive, practical and complete management courses, ever offered to independent business owners and managers with payrolls between three and three hundred or more—and to entrepreneurs who are planning to start a business in the near future.

Can you afford to try it? The truth is you can't afford not to try it! Because now you can get acquainted with SUCCESSFUL BUSINESS MANAGEMENT, the program that can mean the difference between success and failure, between riches and humdrum wages, without risking a cent of your own money!

Between now and the cutoff date shown on the enclosed Free Trial Certificate you can try this landmark program entirely at risk of The Hume Company, Inc.! You'll study and use one of its valuable sections free—receive one of the rugged, permanent binders—plus the authoritative booklet, "How to Cut Government Red Tape," Program Content, Comprehensive Guide to Key Business Terms & Concepts, plus the exclusive Problem-Solving Index that will help melt away business problems for many years to come!

FREE! In addition to the permanent Binder, your Free Trial Certificate will bring you Section 1, the Problem-Solver Index, and "How to Cut Government Red Tape"—all free!

All are yours free and without obligation to continue if you act promptly. Yet our experience tells us that only a tiny fraction of those who receive this no-risk offer will act upon it.

It seems incredible, doesn't it? After all, we take great pains to send this presentation only to business people of good reputation, men and women who are either already running a going business or are seriously considering starting one. Yet many of these entrepreneurs, the cream of the small business crop, will turn down what may be their golden opportunity, their chance to super-manage their businesses into the stratosphere of super sales and profits!

Don't you be one of those nay-sayers. Accept this no-cost, no-risk offer. Now. Today. You'll never be sorry you did!

THE HUME ADVISORY BOARD

Harry W. Colmery, Jr.
Mr. Colmery is a Vice President of Capital Guardian Trust Company, an investment management firm providing domestic and international portfolio management. Before joining Capital, he was Executive Vice President of Glore Forgan, William R. Staats, Inc.; Partner and Managing Director of Lehman Brothers; and Senior Vice President of Crocker National Bank.

Kingman Douglass
Specialist in planning and financial services; previously with the Harris Bank, A.G. Becker & Co., duPont Glore Forgan, Inc., Kuhn, Loeb & Co. and Merrill Lynch, Pierce Fenner & Smith. Mr. Douglass is a corporate counselor, and is on the Boards of several corporations including W.W. Grainger, Inc. and Kewaunee Scientific Corporation.

J. Trevor Eyton
President and Chief Executive Officer of Brascan Ltd., Mr. Eyton was previously a partner with the law firm of Tory, Tory, DesLauriers & Binnington. He also serves as a director and officer of many well-known public corporations including John Labatt, London Life Insurance, Scott Paper Co. and Trizec Corp. He is also Deputy Chairman and a director of Royal Trustco, a major Canadian-based financial institution.

Hon. John C. Stetson
Mr. Stetson, former Secretary of the U.S. Air Force, is a successful investor managing private investments in financial and real estate institutions as well as in industrial and retailing operations. He was past President of A. B. Dick Company and a former partner in Booz Allen & Hamilton. He is a director of NYSE companies including Mercury Finance Company, Lawter International, Helene Curtis Industries, and several large insurance companies and banks.

SOME TYPICAL COMMENTS FROM BUSINESS PEOPLE WHO HAVE TAKEN SUCCESSFUL BUSINESS MANAGEMENT...

■ CALLS IT BEST INVESTMENT EVER!

"I have taken several courses in business management, but nothing has been of such value as Successful Business Management. Every section has so much information that it would be difficult for me to tell you which one is of most value. Any person, whether in business now or just starting, needs this course. I have told people it is the best investment you'll ever make. I want to say thanks to all who put this course together. You have solved all of my problems!"

Lil Baceda

■ INCREASED PROFITABILITY!

"The knowledge I gained in the Successful Business Management course enabled me to increase the productivity and profitability of my company [and] at age 21 to double the business of my company in two years."

Lawrence W. Mathison

■ GAVE HIM CONFIDENCE!

"The course provided me with full confidence in setting standards for all the necessary procedures, and perhaps more importantly, gave me the guidance I needed when unusual problems were encountered."

R. Jeffery Charlton

■ RECOMMENDS COURSE HIGHLY!

"I have taken the Successful Business Management course and I would recommend that course highly to people who are beginning in business but also to business people who want to upgrade themselves…for managers, assistant managers, executives, etc."

Jeanine Hebert

■ WISHES HE'D STARTED EARLIER!

"After taking a look at your first two lessons, all I can say is, 'Where were you six years ago when I started my business?' I not only could have eliminated almost all my costly mistakes, but could also have achieved some realistic goals."

Barry Kavich

■ CLARIFIED HER THINKING!

"I found the course…helped clarify my thinking and made me more aware of what I'm doing as a manager. I use it now as a reference… The Personnel Planning and Training Section is very valuable."

Dorothy Sharp *

*These comments are selected from our files. You may do better than these people—or you may not do as well, but if ever you are not 100% satisfied with your own rate of success, you may drop out of the program at any time.

The 11″ × 22″ inside spread fully opened and the back panel.

A classic message
to those who say
"I decline."

Lift piece 1.

The Hume Company, Inc.

There is a tide in the affairs of men,
Which, taken at the flood, leads on
to fortune;
Omitted, all the voyage of their life
Is bound in shallows and in miseries.
JULIUS CAESAR, Act IV
By William Shakespeare

Dear Entrepreneur,

Mr. Shakespeare appears to predict an unduly bleak future for those who decide to decline our free trial offer of SUCCESSFUL BUSINESS MANAGEMENT.

But I think he is right on target for those who say, "I accept." As Mr. Hume has pointed out, there is no down-side to this offer. And for those who accept -- and only for those who accept -- it may indeed "lead on to fortune."

Just as great oaks from little acorns grow, almost every big, profitable business started out as a small, struggling business.

And when you look into the history of growing, profitable businesses, 99 times out of 100 you will find they were managed in a practical, knowledgeable manner.

In business, as everywhere else, knowledge is power. And SUCCESSFUL BUSINESS MANAGEMENT provides the knowledge your business needs to grow and prosper.

So why don't you change your mind and say, "I accept." You have absolutely nothing to lose. And your potential gain is enormous!

Sincerely,

Benjamin Ordover

Benjamin Ordover
For The Hume Company, Inc.

BO:sbm

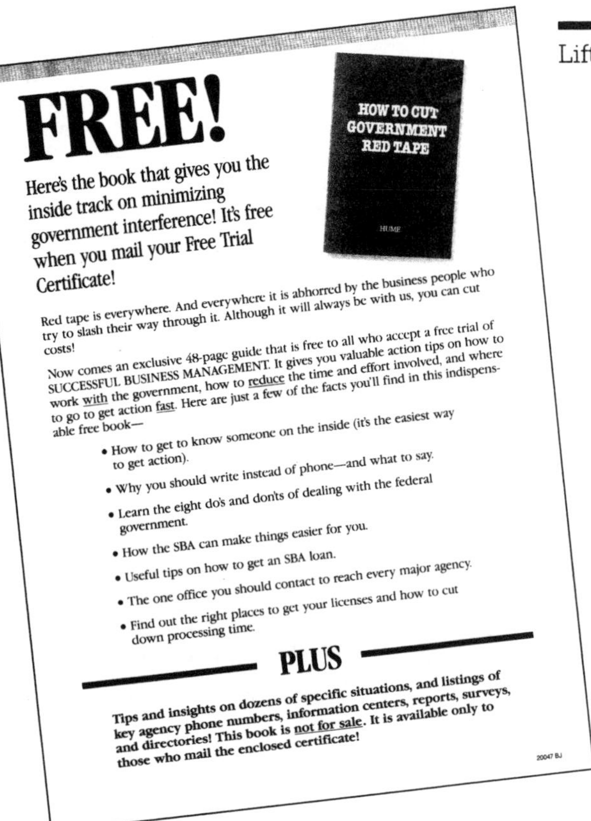
FREE!

Here's the book that gives you the inside track on minimizing government interference! It's free when you mail your Free Trial Certificate!

Red tape is everywhere. And everywhere it is abhorred by the business people who try to slash their way through it. Although it will always be with us, you can cut costs!

Now comes an exclusive 48-page guide that is free to all who accept a free trial of SUCCESSFUL BUSINESS MANAGEMENT. It gives you valuable action tips on how to work with the government, how to reduce the time and effort involved, and where to go to get action fast. Here are just a few of the facts you'll find in this indispensable free book—

- How to get to know someone on the inside (it's the easiest way to get action).
- Why you should write instead of phone—and what to say.
- Learn the eight do's and don'ts of dealing with the federal government.
- How the SBA can make things easier for you.
- Useful tips on how to get an SBA loan.
- The one office you should contact to reach every major agency.
- Find out the right places to get your licenses and how to cut down processing time.

PLUS

Tips and insights on dozens of specific situations, and listings of key agency phone numbers, information centers, reports, surveys, and directories! This book is not for sale. It is available only to those who mail the enclosed certificate!

20047 BJ

Lift piece 2.

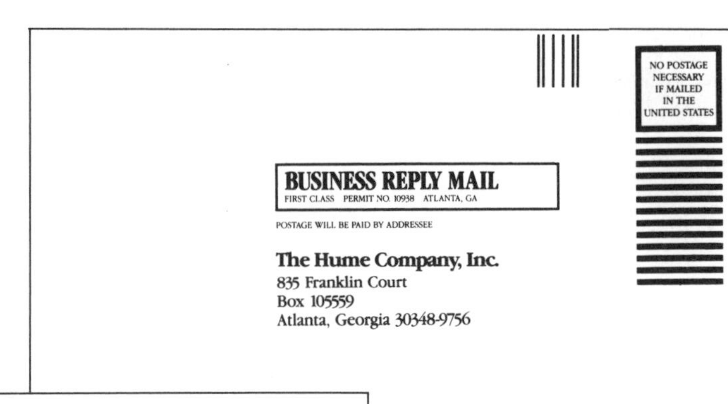

NO POSTAGE NECESSARY IF MAILED IN THE UNITED STATES
BUSINESS REPLY MAIL
FIRST CLASS PERMIT NO. 10938 ATLANTA, GA
POSTAGE WILL BE PAID BY ADDRESSEE
The Hume Company, Inc.
835 Franklin Court
Box 105559
Atlanta, Georgia 30348-9756

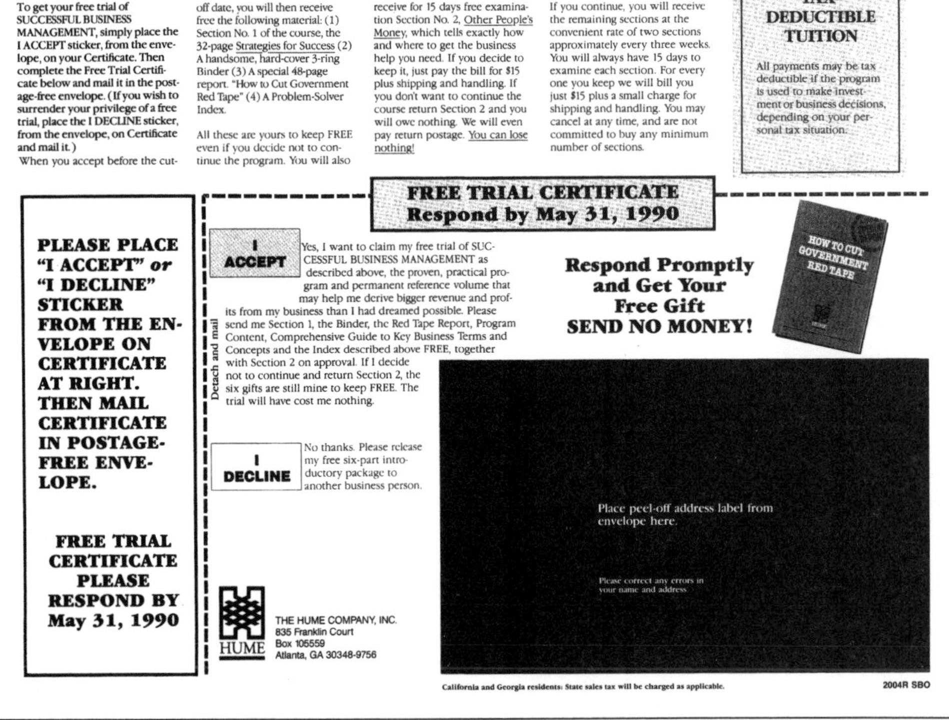
How to get your free trial of SUCCESSFUL BUSINESS MANAGEMENT

To get your free trial of SUCCESSFUL BUSINESS MANAGEMENT, simply place the I ACCEPT sticker, from the envelope, on your Certificate. Then complete the Free Trial Certificate below and mail it in the postage-free envelope. (If you wish to surrender your privilege of a free trial, place the I DECLINE sticker, from the envelope, on Certificate and mail it.)

When you accept before the cut-off date, you will then receive free the following material: (1) Section No. 1 of the course, the 32-page Strategies for Success (2) A handsome, hard-cover 3-ring Binder (3) A special 48-page report. "How to Cut Government Red Tape" (4) A Problem-Solver Index.

All these are yours to keep FREE even if you decide not to continue the program. You will also receive for 15 days free examination Section No. 2, Other People's Money, which tells exactly how and where to get the business help you need. If you decide to keep it, just pay the bill for $15 plus shipping and handling. If you don't want to continue the course return Section 2 and you will owe nothing. We will even pay return postage. You can lose nothing!

If you continue, you will receive the remaining sections at the convenient rate of two sections approximately every three weeks. You will always have 15 days to examine each section. For every one you keep we will bill you just $15 plus a small charge for shipping and handling. You may cancel at any time, and are not committed to buy any minimum number of sections.

TAX-DEDUCTIBLE TUITION

All payments may be tax deductible if the program is used to make investment or business decisions, depending on your personal tax situation.

PLEASE PLACE "I ACCEPT" or "I DECLINE" STICKER FROM THE ENVELOPE ON CERTIFICATE AT RIGHT. THEN MAIL CERTIFICATE IN POSTAGE-FREE ENVELOPE.

FREE TRIAL CERTIFICATE PLEASE RESPOND BY May 31, 1990

FREE TRIAL CERTIFICATE
Respond by May 31, 1990

Detach and mail

I ACCEPT — Yes, I want to claim my free trial of SUCCESSFUL BUSINESS MANAGEMENT as described above, the proven, practical program and permanent reference volume that may help me derive bigger revenue and profits from my business than I had dreamed possible. Please send me Section 1, the Binder, the Red Tape Report, Program Content, Comprehensive Guide to Key Business Terms and Concepts and the Index described above FREE, together with Section 2 on approval. If I decide not to continue and return Section 2, the six gifts are still mine to keep FREE. The trial will have cost me nothing.

I DECLINE — No thanks. Please release my free six-part introductory package to another business person.

Respond Promptly and Get Your Free Gift SEND NO MONEY!

Place peel-off address label from envelope here.

Please correct any errors in your name and address

HUME
THE HUME COMPANY, INC.
835 Franklin Court
Box 105559
Atlanta, GA 30348-9756

California and Georgia residents: State sales tax will be charged as applicable.

2004R SBO

The $8\frac{1}{2}'' \times 11''$ order form. The rectangle in lower right is printed in the same deep blue used on the circular. Also shown here is the BRE.

SuperInvestor Files

This Alan Schwartz package has to rank among the most successful—yet modest—efforts ever sent to investors. There is not even one lift piece. It consists of a #10 envelope, order card, business reply envelope, and six-page letter printed front and back on three nested sheets of paper. The entire mailing is printed in two colors (green and black). This is truly powerful copy:

REMEMBER, TOO, THAT YOUR RISK IN MOST OF THESE INVESTMENTS WILL BE $1,500 OR LESS—OFTEN MUCH LESS. So, even if you are a small or first-time investor, you can still participate in these big-return opportunities and multiply your money faster than you ever imagined possible.

Armed with the SuperInvestor Files, *you really have the opportunity to build a fortune even if you are starting from scratch. My investment capital was $400. I'm sure you've got that much to risk. And the odds are much better for you. Remember, I had to learn these techniques on my own. . . .*

Alan Schwartz has never had a job in his life. He has been a freelancer in the United States and Canada for the past twenty years. His clients have included: Columbia House, GM of Canada, Nightingale-Conant, and the Royal Trust.

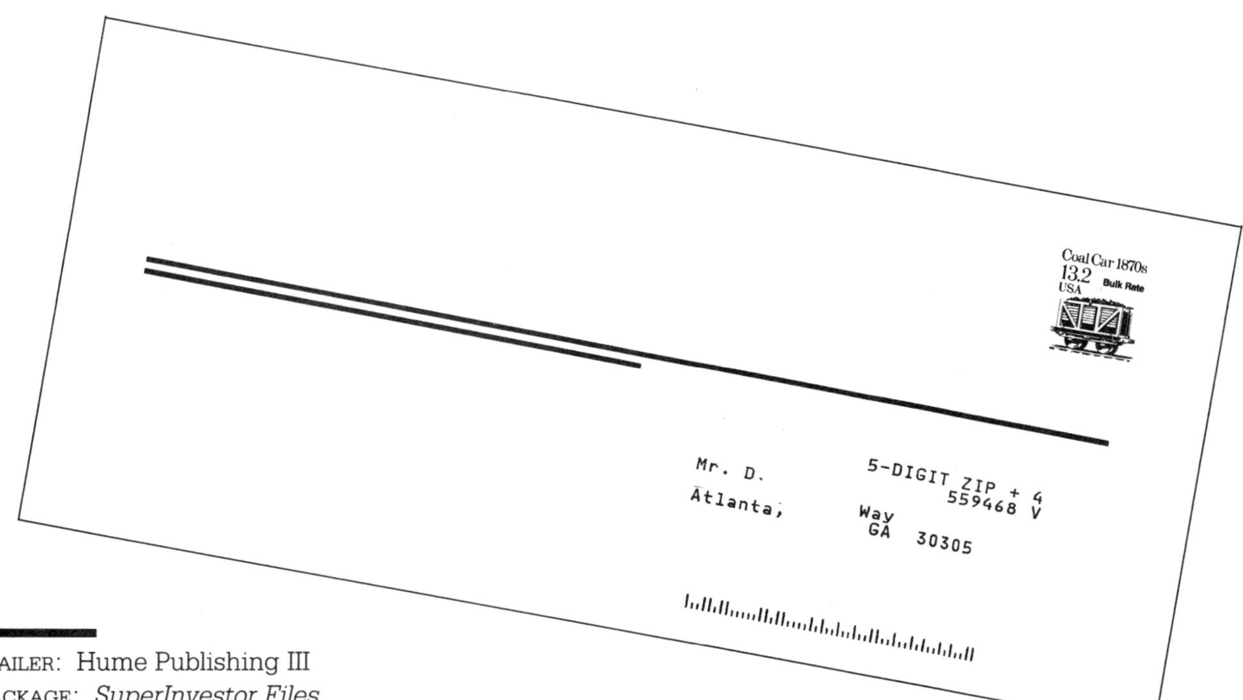

MAILER: Hume Publishing III
PACKAGE: *SuperInvestor Files*
PROJECT MGR.: Suzanne Eastman
WRITER: Alan Schwartz
DESIGNER: Unknown
FIRST MAILED: 1985
The simple #10 outside envelope.

If you think a 12% annual return on your money is good, here's how to set your sights on 100% or more.

Dear Reader,

My name is Morton Shulman. I am a practicing medical doctor. I am also a multi-millionaire. I didn't make my millions by practicing medicine, though. I made them by investing in my spare time.

In this letter I'm going to tell you how I did it. Then I'm going to show you how you can do it, too -- faster than you ever imagined possible -- even if you've never invested before, even if all you can afford to risk is $2,000. It took me four years to make my first million, but with the techniques I'm going to describe, you might well be able to cut that time.

When I first got out of medical school, I had $400. It was all I had to set up my office and get my practice started. (This was back in 1950.) My first investment lost $350 of that $400. It was more than a year before I was ready to try again.

During that year I really burned the midnight oil. I spent months studying finance and the markets. And it paid off. On my second investment, I made $8,000 in just a few weeks. In the following year, I turned that $8,000 into $250,000. Within four years I was a millionaire. Had I known at that time about the techniques I'm going to outline in this letter, I believe I could have cut that four-year period in half. Today, I have many millions -- all the result of using the same kind of strategies I'm going to share with you now.

For example:

> Not long ago, I made an investment that produced a 280% profit in only five weeks. And recently, a friend of mine made nearly 1,000% on his investment in less than a month.

No, I'm not talking about magic. I'm talking about specific investing techniques that have been used again and again by myself and by the world's most successful investors to multiply their money in a matter of weeks or months.

I'm also going to explain why these very same strategies have been among the best kept "secrets" of financial pros. Then

I'll tell you how to unlock these "secrets" and apply them for your own profit. Anyone with an average intelligence and income can do it.

These aren't vague schemes based on "positive thinking" or strategies that require a fortune in investment capital. Nor am I suggesting a particular kind of investment. This isn't a franchise deal. I have no axe to grind. And I have no exotic "system" for successful investing -- just practical, proven techniques that the average person can put to work right now.

But there is a catch.

The strategies I'm going to describe have, until now, been known only to relatively few people who are not very interested or very good at explaining what they know about making money. What's more, unless these techniques are explained very clearly by someone who really knows the ins and outs, few people, even financial professionals, can put them into practice.

That's why you've probably never read about these strategies before, and that's why they are among the best-kept "secrets" of the pros. Not many people know about them -- or know how to use them.

Yet each of these super high-yield investing techniques can be reduced to a simple "recipe" that almost anyone can understand. And that's exactly what Hume and Associates has done. The world's greatest super investments have been outlined in such simple steps that virtually anyone can follow them. I'm not talking about oversimplifications. I am talking about everything the average person will need to know to have the same chance of success as a "SuperInvestor" -- someone who's been utilizing these strategies for years.

The SuperInvestor Files --
your key to annual returns of
100% and more

We call these strategies The SuperInvestor Files. Each File deals with one particular investment technique. Each File will provide you with everything you need to have the same potential for success as myself or any of my "SuperInvestor" colleagues.

The SuperInvestor Files are an absolute "first" in the financial world. Never before have successful SuperInvestors sat down and explained clearly the ins and outs of their most successful trades so that anybody could put them into practice.

Each File explains in plain English how to time, execute and monitor a particular short term investment strategy that is capable of producing returns of more than 100%. Really. And you can get into many of them with as little as $500-$1,500 at risk. In most cases the risk is defined. And nothing has been spared to give you the same chances at success as an experienced SuperInvestor.

The SuperInvestor Files won't require you to spend days and days learning tedious financial facts. Rather, each File is an immediately useful and complete guide to one of the world's most profitable, short-term investment strategies. As soon as you finish reading a File, you will be able to evaluate whether or not the timing is right for that particular trade. If the time is ripe, you will be able to act immediately and with complete confidence -- even if you've never invested before.

And the time will nearly always be ripe for at least some of the strategies contained in The SuperInvestor Files. Novices just don't realize that the opportunities for large, quick investment gains are around all the time. The SuperInvestor Files will show you how, when and where to spot them.

> As a matter of fact, a recent opportunity in silver futures would have enabled anyone to see an effective return of 112%. The trade, begun in August 1989 with approximately $2,075 would have produced $2,325 in profits in just three months! And once you've read The QuickSilver Quest File, you'll be able to pick out similar opportunities.

Each File also shows you how to monitor your investment once it's underway. You'll know exactly what indicators to watch. You'll know when to cash in for maximum profits and safety. To make the Files as easy to use as possible, we've featured a separate 'Key Rules' section in each File that you can remove and carry with you. You'll always be ready to act -- no matter where you are when market conditions indicate the time is right! You'll even be given the phone numbers of qualified brokers familiar with a particular strategy -- and you'll know exactly what to say to them. You will not be hesitant or puzzled about any aspect of a trade -- not even for a moment.

What's more, you'll find out that you don't have to disrupt your regular work or family life in order to monitor or think about your investments. I run a busy medical practice, and even though

my investments amount to millions, I simply can't short change my patients by taking a lot of time away from them.

So now that you have some background on The SuperInvestor Files, I want to describe the first of these ingenious investments.

This is a strategy that made me a 101.25% return on my money in only a month. It's called The TED Spread.

> The TED Spread is based on the movement of interest rates. It works best when rates are moving up -- but the beauty of it is that you can sometimes also make money when rates are moving down. Not so long ago, a TED Spread brought me a 101.25 percent return in only a month. But even more important than these extraordinary potential gains is the fact that, when The TED Spread is done correctly, the risk is controlled and low -- under $1000. That's why we've chosen it as SuperInvestor File #1.

The SuperInvestor File on The TED Spread explains every aspect of the strategy in simple, step-by-step fashion. You'll learn about each of the components of the trade -- you'll see how and why the strategy works. What's even better, you'll be able to breeze through the SuperInvestor File on The TED Spread in a few hours. Once you've finished reading you will be able to look at your newspaper and consult the Key Rules portion of your File. You'll have everything you need to be able to decide if the conditions are right for the trade and to take appropriate action.

If The TED Spread sounds like something you'd like to try, send for a copy of SuperInvestor File #1, The TED Spread. A little later on I'll tell you how to get it. But before I do, I want to describe some of the other techniques in The SuperInvestor Files.

> An investor following the commodities markets in the fall of 1989 would have spotted an exciting opportunity, gone to his arsenal of SuperInvestor trades and headed straight for The Petro Parlay to maximize his profits. It was this heating oil and unleaded gasoline futures spread that produced a gross profit of $2,650 from a $1,000 investment -- in ONLY FOUR MONTHS!

Hypothetical or simulated performance results have certain inherent limitations. Unlike an actual performance record, simulated results do not represent actual trading. Also, since the trades have not actually been executed, the results may have under- or over-compensated for the impact, if any, of certain market factors, such as lack of liquidity. Simulated trading programs in general are also subject to the fact that they are designed with the benefit of hindsight. No representation is being made that any account will or is likely to achieve profits or losses similar to those shown.

The 6-page letter printed front and back on 3 nested pages. The second color is green.

The SuperInvestor Files

Once again, if you had the SuperInvestor File on The Petro Parlay, there is no reason why you couldn't take advantage of similar conditions. You'd know just what to do -- and when to do it. In The SuperInvestor Files, everything is explained -- the history of the trade, why the trade works, and the Key Rules you need to put the trade into action. Nothing is left to your imagination.

The Files assume that you know nothing about finance beyond balancing your own checkbook. Yet, when you are through reading The TED Spread (or any of the Files), you will have expert knowledge on one of the most exciting and clever investments there is. Your knowledge will be practical, not theoretical. Then, each time the opportunity for bonanza profits is there, you will know it, and you will know exactly what to do.

The underlying principle behind these practical investment strategies

Before I go on, I want you to understand that most of the techniques are based on a single principle. Basically, you can create a desirable situation by using the techniques you'll learn in The SuperInvestor Files. You don't have to understand any of them now because you will get a complete explanation in each File.

The point is, with the SuperInvestor strategies, you have the opportunity to make money no matter what is happening. The opportunity may involve changes in interest rates, as in the case of The TED Spread, or movement in the stock market, or in the price of precious metals. In other words, with the full arsenal of SuperInvestor strategies, almost any movement in prices -- UP or DOWN -- can make money for you (there's even one strategy designed to make money when prices don't move).

REMEMBER, TOO, THAT YOUR RISK IN MOST OF THESE INVESTMENTS WILL BE $1,500 OR LESS -- OFTEN MUCH LESS. So, even if you are a small or first-time investor, you can still participate in these big-return opportunities and multiply your money faster than you ever imagined possible.

Armed with The SuperInvestor Files, you really have the opportunity to build a fortune even if you are starting from scratch. My investment capital was $400. I'm sure you've got that much to risk. And the odds are much better for you. Remember, I had to learn these techniques on my own. I had to make all the mistakes before I made my money. You, on the other hand, have it all spelled out for you in The SuperInvestor Files.

Believe me, you don't need any special aptitude. There's no magic involved. It's simply a matter of knowledge -- knowledge that used to be the private preserve of a very few.

How you can become a SuperInvestor

As I said earlier, you can send for the SuperInvestor File on The TED Spread. Study it carefully. If you aren't satisfied that everything I've said about The SuperInvestor Files is absolutely true, return it within two weeks. There's no further obligation and no cost.

The total cost for each File is $35.00. Each File describes in full detail a specific SuperInvestor technique. You never pay for a File before you've had the chance to examine it for a full two weeks. If you send one back, you won't get the next one. You're under no obligation of any kind.

Remember, I'm not asking you to take anything on faith. It costs you nothing to find out whether or not you could become rich through the practical investment strategies spelled out in The SuperInvestor Files. All you have to do is send the enclosed card for your copy of "The TED Spread."

Sincerely,

Morton Shulman

Dr. Morton Shulman

P.S. You may be wondering why I'm involved with The SuperInvestor Files; after all, I've already made my millions. First, my friend Ron Hume and his associates have done such a fine job of putting these powerful techniques on paper. Second, I see no reason why these investment "secrets" should remain secret. In fact I'll be most pleased if you too make your fortune.

MS:eh

Alan Schwartz:

100% Return on Your Investment In Less Than 1 Year

That's why I knew from the very beginning that this promotion couldn't miss. I was able to create an entirely new product *with the built-in features and benefits that I was certain Hume's more sophisticated customers wanted. Since I had been writing for Hume for nearly a decade at the time* SuperInvestors *was born, I was confident of my read of that marketplace.*

I began creating the SuperInvestor Files *product by developing a space ad with all the features and benefits that I wanted the product to have. Then I wrote a prototype* SuperInvestor *lesson, the product itself. The ad never ran and the prototype lesson was never part of the program, but I used them to approach Hume.*

Later, when I wrote the mailing package it was a logical extension of what I had roughed out in the space ad and built into the product. I believe that writing promotional copy first is the best way to do product development for many kinds of companies—especially those that sell editorial products. While the SuperInvestor Files *is the most dramatic success I've had working this way, I've never had a failure when I've created the product and the promotion simultaneously.*

The SuperInvestor Files *actually started with an assignment to write a package for Hume's original advance investment product,* Advanced Strategies for Successful Investing. *Since I know very little about investing, I called a brilliant professor of finance, Eric Kirzner, who had done a lot of editorial work for Hume. I was counting on Eric to help me turn the program's*

REPLY CARD **The SuperInvestor Files**

Yes! **I accept your invitation to examine *SuperInvestor File* #1: The TED Spread, for two weeks, along with future files under the terms described in the enclosed letter.**

Just send in this card!

5-DIGIT ZIP + 4
559468 V

Mr. D.
Way
Atlanta, GA 30305

E Printed in USA

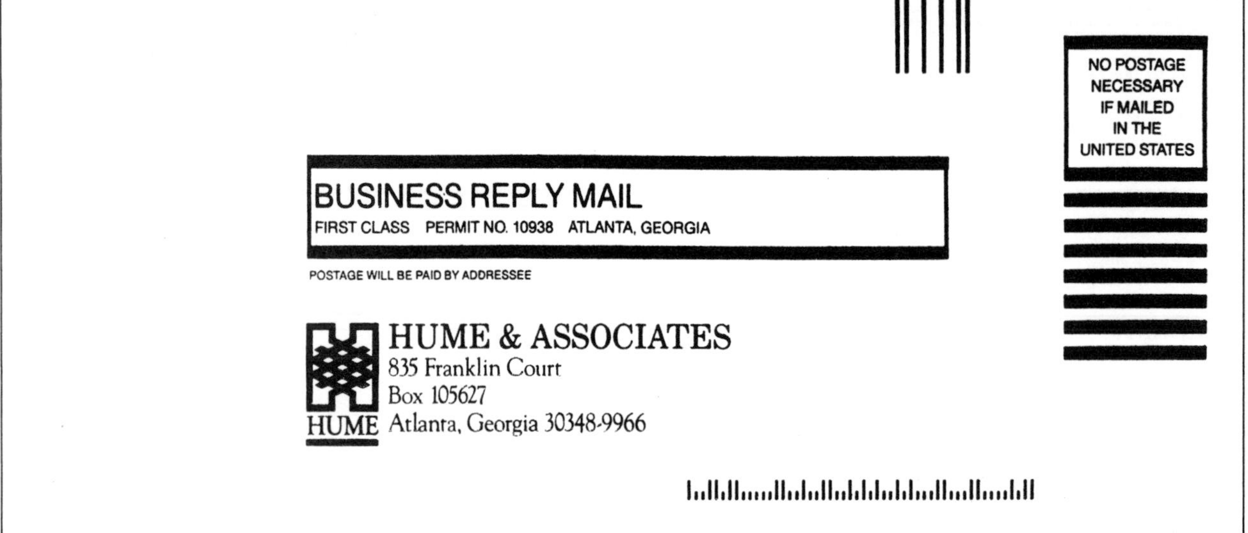

NO POSTAGE NECESSARY IF MAILED IN THE UNITED STATES

BUSINESS REPLY MAIL
FIRST CLASS PERMIT NO. 10938 ATLANTA, GEORGIA

POSTAGE WILL BE PAID BY ADDRESSEE

HUME & ASSOCIATES
835 Franklin Court
Box 105627
HUME Atlanta, Georgia 30348-9966

The order form and business reply envelope.

advanced investment jargon into clear-cut benefits. By the time we finished a half-hour phone call, I was really frustrated. It seems that the existing product was really no good to anyone who had less than $250,000 to invest, and most of Hume's customers had nowhere near that kind of nest egg.

''But, Eric,'' I whined, ''I've read about investors who make $10,000 overnight on a single trade. Those are the kind of advanced investment things I want to write about.''

''You won't find anything like that in this course,'' he said.

''But I've read about them.'' I pleaded.

''Oh, yeah. Sure. It's not easy, but it can be done.''

''But you have to have a fortune first? Right?''

''No. Not really.''

There was a long silence and then I asked, ''How much money would you need to do these super trades?''

''Oh, from fifteen hundred to three thousand to get in.''

''And how many of these trades could you come up with?''

''Oh, I don't know. Maybe twenty.''

''Eric,'' I said, ''I think we've got a great product.''

And that's how the SuperInvestor Files *was born. Of course, the hard part was yet to come. I had to sell the idea to Hume and then prove that I or someone could write the lessons in a way that would be comprehensible to people who had no investment background.*

Writing the prototype lesson was blood, sweat, and tears. Eric would explain financial concepts that would make my head swim. Then I had to write them so that it all sounded fairly easy. After writing the prototype lesson, writing the promotion was simple—especially since I had already written a space ad with all the major copy points in it—points that Eric and I built into the product.

People with money to invest are always looking for financial gurus, and from the beginning I conceived the SuperInvestor Files *as the ultimate guru product. The guy who told you to buy this product had to be someone who had actually done the trades and gotten rich, so the only approach that made sense was to get one of the ''super investors'' to sign a letter describing his own experience with the trades. I interviewed Dr. Morton Shulman, who was on the Hume Advisory Board, got some of his personal background and the letter practically wrote itself. The letter was the only selling piece, though the package was tested with a small brochure. But what could be stronger than a letter from a multimillionaire investment guru who said, ''This is how I made my millions. I'm going to teach you to do it too''?*

Most of the great names in the business have tested against the package but have been unable to beat it. When I was asked to beat it, I said I couldn't. The SuperInvestor Files *was conceived simultaneously as a product and as a promotion, so everything about the product and the mailing was created in ideal terms. The relationship between the mailing and the product was totally seamless, it was totally consistent from a marketing point of view. If my basic assumptions were right about the kind of product the market wanted, everything about the promotion followed with perfect logic. How can you beat that?*

Nightingale-Conant

Another direct mailer who is a giant in testing is Nightingale-Conant; it is not unusual for the archive to receive six or more new and different mailing packages in a month. Like Hume, Nightingale-Conant uses the very best copywriters and designers in the United States and Canada.

Lead the Field

For years Research Institute of America has used 9″ × 12″ kraft envelopes with a prospectus-like report printed on coated stock. A peel-off label is affixed to the blank back cover of the booklet and shows through the window. To order, you peel off the label and place it on an enclosed business reply card.

There are two reasons why this format has worked so well:

1. When a #10 mailing goes into the workplace, it is frequently opened by the secretary or executive assistant. The envelope is discarded and the various elements are flattened out, clipped together, and most probably put into the lowest-priority file. When a secretary unfolds all the pieces and clips them together, you—the sender—have no control over how the various pieces are arranged. The order card might be on top . . . or the letter . . . or whatever.

   With this 9″ × 12″ format, the secretary slips the entire mailing

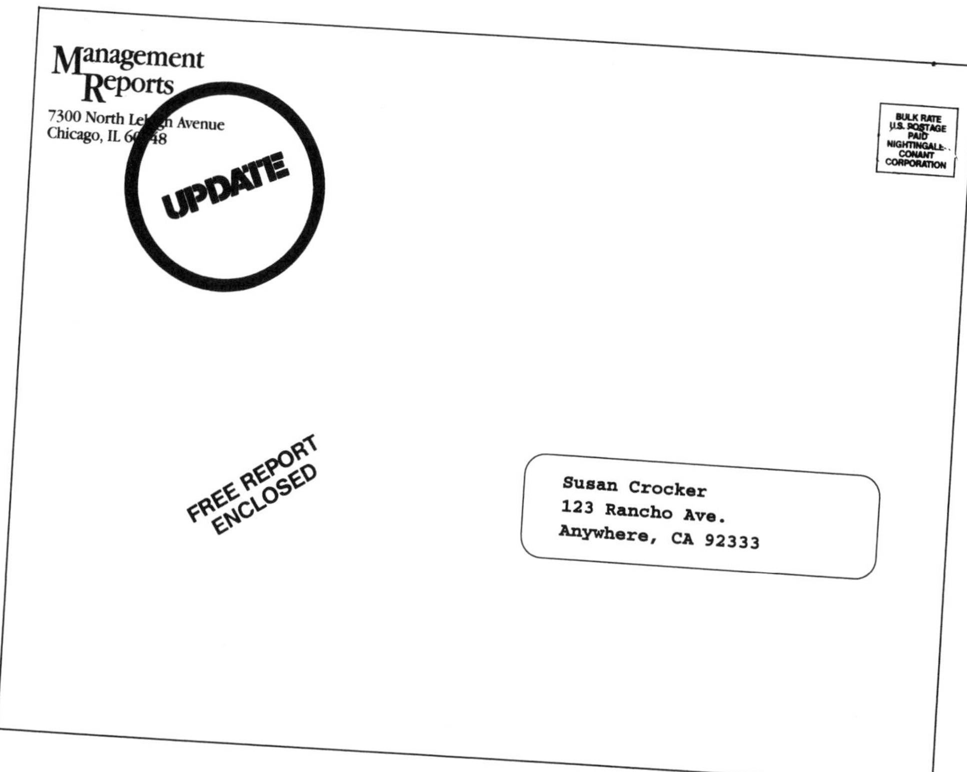

MAILER: Nightingale-Conant I
PACKAGE: *Lead the Field*
PROJECT MGR.: Mark Boyle
WRITER: Bob Matheo
DESIGNER: Chuck Dickinson
FIRST MAILED: 1987
The 9″ × 12″ kraft outer envelope with the circle and "UPDATE" in red and a day-glo "FREE REPORT ENCLOSED" sticker.

out of the envelope and into the file folder; not unfolding or arranging. *You* are in control of what is seen first, no matter whether the person opens the envelope or receives the material from someone else who has opened it.

2. This format resembles a portfolio or special report. It looks as if it might be an internal document that someone created with a desktop publishing program. As a result, the busy executive will start reading it not necessarily thinking it's a promotional ad, but something to do with the business. As Malcolm Decker concluded in Chapter 4: "If you can firmly engage your prospect—and keep *him engaged—through reading, you're on your way to a sale.*"

This Grand Control for Nightingale-Conant was written by Bob Matheo, AdMaker, who has been in advertising for thirty-five years. His clients include Hume Publishing, No-Load Fund Investor, KCI, *Consumer Reports*, BMG Music Service, Time Inc., *Newsweek*, Enterprise Publishing, James Blanchard & Co., Nuveen, Encore Travel, Gaines Dog Food, and (in strictest confidence) various New York advertising agencies.

Bob Matheo:
I have reached a stage in my professional career where colleagues, looking at my work, often ask questions like: "What made you think that would work?" or "How did you dream up that idea?" I usually shrug modestly and say, "I dunno."

Actually, I do know, but I've been reluctant to admit it. I've been a copywriter for thirty-five years, a direct marketer for thirty, and I'll probably be seventy years old when this appears in print. Before that, I had a fifteen-year career as an actor. And I am now trying to launch a new career as a speaker/seminar-giver.

In other words, the answer is experience . . . lots of it . . . in many areas.

A seasoned tennis pro doesn't ponder whether to rush in and volley a return, stand his ground and hit a half-volley, or pull back, wait for the bounce, and hit an overhead slam. He has played often enough that his brain makes thousands of lightning calculations and judgments, causing him to move in the right direction without thinking. Many athletes call this being "in the zone."

I've been told that, during the 1950s, the New York Yankees brought in an expert whose name has since faded into oblivion to instruct the batters what to think when they're batting. Yogi Berra resisted. "I can't bat and think at the same time," he said.

Well, I can't write and think at the same time. My best creative work is done in the zone. *But creating is not thinking—it's a product of all those years of experience.*

The format and content of this mailing for Nightingale-Conant's Lead the Field *came from two things: (1) the client told me he believed that a plain-Jane report format has a certain "magic" for this product (I seldom doubt the wisdom of my clients—after all, they picked me); and (2) I recalled executive how-to-do-it ads and booklets from* Nation's Business *back in the 1960s that used cartoons to fortify their message; I admired the style then, and waited twenty-seven years for an opportunity to use it. The rest is a result of good communications between me and my designer, Chuck Dickinson. And getting* in the zone.

MANAGEMENT REPORTS

SPECIAL UPDATE ON EXECUTIVE SELF-IMPROVEMENT

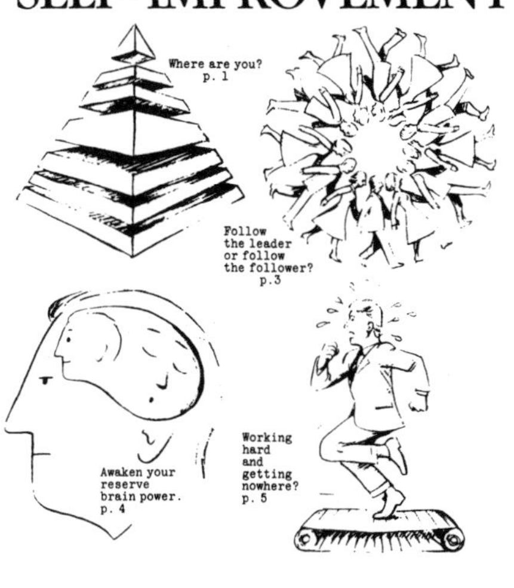

Where are you? p. 1
Follow the leader or follow the follower? p.3
Awaken your reserve brain power. p. 4
Working hard and getting nowhere? p. 5

The 8½″ × 11″ "portfolio cover" printed in black on coated stock. This is purposely designed to look like a special report.

You open the glossy portfolio. At left is the inside panel of the portfolio. At right is the first page of the letter, printed on offset paper. No color here; everything is black and white.

Management Reports
are special reports
published from time to time
by Nightingale-Conant Corporation,
the world's leading publisher
of audio-cassette training programs.
Your comments are welcome.
Write to:
Management Reports Editor
Nightingale-Conant Corporation
7300 North Lehigh Avenue
Chicago, IL 60648.

To acquaint you, your staff and your firm with the benefits to be derived from LEAD THE FIELD, the program described in the enclosed special report, the publisher has authorized a **FREE 30-DAY AUDITION**

An Audition Request Form is enclosed.

Nightingale-Conant Management Reports Page 1

U P D A T E

Dear Executive:

This report will update you on some remarkable new achievements in the field of executive self-improvement.

The program described, we can confidently say, has changed more lives and helped create more millionaires than any other program ever produced. And, because it helps people get their lives and careers on track, it has saved more marriages too.

You may wish to consider it for people in your company -- whether they have achieved executive status or not. You may even wish to consider it for yourself.

To help you reach a decision, we have arranged for you to personally audition and try the program for 30 days without cost or obligation.

WHERE DO YOU STAND?

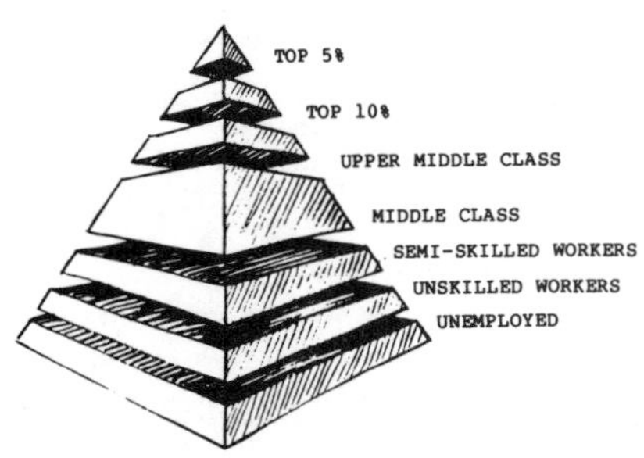

Most people are motivated to take the course because they are dissatisfied with their status in life. They are in the middle or bottom of the earning pyramid, and they long to move up a

Nightingale-Conant Management Reports — Page 2

notch or two.

What most people don't realize until they take the course is that they have the capability of moving to the very top!

Consider your own position for a moment. Where are you now -- and where would you like to be? Do you believe you can reach the very top ... that you can earn more than 95% of the rest of the population ... that you can join the ranks of millionaires?

You're probably shaking your head in doubt. But I say: "Cast your doubts away." If your name belongs on the list of people chosen to receive this report, I can assure you that you can reach the top. Success and wealth are within your grasp!

How We Teach Success

The secrets of success are not really secrets -- they are easy to learn. But most people never bother. Did you know, for example, that you can make yourself lucky? That you can attract good experiences like a magnet? It's one of the very first things the program teaches you.

The program, by the way, is called LEAD THE FIELD. It's been around for years, first on phonograph records -- then on audio cassettes. It was, in fact, the only non-musical recording to become a Gold Record by selling over a million copies.

Now it has been updated and revised -- made more powerful than before -- by incorporating some remarkable new findings on how the brain works.

It was created by Earl Nightingale -- a truly inspiring teacher -- who pioneered recorded learning programs.

Why Recorded Programs Work Better

Earl Nightingale discovered years ago that recorded programs work better than classroom sessions or lectures. The reason is simple: whenever a classroom teacher says something that is especially meaningful to you, your mind wraps itself around the idea so tightly you can hardly hear the next couple of ideas that are spoken. And you miss an important part of the message.

But when the lesson is recorded, you can stop the tape to dwell on any thought that excites you. And, even better, you can play the recording again and again until every subtlety of the message is embedded in your mind.

Listen to our updated and revised LEAD THE FIELD just once and you'll realize how the program can literally catapult you to the

Nightingale-Conant Management Reports — Page 3

top. But you have to listen to each of the 12 sessions many times before they become part of your everyday thinking. Take this concept, for example:

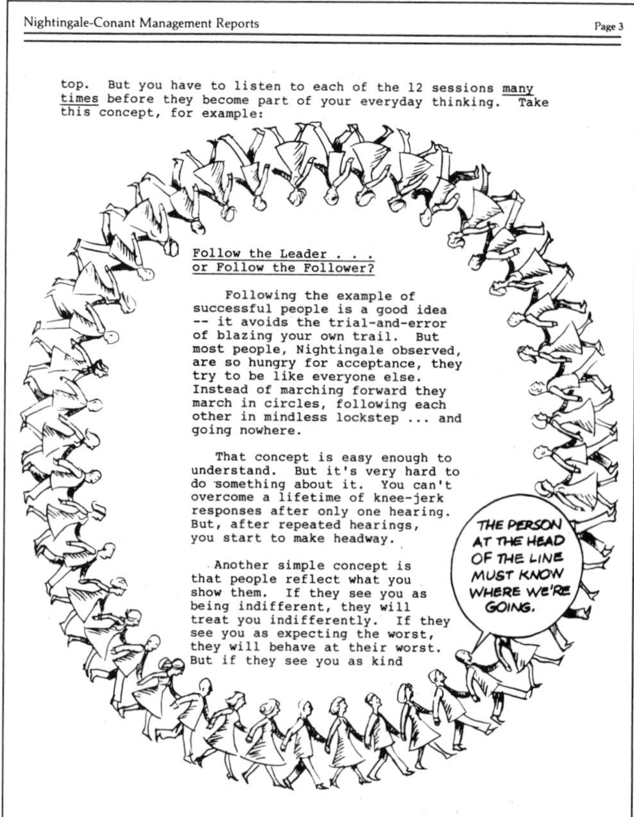

THE PERSON AT THE HEAD OF THE LINE MUST KNOW WHERE WE'RE GOING.

Follow the Leader . . .
or Follow the Follower?

Following the example of successful people is a good idea -- it avoids the trial-and-error of blazing your own trail. But most people, Nightingale observed, are so hungry for acceptance, they try to be like everyone else. Instead of marching forward they march in circles, following each other in mindless lockstep ... and going nowhere.

That concept is easy enough to understand. But it's very hard to do something about it. You can't overcome a lifetime of knee-jerk responses after only one hearing. But, after repeated hearings, you start to make headway.

Another simple concept is that people reflect what you show them. If they see you as being indifferent, they will treat you indifferently. If they see you as expecting the worst, they will behave at their worst. But if they see you as kind

Nightingale-Conant Management Reports — Page 4

and caring, they will treat you with care and kindness.

Could you change the image you present the world after only one hearing? I doubt that anyone could.

Through the miracle of tape recordings, you can hear those messages again and again -- while dressing, while driving, while doing chores -- till they become part of your life. And, in doing so, you can indeed change your life.

Put Your Unused Mental Powers to Work

I can say without hesitation that you are smarter than you think you are. Believe me, most of your capacity for learning, for creating, for memorizing and for profound thinking is fast asleep and almost never used.

There is positive scientific evidence that most people use a mere 5% of their minds. The rest is like a gold mine buried in your own back yard -- a source of unsuspected wealth that already belongs to you ... if only you'd dig it up.

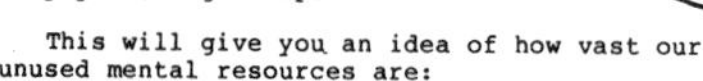

This will give you an idea of how vast our unused mental resources are:

> By using only 50% of our total mental capacity, we could easily learn 40 languages and memorize a 24-volume encyclopedia!
>
> While 50% of mental capacity is not achievable yet, 10% of mental capacity is! I promise that if you diligently perform an exercise described in Session 4 of LEAD THE FIELD, you will within one year be using 10% of your mental capacity ... double the 5% that most of us use.

Money -- How Much Can You Make?

There are two widespread attitudes about money:

1) Money is Nothing; and 2) Money is Everything.

Both attitudes are wrong. To say that money is not important is pretentious and high-falutin'. And please don't split hairs and claim that money is not as important as other things. In areas where money counts, nothing can take its place.

Nightingale-Conant Management Reports — Page 5

It is absolutely essential that you set a goal that is measured in money. It even makes sense, once you reach your goal, to set a new and even higher goal. Session 9 of LEAD THE FIELD shows you how to set goals realistically. More important, it reveals the three factors that determine what you can earn -- factors that you can alter to increase your earning power.

Yes, it's good to have money, and the things money can buy. But you should check every once in a while to make sure you haven't lost the things money can't buy. Fortunately, money, success and spiritual values are all so closely linked, it is almost impossible to achieve the first two and lose the third.

How to Make Your Hard Work Count

Hard work won't hurt you. But it won't get you anywhere either -- not unless it has a special kind of purpose. Without this purpose you're on a treadmill, working up a sweat while going nowhere.

On the other hand, if you do have this special kind of purpose, you don't have to work nearly as hard. And your success is guaranteed. The secret of making your work pay off is revealed in Session 5.

How to Increase Your Efficiency by 50%

Learning how to make your work pay off is a major achievement. Doubling your mental capacity is another. Now, just suppose you then discover how to increase your work efficiency by 50%. Where is your success potential now? Up in the stratosphere!

There's a little-known secret for doing just that. Ivy Lee, America's public relations pioneer and early efficiency expert, developed it at the beginning of the century. He offered it to the president of a small steel company, asked him to try it for six weeks, then pay him whatever he thought it was worth. It wasn't long before he received a check for $25,000 (worth about $300,000 in 1988 dollars). And soon after, that little steel company grew into the giant we call Bethlehem Steel.

The secret is revealed in Session 11. It takes only 3 minutes a day to put it to use. Soon it can be yours.

The Program of Presidents

Many corporate presidents credit their success to Earl Nightingale and this program. Excerpts from their letters are

Four pages of the 6-page letter, printed front and back on 3 sheets 8½″ × 11″.

Nightingale-Conant Management Reports Page 6

enclosed. But even more meaningful is the fact that so many of them wish to share their inspiration with their employees. Typical among the letters we've received is:

> "We've purchased more than 750 cassette albums of 'Lead the Field' ... I can't tell you how pleased we are with the lasting benefits."
> R.W. Butler, CEO
> GTE Directories

Your Free 30-Day Audition Privilege

In Session 2 you learn the danger of being in a rut. (A rut, after all, is really a grave with both ends kicked out.) Also, you learn the importance of taking risks and trying new things.

Well, LEAD THE FIELD is an entirely new thing for you. It will get you out of your rut. And, because you have the right to audition the program for an entire month without charge, there isn't even a risk.

So don't just accept the offer -- leap at it! The peel-off label from the back of your report folder and the enclosed Audition Request Form are all you need.

Respectfully submitted,
Victor Conant, President

EXECUTIVES:

This 12-session cassette program and 64-page progress guide

UNLOCKS YOUR CAPACITY FOR ACHIEVEMENT, SUCCESS AND WEALTH

You will still be harvesting the fruits of this program 20 years from now. But each individual session yields such great profit all by itself, you could stop after just one session and start making a fortune. The very first session teaches you how to become a magnet for good experiences – in other words, how to change your luck.

Even the busiest executive with little or no time to read can profit fully from LEAD THE FIELD because each session is recorded on cassette. Listen and learn while you drive, exercise, shower ...even while waiting for a meeting to start.

Once you hear this program you'll understand why hundreds of U.S. companies routinely give this program to their entire staff.

EARL NIGHTINGALE spent a lifetime researching and studying the phenomenon we call "success." He explains, as only an inspiring teacher can, the simple one-step-at-a-time path that leads to achievement, wealth, and the attainment of happy, rewarding relationships. It's a trail he blazed himself. But he not only shows you the way, he also convinces you that you can complete the journey yourself. And indeed you will – like millions before you.

It Works for Executives and Management Trainees and for the Firms That Employ Them

"I have been a fan of yours for many years since I first purchased your *Lead the Field* album. I listen to your radio show whenever I have the opportunity."

R.M. ALLEN, President
Allen's of Hastings, Inc., Hastings, NB

"It is difficult to express the outstanding benefits I have received as a result of Earl Nightingale's messages. I spend more than 800 hours a year in my car and his programs have opened up a new world for me."

JIM HANSEN, President
J.L. Hansen Associates, Schenectady, NY

"Twenty-seven years ago our company issued me a set of Earl Nightingale's *Lead the Field* on long playing records. Many things have changed in our company over the years, but today we still issue each new sales and management trainee a set of *Lead the Field* on tapes."

GERALD D. REGAN, Director of Dealer Development
Babson Brothers, Oak Brook, IL

"We're into our third year with Nightingale programs, and both veterans and rookies comment on the many valuable, immediately useful ideas they've captured."

JOHN W. HOFFMAN, Sales Training Manager
American Cyanamid, Pearl River, NY

"I believe the success I have achieved can be directly attributed to the ideas, motivations and benefits I have derived from this series. [It] provides me and my family a world of good and a great outlook on life."

PAUL J. McKEEN, President
American Acceptance Corporation, Iowa City, IA

12 SESSIONS TO TOTAL SUCCESS

1. ATTITUDE. Change it and improve your luck. It's easier than you think when Earl Nightingale shows you how.

2. NO MORE RUTS. Ask yourself a certain question each morning and you're on the road to wealth.

3. THOUGHT CONTROL. How to achieve goals by setting them realistically — then thinking about them.

4. MIRACLE OF YOUR MIND. How to tap your mind's hidden resources and double your mental capacity in 30 days.

5. HIGHER REWARDS. Working hard isn't enough. But working in this special way can indeed make you rich.

6. SEED FOR ACHIEVEMENT. How to discover — and exploit — your own unique combination of powers.

7. WINNING MADE EASY. Do you play follow-the-follower instead of follow-the-leader? Switch and start winning.

8. HOW MUCH ARE YOU WORTH? How to assess your potential worth ... and move it up, up, up.

9. MONEY TALK. Where great earning power comes from. Two steps to take to increase yours.

10. WHAT COULD HOLD YOU BACK? The biggest stumbling block to high achievement — and how to overcome it.

11. ACHIEVING GOALS FASTER. The 3-minute-a-day exercise that doubles your efficiency, makes success unavoidable.

12. BECOMING THE LEADER. Tricks and techniques of becoming indispensable, of leading, of holding the lead.

The last page of the letter at left and the inside cover of the portfolio at right. The portfolio—with its illustrations and typeset copy—serves as a kind of lift piece.

This number authorizes

a free 30-day audition of LEAD THE FIELD, the program described in the enclosed Special Report. Please affix it to your Audition Request Form before mailing it.

Susan Crocker
123 Rancho Ave.
Anywhere, CA 92333

The back panel of the portfolio. The name and address are on a pressure-sensitive label that shows through the window of the kraft outer envelope. To order, you peel off the label and affix it to the order form.

The 8½″ × 11″ order form, printed in 4-color. The top portion shows and describes the product itself, acting as a kind of mini-circular.

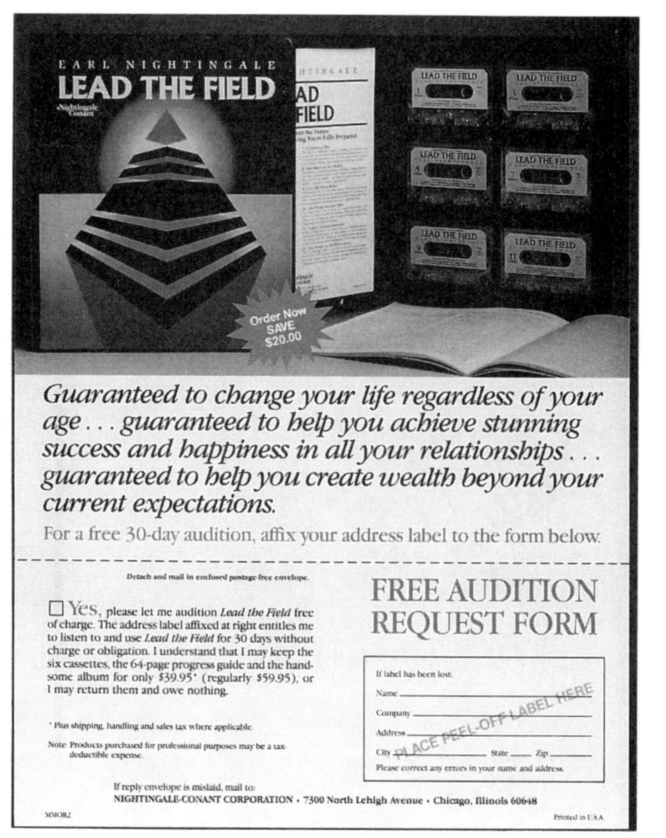

EARL NIGHTINGALE
LEAD THE FIELD
Order Now SAVE $20.00

Guaranteed to change your life regardless of your age . . . guaranteed to help you achieve stunning success and happiness in all your relationships . . . guaranteed to help you create wealth beyond your current expectations.

For a free 30-day audition, affix your address label to the form below.

Detach and mail in enclosed postage-free envelope.

☐ Yes, please let me audition *Lead the Field* free of charge. The address label affixed at right entitles me to listen to and use *Lead the Field* for 30 days without charge or obligation. I understand that I may keep the six cassettes, the 64-page progress guide and the handsome album for only $39.95* (regularly $59.95), or I may return them and owe nothing.

* Plus shipping, handling and sales tax where applicable.

Note: Products purchased for professional purposes may be a tax-deductible expense.

FREE AUDITION REQUEST FORM

If label has been lost:
Name ______
Company ______
Address ______
City ______ State ____ Zip ______
PLACE PEEL-OFF LABEL HERE
Please correct any errors in your name and address.

If reply envelope is mislaid, mail to:
NIGHTINGALE-CONANT CORPORATION • 7300 North Lehigh Avenue • Chicago, Illinois 60648

MMOR2

Printed in U.S.A.

The business reply envelope shown front and back. The address—30-Day FREE TRIAL''—reinforces the offer. The back of the BRE asks for referrals.

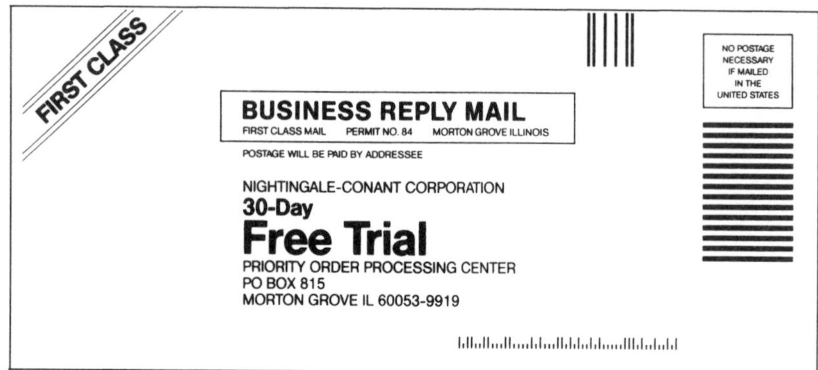

Please let us know of any friends who would like to receive our catalog.

☐ Mr. ☐ Ms. ☐ Mrs.
Name ______
Company ______
Address ______
City ______ State ____ Zip ______
Phone (____) ______

☐ Mr. ☐ Ms. ☐ Mrs.
Name ______
Company ______
Address ______
City ______ State ____ Zip ______
Phone (____) ______

In recent years, Nightingale-Conant has chafed over the excessive size and non-automatability of this mailing. They stepped up efforts to beat it, but haven't succeeded.

They added a tip-on sticker to the envelope which lifted results. But I think the copy on the sticker is wrong.

In my opinion, the mailing owes its longevity to the fact that it's uncolorful and unspectacular. Prospects who don't respond the first time don't remember the second time they see it. So the message has many opportunities to seep into the prospects' minds until they are finally ready to buy.

If a highly successful mailing does have spectacular graphics, however, I urge my client to find new graphics that will work with the same copy. That way, people won't say when they see it for the third or fourth time, ''Oh, I've already seen that,'' and throw it away.

Finally, I would remind all my creative colleagues that getting better is one of the great joys of getting older and urge them not to fight it.

The Secrets of Power Negotiating

Don Kanter, who wrote this Grand Control for Nightingale-Conant, is a native Chicagoan with a degree in editorial journalism. He began in retail advertising and moved to Ward's catalog, where he became copy chief. After stints at Signet Club Plan in Cambridge, Massachusetts, and the legendary Chicago agency Stone & Adler, Kanter went on his own nine years ago. His principal client is Amoco, and he also does work for *Encyclopaedia Britannica,* the Peruvian Connection, Metromail, and others.

Don Kanter:
I never attempt to start creative work until I've done an advertising strategy for the project. The strategy focuses me on what will really sell the product or service. (The format and detail of the strategy were taught to me by Young & Rubicam after they bought Stone & Adler, where I worked for many years.) The client has to approve the strategy before I start creative. That tends to avoid the painful sessions that start: ''Oh, but I wasn't expecting anything like that.''

BULK RATE
U.S. POSTAGE
PAID
NIGHTINGALE-
CONANT
CORPORATION

THE
QUESTION IS NOT:
"AM I A NEGOTIATOR?"
LIKE IT OR NOT,
YOU ARE.

THE REAL QUESTION IS:
"AM I A GOOD
NEGOTIATOR?"

YOU HAVE A
LOT RIDING ON THAT
ANSWER.

NICK
P.O.
Jacksonville, FL 32241

Mailer: Nightingale-Conant
Package: *Power Negotiating*
Project Mgr.: Mark Boyle
Writer: Don Kanter
Designer: Dick Sachs
First Mailed: 1988
The startling 6″ × 9″ outside envelope, printed and addressed vertically. All black and white.

Special introductory price—$20 off!!

Nightingale Conant

> Whether you realize it or not, you negotiate every day: in your business life and your personal life.
>
> Since you must negotiate, why not be good at it? It can make a big difference.

Dear Friend:

It's easy to become a good negotiator. Surprisingly easy.

We'll prove it by sending you, on approval, a "private seminar" by Roger Dawson, one of the world's top negotiators.

This "private seminar" -- a set of six audiocassette tapes -- contains the same material that thousands of people pay $495 to hear in Dawson's seminars and lectures.

It won't cost you $495. It will cost you only $39.95 -- but only if you believe you will profit many times over that $39.95. If you don't believe it, simply return the program within 30 days and it will cost you nothing.

* * *

For starters, Dawson demolishes some myths about negotiating:

Myth: Negotiating is a highly specialized activity for weighty matters like union contracts and nuclear arms control.

Fact: Everybody negotiates. Some negotiations are very important: a new job, a new house, a new car. Some are less important: under what conditions can your teenage son borrow the car? But everybody negotiates, all the time.

Myth: Negotiation involves confrontation. In negotiations, somebody wins and somebody loses.

Fact: A good negotiator will make sure the other guy feels he got a good deal. The good negotiator wants both sides to win.

(over, please)

7300 North Lehigh Avenue • Chicago, Illinois 60648 • Phone 1-800-323-5552

Myth: A good negotiator requires the personality of a dead fish: stern, cold, unbending.

Fact: Negotiations should not be a rigid, stress-laden experience. "Nice guys" do make good negotiators.

After setting you straight on the fundamentals, Dawson proceeds to fill you in on negotiating tactics. Some of these tactics can be rough, and Dawson doesn't necessarily advise you to use them...but because they can be used against you, Dawson wants you to know what they are. He also wants you to know what the counter-tactic is for each tactic. Examples:

Tactic: "Higher Authority." ("It looks good, but I've got to show it to my Board of Directors.")

Counter-tactic: Remove recourse to "higher authority" at the start. ("Now, you do have the authority to make the decision, don't you?")

Tactic: "Nibbling." Get a little bit more after everything has been agreed to.

Counter-tactic: Make the "nibbler" appear petty.

Tactic: "Good Guy/Bad Guy."

Counter-tactic: "I know exactly what you're doing."

...and eight more common negotiating tactics.

But this program is much more than a list of negotiating tactics. Dawson gives you...

...the five key facts that make negotiations essential. (One of them: Everything you'll want in life is owned or controlled by somebody else.)

...the three stages of a good negotiator.(The first one is one that many people never think of).

...the five "training principles" for becoming a good negotiator. (Prime principle: Negotiating is always a two-way affair, and the pressure is on the other party as much as it is on you.)

* * *

Because power is essential to the success of negotiations, Dawson shows you the structure of power as you probably have never seen it before. He enumerates eight different kinds of power, including "information power," which many companies foster by deliberately withholding information from given echelons in the organization...even though the information itself is of no special value to anybody. He then tells you how to manipulate the different types of power, and how to counter or blunt the effect of power.

* * *

Are you an "Amiable"? A "Pragmatic"? An "Analytical"? An Extrovert"?

You'll find out how to evaluate your own personality -- and, more importantly, the personalities of those with whom you're negotiating. To be a successful negotiator, you'll have to make adjustments in the way you "come on." Dawson will tell you what adjustments, and how to make them.

He'll take you into the fascinating world of body language, where the rate of eye blinking is a tipoff to how the negotiations are proceeding. He'll explain why, if you're negotiating with persons who smoke, to wait until they light up before getting down to business.

You'll also learn how to spot hidden meanings in what seems like normal conversation. Sometimes people mean the opposite of what they say. You'll learn the tipoffs to this type of "reverse" language.

* * *

When you finish this program, you will have every tool you need to become at least a good negotiator...and quite probably an expert one.

How long will it take you to finish? Well, that's one of the great things about an audiocassette program: you go at your own pace. Unlike a seminar or lecture, where you have to show up at a certain time, you can "study" Roger Dawson's programs when you wish...and where you wish ...wherever there's a tape player available: in your home, your office, your car.

See for yourself; it's easy and you risk nothing. Simply sign the Free Trial Certificate and mail it back to us in the enclosed postage-paid envelope. Send no money.

We'll send you Roger Dawson's complete audiocassette program: "The Secrets of Power Negotiating."

> Audition it...again and again if you wish. Then, if you don't believe you will profit many times over the special introductory price of $39.95 **(that's $20 off the regular price of $59.95)**, ignore our invoice, return the program within 30 days...and owe nothing.

* * *

Remember that all of us are negotiators, whether we want to be or not. Negotiating is part of life.

If we are bad negotiators, we suffer: in personal feelings, in personal relationships, in growth and in prosperity.

If we are good negotiators, we prosper in these same areas.

This program will help you to become a good negotiator. It will make a major and positive difference in your life.

And you risk nothing to prove it to your own satisfaction. Return the Trial Certificate today.

Yours cordially,

Vic Conant

Vic Conant

P.S. While most people think of "negotiating" in terms of business situations, negotiating occurs regularly in your personal life, too. Being a good negotiator means greater satisfaction, not only in business, but also throughout your life's experiences.

P.P.S. Act now and you'll receive an additional bonus-your FREE POWER PACK of negotiating secrets!

The 4-page letter.

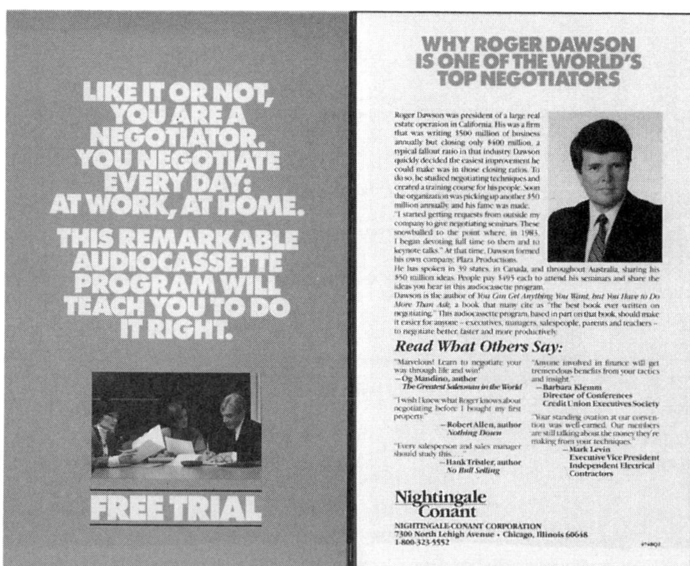

LIKE IT OR NOT, YOU ARE A NEGOTIATOR. YOU NEGOTIATE EVERY DAY: AT WORK, AT HOME.
THIS REMARKABLE AUDIOCASSETTE PROGRAM WILL TEACH YOU TO DO IT RIGHT.
FREE TRIAL
WHY ROGER DAWSON IS ONE OF THE WORLD'S TOP NEGOTIATORS
Read What Others Say:
Nightingale Conant

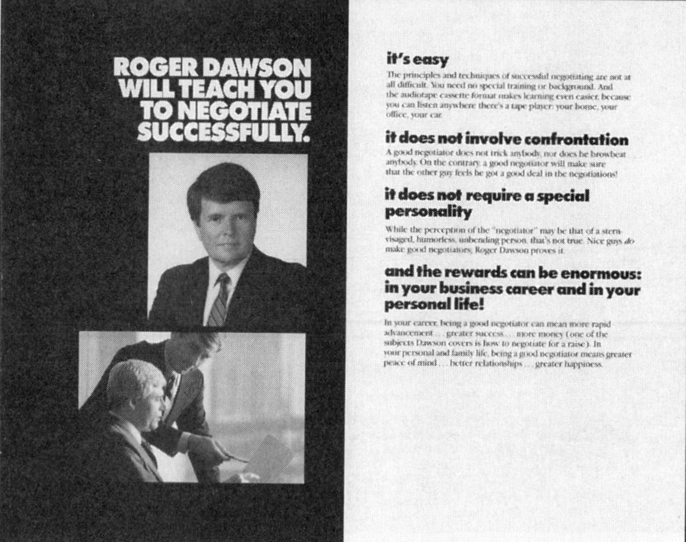

ROGER DAWSON WILL TEACH YOU TO NEGOTIATE SUCCESSFULLY.
it's easy
it does not involve confrontation
it does not require a special personality
and the rewards can be enormous: in your business career and in your personal life!

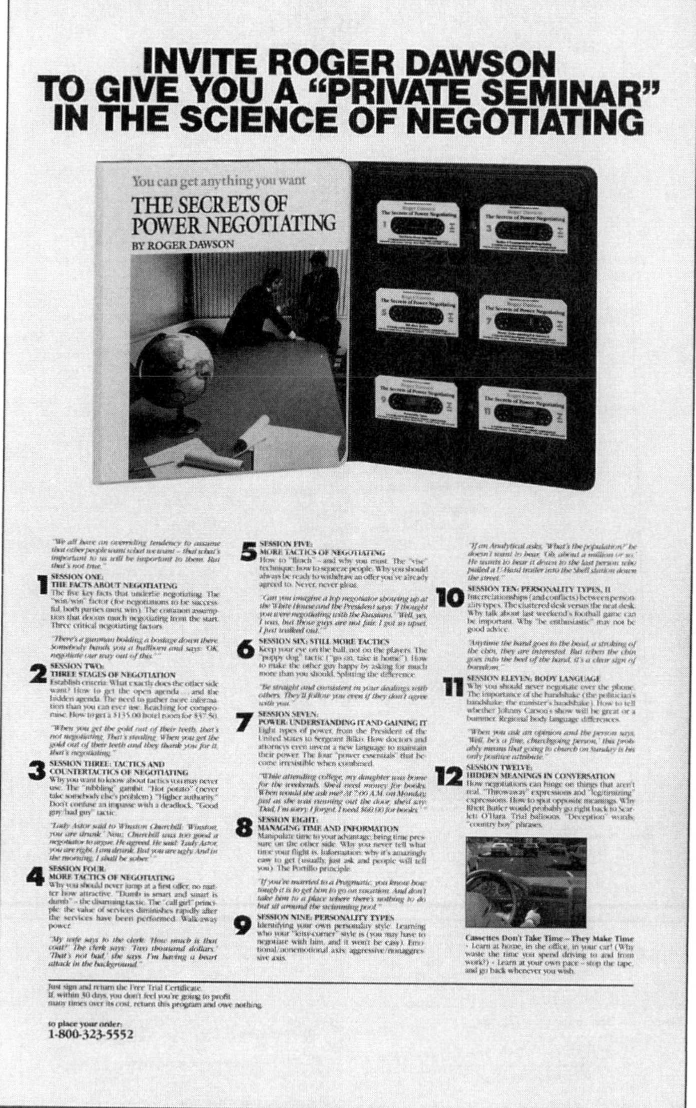

INVITE ROGER DAWSON TO GIVE YOU A "PRIVATE SEMINAR" IN THE SCIENCE OF NEGOTIATING
You can get anything you want
THE SECRETS OF POWER NEGOTIATING
BY ROGER DAWSON
1-800-323-5552

The 4-color brochure that starts out at 5½″ × 8½″ and unfolds twice to an 11″ × 17″ broadside. The back panel contains testimonials.

I look for the best designer I can find, because he or she is going to make or break the mailing. A good designer knows that visual communication is much faster and much stronger than verbal communication, and when he understands what the mailing is supposed to accomplish, he will bring it to life. (Incidentally, Dick Sachs, who designed the Nightingale-Conant mailing, is the best I've ever worked with.)

Ideas on direct mail in general: Maybe it's the recession, and maybe it's advancing age, but I seem to see fewer and fewer "quality" mailings . . . and more and more "formula" or "I know, but it works" type of mailings. It used to be that one prided himself or herself on being a good salesperson; today, the emphasis seems to be on finding gimmicks that work.

FREE GIFT!
POWER PACK 'secrets'
help you come out ahead,
every time.

The lift piece.

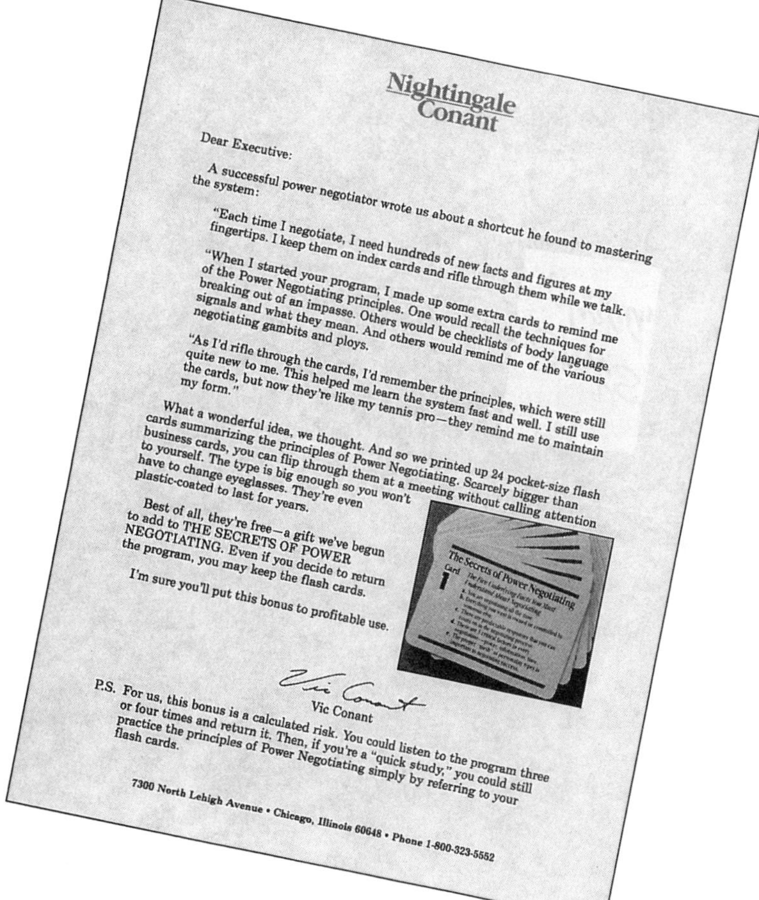

Nightingale
Conant

Dear Executive:

A successful power negotiator wrote us about a shortcut he found to mastering the system:

"Each time I negotiate, I need hundreds of new facts and figures at my fingertips. I keep them on index cards and rifle through them while we talk.

"When I started your program, I made up some extra cards to remind me of the Power Negotiating principles. One would recall the techniques for breaking out of an impasse. Others would be checklists of body language signals and what they mean. And others would remind me of the various negotiating gambits and ploys.

"As I'd rifle through the cards, I'd remember the principles, which were still quite new to me. This helped me learn the system fast and well. I still use the cards, but now they're like my tennis pro—they remind me to maintain my form."

What a wonderful idea, we thought. And so we printed up 24 pocket-size flash cards summarizing the principles of Power Negotiating. Scarcely bigger than business cards, you can flip through them at a meeting without calling attention to yourself. The type is big enough so you won't have to change eyeglasses. They're even plastic-coated to last for years.

Best of all, they're free—a gift we've begun to add to THE SECRETS OF POWER NEGOTIATING. Even if you decide to return the program, you may keep the flash cards.

I'm sure you'll put this bonus to profitable use.

Vic Conant

P.S. For us, this bonus is a calculated risk. You could listen to the program three or four times and return it. Then, if you're a "quick study," you could still practice the principles of Power Negotiating simply by referring to your flash cards.

7300 North Lehigh Avenue • Chicago, Illinois 60648 • Phone 1-800-323-5552

Special introductory price— $20 off!!

Nightingale Conant

30-DAY FREE TRIAL CERTIFICATE

Plus a FREE GIFT— negotiating secrets POWER PACK

ISSUED TO:

NICK HUMPHREYS

This certificate entitles the person named above to audition Roger Dawson's audiocassette program

THE SECRETS OF POWER NEGOTIATING

for 30 days at no cost and with no obligation.

DETACH ALONG PERFORATION AND RETURN LOWER PORTION

DDVXZAS

YES! Please send me THE SECRETS OF POWER NEGOTIATING for my 30-day FREE TRIAL. If I decide to keep the program, I'll save $20 and pay just $39.95. If I am not completely satisfied, I may return the program, PAY NOTHING and keep my complete POWER PACK deck of negotiating secrets.

Signature________________________

FREE POWER PACK

NICK
P.O.
Jacksonville, FL 32241

This special offer expires on: March 21, 1990

7300 North Lehigh Avenue • Chicago, Illinois 60648 • 1-800-323-5552

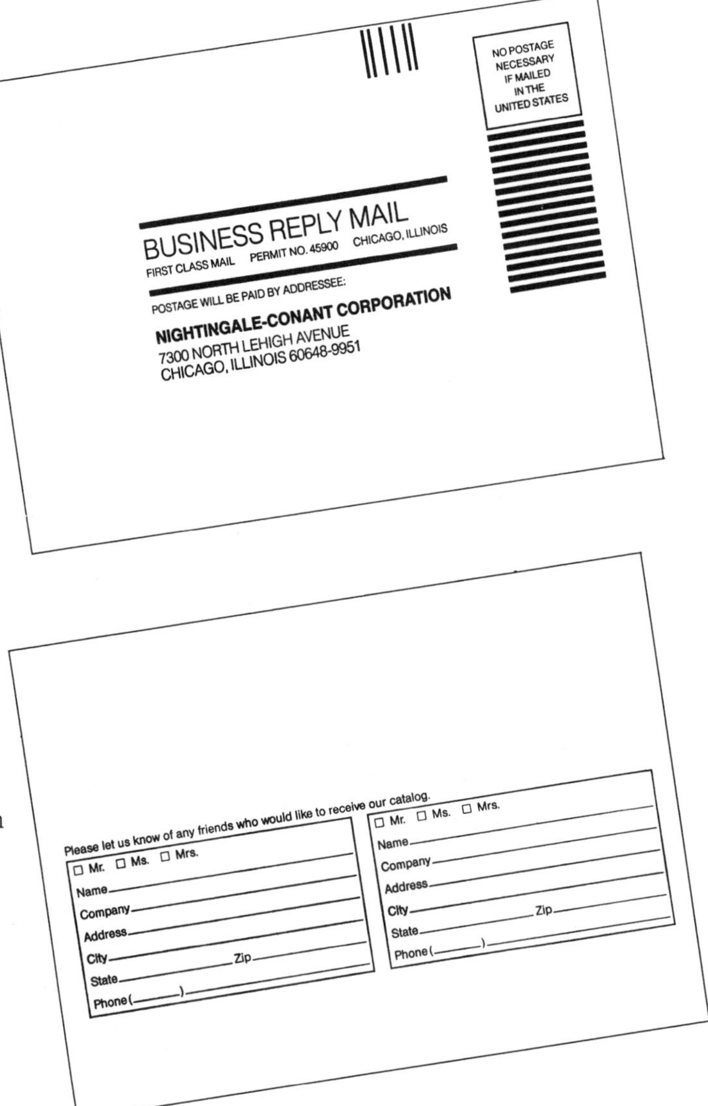

NO POSTAGE NECESSARY IF MAILED IN THE UNITED STATES

BUSINESS REPLY MAIL

FIRST CLASS MAIL PERMIT NO. 45900 CHICAGO, ILLINOIS

POSTAGE WILL BE PAID BY ADDRESSEE:

NIGHTINGALE-CONANT CORPORATION
7300 NORTH LEHIGH AVENUE
CHICAGO, ILLINOIS 60648-9951

Please let us know of any friends who would like to receive our catalog.

☐ Mr. ☐ Ms. ☐ Mrs.
Name____
Company____
Address____
City____ Zip____
State____
Phone (____)____

☐ Mr. ☐ Ms. ☐ Mrs.
Name____
Company____
Address____
City____ Zip____
State____
Phone (____)____

The order card, printed in red and black. Also shown is the business reply envelope, front and back; note the back of the BRE asks for referrals.

23

The Catalog

It was a given that no catalog could possibly win an Axel Andersson Award. Catalogs are constantly changing merchandise and changing covers.

Over the years I have ordered slides for lectures from Cinegraph Slides of Garden Grove, California. Enclosed with every slide order is a catalog. Plus, of course, the *Who's Mailing What!* library of samples continually

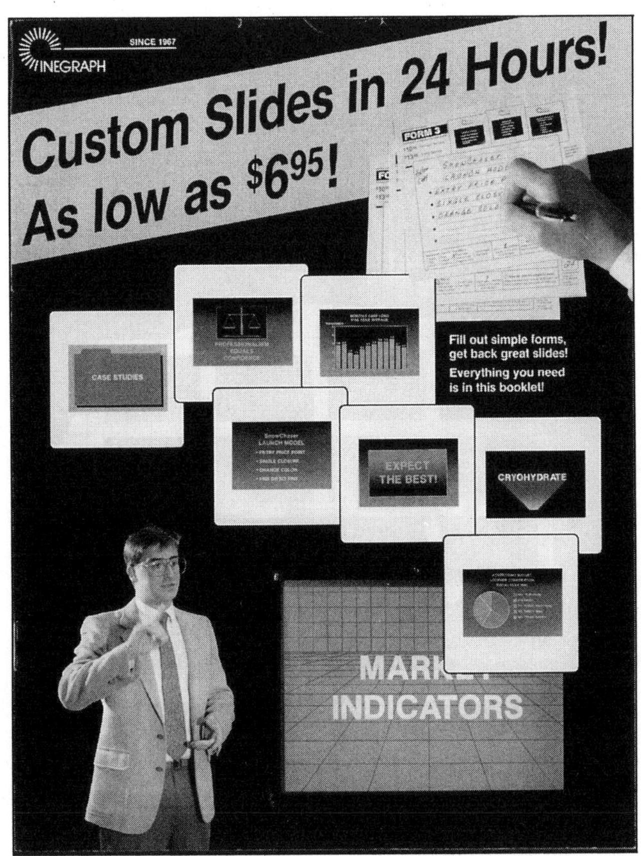

MAILER: Cinegraph Slides, Inc.
PACKAGE: Catalog
PROJECT MGR.: Glen Wolfe
WRITER: Glen Wolfe
DESIGNER: Glen Wolfe
FIRST MAILED: 1987
The cover, inside pages, and back cover of this 4-color, 16-page catalog.

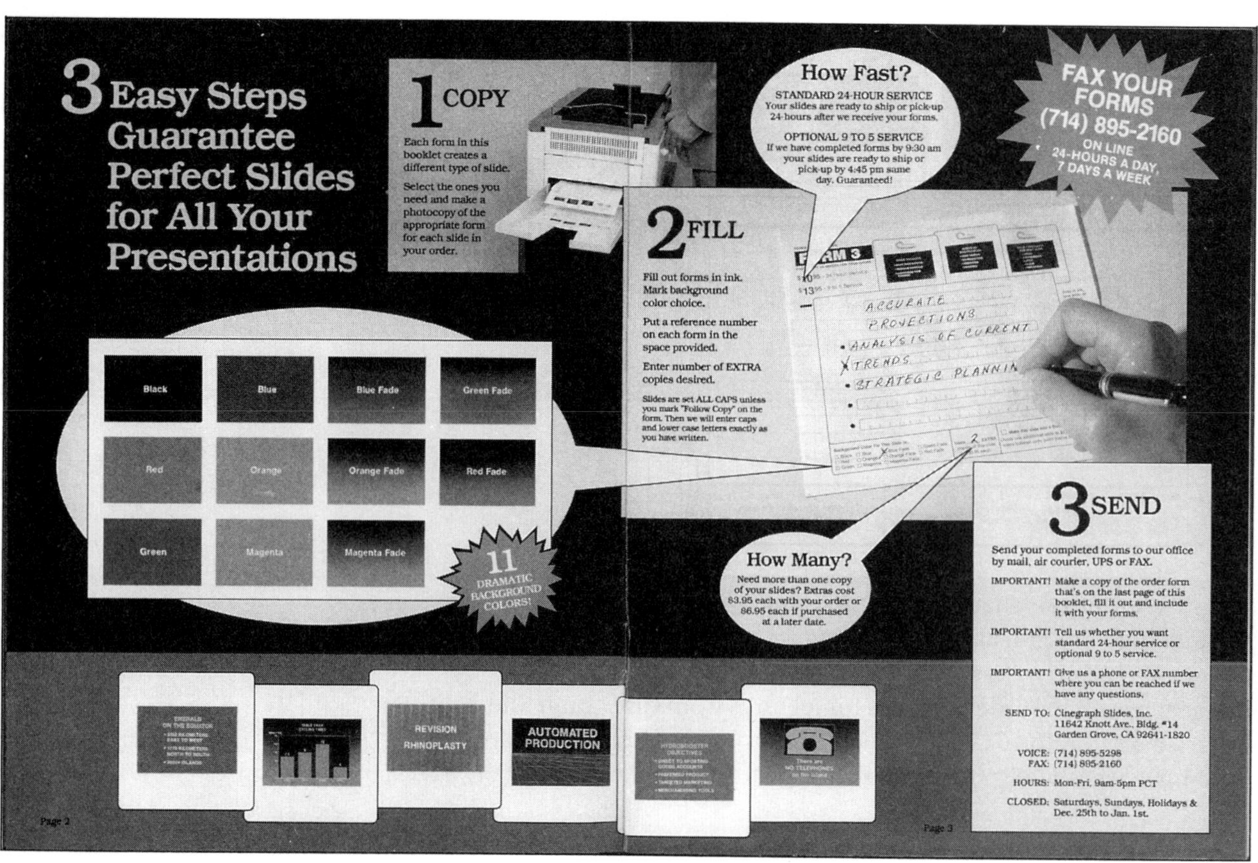
3 Easy Steps Guarantee Perfect Slides for All Your Presentations
1 COPY
Each form in this booklet creates a different type of slide.
Select the ones you need and make a photocopy of the appropriate form for each slide in your order.
How Fast?
STANDARD 24-HOUR SERVICE
Your slides are ready to ship or pick-up 24-hours after we receive your forms.
OPTIONAL 9 TO 5 SERVICE
If we have completed forms by 9:30 am your slides are ready to ship or pick-up by 4:45 pm same day. Guaranteed!
FAX YOUR FORMS
(714) 895-2160
ON LINE 24-HOURS A DAY, 7 DAYS A WEEK
2 FILL
Fill out forms in ink. Mark background color choice.
Put a reference number on each form in the space provided.
Enter number of EXTRA copies desired.
Slides are set ALL CAPS unless you mark "Follow Copy" on the form. Then we will enter caps and lower case letters exactly as you have written.
FORM 3
ACCURATE
PROJECTIONS
ANALYSIS OF CURRENT
TRENDS
STRATEGIC PLANNIN
Black
Blue
Blue Fade
Green Fade
Red
Orange
Orange Fade
Red Fade
Green
Magenta
Magenta Fade
11 DRAMATIC BACKGROUND COLORS!
How Many?
Need more than one copy of your slides? Extras cost $3.95 each with your order or $6.95 each if purchased at a later date.
3 SEND
Send your completed forms to our office by mail, air courier, UPS or FAX.
IMPORTANT! Make a copy of the order form that's on the last page of this booklet, fill it out and include it with your forms.
IMPORTANT! Tell us whether you want standard 24-hour service or optional 9 to 5 service.
IMPORTANT! Give us a phone or FAX number where you can be reached if we have any questions.
SEND TO: Cinegraph Slides, Inc. 11642 Knott Ave., Bldg. #14 Garden Grove, CA 92641-1820
VOICE: (714) 895-5298
FAX: (714) 895-2160
HOURS: Mon-Fri, 9am-5pm PCT
CLOSED: Saturdays, Sundays, Holidays & Dec. 25th to Jan. 1st.
REVISION RHINOPLASTY
AUTOMATED PRODUCTION
Page 2
Page 3

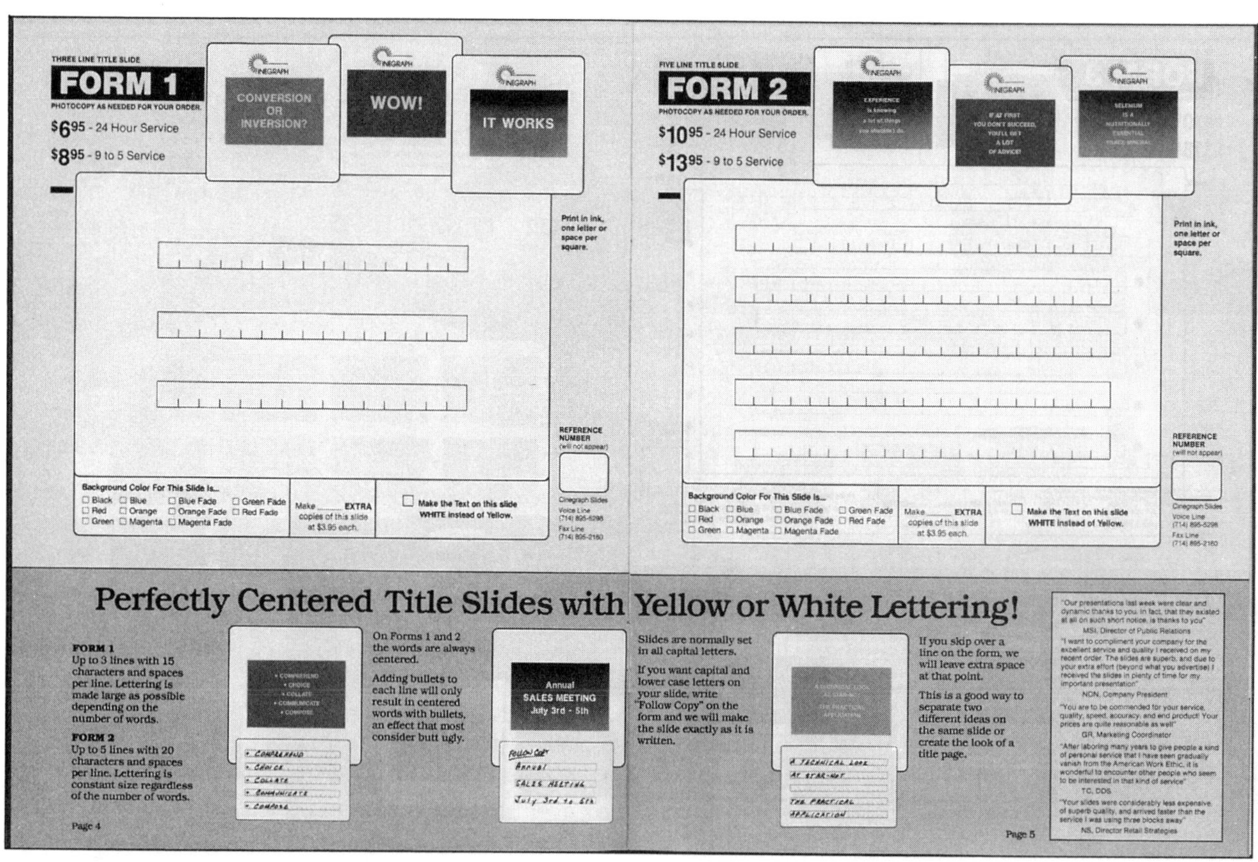
THREE LINE TITLE SLIDE
FORM 1
PHOTOCOPY AS NEEDED FOR YOUR ORDER.
$6.95 - 24 Hour Service
$8.95 - 9 to 5 Service
CONVERSION OR INVERSION?
WOW!
IT WORKS
Print in ink, one letter or space per square.
REFERENCE NUMBER (will not appear)
Background Color For This Slide Is...
Black Blue Blue Fade Green Fade Red Orange Orange Fade Red Fade Green Magenta Magenta Fade
Make ____ EXTRA copies of this slide at $3.95 each.
Make the Text on this slide WHITE instead of Yellow.
Cinegraph Slides Voice Line (714) 895-5298 Fax Line (714) 895-2160
FIVE LINE TITLE SLIDE
FORM 2
PHOTOCOPY AS NEEDED FOR YOUR ORDER.
$10.95 - 24 Hour Service
$13.95 - 9 to 5 Service
Perfectly Centered Title Slides with Yellow or White Lettering!
FORM 1
Up to 3 lines with 15 characters and spaces per line. Lettering is made large as possible depending on the number of words.
FORM 2
Up to 5 lines with 20 characters and spaces per line. Lettering is constant size regardless of the number of words.
On Forms 1 and 2 the words are always centered.
Adding bullets to each line will only result in centered words with bullets, an effect that most consider butt ugly.
Annual SALES MEETING July 3rd - 5th
Slides are normally set in all capital letters.
If you want capital and lower case letters on your slide, write "Follow Copy" on the form and we will make the slide exactly as it is written.
If you skip over a line on the form, we will leave extra space at that point.
This is a good way to separate two different ideas on the same slide or create the look of a title page.
"Our presentations last week were clear and dynamic thanks to you. In fact, that they existed at all on such short notice, is thanks to you"
MSI, Director of Public Relations
"I want to compliment your company for the excellent service and quality I received on my recent order. The slides are superb, and due to your extra effort (beyond what you advertise) I received the slides in plenty of time for my important presentation"
NDN, Company President
"You are to be commended for your service, quality, speed, accuracy, and end product! Your prices are quite reasonable as well"
GR, Marketing Coordinator
"After laboring many years to give people a kind of personal service that I have seen gradually vanish from the American Work Ethic, it is wonderful to encounter other people who seem to be interested in that kind of service"
TC, DDS
"Your slides were considerably less expensive, of superb quality, and arrived faster than the service I was using three blocks away"
NS, Director Retail Strategies
Page 4
Page 5

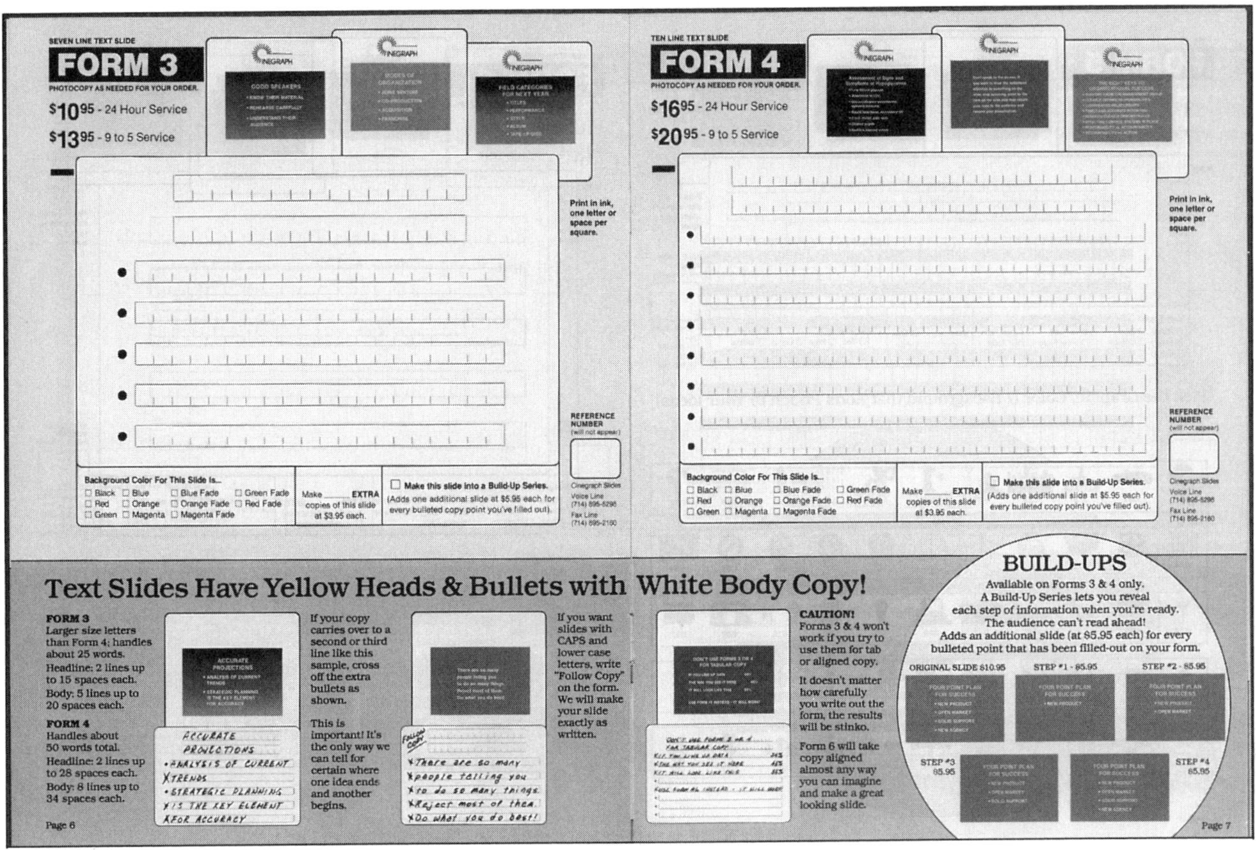
SEVEN LINE TEXT SLIDE
FORM 3
PHOTOCOPY AS NEEDED FOR YOUR ORDER.
$10.95 - 24 Hour Service
$13.95 - 9 to 5 Service
TEN LINE TEXT SLIDE
FORM 4
PHOTOCOPY AS NEEDED FOR YOUR ORDER.
$16.95 - 24 Hour Service
$20.95 - 9 to 5 Service
Text Slides Have Yellow Heads & Bullets with White Body Copy!
FORM 3
Larger size letters than Form 4; handles about 25 words.
Headline: 2 lines up to 15 spaces each.
Body: 5 lines up to 20 spaces each.
FORM 4
Handles about 50 words total.
Headline: 2 lines up to 28 spaces each.
Body: 8 lines up to 34 spaces each.
If your copy carries over to a second or third line like this sample, cross off the extra bullets as shown.
This is important! It's the only way we can tell for certain where one idea ends and another begins.
If you want slides with CAPS and lower case letters, write "Follow Copy" on the form. We will make your slide exactly as written.
CAUTION!
Forms 3 & 4 won't work if you try to use them for tab or aligned copy.
It doesn't matter how carefully you write out the form, the results will be stinko.
Form 6 will take copy aligned almost any way you can imagine and make a great looking slide.
BUILD-UPS
Available on Forms 3 & 4 only.
A Build-Up Series lets you reveal each step of information when you're ready.
The audience can't read ahead!
Adds an additional slide (at $5.95 each) for every bulleted point that has been filled-out on your form.
Page 6
Page 7

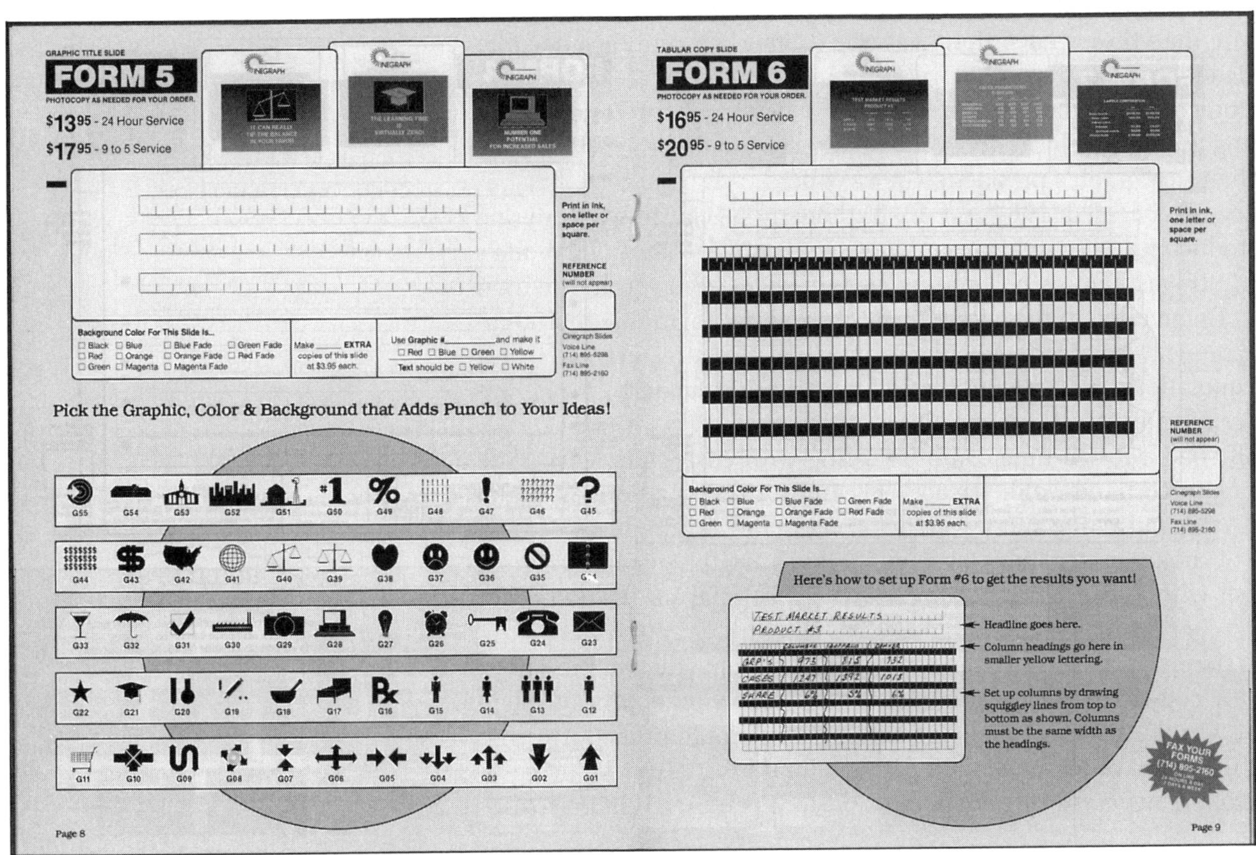
GRAPHIC TITLE SLIDE
FORM 5
PHOTOCOPY AS NEEDED FOR YOUR ORDER.
$13.95 - 24 Hour Service
$17.95 - 9 to 5 Service
Pick the Graphic, Color & Background that Adds Punch to Your Ideas!
TABULAR COPY SLIDE
FORM 6
PHOTOCOPY AS NEEDED FOR YOUR ORDER.
$16.95 - 24 Hour Service
$20.95 - 9 to 5 Service
Here's how to set up Form #6 to get the results you want!
Headline goes here.
Column headings go here in smaller yellow lettering.
Set up columns by drawing squiggley lines from top to bottom as shown. Columns must be the same width as the headings.
Page 8
Page 9

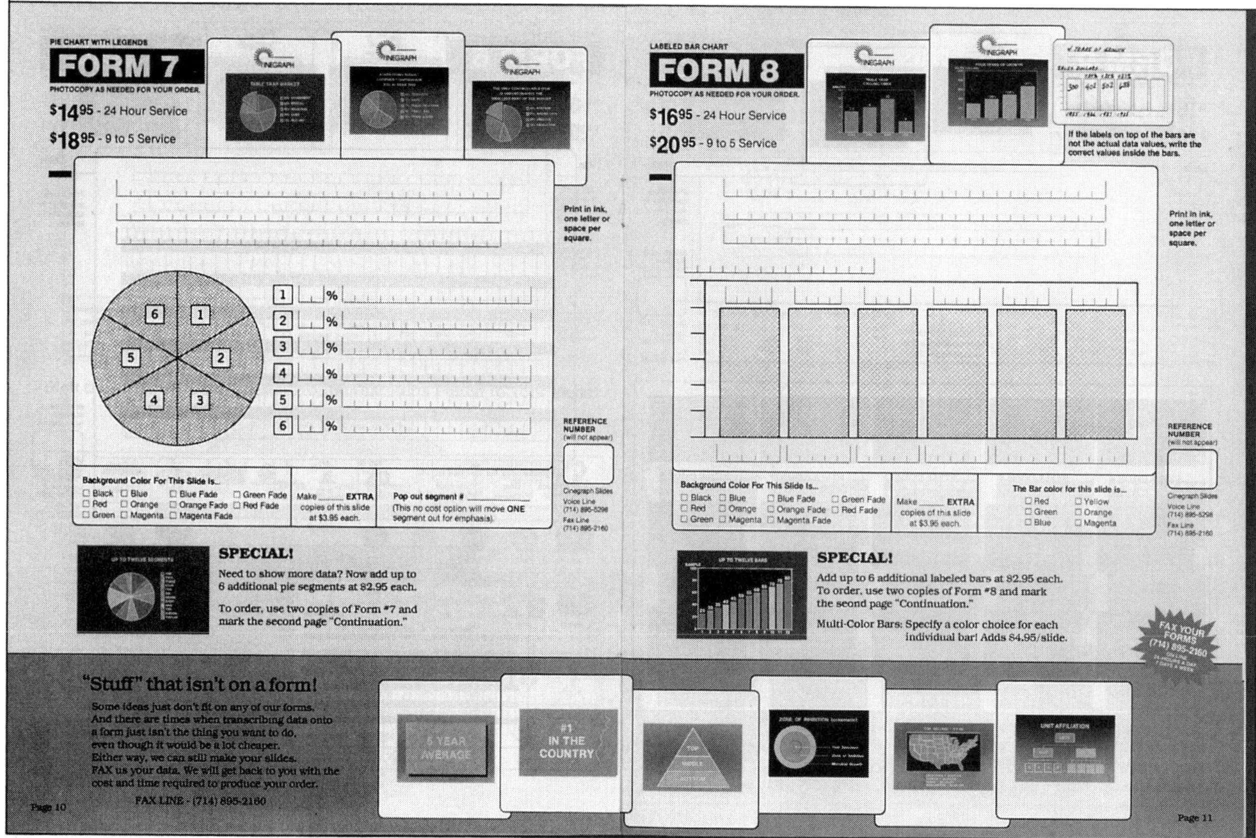

received Cinegraph Slides catalogs through the mail—the same catalog for more than three years. Here was one catalog out of thousands that qualified for an Axel Award!

No other direct marketers have done a better job of conceptually thinking through their products and services or treating their customers well than Cinegraph's president, Glen Wolfe.

Cinegraph began in 1967 as a small company specializing in scripting and producing audiovisual presentations for business clients. In Wolfe's words, "It was hard as hell getting custom slides, so I set up my own shop." He invested in his own typesetting and photographic reproduction systems to be able to create custom slides of charts, graphs, headlines, quotations, etc. Finding himself with an overcapacity, Wolfe put out a catalog offering custom slides to businesses.

Wolfe had a tough time communicating with customers; each slide order required hand-holding and back-and-forth discussions with the client. What put Wolfe's show on the road was the development of a full range of cookie-cutter slides with highly inventive designs in all colors, together with a redesigned catalog in which each page is its own order form.

You simply photocopy a page for each slide design you want to order, write the copy in the spaces provided, and choose your colors and slide format. On the back cover of the catalog is a simple order form that tallies the entire order along with payment options. It's quick and easy. Wolfe offers twenty-four-hour service or, for a surcharge, nine-to-five service.

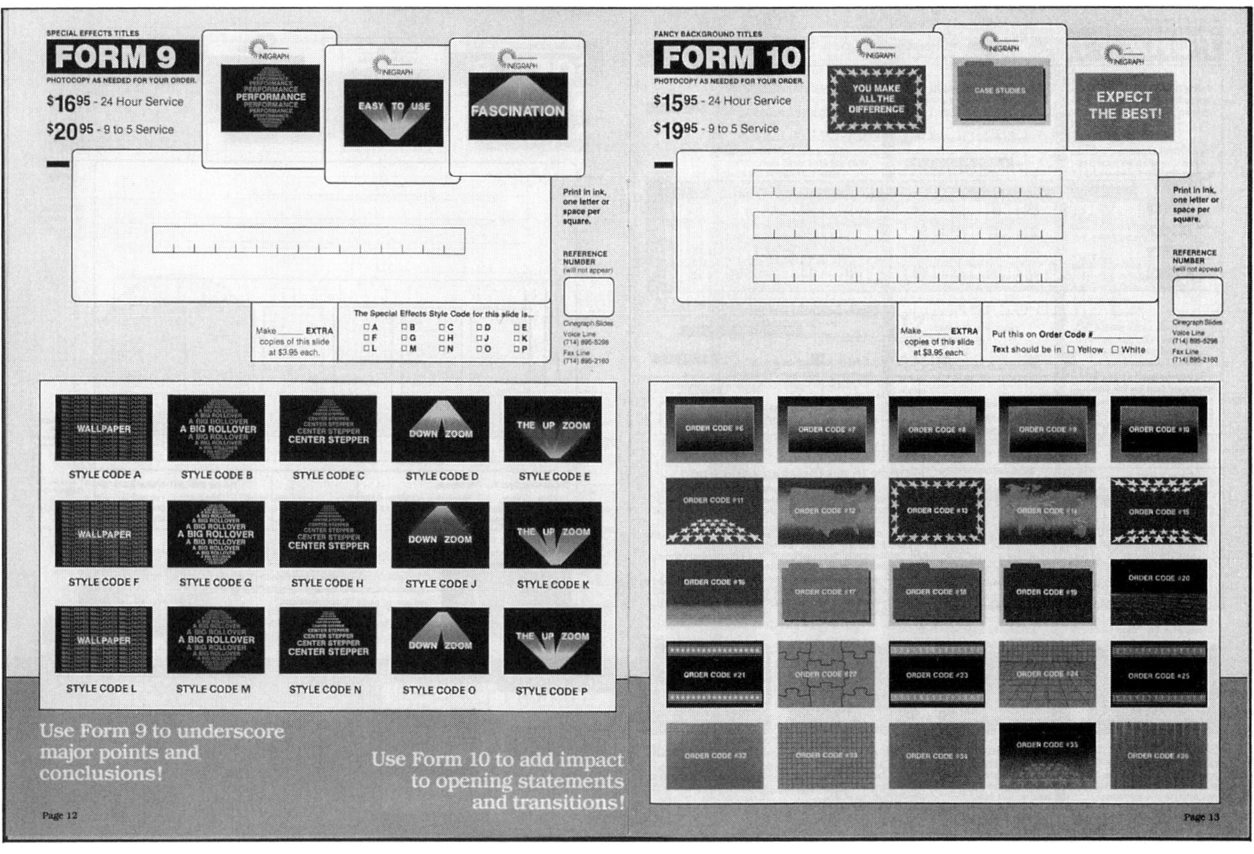

SPECIAL EFFECTS TITLES

FORM 9

PHOTOCOPY AS NEEDED FOR YOUR ORDER.

$16.95 - 24 Hour Service

$20.95 - 9 to 5 Service

Print in ink, one letter or space per square.

REFERENCE NUMBER (will not appear)

Make ____ EXTRA copies of this slide at $3.95 each.

The Special Effects Style Code for this slide is...

☐ A ☐ B ☐ C ☐ D ☐ E
☐ F ☐ G ☐ H ☐ J ☐ K
☐ L ☐ M ☐ N ☐ O ☐ P

Cinegraph Slides
Voice Line (714) 895-5298
Fax Line (714) 895-2160

STYLE CODE A · STYLE CODE B · STYLE CODE C · STYLE CODE D · STYLE CODE E
STYLE CODE F · STYLE CODE G · STYLE CODE H · STYLE CODE J · STYLE CODE K
STYLE CODE L · STYLE CODE M · STYLE CODE N · STYLE CODE O · STYLE CODE P

Use Form 9 to underscore major points and conclusions!

Page 12

FANCY BACKGROUND TITLES

FORM 10

PHOTOCOPY AS NEEDED FOR YOUR ORDER.

$15.95 - 24 Hour Service

$19.95 - 9 to 5 Service

Print in ink, one letter or space per square.

REFERENCE NUMBER (will not appear)

Make ____ EXTRA copies of this slide at $3.95 each.

Put this on Order Code # ______

Text should be in ☐ Yellow ☐ White

Cinegraph Slides
Voice Line (714) 895-5298
Fax Line (714) 895-2160

Use Form 10 to add impact to opening statements and transitions!

Page 13

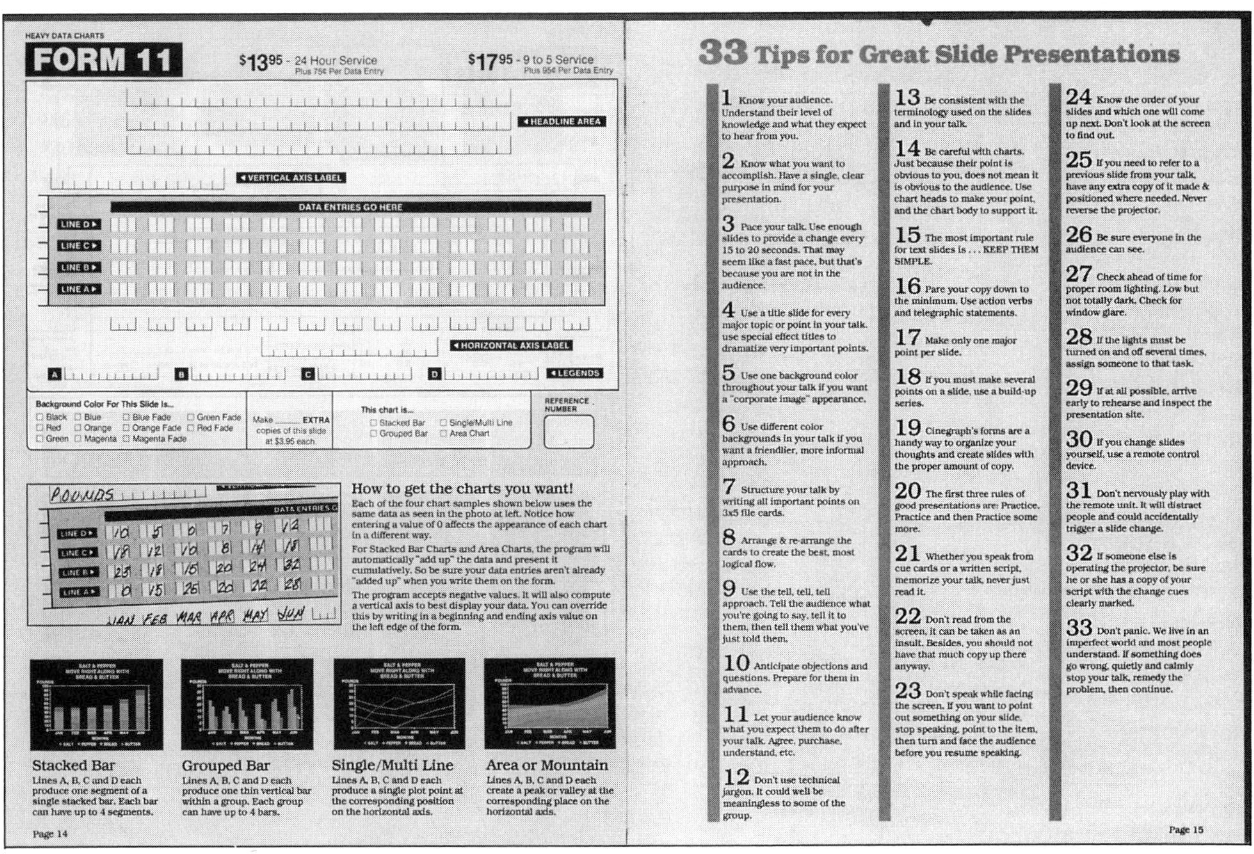

HEAVY DATA CHARTS

FORM 11

$13.95 - 24 Hour Service
Plus 75¢ Per Data Entry

$17.95 - 9 to 5 Service
Plus 95¢ Per Data Entry

◀ HEADLINE AREA

◀ VERTICAL AXIS LABEL

DATA ENTRIES GO HERE

LINE D ▶
LINE C ▶
LINE B ▶
LINE A ▶

◀ HORIZONTAL AXIS LABEL

A B C D ◀ LEGENDS

Background Color For This Slide Is...
☐ Black ☐ Blue ☐ Blue Fade ☐ Green Fade
☐ Red ☐ Orange ☐ Orange Fade ☐ Red Fade
☐ Green ☐ Magenta ☐ Magenta Fade

Make ____ EXTRA copies of this slide at $3.95 each

This chart is...
☐ Stacked Bar ☐ Single/Multi Line
☐ Grouped Bar ☐ Area Chart

REFERENCE NUMBER

How to get the charts you want!

Each of the four chart samples shown below uses the same data as seen in the photo at left. Notice how entering a value of 0 affects the appearance of each chart in a different way.

For Stacked Bar Charts and Area Charts, the program will automatically "add up" the data and present it cumulatively. So be sure your data entries aren't already "added up" when you write them on the form.

The program accepts negative values. It will also compute a vertical axis to best display your data. You can override this by writing in a beginning and ending axis value on the left edge of the form.

Stacked Bar
Lines A, B, C and D each produce one segment of a single stacked bar. Each bar can have up to 4 segments.

Grouped Bar
Lines A, B, C and D each produce one thin vertical bar within a group. Each group can have up to 4 bars.

Single/Multi Line
Lines A, B, C and D each produce a single plot point at the corresponding position on the horizontal axis.

Area or Mountain
Lines A, B, C and D each create a peak or valley at the corresponding place on the horizontal axis.

Page 14

33 Tips for Great Slide Presentations

1 Know your audience. Understand their level of knowledge and what they expect to hear from you.

2 Know what you want to accomplish. Have a single, clear purpose in mind for your presentation.

3 Pace your talk. Use enough slides to provide a change every 15 to 20 seconds. That may seem like a fast pace, but that's because you are not in the audience.

4 Use a title slide for every major topic or point in your talk. use special effect titles to dramatize very important points.

5 Use one background color throughout your talk if you want a "corporate image" appearance.

6 Use different color backgrounds in your talk if you want a friendlier, more informal approach.

7 Structure your talk by writing all important points on 3x5 file cards.

8 Arrange & re-arrange the cards to create the best, most logical flow.

9 Use the tell, tell, tell approach. Tell the audience what you're going to say, tell it to them, then tell them what you've just told them.

10 Anticipate objections and questions. Prepare for them in advance.

11 Let your audience know what you expect them to do after your talk. Agree, purchase, understand, etc.

12 Don't use technical jargon. It could well be meaningless to some of the group.

13 Be consistent with the terminology used on the slides and in your talk.

14 Be careful with charts. Just because their point is obvious to you, does not mean it is obvious to the audience. Use chart heads to make your point, and the chart body to support it.

15 The most important rule for text slides is . . . KEEP THEM SIMPLE.

16 Pare your copy down to the minimum. Use action verbs and telegraphic statements.

17 Make only one major point per slide.

18 If you must make several points on a slide, use a build-up series.

19 Cinegraph's forms are a handy way to organize your thoughts and create slides with the proper amount of copy.

20 The first three rules of good presentations are: Practice, Practice and then Practice some more.

21 Whether you speak from cue cards or a written script, memorize your talk, never just read it.

22 Don't read from the screen, it can be taken as an insult. Besides, you should not have that much copy up there anyway.

23 Don't speak while facing the screen. If you want to point out something on your slide, stop speaking, point to the item, then turn and face the audience before you resume speaking.

24 Know the order of your slides and which one will come up next. Don't look at the screen to find out.

25 If you need to refer to a previous slide from your talk, have any extra copy of it made & positioned where needed. Never reverse the projector.

26 Be sure everyone in the audience can see.

27 Check ahead of time for proper room lighting. Low but not totally dark. Check for window glare.

28 If the lights must be turned on and off several times, assign someone to that task.

29 If at all possible, arrive early to rehearse and inspect the presentation site.

30 If you change slides yourself, use a remote control device.

31 Don't nervously play with the remote unit. It will distract people and could accidentally trigger a slide change.

32 If someone else is operating the projector, be sure he or she has a copy of your script with the change cues clearly marked.

33 Don't panic. We live in an imperfect world and most people understand. If something does go wrong, quietly and calmly stop your talk, remedy the problem, then continue.

Page 15

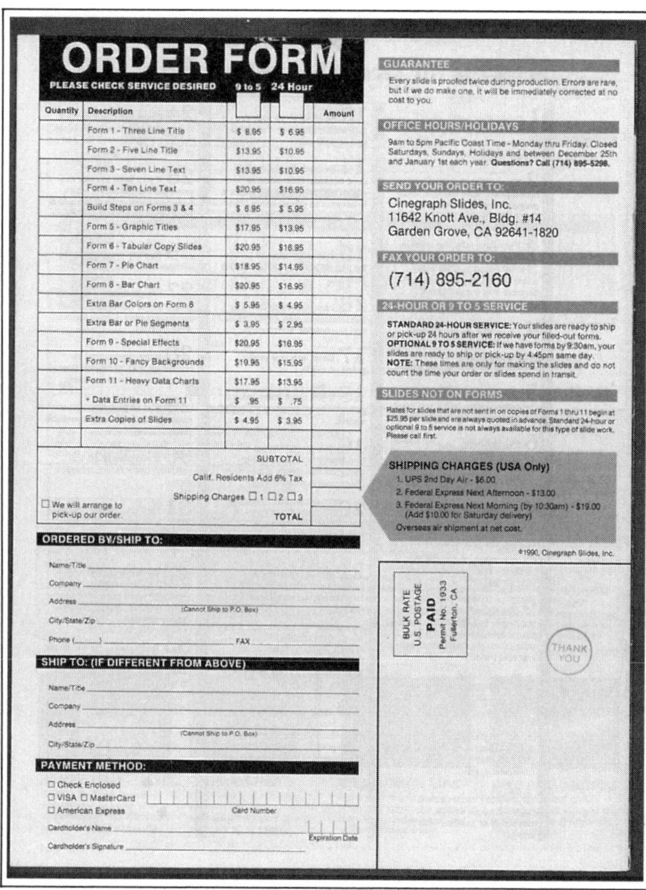

ORDER FORM

PLEASE CHECK SERVICE DESIRED

Quantity	Description	9 to 5	24 Hour	Amount
	Form 1 - Three Line Title	$ 8.95	$ 6.95	
	Form 2 - Five Line Title	$13.95	$10.95	
	Form 3 - Seven Line Text	$13.95	$10.95	
	Form 4 - Ten Line Text	$20.95	$16.95	
	Build Steps on Forms 3 & 4	$ 6.95	$ 5.95	
	Form 5 - Graphic Titles	$17.95	$13.95	
	Form 6 - Tabular Copy Slides	$20.95	$16.95	
	Form 7 - Pie Chart	$18.95	$14.95	
	Form 8 - Bar Chart	$20.95	$16.95	
	Extra Bar Colors on Form 8	$ 5.95	$ 4.95	
	Extra Bar or Pie Segments	$ 3.95	$ 2.95	
	Form 9 - Special Effects	$20.95	$16.95	
	Form 10 - Fancy Backgrounds	$19.95	$15.95	
	Form 11 - Heavy Data Charts	$17.95	$13.95	
	+ Data Entries on Form 11	$ .95	$ .75	
	Extra Copies of Slides	$ 4.95	$ 3.95	
			SUBTOTAL	
			Calif. Residents Add 6% Tax	
			Shipping Charges ☐ 1 ☐ 2 ☐ 3	
	☐ We will arrange to pick-up our order.		TOTAL	

ORDERED BY/SHIP TO:

Name/Title

Company

Address (Cannot Ship to P.O. Box)

City/State/Zip

Phone ( ) FAX

SHIP TO: (IF DIFFERENT FROM ABOVE)

Name/Title

Company

Address (Cannot Ship to P.O. Box)

City/State/Zip

PAYMENT METHOD:

☐ Check Enclosed
☐ VISA ☐ MasterCard Card Number
☐ American Express

Cardholder's Name Expiration Date

Cardholder's Signature

GUARANTEE

Every slide is proofed twice during production. Errors are rare, but if we do make one, it will be immediately corrected at no cost to you.

OFFICE HOURS/HOLIDAYS

9am to 5pm Pacific Coast Time - Monday thru Friday. Closed Saturdays, Sundays, Holidays and between December 25th and January 1st each year. **Questions? Call (714) 895-5298.**

SEND YOUR ORDER TO:

Cinegraph Slides, Inc.
11642 Knott Ave., Bldg. #14
Garden Grove, CA 92641-1820

FAX YOUR ORDER TO:

(714) 895-2160

24-HOUR OR 9 TO 5 SERVICE

STANDARD 24-HOUR SERVICE: Your slides are ready to ship or pick-up 24 hours after we receive your filled-out forms. **OPTIONAL 9 TO 5 SERVICE:** If we have forms by 9:30am, your slides are ready to ship or pick-up by 4:45pm same day. **NOTE:** These times are only for making the slides and do not count the time your order or slides spend in transit.

SLIDES NOT ON FORMS

Rates for slides that are not sent in on copies of Forms 1 thru 11 begin at $25.95 per slide and are always quoted in advance. Standard 24-hour or optional 9 to 5 service is not always available for this type of slide work. Please call first.

SHIPPING CHARGES (USA Only)
1. UPS 2nd Day Air - $6.00
2. Federal Express Next Afternoon - $13.00
3. Federal Express Next Morning (by 10:30am) - $19.00 (Add $10.00 for Saturday delivery)

Overseas air shipment at net cost.

©1990, Cinegraph Slides, Inc.

BULK RATE
U.S. POSTAGE
PAID
Permit No. 1933
Fullerton, CA

THANK YOU

How good is the service Cinegraph Slides provides? For a presentation I hosted at the Direct Marketing Conference in San Francisco, I faxed a slide order (regular twenty-four-hour service) from Connecticut to California on Sunday; the slides were in my hands via UPS that Wednesday, which is truly dazzling. If you order the premium nine-to-five service and Federal Express delivery, you can receive slides the next day.

Cinegraph Slides goes further in great service. Late one evening I put together a slide order and faxed it. I was tired and filled out the form incorrectly. I was going to talk about how great direct mail copywriters are like great actors. I wrote on the form:

> You are
> Merrill Streep
> or
> Dustin Hoffman

When the order arrived, there was a second slide with Meryl Streep's name spelled right. No charge. That's service!

Wolfe has himself a nifty little business with a house file of 50,000 customers and an average order of $240. Wolfe's catalog has basically been unchanged more than four years. Separations are done in Hong Kong; for printing, "the catalog waddles around to the press that gives me the best price." Wolfe has done so well that he is on the prowl for another little direct marketing business to buy.

24

The Dow Jones Story

(Including the single most successful piece of advertising in the history of the world)

The dream of every direct marketer is to have two control efforts for the same product—mailings that can be used interchangeably and bring in low-cost orders at a low cost-per-thousand.

Paul Bell has fulfilled such a dream. Twice! He has two controls each for *Barron's* and the *Wall Street Journal*, both published by Dow Jones & Company, Inc.

The four Dow Jones mailings that follow are classic direct mail efforts. They are not personalized; there is no need for them to be. Nor do they use expensive four-color printing. Nor are there any traditional direct mail bells and whistles: die-cut order form, tokens, scratch-offs, prizes, premiums. Instead, they rely on good offers and beautifully crafted letters. About the only concession to modern direct mail technique is the use of the "fancy" label; instead of plain Cheshire, three of the four efforts are addressed on those printed labels with lines that say "NAME, ADDRESS, CITY, STATE, ZIP" which you almost always find on double postcards.

Paul Bell has been with Dow Jones since 1983 as advertising and promotion manager, mail marketing manager, and subscription national circulation manager for subscription marketing and subscription marketing manager.

Paul Bell:

It's interesting that we are the only mailer with two controls for each of two different publications. But, then again, perhaps we are among the few mailers who are mailing almost fifty-two weeks a year.

The continuous mailing strategy and the tactic of using different subscription offers (which require different letters) come from the premise that it's best to have a variety of subscription marketing programs in the marketplace at the same time (direct mail, television, educational-rate offers, telephone marketing, nontraditional marketing avenues) and that our circulation numbers should not be held hostage to peaks and valleys caused by one or two major subscription drives each year.

We generally like to meet with writers and have a long discussion about our publication. Before anything else, we like to know if the writer reads our publication. We believe that is very important and will ultimately make for a better direct mail letter.

During this initial discussion, we share research findings, failed test letters, successful letters, and our current marketing plan. We want the writer to know where we're ''coming from'' before he/she begins to write.

This initial meeting might last one or two hours, depending on the level of interest the writer has.

We recommend that the writer follow up this meeting by submitting three or four concept statements—short paragraphs indicating possible direct mail letter approaches. Generally, we will choose one of three statements, asking that it be developed into a full-blown direct mail letter. (If none of the concepts is appealing, we ask the writer to try again, but this is usually a sign of trouble ahead; we end up shaking hands and parting company.)

Most times we prefer short copy. It should be sufficient to describe the benefits of our publication. Other publications or products which are less well known (new launches, for example) will likely require more copy.

With the commitment to receive a full draft of a direct mail letter also comes a complete understanding of what the writer's fee will be and, if necessary, what a ''kill fee'' might be. (Sometimes a kill fee is necessary if the publisher decides he doesn't like or can't revise a letter others have found acceptable.)

We always give the writer the option to select the designer. We never want the writer to feel a good letter has been hamstrung by someone else's design. (Some writers decline this option, deciding it's best to use our ''control graphics'' in a head-to-head match against the control letter.)

The entire process—from concept to test letter in the mail—should take between three and six months; but never less than three months.

Barron's I

The "Insurance Against Disaster" effort was created by Joe Vine in 1980 for the Frank Vos Company. Paul Bell describes it as offering *Barron's* at the regular rate or, occasionally, with an annual discount. It has been mailed continuously since 1980.

MAILER: *Barron's I*
PACKAGE: "They trust their luck"
PROJECT MGR.: Paul Bell
AGENCY: Frank Vos Company
ACCOUNT MGR.: Joe Vine
WRITER: Unknown
DESIGNER: Linda Lewis Abedrabbo
FIRST MAILED: 1980
The #7¾ outside envelope with fancy label showing through window. Indicia in black; cornercard with *Barron's* logo reversed out of green.

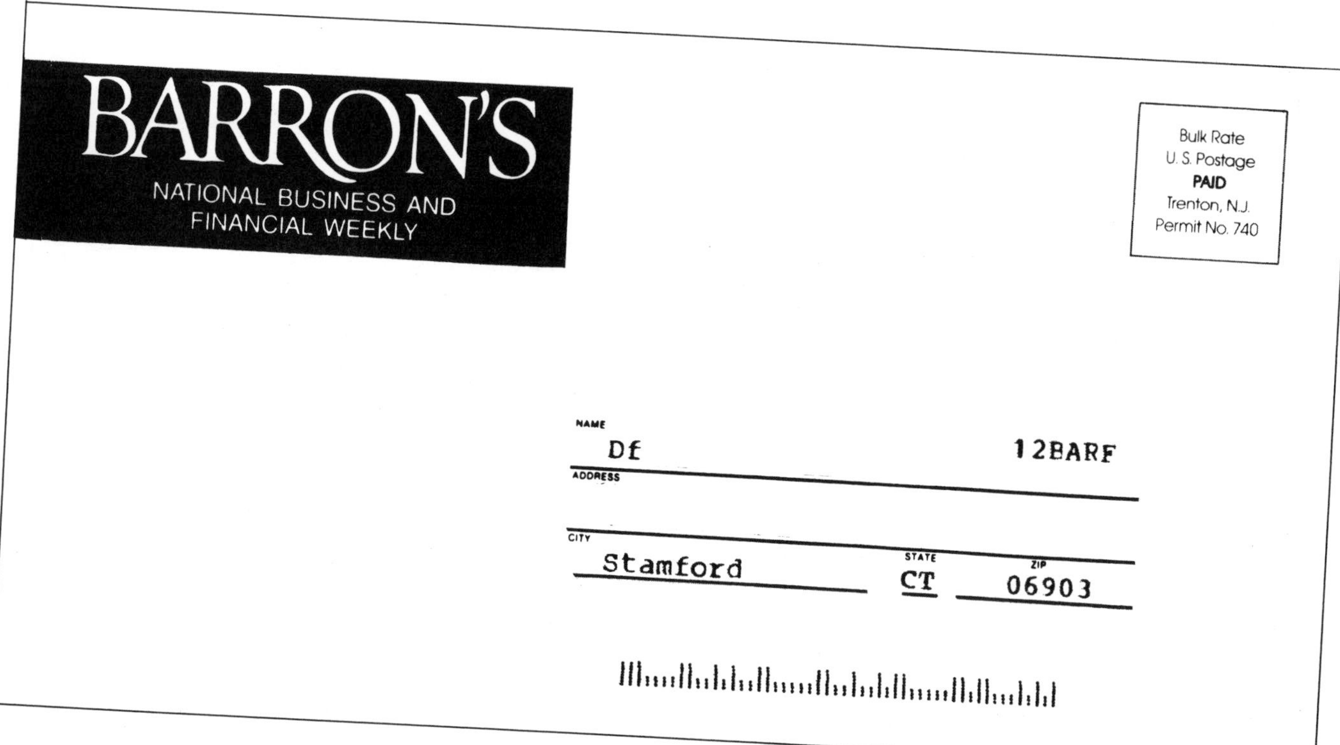

Dear Investor:

Ever notice how some people will insure virtually everything they own against disaster?

Yet when it comes to their investments, they trust their luck.

Does that make sense? Of course not. Especially when, right now, you can get the "investment insurance" more than one million investors like yourself rely on.

Just $28. That's all it takes to begin a subscription to BARRON'S. A full 13 weeks of what's likely to happen in business and the financial markets over the weeks and months ahead. And what you can do about it.

You see, reading BARRON'S is like getting tomorrow's investment news today. And that can be worth a lot more to you than $28.

Just imagine the value of knowing what's likely to happen in the stock market...where interest rates are headed...or what a barrel of oil, an ounce of gold, or a dollar will be worth.

It's precisely this kind of insight that makes BARRON'S unique among today's business and financial publications. Because while the others concentrate on what's already happened or is happening, BARRON'S focuses on what's ahead.

Week after week, BARRON'S reveals the trends and calls the turns in everything from common stocks to commodity futures. From interest rates to the price of gold. From real estate to tax shelters. So you can protect your capital...increase your income...and guide your portfolio toward long-term growth.

For example:

The great business upswing of 1982-199? has now entered its 8th year. Thereby it already ranks as far and away the longest economic expansion in U.S. peacetime history. From day one, the

(inside, please)

readers of BARRON'S were clued in.

Shocked by the recent revelations of manipulation and scandal -- which have led to a belated crackdown by federal authorities -- in penny stocks traded over-the-counter? BARRON'S had the story long ago. On March 16, 1987, "The Abracadabra Man: Turning Pennies Into Millions," the longest and most detailed article the magazine has ever run, blew the whistle on the leading promoters of such scams. Since then, the well-known OTC brokerage firm which dealt in them has gone belly-up, and the principal culprits have either pleaded guilty or been convicted.

By the way, the rigged stocks, some of which traded at $10-$15 per share, once again sell for pennies. While rival publications were pooh-poohing our findings (and the SEC was sitting on its hands), BARRON'S was hard at work protecting investors.

This kind of track record now dates back longer than two-thirds of a century. On May 9, 1986, BARRON'S turned 65, a milestone that only one magazine in 150 ever achieves. At that time we dedicated ourselves anew to the enlightenment of our readers and the hot pursuit of truth.

BARRON'S has an uncanny ability to spot winners. And to accurately project the impact of today's events in the business and financial communities. Plus helping you to make the important decisions about how, when and where you keep your money working for you.

Week after week, BARRON'S brings you financial information you can count on -- the good news and bad news alike. So you can act on it.

A continual flow of reliable information on virtually all investment areas.

In just a single issue BARRON'S has in it over 60 pages of facts, figures, exclusive statistics -- covering every realm of investment. Stocks, Corporate and Municipal Bonds, T-Bills, Mutual Funds, Options, Commodity Futures, Foreign Investments. The whole range of markets.

And BARRON'S lists each week the best rates available from banks and savings and loan associations throughout the country on money market deposit accounts and certificates of deposit, ranging in maturity from six months to five years.

But BARRON'S doesn't stop there. It sharpens the focus and spotlights individual companies and industries. To sort them out of the crowd...zero in on strengths and weaknesses...help you understand where a company is today...and where it's going. So you're in a much better position to evaluate its prospects as an investment.

It's the kind of information you'd dig out for yourself ...if you had the time, the resources, and the know-how.

Our people know. They know Wall Street. And Main Street. Plus the boardrooms. The futures market. The banks. The Fed. The assembly lines. And the check-out counters and breakfast tables. Wherever economic policy -- and buying decisions -- are made. From London's gold market to the coffee plantations in Brazil. From Tokyo's Ginza to the spot oil market in Rotterdam. You've got a ringside seat on the action.

When you read BARRON'S, you sit down with some of the best-informed men and women in the financial world. They're experienced. Knowledgeable. Hard-boiled. And widely respected -- even by those who disagree with them. They're the kind of professionals you'll be glad to have in your corner.

And BARRON'S is published by Dow Jones. The people who set the world's standard for accurate, reliable financial reporting.

What it adds up to is a wealth of vital information on the whole world of investing -- in every issue. You get the information you need to know as an investor. And you get it days, weeks, and even months ahead of any other source. Thanks to BARRON'S unique, incisive reporting. Maybe that explains why, week after week, more than one million investors gather around BARRON'S rather than trust their luck.

And best of all, it doesn't take a major investment to become a BARRON'S subscriber. Just $28 if you act today.

"Just $28 for a trial subscription to BARRON'S? Ridiculous!"

Maybe it IS ridiculous. When you consider the fancy prices of most investment newsletters. Or the fact that BARRON'S reaches you twice as often as most other business or financial magazines.

Which makes our offer (a full 13 weeks) a bargain.

You get 13 information-packed issues of BARRON'S for $28.

(over, please)

see "THE STRIKING PRICE"...if you're thinking about real estate, check "THE GROUND FLOOR."

For those interested in mutual funds, there's Mutual Bonds, where selected fixed-income funds undergo weekly portfolio analysis; and Mutual Choice, where selected fund managers pick their favorite stocks. And of course, there's the comprehensive BARRON'S quarterly mutual fund report, which measures fund performance by the year, five years and ten years, and examines the strategies behind the successes and failures.

To start receiving this invaluable information - and much, much more - simply mail your FREE TRIAL Certificate. We'll send you four weeks of BARRON'S free of cost or obligation on your part.

If you decide that BARRON'S isn't for you, just write "Cancel" on the invoice we'll send you and return it. You'll owe nothing and the four issues are yours to keep with our compliments.

But if you agree that BARRON'S is just what you need in these uncertain times, then we will send you 13 additional weekly issues - making 17 in all - for only $28. That's the regular price of a 13-week subscription, so your first four weeks cost you nothing.

Just mail the FREE TRIAL Certificate in the postage-paid reply envelope. The sooner you do, the sooner we can start sending you BARRON'S.

Since you risk nothing, why not do it now.

Cordially,

Robert M. Blieberg

Robert M. Blieberg
for BARRON'S

RMB:pu
Encs.

P.S. Your subscription to BARRON'S may be a tax-deductible expenditure. Check with your tax advisor.

BARRON'S How the smart money gets that way.

The 4-page letter printed on a 10″ × 14″ sheet of paper.

The order form and business reply envelope.

Our Guarantee

If you decide at any time during your subscription — for any reason whatsoever — that you no longer wish to receive BARRON'S, simply notify us, and the unused portion of your subscription price will be promptly refunded.

RETAIN FOR YOUR RECORDS

SEND ME

BARRON'S

☐ Enter my subscription for one year only $99.
☐ Enter my subscription for 13 weeks only $28.

☐ Payment enclosed ☐ Bill me Charge my: ☐ American Express ☐ VISA ☐ MasterCard ☐ Diners Club

Acct. No. ______

Sig. ______ Exp. ______

NAME Df 12BARF
ADDRESS Rd
CITY Stamford STATE CT ZIP 06903

☐ I'm already a BARRON'S subscriber. Extend my current subscription. Attach BARRON'S label to be assured of fast and correct entry. (Note: This is not a renewal solicitation.) Prices good in continental U.S. for a limited time only. B-27

NO POSTAGE NECESSARY IF MAILED IN THE UNITED STATES

BUSINESS REPLY MAIL
FIRST CLASS PERMIT NO. 26 CHICOPEE, MA

Postage will be paid by Addressee

BARRON'S
National Business and Financial Weekly
P.O. Box 209
Chicopee, MA 01021-9988

Barron's II

Paul Bell:

"Investigate Before You Invest" was written for Barron's *"soft" offer program. It offers four trial issues of* Barron's *followed by thirteen additional weeks. In this case there is no prescreening of zip codes for the "soft" offer. This letter has since been beaten by a double postcard so commonly used by magazines. Postal regulations governing mailings seeking to qualify for automation rates are lowering some of the efficiencies of double postcards, however. Yet, right now, we are still able to mail the double postcard as a first-class piece with pre-sort automation discounts and have a cost-efficient marketing effort.*

Mailer: *Barron's II*
Package: Investigate
Project Mgr.: Paul Bell
Writer: Seymour Zogott
Designer: Stan Greenfield
First Mailed: 1985
The 6″ × 9″ outside envelope printed on pea green stock with blue teaser copy.

The enclosed Certificate is made out in your name and is non-transferable.

It entitles you to receive four weeks of BARRON'S <u>free</u> of cost or obligation.

17BBLS

Ralph
St.
West Orange, NJ 07052

BARRON'S National Business and Financial Weekly
World Financial Center, 200 Liberty Street, New York, NY 10281

Dear Friend:

You are undoubtedly familiar with the old adage about buying securities: "Investigate before you invest."

That is why we are making this extraordinary offer: four weeks of BARRON'S, delivered right to your door, free of cost or obligation on your part.

We want you to "investigate" BARRON'S - first hand - and see for yourself how it can help your investment program, as it helps almost one million investors like you across the country.

Start on the front page with Alan Abelson's "Up & Down Wall Street"...

a column that takes you to the inner sanctums of the securities world...the corporate boardrooms... the corridors of power in Washington...probably the best read column on The Street.

Go on to The Trader...

a detailed examination of what happened in the market during the past week - and what it means for future trends.

Read the feature articles in every issue...

that analyze the prospects for selected companies and industries...where you may discover the latest technological breakthrough, or an interesting turn-around situation.

Study the weekly composite stock and bond tables...

in over 60 pages of facts, figures, exclusive statistics and charts - including the unique "BARRON'S Market Laboratory." You'll have the statistical data and indices you need to make astute investment decisions.

If you're interested in bonds, read "CURRENT YIELD"...for option trading,

(over, please)

see "THE STRIKING PRICE"...if you're thinking about real estate, check "THE GROUND FLOOR."

For those interested in mutual funds, there's Mutual Bonds, where selected fixed-income funds undergo weekly portfolio analysis; and Mutual Choice, where selected fund managers pick their favorite stocks. And of course, there's the comprehensive BARRON'S quarterly mutual fund report, which measures fund performance by the year, five years and ten years, and examines the strategies behind the successes and failures.

To start receiving this invaluable information - and much, much more - simply mail your FREE TRIAL Certificate. We'll send you four weeks of BARRON'S free of cost or obligation on your part.

If you decide that BARRON'S isn't for you, just write "Cancel" on the invoice we'll send you and return it. You'll owe nothing and the four issues are yours to keep with our compliments.

But if you agree that BARRON'S is just what you need in these uncertain times, then we will send you 13 additional weekly issues - making 17 in all - for only $28. That's the regular price of a 13-week subscription, so your first four weeks cost you nothing.

Just mail the FREE TRIAL Certificate in the postage-paid reply envelope. The sooner you do, the sooner we can start sending you BARRON'S.

Since you risk nothing, why not do it now.

Cordially,

Robert M. Blieberg

Robert M. Blieberg
for BARRON'S

RMB:pu
Encs.

P.S. Your subscription to BARRON'S may be a tax-deductible expenditure. Check with your tax advisor.

BARRON'S How the smart money gets that way.

The 2-page letter printed front and back on 1 piece of paper.

SPECIAL BONUS OPPORTUNITY TO INCREASE THE VALUE OF YOUR BARRON'S SUBSCRIPTION

For a limited time only, I am prepared to add **Two Bonus Issues** of BARRON'S to the trial subscription described in my letter. All you have to do is **send payment with your order** in the postage-paid envelope enclosed. Then I'll do these three things for you.

- I'll send four no-risk free issues of BARRON'S for you to read and enjoy.
- PLUS you'll receive 13 regular issues.
- PLUS you'll receive two additional bonus issues.

In all you'll get 19 issues full of detailed information focusing on what's ahead in the worlds of business and finance.

All this just for sending your $28 payment with order.

Robert M. Bleiberg

The lift piece that encourages cash with order.

This mailing was created by Seymour S. Zogott. He and his wife, Mary Clark Zogott, are leading magazine circulation consultants in New York City. Fittingly, the name of their company is The Zogotts. Seymour Zogott also wrote the Axel winning "Extraordinary Offer" effort for the *Wall Street Journal* described later in this chapter.

The Certificate is made out in your name and cannot be redeemed by anyone else. When validated with your initials, it entitles you to receive a no-risk trial to BARRON'S.

Detach and mail the Certificate in the enclosed postage-paid reply envelope.

IMPORTANT TAX NOTE

Your subscription to BARRON'S, when used for business or for your own portfolio management, may be a tax deductible expenditure. Check with your tax advisor.

B-32

NON-TRANSFERABLE

BARRON'S

No-Risk Trial

FOR NEW SUBSCRIBERS ONLY

☐ Please send me four weekly issues of BARRON'S without cost or obligation on my part. If I am not satisfied, I will write "cancel" on the invoice you'll send me, return it and owe nothing. The four issues are mine to keep. Otherwise, I will receive 13 additional weekly issues—making 17 in all—for only $28.
(That's the regular price of a 13-week subscription.)

☐ Payment enclosed gives me two additional bonus issues of BARRON'S—making 19 in all—for just $28.

☐ Charge My Credit Card.

☐ MasterCard ☐ American Express ☐ VISA

Acct. No. ______

Exp. Date ______ Signature ______

Validate Certificate by initialing here ______

17BBLS

Ralph

St.

West Orange, NJ 07052

Price good in U.S. and possessions for a limited time only.

The order certificate.

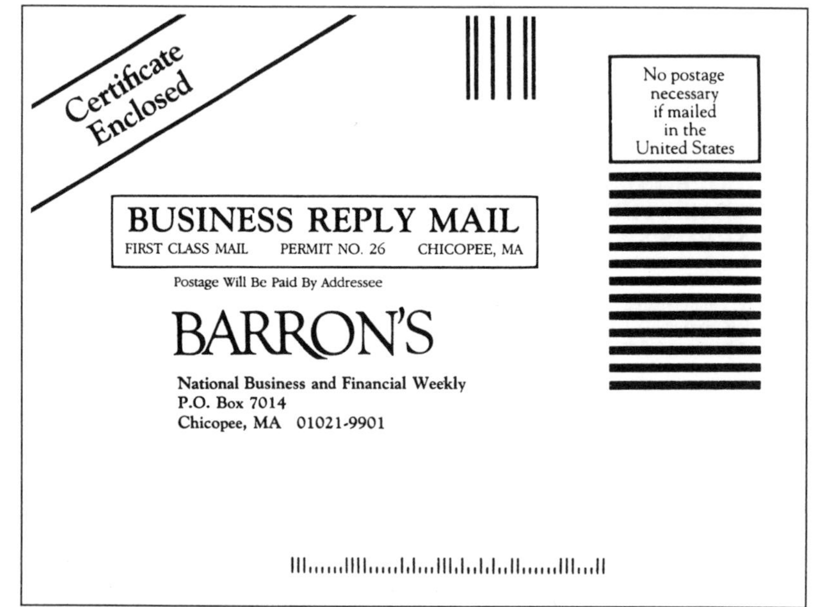

Certificate Enclosed

No postage necessary if mailed in the United States

BUSINESS REPLY MAIL

FIRST CLASS MAIL PERMIT NO. 26 CHICOPEE, MA

Postage Will Be Paid By Addressee

BARRON'S

National Business and Financial Weekly
P.O. Box 7014
Chicopee, MA 01021-9901

The business reply envelope.

Seymour S. Zogott:
I am an instinctive writer. I do not sit down and plot out where each copy point is going to be placed. I get a year's worth of the publication and acquaint myself with the editorials. Letters to the Editor can be quite revealing. I also read any Readers' Surveys that are available and, if possible, find out the type of lists the mailing is going to.

Then I ask myself two questions: (1) What is most likely to get the readers to open the envelope and (2) how do I hook them once I get them inside. (I think a lot of people give lip service to the importance of the envelope treatment, but it is not proven in the execution.)

From that point on, I try to picture the average subscriber (from what I've read) and try to talk to him/her in their own language. I just let my instincts carry me, supported, of course, by years of direct mail experience. This has enabled me to write successfully for such diverse audiences as the Wall Street Journal *and* TV Guide.

I came out of circulation management and still do circulation consulting (in partnership with my lovely wife, Mary). Having had the opportunity to analyze response factors and patterns for many years, and having been exposed to subscriber reaction (particularly in the renewals and billing areas), has been invaluable in helping me decide the best way to get readers to respond.

I also have a secret weapon: my wife, who is my editor. With years of experience in buying creative, she is tougher on me than any client I've come up against. But it works to my advantage.

My pet gripes: (1) Most people coming up the ladder in circulation are not taught how to buy copy and art. (2) Editors who tinker with a writer's copy because they think they know best how to sell their magazine to potential subscribers. They often do not recognize that there is a difference in the perception between what a reader likes *about a magazine and what makes them* buy *the magazine in the first place.*

Wall Street Journal I

Paul Bell:

It's important to understand that we have two distinctly different WSJ *marketing programs. Two different letters (''Two Young Men'' and ''Extraordinary Offer'') are used in the programs. There is no relationship between the two.*

Farmingdale New York

Blk. Rt.
U.S. Postage
PAID
Permit No. 601

Please initial and return your
enclosed Personal Trial Certificate.

Upon receiving it, we will send you
four weeks of THE WALL STREET JOURNAL
free of cost or obligation.

17JDBS
Kathryn
Street
Philadelphia, PA 19103

THE WALL STREET JOURNAL.
World Financial Center
200 Liberty Street
New York, NY 10281-1099

Mailer: *Wall Street Journal I*
Package: ''Extraordinary offer . . .''
Project Mgr.: Paul Bell
Writer: Seymour Zogott
Designer: Stan Greenfield
First Mailed: 1988
The 5½″ × 7″ outer envelope—shown front and back—printed on gray stock with blue teaser copy and blue indicia.

THE WALL STREET JOURNAL.

World Financial Center, 200 Liberty Street, New York, NY 10281

Dear Friend:

Let me repeat our rather extraordinary offer.

The enclosed Personal Trial Certificate is made out in your name and is non-transferable. It can be redeemed only by you.

When you validate it and return it to us, we will send you four weeks of The Wall Street Journal -- FREE of cost or obligation on your part.

Why are we making such an attractive offer on The Journal? Good question - but there's a good answer.

We have a hunch that you read The Journal only once in a while - or that you were a regular reader but haven't seen The Journal on a day-to-day basis for some time.

Either way, we think it's time you knew how reading The Wall Street Journal every business day can keep you better informed and help you get ahead in the business world.

> And we want you to find out for yourself before you commit to becoming a subscriber by accepting this FREE four-week trial of The Journal.

Start on the front page with the What's News column. It's a capsule summary of the most important business news of the day. Check the daily Index to Businesses. Choose the stories that interest you and you'll know which pages to turn to to get all of the details.

Don't miss Who's News - profiles of people at the top and how they got there. You can profit from the experiences of those who took the traditional path - and those who went against tradition to achieve success.

Read Marketplace. It's a complete section with daily reports on marketing, technology, and the law, and issues of concern to people in smaller companies.

Here we aim to cover the fascinating and intensely competitive marketplace -- where companies battle daily to ensure their

(over, please)

success. And where individuals rise -- and sometimes fall -- on the strength of their ideas, talents, and visions.

Keep on top of the markets with our Money & Investing section. Here's where you'll find two of the best read columns on Wall Street: Abreast of the Market and Heard on the Street. And get help with your own investments from the daily feature Your Money Matters.

Money & Investing is a comprehensive report. The Journal's coverage of investments has never been easier, faster, more useful. Better graphics, easy-to-scan stock quotations, a front page summary of the day's market news.

I've just skimmed the surface because there is no way I can tell you, in this short space, all about The Wall Street Journal.

That's why I want you to find out for yourself why there is no other publication like it - by accepting this special trial offer free of cost or obligation.

The enclosed Personal Trial Certificate is made out in your name. (Sorry, it is non-transferable.) When you validate it and return it to us, we will send you The Wall Street Journal - every business day - for four weeks.

Read it...absorb it...use it. If you decide it's not for you, simply write "cancel" on the invoice we'll send you, return it and that will end the matter. Keep your copies with our compliments.

But if you discover - as I bet you will - that The Wall Street Journal can be one of your best sources of ideas and knowledge to help you realize your dream, you'll receive 26 additional weeks - making 30 in all - for only $71. (That's the regular price of a 26-week subscription.)

Don't send any money now.

Just validate and mail your Personal Trial Certificate in the postage-paid reply envelope I have provided.

Since you risk nothing, why not do it today.

Cordially,

Peter R. Kann
Publisher

PRK:gc
Encs.

P.S. Your subscription fee may be tax deductible. Be sure to ask your tax advisor.

The 2-page letter, printed on 1 sheet front and back.

''Extraordinary Offer'' is a letter selling our ''soft'' offer (also referred to as ''no-risk trial'' and ''free issues''). This is basically a knock-off of the soft offers which are used as control mailings by many magazines. The WSJ *has added a slight twist to this offer: we use a zip code pre-screening during the merge/purge to identify prospects whose names/addresses are located in our early-morning carrier delivery areas. If the name/address hits against our zip table, we will send the ''Extraordinary Offer'' letter. If not, we will send the ''Two Young Men'' letter.*

This is the most expensive ''soft'' offer I'm aware of: 4 weeks free (20 issues) followed by 26 additional weeks for $71.

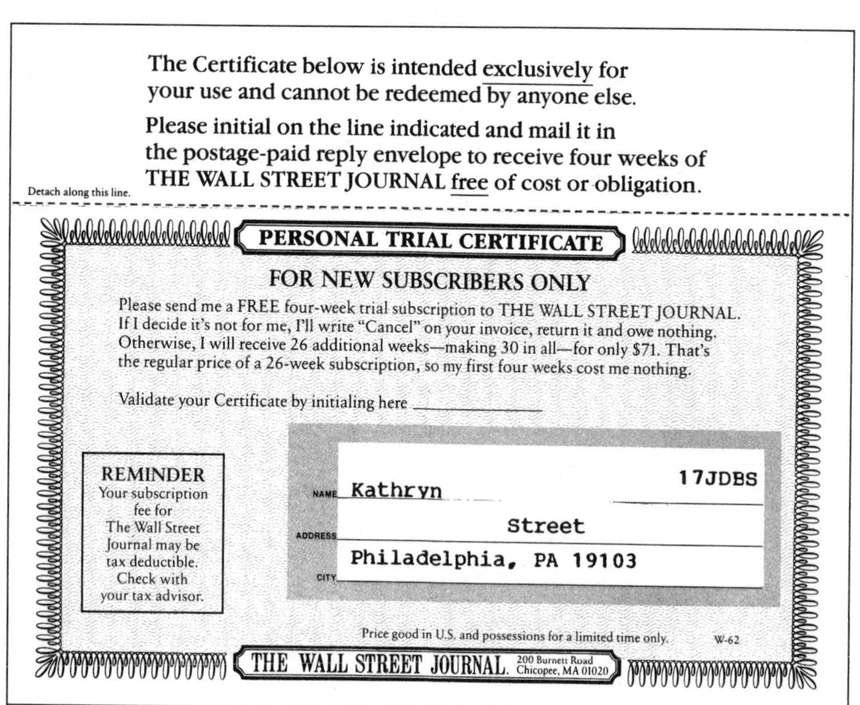

The Certificate below is intended exclusively for your use and cannot be redeemed by anyone else.

Please initial on the line indicated and mail it in the postage-paid reply envelope to receive four weeks of THE WALL STREET JOURNAL free of cost or obligation.

Detach along this line.

PERSONAL TRIAL CERTIFICATE

FOR NEW SUBSCRIBERS ONLY

Please send me a FREE four-week trial subscription to THE WALL STREET JOURNAL. If I decide it's not for me, I'll write "Cancel" on your invoice, return it and owe nothing. Otherwise, I will receive 26 additional weeks—making 30 in all—for only $71. That's the regular price of a 26-week subscription, so my first four weeks cost me nothing.

Validate your Certificate by initialing here ______________

REMINDER
Your subscription fee for The Wall Street Journal may be tax deductible. Check with your tax advisor.

NAME Kathryn 17JDBS
ADDRESS Street
CITY Philadelphia, PA 19103

Price good in U.S. and possessions for a limited time only. W-62

THE WALL STREET JOURNAL. 200 Burnett Road Chicopee, MA 01020

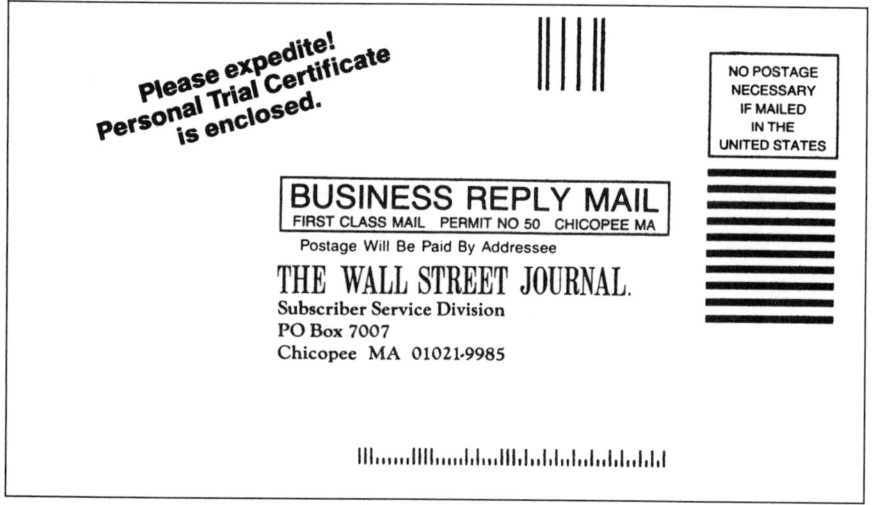

Please expedite!
Personal Trial Certificate
is enclosed.
NO POSTAGE NECESSARY IF MAILED IN THE UNITED STATES

BUSINESS REPLY MAIL
FIRST CLASS MAIL PERMIT NO 50 CHICOPEE MA
Postage Will Be Paid By Addressee

THE WALL STREET JOURNAL.
Subscriber Service Division
PO Box 7007
Chicopee MA 01021-9985

The order form and business reply envelope. Note "Please expedite!" on upper left of the BRE; it makes the whole proposition seem more urgent.

Wall Street Journal II

This mailing, written by freelancer Martin Conroy, is the granddaddy of all the Grand Controls. The highways and byways of North America are littered with the corpses of mailings tested against it by virtually every major (and minor) copywriter and designer in the United States and Canada since it was first mailed in 1974 or 1975. The December 1986 issue of *Who's Mailing What!* featured this effort in a front-page story by freelancer Dennis S. LeBarron of Clear Communications, Wilton, Connecticut, who wrote the Standard Rate and Data Grand Control featured in Chapter 20.

DENNIS S. LEBARRON:
The control direct mail package for the Wall Street Journal *is a circulation manager's dream. It's a low-cost, easy-to-produce package—with a winning offer and winning letter—one that can be mailed almost anytime to any qualified list. It's practically guaranteed to pull in response profitably, year after year.*

The package—with its get-acquainted offer and ''25 years ago'' letter—has been control for more than eighteen years. What makes it so successful?

THE WALL STREET JOURNAL.
World Financial Center
200 Liberty Street
New York, NY 10281-1099

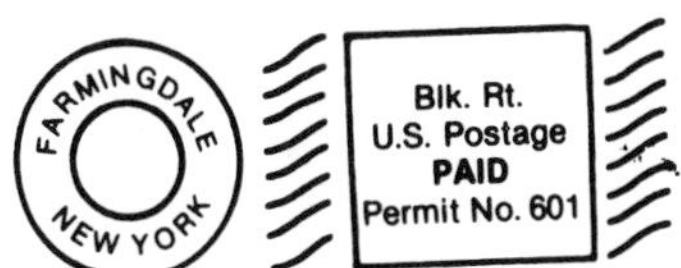

NAME 12JCPW
A. W.
ADDRESS
2200 Comm. St.
CITY
Philadelphia, PA 19103

MAILER: *Wall Street Journal II*
PACKAGE: ''Two Young Men . . .''
PROJECT MGR.: Paul Bell
WRITER: Martin Conroy
DESIGNER: In-house
FIRST MAILED: 1974
The #7¾ outside envelope. This package has been received for over 18 years in an infinite variety of incarnations. This version is the standard.

THE WALL STREET JOURNAL.

World Financial Center, 200 Liberty Street, New York, NY 10281

Dear Reader:

On a beautiful late spring afternoon, twenty-five years ago, two young men graduated from the same college. They were very much alike, these two young men. Both had been better than average students, both were personable and both—as young college graduates are—were filled with ambitious dreams for the future.

Recently, these men returned to their college for their 25th reunion.

They were still very much alike. Both were happily married. Both had three children. And both, it turned out, had gone to work for the same Midwestern manufacturing company after graduation, and were still there.

But there was a difference. One of the men was manager of a small department of that company. The other was its president.

What Made The Difference

Have you ever wondered, as I have, what makes this kind of difference in people's lives? It isn't a native intelligence or talent or dedication. It isn't that one person wants success and the other doesn't.

The difference lies in what each person knows and how he or she makes use of that knowledge.

And that is why I am writing to you and to people like you about The Wall Street Journal. For that is the whole purpose of The Journal: to give its readers knowledge—knowledge that they can use in business.

A Publication Unlike Any Other

You see, The Wall Street Journal is a unique publication. It's the country's only national business daily. Each business day, it is put together by the world's largest staff of business-news experts.

Each business day, The Journal's pages include a broad range of information of interest and significance to business-minded people, no matter where it comes from. Not just stocks and finance, but anything and everything in the whole, fast-moving world of business. . .The Wall Street Journal gives you all the business news you need—when you need it.

Knowledge Is Power

Right now, I am reading page one of The Journal, the best-read front page in America. It combines all the important news of the day with in-depth feature reporting. Every phase of business news is covered, from articles on inflation, wholesale prices, car prices, tax incentives for industries to major developments in Washington, and elsewhere.

(over, please)

And there is page after page inside The Journal, filled with fascinating and significant information that's useful to you. The Marketplace section gives you insights into how consumers are thinking and spending. How companies compete for market share. There is daily coverage of law, technology, media and marketing. Plus daily features on the challenges of managing smaller companies.

The Journal is also the single best source for news and statistics about your money. In the Money & Investing section there are helpful charts, easy-to-scan market quotations, plus "Abreast of the Market," "Heard on the Street" and "Your Money Matters," three of America's most influential and carefully read investment columns.

If you have never read The Wall Street Journal, you cannot imagine how useful it can be to you.

A 13 Week Subscription

Put our statements to the proof by subscribing for the next 13 weeks for just $34. This is the shortest subscription term we offer— and a perfect way to get acquainted with The Journal. Or you may prefer to take advantage of our better buy—one year for $129.

Simply fill out the enclosed order card and mail it in the postage-paid envelope provided. And here's The Journal's guarantee: should The Journal not measure up to your expectations, you may cancel this arrangement at any point and receive a refund for the undelivered portion of your subscription.

If you feel as we do that this is a fair and reasonable proposition, then you will want to find out without delay if The Wall Street Journal can do for you what it is doing for millions of readers. So please mail the enclosed order card now, and we will start serving you immediately.

About those two college classmates I mention at the beginning of this letter: they were graduated from college together and together got started in the business world. So what made their lives in business different?

Knowledge. Useful knowledge. And its application.

An Investment In Success

I cannot promise you that success will be instantly yours if you start reading The Wall Street Journal. But I can guarantee that you will find The Journal always interesting, always reliable, and always useful.

Sincerely,

Peter R. Kann
Publisher

PRK: er
Encs.

P.S. It's important to note that The Journal's subscription price may be tax deductible. Ask your tax advisor.

Martin Conroy's 2-page letter—printed front and back on 1 sheet of paper with no second color—the most successful advertisement in the history of the world.

THE PRODUCT: The Journal *is the best known and most respected business newspaper in America. It's also the largest, with two million circulation. So we don't have to waste time and money educating buyers about the product. It's also used mainly for business and investment purposes, is often paid for by one's company, and is often tax deductible.*

THE OFFER: The short-term (13-week trial) subscription at $37 makes it easy to get acquainted without a big commitment. This is particularly important, since a full year's subscription is up to $185.

The package is simple and inexpensive—monarch-sized (7½" × 3¹⁵⁄₁₆") outside envelope . . . two-page monarch-sized letter . . . 7" order form with small perfed tab featuring the guarantee . . . and business reply envelope. No teaser copy on the outside . . . no brochure . . . no photos . . . no premiums. The design and color of all elements match—to resemble conservative business stationery. The most striking graphics in the entire mailing are the words THE WALL STREET JOURNAL.

To help overcome ''envelope fatigue,'' other formats have been tested, but it has been the solid control in one incarnation or another since 1976.

''The letter is probably so convincing because of its universal appeal. It's something they enjoy reading,'' says Paul D. Bell. ''They can see themselves in the story.''

''They'' are the Journal*'s target prospects: 25 to 54 years old, college grads, with an individual employment income of $30,000+, in a professional/managerial job, and interested in career/financial advancement.*

While the letter may not be true, it's definitely believable. Martin Conroy, the Madison, Connecticut-based freelance copywriter who wrote the original letter back in 1974, says, ''I know guys like that. And I think it works so well because prospects know people like that.''

Conroy and other copywriters have been trying to beat that letter for over fifteen years—with no success yet.

Some notes about the Journal*'s successful effort:*

- *No premium.*
- *Payment option on the order card is ''Payment enclosed/Charge my Amex, Visa, MC, DC /Bill me'' in that order.*
- *Uses a ''fancy'' (lined) label.*
- *Always includes a BRE—they get a large percentage of cash with order.*
- *Simple guarantee: ''Cancel your subscription at any time and receive a refund for the undelivered portion.''*
- *No negative effect on women's lists, even though the letter is about men.*
- *Uses follow-up mailings (monarch envelope, short letter/order form, BRE).*

If, as someone once said, good advertising is a believable promise made to the right audience, then this Martin Conroy effort for the Journal *is a classic.*

Paul Bell:

''Two Young Men'' is mailed in our regular-rate program. The offer involves no discounts, no free issues or premiums of any kind. The offer is sent largely to selected key-response lists that over time have demonstrated good history (response, pay-up, renewal).

We do send follow-up mailing to the ''Two Young Men'' letter with the name/address that has been identified as a multibuyer in the merge/purge.

Late in 1991 I called Paul Bell and ran some numbers by him. This was, in essence, the conversation.

Hatch: Would you say that the average mail order circulation of the *Journal* over the past eighteen years was about one million?

Bell: [Pause.] Yes, that's about right.

Hatch: Am I right in assuming that the average subscription rate of the *Wall Street Journal* over the past eighteen years has been $100 a year?

Bell: [Pause.] Yes, that's about right.

Hatch: Is it safe to assume that 55 percent of all your mail order subscribers over the past eighteen years have come in as a result of Martin Conroy's ''Two Young Men . . . '' letter?

BELL: We have a lot of other sources—telemarketing, subscriptions as a result of newsstand sales, supermarket take-ones, inserts. But, yes, I think 55 percent is a fair estimate.

HATCH: Paul, one million subscribers per year times $100 equals $100 million times 18 years equals $1.8 billion times 55 percent equals $1 billion. If these numbers are correct, the Martin Conroy letter is directly responsible for bringing in $1 billion in revenues to the *Wall Street Journal,* and is therefore THE MOST SUCCESSFUL SINGLE PIECE OF ADVERTISING IN THE HISTORY OF THE WORLD!

BELL: [Long silence. Then in a small voice.] Uh, please don't tell Marty Conroy. He'll raise his prices.

Our Guarantee

If you decide at any time during your subscription—for any reason whatsoever—that you no longer wish to receive The Wall Street Journal, simply notify us, and the unused portion of your subscription price will be promptly refunded.

Retain for your records

THE WALL STREET JOURNAL.

200 Burnett Road, Chicopee, MA 01021

☐ One year for $129 Better Buy!	☐ 13 weeks only $34 Get Acquainted!

☐ Payment enclosed
Charge my:
☐ American Express
☐ VISA
☐ MasterCard
☐ Diners Club
☐ Bill me

Acct. No. ______
Exp. Date ______ Sig. ______

NAME A. W. 12JCPW
ADDRESS 2200 Comm. St.
CITY Philadelphia, PA 19103

☐ I'm already a Journal subscriber. Extend my current subscription. Attach newspaper label to be assured of fast and correct entry. (Note: This is not a renewal solicitation.) Prices good in U.S. and possessions for a limited time only.

W-1

The order form and business reply envelope.

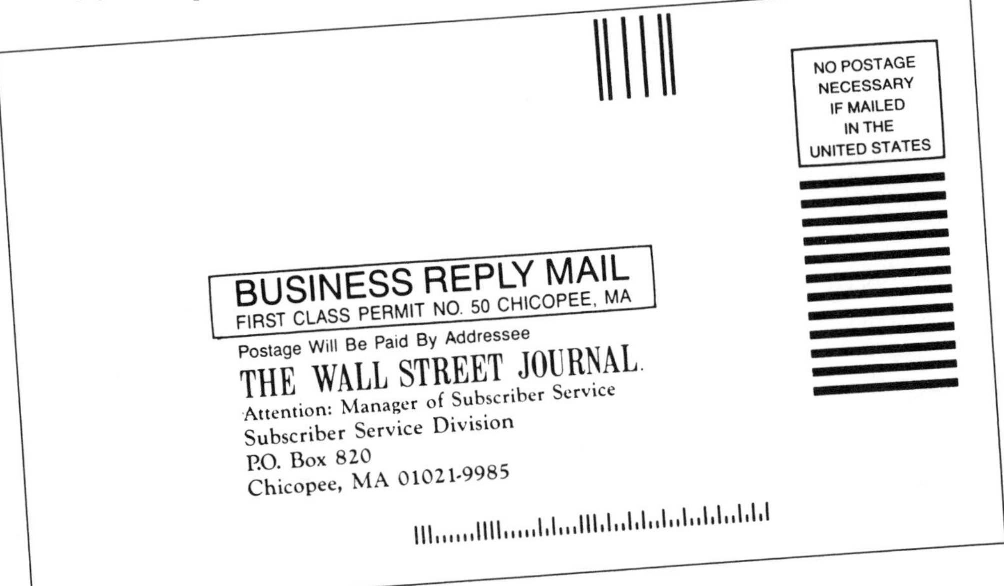

NO POSTAGE NECESSARY IF MAILED IN THE UNITED STATES
BUSINESS REPLY MAIL
FIRST CLASS PERMIT NO. 50 CHICOPEE, MA
Postage Will Be Paid By Addressee
THE WALL STREET JOURNAL.
Attention: Manager of Subscriber Service
Subscriber Service Division
P.O. Box 820
Chicopee, MA 01021-9985

Martin Conroy spent over twenty years writing copy for BBDO with creative responsibility (copy, art, TV production) on a wide variety of national accounts. A freelancer for more than a dozen years, Conroy's other accounts include *People*, Charles Schwab & Co., *Working Woman, Working Mother*, Transamerica Insurance, National Association of Female Executives, Boardroom Reports, *Tennis, American Heritage, Weight Watchers* magazine, and *Child*. He splits his time between homes in Madison, Connecticut, and Captiva Island, Florida.

Conroy asks a lot of questions of the client. What kind of person is your best prospect? What does your product do for that kind of person that's new and/or different and/or better and/or unique? Can you give me sample/samples? May I have your control mailing . . . and another mailing that did well . . . and another mailing that bombed?

Martin Conroy:
I think that some of the direct mail I get is spoiled by the old-fashioned sin of pride. There's really only a handful of us writers, and, face it, we lead pretty nice lives in pretty up-grade places with pretty smart friends and it's all too easy for us to start to feel superior to the great multitude of readers out there. And sometimes, without really meaning to, we write down to them. I think that this shows through in the finished product and turns readers off. So when I'm working on my stuff, I try to keep in mind two things from the Good Book of Direct Response. One: Write unto others as you would have them write unto you. Two: Pride goeth before a flop.

25

Format, Technique, and Offer Grid

I. Consumer Magazines

(1) Mailer	(2) (Complexity)	(3) Size	(4) OE	(5) W	(6) DP	(7) Lttr	(8) Color	(9) Comp	(10) F	(11) Prem	(12) w/o	(13) w/p	(14) Bill	(15) CC	(16) tf	(17) Offer	(18) (Save)	(19) Non-Agy
*Amricn Spectatr	(14)	6x9	p	yes		8								yes		8/$ 11.95	(36%)	yes
Archtrl Digest	(2)	3.5x5	d		yes	½	yes	1	F	1	w/o		yes			8/$ 19.95	(50%)	yes
*Audubon	(15)	6x9	p	yes	yes	4	yes	1	F	1		w/p	yes			12/$ 20.00	(33%)	yes
Bon Appétit	(12)	6x9	p	yes		4	yes	1	F				yes			12/$ 9.00	(50%)	yes
*Condé Nst Travl	(16)	6x9	p	yes		4	yes						yes			12/$ 12.00	(20%)	
Dog Fancy	(5)	#9	p	yes		1							yes			24/$ 21.97	(60%)	yes
*Earthwatch	(16)	6x9	p	yes		4	yes			1		w/p	yes	yes		6/$ 25.00		yes
Economist	(11)	#10		yes		6		3	F				yes			30/$ 39.90	(31%)	yes
*Foreign Affairs	(13)	6x9	p	yes		4							yes	yes		5/$ 16.00	(50%)	yes
*Futurist	(18)	6x9	p	yes		8	yes	1	F	3		w/p		yes		6/$ 30.00		yes
*Harper's	(12)	#10	p		yes	4		1	F				yes			12/$ 12.00	(50%)	yes
House & Garden	(8)	#9	p	yes		2	yes						yes			12/$ 12.00	(50%)	
Islands	(2)	3.5x5	d		yes	½	yes	1	F				yes			6/$ 23.70	(33%)	yes
Lears	(15)	6x9	p	yes		4	yes	1	F				yes			12/$ 18.00	(50%)	yes
M	(14)	6x9	p	yes		4	yes	1	F				yes			12/$ 9.00	(50%)	yes
*Nat'l Wildlife	(10)	#10		yes	yes	2	yes		F	6		w/p	yes			6/$ 15.00		yes
*Natur Consrvncy	(12)	6x9	p	yes		4	yes									6/$ 15.00		yes
Newsweek	(5)	4x8		yes			yes		F	3		w/p	yes			27/$ 15.97	(25%)	yes
Organic Gardng	(13)	#10	p	yes		4	yes		F	3	w/o		yes			10/$ 14.94		yes
Outside	(5)	4x7.5	p	yes		½		2	F	1		w/p	yes			12/$ 12.95	(28%)	yes
*Science News	(9)	#10		yes		4							yes			12/$ 1.00	(13%)	yes
Soviet Life	(12)	5.5x8	p	yes		2	yes						yes			12/$ 12.00	(63%)	yes
Utne Reader	(10)	#10	p	yes		4		1	F				yes			6/$ 18.00	(25%)	yes
W	(16)	6x9	p	yes		4	yes	1					yes			26/$ 16.95	(49%)	yes
Yankee	(2)	3.5x5.5	d		yes	½	yes	1	F	2	w/o	w/p	yes			8/$ 9.97		yes
10 Totals 25 (42%)	10.7 (avg)		21 (84%)	21 (84%)	6 (24%)	3.3 (avg)	17 (68%)	13 (52%)	15 (60%)	9 (36%)			23 (92%)	4 (16%)				23 (92%)

II. Consumer Books

Mailer	(Complexity)	Size	OE	W	DP	Lttr	Color	Comp	F	Prem	w/o	w/p	Bill	CC	tf	Offer	(Save)	Non-Agy
Ins't Improvmnt	(11)	9x12	p	yes		4			F	1		w/p	yes	yes		$ 29.98		yes
Rodale Hom Rems	(18)	9x12	p	yes		6			F	1	w/o		yes			$ 21.96+		yes
Rodale Cntry Fur	(14)	7.5x12	p	yes		4	yes		F	1	w/o		yes			$ 21.96+		yes
Rodale Hlth Tips	(20)	9x12	p	yes		6	yes		F	1	w/o		yes			$ 27.96+		yes
Rodale Hnts Tips	(19)	9x12	p	yes		2	yes		F	1	w/o		yes			$ 21.96+		yes
Totals 5	16.4 (avg)		5 (100%)	5 (100%)		4.4 (avg)	3 (60%)		5 (100%)	5 (100%)			5 (100%)	1 (20%)				5 (100%)

III. Continuity Series

Mailer	(Complexity)	Size	OE	W	DP	Lttr	Color	Comp	F	Prem	w/o	w/p	Bill	CC	tf	Offer	(Save)	Non-Agy
Singer Sewing	(10)	7.5x10.5	p	yes		1	yes		F	1	w/o		yes			$ 13.95+		yes
Time Frame	(22)	9x12	p	yes		4	yes		F	1		w/p	yes			$ 16.99+		yes
Time Mysteries	(20)	6x9	p	yes		4	yes		F	1		w/p	yes			$ 14.99+		yes
Totals 3	17.3		3	3		3.0	3		3	3			3					3
	(avg)		(100%)	(100%)		(avg)	(100%)		(100%)	(100%)			(100%)					(100%)

IV. Negative Option Offers

Mailer	(Complexity)	Size	OE	W	DP	Lttr	Color	Comp	F	Prem	w/o	w/p	Bill	CC	tf	Offer	(Save)	Non-Agy
BMG Compct Disc	(10)	#10	p	yes		1	yes		F				yes			8/$ 8.00+	(94%)	yes
Book of Month	(15)	#10	p	yes	yes	2	yes						yes			4/$ 4.00+	(96%)	
Fortune Bk Club	(11)	#11	p	yes		1	yes			1	w/o		yes			4/$ 4.95+	(95%)	yes
Int'l Previw So	(11)	5x6.5	p	yes		4	yes		F				yes			3/$ 1.00	(98%)	yes
Literary Guild	(16)	6x8.5	p	yes		2	yes		F	1	w/o		yes			5/$ 2.00+	(98%)	
Totals 5	12.6		5	5	1	2.0	5		3	2			5					3
	(avg)		(100%)	(100%)	(20%)	(avg)	(100%)		(60%)	(40%)			(100%)					(60%)

V. Newsletters

Mailer	(Complexity)	Size	OE	W	DP	Lttr	Color	Comp	F	Prem	w/o	w/p	Bill	CC	tf	Offer	(Save)	Non-Agy
Aviation Consumr	(14)	9x12	p	yes		4		2	F	1		w/p	yes			12/$ 16.00	(44%)	yes
Aviation Safety	(12)	#10	p	yes		4	yes	2	F				yes			12/$ 18		yes
Bottom Line Per	(12)	#10	p	yes		4		3	F				yes			NO PRICE		yes
Soundview Exec	(11)	#10	p	yes		4		2	F	1	w/o		yes	yes	t	12/$ 69.50	(28%)	yes
Totals 4	12.3		4	4		4		4	4	2			4	1	1			4
	(avg)		(100%)	(100%)		(avg)		(100%)	(100%)	(50%)			(100%)	(25%)	(25%)			(100%)

VI. Business & Financial Magazines

Mailer	(Complexity)	Size	OE	W	DP	Lttr	Color	Comp	F	Prem	w/o	w/p	Bill	CC	tf	Offer	(Save)	Non-Agy
Advrtsng Age I	(11)	6x9	p	yes	yes	2	yes		F	1		w/p	yes			52/$ 64.00	(24%)	yes
Advrtsng Age II	(10)	#10	p		yes	3	yes		F	1		w/p	yes		t	52/$ 64.00	(24%)	yes
Amrcn Demgrphcs	(12)	9x12		yes		4	yes	1	F				yes			12/$ 58.00		yes
Barron's I	(7)	#7.75		yes		4								yes		13/$ 28.00		yes
Barron's II	(6)	6x9	p	yes		2		4	F				yes	yes		17/$ 28.00	(24%)	yes
Business Week	(4)	5x6	t		yes	½	yes	4	F	1		w/p	yes			32/$ 24.95	(60%)	yes
Financial World	(10)	5.5x8.5	p		yes	4	yes	3	F				yes			26/$ 19.95	(48%)	yes
Fortune	(5)	#10	p	yes		½							yes			14/$ 19.00	(65%)	yes
Inc.	(2)	4.25x6	d		yes	½	yes	1	F	2	w/o	w/p	yes			12/$ 19.00	(47%)	yes
Lotus	(2)	5.5x8.5	d		yes	½	yes	6	F	1		w/p	yes			6 free/18/$18		yes
Std Rate DM List	(11)	#10	p	yes		2							yes			6/$170.00		yes
Success	(4)	4.5x6	p	yes		2		1	F				yes			10/$ 9.97	(50%)	yes
Wall St Jrnl I	(6)	5.5x7	p	yes		2		4	F				yes			30/$ 71.00	(13%)	yes
Wall St Jrnl II	(6)	#7.75		yes		2							yes	yes		13/$ 37.00		yes
Totals 14	6.9		11	9	6	2.1	7	8	10	5			13	3	1			14
	(avg)		(79%)	(64%)	(43%)	(avg)	(50%)	(57%)	(71%)	(35%)			(93%)	(21%)	(7%)			(100%)

VII. Lead Generators

Mailer	(Complexity)	Size	OE	W	DP	Lttr	Color	Comp	F	Prem	w/o	w/p	Bill	CC	tf	Offer	(Save)	Non-Agy
Amer Mgt Assn	(6)	4.5x6.5	p		yes											LEADS		
Ency Britannica	(17)	6x9	p	yes		2	yes		F	1	w/o					LEADS		
Great Expctatns	(4)	#10	p	yes		1										LEADS		yes
Inst Chlds Lit	(9)	#10	p	yes		3			F	1	w/o					LEADS		yes
Totals 4	9.0 (avg)		4 (100%)	3 (75%)	1 (25%)	1.5 (avg)	1 (25%)		2 (50%)	2 (50%)								2 (50%)

VIII. Memberships & Merchandise

Mailer	(Complexity)	Size	OE	W	DP	Lttr	Color	Comp	F	Prem	w/o	w/p	Bill	CC	tf	Offer	(Save)	Non-Agy
CompuServe	(17)	5.5x9.5	p	yes	yes	4	yes		F	1		w/p		yes	t	$ 28.00		yes
Gevalia Kaffe	(8)	5x8	p	yes	yes	2	yes		F	1		w/p		yes	t	$ 3/1 lb.		
Mobil Auto Clb	(19)	6x9	p	yes	yes	5	yes			1		w/p	yes			$ 39.00		
Omaha Steaks	(11)	#10	p	yes		4	yes			1		w/p		yes	t	$ 29.95	(48%)	yes
Totals 4	13.8 (avg)		4 (100%)	4 (100%)	3 (75%)	3.8 (avg)	4 (100%)		2 (50%)	4 (100%)			1 (25%)	3 (75%)	3 (75%)			3 (75%)

IX. Business Book

Mailer	(Complexity)	Size	OE	W	DP	Lttr	Color	Comp	F	Prem	w/o	w/p	Bill	CC	tf	Offer	(Save)	Non-Agy
Brdrm Insid Info	(13)	#10	p	yes		4								yes		$ 29.95	(40%)	yes
Totals 1	13.0 (avg)		1 (100%)	1 (100%)		4.0 (avg)								1 (100%)				1 (100%)

X. Home-Study Courses

Mailer	(Complexity)	Size	OE	W	DP	Lttr	Color	Comp	F	Prem	w/o	w/p	Bill	CC	tf	Offer	(Save)	Non-Agy
Hume I/Biz Mgmt	(17)	9x12	p			6		1	F	5	w/o		yes			$15/Lesson		yes
Hume II/SIMM	(18)	9x12	p	yes		8		1	F	4	w/o		yes			$10/Lesson		yes
Hume III/Suprin	(10)	#10		yes		6							yes			$35/Lesson		yes
Nightngl-Con I	(13)	6x9	p	yes		4	yes		F	1	w/o		yes		t	$ 39.95	(33%)	yes
Nightngl-Con II	(16)	9x12	p	yes		6	yes						yes			$ 39.95	(33%)	yes
Totals 5	14.8 (avg)		4 (80%)	4 (80%)		6.0 (avg)	2 (40%)	2 (40%)	3 (60%)	3 (60%)			5 (100%)		1 (20%)			5 (100%)

XI. Catalog

Mailer	(Complexity)	Size	OE	W	DP	Lttr	Color	Comp	F	Prem	w/o	w/p	Bill	CC	tf	Offer	(Save)	Non-Agy
Cinegraph Sides	(16)	8x11	p				yes							yes	t			yes
Totals 1	16.0		1 (100%)				1 (100%)							1 (100%)	1 (100%)			1 (100%)

Totals

Category	(Complexity)	Size	OE	W	DP	Lttr	Color	Comp	F	Prem	w/o	w/p	Bill	CC	tf	Offer	(Save)	Non-Agy
I. 25	10.7		21	21	6	3.3	17	13	15	9			23	4				23
II. 5	16.4		5	5		4.4	3		5	5			5	1				5
III. 3	17.3		3	3		3.0	3		3	3			3					3
IV. 5	12.6		5	5	1	2.0	5		3	2			5					3
V. 4	12.3		4	4		4.0		4	4	2			4	1	1			4
VI. 14	6.9		11	9	6	2.1	7	8	10	5			13	3	1			14
VII. 4	9.0		4	3	1	1.5	1		2	2								2
VIII. 4	13.8		4	4	4	3.8	4		2	4			1	3	3			3
IX. 1	13.0		1	1		4.0								1				1
X. 5	14.8		4	4		6.0	2	2	3	3			5		1			5
XI. 1	16.0		1				1							1	1			1
Totals 71 (100%)	11.4 (avg)		63 (89%)	59 (83%)	18 (25%)	3.1 (avg)	43 (61%)	27 (38%)	47 (66%)	35 (49%)			59 (83%)	14 (20%)	7 (10%)			64 (90%)

KEY: * = Mails at nonprofit rate. (1) *Mailer.* (2) *Complexity.* The number of ½″ × 11″ single pages it would require to photocopy the mailing package and create a dummy mailing. *2* = double postcard; 20 = complex mailing. (3) *Size.* Dimensions of the piece in the mail. (4) *OE.* Outside envelope. *p* = promotional or teaser copy. *d* = double postcard. *t* = triple postcard. Double and triple postcards are prima facie promotional on the outside. (5) *Window.* (6) *DP.* Data processing or elaborate personalization. Name and/or address is in more than one place in the mailing. (7) *Lttr.* Number of pages in the letter. Blank = no letter. (8) *Color.* Elaborate use of color. (9) *Comp.* Comp copy offer. Number of free issues or lessons or records or books. Totals in this section = the number of mailers who use copy offers (not the average number of free items). (10) *F.* Prominent use of word "Free," e.g., "Free Trial" or "Free Premium" or "Free Issue." (11) *Prem.* Use of premium. (12) *w/o* = premium with order. (13) *w/p* = with payment. (14) *Bill.* Bill-me option. (15) *CC.* Credit card option. (16) *tf.* Telephone number or fax number given for ordering purposes. (17) *Offer.* Take the *Business Week* triple postcard as an example: 4 free issues (Comp: 4); 28 additional issues (for total of 32 issues), $24.95 = 32/$24.95; + = plus shipping & handling. (18) *Save.* If savings are highlighted, the percentage is noted. Many magazines fudge whether savings are on retail or subscription price. (19) *Non-Agy.* Created by freelancer or in-house. Not an agency.

26

Analysis of the Data

By analyzing the data in the "Format, Technique, and Offer Grid," there is much to be learned.

Let me emphasize again that these are not necessarily mailings that I like . . . or would choose to put into a book. The only criterion was longevity—three or more consecutive years in the mail. Of the 50,000 to 60,000 mailings I see every year, these are true rarities. Mailings have been tested against the majority of them—in some cases relentlessly—and the test efforts have been beaten back.

The purpose of this book—and the Analysis Grid—is to ascertain why these mailings are so profitable and successful. What are the common threads or elements that they share that can be adapted and used to boost response?

Please remember, too, that these mailings fall into a fairly narrow range of categories: business and consumer magazines, books, newsletters, services, home-study courses, and one catalog. Most products are relatively low cost; those others that run into hundreds of dollars are either lead generators (where no price is mentioned in the mailing) or sold on a continuity basis at a relatively low cost per month.

Will the various techniques used in these mailings also prove to be successful in other categories, such as fundraising efforts or financial services which are not represented here? Maybe yes, maybe no. Certainly worth a test.

Nonprofit Mailing Rates

I have deep prejudice against mailers who take advantage of nonprofit mailing rates, especially magazine publishers. For years *Harper's* magazine was a notably unprofitable competitor of *Atlantic* and *New Yorker*—competing for the same authors, same advertisers, and same subscribers out of the same universe of prospects. The magazine was bought by John (Rick) MacArthur, whose father made billions in the mail order insurance business and set up the MacArthur Foundation. Young MacArthur promptly set up a nonprofit foundation to enable *Harper's* to mail solicitations at nonprofit rates. It is still in direct competition with *Atlantic* and *New Yorker*—aggressively going after the same advertisers, the same authors, and the same universe of subscribers—but is now viable, because postal customers are paying more so *Harper's* can pay less. In my opinion, *Harper's* nonprofit status gives it a competitive edge over *Atlantic* and *New Yorker*; it can mail more cheaply (or mail more for the same price) and settle for less desirable results; we taxpayers and postal customers are underwriting the deal. In an October 1987 editorial in *Who's Mailing What!* I loudly voiced disapproval and received a letter from MacArthur:

I am compelled to respond to the Opinion column in October's Who's Mailing What! *in which you criticize nonprofit publications for "wantonly undercutting" their worthy profit-making competitors. I think your column misses the real point of nonprofit status. It's not simply a matter of avoiding taxes and getting (for a while longer, at least) a preferential postage rate. The point is that nonprofit publications agree to operate* without a profit, *which is, after all, what allows profit-making magazines to continue publishing.*

Harper's *magazine has renounced profit. If the* New Yorker *is willing to do the same, then by all means give them nonprofit tax and postal status, too. I suspect Condé Nast would feel that the drawbacks of nonprofit publishing far outweigh the benefits . . . I am sorry to see* Who's Mailing What! *jump on the "dump on nonprofit" bandwagon. For every nonprofit publication that founders because of decreased government support (in the form of tax exemptions and postal subsidies), the entire industry loses. Even sadder, in a nation founded on the right of free and varied expression, the loss of each and every publication, nonprofit or otherwise, makes us all the poorer.*

That was 1987. I feel just as strongly today as I did then; in fact, more so, since postage rates have gone through the roof, partly as a result of being forced to underwrite the nonprofit mailings of organizations that are in direct competition with profit-making companies: magazines and newsletters, catalogs, seminar presenters, financial services companies (for example, Prudential insurance offers being mailed under the indicia of the American Association of Retired Persons), and cruise ship owners (those using a nonprofit indicia to offer "educational" cruises to members of the American Museum of Natural History and the Association of Junior Leagues when those same cruises are mailed by others at full rate). If anybody is poorer, it is the direct mail community, especially all those companies forced out of business because postage rates got too high.

In addition, nonprofit organizations are exempt from the obligation to pay taxes as ordinary mortals and profit-oriented companies do. In this respect, they are like the lillies of the field. "They toil not, neither do they spin."

Ten of these consumer magazine Grand Controls mailed at nonprofit rates. They do not compete fairly and squarely against the magazines that pay full postage rates. Perhaps these ten should have been split from the remaining fifteen and analyzed separately.

Plain Envelopes vs. Promotional Envelopes

If a mailing has writing and design on the front, it announces itself as advertising mail.

If a mailing comes in a window, it announces that it is not a personal letter.

Of the seventy-one Grand Controls, sixty-three (89 percent) announce themselves as advertising mail by having words or designs on the carrier. (Double postcards are included in this tally, since the message and reply card are face out and covered with copy and art.)

The amount of promotion on an envelope can range from the discreet line of copy such as "RSVP by June 18, 1991" found on the American Management Association invitation, to Gene Schwartz's wild and woolly screamer:

FREE: HOW TO RUB YOUR STOMACH AWAY . . . "By applying the exercise faithfully, he regularized his bowel movement, lost 40 pounds, and was filled with new energy."

Those that did not have promotional copy (*Economist, National Wildlife, Newsweek, American Demographics, Barron's, Wall Street Journal,* Hume's *SuperInvestor Files*) all had windows; and a window envelope announces itself as nonpersonal mail just as surely as an envelope with promotional copy printed on it.

Not one of these mailings fit the Gary Halbert model of a plain white closed-face (windowless) #10 envelope with the name and address typed on the front, stamp in the upper right corner (or perhaps metered indicia), and no promotional copy. (See Chapter 6.)

If such a mailing arrives, it will indeed be treated like personal mail. Put promotional copy on it, and it is immediately recognized as advertising mail, so, presumably, going to all the trouble to personalize it is pointless.

The conclusion to be drawn: there should be a very good reason to go to the expense of making a mailing seem like a personal letter. Most people are sophisticated; they know that a "personal letter" trying to sell something was written by a computer; they see through the lie, and maybe even are put off by it.

Many practitioners of direct mail will argue convincingly that mailings into the business arena should not look like advertising mail. Yet all these Grand Controls targeted to people in the workplace did not disguise the fact that they were selling something. Eleven of the fourteen business and financial magazine efforts (79 percent) used promotional copy on the envelope. Four of the five home-study courses (80 percent) had a promotional envelope. And the Boardroom business book effort used a strong headline on the outer.

Window Envelopes

A whopping 83 percent of these Grand Controls used window envelopes. If you add to those six double postcards and the single catalog—which by design don't have windows—you arrive at a total of just five efforts (7 percent) that use closed-face envelopes. They are:

- Dave Kelley's *Advertising Age* effort with the personalized cartoon on the envelope (and every other piece in the mailing). This piece is pinned to the personalization.
- Nancy Grady's intriguing mailing for *Harper's*.
- Harry Walsh's *Successful Business Management* package for Hume with a pressure-sensitive label together with "I Accept/I Decline" tokens. These are involvement devices; the package is not clearly personalized; the name and address appear only once in this mailing—on this pressure-sensitive label.
- The fourth is Linda Wells's *Financial World* effort with the abysmal personalization for no apparent reason except that it works.
- The American Management Association invitation.

Putting the prospect's name and address on only one place in the mailing (for example, the reply device which shows through the window) is a lot cheaper than personalizing. And based on the percentages in the grid, there should be good reasons *not* to use a promotional envelope with a window.

Elaborate Data Processing

The question of elaborate use of data processing has been discussed throughout the book. Of all the mailings, only eighteen or 25 percent use elaborate personalization. And of those, there are but five efforts (7 percent) that are personalized for no apparent reason: *Harper's, Financial World, National Wildlife,* Gevalia Kaffe, and Book-of-the-Month. If personalization can be avoided, the mailing costs less.

Letters

Based on the grid, the old saw that "long letters work better than short letters" is no longer true—at least in the business arena. If you compare the average letter length of consumer magazines (3.3 pages) with that of business and financial magazines (2.1 pages), it is immediately obvious that shorter letters to people in the business environment seem to work better.

To sell a newsletter, a four-page letter seems to be the norm; for a home-study course, the average letter is six pages.

Comp and FREE

People who buy by mail like—indeed *expect*—a bargain. More than one-half of all the consumer magazine efforts offer a free issue and 60 percent of them use the word *free* promiscuously (free issue, free premium with order, free premium with payment, etc.).

In the business and financial magazine category, the percentages are higher: 57 percent offer a comp copy and 71 percent feature the word *free*. The idea that people in the workplace don't need a bargain because they are spending other people's money is just plain wrong. Statistically, they like great offers just like anybody else.

Bill-Me Option

Of the seventy-one Grand Controls, 83 percent sell on credit. Delete the four lead generators—where money is not discussed—and only five packages, 11 percent, fail to offer the bill-me option; they are: *American Spectator*, one of the two *Barron's* efforts, CompuServe, the business book effort, and Omaha Steaks. However, all five offer credit card billing, so that in *no case* is the customer forced to write a check for any of these seventy-one products or services.

Credit Card Option

Only fourteen (20 percent) of the Grand Controls allow payment by credit card. With the exception of *American Spectator* ($11.95) and *Foreign Affairs* ($16.00), all other publications and products that offer the credit card option sell for $25.00 or more. The other exception—Gevalia Kaffe—is a continuity program, so while the initial order is small ($3.00), a long-time buyer could spend in the hundreds.

Phone and Fax Orders

So few of the Grand Controls offer the phone or fax order option that we did not even bother to tally them up. For low-price products and services, the cost of inbound telemarketing will eat you alive.

It may be, too, that the phone option makes it *too easy* to order. The act of checking a box and dropping an order into the mail means the person has enough interest in the product to be slightly inconvenienced, and so is better qualified than a spur-of-the-moment tire kicker who takes the free issue and cancels; or worse, he takes a free issue and doesn't bother to cancel, thus putting you through all the time and expense of a series of billing efforts, all of which are ignored.

Offer

A large majority of the magazine offers—business and financial as well as consumer—tout savings. People like a bargain. If they like comp copies and premiums, they also like to save money. The harder the offer . . . the less the saving . . . the poorer the gross results. This is testable, and should be tested.

Non-Agency

One aspect of the Million-Dollar Mailings that shocked and surprised me: the lion's share of them (90 percent) were created by freelancers, tiny boutique agencies, or in-house writers. Only three big direct response agencies are responsible for any of these Grand Controls: Grey Direct, Wunderman, and Rapp Collins Marcoa.

Stamp vs. Metered Indicia vs. Printed Indicia

Not included in the grid were the stats for stamp vs. printed indicia vs. metered indicia. The vast majority of the Grand Controls used a printed indicia. But mailers are always testing stamps and metered indicia.

Michael Moroney of Book-of-the-Month said that the stamp vs. printed indicia was tested eight years and that BOM now operates on the following theory: if a mailing looks remotely like a first-class effort, a stamp will raise response 5 to 7 percent—enough more than to pay for itself. "If the thing looks like a piece of junk mail—a typical 6" × 9" package—a stamp won't help at all," Moroney said. The BOM effort had a personalized letter. But on the line directly above the name and address—the very first thing a person sees when sitting down to read this supposedly personal communication—is:

CAR-RT SORT **RR02

According to Tony Arau, who created the long-term (1983) *Soviet Life* control, a metered indicia increases pull 20 to 30 percent for that publication. Cynthia Folino of *Soundview Executive Book Summaries* reported that the last time she tested metered indicia was in the mid-80s, and it was a clear winner.

When asked about metered indicia, Canadian designer Ted Kikoler—who with Don Hauptman is represented in these pages by *Soundview Executive Book Summaries*—said: "Anything that makes a package look as if a human hand touched it should help."

Inserting Order

When you give a lettershop an inserting job, you must specify exactly in what order the various elements should go into the envelope. With window envelopes, the addressing piece must show through the window, obviously. Most direct mail professionals want the letter folded so that the letterhead and salutation are facing out and the signature is inside, and this face-out letter should be the first piece the prospect sees when removing the contents. So you should specify that the letter should be the piece closest to the back side of the envelope with the letterhead and salutation facing the flap.

The Art of Fulfillment

Million-Dollar Mailing$ has been about the art and science of creating moneymaking direct mail; the emphasis has been on the business of getting subscribers, inquiries, and orders.

What has not been discussed is how mailers treat those who respond.

There are four kinds of advertising: general . . . point-of-sale . . . promotion . . . and direct marketing.

General advertising shoots for awareness. The general agency persuades its clients that it can make such an impression on its intended audience—through TV or print ads—that people will remember the product and buy it at the supermarket or car dealership or airline counter.

At the supermarket, car dealership, and airline counter are point-of-sale reinforcements to remind people of the ad they saw and, it is hoped, fill them with a flood of good feelings so they purchase the product.

In general advertising, then, there are several forces at work: the initial advertisement, the point-of-sale material, and, very often, a salesperson at the place where the item is being purchased. Any one of these elements could be responsible for the sale; as a result, the success of any facet of general advertising is hard to measure.

Promotion is the art of giving a flagging product a quick fix. Sending discount coupons for disposable diapers to young parents . . . the local pizza joint stuffing all the mailboxes in a neighborhood with promises of a free pitcher of beer with every pizza purchased . . . the local radio station running a contest to enhance listenership—all are examples of promotion. Unlike general advertising, the success of a promotion can be precisely tallied; divide the number of discount coupons redeemed by the number of coupons distributed and you have the measure. Print an identifying key on the various coupons and you know exactly how well or poorly each medium performed.

How is direct marketing different? With the exception of the automobile dealer, none of the beneficiaries of the various advertising and promotional campaigns above *keep track of their customers and what they buy*.

The entry of a customer's name into the computer, together with a running history of purchases and perhaps personal information as well (birthday, number of children, income, automobiles, financial information), creates what is known as a database. Direct marketing is database marketing, of which the seventy-one Grand Controls in this book represent the first step.

Direct marketing is not the business of creating awareness or quick fixes; direct marketing is accountable advertising, directly measured by the lifetime value of a customer.

One of the great shortcomings of many mailers is how poorly they treat people once they become customers. An example is the magazine industry. A slew of publishers—including many whose Grand Controls are represented herein—state the following on their order forms:

Please allow 4 to 6 weeks for delivery of your first issue.

or

Please allow 6 to 8 weeks for delivery of your first issue.

or (in the case of Hearst Magazines)

Your first copy will be on its way in 6 to 12 weeks. Watch for it!

Six to twelve weeks for delivery of a magazine is preposterous! Hearst is admitting that the same hardware that put men on the moon is incapable of getting a magazine into someone's hands for one and a half to three months! This is shabby treatment of your brand new and, presumably, most enthusiastic customer.

To be successful in direct marketing, says consultant Lew Smith, you have to "think conceptually." You must think through every step of the relationship from the moment the prospect receives the offer all the way through to receipt of the renewal or reorder check—and beyond.

One critical point in the relationship is the moment of arrival of the merchandise.

The ideal mail order product should be everything promised in the solicitation—and, if possible, even more. It should be immediately usable.

The customer should be able to open the package and start to read it . . . plug it in and watch it . . . stick it in the CD player and listen to it . . . wear it . . . taste it . . . or hang it on the wall.

If batteries don't come with it . . . if it has to go to the picture framer . . . if the sleeves need shortening . . . the enjoyment of the moment is diminished and chances of dissatisfaction and a return of the merchandise are greater.

One way to keep up the excitement level is to provide world-class fulfillment material that *resells* the customer.

Remember, a period of time always elapses between order and receipt . . . between falling in love with the copy and having the product in your hands. In the case of Hearst Magazines, it can be up to three months!

At retail no fulfillment is necessary beyond the instruction booklet; you have seen the actual product and are carting it home on the spot. You have instant gratification.

With mail order sales, the need for excellent fulfillment material is directly proportional to the time it takes for the order to arrive. The longer it takes to deliver the goods, the better the fulfillment material has to be.

In the case of Hearst, a magazine arrives three months later, followed by invoices and statements. Can the average person remember ordering *Town & Country* three months ago? Even if a welcome letter comes in the meantime, the entire transaction is eminently forgettable. Magazines followed by a series of invoices—seemingly out of the blue—can be an irritant.

An Example of Textbook-Perfect Fulfillment

Early in 1992 I ordered a shortwave radio off a page in the *Wall Street Journal*. The seller: Willabee & Ward, a division of MBI (Danbury Mint, Easton Press, Postal Commemorative Society).

I called an 800 number to order the radio and the knowledgeable rep on the other end of the line wasted little of my time as I charged it to my Visa card. The product arrived via UPS *the following afternoon*. It was securely boxed and cushioned in a plastic wrap. Included were—as promised—earphones and a travel case, together with an instruction booklet and shortwave listening guide by Grundig. Not promised were batteries, but they were included as well. I received more than I was expecting. I inserted the batteries, turned on the radio, and in minutes the BBC World Service came in loud and clear.

It's a fact that computer manufacturers, software publishers, watchmakers, and purveyors of electronics are incapable of writing clear instructions on how to use their products.

David Ward of Willabee & Ward knows this. On the outside of the shipping carton was an envelope stuffed with goodies: a warm welcome letter signed by Willabee & Ward's manager, Carl Peru; a tearsheet of the advertisement that I responded to (so I will remember precisely why this thing arrived on my doorstep); notification that my Visa card had been charged, together with a toll-free number in case I had any questions about my account; and a card that gave me Grundig's toll-free "Shortwave Hotline" for assistance in finding shortwave stations.

Knowing full well that most customers are not rocket scientists, Ward wisely included a clearly written, one-page "Quick Guide to Your Grundig RK-709"; it enabled me instantly to set the clock and start using the radio.

Also included were four-color tearsheets of other products—aviator glasses, a bomber jacket, a motorcycle jacket, and a remote-controlled toy car that works on land or water.

Why offer additional merchandise in a shipment? Because if the product lives up to expectations, this is the moment in the relationship that the customer is most disposed to order something else.

Order from Willabee & Ward and discover textbook-correct mail order fulfillment: immediate delivery of a product that is ready to use with easy-to-follow instructions on how to use it and toll-free numbers to call with any questions.

Words to Live By

In Norwalk, Connecticut, is a privately owned supermarket called Stew Leonard's. The store is world renowned for fresh produce and insanely low prices; from the outside it looks like a casino on the Las Vegas strip. Stew Leonard's is a magnet for shoppers from several counties around as well as tourists, students of business, MBAs, and B-School professors. Stew Leonard quotes a statistic that the average person will spend $264,000 in supermarkets over the course of a lifetime; as a result, he sees the number, $264,000, plastered across the forehead of every customer who walks into his store. Stew Leonard is guided by two principles that are carved in stone (literally—on a giant rock just inside the main entrance): OUR POLICY

Rule 1. The customer is always right.
Rule 2. If the customer is ever wrong, reread Rule One.

For one month twenty-five years ago I sold Dictaphones and met a salesman—a huge man, well over six feet tall—whose name was Tiny LaBreque. His motto for treating customers came from a scene in Antoine de Saint Exupéry's beloved children's book, *Le Petit Prince*, wherein the fox tells the Little Prince:

"We are forever responsible for the things we tame."

APPENDICES

Appendix 1

Positioning
by Dennis S. LeBarron

Editor's Note: When taking on a new project or client, you have to learn everything you can about that business quickly before you can put your direct marketing know-how to work.

In the course of writing subscription promotion packages for dozens of newsletters, freelancer Don Hauptman found himself asking similar questions of new clients. As a result, he put together a questionnaire for the client to fill out in advance of their first meeting. The purpose: to save time . . . to get the client's input in writing . . . to be absolutely sure all bases are touched . . . and to have at hand answers to questions that might come up later when the client can't be reached.

This exercise is invaluable in two situations. The first is when a new product or service is being launched and, for the most part, exists only inside the head of one or two people. It gets clients thinking through "their baby" and putting those ideas into writing. The second is when the publisher or editor of a magazine gives you a very precise idea of what they think they are publishing; but when you read the past twelve issues, you find it to be something quite different. If the copy reflects what you believe the magazine to be about—as opposed to what they perceive it to be—there's a good chance the copy will be rejected. By getting their thoughts in writing in advance, this can all be thrashed out before you set fingers to keyboard.

Whereas Hauptman's pioneering questionnaire is slanted toward newsletters and publications, freelancer Denny LeBarron has adapted it to come up with an all-purpose questionnaire; it works for products, publications, and services . . . consumer or business. It should be extremely useful not only for writers, but also for account executives, consultants, and list brokers. In addition, if you are a mailer who uses outside creative help, take some time to fill this form out, and then give it to each new copywriter or agency you hire. You may photocopy the questionnaire and use it as is.

Client Questionnaire

1. CLIENT (Company): Address:

   Phone Number: Contacts:
   Fax Number:

2. DESCRIPTION of Product/Service. (In 50 words or less, what is it we're offering?)

3. PURPOSE of the product. (What does it do? How does it work? How is it used?)

4. PRICE. (How much does it cost?)

5. What is the OFFER? (Is there a special introductory saving? Premium? Limited-time offer? 2-for-1 sale? Free information? Etc.?)

6. What are the FEATURES of the product? (All facts and specs.)

7. What are the main BENEFITS? (What will it do for me? What specific problem does it solve? How will it make or save me money? Save time or work? Make my life easier or better?)

8. OTHER COPY POINTS? (What info/service will it give me that I can't get anywhere else? Or how and why is it new, better than, different from what's already available? Is it unique or exclusive?)

9. What is our ASSIGNMENT? (Ad, direct mail package, brochure, insert, complete campaign?)

10. What is the OBJECTIVE of the project? (Inquiries or leads, direct sales, announcement, image building, etc.?)

11. What's the BUDGET?

12. What's the SCHEDULE? (You want it when?)

13. Who is the main PROSPECT? (In business, what's his or her title/responsibility? What are his biggest concerns, fears, attitudes, possible objections? How will he use your product to get ahead or to keep from falling behind? For consumers, what main interest/desire/fear does it appeal to?

    Who are your SECONDARY PROSPECTS? Are there enough of them to versionalize the copy so the offer appeals more directly to them?)

14. What LISTS/MEDIA will you use? (What have you used in the past? What worked and what did not? What is the performance BY SOURCE?)

15. Do we have a SAMPLE of the product/service?

16. Do you have SAMPLES OF PREVIOUS PROMOTIONS? (Winners and losers?)

17. Do you have any TESTIMONIALS and ENDORSEMENTS? (Letters from happy users? Media coverage? Celebrity endorsements?)

18. Do you have any COMPLAINTS? (Letters from unhappy customers?)

19. Will you be conducting any TESTS? (Copy, price, offer?)

20. What copy points MUST be included?

21. What TABOOS do you have? (Anything that must *never* be said or promised?)

22. What about OUTSIDE COMPETITION? (Why are you better? Product? Price? Service? Can your prospect make price comparisons with others, or do you have an exclusive?)

23. Any IN-HOUSE COMPETITION that might affect positioning, copy approaches, etc.?

24. Any operational RESTRICTIONS? (E.g., no 9″ × 12″ outer envelopes, 4-color, etc.)

25. In the offer, what is the METHOD OF PAYMENT? (Cash with order; bill me; purchase order required? Visa, Mastercard, American Express, Diners, Discover?)

26. What about TELEPHONE ORDERS? (What percent of your business comes in by phone? Do you have a toll-free 800 number? Accept collect calls?)

27. What's the GUARANTEE? (100% money-back anytime? Fifteen-day trial? Other?)

28. What about your COMPANY? (Special history of the company, personality of the owner, authority of the seller, achievements or anything else of sales importance?)

29. ANYTHING ELSE? (As much research and background material as you can supply.)

30. Recommended BACKGROUND READING and OTHER PEOPLE I SHOULD TALK TO.

Appendix 2

The Seventy-one Grand Controls

MAILER: *Advertising Age*
PACKAGE: Coffee Mug Premium
AGENCY: Financial Direct
WRITER: Bill Christensen
DESIGNER: Bill Christensen
FIRST MAILED: 1985

MAILER: *Advertising Age*
PACKAGE: Cartoon Letter
PROJECT MGR.: David Kelley
WRITER: David Kelley
DESIGNER: Stu Heinecke
FIRST MAILED: 1990

MAILER: *American Demographics*
PACKAGE: Yes-No-Maybe
PROJECT MGR.: Michael Edmondson
WRITER: Hank Burnett
DESIGNER: David Gordon
FIRST MAILED: 1987

MAILER: American Management Assn.
PACKAGE: Handwritten Invitation
PROJECT MGR.: Eileen Lewis
AGENCY: Schwab & Beatty
WRITER: Unknown
DESIGNER: Unknown
FIRST MAILED: 1973

MAILER: *American Spectator*
PACKAGE: "Not since the heyday"
PROJECT MGR.: Ron Burr
WRITER: Laurence Jaeger
DESIGNER: Lucy Durand Sikes
FIRST MAILED: 1985

MAILER: *Architectural Digest*
PACKAGE: Double postcard
PROJECT MGR.: Carla Johnson
WRITER: Judith Hannah Weiss
DESIGNER: Theo Pappas
FIRST MAILED: Early 1980s

MAILER: *Audubon*
PACKAGE: Risk-Free Membership
PROJECT MGR.: Trish Edelman (Original)
Celia Tennenbaum (Current)
WRITER: Pete Gelb
DESIGNER: David Gordon
FIRST MAILED: 1985

MAILER: *Aviation Consumer*
PACKAGE: "Which . . . ?"
PROJECT MGR.: Donn E. Smith
WRITER: Donn E. Smith
DESIGNER: John Rettich
FIRST MAILED: 1985

MAILER: *Aviation Safety*
PACKAGE: Piper Cub Sweeps
PROJECT MGR.: Donn E. Smith
WRITER: Donn E. Smith
DESIGNER: John Rettich
FIRST MAILED: 1985

MAILER: *Barron's* I
PACKAGE: "They trust their luck"
PROJECT MGR.: Paul Bell
AGENCY: Frank Vos Company
ACCOUNT MGR.: Joe Vine
WRITER: Unknown
DESIGNER: Linda Lewis Abedrabbo
FIRST MAILED: 1980

MAILER: *Barron's* II
PACKAGE: Investigate
PROJECT MGR.: Paul Bell
WRITER: Seymour Zogott
DESIGNER: Stan Greenfield
FIRST MAILED: 1985

MAILER: BMG Music Service
PACKAGE: 8 CDs for ½
PROJECT MGR.: Ed McCabe
AGENCY: In-house
WRITER: Strat Simon
DESIGNER: Joseph Pontevolpe
FIRST MAILED: 1988

MAILER: Boardroom Reports
PACKAGE: *Book of Inside Information*
PROJECT MGR.: Michael Weil
AGENCY: In-house
WRITER: Declined to reveal
DESIGNER: Declined to reveal
FIRST MAILED: 1987

MAILER: *Bon Appétit*
PACKAGE: "Pick of the crop!"
PROJECT MGR.: Susan Allyn
WRITER: Linda Wells
DESIGNER: R. L. Polk
FIRST MAILED: 1986

MAILER: Book-of-the-Month Club
PACKAGE: "Don't tell your friends"
PROJECT MGR.: Michael Moroney
AGENCY: Wunderman Worldwide
WRITER: Bill Keisler
DESIGNER: Wunderman Worldwide
FIRST MAILED: 1985

MAILER: *Bottom Line/Personal*
PACKAGE: Eat on Airplane
PROJECT MGR.: Laurie Mellon
AGENCY: In-house
WRITER: Declined to reveal
DESIGNER: Declined to reveal
FIRST MAILED: 1987

MAILER: *Business Week*
PACKAGE: Triple postcard
PROJECT MGR.: Kathy Gallagher
WRITER: Judith Hannah Weiss
DESIGNER: Theo Pappas
FIRST MAILED: 1985

MAILER: Cinegraph Slides, Inc.
PACKAGE: Catalog
PROJECT MGR.: Glen Wolfe
WRITER: Glen Wolfe
DESIGNER: Glen Wolfe
FIRST MAILED: 1987

MAILER: CompuServe
PACKAGE: Preferred Acceptance/$25 Cert.
PROJECT MGR.: Regina Brady
WRITER: Sol Blumenfeld
DESIGNER: Sol Blumenfeld
FIRST MAILED: 1987

MAILER: *Condé Nast Traveler*
PACKAGE: Launch effort
PROJECT MGR.: Joanne Wallenstein
AGENCY: Rapp Collins Marcoa
ACCOUNT MGR.: Cindy Abrams
WRITER: Emily Soell
DESIGNER: Jerry Genova
FIRST MAILED: 1987

MAILER: Cy DeCosse Incorporated
PACKAGE: Singer Sewing Reference Library
PROJECT MGR.: Al Anderson
WRITER: Greg Beaupre
DESIGNER: In-house
FIRST MAILED: 1984

MAILER: *Dog Fancy*
PACKAGE: Reply within 10 days
PROJECT MGR.: Penny Stewart
WRITER: Penny Stewart
DESIGNER: Penny Stewart
FIRST MAILED: 1987

MAILER: *Earthwatch*
PACKAGE: "Got some free time?"
PROJECT MGR.: Robin Schweikart
WRITER: Bill Jayme
DESIGNER: Heikki Ratalahti
FIRST MAILED: 1989

MAILER: *Economist*
PACKAGE: 3 Free Issues
PROJECT MGR.: Beth Maher
WRITER: Ken Scheck
DESIGNER: Ken Scheck
FIRST MAILED: 1981

Mailer: *Encyclopaedia Britannica*
Package: "If money were no object"
Project Mgrs.: Ray Markman
Harold Silver
Alan Boyer (Current)
Agency: Frank Vos Company
Project Dir.: Frank Vos
Account Mgr.: Mitch Hisiger
Writer: William A. Butler
Copy Chief: Joe Morrone
Designer: Winnie Young
First Mailed: Mid-1970s

Mailer: *Financial World*
Package: 193,750 Millionaires
Project Mgr.: Laurence Hedblom
Writer: Linda Wells
Designer: John Rettich
First Mailed: 1986

Mailer: *Foreign Affairs*
Package: Should *you* be reading?
Project Mgrs.: Doris Forest
Dave Kellogg
George Fisher
Margaret Kable
Writer: Len Berkowe
Designer: Vincent Gallipani
First Mailed: 1982

Mailer: *Fortune*
Package: Confidential
Project Mgrs.: Ken Godshall
Hala Makowska
Agency: Financial Direct
Writer: Bill Christensen
Designer: Bill Christensen
First Mailed: 1988

Mailer: Fortune Book Club
Package: Interoffice Correspondence
Project Mgr.: Kathy Bloomfield
Writer: Greg Dziuba
Designer: Elizabeth Dipalma
First Mailed: 1988

Mailer: *Futurist*
Package: Forecasts for next 25 yrs.
Project Mgr.: Tony Cornish
Writer: Tony Cornish
Designer: Tony Cornish
First Mailed: 1985

Mailer: Gevalia Kaffe
Package: Free canister
Agency: Wunderman Worldwide
Creative Dir.: Jim Infantino
Writer: Mary Ann Donovan
Designer: Jane Walsh
First Mailed: 1985

Mailer: Great Expectations
Package: Meet Quality Singles
Project Mgr.: Janice Mayo
Writer: Tony Barnard
Designer: Tony Barnard
First Mailed: 1986

Mailer: *Harper's*
Package: Typewriter Type OSE
Project Mgr.: Lynn Carlson
Writer: Nancy Grady
Designer: Nancy Grady
First Mailed: 1987

Mailer: *House & Garden*
Package: Special White Sale
Project Mgr.: Kim Doneker
Agency: Rapp Collins Marcoa
Account Mgr.: Cindy Abrams
Writer: Jerry Ricigliano
Designer: Jerry Genova
First Mailed: 1986

Mailer: Hume Publishing I
Package: *SIMM* Course
Project Mgr.: Kate Bryant
Writer: Joan Throckmorton
Designer: Unknown
First Mailed: 1986

Mailer: Hume Publishing II
Package: *Successful Business Management*
Project Mgr.: Randy Levin
Writer: Harry Walsh
Designer: Gia Felis Watkins/Giagraphics
First Mailed: 1987

Mailer: Hume Publishing III
Package: *SuperInvestor Files*
Project Mgr.: Suzanne Eastman
Writer: Alan Schwartz
Designer: Unknown
First Mailed: 1985

MAILER: *Inc.*
PACKAGE: Double postcard
PROJECT MGR.: Bob LaPointe
WRITER: *Inc.* Staff/Judy Weiss
DESIGNER: Judith Hannah Weiss
FIRST MAILED: 1987

MAILER: Instant Improvement, Inc.
PACKAGE: *Dr. Chang's . . . Exercises*
PROJECT MGR.: Eugene M. Schwartz
WRITER: Eugene M. Schwartz
DESIGNER: Ed Jastrom
FIRST MAILED: 1979

MAILER: Institute of Children's Literature
PACKAGE: Looking for People
PROJECT MGR.: Malcolm Decker
WRITER: Malcolm Decker
DESIGNER: David Gordon
FIRST MAILED: 1977

MAILER: International Preview Society
PACKAGE: Free 10-Day Audition
PROJECT MGR.: Strat Simon
AGENCY: In-house
WRITER: Strat Simon
DESIGNER: Joseph Pontevolpe
FIRST MAILED: 1988

MAILER: *Islands*
PACKAGE: Double postcard
PROJECT MGR.: Tony Theiss (original)
Marcia Scholl (current)
WRITER: Ken Schneider
DESIGNER: Suzette Curtis, A.D.
FIRST MAILED: 1987

MAILER: *Lear's*
PACKAGE: "Congratulations"
PROJECT MGR.: Mirta Soto
CONSULTANT: Dick LaMonica
WRITER: Linda Wells
DESIGNER: John Wagman Design
FIRST MAILED: 1988

MAILER: Literary Guild
PACKAGE: "We're Going to Spoil You"
AGENCY: Grey Direct
CREATIVE DIR.: Karen Henkin
WRITER: Alan Friedenthal
ART SUPVR.: Judi Kolstad
SR. ART DIR.: David Micklewright
FIRST MAILED: 1988

MAILER: *Lotus*
PACKAGE: Double postcard
PROJECT MGR.: Elizabeth Folsom
WRITER: John Klingel
DESIGNER: Paul Baldassini
FIRST MAILED: 1988

MAILER: *M*
PACKAGE: Civilized Man
PROJECT MGR.: Mirta Soto
WRITER: Milt Pierce
DESIGNER: Karen Weinstein
FIRST MAILED: 1988

MAILER: Mobil Auto Club
PACKAGE: Instant Card/Sweeps
PROJECT MGR.: Cynthia Morgan
WRITER: Robert Haydon Jones
DESIGNER: Harold Strauss
FIRST MAILED: 1987

MAILER: *National Wildlife*
PACKAGE: Best Free Bonus Gift
PROJECT MGR.: Susan Hord (original)
Susan Harford (current)
WRITER: Don O'Brien
DESIGNER: Muriel Ebitz
FIRST MAILED: 1988

MAILER: Nature Conservancy
PACKAGE: Crane Package
PROJECT MGR.: Michael Coda
WRITER: Frank H. Johnson
DESIGNER: Frank H. Johnson
FIRST MAILED: 1985

MAILER: *Newsweek*
PACKAGE: Free Gift/Voucher
PROJECT MGR.: Jane Keiffer
DESIGNER: Pierre Volmene
FIRST MAILED: 1988

MAILER: Nightingale-Conant I
PACKAGE: *Lead the Field*
PROJECT MGR.: Mark Boyle
WRITER: Bob Matheo
DESIGNER: Chuck Dickinson
FIRST MAILED: 1987

MAILER: Nightingale-Conant II
PACKAGE: *Power Negotiating*
PROJECT MGR.: Mark Boyle
WRITER: Don Kanter
DESIGNER: Dick Sachs
FIRST MAILED: 1988

MAILER: Omaha Steaks
PACKAGE: Very Special Person . . .
WRITER: Herschell Gordon Lewis
DESIGNER: Jim Spangler
FIRST MAILED: Early 1980s

MAILER: *Organic Gardening*
PACKAGE: "Broccoli Bob Rodale"
PROJECT MGR.: Bob Kaslik
WRITER: Jim Punkre
DESIGNER: Bill Bosler
FIRST MAILED: 1983

MAILER: *Outside*
PACKAGE: Discount Order Form
PROJECT MGR.: Ann Mollo-Christensen
AGENCY: In-house
FIRST MAILED: 1985

MAILER: Rodale Press
PACKAGE: *Country Furniture*
PROJECT MGR.: Brian Carnahan
WRITER: Mark Johnson
DESIGNER: Linda Camana
FIRST MAILED: 1986

MAILER: Rodale Press
PACKAGE: *Ency. of Natural Home Remedies*
PROJECT MGR.: Pat Corpora
WRITER: Eugene M. Schwartz
DESIGNER: Maureen Logan
FIRST MAILED: 1986

MAILER: Rodale Press
PACKAGE: Book of Hints, Tips
PROJECT MGR.: Brian Carnahan
PROMOTION MGR.: Kris Rice
WRITER: Eugene M. Schwartz
DESIGNER: Maureen Logan
FIRST MAILED: 1988

MAILER: Rodale Press
PACKAGE: *Everyday Health Tips*
PROJECT MGR.: Brian Carnahan
WRITER: Josh Manheimer
DESIGNER: David Wise
FIRST MAILED: 1988

MAILER: *Science News*
PACKAGE: 12 for $1
PROJECT MGR.: D. R. Harless
WRITER: Tom McCormick
DESIGNER: Ernie Kunz
FIRST MAILED: 1986

MAILER: *Soundview Executive Book Summaries*
PACKAGE: Stopwatch
PROJECT MGR.: Rob Carter
WRITER: Don Hauptman
DESIGNER: Ted Kikoler
FIRST MAILED: Mid-1980s

MAILER: *Soviet Life*
PACKAGE: Just Say YES!
PROJECT MGR.: Victor Karasin
WRITERS: Tony Arau
Marlene Lewis
DESIGNER: Lonnie Rossi
CONSULTANT: Arau Associates
FIRST MAILED: 1983

MAILER: Standard Rate and Data
PACKAGE: *Direct Mail List Rates and Data*
AGENCY: Tyson Associates, Inc.
PROJECT MGR.: Frank Paulo
WRITER: Dennis S. LeBarron
DESIGNER: Bill Iller
FIRST MAILED: 1985

MAILER: *Success*
PACKAGE: "Got the guts . . ."
PROJECT MGR.: Suzanne Pappas
AGENCY: Clark Direct
ACCOUNT MGR.: Meg Fidler
WRITER: Ken Scheck
DESIGNER: Jerry Simon
FIRST MAILED: 1983

MAILER: Time-Life Books
PACKAGE: *Mysteries of the Unknown*
PROJECT MGR.: Martin Tarratt
WRITER: Len Berkowe
DESIGNER: Ron Wilcox
FIRST MAILED: 1987

MAILER: Time-Life Books
PACKAGE: *Time Frame*
WRITER: Martin Tarratt
DESIGNER: Lynda Chilton
FIRST MAILED: 1988

MAILER: *Utne Reader*
PACKAGE: "Dining Salon"
PROJECT MGR.: Eric Utne
WRITER: Bill Jayme
DESIGNER: Heikki Ratalahti
FIRST MAILED: 1985

Mailer: *W*
Package: Gift Certificate Enclosed
Project Mgr.: Mirta Soto
Writer: Judith Hannah Weiss
Designer: Davidson & Maltz
First Mailed: 1981

Mailer: *Wall Street Journal* I
Package: "Extraordinary offer . . ."
Project Mgr.: Paul Bell
Writer: Seymour Zogott
Designer: Stan Greenfield
First Mailed: 1988

Mailer: *Wall Street Journal* II
Package: "Two Young Men . . ."
Project Mgr.: Paul Bell
Writer: Martin Conroy
Designer: In-house
First Mailed: 1974

Mailer: *Yankee*
Package: Double postcard
Project Mgr.: Joe Timko
Writer: *Yankee* staff
Designer: Bob Johnson
First Mailed: 1985

Appendix 3

Names and Addresses of Writers and Designers

Tony Arau, Arau Associates, P. O. Box 990, Valley Forge, PA 19482. 215/783-6640; fax: 215/783-6616

Paul Baldassini, 234 Clarendon Street, Boston, MA 02116

Tony Barnard, Tony Barnard & Associates, 7033 Sunset Boulevard, Suite 318, Los Angeles, CA 90028. 213/466-9675; fax: 213/466-8295

Greg Beaupre, BBDO Minneapolis, 900 Brotherhood Building, 625 Fourth Avenue South, Minneapolis, MN 55415. 612/338-8401; fax: 612/338-2136

Len Berkowe, 16 Truesdale Drive, Croton-on-Hudson, NY 10520. 914/271-9515; fax: 914/762-8855

Sol Blumenfeld, Sol Blumenfeld Direct Marketing & Advertising, 407 Main Street, Metuchen, NJ 08840. 201/494-1773; fax: 201/494-4699

Bill Bosler, 900 Valley Road—Ste. B102, Melrose Park, PA 19126. 215/635-0856

William A. Butler, 103 Birch Rd., Briarcliff Manor, NY 10510. 914/941-0813

Linda Camana, Rodale Press, 33 East Minor Street, Emmaus, PA 18098. 215/967-5171

Bill Christensen, Financial Direct, Inc., 3444 Ellicott Center Drive, Ellicott City, MD 21043. 301/750-0300

Martin Conroy, 15411 Captiva Drive, 4A, P. O. Box 1089, Captiva, FL 33924. 813/472-0799. June–October: 16 Gull Rock Road, Madison, CT 06443. 203/245-7133

Tony Cornish, World Future Society, 4916 Saint Elmo Avenue, Bethesda, MD 20814. 301/656-8274

Martin Davidson, Davidson & Maltz, Ltd., 24 West 39 Street, New York, NY 10018. 212/221-8080; fax: 212/221-8122

Malcolm Decker, Malcolm Decker Associates, Inc., Box 5093, Westport, CT 06881. 203/227-2775; fax: 203/792-8406

Chuck Dickinson, 17 Hillburn Road, Scarsdale, NY 10583. 914/472-1730

Elizabeth DiPalma, DiPalma Design, 226 West 21st Street, New York, NY 10011. 212/243-5498

Bob Dolman, 17720 Redwood Springs Drive, Fort Bragg, CA 95437. 707/964-9646; fax: 707/964-0134

Mary Ann Donovan, Wunderman Worldwide, 675 Avenue of the Americas, New York, NY 10010. 212/941-3000

Greg Dziuba, 10 Alden Place, Bronxville, NY 10708. 914/779-8507

Muriel Ebitz, Sr. Art Director, National Wildlife Federation, 8925 Leesburg Pike, Vienna, VA 22182. 703/790-4000

Alan Friedenthal, Grey Direct, 875 Third Avenue, New York, NY 10022. 212/303-2300; fax: 212/303-8387

Vincent Gallipani, 44 Judith Drive, Stormville, NY 12582. 914/226-7305

Pete Gelb, 12 Tiskas Path, Water Mill, NY 11976. 516/537-8108; fax: 516/537-0857

Jerry Genova, Rapp Collins Marcoa, 475 Park Avenue South, New York, NY 10016. 212/725-8100; fax: 212/889-5816

David Gordon, David Gordon Associates, Inc., 310 Madison Avenue, Room 1525, New York, NY 10017. 212/687-2753; fax: 212/682-5651

Nancy Grady, 12 Tiskas Path, Water Mill, NY 11976. 516/537-8108; fax: 516/537-0857

Don Hauptman, Don Hauptman, Inc., 61 West 62 Street, New York, NY 10023. 212/246-8229; fax: 212/397-1964

Stu Heinecke, Stu Heinecke Creative Services, Inc., 132 South Rodeo Drive, Beverly Hills, CA 90212. 310/273-8985

Bill Iller, WI Advertising, Inc., 145 Cherry Street, New Canaan, CT 06840. 203/972-0721

Laurence Jaeger, 277 Park Place, Brooklyn, NY 11238. 718/783-0992

Bill Jayme, Jayme, Ratalahti, Inc. (Bill Jayme/copy; Heikki Ratalahti/design), 1033 Bart Road, Sonoma, CA 95476-4707. 707/996-3359

Mark E. Johnson, Direct Response Copywriter, P. O. Box 495, Emmaus, PA 18049-0495. Phone/fax: 215/366-8646

Robert Haydon Jones, Jr., Robert Haydon Jones & Associates, 15 Coleytown Road, Westport, CT 06880. 203/226-9543; fax: 203/226-7581

Don Kanter, Don Kanter, Inc., 3200 N. Lake Shore Drive, Suite 1405, Chicago, IL 60657. 312/472-8797

Bill Keisler, 17 West 67th Street, New York, NY 10023. 212/724-8359

David Kelley, Advertising Age, 965 East Jefferson Avenue, Detroit, MI 48207. 313/446-0452

Ted Kikoler, Ted Kikoler Design, Inc., 43 Beveridge Drive, Don Mills, ON M3A 1P1, Canada. 416/444-6631; fax: 416/444-6632

John D. Klingel, Time Publishing Ventures, 475 Gate Five Road, Suite 225, Sausolito, CA 94965

Ernie Kunz, Kunz & Company, 7331 Ridge Road, Frederick, MD 21701. Phone/fax: 301/293-6862

Dennis S. LeBarron, Clear Communications, P. O. Box 635, Wilton, CT 06897. 203/762-0407; fax: 203/762-5410

Herschell Gordon Lewis, Communicomp, Box 15725, Plantation, FL 33318. 305/587-7500; fax: 305/797-9900

Maureen Logan, Rodale Press, 33 East Minor Street, Emmaus, PA 18098. 215/967-5171

J. C. Manheimer & Co., Ltd., P. O. Box 300, South Strafford, VT 05070. 802/765-4576; fax: 802/765-4262

Bob Matheo, The AdMaker, 529 Almena Avenue, Ardsley, NY 10502. 914/693-4240

Tom McCormick, 9431 Shouse Drive, Vienna, VA 22182. 703/273-2988; 703/356-7242

Don O'Brien, National Wildlife Federation, 8925 Leesburg Pike, Vienna, VA 22184. 703/790-4000

Theo Pappas, Theo Pappas Graphic Design, 301 East 48 Street, New York, NY 10017

Milt Pierce, 162 West 54 Street, New York, NY 10019. 212/246-2325; fax: 212/957-7648

Joseph Pontevolpe, 72 Mulberry Circle, Staten Island, NY 10304. 718/761-5946

Jim Punkre, Brainstorms, Inc., 704 Poppy Avenue, Corona Del Mar, Ca 92626. 714/644-7965; fax: 714/644-8029

Heikki Ratalahti, Jayme, Ratalahti, Inc., 1033 Bart Road, Sonoma, CA 95476-4707. 707/996-3359

John Rettich, 16 Stuyvesant Oval, New York, NY 10009. 212/533-7330

Jerry Ricigliano, Rapp Collins Marcoa, 475 Park Avenue South, New York, NY 10016. 212/725-8100; fax: 212/889-5816

Ken Scheck, P. O. Box 190, Crumpton, MD 21628. 410/778-2267; fax: 410/778-2267 ($1,500–$12,500)

Ken Schneider & Associates, Inc. (Ken Schneider), 3355 West Alabama, Suite 880, Houston, TX 77098. 713/622-2748

Alan Schwartz, 275 Franklin Avenue, Sea Cliff, NY 11579; 516/759-1258; fax: 516/759-2735

Eugene Schwartz, 1160 Park Avenue, New York, NY 10128. 212/439-6904

Lucy Durand Sikes, 231 Washington Avenue, Brooklyn, NY 11205. 718/857-9765

Strat Simon, 78 Chichester Road, Huntington, NY 11743. 516/427-3002

Donn E. Smith, Belvoir Publications, Inc., 75 Holly Hill Lane, P. O. Box 22626, Greenwich, CT 06836. 203/661-6111; fax: 203/661-4802

Emily Soell, Rapp Collins Marcoa, 475 Park Avenue South, New York, NY 10016. 212/725-8100; fax: 212/889-5816

Jim Spangler, Peter James Design, 7520 N.W. FGifth Street, Plantation, FL 33317. 305/587-2842; fax: 305/587-2866

Penny S. Stewart, Fancy Publications, P. O. Box 6040, Mission Viejo, CA 92690. 714/855-8822; fax: 714/855-3045

Martin Tarratt, Time-Life Books, 777 Duke Street, Alexandria, VA 22314. 703/838-7000; fax: 703/548-9564

Joan Throckmorton, Joan Throckmorton, Inc., P. O. Box 452, Trinity Pass, Pound Ridge, NY 10576. 914/764-4036; fax: 914/764-4139

Elaine Tyson, Tyson Associates, Inc., 440 Main Street, Ridgefield, CT 06877. 203/431-8974

Harry B. Walsh, The Walsh Company, 49 Lords Highway, Weston, CT 06883. 203/227-0896

Jane Walsh, Wunderman Worldwide, 675 Avenue of the Americas, New York, NY 10010. 212/941-3000

Gia Felis Watkins, Giagraphics, Inc., 56 Adams Road, Easton, CT 06612. 203/261-7187; fax: 203/261-7127

Karen Weinstein, Karen Weinstein Design, 16 Stuyvesant Oval, New York, NY 10009. 212/533-7330

Judith Hannah Weiss, Judith Hannah Weiss, Inc., 600 W. Saddle River Road, Saddle River, NJ 07458. 201/934-8628

Linda Wells, 10 Smith Street, London SW3 4EE, England. Phone: 011-44-71-730-1429; fax: 011-44-71-259-9163. Also 310 Madison Avenue, New York, NY 10017. 212/687-2753

David Wise, Wise Direct, 242 Main Street, Montpelier, VT 05602. Phone/fax: 802/229-5030

Glen Wolfe, Cinegraph Slides, Inc., 11642 Knott Avenue., Bldg. #14, Garden Grove, CA 92641-1820. 714/895-5298; fax: 714/895-2160

Winnie Young, Lintas: Marketing Communications New York, 1 Dag Hammarskjold Plaza, New York, NY 10017. 212/605-8909

Seymour S. Zogott, The Zogotts, 360 East 65 Street, New York, NY 10021. 212/472-9524

Bibliography

Million-Dollar Mailing$ deals with the art and science of *creating* money-making direct mail. Many other elements go into making a successful direct mail campaign: strategic planning, offers, computer modeling, testing, arithmetic, lists, fulfillment, renewals, and much, much more. For the serious direct mailer, a library of solid, direct marketing information is essential. I'm grateful to Axel Andersson for his invaluable input on this bibliography.

BOOKS

Benson, Richard V., *Secrets of Successful Direct Mail,* 182 pp., NTC Business Books, $29.95.

Bird, Drayton, *Commonsense Direct Marketing* (2nd Edition), 348 pp., NTC Business Books, $29.95.

Bly, Bob, *Ads That Sell,* paperback, 185 pp., Asher-Gallant Press, $43.00.

________, *The Copywriter's Handbook,* paperback, 353 pp., Henry Holt & Co., $12.95.

Bodian, Nat, *Publsher's Direct Mail Handbook,* 256 pp., ISI (dist. by Oryx), $37.95.

Burnett, Ed, *The Complete Direct Mail List Handbook,* 744 pp., Prentice-Hall, $59.95.

Burton, Philip Ward, *Advertising Copywriting* (6th Edition), 333 pp., NTC Business Books, $51.50.

Caples, John, *How to Make Your Advertising Make Money,* 383 pp., Prentice-Hall, $9.95.

________, *Making Ads Pay,* paperback, 248 pp., Prentice-Hall, $6.95.

________, *Tested Advertising Methods* (4th Edition), 318 pp., Prentice-Hall, $14.95.

Cohen, William A., *Building a Mail Order Business,* 584 pp., John Wiley & Sons, $34.95.

Direct Marketing Association, *DMA Manual,* 2 vols., 3-ring binders, free with membership in the DMA.

Emerick, Tracy, and Goldberg, Bernie, *Business-to-Business Direct Marketing,* 490 pp., Direct Marketing, $79.00.

Fenves, Stanley J., *Fenves on Fulfillment,* 285 pp., Hanson Publishing, $49.95.

Gnam, Rene, *Direct Mail Workshop,* 352 pp., Prentice-Hall, $49.95.

Gosden, Freeman F., Jr., *Direct Marketing Success,* 225 pp., John Wiley & Sons, $34.95.

Gross, Martin, *The Direct Marketer's Idea Book,* 256 pp., ANACOM/American Management Association, $19.95.

Hatch, Denison, and Perkins, Russell, *Directory of Major Mailers & What They Mail* (annual), 966 pp., *Who's Mailing What!*/Morgan Rand, $395.

Hodgson, Richard S., *Direct Mail and Mail Order Handbook* (3rd Edition), 1,555 pp., Dartnell, $49.95.

________, *The Greatest Direct Mail Sales Letters of All Time,* 3-ring binder, 450 pp., Dartnell, $91.50.

Hopkins, Claude C., *My Life in Advertising & Scientific Advertising,* 318 pp., NTC Business Books, $9.95.

Jones, Susan K., *Creative Strategy in Direct Marketing,* 436 pp., NTC Business Books, $39.95.

Kobs, Jim, *Profitable Direct Marketing,* 396 pp., NTC Business Books, $47.95.

Kremer, John, *Mail Order Selling Made Easy,* 288 pp., Ad-Lib, $19.95.

Leighton, Richard J., and Regnery, Alfred S., *U.S. Direct Marketing Law: The Complete Handbook for Managers,* 352 pp., Libey Publishing, Incorporated, $70.00.

Lewis, Herschell Gordon, *Direct Mail Copy That Sells!* 416 pp., Prentice-Hall, $49.95.

———, *Herschell Gordon Lewis on the Art of Writing Copy,* 424 pp., Prentice-Hall, $49.95.

Lewis, Herschell Gordon, *Power Copywriting,* 334 pp., Dartnell, $22.95.

Libey, Donald R., *Libey On Customers,* 296 pp., Libey Publishing, Incorporated, $65.00.

Muldoon, Katie, *Catalog Marketing* (2nd Edition), 608 pp., AMACOM/American Management Association, $75.00.

Nash, Edward L., *Direct Marketing Strategy, Planning, Execution,* 454 pp., McGraw-Hill, $44.95.

———, *The Direct Marketing Handbook* (2nd Edition), 827 pp., McGraw-Hill, $69.95.

Ogilvy, David, *Confessions of an Advertising Man,* paperback, 180 pp., Macmillan, $8.95

———, *Ogilvy on Advertising,* 224 pp., Random House, $17.95.

Rapp, Stan, and Collins, Tom, *MaxiMarketing,* 278 pp., McGraw-Hill, $24.95.

Rosenfield, James R., *Financial Services Direct Marketing,* 240 pp., Financial Sourcebooks, $55.00.

Schwartz, Eugene M., *Breakthrough Advertising,* 236 pp., Boardroom Books, $50.00.

———, *Mail Order: How to Get Your Share of the Hidden Profits That Exist in Your Business,* 288 pp., Boardroom, $50.00.

Shepard, David, Associates, *The New Direct Marketing,* 535 pp., Dow Jones, $49.95.

Simon, Julian, *How to Start and Operate a Mail Order Business* (4th Edition), 576 pp., McGraw-Hill, $44.95.

Stone, Bob, *Successful Direct Marketing Methods* (4th Edition), 596 pp., NTC Business Books, $34.95.

Throckmorton, Joan, *Winning Direct Response Advertising,* 397 pp., Prentice-Hall, $39.95.

Warsaw, Steve, *Successful Catalogs: Award Winners That Sell,* 256 pp., Retail Reporting Corp., $49.95.

Weintz, Walter H., *The Solid Gold Mailbox,* 268 pp., John Wiley & Sons, $22.95.

MAGAZINES

Catalog Age, Hanson Publishing Group, P.O. Box 4949, Six River Bend, Stamford, CT 06907. Monthly.

Direct, Hanson Publishing Group, P.O. Box 4949, Six River Bend, Stamford, CT 06907. Monthly.

Direct Marketing, Hoke Communications, 224 Seventh Street, Garden City, NY 11530. Monthly.

DM News, Mill Hollow Corporation, 19 West 21 Street, New York, NY 10010. Weekly.

Target Marketing, North American Communications, 401 North Broad Street, Philadelphia, PA 19108. Monthly.

NEWSLETTERS

Business Mailer's Review, 1813 Shepherd Street, N.W., Washington, DC 20011. 24x/year.

DeLay Letter, 304 Bayberry Lane, Westport, Ct 06880. 24x/year.

Direct Response, Creative Direct Marketing Group, 1815 West 213th Street, 210, Torrance, CA 90501. 12x/year.

The Direct Response Specialist, P.O. Box 1075, Tarpon Springs, FL 34688. 12x/year.

Friday Report, Hoke Communications, 224 Seventh Street, Garden City, NY 11530. 51x/year.

Publisher's Multinational Direct, 150 East 74th Street, New York, NY 10021. 12x/year.

Who's Mailing What! 401 North Broad Street, Philadelphia, PA 19108. 10x/year.

Index

Abedrabbo, Linda Lewis, 427
Abrams, Cindy, 107, 190
Admiral Richard E. Byrd Polar Center, 358, 361
Advanced Strategies for Successful Investing, 403
Advertising Age, 62, 64, 72, 74–75, 348–357, 352, 450
Allyn, Susan, 102
American Demographics, 358–364, 367, 449
American Express Publishing, 64
American Heritage Publishing Co., 147
American Management Association, 289–290, 450
American Spectator, 158–162, 451
Anderson, Al, 205
Andersson, Axel, 5–6, 233, 287–288, 308
Axel Andersson Awards, 8, 9, 379
Angora Marketing, 195
Anyone Can Make a Million, 386
Arau, Tony, 173, 175, 177–178, 452
Arau Associates, 173, 175
Architectural Digest, 45–46, 48, 50–51, 52, 59
Armstrong, Richard, 198
Associations, 8
Atlantic Monthly, 175
Audubon, 120–124, 173, 301
Automatic multiple sales. *See* Continuity series
Aviation Consumer, 328, 329–333, 367
Aviation Safety, 328, 333, 334–337, 367
Awards, 6–8
Axel Andersson Awards, 8, 9, 379

Baird, Bill, 327
Baldassini, Paul, 55
Barnard, Tony, 299–300
Barron's, 425, 427–433, 449, 451
BBDO, 206, 216, 441
Beaupre, Greg, 205–206, 208
Beers, Thomas, 148
Bell, Paul, 425–426, 427, 430, 434–435, 437, 439–440
Belvoir Publications, Inc., 327, 328–331
Benson, Dick, 148, 205, 361
Benson, Stagg & Associates, 358
Berkowe, Len, 168–170, 210, 214–215
Better Homes & Gardens, 175
Bill-me options, 50, 451
Bloom, Carl, 120
Bloom & Gelb, 120
Bloomfield, Kathy, 239
Blumenfeld, Sol, 307, 308, 312
BMG Direct Marketing, 9
BMG Music Service, 225–232
Boardroom Reports, 327, 377–378
The Book of Inside Information, 379, 381–384
Bottom Line/Personal, 327, 377, 379, 381
Bon Appétit, 102–106, 173, 185
Bonner, Bill, 195–196
The Book of Inside Information, 379, 381–384
Book-of-the-Month, 223, 233–238, 348, 450, 452
Bosler, Bill, 93
Bottom Line/Personal, 327, 377, 379, 381
Boyer, Alan, 291
Boyle, Mark, 407, 414
Brady, Regina, 308
Breakthrough Advertising, 255
Broadcast advertising versus direct mail, 11–18
Brochures, circulars, and folders, 23, 26–27
design and copy tips, 29–33
Bryant, Kate, 387
Buckler, Beatrice, 181–182, 184
Build-It-Yourself COUNTRY FURNITURE, 272–276
Burnett, Gretchen Fall, 361, 362
Burnett, Hank, 184, 358–364, 367
Burr, Ron, 158
Business and financial magazines, 345–375, 444. *See also specific titles and publishers*
Business books, 445, 451. *See also specific titles and publishers*
Business services and products, 8
Business-to-business efforts
business and financial magazines, 345–375
postcards, 59
Business Week
snapform, 59, 61–62, 70
triple postcard, 44, 48, 54
Butler, William A., 291, 296

Camana, Linda, 272, 276
Caples, John, 3, 65, 394
Carlson, Lynn, 82, 84
Carnahan, Brian, 267, 272, 277, 278, 280
Carter, Rob, 338
Cartoons, 62, 64
Catalogs, 7, 13–14
format, technique, and offer grid, 445
Charities, 7
Chiat/Day Direct Marketing, 296
Chilton, Lynda, 216, 218, 221
Christensen, Bill, 74–75, 75, 352–357
Chronic comp copy cancel lists, 45
Cinegraph Slides, 419, 422, 424
Clark Direct Marketing, 77, 184
Clear Communications, 437
Client questionnaire, 459–462
Club Med, 44–45
Coda, Michael, 147
Collection problems, 45–46
Colligan Group, 61
Collins, Tom, 190, 198
Color, 32
Compact Disc club, 225
Complimentary copies, 45–46, 451
Components of direct mail. *See* Direct mail packages
CompuServe, 308–312, 451
COMPUTERWORLD, 64
Condé Nast, 190–194, 448
Conroy, Martin, 437, 438, 439–441
Consumer efforts, postcards, 59
Consumer magazines
format, technique, and offer grid, 443
science and nature, 119–156
social and political, 157–178
special interest, 80–100, 328
women's interest, 102–117
Consumer publications
continuity series, 203–221
format, technique, and offer grid, 443
individual titles, 252–285
negative option clubs, 223–250
Consumer Reports, 328, 329
Continuity series, 203–204
encyclopedias and, 292
format, technique, and offer grid, 444
Singer Sewing Reference Library, 205–208
Time-Life Books, 209–221
Controls, 6–7, 8
list of seventy-one grand controls, 463–468
reviving, 30
Conversion (payment), 45–46
bill-me options, 50, 451
credit card options, 50, 451
Copy, 20–21, 27
Cornish, Edward, 131
Cornish, Jeff, 131, 134, 137
Cornish, Tony, 131, 137–139, 179
Corpora, Pat, 255, 259–260, 280
Correspondence courses, 8. *See also* Home study programs
Cost-per-inquiry, 6
Cost-per-order, 6, 22
Cost-per-paid-order, 6
Credit card options, 50, 451
Cruel and Unusual Puns, 339
Cullum, Leo, 350
Curtis, Suzette, 57
Cy DeCosse Incorporated, 205–208
Cycle, 240

Daniels, Judy, 184
Data processing. *See* Personalization
Davidson & Maltz, 111
Davidson, Martin, 114, 116
Decker, Malcolm
on direct mail packages, 23–27, 51, 65, 152, 254, 260, 313, 339, 408
on Institute of Children's Literature, 301, 302, 305
on Schwartz package, 254, 260
Delivery time, 453–454
Design tips to increase response, 29–33
Designers, names and addresses, 469–473
Desktop publishing, 29
Dickie-Raymond, 358
Dickinson, Chuck, 407, 408
Dimension, creating, 33
Dipalma, Elizabeth, 239
Direct mail
beginnings, 3–7
benefits, 13–15
cost-per-order, 22
and environmental issues, 17–18
impulse sales, 19–20
money spent on, 11
versus other media, 11–13
as participatory art form, 19–22
price, service, and exclusivity rule, 15–16
product, offer, list rule, 16, 46
reaction to, 14–15
reasons for, 15–16
response, 22
scams, 12, 15
secrecy of, 14
success of, 16, 195
writing tips, 339–341
Direct mail artists, 19–22. *See also specific persons and organizations*
Direct mail packages, 19–22, 29–33. *See also specific components, e.g.*, Brochures, circulars, and folders; Envelopes; Letters; Lift letters; Mini-packages; Order devices; Postcards
efficiency of, 6
insertion order of components, 452
longevity of, 6, 8
variations, 50–51
"Direct Mail Strip Tease," 128
Direct Mail Writer's Guild, 3
Direct Marketing, 255–256, 258
Dirty load-up, continuity series and, 204
Dog Fancy, 80–81
Domestic Mail Manual, postcard definition and regulation, 43–44
Doneker, Kim, 107
Donovan, Mary Ann, 318–319, 321
Double postcards, 43–59, 449
Doubleday Book Club, 223
Dow Jones & Co., Inc., 425
Barron's, 427–433
The Wall Street Journal, 425, 434–441
Dr. Chang's Book of Internal Exercises, 252–258
Dzuiba, Greg, 239–244

Earth Watch, 125–130
Eastman, Suzanne, 386, 401
Ebitz, Muriel, 140
Economist, 163–167, 168, 179, 449

Edelman, Trish, 120
Edelston, Martin, 377, 379, 381
Edmondson, Michael, 358
Elton, Catherine, 363, 364
Emerson, Andi, 3
Encyclopaedia Brittanica, lead generators, 291–298
The Encyclopedia of Natural Healing, 254
Encyclopedia of Natural Home Remedies, 261–266
Envelopes, 23–24
design and copy tips, 29–33
plain versus promotional, 449–450
prime interrupters, 39–40
reply envelopes, 27, 353–357
window, 450
Environmental issues, direct mail and, 17–18
Everyday Health Tips, 277–285

Fancy labels, 50
Fax orders, 451
Federal Trade Commission, continuity series and, 203–204
Fidler, Meg, 77, 184
Financial Direct, Inc., 74, 75, 352
Financial services, 7
Financial World, 348, 365–369, 450
First class mail, 43–44
Fisher, George, 168
Fishman, Arnold, 11
Folino, Cynthia Langley, 342, 452
Follow-up efforts, 287–288
Folsom, Elizabeth, 55
Forbes, 325
Forbes, Wendell, 331
Foreign Affairs, 168–172
Forest, Doris, 168
Format, technique, and offer grid, 443–445
data analyses, 447–455
totals, 446
Fortune, 72–76, 147, 325
Fortune Book Club, 239–244
Fowles, Jib, 12
Frank Vos Company, 291, 296, 427
Fraud. *See* Scams
Freelancers, 452
Friedenthal, Alan, 245, 278
Fry-Ramsdell, Kathy, 282
Fulfillment, 452–455
Fundraisers, 7, 11, 14–15
Futurist, 131–139, 170

Gallagher, Kathleen, 54, 62
Gallipani, Vincent, 168
Garrard, Pat, 377
Gaylord, Jerry, 4
Gelb, Peter, 120, 122, 301
Genova, Jerry, 107, 109–110, 190
Gevalia Kaffe, 318–321, 450
Giagraphics, 394
Glusker, Irwin, 148
Godshall, Ken, 75
Goldberg, Paul, 181–182
Good Neighbor Centers, 35–38
Gordon, David, 120, 122, 123, 301, 358, 364
Gourmet, 180
Grady & Gelb, 120
Grady, Nancy, 82, 120, 140, 450
Grand control list, 463–468
Great Expectations, 299–300
The Greatest Direct Mail Sales Letters of All Time, 65, 205, 361
Greenfield, Stan, 430, 434
Grey Advertising, 245–247
Grey Direct, 245–247

Haas, Robert K., 223
Hacker, Robert, 287
Hacker Group, 287
Halbert, Gary, 39–40, 198, 449
Handwritten messages, 32, 316
Hardy, Jerome, 209
Harford, Susan, 140
Harless, D. R., 152
Harper's, 82–86, 348, 450
nonprofit status, 448
Harvard Business Review, 329
Haug, Nancy, 345
Hauptman, Don, 338–343, 459
Headlines, 37–38
Hearst, Sheldon, 36
Hearst Magazines, 453–454
Hedblom, Laurence, 365
Heinecke, Stu, 62, 348, 351
Henkin, Karen, 245, 246–247
Hertz, Barbara, 184
Hill, Larry, 35
Hill, Marie, 173
Hints, Tips & Everyday Wisdom, 267–271
Hirsch, George, 331
Hisiger, Mitch, 291
Hodgson, Dick, 65, 205, 301, 361
Holiday, 178
Home-study programs, 385
format, technique, and offer grid, 445
Lead the Field, 407–413
The Secret of Power Negotiating, 414–417
Successful Business Management, 394–400
Successful Investing & Money Management, 387–393
SuperInvestor Files, 401–405
Hord, Susan, 140, 142
House & Garden, 107–110
Hudson, Howard Penn, 341–342
Hume, Ronald, 386
Hume Publishing, 385, 387, 395
Successful Investing & Money Management, 387–393
SuperInvestor Files, 401–405

Iller, Bill, 370
Inc., 48, 52, 53, 59
Indicias versus stamps, 452
Infantino, Jim, 318
Instant Improvements, Inc., 255
Institute of Children's Literature, 300–305
International Masters, 240
International Oceanographic Foundation, 178
International Preview Society, 225–232
International Wildlife, 145
Interruption theory of advertising, 35–40
Involvement, tips to lift response, 29–33
Islands, 48, 56–57, 59

Jaeger, Lawrence, 158
Jastrom, Ed, 252
Jayme, Bill, 4
on disguising advertising mail, 40
Earthwatch, 125–130
launch packages, 181
on personalization, 195
two-page letter, 197
on *Utne Reader*, 198, 200–201
John Wagman Design, 183
Johnson, Bob, 58
Johnson, Carla, 45–46, 50
Johnson, Frank, 147–148, 198
Johnson, Mark, 272, 275–276
Jones, Evan Owen, 317
Jones, Robert Haydon, 4, 313, 316–317, 334
Junk mail, 14, 17

Kable, Margaret, 168
Kaisler, Bill, 233
Kanter, Don, 414, 416
Karasin, Victor, 173
Kaslik, Bob, 93
Keiffer, Jane, 67, 69
Keisler, Bill, 234, 235
Kelley, David, 75, 348, 350, 351, 357, 450
Kellogg, Dave, 168
Kerr, Dorothy, 3
Kikoler, Ted
graphic techniques and design tips, 20, 29–33, 316
print production knowledge, 97–98
Soundview Executive Book Summaries, 338, 339, 340, 343
Kirzner, Eric, 403–405
Klingel, John D., 55
Kolstad, Judi, 245
Kreiser, Joe, 229
Kunz, Ernie, 152

Labels, 50
LaMonica, Dick, 183
LaPointe, Bob, 53
Launch packages, 179–202
client questionnaire, 459–462
Lead generators, 287–288
American Management Association, 289–290
Encyclopaedia Brittanica, 291–298
format, technique, and offer grid, 445
Great Expectations, 299–300
Institute of Children's Literature, 300–305
Lead the Field, 407–413
Lear, Frances, 183–185
Lear's, 183–189, 362
LeBarron, Dennis S., 370, 437–439
client questionnaire, 459–462
Leonard, Stew, 455
Letters, 20–21, 23, 24–26, 65, 450
design and copy tips, 29–33
Levin, Randy, 394
Lewis, Eileen, 289
Lewis, Herschell Gordon, 102, 322, 324–326, 345
Lewis, Marlene, 173
L'Express, 177, 178
Life, 329
Lift letters, 23, 26
design and copy tips, 29–33
Literary Guild, 223, 224, 245–250
Liu, Mark, 184
Load-up, continuity series and, 204
Logan, Maureen, 261, 267
Longman, Harold, 342
Lotus, 44, 48, 55, 59

M, 87–92
MacArthur, John (Rick), 448
Macmillan, 370
Magazines, 13
adversarial actions, 18
business and financial, 345–375, 444
consumer, 80–100, 102–117, 119–178, 443
fulfillment, 454
special interest, 80–100, 328
Maher, Beth, 163
Mail, "A" pile and "B" pile theory, 39–40
Mail Order, 255
Mail order sales, 11, 454
Makowska, Hala, 75
Manheimer, Josh, 277, 279, 282
Manley, Joan, 331
Markman, Ray, 291
Marsh, Penny, 184
Mass media advertising versus direct mail, 11–18
Matheo, Bob, 407, 408, 413
Mayer, Beth, 167, 179
Mayer, Ed, 16, 331
Mayo, Janice, 299
McCabe, Ed, 9
McCall's, 175
McCormick, Tom, 152, 155–156
McGraw-Hill, 48
McLean, Ed, 3, 87, 198
Mellon, Laurie, 377
Memberships, 307
CompuServe, 308–312
format, technique, and offer grid, 445
Gevalia Kaffe, 318–321
Mobil Auto Club, 313–317
Omaha Steaks, 322–326
Merchandisers, 8
Micklewright, David, 245
Mini-packages, 65–78
Misniak, Paul, 317
Mobil Auto Club, 301, 313–317, 334
Moerry, Mariann, 58
Mollo-Christensen, Ann, 70
The MoneyLetter, 386
Morgan, Cynthia, 313
Moroney, Michael, 233, 234–235, 452
Morris, Liz, 3
Morrone, Joe, 291
Mother Jones, 200
Mysteries of the Unknown, 210–215

Nation, 200
National Association of Direct Mail Writers, 3
National Audubon Society, 120–124
National Wildlife, 140–146, 348, 449
National Wildlife Federation, 140–146
The Nature Conservancy, 147–151
Negative option clubs, 223–224
BMG Music Service, 225–232
Book-of-the-Month, 233–238
format, technique, and offer grid, 444
Fortune Book Club, 239–244
Literary Guild, 245–250
Negative option load-up, continuity series and, 204
New England Telephone, 38
New subscriber packages
existing periodicals, 179–180
nonexisting periodicals, 181–182
New Times, 329
New Yorker, 350
Newhouse, S. I., 190
Newsletter on Newsletters, 341–342
Newsletters, 327–343. *See also specific titles and publishers*
format, technique, and offer grid, 444
Newspapers, adversarial actions of, 17–18
Newsweek, 67–69, 70, 179
Nicholas, Don, 49
Nightingale-Conant, 385, 406
Lead the Field, 407–413
The Secret of Power Negotiating, 414–417
Nonprofit mailing rates, 448–449

O'Brien, Donald D., 140–142, 145–146
Offers, 451

product, offer, list rule, 46
Ogilvy, David, 22, 43, 317
Omaha Steaks, 322–326, 451
The 100 Greatest Direct Mail Letters, 301
Order devices, 23, 27
design and copy tips, 29–33
phone and fax orders, 451
prominence, 33
Ordover, Ben, 386
Organic Gardening, 37–38, 93–100, 259
Outside, 70–71

Pappas, Suzanne, 77
Pappas, Theo, 50, 54
Parsons Technology, 20
Paulo, Frank, 370
Perceived quantity of distribution, 30
Perkins/Butler Direct Marketing, 291
Personalization, 195–196, 365, 450
cartoons, 348–351
postcards, 44–45, 62, 64
"reflexive," 196, 198
tricks, 30
Peru, Carl, 455
Phone and fax orders, 451
Pierce, Milt, 87, 88–89, 255–256, 258, 362, 367
Political action committees, 7
Polk, R. L., 102, 105
Pontevolpe, Joseph, 225, 229
Popular Science, 155
Positive option load-up, continuity series and, 204
Postage, 43–44, 448–449
Postcards
additional information requests, 48–49
advantages, 44–45
business-to-business efforts, 59
cartoons on, 62, 64
consumer efforts, 59
definition, 43
disadvantages, 45–46
double, 43–59, 449
four inviolable rules, 46–50
initialing to validate orders, 48
innovations, 60–64
labels, 50
personalization, 44–45, 62, 64
price points, 51–58
snapforms, 61–62
sweepstakes on, 64
triple postcards, 63
variations, 50–51
Power Copywriting, 322
Powerboat Reports, 333
Practical Sailor, 332, 333, 367
Prevention, 259
Price points, 51–58
Prime Time, 184
Product, offer, list rule, 46
Products
products' language, 32
well-known, 46
Publishers, 8
Publishers Clearing House, 346–347
Punkre, Jim, 93, 94–100, 278
Puthukari, Raju, 229

Questionnaire, client, 459–462

Rand McNally Road Atlas, 145
Rapp, Stan, 12, 190, 195
Rapp Collins Marcoa, 107, 190
Ratalahti, Heikki, 125, 127, 148, 198, 200
Reader's Digest, 173–175, 280
Readers' language, use of, 32
Redbook, 175
Research Institute of America, 407
Response, design tips to increase, 29–33
Rettich, John, 334, 365, 367, 368–369
Rice, Kris, 267
Ricigliano, Jerry, 107, 109–110
Riordan, Bob, 331
Ritter, Father Bruce, 198
Rodale, J. I., 259
Rodale, Robert, 280
Rodale Press, 35–38, 259–260
Build-It-Yourself COUNTRY FURNITURE, 272–276
Encyclopedia of Natural Home Remedies, 261–266
Everyday Health Tips, 277–285
Hints, Tips & Everyday Wisdom, 267–271
Organic Gardening, 93–100
Rossi, Lonnie, 173
Ruff, Howard, 198

Sachs, Dick, 414, 416
Sackheim, Maxwell, 223
Sale policy, 455
Sales & Marketing Management, 62–63, 64, 348, 350
"Salvage package," 291
Samuels, Judy, 350
Sassy, 362
Satin, Joan. *See* Throckmorton, Joan
Satin, Shelly, 44
Saturday Evening Post, 175
Savvy, 184
Scams, 12, 15
Scheck, Ken, 77, 163, 164, 167, 168
Scherman, Harry, 223
Schneider, Ken, 56, 57
Scholl, Marcia, 57
Schwab & Beatty, 289
Schwartz, Alan, 401, 403–405
Schwartz, Barbara, 255
Schwartz, Eugene M.
Boardroom Reports, 377, 381
Dr. Chang's Book of Internal Exercises, 252, 254–256, 258, 278
envelope teasers, 449
Rodale Press, 260, 261, 267
Schweikart, Robin, 125
Science and nature magazines, 119–156
Science News, 119, 152–156
The Secret of Power Negotiating, 414–417
Secrets of Executive Success, 254
Shnayerson, Robert, 185
Shulman, Morton, 386, 405
Sikes, Lucy Durand, 158
Silver, Harold, 291
Silverman, Richard, 342
Simon, Jerry, 77
Simon, Strat, 225, 228–229
Simplicity, 33
Sincavage, Mike, 38
Singer Sewing Reference Library, 205–208
Smith, Donn E., 327–333, 334
Smith, Lewis M., 19, 235, 454
Smith, Robin, 347
Smithsonian, 177–178
Smithsonian Institution, 178
Snapforms, 61–62
Social and political magazines, 157–178
Soell, Emily, 190, 194
The Solid Gold Mail Box, 65, 173–175
Soto, Mirta, 87, 111, 183
Soundview Executive Book Summaries, 338–343, 452
Soviet Life, 173–178, 178, 452
Space advertising, 11–18
Spach, Carol, 64
Spangler, Jim, 322
Special interest magazines, 80–100, 328
Sports Illustrated, 332
St. Louis Zoo, 38
Stagg, Christopher, 4, 361, 394
Stamps versus indicias, 452
Standard Rate and Grand Data Control, 370–376, 437
"Stealing smart," 3–5
Stew Leonard's, 455
Stewart, Penny, 80, 81
Stickers. *See* Tokens and stickers
Stone & Adler, 414
Stone, Bob, 65, 301
Strauss, Harold, 313
Strome, Howard, 351
Success, 77–78
Successful Business Management, 386, 394–400, 450
Successful Direct Marketing Methods, 65, 301
Successful Investing & Money Management, 386, 387–393
Sugarman, Joe, 198
SuperInvestor Files, 386, 401–405, 449
Supermarkets
Supermarket Communications Systems, 36
"take-one" literature, 35–38
Sweepstakes, 7–8, 64, 31(
The Synonym Finder, 259

Tarratt, Martin, 210, 215, 216, 219–221
Telemarketing, 12
Television advertising, 11–12
adversarial actions, 18
Temporary membership cards, 301, 316
Tennant, Rich, 64
Tennenbaum, Celia, 120
Testing, 40. *See also* Controls
Teufel, Bob, 259
Theiss, Tony, 57
Throckmorton, Joan, 44, 65, 387, 391–392, 393
Throckmorton/Zolfo, 370
Tighe, John Francis, 4, 367
"Til-forbid" continuity series, 203, 318
Time, 18, 179
Time Frame, 215–221
Time Inc., 329
Time-Life Books, 175, 209, 216
Mysteries of the Unknown, 210–215
Time Frame, 215–221
Time-Life Records, 329
Timko, Joe, 58
Tokens and stickers, 173–178, 301
Audubon, 120–124, 173
Bon Appétit, 102–106, 173
Time-Life packages, 209
Toll-free numbers, 455
Traveler, 190–194
True, 175
TV Guide, 175, 433
Typesize and typestyle, 24–26, 29, 32
Tyson, Elaine, 370–376
Tyson Associates, Inc., 370

U.S. News & World Report, 179
U.S. Postal Service, 43–44
Use charges, 308
Utne, Eric, 198, 202
Utne Reader, 195–202

Vine, Joe, 427
Volmene, Pierre, 67–69
Vos, Frank, 291, 296–298

W, 111–117
The Wall Street Journal, 343, 425, 433, 434–441, 449
Wallenstein, Joanne, 190, 437
Walsh, Harry, 4–5, 394–395, 396, 450
Walsh, Jane, 318, 321
Walsh Company, 394
Wanamaker, John, 13
Ward, David, 455
Watkins, Gia Felis, 394
Weil, Michael, 381
Weinstein, Karen, 87, 90, 92, 367
Weintz, Walter, 20, 65, 173–175
Weiss, Judith Hannah, 50, 52, 53, 54, 111–113, 114, 116
Wellness Encyclopedia, 254
Wells, Linda, 4
Bon Appétit, 102, 103, 105, 106
Financial World, 365, 450
launch packages, 181–182
Lear's, 183, 185
Wilcox, Ron, 210, 215, 221
Wilkinson, David, 22
Willabee & Ward, 454–455
Winning Direct Response Advertising: How to Recognize It, Evaluate It, Inspire It, Create It, 65, 387
Wise, David, 277, 282
Wolfe, Glen, 419, 422, 424
Women's interest magazines, 102–117
Working Woman, 181–182
World Future Society, 131–139
Writers, names and addresses, 469–473
Wunderman Worldwide, 233
WX Wordtronics, 348, 351

Yankee, 48, 58, 59, 60
Young & Rubicam, 414
Young, Winnie, 291

Zogott, Mary Clark, 432, 433
Zogott, Seymour S., 432, 433, 434